Political Economy in Macroeconomics

Political Economy in Macroeconomics

ALLAN DRAZEN

PRINCETON UNIVERSITY PRESS

PRINCETON, NEW JERSEY

Second printing, and first paperback printing, 2002
Paperback ISBN 0-691-09257-5

The Library of Congress has cataloged the cloth edition of this book as follows

Drazen, Allan.
Political economy in macroeconomics / Allan Drazen.
p. cm.
Includes bibliographical references and index.
ISBN 0-691-01670-4 (cl : alk. paper)
1. Macroeconomics. 2. Decision making. 3. Policy sciences. 4. Economics.   I. Title.
HB172.5.D73 2000
339—dc21   99-41735

British Library Cataloging-in-Publication Data is available

This book has been composed in Times Roman and Helvetica

Printed on acid-free paper. ∞

www.pup.princeton.edu

Printed in the United States of America

2   3   4   5   6   7   8   9   10

TO THE MEMORY OF MY FATHER,

A. MICHAEL DRAZEN, ז״ל

MY MOST INFLUENTIAL TEACHER

CONTENTS

POLITICAL ECONOMY is currently one of the most active fields not only in macroeconomics, but also in economics in general. Though the question of how politics affects economic outcomes is one of the oldest in economics, "new" political economy is one of the newest fields in the discipline. The adjective "new" is sometimes added to avoid confusion with use of the term "political economy" to refer to economics itself. This general usage is still popular in some contexts, but political economy as it is used here and among people active in research refers to something more specific. New political economy is defined not simply by renewed interest in the question of how politics affects economics, but more so by its approach to this question, namely, by the use of the conceptual and technical tools of modern economic analysis.

Though the field is quite active, there is no real textbook that covers political economy in macroeconomics broadly at a level suitable for graduate and advanced undergraduate students. There are books of readings and books covering very specific topics, but none of them takes the place of a textbook. The purpose of this book, put simply, is to fill that gap. In deciding how a book could serve this purpose, I have chosen not only to survey recent work, but also to organize and critique the work in the attempt to guide the reader through the wilderness. In so doing, I present a very specific view of the field. The approach is therefore somewhere between a textbook and a monograph. Writing a text in a field where none previously existed presents a special challenge, even more so when the text covers the interaction of two fields. I had no standard with which to compare and could not simply look at previous texts as a starting point, designing a text based on expanding or reducing coverage relative to what was out there, or choosing to treat existing topics from another angle. Instead, I had to start with the question of what I thought a text should include and how I thought topics might be treated. The result is a text that stresses formal economic models, but includes some politics and political philosophy, much conceptual discussion and application, and some empirics. It may seem idiosyncratic in parts, though this must be judged relative to the optimal unwritten texts that others envisage.

What is the intended audience? In writing the book, I was not aiming solely at graduate students in economics, though this is a key audience. I have tried to make large parts of the book accessible to political scientists with some technical background and more generally to anyone interested in more organized exposure to the field. Large parts of the book should also be accessible not only to advanced undergraduates, but also to practitioners with a good background in economics. Some mathematical background is helpful, though it is hoped that the mix of technical and conceptual approaches to a given topic will help readers with different backgrounds. Specific economic and political models that are used heavily are exposited in a self-contained way.

A significant portion of the material in the book is based on courses I have given at the University of Maryland and at the Hebrew University of Jerusalem. The comments and reactions of students in those classes have been invaluable in developing this material. They are owed a greater debt than they realize.

Numerous friends and colleagues have provided comments and suggestions for improving the manuscript. A special thanks goes to Stefan Hubrich, who read the entire manuscript, and made numerous comments on exposition, style, and content. His help was invaluable and greatly improved the book. Larry Ausubel, Avinash Dixit, Bill Easterly, Joram Mayshar, Peter Murrell, Kenneth Rogoff, Arijit Sen, Guido Tabellini, and Mariano Tommasi read all or parts of the book and gave extremely helpful comments. Stefan Hubrich, Esteban Vesperoni, and Devesh Roy provided able research assistance and proofreading of the final galleys.

A significant part of this book was written during a sabbatical at the Hebrew University of Jerusalem, which I thank for its hospitality. I have also benefitted from the hospitality of IGIER, Universita di Bocconi, and MAD, Université de Paris. Some of my own work discussed in the book was supported by the grants from the NSF, which are gratefully acknowledged.

Peter Dougherty and his assistant Linda Chang of Princeton University Press did a superb job of turning a manuscript into a completed book. Technical Typesetting Inc. was similarly superb in typesetting. Peter's advice and encouragement throughout this project was crucial.

The book is dedicated to the memory of my father, Michael Drazen, ז״ל, who was by far the greatest influence on my education. Many years ago, he suggested that I write a textbook in a new field. After I started this project, he always inquired as to how the book was progressing, but passed away not long before its publication. Given the breadth of his interests, he would have found this book interesting as well. I also owe an enormous debt to my wife, Vered, who listened, critiqued, encouraged, and made sure there was a suitable working environment. Without her, the book would be far, far less than what it is. And to Ayelet, who waited.

A BOOK on political economy should be both political and economical. Unfortunately, these two goals often clash if political means polite and economical means frugal and efficient. First of all, there is the problem of coverage of the field. There is just too much to cover if one is to consider all areas in which important contributions have been made. This book concentrates on implications of politics for economic outcomes, rather than politics or public choice *per se*; even more specifically, the coverage is limited to macroeconomics, though macroeconomics broadly defined. Other important areas in which much work has been done are international trade and economic regulation. Neither area is covered here, but not because they are unimportant.

Second, even within macroeconomics, topics that some readers feel are important may have been excluded, or treated only fleetingly. Omissions may be especially glaring given the inclusion of a great deal of material that would not usually be thought of as macroeconomics. The book focuses on theory, rather than empirical work or case studies. However, in some areas where empirical work is quite extensive or key to the field (such as political business cycles or growth), there is significant attention to the empirical research. Beyond that, a key choice criterion was simply personal preference. Cursory treatment of some material reflects not only space constraints but also some of my own judgements, likes, and dislikes. In my decision of what to cover lightly (or perhaps not at all), some areas simply struck me as far less interesting or important than the literature makes them appear. I believe that the coverage of political economy in macroeconomics is quite comprehensive on the whole, but I make no claim for encyclopedic completeness. Anyway, completeness, like beauty, is in the eyes of the beholder.

Third, even in areas covered, there is much extremely good and important published research that is not referenced. This is due in part to space constraints and to the overlap of articles, so that if several articles covered a similar topic, generally only some are discussed or referenced. I have also tried to cover important unpublished work, but there will clearly be many, many gaps. I apologize in advance to those whose work has not received adequate treatment. An oversight on my part should be taken as the main reason. It must be admitted that there is a second reason some work is not mentioned, or mentioned without much comment. As with choice of topics, choice of articles to cover reflects personal preferences. This is unavoidable given the high variability in quality of research in the field, or at least my perceptions of it. If an article is omitted or referenced only in passing, I prefer those affected to think this is due to the first reason given above rather than the second.

Finally, the conflict between being political (that is, politically correct) and economical extends even to writing style. Unfortunately, these two goals often clash in choice of examples or language. Since yet another goal is clarity and simplicity, I often choose a less cumbersome exposition even though it violates "equal-time provisions." Hence, I draw heavily, though not exclusively, on examples from the United States. Similarly, gender neutrality is correct politically, but it is not very economical constantly to write "he (or she)" or "she (or he)." I will use one pronoun to represent both sexes; I take the old-fashioned route of using the male pronoun since, needing to choose, I think using only "she" now sounds a bit affected, rather than refreshing as it once did.

A minor conflict concerns differences in notation between articles. I have attempted the near impossible task of standardizing notation throughout the book. Given the large number of articles, papers, and topics covered and the finite nature of the English and Greek alphabets, such an attempt is necessarily imperfect. Toward the end of trying to be consistent, certain symbols have an unchanged meaning throughout the book, others serve different functions in different chapters or even parts of chapters. I have tried to maximize the number of symbols in the previous category.

PART I

Basic Issues and Tools of Analysis

CHAPTER ONE

What Is Political Economy?

Economists must not only know their economic models,
but also understand politics, interests, conflicts, passions—
the essence of collective life. For a brief period of time you
could make changes by decree; but to let them persist,
you have to build coalitions and bring people around.
You have to be a politician.

—Alejandro Foxley, Chilean Minister of Finance
(quoted in Williamson and Haggard [1994])

1.1. INTRODUCTION

How does politics affect economic outcomes? This question has been
asked probably as long as people have been interested in economics itself.
From Adam Smith's *Wealth of Nations* in 1776 (or perhaps the Physiocrats
even earlier) until at least John Stuart Mill's *Principles of Political Econ-*
omy in 1848, what we now call "economics" was in fact generally referred
to as "political economy."[1] This terminology in large part reflected the
belief that economics was not really separable from politics. This was more
than an administrative classification of disciplines; it arose from the
widespread view that political factors are crucial in determining economic
outcomes. Hence, as a discipline economics historically viewed political
forces not only as influencing economic outcomes, but often as a determining influence.

With the division of economics and political science into distinct disciplines, economists abstracted from political and institutional factors. The
desire for methodological progress and for a more rigorous basis for
economic analysis were important motivations in this separation. The
development of neoclassical economics stressed optimization by consumers
and firms subject to well-defined constraints and a market environment,

---

[1] According to Groenewegen (1987), the term "political economy" for economics originated in France in the 17th century. He attributes the first use to Montchrétien in 1615. Sir
James Steurt (1761) was the first English economist to put the term in the title of a book on
economics, *An Inquiry into the Principles of Political Economy.*

deliberately downplaying more amorphous political factors. Those determinants of economic outcomes easily formalized in this choice-theoretic framework were stressed in the development of neoclassical economics; those not easily formalized were seen as largely the province of other disciplines.

Interest in the question of how politics affects economic outcomes may thus appear new to someone trained solely in modern neoclassical economics; in fact, it is not. One may want to keep the history of this interest in mind in assessing phrases such as "explosion of interest" or "recent flood of work" applied to current research in political economy. Nonetheless, looking at what has been happening in the past few years, such phrases are quite accurate. Of late, there really *has* been an explosion in the number of papers looking at the effect of politics on economic outcomes. Leading journals are filled with articles on the "political economy of" one economic phenomenon or another; specialty journals have been started; conferences on a specific economic issue typically have at least one paper on the politics of the issue, not to mention numerous conferences devoted solely to political economy. In short, it appears justified to speak of the "new political economy" as an important field of current research and to conclude that this is not simply a fad, but an area of analysis that is here to stay.[2] In short, political economy falls into that special class of things that seem quite old and musty and quite young and fresh at the same time.

The "new political economy" is not, however, just a resurrection of an earlier approach to economics. Though characterized by a strong interest in the question of how politics affects economic outcomes, the new political economy is defined more by its way of approaching this question. Specifically, it is defined in large part by its use of the formal and technical tools of modern economic analysis to look at the importance of politics for economics. Modern economic analysis is used not just in the formal sense of a mathematical approach; it is also conceptual, viewing political phenomena in terms of optimization, incentives, constraints, *et cetera*. Hence, what really distinguishes the new political economy is not so much the volume, but the sort of research being done.[3]

Formal technique sometimes clouds, rather than enhances, our understanding of phenomena, and sometimes seems to be used as a substitute for insights into the phenomenon being studied. The relative newness of political economy in its current form may make this problem more acute. It has led some people to the perception, incorrect in my opinion, that the

---

[2] One should, however, note that when asked to assess the significance of the French Revolution, Chinese Premier Chou En-Lai is said to have replied, "It is too soon to tell."

[3] For example, Alt and Shepsle (1990) defined political economy as the study of rational decisions in the context of political and economic institutions, stressing explicit microfoundations based on rational actors.

new political economy is simply a not very insightful formalization of the obvious. Recent research has also been criticized as being too broad, seen as trying to cover everything, with widely differing degrees of success.

Both the strengths and the weaknesses of the new political economy suggest the need for a more organized treatment. In this book, I not only survey recent work on political economy in macroeconomics, but also attempt to organize the work. As such, the approach is somewhere between a textbook and a monograph. It is meant not only to summarize, organize, and critique the existing literature, attempting to guide the reader through the wilderness, but also, like a monograph, to present a very specific view of the field. I argue that heterogeneity and conflict of interests are essential to political economy and should be the organizing principles of the field. However, whether or not a reader finds himself in agreement with this point of view, he should find an organized treatment of the field very useful. Those readers who do agree with the central role of conflict of interests may thereby gain not only an understanding of different parts of the field, but also a better sense of how they fit together.

1.2. POLITICS AND ECONOMICS

What is the new political economy? A general definition is that it is the study of the interaction of politics and economics. Though such a vague definition may have the virtue of being all-inclusive, it gives no real sense of what is being studied. It is like describing the taste of French cooking by saying it results from the interaction of France and cooking. It is technically correct, but one misses the real flavor. Our first task, therefore, is to attempt to provide a definition that will indicate what makes a question one of political economy, and how political economy differs from "straight" economics or from other areas of economics concerned with policy choice. How, for example, is political economy different than the well-developed theories of public finance and public economics? How does it differ from the theory of public choice?

Some Preliminary Definitions

A famous definition of economics is that of Lionel Robbins (1932, p. 16), "Economics is the science which studies human behavior as a relationship between ends and scarce means that have alternative uses." If economics is the study of the optimal use of scarce resources, political economy begins with the political nature of decisionmaking and is concerned with how politics will affect economic choices in a society. Society should be defined broadly to include not only countries or other such jurisdictions, but also firms, social groups, or other organizations.

Obviously, we cannot go much further without being more precise about what we mean by the term "politics." In the political science literature politics is defined as the study of *power* and *authority*, and the exercise of power and authority. Power, in turn, means the ability of an individual (or group) to achieve outcomes which reflect his objectives.[4] Similarly, authority "exists whenever one, several, or many people explicitly or tacitly permit someone else to make decisions for them in some category of acts" (Lindblom, [1977], pp. 17–18). Thus, for example, Lindblom defines politics as the struggle over authority. As he puts it (p. 119), "In an untidy process called politics, people who want authority struggle to get it while others try to control those who hold it."

For our purposes, the most important part of these definitions is what is implicit and taken for granted. Questions of power and authority are relevant only when there is *heterogeneity of interests*, that is, a *conflict* of interests between economic actors in a society. How then does a society make collective policy decisions that affect it as a whole when individual members have conflicting interests? How do individuals, classes, or groups within a larger society gain power or authority to attempt to have the societal choice reflect their preferred course of action? Politics may be thought of generally as the study of mechanisms for making collective choices. Asking how power or authority are attained and exercised can be thought of as a specific form of the general question of what mechanisms are used to make collective decisions.[5]

With this as a basis, we can return to the question of what political economy studies. The view that economics is the study of the *optimal* use of scarce resources contains an implicit, but crucial, assumption when applied to policy choice, namely, that *once the optimal policy is found, it will be implemented*. The problem of policy choice is simply a technical or computational one. Once the optimal policy has been calculated, the policymaker then implements it, where *this* decision is taken as automatic. That is, since the policymaker is a social welfare maximizer, it is taken as given that once an optimal policy is derived, this is the policy that will be carried out. This identity of optimal and actually chosen action implies that a positive economics of policy choice follows almost immediately from the normative economics of policy choice. Note that the process of deciding *technically* what policy to adopt, the decision central to this approach, is very different from the process of deciding on policy which the definition of politics would suggest.

---

[4] For example, Weber (1947, p. 152) defined power as "the probability that an actor in a social relationship will be in a position to carry out his own will despite resistance, regardless of the basis on which this probability rests."

[5] Keohane (1984, p. 21) writes, "wherever, in the economy, actors exert power over one another, the economy is political."

Political economy thus begins with the observation that actual policies are often quite different from "optimal" policies, the latter defined as subject to technical and informational, but not political, constraints. **Political constraints** refer to the constraints due to conflict of interests and the need to make collective choices in the face of these conflicts. Positive political economy thus asks the question how political constraints may explain the choice of policies (and thus economic outcomes) that differ from optimal policies, and the outcomes those policies would imply. To put the same point another way, the mechanisms that societies use in choosing policies in the face of conflicts of interest will imply that the result will often be quite different than what a benign social planner would choose.[6] This positive view implies a normative approach as well: normative political economy would ask the question of how, given the existing political constraints, societies can be led to best achieve specific economic objectives. This includes not only how to "overcome" political constraints within the existing institutional framework, but also the design of political institutions to better achieve economic objectives.

Some Examples

This definition of positive political economy may be better understood by reference to some examples of the questions it addresses. Some phenomena are so clearly in the realm of political economy that little discussion is required as to what are the political influences on the economic outcomes. For example, it is often argued that there is an opportunistic political business cycle, with pre-election economic policies and outcomes influenced by the desire of the incumbent to manipulate the economy in order to improve his re-election prospects. Or, even if incumbents do not, or simply cannot, manipulate the economy before an election, the fact of possible changes in the government after an election may have significant effects on policies and outcomes. If policies were made by an infinitely lived social welfare-maximizing planner who was sure to retain his job (it is, after all, hard to find replacements these days), there would be no effect on policies from the possibility that the policymaker will be replaced. We consider the myriad effects of this possibility in Chapter 7.

In other cases, the role of political constraints may be less in the foreground, but no less important. Consider an economy experiencing hyperinflation, where there is agreement that hyperinflation imposes very large costs on all members of society. The technical problem is how to

---

[6] The importance of conflict of interests is appreciated in some of the literature in public finance. Atkinson and Stiglitz (1980, p. 298), for example, write, "If everyone had identical tastes and endowments, then many public finance questions would lose their significance, and this is particularly true of the behavior of the state. If the interests of the members of society could be treated as those of a 'representative' individual, then the role of the state would be reduced to that of efficiently carrying out agreed decisions."

reduce the inflation at the least possible cost. Experience of many countries which have suffered from hyperinflations indicates that a necessary component of inflation reduction is greatly reducing the government budget deficit. Having this information, a welfare-maximizing policymaker would cut the government budget deficit. What we observe in fact is that in many high-inflation economies, where it is agreed that deficit reduction is a necessary component of an inflation stabilization program, deficit reduction is long delayed while inflation accelerates. The positive political economy question is whether the political constraints on making budgetary decisions can explain this delay, and, furthermore, how the length of delay will reflect different political mechanisms for resolving budgetary conflicts. The normative political economy question is how to design policies or mechanisms for choosing policies which will hasten agreement on how to cut the budget deficit. This approach to the political economy of hyperinflation will be addressed in Chapter 10.

To take another example, consider the question of the transition of the formerly socialist countries of Central and Eastern Europe to market economies. Though it is generally agreed that economic efficiency and social welfare will be substantially higher once a market system of allocation is in place, the transition has been slow, far slower than observers expected at the outset on the basis of the technical constraints. Political opposition from groups that will be hurt in the transition and under the new regime has been a significant factor in determining the pace of reform. Hence, crucial to understanding transition policies and their outcomes are the conflicts between different interest groups in the economy. The relative performance of different transition economies reflects not only their differing economic characteristics, but differing political characteristics as well. We consider the political economy of large-scale economic reform and transition in Chapter 13.

Disciplines Compared

Given the definition of new political economy, one may ask how it differs from the related fields of public economics (or public finance) and of public choice. Public economics is concerned generally with the economics of the public sector, meaning how economic decisions of the government affect economic actors. Positive public economics concerns the effects of tax and expenditure policies on individual and firm behavior. Although positive public economics broadly defined includes political theories of the state, the main focus is on the effect of tax and expenditure policies. To the extent that public economics addresses the question of how tax and expenditure policies are chosen, it is primarily from the perspective of neoclassical welfare economics, that is, taking the government's objective of welfare maximization as given and asking how tax and expenditure policies, rather than direct "command," may be used to achieve the objective of welfare maximization. This is the subject matter of normative public economics. One area of normative public finance is the formulation of simple criteria for government decisionmaking, but this is not in terms of choosing the objective to be maximized, but of choosing criteria and methods to achieve the optimum.[7]

The question of how the objectives are chosen, that is, how collective choices are made, is the subject matter of public choice. That is, public choice is concerned largely with studying decisionmaking mechanisms *per se*, considering not only the positive and normative aspects of different ways of making collective choices, but also the question of how a society can choose over the set of possible choice mechanisms. Public choice differs from political science, in that it stresses the use of tools of economic analysis to study collective choices. As Mueller (1989, p. 1) concisely defines it, "Public choice can be defined as the economic study of nonmarket decision making, or simply the application of economics to political science." We consider the subject matter of public choice in a bit more detail in our treatment of decisionmaking mechanisms in Chapter 3 and again in Chapter 9 in the discussion of problems of collective action.

Public choice and political economy as defined here are clearly closely related. Many treatments of the new political economy would not make a distinction between the fields, arguing that public choice is an integral part of the new political economy. There is much to this argument. First, both public choice and new political economy, namely, the study of the effects of political constraints on economic outcomes using specific analytical tools, are defined not so much by their subject matter as by their analytical and methodological approach. Second, since policy outcomes may depend on the intricacies of the decisionmaking process (consider, for example, the formulation of international trade policy), it may be unproductive to make a distinction between the fields in specific applications. Our distinction is meant more to highlight the subject matter of this book. Our interest is in the *effect* of politics on economic outcomes, not on politics *per se*. Though the stress is on using tools of economic analysis, the interest is not in choice mechanisms themselves. Moreover, there are already excellent textbook treatments of public choice and mathematical political science by practitioners, while there is no comprehensive textbook treatment of the effects of politics on macroeconomic outcomes in any generality.

1.3. TYPES OF HETEROGENEITY

What ties politics, public choice, and political economy together is the centrality of heterogeneity of interests. Were there no heterogeneity of preferences over outcomes, there would be no need for a mechanism to

---

[7] The subject matter of normative public finance will be touched on at many points in the book, especially in the discussion of public goods in Chapter 9.

aggregate individual preferences into a collective choice. Similarly, were there no conflicts of interests whatsoever, the choice of economic policy would be that of the social planner maximizing the utility of the representative individual. (Remember the quote from Atkinson and Stiglitz (1980) in footnote 6.) It is heterogeneity of interests that is the basis of the field of political economy.

At this point, one may argue that heterogeneity of interests is also central to much of economics. Markets are driven by heterogeneity as well, heterogeneity of tastes, of endowments, and of expectations. Why not therefore argue that heterogeneity is the basis not only of the field of political economy, but also of market economics itself? The argument on the importance of heterogeneity for political economy may be summarized in two propositions. First, heterogeneity or conflict of interests is necessary for there to be political constraints. Second, the effect of politics on economics follows from the mechanisms by which these conflicts are resolved. The first point is clear—heterogeneity is a *necessary* condition. It can be read as saying only that without heterogeneity, there would be nothing to study. It is the second which is really our focus, and, to my mind, defines political economy. Heterogeneity is also necessary for there to be markets, but heterogeneity of interests plays out quite differently when addressed through the market than through the political process. For example, the effect of heterogeneity of abilities on distribution of income mediated simply through the market will be quite different than the income distribution which would result when individuals can lobby for transfers, based on their endowed abilities. How much different will depend on the political mechanism by which tax-and-transfer policy is decided.[8] Moreover, there are numerous issues where individuals have a heterogeneity of interests where the market mechanism either cannot be used or simply is not used to determine outcomes, the political choice mechanism being used instead.

Given the necessity of conflict of interests for there to be a political economy problem, one is led to ask: what are important types of heterogeneity for political economy? There are many, which we find useful to separate into two basic classes, giving rise to two crucial types of conflict of interests. The first conflict reflects underlying heterogeneity of actors "coming into" the political arena, implying they have different policy preferences. There are a number of reasons. They may simply have different tastes over goods, broadly defined, or different relative factor endowments. They may find themselves in different situations not easily summarized in terms of tastes or endowments that lead them to prefer different policies. Or, they may just differ in how they think the world works, and hence what policies would best achieve a given aim. In short,

[8] Lindblom (1977) discusses at length the conceptual differences between markets and political institutions as allocation devices, and the implications of these differences.

individuals are heterogeneous in a number of dimensions, leading them to prefer different policies *ex ante*. We apply to this heterogeneity the general term **ex-ante heterogeneity**, which plays a crucial role in political economy.

There is another central type of heterogeneity. Even when political-economic actors have the same "primitives"—endowments, preferences, etc. —there will generally still be a conflict of interests. Actors may all equally value a good, but there is conflict if its distribution (if it is private) or the distribution of the costs of providing it (if it is public) is determined by a collective choice. Economic policies generally have distributional implications. Therefore, when a policy does (or *can*) have distributional consequences, self-interested "representative" agents will be in conflict over distribution. This includes the rents that office-holding may provide to those in office, whether these are pecuniary benefits or simply the "ego rents" associated with holding office. Since "distribution" can also refer to conflicts arising from *ex-ante* heterogeneity of factor endowments, we use the general term **ex-post heterogeneity** for this type of heterogeneity.

These two concepts of heterogeneity will appear in various forms throughout the book. One should note that these are not by any means mutually exclusive. In discussions of supply of a public good, for example, there may be conflict over the importance of the public good relative to other expenditures, reflecting *ex-ante* heterogeneity, as well as conflict over who should bear the cost of supplying the public good, which is *ex-post* heterogeneity. To take another example, conflict over the size of income assistance programs in the budget combines distribution of a private good whose burden may be seen as a public good, not to mention the ideological conflict over the proper role of the state in providing income transfers.

We end this section with two notes on the relevance of our argument that heterogeneity of interests is central to political economy. First, *ex-post* heterogeneity is important not only in questions of income redistribution, but also in understanding the political aspects of some "representative" agent problems, problems where it might initially appear that heterogeneity plays no substantial role. Specifically, consider imperfect credibility of policy due to the possibility of time inconsistency, which is the subject of Chapter 4. Time inconsistency is said to arise if the optimal policy chosen at t_1 for date t_1 differs from the optimal policy for t_1 which was chosen at $t_0 < t_1$, even though technology, preferences, and information are the same at the two dates. Time inconsistency refers to more than a policy-maker announcing a policy for t_1 at t_0 and then enacting a different policy at t_1 if it suits his own interests. Time inconsistency is especially interesting because it can arise even when the planner is maximizing the welfare of a representative individual. Hence, heterogeneity would appear to play no role. We will argue in Chapter 4 that this is not correct. In models where the government is maximizing the welfare of a representative individual, time inconsistency arises only when there is an important *ex-post* heterogeneity. That is, in such models all individuals may be identical *ex ante*, but are not identical *ex post*. In fact, we shall argue that *ex-post* heterogeneity is key to the possibility of time inconsistency in the presence of a "benevolent" government.[9]

Second, the reader may still feel uncomfortable with the argument that the distinction between political and nonpolitical problems turns on the heterogeneity of interests and how they are handled. We had indicated above that markets are also driven by heterogeneity, but that the effects of heterogeneity are quite different when mediated in the market than when addressed by a political process or social planner. What about the study of social welfare maximization with heterogeneous individuals? This is the topic of multiple-agent welfare economics, where *ex-ante* or *ex-post* heterogeneity of actors is central to the analysis of optimal policy choice. How does it differ from political economy? Though heterogeneity is central to both areas, there is a key difference. Welfare economics takes as given the multi-agent objective function, which weights the importance of heterogeneous agents for social welfare. That is, the "say" that different actors have in determining the policy outcome is taken as exogenous, the focus of analysis being the calculation of optimal policy given the objective function. In contrast, in political economy, a main focus is often the endogenous determination of the objective that is to be implicitly maximized. The weights in the implied objective function are not exogenous; they are determined by the political process and in turn determine the economic outcome. In the next section we make this distinction clearer by comparing fields and their approach to heterogeneity through a specific example.

1.4. AN ILLUSTRATION OF APPROACHES

The points of the previous two sections, both on the role of heterogeneity and conflict of interests and on the comparison of disciplines, may be better understood by considering a specific economic problem and asking two questions. First, how might heterogeneity of interests manifest in a specific example and what issues does it raise? Second, how can we better characterize and understand the differences between the disciplines discussed in Section 1.2 by how their focus differs with respect to this problem? Hence, in this section, we consider a basic dynamic optimization problem in economics, namely, the choice between consumption today and consumption tomorrow, and ask what issues it raises with respect to multi-agent welfare economics, public finance, public choice, and political

---

[9] An alternative view of time inconsistency is that it reflects the decisionmaker having different preferences over time, a sort of *ex-ante* heterogeneity. This approach will also be considered in Chapter 4.

economy. The example will also make clear the centrality of heterogeneity to questions of politics and political economy.

The Optimal Saving Problem

Ricardo Smith must decide on how much of his income to consume today and how much to save, that is, accumulate as capital, which produces income next period. He has a two-period horizon, so his decision on how much to save is how much to consume tomorrow. Given his preferences over consumption today and consumption tomorrow, as represented by his utility function, standard maximization techniques, in this case, simple calculus, will allow him to choose saving optimally.

Now, suppose that instead of a two-period horizon, Smith has an infinite horizon. In each period he faces the same decision problem, with the value of saving at any date t depending on the value he assigns to consumption at $t + 1$ (and the return to capital), which in turn depends on the value of consumption at $t + 2$, *et cetera*. His choice problem can be seen as choosing a sequence of optimal consumption levels, one for each date t; though conceptually identical to the two-period problem, the infinite horizon makes this problem technically more difficult. The key point to note is that the "decision problem" is a technical one, that is, how to find an optimal consumption sequence over an infinite horizon, given his preferences. For example, under some fairly unrestrictive conditions, dynamic programming may be used. (An exposition of the method of dynamic programming applied to the optimal saving problem is presented in Chapter 2.)

In an economy composed of a number of identical individuals, the choice problem of a social planner maximizing the utility of a representative individual would be identical, and the same techniques may be used to solve for the consumption sequence that maximizes social welfare. The social planner's problem with a representative agent represents the baseline case in standard welfare economics. The emphasis in welfare economics is on identifying what is the optimal policy, *given* the welfare function to be maximized subject to constraints. Hence, as above, the "decision process" refers only to the *technical* process of solving a set of equations. This may be mathematically difficult (for example, in some dynamic optimization problems), but there is *no* political problem arising from a conflict of objectives.

Ex-Ante Heterogeneity

To introduce *ex-ante* heterogeneity and conflict of interests, suppose that Smith is part of a group that makes collective consumption decisions, where there are several types of individuals in the group with different consumption preferences. For example, the Smith family (all with identical preferences) each summer rents a two-family house together with the family of Robinson Malthus, whose vacation preferences are the same within the family, but differ from those of the Smiths. Hence, a decision must be made on what sort of house to rent. To simplify the exposition, let us begin with a very simple set-up. Suppose there are enough resources left over from previous years for two summers' worth of vacations, and the decision is simply how much to spend on this year's vacation and how much to save and spend on next year's vacation. Suppose there are only two types of individuals in the group—the Smiths prefer a fancier, more expensive house this summer, while the Malthus family prefers a less expensive house this summer, allowing more resources to be saved for next summer. These differences in preferences could be represented by different utility attached to the current summer's consumption, or, in a many-period framework, by a different discount factor β relating the utility of current and future consumption.

Standard welfare economics handles the case of many agents with different preferences by considering a social planner maximizing a weighted sum of individual utilities (a social welfare function), where the weight on each type is *exogenously* given, say α to the preferences of the Smithians, $1 - \alpha$ to the preferences of the Malthusians.[10] A level of current consumption will result from this maximization problem, where it will reflect the value of α. As in the representative agent problem, the planner's decision problem refers to the problem of technically deriving the optimum for any value of α. If α is high, so that the Smithians' utility is more heavily weighted in the social welfare function, the chosen saving rate ("chosen" in the normative, and, therefore, implemented in the positive sense as well) will be closer to their preferred policy, that is, lower. The planner's solution will be **Pareto efficient**, in that neither type of individual could be made better off without the other being made worse off. A typical problem in multi-agent welfare economics would be to ask how the chosen optimum would be affected by an exogenous change in the weights, that is, to derive the **contract curve**, the set of such Pareto-efficient points.

Ex-Post Heterogeneity

The concept of *ex-post* heterogeneity may be easily represented in this example as well. Suppose that both families have exactly the same preferences for what type of house to rent this summer, and hence the same preferences over current and future consumption. However, each family would like to have the nicer half, or perhaps the larger half of the house for itself. That is, they value current consumption equally and care about the distribution of consumption benefits. We could represent this as a problem in welfare economics in which the two types of individuals have

---

[10] The temptation to call the social planner Summers is almost irresistible.

the same utility function and discount rate, but can be assigned different levels of current consumption. The planner's problem can be represented as choosing a level and distribution of current consumption to maximize discounted utility over the two summers. If the distribution of consumption between the Smith and Malthus families could be represented as a continuous variable (let us say, square feet of house space!), standard calculus techniques could be used to find the planner's optimum. As before, the planner's problem is a technical one, finding the optimal consumption vector for given α, with different values of α corresponding to different consumption allocations. The higher α is, the more house space the planner would assign to the Smith family.

Political Economy

By this point, the reader may be a bit amused by this example. The two sorts of conflict of interests between the Smith and Malthus families are easily recognizable, but the social planner is not. Who is this social planner who is making collective consumption decisions for the Smiths and Malthus's? What relation does the social planner's problem with an exogenous weight α on Smithian consumption have to the problem the two families face—resolving the conflict over collective consumption when they have different preferences? The short answer is very little if any. This is not because the multi-agent welfare economics problem is poorly formed, but because it misses key issues we associate with conflicts of interest. How in fact are conflicts of interest resolved? What implications does the need to resolve conflicts (and the way they are resolved) have for economic outcomes? Deriving the optimal policy once society has chosen how to weight the preferences of different groups does not treat these problems.

In the case of two families with different preferences trying to plan a joint vacation, we may think of various ways in which they try to resolve their conflicts. Coming to a joint decision is usually not too difficult, but the problem they face is a political one in microcosm. When we consider not two individuals or families, but an economy as a whole making collective choices on saving and investment, the political problem of resolving conflicts of interests is not so simple, and the economic implications of how the conflicts are resolved are far larger. To continue with our comparison of different disciplines by considering a specific economic problem, the reader should continue thinking of the consumption versus saving problem, but now in an economy composed of many, heterogeneous individuals.

Political economy starts with the problem of choice in a society with heterogeneous agents, but with a very different focus than multi-agent welfare economics. The focus is on the process by which it is decided what policy to adopt, and, more specifically, on what policy choice will emerge from a specific political process. The issue is not the *technical* problem of the implication of different weights, but the *political* problem of how the weights are chosen (representing the question of how conflicts of interests are resolved) and its economic implications. In the consumption versus saving problem with either *ex-ante* heterogeneity (difference in how present and future are weighted) or *ex-post* heterogeneity (the incentive to increase one's share of current consumption at the expense of others), the focus is on the implications for capital accumulation of the society's current aggregate consumption being politically determined. This means both how the political mechanism determines the α in a political-economic equilibrium and how this decision in turn affects capital accumulation and welfare. Heterogeneity of interests is crucial for the problem to be of any political interest. If all individuals had the same discount factor and there was no possibility for consumption to differ across individuals, societal and individual variables would be identical, no matter what the collective choice mechanism, and there would be no political problem.

The idea that the political process may *bias* the result away from a socially preferred solution has at least two aspects to it. First, society as a whole may have preferences over efficient outcomes, but the outcome emerging from the political process, even if Pareto-efficient, may be different from what society finds optimal. For example, given their preferences over income distribution in the society as a whole, individuals may find the political-economic equilibrium far from optimal, even if both exercise of political power and redistribution absorb no economic resources. Second, and more important, the political process by which economic policy is chosen will generally absorb resources in one way or another, leading to an economically inefficient outcome. The most interesting economic implications of heterogeneity and conflict of interests stem not from determining which point on the contract curve is chosen. They stem from the fact that the political process implies the economy is "off the contract curve," that is, in an equilibrium that is economically inefficient, often markedly inefficient.

Public Economics and Public Choice

The optimal saving problem may also be used to sharpen the distinction between political economy (as defined here), on the one hand, and public finance and public choice on the other. Consider first a public finance perspective. In the multi-agent welfare economics problem, the social planner was modeled as choosing consumption levels directly. Alternatively, one may think of a "decentralized" problem, in which the planner does not choose quantities directly; instead, the optimal allocation is achieved via a price system, in which individuals choose their desired levels of consumption and saving on the basis of market prices. The problem is transformed from finding optimal quantities to finding prices that support these quantities. This too is a "technical" problem in the sense set out above. A major question in normative public finance is the derivation of optimal tax and public pricing structures given technological and informational constraints.[11] Positive public finance forms the basis of the normative analysis, where the objective function is taken as given. A public finance "solution" to the multiple-agent decentralized growth problem is a set of tax rates, one on each type of agent at each point of time, that supports the chosen consumption allocation, which itself is derived from the given α.

In contrast, in a political economy model of determination of tax rates, conflict over whose preferences will be reflected in aggregate policy may induce a conflict over tax rates. For example, different preferences over current versus future consumption will induce different preferences over consumption taxes. Conflict over tax policy may also reflect *ex-post* heterogeneity, as individuals use the tax system to try to redistribute resources towards themselves. In both types of cases, conflict over tax structure can lead to grossly inefficient outcomes. Positive public finance forms the basis not of a normative analysis as discussed in the previous paragraph, but of calculating the economic consequences of choosing any particular tax policy, corresponding, for example, to different values of α. The focus would be on what resolution of this conflict of interests is implied by the political mechanism, and, on the basis of positive public finance, the implications for economic magnitudes.

From a public choice perspective, the interesting question is the implications for equilibrium α of different choice mechanisms, more specifically, the formal analysis of how collective choice mechanisms translate into specific policy choices. Relative to the political economy focus in this book, there is far more stress on the positive and normative workings of these mechanisms, far less on the economic consequences. For example, in an economy with many different interests to be weighted in a social welfare function, how will the weights differ under simple majority voting versus more complicated voting procedures? Or, if the weights are chosen in a representative democracy, where the elected representatives then bargain over them, how will a change in election procedures in the first stage, or rules of agenda in the second, affect the equilibrium weights that emerge from this process? In the theory of public choice, the economic implications in terms of an aggregate path of saving are a decidedly secondary consideration (though more important in applied public choice). In fact, the economic application is often not relevant in the analysis of the implication of voting rules, and the analysis often abstracts away from it.

---

[11] In the next chapter we solve a simple, but important public pricing problem under asymmetric information.

1.5. PLAN OF THE BOOK

The book is divided into four parts. The first part of the book, comprising this chapter and the following two, are meant to set the stage for the study of political economy. The next chapter is meant to familiarize readers with a number of useful economic models. Some models and techniques are, however, introduced in chapters as they are used. Chapter 3 concentrates on the subject of "politics" *per se*, concentrating on mechanisms for making collective choices.

In Part II, we investigate the problem of time inconsistency, representing a crucial distortion away from the first-best optimum that can arise even when policy is chosen by a social welfare maximizer with an infinite horizon. Chapter 4 introduces the problem and presents two widely studied models, as well as discussing intuitively why problems of time inconsistency arise. A key argument in the chapter is that time inconsistency reflects heterogeneity of interests and would be absent if such heterogeneity were absent. This view, consistent with the approach of the book, differs from the standard view of time inconsistency. Chapters 5 and 6 consider "solutions" to the problem of time inconsistency. In Chapter 5, we concentrate on how the policymaking environment can make policy credible, that is, how institutions or the creation of external circumstances (broadly defined) can lead to the expectation that announced policies will be carried out. Put simply, we consider mechanisms by which a policymaker can commit himself to a desired policy. In Chapter 6, we consider commitment through repeated interactions, so that policy choice can be made credible. We concentrate on investing policy with credibility by the policymaker building a reputation, that is, by engendering the expectation that certain policies will be followed in the future on the basis of actions that have been observed in the past. These chapters, especially Chapter 6, present much of the game-theoretic basis for analysis so widely used in the new political economy and that will be used repeatedly in the book.

In Part III, we address phenomena of heterogeneity and conflicting interests directly. In Chapter 7, we consider the crucial role in the political economy of macroeconomics of elections, and more generally, expectations of possible changes in policymakers. This includes numerous models of the political business cycle (including a detailed empirical assessment), models of interactions of the executive and the legislature (including discussion of non-American phenomena, such as coalition governments and endogenous timing of elections) and various aspects of "tying the hands" of successor governments. In Chapter 8, we consider numerous aspects of redistribution of income and wealth, including using transfers to court voters, pork-barrel politics, rent-seeking, intergenerational and cross-jurisdictional redistribution. Chapter 9 covers many aspects of public goods, not only the classical theory, but also collective action, clubs, and dynamic models of the supply of public goods. Several of these models form the basis of studying the effects of the political nature of decisionmaking on macroeconomic aspects. Chapter 10 is important both in its own right and as a bridge between Part II and Part IV on applications. We consider four general classes of models in which heterogeneity and conflict of interests lead to the nonadoption or the delayed adoption of socially beneficial policies. We also consider the role of crisis in enabling the adoption of such policies.

Part IV presents applications of the models of earlier chapters to specific areas. Chapter 11 covers the political economy of factor accumulation and growth, including models of redistributive pressures, market imperfections, and the link between political institutions and growth. Given its prominence in the literature, there is also a detailed discussion of empirical determinants of growth. Chapter 12 covers a wide range of political economy issues connected with macroeconomics of the open economy, including exchange rate arrangements, currency crises, international policy cooperation, capital controls, sovereign debt, and foreign aid. Chapter 13 presents a more applied approach to the political economy of large-scale economic reform and transition, with special emphasis on the transition from socialism and central planning to markets. This includes the political economy of labor reallocation, privatization, and price liberalization. Chapter 14 covers a number of topics on the political economy of the size of government (specifically, growth of government) as well as recent work on the size and number of nations.

CHAPTER TWO

Economic Models for Political Analysis

> The economic structure of society [is] the real foundation
> on which arises a legal and political superstructure.
>
> —*Karl Marx*, A Contribution to the Critique of
> Political Economy

> If there ever existed a monarchy strong as granite, it would
> only take the ideas of economists to reduce it to powder.
>
> —*Napoleon, from* Las Cases, Mémorial de Ste-Hélène,
> *June 17, 1816*

2.1. INTRODUCTION

In Chapter 1, we defined political economy as the study of how the political nature of decisionmaking affects policy choices and, ultimately, economic outcomes. This focus is based on the fact that in the real world, economic policy is not chosen by the social planner who safely inhabits economics textbooks, sheltered from agents with conflicting interests while he calculates optimal policy. Economic policy is the result of a decision process that balances conflicting interests so that a collective choice may emerge. This is what we meant by the phrase "the political nature of decisionmaking." In order to study political economy, that is, to study the effects of politics on economic outcomes, we must therefore begin with some political and economic building blocks.

One building block is decisionmaking mechanisms themselves. When there are conflicts of interests over economic policies, so that different groups have different preferred policies, some mechanism must be used for choosing *a* policy. That is what is meant by a *collective* choice mechanism, that is, a mechanism for "aggregating" diverse preferences into a single collective preference or policy not in a technical sense of simply weighting individual preferences to derive a social welfare function, but in the political sense of investing a decision with authority, so that it becomes accepted policy. This is the subject of Chapter 3, where mechanisms for making collective choices are described.

The other building block is an economic model, used to study both the positive question of how policies affect outcomes and the normative question of how to evaluate these effects for individual and social welfare. A number of economic tools and models that are useful in political economy analysis are considered in this chapter. The chapter is not, however, an all-inclusive reference for the techniques that are used in the book. First, it is assumed that readers are familiar with basic mathematical techniques such as simple differentiation and integration of functions and static optimization. Mathematical techniques beyond these basics are covered either in this chapter or when they are used. For example, tools of game theory, which are used throughout the book, will be introduced in Chapter 6 on reputation. Second, when it seems more appropriate, specific models will be introduced when they are used. For example, the expectations-augmented inflation-unemployment trade-off, used repeatedly, is introduced in Chapter 4.

What does this chapter cover? We exposit four models in this chapter, some or all of which should be familiar to someone with graduate training in economics. This chapter is meant to serve a variety of audiences. Those familiar with the models may skip or quickly skim the chapter, concentrating on its discussion of the relation of these techniques to political economy. The detail given in the chapter is meant more for those unfamiliar with the techniques, since lack of familiarity with basic elements of technical economic analysis means that much will be lost in studying the models in the rest of the book.

In Section 2.2, we present the basic principal–agent model and some extensions. The principal–agent relation is highly relevant for political analysis, and after presenting the basic model and results, we discuss the conceptual relation between the model and political economy. Readers familiar with the principal–agent model should skip the basic formal exposition presented here and simply skim the conceptual discussion.

In the subsequent two sections, we present two basic tools for discrete-time analysis. First, we present the method of dynamic programming in Section 2.3. Though we do not use dynamic programming as a direct solution technique extremely often, it provides a way of viewing dynamic problems (as summarized by the "value" function) that is extremely useful in thinking about dynamic optimization. As with the principal–agent model, readers familiar with dynamic programming may skip the basic exposition; those not familiar with the technique, but who are interested mainly in less technical aspects of the analysis in the book, may nonetheless benefit from the intuitive discussion.

In Section 2.4, we present the basic overlapping-generations model with capital accumulation, which in various forms is used throughout the book. Its widespread use reflects the extraordinary combination of tractability and analytical power the model provides. Unlike the other models presented in the chapter, the model is not used to provide deeper intuition for either economic or political analysis. Its inclusion here is motivated simply by its usefulness. Those unfamiliar with the model should work through it, or at least refer back to this section as needed later in the book; those familiar with the model may skip this section.

In Section 2.5, we present a model for continuous-time dynamic analysis. The model is considerably more difficult than the others in this chapter, and the techniques introduced are used only sparingly later in the book. The section is included mainly for two reasons. First, the principal issue discussed, namely, the effects of uncertainty about future government policies on economic decisions, has important political implications. Second, the specific technique for analyzing the effect of uncertainty about future policies on current dynamics will be of interest to students who want to analyze technically this and related questions. However, the model is not crucial to the subsequent development of the book and may be omitted by those less interested in analytical techniques.

Let us expand on the earlier points on the conceptual relevance of these models, especially those in Sections 2.2 and 2.5. In addition to technique, we are interested in the question of how the political nature of policymaking affects economic decisionmaking. When decisionmaking is political, outcomes will differ not only because the policies chosen will be affected. Outcomes will also differ because specific policies emerging from the collective choice mechanism will have different effects than if they were chosen by a social planner. This reflects the fact that the reaction of economic actors to a given policy may depend very much on how that policy was chosen. Why? Economic actors, whether individuals or firms, are both *strategic* and *forward-looking*. They are "strategic" in the sense that they realize policies come not from a social welfare calculator, but from an agent who has his own incentives (or pressures from other agents) in choosing policies. Hence, when policy choice is delegated to policymakers through some mechanism of representative democracy (see Section 3.5 of Chapter 3), individuals and firms must take into account the incentives of their policymaking agent. Actors are forward-looking in that their optimal choice of actions today depends not only on current policies, but also on what they expect their future environment to be, both future policies themselves and the future policymaking environment. Expected future government policies may be especially important in determining behavior. Individuals and firms will use all available information to try to forecast these policies, including their knowledge of the collective choice process itself.

2.2. The Principal–Agent Problem

The delegation of decisions to policymakers with different preferences is pervasive in the making of collective choices. In fact, one may argue it is *inherent* to collective decisionmaking. In any society with a large number of interests, decisionmaking will necessarily be representative, in that individuals will choose representatives to make policy who do *not* have exactly the same preferences as they do over policies. Not every position can be directly represented, so that delegation in the above sense follows almost automatically from heterogeneity of interests in the population as a whole. The relation between the policies that are chosen and the policies individuals desire will depend on the preferences of the representatives and on the incentives that the voters give them. Hence, from a theoretical perspective, representative politics is an example of a *principal–agent problem*. This is true not only in representative democracy as a whole, that is, in the role of voters in choosing their representatives in the legislative and executive branches of government, but also *within* the workings of these organizations. The principal–agent paradigm is also useful, and sometimes central, to other political relationships as well, such as international policy cooperation and gaining support for large-scale economic reform and transition.

Background

The **principal–agent problem** is a general problem of *mechanism* design under incomplete information. In the applications that we use, an "agent" takes actions "on behalf of" a "principal," where the optimal action from the principal's point of view depends on some information known only to the agent. Examples of principal–agent relations include: patient–doctor, where the latter has superior medical knowledge and information affecting the former; depositor–bank, where the latter has superior information on loan riskiness and quality; and, employer–employee, where the latter's effort on the job is unobserved. The relation between a voter and a policymaker is also a principal–agent relation, though it is not the only one of importance in political economy. In some problems, such as taxation under imperfect observability of individual abilities, it is the government that is the principal, and the taxpayer who is the agent. In problems of economic transition and restructuring under asymmetric information, it is also the government that is the principal. The principal–agent relation is characterized by a difference in interests between the principal and an agent, so we should not be surprised by its wide applicability.

In general, an agent will not report crucial information to the principal unless given the incentive to do so. This incentive may be either monetary transfers or some other incentive under the control of the principal. In the case of the voter–policymaker relation, a major tool of control is the electoral mechanism. Providing incentives may be costly, so that the resulting allocation may be inefficient relative to the full-information solution. This should not be automatically equated with political inefficiency, since the "distortion" which may arise from the political nature of decisionmaking is measured relative to the available information.

A key characteristic of the general principal–agent problem is that the relation between the principal and the agent is not exogenous; it is chosen by the principal to maximize his expected utility. This focus on endogenous mechanisms of control will sometimes limit the applicability of the principal–agent paradigm to political problems, but it will not eliminate it. In some problems, such as sovereign borrowing in Section 12.8 of Chapter 12, the paradigm can be applied directly. In others, where a mechanism has been institutionally determined, the principal–agent paradigm may still be a very useful tool of analysis.

An Example

We will illustrate the principal–agent problem with a simple example of nonlinear pricing of government services, following Fudenberg and Tirole (1991). Readers interested in a more general formulation can refer to chapter 7 of their text, or to any reasonably advanced text in microeconomic theory. It may seem more natural to use an example unique to governmental or political relations, such as taxation when individual characteristics are unobserved, so that the government chooses a nonlinear tax schedule to elicit maximum effort or saving from individuals. We choose this example so that participation constraints are not automatically binding, as one might argue they will be in taxation or provision of public goods under some political mechanisms. Another fully worked out example of an optimal contract between principal and agent under incomplete information may be found in Section 12.8 of Chapter 12, giving the optimal contract between a lender and a sovereign borrower.

Suppose the government (the "principal") must finance its services by selling a good it produces at constant marginal cost w to a single consumer (the "agent"). The government prefers more net revenue G to less (the consumer is a foreigner, or the government values the "general welfare," financed by tariff revenues, over the welfare of this consumer). It sells a quantity y to the consumer in exchange for a total payment τ. The consumer's utility may be written

$$\Omega(y, \tau, \theta) = \theta u(y) - \tau, \tag{2.1}$$

where $u(\cdot)$ is an increasing concave function with $u(0) = 0$. The function $u(\cdot)$ is known to both government and consumer (it is *common knowledge*); θ is known only to the consumer, but not to the government (that is, information is *asymmetric*). The government knows only the probability distribution of possible values of θ. For simplicity, suppose θ can take on only two values $\theta^L > 0$ with probability q and $\theta^H > \theta^L$ with probability $1 - q$.

The sale of government output proceeds as follows. The government specifies for each level of output y the size of the tariff τ the consumer is required to pay in exchange. Hence the government can be seen as offering a schedule $\tau(y)$, which the consumer can either accept, buying some level y for a payment of $\tau(y)$, or reject, buying nothing. Without loss of generality, one can assume that one point on this schedule is $\tau(0) = 0$, so that the consumer always accepts the mechanism. If the government knew the consumer's true valuation of the service, that is, knew θ, the consumer's "type", it would offer a given quantity y^0 and charge a tariff $\tau^0 = \theta u(y^0)$, extracting all the consumer surplus. The quantity y^0 would be determined by maximizing net revenue $G = \theta u(y) - wy$, that is, by the condition $\theta u'(y^0) = w$. However, the government does not know the consumer's type. With two types of consumers, it offers a tariff schedule with two points or "bundles": (y^H, τ^H), intended for the type-H consumer; and (y^L, τ^L), intended for the type-L consumer. The "mechanism design" problem is to choose the two possibilities to maximize expected net revenue, which is

$$EG = q(\tau^L - wy^L) + (1 - q)(\tau^H - wy^H). \qquad (2.2)$$

In a principal–agent problem, one generally considers two types of constraints on the principal in designing an optimal mechanism, here, the government in choosing a tariff schedule $\tau(y)$. The first is called a **participation** or **individual-rationality** constraint, which requires that the agent always be willing, that is, find it individually rational, to participate in the relationship. In this example, since the consumer gets zero utility from not purchasing, the individual-rationality constraint requires that each type of consumer is at least as well off purchasing the good as not purchasing it. Assuming temporarily that each type of consumer purchases the quantity designated for him, the individual-rationality constraints can be written

$$\text{IR}_\text{L} \qquad \theta^L u(y^L) - \tau^L \geq 0,$$
$$\qquad\qquad\qquad\qquad\qquad\qquad\qquad (2.3)$$
$$\text{IR}_\text{H} \qquad \theta^H u(y^H) - \tau^H \geq 0.$$

The other type of constraint is called an **incentive compatibility** constraint, implying that each type of agent willingly chooses the bundle intended for him. (It is sometimes termed a "self-selection" criterion, whereby the mechanism induces each agent to reveal his true type by his choice, or selection, of bundle.) In this example, the incentive compatibility constraint requires that each of the two types prefers to consume the bundle designated for him, given his valuation θ, rather than the bundle designated for the other type. The incentive compatibility constraints can be written

$$\text{IC}_L \qquad \theta^L u(y^L) - \tau^L \geq \theta^L u(y^H) - \tau^H,$$

$$\text{IC}_H \qquad \theta^H u(y^H) - \tau^H \geq \theta^H u(y^L) - \tau^L. \qquad (2.4)$$

The government chooses the schedule $\tau(y)$ to maximize its expected net revenue (2.2), subject to the four constraints in (2.3) and (2.4), namely, IR_L, IR_H, IC_L, and IC_H.

Finding the Solution

In a problem such as this, only some of the IR and IC constraints will bind, that is, will hold with equality, and those will be used to calculate the optimal mechanism. The others will be strict inequalities, and will be implied by those constraints that bind. To solve for the schedule, one begins by showing which constraints bind; in this example, only IR_L and IC_H will be binding. Note first that if IR_L and IC_H are satisfied, then IR_H will be satisfied as well. This follows from combining IC_H and IR_L with $\theta^H > \theta^L$ to obtain

$$\theta^H u(y^H) - \tau^H \geq \theta^H u(y^L) - \tau^L \geq \theta^L u(y^L) - \tau^L \geq 0.$$

This result reflects the fact that type θ^H receives a higher surplus from consuming y than does type θ^L. In fact, type θ^L receives no surplus, the last weak inequality in the above expression holding as a strict equality, that is, $\tau^L = \theta^L u(y^L)$. No more than one IR constraint need bind; as long as $y^L > 0$, IR_H is not binding (i.e., it holds with strict inequality). But then, IR_L must be binding. Otherwise, if neither IR constraint were binding, the government could increase its revenue by increasing τ^H and τ^L and still satisfy the IR constraints. If they are increased by the same (small) amount, the IC constraints will be satisfied as well.

Next, note that IC_H will be binding, meaning that the optimal schedule will be such that type θ^H will be indifferent between the bundles (y^H, τ^H) and (y^L, τ^L). The same type of argument that was used for the result that IR_L must bind is used here. If type θ^H were not indifferent, the government could always increase its revenue by raising τ^H until indifference obtained. To see this argument more clearly, consider Figure 2.1, denoting the bundles and indifference curves of the two types drawn through (y^L, τ^L). (Points of higher utility are points to the southeast in the diagram.) Since slope of an indifference curve for a type θ^i is $\theta^i u'(y)$, the indifference curve of type θ^H through any point (y, τ) is always steeper than the indifference curve of type θ^L through the same point. Suppose that type H were not indifferent between the two bundles offered by the

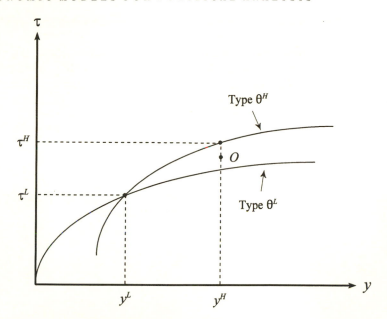

FIGURE 2.1. Indifference curves of the two types.

government, that is, that (y^H, τ^H) was to the southeast of the indifference curve for type H going through (y^L, τ^L), say at point O. The government could then increase its revenue, by moving from point O to (y^H, τ^H).

Figure 2.1 makes clear two crucial characteristics of the optimal schedule. The optimal schedule, from the government's point of view, leaves the low type just indifferent between participating and not participating, that is, he weakly prefers participating. It makes the high type just indifferent between his designated allocation and the allocation designated for the low type, so that he weakly prefers his own allocation. The reason for this should be clear from our discussion in the previous two paragraphs; if not, one should reread them. With more than two types, an optimal mechanism will have the same general characterization—there will be an extreme type, say the "lowest," who is indifferent between participating and not participating. The next highest type is just indifferent between his own allocation and that of the lowest type; the next highest type just indifferent between his allocation and that of the type just below him; and so on. Suitably stated, this could also be used to characterize the nature of the optimal schedule when there is a continuum of types, rather than a discrete number. Moreover, understanding this characterization of the optimal schedule will be useful in understanding the nature of the solution to a number of problems which do not at first glance fit into the principal–agent paradigm. A number of the electoral models in Chapter 7 fit this characterization; the war-of-attrition model in Chapter 9 does as well.

One can now derive the optimal schedule. One solves when IR_L and IC_H are binding, ignoring IC_L, and then verifies that IC_L is satisfied. Maximizing EG in (2.2), subject to IC_H and IR_L binding, is equivalent to maximizing

$$EG = [(q\theta^L - (1 - q)(\theta^H - \theta^L))u(y^L) - qwy^L]$$
$$+ (1 - q)(\theta^H u(y^H) - wy^H). \tag{2.5}$$

Maximizing with respect to y^H and y^L (and assuming that $\theta^L > (1 - q)\theta^H$ and that $u'(0) = 0$), one obtains first-order conditions

$$\theta^L u'(y^L) = \left(1 - \frac{(1 - q)(\theta^H - \theta^L)}{q\theta^L}\right)^{-1} w, \tag{2.6}$$

and

$$\theta^H u'(y^H) = w. \tag{2.7}$$

Equations (2.6) and (2.7), along with IR_L and IC_H, can then be used to compute the optimal schedule.[1]

The quantity of the government-supplied good purchased by the consumer with the high valuation θ^H satisfies the standard optimality condition of marginal utility of consumption equal to the marginal cost of supplying the good. The quantity of the good purchased by the low-valuation consumer, on the other hand, does not satisfy this optimality condition. It is suboptimal. The government must lower the consumption of the low-valuation consumer in order to make it unattractive for the high-valuation consumer to cheat and consume y^L. By so doing, the government can increase τ^H, or, equivalently, reduce the rent the high-valuation consumer receives. (Remember, the low-valuation consumer receives none.) Hence, the government forgoes some efficiency for the purpose of rent extraction.

The Revelation Principle

It is now obvious why the term "self-selection" has been applied to this type of model—the optimal schedule gets types to reveal themselves by their choice of bundles. Put another way, this example illustrates what is

---

[1] One may easily show that under this solution, IC_L is satisfied. We saw above that IR_H is satisfied whenever IR_L is.

known as the **revelation principle**, which states that this game where the principal indirectly elicits the agent's type is equivalent to a "direct revelation game," in which the agent simply announces his type directly. Suppose we denote the optimal tariff schedule as a function of type by $(y^*(\theta), \tau^*(\theta))$ for $\theta = \theta^H, \theta^L$. A direct revelation mechanism would work as follows. The government tells the consumer to announce his type, promising the bundle $(y^*(\theta'), \tau^*(\theta'))$ if he announces that his type is θ'. The incentive constraints IC_H and IC_L imply that both types will find it optimal to truthfully announce their type. Hence, the allocation will be identical to the allocation for the above game. The revelation principle is quite useful in considering more complicated games. We will use it in Chapter 9 to solve the war-of-attrition model, which is a type of principal–agent problem.

Common Agency

One important type of principal–agent problem is that of **common agency**, whereby several principals try to influence the behavior of a single agent. Dixit (1996) argues that common agency is a defining characteristic of many political relationships, such as voters electing a single representative. We will not use formal models of common agency in the book, so we do not exposit them here. Interested readers are referred to Bernheim and Whinston's (1986) seminal paper or to the appendix in Dixit (1996) for a formal treatment. Questions of common agency will arise in a less formal setting, for example in models of politician control, discussed in Section 7.2 of Chapter 7. A general conclusion of models with multiple principals is that the power of incentives to control the agent are very much weakened, sometimes dramatically so.

Application to Political Economy

Analyses of the principal–agent problem stress the effect of asymmetric information between principal and agent on the economic outcome. Equilibrium in a principal–agent relation under incomplete information is characterized by inefficiency relative to a situation of full information. As we have already stressed, however, this inefficiency is not *in itself* evidence of the effect of politics on economic outcomes. In comparing the textbook social planner's to the real-world political solution, we must compare them in the same incomplete information environment. Assuming the social planner has complete information while the political mechanism is subject to incomplete information leads to a false comparison. To use the vernacular, we must compare imperfect-information apples to imperfect-information apples, not to perfect-information oranges.

Keeping this constraint in mind, one can say that the principal–agent nature of many collective choices does have ramifications for economic outcomes, ramifications which reflect the political nature of decisionmaking. First of all, delegation of decisions under imperfect information only has interesting implications if principal and agent do not have identical preferences. If the principal were sure that the agent had exactly the same preferences, there would be no problem of mechanism design. There would be no agency problem. Though this point may seem obvious, it is far from trivial when applied to political economy. The great majority of relationships that define economic life are, in one way or another, agency problems with asymmetric information. The key principal–agent relation in political life, between the governed and those who govern them, has been taken in much of public economics to be characterized by an *identity* of interests between principal and agent. The paradigm is that of a social planner who maximizes the welfare of the representative individual, or of a weighted sum of individuals with different preferences, where the weights are predetermined. Hence, the paradigm of social planner assumes no problem of agency; as argued in the first chapter, the very starting point of political economy is the inapplicability of the paradigm of policy being chosen by a social welfare maximizer. The key fact is heterogeneity of interests that can give rise to agency problems and make the principal–agent paradigm relevant. (As argued in Chapter 4, in contrast to the usual interpretation, heterogeneity of interests is necessary even for the possibility of a time-inconsistency problem under a "benevolent" social welfare maximizer.) In this sense, economic inefficiencies arising from the principal–agent problem are political to the extent that the relevance of the problem is itself political.

There is a second, perhaps more important, sense in which the economic effects of the principal–agent relation under incomplete information reflect more than the information asymmetry itself. Put simply, the political constraint on policymaking is that the policy must have the support of the "electorate," that is, of those who are the source of the policymaker's political authority to make decisions. The principals not only choose to delegate decisions to an agent, but must support the choices he makes, which may significantly affect the policies that can be carried out relative to what is socially optimal. This support constraint implies that under incomplete information, a policymaking agent will often choose policies that are very different from what a social planner would choose under the same information constraint. The need for support at different stages of the relation means that the policies chosen by such an agent may also be very different from what would be chosen under once-and-for-all delegation, even when the mechanism governing this delegation is endogenously determined.

2.3. Discrete-Time Dynamic Models—Dynamic Programming

In this section, we set out some basic principles of optimization in discrete-time models and exposit the solution method of dynamic programming. This treatment is based on Stokey and Lucas (1989), where the interested reader can find further details. The emphasis will be on an intuitive, as opposed to mechanical, understanding. The presentation is also meant to serve as an intuitive introduction to basic concepts of dynamic optimization, concepts that are (or should be) familiar to graduate students in economics. We begin with basic concepts of state and control variables and of transition equations, for those who may be unfamiliar with the conceptual structure of dynamic models.

Some Basic Concepts

A **state variable** is a variable (or one of a set of variables) whose value at a point in time fully determines (along with the values of the other state variables) the state of the system, that is, the values of all the relevant variables in the system. **Control variables** are chosen by the optimizing agent, as a function of the state variable describing the state at the beginning of the period in which the choice is made. The behavior of all other variables either is given exogenously or can be derived from the behavior of the state variables. (For example, in the capital accumulation problem given below, the capital labor ratio k_t is the sole state variable, and k_{t+1} is the control variable. Labor supply is exogenous, while optimal consumption at each t can be derived from k_t. The evolution of the state variables, which determines the dynamic evolution of the system, is determined by **transition equations** for each of the state variables to describe its dynamic behavior. In discrete time, a transition equation gives the value of a state variable at time $t + 1$ as a function of all the state variables at t, known as a *difference equation*, as in the growth example in the previous chapter. In continuous time, the transition equations take the form of *differential equations*, giving the change in a state variable as a function of the state and exogenous equations. The attraction of defining state variables is that by reducing the number of variables one needs to work with, we reduce the complexity of the system.

The concept of the **value function** may be seen as following from the concept of a state variable. Conceptually, the value function represents the fact that the *maximum* present discounted value of the objective function from a point in time onward can be expressed as a function of the state variables at that date. That is, maximum attainable utility from time zero onward is a function of the state of the system at zero, and the value function is the function that summarizes this relation. Since the state variables at a point in time fully determine all other variables both currently and (via the transition equations) at all future dates, including those which enter the objective function, they determine the maximum attainable value of the objective function. For example, in the growth problem below, k_t determines k_{t+1}, which determines k_{t+2}, *et cetera*. The state variable k_t therefore determines the utility-maximizing value of c_t, c_{t+1}, c_{t+2}, *et cetera*, and this maximum attainable value is simply $V(k_t)$. It is important to note that we do not need to know what these values are in order to realize that there is a maximum which is fully determined by k_t. It is simply the *definition* of a value function which will be used in deriving a method of solving dynamic problems.

An Optimal Growth Problem

The use of value functions in solving infinite-horizon problems via dynamic programming may be illustrated by the single-agent optimal growth problem. In any period, output $f(k)$ is divided between current consumption and capital to be carried over to the following period, implying a feasibility constraint of the form

$$c_t + k_{t+1} = f(k_t). \tag{2.8}$$

The planner's objective is to maximize the present discounted value of utility of the individual by choice of sequences of c_t and k_{t+1} from $t = 0$ to infinity. That is, the planner chooses $\{c_t, k_{t+1}\}$ to maximize the individual's present discounted utility:

$$\Omega = \sum_{t=0}^{\infty} \beta^t u(c_t), \tag{2.9}$$

where instantaneous utility $u(\cdot)$ is an increasing, concave function of current consumption and where $0 < \beta < 1$ is the individual's subjective discount factor. Equation (2.9) is maximized subject to the feasibility constraint (2.8) and an initial value of capital at time 0, namely k_0. From the definition of the value function $V(\cdot)$, it should be clear that if the utility-maximizing values of c_t consistent with the feasibility constraint (2.8) and the initial k_0 are substituted into (2.9), the resulting value of (2.9) is simply $V(k_0)$.

From the definition of the value function, two observations lead to the *Bellman equation*. First, it should be clear that in any period t, where the planner begins with k_t, the choice between c_t and k_{t+1} can be represented as maximizing

$$u(c_t) + \beta V(k_{t+1}), \tag{2.10}$$

subject to (2.8). That is, since the maximum utility attainable from k_{t+1} is (by definition of the value function) $V(k_{t+1})$, the maximization of (2.10) subject to (2.8) must represent the optimal choice of c_t and k_{t+1}. Second, also from the definition of the value function, the *maximized* value of (2.10) must obviously be the maximum utility attainable starting with k_t, namely, $V(k_t)$. Combining these two observations, we have

$$V(k_t) = \max_{k_{t+1}} \{ u(f(k_t) - k_{t+1}) + \beta V(k_{t+1}) \}. \tag{2.11}$$

This is the Bellman equation, whose *solution* is a function $V(\cdot)$. Note that this equation applies for any two successive periods. This characteristic of *stationarity* is crucial in solving the infinite-horizon problem.

Before moving from conceptual issues to methodological ones (that is, how to solve this equation), let us consider what can be learned from this method of deriving the Bellman equation. Is not (2.11) sufficiently obvious that we can assert it to be true by simple logic? The basic idea of the above derivation and (2.10) is that the value function allows a nontrivial dynamic problem to be turned into a simple-looking single-period optimization problem. There are two lessons here. The first is technical—it is often useful to try to convert a difficult problem into a form where you can use techniques you have already mastered. The second lesson is more subtle—try to gain intellectual insight into problems by thinking about them in ways that are perhaps nonstandard. Equation (2.10) makes clear that there is a sense in which dynamic problems are two-period problems balancing "today" against "the infinite future," but that this works only when there is consistency between how one treated the future yesterday and how one treats it today. A more general problem with an approach that treats (2.11) as obvious is that we do not then know what to make of cases where it seems that (2.11) should hold, but it does not. When we study the phenomenon of *time inconsistency* in Chapter 4, we will consider dynamic problems where dynamic programming does not work. A clear understanding of what lies behind the Bellman equation is crucial for understanding apparently pathological cases.

Methods of Solution

The Bellman can be solved (in rare cases) by conjecturing a function that solves (2.11) and then verifying that conjecture. If one could figure out the form the value function would take, the method of undetermined coefficients would yield a solution. Alternatively, it could also be solved, in principle, by the "method of successive approximations." One begins with a conjectured function $V_1(\cdot)$ (where the subscript 1 refers not to time but to the first conjecture) which does not solve (2.11). Plugging $V_1(\cdot)$ into the right-hand side of (2.11) would generate a new function on the left-hand side, namely,

$$V_2(k_t) = \max_{k_{t+1}} \{u(f(k_t) - k_{t+1}) + \beta V_1(k_{t+1})\}. \qquad (2.12)$$

Substituting $V_2(\cdot)$ into the right-hand side of (2.12) in place of $V_2(\cdot)$ would generate a third function $V_3(\cdot)$, and so on. Under the conditions that (i) $0 < \beta < 1$ and (ii) $u(\cdot)$ is continuous and bounded, the Contraction Mapping Theorem says that this sequence of functions converges to a unique function, say $V_\infty(\ )$, which "reproduces" itself if plugged into the right-hand side of (2.12). (See Lucas and Stokey for details.) Since the value function is unique (as there must be a maximum value of utility attainable for any k_t), this $V_\infty(\cdot)$ must be the value function $V(\cdot)$. Once one has found the value function, one can derive the optimal path of k_t by solving the maximization problem on the right-hand side of (2.11).

The most useful method for solving a dynamic problem like that in (2.8) and (2.9) via the Bellman equation (2.11) is not to solve for the value function $V(\cdot)$ at all, but to use characteristics of the value function and (2.11) to derive the optimal path without finding $V(\cdot)$ itself. Differentiability of the value function allows us to do this in many cases. Under what conditions would we expect $V(\cdot)$ to be differentiable? First, we would require the underlying functions in the Bellman equation to be differentiable. In the optimal growth problem, if the production function were not differentiable at some k or the utility function were not differentiable at some c, the value function would almost surely not be differentiable at every value of k. Second, we would want the choice variable k_{t+1} not to be a corner solution for some k_t. (Otherwise, an infinitesimal increase in k would imply a different effect on the value function than an infinitesimal decrease.) Our assumptions on preferences and technology imply these conditions are met for the growth problem. Intuitively, with smooth functions and interior solutions, marginal changes in the state variable k imply marginal changes in attainable welfare in the same direction.

With differentiability of $V(\cdot)$, the maximum problem in (2.11) yields the following first-order condition for k_{t+1}:

$$u'(f(k_t) - k_{t+1}) = \beta V'(k_{t+1}). \qquad (2.13)$$

The interpretation of (2.13) is straightforward: choose k_{t+1} so that the loss in utility from "one less unit" of consumption today is just equal to the (discounted) gain in future utility that "one more unit" of capital carried over (i.e., "saving") would allow. What is the utility gain from higher k_{t+1}? This can be calculated by use of the **envelope theorem** applied to $V(\cdot)$ to find the derivative $V'(\cdot)$, namely,

$$V'(k_t) = u'(f(k_t) - k_{t+1})f'(k_t). \qquad (2.14)$$

This equation also has a straightforward interpretation: the value of another unit of beginning-of-period capital along an optimal path is the marginal utility value of the extra product the higher capital allows evaluated at the optimal level of consumption.

To use these expressions, one uses the stationarity of the problem: with an infinite horizon, the planner faces the same form of problem each period, so the form of his solution must be the same. Thus, for a given beginning-of-period value of capital, the level of capital he finds optimal to carry over must be independent of time. Combining (2.13) and (2.14), one obtains

$$u'(f(k_t) - k_{t+1}) = \beta u'(f(k_{t+1}) - \kappa(k_{t+1}))f'(k_{t+1}), \qquad (2.15)$$

where $\kappa(k_{t+1}) \equiv k_{t+2}$.[2] Hence the time-invariant function $\kappa(\cdot)$ giving the optimal level of the control variable as a function of the state, sometimes called the *policy function*, will characterize the optimal path. For many functional forms of $u(\cdot)$ and $f(\cdot)$, it is easy to solve (2.15) to obtain a closed form for $\kappa(\cdot)$.

More generally, we can analyze this equation to obtain certain characteristics of the policy function $\kappa(\cdot)$ and hence the optimal path. For example, one may differentiate (2.15) with respect to k_{t+1} to show $\kappa(\cdot)$ is an increasing function. One learns what characteristics of $\kappa(\cdot)$ can be obtained by "playing around" with (2.15).

2.4. THE OVERLAPPING GENERATIONS MODEL

In this section, we set out an extremely simple, but very useful discrete-time model, the overlapping generations (OLG) model with capital accumulation. The basic OLG model is due to Samuelson (1958); the version with capital accumulation is due to Diamond (1965). We will use variants of the OLG model at many places in the book.

In the simplest version, Samuelson considered a discrete-time model of an infinite-horizon economy populated by individuals who live two periods and then die. A new generation is born in each period, so that in any period, the population consists of only two generations, those born at the beginning of the current period (the current "young") and those born at the beginning of the previous period (the current "old"). To generate saving, Samuelson assumed that the young are endowed with one unit of a nonstorable good ("a chocolate"), while the old have zero (additional) endowment. This simple overlap allows the model to be simultaneously

---

[2] Note that we could also combine (2.13) and (2.14) to get an equation in k_t, k_{t+1}, and k_{t+2} which is exactly the first-order condition we derived in the finite-horizon case. With no endpoint condition, we need stationarity to solve.

highly tractable and quite flexible and powerful in analyzing economic phenomena. In the text, we often consider an even simpler version, in which the economy itself lasts only two periods, with only the first generation alive, as young consumers, in period 1, and both generations, those born in period 2 and those born in period 1, who are now "old," alive in period 2.

Diamond (1965) extended Samuelson's OLG framework to a perfect-certainty discrete-time model with factor accumulation and capital. Let us begin with the life cycle of an individual born at the beginning of period t. He has a labor endowment of one unit when young, which he supplies inelastically, earning a wage of w_t. Denoting the consumption and the saving of the young born at t by c_t^y and s_t, respectively, an individual's budget constraint when young may be written

$$w_t = c_t^y + s_t. \tag{2.16}$$

When old, in period $t + 1$, he has no labor endowment and consumes all of his saving, both principal and interest. If the market interest rate between t and $t + 1$ is r_{t+1}, the individual's budget constraint when old may be written

$$(1 + r_{t+1})s_t = c_{t+1}^o, \tag{2.17}$$

where c_{t+1}^o is consumption when old. (Note that a subscript refers to calendar time, a superscript to the consumer's age.) A representative individual born at t chooses consumption in the two periods to maximize lifetime utility (remember there is no uncertainty):

$$\Omega_t = u(c_t^y, c_{t+1}^o), \tag{2.18}$$

subject to the budget constraints (2.16) and (2.17). This maximization implies functional relations between saving and consumption in the two periods and the wage and interest rates the individual faces, namely,

$$c_t^y = c^y(w_t, r_{t+1}),$$
$$c_{t+1}^o = c^o(w_t, r_{t+1}), \tag{2.19}$$
$$s_t = s(w_t, r_{t+1}).$$

Period-t output Y_t depends on aggregate capital K_t and aggregate labor N_t (which is the number of the young at t) according to

$$Y_t = F(K_t, N_t), \tag{2.20}$$

where the production function $F(\cdot)$ is increasing and concave in both of its arguments displaying constant returns to scale (i.e., it is first-degree homogeneous in K and N, meaning $F(\alpha K, \alpha N) = \alpha F(K, N)$, for any constant α). Capital to be used in production in period t is determined in period $t + 1$. For simplicity, assume no depreciation of capital, so that after production in period t, $Y_t + K_t$ is available for current consumption or capital to be used in production in the next period. The economy's aggregate production constraint may then be written

$$F(K_t, N_t) + K_t = C_t + K_{t+1}, \qquad (2.21)$$

where C_t is aggregate consumption of the two generations. Hence, output is split between aggregate consumption and net investment $K_{t+1} - K_t$, which also is gross investment, given the no-depreciation assumption. Aggregate consumption is the sum of consumption of each generation:

$$C_t = N_t c_t^y + N_{t-1} c_t^o, \qquad (2.22)$$

where N_i is the number of people in generation i. Suppose that population grows at rate n, so that population at any two dates is related by

$$N_{t+1} = (1 + n)N_t. \qquad (2.23)$$

Capital available for production in $t + 1$ is aggregate saving in period t, namely,

$$K_{t+1} = N_t s(w_t, r_{t+1}). \qquad (2.24)$$

Equation (2.24), which represents the supply side of the capital market, will be central to the analysis. The demand side of the capital market is characterized by entrepreneurs, who demand capital until the rate of return r_{t+1} is equal to the marginal product of capital, $F_K(K_{t+1}, N_{t+1})$, where a subscript on F represents the derivative of F with respect to one of its arguments.

More generally, one assumes that factor markets are competitive with the return to a factor equaling its net marginal product. First-degree homogeneity of $F(K, N)$ allows us to express marginal products as functions of the capital–labor ratio $k_t \equiv K_t/N_t$. Note first that given the above definition of first-degree homogeneity, we may express output per worker $y_t \equiv Y_t/N_t$. Dividing both sides of (2.20) by N_t and using first-degree homogeneity, we may write (2.20) as

$$y_t = \frac{F(K_t, N_t)}{N_t} = F\left(\frac{K_t}{N_t}, 1\right)$$

$$\equiv f(k_t), \qquad (2.25)$$

where the properties of the function $f(\cdot)$ can be derived from the properties of $F(\cdot, \cdot)$. For example, one can easily show that $f'(\cdot) = F_K(\cdot, \cdot)$. First-degree homogeneity also implies that $F(K_t, N_t) = K_t F_K(\cdot) + N_t F_N(\cdot)$. Using this relation, the definition of $f(\cdot)$, and the competitive assumption that factor returns are equal to marginal products, we may write

$$w_t = f(k_t) - k_t f'(k_t),$$

$$r_{t+1} = f'(k_t). \tag{2.26}$$

One can now solve for the equilibrium and obtain a transition equation for the state variable k_t. Substituting (2.23) and (2.26) into (2.24) and using the equation for the rate of population growth, we obtain a first-order difference equation in k_t:

$$(1 + n)k_{t+1} = s(f(k_t) - k_t f'(k_t), f'(k_{t+1})). \tag{2.27}$$

This equation, which is the capital market clearing condition, fully characterizes equilibrium and the evolution of the economy.

Since (2.27) is derived given the competitive factor market conditions, it summarizes market clearing in all markets except the market for consumption goods. Since all markets but one clear and consumption demand functions satisfy individual budget constraints, Walras' Law implies that the consumption market clears as well. To confirm that this is the case, note that aggregate demand for consumption is given by (2.22), while aggregate supply of output available for consumption is given by (2.21). Substituting (2.16), (2.17), and (2.23) into (2.22), substituting (2.27) into the resulting expression, and using the first-degree homogeneity result of $F(K_t, N_t) = K_t F_K(\cdot) + N_t F_N(\cdot)$ (or, equivalently, the competitive factor conditions (2.26)), one then shows that (2.22) equals (2.21) when all other markets clear and consumers are obeying their budget constraints.

The OLG model is an extremely useful tool of analysis. We will generally use simplified versions of it in our analysis of political economy problems, but this exposition should allow readers to extend those models if they so desire.

2.5. EFFECTS OF UNCERTAIN FUTURE POLICIES

As discussed in the introduction to this chapter, the political nature of decisionmaking means that outcomes will differ from the social planner's outcome not only because different policies may be chosen, but also because a given policy may have different effects than if it were chosen by a social planner. The key point is that the reaction of economic actors to a given policy may depend very much on how that policy was chosen. One reason is that in a dynamic world, the optimal choice of actions today depends not only on the current environment, but also on expectations of what the future environment may be. Forward-looking optimal behavior is a cornerstone of modern economics. In the modern approach to optimal consumer behavior, for example, current consumption depends not simply on current resources, but on expected future resources, that is, on permanent income. Similarly, investment decisions will clearly depend on future expected sales, rather than simply on current sales. Reaction to government policy is also forward-looking, where expectations of future government policies may be particularly important in determining behavior. In this section, we present a framework for analyzing the effects of future government policy, especially under uncertainty. As indicated in the introduction, this continuous-time model is considerably more difficult than the other models presented in this chapter, and the techniques introduced are used only sparingly later in the book. The section is primarily intended for those who want to learn techniques for analyzing the effects of expected future policies on current dynamics. Others may want to skim the section, for a number of economic concepts (indicated in **bold** type) used in the book are introduced in this section.

The General Problem

How will forward-looking agents behave when expected future government policy is crucial for determining current optimal behavior? They will clearly use currently available information to try to forecast these policies, including their knowledge of the collective choice process itself. To take a simple example, the knowledge that a government may be replaced in an upcoming election by another government with different policy preferences is key to forming expectations of the permanence of current policy, and hence key to understanding the effects of current policy. A large change in the probability that the current government will be re-elected may thus significantly affect the implications of current policy for economic outcomes. This relation is made even more complicated by the fact that current policy may be used to calculate the probability of re-election; more generally, the choice of current policy may be used to form expectations of future policy.

With uncertainty about future policy, the relation between economic policy and economic outcomes may thus be quite complex, even if the incentives of current policymakers are fully known. That is, when information is incomplete but not asymmetric, dynamic feedbacks due to political uncertainty about the future significantly complicate the effects of current policy on outcomes.[3] The complexity of these effects due to political

---

[3] Adding asymmetric information about a policymaker's preferences or information set will only complicate this relation even further. We consider this possibility in future chapters, such as Chapter 6 on unknown policymaker preferences in a dynamic model, some models in Chapter 10 on superior information on the part of policymakers, and applications in Chapter 13 to dynamic models of reform when both types of incompleteness of information may be present.

uncertainty may be roughly divided into three parts. First, there is the information that current policy gives about the likelihood of future policies due to the political process itself—for example, a contractionary policy that results in high unemployment today may increase the probability that a more expansionary government will be elected in the future. Second, there is the information that current policy gives about the likelihood of future policies due to technical constraints—for example, a tax cut today implies the need to raise taxes or cut expenditures in the future to ensure that the government's budget is intertemporally balanced. Third, there is simply the complexity of dynamic paths for exogenously specified uncertainty. To address the first point, we need more institutional detail about the political process. We therefore postpone discussion of it until we have investigated political choice mechanisms themselves and given more institutional detail; we will consider it at great length, both theoretically and empirically, in Chapter 7 in our discussion of the political business cycle. Here, we consider the last two factors.

One way to analyze uncertainty about future policies and get tractable results is to simplify the problem drastically in some dimensions. For example, one may assume a two-period model with only two possible policies in the second period, allowing an easy derivation of optimal individual behavior and equilibrium economic outcomes in the first period. This sort of simplification is very common in the political economy literature, and we will repeatedly look at models of this sort. This approach requires no special dynamic optimization techniques. Moreover, it is not only mathematically simple; it is also very easy to formulate such problems if the technical specification of uncertainty is kept very simple. For many questions, such a simple approach is adequate to illustrate the important phenomenon the model is trying to capture. As is often the case, a simple model is not only adequate, but is actually a virtue: the simplicity of the model makes the crucial driving forces clear in a way that would be obscured by a more complicated model. Sometimes, "less is more."

However, sometimes, less is less. Uncertainty about future economic policy may give rise to complex economic dynamics that cannot be captured or analyzed in a two-period, two-state model. (Of course, the "trick" is to know when simple models will suffice and when they will not, an ability that usually reflects modeling experience.) In this section, we present a general framework for deriving and analyzing the effects of uncertainty about future policy on economic dynamics, based on Drazen and Helpman (1990). Current policy is seen to be unsustainable in the long run, as it violates the government's intertemporal budget constraint. It is therefore known that policy will be changed in the future, but there is uncertainty about exactly how or when it will be changed. What will be the effect on current macroeconomic dynamics? Answering this question requires considering both economic optimization in the face of policy uncertainty and the general equilibrium dynamics implied by economic optimization.

Detailed presentation of the model is justified in part by the fact that, in spite of the importance of policy uncertainty in political economy, general methods for analyzing it are little used and appear not to be widely known. With a few exceptions (not all of them associated with the author of this book), the models presented here have not made their way into the political economy literature. There are a myriad of models relying on policy uncertainty for their conclusions, almost all modeling such uncertainty extremely simply. At the same time, more careful modeling of policy uncertainty does not require use of complex mathematical tools. Only basic calculus is used in the main model presented below. As we shall see, many of the seemingly counterintuitive effects of policies on economic outcomes in the political economy literature are explicable using standard economics carefully applied.

Policy Changes at Known Future Dates

As background, we begin with methodology for analyzing the case of a policy switch at a known date in the future. This was developed by Liviatan (1984) for specific preferences and Drazen (1985) for general preferences for monetary policy, as a continuous-time generalization of Sargent and Wallace's (1981) paper on "Unpleasant Monetarist Arithmetic." The government is running a deficit and accumulating debt, and it is common knowledge that it must be closed at some point in the future. The link between current and future economic policy is thus via the government's intertemporal budget constraint.

The specific policy experiment under certainty is as follows. Consider a continuous-time model of a closed economy[4] in which government policy as of time 0 is described by a vector of per capita government spending, lump-sum taxes, and rate of growth of the nominal money supply (g, τ, μ) such that the government is running a deficit. The deficit implies that debt b_t (also expressed in per capita terms) is growing in an unsustainable way. That is, at given current policy, government debt evolves according to

$$\dot{b}_t = r_t b_t + g_t - \tau_t - \mu_t m_t, \qquad (2.28)$$

where r_t is the real rate of interest (to be determined), m_t is real money balances, and where a "dot" over a variable represents a time derivative. The term $\mu_t m_t$ is thus **seigniorage**, real government revenue from printing money. This term can be understood as follows. The real value of revenue from printing money is simply the nominal value of newly printed money

---

[4] An open-economy version of the model is presented in Drazen and Helpman (1987, 1988), focussing on exchange rate management.

divided by the price level; dividing and multiplying by the level of the nominal money supply yields the last term in (2.28). The last three terms on the right-hand side of (2.28) represent the **primary deficit**, that is, expenditures minus tax revenues. The growth of debt is equal to the government deficit *inclusive* of debt service.

If the primary deficit is positive, debt will be growing at faster than the rate of interest, so that current policy is infeasible in the sense of being inconsistent with intertemporal balance in the government budget. (Formally, one adds a government solvency requirement of the form $\lim_{t \to \infty} e^{-R(t)} b_t \geq 0$, where $R(t)$ is the real interest factor from 0 to t.) We have assumed that prior to T, $(g_t, \tau_t, \mu_t) = (g, \tau, \mu)$, where this latter vector implies infeasible growth in b_t. The level of government debt at some known T in the future, denoted b_T, will be frozen by choice of a new level of government spending g_T, a new level of taxes τ_T, or a new money growth rate μ_T, such that the deficit inclusive of debt service is eliminated and there is no further growth in debt. All debt is held by individuals in the economy.

Individual utility is a function of consumption c_t and real money balances $m_t = M_t/P_t$, given by $u(c_t) + h(m_t)$, where $u(\cdot)$ and $h(\cdot)$ are increasing, concave functions. Separability is assumed for tractability. If a policy switch which implies constant values of all macroeconomic variables is known to occur at T, the consumer's infinite-horizon utility may be written

$$\Omega\left(b_0, \frac{M_0}{P_0}\right) = \int_{t=0}^{T} e^{-\rho t}\left[u(c_t) + h\left(\frac{M_t}{P_t}\right)\right] dt + e^{-\rho T} V^s\left(b_T + \frac{M_T}{P_T^s}; T\right),$$

(2.29)

where ρ is the subjective discount rate and $V^s(\cdot)$ is the discounted flow of utility (as of time T) from T to infinity, which depends positively on wealth at T and possibly T itself. This is the "value" of arriving at time T with wealth of $b_T + M_T/P_T^s$, analogous to the value function introduced in Section 2.3.

We distinguish between magnitudes before and after a policy switch. A superscript S on a function or variable denotes its value at T contingent on a policy switch taking place at that date, while functions or variables without a superscript represent values if no policy switch has taken place at or before this date. Thus, P_T^s is the price level at T if a policy switch has taken place at the date, and P_T is the price level at T if no policy switch has taken place at or before T. In the absence of open-market operations, which we ignore here, there can be no discrete change in nominal money balances or real bond holdings at T. Utility is maximized subject to the individual's budget constraint, which may be written for any $t \leq T$ as

$$b_t = b_0 e^{R(t)} + \int_{x=0}^{t} e^{R(t)-R(x)} \left[y - c_x - \frac{z_x}{P_x} - \tau \right] dx, \qquad (2.30)$$

where b_0 is initial debt holdings, $R(t)$ is the interest factor from 0 to t (that is, $R(t) = \int_0^t r_t \, dt$), y is endowment income, and z_t are flow additions to holdings of nominal cash balances at t. These are related to the stock of nominal balances according to

$$M_t = M_0 + \int_{x=0}^{t} z_x \, dx. \qquad (2.31)$$

The advantage of writing the budget constraints in integral form and defining the flow variable z_t is that ordinary calculus can be used to derive a solution, even though this is a continuous-time model with differential equations of motion. This type of simplification—choosing a slightly more awkward set-up of the problem in order to simplify the mathematics considerably—will be used throughout this book; it is a good "technique" to become familiar with.

In the certainty example, we consider only the case of an anticipated change in the rate of money growth μ at T to stabilize the growth of debt in (2.28), which is the Sargent–Wallace (1981) experiment. A perfectly anticipated increase in μ will imply that there will be no jump in the price level at T (see, however, the discussion in the next paragraph). Constant government spending g before and after T implies that consumption will be constant as well, since in this endowment economy, market clearing requires that $c_t = y - g_t$. Combining individual optimization with market equilibrium conditions thus implies that the marginal utility of consumption, $u'(y - g)$, will be constant as well before and after T, and that the market-clearing real interest rate equals the discount rate for all t, that is, $r_t = \rho$.[5] Individual choice is over consumption (as described in footnote 5) and real money balances. Optimal choice of money balances may be derived by maximizing (2.29) with respect to z_t and M_t subject to (2.30) and (2.31). (Treating flow additions z_t to nominal balances and the stock

---

[5] Substituting (2.30) into (2.29) and differentiating the resulting expression with respect to c_t yields a first-order condition:

$$e^{-\rho t} u'(c_t) = e^{-\rho T} u'(c_T^S) e^{R(T)-R(t)},$$

for each c_t, where $u'(c_T^S) \equiv V^{S'}(b_T + m_T)$. Market clearing with constant y and g for all t implies constant marginal utility of consumption at all dates, which by the above first-order condition, implies $r_t = \rho$ for all t.

M_t as separate variables subject to (2.31) allows the use of ordinary calculus in this continuous-time, dynamic problem.) This yields a relation[6]

$$\frac{h'(m_t)}{u'(y-g)} = i_t = \rho + \pi_t,\qquad(2.32)$$

where i_t is the nominal interest rate and π_t is the inflation rate at t, which under certainty is equal to $\dot{P}_t/P_t$. This condition simply says that the ratio of the marginal utility of money balances to the marginal utility of consumption equals the flow cost of holding money balances, namely, the nominal interest rate.

Though no price level jump occurs at T for this policy change (a change in μ at T) under certainty, it is instructive to see when a perfectly anticipated policy change *can* induce a price level jump. (As is well known, an unanticipated policy change can lead to a jump in the price level.) Suppose that the policy switch at T were a cut in the level of government spending from g to $g_T < g$. In this continuous-time endowment economy, consumption would therefore necessarily jump up at T. In order to make this market-clearing jump consistent with individual optimization (that is, with the continuous-time consumption Euler equation, which will be derived below for the case of uncertainty), the real interest factor must jump discontinuously at T. Since the real interest factor jumps at T, implying an instantaneous infinite return on bonds, arbitrage requires that the price level jumps down at T. This jump is perfectly anticipated, since the cut in g is perfectly anticipated as well. We show this formally below; see footnote 11.[7]

Dynamic Paths

On the basis of individual optimization and market clearing, one can express the evolution of the economy under certainty in terms of dynamic equations for two state variables b_t and m_t. The differential equation for

---

[6] Denoting the multipliers on (2.31) by λ_t (one multiplier for each t as (2.31) must hold at all t), substituting (2.30) into (2.29), and differentiating (2.29) with respect to M_t and z_t subject to the side constraint yields first-order conditions

$$e^{-\rho t}\frac{h'(M_t/P_t)}{P_t} = \lambda_t \quad\text{for each } t,$$

$$e^{-\rho t}V^{S'}(\cdot)\left[e^{R(T)-R(t)}\frac{1}{P_t} - \frac{1}{P_T}\right] = \int_{x=t}^{x=T}\lambda_x\,dx,$$

for the M_t and z_t, respectively. Substituting the first equations into the second, differentiating with respect to t, and using the results in the previous footnote yields (2.32).

[7] Drazen and Helpman (1990) discuss this argument in greater detail in terms of Arrow–Debreu prices.

b_t is given by (2.28) for $r_t = \rho$. To derive a differential equation for the evolution of real money balances m_t in equilibrium, we time-differentiate the definition of real balances, namely, $m_t = M_t/P_t$, to obtain

$$\frac{\dot{m}_t}{m_t} = \frac{\dot{M}_t}{M_t} - \frac{\dot{P}_t}{P_t} = \mu - \pi_t.$$

Using (2.32), one obtains

$$\frac{\dot{m}_t}{m_t} = \mu_t + \rho - \frac{h'(m_t)}{u'(y - g)}. \tag{2.33}$$

Equations (2.28) with $r_t = \rho$ and (2.33) form a system of two first-order differential equations in the variables b_t and m_t, given g_t, τ_t, and μ_t. For future reference, these are *time-autonomous* differential equations, that is, equations where time enters on the right-hand side only through the state variables and not directly. Working with differential equations that are not time autonomous is far more difficult.

We can represent the dynamics which come from these equations in terms of a **phase diagram**, which is a graphical representation of how a dynamic system moves at each possible value of the state variables. For example, consider (2.28). To do a phase diagram analysis, one first derives combinations of b_t and m_t such that $\dot{b}_t = 0$, that is, combinations of b_t and m_t implying a zero deficit (and hence constant b_t) for the specified policy vector (g_t, τ_t, μ_t). On the basis of this, one can then ask whether b_t will be rising or falling for combinations of b_t and m_t not on the $\dot{b}_t = 0$ locus. Inspection of (2.28) reveals that to the right of the $\dot{b}_t = 0$ locus, b_t will be rising, and to the left it will be falling.[8] We represent this by arrows indicating rising or falling debt. A similar analysis may be performed for (2.33), the differential equation for m_t. Such an exercise for both differential equations yields a phase diagram as in Figure 2.2. Note that the steady state (the intersection of the $\dot{b}_t = 0$ and the $\dot{m}_t = 0$ loci) is unstable. This reflects the fact that if the deficit is positive, it can only increase over time; if negative, it can only become more negative for unchanged policy.

An unstable steady state means, for our technical analysis, that if policy (g_t, τ_t, μ_t) is inconsistent with steady state for current b_t and m_t, it will always be inconsistent. Hence, a current policy vector which is infeasible (in the sense just defined) implies that there *must* be a policy change if a steady state is to be attained. Moreover, if policy is changed to achieve a steady state, there is no sense in which the economy will then *converge*

[8] Consider a point on the $\dot{b}_t = 0$ locus. For given m_t, an increase in b_t will imply that $\dot{b}_t > 0$, reflecting higher debt service, all other budget items unchanged.

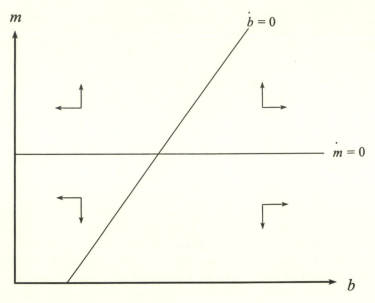

FIGURE 2.2. The basic phase diagram.

to steady state, as in many models (for example, models of growth and capital accumulation). If a policy change at some time T is to make the dynamics consistent with steady state, it must put the economy in steady state immediately; otherwise it will never get there. Therefore, if we are considering a one-time policy change at some future T to assure government budget feasibility, we must consider policy combinations which are consistent with steady state at T.

The steady state consistent with a policy vector (g_T, τ_T, μ_T) and a constant (m_T, b_T) is found by setting $\dot{b}_t = 0$ in (2.28) (consistent with taxes and seigniorage covering government spending and debt service) and $\dot{m}_t = 0$ in (2.33), yielding

$$\frac{h'(m_T)}{u'(y - g)} = \rho + \mu_T, \tag{2.34}$$

$$\rho b_T = \mu_T m_T + \tau_T - g_T.$$

(The first equation reflects the fact that in steady state, with constant m_T, the constant rate of inflation π_T equals the rate of nominal money growth μ_T.) Following the discussion in the previous paragraph, we then ask the following question: suppose a policy switch will take place when debt hits b_T and it will be accomplished via an increase in the rate of nominal money growth from μ to μ_T. For each value of b_T, what value of μ_T must be chosen to put the economy in steady state? That is, while g_t and τ_t are expected to remain unchanged at g and τ, at what value must μ_T be set to satisfy (2.34) for the level of debt b_T that has been reached at T? What value of m_T will be consistent with b_T, given the chosen method of budget stabilization, that is, given unchanged g and τ and the necessary adjustment in μ_T? (An analogous experiment could be performed for a policy switch in other instruments.)

Combining the two equations in (2.34) yields an implicit equation for μ_T. We are really interested, however, in a steady-state relation between m_T and b_T that must hold after a policy switch, which, via (2.34), can be written

$$\rho b_T = m_T \frac{h'(m_T)}{u'(y - g)} - \rho m_T + \tau - g. \qquad (2.35)$$

This may be graphed as in Figure 2.3 as the surface $m^\mu(b_T)$, where its shape reflects the assumption that there is a maximum level of seigniorage μm that can be collected, corresponding to a maximum level of debt that can be serviced and hence a maximum level of feasible steady-state debt, say $\bar{b}$.

We are now in a position to fully specify dynamic paths in anticipation of an expected policy change. We have assumed that b_0, g, τ, and μ are such that $\dot{b}_t > 0$. It is therefore known that policy must be changed. The relation (2.35), as represented by the surface $m^\mu(b_T)$ in Figure 2.3, gives the locus of terminal points for the dynamic paths, while the equation of motion (2.28) and (2.33) give us the dynamic behavior leading to a terminal point. Since we start at b_0 at $t = 0$, and, as indicated above, must hit (b_T, m_T) exactly at T, there is only one possible path. (One way to see this is to think of time "running backwards." If we "start" at some (b_T, m_T) at T as "initial conditions" and let time reverse for length of time T according to (2.28) and (2.33), we will arrive at determinate values of b_0 and m_0.) Since the date of the policy switch is known with certainty and since consumption c does not jump at T, the price level (and hence real balances) also cannot jump at T. Since b_0, b_T, m_T, and the length of time T are all specified, m_0 must be allowed to take whatever value is necessary to put us on the correct dynamic path. Since there can be no instantaneous jump in the value of initial nominal money balances M_0 (as there can be no jump in the value of initial real government debt b_0), the price level P_0 must jump to allow m_0 to hit the correct initial level. An equilibrium path is shown in Figure 2.3. Along this path, b_t is monotonically rising and m_t is monotonically falling. From (2.32), inflation must be monotonically rising along the path.

The initial jump in the price level can be easily understood when one considers money as an asset: the asset price will jump when new information arrives to reflect the effect of the new information on the future

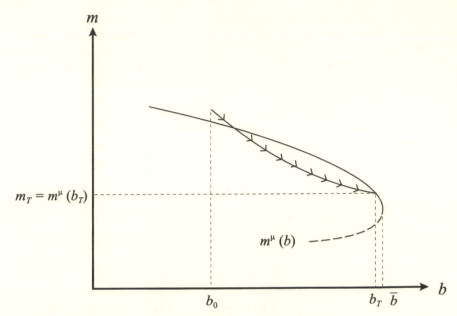

FIGURE 2.3. Perfectly anticipated change in monetary policy.

stream of returns to the asset. Information about future growth rates of
the money supply tell us about the future price level, which affects the
future value of money. When new information arrives, today's value of
money (the inverse of the price level) will jump to reflect this information.
An anticipated event cannot imply a perfectly anticipated jump in the price
level if such an anticipated jump in the value of the asset would allow a
perfect arbitrage opportunity, that is, an opportunity to make infinite
profits by taking an infinite position in the asset for an instant before the
fully anticipated jump.

Uncertainty About the Timing of a Policy Switch

We now ask how these results would be affected by uncertainty about the
date of a policy switch. For simplicity, we assume there is no uncertainty in
the nature of the policy switch, that is, in what policy is changed to achieve
intertemporal government budget balance, only in the timing of a change
in the setting of a given policy. Uncertainty about the composition of a
policy switch will be considered below.

   Following Drazen and Helpman (1990), this uncertainty can be represented by a cumulative distribution function (CDF) as of date 0, denoted
$F(t)$, giving the probability of a switch occurring at or before time t. The
probability of a policy switch at or before a given date will, in general,
represent political considerations. We abstract from any such restrictions
on $F(t)$ and only impose the assumption that there is a latest possible time
at which a policy switch is expected, denoted T_{max}. This date may be less

than the last feasible date of stabilization, that is, the date implied by the maximum level of revenue which can be raised by a tax instrument. By the definition of a CDF, $F(0) = 0$ and $F(T_{max}) = 1$. We assume that $F(t)$ is differentiable, its derivative giving the probability of a switch at each date. The (instantaneous) *conditional* probability of a switch at t, that is, conditional on no switch having previously occurred, is then $F'(t)/(1 - F(t))$, that is, the probability of a switch at t divided by the probability of *no* switch having occurred before t. This conditional probability is called the **hazard rate** for the probabilistic event (policy switch) occurring. Note that the hazard rate goes to infinity as t approaches T_{max}, an observation of great importance below.[9]

With timing uncertainty represented by the CDF $F(t)$, the representative individual's objective function (2.29) may be written

$$\int_{T=0}^{T_{max}} \left[\int_{t=0}^{T} e^{-\rho t} \left[u(c_t) + h\left(\frac{M_t}{P_t} \right) \right] dt \right.$$

$$\left. + e^{-\rho T} V^s \left(b_T + \frac{M_T}{P_T^s} ; T \right) \right] F'(T) \, dT. \qquad (2.36)$$

In the absence of markets for state-contingent securities whose payoffs are contingent on government policy choices, uncertainty about the date of a policy switch does not affect the individual's budget constraints (2.30) and (2.31). The first-order conditions for the individual's optimization problem under uncertainty are found by maximizing (2.36) with respect to c_t, z_t, and M_t, subject to (2.30) and (2.31). Using the fact that the marginal utility of wealth after a policy switch $\partial V^s(\cdot)/\partial(b_T + m_T)$ is equal to the marginal utility of consumption after the policy switch, the first-order conditions imply[10]

$$e^{R(t) - \rho t} u'(c_t) = \int_{T=t}^{T_{max}} e^{R(T) - \rho T} u'(c_T^s) \frac{F'(T)}{1 - F(t)} \, dT, \qquad (2.37)$$

$$\frac{u'(c_t)}{P_t} = \int_{T=t}^{T_{max}} \left[\int_{x=t}^{T} e^{-\rho(x-t)} h'(m_x) \frac{1}{P_x} \, dx \right.$$

$$\left. + e^{-\rho(T-t)} \frac{u'(c_T^s)}{P_T^s} \right] \frac{F'(T)}{1 - F(t)} \, dT, \qquad (2.38)$$

[9] Strictly speaking, this requires there to be no probability "mass" at T_{max}, which we assume here. Probability mass may be thought of as there being a finite probability of the policy switch occurring at a given instant (for example, right after an election), as opposed to an infinitesimal chance at each instant, as is usually assumed for probability density functions. This case is covered in Drazen and Helpman (1990).

[10] Equation (2.37) may be found by substituting (2.30) into (2.36) and differentiating (2.36) with respect to c_t, analogous to the calculation for certainty in footnote 5. Equation (2.38) may be found by differentiating (2.36) with respect to z_t and M_t, using a multiplier on the constraint (2.31) as in footnote 6, and combining the resulting first-order conditions.

where $c_t = y - g$ and where $c_T^s = y - g_T$. Equation (2.37) is a continuous-time Euler equation in the presence of policy uncertainty, relating the marginal utility of consumption at any two dates. Equation (2.38) can be seen as an asset pricing equation for nominal balances. Dividing both sides by $u'(c_t)$, one finds that the value of a unit of nominal balances at t, namely, $1/P_t$, is the expected flow value of the liquidity services of money until T (as measured by the marginal utility of money balances) plus the expected "salvage value" at T, which depends on both the expected price level at T and the expected marginal utility of consumption at T. As we shall see shortly, this asset pricing equation will yield a money demand equation which is the analogue to (2.32).

Differentiation of (2.37) with respect to t yields

$$\frac{dR(t)}{dt} = \rho + \frac{F'(t)}{1 - F(t)} \frac{u'(c_t) - u'(c_t^s)}{u'(c_t)}. \tag{2.39}$$

The left-hand side of (2.39) is the real interest rate as long as no policy switch has taken place. If there is no jump in the marginal utility of consumption when a policy switch takes place (as in the case of a change in the growth rate of the nominal money supply μ with no change in government spending g), the real interest rate will always equal the subjective discount rate ρ. When a policy change may imply a jump in the marginal utility of consumption (as in the case of a discrete change in g in an endowment economy), uncertainty about the timing of a policy change implies that the real interest rate is equal to the discount rate plus a risk premium, the second term on the right-hand side of (2.39). The risk premium is the product of the conditional probability $F'(t)/(1 - F(t))$ of a change in policy at a given date t (i.e., the hazard rate) multiplied by the percentage fall in the marginal utility of consumption that the change in policy at that date would induce. It is this effect that led to the possibility of a perfectly anticipated jump in the price level under certainty, as discussed above.

Differentiating (2.38) with respect to t and rearranging yields

$$\frac{h'(m_t)}{u'(c_t)} = \frac{dR(t)}{dt} + \pi_t + \frac{F'(t)}{1 - F(t)} \frac{1/P_t - 1/P_t^s}{1/P_t} \frac{u'(c_t^s)}{u'(c_t)}. \tag{2.40}$$

The right-hand side of (2.40) is the nominal interest rate, which is the sum of the real interest rate (as defined by (2.39)), the inflation rate π, and a nominal risk premium reflecting both the possibility of a price jump with a policy switch at T, implying a change in the real value of nominal balances, and the possibility of a discrete change in the utility value of nominal real balances. The size of the nominal risk premium is the product of the conditional probability of a change in government policy, the percentage change in the value of nominal balances as a result of a price jump, and the proportional change in the value of these balances. If there is no jump in the marginal utility of consumption from a policy change, there is no real risk premium, but the nominal interest rate still contains a nominal risk premium. The expected capital loss on a unit of nominal balances resulting from an upward price jump, for example, means that an individual must be compensated for the expected capital loss to make him willing to hold money balances in equilibrium. If there is no possibility of a price jump or no uncertainty about the timing of a policy change, the nominal interest rate is simply $\rho + \pi$, as in (2.32).[11]

To understand the effect of uncertainty about the timing of government policy, let us consider the same policy change as above, namely, a change in monetary policy, but with an *uncertain* date of implementation. That is, suppose as in our earlier example that current monetary and fiscal policy is unsustainable and that it is common knowledge that at some date in the future the rate of monetary growth will be increased to ensure intertemporal budget balance by closing the budget deficit and freezing the level of government debt. It is not known, however, when the policy change will occur, this uncertainty about timing being summarized by the CDF $F(t)$ as given above.[12] How will uncertainty about the date of a policy change affect the dynamics?

With no change in resources available for consumption (implied by no change in g_t), equilibrium consumption paths and the real interest rate in (2.39) are unaffected, the real rate always being equal to the subjective discount rate ρ. Given a constant real interest rate, timing uncertainty also has no effect on the government budget constraint (2.28) in the following sense. The intertemporal government budget constraint must hold not simply in expected value, but for actual paths. Uncertainty will affect the demand for real balances, but given the path that real balances follow, the policy vector for g, τ, and μ must be such that the intertemporal budget constraint is satisfied as before.

The effect of uncertain timing of a change in monetary policy will therefore be seen only in the money demand relation (2.40). With no discrete changes in marginal utility of consumption associated with a policy change, it may be written

$$\frac{h'(m_t)}{u'(y - g)} = \rho + \pi_t + \frac{F'(t)}{1 - F(t)} \frac{1/P_t - 1/P_t^s}{1/P_t}. \tag{2.41}$$

---

[11] Note also that (2.38), in conjunction with (2.37), can be used to formally derive the result that a jump in the marginal utility of consumption due to a jump in g at T will induce a jump in the price level even under certainty.

[12] We abstract from any questions of asymmetric information here, that is, whether the government has superior knowledge of the date of the policy change. The government's behavior is assumed to be fully summarized by $F(t)$, with no relevance attached to where this distribution comes from.

As in the certainty case, this equation could be substituted into the equation $\dot{m}/m = \mu - \pi$ to yield a differential equation analogous to (2.33). Note, however, that the dependence of the hazard rate on time would make this a time-*non*autonomous differential equation. Drazen and Helpman (1990) addressed this by *assuming* that any time dependence of the hazard rate $F'/(1 - F)$ comes only through its dependence on the economic state variables, allowing the representation of dynamics under timing uncertainty by time-autonomous differential equations. Since there is a maximum level of debt that can be financed by an increase in the rate of monetary growth (remember the maximum seigniorage assumption), they assumed that higher levels of debt make a change in policy more likely. Specifically, they assumed that the hazard rate is a nondecreasing function of the level of outstanding debt, namely,

$$\frac{F'(t)}{1 - F(t)} \equiv \phi(b_t), \tag{2.42}$$

where $\phi'(b_t) \geq 0$. The constraint that $F(T_{max}) = 1$ implies that the hazard rate $\phi(\cdot)$ approaches infinity as b_t approaches b_{max}, the level of debt associated with T_{max}.

Using (2.42), the differential equation for the evolution of real money balances before a change in policy may be written

$$\frac{\dot{m}_t}{m_t} = \mu + \rho - \frac{h'(m_t)}{u'(y - g)} + \phi(b_t)\left[1 - \frac{m^{\mu}(b_t)}{m_t}\right], \tag{2.43}$$

where we have multiplied the numerator and denominator of the last term in (2.41) by M_t and then rearranged, and where $m^{\mu}(b_t)$ is the same terminal surface as was derived in the certainty case in (2.35). The conditions that policy and m_T and b_T must satisfy for a steady state are independent of how we arrived there. Hence (2.34) still determine the loci of m_T and b_T consistent with steady state. Equations (2.28) with $r_t = \rho$ and (2.43) are the differential equations that describe the evolution of the economy with uncertain timing about a change in the growth rate of the nominal money supply.

What about the paths leading up to the terminal surface $m^{\mu}(b)$? Consider Figure 2.4, which is like the phase diagram for the certainty case but with (2.43) replacing (2.32) in the derivation of the $\dot{m} = 0$ locus. To tie down the path, one considers what happens if the economy has reached T_{max} (strictly speaking, a nanosecond before T_{max}). There is no longer any uncertainty—it is known that a policy switch must occur in the next instant. With full certainty, there can be no jump in the price level, for the timing of such a jump would be known, implying infinite capital gains due to a perfect arbitrage opportunity. Therefore, m_t cannot jump at T_{max}, so that the point $(b_{max}, m^{\mu}(b_{max}))$ must be approached smoothly. (Formally,

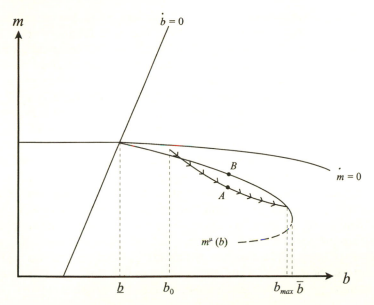

FIGURE 2.4. Uncertain timing of monetary stabilization.

as in the earlier case, the dynamic path as in Figure 2.4 could be derived by "running the differential equations backwards".) Intuitively, this dynamic path can be understood as follows. As of time 0, the path must be consistent with the possibility of no switch until T_{max}, that is, must be consistent with approaching $(b_{max}, m^{\mu}(b_{max}))$ smoothly with no surprises. This is the path that would hold if $(b_{max}, m^{\mu}(b_{max}))$ were *known* to be the terminal point.

If a policy switch occurs at t before T_{max}, we jump from the dynamic path to the terminal surface (point A to point B in the diagram) for whatever the level of debt b_t at t, the jump being accomplished via a jump in m_t induced by a jump in P_t in the opposite direction. Note that this price jump is exactly the phenomenon "built into" the nominal interest rate. Hence the overall dynamic path would follow the arrow curve as before, but with a jump to the terminal surface if stabilization occurs before T_{max}.

Before a policy switch, real money balances will be falling monotonically and the nominal interest rate will be rising monotonically, as in the case of certainty. In sharp contrast to the certainty case, however, the inflation rate *need not* rise monotonically. To see why, let us derive an equation for the inflation rate from (2.43). Solving (2.43) for π_t, one obtains

$$\pi_t = -\rho + \frac{h'(m_t)}{u'(y-g)} - \phi(b_t)\left[1 - \frac{m^{\mu}(b_t)}{m_t}\right]. \qquad (2.44)$$

The first two terms on the right-hand side are as in the certainty case, giving the one-to-one relation between m_t and inflation seen under certainty. The third term, however, need not be so well behaved. If the risk premium rises fast enough, the inflation rate may *decline* along the dynamic path. For example, since the hazard rate approaches infinity as t approaches $T_{\max}$, this last term will dominate the dynamics near $T_{\max}$. If the hazard rate approaches infinity faster than the term in brackets approaches zero, the inflation rate must fall as we get close to $T_{\max}$, and hence will first rise then fall along the dynamic path, "overshooting" its steady-state value. Any cyclical movements in the risk premium will induce similar movements in the rate of inflation.

The results in the last paragraph show that uncertainty *per se* about government policy can have significant effects on macroeconomic dynamics. In comparing the certainty case (where inflation was monotonic) to the case of uncertainty (where it need not be), we see that uncertainty about economic policy itself can induce variability in inflation that would otherwise not be there! This argument is often made, but with little backing. This example gives a formal demonstration of the argument.

Uncertain Timing and Fiscal Policy

Having worked out the implications for inflation dynamics of uncertainty about monetary policy, we quickly summarize results for fiscal policy. The interested reader should be able to work out many of these results on his own. (It will be a good exercise to test one's understanding of the methodology.) Otherwise, he can refer to Drazen and Helpman (1990).

The dynamics associated with a change in lump-sum taxes τ should be straightforward to derive. Consider momentarily the certainty case. Inspection of (2.33) indicates that the $\dot{m} = 0$ locus is unaffected by changes in τ, so that the $\dot{m} = 0$ locus is also the terminal surface $m^\tau(b)$ for intertemporal budget balance brought about by increases in τ. The evolution of the economy is also represented by movements along the $\dot{m} = 0$ locus. To see this, note from the phase diagram, Figure 2.2, that since the system's dynamics always move away from the horizontal $\dot{m} = 0$ locus, the economy can end up along this locus only if it always moves along it. Hence, the evolution of the economy is such that an anticipated change in lump-sum taxes to close the budget deficit at some future date will have no effect on consumption, money balances, inflation, or interest rates. The deficit will be reflected simply in the growth of debt before the date of the policy change, with the present discounted value of nondistortionary taxes being independent of the date of the policy change that eliminates the deficit and any further growth in the debt. This characteristic of macroeconomic dynamics under changes in the timing of lump-sum taxes is termed **Ricardian equivalence**. Note that Ricardian equivalence will *not* hold if the fiscal change involves distortionary taxes, as our discussion of the "inflation tax" above made clear.

Ricardian equivalence *does* hold under uncertain timing of changes in nondistortionary taxes. Formally, one sees that the differential equations are unaffected by timing uncertainty, so the dynamic paths must be unaffected as well. Intuitively, if Ricardian equivalence holds, so that the timing of a tax change is irrelevant (given the present discounted value of taxes), uncertainty about the timing of tax collections cannot matter if there is no uncertainty about the present discounted value of tax payments.

Uncertain timing of changes in government spending is another story entirely, as the discussion in the last few pages suggested. With the real interest factor depending on the timing of policy changes, the government's budget constraint is affected by timing uncertainty about government spending. In integral form, the government's budget constraint may be written

$$\int_{x=t}^{\infty} e^{-[R(x)-R(t)]}[\,\mu(x)m(x) + \tau(x) - g(x)]\,dx = b_t. \qquad (2.45)$$

To obtain a differential equation for b_t, note first that (2.34), which gives b_T and the values of the policy instruments at and after T, can be solved to yield the marginal utility of consumption at and after a policy switch as a function b_T. Denote this quantity by $u'^g(b_T)$ for the case where the policy changed at T is the level of government spending g. Differentiating (2.45) with respect to time and using the quantity $u'^g(b_T)$, (2.39) for the real interest rate, and (2.42) for the hazard rate, one obtains an equation for the evolution of the debt b_t in place of (2.28), namely,

$$\dot{b}_t = \left[\rho + \phi(b_t)\left[1 - \frac{u'^g(b_t)}{u'(y-g)}\right]\right]b_t + g - \tau - \mu m_t. \qquad (2.46)$$

To obtain an equation for the evolution of real balances, one combines (2.40) with $\dot{m}/m = \mu - \pi$, (2.42), and $u'^g(b_T)$ to obtain

$$\frac{\dot{m}_t}{m_t} = \mu + \rho - \frac{h'(m_t)}{u'(y-g)} + \phi(b_t)\left[1 - \frac{m^g(b_t)}{m_t}\frac{u'^g(b_t)}{u'(y-g)}\right]. \qquad (2.47)$$

Equations (2.46) and (2.47) are the differential equations for the case of an uncertain date of a cut in government expenditures to balance the budget. The $\dot{b} = 0$ locus is upward sloping, while the $\dot{m} = 0$ may slope either up or down, or may "wiggle," with both positive and negative slopes at different points. The dynamic paths are further complicated by the jump in the price level and hence in real balances at the date of a policy change even if perfectly anticipated. Hence, the endpoint corresponding to a policy switch at T_{max} is not a point on the terminal surface $m^g(b)$ defined by (2.34), but a point defined by the size of the jump in the price level at T_{max}. A large

56

variety of trajectories are possible. The interested reader may consult Drazen and Helpman (1990), where this case is worked out in detail.

Uncertainty about the Composition of a Policy Change

Consider now the case where the timing of a policy change is known, but there is uncertainty about the form this policy change may take. For example, it may be widely believed that an austerity program will be put in place after an election whose date is known, but the nature of the program is uncertain. Or, if two ideologically different parties are contesting an election, the policy that will be followed after the new administration is in office will be uncertain. Models of this type will be studied in detail in Chapter 7, but where the specification of uncertainty is generally extremely simple. Here, on the basis of the above framework, we consider a more general treatment.

A key component in deriving the dynamic paths induced by changes in a single policy were the terminal surfaces $m^\mu(b)$, $m^\tau(b)$, and $m^g(b)$, corresponding respectively to a change in the nominal money growth rate, lump-sum taxes, and government expenditures at T. For a change in a single policy at a known T, the pre-switch policy vector (μ, τ, g) and the equations (2.28) and (2.33), combined with the relevant terminal surface, determine the dynamics prior to the policy change. The effect of known combinations of changes in μ, τ, and g at a known T can be found by a simple extension of the framework. A terminal surface reflecting the policy mix can be derived from the terminal surfaces $m^\mu(b)$, $m^\tau(b)$, and $m^g(b)$, and the same methodology can then be applied. For example, if the deficit will be closed by a combination of higher lump-sum taxes and higher money growth, the terminal surface will lie between $m^\mu(b)$ and $m^\tau(b)$, its exact location dependent on the precise mix of the two policies that is anticipated. For sake of illustration, denote by $m^s(b_T)$ the terminal surface associated with a specific known combination of policies at T. Given $m^s(\cdot)$, one can derive the value of terminal debt b_T and the level of terminal real balances $m^s(b_T)$ associated with this policy change for known T. More generally, any policy composition (g_T, τ_T, μ_T) at T will induce a pair of terminal values for debt b_T and real balances m_T given the terminal surface corresponding to the mix, where both values will vary as the policy mix varies for given T.[13] Since the nominal money supply cannot jump at T, a locus of terminal values (b_T, m_T) induced by different compositions (g_T, τ_T, μ_T) is equivalent to a locus (b_T, P_T) of terminal debt and the

---

[13] This solution to the problem presented here differs from that presented in Drazen and Helpman (1990), who assumed that T uniquely determines b_T. Though this equivalence holds for a given instrument, it no longer holds as we allow the policy mix at T to vary. Differential equations before T are invariant to the post-switch policy mix, but different terminal surfaces imply different initial values of m_0 and different terminal values of b_T consistent with reaching the surface from the given initial debt b_0 in length of time T.

post-switch price level. Call this surface $b_T = B(P_T)$, each price level corresponding to a different mix of policy changes at T.

The association of different policy compositions with different terminal price levels when the date T of policy switch is known forms the basis of a discussion of uncertain policy composition. Given T and the known surface $b_T = B(P_T)$, uncertainty about policy composition from the point of view of the individual is uncertainty about the post-switch price level P_T. Let $\Gamma(P_T)$ be the distribution of the post-switch price level induced by the subjective probability distribution over possible policy mixes, as well as knowledge of the structure of the economy linking a policy mix to a value of P_T. The representative individual's problem is to maximize expected discounted utility where T is known and $\Gamma(P_T)$ is used to form expectations. His objective function under uncertainty about the composition of policy, analogous to (2.36) for the case of timing uncertainty, may be written

$$\int_{t=0}^{T} e^{-\rho t}\left[u(c_t) + h\left(\frac{M_t}{P_t}\right)\right] dt$$

$$+ e^{-\rho T}\int_{P_T=0}^{P_T=\infty} V^s\left(b_T + \frac{M_T}{P_T};T\right) d\Gamma(P_T) dT. \qquad (2.48)$$

The individual chooses time path for his choice variables, subject to (2.30) and (2.31). The dynamic paths are the same as in the certainty case.

To find the endpoint of the dynamic path, and thus tie down the evolution of b_t and m_t before T, note that once a policy composition is announced at T, the economy must jump to the terminal surface corresponding to that policy mix, meaning to the value $m_T = m^s(b_T)$ for the value of b_T that has been reached, where this value will be reached by a jump in the price level P_T. The expected price level the instant before the price level is announced depends on the probability of different policy compositions. Specifically, it is determined by an asset pricing equation analogous to (2.38):

$$\frac{1}{P_t} = \int_{x=t}^{T} e^{-\rho(x-t)}\frac{h'(m_x)}{u'(y-g)}\frac{1}{P_x} dx + e^{-\rho(T-t)}\int_{P_T}\frac{1}{P_T} d\Gamma(P_T), \quad (2.49)$$

which can be derived from the individual's first-order conditions. Hence, as t approaches T, $1/P_t$ must approach the expected value of $1/P_T$, the last term in (2.49). This ties down the price level the instant before T, and thus the level of terminal debt via $b_T = B(P_T)$ and the associated level of real money balances, m_T. These terminal values tie down the entire path.

Expected Policy Reversals

The crucial link between current and future economic policy in this approach is the government's intertemporal budget constraint. Expectations of policy change reflect the infeasibility of current policy being continued indefinitely. To model uncertain timing of a policy change in this case, we considered the case where the probability of a policy switch was an increasing function of government debt outstanding. Specifically, we simply assumed that the conditional probability of a policy change (the hazard rate) is an increasing function of the level of debt, as in (2.42). This specific representation was motivated by the impossibility of satisfying the government's budget constraint if debt gets too large. The positive dependence of the hazard rate on debt for levels of debt that are consistent with steady state was justified on that basis, but the specific assumption was *ad hoc*.

Bertola and Drazen (1993) suggest an alternative way of modeling an endogenous probability of a policy change flowing from the government's intertemporal budget constraint. The ratio of government spending to output is assumed to follow Brownian motion with an upward drift, so that without a policy change it may be impossible to satisfy the government's intertemporal budget constraint. To maintain intertemporal balance, it is therefore assumed that there is a discrete cut in this ratio when it hits a critical high level, where the level that induces the policy change is known, but the date at which it will be hit is stochastic. We discuss the model and its implications in greater detail in Chapter 14, where we discuss theories of the size and growth of government.[14] It provides another example of how effects of policy which differ from what simple textbook models would predict may reflect the anticipation of policy change engendered by current (infeasible) policy.

One may conclude by noting that all of the models in this section have derived the link between current and future expected policies from the government's intertemporal budget constraint. The alternative is to view expectations of policy change as coming from the political process, which will be our focus in the rest of the book. For example, expectations of a policy change engendered by economic deterioration coming from a political model form the basis of models of the political economy of crisis considered in Chapter 10.

2.6. CONCLUSIONS

In this chapter, we have presented a number of economic models that are useful in political economy. Sometimes, as in the case of the

---

[14] Calvo and Drazen (1998) also focus on dynamics of consumption in a model of uncertain duration of current policy along the lines of Drazen and Helpman (1990).

principal–agent model, a model is useful not only as an analytical tool, but also as the conceptual basis for political models. Other times, as in the case of the overlapping-generations model, a model is useful as an extremely powerful tool of economic analysis, with no political content *per se*. Variants of the OLG model will be used repeatedly in the book. In contrast, the continuous-time model of uncertain future policies presented in the previous section will not be much used directly in this book, though specific concepts and results will be used. It is meant more as a self-contained introduction to the analysis of an important set of issues for students interested in going deeper in the field of political economy. Finally, the material in this chapter may be useful in a more conceptual sense, helping some readers to become more familiar with the way of thinking underlying methods of economic analysis.

At this point, one may find it useful to treat the chapter as one treats an address book. One does not need to become fluent in all the models before continuing, but it helps to know where they are so one can come back to them as needed.

CHAPTER THREE

Decisionmaking Mechanisms

> Robinson Crusoe ... must somehow confront three
> fundamental and interdependent economic problems.
>
> —*Paul Samuelson,* Economics, An Introductory Analysis

> Unlike Robinson Crusoe on his island, human beings in
> society cannot coexist unless a regime and government is
> imposed upon them, or they impose it on themselves.
>
> —*Yeshayahu Leibowitz, "The Religious*
> *Significance of the State"*

3.1. INTRODUCTION

Our study of political economy began with the observation that in the real world, policies are chosen not by an infinitely lived social planner, but by a political mechanism that must balance conflicting interests. This led to the central question of the book—how does the political nature of decision-making affect which policies are chosen and, ultimately, the economic effects that these policies will have? The natural place to begin the study of political economy is thus with the mechanisms themselves by which collective choices are made. In political economy, our interest is in the effects of different policy choice mechanisms on economic outcomes, rather than in the decisionmaking mechanisms *per se*. The latter question is more the province of political science or of public choice; in the latter choice mechanisms are studied using tools of economic analysis. Public choice theory considers not simply the positive and normative aspects of different ways of making collective choices, but also the question of how a society can choose over the set of possible choice mechanisms.

Though the study of choice mechanisms *per se* is not the purpose of this book, one cannot understand the *effects* of different ways of making collective choices without some understanding of the mechanisms themselves. In this chapter, we therefore consider the workings of a number of choice mechanisms. However, the chapter should *not* be seen as an introduction to or summary of the theory of political decisionmaking or public choice. The field is far too broad to be covered in a single chapter, even by a practitioner. For those interested in textbook treatments, there are a number of options. The classic work in public choice is Buchanan and Tullock (1962). An excellent general treatment of public choice, now the standard text, is Mueller (1989). More recent work is covered in Mueller (1997), a collection of survey papers. Ordeshook (1986) presents a mathematical treatment of decisionmaking mechanisms.

While this chapter is designed to be less than a comprehensive introduction to the theory of political choice mechanisms, it is also meant, at the same time, to be something more. In looking at the relation between political economy on the one hand, and political science and public choice on the other, a basic methodological question must be faced, namely, *how much detail about choice mechanisms should the study of political economy include?* This question is far more than one simply of methodology, however, for it gets to some basic conceptual issues about the field of political economy itself. In addition to considering various collective choice mechanisms, the chapter aims to provide perspective on the relation of political economy to the underlying theory of political choice. And, it is meant to present, and perhaps make persuasive, a particular approach.

3.2. How Much Political Detail?

We begin by suggesting why the question on the relation of fields is so important. The methodological question raised in the previous paragraph is, of course, not unique to political economy. It arises whenever one field is based on another. How much atomic physics need a chemist know? (Similarly, how much chemistry need a biologist know? And so on.) To put the question more precisely, in order to understand chemical phenomena, how much of the underlying physics of atomic interactions need a chemist know? The answer clearly depends on the specific phenomenon the chemist is studying.

In the case of political economy, however, the question "underlying detail" is far more central to the field, since we are studying the effect on outcomes of different ways of making collective choices. Can one really study this without studying the details of the political mechanisms themselves? The answer is not quite as obvious as this way of putting the question may suggest. Political institutions clearly matter for outcomes, but that observation alone does not tell us *which* institutional details matter. Legislative rules on when a proposal under consideration may be amended are often crucial to policy outcomes if "when" refers to the stage in the process at which amendments may be proposed. It is unlikely to be important if "when" refers to the time of day the legislature usually meets. That is, in looking at the effect of decisionmaking procedures on outcomes, the question is not whether the decisionmaking process "matters," but which aspects of the process are crucial and which aspects we can abstract away from. One can err in either direction: one can specify institutions and differentiate decisionmaking processes in such detail that no regularities emerge; or, one can represent institutions on so abstract a level that the result tells us little about what to expect from real-world institutions.

An analogy to the methodology of production functions will be useful here. Though we often think of a production function as a structural relation, it is also a reduced form in that it indicates the maximum level of output attainable for a given combination of inputs, without giving the precise details of the production process. For most economic questions concerned, for example, with steel production, we do not need to know the engineering details of how a blast furnace works, the order of combining the inputs, and similar details. We *do* need to know how the level of output changes as we increase inputs. For some questions, it is sufficient to *assume* that the production function has certain "reasonable" basic properties (for example, a positive first derivative), consistent with any production process. For others, it is necessary to know whether a given assumption (such as a negative second derivative) in fact holds. And, for still other questions, much more detail about the shape of the production function is necessary. In each case, the properties reflect underlying production or "institutional" details. How much we need of these details depends on the question being asked. No serious researcher would presume he could understand how employment in the steel industry responds to a cyclical downturn without knowing some of these details. Knowing work rules in terms of how much job protection different workers have might be important; knowing the rules as far as who gets laid off first is probably much less important. Knowing which details are important is not easy; it usually becomes clear only after one is well into a research project.

Analogously, a relation between the political mechanism and economic outcomes, that is, a "production function" relating the desires of heterogeneous interests to collective decisions and final economic outcomes, is necessarily a "reduced form" to someone doing research in political economy.[1] But, the question of how much underlying detail is necessary in order to understand a given phenomenon is at least as complicated as the analogous question for standard production functions presented in the previous paragraph, and the answer to this question will generally be far from clear initially. (It is probably far *more* complicated, not only because

---

[1] "Reduced form" should not be taken in its most literal sense as a functional relation between resources devoted to the political process and final outcomes, but more generally to the idea that one is not interested in all the institutional details in considering, for example, the effect of elections on unemployment. Reduced forms in this literal sense are considered in Section 3.7.

we have far less experience with political economy, but also because the concept of *maximum* output for a given input is clearly inappropriate for a "political production function.") Since this relation is the essence of political economy as we have defined it, the "underlying detail" question is therefore not simply the sort of preliminary question of methodology that must be asked when beginning the study of any field.

Let us continue, for a moment, with the analogy of how to specify the production function for steel. Simply assuming certain "reasonable" properties for a political-economic outcome function by analogy to standard production functions (for example, increased lobbying increases the probability of favorable legislation, but at a decreasing rate) is not uncommon, but has very little to recommend itself *a priori*. One needs more detail as to how lobbying works as part of the political process, and, moreover, great care in making "reasonable" simplifying assumptions. To take an example, in a representative democracy, policy choices resulting from an election of a new legislature depend on the outcome of bargaining among the representatives. What is the relation between vote totals in the election and legislative outcomes? A "reduced form" approach would put certain reasonable restrictions on this relation. But, what is reasonable? Consider the assumption that the higher a party's vote total is, the more influence it will have on outcomes, an assumption which sounds pretty basic. However, in systems with more than two parties where coalition governments are the norm, the coalition is usually not between the two parties with the largest vote totals, but between the party with the largest vote total and a smaller party. (See Section 3.6 below.) Hence, if the changes in vote totals change the ranking of the second- and third-ranked parties, the reality is exactly the opposite of our "reasonable" assumption. Moreover, this example is not a mathematical curiosity, for exactly this possibility often enters into strategic planning before an election.

There is no simple answer to the question of how much underlying detail about choice mechanisms one needs, and what are reasonable restrictions on reduced form relations, since obviously none exists. In later chapters, as we study various models, one question will always be that of how much detail we need. The approach taken in this book is to attempt to find regularities that do not require too fine detail about institutions. The discussion in this section suggests at least three guidelines. First, one should be careful in making assumptions about the "reasonable" characteristics of political behavioral relations. Second, finding out how much detail is necessary may be an iterative process, which suggests that it is probably preferable to give more rather than less detail at this point. Hence, some of what follows is included not because it is directly used in later chapters, but because it may be relevant for alternative models, or simply because it gives useful background. Third, one should be extremely cautious in trying to derive "general" results, and one should be somewhat skeptical of theorems that give the appearance of great generality. In this chapter, we set out details of some choice mechanisms and techniques, without arguing that there is exactly the right amount of detail. We begin with a discussion of public choice.

3.3. CHOOSING DECISIONMAKING MECHANISMS

Public choice applies the methodology of economics to politics, specifically to the study of decisionmaking procedures. Technical tools of analysis are used to discover positive and normative properties of different collective choice mechanisms, for example, majority rule. In addition to studying the mechanisms themselves, public choice is also concerned with the choice of such mechanisms. This includes not simply questions of procedural rules in elections, committees, legislatures, *et cetera*, but also the more general question of how a society chooses the mechanisms for making collective choices, that is, for making specific policy decisions.[2] Issues concerning the choice of mechanisms for making political decisions are often termed *constitutionalism*, though rules concerning the process of making collective choices is but one aspect of constitutions. We therefore begin with constitutionalism more generally, before focusing on the specific question of constitutionalism as defined in the public choice literature. Insightful discussions of constitutions that are accessible without a background in legal or political theory are Elster (1995) and the collection of essays in Elster and Slagstad (1988), especially the introductory essay.

Constitutions

Constitutions are widely seen as containing a society's most basic laws. They may take the form of a specific document (as in the United States Constitution), a group of laws referred to collectively as "the constitution," or laws which are constitutional according to the definitions below, even though no formal written constitution exists. In fact, constitutional laws may even be unwritten, that is, there may be unwritten *conventions* of a constitutional nature, as for example the independence of the Federal Reserve Board in the United States. What defines a law as "basic" is a more difficult question. What is "basic" about the prohibition in the U.S. Constitution against a state using anything other than gold or silver coin as legal tender?[3]

---

[2] There is an "infinite regress" problem here, for, as Buchanan and Tullock (1962, p. 6) put it, "in postulating a decisionmaking rule for constitutional choices, we face the sample problem when we ask: How is the rule itself chosen?" We return to this point shortly.

[3] Article 1, section 10, clause 1. See, however, *The Federalist*, No. 44 for a discussion suggesting what may be "basic" about this provision.

In considering what it is that distinguishes "constitutional" laws from other types of laws, four not entirely distinct characteristics suggest themselves. First, a substantial part of constitutions concerns restrictions on the government's use of authority. To the extent that politics is defined as the struggle over authority (see the discussion of Lindblom [1977] in Chapter 1), control of authority is fundamental to the process of government. Second, a significant part of many constitutions concerns the process of policymaking, that is, laws which are fundamental in the sense that they are laws about how collective choices should be made. This will be the focus of our discussion below. Third, constitutions often treat issues that are fundamental in a deeper conceptual sense, that is, basic rights or liberties, such as freedom of speech or freedom of religion.[4] A fourth characteristic, reflecting the other three, is that constitutions have more stringent amendment procedures than other laws.

In public choice theory, the key characteristic of constitutions is the second, namely, that they concern the choice of rules for making collective decisions. (In Chapter 5, in discussing solutions to the time-consistency problem, we will consider the first and fourth aspects in some detail.) Though it may seem obvious that the choice of such rules is at the heart of public choice, this emphasis may be better understood by considering the view of government in general in public choice theory.

The Creation of Government and Majority Rule

The starting point is that the creation of governments reflects the payoff to cooperation. Consider two statements by leading public choice theorists of the centrality of the benefits of cooperation to the conception of government. In their classic work, *The Calculus of Consent, Logical Foundations of Constitutional Democracy*, Buchanan and Tullock (1962, p. 19) write,

> At base, political or collective action under the individualistic view of the state is much the same [as the mutually beneficial exchange relationship of individuals in the market]. Two or more individuals find it mutually advantageous to join forces to accomplish certain common purposes.

---

[4] Mueller (1997) suggests "fundamental" rights may be defined by very large asymmetries in expected gains and losses to the interested parties. The extreme importance of modes of behavior (such as religious practice) to what is often a minority of the population suggests that decisions on prohibiting those modes of behavior should require far more than a majority. In fact, rights for certain types of behavior may be constitutionalized because it is known *ex ante* that there will be cases in which a majority of the population will be quite agitated by its practice. In Mueller's view (1997, p. 133), "[r]ights, from the perspective of constitutional public choice, are a substitute for the unanimity rule with lower decision costs." Also crucial is the uncertainty of the constitution's drafters about the side of an issue on which they may find themselves. North (1990b) makes a similar argument about the role of self-interest in drafting a constitution.

Along the same lines, Mueller (1997, p. 125) writes,

> The first question public choice asks is why rational self-interested individuals would create the institutions of government. The answer usually given is that there exist situations . . . in which the independent, self-interested actions of each individual lead to outcomes that are Pareto inferior to what could be achieved through cooperative agreement.

However, all individuals will not benefit equally under each possible sort of cooperative agreement, so that the decision about what will be the "rules of cooperation" becomes crucial.

Choosing the rules by which decisions will be made is a conceptually thorny issue. One approach is to argue that since governments are formed by a voluntary agreement among citizens, the rules for choosing government policies should be such that the government chooses to engage in activities that make all citizens better off. This, in part, is the reasoning behind Buchanan and Tullock's (1962) argument that, because of the "infinite regress" problem (see footnote 2), a rule of unanimity be used at the "ultimate constitutional level." This was the view of government of Wicksell (1896), who advocated unanimity for governmental decisions. This may work for very small groups (especially for a group of two!), but it becomes infeasible to reach a decision under this rule in larger communities. The transaction costs of reaching consensus in groups even only of moderate size will become prohibitive.

The high payoff to collective action on the one hand and the infeasibility of unanimity on the other implies that alternative decision rules must be found. How should this be accomplished? The public choice approach to constitutionalism gives a central role to the costs of reaching agreement, in line with the analysis of the problem of choosing decisionmaking mechanisms from an economic point of view. For example, Buchanan and Tullock begin with the recognition that the "attainment of consent is a costly process," so that constitutional choices reflect a balancing of benefits and costs. Choice of rules for making decisions will use a benefit–cost analysis.

For example, if the transaction costs of the unanimity rule are prohibitive, a society must make a constitutional decision on what fraction of the total number of citizens is necessary to enact a policy. What is the optimal fraction N^{maj} of the total vote (that is, the size of the majority) that is needed to enact legislation? Consider the analysis presented in *The Calculus of Consent*. Crucial to the analysis are two effects that changes in the required majority N^{maj} size will have on individual welfare. First, as mentioned above, Buchanan and Tullock assume that decisionmaking costs ζ depend on N^{maj}, where this dependence is increasing and concave. Second, they assume that individuals at the constitutional stage are uncertain whether they would be on the winning or losing side of a policy decision in the future, with q being the probability of gaining from collective action. This probability depends on the size of the majority needed to take an action, with this dependence being increasing and concave $(q'(N^{maj}) > 0, q''(N^{maj}) < 0)$. Also, $q(1) = 1$, since the requirement of unanimity implies that an individual will block any action which does not give him benefit. Since an individual is uncertain whether he will gain from a decision in the future, he chooses the decision *rule* (that is, the required majority) to maximize his expected gain from establishing a decision procedure. Optimization implies that at the constitutional stage, each individual equates the expected marginal gain from increasing the required majority (and thus increasing the probability that he gains from a collective decision) and the marginal cost of increasing N^{maj}, namely, the higher costs of reaching a decision when a larger majority is required for action.

Depending on the nature of the gains (losses) from being on the winning (losing) side, and on the shapes of $q(N^{maj})$ and $\zeta(N^{maj})$, different types of majorities will be optimal in theory for different types of decisions. In practice, a wide variety of types of majority rule is impractical, with there being a limited number of types, such as simple majority, two-thirds majority, *etc.* If every proposal receiving a fraction N^{maj} of the total vote were adopted, no N^{maj} less than one-half is feasible, for it would allow passage of mutually inconsistent proposals.[5] Hence, a simple majority is the smallest possible N^{maj}. For issues which imply relatively small gains and losses to different groups, positive decision costs will imply that a simple majority is optimal, since this is the smallest possible "majority" which will prevent mutually inconsistent proposals from being accepted. When the gains or losses from decisions requiring collective action become significant, or when marginal decision costs become sufficiently low, majorities above the simple majority become optimal.

The choice of the size of the majority necessary to enact a policy has major implications for economic outcomes, our focus in the book. Depending on the distribution of underlying policy preferences, the size of the needed majority may clearly affect what policy is chosen. More relevant is the question of whether there will be *systematic* effects of majority size on policy choice and economic outcomes. As the above discussion suggests, it will be harder to adopt new policies for N^{maj} large; this implication of majority size on outcomes will be a key factor in the failure to adopt, or the delay in adopting socially beneficial policies, discussed in Chapter 10, and in the design of transition programs, discussed in Chapter 13. It will appear, less crucially, in other applications as well.

---

[5] Note that the discussion here is *not* about plurality, which allows the proposal getting the highest total in a single vote to be adopted, even if this fraction is less than one-half. It is about a voting rule for an ongoing legislative process, where *every* proposal getting at least m would be adopted.

Checks and Balances

Another key aspect of rules for collective choices, often embodied in the constitution, is joint or overlapping decisionmaking, allowing different government authorities to be involved in, and hence potentially obstruct, the workings of one another.[6] The first and second aspects of constitutional laws (restriction of government's authority and process of policymaking) clearly interact here. Known informally as "checks and balances," the purpose is to limit the power of any one component of government and of the government as a whole. In the United States, for example, the principle of *separation of powers* of the executive, legislative, and judicial branches of government, as embodied in the U.S. Constitution, is designed to achieve this end. Separation of powers attempts to limit the power of government by "dividing it against itself," specifically, by setting up procedures requiring some decisions to be approved by more than one branch. (*The Federalist*, No. 51, is a very clear discussion of the rationale for separation of powers.)[7] In the U.S. Constitution, limitation of government power via conflict of interests between its parts was stimulated by giving each branch a different base. This followed Montesquieu's precept of a "mixed regime"—each branch, selected in a different way, would represent different interests and views, leading to a welfare-improving competition among them.

One should not confuse this notion of "separation of powers" with simple "division of authority" in which a unit has *sole* authority over a decision, or with the case of multiple units having *independent* jurisdiction in the same area. Though these concepts sound identical, separation of powers and division of authority are, in fact, somewhat the opposite of one another, as is made clear by Neustadt's (1960, p. 33) definition of the former as "separated institutions sharing power."[8] Moreover, these two ways of allocating power across government have very different implications. For example, if the power to print money is given to multiple authorities that can act independently, the result is too great a monetary expansion, relative to the optimum. On the other hand, under separation

---

[6] Or, as Madison put it in *The Federalist*, No. 51, "by so contriving the interior structure of the government as that its several constituent parts may, by their mutual relations, be the means of keeping each other in their proper places."

[7] Persson, Roland, and Tabellini (1997) show formally how a conflict of interests between policymakers based on the separation of powers can improve voters' welfare.

[8] The subtlety of the concept of separating power in order to limit it is illustrated in Madison's response to those who felt that more separation of the branches was necessary for limiting the power of government, when who wrote, "...unless these departments be so far connected and blended as to give each a constitutional control over the others, the degree of separation which the maxim requires, as essential to a free government, can never in practice be duly maintained." (*The Federalist*, No. 48)

of powers, multiple authorities can block the decision of the others in setting the money supply. Thus, independent jurisdiction will often have the opposite effect of checks and balances. This can be formalized as a "common property" model, which is introduced in Section 10.7 of Chapter 10, and will have many applications in the political economy of growth, foreign aid, and transition.

Overlapping authority is important in a number of areas of political economy. As we shall argue in Chapter 4, it underlies some leading models of time inconsistency, as well as being important in possible solutions to the problem of time inconsistency, as discussed in Chapter 5. As Elster (1995) argues, separation of powers is also necessary for effective precommitment. All-powerful dictatorships cannot credibly precommit: since, as he puts it (p. 215, italics in original) "they have all the power, they are unable to make themselves *unable* to interfere." The problem of dictators credibly precommitting themselves not to interfere will be important in understanding the political economy of low growth, as discussed in Section 11.4 of Chapter 11. More generally, overlapping authority comes into play in the political economy of international policy coordination, as discussed in Section 12.5 of Chapter 12.

One should further note that "checks and balances" in the decision process cuts both ways, so that it may either increase or reduce social welfare. In terms of the effect on policy outcomes, choices may be moderated in a socially preferred way, as in the work of Alesina and Rosenthal (1995, 1996), which we will consider in detail in Section 7.7 of Chapter 7. However, the need for consensus among overlapping authorities may thwart policy change, a point central to some explanations of policy delay discussed in Chapter 10.

A Tentative Summing Up

The preceding paragraphs give the reader only a small taste of the approach of public choice theory. Public choice theory has made invaluable contributions to the study of the relation between politics and economics not only in vastly increasing our understanding of specific choice mechanisms, but also, and perhaps far more importantly, in presenting a methodology for analyzing such mechanisms. Not traveling along the route suggested by the public choice literature does not reflect the belief that there are better avenues of analysis, but simply the fact that our destination is different. As already indicated, we are not concerned with the characteristics of decision rules *per se*, but with the implications for economic outcomes. Our discussion of decisionmaking mechanisms will thus be that of a visitor rather than a resident citizen. Subject to the issues raised in Section 3.2 of this chapter, we will try to cover enough detail to help us study the effect of politics on economic outcomes, without studying decisionmaking mechanisms themselves.

3.4. DIRECT DEMOCRACY

In its "purest" form, democracy is direct in that all members of the electorate vote directly on policies. We begin with direct democracy neither because of its Athenian pedigree nor because of any intellectual attraction to purity *per se*, but because it allows us to understand a number of important issues easily, and to illustrate a number of results in the public choice literature. It will also make clear a number of issues in representative systems.

Voting Rules

Except for decisions made by a dictator, all the rules by which choices are made are rules which, in one way or another, concern the voting procedure. These rules may be divided into four (overlapping) categories. First, what are the rules of franchise, that is, who gets to vote? Second, what are the rules determining how proposals come up for a vote, that is, broadly speaking, the rules of agenda? Third, what are the rules by which proposals are adopted, either in the ongoing legislative process (a simple majority versus a "super" majority exceeding fifty percent, up to the point of unanimity), or, in a specific decision over alternatives when more than two options are to be voted on? Fourth, what are the rules determining the information which can be communicated (or is known) when voting takes place? This fourth characteristic is not fully analogous to the first three, to the extent that it also heavily reflects the environment in which voting takes place.

As already stressed numerous times, our focus is not on the rules themselves, but on how different rules may affect economic outcomes. However, the reader should not expect that we will be able to answer this question with a high degree of generality, though we will get nontrivial results in very specific applications. First of all, the number of possible combinations of rules for the different aspects of voting is almost infinite. It will therefore be impossible to specify the effect of any possible combination of rules. Even "holding all other aspects of rules constant," one should not expect general propositions relating one aspect of rules to broad economic outcomes (such as "wider franchises, other things equal, imply more debt accumulation"). The problem here is not so much the technical impossibility of proving propositions of this sort, but the conceptual problem of what meaning can be attached to such propositions. Since voting rules in the real world do not vary one at a time, a *ceteris paribus* statement may tell us about the characteristics of a model, but will probably tell us little about the real world.

Franchise Rules

On the choice of who votes, franchise rules include or exclude potential voters in terms of some identifiable characteristic, such as income, place of residence, hair color, *et cetera*. The effect on political outcomes of a given franchise rule then may be put, in a formal sense, in terms of what are the preferences of those who vote relative to the preferences represented by a social planner choosing policy. Any systematic effect on economic out- comes must reflect a franchise rule based on an economic characteristic, or one significantly correlated with an economic characteristic (such as location in a model of local public finance). For example, if voting is restricted to individuals above a certain income level, then a program of income redistribution chosen under majority voting will most likely be less redistributive than what a social planner would have chosen. Another comparison concerns the preferences of those who vote relative to the group who will be affected. This affects both the reaction to a policy and, when choices can be revisited at a later date, its stability. This latter point becomes relevant in multigenerational models, where some agents are not yet born when decisions are undertaken, as in Section 8.6 of Chapter 8, or in spatial models with migration, as in Section 8.7 of the same chapter.

Rules on Agenda Setting

Agenda setting concerns the rules of how proposals come up for a vote, including the order of voting on proposals, the rules of amendment, and the rules concerning what happens when proposals fail. Agenda setting is crucial to what policies are chosen, so much so that the strength of the effect may be surprising. When several proposals are up for consideration, the order in which they are considered can determine which gets adopted. The rules of amendment and the rules concerning setting the "reversion" level if a policy fails can have similarly significant effects.

To see the importance of the order of voting, consider the following problem of *cycling* in majority voting, first recognized by the Marquis de Condorcet (1785). There are three voters, let us call them A, B, and C, whose preferences over three policies, π_1, π_2, π_3, are as given in Table 3.1, where $\succ$ represents "prefers to." These preferences imply that in pairwise majority voting, π_1 would defeat π_2, π_2 would defeat π_3, and π_3 would defeat π_1. If we use majority voting in which the winner of the first pairwise contest is then pitted against the remaining alternative, with the winner of that contest being the collective choice, the order of voting will determine the ultimate winner. Any of the three outcomes could be the collective outcome, depending on the order of voting. The problem illus- trated by the "Condorcet paradox," better known as **cycling**, is actually quite general. Indeterminacy in general as illustrated by this example is

TABLE 3.1
Voting Preferences Yielding Cycling

Voter	Policy Preference
A	$\pi_1 \succ \pi_2 \succ \pi_3$
B	$\pi_3 \succ \pi_1 \succ \pi_2$
C	$\pi_2 \succ \pi_3 \succ \pi_1$

seen as perhaps the major defect of majority voting as a choice mechanism. We will return to it in detail below.

In direct democracy, agenda setting refers not only to the order of voting on proposals, but also to "reversion" rules, that is, rules on the alternative to voting down a proposal. This is considered by Romer and Rosenthal (1978, 1979). Suppose voters are offered a take-it-or-leave-it proposal; if rejected, there is reversion to a prespecified, institutionally determined outcome, which may be quite undesirable. By presenting voters with such a choice, the agenda setter can have a strong, perhaps determinate influence on final outcomes. The less favorable the reversion level, the more the agenda setter can extract from the voters. Though the result is perhaps unsurprising, it has many important applications. For example, it may be a major factor in the design and management of large-scale transition in formerly socialist economies, as discussed in Chapter 13.

Adoption Rules

Rules affecting under what circumstances proposals are adopted cover several things. On the question of the percentage of the vote necessary for a proposal to be adopted, the key effect on outcomes will reflect Buchanan and Tullock's analysis summarized in the previous section. The size of the majority N^{maj} necessary for a proposal to be adopted will affect the difficulty of adopting the proposal, and, in general, the larger the majority necessary, the harder it will be to adopt a policy. Unanimity (equivalently, consensus) makes it especially difficult to adopt a policy.[9] This need not imply, however, that there will be a monotonic relation between the size N^{maj} of the majority needed and the level of a specific variable in a political-economic equilibrium. The difficulty of reaching an agreement will affect the nature of proposals adopted, as well as the time it takes to reach agreement on a given proposal in a dynamic model. However, since agents know the difficulties of reaching agreement under rules requiring larger majorities, the nature of policies actually proposed will also be affected by N^{maj}.

---

[9] The need for consensus need not be a formal characteristic of the voting process—the ability of groups to block a proposal by making it impossible to implement imposes the need for consensus.

A related issue concerns the choice of a majority or a plurality system when a choice must be made over more than two options. A single vote could be held, with the proposal receiving the most votes, that is, a *plurality*, being adopted, even if this is less than an outright majority. The adoption of a policy favored by perhaps only a fraction of the voters may make it likely that the policy will be reversed in the future. This possibility will be especially important in our discussion of economic reform and transition in Chapter 13. (In the previous chapter, we considered the technical problem of how the expectation of a policy reversal will affect economic outcomes before the fact.) Alternatively, there could be a sequence of pairwise majority votes, with the winning proposal in one vote facing the next proposal in the sequence, the chosen proposal being the one which has not lost a contest.

Information Transmission

The final characteristic of voting rules to be considered are the rules determining the information which can be communicated when voting takes place. The information that voters have when they make their decisions will clearly have a major effect on outcomes, but this in itself is not simply a "political" problem. The degree to which information is incomplete reflects the environment in which voting takes place; incomplete information is a central issue in any study of decisionmaking, independent of the political framework. Hence, in asking what is the effect of incompleteness of information when comparing a political choice mechanism to a social planner, we want to be careful to "control" for the information level due to the environment itself. More precisely, one must assume that the "underlying" information structure is the same for both social planner and collective choosers (such as the unobservability of innate ability in a model of income taxation), and then ask what differences a political mechanism will make. One cannot "bias" the conclusion by assuming that an all-powerful social planner has the ability to extract information unavailable to the participants in a real-world political mechanism.

However, holding the informational environment constant does not mean holding information constant. For the same underlying environment, the political mechanism may imply that the information structure in a political *equilibrium* is quite different than it would be with a social planner.[10] For example, if individuals have different information about the effects of a given proposal, a specific choice mechanism may imply incen-

---

[10] Besley and Coate (1995) analogously point out that one should define a "political failure" subject to the set of feasible allocations, that is, subject to the available policy instruments. They argue, for example, that it is unreasonable to judge a democracy by what can be achieved using lump-sum taxes and transfers when policymakers actually can use only distortionary or uniform taxation. See also Wittman (1989).

tives for better-informed agents to reveal or hide this information from less well-informed agents, incentives that may not exist if decisions were made by a single agent maximizing the sum of individual utilities with predetermined weights. Moreover, different decisionmaking rules may have different informational requirements for their operation, so that a given information structure may lead to different results.

Though rules for communicating information, as well as the incentives to do so, are in theory important in determining the outcomes in a direct democracy, almost all work on information and voting has been concerned with models of representative democracy. Since the questions most studied concern characteristics of representative democracy, we postpone consideration of information transmission and voting until the next section.

Indeterminate and Determinate Outcomes under Majority Voting

We now return to the question of cycling, however with the focus not on the determining role of the agenda setter, but on the inherent instability (and hence indeterminacy) of outcomes under simple majority voting. Under individual preferences implying that the sequence of voting is crucial, as in Table 3.1, instability of the following sort is present. For any proposal that is adopted, for example, in a committee, there is a new coalition that can form to defeat that proposal and adopt another in its stead. As already indicated, the nonexistence of a determinate majority winner is seen as a key defect of majority rule as a choice mechanism. It has generated extensive research in the area of public choice, on both the positive question of why outcomes appear to exhibit stability rather than cycling, and the normative question of what decision rules will eliminate or lessen the cycling problem.

Indeterminacy with Majority Voting

Though we illustrated cycling with a specific example, the problem is quite general. Enelow (1997) presents a survey on cycling under majority rule, in which he points out that it is one of the most heavily researched areas of public choice. The indeterminacy of outcomes under majority voting presents a very serious quandary for the study of political economy as well. If our interest is in the effect of political choice mechanisms on policy outcomes, a major indeterminacy result such as this would appear to make any real progress in the field almost impossible. One "solution" to the problem of indeterminacy under direct majority voting is to consider choice mechanisms that are realistic, but give determinate outcomes more generally. This is a strong attraction of representative democracy, considered in the next section. Alternatively, one can carefully specify assumptions such that results are determinate. One possibility is stronger voting rules, such as Caplin and Nalebuff's (1991) "64% majority rule," such that there is a determinate equilibrium for a broad class of preference distributions. Another possibility is imposing restrictions on preferences such that simple majority rule gives determinate outcomes. As this approach is commonly used in political economy, we consider it in detail.

The Median Voter Theorem

Restricting preferences such that simple majority voting gives a determinate outcome leads to the **Median Voter Theorem**, first put forward by Black (1948). It states that under certain conditions, majority voting leads to a stable equilibrium, with the chosen policy being that favored by the median voter. The two key assumptions are, first, voters' preferences are defined along a single dimension, and, second, that each voter's preferences are single-peaked in that one dimension. Suppose we consider a single dimension π, where voter i's preferences are represented by a utility function u^i over possible values of π. The most preferred point $\tilde{\pi}^i$ is defined by $u^i(\tilde{\pi}^i) > u^i(\pi)$ for all $\pi \neq \tilde{\pi}^i$. **Single-peaked preferences** mean that if two points lie on the same side of $\tilde{\pi}^i$, the point that is closer to $\tilde{\pi}^i$ is preferred to the point that is farther away. Formally, suppose π_1 and π_2 are two points such that either $\pi_1, \pi_2 \leq \tilde{\pi}^i$ or $\pi_1,, \pi_2 \geq \tilde{\pi}^i$. Voter i's preferences are single-peaked if and only if $[u^i(\pi_1) > u^i(\pi_2)] \Leftrightarrow [\,|\pi_1 - \tilde{\pi}^i| < |\pi_2 - \tilde{\pi}^i|\,]$. Voting being determined by the distance from the ideal point leads to the label **spatial voting** for this type of model.

One can derive single-peaked preferences from a model of constrained utility maximization as follows. Suppose that there are two categories of government spending, "guns" and "butter," where the policy choice is over the fraction of spending going to each. Suppose each individual's preferences over guns and butter can be represented by strictly convex indifference curves over the fractions of spending going to the two possible goods, as represented in Figure 3.1a, where a number of indifference curves and a budget line (technically, a two-dimensional simplex) are drawn. One can then represent these same preferences as in Figure 3.1b, giving the most preferred level of spending on guns (as a fraction of the total budget), as well as the relative preferences for other spending levels.

If each voter's preferences can be represented as single-peaked along a single dimension, one can show that the median position (that is, the position with an equal number of voters on each side) along this dimension cannot lose in a majority vote. Formally, suppose there are N voters each with a preferred position $\tilde{\pi}^i$, $i = 1, \ldots, N$. Let π^{med} be a median position in that there are an equal number of voters with preferred points $\tilde{\pi}^i$ above and below π^{med}. (With a finite number of voters, any policy position between the highest policy below π^{med} and the lowest policy above π^{med} also cannot be defeated in a majority vote. As N approaches infinity, so that every point along the π dimension is the most-preferred point of some voter, then π^{med} will be unique.) To see the median voter result,

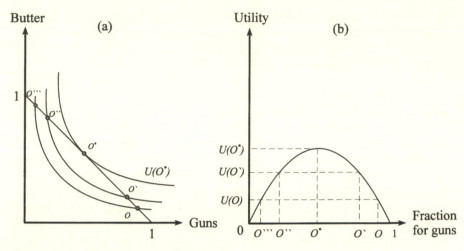

FIGURE 3.1. Single peaked preferences.

consider any $\pi_1 \neq \pi^{med}$ to see it cannot defeat π^{med} in a majority vote. Suppose $\pi_1 < \pi^{med}$. All voters with most-preferred points to the right of π^{med} prefer π^{med} to π_1, as do some to the left of π^{med} but to the right of π_1. Given that half of the voters are to the right of π^{med}, the number of voters preferring π^{med} to π_1 must be at least half of all voters, so that π^{med} could not be defeated in majority voting. An analogous argument holds for $\pi_1 > \pi^{med}$. (A more formal discussion and an extensive treatment of spatial voting may be found in Enelow and Hinich [1984].)

A key attraction of the median voter model is its simplicity. If preferences satisfy the single-peakedness condition in a one-issue world, the result is both intuitive and strong. Moreover, there are political issues where the assumptions are reasonable. For example, if the size of income-based transfers in a world of heterogeneous, observed incomes is the only political question, the conditions necessary for application of the Median Voter model are easily fulfilled. (This issue will be discussed in greater detail in Chapter 8.)

Some Drawbacks of the Median Voter Theorem

Unfortunately, the model has some significant drawbacks in terms of its application to the real world. Voters' decisions are rarely made only on the basis of a single issue, so that their voting preferences cannot generally be represented as one-dimensional. Once one moves to *multiple dimensions*, the conditions are much more restrictive, in that a dominant point under majority rule must be the median in *all* directions. (See Enelow and Hinich, chapter 3.) The theorem loses much of its intuitive attractiveness.

Difficulties also arise with preferences not defined in spatial terms. Moreover, single-peaked preferences is a strong assumption,[11] especially when a single issue has several dimensions. (Consider, for example spending on a public good which displays some economies of scale, so that a voter may prefer either very low spending or very high spending.) In short, the types of preferences needed to bring about the median voter result are quite unlikely. Mueller (1989, chapter 5) presents a good discussion.

3.5. REPRESENTATIVE DEMOCRACY

Direct democracy is not descriptive of how collective choices are usually made. In any system with a large number of voters, democracy is *representative* rather than direct, since the number of citizens becomes too large to assemble directly. That is, in addition to the problem of instability of majority-rule outcomes in a direct democracy discussed in the previous section, there is the inefficiency of requiring voting on every issue by the electorate as a whole. In any group with a sufficiently large number of voters, some sort of delegation or representation will be central to making collective decisions.

Representative democracy, however, does not refer to the size of the decisionmaking body relative to the citizenry. In an electorate where many voters have identical preferences, one could have an elected legislature in which each voter is represented by at least one person whose preferences are identical to his own. When the citizenry becomes so large that a single assembly of all voters is no longer feasible, it is still possible for each citizen's preference to be directly represented in the legislature as long as the number of distinct positions is small enough that the size of the legislature would not be unwieldy. Democracy would be representative only in the sense that a legislator represents a group of identically minded voters.

More likely, as the number of citizens becomes too large to assemble directly, not every position can be directly represented in the legislature. Hence, the essential difference between direct and representative democracy is that, in the latter case, voters, by some mechanism, choose agents who do *not* have exactly the same preferences over policies to choose policies for them. Hence, they are delegating the decision over policies to representatives, and whether their representatives choose policies which the voters favor depends on both the preferences of the representatives and on the incentives that the voters give them. Hence, representative democracy is an example of delegation, that is, of a *principal–agent*

---

[11] In the Condorcet example above, cycling arises because in any spatial arrangement of the policies π_1, π_2, π_3, one voter's preferences will be double-peaked. Draw a picture and try to prove a median voter result!

problem. We discussed the principal–agent problem in the previous chapter, and the general results will be applicable at various points to an understanding of representative democracy. This is especially true when we consider the effects of information transmission in a representative democracy, where the results on the effect of incomplete information when decisions are delegated will be quite relevant.

More generally, delegation of authority can be thought of as characterizing the great majority of choice rules in politics. Representative government is perhaps the leading example of delegation, though certainly not the only one. Legislatures do much of their work in subcommittees; the executive branch is departmentalized. There are several reasons why such delegation from a principal ("the government") to an agent (the "agency" or "authority") might have substantial effects on what decisions are taken, both the agent's decision relative to what the principal might have done, as well as the decision that two different agents may take. One may think of these differences as representing either differences in expertise or differences in objective functions. The inability to specify all contingencies also gives a role to delegation. We discuss a number of these issues in a more applied context in Section 5.3 of Chapter 5.

In a representative democracy, voters, by some mechanism, choose representatives, who in turn choose policy, where the representatives who ultimately make policy decisions do *not* have exactly the same preferences over policies as the voters they represent. Within the legislature composed of these representatives (or at some level of committees within the legislature), direct democracy describes decisionmaking. Hence, one needs to consider decisionmaking in both "stages" (choice of representatives, choice of policy by these representatives), and how these decisions will interact. That is, voters choose representatives based not only on the representative's perceived position on the issues, but also on how decisionmaking at the second stage affects the relation between a representative's positions and policy outcomes; representatives choose policy at the second stage very much aware of how this will affect voters' choices in the next election.[12]

The aspects of voting rules raised in the previous section are relevant at both levels of decisionmaking. In addition, some new issues arise. There are questions of other rules concerning the nature of the legislature, such as its size, whether it is unicameral or bicameral (and, if the latter, how authority is divided between the two legislative bodies), and other legislative rules, beyond those covered by the voting rules, by which representatives choose policy. We consider a number of these points in this and the following section. Another set of issues which are of great interest in the study of representative democracy concern the role of lobbying, or other ways of influencing policymakers. We consider these in Section 3.7.

---

[12] This is analogous, though not identical, to two-level decisionmaking in international policymaking discussed in Section 12.5 of Chapter 12.

Two-Party Competition

The most-studied case of representative democracy is probably that of two parties, each of which cares only about election to office, a single legislative body, and deterministic voting. By "two parties" one means that a voter has a choice of two sets of positions on issues ("platforms"). In saying that a party cares only about election to office, the idea is, first, that there are rents associated with office-holding *per se* (pecuniary rents, "ego rents," *et cetera*), and, second, that parties put no weight on social welfare in choosing their platforms. (We assume for now that parties can be committed to carrying out the platform they announce.) **Deterministic voting** refers to the case where parties know the distribution of voters' preferences so that it is known with certainty how choice of platforms will translate into relative vote totals.

The Median Voter Theorem and Policy Convergence in a Representative Democracy

The key result in this model of two-party competition is due originally to Hotelling (1929) and Downs (1957). With appropriate assumptions paralleling those discussed under direct democracy, a version of the Median Voter Theorem will hold. Specifically, suppose that there is a single issue π with an individual voter's preferences being single-peaked and symmetric around a most-preferred policy $\tilde{\pi}^i$ as defined in Section 3.4 and illustrated in Figure 3.1. Given these preferences, a voter's utility is monotonically decreasing in the distance between his most-preferred policy and the actually chosen policy. The number of voters with each preferred policy may be summarized in a frequency distribution as in Figure 3.2, with the median, that is, the point with half of the voter mass according to most-preferred position to its right and half to its left, being π^{med}. It is assumed that this distribution is known by all candidates and that all individuals vote.

Suppose there are two candidates (or parties) with known positions π^L and π^R to the right of π^L. Let π^{mdpt} be the midpoint between π^L and π^R, that is, the point equidistant between them. Then under the above assumptions about preferences and full participation in elections, party L with position π^L receives the votes of all individuals to the left of π^{mdpt}, and party R with position π^R receives the votes of all individuals with preferred positions to the right of π^{mdpt}. In the example in Figure 3.2, with the midpoint π^{mdpt} (for the positions π^L and π^R) being to the left of the median π^{med}, party R wins the election. This cannot, however, be an equilibrium if parties are free to adjust their policy positions. Since candidates care only about holding office, the left-wing party L will move its position π^L to the right (that is, "invade his opponent's territory"),

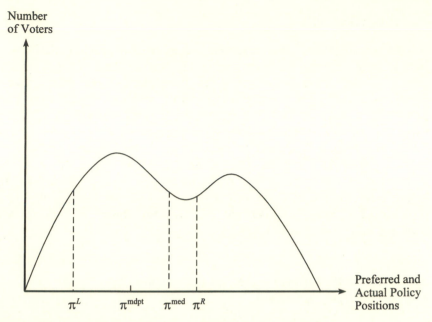

FIGURE 3.2. Frequency distribution of preferred policy position.

moving π^{mdpt} closer to π^{med} and gaining votes.[13] Competition over votes by purely opportunistic candidates will push both their positions to the center, more precisely, to π^{med}, the position favored by the median voter. In equilibrium, there will be convergence of π^{L} and π^{R} to π^{med}. This is the median voter result under two-party competition.

The logic behind the result is really identical to the median voter result in a direct democracy when there is a direct vote over issues. In the two-candidate model, the issue is the policy position of the winning candidate. Note that in this simplest version of the median voter result where all voters vote, the restriction of symmetry and single-peakedness is on individual preferences, not on the frequency distribution of preferred voters' positions. As long as there is full participation, convergence to the median of the frequency distribution will obtain, independent of the population distribution of preferences.

Indifference and Alienation

The complete participation assumption is important to the result, but surely unrealistic in at least two ways. First, voters may be *indifferent* to voting if the two parties' platforms are too close together, which could

---

[13] As Downs (1957, p. 28) put it, "Parties formulate policies in order to win elections, rather than win elections in order to formulate policies."

upset the result of convergence to the median for a general distribution. If, however, the distribution of voters' preferences is symmetric, it is easy to see that the median result will still hold. Second, voters whose desired positions are too far from the common platform may be *alienated* and choose not to vote. If the probability of voting at all is a function of this distance, platforms would converge on the *mode* of the preference distribution, which is identical to the median for a symmetric, unimodal distribution. Hence, convergence of platforms at the median voter's preferences could still describe the outcome of majority voting in a two-party system where nonparticipation is possible, as long as the distribution of preferences is symmetric and unimodal. Once either of these characteristics is no longer assumed, indifference and alienation can upset the median voter result. As in the case of direct democracy, more than one dimension to the issue space causes significant problems.

Probabilistic Voting

There is another disturbing characteristic of voting in the above model that lies behind the median voter result, namely, its deterministic character. Consider a voter infinitesimally to the right of the midpoint π^{mdpt}, given the positions π^L and π^R. He votes for certainty for party R. If party L moves its position infinitesimally to the right, this voter now finds himself to the left of π^{mdpt}, so he votes for L. Hence, the "probability" that he votes for L can be seen as a discontinuous step function. A more realistic view would be that a party's expectation of winning a voter's support is a continuous function of the distance between the party's position and the voter's position as perceived by the party. A small move to the right by L should imply a small increase in the probability that all voters to the right of the original position will vote for L. This is the reasoning behind assuming what is called **probabilistic voting**, as an alternative to deterministic voting. The idea here is not that voters choose probabilistically whether or how to vote, but that the relation between a candidate's relative position and his vote total is no longer deterministic. Instead, candidates perceive only a *probability* that voter i will support him as a function of his relative platform, denoted $q^i(\pi^L, \pi^R)$, which translates into an *expected* vote total. Probabilistic voting will be important in a number of models in Parts III and IV of the book.[14]

Probabilistic voting may be motivated by assuming incomplete information on the part of candidates about voter preferences. Though some voter

---

[14] Probabilistic voting also implies a significant difference between committee voting and electoral competition that, for many purposes, could be analyzed interchangeably under deterministic voting. Voting in committees is inherently deterministic, so a result such as probabilistic voting eliminating the cycling problem under from majority rule is of little comfort in analyzing policy outcomes in committees.

characteristics are observable, others are not, so that a change in a policy position translates only into an increase in the probability of winning an election. With probabilistic voting, the median voter result is not quite as immediate as it was above. However, if the probability functions for all voters are continuous and strictly concave in π^L and π^R over the nonnegative range that probabilities are defined, a unique voting equilibrium exists in which candidates offer the same platform.

Policy Preferences

In fact, we do not see parties' platforms converging, as Downs predicted, and for good reason. Parties are not purely opportunistic, caring only about winning elections; they have preferred policies that they want to implement once in office, and their platforms will reflect these positions. This will imply less than full policy convergence, there being two forces determining where a party's platform will lie on the policy spectrum, forces that may pull in opposing directions. On the one hand, there is the desire to win elections, pushing towards policy convergence, for example, towards the median in a model where the median voter theorem holds. On the other hand, policy preferences (or "ideology") may pull parties away from the median position.

To model the role of policy preferences and its effect on policy nonconvergence, one begins with the observation that parties care about the social welfare in their desire to carry out policies, but that the two parties do not maximize the identical welfare function. This ideological difference reflects (at least one of) two possible phenomena. First, parties may differ in their perception of social welfare, for example putting different weights on opposing policy goals in their objective functions. We will investigate this in a model of unemployment and inflation in Chapter 7, and the implications of this ideological difference for macroeconomic dynamics. Second, parties may propose policies that favor only a subgroup of the population (their "constituency"), such as right-wing parties preferring policies that favor the rich. In Chapter 8, we will consider in greater detail the notion of parties favoring specific constituencies. The effects of the possibly opposing forces of the desire to win elections and of ideology can be studied by considering an objective function that weights both an office-holding motive and an (ideologically determined) social welfare motive.

Voting Rules

We began this section with a very simple model of two-party competition. We now consider variations of the model. Having considered whether opportunism or ideology (or a combination of the two) will determine a party's platform, this means considering voting rules in greater detail—the rules by which votes are won in the initial election for representatives; the nature of voting at different stages of the process; and the rules for proposals to be adopted within the representative body. We concentrate on some issues which are raised by the representative nature of the choice mechanism.

A first crucial issue is the initial election to the legislative body, namely, the type of majority or plurality needed in the initial election for representatives. There are two main systems: proportional and "first-past-the-post" voting. In a system of proportional representation, in its simplest form, parties receive seats in strict proportion to their overall vote total, so that the entire country can be viewed as a single, multiple-seat constituency. In the simplest version of a "first-past-the-post" system, each constituency or district elects a single member by plurality vote. Neither system need be so simple. A proportional representation system can (and typically does) have a minimum percentage vote requirement for a party to enter the legislature, while in a district system, a given district can elect multiple members by some degree of proportionality within the district. Legislatures can also have members elected under both systems.

The nature of legislative voting will imply differences between underlying voter preferences and electoral outcomes. The composition of the legislature will clearly be different for the same underlying voter preferences under proportional and "first-past-the-post" representation. As we shall see in the next section, the relation between underlying voter preferences and electoral outcomes on the one hand and policy influence on the other may be especially subtle when there are more than two parties.

Amendment Rules

On the rules within the legislature, in addition to those concerning adoption and agenda considered in Section 3.4, rules of amendment become important in legislative debate. These are rules about alternatives to the proposal currently "on the floor." Under a "closed" rule, no amendments can be made, so that the proposal on the floor must either be accepted or rejected. Under an "open" rule, once a proposal is made, the relevant voting committee can either accept or amend the proposal. The effects of the rules are not as simple as one may think, since a stricter rule limiting amendments *ex post* may lead to weaker proposals being proposed *ex ante* in order to maximize the probability of passage. The distinction between open and closed rules (or analogous concepts) is important in discussing certain models of nonadoption of socially beneficial policies, as in Section 10.5 of Chapter 10, in the discussion of managing economic reform and transition in Chapter 13, and in budget rules and the growth of the budget, discussed in Chapter 14.

Sincere versus Strategic Voting

If a single vote is taken directly on an issue, one would expect voters to vote simply according to their preferences, that is, to vote *sincerely*. Under delegation, a voter may find it optimal *not* to vote according to his simple preferences in order to maximize his welfare. This is a now standard result in the theory of delegation, whereby it may be optimal for an individual to delegate a decision to someone with preferences other than his own, as in Fershtman and Judd (1987). This possibility will be central to our results on delegation as a solution to the problem of time inconsistency in Chapter 5 and to our analysis of international policy coordination in Chapter 12. In models of voting, it is known as *strategic* voting. In voting for the legislature, voters will take account of how it works. When rational candidates and voters know that legislative bargaining and coalition formation imply that outcomes will not necessarily be a simple reflection of preferences as expressed in vote totals, they should adjust their behavior. As Austen-Smith (1986, p. 85) puts it:

> So, in elections, rational policy-oriented voters will take account not simply of the particular issue positions announced by candidates contesting their district, but also of likely policy outcomes to emerge from the legislature, conditional on electing one or the other of these candidates. This in turn will depend on voters' expectations regarding both coalition formation among elected officials and the bargaining process within such coalitions. Rational office seeking candidates will take account of these voter deliberations in choosing a policy position with which to contest the election.

Strategic voting comes up not only when decisions are delegated, leading to a multistage decision problem, but also when there are multiple decisionmakers at a single stage and the franchise differs across the choice of these decisionmakers. The group of voters who choose a representative to Congress is not identical to the group which chooses a Senator or the President. Differences in the franchise both horizontally (each legislative representative is chosen by a different group) and vertically (a citizen votes for both representative and President) may lead to strategic voting.

Strategic voting may also take place within the legislature, a phenomenon known as *"logrolling."* Logrolling refers to an agreement between two or more voters for mutual support which requires each to vote against his preferences on some issue.[15] Hence, when vote trading occurs,

---

[15] On the origin of the term, Safire (1978, pp. 384–385) traces the term back to the early 1800s, writing:

> Among settlers in the wilderness, cooperation in handling logs for land clearing and construction was a force overriding any differences among neighbors. So too in politics. "If you will vote for my interest," said Congressman B. F. Butler in 1870, "I will vote for yours. That is how these tariffs are log-rolled through."

two proposals that would fail if each legislator voted sincerely may pass. The possibility of an equilibrium depends on the nature of preferences. See Wilson (1996) for an axiomatic treatment. An important result in the public choice literature is that the set of preferences that can result in vote trading would induce cycling under sincere voting. (See, for example, Mueller [1989].) Vote trading has found little application in political economy in macroeconomics. This is not because it is an unimportant idea either theoretically or empirically, but because there are a limited set of economic phenomena where vote trading is *inherent* to economic outcomes, that is, where a vote trading is central to the difference between optimal and politically determined outcomes. One example of such a case is in spending on government projects across geographical localities, as discussed in Section 8.4 of Chapter 8. Vote trading may be important in a number of programs of government redistribution, when two or more interest groups find it optimal to extract resources from general funds. It would seem to be potentially inherent to problems of multipart reform and transition, as discussed in Chapter 13, but so far it has not been formally incorporated into models of reform.

3.6. MULTIPARTY SYSTEMS

The possibility of having more than two parties raises additional issues, the most important of which is the more subtle relation between underlying voter preferences and electoral outcomes on the one hand and policy influence on the other.

Legislative Composition

The difference in legislative composition under proportional and "first-past-the-post" representation for the same underlying voter preferences, first raised in Section 3.5, may be especially striking when there are more than two parties. Under the "first-past-the-post" system, the representation of smaller parties in the legislature will be far below their strength in the electorate as a whole. Though this suggests that policies and hence economic outcomes will be dramatically different under the two systems with multiple parties, the effect is far more subtle for a number of reasons. First, the choice of systems may be endogenous to the degree of underlying policy polarization; sharp underlying differences often spawn new parties. Second, a given degree of underlying policy polarization will simply show up in a different way in a "first-past-the-post" system, affecting the choice of candidates to run in elections. More generally, strategic behavior by both voters and parties suggests caution in deriving simple conclusions.

Given the composition of the legislature, a key issue is the formation of coalitions within the legislature and the implications for policy outcomes.

There are two general approaches to the study of coalitions: the game-theoretic tradition, using game theory to study coalition formation; and, what Laver and Schofield (1991) call the "European politics" tradition, which stresses the empirical attempt to fit actual (largely European) experience of coalition government into an inductive theory.

The Game-Theoretic Approach

As the name implies, this approach uses game theory to study the formation of coalitions. In the public choice literature, the emphasis has been on what determines the formation of coalitions on a general level, that is, not only within the legislature, but in any decisionmaking group. The seminal work here is Riker's (1962) *The Theory of Political Coalitions*, using bargaining theory to study coalition formation. He argued that multiparty systems will in fact converge to two parties or two coalitions of almost equal size. A key concept is the "minimum winning coalition"—members of the governing or winning coalition want it to be as small as possible and still win, as that means the spoils of office can be divided among fewer claimants.

What does this imply for legislative coalitions? As a point of comparison, start with the model, as above, of a two-party proportional system; the party with the most votes has control of the legislature, so that legislative outcomes reflect majoritarian voting. (In fact, the winning party's influence is sometimes monotonic in the size of its majority.) In the case of nonideological parties, both parties adopt the median position, which is thus the legislative outcome as well. Given this relation between votes and outcomes, voters vote sincerely. Two key questions that arise under legislative bargaining in a multiparty system are thus: to what extent will the legislative outcome reflect the majoritarian nature of the original voting process; and, to the extent that it does not fully reflect it, how might voters and candidates adjust their behavior?

On the first question, it is generally accepted that legislative outcomes may look quite different than the underlying voting patterns might suggest. Baron and Ferejohn (1989) suggest that one crucial feature is the nature of the amendment rules, namely, whether there is an "open" or a "closed" rule. Austen-Smith and Banks (1988) consider a specific model of three-party competition under proportional voting, where legislative coalitions may be formed after the election. The main feature of the equilibrium is that, given the policy positions of the parties, only the rank order of the voting matters in determining the coalition. If no party gains a majority in the voting, the first- and third-ranked parties form the governing coalition, so that influence in the legislature is *not* monotonic in the vote share.

Knowing how coalitions are formed, voters should be observed to vote strategically. How might this look? In the three-party proportional voting model of Austen-Smith and Banks (1988) discussed in the previous paragraph, policy positions are symmetrically distributed around the mean voter's preferred position, with one party adopting that mean position. This party receives the fewest votes, but is thus assured of being a member of any coalition government. The expected legislative outcome is the median position, but the actual outcome will be skewed away from this position. Nor will all voters vote sincerely. Hence, neither will the *initial* composition of the legislature reflect the preference distribution of the population at large, nor will legislative outcomes reflect the relative weights of parties in the legislature. Austen-Smith (1986) assumes that voters assign *probabilities* to the formation of post-election coalitions, so that they are voting over lotteries with distributions conditional on district and candidate characteristics. The nature of these lotteries is endogenous, depending on the chosen positions of candidates in all other districts. Each candidate will try to move the expected outcome towards his own district's preferred (i.e., median) position, and at the same time lower the variance of final outcomes, these two objectives most likely involving trade-offs. In general, the position each candidate ends up taking will not be the median of his district, although the median voter's position will be pivotal in determining the candidate's equilibrium position.

The European Politics Approach

The study of coalitions is an important subfield of the study of politics in Europe. As Laver and Schofield put it, in their excellent book on coalition government, this approach is "above all a tradition of empirical theory and research at a cross-national level." (1991, p. 7) To a large extent, there is relatively little really convincing work here on the relation between the coalition nature of governments in proportional democracies and the economic outcomes that result.[16] We discuss some of the results for economic outcomes in this approach in Section 7.8 of Chapter 7. Though we lack models illuminating the mechanisms by which the coalition nature of governments affects economic outcomes, existing work does, however, suggest a number of building blocks.

The basic "player" in the coalition game is the party, which is typically treated as a unitary actor. Though clearly not absolutely correct, with parties being "factional" rather than "coherent," the assumption is basically reasonable for European parties, because they "are, by and large, well disciplined—going into and coming out of coalitions as a single bloc." (p. 34) (This assumption allows application of game theory to coalitions.) Party splits must, however, be considered. As far as the objectives, Laver

---

[16] As Laver and Schofield (1991, p. 194) put it "There can be no doubt...that the development of a much more comprehensive research program to assess the relationship between the policies of a coalition and the preferences of its members remains one of the most important pieces of unfinished business in the political science of government coalitions."

and Schofield argue that either opportunism (office-seeking) or ideology is compatible with notions of coalition government, though the implications for coalition formation will obviously be quite different depending on the motivation for seeking office. Also, the distinction between these two motives is not really so clear-cut.

In discussing empirical inductive results, an obvious place to start is with the theory of legislative bargaining. In a pure parliamentary system, as opposed to a mixed system with both proportional legislature and an independently elected chief executive (for example, as in France), the coalition which controls the legislature *is* the governing coalition. However, Laver and Shepsle (1990) convincingly argue that even in a parliamentary system, theories of outcomes of legislative coalitions and of the governing coalition are not identical, because of the role of the cabinet in making policies. As they put it (p. 874):

> The role of the cabinet in the business of parliamentary government is what makes the formation of government coalitions quite different than the formation of legislative coalitions. This is because the allocation of cabinet portfolios is much more than a mere "payoff".... The cabinet is part of the essential definition of the government that forms.

The emphasis on the central role of the cabinet (and, more generally, of allocation of positions in the government) in coalition bargaining and on policy outcomes is the first general result. That is, policies that are chosen by coalition governments will very much depend on who holds the relevant portfolio, so that the effect of coalition government on outcomes will depend crucially on the bargaining over the allocation of portfolios. The role of the cabinet is also central to the Laver and Schofield (1991) study as well. In discussing the role of opportunism versus policy preferences, they argue that the implications for coalition formation will obviously be quite different depending on the motivation for seeking office. As such, they disagree with the notion beginning with Downs that parties in a two-party system deliberately change their platforms so that they resemble one another, whereas parties in a multiparty system try to remain as ideologically distinct from each other as possible. In considering the payoffs to being in the coalition, they argue that holding office *per se* is important, pointing out that there can be no other explanation for the very close relationship between a party's legislative weight and the number of portfolios that it receives from its coalition partners. They point out that this connection "remains one of the most striking nontrivial empirical relationships in political science."

However, the distinction between implementing one's preferred policy and opportunism is not so clear-cut. In terms of the former, policy "payoffs" may take the form either of control over particular ministries, or of influence over the coalition policy package, but these are related. Laver and Shepsle (1990) present a model which makes this explicit.[17] A government's policy in a given area largely reflects preferences of the relevant cabinet minister, who controls sizable resources and largely determines policy in that area. They argue that it is extremely difficult to implement policy if there is active opposition from the relevant minister, or even to develop a detailed alternative to his desired policy. Hence, if the defense ministry, for example, is given to a conservative, the thrust of military policy decisions will be conservative, even if the conservatives are only a minority in the governing coalition. Second, this model of how policy is made in a coalition cabinet has strong implications for the credibility of a potential coalition's policy proposals. They argue that "a proposal that promises to enact the preferred policy position of the person (party) nominated for each relevant portfolio is *credible* in the sense that it depends only on giving ministers the power to do what they expressly want to do." (p. 874, italics in original)

A second key result on the difference between coalition and single-party governments concerns the stability of such governments, with the conventional wisdom being that the latter are far more stable than the former. As Laver and Schofield (1991, p. 144) argue, this view is too simple:

> One of the most popular misconceptions about coalition government is that it is unstable. As with many popular misconceptions, this contention has an element of truth in it, but can only be sustained on the basis of carefully selected examples. Such examples are typically drawn from Italy or from the French Fourth Republic—both coalition systems in which cabinet instability has, indeed, reached epic proportions. Rarely, however, do those who argue that coalition government is inevitably unstable talk much about Germany, Luxemburg, or Austria, each of which has been ruled more or less continuously, over the post-war period, by stable coalition administrations.

Moreover, many things bear on the durability of coalitions, so relating the durability of coalitions to policy outcomes is not as easy as some papers might lead one to believe.

Lupia and Strøm (1995) stress the importance of "no-confidence" votes in the legislature in understanding the life-expectancy of coalition governments, and perhaps the implied policy outcomes as well. They argue that crucial to a government's ability to remain in office is its ability to win votes of confidence. As they put it (pp. 62–63),

> "The support of the legislature is critical at two key stages in the life of an executive. In the first place it is often necessary for a prospective government to be able to demonstrate its legislative support before it can take office . . . . In the second place it is always necessary for a government to be able to muster

---

[17] Austen-Smith and Banks (1990) explore similar ideas for a theory of coalition governments.

legislative support if challenged. Typically, such a challenge is formalized in the parliamentary procedure of a vote of no confidence tabled by opponents, or a vote of confidence tabled by the government itself."

Having stressed the importance of winning no-confidence votes for government durability, Lupia and Strøm then point out that the ability to survive legislative challenges is *not* equivalent to having a legislative majority. There can be minority or surplus majority governments. In a coalition system where no-confidence votes are key, they argue instead for the importance of a *pivotal* party, though it plays its role in the legislature, not in the executive. They argue that in assessing the importance of such a party, it does not matter whether or not it is in the government coalition.

To take the argument a step further, since the survival of a coalition government will depend on the support of a pivotal party in the legislature, the policy chosen by such a government will thus very much depend on the policy preferences of the pivotal party. This result is analogous to those given above on the crucial role of the allocation of cabinet portfolios in coalition governments (and the close relationship between legislative strength and the number of portfolios controlled). The central role of the cabinet in coalition formation and policymaking meant that policy outcomes will very much depend on the preferences of the minister in charge of making decisions in a given area. Hence, both approaches suggest that policy outcomes in coalitions may strongly reflect the preferences of specific actors (whether in or out of the coalition depending on the specific theory), with the strength of the actor in question reflecting the coalition nature of government, a strength in determining policy that might not be present in two-party majoritarian government.

3.7. INTEREST GROUPS AND LOBBYING

In a representative democracy, a key factor in determining policy outcomes is the attempt of interest groups to influence political outcomes, either electoral outcomes, through contributions or endorsements, or legislative decisions, through lobbying. Given the importance of interest groups, much recent research in political science has been devoted to trying to formalize these effects. Austen-Smith (1997) presents an excellent review of the literature on how interest groups affect outcomes in elections and in legislatures through contributions, lobbying, and other informational activities. This section draws on his survey.

The Influence Function Approach

Early work, of which Becker (1983, 1985) was a pioneer, used a reduced form approach to model the influence of special interest groups. Approaches that entirely abstract from institutional detail have been applied in many areas of political economy. These include models of rent-seeking, presented in Section 8.5 of Chapter 8, common property models, presented in Section 10.7 of Chapter 10 and applied in Chapters 11 and 13, and war-of-attrition models, presented in Section 9.7 of Chapter 9 and applied in Chapter 10.

Austen-Smith presents a simplified version of Becker's approach. A pressure or influence function is posited, which typically depends on the size of the various interest groups and on their spending on political lobbying, with other relevant variables also sometimes being included. It is then argued that a group's influence will be increasing in its own size and spending, and decreasing in the size and spending of other groups. The impact of lobbying in a political equilibrium is then analyzed on the basis of these functions. Specifically, suppose there are two homogeneous interest groups, denoted 1 and 2, of size N_1 and N_2. Political activity could be directed at any purpose; for simplicity, suppose it is simple income redistribution. Group 1 wants to extract resources from group 2 to transfer to its own members. This policy involves deadweight costs with respect both to extracting resources and to distributing them: extracting a dollar yields only γ dollars of revenues, where $0 < \gamma < 1$; a dollar of transfers requires $\zeta > 1$ dollars of revenues. If τ is the amount of tax each member of group 2 pays and ν the transfer each member of group 1 receives, budget balance requires that $N_1 \zeta \nu = N_2 \gamma \tau$.

Each group devotes expenditures to furthering its political aims, namely, high ν by group 1 and low τ by group 2, where per capita expenditures are denoted x_i. Becker posits an exogenous relation (a political technology) between inputs and outcomes that is common knowledge. One defines a political outcome function $D(\cdot)$ such that, in equilibrium,

$$D(N_1 x_1, N_2 x_2, N_1, N_2) = N_1 \zeta \nu = N_2 \gamma \tau, \qquad (3.1)$$

where $D(\cdot)$ is increasing and strictly concave in its first argument, decreasing and strictly convex in its second argument. It is further assumed that $dD_1/dN_1 \leq 0$ and $dD_2/dN_2 \geq 0$ (an increase in group size cannot raise the marginal effectiveness of political expenditures, once all effects are taken into account), and that $D_{14} = D_{23} = 0$ (holding a group's total expenditures constant, a marginal increase in its size has a negligible effect on marginal effectiveness of the other group's political expenditures). Each group chooses its level of per capita political expenditures x_i to maximize the representative member's post-transfer income, net of political expenditures, taking as given the other group's behavior. Becker considers the (Nash) equilibrium that results, arguing for example that an increase in either type of deadweight cost reduces equilibrium τ and that politically successful groups tend to be small relative to the size of those from whom resources are extracted. (These may be derived simply by deriving the conditions defining optimal equilibrium behavior.)

Given the level of abstraction, the importance of these results for economic outcomes will depend on the specific applications. Although the political influence functions seem reasonable, but *ad hoc*, they can be given foundations. Lohmann (1995), for example, provides an informational microfoundation for political pressure and influence functions by modeling competitive political action as a signaling phenomenon.

Campaign Contributions

Most formal models of interest group activity focus on this aspect of political activity. The models may be organized in terms of what contributors hope to gain by contributing to candidates. Snyder (1990) considers an election with two candidates, call them L and R, in which contributors (that is, interest groups) want to receive favors from the winning candidate. Interest groups have no interest in the policy positions of a candidate in general and assume that their contributions have no effect on the likelihood of either candidate being elected. Instead, contributions are seen as a "contract" with recipients—a candidate commits himself to a specific level of services to a contributor if elected in exchange for a specific size contribution. Hence, provision of services in exchange for contributions is an enforceable contingent claims contract. The aggregate amount of contributions received by party j, denoted X^j, depends *inter alia* on the (exogenous) probability of a candidate winning the election. On the basis of this, Snyder derives an equilibrium relation between the election probability of a candidate (say q^L, the election probability of the L party) and both the aggregate services promised to all groups by the candidates (denoted Σ^L and Σ^R) and the fraction of aggregate contributions to each candidate. That is, for given q^L and q^R, he derives that in equilibrium,

$$q^L = \frac{X^L \Sigma^R}{X^L \Sigma^R + X^R \Sigma^L}. \tag{3.2}$$

A number of implications follow. If, for example, both candidates are constrained to give the same maximum level of promised services, then aggregate contributions X^i to a candidate will be an increasing function of his probability of winning q^i; specifically, $q^i = X^i/(X^L + X^R)$. Since services provided are independent of both policy stance and electoral outcomes, the model does not allow one to draw any conclusions about the influence of contributions on electoral outcomes and, hence, on policy and economic outcomes.

Baron (1994) presents a model of campaign contributions in exchange for services, where the optimal contingent claims contract is explicitly derived. Unlike Snyder's model, the probability of a candidate winning the election is taken to be increasing in the aggregate level of contributions he receives and decreasing in the size of contributions his opponent receives. This assumption is motivated by viewing the electoral process as yielding a "vote production function" dependent on campaign contributions. The electoral process is such that candidates differ exogenously in the relation between contributions and votes produced, for example, because of the effect of incumbency. A key result is that the candidate with the exogenously given advantage has, in equilibrium, an electoral advantage, even though he may offer fewer services per dollar of contribution. The contributions he receives are increasing in the exogenously given advantage up to a point, after which further increases in exogenous advantage translate into decreases in campaign contributions. The reason is that for a sufficiently high exogenous advantage, the candidate is so sure of success he offers few services per dollar of contribution; services provided decline fast enough with increases in exogenous advantage that contributions do as well.

An alternative to assuming that campaign contributions are made in exchange for services is to assume that they reflect relative policy stances of candidates. Austen-Smith (1987) considers a two-candidate model in which policy positions are perceived only noisily, so that relative policy platforms determine only *expected* vote totals (i.e., there is probabilistic voting). Contributions are used to reduce the variance with which candidates' positions are perceived, thus increasing their probability of election. Given the election probabilities implied by announced policy positions, interest groups contribute to promote the election of the candidate whose position they prefer, rather than to change that policy. However, since candidates realize that contributions will depend on their policy stance, strategic behavior may lead to candidates' changing their positions. If the positions of the candidates have converged, there will be no contributions. Otherwise, interest groups contribute at most to the candidate whose position is closest to their ideal point. Relative to an equilibrium in which no contributions are allowed, contributions push *both* candidates in the same direction favorable to *one* interest group, usually the largest donor.

Baron (1994) considers a model of combining services-induced and policy-induced voting, in which he derives a "vote production function" dependent on campaign contributions. The key to his model is the distinction between "informed" and "uninformed" voters. A fraction α^{inf} of voters are "informed" about the two candidates' policy positions, denoted π^R and π^L. They may care about these positions directly, or simply about private benefits they can receive from a candidate if he is elected, which are assumed to be a function of his position $\zeta^i = \zeta(\pi^i)$. They vote sincerely on the basis of what a candidate offers, and the fraction of these voters voting for a party depends on its relative position . Uninformed voters, who are a fraction $1 - \alpha^{\text{inf}}$ of the electorate, do not know (or do not care) about candidates' policy positions and respond simply to advertising financed by campaign expenditures, which in turn depend on contributions. The fraction of uninformed votes garnered by the party depends on relative expenditures, as in some of the models above. If aggregate contributions to the two candidates are X^L and X^R, the probability that candidate L wins is

$$q(X^L, X^R, \pi^L, \pi^R) = \alpha^{\text{inf}} D(\pi^L, \pi^R) + (1 - \alpha^{\text{inf}}) \frac{X^L}{X^L + X^R}, \quad (3.3)$$

where the function $D(\cdot)$ depends on a number of factors, including the distribution of voters' preferences over policy issues. The structure of the services-for-contributions function is simply assumed in order to make $D(\cdot)$ tractable. There are a number of possibilities for the effect of expenditures on the relative positions of the two candidates (that is, whether they move closer to or farther away from the median voter's preferred position), where the fraction of voters of the two types is a crucial parameter.

Grossman and Helpman (1996a) use this framework of informed and uninformed voters to study lobbying in a model where contributions are meant both to influence platforms of a given party, where contributions affect policies over which a party has no explicit preferences, and to help the preferred party win an election. The second reflects the role of uninformed (or in their terminology, "impressionable") voters, who are swayed by advertising and other campaign expenditures, financed by contributions. Parties care not simply about winning but about maximizing their vote total, that is, number of seats in legislature, as this gives them more power in bargaining and more patronage ("services") to distribute.[18] The model differs from Baron (1994) in presenting a more sophisticated equilibrium concept, with special interests presenting contribution schedules ("menus"), detailing the contribution they would give for every possible policy.[19] There are two stages in the lobbying process: first, special interests choose these menus of possible contributions to maximize their expected utility; second, on the basis of these menus, parties choose platforms and then elections are held. Differences in platforms and campaign spending determine the election outcome, which in turn determines the probability that a party's platform will be implemented.

As in Austen-Smith (1987), there is platform divergence: the party expected to win more votes gets more contributions from special interests. They cater more to special interest than the "underdog" party, which also receives contributions, but less of them. (As a result, their platform ends

---

[18] Our discussion of the formation of coalition governments in Section 3.6, especially the model of Austen-Smith and Banks (1988), suggests that the relation of vote maximization and power and patronage will be far more complicated when there are more than two parties.

[19] Bernheim and Whinston (1986) introduced this concept of "menu auctions" into the industrial organization literature.

up reflecting more the general interest.) Grossman and Helpman show how the probability of election function (3.3) can be derived from an underlying maximization problem. They further show that with many interest groups, self-fulfilling expectations equilibria are possible. Each group's contributions depend upon its expectations of contributions by other groups. If one group expects other groups to compete strongly for a given party's attention, it will as well. This party does well in elections, but groups pay dearly for this. They would be clearly better off if they could somehow coordinate on a less costly equilibrium.

Though models of campaign contributions are extremely interesting in understanding the workings of the political system in a representative democracy, they have had little impact on studies of political influences on macroeconomic outcomes. This may reflect their relatively recent introduction into the economics literature; more likely, it reflects the fact that special interest groups do not lobby for macroeconomic policies the way they lobby for microeconomic policies. (Income transfers are an exception, as discussed in several contexts in Chapter 8.) They have been more influential in the trade literature, as in Grossman and Helpman (1994).

Electoral Endorsements

Interest groups may also try to influence election outcomes via dissemination of information. This occurs both by providing information to candidates, especially about the importance of various issues to the voters, and information to the electorate about the characteristics of candidates, that is, by providing "endorsements" of candidates meant to affect voter choices. Formal work has concentrated on the latter. Grofman and Norrander (1990), Cameron and Jung (1992), Lupia (1992), and Grossman and Helpman (1996b) present models of endorsements, all with a similar conceptual structure and some similar implications. Some characteristic of candidates or their position is unknown to the voters. Endorsement by an interest group is a statement about which candidate the group (or its leaders) prefer, rather than a statement giving superior information about the candidate's characteristics or positions. Endorsements are meant to affect the behavior of less-informed voters. Endorsements may or may not have an effect in equilibrium, depending on how these voters perceive the interests of the groups making the endorsements relative to their own interests. Very roughly speaking, the greater the similarity of perceived interests is, the more effect endorsements will have. When endorsements can affect votes, candidates will compete for them (and they may have an effect even if never issued). Endorsements may increase voters' expected welfare or may move policies closer to those favored by special interests at the expense of the general public.

Legislative Lobbying

Lobbying for influence in the legislature after an election can be via contributions (for the next campaign) or by transmission of information. Research on the former is heavily empirical; Austen-Smith (1997) argues that the results have been mixed. Two theoretical studies are Denzau and Munger (1986) and Snyder (1991), both of whom find a complex relation between interest group contributions and legislative influence. Legislative lobbying has so far played little role in political economy in macroeconomics because it is much more common to lobby for trade or other "microeconomic" legislation than for macroeconomic policy. This mirrors the argument made above about models of campaign contributions.

The formal literature on interest group influence on legislatures via strategic information transmission is larger, though still in its infancy. Austen-Smith (1997) summarizes a number of papers. Models tend to be quite technical, such as somewhat abstract signaling models under incomplete information. Which legislators are lobbied on a specific issue will often depend on the position *ex ante*. Though models of legislative influence through information transmission are quite interesting, their influence on the politics of macroeconomic policies has also been limited so far, as in the case of legislative lobbying.

3.8. TRANSACTION COST POLITICS

In one of the true classics in economics, Coase (1937), "The Nature of the Firm," made clear the importance of the costs of carrying out transactions in understanding the organization of firms and other hierarchies. Though it took a long time for the seminal importance of the article to be appreciated, there is now a significant amount of work in the industrial organization literature using transaction costs to explain economic phenomena. Williamson (1989) presents an excellent survey of "transaction cost economics," as the field has come to be called.

The concept of "transaction cost" is meant to be quite broad, that is, anything that impedes an economic transaction, be it a technological cost of making the transaction, asymmetry of information between the two parties, or problems of specifying or enforcing the transaction. When nontrivial transaction costs are present, asset specificity is created, meaning difficulties in redeploying the asset to alternative uses and/or alternative users without sacrificing productive value. That is, to reap the gains from a mutually profitable opportunity, at least one party to the transaction must make a less than fully reversible investment. This specificity implies the possibility of "opportunism" (for example, dynamic inconsistency or moral hazard) by self-interested agents in exploiting this relationship. Contractual safeguards may thus be necessary to limit *ex post* opportunism made possible by the existence of transaction costs. These contracts, however, are generally incomplete, given the complexity of and uncertainty about possible states of the world. The need for safeguards (sometimes termed "governance") against opportunism, combined with difficulties in completely specifying such contractual safeguards, is what explains the characteristics of economic relationships which seem inexplicable in the neoclassical model without transactions costs.

Following this work on transaction-cost economics, there has been interesting recent research exploring a transaction cost approach to politics, spearheaded by North (1990b) and explored in a recent book by Dixit (1996). In transaction cost politics, the basic relation is a political transaction, trading votes (or contributions) for promised policies, or sometimes simply votes for votes. North argues that transaction costs—problems of information, specification or enforcement of a political transaction—are even higher in politics than in economics. As North (1990b, p. 362) writes,

> "Political markets are far more prone to inefficiency. The reason is straightforward. It is extraordinarily difficult to measure what is being exchanged in political markets and in consequence to enforce agreements. What is being exchanged are promises for votes. The observable dimensions of the promises are agreements between constituents and their representatives (in a democracy), between the representatives, between representatives and the executive, etc."

Both North and Dixit stress the time dimension of political transactions, so that the problem of dynamic inconsistency is especially acute—votes are given in exchange for promises of policies or votes at a future date, so that a breakdown of exchange due to opportunism seems likely in the absence of safeguards. We will study the problem of time inconsistency in detail in the next chapter.

Given the nature of the political transaction, the notion of a contract plays a central role in transaction cost politics. As in transaction cost economics, contracts are necessarily imperfect, in fact, far more imperfect in the political than the economic realm. Transaction cost politics gives several reasons for this. In politics, complexity and uncertainty are far more pronounced than in transaction cost economics. Contracts are far less explicit and far more difficult to enforce. Hence, while the transaction costs are higher, the contractual safeguards against *ex post* opportunism that are put forward in transaction cost economics are less effective. Forms of governance other than standard contractual remedies become more important.

Governance structures in transaction cost politics are political institutions and organizations, broadly defined. The intertemporal nature of political exchanges makes it necessary, in North's view, to devise a set of institutional arrangements that allow for exchange "over space and time." He argues that the complicated committee systems in legislatures are an example of such arrangements. Similarly, Weingast and Marshall (1988) present a theory of legislative institutions that parallels the transaction

cost theory of the firm and of contractual relations. The committee system
enforces bargains among legislators and limits the sorts of coalitions that
legislators may form, coalitions that raise political transactions costs. For
example, giving a committee monopoly rights over certain types of legislation (i.e., agenda control) means that there is a value to being in a strong
committee position. Rules controlling membership, combined with the
seniority system, thus increase the cost of not keeping bargains and
reneging *ex post*.

Dixit (1996) discusses less formal institutional governance structures,
such as commitment mechanisms to limit the possibility for dynamic
inconsistency, delegation, and structuring political institutions to maximize
repeated interactions. We consider these sorts of solutions to dynamic
inconsistency in Chapters 5 and 6. Though dynamic inconsistency and
solutions to it have not been studied in the macroeconomics literature
using the formalism of transaction cost politics, some of the insights of the
approach may be helpful in understanding these questions.

Overall, though transaction cost politics seems promising in many dimensions, as a formal approach it has so far had relatively little impact on
political macroeconomics. This reflects at least two factors. First, as
applied to the "contract" between voters and their representatives, many
of the conceptual insights have been important without the formal structure itself being applied. This parallels the comments on time inconsistency in the previous paragraph. Second, transaction cost politics seems
most fruitful when applied to legislative interactions, either within the
legislature or between lobbying groups and legislators. As discussed in
Section 3.7, legislative interactions have so far received far less attention
on political macroeconomics than have other types of interactions. It has
played a larger role in the analysis of the politics of trade policy, an area
that Dixit considers in detail. Whether transaction cost politics will prove
similarly fruitful in analyzing the politics of macroeconomic policy is an
interesting, open question.

3.9. CONCLUSIONS

In this chapter, we have summarized a large number of mechanisms for
making collective choices. Some of the material will be used directly in
later chapters; other material is included more to give a more complete
picture of the range of choice mechanisms. As with the models covered in
Chapter 2, even the material that is not used directly may be useful to
strengthen one's conceptual grasp of choice mechanisms and the basic
political problem of making collective choices in the face of conflict of
interests.

With the economic and political building blocks in place, we are now
ready to consider problems of political economy directly.

PART II

Commitment, Credibility, and Reputation

The Time-Consistency Problem

> Like the British Constitution, she owes her success
> in practice to her inconsistencies in principle.
>
> —*Thomas Hardy*, The Hand of Ethelberta

> With consistency a great soul has simply nothing to do.
>
> —*Ralph Waldo Emerson*, Self-Reliance

4.1. INTRODUCTION

In this chapter, we consider the time-consistency problem; in the two subsequent chapters, we consider various "solutions." Time consistency has become an integral part of explanations of many economic phenomena, in large part because of insights it gives into these phenomena. It helps us to formalize and hence better understand a government's incentives to promise that accumulated capital will not be taxed and then weigh the possibility of capital levies in the face of severe revenue shortfalls. The government's incentive toward time-inconsistent behavior in this case also helps explain why capital accumulation may be so low in countries with weak safeguards against such behavior. A second example concerns why there may be an inflationary bias to monetary policy even if governments realize that perfectly anticipated inflation may have little effect on economic activity. More generally, a significant problem of decisionmaking in democracies is potential time inconsistency since majority preferences change over time, and the nature of certain democratic institutions may be better understood as a response to this problem. We organize this chapter around analysis of a number of examples.

Defining Time Inconsistency

Let us begin with a definition of **time inconsistency**. Suppose that a policymaker is responsible for choosing a policy starting at time t for several periods into the future. Consider his choice of the tax rate for time $t + s$, where we denote by $\pi_{t+s}(t + j)$ the policy chosen at time $t + j$ for $t + s, 0 \leq j \leq s$. A forward-looking policymaker can obviously wait until

$t + s$ to choose the tax rate for that date, or he can choose the $t + s$ tax rate at t (where, in a world with uncertainty, he could choose a vector of state-contingent tax rates, one for each state of nature). If there are no changes in his preferences or in technology, nor any unanticipated shocks between t and $t + s$, one would think from basic dynamic programming that it would not matter whether the tax rate for time $t + s$ is chosen at $t + s$ or at t: the value should be the same. Time inconsistency is said to arise if, though nothing has changed (at least ostensibly), these choices are not equal,[1] that is, if

$$\pi_{t+s}(t + s) \neq \pi_{t+s}(t). \tag{4.1}$$

A natural reaction is, "So, what else is new?" Do we not see politicians quite often announcing that they will carry out a specific policy in the future, but then doing something else when the time comes? They are trading a *promise* of future action against a tangible benefit (such as electoral support) today, but not fulfilling their part of the deal. More generally, anyone who makes an agreement to receive something today against the promise of repaying tomorrow would be tempted to renege and not repay, if such an action would increase his utility. If time inconsistency meant simply reneging on a promise or agreement when an individual finds it optimal to do so, one would still ask how such behavior can be prevented, but the phenomenon itself would not occupy us for very long. What makes the phenomenon interesting is that it occurs in cases where time-inconsistent policy is chosen to *maximize the welfare of those who are misled.* Put simply, the policymaker has the incentive to mislead people for their own good! Furthermore, as noted above, the fundamental characteristics of the policymaking environment appear not to have changed. If the environment has changed (for example, due to an exogenous shock to the economy), a change in the optimal policy would not be surprising. With no ostensible change in the fundamental environment, the result in (4.1) appears puzzling.

The Examination Problem

We begin with a simple example, leaving for later an analysis of what lies behind the time-consistency problem. Though it will not be obvious at this point, a conflict of interests of some sort is necessary for time inconsistency in policy choice to arise.

---

[1] The term "time inconsistency" was introduced into economics by Strotz (1956), though the reason for time inconsistency in his model is quite different from the reason here. He considers an individual with a utility function which does not change over time, but where discounting of future utility is not exponential. To take a discrete-time example, suppose individuals treat the current period differently than future periods, in that $\Omega(c_t, c_{t+1}, \ldots) = u(c_t) + \alpha(\beta u(c_{t+1}) + \beta^2 u(c_{t+2}) + \cdots)$, where β is the standard discount factor and $\alpha < 1$. Because of the nature of discounting, c_{t+1} chosen at $t + 1$ will differ from c_{t+1} chosen at t.

This example, a favorite of academics, concerns final examinations. As all students know, professors are interested solely in their students' learning, and give examinations only to induce students to study more. At the beginning of the term, it is thus optimal to announce that there will be a final exam. Otherwise, students will not study hard enough given the demands on their time at the end of the semester. In anticipation of an exam, students will study and hence learn more. On exam day, when the students arrive to the exam having learned the material, everyone is better off if the professor cancels the exam (and simply gives each student a satisfactory grade): students are spared the anxiety associated with finding out about grades and can use the exam time for something else; the professor is spared the trouble of grading the exam. Hence, if the professor's original announcement was believed and students studied, time-inconsistent behavior in canceling the exam is optimal.

Is Time Inconsistency Really a Problem?

Before getting into the technical details, we note and briefly address three arguments suggesting that too much emphasis has been put on the time-consistency problem. First, in specific cases it is argued that, in practice, policymakers really do not have the incentive towards time inconsistency that many economists claim. Blinder (1998), for example, makes this argument with respect to monetary policy and the inflation bias problem mentioned at the beginning of the chapter. We examine his argument further at the end of Section 4.4. However, even if one accepts the view that in some specific cases the incentive towards time inconsistency is less strong than models may suggest, the general concept and its implications nonetheless shed light on a number of economic phenomena. The insights one may gain means that time consistency warrants a careful treatment.

Second, even if there is an incentive towards time inconsistency, it is argued that society has found ways to deal with it when it is significant. Hence, in equilibrium, time inconsistency does not result in a serious policy bias away from the optimum. Taylor (1983) makes this point strongly, suggesting that societies create institutional structures for policy-making that mitigate or eliminate time-consistency problems. It is exactly those sorts of institutional solutions that we consider in the next chapter. Understanding the creation of such institutions means first understanding the problem of time consistency itself.

Finally, a more general criticism is that stressing the importance of finding solutions to the time-consistency problem makes us lose sight of the costs of these solutions. This criticism is not so much in terms of the practical costs, such as a loss of flexibility if policymakers are precommitted to a policy (an issue we take up in Section 4.6), but to a deeper notion of the value judgements a society makes in what is seen as too heavily focusing on the problem of time consistency. Elster (1984), in his brilliant essay on "binding oneself" as a solution to time consistency, argues that values that are worthwhile in and of themselves may be sacrificed in methods of effective precommitment. On a more policy-oriented level, institutional solutions to specific problems, such as central bank independence in the face of pressures for monetary expansion, are seen as contrary to basic democratic principles of accountability.

This criticism runs deeper and cannot be easily ignored. However, because it addresses fundamental issues of the nature of policymaking in a democracy, it also falls somewhat outside the intent of the book. We will return to the issue in our discussion of institutional solutions to the time-consistency problem in Chapter 5, as well as at various points later on, such as in the discussion of democracy and growth in Section 11.4 of Chapter 11. Our approach is to try to illuminate the issues, rather than to give answers. The fundamental importance of the question argues not for putting less stress on the problem of time consistency and its solutions, but in fact for considering the underlying technical issues quite carefully.

4.2. CAPITAL TAXATION

We now consider a more technical example, following the pathbreaking paper of Kydland and Prescott (1977). It concerns capital taxation in a two-period, representative agent model, and will be used to illustrate a number of the issues more precisely.[2] Our presentation follows Fischer (1980).

A Simple Model of Capital Taxation

Individuals consume in both periods, but production and government activity occur only in the second period. In the first period, a representative individual receives an income endowment y which he divides between consumption c_1 and accumulation of capital to be used in the second period k_2. Labor l_2 is also supplied in the second period and the production function is linear in k and l, so that product market equilibrium in the two periods is

$$c_1 + k_2 = y,$$
$$c_2 + g_2 = al_2 + Rk_2,$$

(4.2)

where g_2 is government spending. Finally, the utility of the representative

---

[2] This two-period model is a very simple version of the infinite-horizon overlapping-generations model of capital accumulation, exposited in Section 2.4 of Chapter 2.

individual over the two periods is

$$\Omega = \ln c_1 + \beta[\ln c_2 + \delta \ln(1 - l_2) + \gamma \ln g_2], \qquad (4.3)$$

where β, γ, and δ are given parameters.

The "benevolent" government's objective is to maximize the welfare of the representative individual. The first-best allocation, derived by maximizing the utility function (4.3) over quantities, is

$$c_1 = \frac{y + \dfrac{a}{R}}{1 + \beta(1 + \delta + \gamma)},$$

$$c_2 = \beta R c_1, \qquad (4.4)$$

$$l_2 = 1 - \frac{\delta}{a}\beta R c_1,$$

$$g_2 = \gamma \beta R c_1,$$

which implies that

$$k_2 = \frac{\beta(1 + \delta + \gamma)y - \dfrac{a}{R}}{1 + \beta(1 + \delta + \gamma)}.$$

This is the first-best solution, what Fischer calls the *command optimum*, since with the instruments it has available to it, the government can basically "command" the optimum allocation. To put the same point less dramatically, the command optimum would be achieved if the government had available sufficient nondistortionary fiscal policy tools so that they could hit whatever quantity allocation they desired. In this example, a single lump-sum tax, levied in either period, would be sufficient to achieve the command optimum.

Suppose, however, that the government does not have access to nondistortionary means of financing its expenditures g_2 and must use distortionary taxes in the second period, τ^k on capital and τ^l on labor. What is the decentralized solution, when the government must use price signals to achieve its quantity objectives? The individual's problem is to choose consumption and saving in the first period for the tax rates he expects in the second period (and consumption and labor supply in the second period for the actual tax rates) to maximize his lifetime utility (4.3) subject to his budget constraints:

$$c_1 + k_2 = y,$$
$$c_2 = (1 - \tau^k)R k_2 + (1 - \tau^l)a l_2. \qquad (4.5)$$

The individual also takes government spending g_2 as given, a crucial assumption to which we will shortly return. The fact that the individual does *not* internalize the government's budget constraint reflects the fact that a representative agent is considered (and considers himself) to be atomistic. That is, he assumes his actions have no effect on economywide aggregates, even though all individuals are identical and make identical choices. This is the standard assumption in economics, which, if well understood, causes no problems. Making a clear distinction between a representative (atomistic) agent and a single (nonatomistic) agent who can affect economic aggregates is crucial for an understanding of the time-consistency problem as well.

Individual maximization yields demand and supply functions $c_1(\tau^{ke}, \tau^{le})$, $k_2(\tau^{ke}, \tau^{le})$, $c_2(\tau^k, \tau^l)$, and $l_2(\tau^k, \tau^l)$, where τ^{ke} and τ^{le} are expected tax rates.[3] Given the individual's decision, the government chooses actual tax rates τ^k and τ^l in the second period to maximize individual welfare, subject to the government budget constraint:

$$
\begin{aligned}
g_2 &= \tau^l a l_2 + \tau^k R k_2 \\
&= \tau^l a l_2(\tau^k, \tau^l) + \tau^k R k_2(\tau^{ke}, \tau^{le}).
\end{aligned}
\tag{4.6}
$$

The key question is then how expectations of tax rates are formed, and specifically, whether the vector (τ^k, τ^l) that the government chooses will equal the vector (τ^{ke}, τ^{le}) that the public expected. If not, there is an inherent time-consistency problem, as defined in (4.1).

To see the time-consistency problem in this model of capital taxation, note that as of period 2, with capital k_2 in place, the government has the incentive to minimize distortions by taxing only capital and leaving labor untaxed. Hence, a government interested in maximizing welfare has the incentive to be time inconsistent, announcing a low level of labor taxation *ex ante* and, if that announcement is believed and capital is accumulated, taxing it heavily *ex post*, that is, by announcing a surprise capital levy. This decision reflects a basic optimal tax result that factors whose supply is inelastic should be taxed more heavily. *Ex post*, capital is an inelastically supplied factor. More generally, time inconsistency will characterize factor taxation whenever the *ex-post* elasticity of factor supply is less than the *ex-ante* elasticity.

To derive this result in a slightly more formal way, suppose that individuals fully believed whatever announcement (τ^{ka}, τ^{la}) the government makes, that is, $(\tau^{ke}, \tau^{le}) = (\tau^{ka}, \tau^{la})$, for any announcement (τ^{ka}, τ^{la}). In the first period, the government would maximize the indirect utility function derived from (4.3) using the individual's demand and supply functions $c_1(\tau^{ka}, \tau^{la})$, $k_2(\tau^{ka}, \tau^{la})$, $c_2(\tau^k, \tau^l)$, and $l_2(\tau^k, \tau^l)$ over $\tau^k, \tau^l, \tau^{ka}$,

---

[3] More precisely, c_2 and l_2 will depend on first-period decisions and hence on τ^{ke} and τ^{le}.

and τ^{la} treated as separate choice variables. In the first period, the government will announce the tax vector (τ^{ka}, τ^{la}), where it will be optimal to announce a low tax rate to encourage capital accumulation. In the second period, given the capital stock k_2, the government will carry out (τ^k, τ^l). In general, (τ^k, τ^l) will *not* equal (τ^{ka}, τ^{la}); more specifically, since capital $k_2(\tau^{ka}, \tau^{la})$ is inelastically supplied as of period 2, $\tau^k > \tau^{ka}$. This is a general result in the time-consistency literature. The solution that results can be called the *time-inconsistent* solution; in fact, there are many time-inconsistent solutions, one for each value of the second-period tax rate which was expected. We do *not* call this a time-inconsistent *equilibrium*, since it will not be an equilibrium with rational, forward-looking individuals.

Suppose the government could *commit* itself to whatever policy it announced in the first period, so that $\tau^k = \tau^{ka} (= \tau^{ke})$. The government chooses τ^k to maximize representative agent utility (4.3), knowing the functional relation $k_2(\tau^k, \tau^l)$. It announces (τ^k, τ^l) and has a mechanism to commit to it and not to reoptimize in the second period.[4] The resultant solution is called the *precommitment* solution.[5] In most models, this solution is unique.

The lack of a mechanism for the government to precommit in period 1 to a period-2 fiscal policy does not, however, mean that the equilibrium solution will exhibit time inconsistency. As indicated above, if the public is sophisticated, it realizes that, given capital in place in the second period, the government will have the incentive to tax capital heavily in the second period, that is, to reoptimize and choose $\tau^k > \tau^{ka}$. To choose their optimal saving, individuals would form their expectations (τ^{ke}, τ^{le}) not on the basis of any policy announcement, but according to the government's known incentive to reoptimize. That is, they will use (τ^k, τ^l) as calculated in the next-to-last paragraph as their expectation (τ^{ke}, τ^{le}) in their behavioral functions $c_1(\tau^{ke}, \tau^{le})$ and $k_2(\tau^{ke}, \tau^{le})$. The solution is *time consistent*: when the second period arrives, their expectations about the tax rate the government chooses are fulfilled. This solution is also referred to as the *dynamic programming* solution, since forward-looking agents realize the government is solving a dynamic programming problem and use this fact in forming their expectations. That is, in choosing desired capital

---

[4] These solutions may be characterized in terms of "who moves first." In the precommitment solution, the government fixes tax rates, after which the public chooses k_2. In a time-inconsistent solution, the public chooses k_2, after which the government chooses tax rates.

[5] Semantic quibblers complain that the standard usage of "pre" in "precommitment" (or "pre-existing") is redundant, arguing for use of "commitment" solution instead. I prefer the standard usage, since it emphasizes that the commitment to a policy existed *prior* to the time period in which a change in policy is the central issue (or that the crucial distortion existed prior to the time period of analysis).

accumulation, the public takes account of the government's behavior relating τ^k to capital in place k_2.[6]

We can rank these four solutions in terms of the individual's welfare, temporarily setting aside the question of whether they are all feasible equilibria. Utility can be no higher than at the first-best allocation, that is, at the "command optimum." Utility is next highest for the time-inconsistent solution. (As noted above, there are many such solutions, one for each expected tax rate.) To see why this (weakly) dominates the precommitment and the time-consistent solutions, note that in both of the latter cases, τ^k is correctly anticipated. Hence, if it were possible to fool the public, utility could certainly be no lower, and would in general be higher. For example, call the precommitment solution τ^{kP}. The government would announce τ^{kP} in period 1 and (if it is possible to be time inconsistent) choose whatever capital tax rate was optimal in period 2. Finally, individual utility in the precommitment solution is no lower (and is generally higher) than in the time-consistent solution, since the government could always commit to the time-consistent tax rate. It is the impossibility of precommitment in many environments which implies that the (lower-welfare) time-consistent capital tax rate is the only feasible constant tax rate. (Mechanisms for commitment are studied in detail in the next chapter.)

Explaining Time Inconsistency

In both of the examples of possible time inconsistency, it is not really true that nothing has changed between period 1 and period 2. A key state variable (human capital in the first example, physical capital in the second) has changed, though in a predictable way. The lack of a lump-sum tax to finance government expenditures, combined with the accumulation of capital, makes it optimal for the policymaker to choose a different setting of the policy variable. What is important is not simply this change *per se*, but the reason for the change: expectations of future government policy influence individuals' current investment choices.[7] Government thus has the incentive to lead people to expect one sort of policy, but once

---

[6] This solution may be visualized in terms of reaction functions. The government's choice of tax rates depends on k_2; the representative individual's choice of k_2 depends on (correctly anticipated) tax rates; the intersection of these two reaction functions is the time-consistent solution. (Exactly such a visualization will be presented for the Barro–Gordon model in Section 4.4, where time-inconsistent and precommitment solutions are also displayed.) One sees that the time-consistent equilibrium is a Nash equilibrium.

[7] Hence, a crucial part of the time-consistency phenomenon parallels the role of expectations of future policy influencing current behavior discussed in Section 2.5 of Chapter 2. Note, however, two differences in emphasis. First, in the model of Chapter 2, *uncertainty* about future policy was a key emphasis; here, future policy can be calculated when the public knows the government's objective function. Second, in much of the exposition of Chapter 2, we took expected government policy (or its distribution) as given; here, the use of policy expectations to *manipulate* the public's behavior is central.

individuals act on this expectation, to do something else. Why does the government not try to influence capital accumulation more directly? If the government had sufficient instruments (as indicated above, access to lump-sum taxation in the second example), it would not need to manipulate expectations to induce investment. The optimality of trying to fool people to "invest for their own good" reflects, among other things, insufficient policy instruments.

Though "insufficient instruments" or "lower *ex-post* than *ex-ante* elasticity" are often given as reasons for time inconsistency, and indeed are central to the capital tax example, they really do not *explain* time inconsistency. Why do people "need to be fooled"? Why can they not operate for their own good? The short answer is not that they are irrational, but that they are acting rationally subject to pre-existing constraints or distortions. Focusing on constraints as the essence of the time-consistency problem is a frequent approach to understanding the problem, and is forcefully put forward by Persson and Tabellini (1994a). In their approach to time consistency (and to political economy more generally), they stress "the additional constraints that reflect the specific nature of the policy-making process" (p. 2), which they term "incentive constraints." In the case of time consistency, these incentive constraints "emanate from the sequential nature of policy-making, particularly from the possibility to deviate from earlier plans or announced policy rules" (p. 2). They are correct in stressing the sequential nature of policymaking as a necessary condition for the possibility of time inconsistency. However, this focus leaves unanswered the question of whether an incentive to deviate from previous plans exists whenever policymaking is sequential, or, instead, whether time inconsistency reflects a more basic aspect of the policymaking process.

No problem of time inconsistency would arise if, once a policy were chosen, it were immutable, but the sequential nature of policy choice cannot itself be the essence of the problem. Sequential policymaking is a *necessary* but not a *sufficient* condition for the possibility of time inconsistency to arise. Sequencing, with the possibility of revisiting a decision, is important for most of the decisions we make, but few of our choices exhibit time-consistency problems. For example, dressing for success in business would suggest putting on one's suit after one's morning shower rather than before. This sequencing allows one to choose clothing before entering the shower and then have the option of revising one's choice while in the shower. Nonetheless, no time-consistency problem arises in dressing in the morning.

One may complain that this is not a good example, in that in our examples above, the agent who exhibited time-inconsistent behavior did so in order to influence the behavior of another agent. However, the combination of sequential behavior and the possibility of taking an action in order to manipulate someone else's behavior is also not sufficient in itself to produce a time-inconsistency problem. If my wife chooses her daily wardrobe based on what I wear, setting out one suit on the bed before my shower in the morning and then revising my choice would allow me to manipulate her choice of clothing. But it is not at all clear why I would have the incentive to do so. One could think of numerous examples where decisions are necessarily sequential and where changing one's decision could affect someone else's decision, but where time consistency is not an issue.

We argue, instead, that what is essential to the phenomenon of time inconsistency is conflict of interests, reflecting some *ex-post* heterogeneity as defined in Chapter 1. If government and private sector (or my wife and I) are really maximizing the same function at each stage, then there will be no time-consistency problem. This issue will come up again in other models; it is of sufficient importance to consider it at some length.

4.3. TIME INCONSISTENCY AS A CONFLICT OF INTERESTS

The Conceptual Role of Heterogeneity

Time consistency is generally seen as a problem which can arise even with an infinitely lived, benevolent social planner, benevolent in the sense that his objective is to maximize social welfare.[8] (In the tax example, the utility associated with the time-inconsistent solution is no lower than when the government can commit to a tax rate.) This is certainly the standard view, and with good reason. Some early interpretations of the time-consistency problem following the publication of the Kydland and Prescott (1977) article argued that it reflected a divergence of interests between the social planner and the representative individual. Subsequent papers went to great lengths to stress that time inconsistency did *not* reflect the presence of a policymaker whose objective was to maximize something other than social welfare. Hence, the title of Fischer's (1980) influential paper, "Dynamic Inconsistency, Cooperation and the Benevolent Dissembling Government."

Put another way, the standard view is that there need be no conflict of interests among different individuals, or between individuals and the government, for there to be an incentive for the government to follow time-inconsistent policies.[9] The key point in this section is that this view is

---

[8] If the policymaker is not benevolent, that is, if his objective is *not* to maximize social welfare, then a distortion relative to the social optimum will obviously be present.

[9] A conflict-of-interests interpretation that is widely accepted is that there is a conflict of objectives between policymakers at different points of time. Though the identity of the policymaker has not changed and his objective function is strictly the same over time, his optimal policy is different than that of his time-*t* incarnation, because at time $t + s$ he faces a different set of constraints (due to the changed value of a key state variable). Viewing the time-consistency problem as a conflict of objectives between policymakers at different points of time may be a useful tool for formal analysis, but it is not the key conceptual point being stressed.

incorrect. Conflict of interests is central to time-consistency problems, as it is (albeit in different ways) to the problems of political economy presented elsewhere in the book.[10]

A Formal Demonstration

To understand this view, consider the following problem, where instead of a representative agent, there is only a single individual facing the government. The individual and a government act sequentially, the individual choosing a variable k (say, saving), the government choosing a variable τ (say, the tax rate). The agent who moves first will take the other agent's reaction function into account. Suppose both government and individual are maximizing the same function $u(k, \tau)$. It is simple to show that the sequence of moves has no effect on the outcome. Suppose, for example, the individual first chooses k, after which the government chooses τ. To solve, one works backwards, solving the second-stage problem first, to yield the government's reaction function. That is, the government, taking k as given, chooses τ to maximize $u(k, \tau)$. The resultant first-order condition, $\partial u / \partial \tau = 0$, defines a reaction function $\tau = \Gamma(k)$. On the basis of this reaction function, a rational individual chooses k to maximize the function $u(k, \Gamma(k))$, yielding a first-order condition:

$$\frac{\partial u}{\partial k} + \frac{\partial u}{\partial \tau} \frac{\partial \Gamma}{\partial k} = 0. \tag{4.7}$$

Combining the two first-order conditions, one derives a solution defined by the two conditions:

$$\frac{\partial u}{\partial k} = 0 \quad \text{and} \quad \frac{\partial u}{\partial \tau} = 0. \tag{4.8}$$

Reversing the sequence of moves, one can easily show that the solution is defined by the same two equations in (4.8). In terms of our earlier terminology, the time-consistent solution (as just derived) and the precommitment solution (which would characterize the reverse timing) are the same. There is no problem of time inconsistency.[11]

Why then is there a problem of time inconsistency in the capital tax example in the previous section? It reflects the distinction between a single and a representative agent. To see the importance of this distinction for the time-consistency problem, let us consider a variant of the capital-taxation problem in which the government's choice of τ depends on saving

---

[10] Chari, Kehoe, and Prescott (1989) stress the same point, namely, that the source of the time-consistency problem is in conflict among agents. The formal demonstration follows their paper.

[11] In addition to Chari, Kehoe, and Prescott (1989), Fischer (1980, section 5) makes essentially the same point.

averaged over all individuals, k^{avg} (that is, the tax base), where each individual takes k^{avg} as given in his optimal choice problem. Suppose there are N identical individuals, each individual i maximizing an objective function $u^i(k^i, k^{avg}, \tau)$, subject to the constraint in the previous sentence. The quantity k^{avg} enters the individual's objective function due to his preference for high government expenditures, hence a high tax base, as in (4.6). The government maximizes $\sum_i u^i(k^i, k^{avg}, \tau)$, so that when all individuals are identical, it is maximizing the representative individual's welfare.

When the government moves first (the "precommitment solution"), the second-stage (individual) decision is characterized by first-order condition $\partial u^i / \partial k^i = 0$, which yields k^{avg} as a function of τ, which the government takes account of in its optimization problem. Hence, we obtain first-order conditions[12]

$$\frac{\partial u^i}{\partial k^i} = 0 \quad \text{and} \quad \sum_i \left(\frac{\partial u^i}{\partial k^{avg}} \frac{\partial k^{avg}}{\partial \tau} + \frac{\partial u^i}{\partial \tau} \right) = 0. \qquad (4.9)$$

If the order of the moves is reversed, so that each individual (who does not internalize the government's budget constraint) chooses his saving before the government chooses the tax rate τ (at which point k^{avg} is given), the first-order conditions become:

$$\frac{\partial u^i}{\partial k^i} = 0 \quad \text{and} \quad \sum_i \frac{\partial u^i}{\partial \tau} = 0. \qquad (4.10)$$

The first-order conditions (4.9) and (4.10) in this case are *not* the same under the alternative sequencings. What is key to this result is the effect of k^{avg} on utility; in its absence, (4.9) and (4.10) would be identical. The dependence of utility on aggregate allocations thus induces a source of conflict among agents, which is crucial for the possibility of a time-consistency problem.

The Two Examples Reconsidered

We can now easily understand how the representative agent assumption introduces a conflict of interests into the capital-taxation problem and thus underlies time inconsistency. A representative agent takes the capital tax base k_2, and hence g_2, as given in his maximization; each individual wants a high per capita tax base, so that g_2 is high, but low taxes on himself. In contrast, a single agent would "internalize" the government's budget

---

[12] Assuming that the government also took account of the effect of τ on k^i would not change the basic result.

constraint. In terms of objectives, the government takes account of the individual's demand functions, but the representative individual does not take account of the government's "reaction function." Hence, though the government's objective is the same as the individual's, the actual functions that they maximize are different.

This is what we had called *ex-post heterogeneity* in Chapter 1: individuals are identical *ex ante*, but care about distribution of tax burdens. This "potential" conflict of interests, inherent in a representative agent set-up, is necessary, but not sufficient. To see this, suppose we had multiple agents, but nondistortionary taxation. We could achieve the first-best allocation, and there would be no time-consistency problem. This is what Fischer calls the "insufficient instrument" problem. However, the lack of first-best instruments also does not in itself imply a time-consistency problem, unless time-inconsistent behavior gives an "extra instrument." In the capital tax problem, time-inconsistent behavior gave an extra instrument not simply because of the difference in *ex-ante* and *ex-post* elasticities of substitution in supply of capital, but because the relation between *ex-ante* and *ex-post* elasticities of substitution differed *across* the taxed goods labor and capital.

Now let us consider the examination example again. In the examination example, the pre-existing constraint is that there are other demands on the student's time, such as other exams. If he has exams in all his courses but one, the structure of "payoffs" is such that he will study that subject less during the term, and therefore learn less. To be more precise, suppose the student has two courses, economics and religion. Suppose further that his economics professor has the same preferences as the student as far as the relative importance of the two courses, and that this is known by the student. Hence, the student views the economics professor as a benevolent social planner, and the economics professor acts as one in choosing policy towards exams. Nonetheless, he may need to "fool" the student who has the same objective, but in doing so, he is rationally responding to the current structure of incentives. (If the two professors shared the same objectives, this would not be necessary.) The religion professor's preferences are thus the pre-existing distortions faced by the benevolent policymaker. We will see a similar conflict between policymakers in the model of inflation bias in the next section.

4.4. THE BARRO–GORDON MODEL

The first (and perhaps still the most) influential application of the question of time consistency in macroeconomics was to the use of monetary policy to affect unemployment or real output. As background, suppose, as is often argued, that aggregate unemployment will fall in response to positive inflation only if the inflation is unanticipated. Perfectly anticipated monetary expansions will be reflected in higher nominal wages and prices, with no significant effect on real economic activity. Why then might governments follow inflationary policies to try to lower unemployment if they know such policies will be anticipated and hence largely ineffective in lowering unemployment? That is, why does there appear to be an "inflation bias" in monetary policy in some countries, with the average rate of inflation being above what appears to be socially optimal?

Early proponents of the view that there is no *long-run* trade-off between inflation and unemployment argued that the public adjusts its inflation expectations to actual inflation only slowly (for example, expectations about inflation are formed adaptively), so that in the short run, monetary policy can affect real economic activity (Friedman [1968], Phelps [1970]). The effectiveness of inflationary policy in increasing the level of economic activity is thus dependent on temporarily incorrect inflationary expectations on the part of the public, a phenomenon that would disappear were expectations formed rationally. Hence, in theory there should be no inflationary bias to monetary policy if a rational government knows it is facing agents with rational expectations.

The key result that we derive in this section is that the incentive towards time-inconsistent government behavior can yield an "inflationary bias" to monetary policy. Kydland and Prescott suggested this application, but the development that is best known is due to Barro and Gordon (1983a, 1983b). Governments choose expansionary policies to increase economic activity and reduce unemployment, but once this is recognized, inflation will have little or no effect on economic activity in the long run. Though policymakers realize that anticipated inflation will have no significant positive effect on equilibrium economic activity, time-consistency arguments suggest why they nonetheless succumb to the short-run temptation to inflate in the vain attempt to induce such an effect. Moreover, the argument for the optimality of preannounced rules over discretion in setting monetary policy in the presence of potential time inconsistency is quite different from, and more convincing than, previous arguments. (As noted below, Blinder [1998] strongly argues that this does not describe U.S. Federal Reserve policymaking.)

The Basic Model

In the general Barro–Gordon set-up, the monetary authority (synonymous with the government) chooses a sequence of inflation rates π_t to minimize discounted expected social loss, where the social loss function is assumed to be quadratic in inflation and unemployment[13]:

$$\Lambda_t = \mathrm{E}_t \left[\sum_{s=0}^{T} \beta^s \mathscr{L}_{t+s} \right]$$

$$= \sum_{s=0}^{T} \beta^s \mathrm{E}_t \left[\frac{\left(U_{t+s} - \tilde{U} \right)^2}{2} + \theta \frac{(\pi_{t+s} - \tilde{\pi})^2}{2} \right], \tag{4.11}$$

where T may be infinite, $\tilde{\pi}$ is the socially optimal rate of inflation, and $\tilde{U}$ is the socially optimal unemployment rate, U_{t+s} and $\tilde{U}$ both measured relative to the natural rate of unemployment. We assume that the unemployment rate that the monetary authority finds optimal is below the natural rate of unemployment, so that $\tilde{U}$ is negative. This divergence reflects a "pre-existing distortion" in the natural rate, that is, because of some intervention (such as a distortionary labor income tax), the natural rate is above what the monetary authority considers socially optimal.

The divergence of the unemployment rate U_t in any period from the natural rate of unemployment (zero, by our measurement convention) depends on the difference between the actual rate of inflation and the *economywide* expected rate of inflation π_t^e and on a stochastic unemployment shock ϵ_t:

$$U_t = -(\pi_t - \pi_t^e) + \epsilon_t, \tag{4.12}$$

where ϵ_t is identically and independently distributed (i.i.d.) over time with mean zero and variance σ^2. Equation (4.12) fully describes the determination of unemployment, given π_t and π_t^e. The former is chosen by the monetary authority; the latter reflects individual expectations.

Though (4.11) represents the utility of a representative individual, he does not form his inflation expectations by choosing a sequence of π_t^e to minimize the social loss function. As discussed in the previous section, a representative agent is atomistic, and hence views himself as unable to affect either the inflation rate π_t or the aggregate unemployment rate U_t. As in the capital-taxation problem, it is assumed that an atomistic individual forms his expectations rationally, knowing the government's incentives to inflate, but unable to use π_t^e as a strategic variable. Hence, expected

---

[13] The assumption that the monetary authority controls the inflation rate π as its instrument of policy is made for simplicity of exposition. The assumption is far removed from reality, as Blinder (1998) and many others have stressed.

inflation is[14]

$$\pi_t^e = \mathrm{E}_{t-1}\pi_t, \qquad\qquad (4.13)$$

where the expectation is taken conditional on information in period $t - 1$. This equation is sometimes motivated by describing an individual as choosing his expectation π_t^e to minimize his inflation prediction error, for example, by minimizing the square between actual inflation π_t and his own forecast.[15]

One interpretation of the Phillips curve (4.12) is that it reflects labor supply behavior in which period-t nominal wages are set one period in advance, based on inflation expectations as of period $t - 1$. More specifically, agents set nominal wages to hit a target real wage, and then supply whatever labor is demanded at the realized real wage in period t. This interpretation has been criticized as not reflecting actual behavior in labor markets. (See, for example, Cukierman [1992], chapter 3.) However, none of our basic conclusions depend on this specific interpretation. It is important, however, to note that in this version of the model, agents do not set their expectations strategically.[16]

In the simplest case, there is no connection between periods. This will be true if choice of π_t puts no constraint on future inflation rates π_{t+s}, on future expected rates of inflation π_{t+s}^e, nor on future unemployment rates U_{t+s}. In this case, we have a single-period (that is, one-shot) game, where the policymaker chooses π_t to minimize the single-period loss function $\mathscr{L}_t$ defined over current-period inflation and unemployment.

Inflation Bias

The basic Barro–Gordon result may be seen most clearly if we first consider a nonstochastic world where the loss function is *linear* in *actual* unemployment (rather than quadratic in the *deviation* of unemployment from a target), so that lower unemployment is always better. This simple specification will prove quite useful in the analysis in Chapters 5 and 6.

---

[14] To be precise and consistent with the formal argument in Section 4.3, this expectation should have an individual specific subscript to distinguish it from π_t^e in (4.12).

[15] Rogoff (1987) points out that this standard assumption is not really satisfactory in a stochastic setting, because an individual should also take account of the covariance of his own prediction error with the level of inflation and the aggregate prediction error.

[16] There is a version of the Barro–Gordon model in which the public is thought of as a nonatomistic agent, with wages being set by a large labor union in the wage-setting interpretation. Under this view, strategic behavior would be more plausible, but it is not clear why the union would not use (4.11) to form inflation expectations. This is essentially the problem discussed in Section 4.3 and suggests that some versions of the large labor union interpretation are probably internally inconsistent.

Using (4.12), we may then write a single-period loss function of the form[17]

$$\mathcal{L}(\pi_t, \pi_t^e) = -(\pi_t - \pi_t^e) + \theta\frac{(\pi_t - \tilde{\pi})^2}{2}. \qquad (4.14)$$

The policymaker chooses optimal inflation taking expected inflation as given. Minimizing (4.14) with respect to π_t for given π_t^e, the policymaker chooses $\pi = \tilde{\pi} + 1/\theta$ for any value of π_t^e. Hence, as long as the policymaker does not put an infinite weight on the loss from inflation relative to the loss from unemployment, he will choose an inflation rate above the socially optimal one. Of course, this will be anticipated by rational agents, so that in equilibrium unemployment will be at the natural rate, but inflation will be suboptimally high.

Now let us consider the basic Barro–Gordon model slightly more generally, where we return to a stochastic world and consider a quadratic loss function, as in (4.11). If we continue to assume that there are no intertemporal linkages, and we suppose the government chooses the inflation rate for period t after the stochastic shock ϵ_t has been observed, the loss function is a single-period version of (4.11), namely,

$$\mathcal{L}_t = \frac{(U_t - \tilde{U})^2}{2} + \theta\frac{(\pi_t - \tilde{\pi})^2}{2}. \qquad (4.15)$$

As before, the government chooses optimal inflation taking expected inflation as given. After substituting (4.12) into the loss function and minimizing with respect to π_t for given π_t^e, we obtain a first-order condition:

$$\pi_t = \frac{1}{1+\theta}\pi_t^e + \frac{\theta}{1+\theta}\left(\tilde{\pi} - \frac{1}{\theta}\tilde{U}\right) + \frac{1}{1+\theta}\epsilon_t. \qquad (4.16)$$

In game-theoretic terminology, we could interpret this equation as the government's reaction function to the public's choice of an expected inflation rate. For each value of π_t^e, it tells us what is the socially optimal rate of inflation π_t. If the public expects the government to choose an inflation rate $\tilde{\pi}$ (that is, $\pi_t^e = \tilde{\pi}$), it will be socially optimal for the monetary authority to choose a higher rate of inflation (namely $\pi_t = \tilde{\pi} - \tilde{U}/(1 + \theta) + \epsilon_t/(1 + \theta)$), as long as $\tilde{U}$ is negative, that is, as long as the monetary authority finds it optimal to try to lower the unemployment rate

---

[17] This formulation has conceptual advantages and disadvantages relative to the quadratic formulation. On the one hand, it implies that *given* the inflation rate, lower unemployment is always desirable. On the other, it implies a willingness to tolerate large increases in the variance of unemployment for small reductions in inflation.

below the (distorted, from its point of view) natural rate. (In this solution, the public "moves first" with its choice of π_t^e and the government reacts. If we reverse the order of moves, the solution is quite different, not simply mathematically, but from an economic point of view as well.) For the nonstochastic case with $\epsilon_t = 0$, this solution may be represented in Figure 4.1 as the upper solid line.

To calculate the equilibrium rate of inflation, we use (4.13) to calculate rational expectations of inflation at t by taking expectations of (4.16) as of $t - 1$. That is,

$$\pi_t^e = \mathrm{E}_{t-1}\pi_t = \tilde{\pi} - \frac{1}{\theta}\tilde{U}. \tag{4.17}$$

Substituting this value into (4.16) and solving, we obtain the equilibrium inflation rate:

$$\pi_t = \tilde{\pi} - \frac{1}{\theta}\tilde{U} + \frac{1}{1 + \theta}\epsilon_t. \tag{4.18}$$

One may easily calculate the variance of inflation and unemployment, which are

$$\mathrm{Var}(\pi) = \left(\frac{1}{1 + \theta}\right)^2 \sigma^2, \qquad \mathrm{Var}(U) = \left(\frac{\theta}{1 + \theta}\right)^2 \sigma^2. \tag{4.19}$$

The solution in (4.18) is the time-consistent equilibrium, paralleling the time-consistent solution for the capital-taxation problem in Section 4.2. It is represented for the nonstochastic case as π^{TC} in Figure 4.1. To better understand the figure, note that the 45° line is simply $\pi_t^e = \pi_t$, which can be thought of as the representative agent's "reaction function" giving π_t^e as a function of π_t, analogous to k_2 as a function of (τ^k, τ^l) in the capital-taxation model. The intersection of this line and the government's reaction function gives the time-consistent (Nash) equilibrium.

Equation (4.18) represents the main result of this model. Equilibrium inflation exceeds the socially optimal inflation rate by $-\tilde{U}/\theta$, implying a positive inflation bias as long as $\tilde{U}$ is negative. Unemployment will be equal to the natural rate up to a random error (average unemployment is equal to the natural rate). Hence, even though the government cannot influence the equilibrium rate of unemployment, the temptation to do so when it takes the public's expectations as given will yield an inflationary bias. Note further that this bias depends on the natural rate being too high, that is, it depends on a pre-existing distortion.[18]

---

[18] Given the structure of the economy as summarized by (4.12), the "command optimum" solution for this model could be interpreted as a structural change in the system such that the natural rate of unemployment falls to the government target, i.e., the deviation $\tilde{U} = 0$.

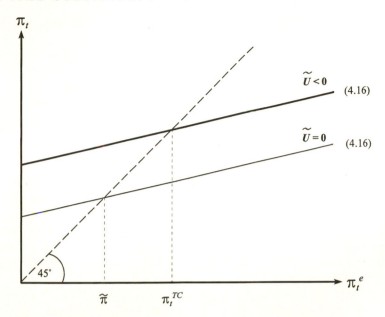

FIGURE 1. The Barro–Gordon model.

To help understand why, in equilibrium, the government chooses π, greater than $\tilde{\pi}$, let us return to the social welfare function (4.15) and suppose, to the contrary, that in a rational expectations equilibrium, the government were to choose $\pi = \tilde{\pi}$. There is obviously no loss from inflation differing from its target, while unemployment is above its target, given the pre-existing distortion. Since the loss from not hitting the optimal target rises with the square of the gap, it is clear that welfare could be increased by increasing inflation infinitesimally relative to its target, thus decreasing unemployment. Hence, $\pi = \tilde{\pi}$ cannot be an equilibrium. The optimal gap in terms of minimizing loss is given by the government's "reaction" function (4.16).

The Conflict-of-Interests Interpretation

How can we characterize the conflict of interests which lies behind the possibility of time inconsistency? There are actually *two* interesting conflicts of interests here. The first, mirroring the capital tax problem, reflects heterogeneity of interests in a representative agent model as discussed in Section 4.3 above. Returning to the question of how individuals form their expectations, each individual wants to minimize his forecast error, but would like everyone else to underpredict inflation, so that the economy-wide average π_t^e in (4.12) implies low unemployment. This parallels the discussion surrounding (4.9). In terms of the notions of heterogeneity introduced in Chapter 1, this conflict of interests reflects *ex-post* hetero-geneity.

There is another conflict of interests in this model, one which was not present in the capital tax example, but was, at least implicitly, in the examination example. It is a conflict of interests between policymakers with different objectives, reflecting perhaps a conflict of interests between the different constituencies they represent. Consider the pre-existing distortion which is crucial for the Barro–Gordon model, namely, a natural rate of unemployment that the monetary authority considers suboptimally high, and thus "distorted." Why is the natural rate of unemployment too high? The answer given in the Barro–Gordon model is that it reflects taxes and transfers, such that labor supply in the competitive solution is below the level the monetary authority considers socially optimal. That is, interventions by the fiscal or other nonmonetary authorities in order to lower the natural rate lead to what the monetary authority views as a distorted market outcome, namely, too high a natural rate. (Formally, the fiscal authority has "moved first" relative to the monetary authority in setting policy and to the public forming inflation expectations.) The "pre-existing distortion" thus reflects a conflict of interests between policymakers; if the natural rate of unemployment that the fiscal authority found optimal was equal to that rate which the monetary authority found optimal, there would be no time-consistency problem.[19] This conflict of interests reflects *ex-ante* heterogeneity as defined in Chapter 1, whereby different groups have different policy objectives.

An Alternative View of the Results

In his description of central banking in theory and practice, Blinder (1998), former vice chairman of the Federal Reserve Board, argues quite forcefully that the description of policymaking in the Barro–Gordon model bears little resemblance to the process of making monetary policy in the United States and many other countries. While agreeing that if politicians made monetary policy there would be a temptation to inflate too much, he argues that this is an inaccurate characterization of central bank behavior. First, central banks do not appear empirically to have an inflationary bias. Second, the description of central banker's behavior and objectives is inaccurate. He argues that policy is *not* viewed in terms of the temptation to move up the short-run Phillips curve in order to lower the rate of unemployment below the natural rate. Just the opposite, with the Fed being extremely concerned about the potential inflationary consequences

---

[19] The conflict of interests we highlight here is closely related to but distinct from a conflict between interest groups on the relative weight put on inflation versus unemployment targets, that is, over θ. We consider some implications of such a conflict in the next two chapters.

of pushing unemployment too low. Hence, a more accurate description is that the Fed targets the natural rate of unemployment (i.e., $\bar{U} = 0$), implying that the problem of time inconsistency flowing from a target below the natural rate does not arise as suggested by the Barro–Gordon model.

Blinder's familiarity with the workings of monetary policy both as an academic and as a central banker means one should take this criticism quite seriously. At the same time, we note that it the model may accurately capture the incentives of a government not constrained by a strong, independent central bank. We return to this question in the next chapter where we draw a distinction between the government and the monetary authority and explore the consequences of this distinction. At that point we will also return to Blinder's evaluation of the realism of various solutions to the problem of possible inflationary bias to monetary policy.

4.5. SEIGNIORAGE REVENUE AND THE OPTIMUM QUANTITY OF MONEY

There are many examples in the macroeconomic literature of time inconsistency. An especially important one concerns the incentive for the government to engineer surprise inflations when the public holds other nominal liabilities. Before seeing a more formal presentation of these results, it may be worthwhile to see them in relation to the earlier results on capital taxation. Inflationary finance is almost exactly identical to the case of capital taxation in terms of the basic issues, and the technical analysis presented there could easily be applied.

Suppose the government uses revenues from money creation (seigniorage) as one way to finance its expenditures. Demand for nominal money balances will be derived from the current price level and the demand for real balances, where the latter depends negatively on the expected rate of inflation. Inflation is a tax on holding money balances, the rate of inflation being the tax rate, and analogously for the expected rate of inflation. For simplicity of exposition, assume zero growth in the economy, so that in a steady state the rate of inflation equals the rate of growth of the nominal money supply.[20] When the actual rate of inflation equals what was expected, consumers are paying a tax at the rate they had anticipated. With positive inflation, moneyholders have reduced their real balances relative to what they would hold if they anticipated zero inflation, in the same way that a positive expected tax on interest earnings in the second period would reduce the demand for capital in the first period in the capital tax example in Section 4.2. Consumers are not being fooled, in that the "tax rate" they expected in choosing their nominal balances is the tax rate

---

[20] For details of how government seigniorage revenue can be seen as a tax on money holders in more complicated cases, see Drazen (1985).

actually realized. The government, however, has an incentive to announce a low rate of money growth and inflation (inducing high demand for real balances if the announcement is believed), and then to choose a higher rate of inflation *ex post*. Knowing the government's incentive, the public would believe only announcements of time-consistent inflation rates unless the government had some mechanism to precommit, exactly as in the case of capital taxation.

The same incentive for time inconsistency in the choice of the inflation rate exists when people hold nominal bonds. Hence, countries which issue nominal claims have an incentive to engineer surprise inflation to reduce the real value of their liabilities. Knowing the incentive for time-inconsistent behavior on the part of governments which issue nominal debt, investors will be unwilling to hold the debt. Hence, indexed or foreign-currency-denominated bonds are a commitment device; the government's inability to issue nominal debt to investors anticipating time-inconsistent behavior explains why it finds it optimal to issue such bonds.

The Calvo Model of Seigniorage

Calvo (1978) was the first to investigate formally the possible time inconsistency of monetary policy in an explicitly monetary model. His conclusion, in the context of a simple deterministic model in which the government was maximizing welfare of the representative consumer, was that, in general, optimal monetary policy will be time inconsistent. He considered a continuous-time monetary economy, where for simplicity, there is no growth. The model is formally very similar to the continuous-time model of government finance in Section 2.5 of Chapter 2, but differs in a number of respects. The government has no consumption expenditures g, as in that model or the capital-taxation model of Section 4.2 above. The government's only function is to create (or destroy) money balances, where it is costless to run the printing presses. The government must fulfill its budget constraint, so that any change in the money supply must be accompanied by a tax or subsidy to maintain budget balance. (A contraction of the money supply would be accomplished by taxing the public, an expansion by a subsidy.) Hence, the government budget constraint is simply

$$\tau_t = -\frac{\dot{M}_t}{P_t} \equiv -\mu_t m_t, \tag{4.20}$$

where τ_t is the level of taxes (or subsidies), M_t the nominal money supply, P_t the price level, m_t the real money supply, and μ_t the rate of growth of the nominal money supply, all at time t.

A representative consumer derives flow utility at each time t from consumption c_t and holding of real balances m_t. The consumer's welfare is the present discounted value of flow utility at each point in time, where discounting is exponential at rate ρ, so that the government's objective function may be written[21]

$$\Omega_0 = \int_{t=0}^{\infty} [u(c_t) + h(m_t)]e^{-\rho t}\, dt. \qquad (4.21)$$

In equilibrium, the real interest rate must equal ρ. The representative consumer's maximization is described by the intertemporal maximization problem under certainty set out in Section 2.5 of Chapter 2, to which the reader may want to refer. For the purposes of Calvo's argument, one needs at this point only a demand for real balances. This is given implicitly by the first-order condition such as (2.32), equating the marginal utility of money balances $h'(m_t)$ to the nominal interest rate, which equals $\rho + \pi^e$, that is, the sum of the real interest rate and the expected rate of inflation. Denote by $\pi^e = \lambda(m)$ the relation between π^e and m consistent with market clearing, given the money demand function.

Calvo considers a *perfect-foresight path* in which expectations are fulfilled and the price level is expected to be a continuous, right-differentiable function from time zero onward. That is, there can be no expected jumps in the price level after time zero.[22] Along a perfect-foresight path, there *can* be a jump at time zero, as this would, by definition, be unanticipated. Hence, though the nominal money supply is a state variable, which cannot jump at *any* point in a continuous-time model, the possibility of a jump in the price level at time zero means that real money balances can jump at time zero as well. The dependence of money demand on the expected rate of inflation, as well as the implications of price jumps, are central to the time-consistency problem in a monetary model.

In the case of *nondistortionary* taxes, policy can easily achieve the first-best (or "command") optimum. Output, which is equal to private consumption c_t, is fixed if there are nondistortionary ways of raising taxes. Consumption will be at its maximum, so that government policy aims to maximize utility from money holding. The nominal money supply is set so that at each point in time, the marginal utility of *real* balances held by the representative consumer is zero, which, by the assumption above, is the marginal cost of producing another unit of money balances. That is, real balances are at the "optimum quantity of money" level $h'(m) = 0$, which

---

[21] Exponential discounting means that time inconsistency does not arise for the reasons of Strotz (1956), as in footnote 1.

[22] The standard argument for no jumps in the price level (except perhaps at the initial instant of time), is that in a perfect-foresight equilibrium with a constant real interest rate, a perfectly anticipated jump would imply an arbitrage opportunity for infinite profits. In the absence of capital or storable output, this argument is less compelling. See Calvo (1978), footnote 4, as well as Section 2.5 in Chapter 2, for a discussion of the issue.

can be denoted m^F. Since the price level can jump at time zero, the economy can immediately jump to a steady state in which real balances equal m^F. Subsequently, the money supply should *contract* at rate ρ, implying an expected inflation rate of $-\rho$, so that the consumer faces a nominal interest rate of 0. (This is Friedman's characterization [1969] of first-best monetary policy.) This can be accomplished without affecting consumption because of the possibility of nondistortionary (negative) taxation. Hence, sufficient instruments allow attainment of the first-best.

Let us now consider what happens when only *distortionary* taxes and transfers are available. If only distortionary financing is available to the government, output is at its maximum (the fixed nondistortionary level) when taxes and transfers are zero. More specifically, Calvo assumes that when taxes and transfers τ_t, are distortionary, output is related to taxes via

$$c_t = f(\tau_t), \quad \text{where } f'(0) = 0, f(0) > 0, \text{and } f''(\tau) < 0. \quad (4.22)$$

It is further assumed that there are upper and lower bounds $\underline{\tau} < 0$ and $\bar{\tau} > 0$ such that

$$f(\underline{\tau}) = f(\bar{\tau}) = 0,$$
$$f(\tau) > 0 \quad \text{for } \underline{\tau} < \tau < \bar{\tau}. \quad (4.23)$$

Equation (4.22) is a simple way of representing the fact that the government may have available only distortionary ways of financing its monetary policy, a crucial ingredient for a possible problem of time inconsistency.

We can now solve for the optimal path. Under perfect foresight, $\pi = \mu = \pi^e$, so that (4.20) implies that $\tau = -\lambda(m)m$. Under perfect foresight, the government's maximization problem (4.21) consistent with satisfying its budget constraint may then be written choosing a sequence of m_t to maximize

$$\int_{t=0}^{\infty} (u[f(-\lambda(m_t)m_t)] + h(m_t))e^{-\rho t} dt, \quad (4.24)$$

subject to $m_0 > 0$ and m_t being continuous and fully differentiable (technically, right-hand and left-hand derivatives being equal) at every $t > 0$. This last point simply says that m_t is not allowed to jump, except at the initial date. The government can be thought of as choosing a path for real balances m_t by choosing a path for expected inflation, that is, choosing a growth rate μ_t for nominal money balances at each point. A crucial feature of the optimal money growth problem is that the optimization problem that the government faces at any date $t > 0$ is identical to the optimization problem that it faces at time zero. Therefore, for the solution to be time consistent, the optimal $\tilde{m}_t$ as seen from time zero must be a constant. The optimal stationary policy maximizes the term inside the large parentheses in (4.24), implying a first-order condition:

$$h'(m) = (\lambda + m\lambda'(m))u'(c)f'(\tau). \qquad (4.25)$$

As argued above, when nondistortionary taxes are available, so that $f'(\tau) = 0$, the first-best solution is easily obtainable. Things are quite different if the government has available only a distortionary tax or transfer, as given in (4.22). First-best optimal policy is characterized, as before, by real balances at the optimum quantity of money level, as well as distortionary taxes equal to zero at each point in time, which will maximize consumption. However, these two requirements for policy to be optimal are not consistent with one another when the government is running a balanced budget. Equations (4.20) and (4.25) cannot in general be simultaneously satisfied for $\tau = 0$ and $m_t = m^F$ along a perfect-foresight path. Zero taxes or transfers means that via the government's budget constraint, the nominal money supply, and hence the price level, must be constant. Thus, with a nominal interest rate equal to ρ, the real money supply will *not* equal m^F. Hence, the government will in general be following a second-best policy. Its inability to hit the first-best reflects a lack of sufficient instruments which characterized our earlier examples.

The lack of sufficient instruments suggests that the government has the incentive to follow a time-inconsistent policy. What form will it take? As pointed out above, in a perfect-foresight equilibrium with a constant real interest rate, there can be no jumps in the price level except *at* time zero. But, at each date, as the government looks forward, a price jump at that date is consistent with a perfect-foresight equilibrium as long as there are no future price jumps. Hence, at each date, the government would engineer a supposedly one-time "surprise" price jump to yield $m_t = m^F$.[23] Of course, such a policy would not be an equilibrium. As in the examples earlier in the chapter, the policy would be fully anticipated, and, instead of achieving the first-best, government behavior would lead to a time-consistent equilibrium with suboptimally high inflation and suboptimally low holdings of real balances.

The incentive for a government to engineer surprise inflations in order to raise revenue reflects a more general phenomenon, namely, the attempt to raise revenue via an unanticipated one-time wealth tax, that is, via a capital levy. After an asset has already been accumulated, it is optimal to raise revenue by taxing it, since, *ex post*, it is inelastically supplied. We saw this in our earlier example on factor taxation. However, the incentive for the government to engage in time-inconsistent behavior is especially acute in the case of nominal assets. In the case of real assets, the political mechanism by which taxes are chosen means that the imposition of a wealth tax is rarely a surprise. The "advance publicity" for a tax means

---

[23] A similar point was raised by Auernheimer (1974).

that asset holders will generally find ways to shield already-accumulated assets from the tax. For this very reason, we rarely see levies on capital used in practice (Eichengreen [1990]). In the case of devaluing the real value of nominal assets via surprise inflation, there is no legislation that need be passed for the "tax" to be imposed, so that there is, at least in theory, a far greater possibility of surprising the public. (One may argue that past inflationary behavior may induce individuals to expect inflation in the future, though this gets us into reputation, which will be covered in Chapter 6.)

4.6. COMMITMENT VERSUS FLEXIBILITY

So far in this chapter we have stressed the gains from a policymaker being able to precommit, leaving largely aside an obvious cost of precommitment, namely, the loss of flexibility to respond to unforseen events. Focusing on the gain from commitment to the exclusion of the loss of flexibility was possible because of the generally nonstochastic nature of the models we considered. (In the general version of the Barro–Gordon model, we assumed that there is a stochastic shock to unemployment, but as we have used that model so far, this had no effects on our qualitative conclusions. In Chapter 5, where we consider institutional solutions to the time-consistency problem, this stochastic element introduces an important trade-off.) If a potential time-consistency problem arises in an environment with no uncertainty, or in one where all contingencies can be fully specified *ex ante*, committing the policymaker to a course of action (defined to include fully specified state-contingent action) may well be optimal. In the real world, however, unforeseen and unforecastable events occur, so that the optimal policy at time $t + s$ cannot always be specified at time t, even on a state-contingent basis. Hence, removing the ability of the monetary authority, for example, to use discretion in setting monetary policy is a two-edged sword. Effective precommitment to a low rate of monetary growth will mean low inflation on average, but may lower social welfare if there are unforseen negative shocks to economic activity.

Conceptually, there are two aspects to the trade-off between commitment and flexibility, which sometimes get confused. One is the question of how much commitment is desirable in a stochastic world; the other is the technical question of how to achieve this desired level of commitment. We consider this second question in the next two chapters. The first question on the optimal degree of commitment in a stochastic world was central to discussions of macroeconomic policy long before the current interest in political economy. (The interested reader is referred to any policy-oriented text on macroeconomics.) The basic conceptual issues are well understood, so there is a low return to a discussion of general principles. Instead, we discuss some specific applications.

Escape Clauses

One way to try to get the benefits of commitment while still retaining flexibility is by the use of **escape clauses**. Under a rule with an escape clause, a policymaker commits himself to the rule under some preannounced circumstances, but announces he will revert to discretion under other circumstances.[24] The policymaker thus tries to gain the advantages of following a rule on average, but still have some flexibility in choosing policy to respond to especially adverse circumstances. If there were no penalty to reverting to discretion, a benevolent policymaker would always invoke the escape clause *ex post*, and there would be no commitment effect. Hence, to avoid problems of time consistency, the standard assumption in escape-clause models is that the policymaker must pay a private fixed cost when choosing discretion. The policymaker is modeled as choosing between a rule and discretion on the basis of the realized state of the world. If all states of the world could be specified *ex ante*, a fully state-contingent rule could be specified (though it might be quite complicated). An escape clause where discretion is the alternative to a simple rule thus captures the notion that all states of the world cannot be specified *ex ante*.

Escape-clause rules with a fixed cost of reneging turn out to be mathematically more complex than the above discussion might suggest, a point stressed by Obstfeld (1997). We sketch out a basic example here that will be examined more closely in Section 12.3 of Chapter 12 in considering fixed versus flexible exchange rates. From a more conceptual point of view, escape-clause models will be discussed further in the next two chapters, with an alternative, more tractable representation presented in Section 6.8 of Chapter 6.

Consider a single-period loss function as in (4.15) with the nonstochastic target $\tilde{\pi} = 0$, but where the policymaker faces a private cost $\zeta > 0$ if he deviates from zero inflation. Hence, the government's objective function may be written

$$\mathscr{L}_t = \frac{\left(U_t - \tilde{U}\right)^2}{2} + \theta\frac{(\pi_t)^2}{2} + \zeta(\pi_t), \qquad (4.26)$$

where for $\zeta(\pi_t) = \zeta$ for $\pi \neq 0$ and equals 0 for $\pi = 0$. Unemployment is determined by (4.12), with the government choosing the inflation rate π_t, after having observed the shock ϵ_t.

As a point of comparison, suppose the government were to choose between pure discretion, with the solution given in (4.18), or a rule of

---

[24] Models with formal escape clauses were introduced by Flood and Isard (1989), and subsequently studied by Lohmann (1990), Persson and Tabellini (1990), Drazen and Masson (1994), and Obstfeld (1997).

$\pi_t = 0$ (a "zero-percent rule"), where for purposes of the example we assume such a rule could be made credible. Comparing the expected loss in the two cases for the loss function (4.15) (that is, without the cost $\zeta(\pi)$), one can easily show that discretion dominates a zero-percent rule (that is, leads to a lower expected loss) if

$$\sigma^2 > \frac{(1 + \theta)^2}{2\theta} \tilde{U}^2, \qquad (4.27)$$

where σ^2 is the variance of ϵ_t. Intuitively, if the variance of the unemployment shock is high enough, then discretion dominates a rule committing the policymaker to zero inflation, even though discretion implies an inflation bias. If the variance is low, a rule dominates discretion. A rule with an escape clause attempts to get the best of both worlds.

To find the optimal escape clause, one must calculate the critical value of ϵ_t such that it is optimal to deviate from zero inflation, pay the cost ζ, and choose π_t according to discretion, that is, according to (4.18). One does this by finding the value of ϵ_t such that the loss from discretion is equal to the loss from following the rule. For tractability of computation, assume that ϵ_t is uniformly distributed over $[-v, v]$. One begins by calculating the loss under the two cases, conditional on π_t^e and ϵ_t. Under discretion, π_t would be chosen to minimize (4.15) subject to (4.12), yielding (4.16). The resulting loss under discretion as a function of π_t^e and ϵ_t is

$$\mathscr{L}^{\text{disc}} = \frac{1}{2} \frac{\theta}{1 + \theta} \left(\epsilon_t - \tilde{U} + \pi_t^e \right)^2 + \zeta \qquad (4.28)$$

while the loss under a zero-percent rule is

$$\mathscr{L}^{\text{rule}} = \frac{1}{2} \left(\epsilon_t - \tilde{U} + \pi_t^e \right)^2. \qquad (4.29)$$

When there is a fixed cost ζ of deviating from zero inflation, the government will inflate only if the shock ϵ_t is large enough that $\mathscr{L}^{\text{disc}} + \zeta < \mathscr{L}^{\text{rule}}$, in which case π_t will be determined by (4.16) as a function of π_t^e. Equating (4.28) and (4.29), one obtains a critical value of the shock, call it $\hat{\epsilon}_t$, as a function of π_t^e:

$$\hat{\epsilon}_t = \tilde{U} - \pi_t^e + (2(1 + \theta)\zeta)^{1/2}. \qquad (4.30)$$

Given this escape-clause rule, the rational expectation of π_t is

$$\text{E}(\pi_t) = 0 + \text{E}(\pi_t \mid \epsilon_t > \hat{\epsilon}_t) \Pr(\epsilon_t > \hat{\epsilon}_t), \qquad (4.31)$$

which, using (4.16) and the uniform distribution of ϵ_t, may be calculated to be

$$
\begin{aligned}
\mathrm{E}(\pi) &= \frac{1}{1+\theta}\left(\frac{v - \hat{\epsilon}_t}{2v}\right)\left(\pi^e - \tilde{U} + \frac{v + \hat{\epsilon}_t}{2}\right) \\
&= \pi_t^e,
\end{aligned}
\tag{4.32}
$$

where the second line follows from the assumption of rational expectations. Solving (4.30) and (4.32) to eliminate π_t^e yields the critical value $\hat{\epsilon}_t$ as a function of $\tilde{U}$, θ, and ζ.

The nature of the optimal policy is as indicated above. When $\epsilon_t \leq \hat{\epsilon}_t$, the zero-percent rule is followed; when $\epsilon_t > \hat{\epsilon}_t$, discretion is invoked, with the chosen rate of inflation being higher the greater the realization of ϵ_t is. The reader may easily show that an escape-clause rule leads to higher welfare than discretion and to higher welfare than a zero-percent rule if σ^2 is sufficiently high. Of course, all this depends on being able to credibly commit to the escape-clause rule.

Flexibility in Seigniorage Policy

Consider the relation between surprise inflation and government revenue discussed in Section 4.5. Suppose the government had a mechanism to commit itself to using surprise inflation *only* for surprise revenue needs (a big if), that is, suppose it could credibly constrain itself not to use surprise inflation to raise revenue *on average*. The nondistortionary nature of price surprises, if in fact they are truly surprises, makes them an excellent tool to meet surprise revenue needs in a nondistortionary manner. Calvo and Guidotti (1993) explore this possibility. They argue that it is *anticipated* inflation which (negatively) affects the demand for money; *unanticipated* inflation has income, but no substitution effects. It can hence be seen as lump-sum tax with no deadweight loss *ex post*, and hence no welfare loss. This implies that optimal monetary policy under precommitment will take advantage of this by being highly responsive *ex post* to states of nature. More specifically, all undesirable randomness in a period is "loaded onto" inflation, replicating a state-contingent lump-sum tax which collects no revenue on average. For example, if government expenditure g were stochastic, fluctuations in g would be financed by unexpected variations in the inflation tax. This would imply, first, high variability of the inflation tax, and, second, a positive correlation between the fiscal deficit and inflation. (A similar argument could be made for optimal random *labor* taxes if labor supply responded only to the expected rate of tax on labor.)

More realistically, governments in general do not have a way to make credible a promise to engineer price surprises only to meet stochastic expenditures needs. The best a government can usually do is to make it difficult, but not impossible, for itself to use surprise inflation to raise revenue, thus trying to get the benefits of low expected inflation on average, but retaining some flexibility for emergencies. This is exactly the trade-off in designing policy discussed above. Reducing flexibility reduces the *temptation* to engineer surprise inflation (via reducing the government's ability to do so), but it also reduces the policymaker's ability to respond to shocks. Generally, the institutional constraints imposed on the monetary authority will reflect the decision on where the optimal point on this trade-off lies. Calvo and Guidotti (1990) discuss this trade-off with respect to the choice of the level of indexation or the debt maturity structure. Cukierman, Kiguel, and Liviatan (1992) present a careful discussion of balancing commitment and flexibility, in the context of choice of an exchange rate rule.

4.7. CONCLUSIONS

In this chapter, we have set out the basic time-consistency problem. By this point, the reader should have a clear sense of how time inconsistency is defined and should be convinced that the problem of time consistency is relevant and useful in explaining a number of key phenomena in macroeconomics. In this respect, the material in this chapter parallels standard treatments of time consistency, though we hope in a way that clarifies a number of issues.

The treatment presented here differs from standard treatments in stressing that conflict of interests is essential to the time-consistency problem. In many works on political economy, the time-consistency problem is distinguished from other issues in this respect. Whereas many problems are seen to reflect heterogeneity of interests, time-consistency problems are seen as arising even when there is no apparent conflict of interests, with the government choosing policy to maximize the welfare of identical representative agents. That is, it is a problem of political economy without explicit political constraints. The explanation of time inconsistency stressed in this chapter removes this dichotomy. Time consistency, like all other problems of political economy, arises because of heterogeneity leading to conflict of interests. It falls squarely within the general framework of our approach to political economy. For students well familiar with the time-consistency problem, this may be the innovation of this chapter.

One should stress, however, that the importance of time consistency is independent of the underlying interpretation given here. In the next two chapters, we consider "solutions" to problems of time inconsistency.

CHAPTER FIVE

Laws, Institutions, and Delegated Authority

> Laws and institutions must go hand in hand
> with the progress of the human mind.
>
> —*Thomas Jefferson, Letter to Samuel Kercheval, 1816*

> There is hardly a political question in the United States
> which does not sooner or later turn into a judicial one.
>
> —*Alexis de Tocqueville,* Democracy in America

5.1. INTRODUCTION

In this chapter and the next, we consider "solutions" to the time-consistency problem, by which we mean the following. As we saw in the previous chapter, when we consider equilibrium solutions, the optimum is achieved when the policymaker is led at $t + s$ to carry out the policy announced at t, rather than some other policy, and it is "common knowledge" that he will indeed carry out the announced policy. That is, his carrying out at $t + s$ the policy announced at t is expected by the public, and the government knows it is expected and can act accordingly. Put more concisely, the optimum is achieved if the announcement at t of first-best policy for the future is *credible*, credible in the sense that the public expects that announced policy will be carried out or adhered to.

Our discussion of how current policy can be made credible is divided into two parts, corresponding to this and the next chapter. One way of investing current policy with credibility is by building a reputation, that is, by engendering the expectation that certain policies will be followed in the future on the basis of actions that have been observed in the past. We consider reputational models in detail in Chapter 6. In this chapter, we concentrate on how the policymaking environment can make policy credible, that is, how institutions or the creation of external circumstances (broadly defined) can lead to the expectation that announced policies will be carried out. An oft-heard claim is that "institutions matter" in determining policy outcomes, but what exactly does this mean? In considering how institutions can put effective constraints on policymakers, we hope to give a more precise meaning to the argument that "institutions matter."

A key issue that arises in modeling institutions or the policymaking environment as commitment mechanisms is: How realistic are these representations of policymaking institutions? That is, how strong is the connection between the theoretical constructs and actual real-world institutions? This is a point of some controversy. Many economists argue that the theoretical constructs well represent real-world institutions (albeit in a schematic way), with the choice of models in fact often being motivated by real-world examples. Others argue that though some of the concepts (such as central bank independence) are measurable (albeit imperfectly), many models of institutions are quite divorced from the real-world counterparts they are meant to represent. In this chapter we espouse both views, depending on the specific model, but generally come down closer to the latter view. The stance is motivated in part as a pedagogical device—a critical attitude towards what are perceived as a model's drawbacks helps a student learn to analyze existing research and ultimately successfully do his or her own research. It is also motivated by a belief that a weakness in the political economy literature is an overreliance on models from other areas of economics (such as industrial organization) because they are formally attractive, rather than really relevant. This issue will come up not only at various places in this chapter, but in subsequent chapters as well. My point of view having been revealed, let us move on to specific institutional mechanisms for commitment.

5.2. LAWS, CONSTITUTIONS, AND SOCIAL CONTRACTS

Laws

In considering institutions that enhance the credibility of policy, a logical place to start is with legal restraints which attempt to "bind" the policymaker, that is, which legally enjoin him to follow a specific course of action. A legal restriction could take several forms. It could be embodied in the country's basic set of laws, that is, in its constitution. For example, many states in the United States are enjoined by their constitutions from issuing debt to cover regular operating expenses; on the federal level, we have seen continued debate on a Balanced-Budget Amendment to the U.S. Constitution.[1] More generally, governmental units on all levels pass laws attempting to regulate their own economic behavior. To take but a few examples, there are restrictions on the financial or commercial agree-

---

[1] At this introductory stage, we ignore the problem of how one interprets the constraining power of laws which give only qualitative targets, or whose escape clauses imply a law has no effective constraints. These issues will be addressed explicitly later in this chapter and in the next chapter.

ments the government is allowed to enter, limits on tax authorities with the effect of disallowing types of tax collection, or, on a more macroeconomic level, mandates concerning the level of economic aggregates. The fiscal authority may be enjoined to achieve full employment, the monetary authority to hit an inflation target $\bar{\pi}$. These injunctions could take the form of specific laws (such as a Full-Employment Act) or of directives which have the force of law. Restrictions could also take the form of unwritten laws, such as norms or "social contracts" which also have much of the force of law. Standards of ethical behavior for public servants may be unwritten, but have a powerful effect on their actions if such standards are widely accepted.

Attempting to invest a policy with credibility by means of a law directing a policymaker to carry out the policy raises a basic question. What forces a policymaker to obey the law, especially in cases where breaking the law *ex post* improves welfare? Or, what prohibits the government from changing a law when it perceives that it is optimal to do so, so that the old law is "broken" in a way which is fully legal? In the absence of any explicit or implicit restrictions to the contrary, a welfare-maximizing policymaker will renege on a promise if it benefits his constituents. If a law is passed directing him to fulfill his promise, the benevolent policymaker should similarly be tempted to break the law if so doing will increase social welfare. By considering laws which direct the policymaker to adopt a policy, are we just moving the problem of time inconsistency one level higher? What makes a $\bar{\pi}$-inflation law any more credible than an announcement of a $\bar{\pi}$-inflation goal? Is there a real, as opposed to a semantic difference?

There *are* important differences between promises which have no legal backing and laws (including widely accepted norms) in analyzing solutions to the time inconsistency problem. The primary difference is that laws have *penalties* attached to them, so that there are explicit costs to breaking the law. Similarly, social norms have recognized costs associated with not following them. (See, for example, Elster [1989], chapter 3.) Secondly, explicit laws or widely recognized social norms make noncompliance more visible and hence more costly.[2] There are also quite explicit costs for changing an existing law. Constitutions specify procedures which must be followed for laws to be changed, including quite restrictive procedures for the constitution itself to be amended. In short, key to understanding how laws can make policy credible is in understanding the specific mechanisms which give laws their force, namely, the penalties or costs of breaking or

---

[2] Formalizing a directive as a law may increase the probability that it is carried out in several ways. Greater visibility makes it easier to monitor compliance, so that visibility is directly related to optimal enforcement. Or, formalizing a directive as a law may make obeying it more of a social norm, to be discussed later in this section. In Section 6.9 in the next chapter, we discuss how visibility may enhance credibility by allowing a policymaker to demonstrate his commitment.

changing the law. The emphasis is (or should be) on concrete as opposed to abstract mechanisms, for example, on restrictive amendment procedures for laws rather than on national governments "posting bond" with mythical supernational organizations.

It is trivial, but besides the point, to argue that with a harsh enough penalty for disobedience, the law will certainly be obeyed. If the penalty for disobedience is so harsh that it implies that the law will be obeyed no matter what, then it is not credible that the penalty will be applied in all circumstances.[3] Decapitation as a penalty for "double-parking" will certainly induce people to obey parking laws if they believe the penalty will always be carried out, but it is unlikely that anyone would believe it will be. Hence, harsh penalties simply shift the credibility problem from whether the law, as written, will be obeyed to whether it will actually be enforced.[4] That is, since individuals know that such a harsh reaction is not optimal *ex post*, the punishment itself is not credible. If laws make policies credible only to the extent that the penalties which enforce the laws are themselves credible, then enhancing credibility depends on choosing the optimum structure of penalties to do this. Penalties should reflect the optimal trade-off between enforcement and flexibility, in this case to give them credibility.

The basic conclusion to be drawn from this discussion can be put as follows. *Laws (and institutions more generally) can enhance credibility by raising the cost and lowering the benefit from deviating from a given policy.*

Constitutions

Having discussed how laws can make policy more credible, we now ask how it can be made credible that existing laws will not be changed. Making credible the expectation that a law will not be changed whenever current circumstances change returns us to the issue of *constitutionalism* first raised in Chapter 3. We suggested four characteristics of laws which make them "constitutional." First, these laws *restrict government's use of authority*. Second, they set out the *basic processes of policymaking*, that is, they are laws about how collective choices should be made. Third, constitutions often treat issues that are more *fundamental* than others, such as basic rights or liberties. Fourth, constitutional laws have more *stringent amend-*

---

[3] To the extent that there is significant leeway in the application of the penalty, as is often the case, the law clearly loses much, if not all, of its force. Issues of whether a penalty will be applied *ex post* are central to the economic analysis of some problems, such as renegotiation-proofness in sovereign debt. In this chapter, when discussing the role of penalties in enforcing time consistent behavior, we assume, in general, that penalties are unambiguous, and unambiguously applied.

[4] McCallum (1995, 1997) makes a similar point in criticizing some of the work on institutional solutions to the time-inconsistency problem. He argues that some of the proposed solutions do not solve the problem, but merely "relocate" it, in that it is not clear why the institutions are themselves credible. This sort of argument will be central to the discussion of institutions in this section.

ment procedures than other laws, this characteristic reflecting in part the previous two characteristics, in that certain types of laws are meant to be more permanent.[5] In our study of choice mechanisms in Chapter 3, we considered the second characteristic in greater detail. Let us consider the third and fourth characteristics, as both are related to the expectation that a law will not be easily changed, though in quite different ways. (The first characteristic, which is related to solutions to the time-inconsistency problem far more directly, is considered below.)

When a law is generally perceived as treating a fundamental issue, this perception, by its nature, will strengthen the expectation that the law will not be quickly changed. That is, to the extent that a law is seen as regulating a basic right, basic in the sense that it is seen as holding across a wide range of circumstances, there is, by definition, the expectation that the law is permanent. Therefore, independent of any implied legal restrictions on changing the law, "constitutionalizing" a law sends the signal that a society sees the law as one not "to be tampered with." That is, while some restrictions (such as freedom of speech) are obviously fundamental and hence permanent, others are not so obviously fundamental, so that constitutionalizing them invests them with an importance they would not otherwise have. For example, zero deficits is not a "fundamental right"; a balanced-budget restriction in the constitution sends the signal that a society attaches fundamental importance to it.[6]

The fourth constitutional characteristic, more stringent amendment procedures, is a concrete, rather than a conceptual, approach to engendering the expectation that a law will not be changed whenever circumstances make it tempting. As already indicated, the last two characteristics of constitutional laws are connected, in that if a law is seen as fundamental, it is natural that it cannot be changed through the ordinary legislative process, but requires a more stringent procedure.[7] Procedures that make it difficult to amend a constitution include: supermajorities; waiting periods; confirmation; referendums; and (in federal systems) ratification by states. Such restrictions are seen as "protecting the electorate against itself," in that a majority may act under the influence of a "momentary passion."[8] In

---

[5] Elster (1988) points out that the second characteristic specifies the operational rules of how majorities operate; the third and the fourth attempt to limit how majorities use their powers.

[6] In discussing constitutions as precommitment devices, one should note that there is often a large difference between what is written on paper and how things actually work.

[7] Many argue (see, for example, Elster [1995] or the discussion of constitutionalism in Chapter 3) that this connection is the heart of constitutionalism.

[8] One may ask *which* time-consistency problem is constitutionalism meant to solve. If we mean weighting the present too heavily relative to the future (as the term "momentary passions" suggests), then it is the implication of nonexponential discounting raised by Strotz (see footnote 1, Chapter 4). Elster (1995) argues that a government may suffer from this type of inconsistency when it chooses investments with low but immediate yields over those with higher but delayed yields, such as investments in education and health care, and suggests that constitutionalizing the right to education and health care could get around the problem.

short, a promise to follow through on a certain action may be made credible by enacting it into a law which itself is difficult to undo, that is, by "constitutionalizing" it. This is the main result and should be stressed. *Effective commitment follows from the extreme difficulty in changing a law once it is given constitutional status.*

One could go a step further and ask what gives the constitution itself credibility. (This is a form of the "infinite-regress" problem already mentioned in Chapter 3.) One view is that giving a constitution credibility requires that the government's power itself be limited, by a system of checks and balances. This was considered in Section 3.3 of Chapter 3 in our discussion of the inability of an all-powerful government to credibly precommit.[9] Thus, following discussions on separation of powers going back to Locke and to the Federalist Papers, constitutions are more credible when power is divided, for example, among an executive, independent judiciary, and democratically elected legislature.[10] The interested reader is also referred to North and Weingast (1989), who present a fascinating discussion of the evolution of institutions in seventeenth century England to solve credibility problems. The credibility of a constitution may also come from the fact that it embodies laws generally agreed upon. To the extent that constitutions are adopted by supermajorities, only laws generally agreed upon will be included.

Are constitutions a good solution to the time-consistency problem, meaning is constitutionalizing a policy action a good way in general to achieve commitment? This depends on what sort of time-consistency problem is being considered. Constitutions are meant as an extreme form of commitment (and hence loss of flexibility), so that this solution should be reserved only for special issues, either issues of great import or those where all else has apparently failed. One time-consistency problem is that in a democracy, the preferences of the majority will change over time. To the extent that fundamental issues are involved, constitutionalism suggests itself.[11] To the extent that we are considering more mundane issues such as the incentive to accumulate capital, less extreme solutions are warranted. This holds even more so when the time-consistency problem does not concern fundamental characteristics of democracy, but operational

---

[9] Schelling (1960) makes the point strongly in viewing bargaining power as the "power to bind oneself." That is, a party that cannot bind itself to honor a commitment cannot enter into an effective agreement.

[10] Persson, Roland, and Tabellini (1997) consider the question of why separation of powers is needed in addition to elections to discipline policymakers. They stress that elections occur only at discrete intervals; once in office, a policymaker can abuse his power. Separation of powers is thus important to ensure greater accountability of elected officials.

[11] "Constitutionalism then stands for the rare moments in a nations's history when deep, principled discussion transcends the logrolling and horse-trading of everyday majority politics, the object of these debates being the principles which are to constrain future majority decisions." (Elster [1988], p. 6)

issues such as the incentive to inflate, unless, as indicated, other solutions have repeatedly failed. Flexibility is one issue; as Elster (1995, p. 220) puts it, "Is it possible to make it easier to unbind constitutional ties in an emergency without at the same time making it possible to yield to temptation—precisely the case for which self-binding was imposed?" A second argument against constitutionalizing too many issues is that it devalues the force that constitutions have.

Another question is whether the process of *writing* a constitution makes this a feasible solution to the time-consistency problem. Relative to the problem of a "momentary passion" mentioned above, constitutionalism is more problematic when a majority is supposed to commit itself against acting on a temptation which is permanent and ongoing, rather than transitory. If the incentive towards time-inconsistent behavior reflects a commonly shared policy goal, it may be unrealistic to expect that a constitution written by individuals who share that goal will eliminate the time-consistency problem. The bottom line is that constitutionalizing promises as solutions to time-consistency problems seems quite limited.

Social Norms

Laws, even those of a constitutional nature need not be written. Even though it is not part of a formal law, independence of the Federal Reserve in the United States has the permanence of a constitutional law, because it is generally agreed upon and thus hard to break. Unwritten agreements that have force because they are generally agreed upon go by several names: social contracts; social conventions; and social norms. Let us begin with a definition. Following Young (1993), a **social norm** is "a pattern of behavior that is customary, expected, and self-enforcing. Everyone conforms, everyone expects others to conform, and everyone wants to conform given that everyone else conforms."[12] The obvious question is: what gives social norms or conventions their force in inducing good behavior in the absence of legal penalties or other legislation? Saying that a social norm is, by *definition*, a mode of social behavior that is generally followed begs the point. The key question is whether following a social norm can be equilibrium behavior.

Most of the formal work showing how adhering to a social norm can be rational from an individual point of view has been either in game theory or in the theory of organizations, looking at incentives for cooperation within an organization. Though the work is quite interesting, we will not concern ourselves with much of it, either because it is highly technical, or because it deals with subjects well outside the realm of macroeconomics. We consider a few relevant examples here.

---

[12] Lewis (1969) and Elster (1989, chapter 3) provide general discussions.

TABLE 5.1
Payoffs in the Cremer Model

	Number who Work		
	≤ 18	= 19	≥ 20
Per-capita payoff to			
working	0	.4	.8
not working	.5	.9	1.3

An early paper that is directly applicable is Hammond (1975), who considered transfers across generations in the basic Samuelson (1958) overlapping generations model.[13] (See Section 2.4 of Chapter 2 for a fuller discussion of the basic overlapping generations model.) In each period t, an individual is born who lives for two periods. In period t, when he is young, he is endowed with one nonstorable chocolate; in the second period of his life in period $t + 1$, when he is old, he has no endowment, but still wants to consume. In Hammond's "pension game," the current young generation decides whether or not to transfer part of his endowment to the current old conditional on the history of transfers made by previous generations when they were young. Consider the strategy of the young giving a "fair" pension (defined as at least half-a-chocolate) to the current old generation either if it was fair to the previous generation as a result of that generation being fair to its elders or if the current old "punished" the previous generation in response to that generation having been unfair to its elders. Otherwise, the current young generation gives nothing to the current old generation. Hammond then shows it is an equilibrium for each generation to follow this strategy and provide for the current old, having the rational belief that if it does so, the next generation will provide for it when it becomes old.[14]

Cremer (1986) presents a simple and extremely clear model of cooperation within a firm. Workers have a working life of thirty years, and firms are made up of thirty workers, each of a different age. In a firm, each year the oldest worker leaves and a new one (of the youngest age) enters. Each year every member of the firm chooses either to work or not to work, with his action observed only *ex post*. The per-worker utility payoffs to each of the actions depends on what other workers are doing, as in Table 5.1. High payoffs depend on enough workers supplying effort (reflecting, for example, a production function with a minimum scale of operation), but workers who shirk obtain the same wage in the period and enjoy their leisure. Hence, the payoffs imply a "prisoner's dilemma," in which not cooperating is a dominant strategy.

---

[13] We consider models of intergenerational transfers in much greater detail in Section 8.6 of Chapter 8.

[14] The reader is referred to Hammond for a more exact description of possible equilibria.

Cremer considers the following two-part norm within the firm. The twenty youngest workers work, the ten oldest do not, and if this behavior is not observed in a given period, in the following period *no one* works. When there is zero discounting, it can be shown that cooperating with this norm is an equilibrium. To see why, note first that if in any period cooperation did not prevail, noncooperation would be an optimal strategy for all agents in all subsequent periods.[15] Conversely, suppose cooperation has prevailed for some time. Then, the ten oldest workers clearly have no incentive to deviate from the social norm and work instead of not working. The twenty youngest workers will also cooperate, since a young worker gains .5 today from not working, but loses at least 8 units of utility ($[1.3 - .5] \times 10$) in his last ten years.[16]

In the political economy literature, Kotlikoff, Persson, and Svensson (1988) apply an overlapping generations model of the type Hammond presented to the problem of time consistency in capital taxation. Analogous to Hammond, the current young agree to provide for the old by transferring tax revenues to them, if the old abide by a social contract not to tax their own capital accumulation. In their terminology, a law not to tax capital that has been honored is "sold" to the young; if the old break the law, it becomes worthless and cannot be sold to the young. Their paper suggests how the idea of self-enforcing social norms can solve the time-consistency problem, but they admit that the institutional structure is contrived. Though the model is quite carefully done, the attractiveness of the result is limited by the difficulty in seeing what are the real-world counterparts of the structures that are central to their model.

Lindbeck, Nyberg, and Weibull (1999) apply Cremer's type of model to the decision of whether or not to work in a model of income redistribution, but where there is a social norm against living on social benefits. The results of their model mirror those of Cremer's model, in that working can be a social norm. Alesina and Spear (1988) have applied this idea to cooperation within political parties, in explaining why candidates who do not plan to run for re-election will keep their campaign promises. We will consider their analysis in greater detail in Chapter 7 on electoral competition.

[15] One should distinguish between the question of how robust is such an equilibrium and the question of how one convention gets chosen, when several are available. On the latter, see Young (1993) and the references therein. On the former, there is the question of "renegotiation-proofness," a forbidding concept (and word) considered very briefly in the next chapter.

[16] It is crucial that there is a lag between when actions are taken and when the action is observed, for otherwise noncooperation would be identified immediately. Such a lag seems realistic for many problems; formally, the discrete time nature of the model guarantees a lag.

5.3. Delegation of Authority

In the Barro–Gordon model of the previous chapter, we considered choice of monetary policy by a monetary authority, though in the context of that model we could use "government" and "monetary authority" interchangeably. That is, though we argued that the pre-existing distortion faced by the monetary authority could reflect the decision of some other agency in the background, the objectives of the monetary authority were identical to the objectives of the government. Calling the decisionmaker the monetary authority reflected rhetorical convenience, but the interpretation in no way affected the results of the model. (One should, however, remember Blinder's [1998] criticism of the model as not representing the behavior of central banks in practice, though it might represent the incentives of politicians.) Hence, delegation was purely semantic and played no substantive role. In this section, we discuss some of the conceptual issues surrounding actual (as opposed to semantic) delegation; very simple models are presented in Section 5.4, where we discuss central bank independence.

Substantial delegation of authority characterizes all governments. There are several reasons why such delegation from a principal ("the government") to an agent (the "agency" or "authority") might have significant effects on what decisions are taken, both the agent's decision relative to what the principal might have done, as well as the decision that two different agents may take. In Chapter 3, we discussed how separation of powers could enhance the government's ability to commit, by putting a constraint on its power. In terms of the principal–agent literature (see Section 2.2 of Chapter 2 for a formal treatment of the principal–agent problem), one may think of the differences in results under delegated versus direct authority as representing either differences in expertise or differences in objective functions.

Expertise, broadly defined, is a major reason why a principal may delegate decisions to an agent. Expertise could reflect experience and knowledge, so that, for example, the Secretary of Defense has better expertise on defense matters than the President. Delegation will also reflect the time constraints on the principal, who does not have the possibility of focusing and concentrating on a subset of his duties the way an agent will. The Secretary may actually not have better expertise than the President, but allowing him to focus on defense matters means that they will get more attention than if the President handled them directly. (Concentrating on a subset of the principal's responsibilities will also allow the agent to acquire expertise.) Governments are required to handle a large number of issues, each of which may be extremely complex. This will make it impossible for a single policymaker to make all decisions, so that the number and complexity of issues makes delegation essential.

Complexity of issues will not only dictate the need for delegation, but also affect the form that delegation will take. For example, in a world with uncertainty, it will be impossible to specify every state of nature or contingency in advance. The impossibility of specifying fully state-contingent rules means that the government must give its agencies some discretion in choosing a policy. Rules with escape clauses, introduced at the end of the previous chapter, would serve this function. Moreover, the need to give agencies discretion will be even more obvious if, in addition to it being impossible to specify fully state-contingent rules, an agency is charged with achieving many objectives relative to the number of instruments it has at its disposal. A policy directive to the central bank charged with maintaining price stability, high economic activity, and a favorable balance-of-payments situation would indicate an overall directive which could not be too detailed.

In earlier chapters, we argued that delegation of decisions to policymakers with different preferences is not only pervasive in the making of collective choices, but probably *inherent* to collective decisionmaking. When there are a large number of interests, decisionmaking is necessarily representative, in that individuals will choose representatives with different preferences to make policy. Since not every position can be directly represented, delegation follows from heterogeneity of interests in the population as a whole.

Here, we want to stress how different objective functions could lead an agent to make different choices than the principal would have made (or lead one agent to make different choices than another agent, even if both are supposed to represent the same principal, and are answerable to the same ultimate authority).[17] As in the standard principal–agent model, the agent may be maximizing a weighted sum of the principal's objectives and his own. Or, the agent may be directed to maximize an objective function different from that of the principal. This is where the issue of delegation becomes most relevant for the problem of time inconsistency. Even if it were possible for the principal to appoint an agent with the same objectives, it may *not* be optimal to do so. That is, in delegating the decision over a specific policy objective, a government may come closer to achieving its preferred objective by having an agent aim for a different objective!

How can a government achieve a given objective by directing its delegated agent to aim for a *different* objective? The key insight is that the government may find it optimal to act strategically when faced with agents who also act strategically. This point is well appreciated in the industrial organization literature. Consider a firm wishing to maximize profits. Fer-

---

[17] Schelling (1960, chapter 2) presents an insightful discussion of using delegation in bargaining, for example, by making it clear to the other side that one's agent is either *unable* to accept an offer below a given level, or *unwilling* to, as he is a principal with his own preferences.

shtman and Judd (1987) show that in a Cournot-quantity competition, for example, owners will direct managers towards high production. This will induce competing managers, who are aware of the incentives given to other managers, to reduce their output. Similarly, in strategic trade policy, Brander and Spencer (1983) consider a government which distorts the incentives faced by local firms in order to change the behavior of the foreign government–foreign firms pair to advance the domestic government's objective.

5.4. CENTRAL BANK INDEPENDENCE

In the vast majority of countries, the most prominent example of delegation of macroeconomic policymaking is the existence of a central bank with varying degrees of independence from other policy authorities in the conduct of monetary policy.[18] Independence can be divided into two components, as in Debelle and Fischer (1994): *goal* independence, meaning the central bank sets its own goals, rather than their being set by another agency; and *instrument* independence, meaning the central bank has control over the instruments of monetary policy, and is allowed to use them. Central bank independence means not only that it has the freedom to decide how to pursue its goals, but also that other government bodies cannot easily reverse the central bank's decisions.

Why is central bank independence (hereafter, CBI) important? Blinder (1998), for example, argues that a key reason is that monetary policy, by its nature, requires a very long time horizon. However, he argues that both politicians and the public have neither such a long time horizon nor an understanding of the long lags of monetary policy. "So, if politicians made monetary policy on a day-to-day basis, the temptation to reach for short-term gains at the expense of the future (that is, to inflate too much) would be hard to resist. Knowing this, many governments wisely try to depoliticize monetary policy by, e.g., putting it in the hands of unelected technocrats with long terms of office and insulation from the hurly-burly of politics." (Blinder, 1998, pp. 56–57). Our primary interest here is this argument, that is, the role of CBI in enhancing the credibility of noninflationary monetary policy. In the next chapter, we will return to other arguments in our discussion of reasons for secrecy, ambiguity, and even optimal imperfect control in monetary policy.[19]

[18] There are other, even stronger, institutional solutions. A currency board requiring that domestic currency be fully backed by foreign assets is considered an even more independent agency. In the extreme, "dollarization," in which the domestic currency is replaced by foreign currency as the medium of exchange, delegates monetary policy to a foreign central bank.

[19] Waller (1989) and Fratianni, von Hagen, and Waller (1997) present formal models of the benefit from central bank independence in partisan models. Eijffinger and De Haan (1996) is an excellent survey of the political economy of central bank independence.

A Framework for Studying Central Bank Independence

Let us now consider the role of CBI in addressing the time-consistency problem. In many countries, especially those with a strong tradition of CBI, it is common to appoint someone with a strong aversion to inflation as head of the central bank in order to enforce a more restrained monetary policy. Rogoff (1985a) was the first to consider in a more formal way how delegation of monetary policy can move the equilibrium closer to the first-best. More recently, work on delegation in order to lessen the inflationary bias of monetary policy has taken two directions. One has been the formal investigation of explicit *inflation targets*, following (or, perhaps, leading) a rethinking of monetary operating procedures by policy-makers. Svensson (1997a, 1997b) presents a very good technical analysis; Leiderman and Svensson (1995) and Bernanke, *et al.* (1999) present excellent overviews, as well as papers on actual country experiences with inflation targeting. A second area of analysis has been the use of incentive contracts for central bankers, whereby their compensation is tied to actual inflation performance. Theoretical analysis was presented by Walsh (1995a) and extended by Persson and Tabellini (1993), influenced by the industrial organization literature on mechanism design; Walsh (1995b) presents an excellent conceptual summary of the issues. We discuss both of these strands below.

All of these papers may be characterized and compared in the following framework, based on Svensson (1997a), though with a different interpretation at points. As in the previous chapter, let the social loss function be given by

$$\mathcal{L}_t = \frac{\left(U_t - \tilde{U}\right)^2}{2} + \theta \frac{(\pi_t - \tilde{\pi})^2}{2}, \tag{5.1}$$

which is (4.11) in the previous chapter. Let us represent the objective function of the central bank by

$$\mathcal{L}_t^B = \frac{\left(U_t - \tilde{U}^B\right)^2}{2} + \theta^B \frac{(\pi_t - \tilde{\pi}^B)^2}{2} + \omega(\pi_t, U_t), \tag{5.2}$$

which may be explained as follows.[20] $\tilde{\pi}^B$ and $\tilde{U}^B$ represent the inflation targets of the central bank, which may or may not differ from those of the government, and θ^B represents the weight the central bank puts on inflation deviations relative to unemployment deviations, which also may or may not differ from that in the social loss function. Finally, $\omega(\pi_t, U_t)$

---

[20] This framework is based on Svensson (1997a), though my interpretation of the results differs from his at points.

represents the private compensation to the central banker as a function of his performance, where the form of $\omega(\cdot)$ is to be determined. As in Section 4.4 of the previous chapter, the policymaker is assumed to choose π to minimize his loss function, subject to the Phillips curve (4.12), reproduced here for convenience:

$$U_t = -(\pi_t - \pi_t^e) + \epsilon_t, \qquad (5.3)$$

where ϵ_t is an unemployment shock that is identically and independently distributed (i.i.d.) over time with mean zero and variance σ^2.

Rogoff's "Conservative" Central Banker

Rogoff (1985a) considered the effect of appointing a monetary authority that places a greater weight than the social planner on the losses from deviations of inflation from optimal rate $\tilde{\pi}$. Since the central bank is free to choose the inflation rate according to its own objective function, some argue that, in this framework, it has both instrument and goal independence. An alternative interpretation, more consistent with the real-world view of why conservative central bankers are appointed, is that the society chooses the inflation goal and, consistent with the inflation bias problem, appoints an inflation-averse central banker with broad policymaking independence to achieve it. How we interpret the choice of objectives is central to interpreting various solutions to the inflation bias problem. Though it may sound like semantics at this point, we make a distinction between a monetary authority that is told to maximize an objective function different from the social objective function and a monetary authority which in fact has different preferences than those of society as a whole. We return to this question below, adopting the second interpretation of the model for now.

The Rogoff analysis can be represented by considering a central banker for whom $\tilde{\pi}^B = \tilde{\pi}$ and $\tilde{U}^B = \tilde{U}$, who has no private incentive schedule, but for whom $\theta^B > \theta$. Following Rogoff, a monetary authority characterized by $\theta^B > \theta$ is termed a "conservative central banker." Deriving the equilibrium in the same way as in the previous chapter, where the government chose the inflation rate π_t after the shock ϵ_t had been observed, a conservative central banker will choose the inflation rate

$$\pi_t = \tilde{\pi} - \frac{1}{\theta^B}\tilde{U} + \frac{1}{1+\theta^B}\epsilon_t. \qquad (5.4a)$$

The implied variances of inflation and unemployment are

$$\text{Var}(\pi) = \left(\frac{1}{1 + \theta^B}\right)^2 \sigma^2, \qquad \text{Var}(U) = \left(\frac{\theta^B}{1 + \theta^B}\right)^2 \sigma^2. \quad (5.4b)$$

Equations (5.4a) and (5.4b) summarize the main implications of appointing a "conservative" central banker, defined as someone with $\theta^B > \theta$. Inflation is lower on average and less variable than it would be if set by a social planner with preferences described by (5.1). (Compare (4.18) and (4.19) to (5.4a) and (5.4b), which are identical, but with θ^B replacing θ.) However, appointment of a conservative central banker does not bring us to the first-best solution. It does not fully eliminate the inflation bias of monetary policy as long as $\theta^B < \infty$, that is, as long as the monetary authority places any weight on unemployment (and, of course, as long as the monetary authority has a target rate of unemployment below the natural rate). This is intuitive, for as long as the monetary authority has any incentive to lower the unemployment rate below the natural rate, there will be some inflationary bias to monetary policy.

Under a conservative central banker, lower variance of inflation is achieved at the cost of a higher variance of unemployment. This should also be intuitive. To the extent that the monetary authority is more averse to deviations of inflation from its target, it will intervene less to offset unemployment shocks, so that a given underlying variance of unemployment shocks will translate into a higher variance of unemployment in equilibrium. These two characteristics of the equilibrium, namely, failure to achieve the first-best solution for $\theta^B < \infty$ and higher unemployment variance, are clearly related. Getting closer to the first-best is achieved at the cost of higher variance of economic activity. In the extreme, if the government appoints a central banker who cares only about inflation, that is, a monetary authority with $\theta^B = \infty$, the first-best inflation rate will be achieved with zero variance, but at the cost of high variance in unemployment. More generally, the result of a trade-off between the average level (and the variance) of inflation and the variance of unemployment or output has been interpreted as indicating that the appointment of a conservative central banker is a necessarily imperfect solution to the problem of inflation bias.

To address this problem, Lohmann (1992) suggests appointing a conservative central banker, but with the option to dismiss him at a cost. Her argument is that the high variance of unemployment with Rogoff's conservative central banker reflects a "distorted" response to output shocks, since the deadweight loss is larger for extreme shocks. The option to dismiss a conservative central banker will lead him to accommodate large shocks. This solution is much like using a rule with an escape clause, discussed in Section 4.6 of the previous chapter, as follows. Under a zero-percent inflation rule with an escape clause as derived in the previous chapter, there is no response to small shocks and a full response to large shocks. Lohmann's conservative central banker has a similar, but nonlinear response. There is a small response to small shocks, but a much larger response to larger shocks.

What Do the Data Say?

What is the empirical evidence on the effect of CBI on economic outcomes? The basic underlying question is: given that it is a multifaceted (and often subtle) concept, how does one measure CBI? The main approach, beginning at least with Bade and Parkin (1988), is to construct an index of CBI based on a set of institutional, legal, and sometimes behavioral characteristics. Cukierman, along with co-authors, has presented the most extensive measures of CBI, for example, in Cukierman, Webb, and Neyapti (1992). This work is summarized in Cukierman (1992), where several measures are presented in chapter 19.[21]

Grilli, Masciandaro, and Tabellini (1991) consider indices of CBI in 18 OECD countries[22] and correlate them with economic outcomes. They consider two types of independence—"economic independence," by which they mean the autonomy of the central bank in choosing the instruments of monetary policy, and "political independence," by which they mean the freedom of the central bank to choose the goals of monetary policy. These correspond to Debelle and Fischer's (1994) concepts of instrument independence and goal independence introduced at the beginning of this section. They construct indices of these two types of independence, using institutional features, but no behavioral indicators, such as rate of growth of the money supply. In making this distinction, they correctly argue that although behavioral characteristics may help define the monetary regime, assessing the role of institutions in ensuring good economic outcomes means that strictly institutional features and economic outcomes need to be kept as distinct as possible.

Instrument independence in Grilli, Masciandaro, and Tabellini is measured by two key institutional factors: the influence of the government in determining how much of the fiscal deficit will be monetized and the nature of monetary instruments under the control of the central bank. The first is measured by both the extent of limitations on direct credit facilities at the central bank available to the government and the extent to which the central bank does *not* participate in the primary market as a buyer of

---

[21] Later in his book, Cukierman discusses theoretical and empirical determinants of differing degrees of CBI.

[22] Australia, Austria, Belgium, Canada, Denmark, France, Germany, Greece, Ireland, Italy, Japan, Netherlands, New Zealand, Portugal, Spain, Switzerland, United Kingdom, and United States.

public debt. They measure the second by looking at whether it is the central bank that sets discount rates and by the extent to which the central bank is *not* responsible (or not solely responsible) for banking supervision, the idea being that giving the central bank control of supervisory instruments on banks (such as portfolio constraints) "facilitates financing of government borrowing by administratively increasing private demand for government securities." By their measures, Canada, Germany, and the United States have the most independent central banks, Greece, Italy, and Portugal the least independent.[23]

Political, or goal, independence in their study is determined by three institutional factors: the procedure for appointing members of the central bank's governing body (representatives of the bank rather than the government appoint the central bank governor and the governing board; the governor and other members of the board are appointed for relatively long terms); the legal relationship of the central bank with the government (no mandatory participation of a government representative on the board; no required government approval of monetary policy); and the formal legal responsibilities of the central bank (maintaining price stability is a statutory goal of the central bank; existence of explicit legal procedures for resolving policy conflicts between the government and the central bank.) Using an index of these provisions, Grilli, Masciandaro, and Tabellini find that Germany, the Netherlands, Switzerland, and the United States have the most independent central banks, Belgium, Japan, New Zealand, Portugal, and the United Kingdom the least independent (but see the previous footnote). Overall, they find that these two indices are positively correlated, but can differ substantially in individual countries.[24]

Cukierman (1992) presents several measures of CBI. First, he uses very similar institutional features, with more detail on some features, to construct a single index of overall legal independence for 68 countries in the 1980. He also takes turnover rates for central bank governors as a measure of independence (high turnover indicating low CBI). A third measure is based on answers to a questionnaire sent to central bankers (giving their assessment of various institutional features). Interestingly, he finds only a modest degree of correlation among these three measures, but argues that this may reflect the wide cross-section coverage of the measures. When he

[23] These institutional data were compiled before New Zealand significantly changed its central bank statutes, giving it probably the most independent central bank in the OECD. More on New Zealand below, whose central bank statutes now contain an explicit clause by which the central bank governor is dismissed for suboptimal inflation performance.

[24] In Section 7.8 of Chapter 7, we discuss Grilli, Masciandaro, and Tabellini's analogous measures of political stability and their relation to fiscal outcomes. To preview those results and relate them to central bank independence, they find that of the four countries with *non*independent central banks in their study (Greece, New Zealand, Portugal, and Spain), three of them (all but New Zealand) also tend to have relatively unstable political systems, high debt accumulation, and high reliance on seigniorage.

considers only developed countries, the correlations are higher (though still far from 1), analogous to the above result of Grilli, Masciandaro, and Tabellini.

There are two key findings from this type of analysis on the relation of central bank independence and economic outcomes. First, high CBI (however measured) is correlated with low-inflation performance, a finding of Grilli, Masciandaro, and Tabellini, of Cukierman, and of others. Grilli, Masciandaro, and Tabellini point out (see footnote 24) that in their sample, there are high-debt countries marked by low political stability (for example, Belgium and the Netherlands) which nonetheless have relatively independent central banks and which maintain low inflation, suggesting that CBI may help induce price stability even when the politics and budgetary pressures are unfavorable.

The second key finding, which is striking given our earlier discussion of the effect of a conservative (and presumably highly independent) central banker, is that a higher degree of CBI brings about lower inflation, but no worse performance in terms of real variables. Grilli, Masciandaro, and Tabellini, for example, find no significant effect of CBI on the level or variance of output growth, and hence no significant trade-off between inflation and the variance of real variables suggested in the modeling of Rogoff's conservative central banker. Similarly, Alesina and Summers (1993) and Alesina and Gatti (1995) find that independent central banks bring about low inflation at no higher variability in growth or unemployment.

The lack of an empirically observed trade-off between the average level of inflation and the variance of economic activity has been interpreted as calling into question the characterization of a "conservative" central banker given above. Leiderman and Svensson (1995) argue this quite strongly, suggesting that a more realistic model may be one where conservatism is reflected not in high θ^B, but in a low target $\tilde{\pi}^B$. We return to this point in the next subsection.

Two critiques of the empirical finding suggesting that CBI leads to lower inflation with no output cost may be mentioned. First, several authors find that the picture is somewhat different if one looks at the dynamics of inflation within a country, rather than at the effect of CBI across countries. Debelle and Fischer (1994), Walsh (1994), Posen (1995a), and Eijffinger and De Haan (1996) all argue that greater CBI is associated with higher costs of disinflation.

A second, more basic critique of the finding that high CBI leads to low inflation is made by Posen (1993, 1995b), who argues that the correlation between CBI and low inflation should not be taken as indicating causation. Monetary institutions are endogenous rather than exogenous, reflecting the preferences of powerful groups within society; countries that are inflation averse, he suggests, *develop* institutions to support these preferences. More precisely, since low inflation (or the move to low inflation) affects groups differentially, a societal preference for low inflation reflects the strength of groups that are inflation averse. In this case, there is support for a strong, independent central bank, which is then able to fight inflation effectively[25]: in the absence of political support, CBI will either be absent or will not translate into strong inflation policy over the long run. In short, monetary institutions reflect the outcome of the conflict of interests over inflation policy.[26]

Posen (1995b) argues that the financial sector is uniquely positioned to provide the political support necessary for CBI, and that central banks are most independent where financial sector support has been strongest. The financial sector lobbies for a strong, independent central bank and supports its anti-inflationary activities, countering the pressure that the government (perhaps representing the median voter) would put on the monetary authority for higher inflation. Posen constructs an index of effective financial sector opposition to inflation, denoted FOI, which attempts to measure both the strength of the financial sector and the extent to which the political system is such that their preferences may be translated into strong monetary institutions.[27] Using Cukierman's (1992) index of legal CBI, he finds that CBI is positively correlated and inflation negatively correlated with FOI for a sample of 32 OECD and developing countries. Once FOI is included in an inflation regression for the same sample of 17 OECD countries used by Grilli, Masciandaro, and Tabellini (1991) discussed above, CBI loses its explanatory power, as it does in a regression including both the OECD and developing countries.

Inflation Targeting

A number of countries (Australia, Canada, New Zealand, Sweden, the United Kingdom, to name a few) have recently instituted explicit "inflation targeting" as the monetary policy regime, and the attraction of inflation targeting appears to be growing. Inflation targeting has several aspects, and different authors often characterize it differently. The crucial characteristic is an explicit quantitative inflation rate or range which is given

---

[25] Garrett (1993) makes a similar argument that German anti-inflation policy reflects the interaction of an independent central bank and a strong anti-inflation constituency. He further argues (see Section 12.4 of Chapter 12) that the German view that this interaction is central to effective anti-inflation policy is crucial to understanding the nature of the transition to a European Monetary Union.

[26] Posen's argument is not that laws and institutions do not matter, but that the effectiveness of these institutions in providing credibility depends on the political support given to their goals.

[27] The latter include measures of the extent to which power is centralized (whether the system is federal or not) and whether the legislature is fractionalized, which enters negatively. It may be argued that these political variables affect inflation for reasons other than their effect on the effectiveness of financial sector lobbying. See, for example, the discussion on the role of political polarization on budget deficits (and ultimately inflation when these budgets are monetized) in Section 7.8 of Chapter 7 and Section 10.6 of Chapter 10.

primacy over other objectives of the independent central bank and is publicly announced. In addition to the target being a range rather than a single number, the inflation target may be made state contingent, as long as the conditionality is common knowledge. There is a greatly reduced role for intermediate targets, such as a money growth target, though they may be used as long as they are subordinate to and supportive of the inflation target. More generally, inflation targeting as a regime means an institutional commitment to price stability as the primary long-term goal of monetary policy, with there being both greater transparency of monetary policy and greater accountability of the central bank in achieving its inflation target. Transparency of policy is enhanced not simply through greater communication with the public and with markets about the plans and objectives of monetary policy, but also because inflation targets are more easily understood than monetary targets. Accountability is enhanced by inflation being specified as the sole or the clearly primary target of monetary policy. Transparency and accountability are seen as strong arguments in favor of the use of inflation targets.

The disadvantages of inflation targeting include problems with implementation, as well as monitoring when inflation is affected by factors outside of the control of the monetary authority. Put simply, the rate of inflation is not easily controlled by the central bank, and outcomes are seen only with a long lag. Imperfect control over inflation makes it more difficult for the public and financial markets to monitor and evaluate the performance of the central bank. Accountability is then lessened, so that a strong argument for inflation targeting is greatly weakened. We return to this point below.

The focus on explicit inflation targets is consistent with the alternative characterization of a "conservative" central banker discussed above, namely, a monetary authority that has a lower target inflation rate than society's preferences (as well as possibly a greater aversion to fluctuations of inflation around a target). How may inflation targeting address the inflationary bias of monetary policy when there exists a temptation to follow shortsighted expansionary policies to hit output or unemployment targets? Intuitively, reducing this bias requires making low inflation the primary target of monetary policy, with unemployment, or some other measure of economic activity, only secondary. More specifically, consider the implications of setting $\tilde{\pi}^B < \tilde{\pi}$ in (5.2), where $\tilde{U}^B$ is given to the central bank and θ^B is set equal to θ. The central bank thus minimizes

$$\mathscr{L}_t^B = \frac{\left(U_t - \tilde{U}^B\right)^2}{2} + \theta \frac{(\pi_t - \tilde{\pi}^B)^2}{2}, \tag{5.5}$$

subject to (5.3). The first-best is achieved by setting $\tilde{\pi}^B = \tilde{\pi} + \tilde{U}^B/\theta$, which will be less than $\tilde{\pi}$ for $\tilde{U}^B < 0$, that is, when the unemployment target is below the natural rate. Actual inflation will then be $\pi_t = \tilde{\pi} + \epsilon_t/(1 + \theta)$, so that the variance of inflation and unemployment are the same as under discretion. This result, that with an inflation target $\tilde{\pi}^B < \tilde{\pi}$, lower average inflation is achieved without an increase in the variance of output, better accords with the empirical evidence discussed above; it is what leads Svensson and others to argue that a "conservative" central banker is empirically better described as someone with an especially low target inflation rate, rather than someone with an especially high aversion to inflation fluctuations around a generally agreed upon (higher) inflation target.

The appearance of an unemployment term in the objective function of a central bank which targets inflation deserves further comment. A literal interpretation of inflation targeting would imply $\theta^B = \infty$, which Svensson terms "strict" inflation targeting. The dynamics of inflation in countries with a regime of inflation targeting indicates this is *not* accurate description of central bank behavior. Real activity has an effect on its policy choices. If the unemployment target of the central bank is the natural rate ($\tilde{U}^B = 0$), a formulation consistent both with Blinder's (1998) characterization of what central bankers do (see Chapter 4) and with the whole rationale of inflation targeting, the monetary authority cannot be said to be using monetary policy to hit a real activity target. The first right-hand-side term in (5.5) then reflects concern about fluctuations of unemployment around the natural rate (or, equivalently, about the "output gap" between actual and potential economic activity). This gap and the size of θ then determine the time horizon over which the central bank attempts to hit the inflation target, which will be longer than the shortest possible time horizon when $\theta < \infty$. This regime is termed "flexible" inflation targeting.

Svensson (1997b) argues that problems of controlling inflation in a stochastic environment may be addressed by inflation *forecast* targeting, with the central bank's inflation forecast becoming an explicit intermediate target. He suggests that countries that use inflation targeting as their monetary regime in fact use inflation forecast targeting. The relevant forecast horizon is lag between the setting of the policy instrument the monetary authority uses (such as a short-term interest rate) and the rate of inflation, generally about two years. The intuition for inflation forecast targeting is as follows. Since the central bank is minimizing a quadratic loss function subject to a linear constraint, one can apply standard certainty equivalence results and model the central bank as choosing the inflation forecast to minimize (5.5) with π_t replaced by the central bank's forecast over the relevant control horizon. The first-order condition is the same, with the inflation target $\tilde{\pi}^B$ chosen as in the discussion after (5.5), thus addressing the inflation bias problem. The central bank cannot in any case prevent deviations from the target $\tilde{\pi}^B$ due to stochastic disturbances occurring within the control lag; it can do no better than inflation forecast targeting.

The problem of monitoring central bank performance (and hence of accountability) is addressed by inflation forecast targeting to the extent that the central bank's inflation forecast can be made known to the public in a credible way. Svensson suggests that this can be achieved if the central bank reveals the details of its forecast to the public, meaning not only the forecast itself, but also the model, information, assumptions, and judgements that went into making this forecast, so that they can be subject to public scrutiny. Hence, successful inflation forecast targeting depends on both central bank instrument independence and on lack of central bank secrecy and ambiguity, the latter being just the opposite of standard operating procedure for the typical central bank.[28] Svensson argues that even if the central bank maintains its tradition of secrecy, there are nonetheless ways to monitor inflation targeting, especially use of inflation forecasts by sophisticated outside observers.

King (1997) interprets inflation targeting as way of committing to an average rate of inflation equal to the optimal $\tilde{\pi}$ while at the same time retaining flexibility to respond to shocks, which is exactly the technical solution given after (5.5). He stresses the transparency and accountability of the inflation targeting regime as the mechanism for achieving this commitment. By providing significant information about its forecasts and the nature of disturbances, and by making itself accountable for meeting these forecasts, the central bank makes its low target credible, while having the ability to offset disturbances which it has credibly made known to the public.

On a conceptual level, the results following (5.5) raise a basic question. The central bank will *consistently* overshoot its target $\tilde{\pi}^B$, instead hitting $\tilde{\pi}$ on average. A central banker who "succeeds" in always overshooting $\tilde{\pi}^B$ will be performing his job exactly as the government that appointed him wishes. He will be retained in office, even though by the simplest possible performance measure of achieving his stated goals, he would appear to be not competent. (In the absence of explicit private incentives, one may assume that the reward for good performance is being retained in office, the punishment for poor performance is being replaced.) In what sense can it credibly be argued that the central bank's target is $\tilde{\pi}^B$? By retaining the central banker who hits $\tilde{\pi}$ rather than $\tilde{\pi}^B$, is not the government sending the signal that it really wants the central bank to hit $\tilde{\pi}$? To understand this better, let us return to the distinction between a monetary authority that is told to maximize an objective function different from the social objective function and a monetary authority that in fact has different preferences than those of society as a whole. If we interpret $\tilde{\pi}^B < \tilde{\pi}$ as a target given to the central bank by the government, then this criticism is valid. If the central banker is told to hit a target $\tilde{\pi}^B$, but is retained when he actually

---

[28] We discuss in Section 6.9 of Chapter 6 arguments for secrecy and ambiguity in models of using monetary policy to affect real economic activity.

hits $\tilde{\pi}$, then $\tilde{\pi}^B$ cannot really be called the monetary authority's target. On the other hand, if we interpret the inflation targets model as the appointment of a central banker with truly different preferences, missing the target $\tilde{\pi}^B$ raises no issues of whether it is really his target. This is the realistic interpretation to give to the model.

Incentive Contracts for Central Bankers

To make sense of the notion that the monetary authority is *assigned* targets different than those of the principal, one must bring in explicit private incentives. This is the approach of Walsh (1995a) and Persson and Tabellini (1993) in studying inflation incentive contracts. The basic conceptual point made here is that if the government can structure a contract that directly affects the incentives faced by the monetary authority in choosing how much to inflate, it may eliminate the inflation bias while still leaving the central bank free to respond to stochastic shocks. The insight is that since the inflation bias reflects the monetary authority underestimating the equilibrium cost of inflation, the bias can be eliminated if it must internalize an additional penalty to higher realized inflation.

The argument may be represented more formally as follows. Suppose the monetary authority shared the social loss function (5.1) but was given a private incentive, whereby its own payoff depended on inflation performance. More specifically, let its payoff be linear in the deviation of actual inflation from society's target $\tilde{\pi}$, so that (5.2) becomes

$$\mathscr{L}_t^B = \frac{\left(U_t - \tilde{U}\right)^2}{2} + \theta\,\frac{(\pi_t - \tilde{\pi})^2}{2} + \omega° \times (\pi_t - \tilde{\pi}), \qquad (5.6)$$

where $\omega°$ is a coefficient to be determined. Minimization of (5.6) by the monetary authority subject to (5.3) yields

$$\pi_t = \tilde{\pi} - \frac{\omega°}{\theta} - \frac{\tilde{U}}{\theta} + \frac{1}{1+\theta}\,\epsilon_t. \qquad (5.7)$$

Setting $\omega°$ equal to $-\tilde{U}$ as the private penalty per unit of inflation will then yield the first-best solution in terms of level and variance of inflation.

An inflation incentive contract appears to be a simple, but very effective solution to the time-consistency problem. By providing the central bank with direct incentives that discourage inflationary monetary policy, the first-best is achieved. In interpreting this result, a number of points should be made. On the positive side, the result suggests that there may be a social benefit from presenting a government agency with the sort of incentives which are standard in the private sector, but which many would consider inappropriate in the government sector. The flavor of the result suggests that types of contracts often deemed "inappropriate" for a government employee may, in fact, be the appropriate type of solution. We return to this point below.

The simplicity of the incentive scheme is striking, but this simplicity is misleading. It reflects the simplicity with which the economy is modeled, namely, the single equation (5.3).[29] Though the model captures the essential temptation to engage in surprise monetary policy, it clearly does not capture the complexity of the unanticipated events to which a monetary authority must respond. The complexity of these events means not only that it will be almost certainly impossible to fully specify all contingencies in advance, but also that it will be quite difficult to write a feasible contract for those events which can be specified. Hence, the simplicity and ease of achieving the first-best solution is quite deceptive. If anything, the lesson of the literature on incentive contracts when applied to other areas is often how *difficult* it is to write such contracts, rather than how easy it is.

Walsh (1995b) stresses this problem, pointing out that getting the incentives right through contracting may be quite difficult in more realistic settings. The absence of state-contingency in the optimal contract also reflects the simplicity of the set-up. It is similarly unlikely to carry over to a more realistic modeling of the economy, where the optimal contract may be state contingent in complicated ways. Even in the simple Barro–Gordon framework, the optimal contract will not be simple if the monetary authority does not have the same preferences as society, as was the case in our mathematical example above. In some cases, however, simple contracts may approximate more complicated optimal contracts. Walsh gives as an example a dismissal rule, whereby the central banker is fired if the inflation rate exceeds a critical value.[30] This arrangement is roughly (but only roughly) representative of that now holding in New Zealand, often cited as an example showing that such contracts are not purely hypothetical. The Governor of the Reserve Bank of New Zealand agrees on a target inflation path with the government, with his job dependent on achieving the target. Adjustments to the target for changes in, for example, the terms-of-trade, are specified in advance. More details of this arrangement may be found in Walsh (1995b) and Archer (1997).

To summarize, the realism of incentive contracts for central bankers is still a point of controversy. Proponents cite the New Zealand example as showing they are not hypothetical; doubters take this as an isolated

---

[29] Lockwood (1997) argues that in the more complicated case where unemployment has an autoregressive component, a linear inflation contract still works if the penalty for incremental inflation depends positively on lagged unemployment. Though the result indicates that for some sorts of persistence, the optimal contract is still quite simple, it does not show that the contract will remain so simple for a significantly more complicated economic structure.

[30] One may compare this with Lohmann's model discussed above where the government has the option of dismissing a conservative central banker depending on his response to shocks.

example. A second issue is the realism of the *simplicity* of such contracts arising in the Barro–Gordon model; to my mind, the result is unrealistic, as argued in the previous two paragraphs. This criticism is distinct from saying that models are stylized, highly simplified representations of reality, a point that is not specific to this model. It is saying that the simplicity of the contracts that arise in these models will not carry over to the real world and hence is a poor description of reality. As stressed above, the literature on optimal contracts indicates how difficult it is to write such contracts in practice.

A second critique of the incentive contract approach concerns the credibility of the government's commitment to the contract *ex post*. McCallum (1996b, 1997) stresses this point, arguing that the question of who enforces the optimal contract means that such contracts simply replace one commitment problem with another. It moves the commitment problem one level higher, an issue raised more generally in Section 5.2 above. Walsh (1995b) suggests these commitment problems are different, since a contract "institutionalizes" the incentives for compliance. That is, he argues that the cost of changing an institutional structure is higher than changing a policy in itself, an argument given in the general discussion of laws and constitutions as commitment devices in Section 5.2 above.

What about the "appropriateness," that is, the acceptability to the public, of incentive contracts of this type? There would likely be the complaint about these contracts to the effect that civil servants should be working for the public good, rather than for their own benefit. That is, a "good" public servant sees his job as maximizing the general welfare, and should need no incentives in that direction. To a certain extent, such a view, though probably common, represents an idealized and unrealistic view of the behavior of public servants. Before one simply dismisses it, however, there are well-founded reasons for some skepticism. First, certain types of monetary rewards could possibly lead to an adverse selection problem for public servants. Second, there may be a suspicion of simple incentive contracts in a world the public views as quite complex. There may also be a disagreement over the goals of policy which would make the electorate hesitant to make goals part of an explicit contract.

Overall, an important contribution of the incentive contract approach (as well as of the inflation targeting literature) is that it forces us to focus more on *accountability* of the central bank. In formal incentive contracts, accountability has a very specific meaning, namely, the existence of an explicit significant punishment for poor performance. More generally, accountability can also mean giving the central bank clearly defined authority, so that politicians and the public know whom to hold accountable for inflation performance. There is general agreement that the central bank should be given a clearly defined goal or goals, be given the power to achieve those goals, and should be held accountable for doing so.

The Central Bank as a Committee

Our discussion so far has considered the central bank as a unitary actor with well-defined preferences. In fact, a prominent feature of many central banks is that policy is made not by a single individual, but by a *committee* made up of individuals with different preferences over monetary policy. In the United States, for example, monetary policy is made by the Federal Open Market Committee (FOMC), consisting of the governors of the Federal Reserve System, appointed by the President of the United States, and five presidents of regional Federal Reserve Banks on a rotating basis. (In practice, a strong central bank head will often dominate policymaking, so that decisions will heavily reflect his or her views.) Decision by committee has a number of implications. According to Blinder (1998), it leads central banks to adopt compromise positions on difficult issues, as well as imparting a certain inertia to monetary policy. On the positive side, he argues that decision by committee means that monetary policy decisions cannot be too idiosyncratic. For example, though the "checks and balances" that characterize much of policymaking in the United States are not present in the case of the Fed, Blinder argues that the structure of the FOMC creates an *internal* system of checks and balances, with the chairman being unable to deviate too far from the view that prevails in the committee.

The political economy implications of the central bank being a committee also depend on the type of diversity that is represented in practice. Many central banks (including the new European Central Bank) have regional representation, which will be important if regions differ in their macroeconomic situation, for example, if some regions are in favor of tighter policy, others in favor of looser policy. (In Section 12.4 of Chapter 12 we consider the implications of this type of heterogeneity in the board of the European Central Bank.) If there is large heterogeneity of preferred policies, it may be easier for members of the central bank's governing board to agree to a policy if this policy is somewhat ambiguous rather than being fully transparent. The need to gain support for a policy in the face of diversity of preferences may therefore affect how much information the central bank chooses to release. We return to the optimality of ambiguity, albeit in a different context in Section 6.9 in the next chapter.

In the political economy literature, there is very little explicit formal discussion of the implications of the committee nature of central banking. Exceptions include Waller (1992) and Faust (1996). Faust suggests that the structure of the FOMC, with different committee members chosen by varied and often elaborate rules, reflects the attempt to achieve superior monetary outcomes by assigning policy decisions to a small group selected to balance interests for and against inflation. Let us examine the argument in more detail. He begins with the view that there is a potential inflationary bias to monetary policy, due not to the time-consistency problems stressed in the previous chapter, but to heterogeneity of interests over the distributional implication of unanticipated inflation. In his view, those who gain from surprise inflation outnumber those who lose, so that if decided by majority vote, steady-state inflation would be positive. As this incentive is known, positive inflation is anticipated, so that in equilibrium it imposes a net cost on everyone. If instead, decisions are made by bargaining in a committee with equal representation of gainers and losers, a lower rate of inflation will generally emerge. Hence, it is the internal structure of the monetary authority that is seen as a commitment device when high inflation represents heterogeneity of interests.

5.5. FISCAL STRUCTURES FOR TIME CONSISTENCY

The Role of State Variables

When policymaking is viewed as a sequence of decisions, so that the government can reoptimize at every point, the problem of time consistency can be viewed as reflecting changes in incentives over time. For example, the decision to impose taxes on capital in a time-inconsistent way reflects the accumulation of capital, an accumulation that was induced by the government's previous policies. Hence, with the policymaker's narrowly defined objective function unchanged over time, time inconsistency may be thought of as due to a change in the environment brought about by the policymaker himself. Put in more formal economic terms, time-t decisions lead to an evolution of state variables which give a policymaker the incentive to deviate at time $t + s$ from his previously optimal policy.

The implication of this view for precommitment is obvious in the abstract, though not quite so simple to implement in practice. Time inconsistency can be avoided if a policymaker at time t can choose policy in such a way that state variables at time $t + s$ imply that it is optimal *not* to deviate at $t + s$ from the previously optimal policy. There are ways a government could do this in theory that are not especially realistic. For example, it has been suggested that a government could credibly commit itself by posting a performance bond, in analogy to the way that individuals might post bond. Unfortunately, the analogy breaks down on the practical level. What does it mean for a sovereign government to post bond? To whom? In short, if one is to argue that there are mechanisms or institutions that can constrain governments not to renege on their promises, these should be realistic ones, corresponding at least in broad terms to the mechanisms that real-world governments actually have at their disposal.

The more convincing work along these lines has taken seriously the constraint of considering real-world state variables that a policymaker can choose to induce next period's policymaker (perhaps himself) to continue previous policies. The most studied state variable has been government debt structure. (Barro [1995] presents an excellent survey of optimal debt management.) The pioneering paper investigating debt structure as a commitment device is that of Lucas and Stokey (1983). The basic idea is that in a model of labor taxation, for example, changing the announced tax structure will affect prices, and more specifically, interest rates, in general equilibrium. Changes in interest rates will in turn induce changes in the value of outstanding debt at all maturities, though by an amount that will depend on the maturity. By bequeathing to its successor government a specific debt structure, the current government can eliminate the incentive for its successor to change tax rates and thus try to (optimally) reduce its debt obligations. Specifically, if the maturing debt in each period is just equal to tax revenue net of government spending, there will be no incentive to devalue the debt. This implies a debt structure such that there is no change over time in the payout due at *future* dates, so that the government neither sells new bonds nor buys back old ones. (Barro [1995] presents a very clear formulation of this.) For this to be successful in general, there must be a sufficiently rich maturity structure of the debt.

The Lucas–Stokey Model of Real Debt Structuring

The Lucas and Stokey (1983) model and its results may be illustrated in a representative-agent model similar to the model presented in Section 4.2 of Chapter 4, with three differences. First, the model will be an infinite-horizon model. Second, there will be no government expenditures on goods and services, only tax-financed transfers. Third, the only factor of production will be labor; there will be no capital. While the first two assumptions are made only for ease of exposition, the third difference is substantive rather than expositional. Were there capital in the model, there would be the incentive to raise revenue by a capital levy, as was discussed in the previous chapter, which would make the analysis quite different.

Consider an infinite-horizon, deterministic[31] model, in which individual welfare as of time 1 is a function of consumption c_t and leisure z_t, according to

$$\Omega_1 = \sum_{t=1}^{\infty} \beta^{t-1} [u(c_t) + h(z_t)], \qquad (5.8)$$

[31] The Lucas and Stokey paper considers a model with stochastic government spending and state-contingent debt. Ensuring time consistency then requires that the set of debt instruments "spans" all states of nature. They assume a complete set of state-contingent securities, where payoff depend on the realizations of stochastic government spending. The main results about debt as a commitment device can be illustrated, however, in a nonstochastic model.

where the discount factor β is between zero and 1. Total labor endowment is equal to one unit, so labor supply at time t is $1 - z_t$. The representative individual's budget constraint as of time 1 over an infinite horizon may be written

$$\sum_{t=1}^{\infty} {}_1R_t^{-1} [w_t(1 - \tau_t)(1 - z_t) + v_t + {}_0b_t - c_t] = 0, \qquad (5.9)$$

where w_t is the wage rate, τ_t is the tax rate on labor income, v_t is the lump-sum transfer from the government, and ${}_0b_t$ are claims upon entering period 1 on goods in period t. That is, ${}_0b_t$ is total debt service (interest payments plus amortization) on debt issued by the time-zero government which comes due at time t. Assume there is no other form of debt. ${}_1R_t$ is a cumulative interest factor defined by

$$ {}_1R_t = \prod_{s=1}^{t-1} (1 + r_s), \qquad (5.10)$$

where r_s is the one-period real interest rate from s to $s + 1$ and where ${}_1R_1 = 1$. Choosing a sequence of c_t and z_t to maximize (5.8) subject to the budget constraint (5.9) yields a set of first-order conditions (one for each $t \geq 1$):

$$u'(c_t) = \frac{\lambda_1}{\beta^{t-1} {}_1R_t} \quad \text{and} \quad h'(z_t) = \frac{\lambda_1(1 - \tau_t)w_t}{\beta^{t-1} {}_1R_t}, \qquad (5.11)$$

where λ_1 is the multiplier on the budget constraint (5.9) for a time-1 consumer.

Production is modeled very simply. As in the model in Section 4.2 of Chapter 4, output is a linear function of labor input alone (remember there is no other factor), where, for simplicity, the (constant) marginal product of labor is equal to 1. The competitive wage will then equal unity as well, that is, $w_t = 1$ for all t. The production side of the economy can then be represented as

$$c_t = 1 - z_t. \qquad (5.12)$$

Suppose the path of transfers v_t is given. In a closed economy with only a tax on labor income, the time-1 government's problem is to find an optimal sequence of tax rates τ_t to finance these given transfers. By optimal, one means a sequence of τ_t that maximizes individual welfare (5.8) subject to the individual first-order conditions (5.11), while satisfying the government budget constraint. This is the optimal commodity-tax problem first studied by Ramsey. (See Atkinson and Stiglitz [1980], chapter

14.) In infinite-horizon form, the time-1 government's budget constraint may be written

$$\sum_{t=1}^{\infty} {}_tR_t^{-1}\left[\tau_t(1 - z_t) - \nu_t - {}_0b_t\right] = 0. \tag{5.13}$$

Given ${}_0b_t$ (inherited from the time-zero government) and the given ν_t, choice of a tax sequence τ_t by the period-1 government implies a debt structure ${}_1b_t$ to be bequeathed to the time-2 government. Hence, the time-1 government restructures the debt, with the new debt structure affecting the successor government's choice of tax rates. The question that Lucas and Stokey pose is whether the time-1 government can find a debt structure ${}_1b_t$ that will induce its successor to choose the same tax rates at all $t \geq 2$ that it (that is, the time-1 government) found optimal.

Formally, the time-1 government's problem is to choose a sequence of tax rates to maximize individual welfare (5.8) subject to its budget constraint (5.13), as well as the individual's first-order conditions (5.11) and the economywide resource constraint (5.12). To solve this problem, we use a standard technique of solving for optimal quantities and then find the (optimal) tax rates that support them from the consumer's first-order conditions. That is, we find an optimal consumption sequence $\tilde{c}_t$, with the associated tax rates derived from (5.11). To do this, we first use (5.11) to eliminate τ_t and ${}_1R_t$ in (5.13), and use (5.12) to eliminate z_t. Denoting by κ_1 the multiplier on the time-1 government's budget constraint (5.13), the government's problem of maximizing (5.8) subject to (5.11), (5.12), and (5.13) may be represented as choosing a sequence $\tilde{c}_t$ to maximize

$$\sum_{t=1}^{\infty} \beta^{t-1}\left\{u(c_t) + h(1 - c_t)\right.$$

$$\left. + \frac{\kappa_1}{\lambda_1}\left[h'(1 - c_t)c_t + u'(c_t)(\nu_t + {}_0b_t - c_t)\right]\right\}. \tag{5.14}$$

The sequence of first-order conditions defining $\tilde{c}_t$ (one for each $t \geq 1$) is then

$$(1 - \mu)(u'(\tilde{c}_t) - h'(1 - \tilde{c}_t))$$

$$+ \frac{\kappa_1}{\lambda_1}\left((\nu_t - {}_0b_t - \tilde{c}_t)\,u''(\tilde{c}_t) - \tilde{c}_t h''\,(1 - \tilde{c}_t)\right) = 0, \tag{5.15}$$

which is the analogue of equation (3.2) in Lucas and Stokey (1983).

The optimal tax rates associated with the optimal consumption sequence $\tilde{c}_t$ are defined by

$$\tilde{\tau}_t = \frac{u'(\tilde{c}_t) - h'(1 - \tilde{c}_t)}{u'(\tilde{c}_t)}. \tag{5.16}$$

The associated optimal interest factors are given by

$$_1\tilde{R}_t = \frac{u'(\tilde{c}_1)}{\beta^{t-1}u'(\tilde{c}_t)}. \tag{5.17}$$

Hence, choosing an optimal tax structure is like choosing a sequence of interest factors. By changing the tax structure, an incoming government can change the real present discounted value of the debt it inherits from a previous government, which can be written as

$$\mathfrak{b}_1 \equiv \sum_{t=1}^{\infty} \frac{_0b_t}{_1R_t}. \tag{5.18}$$

In other words, an incoming government can "devalue" the real value of the debt inherited from its predecessor.

A crucial assumption in the Lucas and Stokey model is that all debt issued by the previous government is honored. That is, a government has no ability to bind successor governments on future taxes, but debt commitments are fully binding. This assumption "does not arise from features that are intrinsic to the theory, ... but because this combination of binding debts and transient tax policies seems to come closest to the institutional arrangements we observe in stable, democratically governed countries." (Lucas and Stokey [1983], p. 69)

Using this framework, one can then understand the time-inconsistency problem and how it can be "solved" if there exists a full maturity structure of debt instruments. Let us consider a number of cases. First, suppose that both government transfers v_t and inherited debt obligations $_0b_t$ are the same in each period, that is, $v_t = v$ and $_0b_t = b$. Then, by the first-order condition (5.15), the consumption sequence $\tilde{c}_t$ that the time-1 government finds optimal over time will be constant as well. By (5.16) and (5.17), the time-1 government will also find optimal a constant tax rate and interest factor between periods for all future periods. The government's budget constraint (5.13) then implies a zero fiscal deficit each period, so that the time-1 government will bequeath to its successor exactly the debt maturity structure it inherited, that is, $_1b_t = {}_0b_t$. The time-2 government will thus find it optimal to continue with the tax plan that the time-1 government found optimal. Therefore, there will be no time-inconsistency problem, as long as each government honors its debt obligations.

A complete maturity structure is necessary for the result of no time inconsistency. Consider, for example, the opposite extreme, namely, one where only one-period debt can be issued. Suppose that all debt the period-1 government inherits has a maturity of only one period, that is, $\mathfrak{b}_0 = {}_0b_1 > 0$ and $_0b_t = 0$ for all $t > 1$, and that it is similarly constrained to leave only one-period maturity debt. Since $_0b_t = 0$ for all $t > 1$, the first-order condition (5.15) implies that optimal consumption sequence $\tilde{c}_t$ will be constant for $t = 2, 3, 4, \ldots$, but that the $\tilde{c}_1$ the time-1 government finds optimal will not equal $\tilde{c}_2$, since $6_0 = {}_0b_1 > 0$. Hence, the optimal tax rates will be constant for all $t > 1$, but $\tilde{\tau}_1$ will not equal $\tilde{\tau}_2$. Moreover, it is almost certain that the time-1 government will find it optimal to bequeath positive debt $6_1 = {}_1b_2$ to its successor. Therefore, by the same reasoning, the successor government will find it optimal to choose a consumption sequence where $\tilde{c}_2$ does not equal $\tilde{c}_3$, with the analogous implication for tax rates. Therefore, optimal (that is, welfare-maximizing) policy will be time inconsistent.

How can restructuring of the debt achieve a time-consistent outcome? Let us consider the same example where all of the debt that the period-1 government inherits has a maturity of only one period, that is, $6_0 = {}_0b_1 > 0$ and ${}_0b_t = 0$ for all $t > 1$. However, let us now suppose that the period-1 government is free to restructure the debt into any maturities it wishes. From the discussion in the previous paragraph, we know that since ${}_0b_t = 0$ for all $t > 1$, the period-1 government's optimal plan will imply constant consumption, and hence constant tax rates, for $t = 2, 3, 4, \ldots$. To induce the period-2 government to choose a flat consumption path, the period-1 government must therefore bequeath a flat maturity structure to its successor, that is, ${}_1b_t$ equals a constant, as implied by the results of the next-to-last paragraph. Hence, by (significantly) changing the maturity structure of the debt it inherits from the time-zero government, the time-1 government can ensure that its successor does not deviate from its desired plan. The time-2 government can similarly ensure that its successor follows the plan it found optimal (which will be the plan the time-1 government found optimal), and so on. This is the essence of the Lucas and Stokey argument on how restructuring the debt can ensure time consistency when there is a sufficiently rich maturity structure.

One can understand the relation between choosing a maturity structure of the debt and the incentive for time-inconsistent behavior in terms of the incentive of the time-2 government to change interest factors ${}_2R_t$ as a function of the debt structure ${}_1b_t$ that it inherits. We argued above that the general characteristic of a debt structure ensuring time consistency is that the maturing debt in each period is just equal to tax revenue net of government spending, so that the government sells no new bonds. Suppose, instead, that the outstanding debt is such that some new debt of short maturities must be sold. The government will then have the incentive to reduce short rates.

Nominal Debt

In the Calvo (1978) model of the previous chapter, we saw that in a model with money, there is an incentive for a benevolent government to engineer a surprise inflation to raise revenue in an *ex-post* nondistortionary manner.

This is, in essence, the capital levy problem which led Lucas and Stokey to consider a model without capital. An obvious question, therefore, is, in a world in which individuals hold money, whether there is a *nominal* debt structure which will eliminate the incentive for surprise inflation. Intuitively, it might appear that there will be no such incentive if the government holds a zero nominal position, that is, it is neither a nominal creditor nor a nominal debtor with respect to the private sector. Persson, Persson, and Svensson (PPS) (1988) present this argument formally. Specifically, they consider the Lucas and Stokey model with money and nominal bonds, where real money balances enter as a third argument in the utility function analogous to (5.8). They argue that if the time-zero government leaves its successor net nominal claims on the private sector whose market value is equal to the nominal money stock, the incentive for surprise inflation will be eliminated. With the market value of the nominal debt defined analogously to real debt in (5.18), the PPS solution is for the time-zero government to bequeath to the time-1 government a nominal debt structure and money balances such that

$$\sum_{t=1}^{\infty} {}_1\tilde{I}_t\, {}_0 B_t + M_0 = 0, \tag{5.19}$$

where ${}_0 B_t$ is nominal debt service, M_0 is the nominal money stock, and ${}_1\tilde{I}_t$ are the nominal interest factors associated with the plan the time-zero government finds optimal. Similarly to the definition of optimal real interest factors in (5.17), the nominal interest factors ${}_1\tilde{I}_t$ will depend on the optimal sequences of consumption and real money balances. (The endogeneity of these interest factors will be crucial in the discussion below.) In short, at these interest factors, the time-1 government should inherit a zero nominal position.

However, as Calvo and Obstfeld (1990) show, the PPS argument, as presented, is not correct. It is not sufficient that the overall present discounted value of the government's nominal claims be equal to the money stock. Even though this ensures that a change in the price level alone will have no effect on government net worth, a simultaneous change in several variables can raise government net worth without violating either the government's budget constraint or the economywide resource constraint, and without lowering the utility of the representative agent. Hence, starting from the debt structure that PPS argue will induce the time-1 government to follow its predecessor's plan, the time-1 government could in fact increase the value of its objective function without violating its constraints. Therefore, the Persson, Persson, and Svensson solution will not necessarily induce time consistency in a monetary economy.

To show this, Calvo and Obstfeld use an infinitesimal variation argument. Consider a small enough variation in consumption and leisure away from the optimum of the form $\Delta\,\tilde{c}_1 = -\Delta\,\tilde{z}_1$ (thus satisfying (5.12)), such that the representative individual stays on the same indifference curve. Since nominal interest factors depend on the $\tilde{c}_t$ sequence, a variation of this sort will, in general, change the value of nominal debt in (5.19). On the basis of this result, they construct a variation in which the time-1 government's nominal net position becomes negative while the government budget constraint is still satisfied. (The key to being able to find such a variation satisfying all the necessary conditions is that the time-1 government changes several variables simultaneously.) This gives the government an incentive for surprise deflation.[32]

One may further understand the failure of what seems like an intuitive prescription to ensure time consistency in a monetary economy by comparing these results to those in the real economy above. In the monetary economy, only a very special maturity structure for nominal debt service, namely, one where all nominal debt matures in the current period, will eliminate the incentive to manipulate the sequence of nominal interest factors $_1\tilde{I}_t$. In the real economy, we similarly saw that for a time-consistent solution, the structure of debt service must also be such as to eliminate the incentive to manipulate the real interest factors $_1\tilde{R}_t$. However, the structure that achieves this is generally achievable with a full range of maturities, rather than being quite special in the case of nominal debt.

5.6. Conclusions

The study of laws, delegation, and institutions to solve the time-consistency problem is an especially attractive avenue for research, because this is how in practice governments often address the problem. Carefully marrying theoretical and institutional analysis should bear much fruit in understanding the political economy of monetary and fiscal policy. Some of the work that has been done so far has limited attractiveness because it considers "institutions" that not only do not exist, but also cannot easily be mapped into real-world institutions. It is yet another example of a problem common in recent work on political economy, namely, applying models from another field because they are formally attractive, rather than really relevant. It may be termed the "looking-for-keys-under-the-lamppost" problem, after a standard joke.[33] Applying existing models from another

---

[32] In more technical terms, Calvo and Obstfeld show that the Persson, Persson, and Svensson argument fails because second-order conditions do not hold. That is, though a change in any single variable will violate the first-order conditions, a simultaneous variation in several variables that satisfies the first-order conditions can improve welfare.

[33] A man walks past a lamppost at night and notices another man searching the ground under the lamppost. "What are you doing?" the first man asks, to which the second replies, "Looking for my keys." "Did you lose them here?" "No," the second man says, "I lost them over there under a tree." "Then, why are you looking here??" the first man asks. The second man replies, "Because there's much more light here. Over there, you can't see a thing."

field is a good place to start in shedding light on political-economic phenomena, but it is only a start. The best models in this institutional literature succeed because they take as a constraint the need to map theoretical institutions into real-world ones. One good way to make sure that institutional research follows this constraint is perhaps to begin with the real-world institutions and build models to represent them, rather than beginning with theoretical constructs and trying to force the institutions that they are meant to represent to fit those constructs.

Credibility and Reputation

> The credibility gap . . . is getting so bad we can't even
> believe our own leaks.
>
> —*Bill Moyers, Lyndon Johnson's press secretary*
> (*as quoted in* Safire *[1978]*)

> For Reputation lost comes not again.
>
> —*Charles Lamb, "Love Death, and Reputation"*

6.1. INTRODUCTION

In the previous chapter, we investigated a number of solutions to the time-consistency problem, that is, how a policy announcement can be made credible, so that people expect it to be carried out. These included institutional and legal constraints, delegation of decisions, contractual arrangements, or manipulating the debt structure to create incentives to adhere to previously chosen policies. In this chapter, we investigate the role of reputation in making announced policy credible, that is, how the policymaker's concern for his reputation will lead to the expectation that he will follow through on policy promises. "Building a reputation" is a common concern of newly elected or appointed policymakers who are often largely unknown quantities and must therefore try to convince the public of their competence or seriousness by their actions.

One should not, however, view the credibility of the policymaker and the credibility of the policy itself as synonymous. Making this distinction means more than recognizing, as we did in the previous chapter, that institutional constraints may make a policy credible, independent of who the current incumbent is. Even in models without institutional constraints, it is important to realize that the policymaker's reputation and credibility of his policy announcements are not the same. One meaning of policymaker credibility is that the policymaker will attempt to do exactly what he says (other meanings are possible as well, and will be considered), while credibility of policy could be thought of as the expectation that policy will be carried out. Using this distinction, a policymaker's credibility will enhance the credibility of his policy announcements, that is, increase the probability the public attaches to the policy being carried out. However, if a policy is widely seen as infeasible, the expectation is that it will *not* be carried out, no matter how "credible" or well-intentioned the policymaker.[1] More generally, a policy may be feasible in one set of circumstances, but not in others. Expectations of how the external environment will develop, rather than the credibility of the policymaker, will then be crucial in assessing whether the policy is credible. By focusing solely on the reputation of the policymaker as a way of solving the problem of time inconsistency, some of the literature in this area leaves the impression that the reputation (or credibility) of the policymaker is synonymous with credibility of the policy itself. It is crucial that in reading this chapter, one keeps these notions conceptually distinct. We will consider this distinction formally in Section 6.8 below.

Game-theoretic models are used extensively in this chapter; the nature of the material makes game theory a natural tool of analysis. The level of analysis will not be especially demanding; no previous exposure to game theory is required to read the chapter, though it probably will be helpful. There are now many excellent texts on game theory, at all different levels. Two more technical texts at the graduate level that are referred to are Fudenberg and Tirole (1991) and Osborne and Rubinstein (1994), but there are many other excellent texts as well. Kreps (1990) is very highly recommended for getting a sense of the success and problems of game theory as a tool of analysis.

The wide use of game theory in political economy leads to a note of caution as well. In the analysis of the time-consistency problem and its solutions, and, more generally, in studying political economy, game theory should be used as a tool in building models to understand phenomena, not as the subject of study itself. Perhaps this seems obvious, and it indeed should be. In reading significant parts of the literature, one could easily get a different impression. Many papers and surveys focus on the question of whether a specific equilibrium concept is satisfied by the model, without asking what is the economic significance of the concept, and whether it is economically relevant to the question at hand.[2] In studying the models in this chapter, as well as other models, one should keep clearly in mind that game theory is a tool and not the subject of study in and of itself. In his superb book, Kreps (1990) makes this point forcefully for economic modeling as a whole, and anyone wanting to use game theory in political

---

[1] Conversely, if a policy promise is seen as trivial to carry out, the policy may be fully credible, but carrying it out will not enhance the policymaker's credibility.

[2] To take but one example, there are discussions in the political economy literature of whether an equilibrium satisfies a condition known as "renegotiation-proofness" without a clear understanding either of the concept itself (there are several competing definitions, and the concept itself is quite controversial), or of what exactly is the negotiation process involved in the model in question. Hoping not to implicate him, I am indebted to Larry Ausubel for conversations leading to this point of view.

economy should be required to read his book before being allowed to toil in the field.

There is a second aspect to the caution of how game theory should be used in studying political economy. We observe that models in the industrial organization and the game theory literature are sometimes simply transferred whole to analyze macroeconomic policy (after the labels on the variables have been changed), without thinking carefully whether the model is economically appropriate. Sometimes it works; sometimes it does not. We saw a crucial problem with this strategy in Chapter 4: models of oligopoly with two nonatomistic competitors cannot be automatically applied to the interaction between the government and a competitive private sector. (Chari and Kehoe [1990], discussed below, give serious consideration to this issue in reputational models.) It is yet another example of the "looking-for-keys-under-the-lamppost" problem first raised at the end of the previous chapter: applying existing models from another field is a good place to start in shedding light on political-economic phenomena, but it is only a start. One should begin with the phenomenon to be explained and ask what models might help to explain it, rather than beginning with the models and asking how can observed phenomena be interpreted so as to fit the model. Having said all this, we now turn to the basic issues.

6.2. REPUTATION

To begin, what exactly is *reputation*? In everyday usage, "reputation" often refers to generally held beliefs about an individual's (or a group's) character or characteristics: "Adam has a reputation for being original; Smith has a reputation for being economical." Economists are not interested in innate characteristics *per se*, but in their implications for behavior, that is, for actions. Reputation can then be thought of in terms of the actions an agent is expected to take—for example, a policymaker may have a reputation for being tough on inflation. One may be tempted to think of reputation as synonymous with predictability, in the sense of always following the same policy. Though perhaps useful if a policymaker faces a static environment, such a simple notion loses attractiveness if the circumstances in which he finds himself change.

A better way to think about reputation is in terms of an inference problem in forming expectations of a policymaker's future actions. To be more exact, individuals form expectations about a policymaker's unobserved characteristics, that is, his preferences and constraints, with reputation referring to beliefs about characteristics. Individuals are ultimately concerned about the policymaker's behavior, which is a manifestation of his characteristics, so we speak of a reputation for behavior. Since we make inferences about future behavior based on what has been observed in the past, the focus is on how past observed actions lead one to expect future behavior of a given sort, that is, serve to build a reputation for future actions. As Fudenberg and Tirole (1991, p. 367) put it, "reputation" reflects

> the notion that a player who plays the same game repeatedly may try to develop a reputation for certain kinds of play. The idea is that if the player always plays in the same way, his opponents will come to expect him to play that way in the future and will adjust their own play accordingly.

The emphasis is on *repeated* interaction between the government and the public, or between two policymakers (to use two examples of the specific actors of interest to us) in forging a link between current policy and expected future policy. The fact that the agents will repeatedly interact is important in two senses: repetition means not only that the public can use the past to forecast the future, but also that the policymaker is concerned about maintaining his reputation, since he wants to influence the behavior of other forward-looking agents.

Though reputation is important in a number of areas in macroeconomics, we will illustrate many points in terms of the welfare cost of inflation in the model of the relation between unanticipated inflation and economic activity introduced in Section 4.4 of Chapter 4. Rogoff (1987) presents an excellent survey of reputation in these models. A key question in assessing models of reputation in the context of the time-inconsistency problem of Chapter 4 is whether reputation can enforce an optimal solution.

6.3. "REPUTATION" UNDER COMPLETE INFORMATION

We begin by showing how repeated interaction between policymaker and public may lead to an equilibrium with a lower rate of inflation than in the Barro and Gordon single-period setting, where the rate of inflation was suboptimally high. We assume there is complete information, in that the public knows the government's objective function. The basic argument comes from the original Barro and Gordon (1983a) paper, following work of Friedman (1971). Persson and Tabellini (1990) present a very clear discussion of these models, and the formal presentation in this and the next two sections draws on their exposition. As indicated in the presentation of the model in Chapter 4, an explicitly multiperiod set-up can be transformed into a "one-shot" game by assuming there is no connection between the government's current choice of inflation today and any relevant future variable. To study reputation, one must therefore drop this assumption with respect to expected inflation, assuming that today's choice of inflation influences tomorrow's expectations.

One should be careful about the use of the term "reputation" in these models. The models in this section address the question of whether repeated interactions enforce good behavior. This is not really a model of "reputation" in the sense discussed above, as the policymaker's preferences are fully known. Since preferences are known, observing actions provides no information about behavior that the public did not already know. More accurately, they are models of how punishment can enforce good behavior of a known "misfit." Nonetheless, the models in this section are useful in addressing repeated interaction as an enforcement mechanism, and thus provide a point of departure for discussing reputation in terms of forming beliefs about a policymaker's future actions. We return to conceptual issues of reputation after setting out the models themselves.

A Basic Model

The basic set-up is as in Chapter 4, where we use the simplified special case of the quadratic loss function. The government chooses a sequence of inflation rates π_s to minimize discounted expected loss:

$$\Lambda_t = \mathrm{E}_t \left[\sum_{s=0}^{T} \beta^s \mathscr{L}_{t+s} \right] = \sum_{s=0}^{T} \beta^s \mathrm{E}_t \left(U_{t+s} + \theta \frac{\pi_{t+s}^2}{2} \right), \qquad (6.1)$$

where the target for inflation π is zero and where T may be finite or infinite. The unemployment rate U_t in any period is below the natural rate of unemployment (taken to be zero) when the actual rate of inflation exceeds the expected rate of inflation π_t^e:

$$U_t = -(\pi_t - \pi_t^e). \qquad (6.2)$$

From (6.2), the single-period loss function $\mathscr{L}_t$ may be written

$$\mathscr{L}(\pi_t, \pi_t^e) = -(\pi_t - \pi_t^e) + \theta \frac{\pi_t^2}{2}. \qquad (6.3)$$

Were there no connections between periods, we would have a one-shot game where the policymaker chooses π_t to minimize the single-period loss function taking π_t^e as given. In this case, the policymaker chooses $\pi = 1/\theta$ for any value of π_t^e.

Now, suppose individuals base their inflation expectations π_t^e on observed past values of inflation π_{t-s}. As indicated, a key assumption is that the public has *complete* information about the policymaker's objectives, meaning here complete information about the relative cost θ he assigns to inflation. To model formation of expectations, we assume that the public expects zero inflation as long as government policy has fulfilled inflationary expectations for a specified period of time in the past. However, if actual inflation exceeded what was expected at any point during this interval, the public anticipates that the policymaker will succumb to his temptation to inflate for a given future period of time. To use the formal game-theoretic terminology, individuals form their expectations according to a **trigger strategy**, whereby observing "good" behavior induces the expectation of continued good behavior and a single observation of "bad" behavior triggers a revision of expectations.

Specifically, consider the following simple modeling of inflation expectations according to a one-period trigger strategy (more generally, the punishment could last several periods):

$$t = 0 \qquad \pi^e = 0,$$
$$t > 0 \qquad \pi_t^e = 0 \quad \text{if } \pi_{t-1} = \pi_{t-1}^e,$$
$$\pi_t^e = \frac{\kappa}{\theta} \quad \text{otherwise,} \tag{6.4}$$

where $\kappa \geq 1$. If T is finite, we have to specify expectations in the last period. We add[3]

$$t > T \qquad \pi_T^e = \frac{1}{\theta} \quad \text{if } \pi_{T-1} = 0,$$
$$\pi_T^e = \frac{\kappa}{\theta} \quad \text{otherwise,} \tag{6.5}$$

where $\kappa > 1$. Hence the public expects zero inflation (except in the last period of a finite-horizon game, where they expect the "one-shot" rate of inflation) as long as last-period's expectations were fulfilled, but "punishes" the government for one period by expecting positive inflation if the government "deviated" by inflating in the previous period.

Nash Equilibrium

Are these expectations rational when the government is choosing inflation optimally to minimize (6.1)? And, can the punishment induce an optimizing government to choose zero inflation? One must show that if the public has these expectations, the government has no incentive to deviate from zero inflation. We begin with the case of a finite horizon. One can show that the zero-inflation outcome in all periods but the last can be a **Nash equilibrium**. (In a Nash equilibrium, the equilibrium strategy of each actor is optimal, given the equilibrium behavior of the other actor.) As we shall see, however, this equilibrium depends on the government's expectation of a harsh punishment if there is a deviation from the zero-inflation equilib-

---

[3] It simplifies the exposition, while being fully consistent with the general form in (6.4), to formulate final-period expectations in this way, rather than as $\pi_T^e = 1/\theta$ if $\pi_{T-1} = \pi_{T-1}^e$.

rium, a punishment that would *not* be carried out if such a deviation actually occurred.

First, let us show the existence of a zero-inflation Nash equilibrium if the punishment for the government deviating from zero inflation is large enough, that is, if expected inflation κ/θ after a deviation is sufficiently large. (The reader may want to keep pencil and paper handy!) One works backwards from T. At T, the government clearly chooses $\pi_T = 1/\theta$, since with no residual horizon, the game is now a one-shot game. Hence, period-T expectations are rational only if $\pi_{T-1} = 0$. Will it be optimal for the government to choose $\pi_{T-1} = 0$, or instead to inflate myopically? (Remember, the optimal myopic rate of inflation for any level of expected inflation is $1/\theta$.) Let us consider the loss associated with different inflation choices, calculated from (6.3). Suppose $\pi_{T-1}^e = 0$. If the government fulfills these expectations, the current-period loss, namely, $\mathscr{L}(0,0)$, is zero, while if it inflates, the loss is $\mathscr{L}(1/\theta, 0) = -1/2\theta$. Therefore, the *gain* from deviating in period $T-1$ is $1/2\theta$. The *loss* from deviating comes from triggering of the punishment in T, namely, expected inflation π_T^e is κ/θ rather than $1/\theta$. Hence, a deviation today triggers a higher loss tomorrow, which, discounted back to today, is

$$\beta\left(\mathscr{L}\left(\frac{1}{\theta}, \frac{\kappa}{\theta}\right) - \mathscr{L}\left(\frac{1}{\theta}, \frac{1}{\theta}\right)\right) = \beta(\kappa - 1)\frac{1}{\theta}. \quad (6.6)$$

It will thus be optimal *not* to deviate (that is, set $\pi_{T-1} = 0$) if

$$\kappa \geq 1 + \frac{1}{2\beta}. \quad (6.7)$$

Working backwards, one can show that this condition ensures the optimality of the government choosing zero inflation in every period but the last, and choosing $\pi_T = 1/\theta$ with the public correctly expecting such an outcome. In short, the expectation of a harsh enough punishment for a deviation enforces the zero-inflation solution. This is the essence of "reputation" enforcing good behavior in a world where the incentive to inflate is fully known.

Sequential Rationality

The problem with this solution is that the public's behavior in forming expectations is not rational if the government in fact deviates. Suppose the government does inflate in period $T - 1$, contrary to what was expected. Since it is known that the government faces a one-period problem at T, it is rational to expect $\pi_T = 1/\theta$, no matter what was observed in period $T - 1$. Since period-T behavior is independent of what occurred at $T - 1$, we can treat it as a one-shot game with no incentive to preserve reputation. We can then move one period backwards and, by the same argument, show that $\pi_{T-1} = 1/\theta$ is optimal, independent of what was expected for $T-1$ or observed in period $T-2$. Hence, the zero-inflation equilibrium *"unravels" backwards*. The expectations in (6.4) and (6.5) which support it are rational only if equilibrium behavior is observed in the past, but not if a deviation was previously observed. That is, they are not **sequentially rational**, which requires that for each information set of each player, his strategy is a best response to the other player's strategies, given his beliefs at that information set. The only sequentially rational equilibrium is the one where the government chooses the one-shot solution $\pi = 1/\theta$ in every period.

This lack of sequential rationality characterizes many models with Nash equilibria, and the weakness it reveals about the concept of Nash equilibrium has an intuitive feel. Suppose I tell my child I will jump out the second-floor window if she does not fulfill her promise to eat all her dinner after having an ice cream, but will hug her if she does. If the threat is believed, she cleans her plate and I hug her. Only equilibrium behavior was observed, and my threat has enforced good behavior. If she does not fulfill her promise, I nonetheless will not jump out the window (which she probably knew). She will see my threat is hollow, calling into question whether such threats can really enforce good behavior. (The announced policy to enforce time-consistent behavior is itself time inconsistent.) Intuitively, "reputational" equilibria break down with a finite horizon since there is no reputation left to protect in the last period and everyone knows it.[4]

If the interaction between government and public extends over an infinite horizon, the expectations embodied in (6.4) can be sequentially rational and can enforce a low-inflation equilibrium.[5] In a multiperiod model, good behavior can be enforced for an arbitrarily long period of time if the horizon is sufficiently long and the discount rate is sufficiently low. This is an application of the **Folk Theorem**, whereby in an infinitely repeated game, any feasible, individually rational payoff can be an equilibrium outcome if players are sufficiently patient, that is, if they have a sufficiently low discount rate. The intuition is that when players are patient, any finite one-period gain from deviation is outweighed by even a small loss in utility in every future period. Hence, when β is close enough to 1, punishment can enforce the desirable behavior.

---

[4] Benoit and Krishna (1985) and Rogoff (1987) argue that if the one-shot game has more than one Nash equilibrium, reputational equilibria may exist which are sequentially rational. Suppose there is a low-inflation and a high-inflation equilibrium. Agents could sustain a sequentially rational low-inflation equilibrium in all periods but the last by reverting to the (sequentially rational) high-inflation equilibrium if they ever observe high inflation.

[5] More generally, a policymaker is more likely to be willing to incur costs to build up his reputation if his horizon is long rather than short.

To formalize these ideas, suppose, in response to (6.4), the government chooses inflation according to

$$
\begin{aligned}
t = 0 \quad & \pi = 0, \\
t > 0 \quad & \pi_t = 0 \quad \text{if } \pi_{t-1} = \pi_{t-1}^e, \\
& \pi_t = \frac{\kappa}{\theta} \quad \text{otherwise.}
\end{aligned}
\tag{6.8}
$$

In words, the government continues to choose zero inflation if it has done so in the past (and thus fulfilled zero-inflation expectations), but ratifies the expectation of high inflation in the current period, induced by unexpectedly high inflation in the previous period. One can show that this is a sequential equilibrium as long as it satisfies two conditions. First, along the equilibrium path (that is, when there is no deviation from zero inflation), the one-period gain from an unexpected deviation is less than the cost of the deviation (in terms of the punishment). Second, off the equilibrium path (that is, after a deviation), the government is willing to accept the punishment of suboptimally high inflation in the current period, rather than engineer a deflationary surprise and thus incur the punishment one more period. In this simple example of a one-period punishment, the first condition will be satisfied as long as $\kappa^2 > 1/\beta$, the second, as long as $\kappa^2 > (\kappa - 1)^2/\beta$.[6]

In essence, what makes this equilibrium work is that the government punishes itself by choosing a suboptimally high rate of inflation if it ever deviates from zero inflation. By punishing itself harshly if it deviates, the government makes it credible that it will not deviate.

Reputation?

As indicated in the introduction to this section, there is a basic conceptual question about this type of model: what does reputation mean under complete information? Put another way, is "reputation" an appropriate term to apply to a situation where the policymaker's incentive to renege on a zero-inflation announcement is fully known? If the public is fully aware of the government's incentive to inflate, why should they revise their expectations if they see an inflationary episode? (This, in essence, is why the finite-horizon, zero-inflation equilibrium breaks down.) If a policymaker's "type" is perfectly known, what reputation does he have to

---

[6] Along the equilibrium path, the gain from a deviation is $|\mathscr{L}(1/\theta, 0) - \mathscr{L}(0, 0)| = 1/2\theta$, the loss is $\beta|\mathscr{L}(\kappa/\theta, \kappa/\theta) - \mathscr{L}(0, 0)| = \beta\kappa^2/2\theta$, so that there will be no deviation if $\beta\kappa^2 > 1$. Off the equilibrium path, the gain from surprise deflation is $|\mathscr{L}(1/\theta, \kappa/\theta) - \mathscr{L}(\kappa/\theta, \kappa/\theta)| = (\kappa - 1)^2/2\theta$, and the loss from one more period of punishment is $\beta|\mathscr{L}(\kappa/\theta, \kappa/\theta) - \mathscr{L}(0, 0)| = \beta\kappa^2/2\theta$, so that the government would incur the punishment if $\beta\kappa^2 > (\kappa - 1)^2$.

protect? One answer to this is to focus on the central role of repeated interactions in these models. The Fudenberg–Tirole definition set out above emphasizes this, rather than uncertainty about the policymaker's preferences. In this sense, the models discussed in this section are models of how reputation can enforce good behavior of a known "misfit": what is crucial for the trigger strategy to enforce the zero-inflation equilibrium is that deviant behavior today can always be punished in the future by behavior that does not go against the punisher's best interests. Nonetheless, if one takes the mechanism of reputation to mean that there is information in current policy actions about future policy choices, so that a positive inflation surprise will lead the public to revise their inflation expectations upward, incomplete information about the policymaker should be central.[7] We now turn to such models.

6.4. REPUTATION UNDER INCOMPLETE INFORMATION—MIMICKING

Models with incomplete information[8] are attractive because uncertainty about policymakers, and hence about the actions they might take, seems central to the notion of reputation. As Fudenberg and Tirole (1991, p. 367) put it:

> To model the possibility that players are concerned about their reputations, we suppose that there is incomplete information about each player's type, with different types expected to play in different ways. Each player's reputation is then summarized by his opponent's current beliefs about his type.

In understanding the concern of politicians with building or maintaining reputation in the real world, uncertainty about some characteristic indeed seems crucial.[9] This is obvious in the case of a newly elected or appointed policymaker whose preferences or abilities are unknown and who must build a reputation through his actions, or for an incumbent who claims that his attitudes towards a given issue have changed but must use actions to make such a claim credible. To a large extent, it is also true for an incumbent who wants to maintain a reputation, since the incentives he faces may change, or, at least, are commonly perceived as always liable to change.

---

[7] Persson and Tabellini (1990) suggest that models of complete information better describe how a reputation is *maintained* than how it is *acquired*, with models of incomplete information more suited to the latter task.

[8] Games of incomplete information can be transformed into games of imperfect information (Harsanyi [1967–8]). We do not distinguish between these terms.

[9] One characteristic which might vary across policymakers is the extent to which they feel it is important to fulfill their promises. Hence, credibility could be a characteristic in itself to be signaled, rather than the result of successful reputation building. We consider such models in Section 6.7.

The basic work on modeling of reputation under incomplete information in the macroeconomics literature is based on the work of Kreps and Wilson (1982) on Selten's (1978) chain-store game. An incumbent firm faces potential entry into its market by a sequence of new firms, each of whom is aware of what has happened in the market in the past. If the new firm chooses not to enter, the incumbent enjoys monopoly rents; if the new firm decides to enter, the incumbent can either fight the entry at a cost, or not fight and forego its monopoly position. The incumbent firm is best off if potential entrants, aware of whether entry has been fought in the past, choose not to enter, since it then keeps its monopoly position without incurring any costs. It thus has the incentive to have a "reputation for toughness," that is, for fighting entry. More exactly, reputation as a way of deterring entry is introduced by assuming that the incumbent's payoffs to fighting or not fighting entry are not observed, with there being some prior probability that the incumbent is a type who fights entry at any cost. If the incumbent is observed as choosing to fight the current entrant, this builds his reputation for toughness in that potential entrants raise the posterior probability that he is the very tough type.

The Backus–Driffill Model

The basic outline of the Kreps–Wilson model was adopted by Backus and Driffill (1985a, 1985b) to the question of building a reputation for toughness against inflation in the context of the Barro–Gordon model. A policymaker who would otherwise choose positive inflation in a single-period setting would choose a lower rate of inflation (zero in their model) in a multiperiod setting for a period of time in order to build a reputation for toughness. This model, or variants of it, has served as the basic framework for modeling of reputation in much subsequent work in macroeconomics. As in the Kreps–Wilson model, what drives their model is not simply the uncertainty about the cost θ the government assigns to inflation in their loss function; it is crucial that a policymaker may assign an *infinite* cost to inflation.

At the beginning of time, the relative cost a government assigns to inflation is unknown to the public. In the simplest version of the Backus and Driffill model, there are two possible types of policymakers, each with a loss function as in (6.1); one, a "tough" policymaker who cares only about inflation, with $\theta^T = \infty$, and the other, a "weak" policymaker who assigns a cost to unemployment as well, that is, with $\theta^W < \infty$. The tough type will therefore always choose a zero rate of inflation, independent of what the weak type does. Therefore, if the weak type ever succumbs to the temptation to inflate, he reveals himself as weak. The public expects him to inflate at rate $\pi^W = 1/\theta^W$ forever after, and it becomes optimal for him to do so. It is this characteristic of the connection between observed policy and public beliefs that is central to the model. Only by choosing zero inflation and not revealing his true nature can a weak type preserve the possibility in the public's mind that he is really tough, implying lower expected inflation in the future. The model is thus one of **mimicking**, with a weak policymaker mimicking a tough policymaker in order to engender expectations of low inflation.

In terms of policy choice, there is no question about the behavior of the tough type, given the extreme assumption about his preferences. (Later on, we will assume he also cares about unemployment and ask whether he can take actions which signal his type, so that he can actively separate himself from weaker types.) There is a question only about a weak policymaker, namely, should he play according to his short-run incentives and reveal himself, or forego short-run gains to invest in reputation by mimicking a tough policymaker? In technical terms, should he take an action that reveals his type, hence **separating** himself from a tough type in equilibrium, or should he take an action that does not reveal his type, so that he is **pooled** with highly anti-inflationary governments in equilibrium?

In considering a mimicking equilibrium, two basic, related questions can be asked. First, how can the desire for a tough reputation enable a "weak" policymaker to make an announcement of low inflation credible? Second, how will reputation develop when the public is uncertain about the policymaker's true preferences and observes zero inflation? Following Persson and Tabellini (1990), these points will be illustrated by a simple two-period example, where the extension to many periods is relatively straightforward. In contrast to the models with complete information, temporary zero inflation can be an equilibrium even when the horizon is finite.

The evolution of reputation over time can be represented by the evolution of the probability the public assigns in each period to the government being tough, denoted p_t. At the beginning of period 1, the public does not know the type of government in office, but has a prior p_1 that the government is tough. The prior is updated by Bayes' rule, with the posterior p_2 being used to form expectations of second-period inflation. Bayesian updating makes concrete the notion of how observed actions affect the reputation for toughness. As in the earlier models, the concept of equilibrium should include a notion of rational beliefs by agents about the strategies of other agents, including rational updating of beliefs. The concept used in this literature is that of **Perfect Bayesian equilibrium**, by which an equilibrium must satisfy the following three intuitive conditions: (i) in each period, the public's strategy is optimal, given their beliefs in that period and the government's equilibrium policies; (ii) in each period, the government's policy is optimal, given its type and the equilibrium strategies of the public; (iii) the public's posterior beliefs at each point are formed using the prior and the currently observed government policy using Bayes' rule, when applicable.[10]

According to **Bayes' rule**, the posterior probability that a government is tough conditional on having observed a rate of inflation π in period t is the prior probability that a government is tough multiplied by the probability that a tough government would choose π, divided by the unconditional probability of observing π. With two types of governments, we have

$$\Pr(\theta = \infty \mid \pi_t = \pi)$$

$$= \frac{\Pr(\pi_t = \pi \mid \theta = \infty) \cdot \Pr(\theta = \infty)}{\Pr(\pi_t = \pi \mid \theta = \infty) \cdot \Pr(\theta = \infty) + \Pr(\pi_t = \pi \mid \theta = \theta^W) \cdot \Pr(\theta = \theta^W)},$$

$$(6.9)$$

where the left-hand side is the posterior p_2 conditional on observed policy. The probability that a tough government will choose anything other than zero inflation (specifically, $\pi = 1/\theta^W$) is zero, while the probability that a weak government will choose zero inflation in period 1 will be denoted q_1. (Strictly speaking, this is the public's *perceived* probability that a weak government will choose zero inflation, which is set equal to the actual probability the weak government will choose zero inflation in equilibrium. For economy of exposition, q_1 is taken to be the true probability, which will be calculated below.) Applying (6.9), for the case where $\pi_1 = \pi^W$ $(= 1/\theta^W)$ is observed, one has

$$p_2(\pi_1 = \pi^W) = \frac{p_1 \cdot 0}{(1 - p_1)(1 - q_1)} = 0, \qquad (6.10)$$

while when $\pi_1 = 0$ is observed, one has

$$p_2(\pi_1 = 0) = \frac{p_1 \cdot 1}{p_1 + (1 - p_1)q_1} \geq p_1, \qquad (6.11)$$

---

[10] Perfect Bayesian equilibrium is similar, but not identical, to sequential equilibrium (though the equilibrium concepts are the same for some games). Like sequential equilibrium, perfect Bayesian equilibrium requires that the public's behavior must be optimal for any set of beliefs which it may hold. However, Bayes' Rule specifies how to update beliefs only in equilibrium, with a zero prior probability assigned to events out of equilibrium. If an out-of-equilibrium event would occur, we could assign an arbitrary probability to the posterior belief. Sequential equilibrium puts stronger restrictions on how posterior beliefs are formed after observing out-of-equilibrium events, so that there are situations which satisfy the requirements of perfect Bayesian equilibrium, but not sequential equilibrium. See Osborne and Rubinstein (1994), chapter 12, or Fudenberg and Tirole (1991), chapter 8, especially the example in 8.3.4.

with strict equality when q_1 is less than 1. In words, when $\pi_1 = \pi^W$ is observed, the government is revealed to be weak. When $\pi_1 = 0$ is chosen, the observation does not reveal the government's type, and the evolution of reputation depends on the value of q_1. When there is a probability that a weak government would have inflated ($q_1 < 1$), observing zero inflation raises the posterior probability that the government is of the tough type, that is, it raises reputation. When the weak type is known to choose zero inflation for sure ($q_1 = 1$), observing zero inflation conveys *no* information and p_t does not change. The expected rate of inflation in any period is

$$\pi_t^e = (1 - p_t)(1 - q_t)\pi^W, \qquad (6.12)$$

since a tough government is known never to inflate.

Equations (6.10) and (6.11) provide part of the answer to the second question above about how reputation evolves as a function of the prior probabilities and the observed action (that is, p_2 as a function of π_1). In a multiperiod model, three cases are present: observing high inflation destroys reputation; observing low inflation builds reputation if it is known a weak government might inflate; observing low inflation leaves reputation unchanged if both types are certain to choose low inflation. One still needs to know what the sequence of these actions might look like in an equilibrium. We will return to this below, after considering the weak government's choice problem in more detail.

When can the desire to be seen as tough lead a weak government to choose zero inflation in the first period and thus lower expected inflation in the second period? Let us consider the loss to the weak government from different choices of π_1. Basically, a government is weighing the gain from surprise inflation today (which by revealing type implies there can be no surprise tomorrow) against the gain from surprise inflation tomorrow (which requires true type not be revealed today). In the first period, the gain from choosing $\pi_1 = \pi^W$ rather than $\pi_1 = 0$ is the reduction in the single-period loss, which is simply

$$|\mathscr{L}(\pi^W, \pi_1^e) - \mathscr{L}(0, \pi_1^e)| = \frac{\pi^W}{2}. \qquad (6.13)$$

The loss of choosing high rather than zero inflation today is that the policymaker is revealed as weak, implying higher loss tomorrow. Specifically, since each type of government is known to choose its myopic optimum in the second period, expected inflation is $\pi_2^e = (1 - p_2)\pi^W$, so that the second-period loss (when the weak government chooses $\pi_2 = \pi^W$ with certainty and reveals itself) is

$$\mathcal{L}(\pi_2, \pi_2^e) = -(\pi^W - (1 - p_2)\pi^W) + \theta^W \frac{(\pi^W)^2}{2}$$

$$= \pi^W \left(\frac{1}{2} - p_2 \right) \tag{6.14}$$

$$= \lambda(p_2).$$

A better reputation (a higher p_2) clearly lowers the second-period loss $\lambda(p_2)$, reflecting the fact that it implies lower expected inflation and hence lower unemployment. The cost of choosing $\pi_1 = \pi^W$ rather than $\pi_1 = 0$ is the increase in second-period loss following a choice of $\pi_1 = \pi^W$, which may then be written

$$| \beta(\lambda(0) - \lambda(p_2))| = \beta p_2 \pi^W. \tag{6.15}$$

The weak policymaker will therefore decide whether or not to inflate depending on the value of (6.15) relative to (6.13): $\pi_1 = 0$ will be optimal if

$$p_2 \geq \frac{1}{2\beta}. \tag{6.16}$$

There are three possibilities, depending on parameter values for β and p_1: (i) if $\beta \geq 1/2p_1$, then a weak policymaker will choose $\pi_1 = 0$ with certainty ($q_1 = 1$), implying $p_2 = p_1$, so that (6.16) is satisfied—we thus have a pooling equilibrium; (ii) if $\beta < 1/2$, no value of $p_2 \leq 1$ can satisfy (6.16), so that no value of p_1 makes it worthwhile to maintain or build a reputation—$\pi_1 = \pi^W$, and we have a separating equilibrium; (iii) if $1/2 \leq \beta < 1/2p_1$, then the weak government plays a mixed strategy, choosing $\pi_1 = 0$ with probability q_1 and $\pi_1 = \pi^W$ with probability $1 - q_1$, where q_1 is chosen so that (6.16) is just satisfied[11]—the policymaker randomizes between $\pi_1 = 0$ and $\pi_1 = \pi^W$, since each gives equal utility. In this last case, reputation is rising over time: $p_2 > p_1$. Hence, even with a finite horizon, for any prior reputation $p_1 > 0$, sufficiently high concern about the future (a high enough discount factor β) will sustain a low-inflation equilibrium.

---

[11] Using (6.11) and (6.16) with equality, one derives $q_1 = (2\beta - 1)p_1/(1 - p_1)$.

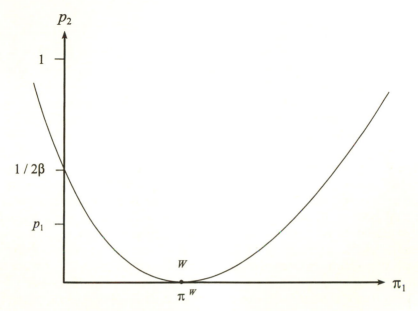

FIGURE 6.1. The indifference curve of the weak type.

The results can be demonstrated in a useful diagram. Using (6.14), the two-period loss function can be written

$$\Lambda = \mathcal{L}(\pi_1, \pi_1^e) + \beta\mathcal{L}(\pi_2, \pi_2^e)$$

$$= -(\pi_1 - \pi_1^e) + \theta^W\frac{\pi_1^2}{2} + \beta\pi^W\left(\frac{1}{2} - p_2\right), \qquad (6.17)$$

allowing us to write Λ as a function of the two endogenous variables π_1 and p_2, given π_1^e. We can then draw an indifference curve as in Figure 6.1, giving combinations of π_1 and p_2 which would yield the same loss as the strategy of inflating in period 1, thereby revealing oneself as weak (so that $p_2 = 0$).[12] This is point W in the diagram. Combinations of π_1 and p_2 which lie above the indifference curve give higher utility, combinations which lie below give lower utility. The indifference curve will intersect the vertical axis at $p_2 = 1/2\beta$. Which of the three cases set out above we obtain depends on the location of this intersection point relative to 1 and p_1. If the intersection point lies below p_1, we have case (i) above, implying a pooling equilibrium; if it lies above 1, we have case (ii), a separating equilibrium; and if it lies between 1 and p_1, we have the weak government playing a mixed strategy.

[12] This figure follows Persson and Tabellini (1990), following Vickers (1986).

Interpreting the Results

A criticism of the results of the model is that the type of equilibrium is dependent on prior beliefs, as summarized by p_1. For a high enough discount factor ($\beta > 1/2$), a high enough prior implies that a weak policymaker plays tough for sure in the first period, so that there is a pooling equilibrium, while a low prior reputation implies that he randomizes, so that he may choose to separate. In my opinion, this is less a problem than a description of reality—with a high enough prior reputation, it makes sense that a policymaker is more likely to play tough to protect that reputation. However, to the extent that the equilibrium is sensitive to prior beliefs, it means that it is determined by something which is exogenous to the model. Economists rightly criticize models that assume what they want to demonstrate; when equilibrium is driven by exogenous factors, such a criticism has a good deal of force. The problem of the sensitivity of equilibria to priors is not unique to this model. It is generic to game theory models, and it arises in other models we consider below.

How does one interpret a government randomizing between two alternatives giving it equal utility, that is, inflating only with some probability? Surely one does not think of monetary policy being made by central bank presidents who flip coins. One interpretation of playing a mixed strategy that is common in the literature is that it really represents there being a continuum of weak types, with the public being unsure of how weak the weak government really is. That is, in each period some weak governments that had not previously inflated would inflate, so that in each period the public assigns a probability to observing positive inflation. We will pursue this interpretation in Section 6.7 below.

Canzoneri (1985) considers a different type of asymmetric information between the central bank and the private sector: the central bank has superior information about shocks hitting the economy, which cannot be observed (or inferred) by individuals. The structure is such that it cannot be fully verified whether or not the central bank reneged on following the announced policy, in that it can argue that high inflation reflected optimal response to an (unobserved) negative shock, rather than suboptimally high inflation. (Canzoneri's framework is much richer than the version presented here, including money demand shocks.) An equilibrium enforcing good behavior on the part of the central bank then has an interesting property not observed in our earlier models. Even if the central bank is following its announced policy, there will be periodic bouts of inflation associated with large negative shocks. This result follows the work of Green and Porter (1984) showing, for example, "price wars" may be necessary to ensure oligopolists do not cheat on collusive agreements. Since the central bank's compliance with its announcements cannot be fully monitored, it will be "punished" following a period of high money growth, *even though such behavior is optimal*, to deter it from reneging on optimal inflation behavior by falsely claiming that an adverse shock occurred. Canzoneri points out that the Barro–Gordon or Rogoff models predict too much stability, in that in their equilibrium we should not see periods of inflation, while his private information model implies periodic inflationary reversions.[13]

The results in the two-period mimicking model could easily be extended to a multiperiod case, as in Backus and Driffill. The nature of the equilibrium would be as follows. In the early periods, the weak policymaker would choose zero inflation for sure, and reputation would not evolve. In the intermediate periods, the weak policymaker would be known to randomize between zero and positive inflation. If zero inflation were observed, reputation would increase over time (that is, $p_t > p_{t-1}$); if positive inflation were observed, the policymaker would be revealed as weak and his reputation would be destroyed. In these intermediate periods when there is zero inflation, the equilibrium probability q_t that the weak policymaker chooses zero inflation will be falling over time and the expected rate of inflation will be rising. Finally, in some period before the end of the horizon, the weak policymaker will inflate for sure if he has not already done so.[14]

In a multiperiod model, the desire to maintain reputation via mimicking can maintain a zero-inflation equilibrium for an arbitrarily long period of time if the horizon is sufficiently long and the discount rate is sufficiently low. This is another application of the Folk Theorem discussed in the previous section, whereby in an infinitely repeated game, any feasible, individually rational payoff can be an equilibrium outcome if players have a sufficiently low discount rate.

6.5. DOES REPUTATION "SOLVE" THE TIME-CONSISTENCY PROBLEM?—THREE CAVEATS

How Bad Is It to Lose Your Reputation?

The result summarized by the Folk Theorem was seen under both complete and incomplete information, namely, once we move to an infinite

---

[13] Zarazaga (1993) suggests an application of the Green–Porter framework to explain why some countries suffer from repeated periods of high, but not hyperinflation. Because government monetary actions cannot be fully monitored, bouts of high inflation ensure that the government does not take actions leading to hyperinflation.

[14] We observe what has been named "the peso problem," because of a decades-long forward premium on the Mexican peso, indicating expectations of a devaluation even though the exchange rate remained fixed. During the time that a weak policymaker would be known to be randomizing, there is positive expected inflation (as in (6.12)), even though only zero inflation has been observed.

horizon, the concern for maintaining a reputation can enforce a solution superior to the time-consistent solution. This is a primary result of models of reputation, and one which is intuitively quite attractive. Unfortunately, it is so intuitively attractive that it is sometimes misapplied, being used to justify arguments where on closer examination it does not hold. One should therefore be careful in arguing that concern for reputation will generally enforce good behavior.

Bulow and Rogoff (1989a) present an excellent illustration concerning the incentives to repay debt. Their model is discussed in detail in Section 12.8 of Chapter 12; here we simply give the flavor of their results. They ask whether the desire to maintain access to international credit markets in the future will induce countries to repay their debt and hence maintain a reputation for repayment. It has long been argued that the threat to a country of not being able to borrow in world credit markets will induce repayment of sovereign debt, even in the absence of other penalties. Bulow and Rogoff show that in a world where countries face income shocks, and borrow in order to smooth the effect of these shocks, this will not be the case. In the absence of sanctions other than loss of reputation in the face of default, the country will default in good times.[15]

Consider a country with a stochastic income stream in which the government borrows abroad to smooth consumption of its citizens. This objective is fully known; that is, there is no uncertainty about a government's "type." Suppose that foreign lenders have no legal recourse in the case of default on loans; they cannot interfere with the country's trade or seize its assets. Only the desire to continue borrowing in the future leads a country to repay its foreign debt, in a "reputation-for-repayment" contract. (With full information about the government's objective function, its incentive to renege on the debt in each state of nature is known.) The only punishment for default is that the country will *not* be allowed to write reputation contracts. However, a country can still borrow abroad to smooth its consumption by writing an *insurance* contract. It makes a cash payout up front in exchange for receiving a (nonnegative), state-contingent payback next period, where the up-front payout is equal to the expected value of the payback it will receive next period. (This payoff structure could arise, for example, if the borrowing country bought foreign assets whose payoffs were state contingent and negatively correlated with home income.)

A simple numerical example will illustrate the idea. In a multiperiod model of stochastic income flows, a country's income is $Y_H = 80$ with probability $1/2$ and $Y_L = 60$ with probability $1/2$, so that expected income is $\bar{Y} = 70$. Suppose that the world interest rate is $r = 1/9$. Rather than consuming its endowment, the country writes a "reputation-for-repayment" contract, according to which it makes payments $\wp_H = 9$ in good times and $\wp_L = -9$ in bad times. It can then achieve aggregate consumption $C_H = Y_H - \wp_H = [1/(1 + r)](\bar{Y} + rY_H) = 71$ in good times and $C_L = Y_L - \wp_L$

---

[15] Chari and Kehoe (1989) present a similar result.

$= [1/(1 + r)](\bar{Y} + rY_L) = 69$ in bad times, where the second equality in each expression comes from realizing that this payment implies consumption of permanent income conditioned on the realization of current Y_t. Its ability to achieve this smoother consumption stream depends on its ability to borrow and repay on these terms.

When a good state occurs, however, the country can do better. It reneges on its reputation-for-repayment contract and, instead, writes an insurance contract of the following sort. It agrees to pay the amount $\wp = 9$ every period in exchange for a state-contingent *gross* payback of $\omega_H = 0$ in good times and $\omega_L = 20$ in bad times (so that $E(\omega) = (1 + r)\wp$). The net payment in bad times, $\wp - \omega_L = 11$, is such that in both good and bad times, the consumption level is 71. Since the country is clearly better off forever by reneging on its reputation-for-repayment contract when a good state occurs, it will certainly do so at the first possible opportunity. But, with lenders aware of this incentive, they will not offer a "reputation-for-repayment" contract to begin with. Therefore, the threat of being prevented from further borrowing (of losing one's reputation) will not in itself enforce "reputation-for-repayment" contracts. (There are ways that repayment of sovereign debt can be enforced, as we shall see when we return to this issue in Chapter 12.)

In contrast to the reputational models discussed in previous sections, the failure of reputation as a mechanism to enforce good behavior does *not* stem from the horizon being finite. Even with an infinite horizon, the desire to maintain access to the consumption-smoothing possibilities of international borrowing and lending is not sufficient to induce a borrower to honor the contract in every state of nature. The reason is that in a good state of nature, a borrower can repudiate the existing contract and write a new contract in which it uses the windfall to pay up-front, that is, to increase its utility by becoming an international lender. The problem with the reputation-for-repayment contract is that it is not *incentive-compatible* in every state of nature.

Atomistic Agents

In chapter 4, we pointed out the importance of the distinction between a single agent and a representative agent in interpreting game-theoretic models of the interaction between the government and the private sector. If government and the private sector are maximizing the same objective function, no time-inconsistency problem exists when the private sector is acting as a single agent. In both the capital-taxation example and the inflation-bias example, the existence of a time-consistency problem reflected the fact that individuals were atomistic, knowing the government's incentive to tax accumulated capital in the first model (or to engineer surprise inflation in the second), but unable to act strategically as a single agent. We showed the importance of this distinction formally in Section

4.3, indicating how a time-consistency problem may be understood as a conflict of interests within the private sector in a representative agent model, a conflict that is absent if the private sector acts as a single agent.

Though the time-consistency problem depends on the private sector being composed of agents who view themselves as unable to affect the government's decisions by their individual choices alone, the game-theoretic techniques and results are often those that apply to games between large agents. A similar criticism can be made of many of the reputational models in this chapter. Techniques are taken from the industrial organization literature, where they were applied to games between oligopolists. One is then led to question whether some of the results from the game theory literature which are often applied (for example, the Folk Theorem) are really applicable.

Chari and Kehoe (1990) address this issue head on. They consider the existence of a trigger-type equilibrium in a general equilibrium model in which private agents are atomistic, and the government is maximizing the welfare of these agents, who are behaving competitively. Towards this end, they develop an equilibrium concept, *sustainable equilibrium*, in which the decision problems of both the government and private agents are sequential. They then ask what sort of results can be obtained, specifically when the government has no commitment technology available to it. In an environment with atomistic, competitive agents, can reputation support a preferred allocation? They show that for an appropriately defined equilibrium concept, trigger-type equilibria do indeed exist, and, in analogy to the Folk Theorem, a preferred allocation can be supported for a sufficiently low discount rate.

What is the relation between the sustainable equilibria in their competitive model and the equilibria of more standard games? To answer this question, Chari and Kehoe consider what is called an *anonymous* game in which there is a continuum of agents, each of whom observes only the government's policies, his own decisions, and the *average* (that is, per capita) outcomes of private agents as a whole. The government observes this per capita outcome and its own decisions. They show that the sustainable outcomes of their competitive model are the same as the set of symmetric perfect Bayesian equilibrium outcomes of the anonymous game.[16]

---

[16] There are no budget constraints in standard games corresponding to the budget constraints of economic models. To capture this feature of a competitive economy in the anonymous game, they define payoffs in the game which are the sum of individual utilities and a function which is zero if the agent's budget constraint is met and is a large negative number if the budget constraint is violated. By making this number large enough in absolute value, they guarantee that all agents satisfy their budget constraints in the anonymous game.

Multiplicity of Equilibria

A third caveat to the conclusion that reputation can "solve" the time-consistency problem concerns the fact that there may be multiple equilibria, so that we cannot talk of reputation enforcing *an* equilibrium. For example, in the complete-information model of the inflation–unemployment trade-off, there were a multiplicity of equilibria in which reputation enforces the zero-inflation equilibrium. Specifically, there is a continuum of values of κ and the length of the punishment period consistent with the zero-inflation equilibrium being sequentially rational. For example, the longer the punishment interval is, the lower is the critical value of κ, with $\kappa = 1$ supporting the zero-inflation equilibrium for a long enough punishment interval. Since these are really choice variables of the government (how strongly it punishes itself) rather than exogenous parameters, there is no reason to argue that the structure of the problem will lead to a unique equilibrium. This problem of multiplicity of equilibria, that is, of there being "too many" equilibria, is common in game theory models, and raises some obvious problems. If there are many possible equilibria, all agents must coordinate on one of the equilibria if a single equilibrium is to be reached.[17] Moreover, with many equilibria, the theory would apparently have no predictive power. We explicitly consider the multiplicity problem, as well as approaches to narrowing down the number of possible equilibria, at the end of the next section, in the context of signaling models.

6.6. SIGNALING

A basic criticism of the mimicking model is that only a weak policymaker acts strategically, deciding under what circumstances to choose zero inflation and hence mimic the tough policymaker. One would think that a tough policymaker would want to signal that he is tough, but the specification of the tough policymaker in the model of Section 6.4 rules out this possibility. Since he places an infinite cost on inflation, and can do no better than choosing zero inflation no matter what the weak policymaker does, there is no scope for signaling. Hence, the assumption that he cares only about inflation is not an innocuous simplification, for it rules out qualitatively different types of equilibria. Moreover, it is not a very realistic assumption—even the "toughest" policymakers would inflate under some

---

[17] Rogoff (1987) presents an excellent discussion of the problem of coordinating on an equilibrium.

circumstances.[18] Once we allow the tough policymaker to assign only a
finite cost to inflation, a number of very different results are possible.

Suppose the tough policymaker assigns a cost to unemployment, represented by a finite weight on inflation in the loss function, namely, $\infty > \theta^T$
$> \theta^W$. His one-shot optimal rate of inflation is no longer 0 but $\pi^T = 1/\theta^T$
> 0. This change in specification of what it means to be tough qualitatively
changes the nature of the solution, for it opens up the possibility that a
tough policymaker may take actions to reveal his type, thus separating
himself from the weak policymaker. That is, it allows him the possibility of
signaling his toughness. Though a weak policymaker still has the incentive
to mimic a tough policymaker under certain circumstances, a tough policymaker can now also act strategically, following a policy tougher than he
otherwise would have in order to make it too costly for the weak type to
mimic him. Specifically, we will show that under parameter values such
that a weak policymaker will mimic a tough policymaker who chooses
$\pi_1 = \pi^T = 1/\theta^T$, the tough type can separate himself by choosing a
higher rate of inflation, sufficiently high that the weak type chooses
$\pi_1 = \pi^W = 1/\theta^W$ and reveals himself.

The Vickers Model

The case we consider was studied by Vickers (1986), following Milgrom
and Roberts' (1982) analysis of limit pricing by oligopolists. As in the case
of mimicking, we derive each type's choice of optimal first-period inflation
(in the second period, each type chooses $\pi^i = 1/\theta^i$) in terms of trading
off the gain from an inflationary surprise today against the gain from a
reputation for toughness carried into the future. Expected inflation in the
second period is

$$\pi_2^e = p_2\pi^T + (1 - p_2)\pi^W, \tag{6.18}$$

implying that the loss for each type in the second period is a decreasing
function of p_2. The two-period loss function for a given type may then be
thought of as a function of π_1 and p_2, analogous to (6.17) in the
mimicking model.

To model the evolution of reputation, suppose the tough type is believed
never to set inflation π above some known level $\hat{\pi}$, to be determined. (As
we shall see, the type of equilibria that are possible will be very much
influenced by the value of $\hat{\pi}$ that is, by beliefs about the tough type.) One

[18] An alternative interpretation of this model is that the tough policymaker places an
infinite cost not on the loss from inflation, but on the cost of reneging on a previous
announcement of zero inflation (so that he acts as if he has infinite θ), while the weak
policymaker places a negligible cost on reneging on his previous announcements. This
interpretation is subject to exactly the same criticism of being unrealistic, since even "tough"
policymakers find it optimal to renege on their announcements under certain circumstances.

can then use Bayes' rule, so that if a first-period inflation rate $\pi_1 > \hat{\pi}$ is observed, second-period reputation is $p_2 = 0$, as in (6.10), while if $\pi_1 \leq \hat{\pi}$ is observed, p_2 is calculated as in (6.11).

One can draw an "indifference" curve (analogous to Figure 6.1) for each type i, showing combinations of π_1 and p_2 which yield the same loss as the pair $\pi_1 = \pi^i$ and $p_2 = 0$. The two indifference curves are represented in Figure 6.2, where the tough type's indifference curve lies to the left of the weak type's indifference curve. The weak type's indifference curve will intersect the vertical axis at the point $p_2 = \pi^W/2\beta(\pi^W - \pi^T)$. We assume this point of intersection lies above unity (as drawn in Figure 6.2), so that if π^T were zero, the weak type would choose to inflate in the first period and reveal himself. That is, we assume parameter values that imply that a weak type would not pool with an infinitely tough type, but might pool with a type $\theta^T < \infty$, so that the tough type has an interest in signaling his type.

With $\pi^T > 0$, there exists a pooling equilibrium, where both types choose $\pi_1 = \pi^T$ (with certainty) and then play their own type in the second period. The observation of low inflation in the first period gives no information about types, so that $p_2 = p_1$ and $\pi_2^e = p_1\pi^T + (1 - p_1)\pi^W$. This equilibrium is represented by point P in the Figure 6.2, representing the case in which the tough type is believed to choose inflation no higher than π^T. The heavy solid lines represent the evolution of reputation as a function of observed inflation via Bayes' rule. To see that this is indeed an

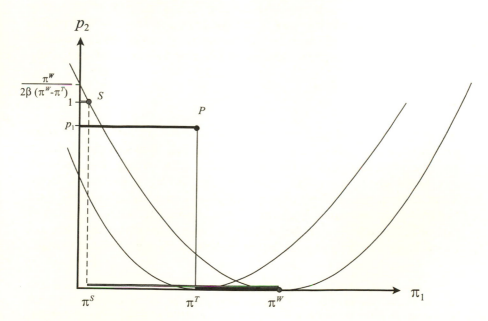

FIGURE 6.2. The Vickers model.

equilibrium, consider first the weak type. First-period inflation above π^T is fully revealing ($p_2 = 0$), implying that an optimal deviation would be at point W, which yields lower utility than point P. What about the tough type? Given the specification of beliefs about the tough type and hence the evolution of reputation, his choosing π_1 below π^T, which is $\hat{\pi}$ in this example, cannot increase his reputation above p_1, but will lower his first-period utility. Choosing higher inflation will clearly destroy his reputation, so P is his preferred point.

The pooling equilibrium is not, however, the only equilibrium consistent with these parameters. A separating equilibrium, in which a tough policy-maker signals his true type, is represented by point S in the figure, in which the tough type is believed to choose and in fact chooses $\pi_1 = \pi^S < \pi^T$ (or an even lower first-period rate of inflation), while a weak type chooses his myopic optimum, π^W. Since the equilibrium is fully revealing, the probability that the policymaker is tough is 1, conditional on observing $\pi_1 = \pi^S$. Expected first-period inflation is $\pi_1^e = p_1\pi^S + (1 - p_1)\pi^W$. To see that this is an equilibrium, note the tough type cannot improve his reputation by choosing a $\pi_1 < \pi^S$, but the greater deflationary surprise will lower welfare; choosing a higher rate of inflation will, via our specification of Bayes' rule, destroy his reputation. A weak policymaker gains nothing by mimicking a tough policymaker (and is strictly worse off if the tough policymaker chooses $\pi_1 < \pi^S$).

To summarize, one can show technically that for the same parameters that yield a pooling equilibrium in which the weak type mimics the tough type, the tough type can signal his toughness and separate himself from weaker policymakers in the eyes of the public by choosing an even tougher policy.[19] (In the case where $\pi^T = 0$, this was ruled out by the fact that the tough policymaker assigned a loss to deflation as well as inflation.)

An Assessment

Intuitively, this modeling of reputation is more attractive than those presented in Sections 6.3 and 6.4. In a signaling model, a tough policy-maker can act strategically, choosing a lower inflation rate than he would in a world where his type is known, in order to signal that he is tough. Thus, the model captures two possible determinants of central bank behavior when the public is unsure of its commitment to fighting inflation: not only the desire of policymakers to appear tougher than they are (mimicking), but also the desire of policymakers who truly are highly

---

[19] Vickers (1986) and Persson and Tabellini (1990) show how equilibrium refinements may allow us to eliminate all of the equilibria except the one with the highest rate of inflation. This approach raises the problem of the economic meaning of refinements, as discussed below.

anti-inflationary to take actions which make this clear to the public.[20] To the extent we think of building reputation in terms of taking actions to convince others of one's true characteristics that are not directly observable, the Vickers model of signaling strikes me as more attractive than the Backus–Driffill model of mimicking. The learning that is key to changes in reputation seems far more realistic in a model of incomplete information than in the model of complete information. One way for a government to reveal just how anti-inflationary it is, is to demonstrate toughness in circumstances in which a weaker policymaker would take other actions. Hence, taking actions to separate oneself seems more consistent with the notion of building reputation.

These models also raise the economic question of the relation between reputation and credibility. First, it is not clear that the credibility of a policy should depend on the policymaker's characteristics and reputation alone. We discuss this issue in detail in Section 6.8 below. Second, even when we restrict ourselves to models in which credibility and reputation are synonymous, these models have the troubling characteristic that reputation, once lost, can never be regained. Persson and Tabellini (1990) argue that this would be eliminated if the private sector could not perfectly monitor the government's action, so that actions are not a perfect indicator of type. (The Canzoneri [1985] model discussed above considers such imperfect monitoring and its implications explicitly.) Imperfect monitoring would certainly complicate the inference problem on which signaling models are based, but it is too simple to say it would eliminate the irreversibility of lost reputation. Even with imperfect monitoring, it may be possible to discern the policymaker's true type; if so, reputation is lost forever.[21] Blinder (1998) makes a similar criticism is assessing the realism of these models.

These models of reputation, whether with complete or incomplete information, have some other drawbacks as well. Some of these drawbacks are not unique to these models, but are problems seen more generally in game-theoretic models. First, equilibria are often sensitive to prior beliefs. We saw this in both the Backus and Driffill model and the Vickers model, where the possibility of pooling and separating equilibria depends on the

---

[20] A tough policymaker taking actions to distinguish himself from weaker types is sometimes referred to as *visibility*. Policymakers with stronger commitment to reform will opt for more visible policies, since greater visibility makes it easier for the public to uncover the true identity of the policymaker, and only those types who are truly committed to reform want this to happen quickly. Canavan and Tommasi (1996) argue, for example, that fixing the nominal exchange rate in an anti-inflation program reflects not the discipline it is supposed to provide, but its visibility, allowing more committed stabilizers to signal their type and gain greater credibility.

[21] Regaining a lost reputation could be possible if a policymaker's type can change. Cukierman and Meltzer (1990) consider a model of this sort, which we will consider in Section 6.9 below. Bartolini and Drazen (1997b), in a stochastic version of the model of the next section, explore this possibility as well.

prior p_1. Second, even for specified prior beliefs, there is often a multiplicity of equilibria, a problem discussed above. For example, in the Vickers model, the same parameter values are consistent with a pooling and with a separating equilibrium.

The Beer-or-Quiche Game

To illustrate the multiplicity problem, as well as approaches to narrowing down the number of possible equilibria, let us consider a simple game of imperfect information with two sequential equilibria, the Beer-or-Quiche game of Cho and Kreps (1987). It may be summarized as follows, as represented in Figure 6.3 from their paper, where the order of the payoffs is that of the players. Player one, whose type is unobserved, may be either "tough" or "weak," where the prior probabilities on the tough and weak type are .9 and .1, respectively. He must choose whether to have a breakfast of beer B (preferred by a tough type) or quiche Q (preferred by a weak type). Player two, after observing player one's breakfast choice, can choose either to fight, F, or not to fight, N. Player one's payoff is the sum of two elements: he receives one unit if he consumes his preferred breakfast (zero otherwise), and two units if he can avoid a fight. Player two's payoff depends on player one's type, but not on player one's observed breakfast: player two gets a payoff of one unit if he fights the weak type or if he does not fight the strong type, and zero otherwise. That is, player two wants to fight if and only if player one is weak.

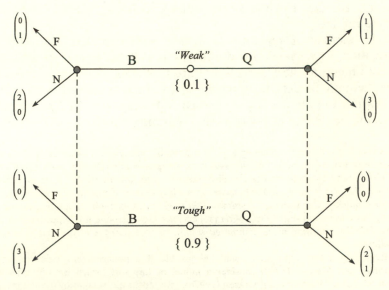

FIGURE 6.3. The Beer-or-Quiche game.

This game has two sequential equilibria. One seems "intuitive," with strategies and the supporting beliefs as follows. Both types of player one have B for breakfast, so that the posterior distribution over types is equivalent to the prior, that is, .9 probability that player one is tough. Player two does not fight if he observes B (consistent with a *posterior* probability of .9 that player one is tough) and fights with probability of at least $\frac{1}{2}$ if he observes Q, which keeps a weak type from having his preferred breakfast. However, there is another set of strategies and supporting beliefs, which may strike one as less sensible, but which also satisfies the restrictions for sequential equilibrium. Both types of player one have Q for breakfast. Player two does not fight if he observes B (which is consistent with the posterior probability he assigns to types) and fights with probability of at least $\frac{1}{2}$ if he observes B, which keeps a tough type from having his preferred breakfast of B. (The reader may want to perform the simple calculation to convince himself this is a sequential equilibrium.) Cho and Kreps point out that this multiplicity is typical of this type of signaling game. Even the requirement of sequential rationality cannot eliminate the seemingly less intuitive equilibria, given the wealth of possible out-of-equilibrium beliefs. What criteria could one use to choose between equilibria?

Eliminating Multiplicity

In the game theory literature, work on eliminating the multiplicity of equilibria has taken two directions: equilibrium refinements and equilibrium selection. There is far too much work to treat here, and much of it is quite technical. Moreover, there is disagreement not only on what are satisfactory solutions to multiplicity from a technical point of view, but also on the more general question of the value of some of these technical concepts. We will simply sketch in the briefest possible way the general approaches.

The approach of **equilibrium refinements** is to strengthen (i.e., refine) the definition of equilibrium in order to eliminate what would be possible equilibria under a weaker condition. The requirement that behavior constitutes a Nash equilibrium is strengthened, generally by putting restrictions on how beliefs are formed. Individuals are restricted from making incredible threats or promises, or from drawing incredible inferences.

To take an example, let us return to the Beer-or-Quiche game. Cho and Kreps suggest that the second equilibrium is not reasonable, even though it satisfies the conditions for a sequential equilibrium. Suppose that player one deviates from the second equilibrium and chooses B. Then player two should conclude that player one is tough with the following reasoning. If player one is weak, then the choice of quiche for breakfast dominates beer, no matter how player two responds. If player one is tough and player two takes B as a signal that player one is tough, then a tough-type player one will indeed be better off by deviating than by following the second equilibrium. It is thus optimal for a tough type to deviate, anticipating that player two will read *B* as a signal that player one is tough. Then player two's belief, namely, that player one is weak with positive probability when *B* is observed, is not reasonable. (A similar argument does *not* apply to the first equilibrium, as player one is playing his preferred type in this case.) Cho and Kreps term this refinement the *intuitive criterion*.

Though some refinements are indeed sensible, others are often convoluted, lacking any apparent economic significance. Kreps (1990) argues that more skepticism is called for in applying equilibrium refinements, for they

> have us and the players employing 'business as usual' arguments following the demonstration that business is very much unusual without giving any reason why. This is not a very satisfactory state of affairs. To get to a more satisfactory state of affairs we must answer the question, What does it mean if some player takes an action that the theory suggests he will not take? Why did it happen, and what does it portend for the future? (p. 114)

The approach of **equilibrium selection** is to retain the definition of equilibrium and, hence, to accept the fact of multiple equilibria, and to ask how agents may choose among them. Perhaps the most influential selection criterion is that of **focal points** introduced by Schelling (1960). He argues that if there is a multiplicity of equilibria, the one selected will have some "natural," "obvious," or "conspicuous" characteristic to it, leading players to focus on it. (In the Beer-or-Quiche game, for example, many readers probably felt that the first equilibrium "seemed more natural," independent of any formal argument about reasonable beliefs.) Numerous informal experiments by Schelling and others convincingly show the existence of focal points. In many games mirroring real-world situations in which there are multiple equilibria (or in many real-world situations mirroring games), players know how to choose among the solutions. To the extent that players do focus on a particular equilibrium even in the absence of communication between them, the problem of coordinating on an equilibrium is far less problematic. Schelling presents an excellent (and nontechnical) discussion of the problem of equilibrium selection and coordination; formal theory has made relatively little progress in following up on his work in studying how players form beliefs about which equilibrium to select.[22] One can hardly do better than reading Schelling (1960), or perhaps some of the work on social norms and conventions mentioned in the previous chapter. The more technically inclined are referred to a game theory text, or to Harsanyi and Selten (1988).

---

[22] As Kreps (1990) puts it, "*formal mathematical game theory has said little or nothing about where these expectations come from, how and why they persist, or when and why we might expect them to arise.*" (p. 101, italics in original)

6.7. REPUTATION FOR NOT RENEGING ON COMMITMENTS

There are, of course, other ways to specify reputation in inflationary surprise models to obtain the result that it can enforce zero inflation in a multiperiod setting in cases where the one-shot result would be positive inflation. For example, policymakers may differ from one another not in the relative cost they assign to inflation versus unemployment, but in their ability to follow through on a low-inflation commitment. Cukierman and Liviatan (1991) consider a single-period model, in which toughness is defined in terms of ability to commit, rather than high θ. In their model of two types with the same objective function, it is optimal under incomplete information for a tough type to accommodate inflationary expectations partially, that is, to inflate by *more* than he would under complete information, rather than by less, as in the Vickers model. A policymaker who is unable to commit (the "weak" type) will inflate at the rate $1/\theta$, no matter what he announces; the tough (that is, dependable) type announces a rate π^a less than $1/\theta$, but greater than zero, the first-best solution. Only by making an announcement *ex ante* can he demonstrate his ability to commit. The expected rate of inflation π^e under imperfect information is between π^a and $1/\theta$, the exact value depending on prior beliefs about types. This explains why the dependable policymaker chooses to announce (and follow through with) an inflation rate greater than zero—choosing a zero-inflation rate implies too large a deflationary surprise *ex post* and hence too high unemployment.

A Model of the Cost of Reneging

Rogoff (1987) considers a dynamic model based on differences across policymakers in the ability to commit, which differs from those of Vickers or Backus and Driffill in two basic assumptions. First, there is a continuum of types. Second, as already indicated, policymakers differ from one another not in the relative cost they assign to inflation versus unemployment, but in the cost they assign to reneging on a low-inflation commitment. The model is worth expositing in some detail.

Consider a policymaker whose horizon is finite and who, at the beginning of his term, announces a commitment to zero inflation. Suppose he maximizes social welfare, represented by the same single-period loss function as in the previous examples, but faces a one-time fixed *private* cost ζ to reneging on his commitment to zero inflation the first time he inflates. Assume that the policymaker's θ is known (and identical across policymakers), where, for simplicity, θ is set equal to 1, but that ζ is not known, so that ζ represents the policymaker's type.[23] The single-period loss function may then be represented as

$$\mathscr{L}(\pi_t, \pi_t^e, \zeta) = -(\pi_t - \pi_t^e) + \frac{\pi_t^2}{2} + \frac{\Psi_t(\zeta, \pi_t, \pi_{t-1}, \ldots)}{2}, \quad (6.19)$$

where $\Psi_t(\ldots) = \zeta$ the first time the policymaker inflates, that is, if $\pi_t \neq 0, \pi_{t-i} = 0$ for all $i > 0$; otherwise, $\Psi_t(\ldots) = 0$. The public knows only the distribution of possible types, and its prior beliefs about ζ are that it is uniformly distributed between 0 and $\bar{\zeta}$, where $\bar{\zeta} > 1$. In each period, the public uses Bayes' rule to update its beliefs.

In equilibrium, the actions of both public and government must be optimal, given the other's actions. We therefore ask two questions. First, given the expectations of the public, what is optimal behavior of policymakers? Second, given optimal policy choices, how are equilibrium expectations formed? We begin with optimal policymaker behavior, for given inflation expectations $\bar{\pi}_t^e$. In answering this question, it will be useful to write an expression for the loss over the whole horizon if the policymaker chooses $\pi = 1$ for the first time in period j (and hence $\pi_t = 0$ in all previous periods and $\pi_t = 1$ in all subsequent periods). Taking $\bar{\pi}_t^e$ as given, one has

$$\Lambda(j, \zeta) = \sum_0^{j-1} \beta^s \bar{\pi}_s^e + \beta^j \left[\bar{\pi}_j^e + \frac{\zeta - 1}{2} \right] + \sum_{j+1}^T \beta^s \frac{1}{2}. \quad (6.20)$$

The following three observations allow us to characterize the form of the equilibrium solution.

First, the policymaker will choose $\pi_t = 0$ before he reneges; $\pi_t = 1$ the period he first reneges; and $\pi_t = 1$ in all subsequent periods. The first part of the statement is trivial, given the assumptions. The second part follows from observing that since he will incur a cost and "lose his reputation" the first time he chooses to inflate, he will choose his myopic optimum, $\pi_t = 1$. Once he has inflated, there is no further cost to inflating, so he will choose his myopic optimum from then on.

Second, if the policymaker has chosen zero inflation until period T, he will choose $\pi_T = 0$ if $\zeta \geq 1$, and $\pi_T = 1$ if $\zeta < 1$. If the policymaker has chosen zero inflation until period T, (6.20) becomes

$$\Lambda(T, \zeta) = \sum_0^T \beta^s \bar{\pi}_s^e + \beta^T \frac{\zeta - 1}{2}, \quad (6.21)$$

---

[23] This cost may represent penalties (including "loss of face") assessed directly on the central bank if it reneges on its low-inflation commitment. The public may know what these penalties are, but not know the cost the central bank associates with them.

from which the observation immediately follows. Note that this result indicates why the assumption that $\bar{\zeta} > 1$ is crucial for the result that reputation may induce otherwise inflationary types to fulfill their zero-inflation commitment for some period of time. If $\bar{\zeta} \leq 1$, people will expect $\pi_T = 1$ with certainty. There would then be no incentive for types who had not inflated before period $T - 1$ to choose zero inflation in that period, as there would be no reputation to preserve. Hence, as we saw in an earlier model, the equilibrium would unravel backwards.

Third, a given cost type will never begin inflating earlier than a type with a lower cost. To see this, note first that from the definition of $\Lambda(t, \zeta)$, the condition for a type ζ to prefer to wait at least until $t + 1$ rather than inflate at t is that $\Lambda(t + 1, \zeta) < \Lambda(t, \zeta)$, or $\Lambda(t, \zeta) - \Lambda(t + 1, \zeta) > 0$. Using (6.21), we may write this latter expression as

$$\Lambda(t, \zeta) - \Lambda(t + 1, \zeta) = \beta^t \left[\beta \left(\frac{1}{2} - \pi_{t+1}^e \right) + (1 - \beta) \frac{\zeta - 1}{2} \right], \quad (6.22)$$

which immediately implies that the gain from waiting to renege is increasing in ζ.

These three results taken together allow us to characterize the form of the equilibrium solution. All types with $\zeta < 1$ inflate at or before T, in groups given by their relative cost, higher cost groups inflating no earlier than lower cost groups; all types with $\zeta \geq 1$ never inflate. Define by ζ_t^0 the lowest type which inflates at $t + 1$ or later (that is, all types for whom $\zeta < \zeta_t^0$ inflate at t or before).[24] We may represent the equilibrium in terms of who inflates when as in Figure 6.4, which divides the whole space of possible types into groups which inflate in the same period.

To solve for the actual values of the ζ_t^0, note that a cut-off type must be indifferent between inflating at t and at $t + 1$ for any $\zeta_t^0 > 0$. Formally, one must have

$$\Lambda(t, \zeta_t^0) = \Lambda(t + 1, \zeta_t^0) \quad \text{if } \zeta_t^0 > 0. \quad (6.23)$$

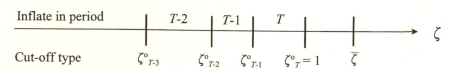

FIGURE 6.4. The sequence of cut-off types.

[24] Defining ζ_t^0 in this way, rather than as the highest type which inflates at t, simply reflects the assumption that if a type is indifferent between inflating and not inflating in a period, it chooses not to inflate.

To see why, suppose this is not the case. If $\Lambda(t, \zeta_t^0) < \Lambda(t + 1, \zeta_t^0)$, then type ζ_t^0 will inflate at t rather than at $t + 1$. If $\Lambda(t, \zeta_t^0) > \Lambda(t + 1, \zeta_t^0)$, there must then be a lower type who would also wait until $t + 1$, so that ζ_t^0 would not be the cut-off type. (When $\zeta_t^0 = 0$, so that no type inflates at t, it must be the case that $\Lambda(t + 1, \zeta_t^0) < \Lambda(t, \zeta_t^0)$, so that it is preferable for every type to wait until at least the next period. This will be true in sufficiently early periods.)

We now can solve for the equilibrium, that is, the sequence of optimal ζ_t^0 which is consistent with rational expectations (rather than with exogenously given expectations $\overline{\pi}_t^e$). Given the ζ_t^0 and the uniform distribution of ζ, Bayes' rule implies that rationally expected inflation must evolve according to

$$\pi_t^e = \frac{\zeta_t^0 - \zeta_{t-1}^0}{\overline{\zeta} - \zeta_{t-1}^0}. \tag{6.24}$$

Put simply, if zero inflation has been observed until period t, the public truncates the distribution of possible types at ζ_{t-1}^0, knowing that the type does not lie below this point. Given the two possible inflation choices, the expected rate of inflation is simply the conditional probability that the policymaker's type lies between ζ_{t-1}^0 and ζ_t^0, which is (6.24). Combining this equation with (6.23) and the definition of $\Lambda(t, \zeta)$, we may derive a difference equation for the ζ_t^0, namely,

$$\zeta_{t+1}^0 = \frac{\beta - 1}{2\beta} \zeta_t^{0^2} + \frac{\overline{\zeta}(1 - \beta) + 1}{2\beta} \zeta_t^0 + \overline{\zeta}\left(1 - \frac{1}{2\beta}\right) \tag{6.25}$$

$$= A(\zeta_t^0),$$

which, together with the boundary condition $\zeta_T^0 = 1$, can be solved for the path of optimal ζ_t^0. Based on the characteristics of $A(\zeta_t^0)$,[25] Rogoff uses this first-order difference equation to construct an equilibrium. With a long enough horizon, there will be no inflation in early periods.

Following Barro (1986), Rogoff points out that, on the one hand, the public may actually be better off facing a type who assigns a low cost to reneging, since the objective function being maximized is close to the social welfare function. However, the public is also better off the higher the likelihood it assigns, *ex ante*, to the policymaker being a high cost type (the higher the prior probability that the cost lies above 1, which means $\overline{\zeta}$ is high), for this means lower expectations of inflation.

[25] It is increasing, concave, lies above the 45° line, and $A(0) > 0$ for $\beta > 1/2$. These properties allow us to draw a simple dynamic diagram to represent the equilibrium. See Figure 1 in Rogoff (1987).

A Stochastic Version of the Model

Bartolini and Drazen (1997b) and Drazen (1999b) extend the model to a stochastic environment, where the cut-off value ζ_t^0 in any period depends on the realization of an external shock that affects the relative values of reneging and not reneging. This opens the interesting possibility of two types of equilibria in any period. There may either be a separating equilibrium as above, in which some types that have not previously inflated inflate in period t, or a pooling equilibrium, in which no type that has not previously inflated inflates for the first time at t. Hence, the evolution of reputation will depend not only on history, but also on the circumstances in which a policymaker inflates.

The basic outline of a stochastic version of the Rogoff model may be illustrated as follows. Suppose the single-period loss depends on a stochastic term ϵ_t, so that we may write the loss function in general terms as $\mathcal{L}(\pi_t, \pi_t^e, \zeta, \epsilon_t)$, where higher ϵ_t implies a higher loss from not inflating in period t. Expected inflation in equilibrium is determined by an equation such as (6.24), with one modification. If equilibrium in period $t-1$ was characterized by separation, with all types below ζ_{t-1}^0 inflating, the observation of no inflation in period $t-1$ means the lowest possible type in t is ζ_{t-1}^0. Call this type $\underline{\zeta}_{t-1}$; the subscript indicating it is inherited from $t-1$. If, however, the equilibrium in $t-1$ was a pooling equilibrium, in which no type devalued given the realization of ϵ_{t-1}, then no inflation in $t-1$ reveals nothing about possible type, so the lowest possible type in t is equal to the lowest type in $t-1$, that is, $\underline{\zeta}_{t-1} = \underline{\zeta}_{t-2}$. Hence, expectations of inflation π_t^e are described by (6.24), but with ζ_{t-1}^0. replaced by $\underline{\zeta}_{t-1}$, where $\underline{\zeta}_{t-1} = \max(\zeta_{t-1}^0, \underline{\zeta}_{t-2})$, as in Figure 6.5.

To solve for the cut-off types in a stochastic model, one begins, as above, with period T. Suppose, for simplicity, that the inflation choices are either $\pi_T = 0$ or $\pi_T = 1$ as in the nonstochastic model. Using the function $\mathcal{L}(\pi_t, \pi_t^e, \zeta, \epsilon_t)$, the cut-off type is then described by

$$\mathcal{L}(1, \pi_T^e, \zeta_T^0, \epsilon_T) = \mathcal{L}(0, \pi_T^e, \zeta_T^0, \epsilon_T), \tag{6.26}$$

where $\pi_T^e = \dfrac{\zeta_T^0 - \underline{\zeta}_{T-1}}{\bar{\zeta} - \underline{\zeta}_{T-1}}$ for $\zeta_T^0 \geq \underline{\zeta}_{T-1}$, and $\pi_T^e = 0$ otherwise. Since lower ϵ_T lowers the cost of $\pi_T = 0$ relative to $\pi_T = 1$, it causes the cut-off value ζ_T^0 to fall. Therefore, for ϵ_T below a critical value $\hat{\epsilon}_T$, $\zeta_T^0 < \underline{\zeta}_{T-1}$, and there is a pooling equilibrium in which all possible types at T choose not to inflate. For $\epsilon_T > \hat{\epsilon}_T$, $\zeta_T^0 > \underline{\zeta}_{T-1}$ so that the equilibrium is separating, in which all types $\zeta > \zeta_T^0$ choose not to inflate at T, while all types $\zeta_T^0 > \zeta \geq \underline{\zeta}_{T-1}$ inflate for the first time at T.

Equilibria in interior periods are similarly characterized. In any period t, there is a cut-off type ζ_t^0 who is just indifferent between inflating and not

Separating Equilibrium: $\zeta^{o}_{t\text{-}1} > \zeta_{t\text{-}2}$. Observing zero inflation implies $\zeta_{t\text{-}1} = \zeta^{o}_{t\text{-}1}$, so that the distribution is updated.

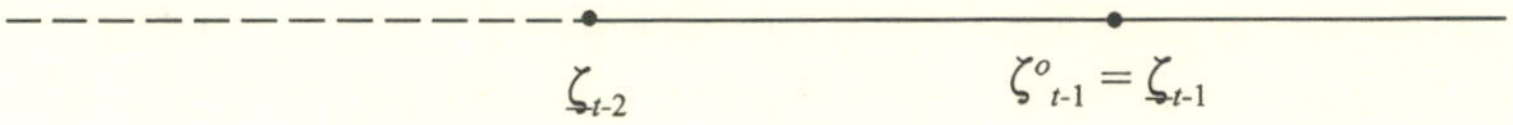

$$\zeta_{t\text{-}2} \qquad\qquad\qquad \zeta^{o}_{t\text{-}1} = \zeta_{t\text{-}1}$$

Pooling Equilibrium: $\zeta^{o}_{t\text{-}1} < \zeta_{t\text{-}2}$. All feasible types choose zero inflation, so that observing zero inflation gives no information. $\zeta_{t\text{-}2} = \zeta_{t\text{-}1}$, so that there is no updating of the distribution.

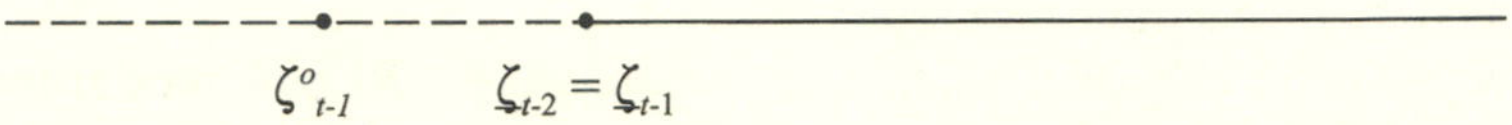

$$\zeta^{o}_{t\text{-}1} \qquad\qquad \zeta_{t\text{-}2} = \zeta_{t\text{-}1}$$

FIGURE 6.5. Separating and pooling equilibria in a stochastic model.

inflating at t (conditional on having not previously inflated), conditional on the realization of ϵ_{t}. All types with ζ less than ζ_{t}^{0} who have not previously inflated will certainly inflate in period t; all types with ζ equal to or greater than ζ_{t}^{0} will not inflate. The equilibrium in t may be either separating or pooling, depending on the relation of ζ_{t}^{0} to ζ_{t-1}, exactly as described in the previous paragraph. (Refer to Figure 6.5.) The only difference from the period-T case is that ζ_{t}^{0} is derived by equating the present discounted expected loss from t to T from inflating for the first time at t to the present discounted expected loss from t to T from not inflating at t, and hence maintaining an anti-inflation reputation. Both of these present discounted expected losses can be easily calculated from the single-period loss function $\mathscr{L}(\cdot)$ and the distribution of ϵ_{t}. Worked-out examples of such calculations for models of capital-account liberalization and devaluation may be found in Bartolini and Drazen (1997b) and Drazen (1999b), respectively.

A Comparison of Models

How does the Rogoff model compare with the other two models of reputation under imperfect information we have studied? Technically, the equilibrium depends on the existence of an "inflation nut," as in the Backus–Driffill (1985b) model. Economically, it is closer to the Vickers (1986) model, in that "tough" types care about both inflation and unemployment, but what distinguishes types is their cost of breaking a zero-inflation commitment. This may be a more realistic specification of the unobserved difference between policymakers. Moreover, whether more realistic or not, it provides an important alternative specification.

Another nice aspect of the model is its characterization of the dynamic learning process, and the implications for inflation dynamics. Based on the underlying distribution of types, in any period for which only zero inflation has previously been observed, there is a probability between zero and 1 of observing positive inflation for the first time. Hence, the evolution of expected inflation is qualitatively identical to the dynamics of expected inflation in the "interior" periods of the multiperiod Backus and Driffill model described at the end of Section 6.4 above, but without relying on the economically unattractive assumption of a central banker randomizing between two alternative policies. Hence, as indicated in that section, a model of a continuum of policymaker types, in which some information is potentially revealed each period, can "justify" a model of a single policy-maker playing a mixed strategy.

The stochastic version of the model enriches the characterization of the learning process, since the inference problem of the private sector about types depends on the external environment and how a policymaker reacts to this environment. This has a number of interesting implications. It makes the building of reputation conditional on the circumstances in which a policymaker finds himself. It also suggests a way to formalize the notion that "tough" policymakers welcome tough times, in order to sepa-rate themselves from weaker policymakers.[26] We now investigate more explicitly the importance of the policymaker's environment in the attempt to establish credibility.

6.8. CREDIBILITY AND EXTERNAL CIRCUMSTANCES

Credibility Versus Reputation

So far in this chapter, we have considered how the belief that the policymaker may have strong anti-inflationary preferences can lend credi-bility to the announcement of a low-inflation policy. The essence of the reputational model is that current policy signals type and a policymaker's type determines what he will do, so that tough policy signals that the policymaker is tough, and *therefore* will follow tough policies in the future. Whether or not an announced policy is carried out, however, reflects more than the policymaker's intentions. The environment in which he finds himself can be as important. Since even a "tough" policymaker cannot ignore the cost of very high unemployment, he may renege on an anti-in-

---

[26] This point suggests that discretion allows a policymaker to establish credibility in a way that a regime of rules cannot. Under discretion, policymakers must make choices in response to the environment, implying that the public can separate tough from weak policymakers; under rules, no such information is generated.

flation commitment in sufficiently adverse circumstances, that is, in times of weak economic activity, when pressures to restore high employment are strong.[27] Hence, in the models of the previous two sections, where tough policymakers are not infinitely tough, the credibility the public assigns to an announced policy should therefore reflect not only the characteristics of the policymaker, but the economic environment as well.

Taking account of the environment in which policy is chosen has a number of important implications. In terms of reputation, the most obvious is that reneging on a no-inflation pledge need not harm reputation. If a policymaker inflates when external circumstances are known to be especially adverse, then this action will not reveal that he will inflate in more normal times. Therefore, inflating under extreme circumstances need not lessen the credibility of a commitment to low inflation. To put the point another way (a related formal model is presented in Section 12.7 of Chapter 12), the signaling content of inflating will be low when circumstances are such that it is known that all types would inflate, and vice versa.

Less obviously, the converse is *not* true: not inflating in adverse circumstances need not enhance the credibility of an anti-inflation announcement, as the basic reputational model suggests. Not inflating when times are bad will, in general, enhance the *reputation* of the policymaker, that is, will strengthen the public's belief that he puts a high weight on the cost of inflation. However, the public knows that his inflation decision tomorrow will depend on the circumstances in which he will find himself as well as on his preferences. If not inflating today raises unemployment tomorrow (and hence worsens the future trade-off between inflation and unemployment), observing tough policy today could increase the probability the public assigns to observing inflation tomorrow at the same time it strengthens the policymaker's reputation. When the policymaking environment is explicitly considered, it becomes crucial, therefore, to distinguish between the reputation of the policymaker and the credibility of the policy.

In a nonstochastic setting with complete information (so that signaling and reputation building are not present), it is well known that policy choices today may constrain the environment tomorrow in such a way that current policy has seemingly counterintuitive effects. This is the essence of the argument first made by Sargent and Wallace in their now classic article, "Unpleasant Monetarist Arithmetic" (1981). Reducing growth of the money supply today will reduce seigniorage today, assuming the economy is on the "good" side of the seigniorage Laffer curve. If no other fiscal changes are made, this will require the government to raise additional revenues at some point in the future to meet its intertemporal

---

[27] A related point is that if policies are too tough, the current policymakers may be removed from power, leading to an easing of policies. See, for example, Flood (1983) or Blanchard (1985).

budget constraint. If the higher revenue needs tomorrow are met by increasing money growth tomorrow, then agents will take a cut in money growth today as indicating an increase in money growth tomorrow. With forward-looking expectations, higher expected money growth tomorrow will positively affect expected and thus actual inflation today. Sargent and Wallace pointed out that this expectational effect may be so strong that a cut in the rate of monetary growth today induces an increase, rather than a fall, in today's inflation rate. In short, "tight" monetary policy can have the opposite effect from what one would naively expect due to today's policy affecting the trade-off the policymaker faces tomorrow. This argument was derived formally in both a nonstochastic and a stochastic setting in Section 2.5 of Chapter 2 in the model of Drazen and Helpman (1990), to which the interested reader may refer.

A Formal Model

Drazen and Masson (1994) examine this possibility in a Vickers-type model of reputation under incomplete information. Key to the argument is persistence in the effects of policy, in that a tough anti-inflation policy raises not only current unemployment, but also unemployment in the future. They argued that if the effects of tough policy on the economic environment are sufficiently persistent, the basic conceptual result in the above reputational models, namely, that observing a tough policy today raises the credibility of announced low-inflation policy and lowers the expected rate of inflation, can be reversed. Following a tough policy may actually harm rather than enhance credibility: for example, a tough anti-inflation policy today may raise unemployment well into the future, making the commitment to future anti-inflation policy less credible.

In the context of signaling, the point may be understood intuitively as follows. Suppose that one afternoon, a colleague announces to you that he is serious about losing weight and plans to skip dinner. He adds that he has not eaten for two days. Does this information make it more or less credible that he really will skip dinner? The model of unobserved types used in previous sections would imply that with each meal he skips, the "tough policy" of skipping the next meal becomes *more* credible, as each observation of playing tough raises the probability we assign to his being a fanatical dieter. Once we realize that his skipping one meal makes him hungrier at the next mealtime (i.e., that policy has persistent effects), we are led to the opposite conclusion, namely, that it becomes less likely he will stick to his diet the more meals he has skipped. Now, let us consider this point more formally.

Drazen and Masson consider a two-period stochastic model, where in the first period the relation between unemployment and inflation is as in (4.12), but where a is a parameter measuring the slope of the short-run

Phillips curve (previously assumed equal to 1):

$$U_1 = -a(\pi_1 - \pi_1^e) + \epsilon_1. \tag{6.27a}$$

In the second period, there is persistence in the rate of unemployment: all else equal, the higher is U_1, the higher will be U_2. This may be represented by

$$U_2 = -a(\pi_2 - \pi_2^e) + a\delta U_1 + \epsilon_2, \tag{6.27b}$$

where $\delta \geq 0$ is a measure of persistence in unemployment fluctuations.[28]

The government's objective is to minimize an expected discounted loss function, where each period's loss is quadratic in actual inflation and in the deviation of actual unemployment from a target level below the natural rate. That is, the unemployment target is not 0, but $\tilde{U} < 0$, so that the loss is quadratic in $U_t - \tilde{U}$. The specification of possible types of governments is identical to that in Section 6.6, with uncertainty about the government's objective function.[29] The type-i ($i = W, T$) government's objective function conditioned on information available at $t = 1$ is

$$
\begin{aligned}
\Lambda^i &= \mathscr{L}_1^i + \beta\, \mathrm{E}\mathscr{L}_2^i \\
&= \left(U_1 - \tilde{U}\right)^2 + \theta^i(\pi_1)^2 + \beta\, \mathrm{E}_1\!\left[\left(U_2 - \tilde{U}\right)^2 + \theta^i(\pi_2)^2\right].
\end{aligned}
\tag{6.28}
$$

To show formally that when anti-inflation policy has persistent effects, a tough policy today can lower the credibility of anti-inflation policy in the future, Drazen and Masson consider a policy rule with an escape clause, where a policymaker chooses between a "rule" of zero inflation and a fixed positive rate of inflation, $\bar{\pi}$.[30] (The more general model of rules with

---

[28] An alternative way to model persistent effects of policy would be in the government's objective function (6.28), by assuming that, all else equal, the *second*-period loss is higher the higher is *first*-period unemployment. This may be a better representation of the political constraint on policymakers when recent unemployment rates have been especially high. The result would be the same under this alternative specification, the key point being that the probability of a devaluation in the second period may depend positively on first-period unemployment.

[29] An alternative approach is to use a trigger-strategy model of expectations with uncertainty, along the lines of Canzoneri (1985). Though this allows the government to depart from tough monetary policy in response to observable adverse shocks without losing credibility and may be simpler than the Kreps–Wilson (1982) framework for some purposes, it does not allow a simple comparison with the signaling-of-type motive for tough policy.

[30] Fomally, this is a state-contingent, two-part rule, rather than a rule with an escape clause *per se*. Inflating at the preannounced trigger could thus be characterized as carrying out the prespecified, state-contingent policy. Though semantically correct, this view misses the key point of this section—that in a stochastic world, even an extremely tough policymaker, who plans *ex ante* to maintain a constant price level (and makes public statements to that effect), will inflate in sufficiently adverse circumstances. Conceptually, therefore, it seems reasonable to think of inflating as departing from the announced, no-inflation rule.

escape clauses, in which a policymaker commits himself to the rule under some preannounced circumstances, but announces he will revert to discretion under other circumstances, was presented in Section 4.6 of Chapter 4.)[31] More specifically, the question is how the probability μ_2 of positive inflation in the second period depends on the observed first-period inflation choice π_1, once we consider not only the standard signaling of unknown government type, but also the effect of persistence. With uncertainty about types, we may write μ_2 as

$$\mu_2(\pi_1) = p_2(\pi_1)q_2^T(\pi_1) + (1 - p_2(\pi_1))q_2^W(\pi_1), \qquad (6.29)$$

where, as in the model of Section 6.6, p_2 is the probability the government is tough and q_2^i is the probability a government of type i will inflate in period 2, where we make explicit the dependence of both probabilities on the first-period inflation rate π_1. Why does the probability that a government of a *given* type will inflate in period 2 depend on the action observed in the first period? This probability is determined by the critical value of the shock ϵ_2 which makes a type indifferent between inflating and not inflating in period 2. Since the loss from a policy depends on the expected rate of inflation, which is simply $\mu_2(\pi_1)\bar{\pi}$, the critical value of the shock for type i will depend on π_1, as will q_2^i as well.

To make the dependence of q_2^i on π_1 specific, one first solves for the value of the second-period shock which makes a government of type i indifferent between inflating and not inflating. This is the value of ϵ_2 such that the loss in the second period from inflating and that from not inflating are equal. One obtains a critical value $\hat{\epsilon}_2^i(\pi_1)$, namely,

$$\hat{\epsilon}_2^i(\pi_1) = \frac{(a^2 + \theta^i)\bar{\pi}}{2a} + \tilde{U} - a\mu_2(\pi_1)\bar{\pi} - a\delta U_1, \qquad (6.30)$$

for $i = W, T$. If the realization of ϵ_2 is below this critical value, zero inflation is optimal; if it is above, an inflation rate of $\bar{\pi} > 0$ is optimal. Using (6.30) and the distribution of ϵ_2, one can then derive q_2^i as a function of $\hat{\epsilon}_2^i(\pi_1)$. For example, if the distribution of ϵ_2 is uniform between $-v$ and $+v$, we have

$$q_2^i(\pi_1) = \text{prob}(\epsilon_2 > \hat{\epsilon}_2^i(\pi_1)) = (v - \hat{\epsilon}_2^i(\pi_1))/2v. \qquad (6.31)$$

---

[31] The problem of discretion always dominating the rule in the absence of a private cost does not arise for this modeling of escape clauses, since for small enough shocks, maintaining a constant price level will be preferred to a discrete devaluation. Another key difference from the Obstfeld (1997) model is that there, multiple equilibria are inherent to the use of escape clauses. Intuitively, this can occur because expected inflation π^e depends on how often the escape clause is invoked, but the decision of whether to invoke the escape clause also depends on π^e, since higher π^e makes it optimal to abandon a fixed exchange rate for smaller shocks. Hence, higher inflationary expectations can be self-fulfilling.

Using (6.30), one sees that (6.31) gives $q_2^i(\pi_1)$ as a function of $\mu_2(\pi_1)$, which itself depends on $q_2^i(\pi_1)$ via (6.29). To complete the calculation, one must calculate the probabilities $p_2(\pi_1)$ of the government being weak, conditional on the first-period action. As in previous sections, one uses Bayes' rule, based on the probability q_1^i that a government of type i will inflate in the first period. For example, if one started with uniform priors and assumed that the public does not observe the shock ϵ_1, the probabilities would be[32]

$$p_2(\pi_1 = \overline{\pi}) = \frac{q_1^T}{q_1^W + q_1^T}, \, p_2(\pi_1 = 0) = \frac{1 - q_1^T}{2 - q_1^W - q_1^T}. \qquad (6.32)$$

The calculation of q_1^i, the probability that a type i would inflate in the first period, is analogous to the calculation for q_2^i. One calculates a critical value of the first-period shock $\hat{\epsilon}_1^i$ such that $\Lambda^i(\pi = 0) = \Lambda^i(\pi = \overline{\pi})$. q_1^i, the probability that $\epsilon_1 > \hat{\epsilon}_1^i$, can then be calculated as above.

To calculate whether observing positive inflation in the first period will in fact raise the probability of inflation in the second period (analogous to a stochastic version with persistent policy effects of the Vickers model), one can calculate the sign of $\mu_2(\pi = \overline{\pi}) - \mu_2(\pi = 0)$. Combining (6.29) through (6.32), one obtains, after some manipulation,

$$\mu_2(\pi = \overline{\pi}) - \mu_2(\pi = 0)$$

$$= \frac{1}{1 - \overline{\pi}/2v} \left[-\frac{a\delta\overline{\pi}}{2v} + \frac{(q_1^W - q_1^T)(\theta^T - \theta^W)\dfrac{\overline{\pi}}{4av}}{(q_1^W + q_1^T)(2 - q_1^W - q_1^T)} \right]. \qquad (6.33)$$

(Note that $1 - \overline{\pi}/2v > 0$, for otherwise the inflation size would exceed twice the maximum size of the shock it was aimed to offset.) The effect of persistence on this expression is not quite as simple as it looks, since the persistence parameter δ will affect both terms inside the brackets. The effect on the second term is via q_1^i ($i = T, W$), which arises because the critical level of the first-period shock depends on welfare in *both* periods and hence on δ.

---

[32] We could perform an analogous calculation in the case where the shock ϵ_1 is observed (or can be inferred). The only difference would be that for some realizations of ϵ_1, action would be fully revealing, a weak government finding it optimal to devalue, a strong government finding it optimal not to. Hence we would have pooling and separating equilibria, with $1 - p_2$ equal to zero or 1 in the relevant regions of separation and equal to the prior in the region of pooling.

In the case of *no* persistence of unemployment effects across periods ($\delta = 0$), so that there is only a signaling effect, the first term in brackets disappears and the expression in (6.33) is unambiguously positive. (This follows from $q_1^W > q_1^T$, that is, a weak government being more likely to inflate in the first period, which follows from $\theta^T > \theta^W$.) Thus, the standard result on signaling of types holds: observing a tough policy (zero inflation) in the first period will raise the probability of observing no inflation in the second period. Hence, in the absence of persistence in the effects of policy, a signaling motive contributes to the credibility of a no-inflation announcement—the credibility of a zero-inflation policy is enhanced in the second period if no inflation was observed in the first period.

However, when $\delta > 0$, that is, when there is persistence in the effects of policy across periods, the expression in (6.33) can be negative. Drazen and Masson (1994) show that the dependence of $\mu_2(\pi = \bar{\pi}) - \mu_2(\pi = 0)$ on δ can be quite complicated; however, by simulation they show that for δ sufficiently large, the persistence effect will dominate the signaling effect and (6.33) will become negative. Hence, positive persistence of unemployment implies that a tough anti-inflationary policy may *raise*, rather than lower, the public's expectation of inflation in future periods. Shocks that are not offset through a surprise inflation in the first period have further unfavorable effects in the second period, increasing the probability that a government of either type will inflate. Thus, credibility will not necessarily be enhanced by "playing tough" in period 1.[33]

Given that a tough anti-inflationary policy has persistent effects which often *lower* the probability that the public assigns to the policy being maintained in the future, why do governments often "nail themselves to the mast" and so singlemindedly pursue such a policy? The most common argument is that by playing tough for a long enough period of time, the government hopes it can change the structure of the economy, a possibility not explicitly considered in the model. Theoretically, this is an implication of the argument presented by Lucas (1976) in his famous critique of economic models which assume that policy parameters are invariant to changes in the monetary policy *regime*. In the second-period Phillips curve (6.27) above, the parameter a may itself be a function of the policy rule the government is following, with the aim of a tough anti-inflationary policy to raise the value of a, so that reduced inflation can be achieved at a lower unemployment cost.[34]

---

[33] Drazen and Masson argue that this type of model is descriptive of the sometimes failed attempts of governments to defend a fixed exchange rate via displays of toughness, as in the case of the United Kingdom or Sweden in 1992. See Section 12.3 of Chapter 12.

[34] An alternative view, that policymakers want to affect the way in which market participants form expectations, is implicit in Bayesian updating in the Vickers model.

6.9. Ambiguity, Secrecy, and Imprecise Control

When the policymaker's type is unknown, a central result is that certain types may have the incentive to disguise their type, at least temporarily. It was assumed that the policymaker has perfect control over monetary policy, so that disguising meant choosing a rate of inflation different from the myopic optimum. The public solved its inference problem of learning the policymaker's true type on the basis of observed inflation, knowing that the rate of inflation observed is the rate of inflation chosen.

There are other ways policymakers try to disguise their intentions. One is to try to hide what they are doing, or, if pushed to reveal their actions or intentions, to make vague and imprecise announcements about policies or goals. Central banks throughout the world appear to have a strong penchant for secrecy and obfuscation. A key reason for secrecy is the view that monetary policy has real effects only if it is unanticipated.[35] This argument requires the further assumption that information about past central bank policy deliberations gives information about what future policy may be beyond the information contained in observed monetary aggregates. This is where imperfect control enters in. In the attempt to disguise its true preferences, might the central bank find it optimal actually to choose *less* precise control over some policy variables in order to make the public's inference problem more difficult? By making learning more difficult, the central bank gains a greater ability to engineer monetary surprises and hence reduce unemployment. The loss of control over the inflation rate has a direct cost; can the indirect benefit due to a greater capacity to surprise outweigh this cost, so that welfare actually rises?[36]

Imprecise Control and Slow Learning

Cukierman and Meltzer (1990) consider models in which more imprecise control of the money supply may be optimal, since imprecise control allows

---

[35] There are other, more bureaucratic reasons for secrecy. Havrilesky (1987, 1993) suggests that secrecy serves to mask the redistribution of income effected by policy. It has also been argued (for example, Kane [1990]) that the U.S. Federal Reserve Bank is given substantial independence because it performs a scapegoat function for incumbent politicians. As Cukierman (1992, p. 213) puts it in his comprehensive study of central bank behavior, "If this [scapegoat] device is to work in credible manner the Fed must be endowed with a sufficient amount of independence so that policies enacted in response to the demands of incumbent politicians are not clearly identifiable as such."

[36] The question here of the optimality of imprecise control is not identical to the question of the optimality of precommitment *per se*, discussed in Section 4.6 of Chapter 4. In the optimality of constraining oneself, the issue was the correctly perceived temptation for a policymaker to be time-inconsistent, even a policymaker with *known* preferences. Here, the basic issue is making it harder for the public to infer the *unknown* preferences of a policymaker from his observed actions.

the central bank to obscure its preferences. It is assumed that these preferences change over time, with the policymaker having better information than the public about his current trade-off between the costs of inflation and the costs of unemployment. Why is it optimal for the policymaker to obscure his current preferences in their model? If the policymaker's preferences change over time, some periods he will be very concerned about unemployment (and hence weak on inflation), other periods less concerned about unemployment (and hence highly anti-inflationary). In those periods in which the policymaker is most concerned about unemployment, inflationary surprises are most valuable. If preferences were known period by period, so it were known when the policymaker was relatively anti-unemployment (low θ), he could not surprise the public any more in these periods than in periods when he was anti-inflationary. Hence, the policymaker's expected loss (that is, averaged over periods with different θ) would be lower if he could disguise his preferences.

Mathematically, this may be seen by taking a variant of the basic model used in this chapter, but where θ is stochastic, drawn independently every period from a known, unchanging distribution. This stochastic structure (including the absence of a reputational component) allows us to treat the problem as a sequence of single-period problems. Let preferences be written as

$$\mathscr{L} = \frac{\pi^e - \pi}{\theta} + \frac{\pi^2}{2}, \tag{6.34}$$

so that chosen $\pi = 1/\theta$, implying $\mathscr{L} = \pi^e/\theta - 1/2\theta^2$. The expectation of $\mathscr{L}$ before θ is known can be written

$$\mathrm{E}_{t-1}\mathscr{L} = \sum p(\theta)\mathscr{L}\left(\frac{1}{\theta}, \pi^e(\theta)\right), \tag{6.35}$$

where $p(\theta)$ is the probability of observing θ. In the case where θ is known when π^e is chosen, $\pi^e = \pi = 1/\theta$, implying a single-period loss of $1/2\theta^2$, so that the *ex-ante* expected loss is $\sum p(\theta)/2\theta^2$. Call this expected loss $\mathrm{E}\mathscr{L}^\theta$. When θ is not known when π^e is chosen, $\pi^e = \mathrm{E}(1/\theta)$. The associated expected loss is easily calculated to be

$$\mathrm{E}\mathscr{L}^{\mathrm{E}(1/\theta)} = \sum p(\theta)\left(\frac{\mathrm{E}(1/\theta)}{\theta} - \frac{1}{2\theta^2}\right).$$

It follows immediately that

$$\mathrm{E}\mathscr{L}^{\theta} - \mathrm{E}\mathscr{L}^{\mathrm{E}(1/\theta)} = \sum p(\theta)\frac{1}{\theta}\left(\frac{1}{\theta} - \mathrm{E}\left(\frac{1}{\theta}\right)\right) > 0, \qquad (6.36)$$

where the right-hand side is simply the variance of $1/\theta$.

To understand the economics of this inequality, note that in the case where θ is not known when π^e is chosen, a low realization of θ will mean that, $1/\theta > \mathrm{E}(1/\theta)$, so that $\pi > \pi^e$, while a high realization of θ will mean that $1/\theta < \mathrm{E}(1/\theta)$, so that $\pi < \pi^e$. Thus, inflationary surprises occur when the unemployment target is relatively more important, deflationary surprises when it is relatively less important.

In this example, the fact that preference shocks are i.i.d. means that past observations of inflation give no information about current preferences. Thus, though it would be socially beneficial for the policymaker to disguise his preferences, obscuring the information that can be extracted from past policies (for example, by claiming he has imperfect control of inflation) will be irrelevant. For there to be a benefit to obscuring the information content of past policy, there must be some serial correlation of the preference shocks over time. What role does imperfect control of inflation then play? If a policymaker faces rational agents who know the form of his decision problem, he cannot simply "be ambiguous" and make that credible. If it is known he has perfect control over the relevant policy variables, agents will see through that. With only a one-time shock to preferences, learning could be quite rapid. If policymakers were known to choose their myopic rate of inflation, a single observation after a known shock occurred would be fully revealing; if there were uncertainty about whether a shock had occurred, the inference problem under these circumstances would be only slightly more difficult. With repeated shocks but perfect control, the inference problem would be more difficult, but the policymaker could not control the speed with which agents learn. However, *precommitting* to imprecise control may help him to disguise his current θ.[37] When the policymaker can choose the degree of precision, less precise control, meaning a looser connection between actual and desired money growth rates, will imply the public will learn more slowly about the policymaker's true preferences.

Alesina and Cukierman (1990) consider the benefits of ambiguity in an electoral model, where the preferences of the parties are subject to stochastic taste shocks. Voters do not know the preferences of the party in power, which cares both about remaining in power and about implement-

---

[37] To take a related point, when a politician is asked to use his power to deliver a favor he would prefer not to deliver, he often claims he would like to help but is unable to do so. To the extent he actually has accumulated power, this excuse is not credible, so he may want to voluntarily forgo some power.

ing its preferred program. (In Chapter 7, these sorts of models, in which elected policymakers care both about implementing their preferred policy and about re-election, are studied in detail.) They show that incumbents will moderate their choices relative to those policies they most prefer in order to make themselves more appealing to voters and increase their chances of re-election. On the basis of this, it may be optimal for an incumbent to precommit to less precise control over policy variables than is technologically feasible. The less precise is control over policy variables, the less informative is a current observation in the eyes of the public. Hence, an incumbent can choose a policy closer to his ideologically preferred one without incurring the wrath of the voters. There are, however, costs to imprecise control. The more risk averse are the voters, the more they dislike policy "slippage," thus reducing (or possibly eliminating) the incentive towards imprecise control.

Secrecy, Ambiguity and Cheap Talk

In the Cukierman and Meltzer model, ambiguity is optimal because of the slow learning it implies. An even more intriguing possibility is that the ambiguity may actually convey more information than precise announcements. The optimality of imprecise announcements about monetary policy in the surprise-inflation model has been studied by Stein (1989) in a model of "cheap talk," where he demonstrates that if the monetary authority is constrained to make imprecise announcements, policy announcements can be informative.

Cheap talk refers to the use of signals that do not directly affect payoffs, which in this context, means announcements that are costless to make. If an announcement can be made costlessly, one would think that it would contain no information. Crawford and Sobel (1982), however, demonstrated the possibility of equilibria in which cheap talk can convey information.[38] Suppose a sender of such messages has preferences over the receiver's beliefs about the sender's type. For example, suppose the receiver's actions depend on what he believes about the sender's "type," where type cannot be observed directly and the receiver's actions affect the sender's utility. If the sender's and receiver's interests are not aligned, the sender's incentive to lie is too great, and cheap talk will be meaningless. If, however, the interests of sender and receiver are correlated, there may be a cheap talk equilibrium that conveys information, where (roughly speaking) the amount of information conveyed is greater the more the interests of sender and receiver are correlated. In fact, there may be a "self-signaling" equilibrium in which there is no incentive to lie, and cheap talk will fully convey private information. (For example, given the choice of two discrete policies that are socially optimal in different states of the

---

[38] An far less technical introduction to cheap talk models is Farell and Rabin (1996).

world, a better-informed incumbent may prefer policy π_A in states of the world where it is in fact socially optimal and prefer policy π_B when it is socially optimal.) Even with some incentive to lie, cheap talk may convey information, as long as the incentive to lie is not too great (that is, there is a correlation of interests) and the sender is constrained to send imprecise messages.

Let us consider a model analogous to Stein's to show how policy announcements can be informative if the monetary authority is constrained to make imprecise announcements.[39] Consider a single-period model of unknown type where a policymaker's type is given by his inflation target $\tilde{\pi}$, rather than by the relative weight he places on inflation. Assume that types (that is, values of $\tilde{\pi}$) are uniformly distributed over $(-v, +v)$. Suppose further that the policymaker assigns a loss not only to the deviation of actual inflation from a target (as before), reflecting a cost to unanticipated inflation, but also to the deviation of *expected* inflation from a target level, reflecting the cost of expected inflation (such as economizing on cash balances). Given a policymaker's incentive for surprise inflation to lower unemployment, precise announcements of his target will not be credible, and hence will be uninformative. In contrast, imprecise announcements, in the sense of announcing a target range, can be credible and hence informative. Let the policymaker minimize the single-period loss subject to constraint (6.2), so that the loss function (analogous to (6.3)) becomes

$$\mathscr{L}(\pi, \pi^e; \tilde{\pi}) = -(\pi - \pi^e) + (\pi - \tilde{\pi})^2 + (\pi^e - \tilde{\pi})^2. \quad (6.37)$$

Note that the monetary authority's optimal inflation rate is $\tilde{\pi} + \frac{1}{2}$, but they would like people to expect a lower rate of inflation $\pi^e = \tilde{\pi} - \frac{1}{2}$, reflecting the incentive towards surprise inflation. Hence, no announcement of a (single-number) inflation target would be credible. Given the uniform distribution of $\tilde{\pi}$ over $(-v, +v)$ and the known inflationary preference of the government, the expected rate of inflation in the absence of an announcement is $\pi^e = \frac{1}{2}$. In this case, the loss of a government of type $\tilde{\pi}$ would be

$$\mathscr{L}(\tilde{\pi} + 1/2, 1/2; \tilde{\pi}) = \tilde{\pi}^2 - 2\tilde{\pi} + 1/2. \quad (6.38)$$

Can the monetary authority do better by announcing a range for its target rather than announcing no target (or announcing a single-number target

---

[39] We return to cheap talk models in Section 10.5 of Chapter 10 where we consider why a socially beneficial reform may not be adopted due to a policymaker being unable to convey to the public that the reform is really socially optimal.

which is not credible[40])? Yes and no. Target ranges can lead to announcements which are credible and partially revealing; there are types who would nonetheless prefer secrecy to announcing a target range.

Let us consider the case where a policymaker must announce that his target rate of inflation is either high or low. (In formal terms, we are considering a *partition equilibrium* with a single partition.) That is, there is some value $\hat{\pi}$ such that the monetary authority must announce either that its target rate of inflation is greater than $\hat{\pi}$ or that it is less than $\hat{\pi}$. Truthful announcements require that, given this choice, types with $\tilde{\pi} > \hat{\pi}$ strictly prefer to announce "$\tilde{\pi}$ is greater than $\hat{\pi}$," while all types $\tilde{\pi} < \hat{\pi}$ strictly prefer to announce "$\tilde{\pi}$ is less than $\hat{\pi}$," with the public forming its expectations of inflation accordingly. An announcement "$\tilde{\pi} < \hat{\pi}$" would lead to an expected rate of inflation $(\hat{\pi} - v)/2 + 1/2$ (that is, $\mathrm{E}(\tilde{\pi} \mid \text{"}\tilde{\pi} < \hat{\pi}\text{"}) + 1/2$), while an announcement "$\tilde{\pi} > \hat{\pi}$" would lead to an expected rate of inflation $(\hat{\pi} + v)/2 + 1/2$ (that is, $\mathrm{E}(\tilde{\pi} \mid \text{"}\tilde{\pi} > \hat{\pi}\text{"}) + 1/2$). A single-partition equilibrium requires that we find a type who is indifferent between announcing "high" or "low," that is, the type $\hat{\pi}$ for whom $\mathscr{L}(\hat{\pi} + 1/2, (\hat{\pi} + v)/2 + 1/2, \hat{\pi}) = \mathscr{L}(\hat{\pi} + 1/2, (\hat{\pi} - v)/2 + 1/2, \hat{\pi})$. One can easily calculate that the value of $\hat{\pi}$ such that this condition holds is $\hat{\pi} = 2$. Hence, if the policymaker can announce either that his target inflation rate is in the range $[-v, 2]$ or in the range $[2, +v]$, his announcement will be truthful. Hence, imprecise announcements can convey information in a world where precise announcements would not.

Why do imprecise announcements convey more information than precise announcements? Since a policymaker finds it optimal to engineer a monetary surprise, he has the incentive to try to manipulate inflation expectations. He will use inflation announcements in the attempt to induce the public to expect an inflation rate which is below the rate that will actually obtain. As long as the public uses the inflation announcements in forming their expectations, the policymaker has the incentive to understate his target. The problem with precise announcements is that they are continuous rather than discrete. With continuous announcements, the policymaker will always have the incentive to (at least) marginally reduce his announced target, that is, to "shade" his announcement downward. Since the public is aware of this incentive, they will be skeptical about inflation announcements. When announcements must be for discrete ranges, policymakers who lie about their intentions must lie by a discrete amount. The impossibility of "marginal lying" means that truthtelling may be preferred to lying, since a large lie may reduce welfare relative to telling the truth (though would be dominated by a small lie).

---

[40] In Section 5.4 of Chapter 5, we considered achieving the optimal rate of inflation via delegation to a monetary authority who is penalized for not hitting his target. Correct structuring of the penalties could induce the monetary authority to make credible announcements. Here, it is assumed there are no explicit penalties for not hitting the target $\tilde{\pi}$.

What happens if announcements are less imprecise, in the sense of allowing the policymaker more choices of ranges to announce? (That is, there is a larger, but still finite, number of partitions of the range $[-v, +v]$.) Will the size of ranges converge to infinitesimally small, so that in the limit, announcing a range will be equivalent to a precise announcement? By repeating the above exercise in finding the optimal dividing line for partitions when there are many of them, one can show that as the number of partitions becomes large, target ranges will become very fine close to 2 but be progressively coarser as one moves towards $+v$ or $-v$.

Central banks, in fact, generally announce target ranges for monetary aggregates and interest rates, rather than precise targets. The standard argument is that uncertainty about future economic developments combined with less than perfect control over both aggregates and interest rates means that it makes little sense to give precise targets; announcing target ranges reflects the reality of imprecise control over the economy. The "cheap talk" result given above suggests a very different rationale. Even when there is no problem of uncertainty or imperfect control, so that the central bank could (and does, in this model) achieve its desired inflation rate, announcement of target ranges may be optimal in the sense that precise announcements actually convey less information.[41]

One major caveat to the result must be noted. In a single-partition equilibrium, for example, a type near $\hat{\pi}$ prefers total secrecy. If the choice is one or the other, he will make a credible announcement. But he prefers no announcement and $\pi^e = 1/2$. We leave it to the reader to demonstrate that, in the single-partition case, any type for whom $\tilde{\pi}$ is sufficiently close to $\hat{\pi}$ will prefer secrecy to making an announcement.

6.10. CONCLUSIONS

In this chapter, we have studied in detail the use of policy to demonstrate one's intentions for future policy choices, and thus to influence expectations. Though issues of reputation and credibility are much broader than monetary policy, we concentrated on the single issue of inflation policy for two reasons. First, focusing on a single type of model clarifies the exposition and is probably an aid to understanding difficult concepts. Second, the majority of the literature on reputation in macroeconomics has looked at monetary policy. Specifically, we looked at a number of models of building a reputation for anti-inflationary behavior, realizing, however, that reputation is not the full story. Our concentration on monetary policy means that this chapter could also be considered an applications chapter, somewhat

---

[41] Bhattacharya and Weller (1997) present a model of intervention in the foreign exchange market and argue that secrecy about the scale of an intervention is always desirable, whereas secrecy about the target is only sometimes desirable.

analogous to those in Part IV of the book, where we concentrate on a number of applications of political economy to specific fields.

On a more technical rather than conceptual level, the chapter has served as an introduction to concepts in game theory, many of which are central to modern political economy and which we will encounter again and again in the book. The chapter has been quite technical, as the concepts and methods it has introduced are themselves quite technical. It is difficult if not impossible to understand questions of credibility and reputation without a technical understanding of game-theoretic concepts, at least on a basic level. We will be concerned with questions of reputation and credibility repeatedly in the rest of the book. The importance of credibility justified the space devoted to it here.

PART III

Heterogeneity and Conflicting Interests

Elections and Changes of Policymakers

> Let me now ... warn you in the most solemn manner
> against the baneful effects of the spirit of party.
>
> —*George Washington, Farewell Address, 1796*

> Long before the appointed day [of a Presidential election]
> arrives, the election becomes the greatest, and one might
> say the only, affair occupying men's minds....
> The President ... no longer rules in the interest of the state,
> but in that of his own reelection; he prostrates himself
> before the majority, and often, instead of resisting their
> passions as duty requires, he hastens to anticipate
> their caprices.
>
> —*Alexis de Tocqueville,* Democracy in America, 1848

7.1. INTRODUCTION

The standard model of optimal policy choice has a single planner who chooses policies over the entire lifetime of the economy, whether infinite or finite. Much as policymakers might like to stay in office forever (and some politicians indeed make heroic efforts to do so), a policymaker is generally chosen for a finite term and knows he will eventually be replaced by another policymaker. The possibility that there will be a change in policymakers has a number of effects on macroeconomic variables. What is crucial from the point of view of an incumbent policymaker is not the finite length of his term *per se*, but the knowledge that he may be replaced in the future by another policymaker. We thus begin with the probability of being retained in office q as the key variable, where q may vary from 1 (as in the models of Part II of the book) to zero, representing the case where a policymaker knows with certainty that he will be replaced.[1]

There are three main ways a policymaker's behavior may be affected by uncertainty about his prospects of being retained in office. First, he may choose policies to *influence* the probability q of remaining in office. If a policymaker can influence this probability, he will be led to choose policies to try to increase q, which may have significant effects on economic outcomes. Second, when there is a possibility that a policymaker will be replaced by someone with different preferences (including a certainty of replacement in the next election, that is, $q = 0$), he will have the incentive to choose policies in such a way as to influence his successor's policy choices. Finally, even if the policymaker can affect neither the probability of being retained nor the policies of his successor, uncertainty about who holds office can have significant effects on economic outcomes. We discuss these in turn.

When a policymaker can influence his chances of remaining in power, a key question is whether the objective of the policymaker simply to remain in office, or to implement a specific program. A policymaker who has objectives which differ from other potential policymakers is termed *partisan*, while one whose primary goal is to remain in office is usually termed *opportunistic* or *office-motivated*. If two policymakers are both purely office-motivated, then they care simply about the distribution of the rents associated with holding office. These rents may be as direct as payoffs and other tangible perks, or more subtle things such as the boost to one's ego that derives from the adulation accorded to leaders. When in office, office-motivated policymakers will choose identical policies if faced with identical circumstances. Partisan policymakers, in contrast, will choose different policies on issues they care about even in identical circumstances. The distinction between partisan and opportunistic motivations for seeking office parallels the distinction made in Chapter 1 between two types of heterogeneity and the conflicts they induce: *ex-ante* heterogeneity, implying conflict over preferred policies, and *ex-post* heterogeneity, implying a conflict over the spoils of office.

These polar characterizations are inaccurate. On the one hand, few officeholders care simply about clinging to power with no concern about what policies are implemented. To put it a bit differently, it makes little sense to *always* conserve one's political resources or popularity for another day or another battle. On the other hand, politicians must win elections in order to implement their preferred policies, so that even the most partisan

---

[1] Knowing that one will be replaced is not identical to knowing the length of one's term in a model of finite terms of office, since a policymaker may be certain of losing the next election, but be uncertain of when it will be. (For example, in the most recent election in Britain, the incumbent Conservatives were seen as sure to lose the election, well before the date of the election was known.) If we define q as the probability of being in office in the next "period," the analysis encompasses both an uncertain date of election and an uncertain election outcome.

policymaker will sometimes display opportunistic or office-motivated be-havior. Hence, one may argue that policymakers are opportunistic at some points in order to be in a position to implement their preferred policies later on. This second view seems far more convincing in the majority of cases, and suggests that in reality policymakers should be viewed as combining opportunistic and partisan motivations.

The mechanism most studied for choosing policymakers is elections. This need not be the only mechanism, since the authority to make decisions may be vested in a policymaker by a single individual, or by a small group. Many government officials, for example, serve at the discre-tion of a single superior. No matter who chooses the policymaker, his ability to remain in office will depend on his ability to carry out policies which maximize the utility of those who choose him. Thus, we have a principal–agent problem, that is, a situation in which decisions affecting the welfare of one individual or group (the principal) are made by someone else (the agent); the key question in a principal–agent problem is how the agent can be led to make decisions beneficial to the principal. Applied to elections, for example, in which the voter is the principal and the elected official the agent, one would ask: what determines the repre-sentative principal's decision to retain (that is, re-elect) the agent; how do the actions of the agent affect this choice of the principal; when is the threat of electoral defeat effective in inducing the agent to act in the best interests of the principals? Viewing the question of how politicians can influence the probability that they are kept in office as a principal–agent problem is extremely useful in some cases, less so in others.

The principal–agent paradigm is most useful when there is a single principal (or a group of principals that can be easily represented as a single principal) evaluating the behavior of a single agent, as in the case of a government official whose sole goal is to "please" his superior. The common question of whether he is both willing and able to do so becomes, in more formal terms, a question of the agent's objective function in comparison with the principal's, and of his ability to translate actions into outcomes. Under imperfect information, one then has the standard incen-tive and monitoring problems from the principal–agent literature. Such problems are not always easy, but there is a well-developed theory, which was discussed in brief in Chapter 2. The reader interested in further detail is referred to chapter 7 of Fudenberg and Tirole (1991), among many possible references.

When there are many principals whose preferences are not fully known and whose behavior cannot easily be collapsed to that of a single principal, and when the principals choose among different possible agents, applying the standard principal–agent models is more difficult. But this description is the essence of elections. The same issues arise, such as the policymaker's "competence," and the extent to which he is partisan as opposed to purely opportunistic; elections have the role of choosing the agent who is the most competent and/or whose objectives best match those of the electorate, and of disciplining officeholders who fail to perform according to either of these criteria. But the analysis is far more complicated: what determines how each individual votes; and, given how votes are aggregated, how can the "principal" control the actions of the policymaker? Put another way, what is the relation between the actions of the policymaker and his electoral success? One must be careful not to let the paradigm of the principal–agent problem conceal more than it reveals. To summarize the discussion of the last several paragraphs, in analyzing models where a policymaker can influence his chances of remaining in office, there are many modeling choices to be made on the nature of the policymaker, the principal who chooses him, and the choice mechanism.

A policymaker who concentrates not on the possibility of remaining in office, but on the possibility that he will be replaced, faces a different set of incentives in choosing policy. If he is both partisan and interested in outcomes after his term ends, he is concerned about being replaced by someone with different preferences. He therefore has the incentive to choose policies in order to influence the policies of his successors. Generally speaking, there are two ways this can be done, both of which are widely observed in practice. First, he can choose policies to try to increase the probability that a successor with similar preferences will be elected. Since this will almost certainly be someone from his own party (or perhaps even someone from his own administration), the issues are very similar to those discussed above, namely, incentives to maximize the probability of re-election. Second, even if the incumbent cannot affect what kind of successor will be chosen, he can attempt to influence his policy choices. How can this be done? A policymaker can influence the choices of a future policymaker by altering the constraints he will face. More specifically, his choice of specific state variables, such as the level of government debt, will affect the constraints faced by a future policymaker. Models of this sort can be seen as an application of the results on debt as a commitment device discussed in Chapter 5 to the case of multiple policymakers.

If a policymaker can affect neither the probability of being retained nor the policies of his successor, uncertainty about who holds office can nonetheless affect policy choices, though in a less direct way. When potential officeholders differ in the policies they would carry out, uncertainty about who will be in power implies uncertainty about what future policy will be. If the effects of policy depend on the extent to which it is not fully anticipated, uncertainty about the outcomes of elections may affect the choice of policy *after* an election is decided. That is, uncertainty about electoral outcomes may itself affect the constraint set a policymaker faces when he takes office. This possibility is crucial to the workings of many models of the political business cycle which rely on the notion that only unanticipated policy matters. Moreover, since uncertainty about future policies, and hence economic outcomes, may greatly affect the consequences of current policy, such uncertainty can influence current policy choices. The effect of uncertainty about future policies on current outcomes was analyzed at length in Chapter 2. On a general level, the results of that analysis will have implications for the policy choices of forward-looking policymakers who are uncertain about who their successors may be.

7.2. ELECTIONS AND POLICYMAKER PERFORMANCE

Elections as a Disciplining Device

Elections are meant to make officeholders accountable to the electorate. They allow voters to choose the candidate they see as "best," either in the sense of being most competent or as being closest to a voter's preferred ideological positions. They may also serve as a disciplining device: if an incumbent's poor performance is punished by a subsequent electoral loss, elections can help to control a policymaker's performance while he is in office. That is, if performance reflects not simply innate characteristics (such as ideology and competence) or external events, but also lack of opportunistic behavior by policymakers, the threat of no re-election may serve to limit such opportunism. Put more formally, an officeholder may be thought of as the agent of the voters, the principals. If there is asymmetric information about some aspect of the relation between an incumbent's actions and performance, there is a *moral hazard* problem once a candidate is elected; the voters, as principals, may try to control the agent's behavior by threatening to replace him.

Barro (1973) is an early paper that considers formally how the possibility of re-election may induce an incumbent to act in the interest of the voters rather than in his own interests. Barro presents a perfect-information, finite-horizon model, similar to the models presented in Section 6.3 in Chapter 6. The basic economic problem is the provision of a public good g financed by taxation, where the optimal level of the public good is $\tilde{g}$. The level of the public good is chosen by a self-interested policymaker, who, in the absence of any electoral control, would choose a level of spending on the public good $\hat{g}$ which is too large from the point of view of the representative voter (that is, $\hat{g} > \tilde{g}$). Electoral control takes the form of setting a level $\bar{g} < \hat{g}$, such that the incumbent is re-elected if he chooses public spending $g \leq \bar{g}$ and is not re-elected if $g > \bar{g}$, where $\bar{g}$ is chosen by the voters. $\bar{g}$ is chosen to be high enough to ensure that the incumbent chooses a level of public good supply $\bar{g}$ rather than $\hat{g}$, where the critical value of $\bar{g}$ will depend on the length of the term of office, the number of terms the incumbent would like to stay in office (representing the value of re-election), the incumbent's discount rate, and the difference between his pay while in office and what he could earn out of office. (A formal representation of this approach is presented in the next subsection.) Barro then considers how both equilibrium behavior and utility of the representative voter would change with changes in the structural parameters of the model, such as the frequency of elections.

Though Barro's model was seminal for modeling the effect of electoral control on economic outcomes, a number of assumptions limit its applicability. First, the assumption that a policymaker desires only a finite number of terms in office would seem to imply that elections play no disciplining role in his last desired term of office. (This is identical to the problem of the equilibrium "unraveling" from the last period, as discussed in Chapter 6.) To address this problem, Barro suggests either the possibility of appointment to some other office after his final term, dependent on his behavior in the final term, or (following Becker and Stigler [1974]), the loss of his pension if an incumbent misbehaves in his final term. Second, the assumption of a "representative" voter may seem to be a logical modeling strategy, but it actually has significant implications, as we discuss below. We shall see in our discussion of the Ferejohn model below that having multiple principals and distributional conflict between them (*ex-post* heterogeneity) may completely change the results. Hence, modeling the electorate as a single representative voter may lead to misleading conclusions. This point is especially relevant in studying the implications of elections for economic outcomes, since the whole point of choice mechanisms is the aggregation of nonhomogeneous preferences into a single policy choice. Hence, as discussed in the introduction, though it is tempting to apply many of the results of the principal–agent literature to elections, one should be quite cautious in this respect.

Ferejohn's Model of Electoral Control

Ferejohn (1986) presents a model of how elections may control incumbent performance which addresses some of the shortcomings of Barro's model. Policymakers have an explicitly infinite horizon (so there is no problem of the equilibrium "unraveling" from the last period), based on the argument given at the end of the previous paragraph that policymakers may look beyond the end of their possible terms of office. Only the performance, and not the actions, of the officeholder is observable, so that the model is one of imperfect monitoring. All candidates are identical in their competence and ideology, so that not re-electing a candidate means that he will be replaced by another candidate of the same "type," meaning the same competence and ideology. The problem is one of policing moral hazard, that is, ensuring good behavior. All voters are identical both *ex ante* and *ex post*, an assumption Ferejohn later shows to be crucial.

With homogeneous voters, the problem can be set up using the basic principal–agent paradigm. The set-up is simple. The current officeholder observes the realization of a bounded random variable $\xi > 0$, drawn from a known cumulative distribution $F(\xi)$. This realization is observed only by the policymaker. On the basis of ξ, he then chooses a level of effort l. The policymaker single-period payoff is

$$U^P(l_t, \xi_t) = \chi - \phi(l_t), \tag{7.1}$$

where χ is the utility of holding office for a single term, effort l will depend on ξ, and $\phi(\cdot)$ is a positive, convex function, where $\phi(0) = 0$. The single-period utility of the representative voter is

$$U^V(l_t, \xi_t) = l_t \xi_t, \tag{7.2}$$

where the voter observes only the product $l\xi$, that is, the performance of the policymaker. The key idea is that performance depends on two factors, one random and one reflecting policymaker effort, with voters being unable to distinguish which accounts for a good outcome.

The optimal decision rules for both representative voter and incumbent are straightforward. If the utility $l_t \xi_t$ in period t is high enough, the representative voter returns the incumbent to office, where the cutoff levels of utility are $\hat{U}_t^V, \hat{U}_{t+1}^V, \ldots$. The voter employs what is known as a **retrospective voting** rule, in that his vote depends on past observed performance. The incumbent's decision rule is a similar cut-off rule, where the lower is ξ_t, the higher must be (costly) effort. Hence, if ξ_t is below some cut-off $\hat{\xi}_t$, the policymaker supplies no effort (that is, $l(\xi_t) = 0$) and is sure to be turned out of office. Otherwise, he supplies the minimal amount of effort to be retained, namely, $l(\xi_t) = \hat{U}_t^V / \xi_t$.

To characterize the equilibrium, the cut-off levels $\hat{\xi}_t$ and $\hat{U}_t^V$ must be specified for all t. To specify $\hat{\xi}_t$, note that the incumbent will supply positive effort as long as this gives him higher utility than supplying zero effort. Denoting the present discounted utility of being in office in $t + 1$ by $\Omega_{t+1}^P[\text{in}]$, and the utility of being out of office in $t + 1$ by $\Omega_{t+1}^P[\text{out}]$, effort will be supplied as long as

$$\chi - \phi\left(\frac{\hat{U}_t^V}{\xi_t}\right) + \beta \Omega_{t+1}^P[\text{in}] \geq \chi - \phi(0) + \beta \Omega_{t+1}^P[\text{out}], \tag{7.3}$$

where β is the discount factor. Rearranging (7.3), one derives a value $\hat{\xi}_t$ such that the disutility of supplying the minimal level of effort needed to be re-elected is just equal to the discounted value of being in office rather than out of office next period. This implies

$$\hat{\xi}_t = \frac{\hat{U}_t^V}{\kappa_t^{\text{INC}}}, \tag{7.4}$$

where $\kappa_t^{\text{INC}} = \phi^{(-1)}[\beta(\Omega_{t+1}^P[\text{in}] - \Omega_{t+1}^P[\text{out}])]$. One intuitive implication of (7.4) is that if the incumbent assigns a low marginal value to staying in office, so that $\hat{\xi}_t$ is large, he will act opportunistically and ensure his own defeat even if re-election were possible. We return to this observation below.

On the basis of (7.4), the cut-off levels $\hat{U}_t^V$, that is, the optimal retrospective voting rule, can be found by the voter maximizing his expected utility. All potential officeholders are the same, so expected utility depends not on whether the incumbent is re-elected, but only on the effort that the incumbent puts in, which, in turn, depends on the realization of ξ_t relative to $\hat{\xi}_t$. When $\xi_t < \hat{\xi}_t$, policymaker effort is zero, so that voter utility U_t^V is zero as well. When $\xi_t \geq \hat{\xi}_t$, which occurs with probability $1 - F(\hat{\xi}_t)$, the policymaker exerts the minimum effort needed for re-election. Using (7.4), expected present discounted utility may thus be written

$$\Omega_t^V = \sum_{s=0}^{\infty} \beta^s \left(1 - F\left[\hat{U}_{t+s}^V / \kappa_{t+s}^{\mathrm{INC}}\right]\right)\hat{U}_{t+s}^V. \tag{7.5}$$

The optimal sequence $\hat{U}_t^V, \hat{U}_{t+1}^V, \dots$ is then found from the first-order conditions implied by differentiating expected utility (7.5) with respect to the $\hat{U}_t^V$. This yields the cut-off utility levels as functions of the cumulative distribution $F(\xi)$ and the κ_t^{INC}, which in turn depends on β, the function $\phi(\cdot)$, and the difference $\Omega_{t+1}^P[\mathrm{in}] - \Omega_{t+1}^P[\mathrm{out}]$. The last is especially important in relating the value of holding office with the ability of voters to discipline policymakers for poor performance. For example, if the ξ_t are independent, identically distributed random variables, the optimal retrospective voting rule is given by

$$\hat{U}_t^V = \frac{1 - F(\hat{\xi}_t)}{F'(\hat{\xi}_t)} \kappa_t^{\mathrm{INC}}$$

$$= \frac{1 - F(\hat{\xi}_t)}{F'(\hat{\xi}_t)} \phi^{(-1)}\left[\beta\left(\Omega_{t+1}^P[\mathrm{in}] - \Omega_{t+1}^P[\mathrm{out}]\right)\right], \tag{7.6}$$

where $F'(\xi)$ is the density function associated with $F(\xi)$.

As already indicated, the equilibrium depends crucially on $\Omega_{t+1}^P[\mathrm{in}] - \Omega_{t+1}^P[\mathrm{out}]$. This difference depends not only on the value of holding office χ, but also on the probability of regaining office once voted out. The electorate's utility is higher the higher is χ, the simple value of holding office in any period. Hence, providing higher "perks" for an officeholder may end up eliciting better behavior as far as the voters are concerned, a proposition which should be intuitive. The higher is the probability of regaining office once voted out, the lower is the difference $\Omega_{t+1}^P[\mathrm{in}] - \Omega_{t+1}^P[\mathrm{out}]$, so the *worse off* are the voters. Intuitively, it is the fear of losing office that disciplines an incumbent. The easier it is to regain office once it is lost, the lower is this fear, and hence the lower is the electorate's control of incumbents.

Given our assumptions about infinitely lived politicians, the formulation of the problem implies that the $\hat{U}_t^V$ are stationary. Combining stationary versions of (7.4) and, for example, (7.6) would yield the stationary values of $\hat{U}^V$ and $\hat{\xi}$. Ferejohn (1986) presents some specific examples.

When the electorate is heterogeneous, the results may be quite different. Ferejohn shows that in the presence of what we term *ex-post* heterogeneity, an incumbent may be able to play voters off against one another. Suppose there are N voters and that each voter cares not about total performance $l\xi$, but only about his share of the pie, call it ν^i, where the sum of the ν^i equals $l\xi$. Each voter then has a cut-off level $\hat{U}^i$ (assumed stationary without loss of generality) and votes to re-elect the incumbent only if $\nu^i \geq \hat{U}^i$. Ferejohn argues that in a majority voting equilibrium, all the $\hat{U}^i$ will equal zero, as will the incumbent's effort level l. The argument runs as follows. Given the voters' choices of the $\hat{U}^i$, the incumbent will distribute the ν^i to assemble a majority coalition N^{maj} that minimizes the sum of payouts to members of the coalition, subject to the constraint that $\nu^i \geq \hat{U}^i$ for all $i \in N^{\mathrm{maj}}$. (Obviously, this constraint will hold with equality.) Then any voter j *not* in the majority coalition would have been better off to offer $\hat{U}^j < \max\{\hat{U}^i \mid i \in N^{\mathrm{maj}}\}$. Hence, the equilibrium will be such that $\hat{U}^i = 0$ for all i, so that effort l supplied by the incumbent will also equal zero. Hence, if voters cannot collude, the incumbent can play them off against each other, so that he is entirely uncontrolled by the electorate. The distributive conflict among the voters leads to an outcome where all of them suffer, relative to where the incumbent is induced to provide satisfactory performance. Moreover, since challengers for office are unable to make binding commitments, any promise by a challenger to provide positive performance would not be credible; once in office, he would face the same motivation to provide zero effort as the current incumbent.

Though the conclusion looks quite bleak for the ability of voters to control incumbent performance through elections, things are not quite as bad as they seem. The problem in the previous paragraph arises because voters base their choices on their *individual* benefit from incumbent performance, allowing the incumbent to exploit the ever-present conflict over distribution.[2] To use the political vernacular, voters "vote [according to] their own pocketbooks." However, suppose that individuals vote on the basis of aggregate performance (that is, use a **sociotropic** voting rule), rather than individual benefits. This reduces the ability of the incumbent to exploit distributional conflict. Then, retrospective voting strategies can have a disciplining effect. Ferejohn formalizes this idea by showing that if

---

[2] In Section 8.3 of Chapter 8, we consider the related issue of how incumbents can maximize their electoral support by targeting transfers to specific interest groups.

voters use expected aggregate output as their voting criterion, so that each voter acts as if he were representative, the equilibrium performance levels derived above can be induced. There appears to be significant evidence that voters do vote retrospectively on the basis of aggregate macroeconomic performance. A number of researchers, starting with Fair (1978) for the United States, present evidence that aggregate economic conditions strongly affect voting in presidential and legislative elections. Using survey data which asks about the influence of individual and aggregate economic conditions, Lewis-Beck (1988) argues persuasively that the latter more strongly influences voting than the former, that is, that voters are more likely to vote sociotropically than on the basis of their own pocketbooks. We return to this phenomenon in the next section.

7.3. THE OPPORTUNISTIC POLITICAL BUSINESS CYCLE

For better or worse (most probably the latter), a politician's desire to win the next election sometimes seems to swamp all other considerations in choosing policy. Hence, while the changes in policy induced by elections (or the fear of losing them) can be viewed as demonstrating accountability in a democratic system, they can also be seen as introducing significant inefficiencies into policymaking. Though the first formal models of pre-electoral manipulation of the economy appeared only twenty-five years ago, both politicians and voters have been aware of the phenomenon probably for as long as there have been elections. Models of economic cycles induced by the political cycle are termed models of the **political business cycle** (PBC); models which focus on the desire to win elections as determinants of policy and the expected effect of such policies are termed models of the **opportunistic** PBC.[3] However, the phenomenon of the desire for popular support largely determining policy choice is not limited to models of political cycles, nor are all PBC models driven by this factor. For example, the design of comprehensive reform and transition programs is similarly heavily influenced by the need to ensure popular support, as will be considered in detail in Chapters 10 and 13; uncertainty about the outcome of elections in itself is an important part of the literature on political cycles. Nonetheless, the opportunistic desire to influence election outcomes is a good place to start. The key question is in terms of outcomes: how does electoral competition between incumbents and challengers influence aggregate measures of economic activity?

---

[3] In some of the literature, the term "political business cycle" is used to refer to opportunistic manipulation of the economy by incumbents before an election, with the terms "political business cycle" and "opportunistic political business cycle" being synonymous. We use the term to mean any economic cycle induced by the electoral cycle, whether due to opportunistic or partisan factors.

Early Empirical Work

As already indicated, the view that economic activity around elections is influenced by the incumbent's desire to be re-elected is by no means new.[4] However, current interest in politically induced business cycles began in the early to mid-1970s, stimulated by Kramer's (1971) study of economic determinants of United States congressional voting, Tufte's (1975, 1978) influential studies, Nordhaus's (1975) theoretical model of the political business cycle, and most probably, the 1972 presidential election in the United States.[5] We begin with a review of the early empirical evidence in support of opportunistic electoral behavior by politicians, deferring until later discussion of underlying theoretical models and subsequent econometric analysis.

The classic study in this area is Tufte's (1978) *Political Control of the Economy*, a book that should be read by any student of political business cycles. Following Tufte, one can summarize the basis of the opportunistic PBC model by two premises: economic conditions before an election significantly affect voters' choices; and, politicians, being well aware of this fact, attempt to take advantage of it. The latter will be evidenced by cyclical movements in policy instruments and in measures of economic activity that correlate with the political cycle and peak around election time. Early studies argued that there is significant empirical support for both premises.

Economic Conditions and Election Outcomes

Kramer (1971) is perhaps the first careful empirical study of how economic conditions affect voting behavior. He concluded that economic fluctuations have an important influence on the results of U.S. congressional elections, a result confirmed by Tufte (1975).[6] Specifically, Kramer regressed votes received by the incumbent party on two measures of performance in the year of the election, the growth rate of real per capita income and the rate of inflation in that year, and found they were both significant determinants of vote totals. The most influential early work is probably that of Fair (1978), who finds similar results for the United States in this and subsequent articles (1982, 1988). In his original article, Fair looked at presidential elections from 1916 through 1976, arguing that if voters hold the party that holds the presidency accountable for economic events, their influence should be seen most strongly in presidential elections. He considers 16

[4] Tufte (1978, p. 3) begins his book with a quote from 1814, "A Government is not supported a hundredth part so much by the constant, uniform, quiet prosperity of the country as by those damned spurts which Pitt used to have just in the nick of time."

[5] Kramer (1971) presents a review of various early papers on the connections between politics and fluctuations in economic activity.

[6] Though most studies confirm the basic results, Stigler (1973) concluded that congressional election results are not affected by economic fluctuations. See also Okun's (1973) comment on Stigler, as well as Arcelus and Meltzer (1975) and Bloom and Price (1975).

possible measures of economic performance in a presidential term: four basic measures of economic performance—the growth rate of real per capita GNP, the change in the GNP deflator, the level of unemployment, and the change in unemployment—over four retrospective horizons: the year of the election, the two-year period before the election, the three-year period before the election, and the entire four-year period before the election. He then regresses Democratic vote totals in the 16 presidential elections in his sample on one or two of these variables at a time, as well as a time trend and a party dummy. (Testing only one or two measures at a time is dictated by a lack of degrees of freedom, a recurring problem in empirical tests of PBC models.)

Fair's (1978) results may be summarized as follows. Economic performance before an election does matter for voting outcomes. The change in real economic activity in the year of the election, as measured either by the change in real per capita GNP or the change in unemployment in the election year, appear to have an important effect on votes for president. He finds that a 1% increase in the growth rate increases the incumbent's vote total by about 1%. (Further evidence suggests it may be the growth of real per capita GNP in the second and third quarters of the election year, but data limitations prevent him from drawing any definitive conclusions about what part of the election year is most important in determining voter behavior.) Given the growth of economic activity, he finds that the other 14 measures of macroeconomic performance contribute little, though the best of the other measures is the inflation rate in the two-year period before the election, as measured by the change in the GNP deflator. A second key finding is that voters appear to have a high discount rate on past economic performance; they do not look back more than a year or two. Finally, Fair argues that statistically, the effect of variables on votes is the same for Democratic or Republican incumbents.

Numerous other articles find similar results on the importance of pre-election conditions on voting patterns in both the United States and other countries. Looking at voting or popularity functions, Lewis-Beck (1988) finds that the sort of results that Kramer and Fair report for the United States hold in Britain, France, West Germany, Italy, and Spain as well. Madsen (1980) reports similar results for Denmark, Norway, and Sweden. Many studies are summarized in Tufte (1978) and in Alesina and Rosenthal (1995).[7]

---

[7] One early study which disputes this point is by Golden and Poterba (1980), who look at the effect of economic conditions on the president's popularity, as measured by the response to the Gallup poll question, "Do you approve or disapprove of the way Mr. _____ is handling his job as president?" By regressing the within-quarter averages of the responses on measures of economic activity in the previous three to six quarters (as well as on some incumbency variables), they find that increasing popularity by one point requires substantial stimulus. Two key differences should be noted between this study and those of Fair and others: first, popularity in opinion polls is not equivalent to actual votes; more importantly, the Golden and Poterba results concern the whole presidential term, not just the period before elections, so that it may have less relevance for pre-electoral manipulation *per se.*

In discussing the effects of economic conditions on election outcomes, one final point concerns the influence of aggregate versus individual economic conditions on voting. Lewis-Beck (1988) argues that though economic influences are important, individuals do not appear to vote on the basis of their own personal economic situation ("narrow pocketbook" voting) but rather on the basis of national economic performance (socio-tropic voting). On the basis of careful analysis of survey data, he finds this both for the United States and for legislative elections in the Western European countries he examines. Given aggregate economic conditions, he argues that "simple pocketbook evaluations have a negligible impact on individual vote choice." (1988, p. 57) He suggests that in judging performance or competence of an incumbent, a voter realizes that aggregate economic outcomes give more accurate information than one's own economic situation.

Opportunistic Manipulation

As far as the response of politicians to these voting patterns, early studies considered the variability of both policies and outcomes in response to election timing. Let us consider them in turn. There appear to be many indicators (often anecdotal) that politicians often try to manipulate the economy to improve their electoral prospects.[8] (To what extent it is successful is less clear, a point to which we return below.) Tufte (1978, chapter 2) presents a good bit of case-study type evidence on the timing of transfer payments, with governments moving the distribution of checks one or two months forward in election years to arrive just before the election. Most striking is the case of Richard Nixon (whom Rogoff [1988] termed "the all-time hero of political business cycles"[9]) prior to the 1972 election. The full-employment budget deficit, in balance in 1970, rose to $10 billion in 1971 and $12 billion in 1972. In 1971, Social Security benefits and personal tax exemptions were increased, while the investment tax credit was restored. Manipulation in 1972 appears even more striking: two weeks prior to the election, there was a 20% increase in Social Security benefits, announced in a letter from President Nixon to 24,760,000 Social Security recipients.[10] The fiscal overdose can be better understood against the

[8] "Election year economics," or its equivalent, has become a common term in many languages.

[9] Rogoff may be unfair to earlier politicians—consider the quote from Tufte (1978) in footnote 4.

[10] Under the headline "Higher social security payments" it was written: "Your social security payment has been increased by 20 percent, starting with this month's check, by a new statute enacted by the Congress and signed into law by President Richard Nixon on July 1, 1972. The President also signed into law a provision which will allow your social security benefits to increase automatically if the cost of living goes up. Automatic benefit increases will be added to your check in future years according to the conditions set out in that law." One should note that the Democrats were strong supporters of this stimulus. The increase in Social Security benefits, for example, was passed by a Democratic Congress.

backdrop of the 1960 elections, when Nixon narrowly lost the race for president, in his eyes because of a weak economy. (See Nixon's *Six Crises*, as quoted by Tufte, 1978, p. 6.) Given his experience in 1960, Nixon was taking no chances in 1972.

Tufte also argues strongly that in industrialized countries, economic activity exhibits a clear political cycle. For the United States from 1948 to 1976, he asserts that, with the exception of the Eisenhower years in the 1950s, political business cycles have consisted of a two-year cycle in "real disposable income, with accelerations in even-numbered years and decelerations in odd-numbered years," as well as a four-year cycle "in the unemployment rate, with downturns in unemployment in the months before a presidential election and upturns in the unemployment rate usually beginning from twelve to eighteen months after the election." (1978, p. 27) He similarly argues there is clear evidence of a political cycle in outcomes in other democratic countries as well, in that "short-run accelerations in real disposable income per capita were more likely to occur in election years than in years without elections" (1978, p. 11) in a sample of 27 countries.[11]

The Nordhaus Model of the Political Business Cycle

Opportunistic PBC models generally assume that all voters are identical, so that the electoral manipulation on which the cycle depends is aimed at the representative voter. With no conflict of interests between voters, it makes sense to model the representative voter as basing his decisions on macroeconomic aggregates. Opportunistic PBC models stress another conflict of interests, namely, between a less-than-fully informed (or fully rational) electorate on the one hand, and a self-interested incumbent on the other. Nordhaus (1975) presented one of the first formal models of the Political Business Cycle in which opportunistic policymakers stimulate the economy before the election to reduce unemployment, with the inflationary cost of such a policy coming only after.[12] Opportunism means that the

---

[11] The behavior of the incumbent Likud prior to the Israeli elections of 1982 would appear to provide another good example of especially strong pre-electoral fiscal manipulation. In the months before the election, there were sharp but temporary reductions in previously heavy taxes on imported durables. Imports of durable goods grew in 1982 by 24%, after what was already a sharp growth of 80% in 1981. Ben-Porath (1975) shows convincingly that opportunistic policymaking in light of elections was quite consistent over the period 1952–1973. Devaluations were postponed until after elections; often tax cuts were implemented before, but tax increases only after elections.

[12] Kalecki (1943) presented an early explicit model of the political business cycle; the political nature of economic fluctuations was recognized by Schumpeter (1939) in his monumental work on business cycles. Simultaneously with Nordhaus, Lindbeck (1976) presented a similar idea; soon after, McRae (1977) also presented a formal model of the political business cycle.

policymaker himself has no preferences over inflation and unemployment. The structure of the economy is summarized by a downward-sloping Phillips curve, yielding a trade-off between unemployment and unexpected inflation, and slow adjustment of inflation expectations. Voters have a preference for both low unemployment and low inflation, but in evaluating incumbents on the basis of macroeconomic performance they have short memories and no foresight. The slow adjustment of inflation expectations to economic stimulation, combined with myopic voters, allows an opportunistic incumbent to manipulate macroeconomic time paths to his electoral benefit.

The Basic Model

The Nordhaus model, as well as many similar models, is based on the same two-equation model as the Barro–Gordon example in Section 4.4 of Chapter 4, though the loss function enters the analysis somewhat differently.[13] The objective of the policymaker is to maximize his probability of re-election, where voting behavior is retrospective, in that it depends on economic performance under the incumbent in the past. Economic performance in a period is measured by the behavior of inflation and unemployment, so that voter dissatisfaction in any period can be represented by a loss function, as in the Barro–Gordon model. For computational purposes, it will be easier to use the linear version of the loss function presented in Chapters 4 and 5, namely,

$$\mathscr{L}_t = U_t + \theta \frac{(\pi_t - \tilde{\pi})^2}{2}, \tag{7.7}$$

where $\tilde{\pi}$ is the electorate's target rate of inflation and θ is the relative weight the electorate puts on inflation deviations relative to unemployment. Though this looks technically identical to the social loss function in the Barro–Gordon model, the interpretation in the Political Business Cycle model is different; in the latter, the parameters $\tilde{\pi}$ and θ are interpreted as representing voters' preferences. (More exactly, an opportunistic policymaker will choose the policy that attracts most voters, so that these parameters could be thought of as representing the preferences of the median voter.) For economy of exposition, we assume that $\tilde{\pi} = 0$.

---

[13] The Nordhaus model uses continuous time, but the basic results are easily represented by a discrete-time model.

In the basic model, one then posits a retrospective voting function for an election at the end of period t, of the form

$$N_t = \mathrm{N}\left[\sum_{s=0}^{3} \beta^s \mathscr{L}_{t-s}\right] + \epsilon_t, \qquad (7.8)$$

yielding the number of votes N_t as a function of voters' well-being. The exogenous length of time between elections is 4 periods, $0 < \beta < 1$ is the discount factor on past incumbent performance, $\mathrm{N}'(\cdot) < 0$, and ϵ_t is a mean-zero stochastic term relating economic performance to electoral outcomes. The electoral mechanism is not made more specific. The standard opportunistic PBC model assumes that β is small, in the sense that recent economic performance counts far more heavily in influencing voter choices than economic performance in the more distant past. The stochastic element is added to allow for the possibility of an incumbent losing the election. Otherwise, if he cared *only* about staying in office, he could choose policies to assure re-election. (Alternatively, if policymakers not only care about being re-elected, but also put some weight on social welfare, they may choose policies which do not necessarily maximize their chances of re-election. We consider this issue explicitly in Section 7.5 below, where we discuss models of policymaker competence.)

The structure of the economy is summarized by a nonstochastic, expectations-adjusted Phillips curve. We slightly modify the basic model of the inflation–unemployment trade-off in order to reproduce the "regularity" of high inflation in the period after an election reflecting a high money growth rate μ_t just before an election. To do this, one must "decouple" money growth and inflation. A simple assumption along these lines is that inflation reflects money growth in the previous period, that is, $\pi_t = \mu_{t-1}$. The divergence of the unemployment rate U_t in any period from the natural rate of unemployment (zero, by our measurement convention) then depends on the difference between the actual rate of money growth and the economywide expected rate of money growth μ_t^e:

$$U_t = -(\mu_t - \mu_t^e), \qquad (7.9)$$

where the monetary authority's control variable is μ_t. The loss function is defined over π_{t+1} and U_t as in (7.7).

To close the model, one must specify the formation of expectations. Crucial to the main results of the Nordhaus model is some form of adaptive expectations. A standard formulation of adaptive determination of the expected rate of money growth μ_t^e is

$$\mu_t^e = \mu_{t-1} + \alpha(\mu_{t-1}^e - \mu_{t-1}), \tag{7.10}$$

where α is a coefficient between 0 and 1 representing the speed with which expectations adapt to past money growth rates. This may be rewritten as

$$\mu_t^e = (1 - \alpha) \sum_{i=1}^{\infty} \alpha^{i-1} \mu_{t-i}. \tag{7.11}$$

To derive an explicit solution, let us assume that elections occur every four periods and that α is close to zero, so that terms in α^2 and higher are approximately zero, implying that (7.11) may be approximated by

$$\mu_t^e = (1 - \alpha)\mu_{t-1} + \alpha\mu_{t-2}. \tag{7.12}$$

What is crucial in the formation of expectations is that μ_t^e does *not* depend on the expectation of future policies, so that expectations are not rational. It is this characteristic (combined with the absence of any other connections between periods) which gives the incumbent policymaker an exploitable trade-off between inflation and unemployment in the attempt to affect election outcomes.

To derive the cyclical behavior of macroeconomic variables, one begins with expected vote totals as a function of economic performance. Combining (7.7) through (7.9) and (7.12), the term in brackets in (7.8) as a function of current and past inflation policy is given by

$$\begin{aligned}
\Sigma \beta^s \mathscr{L}_{t-s} = \;&\frac{\theta}{2} \mu_t^2 - \mu_t + (1 - \alpha)\mu_{t-1} + \alpha\mu_{t-2} \\
&+ \beta\left(\frac{\theta}{2} \mu_{t-1}^2 - \mu_{t-1} + (1 - \alpha)\mu_{t-2} + \alpha\mu_{t-3}\right) \\
&+ \beta^2\left(\frac{\theta}{2} \mu_{t-2}^2 - \mu_{t-2} + (1 - \alpha)\mu_{t-3} + \alpha\mu_{t-4}\right) \\
&+ \beta^3\left(\frac{\theta}{2} \mu_{t-3}^2 - \mu_{t-3} + (1 - \alpha)\mu_{t-4} + \alpha\mu_{t-5}\right).
\end{aligned} \tag{7.13}$$

Note that voter behavior in the Nordhaus model is backward-looking in two dimensions: voting depends on past incumbent performance; and, expectations of money growth depend only on past money growth rates. We return to a discussion of this backward-looking behavior below. The incumbent policymaker elected at $t - 3$ chooses money growth rates

$\mu_{t-3}, \mu_{t-2}, \mu_{t-1}$, and μ_t to maximize his expected vote in the next election, yielding the policy sequence

$$\mu_{t-3} = \frac{(\beta - 1)(\beta + \alpha)}{\beta^2} \frac{1}{\theta},$$

$$\mu_{t-2} = \frac{(\beta - 1)(\beta + \alpha)}{\beta^2} \frac{1}{\theta}, \qquad (7.14)$$

$$\mu_{t-1} = \frac{\beta + \alpha - 1}{\beta} \frac{1}{\theta},$$

$$\mu_t = \frac{1}{\theta}.$$

(Note that the optimal choices of μ are independent of expected money growth rates μ^e due to the nature of the loss function (7.7).) The behavior of inflation, under our assumptions, follows by one period. If money growth and inflation were connected by "long and variable" lags, it would be more difficult to derive simple predictions.

This simple structure yields the following behavior of incumbents who wish to maximize the probability of remaining in office. Immediately preceding an election, the government stimulates the economy via expansionary monetary policy, unemployment falling due to high unanticipated money growth. The levels of monetary expansion and unemployment are those which maximize voter satisfaction in an election period taken alone. In the period immediately after the election, when high inflation kicks in, the government reverses course. It engineers a recession via contractionary monetary policy to bring down inflationary expectations. The incumbent keeps economic activity low to keep expected inflation low until the period immediately before the next election, so that a given rate of economic expansion (induced by a monetary surprise) can be obtained at a relatively low rate of inflation. In the next election cycle, the same behavior is repeated. Hence, we have a simple example in which the possibility of influencing the probability of re-election, combined with the structure of the economy, yields a cycle in economic activity which would not be present with a planner with an infinite horizon.

A Conceptual Assessment of the Model

A first criticism of this approach is that it assumes that incumbents running for re-election control monetary policy, an assumption inconsistent with a central bank independence. Some authors, notably Havrilesky (1993), argue that decisions on monetary policy in the United States are strongly influenced by the executive branch. A more subtle argument, following Woolley (1986) and Beck (1987), is that an independent Federal Reserve may be especially willing to accommodate the executive branch's pressures for monetary policy during election years in order to prevent sharp movements in interest rates. We discuss this argument in greater detail at the end of this section.

A more serious problem with the Nordhaus model is its reliance on *irrational* behavior on the part of voters. Voters are naive, not simply in the way they form expectations of inflation, but also in the way they assess government performance. Any voter who has lived through an election cycle in Nordhaus's world should not be fooled into voting for an opportunistic, manipulative policymaker. He will know that the pre-election period of low inflation and low unemployment will be followed by a post-election period of both high inflation and high unemployment. His voting behavior should be forward-looking, rather than retrospective, and voters should punish an incumbent who engages in pre-election shenanigans, rather than reward him. If voters are not fooled into voting for a policymaker who chooses short-run stimulation, policymakers will not engage in such policies and the electoral business cycle disappears.

One response to the criticism of irrational voter behavior is that we observe voters apparently being fooled and responding to manipulative policies. Therefore, though we cannot explain why voters do not act rationally, we take it as an empirical fact and simply derive the implications of voter irrationality for behavior of policymakers. Though it is common in macroeconomics to study the positive implications of certain features of the economy that cannot themselves be explained, it is not a fruitful approach in this case. Simply because behavior appears to be irrational to an outside observer docs not mean that it is irrational; it may simply mean that we do not understand the decision process of the voters. A far better approach would be to ask whether political business cycles can be consistent with rational behavior.

Two lines of research can be identified here, following the two motivations for policy choice, namely, partisan and opportunistic. (Nordhaus [1989] gives a clear, concise summary of basic opportunistic and partisan PBC models, as well as a good discussion of the role of rationality in these models.) On the first, given the importance of ideology, the strategy is to see whether alternation of parties with different preferred policies can lead to a cycle when voters are rational. Here, two approaches are presented by Alesina (1987, 1988b)[14] and by Hibbs (1994), following Hibbs's (1977) model of partisan policymakers in an environment similar to that of Nordhaus. In the Alesina model, uncertainty about who will win the election implies uncertainty about post-election monetary policy, which can have real effects; in the later Hibbs model, parties' objectives evolve

---

[14] Chappell and Keech (1986) suggested a similar approach at the same time, but without the detailed modeling of Alesina's work.

over time in response to the evolution of the economy. We consider the partisan approach in the next section.

Alternatively, one can investigate whether some further aspect of the environment can lead to seemingly opportunistic policies having an effect even when voters are rational, as in the work of Rogoff and Sibert (1988), Rogoff (1990), and Cukierman and Meltzer (1986). Opportunistic behavior by politicians before elections is so widespread that it would be a mistake to dismiss the phenomenon (and models based on such behavior) as reflecting simply the stupidity of voters. For opportunistic policymaking to affect the choices of rational voters, one may assume that voters have less than full information and that favorable past economic performance reveals something, leading to retrospective voting reflecting a rational inference problem. (Some authors, notably Alesina and Rosenthal [1995], use the term "rational retrospective voting" for voting reflecting this type of inference problem. I prefer not to apply the term solely to this phenomenon, because retrospective voting in the Ferejohn (1986) model of disciplining incumbents, discussed in Section 7.2, is also fully rational even though no problem of inferring unobserved characteristics is involved.) The crucial assumption in these imperfect-information models is that past performance of an incumbent reveals something about his *competence* or ability, so that incumbents who performed well in the past are expected to perform well in the future as well. In my opinion, voters taking good economic performance as indicating ability is one of the keys to understanding electoral cycles. This approach will be considered in detail in Section 7.5 of this chapter.

Another serious problem with the basic Nordhaus model is the lack of empirical support for it, at least in its basic form. We now turn to this issue.

Empirical Studies of the Opportunistic Political Business Cycle

There have been scores of articles testing for the opportunistic PBC in a more formal way than in Tufte's (1978) study, both for economic outcomes and for policy instruments. Starting with McCallum's (1978) study of unemployment fluctuations in the United States before elections, the opportunistic model has been widely tested econometrically both for the United States and for other countries, with the bulk of studies finding little support for the basic Nordhaus model of a political cycle in economic activity and (to a lesser extent) for inflation. It is neither possible nor useful to summarize all of the studies except to say there is fairly clear rejection of the simple model for the United States.[15] Similarly, no

---

[15] See, for example, Alt and Chrystal (1983) or Hibbs (1987). Alesina, Roubini, and Cohen (1997) present a good, though not entirely unbiased, summary of empirical research on opportunistic models. A very clear, shorter summary, on which parts of the later work are based, is Alesina, Cohen, and Roubini (1992).

evidence is found for a Nordhaus-style PBC for unemployment, inflation, and economic growth by Paldam (1979) for 17 OECD countries, nor by Lewis-Beck (1988) for any of the European countries he considers. Alesina, Cohen, and Roubini (1992) reject an opportunistic cycle in real activity for a sample of 18 OECD countries, but not for inflation.

There is less consensus on whether there is empirical support for an opportunistic political business cycle in policy instruments. Several authors find evidence over specific time periods, while others, such as Lewis-Beck (1988) and Alesina, Roubini, and Cohen (1997), argue that the evidence is quite weak. My reading of the results suggests there is some econometric evidence of opportunistic behavior in policy instruments, especially in fiscal transfers, so that, on the whole, the evidence for opportunistic manipulation of macroeconomic policy is stronger than for macroeconomic outcomes. This distinction is important not only for getting a clearer empirical picture, but also for making conceptual sense of the welter of seemingly contradictory evidence.

The empirical predictions of the Nordhaus model can be summarized as follows: before an election, unemployment will be below normal and economic activity above normal, whereas after an election, inflation will begin to increase and a recession will set in. Low unemployment and high economic activity in an election year should help the incumbent. Moreover, there should be no significant difference between parties in the policies they choose before elections and in the behavior of unemployment and inflation before and after elections. To better understand the nature of the tests of the model and their results, and why there are significant differences in opinion about how much empirical support it receives, it is useful to divide these studies into those concerning outcomes (such as disposable income, unemployment, or inflation), as summarized at the beginning of the paragraph, and those concerning policy instruments (such as transfers, other fiscal instruments, or money growth). We begin with the former type of study.

Opportunistic Cycles in Macroeconomic Outcomes

To begin, let us take a quick look at nonparametric evidence of cycles in economic activity similar to Tufte's evidence. Alesina, Roubini, and Cohen (1997, Tables 4.1 to 4.3) present yearly averages for real GDP growth, unemployment, and inflation rates for the period 1949–1994 for the United States, both averaged across all administrations and divided between Republican and Democratic administrations. For the whole sample, independent of which party is in power, the average growth rate of GDP in the fourth year of the administration, that is, the presidential election year, is only slightly higher than the sample average (3.66% versus 3.17%), the unemployment rate only slightly lower (5.66% in the fourth year of an administration versus 5.81% averaged over all years), and the inflation rate basically identical (4.07% versus 4.03%). They point out that this simple comparison suggests the absence of any large systematic manipulation. One does see a difference in average real GDP growth rates between the second half of presidential terms (3.59%) and the first half (2.76%), averaged over both parties (they present no standard deviations for these figures), so one cannot totally reject the possibility of opportunistic manipulation, though no similar first-half versus second-half difference exists in unemployment. They do find an intriguing difference in economic activity between Democratic and Republican administrations. Real GDP growth is substantially higher under Democrats than Republicans in years 2 (5.73% versus .03%) and 3 of their administrations (4.8% versus 2.79%). Unemployment is substantially lower under Democrats than Republicans in years 2, 3, and 4 of their terms, with the difference especially striking in the second half of their terms (4.69% under Democrats versus 6.43% under Republicans). We return to these partisan differences in Section 7.4.

The most common form of econometric test of these models in terms of outcomes is to run an autoregression of an economic performance measure on itself, a small set of economic variables, and political dummies to test a specific theory. Consider a regression of the form

$$y_t = \sum_{i=1}^{s} a_i y_{t-i} + b_0 + \sum_j b_j x_{jt} + dPDUM_t + \epsilon_t, \qquad (7.15)$$

where y is an outcome variable such as GDP, x_j are other economic variables that may also affect y, such as world economic activity, and *PDUM* is a political dummy variable (or set of variables) meant to represent a given political model. The autoregressive specification for the y_t is adopted as a parsimonious representation of the time-series behavior of y_t, instead of using a structural model. Equation (7.15) is usually tested on a country-by-country basis, but there are also studies that use pooled time-series cross-section data, so that y_t represents a vector of observations at a point in time across countries. The difference in results across models may stem from a number of factors, such as different definitions of economic activity and different samples, but the main differences in results appear to stem from different data periods and, especially, different specifications of the political dummies.

As a test of the Nordhaus model on quarterly data, Alesina and Roubini (1992), Alesina, Cohen, and Roubini (1992), and subsequently Alesina, Roubini, and Cohen (1997), use a dummy variable that equals 1 in the election quarter and in the $T - 1$ quarters before the election, and 0 otherwise, where T may equal 4, 6, or 8. As the measure of economic activity y they take the year-over-year growth rate of GNP or U^{DIF}, the difference between the domestic unemployment rate and an OECD average (this unemployment specification is to try to address a possible problem with "unit roots" in the unemployment data); as an additional explanatory variable x, they take the average output growth rate of the seven largest OECD economies in the GNP growth regression. Their sample consists of 18 OECD democracies[16] over the period 1960–1993 in the 1997 study, over 1960–1987 in the earlier studies. They estimate both a single pooled regression with country fixed effects, and (in the earlier studies) 18 individual country regressions, both with a lag length of $i = 2$ in the y_{t-i} in (7.15). Their evidence is quite negative. They find no significant effects for either measure of economic activity in the pooled regression, no matter what lag length T is used for the *PDUM* variable. In the country regressions for GNP growth, taking the lag T that gives the best results, they find significant effects of the correct sign for only four of the 18 OECD economies: Germany, Japan, New Zealand, and the United Kingdom. (For the U^{DIF}, they find no significant signs.) In no specification do they find a significant coefficient d for the United States. Further tests focusing on the United States can be found in Alesina, Roubini, and Cohen (1997), where they also find no support for the basic Nordhaus model.

One criticism of the work of Alesina and co-authors in their tests of pre-electoral effects is on their specification of the timing of political effects, specifically, the discontinuous nature of their *PDUM*, which drops from 1 to 0 after $T - 1$ quarters. This argument has been put forward by Grier (1989) and Williams (1990), who argue that there is significant uncertainty about the shape of an economy's response to pre-electoral economic stimulation, with no reason to expect a discontinuous fall-off immediately after the election. The problem of imposing an arbitrary response function would seem especially problematic in regressions pooling eighteen different economies. Williams suggests using a simple counter for the dummy, rising from 1 to 16 over the president's term, this specification imposing the restriction that the economic effect of political manipulation is linearly related to the distance from the next election. Using a vector autoregression (VAR) of the form of (7.15) on quarterly data from 1953 to 1984, but with the political dummy specified as in the previous sentence, he finds that the three-month Treasury bill rate is in part explained by a political cycle, with no significant effect for other macroeconomic outcomes, except perhaps a marginally significant effect for real GNP.

Among sophisticated econometric studies, Haynes and Stone (1989) probably find the strongest evidence for a political business cycle in macroeconomic outcomes, using a somewhat different methodology than that of most papers. Rather than parameterizing the shape of the political

---

[16] Australia, Austria, Belgium, Canada, Denmark, Finland, France, Germany, Ireland, Italy, Japan, Netherlands, New Zealand, Norway, Sweden, Switzerland, United Kingdom, and United States.

effects in *PDUM* in an equation such as (7.15) with estimated a_i coefficients, they parameterize the time-series process for GNP and unemployment as sine waves, and they investigate how such waves are correlated with the electoral cycle. They find a four-year cycle in both GNP and unemployment, with GNP reaching its peak in the quarter of the presidential election and unemployment hitting its trough in the quarter after the election. However, the Haynes and Stone study is an exception in the strength of its results. The general consensus is that the opportunistic PBC model receives little support in the pre-electoral behavior of GNP or unemployment.

Evidence consistent with the Nordhaus PBC model can be found in the behavior of inflation, where the prediction of the model is that after an election, inflation will begin to increase. Alesina, Cohen, and Roubini (1992) test for a political cycle in inflation (measured as the growth rate of the CPI over the previous four quarters), using the same data set and methodology they used for GNP growth and defining a political dummy as equal to 1 in the election quarter and in the three quarters *following* the election, and 0 otherwise. In a pooled cross-section, time-series regression, they find a highly significant coefficient of the correct sign on the political dummy; in the individual country regressions, they find the coefficient is of the correct sign in almost all the regressions, and significant at the 10% or higher level for Denmark, France, Germany, Italy, and New Zealand. Overall, they conclude the PBC effect on inflation is widespread across countries (on the basis of their pooled regression) and on a much stronger empirical footing than the GNP and unemployment results. Similarly, Haynes and Stone (1989) find a four-year component to inflation cycles, with the peak coming five years after the quarter of the presidential election. Overall, there is evidence in support of a political cycle in inflation, with the inflation rate exhibiting a post-electoral jump in many countries. Hence, to summarize the discussion so far, there is a contradiction between the inflation and economic activity results in terms of the predictions of the Nordhaus model.

Opportunistic Cycles in Policy Instruments

We now turn to the results for policy instruments. In part, they will help us understand the difference in the results for economic activity and inflation, and the implications of this difference for opportunistic models. We begin with monetary policy. Using the same political dummy they did for inflation, Alesina, Cohen, and Roubini (1992) find a significant political effect for the yearly M1 growth rates in pooled cross-section, time-series regressions in their sample of OECD countries, with money growth being higher for the year to year-and-a-half before elections. In the country regressions, the results are less strong, though a number of countries display significant effects. They find that the evidence of a political monetary cycle is weak for the United States, a conclusion reinforced in Alesina, Roubini, and Cohen (1997), a point to which we will return. (See the discussion surrounding footnote 17 below.) They further argue that there is no significant difference between Republicans and Democrats in their pre-election choices for monetary policy.

Grier (1989) and Williams (1990) both find significant support for an office-motivated model of monetary policy in the United States. Williams's methodology is as described above. Grier, using U.S. quarterly data from 1961 to 1982, regresses M1 growth on its previous value, the full-employment deficit, and a political dummy specified as a fifteen-quarter second-degree polynomial distributed lag on a dummy which takes a value of 1 in the election quarter and zero otherwise. (The polynomial distributed lag is chosen to conserve on degrees of freedom.) He finds that the timing of an election significantly influences money growth, even when fluctuations in output, interest rates, and the deficit are held constant.

How should one interpret the results of a significant cycle in money growth? What light, if any, might be shed on the apparent contradiction, at least as far as the Nordhaus model is concerned, between the results on a post-electoral inflation cycle, but the absence of pre-electoral output effects? The key is in distinguishing between active monetary policy and money growth *per se*, especially in view of the apparent pre-electoral manipulation of fiscal instruments reported by Tufte (1978), which we will see is confirmed by more rigorous statistical tests. The distinction between active and passive monetary policy follows Beck's (1987) discussion of Grier's results. Beck argues that there is a political cycle in the money supply in the United States, but no cycle in monetary instruments, such as reserves or the Federal Fund rate. The reason is that the Federal Reserve accommodates fiscal policy in an election year, so that there is a passive political monetary cycle caused by a political cycle in fiscal instruments, but the Fed does not actively induce a political cycle. Beck argues that this accommodation is why the monetary cycle that both he and Grier find peaks in the election quarter itself, when the monetary expansion should not affect outcomes. Beck regresses M1 on its lags and on fiscal indicators to confirm this argument.

Why does the Fed accommodate shock during an election year? The argument, put forward by several authors, is that the Fed is not so much interested in pushing the re-election of the incumbent as in simply "laying low" during the election so as not to be subsequently criticized. Williams (1990), for example, quotes Woolley (1986) as arguing that during election years, highly visible monetary policy actions are much more likely to be expansionary than contractionary. In short, monetary aggregates before an election (and inflation after the election) exhibit behavior consistent with an opportunistic cycle, but only because monetary policy is accommodating fiscal policy, so that the Fed is not criticized during the election period.

What then is the evidence on an electoral cycle in fiscal policy? In fact, the strongest econometric evidence by far supporting an opportunistic political business cycle is in the behavior of fiscal policy, both in the post-war United States as well as in a number of OECD economies. Several papers find evidence of a political budget cycle. Tufte (1978), for example, documents a number of clear incidents of pre-electoral opportunistic manipulation of fiscal transfers, both Social Security payments and veterans benefits. Keech and Pak (1989) found an electoral cycle for veterans' benefits in the United States between 1961 and 1978, but argue that it has subsequently disappeared.[17] Alesina, Cohen, and Roubini (1992), as well as Alesina and Roubini (1992), similarly find evidence for an opportunistic cycle in transfers, though they argue that there is no evidence of fiscal cycle for instruments other than transfers. As with monetary policy, they find no significant difference between Republicans and Democrats in their pre-election choices for fiscal policy.

Making Sense of the Results

What can one make of this welter of results? Taken as a whole, the econometric evidence presents a case for the existence of some opportunistic, pre-electoral manipulation of economic policy, and for the effects of that manipulation perhaps on inflation, but not on economic activity. There is disagreement on how strong the case is. The evidence is quite weak that this cycle is of the form suggested by Nordhaus, in which expansionary monetary policy and high inflation before an election reduce pre-election unemployment, followed by a post-election contraction to cool down the economy. Instead, to the extent that manipulation occurs, it is via transfer payments, a policy most likely to affect disposable income before an election, as originally argued by Tufte (1978). Monetary policy does not appear to be the driving force for the politically induced cycle, but money growth moves before an election to accommodate fiscal policy, the inflationary effects being seen in the quarter of the election and subsequently.

But, if there is an opportunistic cycle in some policy instruments, why do we not see an effect on real economic activity? One answer to this crucial question starts with the argument that, in fact, there is no cycle in monetary and fiscal policy. For example, Lewis-Beck (1988) argues that there is no evidence of a significant opportunistic cycle either in outcomes or in instruments. He finds this lack of evidence paradoxical, given the

---

[17] The disappearance of a political cycle for veteran's benefits after the late 1970s may help explain why Grier (1989) and Williams (1990) find a significant political monetary cycle in data up to or through the early 1980s, while Alesina, Cohen, and Roubini (1992), using a longer time series, find weaker evidence. To the extent that the political monetary cycle is induced by a political fiscal cycle, a weakening of the latter would weaken the former as well.

apparent importance of aggregate economic performance in determining the way people vote. That is, if voters are motivated by economic benefits and governments want to win re-election, why do we not observe a clear opportunistic PBC? He suggests that the reason we do not observe a cycle is that it is exceedingly hard to time economic manipulation. Monetary and fiscal policy can be used only with great imprecision, so that politicians cannot expect to time the stimulus to come right before an election, with the risks associated with the benefits of expansion reaching the voters too early or too late being unacceptably high. As a result, he argues, opportunistic politicians will try to provide for continual good economic news, suggesting how to reconcile the sensitivity of voters to macroeconomic outcomes with the failure to observe pre-electoral manipulation, except perhaps by the most desperate incumbents.

An alternative approach is to accept the evidence for an opportunistic cycle in some policy instruments and focus on why it does not translate into observed economic activity. This raises a further question: if manipulation of policy instruments does not have a significant effect on aggregate economic activity, how does it affect election outcomes? Numerous authors have argued that our current views on the relation of inflation to economic activity make it doubtful that the political effects are via moving along the Phillips curve to reduce unemployment. Though inflation fluctuations may not have significant effects on real economic activity, especially if they are anticipated, fluctuations in fiscal policy will have real effects, whether anticipated or not. (This point will come up again in our evaluation of partisan models in the next section.) There are several ways to explain the apparent lack of a cycle in aggregate economic activity in the face of fiscal manipulation. One explanation, following from the fact that the results are neither uniformly negative or positive, is that there may be aggregate effects in the correct direction, but that they are statistically weak. Second, the fact that manipulation of fiscal instruments before an election has no effect on output, but only on inflation after the election, is fully consistent with the Rogoff and Sibert (1988) and Rogoff (1990) models of using pre-electoral (nondistortionary) transfers to signal competence, and hence affect election outcomes. We return to evaluating the empirical plausibility of this explanation in Section 7.5 where these models are exposited.

A final line of explanation concentrates on individual rather than aggregate benefits of manipulation. The argument is that policy manipulation that has real effects on the economic well-being of subsets of voters can affect election outcomes, even if it has no significant effects on *aggregate* economic activity. (Remember, however, our above results on the prevalence of sociotropic versus pocketbook voting.) An increase in Social Security benefits for the elderly, for example, may have significant effects on voting independent of its effects on economic aggregates. The very nature of transfers, in fact, suggests they should be targeted to subgroups of voters for maximum electoral impact, and the vote-maximizing structure of transfers is considered in detail in Section 8.3 of Chapter 8. Incumbents would then target fiscal policy in a clear partisan way, and the nature of the political business cycle would depend on the nature of partisan differences, a subject to which we now turn.

7.4. PARTISAN POLITICAL CYCLES

The opportunistic models of the previous section assumed that all voters are identical. This assumption is, of course, unrealistic in the extreme. A realistic view of the electoral process might well start at the opposite extreme, stressing the fact that *ex-ante* heterogeneity will lead voters to have different preferences. In fact, as discussed in Chapter 3, elections may be seen as a generally agreed upon way to aggregate the preferences of voters with conflicting interests. Hence, voter heterogeneity, and the partisan nature of elections that follows from this heterogeneity, should be an important component of explanations of the political business cycle. Analysis of the effects of elections on any economic phenomenon would be seriously incomplete if the effects of heterogeneous interests were not taken into account.

Models whose basic assumptions are an incomplete description of reality are nonetheless often quite useful if their predictions conform to reality and shed light on the phenomena they were built to explain. In terms of realistically predicting the policy platforms adopted by parties seeking election, however, the purely opportunistic model definitely comes up short. (We defer to Section 7.6 a fuller discussion of the credibility of electoral platforms.) If all parties are purely opportunistic, so that they choose platforms that will attract most voters, platforms should converge to the same policy, that preferred by the median voter. This is simply an application of the median voter theorem for two-party politics derived in Section 3.5 of Chapter 3. Policy convergence was the prediction of Downs (1957). As he put it (p. 115), "Parties in a two-party system deliberately change their platforms so that they resemble one another." However, we have not seen policy convergence to the extent that Downs and other writers at the time predicted. That we have not seen more policy convergence is taken as evidence of the importance of partisan preferences.[18]

In this section, we consider models which stress the role of partisan differences as a possible driving force in political business cycles, models known in the PBC literature as *partisan models*. The most basic partisan

---

[18] Tufte (1978, chapter 4) presents a good conceptual discussion of the importance of ideology in light of the presumption of policy convergence.

model considers differences in preferred policies as the only driving force; there is no room for opportunism. (More complex models, for example, Frey and Schneider [1978], consider possible interactions of opportunism and partisan differences.) This characterization, meant to highlight the role that partisan differences may play, is extreme. Independent of empirical results suggesting that the desire to be elected is important in the formulation of policy, there is a strong argument that even theoretically, partisan differences and the desire to be elected cannot be so easily separated. With few (perhaps notable) exceptions, strongly partisan candidates are not interested in simply espousing their positions, but in getting elected so that they can enact them. Hence, to argue that a candidate is either strongly partisan or strongly opportunistic may miss the point—a candidate whose basic positions mark him as strongly partisan may be especially willing to compromise on some positions in order to get elected to follow through on others. There may be a tension between partisanship and opportunism, a tension which is absent in the partisan models summarized below, but which (as we shall argue) may affect their workings and implications for economic fluctuations. The interaction between partisanship and opportunism may also significantly affect how we interpret the empirical evidence presented in favor of those models.

Hibbs's Model of Partisan Political Business Cycles

The basic partisan model is due to Hibbs (1977, 1987), who started from the observation that the two parties in the United States have different positions on economic issues. In terms of the business cycle, they have different preferences over inflation and unemployment, both in inflation and unemployment targets and in the relative dislike of inflation versus unemployment. These party-specific differences reflect the fact that the Democratic and Republican parties in the United States represent constituencies with different views about the costs of inflation and unemployment; as Hibbs (1987, p. 66) summarizes it:

> the core constituency of the Democratic party consists of the down-scale classes, who primarily hold human capital and bear a disproportionate share of the economic and broader social costs of extra unemployment. Up-scale groups form the core constituency of the Republican party; they hold financial capital and absorb the greatest losses from extra inflation. For this reason Democratic voters generally express greater aversion to unemployment and less aversion to inflation than Republican voters.

This difference in the interests of their constituencies leads the parties to prefer different policies. Obviously, the same type of argument applies to left-wing and right-wing parties in other countries as well.

To represent this difference in interests, we replace the social loss function (7.7) by a partisan loss function:

$$\mathscr{L}_t^j = \frac{\left(U_t - \tilde{U}^j\right)^2}{2} + \theta^j \frac{\left(\pi_t - \tilde{\pi}^j\right)^2}{2}, \qquad (7.16a)$$

for party j, where $\tilde{\pi}^j$ is party j's target rate of inflation, $\tilde{U}^j$ is party j's target unemployment rate, and θ^j is the relative weight put on inflation deviations relative to unemployment deviations by party j. There are two parties, a left-wing party, denoted L, and a right-wing party, denoted R. The two parties are characterized by the following possible differences in their objectives. First, the left-wing party may have a lower unemployment target than the right-wing party. Second, the left-wing party may assign a larger cost to deviations of unemployment from their target level than to deviations of inflation from the target. Finally, the left-wing party may have a higher inflation target than the right-wing party, *independent* of the effects on unemployment via the Phillips curve, which could reflect other effects of inflation viewed differently by the two parties. To summarize the difference between the parties:

$$\tilde{U}^L \leq \tilde{U}^R,$$
$$\theta^L \leq \theta^R, \qquad (7.16b)$$
$$\tilde{\pi}^L \geq \tilde{\pi}^R.$$

To obtain the partisan cycles, at least one of these must hold with strict inequality.

Fluctuations in economic activity induced by these partisan differences are generated in the basic Hibbs model by movements along an exploitable Phillips curve, where it is assumed, as in the basic Nordhaus model, that expectations are not rational. Thus, the left-wing party will pursue a more expansionary monetary policy throughout its term.[19] Moreover, the expansionary effect can continue even when the policy the policymaker will pursue is known. Though the economic working of the model could be represented in terms of the expectations-adjusted Phillips curve (7.9) combined with adaptive expectations as in (7.12), the effects that the Hibbs model stresses are most easily seen using a Phillips curve where there is a trade-off between unemployment and *anticipated* inflation, such as

$$U_t = -\pi_t. \qquad (7.17)$$

---

[19] As in the Nordhaus model, the key assumption here is that, in spite of the Federal Reserve's formal autonomy in the U.S., monetary policy reflects the administration's macroeconomic goals.

Substituting (7.17) into the partisan objective function (7.16), one can derive the unemployment and inflation rates that obtain over the whole term of office when each party is in power. For simplicity, suppose in (7.16b) that $\tilde{U}^L < \tilde{U}^R$ and $\tilde{\pi}^L > \tilde{\pi}^R$, with θ being the same across parties. The unemployment rates which characterize left-wing and right-wing administrations are

$$U^L = \frac{1}{1+\theta}(\tilde{U}^L - \theta\tilde{\pi}^L),$$

$$U^R = \frac{1}{1+\theta}(\tilde{U}^R - \theta\tilde{\pi}^R),$$

(7.18)

so that $U^L < U^R$. Hence, there will be a cycle in unemployment and inflation mirroring the cycle of office-holding across the two parties, with unemployment being high and inflation low whenever the right is in office for the duration of their terms, and vice versa whenever the left is in office, for the duration of their terms. To summarize the driving principle in Hibbs's approach, parties have different goals for macroeconomic outcomes, and cycles in these outcomes reflect cycles in which party holds office.

A basic criticism of the original Hibbs model is the same critique that was applied to the Nordhaus model, namely, that it relies (in the general case of a Phillips curve relying on inflation surprises) on mistaken expectations of what policy will be in order to get real effects. Hence, to the extent that it is assumed that monetary policy is used to hit partisan unemployment and growth targets, the explanation of the political business cycle is unsatisfactory. However, a partisan PBC model, in which the cycle reflects parties having different policy goals and alternating in office, need not depend on exploiting mistaken expectations to generate movements along the Phillips curve. Suppose that instead of using monetary policy to influence economic activity, a partisan policymaker used *fiscal* variables such as transfers. Perfectly anticipated fiscal policy can have real effects. As with an opportunistic PBC relying on transfers, the economic mechanism driving the cycle would not be suspect. Moreover, unlike the opportunistic PBC, there would also be no question of why rational voters re-elect incumbents who successfully manipulate the economy. Since partisan incumbents manipulate the economy for the good of their own supporters (at the presumed expense of the other party's supporters), those constituents will gladly vote to re-elect the incumbent.

Another early partisan theory is that of Frey and Schneider (1978), which focuses on the interaction of opportunistic and partisan motives. They argue that the party in power will pursue its ideological goals as long as it has favorable approval ratings and does not see itself in electoral danger. However, if its approval ratings decline as an election approaches, indicating possible problems in being re-elected, its policy choices will be driven by primarily opportunistic electoral motives. This view of *contingent partisanship* (to use Keech's [1995] term), whereby parties pursue their partisan goals contingent on economic or other conditions guaranteeing support, can be seen as analogous to the models of credibility being contingent on external circumstances discussed in Section 6.8 of the previous chapter. The relation of objectives to actual economic conditions will also form the basis of Hibbs's (1994) model, cycles reflecting changing partisan objectives.

Alesina's Rational Partisan Model

Hibbs's basic partisan model captures a key driving force in economic fluctuations, but relies on parties inducing these fluctuations by moving along a long-run, downward-sloping Phillips curve. This raises the question of what sort of partisan fluctuations would be observed in a world of rational expectations. An alternative approach to modeling partisan cycles is to retain monetary policy as the driving force, but to assume rational expectations, combined with a Phillips curve where only unanticipated inflation affects output. This is the approach of Alesina (1987, 1988b), who introduces rational formation of expectations into the original Hibbs model, hence the name *rational partisan* model. The driving force for fluctuations in inflation and unemployment is not partisan differences *per se*, but these differences combined with uncertainty about election outcomes. The change is significant, for the aggregate fluctuations implied by the model are, as we shall shortly see, quite different from the original partisan model.

The rational partisan model can be represented by a three-equation model similar to that used by Nordhaus, retaining the expectations-augmented Phillips curve (7.9), but changing the other two components. First, following Hibbs, the motivation of policymakers is quite different than in the Nordhaus model: they are purely partisan, with no opportunistic motives and hence no desire to manipulate outcomes. To represent the difference between economic effects in the early part and the latter part of an incumbent's term of office, Alesina divides a term of office into two periods and assumes that there is an election every other period, say at $t, t + 2, t + 4$, *et cetera*. It is assumed that a party cares only about its own term of office,[20] so that the objective function of party j at time t may then

---

[20] Using a model similar to Cremer (1986) studied in Chapter 5, Alesina and Spear (1988) consider a model where a politician cares about his party after his own term. We consider this below.

be represented by an extended version of (7.16a), namely,

$$\Lambda_t^j = \frac{\left(U_t - \tilde{U}^j\right)^2}{2} + \theta^j \frac{(\pi_t - \tilde{\pi}^j)^2}{2}$$
$$+ \beta \left[\frac{\left(U_{t+1} - \tilde{U}^j\right)^2}{2} + \theta^j \frac{(\pi_{t+1} - \tilde{\pi}^j)^2}{2} \right] \qquad (7.19)$$

for party j, where $\tilde{\pi}^j$ and $\tilde{U}^j$ are the partisan targets and θ^j the relative weight put on inflation deviations relative to unemployment deviations by party j. These are characterized, as in the Hibbs model, by (7.16b) above. To obtain the cycles in the rational-partisan model, at least one of the inequalities in (7.16b) must be strict.

The other crucial change, relative to both the Nordhaus and the Hibbs models, is that Alesina replaces the assumption of adaptive expectations by rational expectations, so instead of (7.10), expected inflation π_t^e is given by

$$\pi_t^e = \mathrm{E}_{t-1}(\pi_t). \qquad (7.20)$$

In determining the evolution of inflation and unemployment during a term of office, say t and $t + 1$, the key variable in the model is expected inflation in those periods, this expectation formed before the election in period t. Conditional on expected inflation in each half-term, the party in power chooses its optimal policy, denoted π_t^L and π_t^R for the left-wing and right-wing party, respectively, by maximizing (7.19) subject to (7.9) defined over π rather than μ, retaining the assumption from earlier models that the government has perfect control over inflation. In turn, expectations of inflation depend on the expectation of who will win the upcoming election. If outcomes were fully known, there would be *no* cycle. For example, if the left-wing party is believed certain to win the upcoming election, their policy choice would be fully anticipated, so that $\pi_t^e = \pi_{t+1}^e = \pi^{*L}$, where π^{*L} is the inflation rate that maximizes the single-period loss function (7.16a) for $j = L$, namely, $\pi^{*L} = \tilde{\pi}^L - \tilde{U}^L/\theta^L$.[21] (Since the party in power is known at the beginning of the second half of the term and desired policy at $t + 1$ is independent of election uncertainty at t, π^{*L} and π^{*R} are the inflation rates chosen by the two parties in the second half of their terms even when election outcomes are uncertain.) With certain election outcomes, unemployment will therefore also be constant (equal to the natural rate of unemployment) over the term of office.

The existence of a cycle thus depends on uncertainty about election outcomes. Alesina analyzes the implications of a probability q^L that the

---

[21] As in the basic Barro–Gordon model of Chapter 4, there is no connection between choice of inflation in a period and inflation or unemployment in the following period.

left-wing party wins the election at t, where q^L is taken as exogenous, restricted only to be between zero and 1. Before the election at t, expected inflation over the upcoming term can then be specified:

$$\pi_t^e = q^L \pi_t^L + (1 - q^L) \pi_t^R$$

$$\pi_{t+1}^e = \pi^{*L} \quad \text{if } L \text{ wins at } t, \tag{7.21}$$

$$\pi_{t+1}^e = \pi^{*R} \quad \text{if } R \text{ wins at } t.$$

To calculate π_t^L and π_t^R, one substitutes (7.9) and the first equation in (7.21) into (7.19) for both $j = L$ and $j = R$ and then differentiates each loss function with respect to the associated choice variable π_t^j. Solving these two equations simultaneously, one obtains

$$\pi_t^L = \kappa^L \pi^{*L} + (1 - \kappa^L) \pi^{*R},$$
$$\pi_t^R = (1 - \kappa^R) \pi^{*L} + \kappa^R \pi^{*R}, \tag{7.22a}$$

where

$$\kappa^L \equiv \frac{\theta^R \theta^L + q^L \theta^L}{\theta^R \theta^L + q^L \theta^L + (1 - q^L) \theta^R},$$

$$\kappa^R \equiv \frac{\theta^R \theta^L + (1 - q^L) \theta^R}{\theta^R \theta^L + q^L \theta^L + (1 - q^L) \theta^R}, \tag{7.22b}$$

$$\pi^{*j} = \tilde{\pi}^j - \tilde{U}^j / \theta^j.$$

One may then easily show that, for any $0 < q^L < 1$, one has

$$\pi_t^L > \pi_t^e > \pi_t^R, \tag{7.23}$$

as long as at least one of the equalities in (7.16b) is strict. (If q^L equals 1 or zero, there is no cycle.) Hence, at the beginning of a left-wing party's term there will be a "boom," with high inflation and unemployment below the natural rate (specifically, $U_t^L = \pi_t^e - \pi_t^L = (1 - q^L)(\pi_t^R - \pi_t^L) < 0$, where U_t^j measures deviations from the natural rate), while at the beginning of a right-wing party's term there will be a recession, characterized by low inflation and by unemployment above the natural rate (that is, $U_t^R = \pi_t^e - \pi_t^R = q^L(\pi_t^R - \pi_t^L) > 0$). In the second part of the term, there will be no partisan differences in real economic activity. With expected inflation equal to actual inflation (higher under left-wing than right-wing governments), unemployment will be equal to the natural rate no matter which party is in power. A right-wing government "delivers" a recession in the first part of its term not because it prefers this outcome (if $\tilde{U}^R < 0$, it has an incentive towards surprise expansionary policy as in the basic Barro–Gordon model of Chapter 4), but because it prefers a *less* expansionary policy than does a left-wing government. Note also that there are no effects just *before* an election, that is, no pumping up of the economy by the incumbent party in the attempt to win an election. Put formally, the probability of winning an election (q^L for a left-wing party) is *independent* of the incumbent's policy. Parties are purely partisan; there is no room for opportunism.

There is a crucial difference in implications between Hibbs's (1977) basic partisan model and Alesina's rational partisan theory. In the former model, differences in unemployment and inflation persist for the party's entire term; in the latter model, unemployment differences are not persistent, characterizing only the first part of a president's term. This difference is crucial in the formulation of Hibbs's (1994) model of contingent goal formation, discussed below, as well as in some of the empirical tests that attempt to discriminate between the two models, discussed in the next subsection.

Alesina (1987, 1988a) considers the welfare properties of electoral competition in a partisan model and argues that the outcome is suboptimal in the sense that if the parties could agree to follow a common policy, fluctuations in unemployment could be eliminated. Is there such a policy $\hat{\pi}$ (such that $\tilde{\pi}^R < \hat{\pi} < \tilde{\pi}^L$) that the two parties will agree to follow? Given the convexity of the loss function (7.19), each party also dislikes fluctuations in unemployment and inflation, so that there will be a range of policies $\hat{\pi}$ which each party would agree to follow, conditional on the other party following the same policy. Alesina considers the Nash bargaining solution, and shows that in this solution, $\hat{\pi}$ is increasing in q^L. The reason is straightforward. The higher is q^L, the better off a left-wing party would be in the absence of cooperation, that is, the higher is its threat point. Hence, the higher is q^L, the more bargaining power the left-wing party has, so that the cooperative solution will be closer to its desired solution.

Preferring a cooperative solution, however, is only part of the story. Analogous to the time-consistency problem raised in Chapter 4, one must ask how it can be made credible that both parties will honor the agreement once in office and carry out $\hat{\pi}$, rather than reverting to their preferred policy. Solutions to the problem of making the choice of $\hat{\pi}$ credible are parallel to solutions to the problem of time inconsistency given in Chapters 5 and 6. The choice of $\hat{\pi}$ could be "constitutionalized," as discussed in Section 5.2 of Chapter 5, with, however, the problem of flexibility versus commitment discussed there. The choice could be delegated, for example to an independent central bank, as in Section 5.4 of Chapter 5. Or, as Alesina (1988a) discusses in detail, it could be enforced by reputational considerations, if there is repeated interaction between the parties and q^L is near neither zero nor 1. All three solutions are seen in practice to the problem of certain types of socially suboptimal party "warfare." An increasing number of countries have inflation targets written into laws for politically independent central banks, as discussed in Chapter 5. When parties know they will face one another repeatedly in elections, certain issues are "taken off the table," with the parties implicitly agreeing on common compromise policies.

A Theoretical Assesment of the Rational Partisan Model

The theoretical structure of the model raises at least three main questions about the underlying driving forces. The most difficult question has to do with the underlying microeconomic structure such that unanticipated monetary policy can have a real effect. The question of microfoundations is often raised about models in which policymakers exploit an expectations-augmented Phillips curve, but the importance of electoral effects gives it added "bite" here. A standard argument, used also by Alesina, is that nominal wage contracts are signed at discrete intervals (due perhaps to costs of negotiating such contracts). Nominal wage increases reflect rationally anticipated inflation at the time the contract is signed, so that surprise inflation between contract dates can have real effects even when agents are rational.[22] Hours of work are demand determined, so that the fall in the real wage induced by surprise inflation implies that workers are supplying a different level of labor than they would under full information, ostensibly leading to lower utility.

This micro-foundation for surprise inflation lowering unemployment is used by Alesina as the basis for a Phillips curve such as (7.9). The basic problem, as Rogoff (1988) points out, is that, on the one hand, elections are an important source of fluctuations due to their outcomes being less than fully anticipated, but, on the other, the election date is fully known. The changes in inflation and unemployment the model is meant to explain are sufficiently large that there should be a large utility payoff to eliminating the uncertainty that leads to these fluctuations. But, that is easy to do. To the extent there is a significant effect on unemployment, old contracts should be timed to expire and new contract signing postponed until just after an election, so that they can reflect the election results. (Of course in industries where fluctuations in aggregate economic activity and inflation have little effect, election uncertainty would not induce significant employment fluctuations, so that there would be no similar incentive to postpone the signing of contracts until after the election.) If a contract had to be signed before an election whose outcome were highly uncertain and hence

---

[22] There are many theoretical objections that have been raised to this framework. Our goal is not to defend (or attack) the basic structure, but to ask what special issues arise in a political economy context. See Cukierman (1992) for a strong critique of the microfoundations of the expectations-adjusted Phillips curve when applied to political models.

likely to have large real effects, a simple state-contingent contract would similarly eliminate unemployment fluctuations. Though one does not observe textbook-style state-contingent contracts in labor markets, actual contracts may be able to mimic some of the necessary contingent features to reduce the firm's employment fluctuations due to aggregate surprises. Hence, the main driving force of the model would seem to depend on behavior of workers and unions that is less than rational, not in the formation of their expectations *per se*, but in their labor supply behavior. A simple change in the timing of contract behavior would eliminate the political cycle.

Garfinkel and Glazer (1994) present empirical evidence that for labor contracts of less than two years signed in a presidential election year, there is a clear tendency to move the signing of labor contracts until after the election. They considered labor contracts in the United States affecting more than 3,000 workers signed between 1960 and 1992 for which the month of signing was available. For contracts of two years or less signed in this period, 39% of all contracts were signed in November or later in a year without a presidential election, versus 50% of contracts signed in November or later in a year with a presidential election. (A chi-square test indicates the difference in the time-distribution of contracts is significant at the 5% level.) Though one might expect to see a larger fraction of contract signings postponed until after elections if parties differ significantly in their desired economic policies, remember that it is only in election years with significant uncertainty about outcomes and in industries highly susceptible to aggregate fluctuations that there would be an incentive to postpone signings. Garfinkel and Glazer note that for labor contracts lasting more than two years, the time of signing appears independent of presidential elections; they hypothesize that these may cover industries which are relatively insensitive to changes in aggregate demand, implying a greater willingness of firms and unions to enter into long-term contracts. In short, there appears to be evidence of changes in the timing of labor contracts that casts some doubt on a basic building block of the rational partisan theory.[23] In summarizing the theory, Alesina (1995) admits the potential importance of this line of criticism, calling the exogeneity of the crucial wage-setting mechanism the "Achilles' heel" of the rational partisan theory.

A second crucial question about the basic driving forces in the model has to do with the probability of a party being elected, q^L for the left-wing party and $1 - q^L$ for the right-wing party. These probabilities drive the model, but they are given exogenously. While it is true that there will be a

---

[23] Alesina, Roubini, and Cohen (1997, p. 63) say that because elections are important in the timing of contract signings and because not all signings adjust, the Garfinkel–Glazer results are "strikingly consistent with the spirit of the rational partisan theory," a claim that is debatable.

political cycle for any interior value of q^L, the nature of the cycle depends on the value q^L and on the difference between π_t^R and π_t^L, which themselves depend on q^L (as well as the underlying objectives $\tilde{\pi}^R$ and $\tilde{\pi}^L$).[24] As q^L approaches zero or 1, the magnitude of the fluctuations will approach zero. (We discuss below the empirical implications of this observation in testing the model.) Hence, another key driving force, determining the empirical magnitude of politically induced fluctuations, and how this magnitude may change over time, is simply specified exogenously.

The easiest way to interpret the election probabilities q^L is that there is some underlying, exogenous stochastic process that makes the outcomes of elections uncertain. An example of such an approach is given in the Rogoff–Sibert model in the next section. In a partisan model of this type, however, specifying a stochastic structure such that election outcomes are uncertain is more complicated, as there should be a connection in both directions between the positions that parties take and the probability of winning the election. There should be a feedback from the positions the parties adopt to the probability of winning an election, especially under the interpretation that party positions represent the desires of their constituents. Moreover, if parties care about winning elections in order to implement their desired policies, a view fully consistent with parties being ideologically motivated, there should be a feedback from probabilities of winning elections to the positions that parties adopt. To make the outcomes of elections probabilistic and dependent on the policy positions that a party takes, one could assume there is uncertainty about the underlying preferred positions of the heterogeneous electorate. Positions then translate only probabilistically into election outcomes, and a change in a party's position in a given direction will change its probability of winning the election. Alesina, Roubini, and Cohen (1997) suggest how probabilities of elections could be derived from an underlying distribution of voter preferences, but do not explore how parties might change their positions in a partisan model to affect their electoral chances. It should be easy to analyze the full equilibrium effects of endogenous election probabilities in the rational partisan model, but in the absence of such an analysis, one is left with the question of how important an exogenous specification of these probabilities is for the workings of the model. Since policy choice and probabilities of winning interact in driving the dynamics, one must be careful in interpreting the results of models that treat them as independent.

---

[24] The objectives $\tilde{\pi}^R$ and $\tilde{\pi}^L$, as well as other parameters of each party's loss functions, are themselves exogenous. But the difference in the two parties' loss functions represents the basic insight of the partisan approach, reflecting the fact that each party represents a different constituency, with the loss function representing the preferences of their own constituency.

A final basic question about the driving forces in the rational partisan model has to do with the underlying party preferences themselves. If one takes the election probability q^L as given, the larger is the difference between the goals of the two parties in (7.16b), the greater will be the size of economic fluctuations induced by electoral uncertainty. (This characteristic was, in fact, a motivation for Alesina's work on common platforms discussed above.) One response to this question is to argue simply, following Hibbs (1977) and Tufte (1978), that partisan differences are a "primitive" of democratic systems, and that the degree of polarization in a society will determine the magnitude of politically induced fluctuations. This seems too simple an answer for two reasons. First, the relation between the degree of underlying polarization of positions and the magnitude of policy change accompanying a change in governments is not so simple. The discussion of executive–legislative interaction in Section 7.7 below and of coalition government in Section 7.8 will make this clear.

A second reason not to treat the partisan differences as represented by (7.16b) simply as primitives is that a party's objectives may change, even in the short run, in response to economic conditions. As already discussed in our criticism of exogenous q^L above, parties that lose elections will be induced to change their positions. Moreover, parties may adjust their objectives not only to political "realities," but to economic "realities" as well. Popular but unrealistic economic goals, such as aiming for too low a rate of unemployment, may be as damaging for ultimate electoral success as goals which are themselves unpopular.[25] As Okun (1973, p. 175) points out in an often quoted observation:

> For a generation, every major mistake in economic policy under a Democratic president has taken the form of overstimulating the economy and every major mistake under a Republican of overrestraining it.

To the extent that parties are punished at the polls for the mistake of pushing their goals too far, too much partisanship can be electorally dangerous.

This simple observation, combined with the differences in the goals of left-wing and right-wing parties, yields a theory of endogenous election outcomes consistent with the observed differences in economic outcomes between, for example, Democratic and Republican administrations in the United States. As Hibbs (1987) and others have suggested, electoral defeats of the incumbent party may be due to economic mismanagement due to their overzealousness in trying to achieve their goals, with the opposition elected with a mandate to correct those mistakes. As Keech (1995) points out, Republican victories in 1968 and 1980 followed infla-

---

[25] The political failure of "populism" in many Latin American countries as a result of its economic failures is a case in point. See Dornbusch and Edwards (1990). We return to this point in Chapter 13 in our discussion of economic reform.

tionary outbursts due to Democratic administrations having pursued highly expansionary policies, with the incoming administrations deliberately restraining the economy. Analogously, Democratic victories in 1960, 1976, and 1992 followed Republican administrations bedeviled by the problem of low economic activity. If parties learn from their mistakes of overzealous pursuit of their partisan targets, we should see an incumbent party that desires to be re-elected change its policies in response to realized outcomes, yielding an interaction between partisanship and opportunism subtler than that suggested by Frey and Schneider (1978), as discussed above. As Keech (1995) sums it up, this interaction implies that partisan strategies are likely to be contingent on economic conditions.

Hibbs's Model of Changing Objectives

Hibbs (1994) presents such a theory of adjustment of partisan objectives contingent on economic outcomes. As in Alesina's rational partisan theory, this theory predicts that unemployment and inflation outcomes across the two parties may diverge more in the first part of their terms than in the second, though not because of the uncertainty about electoral outcomes that drives this result in Alesina's models. Even without electoral uncertainty, there will be partisan differences that diminish as a president's term progresses. The key to Hibbs's model of changing objectives (and to the result on time-varying outcomes) is that *policymakers* are uncertain about the structure of the economy and the effects of policies. They use outcomes to refine their beliefs about attainable targets, leading to a feedback from outcomes to partisan objectives and thus policies.

The basic driving force in Hibbs's model can be represented as follows.[26] Suppose that policymakers are uncertain about the natural rate of unemployment, with the Phillips curve (7.17) becoming

$$U_t = \hat{U}^{NAT} - \pi_t + \epsilon_t, \tag{7.17a}$$

where $\hat{U}^{NAT}$ is the uncertain natural rate of unemployment and where ϵ_t is an unobserved i.i.d. random variable, with unemployment measured relative to zero, rather than the natural rate as in earlier specifications. A government chooses monetary policy based on its prior on $\hat{U}^{NAT}$, observes the outcomes U_t and π_t, based on which it forms a posterior estimate of $\hat{U}^{NAT}$. (Remember that ϵ_t is unobserved.) Consistent with Okun's argument above, one might argue that left-wingers have a tendency to underes-

---

[26] The simple representation of the argument differs from Hibbs's formulation, but I suggest that this characterization of uncertainty about the workings of the economy and the implied evolution of the time-varying target capture Hibbs's basic argument. The heart of the Hibbs model is a negative relation between partisan output targets and past observed inflation (i.e., a positive relation between unemployment targets and inflation). Hibbs assumes this relation, which we derive, based on the sort of learning arguments suggested in the text.

timate the natural rate (which will lead to too expansionary a policy) and right-wingers have a tendency to overestimate the natural rate (which will lead to too contractionary a policy). For simple, general assumptions about the distributions of $\hat{U}^{NAT}$ and ϵ_t, the estimate of $\hat{U}^{NAT}$ will be increasing in the observed value of π_t relative to its prior.[27] Hence, inflation higher than expected (consistent with an initial underestimate of $\hat{U}^{NAT}$) would raise the estimate of the natural rate; inflation lower than expected (consistent with an initial overestimate of $\hat{U}^{NAT}$) would lower it.

A party elected in t is in office for t and $t + 1$ and chooses policy to minimize a loss function such as (7.19), but with a crucial difference from other partisan models, in the specification of its unemployment objective. Suppose that the two parties have the same inflation target $\tilde{\pi}$ and inflation aversion θ, but differ in both their estimates of the natural rate (as discussed above) and their unemployment targets. Uncertainty about the natural rate implies that a party's unemployment target will depend on its estimate of the natural rate; updating this estimate depending on observations of inflation (and unemployment) implies that this target will be time varying. Hence, in (7.19), party j's target in the second half of its term would depend on the inflation observation in the first half of the term. It would not be simply $\tilde{U}^j$ as in the basic partisan model, but would be a target $U_{t+1}^{\text{tar} j}$ which depends on "underlying" preferences $\tilde{U}^j$ and its beliefs about $\hat{U}^{NAT}$. Expressing the target relative to the natural rate would yield

$$U_{t+1}^{\text{tar} j} = \tilde{U}^j + \mathrm{E}\left(\hat{U}^{NAT} \mid \pi_t\right). \tag{7.24}$$

(The unemployment objective in (7.19) may be seen as a "special case" of this specification, where the natural rate of unemployment is known and the target is expressed relative to the natural rate.) A rational inference process as discussed in the previous paragraph, whereby a government updates its estimate of $\hat{U}^{NAT}$ based on observation of actual economic conditions, would thus imply that the target unemployment rate will evolve according to the evolution of economic conditions.

The implications for policy choices and economic outcomes follow from substituting (7.24) into (7.19), using the inference on $\hat{U}^{NAT}$ based on (7.17a). If, for example, a left-wing party enters office with a low target unemployment rate (reflecting both their underlying preferences and perhaps a low estimate of $\hat{U}^{NAT}$), they will choose an expansionary policy with a resultant high rate of inflation. If their estimate of the natural rate of unemployment is overly optimistic (that is, below the true natural rate), the unexpectedly high inflation that results will lead them to raise their unemployment target over time, which in turn leads them to choose a

---

[27] To take an extremely simple example, suppose both $\hat{U}^{NAT}$ and ϵ_t are mean-zero normally distributed random variables, with variances σ_N^2 and σ_ϵ^2, respectively. The expectation of $\hat{U}^{NAT}$ conditional on π_t is $\mathrm{E}(\hat{U}^{NAT} \mid \pi_t) = ((\pi_t - \mathrm{E}(\pi_t))\sigma_N^2)/(\sigma_\epsilon^2 + \sigma_N^2)$.

policy of lower inflation and higher unemployment in the second half of their terms. In contrast, if a right-wing party enters office with a relatively high target unemployment rate, they will choose a relatively contractionary policy with resultant low inflation and high unemployment. To the extent that their estimate of the natural rate of unemployment is overly pessimistic, they will be led to lower their unemployment target over time, implying a policy of higher inflation and lower unemployment in the second half of their terms. Thus, unemployment rates would converge in the latter part of administrations, as in the rational partisan model, but for a very different reason. This argument depends on left-wing governments on average tending to err towards underestimating the natural rate and their ability to expand the economy and right-wing governments tending to err towards overestimating the natural rate and the optimal degree of economic contraction.

The Hibbs model of contingent partisan objectives is preliminary. A more robust optimal learning process needs to be specified, as this is the heart of the model (see footnote 26). Furthermore, as Hibbs argues at the end of the paper, the mechanisms by which a policymaker attempts to influence economic activity away from an underlying natural rate must be better specified under rational expectations. Finally, the model must be subjected to more rigorous empirical testing. All these caveats notwithstanding, the theory of contingent partisan objectives seems promising for at least two reasons. First, since parties' objectives are not static and do appear to respond to changes in economic conditions, such a theory would significantly enrich the partisan approach to political business cycles. Second, such a theory suggests how reduced partisan differences in economic activity over the duration of the term of office may be explained without invoking uncertainty about election outcomes or special assumptions about the timing of labor contracts. We now turn to empirical evidence on partisan models.

Empirical Studies of the Partisan Political Business Cycle

Both the basic partisan model and the extensions represent important steps in the study of political business cycles. The rational partisan model, for example, shows that differences in desired policies of parties of the sorts that are actually observed, combined with uncertainty about who will win the election, can give rise to cyclical behavior of economic activity even when expectations of inflation are formed rationally. One crucial aspect that is less clear is to what extent this is due to unanticipated monetary shocks. More generally, one may ask how convincingly the models explain actual fluctuations in economic activity.

The partisan PBC model has been tested less than the opportunistic model. Though there is general agreement on the existence of partisan effects *per se*, there is far less consensus on which of the possible mechanisms discussed in this section is or is not supported by the data. Alesina and co-authors find the strongest empirical support for the rational partisan model and against both the opportunistic model and the basic Hibbs partisan model. (As of yet, there is little work comparing the Alesina and the more recent Hibbs partisan model.) Other authors find less support for partisan models based on trading off inflation and aggregate economic activity and argue for a more eclectic stance. Alesina, Roubini, and Cohen (1997) present a summary of the empirical work.

The basic partisan model suggests higher economic activity in left-wing (Democratic, in the U.S.) administrations than in right-wing (Republican in the U.S.) administrations. In contrast, the basic empirical predictions of the rational partisan model are as follows: an expansion at the beginning of a Democratic administration, a recession at the beginning of a Republican administration; the deviation of unemployment from the natural rate being greater the greater is the electoral surprise, with no effect at the beginning of a party's term if the electoral outcome is not in doubt; and, no unemployment effect in the latter part of either party's term. Inflation is higher under Democrats than Republicans over the whole term.

Summary Statistics

Let us begin with the nonparametric evidence for the United States. As reported in Section 7.3 above, real GDP growth is substantially higher under Democrats than Republicans in years 2 and 3 of their administrations. The evidence of differences is especially striking in the average quarterly values of real GDP growth during the term of administrations (16 quarters) over the period from the first quarter of 1949 through the second quarter of 1994, as reported in Alesina, Roubini, and Cohen (1997). Starting about the third quarter after the election, the growth rates in Democratic and Republican administrations sharply diverge. The quarterly growth rate averaged over Democratic administrations rises from about 3% per annum in quarter 3 to about 6% per annum by quarter 6 or 7 in the administration's term of office and falls from the same level to zero by quarter 6 or 7 in the administration's term averaged over Republican administrations; real GDP growth rates then improve under Republican and worsen under Democratic administrations, so that in the fourth year of the administration (quarters 13 through 16), the growth performance under the two parties is identical. The unemployment averages are also favorable for the rational partisan theory, though somewhat less so. Unemployment is substantially lower under Democrats than Republicans in years 2, 3, and 4 of their terms, with the difference especially striking in the second half of their terms, rather than in the first half, as the rational partisan theory would suggest.

On the other hand, the basic inflation figures (as measured by the rate of change in the Consumer Price Index) do not conform to the partisan theory, especially the rational partisan theory. Democratic administrations have *lower* average inflation than Republican administrations in the first half of their terms, exactly the opposite of what the rational partisan theory of inflation surprises predicts. (If one argues, as we did for the Nordhaus model, that inflation follows economic stimulation with a lag, the data appear more favorable; however, this is not really consistent with the model's stress on inflation surprises as the driving force.) In interpreting these data, Alesina, Roubini, and Cohen (1997) argue that they are consistent with the theory, as inflation is rising starting in the second year of a Democratic administration and falling starting in the second year of a Republican administration. Such an argument is only partially convincing, since the rational partisan theory based on the expectations-augmented Phillips curve is built on the rate of inflation, not on changes in that rate. They further argue that the inflation data is strongly influenced by external events, such as the oil shocks of 1973 and 1979, and hence its patterns should not be read as evidence against the rational partisan theory. On the whole, one would say that the nonparametric evidence on real GDP growth rates is quite favorable to the rational partisan theory, the unemployment data more mixed, while the inflation data at the very least raises some questions about its validity.

Econometric Tests for the United States

Alesina, Roubini, and Cohen (1997) present more formal econometric tests for the United States using autoregressive equations such as (7.15) in quarterly data from 1947: I through 1993: IV. They use a *PDUM* political dummy variable that equals $+1$ in the first T quarters of a Republican administration, -1 in the first T quarters of a Democratic administration (whether a change in party or a re-election of the incumbent party), and 0 otherwise, where T may equal 4, 6, or 8. In equations for real GDP growth, the political dummy is statistically significant and of the correct sign for all values of N, the strongest results being those for $T = 6$. They report similar results supporting the rational partisan model in unemployment regressions. (They also performed tests with a dummy which was nonzero only after changes in party, with similar supportive results.)

To test for permanent partisan effects, they consider a political dummy that equals $+1$ over an entire Republican administration and -1 over an entire Democratic administration. In GDP growth regressions, the variable enters significantly and is of the right sign. However, by dividing this political dummy into two variables—one, as in the previous paragraph, equals $+1$ in the first six quarters of a Republican administration, -1 in the first six quarters of a Democratic administration, 0 thereafter; the other, its complement, equaling zero until quarter $T + 1$ and $+1$ or -1 thereafter, they show the partisan effect on measures of economic activity is strongest in the first half of the term.

The econometric tests for inflation cycles in the United States are far less favorable to partisan models, paralleling the nonparametric tests discussed above. They find that after 1973 (and the move to floating rates after the collapse of Bretton Woods), the difference in average inflation rates between Democratic and Republican administrations is (only) about 1.8% per year. Alesina, Roubini, and Cohen (1997) present no formal tests of the timing of inflation within administrations, that is, whether inflation rates are higher in the first half of Democratic than Republican administrations, with these differences narrowing in the second half.

To test for partisan cycles in monetary policy, Alesina, Roubini, and Cohen (1997) consider a reaction function of the form of (7.15) in which money growth rates are regressed on lagged money growth rates, lagged unemployment, and a political dummy. Over the entire sample, there are no significant partisan differences in quarterly data for money growth rates. The results are more favorable for partisan theories, especially when M_1 rather than the monetary base M_0 is used, over the period 1949–1987. They attribute this difference to the instability of money demand starting in the early 1980s found by many researchers. They also find no significant partisan differences in fiscal policy, specifically in transfers to individuals relative to GNP, although (paralleling the results for opportunistic models) this depends on the time period considered. Alesina (1988b) finds a significant effect over the period 1961–1985, which, however, disappears if the period 1949–1961 or 1985–1994 is added, or the entire sample period is considered.

Econometric Results for the OECD

Following Alesina and Roubini (1992), Alesina, Roubini, and Cohen (1997) run similar tests on a sample of 18 OECD countries over the period 1960–1993. To test the rational partisan model, they use the dummy variable that equals $+1$ in the quarter of the change to a right-wing party and in the $T-1$ subsequent quarters, -1 in the quarter of the change to a left-wing party and in the $T-1$ subsequent quarters, and 0 otherwise, where T may equal 4, 6, or 8. In a pooled cross-section time-series regression of year-over-year real GDP growth rate regression with country dummies, the later paper reports that the rational partisan dummy with $T=6$ has the correct (negative) sign and is significant at the 1% level, with a point estimate of -0.35, confirming results found in the earlier paper for the period 1960–1987. They report similar results for U^{DIF}, the difference between the domestic unemployment rate and an OECD average, as the measure of economic activity. In individual country regressions, they find the evidence strong for a number of countries, but only marginally significant in others.

To test for partisan monetary effects in their sample of OECD countries, they use a political dummy variable that is $+1$ if a right-wing government is in office (including the quarter of the change in government) and is -1 if a left-wing government is in office (including the quarter of the change in government). In similar pooled cross-section time-series regressions for year-over-year CPI growth with country dummies, they find the coefficient on the political dummy is insignificant when the entire sample is used, but is significant at the 5% level in a subsample of countries they consider more partisan, having either a "pure" two-party system or (in their estimation) more clearly identifiable left-wing and right-wing coalitions.[28] Money growth rates show similar patterns—partisan effects being significant in some cases, not in others. In a pooled regression, Alesina, Roubini, and Cohen (1997) also test a political dummy that distinguishes not only right-wing versus left-wing governments, but also center-left and center-right governments from more extreme governments. They similarly find it to be insignificant in inflation regressions. Finally, paralleling their results for fiscal policy in the United States, Alesina, Roubini, and Cohen (1997) find no evidence of systematic partisan effects on budget deficits in their sample of OECD countries.

Alesina and co-authors, for example, Alesina, Roubini, and Cohen (1997), also test Hibbs's original partisan theory for economic activity in the OECD sample as they did for the United States and find similar results. They run the basic type of regression for real GDP growth using a political dummy that equals $+1$ over the entire life of a right-wing government and -1 over the entire life of a left-wing government. The variable enters quite significantly and of the right sign. However, by dividing this political dummy into two variables as they did for the United States—one that equals $+1$ in the first part of a right-wing administration, -1 in the first part of a left-wing administration, 0 thereafter; the other, its complement, equaling zero in the first part and $+1$ or -1 thereafter, they show the partisan effect on measures of economic activity is strongest in the first half of the term.

Both Hibbs (1992) and Gärtner (1994) question the possibility of econometrically distinguishing the original partisan theory from the rational partisan theory on the basis of persistent versus temporary effects of elections on real economic activity. The problem is in the unemployment and GNP series themselves. Since one cannot reject the hypothesis of a unit root in the unemployment data for many countries over the period of analysis, one cannot confidently base a rejection of one model and acceptance of the other on tests of persistence. (The Alesina–Roubini unemployment correction embodied in U^{DIF} does not solve the problem.) In short, they argue that the test Alesina and Roubini (1992) design to discriminate between the two models does not have the power to do so.

---

[28] Australian, Canada, France, Germany, New Zealand, Sweden, the U.K., and the U.S.

Summary and Assessment

As with the opportunistic model, one can ask: what is one to make of all the results? We begin with a "bottom-line" summary of the statistical evidence, both nonparametric and parametric, and then consider some of the critiques that have been made. What is unmistakable is a partisan pattern for real GDP growth rates both in the United States and in numerous other countries. There are also partisan patterns in inflation and in money growth rates. The effects on unemployment are a bit weaker, but often observed. What is more open to question is what sort of partisan model these results support. Alesina and co-authors, not surprisingly, summarize the statistical tests as quite favorable for the rational partisan theory and unfavorable to Hibbs's original partisan theory, though I think an unbiased assessment is that even without deeper analysis, the conclusions to be drawn from the empirical results are less clear. (Obviously, these tests cannot discriminate between the rational partisan theory and Hibbs's more recent contingent partisan objectives theory.) The strongest evidence in favor of the rational partisan theory comes from the nonparametric and econometric results on economic growth, where growth effects in both the United States and other OECD countries are concentrated in the early part of a government's term. This evidence is quite impressive. Both the nonparametric and parametric results for unemployment are a bit less impressive in this respect.

Much more damaging for the rational partisan theory is the inflation evidence. For the United States, the timing of partisan inflation differences does not conform to the rational partisan theory in nonparametric tests. In spite of the wealth of empirical evidence that Alesina and co-authors present on political business cycles, they present no formal tests of the timing of inflation that the theory would predict within government terms. For the OECD, Alesina and Roubini (1992) present individual country regressions for the OECD in which output growth, unemployment, and inflation regressions in seven countries[29] yield support for the rational partisan theory (though sometimes with marginal significance). In the rest of the countries, the evidence is fairly negative: the coefficient on the political dummy in the inflation regressions is always insignificant, while the political dummy coefficients in the GNP growth or unemployment are at best only marginally significant.

The lack of unqualified support to a single partisan theory suggests the need for further analysis. Most fruitful is probably analysis of the underlying components of the theories. Much work remains to be done, but in this respect, a number of researchers argue that the empirical evidence is not especially favorable to the rational partisan theory. As already discussed in connection with the Nordhaus model, there are doubts about the central

---

[29] Australia, Denmark, France, Germany, New Zealand, the U.K., and the U.S.

role assigned to moving along the Phillips curve to reduce unemployment via inflation surprises. Sheffrin (1989) finds the empirical evidence in favor of the rational partisan theory to be weak for both the United States and other countries. For example, he argues that economic fluctuations following Republican presidential victories in the United States are generally inconsistent with the rational partisan theory, post-electoral recessions often coming as a surprise. He argues that his weak results are due to, among other things, the importance for macroeconomic fluctuations of factors other than unanticipated monetary policy. Hibbs (1994) echoes this point.

Considering a wider set of influences than simply unanticipated monetary policy suggests a "reverse causation" argument, namely, that the desire for specific economic outcomes "causes" partisan electoral victories, rather than elections causing economic outcomes. The real effects of fiscal policy, even when expected, mean that an administration can exercise its taste even if a victory is anticipated. If Democrats have a known preference for expansionary policies and Republicans a known preference for anti-inflationary policies, the observed difference in outcomes across Democratic and Republican administrations may simply reflect parties fulfilling their mandates when elected.

Three other basic empirical criticisms of the rational partisan theory's reliance on inflation surprises may be mentioned.[30] The first is the crucial assumption that wage contracts are signed before the election, discussed in our theoretical analysis of the rational partisan model earlier in this section. The second concerns the partisan differences necessary to drive the model. Sheffrin suggested that his results unfavorable to the rational partisan model also reflect the fact that in the United States, partisan differences are simply not that strong. The results of Romer and Romer's (1989) careful study of monetary policy cast similar doubt on political differences there.

The final criticism concerns the central role played by uncertainty about who will win an election. The rational partisan model predicts a positive correlation between the extent of the electoral surprise and the size of post-electoral movements in real economic activity. If an election outcome can be well predicted, there should be little uncertainty about monetary policy after the election, and hence little effect on economic activity. Hibbs (1992), among others, has argued that this prediction is not consistent with the empirical evidence for the United States. Consideration of individual elections reveals the problem. For example, the outcome of the 1964 presidential election is probably the closest we have seen to a sure thing in the post-war era, with Lyndon Johnson's victory widely anticipated. Yet the rate of real GNP growth in the first two years of the Johnson administration averaged 5.8% per year, the highest figure of any Democratic adminis-

---

[30] Hibbs (1992) presents a good critical assessement of the rational partisan model.

tration. In contrast, considering post-war Republican victories through Reagan's first election, Nixon's victory in 1968 was the closest and least certain, but corresponds to the smallest drop in real output in the critical second year of the administration. On the other hand, Alesina, Roubini, and Cohen (1997, chapter 5) construct an index of electoral surprise for the U.S. presidential elections from 1948 to 1992, with Republican victories entering as negative surprises. They use different variants as an explanatory variable in a real GDP growth regression of the form of (7.15) and find that the coefficient on the surprise variable is significantly positive, meaning that larger Democratic (Republican) surprises imply higher (lower) post-election real growth rates. The construction of the variable is ingenious but complicated, so that it is not easy to see why the regression results and simple case study results do not agree. The relation of pre-electoral uncertainty and post-electoral fluctuations is an important question deserving further research.

Finally, one may note an alternative empirical explanation for some of the results on the difference between outcomes under Democratic and Republican administrations in the United States. The high growth rates after the 1964 election reflect not a monetary surprise, but the military build-up associated with the Vietnam war, on top of ambitious social programs. The highest post-war output growth rates were in the second and third years of the Truman administration in 1950–1951. While this is consistent with the Truman victory in 1948 being the biggest surprise in modern U.S. electoral history, there is a simpler, more convincing explanation, namely, the Korean War and the high expenditures associated with it. More generally, Democrats have been in power more often than Republicans during wars, which may account for their tenures being associated with booms. Hence, partisan cyclical behavior may reflect noneconomically motivated policy choices. This too merits further research.

To summarize, the empirical results indicate that there is significant empirical evidence in favor of systematic partisan effects, but the evidence on how important these differences are and which partisan model they support is less clear. The combination of theoretical and empirical problems raises significant questions about the rational partisan model, as similar problems cast doubt on the specific Nordhaus model of opportunistic political business cycles. In my opinion, there is still much interesting work to be done, including investigation of partisan goals which change in response to economic circumstances, and of reverse causation as discussed above, and of the possibility that partisan factors other than basic macroeconomic goals may help explain partisan differences.

To the extent that pre-electoral manipulation is at least a part of the theory of the political business cycle and of the distortions that are induced by elections, we return to the questions posed at the end of the previous section. Why do politicians make promises during campaigns that it would appear they know they cannot fulfill or, in the case of incumbents, enact policies which appear to be opportunistically shortsighted; and, why do voters appear to be influenced by such promises and policies? If we are to reject irrationality as an explanation, such behavior suggests a *signaling* effect: voters have imperfect information about relevant characteristics of potential policymakers, and what appear to be gimmicks have an effect because they are taken to provide relevant information about candidates for office. We now turn to such models.

7.5. COMPETENCE AND PROSPECTIVE VOTING

Some of the most convincing models of the rationality of pre-electoral manipulation turn on the issue of imperfect information about how *competent* the policymaker is. The basic work is due to Rogoff and Sibert (1988) and Rogoff (1990) in models where opportunistic incumbents use fiscal policy to signal good information on competence. The work is designed to address some of the more serious criticisms of political business cycle models based on the Phillips curve, in which incumbents try to influence the outcomes of elections by surprise inflation. First, both the Nordhaus and Alesina models concentrate on monetary policy to the exclusion of fiscal policy, though much of the cyclical behavior is seen in fiscal variables.[31] Monetary policy works via surprises in these models; however, as indicated above, irrationality of inflation expectations is only part of the problem. The more serious problem is the response of voters to electoral manipulation. Why should voters respond positively to officeholders engaging in distortionary policy? The above papers present models where more expansionary fiscal policy signals that the incumbent policymaker is more competent, a fact not directly observable by voters. Hence, as in the signaling models of Section 6.6 of Chapter 6, the policymaker's type is not observed. Voters face a standard inference problem of predicting unobservable type from observable policy, while a government uses policy to signal its type and separate itself from other types. Competence has some persistence, which justifies retrospective voting.

How does a government signal its type? The basic idea is that a policymaker engages in a sort of brinkmanship—he takes actions which worsen his budget situation with the notion that only someone who is very competent would put himself in that situation. It bears a resemblance to the policymaker who chooses current actions to constrain his successor (see Section 7.9 below), only here he hopes that by putting on constraints that would greatly constrain an incompetent policymaker, he can credibly signal his own competence.

---

[31] As already mentioned, Tufte (1978) argues that increasing transfers and cutting taxes before an election is the most robust empirical characteristic of the political business cycle.

The Rogoff–Sibert and Rogoff Models of Signaling Competence

These points can be illustrated in a simplified version of the Rogoff and Sibert model. As in many partisan models, there are elections every other period (say in even-numbered periods), in which two parties, L and R, compete for power. The government in power provides a known fixed level of services g.[32] Policymakers differ, however, in the amount of taxes that must be levied to provide g—more competent governments need to raise less revenues to provide the same g:

$$g - \xi = \tau + \pi, \tag{7.25}$$

where ξ is a measure of the government's competency, τ is a nondistortionary tax, and π is a distortionary tax.

The basic building block of voter choice is individual utility, which depends on after-tax income, the loss from the distortionary tax, and a nonpecuniary party preference shock. All voters are identical, so we can write the social welfare function at t, which is the utility of the representative voter at t, as

$$\Omega_t^V = y - \tau_t - \pi_t - \mathscr{L}(\pi_t) + \eta_t, \tag{7.26}$$

where y is (constant) income inclusive of government spending, η_t is the party-preference shock, and $\mathscr{L}(\pi)$ represents the loss from use of distortionary financing. It is assumed that the distortions are zero when $\pi = 0$ and are positive when $\pi > 0$, and that $\mathscr{L}(\pi)$ is a convex function. Taking the tax mix as given, voters clearly prefer a more competent policymaker to a less competent one. It is also clear that the efficient solution would be to rely only on nondistortionary taxes τ to finance $g - \xi$. If there were full information about competence, policymakers would do this; under imperfect information, the tax mix must be used to signal competence.

Two factors are crucial in modeling competence. First, the incumbent must have better information about his competence than the voters, so that there is something to be signaled. That is, there must be asymmetric information. Second, there must be some persistence to the incumbent's competence, so that information about competence that is learned before an election is relevant after the election. This is captured by assuming there is a shock to competence each period, where the current shock is observed by voters only with a lag, with current competence being the sum of this period's and last period's shock:

$$\xi_t^j = \gamma_t^j + \gamma_{t-1}^j, \tag{7.27}$$

---

[32] Rogoff (1990) presents a model where the government provides two goods, with choice over the quantities provided of each good.

for $j = L, R$ where γ is an nonnegative i.i.d. shock with maximum value $\gamma^{\max} < \infty$, distributed according to a cumulative distribution $\Gamma(\gamma)$ with mean $\bar{\gamma}$. Note that modeling competence ξ as following a first-order moving average (MA(1)) process implies that elections are independent (they take place every *second* period), and that any information from a party's previous terms in office gives no information about current competence. In reality, of course, competence is much longer-lived so that performance in past terms of office provides information, but the assumption of an MA(1) process is necessary to solve the model so simply. Note also that the party out of power has no way of signaling competence in the Rogoff and Sibert model. Promises of what they might do once in office have no effect on voters, as candidates have no incentive to be honest. (We return to this issue in the next section.) Voters assign to the out-of-power party the unconditional mean of competence, namely, $\bar{\xi} = 2\bar{\gamma}$. An alternative, more realistic assumption would be that a nonincumbent signals his competence via his performance in a similar job.

What does competence represent? It cannot be simply a characteristic of the policymaker himself, for in that case it makes little sense that he is always learning new things about himself. It makes more sense to think of competence as representing the interaction between the policymaker and his environment, for example, how well a president interacts with Congress. That is, the ability of an executive to achieve his goals in a representative democracy will depend on his relationship with the legislature; this will change over time, albeit slowly, with the executive himself having incomplete information about how this relationship, and hence how his "competence," will evolve.

The other stochastic variable in the model is the party-preference shock η. Its role is to make the outcome of elections stochastic from the point of view of the government. Rogoff and Sibert also model this variable as a first-order moving average:

$$\eta_t^R - \eta_t^L = \sigma_t + \sigma_{t-1}, \tag{7.28}$$

where ζ_t is a mean-zero i.i.d. stochastic process. η may be thought of as capturing factors which influence election outcomes which are independent of policies which could signal competence and are unknown to the incumbent government when policies are chosen (such as election-day turnout).

As in all models of asymmetric information, the sequencing of who knows what when is crucial. The timing and information structure are as follows. At the beginning of a period in which election will be held (say t), the incumbent government observes its current competence shock γ_t and, before the election is held, commits itself to nondistortionary taxes τ_t for the current period. One interpretation, which has the virtue of sidestepping the issue of how campaign promises can be made credible (see

Section 7.6 below), is that this tax is somehow implemented before the election. When it chooses τ_t, the incumbent government does not know σ_t and hence does not know for certain the election outcome as a function of τ_t. Voters do not observe γ_t, but can draw inferences about it from τ_t. After τ_t is set, voters observe σ_t and the election is held to choose the government for periods $t + 1$ and $t + 2$. The period-t government then supplies g, using distortionary taxes π_t to make up any shortfall. Knowing the level of both types of taxes, voters can thus deduce γ_t from the government's budget constraint (7.25). In an off-election year, say $t + 1$, there is no role for signaling the new competence shock γ_{t+1} since it will be irrelevant in the term of office beginning in $t + 3$ and hence in the next election. The government therefore uses only nondistortionary taxes τ to finance its expenditures $g - \xi_{t+1}$.

The "voting mechanism" is modeled simply as follows. Voters prefer the party which will give them higher expected utility over their term of office. Hence, party R will win at t if

$$E_t^V\left[(\Omega_{t+1}^V[R] + \Omega_{t+2}^V[R]) - (\Omega_{t+1}^V[L] + \Omega_{t+2}[L])\right] \geq 0, \quad (7.29)$$

where $E_t^V(\cdot)$ is the expectation operator of the representative voter conditional on his information at the time of election and $\Omega_t^V[j]$ is voter utility if party j is in power. Since governments do not use distortionary taxes in off-election years, $\pi_{t+1} = 0$ for both parties. The MA(1) structure of ξ implies that information on ξ_t provides no information on ξ_{t+2} for either party; voters assign the same unconditional mean $\bar{\xi}$ to each party's expected competence, implying they have the same expectation of π_{t+2} for each party, so that $E_t^V(\Omega_{t+2}^V[R]) = E_t^V(\Omega_{t+2}^V[L])$. Using (7.25) and the definition of Ω_t^V in (7.26), (7.29) simplifies to

$$E_t^V\left[(\xi_{t+1}^R + \eta_{t+1}^R) - (\xi_{t+1}^L + \eta_{t+1}^L)\right] \geq 0. \quad (7.30)$$

Suppose party R is in power. Since L has no way to signal, and since σ is mean zero, the above equation becomes

$$E_t^V\left[(\xi_{t+1}^R - \xi_{t+1}^L) + (\eta_{t+1}^R - \eta_{t+1}^L)\right] = E_t^V(\gamma_t^R|\tau_t^R) + \bar{\gamma} - 2\bar{\gamma} + \sigma_t. \quad (7.31)$$

The probability that the incumbent R will win the election is then the probability that (7.31) is positive (meaning the party-preference shock favoring the right-wing party outweighs the voter's expectation of the competence difference), that is, the probability that $\sigma_t \geq \bar{\gamma} - E_t^V(\gamma_t^R|\tau_t^R)$. (Remember that the incumbent does not know σ_t when he sets τ.) Call the right-wing incumbent's estimate of this probability q^R (where the probability that the left-wing party will win the election is $q^L = 1 - q^R$). The function $q^R[E_t^V(\gamma_t^R|\tau_t^R)]$ is assumed to be twice differentiable, with a positive first derivative, which approaches zero as $E_t^V(\gamma_t^R|\tau_t^R)$ approaches

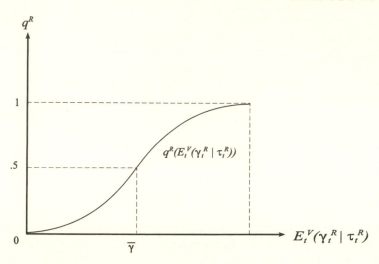

FIGURE 7.1. The probability of election function.

infinity, and a positive (negative) second derivative as $E_t^V(\gamma_t^R|\tau_t^R) < (>)\bar{\gamma}$. These characteristics follow from the underlying distribution of σ; the function $q^R[E_t^V(\gamma_t^R|\tau_t^R)]$ is illustrated in Figure 7.1.

The objective function of the incumbent in choosing period-t policy is to maximize a weighted sum of the probability of winning the upcoming election and of the social welfare loss from distortionary taxation, with weights χ and $1 - \chi$, respectively. (The MA(1) nature of the shocks and the absence of any other determinants of electoral success mean the policymaker need consider only the current election, even if he has a longer horizon.) For example, party R's objective function is

$$\Omega_t^R = \chi q^R\big[E_t^V(\gamma_t^R|\tau_t^R)\big] + (1 - \chi)\big[-\mathscr{L}(\pi_t^R)\big]. \qquad (7.32)$$

(Party L maximizes the corresponding function when in power.) Crucial to the results is that a party put some weight on social welfare (that is, $\chi < 1$). Otherwise, the incumbent would always set the nondistortionary tax τ at a minimum since he would not care about the magnitude of distortions that might result. The signaling equilibrium would then break down.

In a fully revealing signaling equilibrium, the choice of τ will perfectly signal γ, but the optimal τ will be less than $g - \xi$. That is, in a signaling equilibrium, $\pi(\gamma) > 0$ for all $\gamma > 0.$[33] In the separating equilibrium, by

---

[33] The reader should note the difference between a fully revealing equilibrium, as derived here, and an equilibrium in which there is full information about types *ex ante*. In a fully revealing equilibrium, there is full information about types only *ex post*, that is, after types have expended costly resources to communicate this information. The costliness of revealing information in one case, compared with the costlessness of having full information in the other, make the economic outcomes qualitatively different.

definition of an equilibrium, each type prefers his own tax rate. With a continuum of types, the representative voter conjectures an equilibrium $\tau^*(\gamma)$, forms $E_t^V(\gamma_t^R|\tau_t^R)$ using this conjecture, which yields q^R as a function of voters' conjectures. Given the $q^R(\cdot)$ function, each type γ chooses actual τ to maximize the objective function. In equilibrium, $\tau(\gamma) = \tau^*(\gamma)$.[34] In the next paragraph, we show formally how this equilibrium function is derived. Readers not interested in the technical details may skip the paragraph.

To derive the self-confirming equilibrium function $\tau(\gamma)$, suppose, as will turn out to be the case, that the conjecture $\tau^*(\gamma)$ is continuous and monotonic in γ, so that it can be inverted, yielding an inference on γ for any observed τ. This inference is simply $E_t^V(\gamma_t^R|\tau_t^R) = (\tau^*)^{-1}(\tau_t)$. Using $\tau^* = \tau$ (that is, assuming that voters know the government's incentives), and the function $(\tau^*)^{-1}(\cdot)$, one can use (7.32) to write the maximization problem for a right-wing incumbent who has drawn a competence shock γ_t as

$$\max_{\tau_t} \chi q^R\left[(\tau^*)^{-1}(\tau_t)\right] - (1 - \chi)[\mathscr{L}(\hat{g}_t - \gamma_t - \tau_t)],$$

where $\hat{g}_t = g - \gamma_{t-1}$. Differentiating with respect to τ_t and using the equilibrium relation $(\tau^*)^{-1}(\tau) = \gamma$ to define $d\tau/d\gamma$ one obtains a first-order condition which may be solved for $\tau'(\gamma)$ and thus for $\tau(\gamma)$. It may be more illuminating to consider the associated equation for $\pi'(\gamma)$, which follows from differentiating the budget constraint $\hat{g}_t - \gamma_t = \tau(\gamma_t) + \pi(\gamma_t)$, which implies that $\pi'(\gamma) = -1 - \tau'(\gamma)$. On substituting in the expression for $\tau'(\gamma)$, one obtains

$$\pi'(\gamma) = \frac{\chi q'(\gamma)}{(1 - \chi)\mathscr{L}'(\pi(\gamma))} - 1, \tag{7.33}$$

where we have suppressed the R superscript on the function $q^R(\cdot)$ for expositional clarity. This is a first-order differential equation in the function $\pi(\gamma)$. To solve it, one adds the boundary condition $\pi(0) = 0$. This boundary condition comes from the fact that in an equilibrium, however much the least competent type "cheats," that is, chooses $\pi > 0$, more competent types will cheat by more; since the least competent type will

---

[34] In the absence of a stochastic factor, governments of low enough competence would choose policies which they know would lead them to lose elections for sure, since all types put weight on social welfare. Though this may seem strange, it reflects a basic function of elections, namely, to replace low-competence governments by ones whose expected competence is higher.

be revealed for any level of cheating, it will be optimal for him not to cheat at all.[35]

In the previous paragraph, we derived the differential equation determining the equilibrium function $\pi(\gamma)$ (and the associated nondistortionary tax function $\tau(\gamma)$). Its two main characteristics are: $\pi(0) = 0$, that is, the least competent type does not use distortionary taxes; and $\pi(\gamma) > 0$ for $\gamma > 0$, that is, all competence types above 0 choose some (perhaps minimal) level of cheating in equilibrium, that is, choose $\tau_t < \hat{g}_t - \gamma_t$.[36] The function $\pi(\gamma)$ is illustrated in Figure 7.2a with the associated tax function $\tau(\gamma)$ shown in Figure 7.2b, based on similar diagrams from Rogoff and Sibert.

A main innovation of Rogoff (1990) relative to Rogoff and Sibert (1988) is to examine what institutional mechanisms may mitigate the tendency towards cycles in fiscal policy in the signaling model we considered above. One obvious suggestion is to remove choice of fiscal policy from politicians running for re-election. Rogoff considers mandating that fiscal policy decisions be made biennially in off-election years. An alternative would be to vest the decision with another authority, as in the discussion in Chapter 5 of appointing an independent conservative central banker to solve the time-consistency problem in choice of monetary policy. Though such a move would mitigate the political business cycle, Rogoff correctly points out that it has costs: it prevents information about high competence from being usefully transmitted to voters, and it prevents a highly competent incumbent from using this information in setting fiscal policy.[37] The net gain from such a proposal depends on the loss from smaller transmission of information against the benefits from smoothing the political cycle. Moreover, such fiscal restrictions might only worsen the distortions caused by the political cycle. Prevented from signaling in one way, an incumbent

---

[35] Suppose a policymaker with $\gamma_t = 0$ chooses $\pi(0) = \pi^\circ > 0$, implying an *ex-post* social welfare cost $\mathscr{L}(\pi^\circ) > 0$ and a pre-election tax $\tau_t = g_t - \pi^\circ$. Any type with $\gamma_t > 0$ can choose a lower τ_t with no higher social loss (that is, with $\pi \leq \pi^\circ$) and so can separate himself from type $\gamma_t = 0$. Hence, there will be a separating equilibrium for any $\pi \geq 0$ that type $\gamma_t = 0$ chooses. Choosing $\pi > 0$ rather than $\pi = 0$ thus provides no benefit as far as a higher probability of election, but incurs a social loss and cannot be an equilibrium. A formal proof is constructed along these lines.

[36] The second-order condition associated with minimizing (7.32) with respect to τ is

$$\frac{\chi q''(\gamma)}{(1 + \pi'(\gamma))^2} - \frac{\chi q'(\gamma)\pi''(\gamma)}{(1 + \pi'(\gamma))^3} - (1 - \chi)\mathscr{L}''(\pi(\gamma)) < 0,$$

where we have suppressed the R superscript on the function $q^R(\cdot)$. Differentiating (7.33) with respect to γ and substituting the resulting expression into the above equation shows that fulfillment of the second-order condition requires $\mathscr{L}''(\cdot)/(1 + \pi'(\cdot)) > 0$, that is, $1 + \pi'(\cdot) > 0$. By (7.33), this implies $\mathscr{L}'(\pi) > 0$, that is, $\pi > 0$.

[37] This cost did not arise in the case of a policymaker *choosing* to give up full control over monetary policy in Chapter 6, since his competence was effectively known.

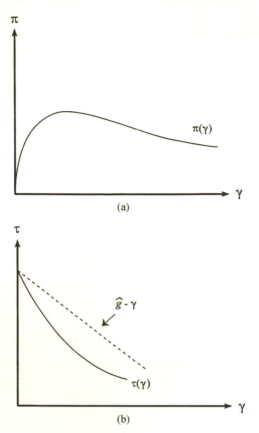

FIGURE 7.2. Equilibrium inflation and lump-sum taxes. (a) Inflation. (b) Taxes.

will no doubt search for other ways to signal. To the extent that the incumbent is forced to signal in an even more distortionary way, the problem inherent in the political cycle will only be worsened.

In a system where elections take place at fixed intervals, giving the incumbent the option of calling early elections may serve as an efficient signal of competence. Rogoff argues that in his model this type of signal will be nondistortionary. We consider the signal content of calling early elections in Section 7.8 below. As that discussion will suggest, such a signal may not, in general, be nondistortionary. For example, if performance has a stochastic component, an incompetent policymaker would call an election when things temporarily break his way. Signaling via calling early elections is an important, but basically unexplored topic. Since adding a stochastic component to competence would yield a model that is qualitatively different than Rogoff's, one cannot draw any simple conclusions about the implications of endogenous election dates in a formal model of incomplete information.

Rogoff also considers the possibility of an incumbent signaling via imposing costs on himself, an idea that is often used in game-theoretic models of behavior. Formally, Rogoff allows a policymaker to publicly destroy some part of his own endowment of a private consumption good, and then shows how "self-denial" could be revealing in the context of his model. However, it is not clear what would be the corresponding behavior in the real world. Perhaps this would correspond to giving up voluntarily some of the perks of office, or, in a scandal-ridden government, a policy-maker allowing himself to be investigated.

Some Extensions

In my opinion, the Rogoff–Sibert and Rogoff papers represent the strongest research in the area of political business cycles. They aim to explain the key characteristic with which this literature began, namely, the *pre*-electoral manipulation of the economy,[38] and to explain it in a way which is consistent with voters behaving rationally. The models are highly stylized, but in the way that successful models are—they capture what appear to be the key phenomena in a simple, tractable way in order to focus on them to the exclusion of secondary factors.

A related, but distinct approach would consider how an incumbent government could demonstrate its competence by how it handles difficult situations. The simplest case would be response to external shocks, that is, shocks which are fully exogenous to the government's behavior. A signaling model of this sort is presented by Bartolini and Drazen (1997b), who study the information contained in capital-account liberalization in response to the stochastic evolution of the world interest rate. This model will be considered in greater detail in Section 12.7 of Chapter 12. A more interesting possibility in the context of pre-electoral manipulations is where the government may find it optimal somehow to induce a crisis in order to demonstrate its competence, an even more graphic sort of "brinkmanship" than in Rogoff and Sibert. Hess and Orphanides (1995) consider such a model of politically motivated uses of discretion in policy-making, but looking at war, rather than macroeconomic policy.

Hess and Orphanides consider a world in which incumbents (and potential incumbents) may differ not only in their economic ability ξ^{econ}, but also in their wartime ability ξ^{war}, this latter characteristic being unobservable to voters until a war begins. Unlike the Rogoff–Sibert model, these abilities are assumed to have some persistence across terms of office. Though some wars are avoidable, others are unavoidable, so that forward-

---

[38] It also explains why an incumbent might hesitate to "pull out all stops" in electoral manipulation, as he knows he may have to live with the consequences of his choices.

looking voters care about ξ^{war}. Hence, an incumbent with a low probability of re-election due to his being revealed as incompetent in handling domestic economic affairs (low ξ^{econ}) has the incentive to start a war for his political advantage. In the absence of war, his defeat might be inevitable, but if sufficiently good wartime ability is revealed (high ξ^{war}), he may be re-elected by voters concerned about possible future unavoidable wars.

The model works out this sort of equilibrium formally, and it has an (unfortunate) realism to it—incumbents in trouble because of a poorly performing economy often put their faith in the maxim, "Nothing unites a country like a good war." Hess and Orphanides find supportive econometric evidence that "avoidable" wars are more likely when an otherwise poorly performing incumbent faces re-election. Specifically, they find that in the United States, the probability of "conflict initiation or escalation" exceeds 60% when the president is up for re-election and the economy is doing poorly, but is only 30% in years in which either the economy is healthy or the president is not up for re-election.

Retrospective versus Prospective Voting

Models on signaling competence bring into sharp focus the connection between *retrospective* voting, whereby the electorate votes on the basis of past events, and *prospective* voting, whereby they vote on the basis of expected future events. A model of retrospective voting with no uncertainty about government types, but where such behavior is fully rational, is that of Ferejohn (1986), discussed in Section 7.2 above. The models of inferring competence presented earlier in this section provide another example of retrospective voting being rational.

In the literature on voting, there is a debate over whether voters vote retrospectively or prospectively. (Keech [1995, chapter 6] provides a nice summary of the issues and the economic implications.) Key (1966) argued strongly that voting was retrospective, with voting patterns reflecting approval or disapproval of past performance or past actions. He viewed prospective voting as voters responding to campaign promises, a view he explicitly rejected. (We consider campaign promises in Section 7.6; both that discussion and the discussion in the remainder of this section make clear that voting prospectively and voting on the basis of promises are not identical.) Fiorina (1981a) has studied retrospective voting in United States elections in detail, and views retrospective voting in a way consistent with the Ferejohn approach, whereby voters reward or punish past policymaker behavior. In contrast, Downs (1957) has argued that voting is largely prospective, since the whole purpose of voting is to select a future government, with voters caring about what their future utility is when they decide how to vote. Downs's book suggests the connection between past and future that the models of inference in this section stress: voters use past observed events to infer the future. It is in this sense that one can argue that rational prospective voting when there is imperfect information *is* necessarily retrospective. In fact, this connection is simply the description of an inference problem under imperfect information, whereby a rational agent forecasts unobserved variables as a projection of observed variables.

Lewis-Beck (1988) does not fully accept this simple formula linking retrospective and prospective voting via inference, and suggests that empirically there is evidence for both types of behavior. For example, he considers survey data of voters in five European countries (see Section 7.3 above) in which voters were asked both to evaluate past economic performance and to give their expectations of future economic conditions. On the basis of survey data, he argues that even after controlling for the effect of retrospective variables, we still observe an influence of prospective voting, as voters vote on the basis of how they think the economic situation will be after the election, but do *not* base this inference on past economic performance.[39]

7.6. CAMPAIGN PROMISES

So far, we have ignored the role of campaign promises in affecting election outcomes. In the opportunistic models of Section 7.3, the focus was on manipulation of policy and economic outcomes to affect voting; the implicit assumption was that promises *per se* would have no effect on voters. In a model of rational voters, the argument is even stronger—unless candidates can find a way to credibly bind themselves to carry out their campaign promises once elected, these promises have no effect on rational voting behavior. In the Rogoff–Sibert model discussed in the previous section, the incumbent government was assumed to have the ability to credibly commit itself to a tax rate. In the partisan models of Section 7.4, candidates' preferred positions were common knowledge, and campaign promises of what a candidate would do if elected had no relevance.

In practice, candidates' making promises during campaigns is a worldwide phenomenon; their breaking of their campaign promises by one means or another once they are elected appears to be almost as frequent,

---

[39] One nice example he gives (Lewis-Beck, 1988, pp. 134–135) is of Iowa farmers in the 1984 U.S. Presidential election—though they "were in the midst of their worst economic crisis since the Great Depression" and reported right before the election "by a ratio of two to one . . . that economically matters were worse than four years ago," they voted overwhelmingly for Reagan over Mondale. "These Iowa farmers, when queried about the future of the farm economy, were more likely to feel that Reagan, rather than Mondale, would solve things. Hence, in voting for President Reagan, they ignored their negative retrospective economic evaluation, following instead their favorable prospective assessment."

so much so that the common view is that a politician's promises are often worthless. George Bush's subsequently broken pledge of "Read my Lips. No New Taxes." in the 1988 U.S. presidential campaign is the most often-cited example of recent times, but by far not the only one.[40] In this section, we consider how (and whether) campaign promises can be made credible and convey information.

Some General Issues and Results

What makes campaign promises credible; and, how can candidates make credible commitments to deliver on their promises? Put in this way, the question becomes very similar to the question of credibility of policy announcements studied in the last chapter; hence, many of the lessons of the models studied in that chapter should be useful in studying the credibility of campaign promises. One should note that breaking promises made simply to get elected is not the same phenomena of time inconsistency stressed in Chapter 6, as candidates are not doing so for the public good. However, the analogue so strongly suggests itself that it is not surprising that the material of the previous chapter is relevant. There is relatively little research that uses these models directly, so it is useful to sketch how they may be applied.

One obvious mechanism for making promises credible is "reputation": candidates who fail to deliver on a campaign promise are somehow punished (as Bush was—his broken tax promise, and the perceptions of him it created, were seen by many commentators as significantly contributing to his loss in the 1992 election). Models of "reputation" under certainty, as discussed in Section 6.3 of Chapter 6, are relevant here. The incentive of an incumbent to deviate from what he promised is known. A trigger strategy that punishes the failure to fulfill a promise can enforce good behavior if deviant behavior can always be punished in the future in a way that does not go against the punisher's best interests. Hence, in a "repeated electoral game" with a low enough discount rate and an infinite horizon, reputation may lead politicians to deliver on their promises, even with no formal commitment mechanism. In such a case, convergence of platforms might be observed; in fact, as Alesina (1988a) shows, there may even be full convergence to the most preferred policy.

However, both of the key assumptions, namely, a low enough discount rate and an infinite horizon, would appear to be not very descriptive of politicians. Alesina and Spear (1988) address this issue in an overlapping generations model of politicians, following the work of Cremer (1986) discussed in Section 5.2 of Chapter 5. An elected president can serve only one term, so that an incumbent would appear to have no incentive to

---

[40] As the joke goes, "Question: How can you tell when a politician is lying? Answer: When he is moving his lips."

follow through on his campaign promise. Specifically, suppose a right-wing party has ideological preferences over policy π represented by $\Omega^R(\pi)$, so that once in office it will choose the policy $\tilde{\pi}^R$ which maximizes $\Omega^R(\pi)$. With no incentives or constraints on the president to choose another policy once in office, no campaign promise other than $\tilde{\pi}^R$ will be believed.

In the absence of some pre-electoral commitment mechanism, how can an elected (right-wing) president, who knows he will leave the political scene after his term of office, be induced to follow through on a campaign promise other than $\tilde{\pi}^R$? Alesina and Spear suggest that he may be given an incentive to do so by members of his party who will compete for the presidency in the future. They assume there is a member of the president's party (the "heir apparent") who, first, knows that he will be the party's candidate in the next election, and, second, who is in a position to provide help or favors for the president while he is in office. They suggest that there is a norm which will induce an elected president to promise a policy other than $\tilde{\pi}^R$ in a campaign and to follow through on his promise once in office, due to the influence of the "heir apparent."

To make the argument more specific, consider the following set-up. Presidential candidates of the two parties run for office, where *ex ante* they care about the probability of being elected; the only credible platform promises are those that it is known they will be induced to carry out *ex post*. After the election, the winning presidential candidate carries out his preferred policy, no longer subject to the need to win an election, but affected by any transfers the heir apparent may make to him. Suppose, analogous to the Rogoff and Sibert model, that a presidential *candidate*'s objective can be represented by a weighted sum of the probability of winning the upcoming election and of having his ideological preferred policies implemented, with weights χ and $1 - \chi$, respectively. Let us limit attention to credible policy promises, $\hat{\pi}^R$ for party R and $\hat{\pi}^L$ for party L, where we discuss below how campaign promises are made credible. The probability of a party-R victory as a function of (credible) electoral promises can be represented as $q^R(\hat{\pi}^R, \hat{\pi}^L)$. When running for office, a presidential candidate of party R would then choose an electoral platform $\hat{\pi}^R$ to maximize

$$\Omega_C^R = (1 - \chi)\left[q^R(\hat{\pi}^R, \hat{\pi}^L)\,\Omega^R(\hat{\pi}^R) + (1 - q^R(\hat{\pi}^R, \hat{\pi}^L))\Omega^R(\hat{\pi}^L)\right]$$
$$+ \chi q^R(\hat{\pi}^R, \hat{\pi}^L), \tag{7.34}$$

where Ω_C^R represents preferences before an election and $\Omega^R(\cdot)$ ("true") preferences after an election, when re-election is not an option. The optimal campaign platform for a right-wing candidate, chosen from the set of credible platform promises, is $\hat{\pi}^{*R}(\hat{\pi}^L)$. A left-wing presidential candidate would maximize an analogous function, implying an analogous maximizing promise $\hat{\pi}^{*L}(\hat{\pi}^R)$. Taking these two "reaction functions" simultaneously would yield a Nash equilibrium in campaign platforms.

How are these campaign promises made credible? Suppose the right-wing party wins. Once in office, suppose the R "heir apparent" makes a transfer of $\nu(\hat{\pi}^{*R}) = \Omega(\hat{\pi}^R) - \Omega(\hat{\pi}^{*R})$ if the president chooses the policy $\hat{\pi}^{*R}$. Given this transfer, the president will choose the policy $\hat{\pi}^{*R}$ under weak indifference. To support such a transfer, consider the following norm: (1) if the chain of transfers has been broken in the past, the heir apparent expects to receive no transfers when he becomes president; (2) if the chain of transfers has never been broken in the past, the heir apparent expects transfers in the next period equal to the transfer he paid. One can then easily show that this norm is an equilibrium (Alesina and Spear present a formal proof); in this equilibrium, campaign promises will be kept. Though candidates have a known incentive to break campaign promises once they are elected, the equilibrium transfers make credible their pre-election announcements.

Incomplete Information about Policymakers

The more satisfactory model of reputation discussed in Chapter 6 was one of incomplete information about a policymaker, two important examples being mimicking and signaling models. Cukierman and Liviatan (1991) present a single-period mimicking model of two types of policymakers who have the same objective function, but differ in their ability to commit to carrying out their promises. The framework is a nonelectoral one, of the sort presented in Part II of the book. Hence, the common preferences of the two types may be represented by a loss function such as (7.7) over inflation and unemployment, where both types have the same θ and $\tilde{\pi}$, the latter set equal to 0 for ease of exposition. A "dependable" type can commit to follow through with an announcement or promise; an "undependable" type cannot, and will always choose the discretionary inflation rate $1/\theta$. The dependable type will find it optimal to make an announcement π^a, since otherwise he has no way of actually demonstrating his ability to keep his promises *ex post*. The undependable type will mimic the dependable type and also announce π^a, since any other announcement (or no announcement) would reveal his type. Given the announcement π^a, the public expects an inflation rate

$$\pi^a = p\pi^a + (1-p)\frac{1}{\theta}, \tag{7.35}$$

where p is the prior probability assigned to the policymaker being dependable.

Under incomplete information, the dependable type partially accommodates inflationary expectations, a result in contrast, for example, to the

Vickers (1986) model discussed in Section 6.6 of Chapter 6, where a "strong" type underinflates to signal his type. Specifically, given (7.35) and the determination of unemployment as in (7.9), the dependable type chooses π^a to minimize the standard one-period loss function:

$$\mathscr{L} = \left(p\pi^a + (1 - p)\frac{1}{\theta} \right) - \pi + \theta\,\frac{\pi^2}{2}, \qquad (7.36)$$

subject to the constraint that π equals π^a. Hence, a dependable policy-maker promises (and delivers) a rate of inflation of $(1 - p)/\theta$, rather than zero, the inflation rate he would choose if he were known to be dependable. Intuitively, the reason for his choosing a positive inflation rate when it is uncertain whether a promise will be carried out is that promising and delivering zero inflation creates suboptimally high unemployment; this is due to the deflationary surprise when the announced policy is actually carried out.

To summarize, when it is common knowledge that campaign promises are less than fully credible, since candidates who will not carry out their promises will mimic those who will, dependable candidates may choose to soften their promises in the direction of what the undependable candidates will do *ex post*, in order to lessen the macroeconomic fluctuations that imperfect credibility of promises implies. Interesting as this result is, the Cukierman–Liviatan model has a crucial drawback in helping us understand how and why campaign promises may be credible. The model treats keeping promises as an underlying *characteristic* of a policymaker, rather than as an outcome. While this may be relevant in some cases, it would be more appealing as a general approach to see whether II candidates' keeping their promises can be shown to follow from the incentives they face.

The main approach to showing why a candidate may find it optimal to keep his campaign promises relies on such announcements being used to signal an unobserved characteristic of the candidate; to the extent that the signal conveys information, it can affect election outcomes. For signaling to work, each type must find it preferable to truthfully reveal his own type, rather than masquerade as another type. Harrington (1993) presents a nice, carefully worked out model of this sort illustrating one way in which information transmission is important. Here, we simply go over the main driving force of the model, which is two-sided asymmetric information—not only do voters not fully know a candidate's true preferences, but candidates are unsure of the voters' policy preferences. Suppose re-election is possible, and, analogous to the Alesina–Spear model, candidates care both about implementing their preferred policy and about getting not only elected, but also re-elected. Harrington shows that under these circumstances, a candidate who is unsure of the policy preferences of the electorate may be best off to announce his true preferences—if they match those of the electorate, he will be elected; when he implements his preferred policy once in office, and the voters believe that his policy choices reflect his preferences (and thus signal what he will do in the future), they will re-elect him. Were he to misrepresent his preferences and gain election, he would have to forego either implementing his preferred policy or getting re-elected; misrepresenting one's preferences and not being elected (meaning the electorate shares the candidate's true preferences) is the worst of all worlds. With sufficient uncertainty about the electorate's preferences, the equilibrium may be truthful revelation. Intuitively, the Harrington model is like a model of optimal behavior in finding a suitable mate. If an individual is happiest with his own type and wants a long-term relationship ("continued re-election"), he announces his type truthfully to maximize the probability of a *successful* match. Harrington (1992) presents a similar model, but focuses on the implications of limited ability of an incumbent to carry out his preferred policies. More specifically, the more voters favor his policy, the more of a mandate the candidate has to carry it out. Getting votes on the basis of promising something thus means a successful candidate has the power only to carry out the promised policy. Therefore, to achieve a mandate to carry out his preferred policy, a candidate has the incentive to be honest. Assuming that the support of the electorate is crucial not only in getting elected, but also in carrying out policy strengthens the incentives for matching that support Harrington's approach to credible campaign promises.

7.7. INTERACTIONS OF THE EXECUTIVE AND THE LEGISLATURE

All of the models we have considered so far assume that a single policy-maker is elected, who then controls the setting of policy. In the opportunistic models, he manipulates policy to maximize his electoral prospects. In the partisan models, expectations of future policy are based on the rational belief that whoever is elected will carry out his own preferred policy. This approach ignores a key institutional fact of policymaking in all democracies—the institutional structure is such that numerous political actors affect the choice of policy, so that final policies reflect their interaction. The literature has concentrated on two types of interactions in determining policy outcomes: the interaction among legislators within the legislature; and the interaction between the legislature and the executive. We consider them in turn.

Interaction within the Legislature

The work on interactions between legislators within the legislature is found primarily in the public choice or political science literature, looking at formation of coalitions. In the political science literature, the emphasis is on the effects on policy of bargaining within legislatures, concentrating on bargaining among parties in a system with more than two parties. We refer the reader back to Section 3.6 of Chapter 3 for a discussion of some of these results. There is relatively little theoretical work in this literature on how legislative coalitions affect economic outcomes; we discuss some of the empirical work from a broader perspective in Section 7.8 below.

Interaction between the Legislature and the Executive

Alesina and Rosenthal (1995, 1996) present a formal model of the interaction of the legislature and executive in determining policy outcomes, and the implications of that interaction for political-economic cycles. Policy becomes a compromise between the executive and the legislature, where divided government puts a rein on the president. (They note that repeated polls have documented the preference of American voters for a divided government.) They begin with two facts about choices in legislative systems that we first encountered in Chapter 3: policy outcomes are the result of legislative bargaining; and, voters, being aware of the first fact, may vote strategically.

Their modeling of these phenomena is as follows. As in Section 7.4, there are two parties L and R, with different preferred policies, $\tilde{\pi}^R$ and $\tilde{\pi}^L < \tilde{\pi}^R$. (The variable π represents a general policy, *not* inflation.) For simplicity, assume that the parties differ only along this dimension, and that a party's "ideological utility" is quadratic in the difference between the actual policy π^j and the preferred policy $\tilde{\pi}^j$, that is, of the form $(\pi^j - \tilde{\pi}^j)^2$. Parties may also be opportunistic, that is, they assign a value to holding office *per se*. Alesina and Rosenthal assume that parties *cannot* make binding campaign promises, and that voters know the true preferences $\tilde{\pi}^R$ and $\tilde{\pi}^L$ of the two parties, so that they vote on the basis of those.

Individual voters have preferred positions as well, which can be represented as simply π^i, distributed in the population as $F(\pi^i)$. The utility that a voter i assigns to a policy π^j is quadratic in the distance between π^j and π^i, namely, $(\pi^j - \pi^i)^2$. Hence, a voter's utility from a policy is standard, allowing us to focus on the implications of the institutional structure. Suppose that individual voter-desired positions are uniformly distributed over the interval $(0, 1)$, an assumption that greatly simplifies the algebra. Then, if a voter π° was indifferent between the two parties, so that all voters to his left voted for the left-wing party and all voters to his right voted for the right-wing party, the two parties' vote totals would be π° and $1 - \pi^\circ$, respectively.

The determination of the legislature and the executive, and the implications of the interaction between them for policy outcomes, is modeled simply. The executive is elected by majority vote from one of the two parties every even-numbered period (an "on-year" election), while the legislature is chosen every period (that is, both "on-year" and "off-year," when there are only legislative elections). That is, in even-numbered years, both an executive and a legislature are elected, while in odd-numbered years, only the legislature is elected. Legislative representation is assumed to be proportional to vote totals, rather than based on plurality in geographically separate districts, as in the United States. Hence, if N^R and $N^L (= 1 - N^R)$ are the proportion of votes in the legislative elections received by the two parties, they are also the share of seats in the legislature. (See, however, the discussion in Chapter 3 on the complexity of interactions within the legislature.) Policy choice is assumed to be determined according to

$$\pi^j = \alpha\tilde{\pi}^j + (1 - \alpha)[N^R\tilde{\pi}^R + (1 - N^R)\tilde{\pi}^L] \qquad (7.37)$$

when the executive is from party j, where α represents the weight of the executive in policymaking. (α close to 1 represents a strong executive, with the legislature having little power.) The term in square brackets is the position of the legislature, which itself reflects the strength of the two parties.

The focus of the Alesina and Rosenthal analysis is to determine the outcome of elections in a system with both a legislature and an executive, and to show how it differs from a system with policy determined by either one or the other. It may at first seem strange to *assume* a formulation such as (7.37) if the goal is to study how the interaction between the legislature and the executive determines policy outcomes. However, the formulation in (7.37), which is both reasonable and flexible as a specification of outcomes given the results of an election, yields a number of interesting and sensible results. The main result of the analysis is that electoral outcomes (and hence the policy outcomes that follow from them) will reflect voters realizing the interactive nature of policymaking and taking advantage of it. When policies of the two parties are ideologically different, voters take advantage of the "checks and balances" implicit in the executive–legislative interaction to bring about moderate policies. The key to this result is that the outcome of the presidential vote is discrete in the inputs, whereas the outcome of the legislative vote is continuous in the inputs. Suppose that $\tilde{\pi}^L$ and $\tilde{\pi}^R$ are not "close" to one another. Voters in the interval $(\tilde{\pi}^R, \tilde{\pi}^L)$ would prefer an intermediate policy to that of the two possible presidents. If policy were made solely by the president, they would be "stuck." However, the nature of the policymaking process means that they can *moderate* presidential policy preferences by voting for a legislature dominated by the opposing party.

To derive the results more specifically, we begin by assuming that the voters know the outcome of the presidential election when they vote for the legislature in an on-year election, that is, when both the executive and the legislature are elected simultaneously. This would be the case if both the distribution of voter preferences and the party platforms $\tilde{\pi}^L$ and $\tilde{\pi}^R$ are known. Then voting for the legislature will be the same in both on-year and off-year elections, conditional on the identity of the president, and the question becomes simply what the result of the legislative election will be, conditional on the party affiliation of the president. Without lack of generality, suppose it is known that L will be president. Then each individual i will vote so that the policy outcome π^L will be as close as possible to his desired policy π^i, given the policy process as summarized by (7.37) above. Voters to the left of $\tilde{\pi}^L$ will always vote for the left-wing party, no matter who is president; similarly, voters to the right of $\tilde{\pi}^R$ will always vote for the right-wing party, no matter who is president. In the interval $(\tilde{\pi}^L, \tilde{\pi}^R)$, however, the choice of how to vote will depend on the identity of the president, as well as the value of α. The behavior of these voters can be summarized by what Alesina and Rosenthal term a "pivotal voter" theorem, which can be summarized as follows. Voting behavior is described by a critical value Π^j ($j = L, R$), such that (a) all voters with $\pi^i < \Pi^j$ will vote for the left-wing party, while all voters with $\pi^i > \Pi^j$ will vote for the right-wing party; and (b) the critical value Π^j is equal to the equilibrium policy π^j.

A sketch of the proof of this proposition is as follows. To see part (a), note first that if a voter π' finds it optimal to vote for the left-wing party, any voter to his left (i.e., $\pi^i < \pi'$) will find it optimal to vote for the left-wing party as well. (Otherwise, π' would not have found it optimal to vote as he did.) Similarly, if a voter π'' finds it optimal to vote for the right-wing party, any voter to his right (i.e., $\pi^i > \pi''$) will find it optimal to vote for the right-wing party as well. This is equivalent to part (a) of the proposition. The equality of Π^j and the equilibrium policy π^j may be shown by contradiction. Without loss of generality, suppose a left-winger is president. Suppose, contrary to part (b) of the proposition, $\Pi^L < \pi^L$. This implies there is a group of voters, namely, those in the interval (Π^L, π^L), who are voting for the right-wing party, even though they favor a policy to the left of the equilibrium policy π^L. Thus, they cannot be voting optimally, so that $\Pi^L < \pi^L$ cannot be the equilibrium critical value. Similarly, suppose, contrary to part (b) of the proposition, $\Pi^L > \pi^L$. This implies there is a group of voters, namely, those in the interval (π^L, Π^L), who are voting for the left-wing party, even though they favor a policy to the right of the equilibrium policy π^L. Thus, they cannot be voting optimally, so that $\Pi^L > \pi^L$ cannot be the equilibrium critical value. Thus, the critical value must be $\Pi^L = \pi^L$.

To calculate the critical value (and hence the equilibrium policy), note that the assumption of a uniform distribution over $(0, 1)$ implies that $N^L = \Pi^j$ and thus $N^R = 1 - \Pi^j$ for $j = L, R$. Substituting this into (7.37), one obtains the equilibrium legislative voting results and the equilibrium policies when there is a left-wing president (π^L) and when there is a right-wing president (π^R). These are

$$\pi^L = \Pi^L = \frac{\alpha\tilde{\pi}^L + (1-\alpha)\tilde{\pi}^R}{1 + (1-\alpha)(\tilde{\pi}^R - \tilde{\pi}^L)},$$

$$\pi^R = \Pi^R = \frac{\tilde{\pi}^R}{1 + (1-\alpha)(\tilde{\pi}^R - \tilde{\pi}^L)}. \tag{7.38}$$

Under the assumption of certainty about the results of the presidential election, the voting results embodied in (7.38) will obtain both for on-year and off-year elections.

The result on the value of the adopted policy π^j relative to the optimal policy $\tilde{\pi}^j$ for each party given in (7.38) yields Alesina and Rosenthal's main propositions on election and policy outcomes when individual voters know the characteristics of the voting distribution. First, there is a range of parameters such that there will be a *divided government*, in the sense that the party which has a majority in the legislature and the party which wins the presidency will be different. Whether this outcome obtains will depend on the values of the two parties' ideal policies (that is, $\tilde{\pi}^R$ and $\tilde{\pi}^L$) relative to $\frac{1}{2}$, which is the mean and the midpoint of the distribution of π, as well as the value of α. For given α, divided government will generally obtain if both parties' positions are close to, but on different sides of $\frac{1}{2}$. (If both parties are on the same side of the median $\frac{1}{2}$, then there will be no divided government no matter what the value of α, with the party closer to $\frac{1}{2}$ controlling both the legislature and the executive.) When α is large, meaning the executive is powerful relative to the legislature, the government will generally be divided, unless the parties' location around the median is very asymmetric, implying that a large majority of the electorate clearly prefers one party over the other.

If voters are uncertain about the outcome of the presidential election when they vote for the legislature in the on-year elections, the outcome of legislative outcomes will be different in on-year elections and off-year elections (when the identity of the president is known). We now discuss this as part of the general phenomenon known as the "midterm" cycle.

Midterm Cycles

When policymaking reflects the interaction between an elected executive and an elected legislature, a policy cycle (and the implied political business cycle, to use our earlier terminology) could occur if the elections for these two branches of government occur at different times. In a system where the legislature is elected more frequently than the executive (as in the United States, with the president elected every four years and the House of Representatives every two years), a policy cycle over the term of a president would occur if the on-year and off-year legislative vote totals were different. In the Alesina–Rosenthal model under certainty in the previous subsection, there will be *no* such midterm cycle. Since voters know the characteristics of the voting distribution, they know the outcome of the presidential election in an on-year election, and, as already indicated, the voting behavior of each voter will be the same in an on-year and in an off-year election. Hence, in the absence of changes in the composition of the electorate between the on-year and the off-year election, there will be no change in the composition of the legislature. This implies, in turn, that the nature of the political and electoral system, in which power is divided between the executive and the legislature, and the associated electoral system, in which the latter is elected more frequently than the former, would not, in itself, give rise to a regular political business cycle in the Alesina–Rosenthal model under certainty. In fact, it gives rise to no policy cycle whatsoever within a president's term.

This result for legislative composition stands in very sharp contrast to what is actually observed in the United States. Off-year United States congressional elections are characterized by an extremely striking fact—in every off-year election since 1862 (except 1934 and 1998[41]), the president's party has lost seats in the legislative elections, a phenomenon known as the **midterm cycle**. Though an explanation of the midterm cycle *per se* is beyond the scope of this book, the remarkable regularity of the cycle suggests that it cannot be totally ignored by any serious student of politically induced cycles in economic policy. Erikson (1988) presents a good summary of a number of theories; Campbell (1993) presents a comprehensive book-length treatment, examining a number of theories in detail.

Many explanations of the midterm cycle have been put forward, but we will limit discussion to those which address the systematic nature of the midterm loss for the president's party, and/or those focusing on economic outcomes. Hence, we reject as too simple the argument that there is a stochastic element in voting, with off-year election results reflecting mean reversion, since it does not explain why voting shifts should almost *always* go against the party of the president. There are four main explanations, including that of Alesina and Rosenthal.

Kramer (1971) and Tufte (1975, 1978), in their work on economic determinants of election outcomes, argue that the midterm election is primarily a *referendum* on the performance of the president midway through his term. The public's satisfaction or dissatisfaction with the president is expressed by their votes for or against congressional candi-

---

[41] In the 1902 election, the president's party appeared to gain seats, but only because the size of the House of Representatives was increased in that election. Campbell (1993) calculates that if the size of the House were held constant at its current size of 435, the midterm election results would have translated into a 12-seat *loss* for the Republican party.

dates of the president's party. Tufte proposes two indicators of sentiment about presidential performance: president's popularity, as measured by the response to the monthly Gallup poll question on whether or not those questioned approve of how the president is handling his job (see footnote 7); and the change in real personal disposable income per capita as a measure of economic performance (see the discussion in Section 7.3 above). Tufte (1975, p. 817) hypothesizes, "the lower the approval rating of the incumbent president and the less prosperous the economy, the greater the loss of support for the president's party in midterm congressional elections." To test this hypothesis, Tufte (1978) regressed the midterm "standardized" vote loss (difference between the party's congressional vote in that election and their normal congressional vote) on these two variables over the eight midterm elections from 1946 to 1974, and found significant coefficients of the correct sign on both variables with an R^2 of .83. Campbell (1993) found that if the equation is estimated over the period from 1946 to 1990, the R^2 drops to .59 (and the adjusted R^2 to .5), while if the dependent variable is the actual seat loss, the adjusted R^2 is .39 and the coefficient on income is no longer significant.

The results taken as a whole suggest that the midterm cycle can be explained in part by viewing the elections as referenda, with the loss in seats reflecting dissatisfaction with the incumbent president's performance, but this shifts the question to why there is regular dissatisfaction at midterm. Kernell (1977) suggests two factors. First, newly inaugurated presidents begin with a "honeymoon" period, as evidenced by extremely high approval ratings at the beginning of the term; at that point, voters on average have overly high expectations of the newly inaugurated president, which are regularly disappointed. Second, disgruntled voters are more likely to turn out at midterm. Jacobson and Kernell (1981), taking the drop in approval ratings as given, suggest a subtler connection between approval ratings and congressional results, focusing on candidate characteristics. A party's strongest candidates are those who are the most ambitious career politicians and view themselves as having the most to lose by electoral defeat; they choose to run only when they view the political climate as especially favorable, which for candidates of the president's party is when his approval rating is relatively high (and, conversely, when it is relatively low for candidates of the opposing party).

A far more convincing theory, to my mind, is the *"surge and decline"* theory first put forward by Angus Campbell (1960, 1964; see also Campbell, Converse, Miller, and Stokes [1966]) and extended by James Campbell (1987, 1993), who stresses, among other things, that he is not related. This theory begins with another regularity in United States elections—voter turnout surges in presidential elections and declines precipitously at midterm. To explain the connection with the midterm cycle, the original theory considered two distinctions, one between types of elections and the other between types of voters. First, presidential on-year elections generate far more campaign activity and interest than off-year elections, which Campbell et al. (1966) summarize as more "political information." The second distinction is between "core" voters, who have a stronger commitment to one party or the other and who in general turn out for both on-year and off-year elections,[42] and "peripheral" voters, who have a lower level of interest in political outcomes in general, and who are more likely to vote only when they view an election as special. Hence, the far higher turnout in presidential elections reflects a far higher turnout of peripheral voters than in midterm elections, so that their votes constitute a significantly higher proportion of the total vote on-year than off-year.

The theory explains the midterm cycle by combining the different propensity of the types to vote with a difference in the way the two types vote. Whereas core voters have a stronger party attachment, peripheral voters respond to "short-term forces" and individual campaign-specific events, voting disproportionately for the winning presidential candidate's party. Hence, the "surge-and-decline" theory yields a systematic midterm reversal of the fortunes of the president's party due to the significantly different composition of the overall electorate between on-year and off-year elections. The surge in turnout of peripheral voters on-year gives them a higher percentage of the total vote (relative to core voters) than in off-years, implying that the party that benefitted from that surge on-year will systematically do worse off-year. Such a theory could easily be represented by a formal model of types along the lines of those of Chapter 6. One especially attractive feature of the model is the central role of voter turnout. Most voting models not only assume full voter participation—in spite of the oft-discussed "paradox" of why people bother voting since the probability that their vote will affect the outcome is effectively zero—but actually need such an assumption to derive their results. (Consider models relying on the median voter.) In contrast, the surge-and-decline theory begins with the argument that some voters have a higher propensity to vote than others, because of underlying characteristics or interests, and shows how this difference yields important results.

James Campbell (1987, 1993) integrates the surge-and-decline theory with the midterms-as-referenda theory discussed above, arguing that midterm losses reflect both political conditions at midterm and the loss of factors which favored the president's party in the on-year election. While the latter theory also relies on different voting patterns across types of voters, combined with changes in the composition of the electorate on-year and off-year to explain the midterm cycle, the characterization of types of voters is richer, and the decision of whether to vote in both on-year and off-year elections is more complicated for all types of voters. Interested readers are referred to Campbell (1993) for the details.

---

[42] In Chapter 8, in our discussion of targeting transfers to groups of voters, we consider an alternative definition of core voters.

In comparing the original and the revised theory of surge and decline, James Campbell stresses that in explaining the midterm cycle, both theories assign the main role to the favorable effect for the winner of election-specific circumstances (Angus Campbell's "short-term forces") in the presidential election. This suggests that the midterm losses for the president's party should be positively related to the magnitude of the president's victory on-year. To test this presumption, Campbell (1993) first divides all midterm elections from 1902 to 1990[43] into those where the president received less than 57% of the vote in the previous presidential election, and to those where he received 57% or more of the vote in the previous election (the latter being presidential "landslides"). He shows that the loss of seats was far greater in elections in the latter category, the median loss of seats being over twice as high. He confirms this in a simple regression of the midterm seat loss for the president's party in the House of Representatives relative to the previous election on the president's share of the two-party vote in the previous election over the same sample. He finds that the coefficient on the prior presidential vote is significantly negative, that is, the larger the president's win in the on-year elections, the greater the midterm seat loss in the off-year elections. We return to implications of this result below.

A third, related theory is that of a *"coattail effect"* in on-year elections. The "coattail" effect refers to the phenomenon that a winning candidate at the top of the ticket increases the vote totals for candidates lower down on the ticket, relative to what they would get if they were running alone.[44] (See, for example, Calvert and Ferejohn [1983].) According to this argument, the midterm cycle reflects the absence of coattails for candidates of the previously victorious president's party. The central role played by the unfavorable circumstances for the incumbent president's party relative to the last election makes the theory similar to the surge-and-decline theory. Unlike that theory, however, the absence-of-coattails theory does not give an underlying argument of why voters vote as they do in presidential elections and withdraw support at midterm, nor does it simultaneously explain the cycle in voter turnout. Campbell's regression results reported in the last paragraph are consistent with this theory.

---

[43] The 1914 election is omitted, because of the extremely strong showing of Theodore Roosevelt in the previous presidential election.

[44] In explaining the origin of the phrase, Safire (1978, p. 125) writes, "Congressman Abraham Lincoln popularized the phrase in a speech in the House on July 27, 1848, after the metaphor had been introduced by Alfred Iverson of Georgia:

> But the gentleman from Georgia further says, we have deserted all our principles, and taken shelter under General Taylor's military coat tail.... Has he no acquaintance with the ample military coat tail of General Jackson? Does he not know that his own party have run the last five Presidential races under that coat tail, and that they are now running the sixth, under the same cover?... Mr. Speaker, old horses and military coat tails, or tails of any sort, are not figures of speech, such as I would be the first to introduce into discussion here, but ... "

Lastly, Alesina and Rosenthal (1995, 1996) present a very different explanation of the midterm cycle. They argue that uncertainty about the outcome of the presidential election when voters choose the on-year legislature can yield a bias which always goes in the direction of a midterm loss for the president's party. To see the argument intuitively, consider a voter slightly to the left of $\tilde{\pi}^R$, that is, a voter who favors a policy slightly more moderate than a right-wing (i.e., Republican) president would enact on his own. If he knew the president would be Republican, he would vote for the left-wing (i.e., Democratic) party in the legislative election. However, not knowing the outcome of the presidential race, he votes Republican in the legislative election, since a Democratic president combined with a legislature tilted towards Democrats would produce a policy outcome significantly to the left of what he desires. If a Republican wins on-year, he then votes Democratic off-year. Technically, the critical values Π^j in the off-year legislative elections, when the identity of the president is known, are the same as in the certainty model, namely, Π^R and Π^L in (7.38); in an on-year election, when voters vote for the legislature not knowing the identity of the president, the legislative critical value, call it Π^{ON}, is to the left of Π^R and to the right of Π^L. Since $\Pi^L < \Pi^{ON} < \Pi^R$, the off-year election will always be characterized by a swing away from the party that won the presidency in the previous on-year election.

The Alesina–Rosenthal model, though it may be attractive to model strategic voting when several elected branches of government can affect policy, does not give a convincing explanation of the midterm cycle. The basic problem is the crucial importance of uncertainty about the presidential electoral outcome before the election itself, and its implications for the midterm effect. There are elections in which the presidential outcome is fairly certain before election day. The Alesina–Rosenthal model implies that if the outcome of an on-year election is fairly certain before the voting, the off-year should show relatively little midterm loss. The data do not give this implication much support. The post-war presidential elections in which the outcome was least in doubt before the voting took place are probably the elections of 1956, 1964, 1972, and 1984, a view strengthened by the "landslide" dimensions of the president's margin of victory in each of these elections. The three largest post-war midterm reversals by far (each over 40 seats in the House) occurred after these elections, in 1958, 1966, and 1974. (The Republican loss in 1986 was one of the smallest midterm reversals, consistent with their model.) The closest post-war presidential election was the 1960 election with Kennedy winning just over 50% of the vote; the 1962 midterm loss of four seats for the Democrats was the smallest in the post-war period. If uncertainty about the on-year presidential results is the driving force of the midterm cycle, the results should be just the opposite. (Of course, in any one of these off-year elections, one could probably find specific events since the previous election that could explain the result, though repeated use of this type of argument renders a theory nonfalsifiable.) This may be considered more formally in terms of the regression results reported above, in which the size of the midterm loss was negatively related to the size of the president's victory in the previous election. If we take the president's winning margin in an election as a rough measure of the degree of certainty of the victory *ex ante*, these results are the opposite of the positive coefficient the Alesina–Rosenthal theory would predict. In short, the data clearly favor a model such as surge-and-decline over one stressing uncertainty about presidential outcomes in on-year elections. Working out the full implications of such a model for policy cycles remains to be done.

7.8. MULTIPARTY SYSTEMS AND ENDOGENOUS ELECTION DATES

Almost all models of the political business cycle in particular and electoral effects more generally assume a political system as in the United States, namely, a two-party system with fixed election dates. However, in these respects, the United States is the exception rather than the rule among democracies: most are characterized by more than two parties (often many more), so that governments are usually comprised of a coalition of parties[45]; furthermore, in many democracies the election date is endogenous, rather than exogenously fixed, with the executive or the legislature having at least partial ability to call an early election on relatively short notice. What are the effects of multiparty systems and endogenous election dates on economic outcomes?[46] In this section we consider these questions of comparative politics.

Coalition Government—The Empirical Approach

There is very little rigorous modeling of how economic outcomes are affected if the executive is controlled by a coalition of parties, rather than by a single party. Whereas at the beginning of the previous section we raised the issue of the implication of coalitions for *legislative* outcomes, understanding ultimate policy choices in a many-party government requires looking at the question more broadly. The main reason for the absence of models on the policy implications of coalition government is

---

[45] "For most of Western Europe, the politics of coalition lie at the heart of the business of representative government. Every West European state has been governed by a coalition for at least some time this century; many have been governed by coalitions for most of this time." Laver and Schofield (1991, p. 1)

[46] The existence of multiple parties rather than just two does *not* mean that the society is more polarized or fragmented, but simply that given the nature of the electoral system, such differences of opinion show up in formation and representation of many parties, rather than in conflicts within a party. It may be, however, that in more polarized societies, a proportional rather than a "winner-take-all" legislative electoral system is chosen, so that diverse views can be better represented.

that research on coalitions has focused on what determines the formation of governing coalitions, rather than on what effects this will have on outcomes. As Laver and Shepsle (1990, p. 873, italics in original) put it, "discussions of government coalitions have concentrated on the fact that they are *coalitions* and more or less have ignored the fact that they are *governments*. Little attention has been devoted to what happens *after* a coalition has been formed..." The work that has been done on the effect of coalition government on economic outcomes has been largely empirical, in what Laver and Schofield (1991) call the "European Politics Tradition." We discussed some underpinnings of this approach in Section 3.6 of Chapter 3; here we discuss some results.

There are two main types of results in the literature, largely empirical; their theoretical underpinnings are largely intuitive, rather than based on formal models. First, coalition governments are more moderate than the single-party governments which characterize majoritarian electoral systems, so that sharp policy changes are far less likely. This implies less of a partisan cycle. Second, coalition governments, by their nature, are less able than single-party governments to adopt fiscal adjustment programs, so that countries with electoral systems leading to coalitions have higher deficits and debts. To distinguish these two points from one another, note that the second concerns the inability of coalition governments to adopt difficult policy changes, while the first argues that the policies which *are* adopted will vary less across changes in governments.

To evaluate the first point, one must distinguish two different arguments by considering policy choice *conditional* on government composition. One argument is that sharp policy changes are less likely simply because government composition varies less across different governments in coalition systems. The other is that, *given* changes in the composition of government, policy changes less in coalition systems because of the nature of coalition government. The empirical support is mixed for both arguments; the theoretical basis for the second, more interesting argument is doubtful, as small, extreme parties often have inordinate weight in coalition systems. We return to this question below. The point that coalition government leads to less variable policy implies that partisan political business cycles should be smaller in countries with a tendency towards coalition government; from this perspective, empirical support for the point is also not clear-cut. In short, more empirical work needs to be done before one can draw clear conclusions. Moreover, although it seems intuitive that coalitions may lead to more moderate policy outcomes, proponents of this view have yet to present a solid, convincing theoretical basis to support it.

The empirical basis of the relation of coalitions to fiscal outcomes is clearer. Grilli, Masciandaro, and Tabellini (1991) present a clear summary of the argument. Following Roubini and Sachs (1989a, 1989b), they consider the relationship between the nature of the party system and the government, on the one hand, and the characteristics of government deficits and debt accumulation, on the other. They begin with a sample of 18 OECD democracies (the same countries listed in footnote 16, but including Greece, Portugal, and Spain, and excluding Finland, Norway, and Sweden), and classify the nature of the political system, the party system, and the resulting nature of observed government itself in a number of dimensions. On the nature of the political system, they consider: first, the extent to which the systems are "presidential," in that the president is elected directly into office and has significant independent authority, versus "parliamentary," in which the prime minister is accountable to the legislature; and, second, within parliamentary systems, the degree to which they are proportional. This is measured by the number of representatives per district, measured by dividing the number of legislators in the popular house of the legislature by the number of electoral districts in the country. Systems with less than five representatives per district are classified as "majoritarian"; those with five or more as "representational." On the nature of the party system, they consider the number of parties and the degree of "fractionalization" in the legislature at various dates from 1960 to 1990, the latter measured by the probability that two legislators chosen at random belong to different parties. The index of fractionalization ranges between 0 and 1, with a value of $\frac{1}{2}$ being associated with, in their words, "a perfectly balanced two-party system." Finally, on the resulting nature of observed government, they consider a number of indicators of government "weakness": the fraction of time between 1950 and 1990 that the government was a majority (that is, the executive is supported by a single party that has a majority in the legislature), a coalition (the executive is supported by a coalition of parties that together have a majority in the legislature), or a minority (the executive is supported by a single party or coalition with no legislative majority); the average "durability" of governments, as measured by the average number of years between one government change and the next; and the "stability" of governments, measured as the average number of years between "significant" change in governments, meaning those where the change is a change in parties or coalitions of parties supporting the government, not just in personalities.[47]

Grilli, Masciandaro, and Tabellini then relate these measures to the level of debt accumulation. For those measures which are nonnumerical (such as the nature of the political system), they simply report associations. For example, they report a strong association between representational political systems and a lack of fiscal discipline: "All the countries that seem

---

[47] For example, over the period 1950–1989, according to Grilli, Masciandaro, and Tabellini, governments in Japan had an average life of 1.67 years and those in Austria an average life of 2.67 years, but neither country had a significant party change over the entire period. In contrast, average government durability in the United States was 5 years, with a significant change in government over the period occurring once every eight years.

to have unsustainable debt, except Ireland and Portugal, are governed by representational systems...[and] all representational democracies except Denmark have unsustainable fiscal policies." On the measures of the nature of observed government itself that are numerical, they perform statistical tests. For a cross-section of fifteen of the countries (data were unavailable for Spain, Switzerland, and New Zealand), they regress the change in net debt to GNP ratios over 1970–1989 on the percentage of governments supported by a single-party majority, the average durability, and the index of stability over the period. They find that average durability of the government has a significant negative effect on debt accumulation, while the majority support and stability measures were insignificant. They also present similar regressions of primary government budget deficits (as a percent of GNP) on government attributes, dividing the sample into four decade-long subsamples over the period 1950–1989 (dropping countries in periods in which they were nondemocratic) and find similar results. The frequency of government changes always implies higher deficit-to-GNP ratios, with the coefficient being significant in three of the four decades, while measures of majority support and stability (significant government changes) are insignificant and often of the wrong sign.

The findings of Grilli, Masciandaro, and Tabellini (1991) and similar papers using a purely empirical approach are quite important in documenting possible effects on economic outcomes of having a proportional political system, leading to short-lived and/or coalition governments. However, these studies shed relatively little light on the mechanisms underlying these effects, nor do they, in themselves, provide a basis for modeling the effects of coalition governments on economic outcomes. The results reported above, for example, cannot discriminate between the view that the effects of durability reflect the importance of a strong versus a weak executive for fiscal outcomes and the view that short durability is simply an indicator of underlying political instability.

As a theoretical basis for a relation between coalition governments and/or political instability on the one hand and fiscal laxity on the other, empirical papers often cite Alesina and Drazen (1991), who use the "war of attrition" as a model of how conflict of interests may lead to a delay in eliminating persistent fiscal deficits. No formal models are generally presented, but the paper is mentioned as making rigorous the intuitive notion that large and fragmented coalitions may lead to large budget deficits and growing debt. The general idea underlying the war-of-attrition model is that when there are a number of individuals who can supply a public good, the good may not be supplied, or may be supplied only with a significant delay, as each individual waits in the hope that some other individual may supply the good. (The war of attrition is covered in detail in Chapter 9 and applied to suboptimal policy performance in Chapter 10. Other comparative politics models of government are discussed in Chapter 14.)

Alesina and Drazen (1991) applied the idea to delay in fiscal stabilization, where the public good is deficit reduction. The decision mechanism may be thought of as consensus, with each interest group having the possibility to block or "veto" the deficit reduction plan. One obvious question, especially relevant for the application to coalition governments, is whether the delay in supplying the public good will increase or decrease with the number of interest groups.[48] In the general war of attrition, either outcome is possible, depending on the details of the situation, as a careful analysis of the problem will make clear.

Though a fuller discussion of the implications of the war-of-attrition model for fiscal stabilization must be postponed until we consider the model explicitly, one should be careful in arguing that the basic model clearly predicts the results found in the above empirical studies. The problem is not simply (or even primarily) the fact that delay could either rise or fall as the number of parties rises. It is that the interactions, and subsequent dynamics, within a coalition government are far more complicated than in the war-of-attrition model. If the only possible options for a coalition partner are either to accept a proposal on the table, or to veto it, an increase in the number of partners may in fact increase delay. On the other hand, in practice, the range of behavior is far wider. For example, as the number of parties increases (both within and outside of the coalition), the possibility of forming alliances, that is, subcoalitions, within the coalition may increase as well, as shown in the theoretical literature.

Endogenous Timing of Elections

Another feature of political business cycle models which reflects the form of the U.S. political system is fixed election dates, known in advance. Many democracies are characterized instead by election dates which are partially endogenous, in that the executive or the legislature can call an election before the maximum interval between elections has elapsed. We considered some policy implications of such a system in our discussion of the work of Lupia and Strøm (1995) in Section 3.6 of Chapter 3, specifically, the importance of winning no-confidence votes for the durability of coalition governments and the role that this implies for specific actors in determining policy. In this subsection, we consider another aspect, namely, the implications of endogenous election dates for the political business cycle not present when election dates are fixed exogenously.

Models of opportunistic political business cycles argue that economic activity will boom before an election because of a causal link from the timing of an election to pre-electoral activity, via policy actions to stimu-

---

[48] Spolaore (1993) uses a war-of-attrition model to show formally that the length of delay in fiscal adjustment may increase with an increase in the number of parties in a coalition government.

late the economy before the election. Endogenous timing suggests the possibility of reverse causation—a government can call an election when economic conditions are exogenously good (for example, when a stochastic component is dominant in macroeconomic performance), so they need *not* manipulate economic conditions.

A simple model of unobserved competence (i.e., a variant of the Rogoff–Sibert model presented in Section 7.5 above) can deliver the result. A newly elected government's competence is ξ, where, without loss of generality, we assume ξ is discrete rather than continuous, equaling ξ_H with probability p and ξ_L with probability $1 - p$, with a mean value $\bar{\xi} = p\xi_H + (1 - p)\xi_L$. For simplicity, suppose ξ is constant over the next T (> 2) periods. Voters cannot observe ξ, but only an indicator y_t of economic activity, which is given by

$$y_t = \xi + \eta_t, \tag{7.39}$$

where η_t is a mean-zero i.i.d. random variable with a known distribution $F(\eta)$. Voters cannot observe η, while the incumbent government knows the current-period η_t.

Elections must be held at least every other period, but a government can call an early election after it has been in office only a single period. More precisely, the timing of events within a period is as follows. At the beginning of the period, the government observes both ξ and η_t, implying an economic outcome of y_t. If the government has been in office two periods, there is an election at the end of the period. If it has been in office only one period, it may either call an election at the end of the period or wait till the end of the next period. If it calls an early election and wins, its term of office is renewed for two more periods.

Voters vote for the candidate whom they believe will maximize their expected utility, where the utility of the representative voter is linear in y_t. Given the assumptions on η, this means that voters will re-elect a government in office for n ($\leq T - 2$) periods if

$$E_t(\xi \mid y_t, y_{t-1}, \ldots, y_{t-n-1}, \text{HIST}) \geq \bar{\xi}, \tag{7.40}$$

where HIST refers to the history of the government in calling or not calling elections, since that itself may signal competence. Suppose, as in the Rogoff and Sibert model, that there is a stochastic element to election outcomes, so that a government's probability of re-election is $q[E_t(\xi \mid y_t, \ldots, \text{HIST})]$, where $q[E_t(\xi \mid y_t, \ldots, \text{HIST})]$ is twice differentiable, with a positive first derivative, which approaches zero as $E_t(\xi \mid \ldots)$ approaches infinity, and a positive (negative) second derivative as $E_t(\xi \mid \ldots) < (>)\bar{\xi}$.

The nature of the voters' inference problem and the information content of a decision to call an early election may be better understood if we consider a government's decision of whether or not to call an early election. The inability of voters to distinguish whether a high current economic activity reflects high competence ξ_H or a favorable shock η_t immediately suggests that governments will call early elections when economic times are good. However, the argument is not quite so simple. A low-competence government knows that the more observations on y that voters have, the more it is likely to be revealed as low competence; a high-competence government can, on average, only be helped by the accumulation of more information, especially since there is a stochastic component to elections. However, since the decision process is common knowledge, it cannot be an equilibrium for a first-period low-competence government to call an election unless η is low, for this would reveal its type. Hence, the equilibrium must be a pooling equilibrium, where both types call an early election if η is at or above a critical level, and call no election if η is below that level. The critical value of η will depend on the probabilities p and q, as well as on the characteristics of the distribution $F(\eta)$. One can prove the existence of a pooling equilibrium with a critical value of η for a government in its very first period of office, such that elections will be called when economic activity is sufficiently high, but not otherwise. This is shown formally in Smith (1996), but the interested reader may want to work this out on his own. (One may refer back to the Rogoff–Sibert (1988) model above for general guidance; this problem is far easier.)

Ito (1990) finds evidence that governments in Japan do not manipulate policies in anticipation of upcoming elections, but that they opportunistically manipulate the timing of elections to take advantage of autonomous economic expansions. To demonstrate the latter proposition, he estimates the probability of an election in a quarter as a function of the growth rate of GNP in the quarter, the inflation rate in the quarter, and the time since the last election. Using both PROBIT and LOGIT techniques, he finds that high growth significantly increases the probability of an election, while high inflation significantly reduces it. Chowdhury (1993) reports similar results for India, with the government more likely to call early elections when economic times are good. On the other hand, Alesina, Cohen, and Roubini (1993), using techniques similar to Ito's for a sample of 14 OECD countries with endogenous election timing, claim that there is no evidence of such governmental behavior in countries other than Japan. As they point out, one problem in finding a strong empirical connection between economic conditions and the timing of elections is that governments may call elections when they perceive that poor as conditions are, they will only get worse before the latest date at which they may call elections. The empirical evidence taken as a whole suggests that the political business cycle effects running from economic conditions to early elections are not universal, but are almost definitely present in a number of countries.

7.9. TYING THE HANDS OF ONE'S REPLACEMENT

In this section, we consider a second key mechanism by which an incumbent's uncertainty about whether he will be retained in office may distort policy choices. In the models so far, we have considered either incumbents who take actions to try to influence the probability of remaining in office, or politicians whose partisan positions are independent of elections, focusing on the implications of electoral uncertainty. In this section, we investigate another implication of uncertain retention: given that he might not be retained, a policymaker will take actions to constrain his successor.[49]

Models of constraining one's possible electoral successor are obviously closely related to the work discussed in Section 5.5 of Chapter 5 on using policy to bind one's successors as a solution to the time-consistency problem. But there is a key difference. In models of time inconsistency, though the identity of the policymaker does not literally change over time, the current government knows *with certainty* that future governments will have a different objective function, due to their facing constraints different than those faced by the current government. To put it somewhat broadly, in models of time inconsistency, a policymaker knew he would be "replaced" with certainty. Here, the policymaker is replaced only with some probability, and the focus will be on the implications of this probability being neither zero nor 1. Given the technical similarity of these models with the earlier ones, a number of formal results will not be rederived, and the space devoted to these models will be far less than what was devoted to models of the political business cycle.

The starting point of analysis is the partisan, not the opportunistic, side of policymakers. Because the incumbent knows that if he is replaced, his successor will have different objectives, he would like to constrain his successor's choices as much as possible to match the choices that he (that is, the incumbent) would have made if retained. As in the models of Chapter 5, the incumbent government must have control of some *state* variable which is bequeathed to a successor government in order to influence these choices. Generally, models have focused on government debt, either its level or its maturity structure, as the relevant state variable. In most of the models, it is assumed that there is no repudiation of the debt by a successor government. As in the models of Chapter 5, this assumption is crucial for the results. Aghion and Bolton (1990), however,

---

[49] One may contrast the common attempt to constrain one's successor with President Thomas Jefferson's sentiment expressed in a letter to James Monroe, six weeks before Jefferson was to leave office. "I am now so near the moment of retiring that I take no part in affairs beyond the expression of an opinion. I think it fair that my successor should now originate those measures of which he will be charged with the execution and responsibility and that it is my duty to cloth them with the forms of authority." (*Letters to James Monroe*, January 21, 1809)

make the possibility of debt repudiation central to their results. We discuss their paper below.

Overissuance (and Underissuance) of Debt

One of the basic results in the literature is that the incentive to "tie the hands" of a possible successor with different preferences will often lead to an overissuance of government debt relative to what is optimal, as in Persson and Svensson (1989) and Alesina and Tabellini (1990) (and its follow-up, Tabellini and Alesina [1990]). In both papers (which were written independently, at about the same time), policymakers, though partisan, care about social welfare. Only distortionary taxes are available to finance public spending and to service the debt, with the level of distortion rising with the tax burden. Hence, the level of spending a government would find optimal would depend on the level of debt (via debt service) existing when it began office: the higher is the level of debt, the lower will be desired spending for given preferences.

Persson and Svensson consider policymakers who are concerned both with individual welfare, which is decreasing in the level of distortionary taxation, and with the level of public spending. Governments differ in terms of the desired *level* of public spending, with right-wing (i.e., conservative) governments preferring a lower level than left-wing governments. Suppose that a conservative government fears it will be replaced by a left-wing successor with a taste for higher spending. Whereas it would choose a balanced budget if it were certain to remain in power, the likelihood of being replaced means that its choice of debt will reflect two conflicting forces. On the one hand, the desire to smooth individual utility over time would lead it to run a surplus, reducing the level of distortionary taxation its successor would choose to finance higher desired spending. On the other, leaving positive debt will induce a successor who cares about tax distortions himself to choose a lower level of government spending than he would have if he inherited zero debt. If the current conservative government has a relatively steep marginal utility curve for public spending (which Persson and Svensson term a "stubborn" conservative), the latter effect will dominate and it will issue more debt than it would have if it knew it would remain in power.[50] They show that the greater is the ideological gap between the incumbent conservative government and its possible successor, the greater will be the debt issue.

---

[50] They suggest this argument may help explain why government debt in the United States rose so precipitously in the 1980s under the very conservative Reagan administration. It is probably more accurate to say that the Reagan administration may have seen deficits as a way of putting political pressure on policymakers with different objectives, but that they were not thinking primarily of successor governments. Rather, the deficits induced by sharp tax cuts may have been intended to force Congress to cut spending.

One problem with this explanation of a government bias towards deficits is that one gets the reverse result if a left-wing government is in power. That is, the same line of argument indicates that a left-wing government with a taste for large public spending which fears its successor will be more conservative will run a budget *surplus*, in order to retire government debt and thus induce its successor to spend more than it otherwise would have. This prediction is at odds with the behavior of many very left-wing governments we observe, for example, in Latin America in the 1970s and 1980s.

Alesina and Tabellini consider a similar model, but in their papers policymakers differ in terms of the desired *composition* of public spending —there are two types of public expenditure, say g^A and g^X, with different potential policymakers differing in the weights they put on these goods in their objective functions. We use this set-up to exposit the basic results on deficit bias, in a version of the model presented by Tabellini and Alesina (1990). Rather than model directly the notion that government can extract more resources only at the cost of greater distortions, Tabellini and Alesina assume that total resources are fixed at unity in each period, but can be transferred across periods. This assumption has the same effect as ruling out lump-sum taxation, and simplifies the exposition. One may further simplify the exposition by assuming that there are only two parties, right-wing R and left-wing L as in previous sections, rather than a continuum, as in their original paper. Consider a two-period model with no discounting, so that as of period 1, the expected welfare as seen by party j may be written

$$\alpha^j u(g_1^A) + (1 - \alpha^j) u(g_1^X) + \mathrm{E}_1 \big[\alpha^j u(g_2^A) + (1 - \alpha^j) u(g_2^X) \big],$$

$$j = L, R, \tag{7.41}$$

where $u(\cdot)$ is assumed to be an increasing, concave, twice-differentiable function which satisfies the Inada conditions. α^j is the relative importance that party j attaches to g_t^A (so that $1 - \alpha^j$ is the weight it attaches to g_t^X), and the expectation E_1 is taken over g_2^A and g_2^X, which are uncertain because the identity of the party in power at $t = 2$ is uncertain. Assume that, other things equal, R prefers g^A and L prefers g^X, so that $\alpha^R > \alpha^L$. Party j chooses g_1^A and g_1^X, planned g_2^A and g_2^X, as well as debt b to maximize (7.41), subject to

$$g_1^A + g_1^X = 1 + b,$$

$$g_2^A + g_2^X = 1 - b. \tag{7.42}$$

One solves the problem by backward recursion. The quantities of expenditure each party would choose in the second period are found by maximizing the term inside brackets in (7.41), subject to the second-period budget constraint and the given level of debt. This yields a first-order condition:

$$\alpha^j u'(g_2^A) = (1 - \alpha^j)u'(1 - b - g_2^A), \tag{7.43}$$

which implicitly defines second-period quantities as functions of preferences and inherited level of debt for each party $j = L, R$, namely,

$$g_2^A(j) = A(\alpha^j, b), \qquad g_2^X = X(\alpha^j, b). \tag{7.44}$$

Suppose that party R is in power in period 1 and that there is a probability $1 - q^L$ that it will be retained in office in period 2 and a probability q^L that it will be replaced by party L. Substituting (7.44) into (7.41), the solution to the first-period problem for R is then characterized by first-order conditions:

$$\alpha^R u'(g_1^A) = (1 - \alpha^R)u'(1 + b - g_1^A), \tag{7.45}$$

for g_1^A and,

$$
\begin{aligned}
\alpha^R u'(g_1^A) + q^L \Bigg[&\alpha^R u'(A(\alpha^L, b)) \frac{\partial A(\alpha^L, b)}{\partial b} \\
&+ (1 - \alpha^R)u'(X(\alpha^L, b)) \frac{\partial X(\alpha^L, b)}{\partial b} \Bigg] \\
+ (1 - q^L) \Bigg[&\alpha^R u'(A(\alpha^R, b)) \frac{\partial A(\alpha^R, b)}{\partial b} \\
&+ (1 - \alpha^R)u'(X(\alpha^R, b)) \frac{\partial X(\alpha^R, b)}{\partial b} \Bigg] = 0
\end{aligned}
\tag{7.46}
$$

for b. The first term on the left-hand side of (7.46) is the gain to R from issuing one more unit of debt in terms of higher current expenditure; the second and third terms represent the expected cost of increased debt in terms of the need to cut expenditure tomorrow.

As a benchmark, consider first the case where R anticipates remaining in power in the second period with certainty. Since the policymaker faces the same problem each period, he wants to smooth utility, that is, to smooth taxes in the face of explicit distortionary taxes. Formally, comparison of (7.45) and (7.43) for $j = R$ shows that in this case, optimal debt issuance is zero. Hence, as in Persson and Svensson, the cost of debt issuance is the intertemporal "unsmoothing" of utility.

To see the consequences of uncertainty about remaining in power, consider first the simple case where party R cares only about g^A and party L cares only about g^X (that is, $\alpha^R = 1$ and $\alpha^L = 0$). Equation (7.46) becomes

$$u'(1 + b) - (1 - q^L)u'(1 - b) = 0. \tag{7.47}$$

Since the left-hand side will be strictly positive at $b = 0$ as long as $q^L < 1$, the party in power will always issue debt if it believes there is some probability that it will be turned out of office. This is the basic result of overissuance of debt to constrain one's possible successor. Intuitively, the policymaker is better off consuming according to his own preferences than transferring resources forward to an "unknown" future.

This result of an unambiguous deficit bias due to a probability of being turned out of office does *not* carry over if both parties care about both goods, albeit differentially, that is, when $1 > \alpha^R > \alpha^L > 0$. As Tabellini and Alesina make clear, the tendency towards deficit bias is now ambiguous, depending on the relative strengths of two effects, a "desired composition" effect and a "level" effect. The desired composition effect is what was operating in the previous example—given that an L government prefers a different composition of spending than the current R government, the R government finds it optimal to spend more resources today according to its own preferences, leaving a deficit so the future government can spend less. However, since a future L government would spend less on g^A than the R government would like, leaving a surplus to the next government will bring its desired spending on g^A closer to the R government's desired level and raise second-period utility, as evaluated by R. The extreme nature of preferences in the previous example meant that this effect was absent.

This point may be seen by considering Figure 7.3, taken with minor changes from the Tabellini–Alesina paper, drawn in g^A–g^X space. The downward-sloping straight line represents the opportunity set (7.42), drawn for the case of $b = 0$. A first-period deficit ($b > 0$) causes this line to shift out in the first period, and to shift inward in the second period. A first-period surplus has the opposite effect. R_1 represents R's optimal bundle in the first period, L_2 the optimal bundle that L would choose in the second period if in power. The relative position of these two points reflects the assumption that $1 > \alpha^R > \alpha^L > 0$. The downward-sloping curves are R's indifference curves, and the upward-sloping lines passing through R_1 and L_2 are the income expansion paths of R and L, respectively. By assumption, the expansion paths diverge as government resources rise, so that disagreement about the composition of spending rises as the overall level of spending rises. This is a key assumption, to which we return shortly.

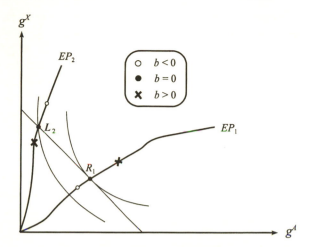

FIGURE 7.3. Composition and level effects in deficit bias.

If R chooses to run a surplus in the first period, R_1 will move to the left on EP_1 and L_2 will move to the right on EP_2 to the circled points. The composition of spending will diverge, but the two indifference curves will move closer to one another, allowing R to smooth expected utility. This is the "level" effect. If R chooses to run a deficit in period 1, R_1 will move to the right on EP_1 and L_2 will move to the left on EP_2 to the points marked by x's. Second-period expected utility will fall, as utility is "unsmoothed," but more spending is undertaken, in the first period, at the composition that R prefers. This is what we labeled the "desired composition" effect. Whether it is optimal to run a deficit or a surplus will depend on which effect dominates. If the income expansion paths are highly divergent (for example, if α^R and α^L were very different), the desired composition effect will dominate and the result of deficit bias will hold. On the other hand, if the utility function is highly concave, the level effect would dominate and there would be a surplus bias. Tabellini and Alesina (1990) show that a sufficient condition for the desired composition effect to dominate is that the "concavity index" of $u(c)$, defined as $-u''(c)/[u(c)]^2$, is decreasing in c.

To summarize, though a bias towards higher deficits can easily arise from differences in parties' spending preferences, the conventional wisdom that such a difference in itself implies a deficit bias is unfounded.[51] One clear difference between the Persson and Svensson and the Alesina and

---

[51] Chari and Cole (1993) present a different argument for why an optimizing government would overaccumulate debt. Because free rider problems in legislatures lead to excessive spending, the current legislature prefers a higher level of debt than would otherwise be optimal in order to restrain excessive spending by future legislatures. This result is independent of any partisan bias of the current legislature.

Tabellini papers emerges in the results: in the former paper, the direction of the bias (i.e., towards deficits or surpluses) depends on the identity of the incumbent government; in the latter paper, both types of governments have an incentive to overissue debt under certain parameter values. If overissuance of debt occurs, its magnitude will depend on the partisan gap between the two parties, and not on which party is currently in power. Hence, the Alesina and Tabellini paper implies that partisan difference *per se* yields a "deficit bias," the bias being larger the greater the instability of the system, defined as the probability there will be a change in government. The paper may thus serve as a partial theoretical basis for the empirical work on coalition government discussed in Section 7.8 above. We will return to it in our discussion of the growth of government in Chapter 14.

Endogenous Election Outcomes and Strategic Inefficiencies

One extremely interesting strand of recent research has combined the above type of model of manipulating the policies of one's successor via strategic choice of some state variable with the models of endogenous election outcomes. The basic idea is that by choosing the environment that one's electoral opponent will inherit if he is elected (thus constraining his policy choices), an opportunistic incumbent can affect the electorate's expectations of macroeconomic performance under that opponent. Strategic choice of state variables will thus influence an incumbent's re-election chances not because they affect the current state of the economy, but because they affect a voter's perceptions of what the post-election state of the economy will be under possible election outcomes. For such a strategy to work and increase the probability of his re-election, the incumbent must engineer a change in the environment which is viewed by the voters as affecting his attractiveness *relative* to his opponent. That is, he chooses state variables to make his opponent "look bad" as an alternative. Formally, this research studies the incentive of an incumbent to create *strategic inefficiencies*. A strategic inefficiency is, put simply, a policy choice that is welfare reducing, but that may nonetheless increase the likelihood of the incumbent's re-election.

Aghion and Bolton (1990) consider a model in which partisan differences among policymakers lead to different predilections to default on the debt. As we will consider models of endogenous default in detail in Chapters 8 and 12, we do not present the formal details of such an argument here, presenting only the main type of results they obtain, and the intuition underlying these results. Suppose that the left-wing party L represents voters of below-average income and that the right-wing party R represents voters of above-average income, with richer voters more likely to hold debt than poorer voters for a given size debt issue. Hence, party L is perceived as more likely to default on the debt than party R, a perception that R can exploit when in office to influence election outcomes. By issuing more debt when in power, R will shift the preferences of moderate voters since they now face a greater loss from default. In a median voter model, issuance of more debt will make the median voter more likely to vote for R.[52]

Milesi-Ferretti (1995a) considers the optimality of constraining possible successor governments when the two parties are seen as differing in their relative competence in different areas. (See also Milesi-Ferretti [1995b]) His intriguing result is that when election outcomes are endogenous, it may be optimal *not* to tie the hands of a successor government in an area where he is perceived to be weak relative to the incumbent! Low competence should be thought of as including competence both in the sense that Rogoff and Sibert use it and in an ideological sense—weakness in controlling inflation, for example, may reflect either lower ability or policymaker preferences which assign a lower loss to inflation. Consider first the latter interpretation, where, in a median voter model, the incumbent party R is seen as being highly inflation averse, relative both to party L and to the median voter. If there were no possibility of influencing election outcomes, R would have the incentive to constrain the inflation choice of a successor, for example, by appointing a conservative Central Banker (see Section 5.4 of Chapter 5). With the election outcome being endogenous, however, the desire to remain in office works against this incentive. By taking actions which ensure that the inflation rate will remain relatively low, R is basically removing as an influence on voters a potential election issue where its opponent is perceived as weak. If the opportunistic motivation is strong enough relative to the partisan one, R will thus choose not to tie the hands of possible successors.

Technically, the nature of the result that an incumbent will find it optimal not to constrain his successor in an electoral framework is easy to see using a slight modification of the Tabellini and Alesina (1990) model discussed above. Suppose the perception that L will provide less of some government output than R would reflects a perception of low competence. Specifically, while R governments are seen as able to provide both goods according to (7.42), an L government is perceived as supplying g_2^A according to $g_2^A = z(1 - b - g_2^X)$, where $z(\cdot) < 1$, for all values of $1 - b$, representing low competence in providing g_2^A. Hence, a surplus inherited by an L government does not correspond one-to-one to higher spending, as in (7.42). Suppose that if the election probability q^L were exogenous, the incumbent R government would find it optimal to manipulate a possible L successor to provide more of R's desired good g by bequeathing a higher surplus. For $z(\cdot) \ll 1$, this would be highly likely. However, with the

---

[52] When an incoming government cannot default on the debt, there is no possibility for affecting election outcomes by debt issuance and Aghion and Bolton obtain the results of the earlier papers.

probability of election dependent on which party is expected to provide higher welfare, the incumbent R government would find it optimal to provide few resources to its possible successor, ensuring that voters concerned about efficient supply of both goods re-elect R. In short, it may be optimal to "play to an opponent's weakness" in an electoral system.

Milesi-Ferretti and Spolaore (1993) present an interesting "twist" on the use of state variables to influence election results. They consider a world in which an incumbent may use resources "productively," that is, for the benefit of all voters, or "unproductively," that is, for the sole benefit of the ruling party's constituency. (In Sections 8.3 and 8.4 of Chapter 8, we discuss, respectively, the phenomena of a government directing transfers to its "core" supporters, and "pork barrel" politics more generally.) They show that under certain circumstances, an incumbent government may choose to introduce a commitment technology that constrains a government's partisan use of resources. By putting a constraint on the ability of a government to reward its own supporters, that is, in dividing the "spoils of office," the incumbent limits the role of expected spoils of office in voters' decisions. Hence, if limited ability of an incumbent to direct transfers to its supporters harms the party out of office more than the party in office, an incumbent may adopt a socially beneficial reform for purely opportunistic purposes. That is, rather than accumulating debt as in the Aghion and Bolton model, the current government uses institutional reform to increase its attractiveness to the voters, relative to its opponents. Such an argument is far from fanciful: political history is full of examples where reforms in the name of "good government" were adopted in large part because of the relative advantage they were seen as giving those in power.

7.10. CONCLUSIONS

Electoral economics, and more generally the implications of endogenous and exogenous changes in policymakers, is one of the most important topics in the political economy of macroeconomics. This chapter has covered a large amount of material, reflecting the importance of the topic. The macroeconomic implications of electoral politics is not, however, synonymous with political macroeconomics, and in the next several chapters we cover other major topics that are at the heart of political economy in macroeconomics.

Redistribution

> But the most common and durable source of factions has
> been the various and unequal distribution of property.
>
> —*James Madison,* The Federalist, no. 10

8.1. INTRODUCTION

Redistribution, whether of income, wealth, or private goods, is a major area of political debate in most economies. Redistribution certainly looms large in discussions of fiscal policy, especially in issues of taxation, where the equity of a given tax structure is a major focus. On the expenditure side, it is widely recognized that many government programs have strong redistributive implications. More generally, redistribution is debated not simply as an implication of many government policies whose purpose may be to achieve other goals, but as an end in itself. This chapter, and the one that follows, discuss a number of basic issues related to distribution and the conflict over distribution. In this chapter, we focus on redistribution of private goods, where the conflict of interests concerns both the magnitude and the distribution of transfers of the good across the population. In the next chapter, the focus is on public goods, both decisions on the level and on how the burden of financing public goods will be distributed across the population.

There is no simple division between the question of redistribution of pure private goods and distributing the burden of financing public goods. There are a number of reasons for the difficulty of separating redistribution and provision of public goods. First, there are conceptual questions. Redistribution of income, or more precisely, the increase in equality or alleviation of poverty it is meant to achieve, may itself be considered a public good. The question of the optimal amount of redistribution could be then framed as how the cost of providing this public good be divided among the taxpayers.

A second, more prosaic, reason why redistribution of private goods and supply of public goods are related is simply that the allocation of taxes between groups to finance a public good has, by definition, redistributive implications. Consider an economy with two types of individuals, rich and poor, whose utilities in the absence of a public good are U^R and U^P, respectively. A public good g benefits both types, where taxes on the two types are τ^R and τ^P, which, aggregated over all individuals of both types, must equal g. The choice of τ^R and τ^P, for given g, is a clear distributive issue. Moreover, while a decision rule of unanimity would imply choices of τ^R and τ^P which would leave individuals of each type at least as well off as they were with no public good (that is, allocations on the "contract curve" whose endpoints are defined by U^R and U^P), this need not be the case under alternative decision rules. If one group has enough power under the choice mechanism by which the allocation is chosen, it could impose taxes on the other group greater than the amount to be financed, the excess being a transfer to itself. This would be the case if, for example, decisions on the financing of the public good were made by majority rule, with one group outnumbering the other.

Mueller (1989, chapter 5) goes a step further and argues that under majority rule, one should *expect* that such redistribution will take place. Members of the majority coalition will attempt to redefine the issue at hand to increase their benefits relative to the minority, through a change in the amount of the public good provided, through a change in the tax shares, or both. As Mueller puts it (p. 59), "As long as the issue could be continually redefined in such a way that a majority still benefitted, it would pass, and a stable majority coalition could, in principle, push a minority back as far along the Pareto-possibility frontier as their consciences or the constitution allowed."[1]

Finally, redistribution and provision of public goods may be related when it is the provision of the public good which *enables* one group to enrich itself at the expense of others. That is, provision of public goods is integral to redistribution, in that the latter might not otherwise take place. Redistribution which would be politically unacceptable if it were done openly can often be accomplished if it is disguised. To the extent that provision of a public good benefits some more than others in ways that are difficult to discover, such provision can be the mechanism by which transfers take place. A simple, but very realistic, example is the wealth-enhancing effect of a highway for owners of commercial land near that highway. Tullock (1959) was probably the first to model this explicitly under majority rule.

To separate the issues of redistribution of private goods and provision and financing of public goods, we proceed as follows. If the question is primarily one of distribution, it will be treated in this chapter. The primacy of distribution as the issue may reflect the very nature of the question, for

---

[1] Muller points out a similarity with Riker's (1962) argument whereby large coalitions are transformed into minimum winning coalitions. Riker assumes that issues of allocational efficiency are "optimally resolved as a matter of course," so that only redistributional questions remain. Political decisions then amount to transferring income from the losing to the winning coalition, by redefining issues so that the size of the losing coalition is increased and the benefits to the majority increase, until proposals pass by only a bare majority. See also the discussion in Chapter 3.

example, transfer programs to alleviate poverty or programs whose disguised transfer aspect is central to the decision of some supporters. If the question is instead primarily one of provision of public goods, analysis will be deferred to the next chapter. This includes, for example, the failure to provide public goods due to the distributional conflict over how they should be financed. That is, even though distributional issues may be central to the failure to provide the good, when the focus is on the result rather than the cause, the material will be covered in the next chapter. Of course, the division of material between this chapter and the next must nonetheless be arbitrary at some points. Instances of public provision of private goods in order to effect redistribution, as in Buchanan (1970), will appear in both chapters.

We begin the chapter with the simplest question, namely redistribution of income in a world where all affected individuals are included in the decisionmaking process. In the basic model in the next section, all individuals face the same tax-transfer schedule. In Section 8.3, we drop the "equal treatment" assumption for income redistribution and assume instead transfers can be given differentially. The focus in this section is then what characteristics of individuals or groups will make them likely targets of taxes and transfers in a political-economic equilibrium. In Section 8.4, we relax the assumptions of the basic model in another direction and consider nonmonetary redistribution. Nonmonetary redistribution raises a host of issues, some present in the case of monetary transfers but to a far lesser extent, that are central to the operation and institutional detail of real-world redistributive programs. In Section 8.5, we move in the opposite direction, considering models that abstract from institutional detail and concentrate instead on the general phenomenon of expending resources to gain a larger share of transferable private goods. The final sections of the chapter concern two types of redistribution that are conceptually and empirically quite important, namely redistribution across generations in Section 8.6 and geographically-based redistribution in Section 8.6.

8.2. REDISTRIBUTION OF INCOME

We begin with redistribution of income in a world where all affected individuals are included in the decisionmaking process. The important heterogeneity across individuals is in the level of income, the focus of analysis being the amount of redistribution that emerges from the political process. The outcome depends on whether an individual knows his position in the income distribution (and hence how he will be affected) before a redistribution program is adopted.[2] When individuals are uncertain

---

[2] To take a trivial example, if individuals know their position in the income distribution and there is a unanimity requirement, no redistribution program will ever be adopted.

about their income in the absence of an income redistribution program, the program will have an insurance aspect not present in the certainty case, and this may dominate other considerations. In reality, of course, individuals are neither totally informed nor totally ignorant about their future income, so tax-transfer schemes have both redistribution-of-income and insurance aspects.

A Basic Model

We begin with the case in which individuals know their income when they choose a tax-transfer scheme. Romer (1975), Roberts (1977), and Meltzer and Richard (1981) all present such models of majority voting over simple income tax schedules meant to finance redistributive transfers. We consider the model of Meltzer and Richard, which illustrates some of the fundamental results on the connection between the characteristics of the income distribution and the nature of tax-transfer programs in the context of a simple model in which all individuals face the same linear tax rate and receive the same transfer. Thus, politicians cannot pander to one group of voters, designing tax-and-transfer policy to win their votes, which is a salient characteristic of redistribution in most, if not all, societies. We consider such pandering in Section 8.3. Equal treatment of individuals with the same income does not, however, necessarily imply a single tax rate. A progressive tax structure where the tax rate an individual faces depends only on his net income (but not on his "political clout") would satisfy such an equal-treatment assumption, but it is harder to solve for both the optimal tax structure and the political equilibrium. Moreover, in the absence of any restrictions about the shape of the function relating tax rates to income (other than it being nondecreasing), it is difficult to derive definite results.[3] A second key assumption in the Meltzer and Richard model is that voters are purely opportunistic, caring only about their net income and not at all about ideology, either issues that individuals can "trade off" against transfers in deciding which party to support, or ideological concerns about income redistribution itself.

A **political-economic equilibrium** is found in three steps. First, individuals optimize over their choice variables for a given fiscal policy. Second, on the basis of their individual optimization, each individual determines his preferred fiscal policy. Third, these preferences are "aggregated" into a economywide fiscal policy via the collective choice mechanism in place.

The Meltzer and Richard model may be represented as follows. Consider first optimal individual behavior as a function of the fiscal variables, namely, the tax rate τ and the level of transfers ν. Individuals differ in their innate productivity ξ, which is unobservable to the government, where $F(\xi)$ is the cumulative distribution of productivity types in the

---

[3] Rodriguez (1998) presents such a model and shows that the key relation between the characteristics of the income distribution and the degree of redistribution need not hold.

population. Before-tax income, which is observable, is the product of productivity ξ and hours worked l, which will depend on ξ:

$$y(\xi) = \xi l(\xi).\tag{8.1}$$

The individual maximizes utility, which is an increasing, concave function of consumption c and leisure z, denoted $u(c, z)$, where $z = 1 - l$, subject to a budget constraint:

$$c = (1 - \tau)l\xi + \nu.\tag{8.2}$$

The first-order condition determining supply of labor l may be written

$$(1 - \tau)\xi u_c[(1 - \tau)l\xi + \nu, 1 - l] - u_z[(1 - \tau)l\xi + \nu, 1 - l] = 0.\tag{8.3}$$

With a strictly positive tax rate and level of transfers, (8.3) will not have an interior solution for l for individuals with productivity below a certain level, implying that they do not work. The level of productivity for which (8.3) is just satisfied for $l = 0$ is

$$\xi_0 = \frac{u_z[\nu, 1]}{(1 - \tau)u_c[\nu, 1]},\tag{8.4}$$

with all individuals with $\xi \le \xi_0$ supplying no labor.

A tax-transfer policy (τ, ν) must satisfy the government's budget constraint:

$$\tau \bar{y} = \nu,\tag{8.5}$$

where economywide per capita income $\bar{y}$ is defined by

$$\bar{y} = \int_{\xi_0}^{\infty} \xi l[(1 - \tau)\xi, \nu]\, dF(\xi).\tag{8.6}$$

Under the assumption that consumption and leisure are normal goods, so that c is monotonically increasing and l is monotonically decreasing in ν, one can easily show that y is monotonically increasing in ξ for those individuals with positive l. To show that choice of τ implies unique values of ν, c, y, and $\bar{y}$, one uses these characteristics and the government budget constraint (8.5). Normality of leisure implies that $\bar{y}$ is decreasing in ν, so that there is a unique ν which solves (8.5) for each τ. Since c, l, y, and $\bar{y}$ are all monotonic in ν, the individual choice problem thus has a unique solution for each value of τ. One may easily show that $\bar{y}$ is decreasing in τ.

If each individual is self-interested and has no preference for redistribution *per se*, his preferred tax rate $\tilde{\tau}$ is that which maximizes his utility $u(c, 1 - l)$. This optimization yields (making use of (8.2), (8.5) to replace v, and (8.3) to eliminate terms)

$$\tilde{\tau}(\xi) = \max\left(\frac{y(\xi) - \bar{y}}{d\bar{y}/d\tau}, 0\right), \tag{8.7}$$

including the constraint that the tax rate must be nonnegative. This implies that an individual's desired tax rate will be a non-increasing function of his pre-tax income.

The median voter theorem may then be applied if the ordering of pre-tax incomes is independent of the tax-transfer policy. Since all individuals have identical preferences and differ only in their innate productivity ξ, pre-tax income (and hence desired tax rates) will be ordered by ξ as long as $dy/d\xi > 0$ for all redistributive policies.[4]

From (8.7), the shape of the preferred tax schedule as a function of ξ is easy to derive. An individual whose pre-tax income is at or above the mean income $\bar{y}$ will prefer a zero tax rate and no lump-sum redistribution; intuitively, he cannot gain from a positive tax-transfer scheme. Individuals with $\xi \le \xi_0$ will derive income only from transfers v and will prefer the tax rate which maximizes v (where the elasticity of $\bar{y}$ with respect to τ is -1). Denote this tax rate τ^v. Since y is monotonically increasing in ξ, preferred tax rates can be ordered by ξ, as in Figure 8.1 (adapted from Meltzer and Richard), where $\bar{\xi}$ is the productivity of an individual with pre-tax income equal to $\bar{y}$.

The tax-transfer policy actually chosen will depend on the political mechanism by which preferences are aggregated. Meltzer and Richard consider a median voter rule, by which the median voter chooses the economywide tax rate (and level of transfers consistent with government budget balance). The equilibrium tax rate will thus be that corresponding to the productivity of the median voter.

In a fundamental model like this, a key sort of question arises. For a given decision rule, such as the median voter's preferences being determinate, how will the nature of the redistribution program be related to the characteristics of the electorate? An obvious place to start is the distribution of income, and the obvious question is: what is the effect of greater inequality on redistribution, when tax-transfer programs are chosen via political processes rather than by a social planner? Consider the effects in the basic Meltzer and Richard median voter model. As indicated above, if the median voter's income is above the mean, there will be no program of redistribution, no matter how unequal the income distribution. Changes in

---

[4] The details of this type of argument may be found in Roberts (1977).

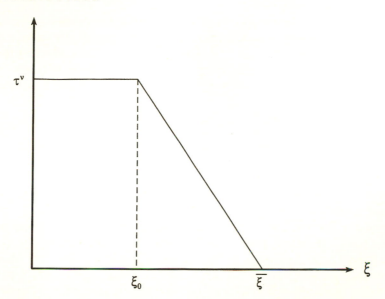

FIGURE 8.1. Preferred tax rates.

the income distribution will have no effect on the amount of redistribution if the change does not reduce the median income below the mean. On the other hand, if the median voter's income is below the mean, he will choose a positive tax-transfer program, and a change in the distribution of income which lowers the median relative to the mean (which can be thought of as an increase in income inequality) will result in a higher tax rate and greater redistribution.

Uncertainty about One's Position

Redistribution of income *ex post* may be motivated by the desire to share risk *ex ante* if voters are uncertain about their income at the time they choose a tax-transfer program. In this case, the program has an insurance aspect, and insuring against bad outcomes may dominate a voter's thinking in deciding which program he finds optimal. In this subsection, we consider the influence of risk sharing on the nature of the redistributive program emerging from a political equilibrium. Some basic results may be illustrated by considering an extension of the basic Meltzer–Richard model in the previous subsection to a world of income uncertainty. Specifically, consider that model, but where individuals learn their productivity ξ only after they vote on a tax-transfer program. Individual i believes his possible productivity type is taken from a set Ξ_i, with an *ex-ante* distribution $F_i(\xi)$, where the distribution of possible types may be the distribution of types in the population. Assume that individuals learn their productivity before they choose their labor supply l and consumption c, so that the first-order condition for optimal l is the same as (8.3), implying the demand and supply functions are the same for a given tax rate. Each voter, however, maximizes his *expected* utility over possible productivity in choosing his desired tax rate. Instead of (8.7), the first-order condition for individual i's desired tax rate is

$$\int_{\Xi_i} u_c[\ ] \cdot \left(\bar{y} + \tau \frac{d\bar{y}}{d\tau} - y(\xi) \right) dF_i(\xi) = 0, \qquad (8.8)$$

where $\bar{y}$ is, as above, per capita income averaged over the whole economy, so that $\bar{y}$ and $d\bar{y}/d\tau$ are nonstochastic. As before, $d\bar{y}/d\tau < 0$.

Consider first the case where all individuals are identical *ex ante*, in that they all have the same prior distribution over productivities, which must then simply be the population distribution, $F(\xi)$. With all voters identical *ex ante*, the median voter is the representative voter, with expected income $\bar{y}$. If utility were linear in consumption, so that marginal utility of consumption were constant and could be factored out of the left-hand side of (8.8), the first-order condition for the median voter's preferred tax rate would simplify to

$$\tau \frac{dy}{d\tau} = 0, \qquad (8.9)$$

so that the preferred tax rate is zero. The intuition is simple: since an individual is risk neutral and his expected income is the mean $\bar{y}$, there is no expected gain from a redistribution program; however, since positive taxes lower $\bar{y}$ *ex post*, there is a cost, so that *ex ante*, the representative individual prefers no redistributive program.

When all voters are identical *ex ante* in terms of expected income, but utility is concave, so that voters are risk averse, the results will obviously be quite different. The first-order condition (8.8) may be written

$$\tau = \left(\frac{d\bar{y}}{d\tau} \right)^{-1} \frac{\int u_c[\ ] \cdot (y(\xi) - \bar{y}) \, dF(\xi)}{\int u_c[\ ] \, dF(\xi)}. \qquad (8.10)$$

With diminishing marginal utility, the negative terms (income below the mean) in the numerator are weighted more heavily than the positive terms, so the numerator of this expression is negative. Therefore, the preferred tax rate for the median voter is positive. This illustrates the role of risk aversion in design of a tax-transfer program. In the Meltzer–Richard model under certainty, if the median voter has income equal to the mean, he prefers a zero tax rate; here we see that under uncertainty, if the median voter has *expected* income equal to the mean, risk aversion will lead him to prefer a positive tax rate.

A more realistic assumption on income expectations is that individuals are not identical *ex ante*, having different prior distributions over their income prospects. If individuals have differing expected mean income *ex ante*, one can easily show by considering (8.10) for a subset Ξ_i of the population income distribution that one gets a result analogous to the certainty case: an individual whose expected income is below the population mean will favor a positive tax rate, while one whose expected income is sufficiently above the mean will prefer a zero tax rate. The difference, as indicated above, is that a voter whose expected income is at or slightly above the mean will prefer a tax-transfer program because of its insurance aspects. This last point makes clear the importance of the timing of the political decision relative to when uncertainty about income is resolved. As is well known in other contexts, voters may be far more willing to "buy into" an income redistribution program if they must decide before they know their position in the income distribution than if they can decide (or recontract) after they know their position.

More generally, different prior distributions of income across individuals suggests the realistic assumption that some individuals have far higher uncertainty about their income than do others. To abstract from desired redistribution due to differences in mean income, suppose, for simplicity, that all voters had the same expected income, but differed in the variance of their possible income. Individuals with high variance (or low precision) of income are low in the *variance-of-income distribution*. With risk aversion, voters with high uncertainty about income would be in favor of positive taxes; those with little or no uncertainty about their income would prefer zero taxes, given the distortionary nature of taxation. If only a small fraction of voters fell in the first class, the median voter would choose little or no redistribution. If income risk is pervasive in the population, political equilibrium will lead to a larger tax-transfer scheme. These results are in a sense analogous to the results under certainty once one realizes that the analogue to high income under certainty is *low* variance of income in this model. If the median voter is high up in the distribution, in the sense of having highly precise income expectations, political equilibrium leads to little redistribution, while if the median voter is low in the distribution (little precision of his income estimates), there will be more extensive redistribution.

Alternative Decision Mechanisms

Another type of question which arises in models of redistribution is how will changes in the decision rule affect the nature of the redistribution program? One simple change is greater enfranchisement, that is, broadening the electorate in the context of the basic median voter model. That is, one can ask how changing the decision of who gets to vote will affect the results, a question addressed by Meltzer and Richard.[5] In the realistic case that it is poorer voters who become enfranchised, their model predicts that the size of redistribution programs and tax rates will increase, an empirical prediction which is supportive of their model.

One might argue that in the case of redistribution of income from rich to poor, the median voter model may be especially inappropriate. If large income transfers are being discussed, for example, the very well-off have an incentive to use their income or wealth to lobby against such a program, so that a lobbying model would be more appropriate. Hence, the program that would emerge would reflect not only who the median voter is, but how wealthy is the upper tail. One must then ask what is the ability of the richest citizens to block the program. We consider some models in which relative wealth affects the nature of politically determined redistribution programs in subsequent sections.

8.3. DIFFERENTIAL TRANSFERS

A key feature of the Meltzer and Richard model is that all individuals face the same tax schedule and receive the same transfer. In reality, transfers are targeted to groups of individuals, often with the goal of increasing political support for the policymaker giving the transfers. Once we drop the equal-treatment assumption, so that the government is not constrained to give the same transfer to all voters, one may ask what characteristics make a specific group of voters likely targets of redistributive efforts. For example, will parties direct their efforts towards their most loyal supporters, or will they court "swing" voters, whose loyalties are most up for grabs? The first approach need not reflect backward-looking politicians who are simply rewarding past supporters; opportunistic politicians will direct transfers towards their "core" supporters if they believe that this is the cheapest way to buy votes. Such behavior would represent the "machine" politics that once characterized many large cities in the United States, such as Boston, Chicago, or New York. Cox and McCubbins (1986) present a model of political determinants of redistributive policy which stresses machine politics, where transfers go to core supporters. The alternative view starts with the observation that politicians often take their core supporters for granted, directing their efforts to voters who are not so ideologically committed and hence most likely to switch their votes in exchange for favors.[6] Lindbeck and Weibull (1987) present a model

[5] In Section 11.4 of Chapter 11, we discuss a number of models of *endogenous* changes in the extent of the franchise due to growth and rising incomes.

[6] Note that "core" constituency is used differently in these two statements, reflecting different meanings. Core can refer either to those voters the party can target most effectively with transfers, due to great familiarity with their needs, or to those voters ideologically most committed to the party's positions. These need not overlap, though they often do.

stressing this view in which transfers are directed to "swing" voters. Dixit and Londregan (1996) present a general approach that encompasses both of these approaches, with voters who care both about positions on issues (or other candidate-specific characteristics) and about transfers of private goods.

The Dixit-Londregan Model

In the Dixit and Londregan model, two parties with different policy preferences compete for the votes of the electorate. As in the previous chapter, call the two parties L (the left-wing party) and R (the right-wing party), with positions on a policy issue of π^L and π^R ($> \pi^L$), where it is assumed these positions are fixed. For ease of exposition we assume, without loss of generality, that $\pi^L = -\frac{1}{2}$ and $\pi^R = \frac{1}{2}$. Parties compete in the vector of transfers they give to each group of voters. A group is defined as a subset of voters who all must receive the same transfers and pay the same taxes, where groups may be identified by location, age, gender, *et cetera*.[7]

The utility of a voter i in group h depends on two factors: the distance between his desired position $\tilde{\pi}^i$ and the position of the party in power; and on his consumption c^{ih}, which depends on the transfer he receives. Policy preference i cuts across "transfer groups" h, though not every type i need be represented in every group h. Utility is concave in consumption and may be written

$$u^{ih}(j) = -\frac{1}{2}(\tilde{\pi}^i - \pi^j)^2 + \kappa_h \frac{\sigma}{\sigma - 1}(c^{ih})^{(\sigma - 1)/\sigma}, \qquad (8.11)$$

when party j is in power. The parameter κ_h, which Dixit and Londregan call the "greed" parameter, is central to their analysis. It represents the degree to which a voter who is a member of group h is willing to trade off utility from consumption (amenable to transfers) and policy preferences (assumed an immutable characteristic of a voter).

Consumption c^{ih} of voter i who is a member of group h is the sum of (given) pre-transfer income y^i and the transfer delivered by party j if in power:

$$c^{ih}(j) = y^i + A^j(h, v_j^h), \qquad (8.12)$$

where the party- and group-specific function $A^j(\cdot, \cdot)$ is meant to capture the fact that transfers v_j^h (positive or negative) need not affect consumption one-for-one. A party may be especially effective in transferring resources to a specific group, in that the consumption benefit the group

---

[7] Programs which redistribute income across age groups are discussed specifically in Section 8.6.

receives from spending on them by the party is greater than what another group would receive from the same amount spent. This arises either because parties have special abilities (or handicaps) in transferring income to particular groups of voters, or because loyal followers of a party are more willing to bear taxes on them levied by the party. (This latter assumption is important in Dixit and Londregan's analysis of programs affecting "core" supporters.) The transfer function need not be symmetric for positive and negative transfers (that is, taxes). Characteristics of the transfer function $A^j(\cdot,\cdot)$ include:

$$
\begin{aligned}
&\text{(a)} \quad A^j(h,0) = 0, \\[4pt]
&\text{(b)} \quad A^j(h,v) > -y^i, \quad \text{for } i \in h, \\[4pt]
&\text{(c)} \quad A^j_v(h,v) > 0, \\[4pt]
&\text{(d)} \quad A^j_{vv}(h,v) \le 0,
\end{aligned}
\qquad (8.13)
$$

for all i, h, and v, and for both parties $j = L, R$. These characteristics may be explained as follows: (a) zero transfers or taxes have no effect on consumption; (b) a party cannot tax away more than an individual's pre-transfer income; (c) transfers and taxes are used effectively, so that higher expenditures translate into higher consumption; with (d) more effective tax-transfer allocations being used before less effective means.

Voters within a group (receiving uniform transfers) can differ as to their preferred policy, where the distribution of policy preferences is assumed to differ systematically across groups. Call this cumulative distribution $F_h(\pi)$. Groups may also differ in size. Hence, if the number of members of group h is N_h, the number of voters with a preferred position at or to the left of π is $N_h F_h(\pi)$. It is assumed that all individuals vote.

A voter supports the party whose platform (both policy position and promised transfers) yields him the most utility. Voter i will vote for the left- rather than the right-wing party if $u^{ih}(L) > u^{ih}(R)$. Substituting (8.12) into (8.11), using the numerical values for π^L and π^R, and rearranging yields

$$
\tilde{\pi}^i < \frac{\kappa_h \sigma}{\sigma - 1} \left[\left(y^i + A^L(h, v_L^h) \right)^{(\sigma-1)/\sigma} - \left(y^i + A^R(h, v_R^h) \right)^{(\sigma-1)/\sigma} \right]
$$

$$
\equiv \hat{\pi}^h(v_L, v_R). \qquad (8.14)
$$

The term $\hat{\pi}^h(v_L, v_R)$ represents the type of voter in group h who is just indifferent between the two parties given the transfer vectors over all groups, v_L and v_R, that the parties propose.

Given the transfer vectors v_L, and v_R, vote totals for the two parties follow from the voter distribution $F_h(\pi)$ and the definition of $\hat{\pi}^h(v_L, v_R)$

from (8.14). Vote totals may be written

$$N_L(\nu_L, \nu_R) = \sum_{h=1}^{H} N_h F_h\big[\hat{\pi}^h(\nu_L, \nu_R)\big],$$

$$N_R(\nu_L, \nu_R) = \sum_{h=1}^{H} N_h\big(1 - F_h\big[\hat{\pi}^h(\nu_L, \nu_R)\big]\big). \tag{8.15}$$

In equilibrium, each party offers a vector of transfers which maximizes its vote total as given in (8.15), taking the other party's equilibrium transfer vector as given, subject to a balanced budget constraint on transfers (and a prohibition of taxing individuals beyond their ability to pay). The budget constraint may be written

$$\sum_{h=1}^{H} N_h \nu_j^h = 0, \tag{8.16}$$

for $j = L, R$. In an equilibrium, neither party is able to increase its expected vote total, given the transfers chosen by the other party. That is, the equilibrium concept is Nash in pure strategies. More formally, an equilibrium is a pair of transfer vectors (ν_L, ν_R) such that: (i) L's choice of the vector ν_L maximizes $N_L(\nu_L, \nu_R)$ in (8.15) taking R's equilibrium choice of ν_R as given, subject to (8.13b) and (8.16) for L; and, (ii) R's choice of the vector ν_R maximizes $N_R(\nu_L, \nu_R)$ in (8.15) taking L's equilibrium choice of ν_L as given, subject to (8.13b) and (8.16) for R.

To derive equilibrium transfer vectors, Dixit and Londregan write the problem as a Lagrangian for each party, maximizing the relevant expression in (8.15) with a Lagrange multiplier λ_j on the party's budget constraint (8.16). The Lagrange multiplier measures the value to party j, in terms of votes, of an additional dollar available to give as transfers. Its reciprocal is the marginal cost to the party of "buying" another vote. The key first-order condition for each party j becomes

$$f_h(\hat{\pi}^h(\nu_L, \nu_R)) \cdot \kappa_h \cdot \big(y^i + A^j(h, \nu_j^h)\big)^{-1/\sigma} \frac{\partial A^j(h, \nu_j^h)}{\partial \nu_j^h} = \lambda_j \tag{8.17}$$

for each group h and party j, where $f_h(\cdot)$ is the density function associated with the cdf $F_h(\cdot)$.[8] This condition says that in equilibrium, a party chooses its promised transfers and taxes so that a change in the net transfers offered to any group will produce the same number of votes.

---

[8] Sufficient conditions for the existence of a Nash equilibrium are that each party's payoff is a quasi-concave function of his own strategy, and a continuous function of the other party's strategy. For details, see Dixit and Londregan (1996).

Core versus Swing Voters—Who Gets Courted?

Equation (8.17) and its implications are the heart of the Dixit–Londregan model. The equation makes clear which groups of voters will be targeted in a vote-maximizing transfer scheme under different assumptions about the distribution of voters, the susceptibility of groups to transfers, and the effectiveness of delivering (or extracting) income from voters. A group will be a likely recipient of transfers in equilibrium if there is: a large relative density of voters at the indifference point $\hat{\pi}^h(\nu_L, \nu_R)$, giving the fraction of group h that is just indifferent ideologically between the two parties, and hence especially susceptible to switching their votes in response to a marginal increase in transfers or a marginal decrease in taxes; a high marginal utility of private consumption $\kappa_h(y^i + A^j(h, v_j^h))^{-1/\sigma}$, where the marginal utility term includes the factor κ_h, the degree to which the group members are willing to trade a preferred policy position for extra consumption; and, high productivity of the party in taxing and subsidizing a group, as measured by the derivative of the transfer function with respect to v_j^h. Dixit and Londregan show that a rich variety of results is possible, depending on how these characteristics interact. The model is attractive, for it provides a structure to see what factors account for different types of voters being favored in the political process of redistribution. For example, when will transfer activity be targeted at "swing voters," whose party loyalty is most fluid, versus "core supporters," with whom the party is most familiar?

Dixit and Londregan show that swing voters are likely to be targeted if parties are identical in their ability to subsidize or tax different groups, who differ in their distribution of preferred positions. Specifically, suppose the transfer function is simply

$$A^j\left(h, v_j^h\right) = v_j^h, \tag{8.18}$$

so that $\partial A^j(\cdot)/\partial v_j^h = 1$, for both parties. (Under the definition of "core supporters" used in their paper, the lack of differential ability to target transfers means that neither party has such supporters.) Both parties then equally court the voters most likely to change their support in exchange for favors, each offering the same redistributive package to a given group.[9] This follows from both parties having the same price of an additional vote in equilibrium, that is, $\lambda_L = \lambda_R$,[10] which, using (8.17) for the two parties,

---

[9] Lindbeck and Weibull (1987) similarly show that in equilibrium, groups are offered identical transfers from the two parties, though they do not focus on how these transfers will differ across groups.

[10] To see this formally, use (8.18) in (8.17) for both parties, yielding the condition $\lambda_L^\sigma(y^i + v_L^h) = \lambda_R^\sigma(y^i + v_R^h)$. Multiplying by N_h, summing over h, and using the budget constraints (8.16) for each party, one obtains $\lambda_L = \lambda_R$.

implies that $\nu_L^h = \nu_R^h$. The groups of voters who are offered the highest transfers are either those who have high κ_h or those with relatively many members who are relatively indifferent between the candidates. In a political equilibrium, the parties neutralize the electoral effects of each other's redistribution strategies, so that the vote is the same as in a world where there were no transfers. However, unless parties are constrained to give no transfers, zero transfers is not an equilibrium: starting from this point, each party will offer transfers in the attempt to win voters, and we reach the above "inefficient" equilibrium.

When parties differ in their ability to transfer resources to specific groups, then it may be core supporters, that is, those whom the party knows well and therefore can target most effectively, rather than swing voters who are courted. (More precisely, core supporters of each party are those voters whom it can tax or subsidize with relatively small deadweight losses.) If voters cared only about the private goods that a party could provide them, and not at all about ideology, the equilibrium outcome would have those voters most easily targeted benefitting disproportionately from redistributive policies. (Of course, concave utility will temper this result, since the value of a unit of transfers will fall the more transfers individuals in the group receive.) When both ideology and private consumption matter, all of the factors mentioned in the discussion of (8.17) will come into play. That is, groups to whom the party can deliver subsidies are most likely to receive positive transfers, but this is conditioned on other characteristics, such as the group containing a relatively high density of members who have low incomes or are indifferent between the parties ideologically.

One especially interesting result of Dixit and Londregan is that core supporters may be singled out for *negative* transfers if they are core in both senses of footnote 6. That is, suppose a group of voters whom a party can easily target for redistribution are strongly partisan, either in the sense of having many members who are far from the margin of indifference about the party's policies, or in the sense of heavily weighting partisan issues relative to pecuniary benefits (low κ_h). They will then clearly be seen as targets for taxation, since the party knows how to extract resources from them effectively (that is, with low deadweight loss) and further knows they will remain loyal nonetheless.

Opportunism, Ideology, and Social Welfare

Both governments and voters in the Dixit–Londregan political world are motivated solely by selfish concerns: governments care simply about getting votes and not about social welfare and are willing to "soak people for all they're worth" towards this end; voters respond to the benefits (both pecuniary and policy) that politicians are expected to give them. This feature reflects the purpose of the model, namely, to give a general discussion of what motivates vote-maximizing transfers under a wide range of circumstances. The model is quite successful in this regard. The fact that governments do not exploit the politically disadvantaged all the time suggests they also care about social welfare, or at least about their reputations.

Dixit and Londregan (1998) consider how the results are affected when voters and parties are also motivated by concern over income inequality and view distributive equity as a desirable public good. Though each individual would be unwilling to sacrifice his own benefits on an individual basis, he might favor a general policy of redistribution that would require all individuals to sacrifice some individual benefits. They add a desire for lower income inequality to the preferences of individuals in the model in the first part of this section. In their set-up, this change has a significant effect on the structure of the tax-transfer programs offered by the two competing parties. In equilibrium, each party offers a marginal tax rate that is uniform for all groups, augmented by lump-sum group-specific transfers that depend on the same factors discussed earlier. Parties court pivotal voters by adjusting both the social welfare component of tax-transfer policy (absent in the previous model) and the particular benefits these voters receive.

8.4. NONMONETARY REDISTRIBUTION

Many government programs that are not explicitly redistributive nonetheless provide benefits to some groups and impose costs on other groups, and hence have distributive implications. Even if we ignore those programs for which the redistributive aspect is tangential (even replacing a stop sign by a stoplight at a busy intersection will impact citizens differently) and restrict attention to those programs for which the distributive aspect is an important component, the list of programs is nontrivial. One example is regulations restricting competition, such as import tariffs, quotas, or licensing requirements; such regulations redistribute income in a recognizable way towards those who produce the restricted good or obtain the license. Another leading example is public works programs, such as highway, dams, mass transit, or other construction projects, where the redistributive effects are heavily geographical. A third example is publicly financed education with limited access. Though some of these programs have more equitable distribution of income or wealth as one of their goals (for example, this argument could be made in relation to public education), most are targeted at special interest groups (an industry, sector profession, or demographic group that has significant lobbying or electoral power) or a geographical constituency defined by a legislative district. To the extent that a program targets some groups for net benefits, others for net costs, the general Dixit–Londregan analysis in the previous section is relevant.

In this section, we consider additional issues raised (or at least highlighted) by nonmonetary transfers or by programs in which the transfer is implicit. Many of these issues are not associated only with in-kind transfers, but they are more common or pronounced than with monetary transfers, so this seems a logical place to discuss them.

General Issues

Government programs, projects, or regulations with significant redistributive aspects share a number of characteristics. First, as already indicated, in the typical program *benefits are concentrated in a small group, while the costs are spread over a much larger group.* Following Lowi (1964), writers such as Baron, Shepsle, and Weingast use the term "distributive" to describe programs with this characteristic; Wilson (1989a, 1989b) uses the term "client politics" to characterize such programs (or government agencies) in his taxonomy of government programs in terms of the distribution of per capita benefits and costs. Collectively financed programs that serve narrow interests thus are characterized by benefits that have a high per capita value to a small group and costs that have a low per capita value. While this may also describe monetary redistribution, it seems stronger when redistribution takes the form of very specific goods, since those who receive the benefits may put a very different valuation on a specific program than those who pay the dollar cost. A project that creates jobs in an economically depressed area is a good example—even if those who paid for the program were similarly concentrated, the valuation they would put on the loss of income would probably be far less than the gain the recipients would perceive.

The possibility of different valuations of a dollar of transfers is certainly present in the Dixit–Londregan model applied to monetary transfers: an individual with a low "greed parameter" or high income will put lower value on a dollar of transfers received or taxes paid. However, the possibility of extremely large differences in the valuation of net benefits appears greater with in-kind transfers, and such large differences are important in the adoption of many programs with particularist benefits.

A second important characteristic of many in-kind redistribution programs, especially when targeted at geographically defined legislative districts, is their *universalism.* Public works programs, for example, are given to the vast majority of (if not all) legislative districts represented in the legislature, well in excess of the minimal size coalition needed to ensure passage of an omnibus bill. Though each individual program benefits a small group at the expense of the whole, in a political equilibrium, each group gets a benefit from the set of programs taken as a whole. If redistribution is distortionary, this equilibrium may leave all individuals worse off than the case where there is no redistribution. Here too, universalism may apply to monetary as well as nonmonetary transfers,[11] but is extremely pervasive with geographical redistribution via public works programs.

Third, and perhaps most important, nonmonetary transfers are characterized by *inefficiency*. There are several related aspects. Total economic costs often exceed economic benefits, with the economic inefficiency often being quite large. (Anyone who has driven through a sparsely populated area represented by a powerful congressman and wondered why the little-used highways are so good is certainly aware of this. Numerous other examples of wasteful public works projects could be given.) There is not only Pareto inefficiency in individual projects, but general overprovision, a phenomenon related to universalism. Inefficiency of individual projects combined with universalism means redistribution may be particularly inefficient.

Transparency of the redistribution is another characteristic separating nonmonetary redistribution from cash transfers, and, it may be argued, the *lack of transparency* plays a crucial role in explaining why nonmonetary transfers are prevalent. On the assumption that redistribution to some special interest groups would elicit majority disapproval by voters who had to foot the bill if they were fully aware of it, politicians who want to transfer resources to these groups must find less than transparent ways of doing so. Transparency (or lack of it) has several aspects. First, nontransparent redistributions are those with concealed benefits and costs. Policies which have no explicit tax and expenditure aspect but which change market prices by reducing supply or inflating demand fall squarely in this category. Second, policies which have a socially beneficial as well as a redistributive aspect (what Tullock [1983] calls *disguised* transfers) lack transparency. Location of a public works project which will increase the value of surrounding land is a good example: since voters probably do not have a strong sense of the optimal location, the implicit transfer in choosing one location over another is well hidden. In both of these cases, the same transfer made in cash would be far more transparent.

Finally, in-kind redistribution may be special if consumption of the goods provided requires a private resource input of the consumer. Consider, for example, public education, which requires not only some expenditure of individuals to attend school, but also, for some, forgoing much needed income when they attend school. Hence, the need to put in one's own resources means the poor may be excluded from benefitting from the program. The importance of this is that it raises the possibility that the

---

[11] Arnold (1979, 1990), for example, discusses how a 1965 United States government program of revenue sharing originally targeted at a very small number of cities grew to include 227 congressional districts.

program may lead to redistribution from the poor to the rich, rather than vice versa.

"Pork-Barrel" Politics

When a collectively financed program whose benefits are concentrated in a small group is thought to have social costs that exceed the social benefits, it is commonly referred to as a "pork-barrel" program.[12] There is the widespread view that there is overprovision of such projects, referring either to the excess of social costs over social benefits or to universalism in their provision, or both. Public works projects benefitting a single legislative district, but paid for by the electorate as a whole provide a prime example, the rivers and harbors bills coming out of the United States. Congress being the classic example of "pork."

There are three general types of arguments that have been advanced for the overprovision of programs which are characterized by concentrated benefits and dispersed costs. The first type of argument focuses on the very different per capita benefits and costs that define client politics—the costs of the projects are perceived to be low, so that those who bear the costs have no great incentive to oppose them (whereas the beneficiaries have a strong incentive to push hard for their adoption).[13] However intuitively appealing, this argument for overprovision is incomplete. Why should a legislator or a group of voters acquiesce to a program that yields only costs for them, albeit small ones? The argument often turns on some sort of illusion, with voters underestimating the costs. Alternatively, one may argue that there is lack of information about the costs of pork-barrel projects. While the beneficiaries of a program arc well aware of its effects, those who bear the costs are largely ignorant of what those costs are, either in terms of taxes they pay or other distortions induced. However, this argument is subject to a basic criticism. Ambitious politicians or journalists have an incentive to reveal to otherwise uninformed voters the true burden of projects whose costs they might ignore and of the decision-making process which leads to overprovision of pork-barrel projects. Politicians can go a step further to garner votes, by opposing such projects and offering alternative programs the general mass of voters would prefer.

---

[12] According to Safire (1978, p. 553), the phrase *pork barrel* is "probably derived from the pre-Civil War practice of [slave-owners] periodically distributing salt pork to the slaves from huge barrels." The "stampede of congressmen to get their local appropriations into omnibus river and harbor bills" led to the analogy to attempts to "strive to grab as much as possible" from the pork barrel, hence the term "pork-barrel" bills. "By the 1870's," Safire writes, "congressmen were regularly referring to 'pork' and the word became part of the United States political lexicon."

[13] This is sometimes viewed as a "collective action" problem in organizing interest groups, following the pioneering work of Olson (1965). Collective action problems are discussed in detail in the next chapter.

Arnold (1990) argues this point quite forcefully and contends that this possibility limits the ability of members of the United States. Congress to enact programs or laws favoring a specific constituency.

A second type of argument is that, in addition to economic benefits, the programs provide political benefits, leading to a greater number and scale of projects than would be chosen on purely economic grounds. Shepsle and Weingast (1981, 1984) and Weingast, Shepsle, and Johnsen (1981) make this argument when considering geographically concentrated projects. For example, they argue that the expenditures to build public projects are often disproportionately targeted to the district as well, and that these expenditures are seen as a benefit. The argument is that factors of production are not always fully employed, so that the jobs created by the government programs generate employment and income, rather than bidding away scarce resources from other uses. This employment-generating effect for the targeted voters is seen as strengthening the bias towards pork-barrel projects flowing from the asymmetric perception of costs and benefits outlined above.

To make the point more precise, let us consider the basic Weingast–Shepsle–Johnsen model. Projects are targeted to geographically defined legislative districts, reflecting the geographical nature of representation in legislatures. Suppose there are J legislative districts. A project of size g in a legislative district provides economic benefits to the district of $u(g)$, where $u(\cdot)$ is an increasing, concave function. For simplicity, the time dimension of the flow of benefits (and costs) is ignored, so that $u(g)$ could be thought of as a present discounted value. The total resource cost of the project $\zeta(g)$ is decomposed into three components, $\zeta(g) = \zeta_1(g) + \zeta_2(g) + \zeta_3(g)$, where $\zeta_1(g)$ = real resource expenditure on inputs spent within the district; $\zeta_2(g)$ = real resource expenditure on inputs spent outside the district; and, $\zeta_3(g)$ = real resource costs other than input expenditure imposed on the district by the project. This last type of cost would be things such as the possible destruction of natural resources or the increase in consumer prices due to higher economic activity within the district. Each of the cost components is assumed to be an increasing convex function of project size. The benefit and cost functions are assumed to be identical across districts.

Projects are financed by tax revenues, where the total tax bill for a project is $T(g) = \zeta_1(g) + \zeta_2(g)$. This is apportioned across districts according to tax shares τ^j for each of the $j \in J$ districts, where $\sum_J \tau^j = 1$. As a benchmark, suppose that the tax costs of a single project are fully internalized, so that the beneficiaries of a project see themselves as paying the full resource cost. Project size will be chosen to maximize

$$u(g) - \zeta_3(g) - T(g) = u(g) - \zeta(g), \qquad (8.19)$$

so that project size is chosen such that marginal benefit equals marginal cost $(u'(g) = \zeta'(g))$. Hence, the solution is one of economic efficiency. Given the characteristics of the functions $u(\cdot)$ and $\zeta(\cdot)$, this leads to a determinate project size, which we denote g^{eff}. Note that the same solution would obtain if each district sees itself as paying $1/J$th of the tax cost of J identical projects.

In a political world, legislators represent specific geographical constituencies. This has two important effects. First, in district j, the tax cost of the typical project is then seen not as $T(g)$, but as $\tau^j T(g)$. Second, expenditures on project inputs are often earmarked for the district in which the project is built, with these resource costs seen as a benefit of the project for the reasons mentioned above. They represent a gain to owners of factor inputs within the district. This is the political benefit crucial to the Weingast–Shepsle–Johnsen model. In this political set-up, they begin with the case of "universalism in the extreme," where each legislator independently determines whether and at what scale to build a project. The two political effects imply that in choosing a project for his district, a legislator in district j maximizes not (8.19), but the objective:

$$[u(g) + \zeta_1(g)] - [\zeta_3(g) + \tau^j T(g)], \tag{8.19a}$$

where the first term in brackets is the district's private benefits, inclusive of resources spent in the district, and the second is nonresource, plus tax costs. This leads to a first-order condition that may be written

$$u'(g) + \zeta_1'(g) = \tau^j(\zeta_1'(g) + \zeta_2'(g)) + \zeta_3'(g). \tag{8.20}$$

Call the solution to this condition g^{pol}. One may easily show (since $u'(g^{\text{eff}}) > \zeta_3'(g^{\text{eff}})$) that if $\zeta_1'(g) > \tau^j(\zeta_1'(g) + \zeta_2'(g))$, that is, if local expenditures on a project grow more rapidly than locally paid taxes as the project size increases, then $g^{\text{pol}} > g^{\text{eff}}$. Weingast, Shepsle, and Johnsen argue that this condition is likely to hold as τ_j is generally quite small, so that "imaginative" legislators will find projects that satisfy it. Hence, they conclude that with fully decentralized choice of projects by legislators and dispersed taxation, the political benefits that legislators associate with projects will lead to provision of projects above the economically efficient level. As Baron (1991) points out, the distinction between economic and political benefits crucial for the results does not involve double counting, as the expenditures serve as a substitute for targeted transfers and patronage that gives legislators electoral benefits.

Though this example well represents the role of political benefits in explaining the pork barrel, its simplicity reflects the assumption that each legislator makes his computations independently and, by the rules of the game, can ignore the political decisions of other legislators. Universalism (and, implicitly, reciprocity) is therefore built into the model, rather than coming out of the nature of legislative interactions. One is thus led to the third type of argument used to explain overprovision, focusing on the decisionmaking process within the legislature. We simply summarize some of the main arguments.

The basic argument on the role of decisionmaking mechanisms follows Buchanan and Tullock's (1962, chapters 10 and 11) analysis of vote trading (or "logrolling") in majority systems, a phenomenon first discussed in Section 3.5 of Chapter 3. The key point is that decisions are made with *reciprocity* in mind. Each legislator represents a district which wants a project for itself and legislators tell one another, "You support my project and I'll support yours." There is abundant empirical evidence that such "logrolling" takes place in legislatures; from a theoretical point of view, the reciprocal behavior which permits the existence of logrolling equilibria must be shown to be consistent with individual optimization.

The central idea can be represented using the above model. The discussion following (8.19) indicates that if only economic benefits are considered for a package of J identical projects in which each district pays $1/J$th of the tax cost, the efficient solution would still obtain. On the other hand, when the resource input $\zeta_1(g)$ is seen as a benefit, the same calculation for the package of J projects implies an objective of $u(g) + \zeta_1(g) - (1/J)(J\zeta_1(g) + J\zeta_2(g)) - \zeta_3(g)$, yielding a first-order condition:

$$u'(g) = \zeta_2'(g) + \zeta_3'(g). \tag{8.20a}$$

The solution, call it g^{rec}, will clearly exceed g^{eff}.

Buchanan and Tullock (1962) present a simple but insightful analysis based on cooperative game theory. The temporal nature of vote trading suggests a repeated game model with reputational considerations, as in Chapter 6, where a legislator who promises to support other programs in the future in exchange for support he receives today and subsequently reneges is punished. Chari and Cole (1993) present a formal model in which vote trading within a legislature leads to excessive spending on projects with concentrated benefits and diffuse costs.

The argument that majority rule leads to universalism appears, however, to violate Riker's (1962) prediction that programs will be adopted by the minimal-size coalition needed to gain a majority. Weingast (1979) shows that in a one-shot game in which economic benefits of a project exceed costs and where each district pays $1/N$th of the cost if $N \leq J$ projects are adopted, the set of packages that cannot be defeated consists of those giving projects to a bare majority of districts (i.e., the "core" of the game is the set of minimal winning coalitions). There are, of course, many such coalitions. Weingast then considers the choice problem of legislators if they must vote not knowing which of the minimal winning coalitions will form, that is, if their district will be a member of the winning coalition or not. In this case, legislators will prefer a universalist program that includes all districts to a "lottery" over minimal winning coalitions. This result requires, however, that economic costs are less than economic benefits. Shepsle and Weingast (1981) use the model presented above to add political benefits and extend Weingast's universalism result to the case where costs exceed pure economic benefits, but where the political benefits (the ζ_1 of the above model) support the result. Hence, universalism in majority-rule legislatures is extended to economically inefficient projects.

Fiorina (1981b) and Baron (1991) model the importance of legislative procedures in even more detail by considering the role of amendment procedures whereby a given project can be added or deleted from a legislative package. Specifically, procedures limiting such amendments are considered. Fiorina finds that once amendment control procedures are considered explicitly, the conditions for a universalist result are stricter than in Weingast's models. Baron considers the effects of using open versus closed amendment rules on the types of programs that will be adopted, and shows that open rules may limit the inefficiency of programs adopted.

Inefficiency

Another aspect of inefficiency is in the type of program used to make a given transfer. A common argument concerning nonmonetary transfers is that they are an inefficient means of redistribution relative to cash transfers. In the public finance literature, there is an extensive discussion of conditions under which nonmonetary transfers may be less efficient economically than monetary transfers in effecting redistribution. The basic results support the common presumption that monetary transfers are generally preferred on efficiency grounds. From a political economy perspective, therefore, the emphasis is then on why such transfers may be used, even though they are less efficient. This question has been considered, for example, in papers by Olsen (1969) and Bruce and Waldman (1991).

Coate and Morris (1995) address this issue, putting special emphasis on the lack of transparency in generating redistribution via nonmonetary transfers as opposed to more efficient cash transfers. In so doing, they formalize the role of lack of voter information in explaining the prevalence of pork-barrel projects, an explanation suggested in the previous subsection. They consider a model of disguised transfers in which politicians may make transfers to special interests either in cash or via building public projects (or both), where a project benefits the special interests and may or may not benefit the representative citizen, that is, the population as a whole.

The utility of a representative citizen is the sum of his post-tax income and the benefit from public projects, denoted g. The special interest derives income indirectly from public projects as well as receiving direct cash transfers ν, so that the special interest's income in any period is the sum of these two. In each period, the politician gives a cash transfer $\nu \geq 0$ to the special interest, and may also build a public project. A project costs ζ and is financed by taxes on the representative citizen. A project may either yield high benefits g_H or low benefits g_L to the citizen, where the probability of high benefits is p, which can take on two values, p_0 or p_1, where $0 < p_0 < p_1 < 1$. It is assumed that the parameter values are such that the expected net benefits of the project (expected benefits minus costs) are positive when $p = p_1$, while when $p = p_0$, ordinary citizens would actually be better off with a tax-financed transfer ν to special interests than with the project being built. Hence, it is socially optimal (in an expected sense) to build the project when $p = p_1$, and inefficient otherwise. (Obviously, an outcome of g_L does not mean the decision was wrong, as $p_1 < 1$.)

The model has two periods with an election at the end of the first period, in which the incumbent runs against a randomly drawn challenger. Elections are meant to control politicians, as in the models of Barro (1973) and Ferejohn (1986), considered in Section 7.2 of Chapter 7. The type of both incumbent and challenger is not known with certainty. There are two types of politicians. "Good" politicians care both about remaining in office (they are opportunistic, in the language of Chapter 7) and about social welfare. Both aims are crucial, as in the Rogoff and Sibert (1987) model in the previous chapter. "Bad" politicians care about these two aims, and about making transfers to special interests as well. Hence, in the election at the end of the first period, voters will vote for the candidate whom they believe is more likely to be good. Crucial to the possibility of inefficiency in choice of public projects are two types of asymmetric information. One is the "politician uncertainty" already mentioned. The second is "policy uncertainty": incumbents observe p while voters do not, having only a prior probability that the project is likely to yield high benefits, that is, that $p = p_1$. Since the p's are interior, observing high benefits *ex post* is not a perfect indicator that the socially optimal policy (in an expected sense) was to build the project. Thus, voters must try to infer the likelihood the incumbent is "good" from the policies he adopts and from the outcome of the project if built, where neither will be a perfect indicator. Incumbents have the incentive to choose policies which maximize the posterior probability that voters assign to their being "good," where the prior probability that they are good (their *reputation*) is denoted q_I and the posterior is derived from Bayes' rule conditional on the policies and outcomes observed. The probability that the challenger is of the good type is some observed q_C drawn from a known distribution $\Gamma(q_C)$.

Coate and Morris solve for a perfect Bayesian equilibrium. Under the restriction on beliefs that observing a lower cash transfer cannot lead to more pessimistic beliefs about the incumbent, they show first the intuitive result that a good incumbent will never make cash transfers in the first period. Therefore, if a bad incumbent has a high enough initial reputation q_I, he will also make no cash transfers, meaning he will transfer resources to special interests by building a project even when it is bad, that is, when $p = p_0$. Hence, there may be inefficient overprovision of public projects, arising from the lack of transparency of redistribution via public works in contrast to the transparency via cash transfers. Both types of asymmetric information are necessary for this result. If either it were known with certainty that politicians protect special interests or if voters knew or could infer *ex post* whether a project should have been undertaken, a bad politician would use cash transfers when that was the most efficient way to give resources to special interests. Interestingly, reputational considerations can also lead to underprovision of public projects, that is, no incumbent building the project even when $p = p_1$. This arises if the weight a politician puts on staying in office is high enough relative to the weight put on social welfare that he does not undertake the project even when it is good for fear of sending a negative signal.

Dixit and Londregan (1995) present an alternative explanation of why the possibility of targeting expenditures may lead to inefficient programs being adopted. They consider a world where transfers are decided *solely* on political grounds, as set out in their paper discussed above. How the benefits of government expenditures are divided (they actually consider income transfers, but the argument is general) will thus depend on political characteristics, that is, on how many votes a party can get per dollar of project expenditure. These political characteristics may be distributed quite differently from the economic characteristics which an efficient government program would reward. To use the example they present, programs to support declining industries (including placing projects in declining geographical areas) may be inefficient relative to programs which encourage movement of factors out of declining regions or industries. But if voters satisfy the political conditions which make them likely recipients of largesse, economic inefficiencies can result from policy being motivated simply by the attempt to gain votes. Dixit and Londregan present a dynamic model of the interaction of political and economic decisions in a declining industry, where the former are motivated solely by vote maximization. Individuals, in deciding whether to pay any costs of adjustment, must consider the possibility that their gains from adjusting may be taxed away to support programs benefitting others, that is, must consider the possibility that their income gains may well make them likely candidates for taxation.[14] Promises by politicians to ignore such character-

---

[14] However, the willingness to move may signal favorable political characteristics, namely, that such individuals will be able to adapt to future shocks and hence will continue to earn high income. Thus, a forward-looking government would not necessarily tax such individuals heavily in response to their efficient choices.

istics will not be credible. Hence, in a dynamic adjustment problem, agents will not pay any nonnegligible costs of adjustment (provided that their "political characteristics" do not change), knowing that any private gains they make by undergoing the adjustment will be taxed away. Hence, when expenditures can be targeted and the costs of such programs are not borne by the beneficiaries, not only will the political nature of expenditure decisions mean inefficiency in choice of programs is possible; it will also lead to inefficient private behavior in anticipation of government's response to efficient individual choices.

The Interaction of Nonmonetary Transfers and Private Goods

When redistribution is in kind or in indirect ways, the form of the transfer can affect consumption patterns by more than a simple income effect coming from the cash value of the transfer. One important case is that of government-provided goods whose consumption requires a resource input by the consumer. Consider an example of Fernandez and Rogerson (1995) concerning partial public funding of education. If all costs of education were fully provided by government, so that no private resource input was required, with this subsidy being covered by a linear tax of the sort considered by Meltzer and Richard, public provision of education would act like a transfer from rich to poor. However, when individuals must spend some of their own resources to get educated and capital markets are imperfect, there can be a transfer in the opposite direction. When consuming public education requires a private input, imperfect capital markets imply that only children of families whose income is above a certain level will be able to benefit from publicly provided education. Thus, wealthier individuals prefer only partial subsidization of education, since this excludes the poor from receiving the subsidy and thus serves to transfer resources from the poor to themselves. Fernandez and Rogerson show that such a program of partial subsidization can develop endogenously in a political equilibrium. They consider a world with several income classes where the tax rate and education subsidy are endogenous, subject to a government balanced budget constraint, and show how a partial subsidy, implying a transfer from poor to rich, could arise under majority voting. This is consistent with Director's law that in a democracy, redistribution will be from the tails of the income distribution to the center.

8.5. Rent Seeking and Predation

In the previous sections, all redistribution of private goods was accomplished via some explicitly specified tax-transfer, government expenditure, or regulatory program. Both the specific program and the decisionmaking mechanism were crucial in understanding the political-economic equilibrium. An alternative approach to the political economy of redistribution is to abstract from the specific policy mechanism which is the vehicle for redistribution and instead consider more generally the phenomenon of expending resources in the attempt to redistribute resources. This is generally labeled the theory of **rent seeking**, though the term is used not only in the broad sense as referring to the socially costly pursuit of income and wealth transfers, but also in the more narrow sense of the pursuit of the monopoly rents that a government can create or increase. (Mueller [1989, chapter 13] presents a good summary of this latter approach.) In this section, we consider this type of model of redistribution that largely abstracts from institutional or political details. Under this approach, specific redistributive mechanisms are replaced by a more general specification of the "technology" of redistribution, this specification limited only by reasonable assumptions characterizing the relation between resources devoted to appropriating wealth and the outcome of the process.

The Theory of Rent Seeking

The concept of rent seeking, referring generally to expenditure of resources to win a contestable prize, was introduced by Tullock (1967); the term was introduced by Krueger (1974), in a paper entitled "The Political Economy of the Rent-Seeking Society." Bhagwati's (1982) concept of Directly Unprofitable Profit Seeking is analogous. Buchanan, Tollison, and Tullock (1980) present a survey of the literature and collection of papers, including a number of the classic articles. The basic idea is well summed up in the introduction to Krueger's paper (p. 291):

> In many market-oriented economies, government restrictions upon economic activity are pervasive facts of life. These restrictions give rise to rents of a variety of forms, and people often compete for the rents. Sometimes, such competition is perfectly legal. In other instances, rent seeking takes other forms, such as bribery, corruption, smuggling and black markets.

As any romantic suitor can attest, rent seeking defined as the "expenditure of resources to win a contestable prize" can take place outside of the political arena, but we restrict our attention to political applications. Specifically, we consider the use of costly resources to influence some government policy choice, where government policy can create rents.[15] By focusing on the use of costly resources, the rent-seeking literature highlights socially undesirable consequences of contesting rents.

The activity of rent seeking is closely connected to lobbying, but the emphasis is not on the process of lobbying itself, but on the implications

---

[15] Much of the literature on rent seeking is even more specific, concentrating on the rents created by government programs which create artificial scarcity, and the attempt to secure the rights to those artificially scarce opportunities. See, for example, Buchanan's introductory essay in Buchanan, Tollison, and Tullock (1980).

for waste (or "dissipation") of resources. (A discussion focusing more on the implications of the process of lobbying is found in Section 3.7 of Chapter 3.) Hence, a rent-seeking analysis measures the social cost of an activity such as lobbying not by comparing the policy outcome under lobbying to the social planner's solution, but more directly by attempting to measure the resource cost of the attempt to affect policy outcomes. Moreover, as argued in Buchanan, Tollison, and Tullock (1980), rent seeking is broader than lobbying, there being three levels of rent seeking: *lobbying* to affect the decisionmaking process; direct engagement in *politics* to secure access to decisionmaking power; and, *shifting* in or out of the affected activity. All three types of activities waste resources.

In his pioneering paper, Tullock argued that the social costs of monopoly may be far higher than suggested by the analysis of Harberger (1954) and others, who concluded that these costs were small. Harberger's argument focused on the welfare triangle of lost consumer surplus, as represented in Figure 8.2. With a monopoly price of P_{mnp} greater than the competitive price P_{cmp} (equal to marginal cost), the social or deadweight loss from monopoly is given by the triangular area L under the demand curve, representing the loss in consumer surplus if a quantity Y_{mnp} less than Y_{cmp} is consumed. In the standard analysis, the rectangle A of monopoly rents does *not* represent a social loss, but only a pure redistribution of income from consumers to monopoly producers. The argument that the welfare

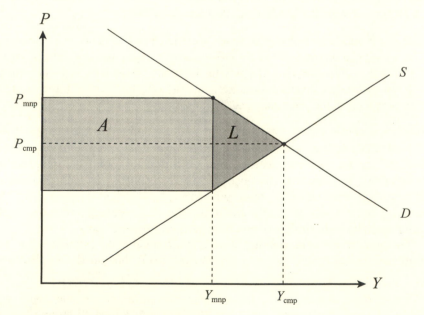

FIGURE 8.2. The social cost of monopoly.

cost of monopolies (or tariffs, to take another example) was small was that, empirically, "Harberger's triangles" (i.e., the L's) were small.

Tullock argued that competition over A will imply that the social cost of monopoly may exceed L, including part, all, or even more than all, of the monopoly rents A themselves. Suppose the monopoly in question was created by the government, to be granted to a single producer, for example, an airline route. If either of two airlines could service the route, they will expend resources to increase their chances of being awarded the route and capturing the rents A. For example, they may hire lobbyists to press their respective cases before the government officials who are responsible for awarding the route. Resources spent on capturing the rents, which would not be expended if the rents did not exist, constitute a social loss in addition to the loss in consumer surplus L.

As already indicated, the socially wasteful expenditures associated with rent seeking may include more than those of the potential monopolists competing for the rents. Several contributors to the important summary volume by Buchanan, Tollison, and Tullock (1980) argue that there are two additional possible types of socially wasteful rent-seeking expenditures: resources expended by government officials hoping to benefit from the expenditures of potential monopolists competing for the rents; and, socially wasteful expenditures by third parties as a result of the actions of both the monopolists and the government. To continue our high-flying example, suppose airline lobbyists attempt to influence the relevant government officials by offering direct bribes to obtain highly lucrative contracts to supply airplanes to the government. Though the bribe itself is a pure transfer, there may be a competition among potential officeholders to gain the power to award the rents, and resources will be expended to gain office and the spoils it carries with it. If the government-created monopoly generates tax revenues, other groups will expend resources to try to capture these revenues.

The above arguments implicitly assume that the economy is starting from a first-best equilibrium, so that rent seeking must lead to lower social welfare. If, however, we begin from a second-best state, rent seeking could improve welfare, a point stressed by Bhagwati and Srinivasan (1980) and Bhagwati (1982). For example, one could consider an economy beginning with a trade barrier which is eliminated due to rent-seeking activities, thus leading to higher social welfare. Another possibility is where imposition of a tariff may be welfare improving for a large country by allowing it to improve its terms of trade at the expense of its trading partners. Though these are potentially important possibilities, we concentrate here on the case where rent dissipation reduces welfare.

A key question in the literature on rent seeking is whether or not the rents are totally dissipated by the socially wasteful expenditure of resources meant to capture them. (Tullock [1980] terms less than full dissipation of rents *"efficient" rent seeking*.) The answer to this question depends on the alternative, productive, use of these resources, and (given the arguments about associated rent-seeking expenditures in the previous paragraph) how broadly we consider rent-seeking expenditures. Early analyses of rent seeking focused on expenditures by potential direct beneficiaries of monopoly rents, and assumed that these resources used to influence policy could be more productively used to increase economywide output. Under these assumptions, the conclusion was that there would be complete dissipation of rents, that is, that the value of the resources used to influence the policy outcome equals the value of the rents.

While complete dissipation might seem an intuitive conclusion of investing resources in rent seeking as long as the marginal benefit exceeds the marginal cost, such a conclusion requires somewhat strong linearity and symmetry assumptions. One would require, among other things (see Hillman [1989] for a set of sufficient conditions): risk-neutral contenders; constant returns to outlays made; common knowledge of the valuations of the rents, as well as identical valuation of the rents by all contenders.[16]. These conditions are quite strong and may well fail to hold. More generally, whether there is full dissipation of rents depends, *inter alia*, on: the nature of the rule for determining the winner in the rent-seeking contest; the degree of risk aversion of the contestants; the extent to which contestants are heterogeneous; and, the extent of their information about each other. Rents not being fully dissipated could also reflect an assumption that the resources used for rent seeking are unproductive in alternative uses. On the other hand, given the arguments presented above about associated rent-seeking expenditures, more than full dissipation is possible, as the resource cost of the three sources of rent seeking could exceed the value of the rents themselves. Nitzan (1994) presents a good technical survey of a number of these issues.

Rent seeking has numerous applications. Trade policy (starting with Krueger's paper) is a major one, as the implementation of tariffs, quotas, and other protectionist measures is a major source of rent creation. Hillman (1989) is an excellent source on the theoretical and conceptual issues; Baldwin (1985) and Magee (1997) are two (of numerous) more empirical analyses. Regulation is another major area of application. Stigler (1971, 1975) was a seminal contribution to the debate on regulation, arguing that regulatory agencies are often "captured" by those they are meant to regulate, so that they become a vehicle for creation and distribution of rents. Posner (1975), in an influential article, attempted to measure the loss from rent seeking in regulated industries by assuming that the rents are given by the rectangle A in Figure 8.2, and that these rents are fully dissipated. He finds that the costs of rent seeking in the regulated

---

[16] One further assumes that the source of the prize to the winner is not transfers from the losers. That is, the contest is one over pre-existing rents, with no further transfers. This is in contrast to the war of attrition discussed in Chapter 9.)

sectors in the United States, such as airlines, medical services, and oil, are substantial.

A Formal Analysis of Rent Seeking

To understand the relation between the characteristics of the rent-seeking contest and the extent of rent dissipation, we now analyze rent-seeking contests more formally. Let us begin with a contest with a small number of risk-neutral contenders, so that each acts strategically, rather than competitively. The probability p^i that an agent i will win the rents will depend both on his own expenditures x^i and on the expenditures x^j of other contenders, this probability being (weakly) increasing in x^j and decreasing in the x^j. The relation between outlays and probabilities of winning will depend not only on the strategy of other contenders, but also on the nature of the political competition. An intuitive specification of the political process is that the rents go to the contender expending the most resources, termed a "perfectly discriminating" contest, though there could be other specifications. If the process of awarding the prize is perfectly discriminating, there will be no equilibrium in pure strategies. To see why, note that if agent i chooses the strategy of spending $x^i = x'$ on the contest, an opponent j can raise his probability of winning discontinuously by raising his spending x^j infinitesimally above x'. But then agent i is better off spending an amount finitely less than x', as his probability of winning is the same. Hence, a pure strategy of spending x' cannot be an equilibrium strategy.[17]. Therefore, in equilibrium, contenders will use mixed strategies, the probabilities of expenditure represented by some cumulative distribution function $\Gamma^i(x^i)$ for each contender i.

What will the mixed strategy look like? Following Hillman (1989), let us consider a perfectly discriminating contest involving an income transfer between two contenders. (We will later show how the case of N contenders can be represented by the two-contender case.) Suppose a risk-neutral contender 1 spends resources x^1 to influence the outcome. Let us denote by u^{1H} his value of being the winner, by u^{1L} his value of being the loser, and, as above, by p^1 the probability of winning as a function of x^1 given agent 2's equilibrium expenditures. Agent 1's expected payoff Ω^1 can then be written

$$\Omega^1(x^1) = p^1 u^{1H} + (1 - p^1)u^{1L} - x^1$$

$$= u^{1L} + p^1 V^1 - x^1, \qquad (8.21)$$

---

[17] By a similar argument, only one player can have zero expenditures in equilibrium (it will turn out to be the player with the lower valuation of the rent), since the other player can guarantee himself a finite positive payoff in this case by spending an infinitesimal positive amount.

where $V^1 = u^{1H} - u^{1L}$, that is, the value of a favorable outcome net of rent-seeking expenditures. Without loss of generality, let agents be ranked by their V^i, so that $V^1 > V^2$. In a perfectly discriminating contest, the probability that agent 1 wins with an expenditure of x^1 is the probability that agent 2 spends less than x^1 (equal expenditure is a zero probability event), so that agent 1's expected payoff (8.21) may be written

$$\Omega^1(x^1) = u^{1L} + \Gamma^2(x^1)V^1 - x^1. \tag{8.22}$$

There is an analogous expression for the expected payoff of agent 2, namely,

$$\Omega^2(x^2) = u^{2L} + \Gamma^1(x^2)V^2 - x^2. \tag{8.23}$$

A mixed strategy in the level of expenditure x^i for each player is characterized by probabilities $\Gamma^i(x^i)$ of spending an amount x^i. For this to be an equilibrium, any level of expenditure undertaken with positive probability must yield the same utility. To calculate the equilibrium probabilities, note first that there will be a maximum level of expenditures, call it $x_{\max}$ with $\Gamma^i(x_{\max}) = 1$, for each player, which will equal V^2 for both players. The player with the lower net valuation (here, player 2) will never spend more than his net valuation V^2, with this level (or more exactly, an infinitesimally greater amount) then being the maximum expenditure for the high-valuation player (i.e., player 1) as well. Since all levels of expenditure, including the maximum level of expenditure, must yield the same utility, (8.22) and (8.23) then imply[18]

$$u^{1L} + \Gamma^2(x^1)V^1 - x^1 = u^{1L} + V^1 - V^2, \tag{8.22a}$$

and

$$u^{2L} + \Gamma^1(x^2)V^2 - x^2 = u^{2L} + V^2 - V^2. \tag{8.23a}$$

One may then write the equilibrium mixed strategies (i.e., the probabilities $\Gamma^i(x)$ for each player i such that the other player is just indifferent

---

[18] Using $\Gamma^i(V^2) = 1$, (8.22) and (8.23) imply that in equilibrium, player 2 realizes utility of u^{2L} and player 1 realizes $u^{1L} + V^1 - V^2$. Intuitively, the high-valuation ("strong") player pushes the low-valuation player down to the latter's reservation payoff, with the strong player capturing the entire difference $V^1 - V^2$ with infinitesimally larger expenditures. One may further conclude that in this perfectly discriminating contest, the high-valuation player will never have zero expenditures in equilibrium, as he can always do better (if this is not obvious, see the previous footnote), while the low-valuation player will have zero expenditures with positive probability.

between two equilibrium expenditure levels) as

$$\Gamma^1(x) = \frac{x}{V^2}, \qquad x \in [0, V^2], \tag{8.24}$$

and

$$\Gamma^2(x) = \frac{x}{V^1} + \left(1 - \frac{V^2}{V^1}\right), \qquad x \in [0, V^2]. \tag{8.25}$$

One can calculate the expected spending levels, namely, $\int_0^{V^2} x^i \, d\Gamma^i$, on the basis of these distributions, and implied expected total spending, which is

$$E(x^1 + x^2) = V^2 \frac{V^1 + V^2}{2V^1}. \tag{8.26}$$

It follows immediately that if the valuations are symmetric, expected expenditures equal the common valuation, so that rents are fully dissipated (in an expected sense). Otherwise, however, expected spending will be lower than *either* of the valuations. Intuitively, when the valuations are common knowledge, the fact that one agent is known to value the rent less puts a limit not only on the expenditures he is willing to make to capture the rent, but also on the expenditures the other agent knows he needs to make.

The results of the two-agent rent-seeking contest are still valid with more than two agents, as long as their *relative* valuations of the rent are common knowledge. Suppose there were a third agent potentially competing for the rent and, without loss of generality, assume that $V^3 \le V^2 \le V^1$. To capture the rent in a perfectly discriminating contest, agent 3's expenditure x^3 must be greater than both x^1 and x^2. Hence, if agents 1 and 2 continue to act as they did before (as in (8.24) and (8.25)), agent 3's expected payoff as a function of x^3 is identical to an expression such as (8.22), evaluated at the probability that x^1 and x^2 are less than x^3:

$$\Omega^3(x^3) = u^{3L} + \Gamma^1(x^3)\Gamma^2(x^3)V^3 - x^3$$

$$= u^{3L} + \frac{V^3}{V^2}x^3\left(1 - \frac{V^2}{V^1} + \frac{x^3}{V^1} - \frac{V^2}{V^3}\right). \tag{8.27}$$

Since agent 3 will never spend more than the value he assigns to the rent (that is, $x^3 \le V^3 \le V^2$), the term in large parentheses in (8.25) is nonpositive, implying that there is no positive spending level x^3 for agent 3 which will generate a positive expected payoff. Hence, his best response to the strategies of agents 1 and 2 is to stay out of the contest, that is, not to engage in rent seeking. More generally, if there are $N \geq 3$ agents for whom it is known that $V^1 \geq V^2 \geq V^3 \geq \ldots \geq V^N$, then agents 1 and 2 act as if there are no other participants in the rent-seeking contest and the other agents do not compete for the rent. To summarize, known *asymmetric* valuations of the rent tend to reduce rent-seeking expenditures. All agents but the two with the highest valuations drop out of the contest; moreover, as we saw above, the agent with the second-highest valuation is inhibited in his rent-seeking activity by the knowledge that there exists another agent with a higher valuation of the contested rent.

How will the extent of rent dissipation change as we change the assumptions? Let us consider only some of the possible changes. Uncertainty about the value of rents can take several forms and have significant implications, even under risk neutrality. If there is uncertainty about whether the rent will actually be awarded to one of the contestants, this will lower its expected value, so that contestants will be willing to spend less to gain the rent. Rent dissipation relative to the original value of the rent will be reduced. More interesting, perhaps, is uncertainty about the value other contestants attach to the rent, which has been considered by Hillman and Riley (1989). Common knowledge about the *relative* valuation of rents was crucial to a number of the arguments made above. In analogy to uncertainty about whether the rent will be awarded, one might think that uncertainty about the valuation of other contestants also reduces the extent of rent dissipation. Hillman and Riley show that this is not the case. This type of uncertainty actually *increases* rent dissipation, because it induces participation by players who would be inactive under full information.[19]

When contestants are risk averse, uncertainty means that they will be unwilling to allocate the expected value of the rents to influencing the outcome. It is easy to show that, in fact, total resources spent will be less than the value of the rents even as the number of contestants becomes large. However, for small rents (relative to the wealth of individual contenders), rent dissipation will be close to complete.

Imperfectly discriminating rent-seeking contests are modeled by characterizing the equilibrium outcome in terms of a probability of success for each contestant as a function of their rent-seeking expenditures, rather than by a winner of the contest. Tullock (1980), in his analysis of "efficient" rent seeking (i.e., where rents are less than fully dissipated), shows that when all contenders value the rent equally, full dissipation of rents occurs only in the limit, as the number of contenders approaches infinity. For any finite number of contenders, total expenditures fall short of the value of the rent. Hillman (1989) shows that when contenders value the rent differentially in an imperfectly discriminating contest, total expenditures

---

[19] There is an analogous result in the war-of-attrition model in the next chapter, a result which is fundamental to that model.

will be approximated by the harmonic mean of their valuations, strictly equal when the number of contenders is infinite.

Predation

Another approach to redistribution that abstracts from specific institutional detail is *predation*, in which individuals and groups may concentrate their activities on appropriating goods from others. Grossman and Kim (1996a) present a general equilibrium model of the potential appropriative interaction between two agents, a predetermined potential "predator" and a predetermined potential "prey." The potential prey divides his resources between production of consumption goods and protecting his property ("defensive fortifications"). The potential predator divides his resources between production of consumption goods and production of offensive weapons that he can use to appropriate the prey's property. They consider three types of equilibria: a *nonaggressive equilibrium*, in which a predator allocates no resources to predation; a *pure predation equilibrium*, in which a predator allocates no resources to productive activity; and a *part-time predation equilibrium*, in which a predator allocates resources to both productive activity and predation.

The prey, with initial endowment e^d, is assumed to move first, choosing expenditures on "*d*efensive fortifications" x^d and productive capital k^d, subject to the budget constraint

$$e^d = x^d + k^d. \tag{8.28}$$

The predator then allocates his initial endowment e^o to expenditures on "*o*ffensive weapons" x^o and productive capital k^o, subject to the budget constraint

$$e^o = x^o + k^o. \tag{8.29}$$

Production then takes place, where it is linear for both agents, with a production coefficient α.

In the event of predation ($x^o > 0$), the prey retains a fraction δ of his endowment (both fortifications and capital are subject to appropriation), where δ depends on the relative allocation of the two agents to offensive weapons and fortifications. (Thus, $\delta = \Psi(x^o/x^d)$ with $\Psi' < 0$.) Final wealth is ω^j ($j = d, o$), and predation may waste resources, so that $\omega^d + \omega^o$ may be strictly less than $e^d + e^o$. An agent's objective is to maximize the sum of produced consumption goods and final wealth, denoted $\Omega^j = \alpha k^j + \omega^j$. Equilibria of the model are Nash equilibria based on best response choices of x^o and x^d.

The possible equilibria will depend on parameter values and initial endowments. More specifically, one wants to consider two variables: relative initial endowments e^d/e^o, denoted ϵ; and κ, the effectiveness of predation against defensive actions. For both ϵ and κ small, there will be no predation. Offensive weapons are so ineffective against defense that allocating resources to predation is not worthwhile. On the other hand, for ϵ large and κ neither too large nor too small, the predator allocates all of his resources to predation, given the high *relative* level of resources to be appropriated. Hence, if a potential predator is poor relative to its prey, the wealth of the prey will induce full-time predation. If κ is small, we will be in the former situation where the ineffectiveness of offensive weapons is key, and there will be nonaggression, even if ϵ is very high. If κ is extremely large, the high effectiveness of offensive against defensive weapons will imply the predator need devote only part of his resources to predation.

Grossman, either alone or with co-authors, has applied the above framework to a large number of issues, two of which will be sketched out here.[20] In Grossman and Kim (1995), it is used to construct a theory of security of claims to property, that is, of property rights. The modeling itself is very similar to the above model, but here both agents can engage in both activities. The motivation is their observation that though it is widespread for people and societies to allocate resources to "appropriative activities," these are generally resources for defense against appropriation, not resources towards predation. A society with fully secure claims to property is "a set of individuals or groups that are nonaggressive with respect to each other." Following the results of the above analysis, in this *nonaggressive equilibrium*, no resources are allocated to predation because individuals allocate enough resources to defense that predation is deterred. Hence, security of property comes at a cost, so that it is not immediately obvious that a society is better off with fully secure property rights.

To analyze whether this is the case, consider the two-agent model where both agents can engage in both activities. For each agent to be nonaggressive, the parameters must be such that the other agent chooses "defensive fortifications" large enough to deter predation. An agent will do so for κ small enough or the resource loss from predation large enough relative to κ. Otherwise, resources devoted to defense will not be sufficient to deter predation, and property rights will not be fully secure. In this type of equilibrium, the security of claims to property is negatively related to the effectiveness of offensive weapons against defensive fortifications and is positively related to the destructiveness of predation. That is, Grossman and Kim show that if an agent is rich, he is always better off the smaller is κ and the larger is the resource loss from predation, and, hence, if claims

---

[20] An application to capital accumulation will be considered in Chapter 11.

to property are more secure. Conversely, if an agent is poor and the equilibrium is predatory, then his welfare is higher the *higher* is κ and the *smaller* is the resource loss, that is, the *less* secure are property rights. The reason is that a predation equilibrium is *relatively* advantageous to the poorer agent "in the sense that the equilibrium ratio of the sum of the production of consumables and final wealth ... to the initial endowment ... is larger for the poorer agent than for the richer agent." (Grossman and Kim [1995], p. 1286)[21] Grossman and Kim suggest that the model may serve as the basis for a theory of legal barriers to appropriation in order to make property rights secure. Another nice feature of the model is that nonaggressive behavior reflects optimal behavior given the underlying parameters (and the optimal reaction to other agents' optimal behavior given the underlying parameters), not simply social norms.

In Grossman (1995), it is argued that redistribution of income from capitalists to workers may be to the advantage of capitalists if it induces productive, rather than predatory, behavior on the part of workers. On a general level, this point is often raised; the attraction of Grossman's analysis is that it gives a specific framework which suggests a specific type of redistribution. Workers have an endowment of *time*, which they must decide how to split between productive and predatory activities. Assuming that wage subsidies are not difficult to administer, capitalists will find it profitable to give such subsidies, as they increase the value of time spent on productive activities relative to predatory activities.

8.6. INTERGENERATIONAL REDISTRIBUTION

An empirically extremely important type of policy-induced redistribution is across generations. Some of this redistribution is the by-product of income transfer programs aimed at alleviating poverty of the sort studied in Section 8.2. Since the incidence of poverty is higher among the elderly than among the general population in many countries, such programs end up redistributing income across generations, even though this is not their explicit intention. The phenomenon of intergenerational redistribution is much wider than income maintenance programs, however, since many other policies have large effects on the distribution of income and wealth across generations. One example would be government-sponsored health maintenance or health insurance programs, since medical services are consumed disproportionately by the elderly. A perhaps more important

---

[21] This result is related to what Hirshleifer (1991) has called the "paradox of power." In power struggles, weaker groups improve their position relative to stronger groups because they fight harder, unless the power differential is so great that they are dissuaded from fighting. Hence, the final distribution of income (or whatever resource the struggle is about) will be less dispersed than the initial distribution.

case, because of its magnitude,[22] is social security or old age assistance, when the program is not fully "funded." Though such programs were originally conceived as government-sponsored (or enforced) savings programs, the "pay-as-you-go" character of many programs, in which the working population is taxed to make payments to older retirees, means there is a strong element of intergenerational redistribution, more specifically, of redistribution from the young to the old. (Decisions of whether or not to repudiate government debt also have the effect of redistributing resources across generations, if holding of the debt is skewed across generations.) The large number of such programs of intergenerational redistribution both within and across economies raises the question, as Breyer (1994) puts it: why is there such a strong tendency to force transfers from young to old?

A further motivation for studying intergenerational redistribution programs is for some new questions they raise. If a program transfers resources across generations, there is an important element that was absent in the earlier models of redistribution within a generation, namely, the possibility of a transfer (positive or negative) to generations yet unborn. Hence, some agents who will be affected by the transfer program do not participate in the political decision on the design of the program. Two key issues arise due to limited participation. First, will the current generation take advantage of a future generation by designing a program that imposes a transfer from the future generation to themselves? The transfer to the current old from the current young and from generations yet unborn in a pay-as-you-go social security system is a good example of such a burden. Second, when the time comes for future generations to pay the transfer that was imposed on them, will they accept the burden even though they did not participate in the initial decision, or will they repudiate it? That is, as the electorate changes, will the program be significantly altered or abolished? For debt held disproportionately by the old, this means repudiating the debt; for a social security system, it means reducing benefits. To summarize these two questions: Will the current generation *be able to* take advantage of the next generation; and, what constraints does the need to gain acceptability put on program design?

Some General Approaches

There has been significant work attempting to answer these and related questions. Breyer (1994) presents an excellent survey of the political economy of intergenerational redistribution; Gustafsson and Klevmarken (1989) present a collection of earlier papers on the political economy of

---

[22] The growing size of health insurance programs, as well as the growing realization that there is a strong across-generation redistributive element involved, suggests that these programs will soon become a major area of the intergenerational political debate.

social security. The seminal paper is probably Browning (1975), who considers a multigeneration model of identical, nonaltruistic individuals, in which a program is chosen by majority rule. Browning asks whether a "pay-as-you-go" social security system will be instituted with the support of a majority of the population. He assumes that the decision of the current generation is believed to be binding forever, so that a number of issues raised in the previous paragraph do not arise. The crucial assumption in the model is that there are more than two generations, implying that *workers* of different generations are alive simultaneously. Thus, workers who would contribute to a social security system differ in the net gain they would gain from the system, measured by the present discounted value of retirement benefits net of pre-retirement contributions. This characteristic of the population distribution implies that even if there is population growth (so that a younger cohort is larger than an older cohort), a majority will favor a social security system which transfers income from workers to retirees. Moreover, the size of the system is greater than what would be preferred by a young worker, who would face the full cost of the system over his lifetime.

The main criticism of the Browning model is that it assumes future voters must abide by the decisions the current generation has made. This criticism, which implies that the key questions at the end of the introduction to this section are not fully answered, applies to much of the literature on intergenerational redistribution and can be put more generally. The standard assumption in the literature is precommitment to honor the explicit or implicit debt associated with a given program: voters cannot repudiate previously made commitments. Such an approach, though useful for some issues,[23] makes the answers to the above questions trivial. To the extent that the currently alive generation is selfish, it will impose a burden on future generations, which they in turn are forced to accept; only altruism will mitigate this tendency. There is really little interesting role for studying the political constraints on intergenerational redistribution if it is assumed that previously adopted policies must be upheld.

In models of direct voting on intergenerational redistribution, there are a number of ways to explain the sustainability of redistribution when it is possible to repudiate the contract.[24] As already indicated, one approach is to assume that the young are highly altruistic towards their elders. A

---

[23] See, for example, the discussion in Chapter 5 on debt as a commitment device.

[24] There is relatively little work on the sustainability of intergenerational redistribution in a representative democracy. Hansson and Stuart (1989) argue that since politicians would be thrown out of office if they changed the existing social security system against the wishes of *either* young or old, subsequent changes must be unanimously approved. This means the initial voters can choose to impose a system subject to a much weaker restriction than majority support by future generations. To my mind, this is simply a slightly weaker no-repudiation assumption, since the no-veto characteristic is not a general characteristic of representative democracy, but an assumption.

second approach is to study a social contract which induces workers to tax themselves to support retirees. This type of social contract was first considered by Hammond (1975) for pensions, and was already discussed explicitly in Section 5.2 of Chapter 5, to which the reader may refer. Sjoblom (1985) presents a similar model, specifically applied to social security, in which the tax rate which workers put on themselves is a function of the tax rate previous generations put on themselves. Sjoblom shows there is an equilibrium strategy in which the young obey the social contract and tax themselves to make contributions to the old if the old themselves obeyed the social contract, while they break the contract and make no contributions if the old themselves broke the contract. The model is elegant, but subject to the same criticism leveled in Chapter 5 against the use of social contracts to explain economic phenomena: it seems to be an extremely unrealistic description of how a real-world social security system actually works.

The third, and probably most realistic, approach to the sustainability (that is, nonrepudiation) of intergenerational redistribution schemes concentrates on heterogeneity of voters *within* a generation, combined with some degree of altruism. In this approach, altruism alone would not be sufficient to keep the young from repudiating a pay-as-you-go social security system (or debt held by the old) if they all had identical interests. However, heterogeneity among the young leads to the formation of a majority coalition between some of the young and some of the old to sustain intergenerational redistribution. We now turn to one such model.

Tabellini's Model of Intergenerational Redistribution

Tabellini (1990b, 1991) considers intergenerational redistribution in models where repayment of explicit or implicit debt by future generations arises out of a political equilibrium, rather than being assumed. That is, there is no precommitment; instead, policy must be supported, according to the political decisionmaking mechanism, by the current electorate. For example, in a majority voting system, a majority of voters currently alive must support the tax-transfer scheme for it to be continued. Such a scheme is "politically viable." In the case of government debt, the old and the children of the wealthy (who hold a quantity of debt above the mean) vote to repay the debt. However, even though some fraction of the young must support a program for it to be continued, the current old *do* take advantage of the fact that the debt was issued without the consent of the current young. If the wealthy young could commit *ex ante* not to repay the debt, they would do so; however, once it is in existence, they favor repayment. Hence, issuance of the debt does "create facts."

Tabellini (1991) specifically considers a two-period model of debt issuance and repayment in a closed economy. (For possible application to social security, see Tabellini [1990b], as discussed in footnote 27 below.) In the first period only "parents" are alive, where each parent lives for both periods. In the second period another generation of "children" is born, who live only one period; each parent has $1 + n$ children. Debt is issued in the first period to finance a uniform transfer to all parents. In the second period, some of the debt may be repudiated, where how much of the debt to repudiate is the key political decision. (Deciding on how much debt to repudiate is identical to choosing an *ex-post* interest rate to pay on the debt.) The identity of the debt holders cannot be observed once the debt is issued; therefore, there can be no selective repudiation which, in essence, would tax debt holders differentially. Repayment of that part of the debt not repudiated is financed by a tax on the wage earnings of all children.

As in the earlier models, a political equilibrium is found in three steps: first, the individual maximization problem is solved (consistent with market clearing) for any tax-transfer policy; second, each individual's desired tax-transfer policy is derived, which in this case means the desired degree of repudiation of the debt; third, these preferences are aggregated via the political decision mechanism to find the equilibrium level of redistribution.

First consider individual optimization, where generations are linked by altruism. A parent maximizes

$$\Omega_P^i = u(c_1^i) + c_2^i + \sigma^P(1 + n)h(s^i), \tag{8.30}$$

and a child maximizes

$$\Omega_C^i = \frac{\sigma^C}{1 + n}c_2^i + h(s^i), \tag{8.31}$$

where c_1^i, c_2^i, and s^i are family i's parent's first-period, parent's second-period, and children's consumption, $1 + n$ is the number of children per parent, and σ^P and σ^C measure the altruistic urges of parents and children, respectively.

Families differ only in the endowment of parents, where the endowment of (parents in) family i is ξ^i. Assume that ξ^i is distributed inside the population according to a known distribution $F(\xi)$. Parents also receive a lump-sum transfer ν from the government, which is the same across families. The budget constraints for families are

$$c_1^i + s^i = \xi^i + \nu, \tag{8.32}$$

for parents in the first period, where s^i is saving and government debt is the only saving vehicle, and

$$c_2^i + d^i = Rs^i + (1 + n)o^i + \hat{\xi}, \tag{8.33}$$

for parents in the second period, where d^i is bequests to children, o^i is gifts from children, R is the *ex-post* (that is, *inclusive* of any repudiation decision) interest rate, and $\hat{\xi}$ is second-period endowment of parents.[25] Finally, a child's budget constraint is

$$s^i + o^i = (1 - \tau)w + \frac{d^i}{1 + n},\qquad(8.34)$$

where $(1 - \tau)w$ is the after-tax wage.

For a parent, individual maximization yields desired saving and bequest, as a function of endowment and the expected after-repudiation rate of return. Since a parent's utility is linear in second-period consumption, saving will be a linear function of endowment above a certain critical endowment level. That is, saving of parent i will be

$$s^i \equiv \max(0, s^\circ + \xi^i),\qquad(8.35)$$

where $s^\circ < 0$ is defined by (subscripts on functions denote derivatives)

$$u_c(\nu - s^\circ) = R,\qquad(8.36)$$

where we have assumed that the second-period interest factor is correctly forseen. Desired bequests will be implicitly defined by

$$6^P h_s\left[(1 - \tau)w - o^i + \frac{d^i}{1 + n}\right] \leq 1,\qquad(8.37)$$

with equality if $d^i > 0$. Tabellini assumes that $6^P h_s(w) < 1$, so that in the absence of any government policy, parents would leave no bequests to children. (More exactly, 6^P is such that in the absence of government policy, desired bequests are negative, but are constrained to be zero as parents cannot enforce liabilities on their children.)

The solution to a child's optimization problem is even simpler. Substituting the parent's second-period budget constraint into the child's objective function, one obtains

$$h_s(s_i) \geq 6^C,\qquad(8.38)$$

with equality if $o^i > 0$, that is, if the child is transferring resources to the parent. Otherwise, all income is consumed. Tabellini assumes, as was assumed for the parents, that in the absence of government policy, 6^C is

---

[25] A large enough second-period endowment ensures that second-period consumption is positive, significantly simplifying the arguments.

low enough that desired transfers, which are constrained to be nonnegative, would be zero in equilibrium.

To close the model, note first that aggregate saving equals (first-period) government debt. Denoting debt averaged across parents by b, one may write

$$\int_0^\infty s^i \, d\Gamma(s^i) = b, \tag{8.39}$$

where $\Gamma(\cdot)$ is the endogenous distribution of saving, which is induced by $F(\cdot)$ and the saving function (8.35). Assuming the government engages in no activities other than issuing debt to finance transfers and then taxing to pay off the (nonrepudiated) debt, the government's budget constraints in the two periods are

$$\begin{aligned} \nu &= b, \\ Rb &= (1+n)\tau w. \end{aligned} \tag{8.40}$$

Having solved the optimization problem of each generation for given government policies, we can now consider the second step, namely each individual's preferred policies and, based on that, the amount of redistribution consistent with political equilibrium. This means, given the simple form of the government's budget constraints, the choice of b in the first period and the choice of a repudiation rate in the second period. Individuals will differ in their desired levels of repudiation due to their parents' different endowments. Wealthy parents are relatively high savers and hence are disproportionately hurt by any degree of repudiation, which must be across-the-board repudiation. Children of wealthy parents will choose less than full repudiation because they weight their parent's utility in their own objective function.

To solve this problem, one works backwards: first, one determines, for each b, what interest factor $R(b)$ would emerge from the political process in the second period; second, given the correctly anticipated function $R(b)$, one solves for the level of debt b that emerges from the political process in the first period, what Tabellini terms the "politically viable" level of debt. We thus begin with determination of the second-period equilibrium repudiation decision.

As indicated above, the choice of a repudiation rate is equivalent to choice of an *ex-post* interest rate. Consider first the optimal interest rate as of the second period for a parent with endowment ξ^i. Differentiating (8.30) with respect to R, note that direct intergenerational transfers will be zero in a political equilibrium in which the median voter chooses R (the nonnegativity constraints will be binding). Using the parent's second-period budget constraint (8.33) and the government budget constraint (8.40) to link the tax on children's wages to debt b, and holding b, c_1^i, and s^i

constant (as they are determined in the first period), one obtains a first-order condition

$$\frac{\partial \Omega_P^i}{\partial R} = b\left(\frac{s^i}{b} - 6^P h_s(\cdot)\right) = 0,\tag{8.41}$$

where s^i is the saving of a parent with endowment ξ^i, so that we can index individuals by their s^i. This condition has the following interpretation. Repayment of the debt affects parent i's welfare in two ways. First, since he holds a fraction s^i/b of the debt, an extra dollar of repayment increases his wealth (and hence his utility) by s^i/b. However, repaying an extra dollar also increases the tax burden on each of his children by $1/(1 + n)$ dollars, giving him an overall disutility of $6^P h_s(\cdot)$. At the optimum, the two effects are equal. One may easily show that more wealthy parents (that is, those with higher saving) prefer higher rates of return.

Similarly, for a child whose parent has endowment ξ^i, using the assumption that the nonnegativity constraints on transfers are binding, we can derive a first-order condition from (8.31) expressed as a function of R and the budget constraints, namely,

$$\frac{\partial \Omega_C^i}{\partial R} = \frac{b}{1 + n}\left(6^C \frac{s^i}{b} - h_s(\cdot)\right) = 0.\tag{8.42}$$

As in the case of a parent, the child weighs his parent's disutility from repayment of one dollar less against his own utility gain from lower taxes.

It is apparent that each parent can be paired with a child (*not* his own) who will vote the same way. Specifically, using (8.41) and (8.42), a child whose parent's saving is $s^i/6^P 6^C$ will vote the same way as a parent with saving s^i. Hence, we can speak of a median voter pair. In order to define a median voter, one uses the fact that voters as indexed by their s^i have preferences over rates of return that satisfy the conditions of the median voter theorem. Therefore, using the distribution of saving $\Gamma(\cdot)$ and denoting the saving of the median parent by s^{med}, one can define the median voter pair (a parent with relative saving s^{med}/b and a child of parents with relative saving $s^{\mathrm{med}}/6^P 6^C b$) by

$$\Gamma\left[\frac{s^{\mathrm{med}}}{b}\right] + (1 + n)\Gamma\left[\frac{s^{\mathrm{med}}}{6^P 6^C b}\right]$$

$$= 1 - \Gamma\left[\frac{s^{\mathrm{med}}}{b}\right] + (1 + n)\left(1 - \Gamma\left[\frac{s^{\mathrm{med}}}{6^P 6^C b}\right]\right).\tag{8.43}$$

This may be simplified to

$$\Gamma\left[\frac{s^{\text{med}}}{b}\right] + (1+n)\Gamma\left[\frac{s^{\text{med}}}{6^P6^Cb}\right] = 1 + \frac{n}{2}. \qquad (8.44)$$

Since $6^P6^C < 1$, s^{med}/b in (8.44) lies to the left of the median value of s^i/b and $s^{\text{med}}/6^P6^Cb$ lies to the right of it. Hence, the coalition in favor of repayment at least as great as that favored by the median voter consists of a majority of parents and a minority of children, namely, those of the wealthiest parents. Note also that this equation defines the relative wealth of the median voter as a function of b, which we denote as $s^{\text{med}}/b = S^{\text{med}}(b)$, where $S^{\text{med}}(b)$ is positive and increasing in b above a certain minimum level of debt.

To complete the discussion of the second-period political decision, note simply that the interest factor R chosen by the median voter pair for each b will be given implicitly by (8.41) with s^i/b replaced by $S^{\text{med}}(b)$, namely,[26]

$$S^{\text{med}}(b) - 6^P h_s\left(w - \frac{Rb}{1+n}\right) = 0. \qquad (8.45)$$

The correctly anticipated interest factor implicitly defined by (8.45) is consistent with both economic and political equilibrium in the second period.

We now consider the first-period problem of parents choosing the equilibrium level of debt. Only debt levels for which the left-hand side of (8.45) is nonnegative will be repaid. Hence, the "politically viable" set of b is given by

$$S^{\text{med}}(b) - 6^P h_s\left(w - \frac{R(b)b}{1+n}\right) \geq 0. \qquad (8.46)$$

This set could be empty, but Tabellini shows that for a uniform distribution of endowments and logarithmic $u(\cdot)$, for example, it is nonempty. It is bounded from above, as too high a level of debt would be fully repudiated by the next generation ($R(b) = 0$). Interestingly, too low a level of debt will also be fully repudiated. The reason is that the smaller the level of debt, the smaller the fraction of parents who hold debt; with b too low, it will be held by a minority of parents and a majority of voters will be in favor of fully repudiating the debt. A nonempty politically viable set yields one of Tabellini's main conclusions: some intergenerational redistribution will take place in equilibrium, even in the absence of a commitment device. Parents will issue debt to redistribute resources away from children

---

[26] There will be full repudiation of the debt, that is, $R = 0$, if $S^{\text{med}}(b) - 6^P h_s(w) < 0$.

and towards themselves, and hence benefit from the ability to issue debt without the consent of the next generation. A coalition of parents and children will support its repayment, even though if children were allowed to vote in the first period, all of them would be against issuing debt. Since they constitute a majority, no debt would be issued.[27] The precise amount of debt issued could also be derived via a median voter mechanism in period 1. As long as the viable set is nonempty, some debt will be issued.

The key to understanding the principal results of the Tabellini model is the strength of the altruism motive, namely, that it exists, but is not too strong. Were there no altruism, repayment of debt could not be supported by majority vote with a growing population. Weak altruism means there is still a conflict of interests between generations, so that parents issue debt to redistribute resources intergenerationally, and children *ex ante* would be in favor of none being issued. However, once the debt is in place, children of parents who hold a lot of the debt support repayment because of their concern about their parents' welfare. Weak altruism means that no direct transfers across generations take place in equilibrium; nonetheless, altruism is crucial in guaranteeing that repayment takes place. Put another way, in the initial decision to issue debt, the *inter*generational implications of debt issuance are decisive. Once the debt is issued, the *intra*generational aspects are crucial in guaranteeing its repayment, for repudiation would imply a redistribution from rich to poor.

As in the static models of redistribution in the previous sections, imperfect information on the part of the government is also crucial to the results. If the government were to undo the "facts" created by parents in the issuance of debt, they would have to tax each parent in a lump-sum fashion according to the debt they hold. But the government does not have the information necessary to do this, by assumption. This leads to imperfect reversibility of the parent's initial decision and to the ability to issue a politically viable level of debt.

8.7. REDISTRIBUTION AND MOBILITY

So far, we have assumed that individuals cannot legally avoid the implications of the decision over redistribution. It may be the case that individuals affected by redistributive policies have no say in the decision on redistribution, as in the previous section, but the converse is not true: in the models we have considered up to now, individuals who participate in the decision

---

[27] Social security might appear identical to debt, but need not be due to differences in political viability. If there was a vote *in the second period* on whether to make a transfer to the old financed by a wage tax on the young, it would not gain a majority in this set-up and hence would not be viable. Alternative ways of modeling social security could lead to political viability, as in Tabellini (1990b).

over redistribution cannot subsequently exclude themselves from the consequences of those decisions. Though this assumption may be largely true on the national level, it is certainly not true on the local level. People may "vote with their feet" if they dislike a decision. The possibility of mobility may be quite important, as the knowledge that there is *ex-post* mobility will put limits on the nature of redistribution programs *ex ante*. The purpose of this section is to examine the implications of mobility of taxed factors for the political economy of redistribution.

The possibility of moving across jurisdictions implies, quite obviously, multiple jurisdictions which provide the same or similar public goods (including income redistribution), though generally in different proportions. In discussing the relation of mobility to redistribution, there is an inescapable connection between redistribution and public goods, bringing us back to an issue first raised at the beginning of the chapter. An income redistribution program is decided upon at the community level, so that it becomes a collective good "supplied" to all residents of that community. Choosing among communities is thus choosing among different public goods bundles, where residency in a given community is the decision to accept the supply of public goods which characterizes that community. This theory of choice of community was originated by Tiebout (1956). It is very much akin to the theory of clubs in the provision of public goods, which will be covered in Section 9.5 of Chapter 9; one may want to read that section in conjunction with this one. Goods provided by local jurisdictions are impure public goods, in that it is possible to exclude some individuals, the consumption of the public good being analogous with the extent of the jurisdiction. In the case of education, some of the redistribution is in goods in kind. As we saw in Section 8.4, this may interact with pure private goods.

The material in this section is also related to the material in Chapter 11 on factor accumulation and growth. An important area of research in the political economy of growth is how the threat of income redistribution may significantly hamper factor accumulation, and hence depress growth. In both this section and in Chapter 11, we are concerned with the implications of the possibility of choosing actions which allow one to avoid redistribution. The difference is that here the concentration will be on moving already existing assets out of reach of the redistributive jurisdiction; in Chapter 11, the focus will be on changing the accumulation of assets and factors in response to the program of redistribution. Obviously, these are closely connected and the material in this section may also be seen as a part of the discussion of issues covered in Chapter 11.

Finally, the material on mobility of taxed voters in this section is clearly related to a much broader literature on community formation more generally. Although some of the results are highly relevant for questions of the formation of communities on the local level, we do not discuss that issue in any comprehensive way. As such, the discussion is incomplete, though necessarily so, for a systematic treatment of this issue would take us too far afield. In Chapter 14, however, in our discussion of the size of government, we will review current literature of the size and number of nations.

Mobility of Taxed Voters

Epple and Romer (1991) present a very lucid model of how mobility of factors subject to taxation will limit the possibilities for redistribution. The model assumes perfect mobility across communities, allowing individuals to choose the community whose tax-transfer program is most to their liking. Though the model abstracts away from a number of factors which are no doubt central to an individual's choice of which community to live in, its simplicity makes clear the basic limitations that mobility may place on redistribution. Its simplicity also makes it easy to compare the results with the fundamental model of Meltzer and Richard in Section 8.2 above. We will consider below how a more realistic description of the decision of whether to switch communities will alter the results.

Epple and Romer consider a metropolitan area in which homogeneous land is divided between J jurisdictions, where both the number and the boundaries of the communities are fixed. Individuals who differ in their income y choose to live in one of the J possible communities, where income, which is common knowledge, is distributed according to a cumulative distribution $F(y)$ over $[0, y^{MAX}]$. Individuals consume two goods, a numeraire consumption good c and a community-specific good x_h, called "housing," where utility is an increasing, concave function of c and x_h, denoted $u(c, x_h)$. What is important about the second good is that it is a taxable good on which an individual is liable for tax if and only if he is a resident of a specific community.

Redistribution within a community j consists of paying a lump-sum per capita grant v^j, financed by a tax on housing. Let the tax rate on housing in community j be τ^j and the pre-tax rental price of housing (to be determined in equilibrium) be P_h^j, so that the gross-of-tax price of housing in community j is $P^j \equiv (1 + \tau^j)P_h^j$. The budget constraint of an individual with income y living in community j is then[28]

$$y + v^j = c + P^j x_h. \tag{8.47}$$

In a given community j, an individual maximizes utility by choice of c and x_h, for given P^j and v^j. This decision can be described by standard

---

[28] The specification assumes no capital gains when housing prices change, so that residents of a community are treated as renters. Epple and Romer also consider the case of owners who purchase housing in a community before voting on a redistributive program, and hence can make capital gains or losses from the introduction of a program that will affect housing prices. By assuming that all transactions take place at equilibrium prices, they show the basic results are unchanged.

first-order condition derived by maximizing $u(c, x_h)$ subject to (8.47). Moreover, the individual also chooses which community to live in by finding the community whose grant and housing price pair (P^j, ν^j) yields maximum utility. Finally, the pair (P^j, ν^j) is determined by majority voting by all members of a community.

The utility of living in a community with a pair (P^j, ν^j) for an individual with income y can be represented by the value of the indirect utility function $V(P, \nu, y)$ associated with (P^j, ν^j), where the indirect function is defined in the standard way. Several aspects of the community choice decision will be made clear by deriving the indifference curve between P and ν for an individual with income y. This indifference curve will be upward sloping in (P, ν) space:

$$\frac{dP}{d\nu}\Big|_{V=\bar{V}} = -\frac{\partial V/\partial \nu}{\partial V/\partial P} = \frac{1}{x^h(P, y + \nu)} > 0, \qquad (8.48)$$

where $x^h(P, y + \nu)$ is the demand for housing as a function of gross-of-tax price and gross-of-grant income. Crucial to the results that follow is the fact that the slope of the indifference curve through any point decreases with y, as long as housing is a normal good:

$$\frac{\partial(dP/d\nu|_{V=\bar{V}})}{\partial y} = -\frac{1}{[x^h(P, y + \nu)]^2} x_2^h(\cdot) < 0, \qquad (8.49)$$

where $x_2^h(\cdot)$ is the partial derivative of $x^h(\cdot)$ with respect to its second argument, income. Intuitively, this characteristic of indifference curves means that richer individuals place less weight on grants relative to lower housing prices.[29]

An equilibrium in the J communities is defined as a set of J pairs (P^j, ν^j), one for each community, which satisfy two sets of conditions. First, each community is in internal equilibrium, meaning that within each jurisdiction j: the housing market clears; the jurisdiction's budget is balanced; and the pair (P^j, ν^j), representing the redistributional decision, is chosen by majority rule. These conditions parallel those for a political-economic equilibrium in the Meltzer–Richard model in Section 8.2. Second, given the equilibrium set of J pairs (P^j, ν^j), no individual wants to move to another community.

---

[29] Equations (8.48) and (8.49) imply that the indifference curves of two individuals with different incomes cross at most once, with the indifference curve of the poorer individual crossing the indifference curve of the richer one from below. This single-crossing property is crucial in models analyzing multiple jurisdictions, and more generally in models of self-selection across alternatives (see the discussion of incentive compatibility in Section 2.2 of Chapter 2). Unlike some models where the crucial single-crossing property is assumed, it here follows from individual maximization.

Following Epple and Romer, it will be simpler to characterize the equilibrium location decision before discussing the conditions for internal equilibrium. The preferences of individuals over communities, as a function of pre-grant income y, follow from the characteristics of indifference curves given in (8.48) and (8.49). Consider two communities, characterized by (P^1, ν^1) and (P^2, ν^2), such that $(\nu^2 > \nu^1)$. Consider the individual y who is just indifferent between these two communities (i.e., $V(P^1, \nu^1, y) = V(P^2, \nu^2, y)$). Then all individuals with higher income $y' > y$ will strictly prefer living in community 1 with the lower grant ν^1, while all individuals with lower income $y'' < y$ will strictly prefer living in community 2 with the higher grant ν^2.[30] As Epple and Romer point out, this ordering of preferences generates considerable structure on the characteristics of communities in equilibrium. Specifically, if we consider an equilibrium in which no two communities have the same housing price P^j (and hence level of grants ν^j), there will be income *stratification* across communities, in that each community is formed by individuals with incomes in a single interval (and all individuals with incomes in that interval will live in that community). Individuals on the boundary of each interval will be indifferent between living in that community and the "adjacent" one, where adjacent is defined by the ordering of communities by incomes from the lowest to the highest.[31] For our discussion, it will be useful to denote each community $j \in J$ under this ordering in terms of the highest income level in that community, y^j (so that y^j is indifferent between living in community j and community $j + 1$), where $y^j < y^{j+1}$ and $y^J = y^{\text{MAX}}$, the highest possible income. A community j consists of all types in the (half-open) interval $(y^{j-1}, y^j]$. A further characteristic of the equilibrium in which no individual wants to move to another community is that higher-income communities are characterized by lower subsidies and lower taxes than lower-income communities.

The key result for our purposes is that mobility leads to stratification of communities across income levels, with higher-income communities being characterized by lower levels of redistribution. Before considering this result in more detail, let us quickly show how the model is closed by considering internal equilibrium conditions. Internal economic equilibrium requires that the housing market clears and that the government's budget is in balance, both on a community level. Community housing demand X^h as a function of the gross-of-tax housing price is found by integrating individual housing demand over the interval of income types in that community. Housing supply is a function of the *pre-tax* housing price P_h^j,

[30] An easy way to see this is to note that this is a self-selection criterion, as in Chapter 2 (or in the previous footnote.) Hence, one may illustrate the result simply by drawing the indifference curves for the three types.

[31] This follows from the assumption that the distribution of incomes is continuous, with no gaps.

as well as the exogenous land characteristics in the community, and is denoted $S^{hj}(P_h^j)$. The clearing of the communitywide housing market in community j is then represented by the condition

$$X^h\big((1 + \tau^j)P_h^j, \nu^j, y^j\big) \equiv \int_{y^{j-1}}^{y^j} x^h\big((1 + \tau^j)P_h^j, y + \nu^j\big)\,dF(y)$$

$$= S^{hj}(P_h^j), \tag{8.50}$$

which determines the pre-tax housing price in community j as a function of the tax-transfer program (τ^j, ν^j) and community demographic and land characteristics.

The tax-transfer program (τ^j, ν^j) in community j must satisfy a balanced budget condition:

$$\nu^j \int_{y^{j-1}}^{y^j} dF(y) = \tau^j P_h^j S^{hj}(P_h^j). \tag{8.51}$$

The program is chosen by majority voting, though its determination is more complicated than in the Meltzer–Richard model of Section 8.2 for a number of reasons. First, the choice of a tax-transfer scheme (τ^j, ν^j) by voters in any community will depend on the policy choice of other communities. Epple and Romer assume that voters in each community choose their preferred tax-transfer program, taking the programs of other communities as given. Second, the choice of a given program (given the programs of other jurisdictions) will change the tax base by inducing in- or outmigration, a complicating factor not found in the Meltzer–Richard model. Epple and Romer assume sophisticated voters, in the sense that voters realize the effect of changes in (τ^j, ν^j) on both the size of their community and on the pre-tax housing price P_h^j.

The implications of the multicommunity nature of the model on the effects of changes in the (τ^j, ν^j) package mean that voter preferences are *not*, in general, single peaked. Hence, the median voter theorem cannot be applied in the straightforward way it was used in the Meltzer–Richard model. Epple and Romer prove, however, based on a result in Roberts (1977), that a majority voting equilibrium nonetheless exists, and that this equilibrium is the preferred point of the median voter in the community. (The interested reader is referred to the proof of Proposition 2 in their article for the precise argument.) The existence of a median voter political equilibrium which satisfies the conditions both of internal equilibrium and of each individual (weakly) preferring his community to any other under costless mobility completes the specification of the model.

As indicated above, the main result for our purposes is that mobility in the presence of majority-rule redistribution induces stratification of communities by income, with higher-income communities choosing lower taxes and lower levels of redistribution. (Remember taxes are used only to finance redistribution, and not to finance some communitywide good, such as public schooling. We consider this below.) Hence, the attempt to redistribute income leads to sorting by income. Put in simpler language, when mobility is possible, redistributive policies will drive the rich away, as suggested by Oates (1977, p. 5), in a passage cited by Epple and Romer: "An aggressive policy to redistribute income from the rich to the poor in a particular locality may, in the end, simply chase the relatively wealthy to other jurisdictions and attract those with low incomes." Oates and others in fact argue that the possibility of out- and inmigration is the central issue in evaluating the optimal level of local government redistributive programs. In short, the possibility of migration introduces a "free rider" problem into redistributive decisions.

Cross-Jurisdictional Taxation and Barriers to Mobility

Our purpose here is not to consider optimal public policy on a local level, but simply to point out implications of the limits on redistribution due to the possibility of mobility out of (and into) the jurisdictions. Foremost are the qualitative implications of mobility in limiting redistribution, though the quantitative effects are important as well. To the extent these limitations are substantial, an obvious response is to internalize the externality implied by migration. That is, a uniform tax system across jurisdictions would eliminate the possibility, and hence the incentive, for escaping taxation via outmigration. Taxation of factors should be at the national level, as suggested by Stigler (1957) and Oates (1972, 1977), with tax revenues distributed to the localities, in a program of fiscal federalism. Wildasin (1991) considers such a scheme when there is a common labor market across localities.

Pauly (1973) challenges this conventional wisdom. He challenges both the normative and the positive implications of an analysis such as Epple and Romer's: the welfare implication that local redistribution will be Pareto-inferior to national redistribution; and the positive proposition that due to the threat of out- and inmigration, local governments would not redistribute income to the poor to the extent that the national government would. His argument for redistribution at the local level, even with labor mobility, is based on *endogenously* different tastes for redistribution across localities. He begins with the assumption of Hochman and Rodgers (1969) that individuals value redistribution *per se*, that is, they value the income gains of other individuals. Suppose that people care primarily about the poor in their own community, but that redistribution at the national level is subject to an equal-treatment constraint, whereby people in all communities must be treated the same. The normative challenge follows from the observation that differences in population composition across communities imply the optimality of different programs of redistribution across communities. The positive challenge follows from considering the voting equilibria consistent with national versus local redistribution. Since a national program requires people to make payments to people other than their neighbors, hence, people for whom they have no concern, there will be less support for a national than for a local program. Hence, in a voting equilibrium, there may be less redistribution under a national program, rather than more.

An alternative response to the implications of the Epple and Romer model is to argue that its key assumption in deriving its results, namely, perfectly costless labor mobility across jurisdictions, is extreme. Once individuals are tied to their communities in various ways, the scope for redistribution presumably becomes larger. On a macroeconomic level, when we look at economies as a whole rather than at localities, one might argue that due to the myriad of factors inducing people to "stay at home," it is uncommon for the wealthy to move to another country simply because of tax-transfer programs (though it is still observed, certainly for the extremely wealthy leaving high-tax countries). Such a view is too sanguine for at least two reasons. First, though generous redistributive programs may imply quantitatively small outmigration by rich taxpayers who must finance them, the inmigration by poor individuals wanting to take advantage of them may be far more significant, unless a country imposes restrictions that limit the ability of the poor to enter. We turn to this issue in the next paragraphs. Second, individuals may choose to move taxable assets out of reach of the jurisdiction without having to move themselves. We consider the implications of capital flight induced by redistributive tax-transfer schemes in the next subsection.

In order to have more flexibility to engage in redistribution, rich jurisdictions may limit entry of the poor who may be attracted by larger grants. Such restrictions take several forms. On the national level, there are restrictions on entry and on obtaining residency status and citizenship. On the local level, one sort of entry barrier often observed is high taxation that finances expenditures *other than* redistributive transfers. If these expenditures are on items that cannot be resold or whose value cannot be capitalized, or if their consumption requires private inputs, choice of expenditures may effectively exclude the poor. The Fernandez and Rogerson (1995) paper concerning partial public funding of education, discussed in Section 8.4, provides an example. If no private resource input was required to consume public education financed by a linear tax, public provision of education would act like a transfer from rich to poor. However, when significant private inputs are required (and capital markets are imperfect), we saw that the transfer may actually go in the opposite direction, as the poor would be required to pay for a program from which they could not benefit. A high level of public education requiring significant input of private resources could then act as an effective barrier to the poor joining a community with such a program.

Zoning laws regulating land use are another common type of endogenously determined barrier used on the local level to exclude the poor. For example, along the lines of the Epple–Romer analysis, Fernandez and Rogerson (1993) consider laws dictating a minimum house size in a model of two communities, where one of them has a rule requiring all of its residents to consume housing services greater than or equal to some specified level. Via simulating a number of examples, they show that such a rule may significantly change Epple and Romer's main results. Specifically, there can be an equilibrium in which the richer community engages in more redistribution, choosing both higher taxes and higher transfers. Hence, the zoning restriction may lead to community stratification going in the opposite direction to what Epple and Romer found. Furthermore, the zoning restriction may make the richer community either smaller or larger than it would be in the absence of the restriction, so that rich communities are *less*, rather than more, exclusive in the presence of such laws.

Capital Mobility

The Epple–Romer model made the polar assumption that the jurisdiction in which an individual resides is identical to the jurisdiction in which his productive factors are taxed. This assumption was motivated by concentrating on labor as the taxed factor. If, however, residency is largely determined by noneconomic considerations, more specifically, by reasons other than tax-transfer programs themselves, the political-economic relevance of the model is limited. Put simply, if there is little mobility because of noneconomic reasons, why worry about the possibility of redistribution-induced mobility limiting the scope of such redistribution? Suppose, however, that we dropped this polar assumption, and assumed instead that some factors can escape taxation, at least partially, without an individual leaving the jurisdiction imposing taxes. Then, even if individuals are tied to communities, mobility of those factors that can be moved would limit the scope for redistribution.

The possibility of easily moving factors out of reach of a jurisdiction's taxation is crucial once we consider redistribution of capital income. In the extreme, if capital were perfectly mobile across jurisdictions and constituted a significant fraction of wealth, the main message of the Epple–Romer argument would remain intact. The threat of capital taxation would induce capital flight, which would severely limit the scope for income redistribution (or for any expenditure program dependent on significant taxation of capital income or wealth). We would, of course, lose any implications for community formation and stratification if the mobile factor were capital rather than labor. But the inverse relation between the possibility for redistribution in one jurisdiction and the ease of locating factors in other jurisdictions would still generally hold.

The tax implications of capital mobility across jurisdictions are especially important in international economics. A "residence principle" of taxation, whereby factors are taxed according to the place of residence of their owners, would suggest that the mobility of capital in the absence of labor mobility is irrelevant. This requires, however, both that different jurisdictions agree to implement the principle (or agree to a cross-jurisdiction uniform tax system, as discussed above) and that moving assets across borders does not affect the possibility of income from those assets being more easily hidden from the relevant tax authorities. Both of these assumptions are probably more likely to hold within a country than across countries. This is why the tax consequences of capital mobility have received the greatest attention in international economics. Because of this, we postpone further consideration of this issue until Chapter 12.

On a political level, there is a crucial qualitative difference between capital mobility and labor mobility in the endogenous determination of redistribution programs. In the Epple–Romer model of mobile labor, the movement of the taxed factor meant the movement of voters who chose the tax. In contrast, when individuals do not move but capital assets do, the constituency of voters is different than the "constituency" of taxed assets. Wealthy voters, for example, will vote on redistribution programs without the individual redistributive implications that drove the Meltzer and Richards model in Section 8.2. The resultant voting equilibrium could therefore be quite "distorted" relative to an equilibrium where individuals have to live with the redistributive consequences of their decisions. There are, to the best of my knowledge, no robust, general models studying this phenomenon. There are, however, some specific models that consider the implications of the identity of those who vote being different than the identity of those who bear the cost of taxation. We saw one such model in Section 8.6, albeit in a different context. In Tabellini's (1991) model of intergenerational redistribution, the difference between the group that voted for redistribution and that who bore its cost arose not because of factor mobility, but because of the latter group not being alive when the vote was taken. We now consider a related type of model.

Labor Mobility and Redistribution over Time

The Epple–Romer model is a single-period model. It assumes that individuals make a one-time location decision, with the level of redistribution endogenously determined by voting within each community. In equilibrium, each community is required to run a balanced budget. With costless mobility, a further key equilibrium condition is that no individual prefers to move to another community, given the equilibrium vector of tax-transfers schemes across communities and the associated housing prices.

Suppose, instead, we consider a multiperiod model in which an individual could change his location at any point in time, but we maintain the assumption of an endowment economy in which no individual can accumulate assets over time. If we retain the requirement that a community is required to run a balanced budget each period, the possibility of changing location would be irrelevant in the absence of some exogenous shock that changed an individual's income. With no asset accumulation or decumulation on either the individual or community level, the constraints faced by both a community and each of its residents would not change over time. There would therefore be no reason to exercise the option to move after the first period. Since no individual would prefer to move to another community in the first-period equilibrium (given the equilibrium vector of tax-transfers schemes across communities), he would have no reason to move in the second period, *et cetera*.

Suppose, however, that, consistent with the multiperiod framework, communities were required to balance their budgets only intertemporally, rather than period by period. This suggests the following possibility. Individuals whose assets were highly mobile might support a redistribution scheme financed by external borrowing, and then flee with their assets before the borrowing had to be repaid. Perotti (1996b) presents a model of this sort. He shows how a coalition of low-income and high-income voters would support a program of redistribution, the rich planning to flee with their wealth when the bills come due. What is especially interesting about Perotti's paper is that he shows that in even a very simple model, the interaction of voting, factor mobility, and income inequality can give extremely rich and complex results.

Though Perotti considers a small open economy that can borrow abroad, the basic idea is applicable to any jurisdiction that can borrow. For ease of exposition, we retain the terminology of "home" to refer to the jurisdiction under consideration and "abroad" to refer to other jurisdictions. The economy lasts two periods, with migration abroad possible only in the second period. The only input is a labor endowment, and there are three types of individuals, high-, middle-, and low-income (denoted by initials H, M, and L, respectively), distinguished by their labor endowments, $e^H > e^M > e^L = 0$. The number of individuals of type i is N_i, where it is assumed for simplicity that $N_L = N_M = 2N_H$ and that $N_H + N_M + N_L = 1$, so that the N_i can be interpreted as population fractions.[32] The key assumption about relative sizes is that no group is large enough to form a majority by itself, even if all the high-income types H outmigrate.

Labor is supplied inelastically, and nonstorable output is produced in the home jurisdiction according to a linear technology:

$$y = ae, \tag{8.52}$$

[32] Perotti's model is strongly parameterized to retain tractability. Given the richness of results even under his strong parameterization, this does not appear to limit its generality.

applying to all types of individuals, where a is a positive parameter that may be either greater than or less than 1. The pre-tax income of any individual i who supplies labor at home is thus ae^i. For tractability, Perotti assumes that total and average output in the economy is a, which requires that $N_M e^M + N_H e^H = 1$. Using the restrictions on N_M and N_H given above, this implies that

$$e^M = \frac{5}{2} - \frac{1}{2}e^H, \tag{8.53}$$

a relation which will be useful below. Equation (8.53) implies that income dispersion between types M and H is at a minimum when $e^H = e^M = 5/3$, and is at a maximum when $e^H = 5$ and $e^M = 0$.

Any individual can migrate "abroad" at the beginning of the second period, but there is a migration cost of one unit. The production function abroad is linear in output with a coefficient of unity. Output abroad is untaxed (representing the possibility of escaping factor taxation by outmigration), so that an individual of type i who moves abroad earns income of $e^i - 1$, rather than the pre-tax income of ae^i he would earn at home. Hence, net of the migration cost, labor is more productive at home than abroad if $a > 1$ and less productive at home than abroad if $a < 1$.

Consumption over the two periods yields utility according to the function

$$u(c_1^i, c_2^i) = \frac{(c_1^i)^{(\sigma-1)/\sigma} + (c_2^i)^{(\sigma-1)/\sigma}}{\sigma/(\sigma-1)}, \tag{8.54}$$

where we have assumed there is no discounting between periods, and where the elasticity of intertemporal substitution σ is greater than 1. The concavity of the utility function indicates that, all else equal, there is a desire for consumption smoothing. $\sigma > 1$ indicates a willingness to substitute consumption between the two periods.

Redistribution programs take a very simple form: there is a proportional tax τ_t on income, the proceeds redistributed lump-sum to all individuals in the economy. If all individuals are present in the economy, total tax revenues are $\tau_t a$, which is also the lump-sum, per capita subsidy financed by tax revenues. However, the possibility of borrowing abroad means that the total transfer may differ from this amount. It is assumed that individuals cannot borrow abroad, but that the government can, at an exogenously given interest rate. (If the jurisdiction were interpreted as a small, open economy, this rate would be the world rate of interest.) Perotti assumes that the interest rate equals the discount rate, namely zero, given the assumption of no discounting in (8.54). This assumption is made to eliminate any incentive for borrowing or lending starting from a point of equal consumption over the two periods. Let D denote the government budget deficit in period 1, which is also the jurisdiction's external deficit, where a negative value of D indicates a surplus in the first period. The government's budget must be balanced over the two periods, so that a budget deficit of D in the first period must be matched (under the zero interest rate assumption) by an equal budget surplus in the second period. Given that total population equals 1, D is also the per capita first-period budget deficit. Any government borrowing in the first period is redistributed in a lump-sum fashion, with the second-period transfer reduced by an equal amount. For given D and tax rates τ_1 and τ_2 in the two periods, the consumption of a type-i individual ($i = $ H, M, L) in the two periods is

$$c_1^i = (1 - \tau_1)ae^i + \tau_1 a \sum_i N_i e^i + D,$$

$$c_2^i = (1 - \tau_2)ae^i + \tau_2 a \sum_i N_i e^i - D,$$

(8.55)

where the summation in each of the expressions is taken over the types present in the economy at that date, so that $\sum_i N_i e^i = 1$ in the first period and equals 1 in the second period if there has been no outmigration, and is less than 1 otherwise. These expressions make clear that the tax rate which maximizes an individual's consumption depends on the value of his endowment e^i relative to 1: if the individual has an above-average endowment, his optimal tax rate is 0; if it is below average, his optimal tax rate is 1.

The determination of fiscal policy is by majority vote in each period, over the preferred policies of each of the three types of individuals, where "preferred" means the policy that is utility maximizing for each of the types. (There is no bargaining over policy proposals.) The first-period policy consists of the pair (τ_1, D); the second-period policy choice is simply over τ_2. The winning policy proposal is the one that beats the other two in pairwise comparisons. Since the first-period policy has two dimensions, there is no guarantee that a winner will emerge from such a process. (One may refer back to the discussion of problems of cycling in voting in Chapter 3.) However, as there are only three possible proposals, one is able to identify majority winners. Given the equilibrium tax structures, an individual's migration decision will be made by comparing income net of migration costs which could be earned abroad with income net of taxes and transfers which could be earned at home.

To understand the role of income distribution in driving the results, it is useful to consider what the political-economic equilibrium would look like if there were no dispersion in income. That is, suppose there were no dispersion in endowments, so that $e^L = e^M = e^H = 1$. (The last equality comes from normalizing average labor endowment at unity.) Two conclusions are immediate. First, the structure of fiscal policy will be simple: there will be no redistribution and agents will unanimously agree on a balanced budget in each period. With all individuals identical, a tax-transfer system cannot transfer income across individuals. A government deficit will simply unsmooth consumption, which by the concavity of utility and the assumption of an interest rate equal to the discount rate cannot be optimal. Hence, there will be no redistribution across periods as well. Second, given this fiscal policy, there will be no migration abroad in the second period, as $a > 0$. The predictions of the model are neoclassical.

In the case of a sufficiently rich economy, the results are identical both for the optimality of a balanced budget in each period and for the absence of migration by the high-income individuals. There may, however, be redistribution in a political equilibrium, depending on the endowments of the middle class, which will determine the majority coalition. For a sufficiently high, a high-income individual will consume more at home than abroad, even if the tax rate on his income is 1 (remember that he receives the average income of the economy as a transfer). If high-income individuals do not move abroad in the second period, *a fortiori*, neither will middle-income individuals. All agents will be in favor of a balanced budget in order to smooth consumption across periods. With no migration and a balanced budget, the optimal tax rate of each type will be determined by (8.55) with $D = 0$ and $\sum_i N_i e^i = 1$ in each period. Types with $e^i \geq 1$ will prefer $\tau = 0$, while types with $e^i < 1$ will prefer $\tau = 1$. Therefore, the tax rate consistent with a political-economic equilibrium will be $\tau = 0$, supported by middle- and high-income voters (i.e., groups M and H), if $e^M \geq 1$, and will be $\tau = 1$, supported by low- and middle-income voters (groups L and M), if $e^M < 1$. As noted, in each case there will be no external borrowing and no out-migration, even though income is unequally distributed across groups.

The situation is entirely different in a jurisdiction which is very poor relative to other jurisdictions, as measured by a value of a significantly less than 1. The low productivity of the economy may result in high-income individuals leaving in period 2. This can lead to extremely large redistribution in period 1, financed largely by heavy borrowing from "abroad." Interestingly, this redistributive program is supported by a coalition of low- and high-income voters. High-income voters support a high level of income redistribution because it is financed by external borrowing, for which they will not bear the burden because they will migrate before the borrowing must be repaid. More generally, the type of equilibrium that will obtain will depend on both the level of economic productivity in the jurisdiction relative to that abroad, as measured by a, and by the degree of inequality in the distribution of income between the high-and middle-income voters. Following Perotti, we set $a = 1/2$ in order to concentrate on how the political-economic equilibrium changes as the degree of income inequality between high- and middle-income individuals changes.

As the distribution of income between the rich and the middle class becomes less and less equal, the nature of the equilibrium will change significantly and discontinuously. The reason for the discontinuous changes is the discreteness in three types of decisions, discreteness that implies that small changes in the income distribution may have extremely large effects. The three sources of discreteness are: the migration decision of high- and middle-income individuals; the voting decision in choosing between minimum and maximum tax rates and minimum and maximum deficits; and the discrete shifts in coalitions among the three groups of voters in the formation of the majority coalitions. The interaction of these sources of the discreteness is what allows such a simple model of endogenous migration and politically determined redistribution to yield a complexity of results for a poor economy. We consider only some of the possibilities, referring the interested reader to Perotti for a more complete characterization.

When inequality of income distribution between high- and middle-income types is at or near the minimum (e^H at or slightly above $5/3$, with e^M determined by (8.53)), high-income individuals will remain in the economy in period 2 (as will, *a fortiori*, middle-income individuals). The reason is that since middle-income voters have an endowment greater than 1, they will support a program of no redistribution, so that the majority coalition will be one of groups H and M adopting a program of $\tau_1 = \tau_2 = D = 0$. Thus, both high- and middle-income voters earn more at home than abroad and do not migrate, even for a value of a as low as $1/2$. Their utility is maximized when consumption is smoothed across periods. Hence, a low-productivity jurisdiction with equal (or close to equal) income between the rich and the middle class will look like a representative-agent economy, or an (exogenously) high-productivity jurisdiction with a relatively wealthy middle class ($e^M > 1$).

If the distribution of income between the high- and middle-income types becomes sufficiently unequal (that is, as e^H rises with e^M falling, as determined by (8.53)), the nature of the political equilibrium will undergo a discrete shift. When e^H becomes just large enough, high-income individuals will plan to migrate in period 2, and hence support the *maximum* feasible per capita deficit in period 1, call it D_{max}, rather than the minimum possible deficit, namely, 0. More specifically, the utility of the rich will be maximized by a first-period policy of $\tau_1 = 0$ and $D = D_{max}$. Though the consumption of high-income individuals will fall from ae^H to $e^H - 1$ in period 2, this loss is more than compensated in utility terms by the increase in consumption from ae^H to $ae^H + D_{max}$ in period 1. If e^M is greater than 1, the value of D_{max} is the value of the first-period deficit such that middle-class voters are just indifferent between migrating in period 2 and consuming $e^M - 1$, or staying and repaying the debt D_{max}. Given the requirement of intertemporal solvency, it is assumed that voters will of necessity support repayment of the debt, which will be no greater than what can be feasibly repaid. If the only productive workers in the economy in the second period are middle-income, there will be no redistribution in the second period, and, for a first-period deficit of D, the second-period tax rate will be such that $.4\tau_2 ae^M = D$. Substituting the implied tax rate into the second part of (8.55) to find possible second-period consumption of the middle class at home, that is, c_2^M, one obtains a no-migration condition that c_2^M is no less than $e^M - 1$, that is,

$$ae^M - \tfrac{5}{2}D \geq e^M - 1. \tag{8.56}$$

D_{max} is the value of D which satisfies (8.56) with equality if such a value is positive, and is zero otherwise. The critical value of e^H such that the political equilibrium changes is found by solving a simple linear programming problem, using (8.54) and (8.55) to find the value of e^H yielding equal-utility consumption vectors for type H under the two possible second-period location decisions, where (8.53) and (8.56) with equality yield the associated value of D_{max}.

To complete the argument, in pairwise voting, high-income voters' preferred first-period policy of $\tau_1 = 0$ and $D = D_{max}$ will beat the preferred policies of both of the other two types in pairwise voting. Low-income individuals will propose a policy of $\tau_1 = 1$ and $D = D_{max}$, so that given the choice of the two proposed policies, the middle class will prefer the proposal of the high-income voter (since $e^M > 1$); the middle class will propose a policy of $\tau_1 = 0$ and $D = 0$, so that given the choice between the policy of high-income and middle-income individuals, low-income voters will prefer the policy proposed by the former. Crucial to the sharp change in the political-economic equilibrium is the fact that high-income individuals are mobile and migrate in period 2, inducing them to support deficit-financed redistribution in the first period, their interests in this respect being allied with those of low-income voters.

For higher inequality between high- and middle-income individuals, that is, an even higher value of e^H such that $e^M < 1$, high-income voters will have an even greater incentive to leave in the second period, so they support a policy of $D = D_{max}$ in the first. Hence, as before, their interests are allied with those of low-income voters in this respect. However, now middle-income voters will be in favor of a policy of $\tau_1 = 1$ rather than $\tau_1 = 0$. Hence, the political equilibrium will be one with redistribution from both tax revenues and borrowing, as both high- and middle-income voters support the low-income voter's proposal of $\tau_1 = 1$ and $D = D_{max}$, if they cannot have their own preferred proposal. One should further note, however, that if inequality between the rich and the middle class becomes too large, the nature of the equilibrium switches again: with e^M sufficiently small, D_{max} will be too small to make it worthwhile to unsmooth consumption by borrowing in the first period. Both the low- and middle-income voters will support a policy of $\tau_1 = 1$ and $D < 0$ in the first period, building up a surplus for the second period, when the high-income individuals leave and can no longer be taxed.

Hence, the possibility of mobility significantly alters the nature of redistributive policies (remember that when the rich remained, there was a coalition in favor of no redistribution), but in a way quite different than the Epple and Romer model suggests. It may induce redistribution where none would be present in the absence of mobility, that is, where in the absence of mobility, the median voter would oppose redistribution. In a dynamic model, it may be rich voters who support redistributive policies currently if they know that they will be able to escape the consequences of that policy when it must be paid for by leaving the jurisdiction that imposed the policy. Mobility is central to the result, but the result is far more complicated than the intuitive one that mobility limits redistribution.

Though the model looks quite stylized, it may help explain important phenomena. Dornbusch and Edwards (1990), for example, argue that the shifting coalitions combined with capital mobility help to explain the failure of populist programs. Expansions associated with the initial phases of a populist program draw wide approval from both unions and industrialists because of the (temporary) increase in real wages and profitability they bring. However, when the program fails, there is a dramatic shift in coalitions, with industrialists now on one side and labor on the other, as the rich, who own more mobile factors, can escape the costs of adjustment. Dornbusch and Edwards (1990) point out that the massive decline in real wages as the program continues reflects the fact that capital is highly mobile across borders but labor is not. The Perotti model incorporates in a stylized way four key features that give rise to cycles in populist stabilization programs: the formation and subsequent shifting of coalitions among different groups; endogenous fiscal policy; the accumulation and repayment of foreign debt; and the mobility of some factors, but not others.

8.8. Conclusions

Redistribution of income or wealth is certainly a major issue in political economy. The conflict of interests that drives redistribution may seem simple, in that opportunistic individuals use the political mechanisms available to them to maximize their income. As this chapter demonstrates, however, the implications of conflict of interests over private goods and the resultant redistribution are often far from simple, as there are many dimensions for complexity. One must consider who are the participants—whether within a generation, across generations, "present" at some points but not others. One must consider what are the mechanisms by which redistribution takes place—open or disguised—as well as considering what is redistributed, whether income or goods. There are also related issues, such as the insurance aspects of redistribution. As complicated as the story already is, there are a number of issues related to redistribution yet to be covered. To name but a few that will be covered in greater depth, there is: the relation of distributional issues to the supply (or nonsupply) of public goods; the effect of pressures for redistribution on factor accumulation and growth; and the effect of the growth of programs of redistribution on the growth of government. These issues will be treated in upcoming chapters.

Public Goods

> "Would you like to see our country lose?"
>
> Major Major asked.
>
> "We won't lose. We've got more men, more money and
> more material. There are ten million men in uniform who
> could replace me. Some people are getting killed and
> a lot more are making money and having fun.
> Let someone else get killed."
>
> "But suppose everybody on our side felt that way."
>
> "Then I'd certainly be a damned fool to feel any
> other way. Wouldn't I?"
>
> —*Joseph Heller,* Catch-22

9.1. INTRODUCTION

The previous chapter was concerned with conflict of interests due to redistribution of divisible private goods and the consequences of such redistribution. Though some of the goods considered were not purely private, the focus was on transferring resources from one group to another. That is, the emphasis was on the rival aspect of the goods in question, in that income, wealth, or consumption, or welfare of one individual could be increased only by reducing income, wealth, or consumption, of another individual. In this chapter, we study public goods, that is, goods for which consumption of the good by one agent does not necessarily subtract from the consumption of the good by another agent. We focus on the theory of public goods, on models of their provision, and on general implications of the public nature of certain goods. Applications to specific political environments are numerous, but will be considered primarily in subsequent chapters.

The study of public goods is one of the classic topics in public economics.[1] We begin the chapter by reviewing the neoclassical approach to

---

[1] There are many excellent expositions of the modern public finance approach to public goods; one may be found in Atkinson and Stiglitz (1980).

the determination of the supply of public goods and their provision in Sections 9.2 and 9.3. In Section 9.2, we consider the basic neoclassical theory of public goods, leading to a condition determining the optimal supply of such goods. A key problem in the determination of the optimal supply of public goods stems from their very nature. There is a clear incentive to let someone else bear the burden of providing the public good which all enjoy, that is, to "free ride." This may be as simple as not contributing to the cost of the public good. Or, if the public good is tax-financed and if tax burden is positively related to expressed demand, there is the incentive to understate one's preference for the public good. In Section 9.2, we therefore also consider how people may be induced to reveal those preferences. In Section 9.3, we consider some classical mechanisms in practice for provision of public goods.

The neoclassical theory of public goods assigns a central role to the government in their provision. In fact, it is often argued, especially in the public choice literature, that a key reason that governments are instituted is for the provision of public goods.[2] On the face of it, however, it is not self-evident that simply because a good is "public" in the sense defined above, it should be provided by the government. One argument for government provision is that, for many goods whose purchase by some individuals benefits a wider group, it is difficult to exclude free riders. For the good to be provided at all, or for the burden of providing it across individuals to be perceived as fair, some type of coercion may be necessary. Since governments are defined as having a monopoly on coercion,[3] government becomes the natural provider of public goods. A second argument for government provision is that even if excludability were possible, efficiency may imply that it is not desirable to use a price system to govern usage (for example, for goods with highly inelastic demand). Finally, provision of some public goods has strong distributional consequences. Hence, the view of the role of government as provider of public goods overlaps with the role of government in redistribution of private goods considered in the previous chapter.

Though government may be the most obvious provider of public goods, there is a considerable body of research on how public goods may be provided in its absence. The interest in this area reflects the fact that in practice we do see public goods being provided without governmental

---

[2] For example, in Mueller's (1989, p. 3) standard text on Public Choice, "The existence of these forms of market failure [namely, public goods, externalities, and economies of scale] provides a natural explanation for why government exists, and thus for a theory of the origins of the state." One may compare this with the discussion in Chapter 3 on creation of government.

[3] For example, Weber (1946a, p. 78, italics in original) writes, "We have to say that a state is a human community that (successfully) claims the *monopoly on the legitimate use of physical force* within a given territory. ...[T]he right to use physical force is ascribed to other institutions or to individuals only to the extent to which the state permits it."

action. How might the free-rider problem be solved without the means of coercion available only to governments, so that provision of a public good is voluntary? To use Olson's (1965) well-known formulation, how can the problem of "collective action" be solved without coercion? In Section 9.4, we consider the collective action problem in detail, and answers to these questions based on characteristics of groups facing the problem. In Section 9.5, we consider one specific mechanism for voluntary provision of public goods, namely, the formation of "clubs" to provide public goods.[4] Some of the issues involved were considered implicitly in our discussion of mobility across communities in the previous chapter, where the public good was income redistribution. In this chapter, we consider the issue more generally.

The study of public goods is relevant for political economy, not simply because government is often considered the natural provider of such goods. There is a more basic reason. Conflict of interests, which is central to our approach to political economy, is inherent in the provision of public goods. As already indicated, since individuals may benefit even if they contribute nothing to the cost of providing the good, there is the incentive to have someone else bear the burden of financing the good. Hence, *ex-post* heterogeneity as defined in Chapter 1, arising here as conflict of interests over the distribution of the cost of supplying the public good, is essential to public goods problems. In the above paragraphs, we touched briefly on ways to resolve this conflict so that the public good is provided. Our interest, however, is not simply in asking how this conflict gets resolved, but also, and perhaps more importantly, in discovering the economic implications of the conflict. That is, a key question is how the political nature of decisionmaking may result in the good either not being provided at all, or being provided only with a long delay after its benefits become apparent. Formal models of the problem of nonprovision or delayed provision will be presented in Sections 9.6 and 9.7.

These positive implications are especially relevant in the political economy of policymaking, since socially beneficial policy changes which are initially costly to adopt can be thought of as public goods. (Consider, for example, a program to stabilize inflation whose success requires a large cut in the government budget deficit. Though the benefits may be significant and widespread, there will be a conflict over who bears the cost of the budget cuts.) Hence, the study of public goods will form an important basis for the study of delay in adopting optimal policies in Chapter 10 and economic reform and transition in Chapter 13.

If one extends the arguments of the last two paragraphs a bit, the study of public goods leads easily to the study of the size of government. The models of the previous chapter (for example, those of Meltzer and Richard

---

[4] Cornes and Sandler (1986) cover a large number of topics in the theory of public goods from a public choice perspective, including problems of collective action and clubs.

and of Tabellini) considered this issue in the context of redistribution. In Chapter 14, we return to the political economy of government size and consider some of the literature on the growth of government, considering explanations of the size of government with special emphasis on the material of this and the previous two chapters.

9.2. Public Goods—The Neoclassical Approach

We begin with the neoclassical approach to determining the optimal quantity of a public good by a planner who has full information about preferences and power to levy lump-sum taxes. We will then briefly discuss how this solution is modified by relaxing these two assumptions, considering how people can be induced to reveal their preferences for the public good, and how to allocate the burden of financing public goods. This will serve as a benchmark for later results.

The Samuelson Analysis

The neoclassical approach is associated with Samuelson and his two classic articles (1954, 1955) on the first-best allocation. Samuelson (1954, p. 387) defined a "pure" public good as a good where "each individual's consumption of such a good leads to no subtraction from any other individual's consumption." More generally, one can think of goods where consumption of the good by one person does not reduce another person's consumption by an equal amount.

To make these ideas more precise, we can consider two characteristics of goods: rivalness and excludability. Two goods are **rival** if consumption by one agent technically precludes consumption by another; for nonrival goods, the consumption benefits of any one individual do not depend on the benefits derived by others. Cable television broadcasts, sunshine, and technical know-how are examples of nonrival goods. A separate characteristic is **excludability**, meaning whether an individual can be prevented from consuming a good, specifically a nonrival good. Cable television broadcasts are excludable, while sunshine is nonexcludable (though a place in the sun, more prosaically called "beach space," is neither fully non-rival nor nonexcludable). A pure public good is both nonrival and nonexcludable.[5]

The basic social planner's solution of how much of a public good should be provided and how the burden of financing should be allocated follows

---

[5] Alternatively, one could think of public goods in terms of consumption externalities: consumption of the good by one individual may affect the utility of other individuals, with the characteristics of rivalness and excludability being reflected in the specification of the nature of the externality. Which concept is more useful in a political economy application will depend on the application itself.

Samuelson's (1954) classic paper. The result may be represented as follows. Consider an economy in which a private good c and a pure public good g are produced subject to a production possibility frontier. For simplicity, assume this production constraint is linear, of the form

$$\sum_i c^i + P_g g = \sum_i e^i, \qquad (9.1)$$

where c^i is individual i's consumption of the private good, e^i is the resource endowment of individual i (in terms of the numeraire private good), and P_g is the producer price of the public good. Suppose a social planner can fully control the allocation of private goods across individuals i, as well as the level of the public good. (Equivalently, suppose he has access to lump-sum taxes to finance the provision of the public good, and these taxes can vary across individuals.) His objective is to maximize a social welfare function defined over individual utilities $u^i(c^i, g)$ denoted $\Omega[u^1, \ldots, u^i, \ldots]$. The first-order conditions for this problem are

$$\Omega_i u_c^i = \lambda, \qquad (9.2)$$

for the private good, and

$$\sum_i \Omega_i u_g^i = \lambda P_g, \qquad (9.3)$$

for the public good, where subscripts represent partial derivatives and where λ is the multiplier on the production constraint. In the case of the private good in (9.2), we get the familiar equality of marginal rates of substitution and transformation, where the latter is linear as in (9.1) by assumption. To derive a condition for optimum supply of the public good, we substitute (9.2) into (9.3) to obtain

$$\sum_i \frac{u_g^i}{u_c^i} = P_g. \qquad (9.4)$$

This is the well-known Samuelson Rule for the optimal supply of public goods: the *sum* of the marginal rates of substitution between the public good and a private good must be equal to the marginal rates of transformation between the two goods. Intuitively, when a good is a pure public good, so that consumption of the good by one individual in no way excludes consumption by another individual, the social planner will sum the benefits across individuals in calculating the optimum. The allocation of (lump-sum) taxes τ^i across individuals may be found by solving for the allocation of c^i across individuals and noting that the individual's budget constraint is $c^i + \tau^i = e^i$, which allows calculation of the τ^i.

Distortionary Taxes

When there are restrictions on the types of taxes that can be levied, the Samuelson Rule for optimal allocation must be modified. (For details of these arguments, see Atkinson and Stiglitz [1980].) If the government is limited to a lump-sum tax which is uniform across individuals, one may show that the optimal allocation rule is to equate a weighted sum of the marginal rates of substitution to the marginal rate of transformation, the weights being proportional to the social marginal utility of income and summing to 1. Mathematically, (9.4) becomes

$$\sum_i \left(\frac{\Omega_i u_c^i}{\overline{\Omega}} \right) \frac{u_g^i}{u_c^i} = P_g, \tag{9.5}$$

where $\overline{\Omega}$ is the mean of the $\Omega_i u_c^i$. When lump-sum taxes are unavailable, and the provision of public goods is financed by distortionary taxation, this condition must be modified. One might think that a rule equating the sum of marginal rates of substitution to marginal rates of transformation would imply too high a level of public spending, that is, that distortionary financing will move the optimum towards a lower provision of public goods once the distortionary burden is taken into account. This intuitive argument need not be correct, as Atkinson and Stern (1974) have shown. If an increase in provision of the public good leads to increased demand for the taxed goods (e.g., provision of public swimming pools increasing demand for taxed swimsuits), the optimal amount of the public good may be *higher* than under nonuniform, lump-sum taxes. If the government has distributional goals when distortionary taxes must be used to finance the public good, the Samuelson Rule must be further modified to take account of the distributional effect of these taxes.

Revelation of Preferences

The other crucial issue in the public finance approach is what information about preferences the government has. The social planner's solution assumes that the government knows the preferences of individuals, which is a heroic assumption, especially in the case of public goods. Will individuals have an incentive to correctly reveal their preferences? If the amount of taxes an individual must pay is positively related to the demand he reveals (as was the case in the example above when preferences were known), individuals have every incentive to understate their demand for public goods. To quote Samuelson (1954, pp. 888–889), "it is in the selfish interest of each person to give *false* signals, to pretend to have less interest in a given collective consumption activity than he really has." An individual revealing his preferences when the public good is financed via the Samuelson Rule is analogous to his making a voluntary contribution to the provision of the public good, as in Section 9.4 below. Hence, there is the "free-rider problem," as discussed in greater detail in that section.

How can the planner learn the true preferences of individuals? As the problem is not of direct importance to the political analysis that follows, we simply give a general outline of a mechanism suggested by Clarke (1971, 1972) and Groves (1970, 1973)[6] that will lead to truthful revelation, referring the interested reader to the exposition in Atkinson and Stiglitz (1980) and the references therein. Suppose an individual's utility is linear in the private good c, so that it may be written, using the individual's budget constraint $c^i + \tau^i = e^i$, as

$$u^i(c^i, g) = h^i(g) + e^i - \tau^i. \tag{9.6}$$

Each individual is required to announce a valuation of public goods $\omega^i(g)$. The tax shares and the supply of the public good will then be a function of the announcements. Specifically, the supply of the public good g is chosen to maximize $\sum_i \omega^i(g) - P_g g$. Denote by g^* the maximized value of g. Given g^*, in the Clarke–Groves mechanism, the lump-sum tax τ^i on individual i will be, up to an arbitrary constant, the cost of the public good $P_g g^*$ minus the sum of valuations $\omega^j(g^*)$ taken over all individuals j *other* than i, that is,

$$\tau^i(\omega^i) = P_g g^* - \sum_{j \neq i} \omega^j(g^*) + \kappa(\boldsymbol{\omega}^{-i}), \tag{9.7}$$

where $\kappa(\boldsymbol{\omega}^{-i})$ is an arbitrary function of the vector of all announcements other than i's. The utility function in (9.6) may then be written as

$$u^i(c^i, g^*) = h^i(g^*) - \omega^i(g^*)$$
$$+ \sum_j \omega^j(g^*) - P_g g^* - \kappa(\boldsymbol{\omega}^{-i}) + e^i. \tag{9.8}$$

With this tax schedule, individuals have the incentive to report accurately their valuations $\omega^i(g)$ for any g, independent of the announcements of others. Why is truthful reporting a dominant strategy (in that each individual prefers to report his preferences correctly, independent of announcements other individuals may make)? An individual has no *direct* effect on his utility by varying his announcement $\omega^i(g)$, since the terms in $\omega^i(g)$ will

---

[6] Vickrey (1961) was actually the first to propose this mechanism, but in a different context, namely, for a public marketing agency facing monopolistic buyers and sellers. Both Clarke and Groves were unaware of the connection of their work to Vickrey's when they proposed their demand-revealing tax mechanisms.

cancel in (9.8). There is an indirect effect, since announcements affect g^*, and hence utility. However, by the optimal condition for g^*, this has no effect on $\sum_j \omega^j(g) - P_g g$ in (9.8). The variation in utility from a different announcement is thus proportional to the derivative of the first two terms in (9.8), that is, to $\partial h^i(g^*)/\partial g - \partial \omega^i(g^*)/\partial g$, which thus must be zero at the optimum. Therefore, $\omega^i(g^*)$ equals $h^i(g^*)$ (up to the addition of a constant). Green and Laffont (1977) show that this is the only class of mechanisms such that truthtelling is a dominant strategy and the outcome is Pareto efficient. It would appear that the major problem limiting the applicability of the Samuelson Rule can in fact be overcome.

However, all is not well in paradise, for this mechanism has several, sometimes severe, limitations. It does not guarantee that the government budget will be balanced. Groves and Ledyard (1977) argue that it will typically lead to a budget surplus, thereby wasting resources. It ignores collusion between individuals. In fact, coalitions might find it optimal to misrepresent their preferences, in the attempt to manipulate the mechanism. Finally, it also ignores issues of equity. Groves and Ledyard suggest that tax levels may sometimes be so high as to be confiscatory.

To summarize, the neoclassical treatment of public goods is a largely *technical* one—a planner chooses expenditure and tax policies to reach an optimum, where in the case in which individual preferences are unknown, these policies must be designed to elicit truthful revelation of information. There may be constraints on the type of taxes the government can levy (for example, only distortionary taxes may be available), but the emphasis is on calculating the optimal policy (perhaps subject to information constraints) rather than on problems of adopting and implementing the optimal policy. Once the optimal policy is calculated, it is agreed to and implemented. Putting the same point another way, the *positive* theory of public goods provision embodied in the approach outlined above is that of standard welfare economics: the policy actually implemented will be the social planner's optimum. The government is assumed to have the ability to adopt what is optimal and to induce people to pay their calculated share of the cost.

9.3. Provision of Public Goods in Practice

Having considered in detail the optimal provision of public goods that a social planner would choose, in this section and the next we ask what are the actual levels of public goods provision that would emerge under alternative decisionmaking mechanisms. In this section, we consider two general mechanisms: voting and a sort of a price system. In the next section, we consider the implications of public goods provision being financed by voluntary contributions.

Voting on Public Goods

Consider first the implications of voting on the level of public goods. The specific question we ask is whether majority voting leads to a *systematic* bias in the provision of public goods, as is often argued, relative to the social planner's optimum. As discussed in Section 3.4 of Chapter 3, the nature of preferences may imply that no voting equilibrium exists. Therefore, in order to derive results on the implications of majority voting, let us consider a case where preferences are single peaked, so that the Median Voter Theorem may be applied. Specifically, suppose the only decision subject to voting is on the level of a single public good g, financed by a uniform lump-sum tax, when individuals differ in the utility they attach to the public good g.

Suppose there are N individuals, each with endowment e^i, so that individual i's utility from the private and the public good may be written

$$u^i\left(e^i - \frac{P_g g}{N}, g\right).$$ (9.9)

This implies that preferences over g will indeed be single peaked. Denoting the median voter's utility by $u^{\mathrm{med}}(\cdot)$, his preferred level of expenditure is characterized by

$$\frac{u_g^{\mathrm{med}}}{u_c^{\mathrm{med}}} = \frac{P_g}{N}.$$ (9.10)

How will this compare with the social planner's allocation? To see whether social welfare can be locally increased above the level chosen by the median voter, consider a marginal increase in g above that level. The effect on social welfare can be written

$$\sum_i \Omega_i u_c^i\left(\frac{u_g^i}{u_c^i} - \frac{P_g}{N}\right).$$ (9.11)

This expression can be either positive or negative, indicating that there is no presumption about whether decisionmaking by majority voting leads to a level of public goods provision either systematically above or below the optimum level. To draw conclusions about the effect of voting, one would need to limit even further either the nature of preferences or the mechanism for making political decisions. Specifically, since the overall level of public spending very much reflects vote trading in legislatures, the nature of legislative decisionmaking has to be specified more fully. Such an approach obviously has much in common with the discussion of "pork-barrel" spending in Section 8.4 of Chapter 8.

The Lindahl Solution

An alternative decision mechanism is one that would imitate the market allocation system. That is, in a competitive market for private goods, individuals face the same prices but consume different amounts, with an equilibrium being a price vector that clears the market. In the case of public goods, an intriguing analogue would be a situation in which individuals consume the same amount, but face different prices. Technically, this could be achieved by a set of individual-specific subsidies to the price of cost of the public good. Based on the (different) price that each individual faces ("personalized prices"), he calculates a demand for the public good. An equilibrium is achieved when a vector of personalized prices is found that leads all individuals to demand the same quantity of the public good, subject to an appropriate government budget constraint. This is the "Lindahl equilibrium" (1919), named for the proposer of the mechanism as an actual allocation process.

Central to the Lindahl mechanism is the distribution of the burden of financing the public good g across individuals. Each individual i faces a tax *share* τ^i of the expenditure on g, where the τ^i sum to 1, ensuring budget balance. The tax shares are referred to as "Lindahl prices." Considering the case of a single private and a single public good as above, an individual maximizes a utility function of the form

$$u^i\!\left(e^i - \tau^i P_g g, g\right), \tag{9.12}$$

implying a first-order condition

$$\frac{u^i_g}{u^i_c} = \tau^i P_g. \tag{9.13}$$

If we then sum over i and use the government budget constraint, implying that $\sum_i \tau^i = 1$, we obtain the Samuelson Rule (9.4).

The mechanism indeed bears a strong resemblance to a competitive equilibrium for private goods, and much of the extensive analysis of the Lindahl solution to the public goods problem parallels the analysis of general competitive equilibrium. The existence of a Lindahl equilibrium is often demonstrated by the sort of fixed-point argument used to show the existence of a general competitive equilibrium in an economy with private goods. Similarly, properties of the Lindahl equilibrium are discussed in an analogous way to those of a competitive equilibrium, with emphasis on the analogues of the two basic theorems of welfare economics: the Pareto efficiency of the Lindahl equilibrium; and the conditions under which any Pareto-efficient allocation can be generated as a Lindahl equilibrium for suitable lump-sum taxes and transfers. The first can be demonstrated for certain general conditions, as was shown above as an implication of the first-order condition (9.13). The second proposition generally does not hold. In the analysis of the efficiency properties of the Lindahl equilibrium, there has been considerable work on its relation to the **core**, which is the set of allocations such that no coalition of individuals can propose an alternative allocation of its own resources which is weakly Pareto superior. For a fuller discussion of this point, as well as the other results given in this paragraph, the interested reader is referred to Atkinson and Stiglitz (1980), and the references therein.

9.4. Voluntary Provision of Public Goods— Free Riders and Collective Action

Both of the mechanisms listed in the previous section considered some sort of government intervention, either via economywide voting or via the tax system. There are numerous examples of public goods whose provision depends on voluntary contributions or participation. Charitable organizations supporting medical research will benefit many more people than simply those who contribute. Keeping the sidewalk clean in front of my house can significantly improve the appearance of my neighborhood, but only if my neighbors act similarly. Accepting committee assignments in my department or school is necessary for various sorts of administrative work to get done. Note the crucial difference between public goods whose supply depends on voluntary contributions and public goods financed by taxation, as discussed in the previous section. In the latter case, the government has the power to induce people to contribute; in the examples of voluntary provision of a public good, someone who benefits cannot really be forced to contribute his "fair share." Self-interested individuals thus have an incentive to "**free ride**," that is, enjoy the benefits of the nonrival good without contributing, as exclusion is infeasible. The free-rider problem is central to public goods provision dependent on voluntary behavior.[7] The problem of providing such goods has been termed the problem of **collective action**, following Olson's (1965) classic *The Logic of Collective Action*.

The Collective Action Problem in General

The problem of collective action has long been recognized. It is certainly present in Rousseau's famous parable about the stag hunt in his *Second*

---

[7] This contrast between public goods financed by taxation and those dependent on voluntary contributions is perhaps too sharp. When a tax must be changed in order to provide a public good, individuals must agree on the new system. When a group has the power to block a tax reform, there is a voluntary nature to public good provision. This will be important in considering the application of this model to nonadoption of policy in Chapter 10, based on the model in Section 9.7 below.

Discourse. Hardin (1982, p. 8), in his excellent study of collective action, argues that it can be found in the writings of many political philosophers from Hobbes onward with "especially elegant examples" given by Hume (his example of draining a swamp in *A Treatise on Human Nature*) and J. S. Mill (in *Principles of Political Economy*). Pareto (1935, pp. 946–947, sect. 1496, italics in original) presents an especially clear statement of the problem in considering a situation in which "if *all* individuals refrained from doing A, every individual as a member of the community would derive a certain advantage. But now if all individuals *less one* continue refraining from doing A, the community loss is very slight, whereas the one individual doing A makes a personal gain far greater than the loss that he incurs as a member of the community." Hence, for any one individual it is optimal, or one may say, rational, to pursue his self-interest rather than act in the collective interest. If all individuals act rationally, they will all do A, and all will be worse off. Hardin also argues that the general argument is clearly spelled out in Baumol (1952), but the strength of Olson's (1965) treatment is that he generalized the problem, rather than presenting specific examples.

Olson considered the behavior of groups and demolished the conventional wisdom that a group of people with a common interest will necessarily take action to further that interest. Instead, he convincingly argued that the self-interest of individuals in groups may mean that a group is unsuccessful in collective endeavors. He then asked why some groups are nonetheless successful, while others are not. Olson's central hypothesis is that the size of the group will be crucial in determining the likelihood of successful collective action. Put simply, he argues that large groups will fail to provide the collective good, while small groups may succeed. He is careful to point out, however, that what is important is not the number of members in a group *per se*, but the size of the benefit an individual member receives from the public good relative to its cost to him.[8] Formally, for each member i, Olson considers A^i, the return to contributing, net of the cost. A group in which A^i is positive for some members is termed a **privileged group**, and is likely to succeed in collective action. In contrast, a **latent group** is defined as one in which the return to contributing to provision of the public good is negative for all members, that is, $A^i < 0$ for all members i. The possible "latency" of a group is key to the problem of collective action, as latent groups, it is argued, are likely to be unsuccessful in providing public goods. Size affects the A^i, in that the larger the group, Olson argues the more likely it is to be latent, in the absence of special incentives to group members. As he puts it, (pp. 49–51,

---

[8] A similar notion is involved in Wilson's (1989a, 1989b) characterization of different types of government programs in terms of the distribution of per capita benefits and costs, as discussed in Section 8.4 of Chapter 8, used to better understand "pork-barrel" politics.

italics in original):

> A "privileged" group is a group such that each of its members, or at least some
> one of them, has an incentive to see that the collective good is provided, even if
> he has to bear the full burden of providing it himself. In such a group there is a
> presumption that the collective good will be obtained, and it may be obtained
> without any group organization or coordination whatever.... large or "latent"
> groups have no incentive to act to obtain a collective good because, however
> valuable the collective good might be to the group as a whole, it does not offer
> the individual any incentive...to bear...any of the costs of the necessary
> collective action. Only a *separate and "selective" incentive* will stimulate a
> rational individual in a latent group to act in a group oriented way.

Though the conclusions are intuitively attractive, the relation between
group size and success in providing collective goods is one of the most
controversial issues in the theory of collective action. The general conclusion that small groups may succeed but large groups will fail has been
challenged by many authors who show examples where this conclusion
does not hold. In summarizing many of the arguments, Hardin (1982, p. 41)
concludes that there is no logical connection between the size of a group
and whether it is privileged or latent: a two-member group could be latent,
while a small, privileged group could be expanded to any size and still
remain a privileged group. We shall see examples of both below; moreover,
it will be argued that the "latency" of *small* groups is central to many
problems of political economy.

Hence, we are left with the question of when a group will be latent. Or,
to put the question another way: When provision of public goods depends
on voluntary contributions, when is there a collective action problem? To
answer this question, two arguments will be made. First, many examples of
voluntary provision of collective goods are *not* fruitfully characterized as
collective action problems, in the sense discussed by Olson and others. A
careful differentiation between cases, sometimes lacking in the literature,
is central to understanding collective action failures. Second, crucial to
understanding the effect of group size is the question of what is held
constant in comparing groups of different sizes. We consider these two
points in turn.

Does Voluntary Provision Imply the Collective Action Problem?

There is a temptation to label any situation characterized by voluntary
provision of a public good as a potential collective action problem. In my
opinion, the generality that one appears to obtain by doing this is false,
and probably only confuses the issue. To clarify this point, let us consider
three simple games: the Prisoner's Dilemma, the Coordination Game, and
the Public Goods Game. The Prisoner's Dilemma is so well known that a
quick characterization is sufficient. (A form of the Prisoner's Dilemma was

TABLE 9.1
The Prisoner's Dilemma

	Cooperate	*Defect*
Cooperate	1, 1	−2, 2
Defect	2, −2	0, 0

already presented in Table 5.1 in Chapter 5.) In its simplest form, the game has two players who make their choices independently, each of whom has two possible strategies: he can either cooperate or defect (not cooperate). The structure of payoffs has two crucial characteristics: first, defection is a dominant strategy for both players, in that no matter what action one's opponent takes, the defection yields a higher (or at least no lower) payoff than cooperation; second, the payoff to each player is higher if both cooperate than if both defect. A matrix of payoffs representing the Prisoner's Dilemma is given in Table 9.1.[9]

Since defection is a dominant strategy, the equilibrium in a one-shot Prisoner's Dilemma is that both players defect. The equilibrium payoff is (0, 0), so that both individuals are worse off than if they both cooperated. Behavior is individually rational, though collectively disastrous. The Prisoner's Dilemma captures the essential features of the collective action problem: *an individual acting alone is always better off if he free rides, implying the public good will not be provided, even though all individuals would be better off if it were.*

There are cases of voluntarily provided public goods, however, which do *not* provide examples of collective action problems. Consider first the problem of *coordinating* behavior, often termed a collective action problem. Coordination games are numerous in everyday life, as discussed in Schelling's (1960) brilliant book. A simple example is the benefit of having everyone drive on the same side of the street, whether right or left. This may be represented by the payoff matrix in Table 9.2. The key conclusion is that either action is equally good, as long as everyone else acts the same way. The problem is simply how to get individuals to coordinate their

[9] Following the standard convention, the players "row" and "column" receive the first and second payoffs in each payoff pair.

TABLE 9.2
A Coordination Game

	Right	*Left*
Right	1, 1	0, 0
Left	0, 0	1, 1

choices. One possibility is the use of conventions, as discussed in Section 5.2 of Chapter 5. Our interest here, however, is not so much in considering mechanisms to reach the good outcome, but in pointing out essential differences between problems of coordination and of collective action.

In the coordination game, one may think of the superior outcome as a collective good. (In the strict economic sense, one definition of a public good is satisfied, as the utility an individual derives from his choice depends directly on the choices that others make.) However, there is not really a "collective action problem" as defined in the first paragraph of this section. Defection from what others are doing is *not* a dominant strategy. Just the opposite—if everyone else drives on the right, I will want to as well. There is no free-rider problem here, crucial to the existence of collective action problems. Roughly speaking, self-interested behavior supports a good equilibrium (there may be one, or many, in more complicated situations), rather than potentially destroying it. The problem is simply coordinating on a good equilibrium, as Schelling shows, which is often a problem of communication.

The second case of public goods that should *not* be considered as necessarily giving rise to collective action problems is closer to the Prisoner's Dilemma, and the qualitative argument may be more controversial. The importance of this case, however, means that a careful differentiation of the two cases is crucial. Specifically, consider the case where there is an incentive to free ride, *but only* if the public good is provided by someone else. This might seem semantic, but it is not. In the Prisoner's Dilemma, noncooperation is a dominant strategy, in that it is better for an agent to choose the selfish, noncooperative action, whether other players are selfish or not. In contrast, there are many situations in which it is optimal to free ride if others are providing the good, but to contribute if the good would not otherwise be provided. (Hence, noncooperation is *not* a dominant strategy.) This describes many public goods, and is important in public finance; the game which represents this situation is often termed "the public goods game." The public goods game is extremely important in political economy, with very different implications than the Prisoner's Dilemma. The static version of the game is analyzed in detail in Section 9.6 below, the dynamic version in Section 9.7.

To illustrate the public goods game, consider the following simple situation. There is a good which provides two units of utility if either individual provides it ("cooperates"), but costs the provider one unit of utility. Hence, an individual has an incentive to free ride ("defect"), if the other individual will provide the good. If neither provides the good, both get zero utility. A symmetric payoff version is shown in Table 9.3.

In isolation, either agent would provide the good. Hence, in this case the provision of a public good is parallel to Olson's privileged group as described in the passage quoted above, not to a latent group to which the "collective action problem" applies. If an agent believed there was a low

TABLE 9.3
A Public Goods Game

	Cooperate	Defect
Cooperate	1, 1	1, 2
Defect	2, 1	0, 0

probability that the other agent would provide the good (i.e., a high probability he would play "Defect"), he would provide the good, with there being no collective action problem even though the good is costly to provide.

Note, however, that though the group is "privileged," it could act like a latent group—if each individual believed that there was a high enough probability that the other would supply the good (i.e., a high probability he would play "Cooperate"), neither would supply it. In Section 9.6, this possibility is studied in detail, calling into question Olson's "presumption" in the citation quoted several paragraphs above.[10] Hence, we need to consider more carefully the relation between the size of a group and whether it is latent or privileged.

The Role of Group Size

To understand the effect of size on collective action, that is, to look at success or failure in provision when there are many players, one must ask how the benefits and costs change as the size of the group changes. Different conclusions about the effect of group size on the likelihood of group action reflect different assumptions. Olson's conclusion would reflect, for example, a case where the total cost and the *sum* of individual benefits remain the same as the size of the group increases, so that the ratio of individual benefit to total cost of the good *falls* as the group size rises. For a small enough group, this ratio could be larger than 1 and the group would be "privileged," by Olson's definition; for a large enough group, this ratio will be small and the group will be latent.

Olson's case, however, is not the only possibility. If, for given total cost, *per capita* benefits stay constant as group size changes, the ratio of individual benefit to total cost of the good would stay *constant* as the group size rises, so a large group would be as likely to be privileged as a small one. Consider, for example, an organization formed to lobby Congress for a cause that has a given value for all members of the group, while the cost of influencing Congress should be largely independent of the size of the group. More generally, a constant ratio of individual benefit to total cost

---

[10] It should be noted that Olson is aware of this possibility, as discussed in footnote 70 in chapter 1 of *The Logic of Collective Action*, where he also considers the war of attrition.

will hold strictly for any pure, that is, nonrival, public good, calling into question any simple presumption on size effects on the latency of a group. Congestion effects will lead to the ratio falling with group size, but the exact nature of these effects must be specified before concluding that large groups are likely to be latent.

In short, there appears to be no simple relation between the size of a group and whether it is latent or privileged. An especially clear discussion of this issue, including analysis of a number of cases, is found in Chapter 3 of Hardin (1982). Hardin suggests that a useful concept in understanding the relation of group size to latency is that of an "efficacious subgroup." (See also the discussion of Schelling in the next paragraph.) This is a subgroup within the group that just barely stands to benefit from providing the public good, even without cooperation from the rest of the group as a whole, and hence would provide the good. Denote the size of this group by $\hat{N}$, where if the group is heterogeneous in their valuation of the public good, $\hat{N}$ may have a range of values. If $\hat{N} = 1$, the group is privileged in Olson's terminology. A group is latent if the smallest efficacious subgroup has more than one member, that is, when $\hat{N} > 1$. The size of the smallest efficacious subgroup may rise as overall group size rises, but there is no necessary connection. It will very much depend on the nature of the public good and the nature of payoffs in providing the good. For example, in the two-person Prisoner's Dilemma, represented in Table 9.1, $\hat{N} = 2$.

An especially relevant case for size effects is that of "threshold goods," where the nature of the good defines a minimum level of contributors which is needed for the good to be provided.[11] More generally, following Schelling's (1978) analysis of situations with binary choices, one may think of situations where it is key how many individuals make one choice or the other. He considers a situation of identical individuals, where only the number (but not the identities) of other players matter for payoffs. By assuming that individuals are better off the larger the number of other individuals who "cooperate" and that the individual's own preferences remain constant no matter how many others cooperate or defect, he presents a uniform multiperson Prisoner's Dilemma. Analogous to Hardin, Schelling considers a crucial parameter $\hat{N} > 1$, such that if (and only if) $\hat{N}$ or more individuals choose their unpreferred (that is, the cooperative) alternative and the rest do not, those who do are better off than if they had all chosen their preferred alternative. Hence, Schelling's $\hat{N}$ performs the same function as did the discussion of efficacious subgroups in the previous paragraph, serving as a key to determining the latency of a group.

---

[11] Hardin (1982, pp. 55–61) discusses such cases under the name of "step" goods. A key problem he raises is that with a pure "step" good, there is no dominant strategy in exactly the way there was no dominant strategy in the public goods game above. One way to address this problem is to consider individual strategies defined over expected values.

Can Latent Groups Provide Public Goods?

How can a latent group be led to act? Olson's original analysis also asks how participation can be induced in an otherwise latent group, that is, what mechanisms can be created to ensure contributions to the provision of collective goods. He suggests several possibilities. One possibility is "selective incentives," whereby some members of the group might be able to induce others to cooperate, by providing them with positive or negative selective incentives. Incentives are selective in that they depend on the behavior of the individual agent. Olson argues that such incentives are often seen, for example, in trade unions. Elster (1989), for one, argues, however, that selective incentives cannot be a general solution to the collective action problem. The reason is that the provision of such incentives assumes that a "second-order" collective action problem has been solved by the central authority offering such incentives. Consider negative selective incentives, whereby failure to cooperate in providing the public good induces some sort of individual punishment. Why would an individual group member find it individually optimal to punish noncooperators? A collective action problem is present, in that punishment is individually costly to the punisher, but benefits the group as a whole. In short, the provision of selective incentives to ensure cooperation is itself a public good.

A second possibility that Olson presents is what he calls "by-product theory." The argument is that groups originally organized for other purposes can sometimes cooperate to act collectively, as a by-product. (This argument is actually closely connected to the discussion of selective incentives in the previous paragraph. To the extent that the "other purposes" for which groups may be organized provide individual payoffs to joining the group, they play the role of selective incentives.) Organizing a group means that a structure is in place to provide collective goods, lowering the cost of collective goods, which may push the net benefit A^i into the positive range for many members. Moreover, the creation of a group may create a sense of solidarity among its members, allowing the collective action problem to be solved. Many interest groups do, in fact, succeed in providing public goods as a by-product of being organized for other purposes, and remain operating over long periods of time, so that they can continue providing such collective goods. Hence, the by-product theory can explain, in some cases, why groups that are latent with respect to collective action nonetheless do solve the collective action problem.

The by-product theory does not, however, appear to be a general solution to the problem of collective action, for at least two reasons. First, the other purposes for which groups are organized are sometimes only very weak incentives as far as collective action problems are concerned. Many groups are essentially "buying clubs," formed basically to take advantage of the economies of scale involved in purchasing private goods in bulk. (This includes organizations which on the surface do not appear to be such groups.) We will formally analyze such clubs in the next section. To the extent they are organizations of convenience, little solidarity is created, and it is unlikely that any collective action problem could be addressed as a by-product.

A deeper problem is that though organizations may provide collective goods as a by-product, the by-product theory does not explain how these groups came to be formed in the first place. In fact, the history of many organizations (including unions) suggests that the by-product theory may have it backwards. Groups formed specifically to supply collective goods later provided for other interests as a by-product. Hence, at best, as with the theory of selective incentives, the by-product theory solves one collective action problem by creating another one. More generally, to the extent that the groups were formed to provide collective goods, the problem of collective action remains.

A third possibility is that agents who interact repeatedly will learn to cooperate as they see noncooperation is in no one's interest. Formally, the argument is that in repeated play of the Prisoner's Dilemma Game, cooperation may emerge. How the equilibria of repeated games may differ from one-shot games was discussed in the reputational models of Chapter 6, and the interested reader is referred back to that chapter to review the strengths and weaknesses of this approach to enforcing good behavior. Elster (1989, pp. 42–44) briefly discusses this solution to the collective action problem, but rejects it for some of the reasons discussed in Chapter 6. He argues that the relevant game is the N-person Prisoner's Dilemma (rather than the two-person Prisoner's Dilemma), for which robust results are rare.

To summarize, much work subsequent to Olson's pioneering contribution has argued that rational behavior alone cannot explain why collective goods are provided. Elster (1989) and Hardin (1982) provide in-depth treatments of the shortcomings of relying on rational behavior alone as an explanation of why collective action problems get solved, as well as discussing the importance of alternative approaches. Such work is far too extensive to cover here, so we simply mention some approaches, giving occasional references. A *contractarian* approach says that people "play fair," trying to cooperate if others do. The success of this approach to solving the collective action problem depends on there being a clear notion of what is fair (Hardin [1982, chapter 6], Schelling [1978]). A related idea is a *convention* ensuring cooperation with provision of the public good. The outstanding work on conventions is by Lewis (1969). A shortened version of his definition of **convention** may be summarized as a regularity R in the behavior of members of a given population P in recurrent situations S such that, in almost any instance of S among members of P: almost everyone conforms to R; almost everyone expects almost everyone else to conform to R; almost everyone prefers that any additional person conform to R, on the condition that almost everyone conforms to R; and, that these are common knowledge (Lewis [1969, p. 14]). This notion is clearly very close to the existence of a *social norm* of the type considered in Chapter 5, where the norm is to contribute to the public good, even though contributing does not seem individually rational. Conventions as a solution to the collective action problem are considered in Chapters 10–14 of Hardin (1982) and Sugden (1984, 1986). An insightful discussion of social norms as a solution to the collective action problem can be found in Chapter 5 of Elster (1989). He includes a discussion of moral norms and of what he calls "everyday Kantianism," whereby "one should cooperate if and only if universal cooperation is better for everybody than universal defection." (p.193) Similarly, Hardin suggests a "modified theory of collective action," taking account of psychological and sociological variables in trying to explain voluntary contributions.

Finally, one should note that there are those who argue that there really is not a problem of collective action, in the sense that it is not a problem empirically. Hardin (1982) argues that since the publication of *The Logic of Collective Action*, successful collective action has become far more commonplace, perhaps, he argues, because of technological developments that make collective action easier. Johansen (1977) also suggests that empirically, free riding may not be a serious problem. He argues, first, that honesty may be a social norm, in line with the above arguments. Second, decisions on the provision of public goods are in fact not typically made by individuals, but by their elected representatives, who face a very different set of incentives.

9.5. VOLUNTARY PROVISION OF PUBLIC GOODS—CLUBS

Central to the free-rider problem discussed in the previous section was the nonexcludability of the public good. However, for many nonrival goods, excludability may be an option. A country club which offers some goods and services which are not fully rival (such as a golf course and clubhouse) can charge a fee for members and can exclude nonmembers. Since the average cost of supplying the good to the existing members falls when a new member joins, at least over some range, it will be optimal to exploit the nonrival nature of the good supplied over that range.[12] There will be an optimal size of the consumption group, which will be smaller than the population if congestion eventually sets in. Hence, with the possibility of excludability, a group of individuals may find it optimal to voluntarily form

---

[12] Since the argument made here can apply to goods with economies of scale in their provision, it will have broad applicability. Consider "buying clubs" for pure private goods where unit costs fall with bulk sales. We return to this point below.

an association or a **club** to provide the good only to themselves.[13] Buchanan (1965) was the first to consider the efficiency properties of voluntary clubs, though many of the basic ideas can also be found in Olson (1965). Numerous papers have followed. Sandler and Tschirhart (1980) provide a survey.

Looked at very generally, the theory of clubs may be thought of as complementary to Lindahl's tax solution in Section 9.3 above. If a good is a pure public good, in that nonrivalry and nonexcludability are complete, revelation of preferences and optimal allocation require nonmarket decision processes, as in the Samuelson (1954) treatment. These are "voice" solutions, to use Hirschman's (1970) term, whereby preferences are expressed by some sort of verbal, written, or other standard means of communication, including voting. Following Hirschman, one may then ask whether there are "exit" solutions, where preferences are expressed via entry or exit, the market being the prime example. In the case of public goods, we would include quasi-market solutions: the Lindahl tax equilibrium provides one such solution; the theory of clubs provides another.

Olson (1965, pp. 33–43) considers clubs formed to exploit economies of scale and share public goods, as a solution to problems of collective action. He argues that certain small groups can provide themselves with collective goods without relying on coercion or any positive inducements apart from the collective good itself. Each member, or at least one, will find it optimal to provide the good, even if he had to pay the entire cost himself. Olson then considers inclusive and exclusive groups, the former sharing pure public goods and hence requiring no membership restrictions, the latter sharing impure public goods and thus requiring membership restrictions, due to crowding and congestion.

Buchanan (1965) is credited with being the first to formalize a number of these ideas. In the basic Buchanan model, homogeneous members *equally share* an impure public good and its associated costs. Nonmembers can be costlessly excluded, and there are no transaction costs in the exclusion process. Buchanan thus considered a utility function similar to that in the Samuelson model in Section 9.2, but where the public good g is impure, so that the number of members N of the club enters into individual utility. The novel aspect of the analysis is a first-order condition on the number of members in the club. In Buchanan, the provision and membership conditions must *simultaneously* be determined, and it is the utility of the *representative* member that is maximized.

An alternative is to consider "mixed" clubs, namely, clubs with heterogeneous members. With heterogeneous members, an issue is *utilization* in

---

[13] There is the collective action problem in *setting up* a club, as discussed in our criticism of by-product theory above. However, we ignore this question, for it misses the basic point of analysis of clubs. Excludability in the provision of the good itself eliminates the general collective action problem in the previous section.

addition to membership since each member can utilize a different amount of the shared good. One may therefore consider *utilization* charges ("tolls") as part of the optimal equilibrium. A key question is whether and when mixed clubs may be optimal, with some papers in the literature arguing against the optimality of mixed clubs, others arguing in favor. Sandler and Tschirhart (1980) show mixed clubs to be optimal unless a second-best constraint is imposed, whereby all members must share costs equally regardless of their utilization of the public good.

A Formal Treatment

To demonstrate a number of basic results, we extend the Samuelson analysis in Section 9.2 to the theory of clubs. We consider first homogeneous clubs, where both club size and the quantity of the collective consumption good to be provided are optimally chosen to maximize the utility of the representative member. The utility of the representative member may be written as $u(c, g, N)$, where c is a numeraire private good, g is an (excludable) public good, and N is club size. Each individual has an identical endowment e and must pay a fee τ for membership in the club, which allows him to consume the good in the quantity optimally determined by the club, so that we may write his utility function as

$$u(e - \tau, g, N). \tag{9.14}$$

Suppose the cost of providing the public good includes a fixed cost ζ^0, in addition to a fixed producer price P_g. The club operates under a balanced budget condition, whereby fees must cover the cost of providing the public good to club members, that is,

$$\tau N = \zeta^0 + P_g g. \tag{9.15}$$

The club's maximization problem may be represented as maximizing (9.14) subject to (9.15). This yields optimality conditions

$$N \frac{u_g}{u_c} = P_g, \tag{9.16}$$

and

$$N = -\frac{u_g}{u_N} \frac{\zeta^0 + P_g g}{P_g}. \tag{9.17}$$

The first condition (9.16) is simply the Samuelson condition for optimal supply of public goods for a group of N identical individuals. The second condition (9.17) is the novel aspect of the club analysis, giving the optimal number of club members. In equilibrium, $u_N < 0$, as a club will expand until crowding sets in. The larger is the disutility from crowding relative to the marginal utility from the private good, the smaller is the optimal size of the club. The larger is the fixed cost of providing the public good, the larger is the optimal size of the club, as fixed cost can be spread over a larger number of members.

We may now consider the possibility of mixed clubs, that is, the possibility of forming clubs consisting of members with different tastes or different endowments. From the limited standpoint of simple economic efficiency, is it better to restrict a club to individuals with identical preferences, or not to impose such a restriction? Intuitively, it does seem more efficient to have clubs composed of individuals with the same preferences. This may be shown technically, if the same user fee is imposed on all individuals. If members differ along a simple utilization dimension (such as hours per week they use a swimming pool), and the costs of providing the collective good are positively related to utilization, then efficiency is consistent with a mixed club if the membership fees are also allowed to vary positively with utilization. This may be shown in an extended version of the model above, where the additional optimality condition will determine the price per unit of utilization.

Once differences in utilization are not so easily characterized, the design of membership fees as a function of utilization is more complicated. Mixed clubs may then be able to achieve efficiencies that homogeneous clubs cannot, as for example, when individuals differ not in how intensively they use the collective good, but when they use it. Off-peak and on-peak pricing would be necessary for efficiency; moreover, only heterogeneous clubs would be able to ensure full-time utilization of the collective good most efficiently. Mixed clubs may also be desirable on efficiency grounds if scale economies imply a larger optimal membership than possible with a homogeneous membership, when the collective good is necessarily multidimensional, or when heterogeneous member skills are an important input into the production of the collective good. For references on some of these issues, the reader is referred to Sandler and Tschirhart (1980) or Cornes and Sandler (1986).

Of course, many would argue that the desirability of mixed clubs is not a question primarily of economic efficiency, for example, in considering the desirability of racially integrated neighborhoods. The strength of the analysis in this and the previous chapter is not that it gives us answers to difficult policy questions, but that it gives us the tools with which to analyze them. To be weighed against simple economic efficiency discussed in the previous paragraphs are the benefits of diversity, as well as the redistributive aspects associated with mixed neighborhoods. The analysis in Section 8.7 of the previous chapter indicated how some of these concerns can be formalized, for example, in Pauly's model of local redistribution. As discussed in that section, the theory of community formation associated with Tiebout (1956), on which the Epple and Romer (1991) model of local redistribution is based, is essentially a theory of geographically distinct clubs.

9.6. THE STATIC PUBLIC GOODS GAME

We now return to the problem of provision of a public good in a static setting, studying the static public goods game presented in Table 9.3 more formally. The goal is to show how the public good might not be provided even in a small group, though the benefit to each player exceeds his cost. (To use the terminology of Section 9.4, $A^i > 0$ for all i, but the collective good is nonetheless not provided.) In Section 9.7, we extend the analysis to a dynamic setting, yielding the "war of attrition."

To make the problem and its implications as clear as possible, we will model the problem as a game between two players, where the economic framework is kept very simple. We illustrate the nature of the collective action problem by first considering whether a public good would be provided in a world where each individual decides whether or not to purchase the good himself. Hence, the results set the stage for a public choice analysis of decisionmaking mechanisms which may overcome the free-rider problem. As we shall see, the results can also be interpreted as representing the distortion caused by the conflict of interests inherent in public goods when the decisionmaking mechanism is consensus.

Suppose an individual must decide whether or not to make a one-time purchase of a good that costs ζ. He gets utility of 1 if he buys the good and utility zero if he does not. If the good were a pure private good, the solution to this problem would be trivial: buy the good if the cost ζ was less than 1; otherwise, do not buy the good.

Now consider the problem where the good is a public good, in that if any individual buys the good, everyone has utility equal to 1; if no one buys the good, everyone has utility of zero. Suppose, for concreteness, there are two individuals, call them i and j, who have costs ζ^i and ζ^j, respectively. Hence, if, for example, individual i pays the cost of the public good being provided, he receives net utility $1 - \zeta^i$. The conflict of interests is simple: each individual would like the other to pay the cost of the good being provided. The Samuelson social planner's solution to this problem is also simple—the good should be provided if the total gain from provision is at least as great as the minimum cost of providing the good, which is $\min\{\zeta^i, \zeta^j\}$. This further implies that the individual with the lower cost should provide the good. In terms of the distribution of costs, the government may choose to give this individual a subsidy financed by a lump-sum tax on the other individual.

In deriving the equilibrium in the absence of a social planner, the individual information structure is crucial. Suppose each individual knows his own cost, but not that of the other individual. He only knows the other individual's cost is distributed as $F(\zeta)$ over $[\underline{\zeta}, \bar{\zeta}]$, where $F(\zeta)$ is common knowledge, meaning that each individual knows $F(\zeta)$, knows that the other individual knows $F(\zeta)$, knows that the other individual knows that he knows $F(\zeta)$, etc.[14] Under these assumptions, one may ask whether the good will be provided in the absence of collective action.

We begin with each individual's "strategy." For example, for i, a strategy is to provide or not to provide the good as a function of his cost ζ^i. For ease of exposition, let us denote these two actions by 1 and 0. Formally, the strategy $s_i(\zeta^i)$ of individual i assigns to each ζ^i an action 1 or 0. The payoff of individual i depends on his cost, his strategy (that is, choice of whether or not to pay the cost of providing), and the other individual's strategy. Formally, we may write the payoff as

$$u^j(s^j, s^i, \zeta^j) = \max(s^j, s^i) - s^j \zeta^j, \tag{9.18}$$

where s^i and s^j are the actions implied by the strategies $s_i(\zeta^i)$ and $s_j(\zeta^j)$.

Consider an equilibrium in which we solve for a pair of strategies $\{\bar{s}_i(\zeta^i), \bar{s}_j(\zeta^j)\}$ for each possible value of ζ^i and ζ^j such that each individual's behavior is optimal given the other individual's strategy. The solution to this problem is simple. If we define by p^i the equilibrium probability that player i pays the cost of providing the public good (that is, $p^i = \Pr(\bar{s}_i(\zeta^i) = 1)$), player j's optimal behavior is[15]

$$\bar{s}^j = 1 \quad \text{if } \zeta^j \leq 1 - p^i,$$
$$\bar{s}^j = 0 \quad \text{if } \zeta^j > 1 - p^i, \tag{9.19}$$

where $\bar{s}^j = 1$ corresponds to the (optimal) action for player j of paying the cost of the public good being provided and $\bar{s}^j = 0$ corresponds to the (optimal) action for player j of not paying this cost.

---

[14] This version of the well-known "public goods game" follows Fudenberg and Tirole (1991).

[15] Let individual i's decision be characterized by a reservation cost $\bar{\zeta}^i$ such that $\bar{s}^i = 1$ if $\zeta^i < \bar{\zeta}^i$. Individual j chooses action s^j to maximize his expected utility, which can be written

$$E\Omega^j = \int_{\zeta^i = \underline{\zeta}}^{\bar{\zeta}^i} u^j(s^j, \bar{s}^i = 1, \zeta^j) \, dF(\zeta) + \int_{\bar{\zeta}^i}^{\bar{\zeta}} u^j(s^j, \bar{s}^i = 0, \zeta^j) \, dF(\zeta)$$

$$= \int_{\zeta^i = \underline{\zeta}}^{\bar{\zeta}^i} (1 - \zeta^j s^j) \, dF(\zeta) + \int_{\bar{\zeta}^i}^{\bar{\zeta}} (s^j - \zeta^j s^j) \, dF(\zeta)$$

$$= p^i(1 - \zeta^j s^j) + (1 - p^i)(s^j - \zeta^j s^j).$$

It follows that a choice of $s^j = 0$ implies that $E\Omega^j = p^i$, and a choice of $s^j = 1$ implies that $E\Omega^j = 1 - \zeta^j$. Therefore, $s^j = 1$ if and only if $1 - \zeta^j > p^i$.

What the solution indicates is that because of the public nature of the good, an individual will not be willing to provide the good if he thinks that the probability is high enough that someone else will do so, even though the benefit exceeds the cost of provision. In the optimal solution, an individual equates his cost not to the net benefit of providing over not providing the good, but to the expected net benefit. In equilibrium, if both individuals are known to act according to this rule, the equilibrium probability and reservation level of cost can be derived. If $\tilde{\zeta}^i$ is i's reservation cost, so that $p^i = \Pr(\underline{\zeta} < \zeta^i \le \tilde{\zeta}^i) = F(\tilde{\zeta}^i)$, we have

$$\tilde{\zeta}^j = 1 - F(\tilde{\zeta}^i) = 1 - F(1 - F(\tilde{\zeta}^j)), \tag{9.20}$$

with an identical equation for $\tilde{\zeta}^i$. If there is a unique $\tilde{\zeta}$ which solves this equation, this is the solution, that is, the reservation cost for both players.

To take an example, if $F(\zeta)$ is uniform on $[0, 2]$, we may derive $\tilde{\zeta} = 2/3$ and $F(\tilde{\zeta}) = 1/3$. Hence, if both individuals have costs that lie between $2/3$ and 1, the good will not be provided in equilibrium, even though each individual would be better off if he provided the good himself. Though each individual would benefit, each decides not to pay the cost of provision, given his cost and the probability that the other individual will provide the good. Therefore, in equilibrium, the good is not provided.

9.7. The War of Attrition in Public Goods Provision

We now consider the same problem of provision of public goods in a dynamic setting. This will yield a "war of attrition," with each individual playing a waiting game in the hope that the other individual will give in first and be the one who provides the public good. Formally, a **war of attrition** is a game of timing with the following two characteristics: (1) the payoff to the "winner" exceeds the payoff to the "loser"; and (2) the payoffs to both winner and loser are declining over time. The dynamic version of the public goods game of the previous section fits easily into this framework: the individual who provides the good has lower net utility than the other individual, and hence is the "loser" in the dynamic game; the longer the individuals go without consuming the public good, the lower is their utility taken over the whole horizon. As before, we can ask what distortion will result from the provision of public goods being determined by a war of attrition between self-interested individuals rather than a social planner. The war of attrition will form the basis of one of the main approaches to explaining delay in adopting socially optimal reforms, to be discussed in detail in Chapter 10. For example, Alesina and Drazen (1991) use the war-of-attrition model to explain why deficit reduction may be delayed, even if viewed as socially beneficial by all interest groups.

One way to make the public goods game dynamic is to consider a multiperiod discrete-time version of the above static problem, in which each individual maximizes the discounted sum of expected payoffs, with the single-period payoff being defined as above. Consider, for example, a two-period version of the game. If p_2^i were independent of what happened in the first period, simply reflecting $F(\zeta)$ as above, optimal behavior would be independent across periods; each period's problem can be solved as above, yielding the same reservation cost in each period, namely, $\tilde{\zeta}$ as above. What is crucial in a dynamic framework is that the probability of i's providing the public good in period 2, p_2^i, depends on the action that j took in the first period. This occurs because observing the other individual *not* providing the good reveals information about his cost, since it is known that he uses a reservation cost rule. If individual j believes that i's equilibrium reservation cost in period 1 is $\tilde{\zeta}_1^i$, observing no provision leads j to update the distribution of possible costs by truncating the distribution $F(\zeta)$ below $\tilde{\zeta}_1^i$. Hence, j updates the probability p_2^i. Knowing that the other individual is solving this inference problem leads each individual to "shade" his reservation cost downward in the first period, relative to what he would choose in the absence of such an inference. This lower reservation cost represents the incentive to not provide the good because he hopes that the other individual will provide it.

Alternatively, one could consider a continuous-time, infinite-horizon version of the static game. Consider a set-up in continuous time which is identical to that in the static problem, including payoffs, costs, and information structure.[16] Individual j's strategy, for example, is to choose a date $T^j(\zeta^j)$ to agree to pay for the public good as a function of his cost, conditional on individual i not yet having agreed to pay for provision of the public good. Individual i chooses a similar function. Each individual chooses his optimal date to pay the cost of supplying the good (to "concede") in order to maximize discounted expected payoff, where the discount rate is ρ.

Let us consider individual j's decision problem. For concreteness, call the individual who concedes first (that is, who agrees to pay the cost of supplying the public good) the "loser," and denote his payoffs by L for "low." Call the other individual the "winner," with his payoffs denoted by H for "high." Suppose that j concedes at time T, so that he is the loser. He has zero flow utility until T, flow utility of $1 - \zeta^j$ thereafter. His

---

[16] More generally, we could have a game where the good is supplied as soon as one individual agrees to pay a disproportionate share of the cost of the public good, with the other then agreeing to pay the remainder.

discounted utility would then be

$$\Omega^L(T, \zeta^j) = \int_{z=0}^{T} 0 e^{-\rho z} \, dz + e^{-\rho T} \int_{z=T}^{\infty} (1 - \zeta^j) e^{-\rho(z-T)} \, dz$$

$$= \frac{1 - \zeta^j}{\rho} e^{-\rho T}.$$

(9.21)

If individual i concedes first, so that j is the winner, j's discounted utility would be

$$\Omega^H(T, \zeta^j) = \int_{z=0}^{T} 0 e^{-\rho z} \, dz + e^{-\rho T} \int_{z=T}^{\infty} 1 e^{-\rho(z-T)} \, dz$$

$$= \frac{1}{\rho} e^{-\rho T}.$$

(9.22)

To solve for j's optimal behavior, we begin, as in the static public goods game, by representing i's optimal behavior simply in terms of his probability of conceding. In continuous time, this is represented by a cumulative distribution function $\Gamma^i(T)$, giving the probability of i's conceding at or before T, with an associated density function $\gamma^i(T)$. One may then calculate individual j's expected utility as a function of possible concession time T^j. With probability $1 - \Gamma^i(T^j)$ individual j concedes, his infinite-horizon utility being $\Omega^L(T^j)$; if, however, i's optimal concession time T^i is less than T^j, then j's infinite-horizon utility is $\Omega^H(T^i)$, where for each T^i less than T^j, there is an associated probability $\gamma^i(T^i)$. Expected utility of individual j as a function of T^j and his cost ζ^j may then be written

$$\mathrm{E}\Omega^j(T^j) = (1 - \Gamma^i(T^j))\Omega^L(T^j, \zeta^j)$$

$$+ \int_{z=0}^{T^j} \Omega^H(z, \zeta^j)\gamma^i(z) \, dz.$$

(9.23)

To calculate optimal T^j, substitute (9.21) and (9.22) into (9.23), and set the derivative with respect to T^j equal to zero to obtain[17]

$$\frac{\gamma^i(T^j)}{1 - \Gamma^i(T^j)} \frac{\zeta^j}{\rho} = 1 - \zeta^j.$$

(9.24)

This equation has a simple interpretation. Consider first the left-hand side. The first term is the probability that individual i concedes at T^j, condi-

---

[17] One may easily verify that the second-order condition holds, so that the solution is a maximum.

tional on his not having yet conceded. The second term is the gain in utility to individual j from T^j onwards if the public good is supplied by his opponent rather than himself, which is the cost saving over the infinite horizon. This second term is simply $\Omega^H(T^j) - \Omega^L(T^j)$ as of time T^j. Thus, the left-hand side represents the expected *gain* to j of waiting another instant to concede. The right-hand side is the cost of waiting another instant to concede, which is the foregone utility associated with not having the good for another instant minus the cost of providing that he saves over the instant. Hence, (9.24) indicates that individual j concedes and agrees to pay the cost of providing the public good when the expected gain from waiting just equals the cost from waiting, the latter being the loss in utility from waiting another instant to concede. This solution, as represented by the above equation, is analogous to the solution to the static public goods game conditional on p^i given by (9.19), namely, provide the good if $\zeta^j \leq 1 - p^i$. As in the static case, each individual i and j can derive the optimal concession time as a function of his cost, depending on his beliefs about his opponent's probability of conceding.

However, (9.24) cannot be used directly to calculate an equilibrium $T^j(\zeta^j)$ for j, since the distribution $\Gamma^i(T)$ is unknown. Analogous to the discussion of equilibrium in the static game which followed the characterization of optimal behavior conditional on p^i, we must derive equilibrium $\Gamma^i(T)$. Since individual i is solving the same sort of problem as j is, individual j assumes that i follows a reservation rule for time of concession, where this time is increasing in his cost. As in the static game, let us consider the symmetric solution, where both individuals concede according to the same function $T(\zeta)$, where T is increasing in ζ.[18] This implies that the probability that individual i concedes before a time T^0 is the probability that his cost ζ^i is less than the associated ζ^0, namely, $F(\zeta^0)$, so that we may write

$$\Gamma^i(T^0) = \Gamma^i(T(\zeta^0)) = F(\zeta^0). \tag{9.25}$$

Differentiating (9.25), one derives, for any value of T, that $\gamma^i(T) \cdot T'(\zeta) = f(\zeta)$. This allows us to write $\gamma^i(T)/(1 - \Gamma^i(T))$ in (9.24) as $f(\zeta)/[(1 - F(\zeta))T'(\zeta)]$. Equation (9.24) can then be written, for any value of ζ,

$$T'(\zeta^j) = \frac{f(\zeta^j)}{1 - F(\zeta^j)} \frac{1}{\rho} \frac{\zeta^j}{1 - \zeta^j}, \tag{9.26}$$

which is relevant for $\zeta^j < 1$. (Individuals with a cost greater than 1 would never find it optimal to provide the public good.) The identical equation

---

[18] $T(\zeta)$ monotonically increasing in ζ follows from the nature of the optimization problem, as we will shortly verify.

will describe the behavior of individual i. Equation (9.26) is a differential equation in the function $T(\zeta)$ which, combined with the boundary condition $T(0) = 0$, can be solved for the optimal concession time $T(\zeta)$ for each individual. (The boundary condition should be obvious, since an individual who has no cost of providing the good will choose to do so immediately.) Hence, we get a model where the public good is provided with a delay.

With both individuals i and j behaving according to $T(\zeta)$, the expected date T^ϵ of provision of the public good may be calculated as the expected minimum T, which reflects the expected minimum ζ. This probability associated with this minimum value is the density multiplied by the probability that no other ζ is lower. For the case of only two individuals, one obtains

$$T^E = 2\int_{z=0}^{\bar{\zeta}} T(z)(1 - F(z))\,f(z)\,dz. \tag{9.27}$$

The solution to this dynamic problem represents the basic result of how the public goods nature of socially beneficial government programs may lead to their being delayed relative to what is socially optimal. This model will be one of the basic models used in our study of the political economy of inaction and delay in policy adoption in the next chapter.

9.8. CONCLUSIONS

In this chapter, we have presented the theory of public goods, concentrating on models of their provision, and on general implications of the public nature of certain goods. The study of public goods is one of the classic topics in public economics, and it has relevance to political economy for a number of reasons. The simplest reason is that the importance of the topic in public economics makes it important for students of political economy to be familiar with the basic issues. A second reason is the public choice argument that a theory of the provision of public goods is a theory of government, following the view that a key reason that governments are instituted is for the provision of public goods.

A third reason why studying public goods is important in political economy is that problems in their provision (such as "collective action" problems) provide significant insight into basic driving forces of political economy, specifically, *ex-post* heterogeneity arising as conflict of interests over the distribution of the cost of supplying the public good. Finally, and perhaps most importantly, these conflicts have important positive implications. When a good has public aspects, it may be underprovided, not provided at all, or provided only after significant delay. Whether any of these outcomes occur depends on the mechanisms for making collective choices about the provision of the public good. A number of such mechanisms were considered in general terms in this chapter. Hence, public goods problems fall squarely in the realm of political economy, defined as studying the implications for outcomes of mechanisms for making collective choices when there is heterogeneity of interests. Moreover, when one realizes how many economic policies have the characteristic of public goods, the positive implications of the public goods problem are not only at the heart of political economy, but throughout the whole body of the field as well.

We have not included extensive discussion of these positive implications of the public goods problem, that is, of more specific applications of the problem, in this chapter. The primary reason is the ubiquitousness of applications in political economy, as indicated at the end of the previous paragraph. In the coming chapters, we do present extensive applications. A primary application is in the failure or delay of adoption of reform, which will be considered in detail in the next chapter. More applied issues related to specific economic reform and transition will be considered in Chapter 13. There are many other applications. Incentive problems leading to underaccumulation of public goods will also be important in studying the political economy of factor accumulation and growth, treated in Chapter 11. Problems of international policy coordination when, for example, good macroeconomic policy is a public good will be discussed in Chapter 12. Finally, questions of the size of government (and the number of nations), discussed in Chapter 14, reflect public goods considerations, as well as many of the redistributional issues considered in the previous chapter.

Inaction, Delay, and Crisis

> I was ... a great reformist; but never suspected that the people in power were against reform. I supposed they only wanted to know what was good in order to embrace it.
>
> —*Jeremy Bentham*

> HURRY UP PLEASE IT'S TIME
>
> —*T. S. Eliot, "The Waste Land"*

10.1. INTRODUCTION

The failure to adopt socially beneficial economic reforms, their adoption only after long delays, or their being sustained only after repeated attempts certainly constitute prime examples of the divergence between the simple textbook models of economic policymaking and real-world experience. The textbook social planner would adopt any policy change that is perceived as raising social welfare. In reality, changes that are socially beneficial are often delayed for long periods of time, especially when one includes policy changes that are sustained rather than adopted and subsequently reversed. The divergence between prescription and practice is particularly true if we consider significant economic reform. Quick enactment of a lasting program of broad but necessary reform is rare. Hence, in situations in which the economic arguments clearly favor reform, one must look to the political constraints to understand why reforms are not enacted or sustained, or are only enacted after long delay.

The question of why optimal policies are not enacted has been a primary focus of this book. The political economy of nonadoption, delay, or reversal of reform gets special attention for at least two reasons. First, if reform is taken to mean the move away from clearly inferior policy, the continuation of such policies is especially puzzling. Second, if reform means more specifically a sweeping change in a whole set of policies held responsible for a country's very poor economic performance, explaining the failure to reform is of paramount importance in terms of economic welfare.

Our discussion of "reform" is divided between this chapter and Chapter 13. There are two key differences between the material covered in this chapter and in Chapter 13. First, on a theoretical level, we concentrate in this chapter on single policy changes, focusing on nonadoption or delay of such changes; in Chapter 13, we argue that the number and magnitude of policy changes is the essence of large-scale reform and transition, and hence consider policy *packages*. The focus there is on how reform and transition programs can be structured to overcome political constraints, rather than on nonadoption. Second, in this chapter, we present general theoretical models that can be applied to a wide range of policy changes; in Chapter 13, we consider specific applications, such as labor market restructuring or price decontrol, consistent with the general focus of Part IV of the book.

Concentrating on general models in this chapter is consistent with the nature of Part III of the book, where our focus has been on political factors and mechanisms that cut across specific topics or applications. Though the general explanations for nonadoption that we study here are quite diverse, they share a common feature that is crucial to each explanation. This common feature is heterogeneity and conflict of interests, which we have argued throughout the book to be the defining characteristic of political economy explanations of economic outcomes.[1]

Why divide material on reform into two separate chapters? Paradoxical as it may sound, this division is made in the attempt to help bridge the often wide gap between the theory of reform and the practice. To theorists, practical discussions of real-world problems in implementing reform programs often seem both enormously confusing and confused. Confusing, in that so many factors are at play that seriously modeling them with any degree of technical rigor appears hopeless. Confused, in that practitioners often seem not only to be speaking a totally different language, but also to be using modes of analysis that appear to be quite at odds with standard modes of economic analysis. To practitioners, on the other hand, theoretical treatments of reform sometimes appear to be hopelessly out of touch with reality. The work is admittedly elegant, but in its search for rigor, it is often correctly seen as missing the point. In this chapter and in Chapter 13, we attempt to help bridge the gap between theory and practice. The hope is that it can be bridged by understanding the theoretical models *per se*, be it at a conceptual or a more technical level, and, on the basis of this understanding, by being careful in applying them.

---

[1] Romer (1997) suggests an alternative explanation of economically inefficient political decisions, namely, that individuals' errors in assessing the likely effects of a proposed policy are correlated, so that democratic decisionmaking can produce inefficient outcomes even in the absence of distributional conflicts or heterogeneous preferences. He terms correlated errors "misconceptions," which may arise from small incentives of individuals to gather information.

Three further observations on the subject matter of this chapter will be useful. First, in this chapter, we will take "reform" generally to mean simply the adoption of a superior policy, whether a single policy or a package as a whole. The technical definition used here allows us to focus on political determinants of suboptimal economic policies more generally. Issues in the political economy of reform which are connected *specifically* with reform being a package rather than a single policy will be covered in Chapter 13. However, the approach taken here is not necessarily at odds with viewing reform as a comprehensive package of policy changes, since a package could be treated as a single policy if there is agreement about the elements of the package. In fact, those who stress the importance of comprehensive reform (Williamson [1994b], Rodrik [1996], to name but two) suggest there is agreement on the broad outline of comprehensive policy reform, though of course it is not total.[2] Such agreement highlights the puzzle of suboptimal policy choice. As Williamson and Haggard (1994, p. 531) write, in discussing the "Washington consensus" of agreed-upon components for successful reform,[3] "Yet this raises the following puzzle: if the consensus is in fact widely endorsed, why is it not more widely implemented?" Therefore, studying the basic question of adoption of suboptimal policies does not hinge on whether we mean an individual policy or an entire package.

Second, it is useful to distinguish those reforms which are expected to be of general benefit (for example, macroeconomic stabilization) from those for which there are clearly defined losers *ex ante* (for example, breaking up a monopoly). Naim (1994) has made a closely related distinction between "stage-one" and "stage-two" reforms. The former, associated with the launching of reform programs, have more immediate payoffs and widely distributed political costs; from an economic and political point of view, they are easier to implement. The latter are associated with the consolidation of a reform program and generally concern deeper structural reform. Their benefits accrue only over the longer term and require the elimination of advantages to some special interests; from both a technical and a political standpoint, they are far more difficult. To the extent that our focus in this chapter is on models formulated to answer the basic question of why socially beneficial economic policy changes are not adopted, the policy changes we consider are more like "stage-one" reforms, but one should be careful about such a simple dichotomy. We also consider problems of vested interests, a typical problem for "stage-two" reforms; moreover, the main message of the chapter is that policies which are socially beneficial may nonetheless face severe political constraints.

---

[2] One should distinguish between economists and noneconomists, the former generally being in greater agreement about the components of successful reform than the latter.

[3] We discuss the "Washington consensus" in Chapter 13.

Third, "reform" focuses our attention on policy *change*. The question of why beneficial policy changes are not made is closely related to the question of why an economy finds itself in a bad equilibrium to begin with. They are not identical from a political economy point of view, as the forces which help explain the failure to change policy may differ from those which explain the current suboptimal policy, especially when current policy is viewed in historical perspective. Moreover, the answer to the former question will generally very much depend on the answer to the latter question. In this sense, our approach here will necessarily be incomplete. One should, however, not overemphasize the difference, as many of the same factors will come into play, as the models will make clear.

Categories of Models

The models of the failure to make socially optimal policy changes that we study fall into four general categories, all reflecting some conflict between interest groups. First, there are models of the role of powerful vested interest groups who block socially beneficial policy change because it is not in their individual interest. These are discussed in Section 10.3. Though not developed as formally as some of the other models, this approach, often associated with Olson (1982), forms an important component of general approaches to the failure to adopt socially beneficial policy changes. Second, there are models in which this failure reflects the public goods of socially beneficial policy. In one strand of this approach, inaction or delay may arise because individuals view the policy change as desirable, but, since this benefit accrues to a group far wider than those who bear the costs of the change, everyone wants someone else to bear the cost. These models, discussed in Section 10.6, follow the discussion of the static and dynamic public goods games in Chapter 9. Another public goods approach is more abstract, stressing the phenomenon of "fishing from a common pool," a mutually destructive form of behavior which stops only when the common pool falls low enough in size. Such models are presented in Section 10.7. Third, there are models which stress *ex-ante* uncertainty about private benefits. Though a policy change is beneficial for a majority of individuals, there are still losers. Individual uncertainty about whether he will be a net gainer or loser may then imply that a policy that would benefit a majority of the population *ex post* may nonetheless be opposed by a majority *ex ante*. These models are discussed in Section 10.4. Finally, there are models which stress the decisionmaking process itself, with the failure to reform arising from asymmetric information between policymakers and the electorate (the decisionmakers) which must support the reforms. If voters are less well informed than politicians about the benefits of a policy change, they may reject a change because they are unsure whether the new policy is to their benefit or only to the benefit of the politician (or his specific constituency). Hence, the problem may be seen as one of an inability to communicate the socially beneficial nature of reform. We consider such models in Section 10.5.

10.2. ECONOMIC ARGUMENTS

To make the political nature of nonadoption, delayed adoption, or reversal of reforms clear, we begin with a discussion of nonpolitical reasons for such failures. For the most part, the discussion will be quite cursory, though this is not because these arguments are empirically irrelevant. In fact, the economic arguments we review often play a major role in explaining the failure (or delay) to change policies. We do not concentrate on arguments that are largely nonpolitical because our focus is on political explanations of inaction and delay.

Lack of Knowledge and Expertise

The first general line of explanation for failure to change policy is ignorance of how to do so. There are several important variants of the argument. First, and most simply, failure or delay in changing a policy that does not work simply reflects the fact that policymakers do not know what policy will work better. That is, there are cases where the stumbling block appears to be the absence of a clearly superior alternative to current policy. One may go a step further and include the argument that there are many alternatives, but none clearly dominates from a social welfare point of view. This refers to the oft-observed phenomenon of disagreement by social welfare-maximizing policymakers about what policies should be adopted.[4] Though it is far from easy to design highly effective policy, so that this argument has empirical importance, it misses the key point we want to consider. When policymakers do not know what to do, the failure to take action is not surprising; inaction or delay is puzzling when there is agreement about what measures must be taken but, nonetheless, nothing is done.[5]

Another aspect of ignorance or lack of knowledge is more on tactics or logistics than on overall policy design. One form of this explanation is that in spite of agreement on what to do, a country lacks the technical inputs to carry it out. This could refer to various types of capital or infrastructure; however, one usually thinks of a lack of human capital necessary to carry out the desired program successfully. Lack of expertise may be a lack of

---

[4] Consider, for example, the following quote from Nelson (1990, p. 347), "The cases of clear failure [of reform] all traced collapse in large part to deeply divided economic teams."

[5] One should note, however, that clever (and often not-so-clever) politicians try to avoid taking action when it is clear what should be done by claiming that the correct course of action is in fact far from clear. Hence, pleading ignorance about what needs to be done is often a smokescreen for unwillingness to take actions.

technical knowledge *per se,* or a lack of the necessary technicians, managers, or bureaucrats. Many studies of economic crisis assign a crucial role to this lack of technical knowledge, as for example in the Williamson (1994b) hypotheses on why reforms are not adopted. This may also explain optimal delay, as the necessary capital is accumulated.[6] The need to accumulate the necessary capital may also influence the optimal sequencing of multipart reform, a topic that we explore in Chapter 13.

Here too, though lack of necessary capital or expertise may be an important factor in delaying the implementation of a policy change, there is nothing political nor puzzling about it. Moreover, though this may be a constraint in some cases, it does not explain the failure to carry out many programs, such as deficit reduction. If lack of expertise refers to the inability to explain or communicate the need for policy reform, as analyzed in Section 10.5 this has a more political dimension.

Optimal Waiting

A second line of explanation for inaction may be termed "benign neglect": given time, the problem will solve itself, so the response of "mañana" is optimal. To make sense of such a response in a world of rational agents, one may draw the distinction between transitory and permanent conditions. If a problem results from a shock which is perceived to be a transitory shock, policy lags mean that doing nothing may be the best response. Any lag in the ability to implement a policy, or in the effects the policy will have once put in place, means that activism may make things worse rather than better. Similarly, if a problem is "on the way" to being solved, so that what we are observing is a transitional period, taking no action may be the optimal action. (One should note, however, that arguing for "benign neglect" may simply be an excuse for unwillingness to act.) Here too, the argument has empirical relevance as an explanation for policy delay, but does not answer the question of why there are delays when it is agreed that problems will not solve themselves.

A variant of the argument for optimal waiting is that though a problem will not solve itself without a change in policy, external circumstances are currently not economically favorable for a major policy change. That is, some situations are more favorable than others to implement a new policy, so that it may be optimal to wait for more favorable circumstances if there is a cost of failure. This argument has been formalized by Orphanides

---

[6] Glazer (1991) argues that a policy may be politically unpopular if implemented immediately, but may attract support later if its implementation was expected, so that individuals adjust their behavior accordingly and would suffer losses were the policy not implemented. Political leaders may therefore announce an intention to implement a policy later, rather than pushing for its immediate adoption, thereby building a constituency for a policy change.

(1992), who applied it to inflation stabilization via exchange rate management, which required a sufficient stock of foreign exchange reserves. The level of reserves is subject to stochastic influences once a reform program is put in place, and too low a level of reserves will require program abandonment. Not surprisingly, the optimal decision on when to undertake a stabilization program is summarized by a reservation level of reserves; if reserves are below that level, waiting is optimal.[7]

This is an optimal stopping problem that may be represented as follows. Suppose the social cost to enacting the policy change at time t is simply ζ_t, where there is a new draw of ζ each period from a known distribution $F(\zeta)$. If the new policy is adopted at time t at a cost ζ_t, aggregate welfare is $\bar{u} - \zeta_t$ in every period thereafter; until it is adopted, aggregate welfare is u^{SQ} per period. Hence, in any period the policymaker's choice is to adopt the new policy or to wait, implying welfare u^{SQ} in the current period, and draw ζ_{t+1} next period. The solution is a reservation cost ζ^0, with the policymaker choosing to adopt the policy if $\zeta_t \leq \zeta^0$, and to wait if $\zeta_t > \zeta^0$.

The model thus yields the result that the adoption of new policies will take place when conditions are favorable, that is, when ζ_t is relatively low. There will be optimal delay of beneficial policy changes, in the sense that there can be periods when no reform will take place, even though the net benefit from the policy change $\bar{u} - u^{SQ}$ exceeds the current cost ζ_t, since $\zeta_t < \zeta^0$. However, there will be no *bias* towards delay, in the sense of waiting though times are good. This view of delay is sensible (it explains why delays may occur if policymakers believe bad times are transitory and conditions will improve), and it has some empirical relevance. It suggests, however, that difficult policy changes should be adopted mostly in good times. In fact, we often see the opposite: there is delay even though the economic situation is deteriorating and expected only to get worse, with difficult reforms adopted only in a time of crisis. This chapter suggests a number of models that yield this result.

This formalization could also be extended to include the other variant of optimal procrastination, namely, "benign neglect" in the expectation that things will get better by themselves. Suppose we extended the war of attrition model at the end of the previous chapter to include a probability that in each period the public good will be costlessly supplied by nature. This will increase the return to doing nothing. If this probability is high enough, continual delay may be the optimal solution.

---

[7] When programs are multistage, there is also a stopping rule whereby it is optimal to abandon a program already in place if reserves fall too sharply after a stabilization program has been started.

Irrationality

A final explanation for the failure to adopt necessary policy changes is simple (or not so simple) irrationality: societies, like individuals, put off making difficult choices, even though they know they must be faced and will only become more difficult with time. To what extent should we include irrationality as an important cause of the failure to change inferior policies? On the one hand, there seem to be economic phenomena for which irrationality may be the most compelling explanation and thus be empirically important. Especially in the study of reform, there are policy choices which are difficult to reconcile with rational behavior. For example, Krueger (1993b, p. 19), among others, argues that myopic deficit spending and exchange rate policies are widespread in developing economies. "Regardless of the form of government ... the political process typically demanded more resources than were available from tax revenues in the early stages of growth." The extremely adverse implications of such policies are well known to economists, but, Krueger argues, were largely unanticipated by the relevant groups themselves.

However, attributing economic phenomena to irrational behavior strikes at the whole basis of economic analysis. Instead, we want to take phenomena which appear to have no logical explanation and to present such an explanation.[8] Of course, some explanations are more successful than others. In some cases, we can show that seemingly irrational behavior is fully consistent with individual optimization, so that the phenomenon can be explained in a coherent framework. A goal of political economy analysis is to show how policies which seem suboptimal (hence, irrational in terms of basic welfare economics) can in fact be shown to be the result of the political mechanism under which the decisions of rational, self-interested agents are aggregated. In other cases, putting phenomena in a fully rational framework may be beyond our grasp, but economic analysis can limit the role played by irrational decisions.[9] The models presented in this chapter attempt to show how inefficient outcomes are the result of individually rational behavior, given their information and the political system under which they operate.

[8] Simon (1969) quotes the Dutch physicist Simon Stevin's epigram on illustrating the law of the inclined plane, "Wonderful, but not incomprehensible," as illustrating the task of natural science, to show that intriguing and complex aspects of experience can be comprehended without destroying what makes them intriguing.

[9] Akerlof (1991) presents an insightful discussion and modeling of procrastination. His arguments are also relevant to explaining inaction in terms of the perception of a need to act, that is, to the *salience* of a problem. We return to this issue in Section 10.8.

10.3. VESTED INTERESTS

In some ways, the easiest explanation for the nonadoption of a policy beneficial to the population as a whole is that policies are chosen by a minority whose interests are different and who would be hurt by the change. If we take this unequal distribution of power as given, there is no real puzzle to nonadoption: the policies chosen are in the best interests of those who choose. It seems obvious that when different groups have conflicting interests, some policy changes that are beneficial on average may nonetheless harm certain groups; if those groups hold the reins of power, nonadoption results. They have a vested interest in remaining with the status quo.

Theories of vested interests, however, often make a stronger claim. The argument is not simply that groups in power may sometimes be hurt by the adoption of socially beneficial policy changes, but that this possibility is likely to be a common outcome. That is, given economic and political dynamics, one should expect that, in general, politically powerful groups may try to block the adoption of socially beneficial changes because they have a vested interest in no change. Hence, this explanation of nonadoption is important not only because it seems empirically relevant to so many cases of delay or nonadoption of reforms, but also because its proponents suggest that it explains theoretically why this is the case.

Models of Stagnation

A dynamic view of the emergence of vested interests is probably most strongly associated with Olson's (1982) *The Rise and Decline of Nations*, in which he presents a theory of stagnation and decline as a consequence of previous economic success. Consider a country enjoying economic prosperity. Even if widespread, some groups may prosper more than others, which not only puts them in a position to increase their political influence, but gives them the incentive to do so in order to protect their gains. Hence, economic success creates powerful groups with vested interests who may naturally be against further policy changes which would be to their detriment.[10] That is, success creates groups who block further change. In Olson's terminology, societies have a tendency to become "sclerotic" and further policy change becomes especially difficult. Olson suggests that this effect can be seen in the success and subsequent decline of nations. Hence, the theory is not simply one of nonadoption of necessary policies,

---

[10] Not surprisingly, Olson relates part of this problem to problems of collective action in group behavior, as discussed in detail in Section 9.4 of Chapter 9. His argument may be seen as a logical continuation of the arguments first advanced in *The Logic of Collective Action*.

but a theory of longer-run economic dynamics. This is evidenced in part, he argues, by the decline of growth rates in mature societies.

Though the Olson "stagnation" hypothesis has been quite influential, there has been little formal modeling. Benhabib and Rustichini (1996) present a "common property" of appropriation in which optimal behavior depends on the value of a state variable and can change discretely. More specifically, appropriation strategies depend on the level of wealth in the economy. They show that one possibility in such a model of wealth-dependent appropriation and growth is that cooperative behavior will be observed when the economy is poor, as capital is too valuable to risk the retaliation that appropriation will trigger, but that as capital becomes more plentiful, fully cooperative behavior can no longer be sustained, and inefficiency will set in. They interpret this equilibrium as representing Olson's argument of stagnation arising in a mature economy due to pressure from organized interest groups. In the Benhabib and Rustichini model, the sclerosis that Olson argued characterizes many mature economies can be modeled by interest groups trying to appropriate resources to themselves. We consider common property models in Section 10.7 and present the Benhabib–Rustichini model in detail in Section 11.5 of Chapter 11.

Krusell and Rios-Rull (1996) present a formal model of vested interest groups and stagnation in the process of growth. In their model, growth is driven by the adoption of new technologies. With the passage of time, new superior production technologies can continually be created; the adoption of a new technology makes previous technologies obsolete. Investment in technology has a degree of irreversibility, so that once individuals have invested in a technology, they have a vested interest in blocking the emergence of a newer superior technology. They attempt to do this via the political process.

"Reform from Within"

Tornell (1998) presents a common property model where only powerful groups ("elites") have the power to appropriate common property. His model is crucially different from standard common property models in that this power can be removed only if some other elite takes costly actions to destroy its opponent's ability to appropriate common property (rather than a group simply ceasing to engage in appropriation). Hence, the key discrete change to behavior is to predatory behavior, meaning the taking of costly action to destroy an opponent's appropriative ability, analogous to the models of Grossman in Chapter 8. Given the assumption that the failure to act this way when one's opponent does implies a permanent disadvantage (a "follower" status), powerful groups take *preemptive* destructive actions.

Tornell's choice of model follows from his view of the reform process. Following the work of historians and sociologists of structural change, he argues that major structural change or reform is induced by vested interests or elites themselves rather than being imposed by forces external to the privileged elite, including severe crisis. He terms this "reform from within." However, he rejects the simple argument that in a reform from within, powerful elites abandon the status quo because they gain from reform. Some privileged groups are hurt: why do they block reform in good times, but not during crisis? He argues that reform is an outcome not wanted by the elites that occurs because one vested interest induces a change in the status quo to weaken other elites. The change is costly to this group, but it induces the change to neutralize the harmful effects of changes already induced by other groups, or to prevent these changes.

More specifically, consider an economy dominated by groups with the power to extract resources from the rest of the economy. Each group can induce a change in the status quo, but only at a short-run cost to itself, because it must divert some of its assets to nonproductive activities. The long-term benefit is that if other groups do not respond, the post-reform regime will be more favorable to this group than to the others. If the economy is booming, this diversion will be especially costly, perhaps more so than the future benefits, so that no group has incentives to unilaterally induce a change nor fears that other groups will do so. However, as the economy deteriorates, there is a fall in the opportunity cost of diverting productive factors to destroy the power of rival groups. There is an increased incentive to become the "leader" and capture a greater share of future resources. As a result, tacit cooperation among vested interests breaks down and preemptive reforms take place, with some or all groups ending up worse off.[11]

Politicians as a Vested Interest

As discussed at length in Chapter 7, opportunistic politicians whose primary motivation is to remain in office may adopt policies with the primary goal of getting re-elected (or otherwise retained in office) rather

---

[11] Formally, Tornell (1998) combines the common property model of Lane and Tornell (1996), discussed in Section 11.5 of the next chapter, with the possibility of preemptive destruction of one's rival, as in Grossman and Kim (1996a), discussed in Section 8.5 of Chapter 8. Each vested interest chooses an optimal date at which to take preemptive action (and hence initiate reform) if no other vested interest has previously done so. (This characteristic makes it similar to the war-of-attrition model, set out at the end of the previous chapter and applied to reform in Section 10.6 below.) In a Markov perfect equilibrium, interest groups choose Markov strategies, dependent on the state of the economy. (See Section 10.7 below for a formal exposition of these ideas.) Depending on parameter values, there can either be eventual reform, when the economy's wealth becomes low enough, or a no-reform equilibrium, in which the status quo prevails forever.

than with the goal of social welfare maximization. As such, they may be the most important vested interest blocking the adoption of socially beneficial reform. Since models of opportunistic politicians were analyzed in detail in Chapter 7, we simply mention this point here without much elaboration, even though it may be empirically quite important. In line with our focus in this chapter in showing how inefficient outcomes may be the result of individually rational behavior, models stressing how electoral manipulation may be consistent with voter rationality, given their information and political constraints, are especially relevant. For example, suppose the present discounted value of a policy change is positive, given the social discount rate, but the benefits accrue in the long run, while the costs are borne in the short run. An oft-heard argument is that the policy change is not adopted because politicians have high discount rates, reflecting their short horizons until the next election. One need then ask why voters re-elect policymakers who don't adopt socially beneficial reforms, with the models in Chapter 7 providing some answers. In Section 10.5 in the chapter, we consider the mirror image of this question in the case where policymaking is delegated: why might voters fail to support a socially optimal policy change proposed by a delegated agent because of suspicion of his motives?

10.4. Nonadoption Due to Uncertainty About Individual Benefits

Explanations of nonadoption due to vested interests are generally based on individuals or groups knowing whether they stand to gain or lose via the adoption of a policy change. For a policy that benefits the majority not to be adopted, the power to choose policy must be in the hands of a minority. However, a puzzle of nonadoption is that groups who end up benefiting from superior policies often do not support adoption of these policies. The conceptually simplest argument to explain nonadoption is that the public is unaware of or uncertain about their benefits. Models relying on uncertain benefits go further than simply saying that a potentially beneficial reform is not adopted because the expected value of the net benefits is negative. If this were the story, uncertainty about benefits would be another way of saying that the failure to adopt a reform stems from the general belief that the reform is expected *not* to be welfare improving relative to the status quo. This argument is a variant of the above argument that the failure to change policy is due to policymakers not knowing what policy will work better. To the extent that we are interested in explanations based on rational beliefs, nonadoption is fully rational and there is really little further to be explained.

Political explanations of the nonadoption of reform based on imperfect information about the benefits become interesting when it is *known* that the reforms are socially optimal, that is, when it is known that a majority would benefit from the reform. Two strands of literature have emerged, one based on uncertainty about individual benefits in a majority voting model, the other based on the combination of a distinction between the policymaker and the electorate and asymmetric information, so that the better-informed policymaker has private information about the social benefits of a policy change which is unavailable to the electorate, the ultimate decisionmakers. We consider the first strand in this section, the second in the next section.

Status-Quo Bias

In the approach stressing uncertainty about individual benefits, the central idea is that individuals or interest groups are uncertain about the benefits they will enjoy if a reform is adopted, and hence may oppose the policy change. Key papers include Fernandez and Rodrik (1991) and Rodrik (1993), where nonadoption of beneficial reforms in a static context, rather than delay over time, is the focus.

Fernandez and Rodrik (1991) is concerned with trade reform. In a two-sector model, a trade liberalization will lower real wages in one sector, but raise them in the other sector, with the size of the change being known. Workers in the first sector can move to the second sector, but at a cost. The key point is that the cost of moving is not fully known *ex ante*, so that the net benefit of higher wages is not known *ex ante*. More specifically, the cost of moving has two parts: there is a general investment cost that is known prior to switching sectors and an individual-specific cost, incurred on switching sectors and known only after the liberalization is in place and the general cost has been incurred. Individuals in the first sector know the distribution of individual-specific costs, but not the cost they will actually face if they decide to move. Individuals in the first sector support the liberalization only if they believe their net utility will rise as a result of its being adopted; individuals in the second sector unconditionally support the reform. Reforms are adopted by majority vote, so passage of a reform requires a majority of voters to expect a net benefit.

To better understand the role of uncertainty about individual economic benefits in general and the role of various components of the Fernandez–Rodrik model in particular, let us start with a very simple model of policy choice under uncertainty. Suppose that consumption ($\equiv$ income) of a representative individual in the absence of a policy change (the *status quo*) is a known quantity y^{SQ}, with associated known utility $u(y^{SQ})$. The outcome of the policy change is uncertain, as represented by post-reform consumption being a random variable $y^{SQ} - \zeta$, where ζ (which may be positive or negative) has a cumulative distribution $F(\zeta)$. The expected benefit of the policy change to the representative individual is $\int_\zeta u(y^{SQ} - \zeta)\,dF(\zeta)$. Adoption of the policy change corresponds to

$$\int_\zeta u(y^{SQ} - \zeta)\,dF(\zeta) \geq u(y^{SQ}), \qquad (10.1)$$

where we have assumed, without loss of generality, that equality implies adoption of the policy change.

The role of risk aversion in a model of individual uncertainty about outcomes can be easily seen from (10.1). If expected consumption is the same before and after the policy change, that is, if $E(\zeta) = 0$, then risk neutrality would imply adoption of the policy change (as (10.1) would hold with equality), while risk aversion would imply nonadoption (as the left-hand side of (10.1) would be strictly less than the right-hand side). Moreover, the greater the degree of risk aversion (the greater the curvature of $u(\cdot)$), the greater must be the excess of $E(y^{SQ} - \zeta)$ over y^{SQ} for the policy change to be adopted.

Note further that there is a nonconvexity introduced by majority voting. Small differences in the expected utility associated with adopting or not adopting the policy change are translated to 100% support or rejection of the change in a voting model under uncertainty with *ex-ante* identical individuals. This nonconvexity induced by a system of majority voting was partially responsible for sharp changes in the effects of income distribution on equilibrium outcomes in the model of labor mobility in Section 8.7 of Chapter 8. It will come up again in a number of examples in Part IV of the book.

In the model as it stands, though a majority voting system "magnifies" differences in the expected utility from policies into unanimous approval or disapproval, policies that benefit a majority are adopted, while those that hurt the majority are not. This simple representative-agent example will not, however, yield nonadoption of a policy change that is expected to be socially beneficial, that is, nonadoption when (10.1) holds. If all individuals are identical, a reform will be adopted under majority voting if it is expected to be beneficial and rejected if it yields expected utility below the utility associated with the status quo. This is why Fernandez and Rodrik add a second sector certain to benefit from reform.

The importance of having two sectors for the political equilibrium may be seen as follows. Suppose that all individuals in the first sector are described as in the above problem with $E(\zeta) = 0$, but where the inequality in (10.1) is reversed due to risk aversion. Then all individuals in the sector are against the policy change *ex ante*, even though it is known that some will benefit *ex post*. The addition of a second sector that favors the reform, due either to known benefits, as in Fernandez–Rodrik, or simply to positive expected benefits, means that there could be a situation in which a majority of voters in the economy as a whole oppose a policy change *ex ante* that benefits a majority *ex post*. The result is driven by *ex-ante* individual uncertainty, but must be combined with the impossibility of *ex-post* compensation of the losers (i.e., some economically feasible way of insuring against uncertainty) in order for the socially beneficial policy change not to be undertaken. This is the essence of the Fernandez–Rodrik result.

The specific modeling in the Fernandez–Rodrik model of uncertainty in sector 1 is different, based on uncertainty about adjusting to trade reform, but it can be represented more generally. Continuing with the above example, suppose that in the absence of a policy change, known consumption is y^{SQ} for all individuals. If a policy change is enacted, individuals in the second sector consume $y^H > y^{SQ}$. Individuals in the first sector can move to the second sector but only at a cost ζ, so that their net income would be $y^H - \zeta$, where ζ is learned only after the policy change has been adopted. *Ex ante*, it is known only that ζ is drawn from a cumulative distribution $F(\zeta)$, defined over $[\underline{\zeta}, \bar{\zeta}]$. If an individual chooses not to switch sectors after learning ζ, he receives $y^L < y^{SQ}$. An individual in sector 1 thus has a two-stage political-economic decision: first, whether or not to support adoption of the policy change; and, second, if the policy change is enacted, whether or not to switch sectors.[12]

The solution to this two-stage problem faced by sector-1 individuals is not difficult. In the second stage, after the policy change has been adopted and an individual has learned his private cost ζ, he will switch sectors if $\zeta \leq y^H - y^L$. In the first stage, the individual will support the policy change as long as the expected utility from adoption is at least as great as $u(y^{SQ})$. Using the second-stage result, an individual is in favor of enacting the change in policy if

$$\int_{\zeta=\underline{\zeta}}^{y^H-y^L} u(y^H - \zeta) \, dF(\zeta) + \int_{y^H-y^L}^{\zeta=\bar{\zeta}} u(y^L) \, dF(\zeta) \geq u(y^{SQ}). \quad (10.2)$$

The left-hand side is the expected benefit from adopting the policy change, the right-hand side, the benefit from remaining with the status quo, which may be thought of as the opportunity cost of adoption.

Equation (10.2) highlights a number of points about the failure to adopt a policy change due to individual uncertainty about its potential net benefits. Consider individuals in sector 1, all drawing from the same distribution $F(\zeta)$ and thus facing the same choice problem *ex ante*, who

---

[12] This problem can be represented as the purchase of a private good with a two-part cost, as in Drazen (1996), where the individual is uncertain about the second part of the cost when making the decision of whether or not to pay the first part.

will draw different values of ζ in the second stage.[13] If the gainers clearly benefit, but the losers end up no better off than the status quo, uncertainty about who will be a gainer is crucial. If the losers are actually worse off under the new policy, very large gains to the winners may not be enough to offset the effects of this uncertainty. Though we have a representative individual *ex ante* in sector 1, as all draw from the same distribution, individuals are different *ex post*, once they have discovered their private cost ζ.

To summarize, there are two crucial types of heterogeneity in the uncertainty-about-individual-benefits model, both crucial to the possibility of nonadoption of a socially beneficial reform. These are the two types of heterogeneity, or conflict of interests, stressed in Chapter 1 as key to political economy. There is *ex-ante* heterogeneity between individuals in sector 1 and those in sector 2 in terms of their *ex-ante* expected benefit from reform. This yields a conflict of interests between individuals in the two sectors as to whether to support adoption (when the inequality in (10.1) is reversed). As we saw, this heterogeneity is necessary for the result of nonadoption of a socially beneficial reform. There is also *ex-post* heterogeneity in sector 1, as the reform affects individuals in that sector differentially, even though they are identical *ex ante*. This heterogeneity is crucial to the result that individuals who benefit from reform *ex post* may rationally oppose it *ex ante*. It also explains why reforms that are initially unpopular (here meaning unable to garner majority support) may be sustained rather than reversed once they are adopted.

Impossibility of *ex-post* compensation from gainers to losers is also crucial to the result of failing to adopt a policy that benefits more than half of the population. (The impossibility of compensating losers *ex post* is also central to the static public goods game and the war-of-attrition model in the previous chapter.) It is, of course, technically true that the nature of the solution would change radically if we allowed such *ex-post* compensation. However, the argument that these results are therefore not robust misses the whole point, which is to study how private uncertainty about benefits can lead to nonadoption in the presence of *ex-post* heterogeneity. Empirically, one should simply note the general absence of institutions which mandate *ex-post* compensation which is sufficient to imply that a distributional conflict is absent.

The difference between support for a policy change before and after individual uncertainty has been resolved leads to what Fernandez and Rodrik term **status quo bias**, a result they stress. It may be easily explained. We have so far stressed the result that a reform that benefits a majority *ex post* may not be adopted. Conversely, using the above model,

---

[13] It is assumed here that individuals *view* themselves as identical *ex ante*, that is, they have no prior knowledge about the likelihood that they will be among those who gain from the change.

one can easily show that a policy change that ends up hurting a majority of the population *ex post* may be adopted, if enough people believe *ex ante* that they will benefit. However, once uncertainty is resolved, the majority will see that they are hurt and vote to reverse the reform. These two possibilities taken together imply a "bias" towards the status quo. Policy changes that have been adopted can be reversed (perhaps at a cost) once individuals gain information about the actual benefits; however, reforms that are not adopted even though they would benefit the majority *ex post* will never be adopted in the Fernandez–Rodrik world, since this information cannot be discovered.

The status quo bias in the Fernandez and Rodrik model cuts two ways in terms of explaining policy nonadoption and policy delay. It gives a convincing argument as to why socially beneficial policies are not adopted. However, to the extent that it explains nonadoption, the model *per se* cannot explain delay. Socially beneficial policy changes not enacted at a given date will not be enacted later, since this information that they are socially beneficial cannot be discovered. Hence, the uncertainty which generates a bias towards the status quo means that the model will not generate a delay in adopting a socially optimal policy. One needs an explanation of two observations: why socially beneficial policy is *not* adopted today; and why it *is* adopted at a later date.

Deteriorating Conditions

Labán and Sturzenegger [(1994a), see also (1994b)] have applied a dynamic version of the Fernandez–Rodrik model to the case of inflation stabilization. Thus, they address precisely the question addressed by Alesina and Drazen (1991) discussed in Section 10.6 below, namely, why do countries delay the fiscal adjustment they realize is necessary for reducing very high inflation; their answer, however, is different. Labán and Sturzenegger consider an economy with two groups, rich and poor. The groups live in an inflationary environment, reflecting the use of seigniorage to finance government expenditures in the absence of an agreement on allocating the burden of nondistortionary taxation. As in Fernandez and Rodrik (and in contrast to Alesina and Drazen), there is uncertainty about the net benefits of stabilization.

The dynamics in the two-period, discrete-time model come from the ability of the rich in the first period to invest in a "financial technology" which partially shields them from costly inflation (for example, converting domestic currency assets into assets denominated in foreign currency), which is unavailable to the poor. "Dollarizing" assets reduces the domestic monetary base and increases inflation in the second period. Hence, the failure to reach agreement on a fiscal retrenchment in the first period leads to an endogenous deterioration in the economy (as the rich increase their utilization of the financial technology), so that the poor face even higher costs from inflation in the second period. Labán and Sturzenegger demonstrate that this model driven by uncertainty about the post-stabilization environment can generate delay, with the poor agreeing to unfavorable terms in the second period which are worse than those they rejected in the first period. What is especially intriguing in their result is that the poor reject an agreement in the first period *even though they know* that they will suffer an extra period of inflation and then stabilize on even worse terms.

To see how this may come about, let us consider a two-period version of the Fernandez and Rodrik problem in the previous subsection in which the costs and benefits of changing policy change over time. That is, consider individuals in sector 1 whose choice problem is as in the discussion surrounding (10.2), but where the utility of both reform and the status quo are falling over time. Letting the subscripts 1 and 2 represent the two periods, suppose that $y_2^H < y_1^H$ and that $y_2^L < y_1^L$, so that delaying reform leads to lower expected benefits. Suppose also that $y_2^{SQ} \ll y_1^{SQ}$, representing an extreme deterioration of the welfare associated with not reforming between periods 1 and 2. (For simplicity of exposition, we assume that the distribution $F(\zeta)$ does not change over time. This possibility would not affect the qualitative results.) If this deterioration is large enough (that is, if $u(y_2^{SQ})$ is very much smaller than $u(y_1^{SQ})$), then it may be optimal to enact a reform only with delay, even though the expected benefit from reform is falling as well.

To see this, let us consider a number of options. For adoption in the second period to dominate never adopting the policy change (both options yield utility $u(y_1^{SQ})$ in the first period), one requires

$$E\Omega_2^{REF} \equiv \int_{\zeta=\underline{\zeta}}^{y_2^H - y_2^L} u(y_2^H - \zeta)\,dF(\zeta) + \int_{y_2^H - y_2^L}^{\zeta=\bar{\zeta}} u(y_2^L)\,dF(\zeta) \tag{10.3}$$

$$> u(y_2^{SQ}).$$

This will hold for $u(y_2^{SQ})$ sufficiently small. (Assuming that reversal of reform can occur only with a lag of one period and that the status quo only deteriorates over time, this condition also ensures that the reform will not be reversed if adopted in the second period.) Now consider the choice between adopting in period 1 versus delaying and adopting in period 2. For delay to dominate immediate adoption, one requires (using the definition of $E\Omega_t^{REF}$ in (10.3)) that[14]

$$E\Omega_1^{REF} + \beta E\Omega_1^{REF} < u(y_1^{SQ}) + \beta E\Omega_2^{REF}. \tag{10.4}$$

[14] The assumption that reversal can occur only with a one-period lag combined with (10.3) implies that a reform adopted in period 1 will not be reversed in period 2.

Combining (10.3) and (10.4), one finds that for delayed adoption to dominate both adopting the reform immediately and never adopting the reform, one requires

$$u(y_1^{SQ}) - \mathrm{E}\Omega_1^{REF} > \beta(\mathrm{E}\Omega_1^{REF} - \mathrm{E}\Omega_2^{REF}) > 0 > \beta\big(u(y_2^{SQ}) - \mathrm{E}\Omega_2^{REF}\big).$$
$$(10.5)$$

One may easily find parameter values for the y_t^H, y_t^L, y_t^{SQ}, a utility function $u(\cdot)$, and a distribution $\mathrm{F}(\zeta)$ such that all the inequalities in (10.5) hold. In this case, postponement is optimal, even though it is known that it implies that reform will be undertaken on less favorable terms.

Understanding the technical conditions such that (10.5) holds will help to understand the conceptual basis of the Labán–Sturzenegger result. The second inequality in (10.5) follows from the assumption that the expected benefit from reform is falling over time; a sufficient condition for the third inequality, as argued above, is that $u(y_2^{SQ})$ is small relative to the expected benefit from the reform. Though the first inequality will hold for a small enough value of the discount factor β, the Labán–Sturzenegger argument does not depend on heavy discounting of the future. Hence, one wants to find conditions for the first inequality to hold independent of the value of the discount factor (and to be consistent with the third inequality). This will depend on both the value of $u(y_t^{SQ})$ and on the uncertainty associated with reform. $\mathrm{E}\Omega_1^{REF}\ (\equiv \int u(y_1^H - \zeta)\,d\mathrm{F}(\zeta) + \int u(y_2^L)\,d\mathrm{F}(\zeta))$ will be less than $u(y_1^{SQ})$ even for y_1^H large relative to y_1^{SQ} if the distribution of costs $\mathrm{F}(\zeta)$ is disperse or utility is very concave. (Remember the discussion in the paragraph following (10.1).) Given the dispersion of $\mathrm{F}(\zeta)$ and the degree of risk aversion, one can simultaneously have $\mathrm{E}\Omega_1^{REF} < u(y_1^{SQ})$ and $\mathrm{E}\Omega_2^{REF} > u(y_2^{SQ})$ if $y_2^{SQ} \ll y_1^{SQ}$, that is, for large enough deterioration of the pre-reform environment.

To summarize, the Labán–Sturzenegger model depends on two general features: sufficiently large uncertainty about the post-reform environment to make it worthwhile to put up with the status quo temporarily; and, sufficiently large deterioration in the status quo to make adoption of a reform eventually optimal. An analogy would be to the need for a patient whose health is poor and getting worse to undergo a very risky operation. Though his chances of surviving the operation may decrease the longer he waits and though he may know he eventually has no choice, he may prefer to remain in the certain state of poor health and put off taking the chance of an unsuccessful operation as long as possible.

Technically, the driving force in the model of multiperiod uncertainty with deterioration is basically the same as in the model of optimal waiting discussed in Section 10.2 above. The difference is that one looks not at the benefit from agreeing to reform net of its cost, but at the net benefit relative to that of *no* reform. In the optimal waiting model, the utility associated with the status quo is constant over time and reform occurs when the cost of reform is low. In contrast, in the Labán and Sturzenegger model, the key driving force is the deterioration of the status quo. Though the cost of reform is rising over time, the utility associated with the status quo is falling even faster. Therefore, even though reform occurs when the cost is high relative to the benefit (addressing our criticism of the optimal waiting model), it could be better characterized as occurring when the net benefit of reform *relative* to the status quo is high.[15]

Though the basic argument as to why a socially beneficial reform is delayed is the same in a technical sense, the underlying economics are quite different. One model has reform occurring at good times, the other at bad times. Moreover, the deterioration is endogenous, rather than reflecting exogenous factors: in Labán–Sturzenegger, endogenous deterioration captures the financial adaptation to inflation often seen in high inflation countries. (This aspect was absent in the simple example set out above; it could be formally represented by the sharp fall in y_2^{SQ} relative to y_1^{SQ} resulting from actions taken in the first period by individuals certain to benefit from a reform.) This adaptation is beneficial for the individual, but there is a negative externality in that it further drives up inflation, which is costly to society.[16]

Viewed generally, models stressing individual uncertainty capture a key aspect of the failure to adopt large reform programs. The large risk associated with a significant reform leads to a desire to postpone adoption, even though it is generally conceded that things will only get more difficult with the passage of time. The role of very large uncertainty associated with significant reforms is a major theme of Chapter 13, where we consider how reform programs may be structured to overcome the political constraints implied by such uncertainty.

---

[15] The structure of both models also implies that reform occurs when it is socially optimal, in the sense of maximizing expected welfare. Hence, the Labán–Sturzenegger model is more like the optimal waiting problem than the Fernandez–Rodrik·model *per se*, since, as was noted above, the results of the Fernandez–Rodrik model depended on the existence of another type of agent who benefits from reform with certainty. Adding such agents to the Labán–Sturzenegger model would make it strictly analogous to Fernandez–Rodrik; specifically, a reform that is expected to benefit more than half of the population could be rejected by majority vote.

[16] Mondino, Sturzenegger, and Tommasi (1996) present a model where dynamic financial adaptation combined with noncooperative behavior in demanding subsidies (which are covered by inflationary finance) lead to recurrent cycles in inflation acceleration followed by stabilization. Zarazaga (1993) suggests that the pattern of alternating between low chronic inflation and short bursts of very high inflation ("megainflation") arises because the latter are necessary to discipline appropriative groups to keep their inflationary demands from getting too high, much like the explanation for "price wars" as a disciplining device in the industrial organization literature. A crucial ingredient of this sort of story is imperfect monitoring.

10.5. "COMMUNICATION" FAILURES

Another type of model based on imperfect information takes a very different approach, namely, a problem of *communicating* the socially beneficial nature of the policy change. Models of this type are based on crucial *institutional* details of the policymaking process, whereby policymaking may be delegated, as in representative democracies, as well as being shared between different policymakers. Delegation or division of authority introduces another facet of imperfect information about the optimality of different policies, namely, the possibility that agents are *differentially* informed. Models of this type have two key features. First, there is a distinction between the *proposer* of policies and the ultimate *chooser* of policies. This distinction may be between a policymaker as the proposer and the electorate as the ultimate chooser of policy, or between two different branches of government, for example, a legislature as the proposer, with the executive having veto power. In short, there is a principal–agent problem, where the exact details reflect the specification of the political mechanism. Second, there is asymmetric information between proposer and chooser, with the proposer being limited in his ability to convey the optimality of a given policy to the chooser.

Though there are many possibilities in modeling the role of asymmetric information, two cases seem especially relevant. The most obvious specification of asymmetric information in this type of model is one where the better-informed policymaker has private information about the social benefits of a policy change which is unavailable to the electorate, the ultimate decisionmakers. Under this specification, the failure to adopt a reform reflects the inability of the policymaker to communicate this information credibly to the voters. A second leading case is one where the proposer and the chooser have different policy preferences, with severe limitations both on the amount of information that can be communicated and on the "give-and-take" of formulating policies. More specifically, suppose it is the chooser's, rather than the proposer's, preferences that are unknown, where the proposer is an agenda setter. Alternative, less obvious specifications of informational asymmetries may also give rise to nonadoption of socially beneficial changes. In all cases, the inability of one agent to communicate information credibly to the other agent is key to the result.

Models of this type, which we term *"communication failure"* models, follow work in the political science literature. There is relatively little work on this approach in economics (though the asymmetric information and delegation problems on which they are based are widely studied). In fact, there is probably not even a consensus that this is a main approach to nonadoption of reform. Nor is there any unified treatment, at least that I am aware of. Nonetheless, I believe that work in this area is especially important, as it may allow us to formalize a number of hypotheses about the role of effective communication in successful reform, including issues such as the importance of "visionary leaders" or effective "use of the media." Interesting as these more conceptual issues are, I will concentrate on more formal models, a concentration dictated largely by comparative advantage.

Cheap Talk and Agenda Setting

"Cheap talk" refers to the use of signals that do not directly affect payoffs. That is, in our context, we may think of announcements that are costless to make. If an announcement can be made costlessly, one would think that it would contain no information. This has an obvious application to the problem of the failure to adopt a socially beneficial policy change, as it reflects the great difficulty that a policymaker may have in communicating the policy's value to the electorate. A policymaker who has no concern about social welfare may find it to his private benefit to announce that a given policy change is socially optimal, for example, if he is running for re-election. If announcements are costless, it may therefore be difficult for a policymaker who is concerned about social welfare to make credible an announcement that a policy really is socially beneficial. In the language of Chapter 6 on credibility and reputation, if talk is cheap, it would appear that an opportunistic policymaker can mimic a social welfare-maximizing one, so that there is a pooling equilibrium where the social value of policy cannot be communicated simply by announcement.

As discussed in Section 6.9 of Chapter 6 where we first introduced models of "cheap talk," Crawford and Sobel (1982) demonstrated the possibility of equilibria in which cheap talk can convey information. Consider a case in which the sender of a cheap talk message has preferences over the receiver's beliefs about the sender's type. For example, suppose the receiver's actions depend on what he believes about the sender's "type," where type cannot be observed directly, and the receiver's actions affect the sender's utility. When the sender's and receiver's interests are not aligned, the sender's incentive to lie is too great, and cheap talk will be meaningless. (For example, suppose the electorate as receiver of messages want to elect the most competent candidate, while the sender, an incumbent up for re-election, cares only about staying in office and not at all about social welfare. Campaign promises will then be "meaningless cheap talk" in both the technical and the everyday sense, as was discussed in Section 7.6 of Chapter 7.) When, however, their interests are correlated, there may be a cheap talk equilibrium that conveys information, with the amount of information conveyed being greater the more the interests of sender and receiver are correlated. Even with some incentive to lie, cheap talk may convey information, as long as the incentive to lie is not too great (that is, there is a correlation of interests) and the sender is constrained to send imprecise messages.

We considered this type of "cheap talk" model applied to monetary policy in Section 6.9 of Chapter 6. Stein (1989) demonstrates that if the monetary authority is constrained to make imprecise announcements, policy announcements can be informative. In his model, imprecise announcements convey more information than precise announcements because of their discreteness. Stein considers a case in which a policymaker has the incentive to try to manipulate inflation expectations, that is, to induce the public to expect an inflation rate that is below the rate that will actually obtain. The problem with precise announcements is that they are continuous rather than discrete. With continuous announcements, the policymaker always has the incentive to (at least) marginally reduce his announced target, that is, to "shade" his announcement downward. Since the public is aware of this incentive, they are skeptical about inflation announcements. However, when announcements must be for discrete ranges, policymakers who lie about their intentions must lie by a discrete amount. The impossibility of "marginal lying" means that truthtelling may be preferred to lying, since a large lie may reduce welfare relative to telling the truth (though would be dominated by a small lie).

Austen-Smith (1990, 1993) has considered applications of cheap talk to political debate where a proposer of a policy must persuade potential choosers of the importance or validity of his position. Failure to do so may mean that an optimal policy is not adopted. The amount of information a speaker can communicate in his models depends on the similarity of preferences of the speaker and his listeners. Lupia (1992) applies this type of model to agenda setting under imperfect information. The combination of monopoly agenda control and voter uncertainty forces voters who choose legislation directly into having to choose between the status quo and the agenda setter's most preferred policy.[17] Under these conditions, neither alternative need be closely related to the median voter's preferences. The policy that is the electoral winner between these two choices may not be the alternative that an informed electorate would have chosen.

Matthews (1989) considers exactly this sort of possibility in a model of veto threats when the proposer of a policy does not know the preferences of the agent who will choose the policy. He considers the following three-stage game. In stage 1, the policy chooser (call him C) sends a costless message. In stage 2, the policy proposer (call him P) proposes a policy outcome, where we suppose that policies can be represented along a single dimension. In stage 3, the chooser C either accepts or rejects (vetoes) P's proposal. If he rejects the proposed policy, the status quo π^{SQ} stays in force. The preferences of the proposer are represented by a utility

---

[17] As discussed in Chapter 3, Romer and Rosenthal (1978, 1979) similarly show that in referenda, control of initial proposals may significantly affect final outcomes. Voters choose between an agenda setter's proposal and some "reversion level." The lower the reversion level, the more the agenda setter can extract from the voters.

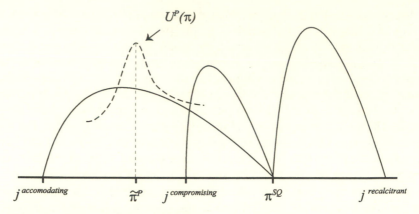

FIGURE 10.1. Types of policy choosers.

function u^P over outcomes, which is single peaked with a most preferred policy $\tilde{\pi}^P$. Assume, for simplicity, that $\tilde{\pi}^P < \pi^{SQ}$. The proposer P does not know the chooser C's utility function, which depends on his unobserved type j. The utility function u^j of type j is single peaked with a most preferred policy $\tilde{\pi}^j$, where we assume $\tilde{\pi}^j$ is increasing in j. A "single crossing of utility curves" property is also assumed.[18] Under these assumptions, there exists a policy $\check{\pi}^j$ such that C is indifferent between $\check{\pi}^j$ and π^{SQ}, where $\check{\pi}^j$ is strictly increasing in j. We may then transform the type variable, so that $\check{\pi}^j = j$.

This characterization of C's preferences allows a simple classification of possible types of policy choosers. The single-peaked property of utility functions implies that type j prefers outcomes located between j and π^{SQ} to the status quo π^{SQ}. Types for whom $j < \tilde{\pi}^P$ prefer P's most preferred outcome $\tilde{\pi}^P$ to the status quo π^{SQ}. Matthews calls these types *accommodating*. Types for whom $j > \pi^{SQ}$ prefer the status quo to any outcome that P prefers to the status quo. Matthews terms these types *recalcitrant*. Finally, types for whom j lies between $\tilde{\pi}^P$ and π^{SQ} will find themselves in agreement with P that outcomes in the interval (j, π^{SQ}) are preferred to π^{SQ}. These types are called *compromising*. The possibilities are illustrated in Figure 10.1, based on the analogous diagram in Matthews, showing the utility of policies relative to the status quo. Assume that the distribution of types is such that there is a positive probability that the chooser C is compromising.

In the first stage, C can send one of a finite set of messages. The first-stage strategy of a chooser of type j is then a *rhetoric rule* that

---

[18] The single crossing property is that if a proposer of type j is indifferent between π^1 and $\pi^2 > \pi^1$, then higher types prefer π^2 and lower types prefer π^1. That is, for all π^1, π^2, j and j', if $\pi^1 < \pi^2$ and $u^j(\pi^1) = u^j(\pi^2)$, then $(j' - j)(u^{j'}(\pi^2) - u^{j'}(\pi^1)) > 0$.

specifies for each possible message a probability of its being sent by j. In the second stage, P's strategy is a *proposal rule*, mapping messages received into policies proposed. (Remember that P does not observe C's type.) In the third stage, C has an *acceptance rule*, assigning the outcome "accept" or "veto" to proposed policies.

This three-stage game has many equilibria, some of which Matthews points out are not very plausible. Some are rejected because they are not subgame perfect, such as an equilibrium in which C announces his true type j and promises to veto any proposal other than $\tilde{\pi}^j$, which P proposes as long as he prefers it to π^{SQ} (and proposes π^{SQ} otherwise). Matthews further narrows down the set of possible equilibria by using the equilibrium refinement corresponding to Selten's (1975) "trembling-hand perfection." Within this set, he shows that only two kinds of equilibria exist. In the first kind, P always makes the same proposal independent of the message that C sent in stage 1. It is a compromise proposal between $\tilde{\pi}^P$ and π^{SQ}, which, in general, has a positive probability of being accepted and of being rejected. In this type of equilibrium, cheap talk plays no role and a policy that would be preferred *ex post* to the status quo by both P and C may be rejected in favor of the status quo. That is, an optimal policy may be rejected.

In the second kind of equilibrium, C may send one of two messages, an "accommodating" message, conveying the information that he will accept P's preferred policy, or a "threatening" message, indicating he will veto any proposal too far below his own preferred policy. P responds to an accommodating message by proposing his preferred policy $\tilde{\pi}^P$, which is accepted. In response to a threatening message, P proposes a compromise policy as in the first type of equilibrium, which is accepted by some types of choosers and rejected by other types. Matthews's interest is in when veto rhetoric can be meaningful and when proposals will actually be vetoed. (He gives structure to the model by considering the President as the chooser and Congress as the proposer.) Hence, a key result is that only compromise proposals are ever vetoed.

Nonadoption When Policymakers Have Superior Information

The basic idea here is that when there is delegation of decisions to policymakers and they are better informed than the electorate, policymakers must convince the electorate of the benefits of policy change for the change to be adopted. Hence, informational asymmetries between policymakers and the electorate become crucial. A policy change that is optimal may not be adopted because the policymaker cannot credibly demonstrate this fact to the electorate.

This idea is explored by Cukierman and Tommasi (1998a, 1998b), in models in which policymakers in office have superior information about the state of the world, and hence about socially optimal policies, than does the public. However, because of the government's partisan preferences, the public cannot be certain whether a given policy is motivated by concern over social welfare or by the government's desire to implement its own partisan preferences. Hence, uncertainty about the policymaker's motivations makes it impossible to fully communicate the superiority of certain policies. Among other things, this will have implications for the likelihood of their adoption as a function of the partisan bent of the government that proposes the policy. If a left-wing party proposes a right-wing policy, voters assign higher probability to the possibility that the policy represents the social optimum as a function of the unobserved state of the world than if a right-wing party would propose the same policy.

Cukierman and Tommasi (1998a) present a voting model, in which voters elect either an incumbent, who is committed to carry out his announced policy, or a challenger, the winner of the election choosing a policy. Policymakers are motivated by the desire to hold office, in addition to both social welfare and partisan considerations. Voters are uncertain both about the optimal policy (the "state of the world") and about the incumbent's preferences, using the incumbent's policy announcement to form an expectation of the optimal policy and, on the basis of the incumbent's announced policy and their expectation of the optimum, to choose between incumbent and challenger.[19]

Cukierman and Tommasi (1998b) consider a simpler model in which the public votes directly on the policy on the basis of a policymaker's announcement, and we will exposit this model. The economy is composed of voters and a left-wing (L) and a right-wing (R) policymaker with preferences over a single policy issue and whose utility from a policy depends on the distance of that policy from their preferred position. Specifically, the utility of a type j is given by

$$\Omega^j = -| z - (\tilde{\pi}^j + \gamma)|, \tag{10.6}$$

where z is the implemented policy, $\tilde{\pi}^i$ is the agent's most preferred policy position, and γ is a random variable meant to capture a unidirectional shift in the preferred position of *all* voters and parties, due to a change in external circumstances, that is, in the "state of the world." Following Cukierman and Tommasi, we assume, without loss of generality, that $\tilde{\pi}^L = -\kappa$, $\tilde{\pi}^R = \kappa$, and that the preferred position of the median voter $\tilde{\pi}^{\text{med}} = 0$.

The sequencing of events is as follows. Suppose that the incumbent policymaker is left-wing. He, but not the public, observes γ, after which he

---

[19] In Cukierman and Tommasi (1998a), the incumbent observes a shock to preferences and to the state of the world and chooses optimal policy as a *linear* function of the shocks. Drazen and Hubrich (1999) suggest that the optimal solution must be a nonlinear function of the shocks.

chooses between remaining with the status quo (normalized to 0) or proposing a change in policy. He has a choice of only two new policies, namely, $\pi^L \in \{-\pi, \pi\}$ for $\pi > 0$, with $-\pi$ interpreted as a left-of-center policy, π as a right-of-center policy. After π^L is proposed, voters either vote against the policy ($v = 0$) or in favor ($v = 1$). With the normalization of the status quo policy, the implemented policy is simply $z = v\pi^L$. Equation (10.6) implies that voters have single-peaked preferences, so that the outcome is decided by the median voter.

The prior distribution of γ is given by

$$\gamma = \begin{cases} -a & \text{with probability } p, \\ 0 & \text{with probability } 1 - 2p, \\ a & \text{with probability } p, \end{cases} \tag{10.7}$$

where $a > 0$. If, for example, $\gamma = a$, right-of-center policies become more desirable for everyone.

The following three assumptions are made about the parameters to yield the result that a right-of-center policy can be implemented only by a left-wing party:

$$\begin{array}{ll} \text{(a)} & a > \kappa + \pi/2, \\ \text{(b)} & \kappa > \pi/2, \\ \text{(c)} & p < 1/3. \end{array} \tag{10.8}$$

These assumptions may be explained as follows. Assumption (10.8a) implies that the state-of-the world shock is large enough to overcome the left-wing policymaker's partisan preference. Assumption (10.8b) implies that partisan preferences are sufficiently dispersed that each party chooses its preferred policy when $\gamma = 0$. Assumption (10.8c) means there is relatively low probability of state-of-the-world shocks that would lead a party to propose a policy against its partisan preferences. Assumptions (10.8b) and (10.8c) together are the source of a party's credibility problem in convincing voters that its ideologically most preferred policy is in fact a social optimum. Since the left-wing party chooses $-\pi$ when the status quo is socially optimal and since the probability of $\gamma = -a$ is small enough, the left-wing party chooses policies that are purely ideologically motivated often enough that the median voter will vote against $-\pi$ when it is proposed by a left-wing party but accept it when it is proposed by a right-wing party. (If the probability of $-a$ were sufficiently large, it might be optimal for the median voter to accept it, no matter which party proposed it.)

To formalize these ideas, Cukierman and Tommasi consider a set of strategies and beliefs which constitute a Perfect Bayesian Equilibrium (PBE) for the parameter values in (10.8). The strategies are given by s^L:

$\{-a, 0, a\} \to \{-\pi, -\pi, \pi\}$ for the left-wing party, mapping state-of-the-world shocks into policy proposals, and $s^{\text{med}}: \{-\pi, \pi\} \to \{0, 1\}$ for the median voter, mapping policy proposals into adoption or nonadoption. The beliefs of the voters on the posterior probabilities of a particular state of the world after observing a left-wing policy proposal are denoted $\Pr(\gamma \mid \pi^L)$. In a PBE: the strategy of the left-wing party must be optimal, given the voter's strategies and beliefs; the voter's strategy must be optimal, given his beliefs and the party's strategies; and beliefs are derived from Bayesian updating wherever possible. The strategies given above can be supported as a PBE by the following set of beliefs:

$$\Pr(-a \mid -\pi) = p/(1-p), \qquad \Pr(-a \mid \pi) = 0,$$

$$\Pr(0 \mid -\pi) = (1-2p)/(1-p), \qquad \Pr(0 \mid \pi) = 0, \qquad (10.9)$$

$$\Pr(a \mid -\pi) = 0, \qquad \Pr(a \mid \pi) = 1.$$

We leave to the reader to prove that the strategies given above and the posterior beliefs given in (10.9) indeed constitute a PBE. An analogous PBE can be derived for the case of a right-wing incumbent, which the reader can easily convince himself is the mirror image of (10.9).

Credibility of Policy Proposals and the Implementation of Extreme Policies

One especially interesting result of this model (which in fact is the focus of the Cukierman and Tommasi paper) is that it formalizes the observation that substantial policy changes in a given direction may be most likely to be implemented by parties which *ex ante* would appear to be the most opposed to these policies ideologically. That is, very left-wing policies are more likely to be implemented by a right-wing incumbent and very right-wing policies are more likely to be implemented by a left-wing incumbent. As the title of Cukierman and Tommasi (1998a) puts it, "When Does it Take Nixon to Go to China?", referring to the fact that it was Richard Nixon, a president with staunch anti-communist credentials, who established diplomatic relations with the People's Republic of China, a policy that had long been anathema to the right-of-center politicians in the United States.[20]

This result may be seen immediately from considering the equilibrium strategies supported by the beliefs in (10.9) and the analogous equilibrium for the case of a right-wing incumbent. Because the electorate thinks a left-of-center policy is ideologically motivated if proposed by a left-wing

---

[20] A seemingly related issue is whether authoritarian governments are more likely to carry out successful reforms. We discuss this issue both in Chapter 11, where we discuss the susceptibility of types of governments to pressure groups, and in Chapter 13, where we return to the role of agenda setting to overcome political constraints in the successful design of multipart reform and transition programs.

party, it will be voted down, while the same left-of-center policy would be seen as unquestionably motivated by concern for social welfare if it were proposed by a right-wing party and accepted. Analogously, the right-of-center policy π will be accepted by voters only if proposed by a left-wing party.

This same result can be framed in terms of the nonadoption of optimal policy changes that is the focus of this chapter. A left-of-center policy that is socially optimal because of a realization of $-a$ will not be adopted if proposed by a left-wing policymaker, and similarly for a socially optimal right-of-center policy proposed by a right-winger. Policymakers cannot always credibly communicate their superior information about the state of the world to the public because of their perceived partisan bias, so socially optimal policies will not always be adopted. This partisan bias means they simply cannot make it credible that a proposed policy is in the social interest.

Put more generally, an ideologically extreme policy is more "credible" if it is proposed by someone on the other side of the political spectrum, where Cukierman and Tommasi define the credibility of a policy as the probability that the policy is proposed because it is socially optimal. Though not a standard definition of credibility, it is the natural one in this model, since the central question is whether a policy is undertaken for the social good, as opposed to partisan reasons. This definition of credibility applies to policymakers as well as policies. A left-wing policymaker, for example, has higher credibility when he proposes a large policy shift to the right than when he proposes a large policy shift to the left. Hence, one should think of the credibility of a policy–policymaker pair, that is, the credibility of a policy conditional on the policymaker's type. It is useful to contrast the results on credibility in this model with those in the model of Drazen and Masson (1994) considered in Section 6.8 of Chapter 6. In the Drazen–Masson paper, credibility is the likelihood that an announced policy will be carried out, where there is no precommitment to policy announcements.[21] Uncertainty about what policy will be carried out reflects both uncertainty about the policymaker's type and the possibility of a shock *after* policy is announced, leading to a change in the *ex-post* preferred policy. The notions of credibility are different in the two papers (each appropriate to the specific question studied), though in each paper, credibility does depend on the policymaker–policy pair. In Drazen–Masson, the probability that the announced policy will be carried out in the future will depend on both the prior over policymaker type and what policy is actually implemented in the current period.

---

[21] Rodrik (1989) presents a signaling model in which a committed reformer demonstrates his commitment by the magnitude of the reform he is willing to enact. Committed reformers enact larger reforms than may be necessary to signal their type, suggesting why "overshooting" in the reform process is sometimes observed.

10.6. Conflict over the Burden of Reform

An alternative approach to explaining failure or delay in adopting reform is based on the observation that reform is a public good, so that individuals or groups can reap the benefits without bearing all the costs. Each interest group would therefore want some other group to bear the costs of adopting a socially beneficial policy change, implying it might not be adopted even though it is known that all groups would gain. This approach is in contrast to the models of Section 10.4, which concentrated on uncertainty about the benefits that the policy change will yield. Though both approaches are based on heterogeneity of interests and uncertainty, these factors enter quite differently. In this approach stressing conflict over how the burden of reform is divided among interest groups, *ex-post* heterogeneity is the key concept, in that an agreement to enact a reform carries with it a distribution of the costs of reform.[22] Uncertainty enters in because each interest group knows the net benefit it would receive from the change under a proposed allocation of costs, but is uncertain about the net benefits other groups will enjoy and hence about their willingness to bear the costs of reform.

The failure to adopt a socially beneficial policy change due to a conflict over who bears its cost can be formalized as the static public goods game discussed in Section 9.6 of Chapter 9; delay in adopting a socially beneficial policy change due to the sort of conflict can be formalized as a war of attrition, derived in Section 9.7 of Chapter 9. Having exposited the basic models in the previous chapter, we consider a more specific application of this approach to an example of policy delay. Since this application is quite direct, it may be useful to review the exposition of the two models in Chapter 9 as the basis for the discussion that follows. We concentrate on the dynamic problem of delay, rather than the static problem of non-adoption.

An influential application of the war of attrition is to delayed stabilization in Alesina and Drazen (1991) and Drazen and Grilli (1993). The basic model is one of an economy in which the government is running a deficit due to the failure of interest groups to agree on a deficit reduction program. In the absence of a consensus, only highly distortionary taxes can be used to finance government expenditures, and the revenue from those taxes is insufficient to fully cover expenditures. A fiscal reform program replaces highly distortionary taxes with less distortionary taxes large enough to cover government expenditures and close the deficit. There is disagree-

---

[22] Compare the statement in Williamson and Haggard (1994, p. 531), summarizing their answer to why beneficial reforms are not adopted: "[Policy reform] is like an investment that should ultimately benefit the majority by enough to make them happy they made it, but that in the short run will—like all investments—involve sacrifices. The distribution of these sacrifices over time and across groups is at the heart of the politics of economic reform."

ment, however, on how the burden of these higher taxes should be distributed across groups in the economy: each group would like the burden of higher taxes placed elsewhere and refuses to agree to bearing a large fraction of the taxes in the hope that some other group will concede and accept (or no longer block) a fiscal reform placing a high burden on itself. As groups can obstruct programs they dislike, fiscal reform requires consensus. Only when a group realizes that it can only do worse by waiting (for example, when they realize their opponents are far more able politically or economically to withstand the distortions of the current tax regime) will they concede and accept a reform with unfavorable distributional implications.

A Formal Model of Delayed Fiscal Stabilization

The war-of-attrition model presented in Section 9.7 of Chapter 9 need be modified only slightly to represent the Alesina–Drazen model of delayed inflation stabilization. We use the version of the model presented in Drazen and Grilli (1993) in which inflation appears explicitly. Unlike the original Alesina–Drazen model in which debt evolved over time, this later version has no explicit evolution of government debt, as government expenditures are always covered by some sort of taxation. However, it yields exactly the same type of equilibrium as the original model, since the choice of functional forms implied that growth of debt actually played no real role in the earlier model. The lack of explicit macroeconomic dynamics actually has an advantage, as it makes clear that what is crucial for the stabilization result is the evolution of beliefs about one's opponent, as in the general model presented in Chapter 9.

Consider a country in which some fraction a of government expenditures are covered by monetization of the deficit, the remainder covered by regular taxation, assumed to be nondistortionary. Hence, government debt is constant, for simplicity set to zero. The presence of an outstanding deficit would not change the basic argument—if we think of bond financing covered by nondistortionary taxation in the future, this set-up captures the choice between distortionary and nondistortionary taxation implied by a choice between bond financing and monetization. Monetization of a fraction a of the government budget is due to an inability to agree on the distribution of the burden of nondistortionary (or less distortionary) taxes. A "stabilization" is thus an agreement on the allocation of regular taxation across interest groups which allows government expenditures to be financed without inflation. (This notion of inflation stabilization corresponds to many historical experiences.) Such a financing agreement occurs when some groups agree to bear a high enough portion of taxation, that the remaining groups agree to bear the remainder. For simplicity, assume there are only two groups, each sharing the tax burden equally before a stabilization at time T and the group agreeing to bear the higher fraction (the group that "concedes") paying the fraction $\alpha > 1/2$ in a financing agreement, the other group paying a fraction $1 - \alpha$.[23] As in Alesina and Drazen, α is taken as an exogenous parameter, a higher α representing greater "polarization" in the society.

Before a stabilization, the government budget constraint is

$$i_t m_t + \tau_t = g, \tag{10.10}$$

where i_t is the nominal interest rate at t, m_t is real money balances, τ_t is nondistortionary taxation, and g is government expenditure, assumed constant for simplicity. The first revenue term is seigniorage with a constant real money supply. As already indicated, the government finances a fraction a of expenditures via seigniorage, that is,

$$i_t m_t = ag. \tag{10.11}$$

If a is constant over time before a stabilization, im and τ will be as well. After a stabilization, $a = 0$, so that $g = \tau$.

In each interest group, the utility of the representative individual in the group depends positively on consumption c_t and negatively on inflation π_t according to

$$u^\theta(c_t, \pi_t) = c_t - \mathscr{L}(\pi_t, \theta), \tag{10.12}$$

where the loss from inflation $\mathscr{L}(\pi_t, \theta)$ is increasing in both its arguments and equals $\mathscr{L}_0$ for $\pi = 0$. θ, the group's type, is a constant group-specific component indexing the loss it assigns to inflation. The preferences represented in (10.12) could be derived from an underlying utility function over consumption and real balances. Instead, Drazen and Grilli assume a simple *aggregate* money demand function which, expressed in per capita terms, is of the form

$$m^d = e^{-i/(1+i)}, \tag{10.13}$$

where time subscripts have been suppressed, since the nominal interest rate i is constant for constant a. (See Section 2.5 of Chapter 2 for the derivation of such a function from utility maximization.) There is asymmetric information on θ—each group knows its own θ, but only the distribution of its opponent's θ, drawn from a common, known cumulative distribution $F(\theta)$ defined over $[\underline{\theta}, \overline{\theta}]$. This is the unobserved cost, crucial to the war of attrition.

---

[23] As in the earlier papers, we ignore any collective action problems within groups. This would introduce a "second-level" war of attrition, but would not change the general point we are making. In Section 12.5 of Chapter 12, we consider "two-level" bargaining in international agreements, albeit in a very different model.

Combining (10.11), which gives real money supply as a function of i and g, with (10.13), we can specify money market equilibrium in order to relate the rate of inflation to the government budget. Assuming a constant real interest rate r, this yields

$$(r + \pi)e^{-(r+\pi)/(1+r+\pi)} = ag, \qquad (10.14)$$

which implicitly defines the equilibrium rate of inflation π before stabilization as a function of a.

The infinitely lived individual's objective is to maximize expected present discounted value of utility by choice of a time path of consumption c_t and a date to "concede", that is, to agree to bear the disproportionate flow tax burden αg, at which point the other group agrees to bear the burden $(1 - \alpha)g < \alpha g$. The choice of concession date will depend on θ, the parameter measuring the loss from inflation prior to a stabilization. Denote this optimal concession time $T(\theta)$.

The linearity of flow utility in c_t means that any feasible consumption path yields the same utility. Drazen and Grilli then simply assume that individuals consume their current after-tax income. If each individual has a flow endowment w, equal sharing of taxes before a stabilization combined with the budget constraint (10.10) thus implies that consumption for each individual before a stabilization (i.e., in the status quo) is

$$c^{SQ} = w - \frac{g}{2}, \qquad (10.15a)$$

while consumption after a stabilization for individuals in the group that concedes (denoted L, for relatively low consumption and utility) and for individuals in the other group (denoted H, for higher consumption and utility) are, respectively,

$$c^L = w - \alpha g,$$
$$c^H = w - (1 - \alpha)g. \qquad (10.15b)$$

The associated flow utility for a type-θ individual is found by substituting (10.15) into (10.12) for equilibrium inflation π.

The optimal concession time $T(\theta)$ for type θ may then be derived exactly as in the war-of-attrition model of Section 9.7 of Chapter 9. Rather than rederiving the solution, we refer the reader back to that derivation, with some guidance. We want to find a symmetric solution in the function $T(\cdot)$, such that a group with inflation cost θ finds it optimal to concede at $T(\theta)$ if the other group is behaving according to the same $T(\cdot)$. To derive this solution, the instantaneous utility function (10.12) combined with (10.15) yields expected utility over an infinite horizon as a function of the chosen concession time, the type θ, and the exogenous parameters.

(Following (9.21) through (9.23) in Chapter 9, one uses expressions for $u^\theta(c^{SQ}, \pi)$, $u^\theta(c^L, \pi)$, and $u^\theta(c^H, \pi)$ to derive present discounted utility for individuals in both the conceding and the non-conceding group and then expected utility as a function of $T(\theta)$.) Differentiating expected utility with respect to optimal concession time, as in the derivation of (9.24), one derives a first-order condition for the optimal concession time, as in the derivation of (9.26), which can be written

$$\left[-\frac{f(\theta)}{F(\theta)} \frac{1}{T'(\theta)} \right] (2\alpha - 1)\frac{g}{r} = \mathscr{L}(\theta, \pi) - \left(\alpha - \frac{1}{2} \right)g, \quad (10.16a)$$

where $f(\theta)$ is the density function associated with $F(\theta)$ and r is the discount rate. As explained following (9.24), this equation equates the expected benefit from waiting another instant to concede (the left-hand side) with the expected cost (the right-hand side). Consider first the left-hand side. The term in brackets is the probability that the other group concedes at time $T(\theta)$, conditional on their not having yet conceded, that is, the hazard rate (note that $T'(\theta)$ is negative). The other term on the left-hand side is the present discounted value from $T(\theta)$. The second term is the gain in utility from $T(\theta)$ onwards if the other group concedes; it is the present discounted value of lower taxes over the infinite horizon. Thus, the left-hand side represents the expected gain from waiting another instant to concede. The right-hand side is the cost of waiting another instant to concede, which is the loss due to inflation if there is no stabilization minus the flow net increase in taxes implied by concession. Hence, (10.16a) indicates that the optimal time of concession is when the expected gain from waiting just equals the cost from waiting.

   This condition may be rearranged to yield a differential equation for the optimal concession time $T(\theta)$, namely,

$$T'(\theta) = -\frac{f(\theta)}{F(\theta)} \frac{(2\alpha - 1)g/r}{\mathscr{L}(\theta, \pi) - (\alpha - 1/2)g}, \quad (10.16b)$$

with the associated boundary condition $T(\bar{\theta}) = 0$. The boundary condition says simply that a type who knows he suffers more from inflation than any other will concede immediately. This should be obvious from the set-up of the problem with both groups acting according to $T(\cdot)$, since a type who knows he suffers more than any other type knows that they can always "wait him out." The differential equation could then be solved for the optimal concession time $T(\theta)$ for each agent. With both groups behaving according to $T(\theta)$, the expected date of stabilization T^E is calculated as in (9.27), namely,

$$T^E = 2 \int_{s=0}^{\bar{\theta}} T(s)(1 - F(s)) f(s) \, ds. \tag{10.17}$$

The solution to the individual's optimization problem as given in (10.16b) and its implications represents the basic result of the war-of-attrition approach to delay in adopting a socially beneficial policy change. Interest groups who would benefit from the change refuse to bear the cost in the hope that someone else who may benefit even more will do so, as in a static public goods game. The dynamic element reflects learning about the net benefit that other groups assign to the new policy or, equivalently, the cost that other groups assign to the distortions associated with the status quo. (This is the specific interpretation that Alesina and Drazen give to the relative costs across agents.) Hence, delay reflects a war of attrition, as each interest group tries to "wait out" other groups in the hope that they will concede first. Delay ends and reform takes place when some group realizes that it is relatively weaker than other groups and agrees to bear a disproportionate burden of the reform program.

The formalization of the problem allows one to derive the implications for the expected length of delay of changes in some basic parameters. For example, higher pre-reform distortions, represented here by a higher value of inflation π, implying a high $\mathscr{L}(\cdot)$ for each type θ, clearly lowers $T'(\theta)$ in (10.16b). Since the highest cost type concedes at time 0 for any value of π, a smaller slope of the $T(\theta)$ curve means the new curve lies below the old one (see Figure 10.2), so each type chooses to concede earlier. From (10.17), the expected date of reform is thus earlier. Similarly, one could calculate the effect of a change in α on the expected date of a policy change. For example, a more unequal sharing of the burden of policy change (a higher α) will result in a later expected date of reform. This follows immediately from the previous result and inspection of (10.15). When the burden is shared equally ($\alpha = 1/2$), there will be no delay ($T'(\theta) = 0$, so that $T(\theta) = 0$): since the group that concedes pays the same share as the one that does not, any agent for whom the reform is beneficial will immediately agree to pay half of the cost if his opponent will pay the other half. Equal sharing of the burden removes the public good aspect of reform, and therefore removes the basic reason for reform to be delayed. As the disproportionate burden the conceding group pays rises, there is an increase in an agent's gain from waiting to see if his opponent will bear this burden. These comparative statics exercises are important, as changes in these parameters have intuitive economic analogues. We return to this in our discussion of crisis in Section 10.8 below.

As in the models of uncertainty about net benefits in Section 10.4, impossibility of *ex-post* compensation from "winners" to "losers" is crucial

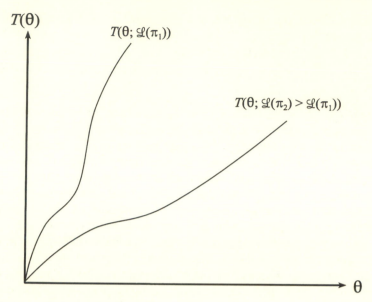

FIGURE 10.2. Time of concession.

to the results. If there were full compensation of this sort, it would be equivalent to the burden of reform being shared equally ($\alpha = 1/2$), so that there would be no delay. As indicated in the previous paragraph, equal sharing of the burden removes the public good aspect of reform, and therefore removes the basic reason for reform to be delayed. That is, the whole rationale of these models is to study the implications of the public good aspect of reform, a defining aspect which *ex-post* compensation removes.

One should note how an optimal stopping problem, for example in Section 10.2, is related to the war-of-attrition approach. Consider extending the optimal stopping problem to include the other variant of optimal procrastination, namely, "benign neglect" in the expectation that things will get better by themselves. A simple way to do this is to include a probability that in each period the reform will be costlessly "supplied" by nature. This will increase the return to doing nothing. Thus, as in the war of attrition, in the optimal stopping problem the higher is the probability that things will improve without the need for costly action, the less likely is an agent to take action. Delay reflects the hope on the part of each agent for improvement without his having to bear any cost. But, there is a crucial difference between the two problems. In the optimal stopping problem, this key probability was *exogenous*, so that delay based on perceiving a very high probability of no need for action could be judged to be irrational in light of subsequent developments. In the public goods game, the same probability is *endogenous*: with a small number of agents, the probability that one agent will take action depends on his beliefs about the probability of other agents acting; delaying could therefore be interpreted as a rational attempt to force someone else to act.

Bargaining over Shares

Hsieh (1997) presents a model of delayed stabilization, building on the Alesina–Drazen model, but where the shares of the stabilization cost that the two parties pay (that is, α) are determined endogenously via bargaining, rather than being exogenously fixed. A two-period model of a conflict between workers and capitalists is presented in which workers' income is known, but capitalists' income is not. Hence the capitalists' income is their type, with workers in the first period knowing only the distribution of capitalists' income. Workers make an offer that capitalists pay a share α_1 of the higher taxes needed to close the budget deficit. If the offer is accepted, stabilization takes place and the game ends. If it is rejected, workers make an offer in the second period that capitalists pay a share α_2 of the tax bill, which capitalists can either accept or reject; if they reject the offer, the game ends with no stabilization.

The endogenous determination of the cost shares and the possibility of it changing over time is central to Hsieh's model. By rejecting the first offer, capitalists provide information about their income, which induces workers to adjust their second offer upward. The argument is that the lower is capitalists' income, the less they suffer from no stabilization, so that capitalists with a high enough income will accept an offer in the first period. Rejecting an offer signals income is below some critical level and that the offer was not good enough to induce acceptance; since workers benefit from a stabilization, they will make a better offer in the second period. Delay acts as a screening device in separating types of capitalists.

10.7. COMMON PROPERTY MODELS

Another public goods approach to delay in adopting policy changes is based on the implications of some government assets being common property. Economic policy reflects the sum of behavior of the interest groups with respect to the common property: nonoptimal policy results from the attempt of interest groups to appropriate these assets; cooperative, nonappropriative behavior on the part of interest groups, which may lead to an identical division of a larger pie, is associated with socially beneficial policy. The idea is an application of the problem of "fishing from a common pool," where common access to a resource implies overuse. Delay in adopting a socially beneficial policy arises because the individual optimality of the appropriative strategy by interest groups depends on the stock of assets or wealth to be appropriated, as in the approach of Benhabib and Rustichini (1996) mentioned in Section 10.3. Delay results from wealth-dependent strategies if appropriative behavior is optimal when the asset stock is high (and government debt is low), nonappropriative behavior is optimal when the stock of appropriable assets becomes low, with appropriation inducing this fall.

Velasco (1999) has applied this idea to fiscal reform, as in the Alesina–Drazen model in the previous section. He uses a common prop- erty model with wealth-dependent appropriative strategies to yield delay in eliminating a fiscal deficit: common access to government revenues by a number of interest groups implies total expenditures in excess of revenues, with government debt growing over time; appropriative behavior is optimal when government debt is low, with cooperative behavior becoming optimal only when debt becomes too high. Whether cooperative behavior is opti- mal when assets to be appropriated are low (as in Velasco), high (as in the Benhabib and Rustichini model of Olson's stagnation argument in Section 10.3), or independent of the level of wealth depends very much on the specification of the model, including functional forms. We present a version of the Velasco model here, with alternatives as applied to growth in the next chapter.

Consider a discrete-time model of J symmetric interest groups, where an interest group j can extract net transfers v^j subject to restrictions given below. Transfers v^j can be positive or negative (i.e., groups can be taxed), but it is assumed there is a maximum negative transfer $\underline{v}$ that can be extracted from any group. The government has exogenous nontax revenue y; any excess of total transfers over revenue is financed by issuing interna- tional debt. There is a deadweight cost of d_t per period, which is equal to $d > 0$ if there are interest groups engaging in appropriative behavior and equal to 0 if all groups cooperate such that total transfers imply that debt is constant (a "stabilization"). This cost is analogous to the cost $\mathscr{L}(\cdot)$ in (10.12) in the Alesina and Drazen model, and it plays a central role in Velasco's model. Hence, the government budget constraint may be written

$$A_{t+1} = RA_t + y - d_t - \sum_{j=1}^{J} v_t^j, \qquad (10.18)$$

where A is the government's stock of interest-bearing assets (for example, international reserves minus debt) and R is the exogenous interest factor. The government is assumed to satisfy a solvency condition, $\lim_{t \to \infty} R^{-t} A_t \geq 0$, implying that debt does not grow without bound. This solvency condition combined with (10.18) puts a limit on the v^j, namely, that the present discounted value of all transfers cannot be greater than maximum government wealth, which is the sum of current assets plus the present discounted value of government income net of deadweight costs. In order to ensure that this condition is satisfied, it is assumed there is a limit on the transfer that the government will pay to an interest group at any point in time. Specifically, Velasco assumes that a group's transfer demand v_t^j at time t is paid out by the government if and only if it does not exceed $1/J$th of the income flow from maximum wealth:

$$v_t^j \le \frac{1}{J}R\left[A_t + \frac{y - J\underline{v}}{R - 1} - \frac{1}{R}\sum_{s=t}^{\infty}\frac{d_s}{R^{s-t}}\right], \quad \forall j, t, \qquad (10.19)$$

where the term in brackets is maximum possible government wealth starting at any A_t for an expected sequence $\{d_s\}$ from $s = t$ to ∞.

The objective of each interest group j may be written

$$\Omega^j = \sum_{s=t}^{\infty} \beta^{s-t} \ln v_t^j, \qquad (10.20)$$

where it is assumed that the discount factor β is equal to $1/R$. Each interest group chooses a sequence $\{v_t^j\}$ to maximize (10.20) subject to the evolution of A_t, the constraint (10.19), and the strategies of the other groups. Velasco focuses on **Markov strategies**, that is, strategies that are restricted to be functions only of the payoff-relevant state variables and are not allowed to be history dependent. Specifically, this means that the transfer demanded is a function of the state variable A_t. The equilibrium concept is Markov Perfect Equilibrium (MPE). A J-component vector of Markov strategies $\{\tilde{v}^j(A_t)\}$ for $j = 1, \dots, J$ and all t forms a **Markov Perfect Equilibrium** if it is a subgame-perfect equilibrium for every value of A_t.

Given the form of the objective function, the Nash–Markov appropriative equilibrium strategy can be shown to be of the form

$$v_t^j = v^0 + \phi RA_t, \qquad (10.21a)$$

where

$$v^0 = \frac{R(y - d)}{1 + J(R - 1)} \quad \text{and} \quad \phi = \frac{R - 1}{1 + J(R - 1)}. \qquad (10.21b)$$

This is demonstrated by assuming the linear strategy (10.21a) with coefficients to be determined, and then verifying this conjecture for coefficients (10.21b). We now show this. Assuming that all other groups follow (10.21a), government assets evolve according to

$$A_{t+1} = RA_t[1 - (J - 1)\phi] - (J - 1)v^0 + y - d_t - v_t^j. \qquad (10.22)$$

Group j's optimal decision is to choose sequences of v_t^j to maximize its infinite-horizon objective (10.20) subject to (10.19) and (10.22). Using a dynamic programming set-up, taking first-order conditions over ν_t^j, and using the envelope theorem (see Chapter 2), one obtains a dynamic equation for ν_t^j:

$$\nu_{t+1}^j = (1 - (J - 1)\phi)\nu_t^j. \tag{10.23}$$

Substituting (10.21a) into (10.23), one obtains a difference equation in A_t. Substituting (10.21a) into (10.17) for all J groups, one also obtains a difference equation in A_t. Equating coefficients yields (10.21b).

One may easily show that under appropriation, as in (10.21a), total demand exceeds revenues, so that assets are falling over time. The utility associated with this Markov appropriative path can be easily calculated. It is

$$\Omega^M(A_t) = \frac{R}{R - 1} \ln\left((R - 1)A_t + y - d\right)$$

$$+ \frac{R}{R - 1} \ln\left(\frac{R}{1 + J(R - 1)}\right), \tag{10.24}$$

where M stands for "Markov." This quantity $\Omega^M(A_t)$ will be used to determine the value of "defecting" from cooperative behavior.

In contrast, if each group were to accept a transfer of $((R - 1)A_t + y)/J$ consistent with a balanced budget, so that debt is stabilized at A_t, lifetime utility would be

$$\Omega^C(A_t) = \frac{R}{R - 1} \ln\left(\frac{y + (R - 1)A_t}{J}\right), \tag{10.25}$$

where C stands for "cooperative." (Cooperation means that $d_t = 0$.) $\Omega^C(A_t) > \Omega^M(A_t)$ for all A_t, implying that all groups would be better off in a cooperative equilibrium. A policy change away from appropriative behavior would indeed be optimal if it could be sustained.

However, the optimality of a cooperative equilibrium does not in itself mean that it can be sustained. Even if all other groups are cooperating and are willing to accept a transfer of $((R - 1)A_t + y)/J$, a single group may find it optimal to defect and appropriate more. Cooperation is preferred to appropriation only if all potential appropriators cooperate. If a group knew that its nonappropriative behavior would be met by appropriation on the part of other interests, cooperation would not be in its interest. To sustain a cooperative equilibrium, one considers punishment against defection. Whether or not an interest group will find it optimal to defect will depend crucially on the "punishment" for defection, that is, on the behavior of other agents in response to unilateral selfish behavior on its part. Velasco follows a standard assumption in Markov models with switching. He assumes that starting from a situation in which no appropriation is taking place, defection from the cooperative equilibrium triggers no change in behavior in the current period t, but a reversion to appropriative behavior by all groups forever after starting in the next period. Hence, in a Markov switching equilibrium, each interest group acts in a cooperative way as long as all others do, but switches to appropriation if it sees some other group doing so. That is, it is an equilibrium where each interest group follows a "trigger strategy," as in some of the models of Section 6.3 of Chapter 6.[24]

The maximization problem faced by an interest group in choosing whether to deviate from the cooperative equilibrium may thus be represented by

$$\Omega^D(A_t) = \max_{\nu_t^j} \left\{ \ln \nu_t^j + \frac{1}{R} \Omega^M(A_{t+1}) \right\}, \tag{10.26}$$

subject to (10.19) and

$$A_{t+1} = \left(1 - \frac{J-1}{J}\frac{R-1}{R}\right)RA_t + \frac{y}{J} - d - \nu_t^j. \tag{10.27}$$

Substituting (10.27) into the right-hand side of (10.26) and using (10.24), one may derive the term in braces on the right-hand side of (10.26) as a function of ν_t^j and A_t. Maximizing this expression, one obtains the optimal transfer demand under defection:

$$\nu_t^j = \frac{R-1}{R}\frac{R+J-1}{J}A_t + \frac{R+J-1}{J}\frac{y}{R} - d. \tag{10.28}$$

Substituting (10.28) along with (10.24) into (10.26), one obtains the infinite-horizon expected utility from defection, namely,

$$\Omega^D(A_t) = \frac{R}{R-1} \ln \left(\frac{R-1}{R}\frac{R+J-1}{J}A_t + \frac{R+J-1}{J}\frac{y}{R} - d \right)$$

$$+ \frac{R}{(R-1)^2} \ln \left(\frac{R}{1 + J(R-1)} \right). \tag{10.29}$$

One can now study whether cooperation is sustainable. Defection will take place as long as $\Omega^D(A_t) > \Omega^C(A_t)$; otherwise, cooperation is sustain-

---

[24] Note that in this trigger strategy equilibrium, it is assumed that there is no switch back to cooperative behavior, groups following the Nash–Markov strategy forever even though A_t is falling to zero over time as a result. That is, though A_t falls below the level that would make cooperation sustainable, the punishment assumption is that behavior is nonetheless Nash–Markov forever after.

able. Comparing (10.25) and (10.29), one sees that if d is not too large, there will be a unique level of A_t, call it $\hat{A}$, at which they are just equal. For $A_t > \hat{A}$, cooperation is not sustainable, and interest groups will follow the Markov strategy (10.21), with the implication that A_t will be falling over time. When A_t falls to the level $\hat{A}$, there is a switch to cooperative behavior, as evidenced by a switch from an unsustainable to a sustainable fiscal policy. Thus, this is a model of delay in adopting the socially optimal policy.

Common property models share some important similarities with the war-of-attrition model, over and above the centrality of public goods to explaining socially nonoptimal behavior. In both models, there is economic deterioration, which ends endogenously only after a period of time. Also, in both models, agents would be better off if they would cooperate. But in a common property model, the uncertainty about the preferences of other interest groups, central to the war-of-attrition model in the previous section, plays no role. (In fact, it is the knowledge of what other groups will do which is central to the noncooperative equilibrium.) Instead, the failure may be seen as *institutional* in the sense that it is the lack of defined property rights which leads to the socially unproductive behavior.

10.8. ECONOMIC CRISES

The hypothesis that crisis induces policy change (or that crisis is necessary for a reform) has become, in the eyes of many, the new orthodoxy. Numerous references could be given; see, for example, the articles in Nelson (1990) or Williamson (1994a). As Tommasi and Velasco (1996, p. 197) write, "That economic crises seem either to facilitate or outright cause economic reforms is part of the new conventional wisdom on reform." On the other hand, it has been argued that, like most conventional wisdom, this view is a tautology. Rodrik (1996, p. 27) puts the problem clearly:

> "Reform naturally becomes an issue only when policies are perceived not to be working. A crisis is just an extreme case of policy failure. That reform should follow crisis, then, is no more surprising than smoke following fire."

In this section, we review some theoretical models of the role of crisis in policy change, that is, of the mechanisms by which a crisis induces a change in policy. First, however, in light of these two conflicting views, we discuss more carefully what it means to say that crisis is necessary or sufficient for reform in order to give substance to the "crisis hypothesis."

The Relation of Crisis and Policy Change

To understand the relation between crises and policy change, one should distinguish between two related, but not identical, hypotheses. The first is that reform is more likely to be adopted in bad than in good times. The second is that things need to get *very* bad (and not just bad) to induce reform. Variants of both arguments have been presented as a "crisis hypothesis," though we argue that the term should be reserved for the latter argument. To clarify the "crisis hypothesis," let us begin by examining the former argument.

The basic answer to the question of whether policy change is more likely to be adopted in good times or bad times[25] may be put in terms of the answer to the following question, where we consider the effects of a negative shock. What is the effect of a negative shock on the net benefit of adopting a policy change versus staying with the status quo? If the shock raises the cost of not reforming (for example, a fall in u^{SQ} in the Fernandez–Rodrik model in Section 10.4 or the Alesina–Drazen model in Section 10.6), then it will make a reform more likely. Or, if it lowers the cost of reforming (for example, a fall in the world interest rate making it less risky to open the capital account, as in the model of Bartolini and Drazen [1997b]), then it will make a reform more likely. If the shock lowers both the costs of reforming and of staying with the status quo, then the effect on the likelihood of reform will depend on the relative effect on costs.

To say that bad times encourage reform because the *relative* deterioration of the status quo changes the net benefit of reform does not, in itself, address the second argument given above. Why may there need to be an *extreme* deterioration (or simply an extremely low level) of the status quo, that is, a "crisis," before a reform is adopted? Why is it "business as usual" until times get really bad? It is the magnitude of the deterioration in the status quo which makes the role of crisis nontrivial. Hence, the question inherent in the crisis hypothesis may be put as follows: why do times need to get *very* bad (and not just bad) to induce reform? Stating it in this way makes clear that the hypothesis is *not* a tautology. That smoke follows fire is not surprising; if, however, one were to observe that small or medium size fires produce no smoke, while large fires do, there is indeed something to be explained.

A more difficult point is whether the role of crisis should be seen as "necessary," "sufficient," or simply "facilitating" reform. To the extent that one argues that a crisis is sufficient to induce a policy change, there is a tautological character to the crisis hypothesis. As Rodrik (1996, p. 27) puts it, "...the hypothesis is virtually non-falsifiable: if an economy in crisis has not yet reformed, the frequently proffered explanation is that the

---

[25] Note a crucial distinction between it being more likely that the need for new policies is *perceived* in bad times (as the above Rodrik quote suggests) and it being more likely that new policies are *adopted* in bad times. Though failure may be necessary to realize the need for change, this change need not *occur* in times of crisis, but may be postponed till more favorable times. Though I realize that my roof leaks only if it rains, do I fix it on the next sunny day, or worry about it again only during the next rain?

crisis has not yet become 'severe enough'." To the extent that one argues that a crisis is necessary to induce a reform, the hypothesis is too easily falsifiable (unless one similarly defines any situation leading to reform as a crisis). The variety of episodes of crisis suggests that no simple formulation will be correct. In this section, we therefore simply investigate mechanisms by which crisis helps facilitate policy change. To repeat a key point, we take the "crisis hypothesis" to mean that the economic situation must deteriorate significantly to induce or facilitate reform.

Reshuffling of Interest Groups

The first political theory in this chapter of nonadoption of socially beneficial policies focused on the ability of powerful vested interests to block policy change. According to Olson (1982), economic success creates powerful groups with vested interests who may naturally be against further policy changes which would be to their detriment. Their ability to block socially beneficial reform leads to the society becoming "sclerotic," as Olson terms it. A theory of nonadoption based on vested interests gives a straightforward answer to the question of why a crisis may be necessary to enact reform. If reform requires a significant weakening of the power of some interest groups, only a severe economic deterioration may be sufficient to weaken their power and bring about reform. A crisis is thus necessary to "reshuffle" interest groups in sclerotic societies. This argument has received no formal treatment to my knowledge, but is discussed in the reform literature; see, for example, Nelson (1990, 1994).

Perception of the Need for Change

A second argument on why a crisis may be necessary to enact significant reforms concerns perception of the need for reform. Only when things get quite bad do we realize there is a permanent problem that will not go away on its own, rather than a transitory problem. The *salience* view of the role of crisis (see also Akerlof [1991], mentioned in footnote 9) may be thought of as a deterioration or shock *strongly* affecting the perception of utility of the status quo. It is not simply the view that the current situation is unacceptable, but that different types of policies must be tried. As Harberger (1993b) puts it:

> ... practitioners go around with a certain world view in their heads. All sorts of crazy things can happen—like hyperinflations and huge recessions and wrenching debt or exchange rate crises. All of these ... can occur and still leave seasoned practitioners unruffled, because their world view already contains sensible explanations for them. Every now and then, however, something happens that does not fit the previous image—something that shakes our Bayesian faith in what we used to think.

The role of crisis in inducing a change in policy by inducing a change in one's model of the economy has apparently received no formal modeling, but there are many models that are applicable. The models of Section 10.5 on "communication failures" suggest one possible path of analysis. By significantly changing priors, a crisis may make voters (or policy choosers in the terminology of the Matthews [1989] model) more likely to overcome ideological skepticism and accept proposed policy changes. There is also much work on Bayesian learning about the "correct" model of the world which may be relevant.

Acceptance of Uncertainty

A third argument for the role of crisis in enabling reform follows the models of uncertainty about individual benefits in Section 10.4 above. In the Labán and Sturzenegger (1994a) model in that section, socially beneficial policy change was delayed by high uncertainty about who will be the winners and who the losers from the change. What made reform possible was a sufficiently large deterioration of the status quo. The greater the uncertainty about the post-reform environment, the greater the deterioration of the status quo must be to induce acceptance of uncertain reform. Hence, a crisis, defined as an extremely large deterioration of the status quo, may be necessary for reform. A formal demonstration of this can easily be shown using the formal model presented in Section 10.4.

Suspension of Selfish Interest

When the benefit from a policy change has the aspect of a public good as in the war-of-attrition model in Section 10.6, each individual perceives the possibility of large gain at small cost if someone else acts. There will thus be a large incentive to inaction. Given the large gap between the gain from acting and from someone else acting, a significant deterioration of the status quo may be necessary to induce an interest group to accept a disproportionate part of the cost of a policy change and thus enable a reform to be enacted.

This result forms the basis of the argument of Drazen and Grilli (1993) on the benefit of crises in inducing policy reform. Since higher pre-reform distortions induce an earlier expected reform, the government, by inducing a crisis, can hasten the expected date of reform. Intuitively, if what is blocking a reform is the inability to gain consensus on how the burden of reform is to be divided among interest groups, a crisis can hasten agreement by increasing the distortion associated with the status quo, thus raising the cost of not agreeing to reform. That is, a crisis can make each interest group more amenable to reform, and hence shorten the expected delay in adopting a reform. (The focus on a highly distorted status quo, where these distortions may rise over time, makes the argument similar to that applied to the model of Labán and Sturzenegger [1994a].) In fact, as Drazen and Grilli show, if the expected date of reform is significantly brought forward, lower pre-reform utility implies that expected welfare can actually rise.[26]

In the context of his two-period model discussed at the end of Section 10.6, Hsieh (1997), however, argues that once the shares of the stabilization cost that the two parties pay is determined endogenously via bargaining, "crisis" may actually delay rather than hasten reform. With the size of the offer one group makes to the other being endogenous, there are offsetting effects. There is a cost of higher delay, which hastens reform as in Drazen–Grilli. Holding the share α fixed, an increase in the cost of delay will increase the probability of early agreement. However, the proposer of α takes advantage of economic deterioration to make a less attractive offer, which taken alone reduces the probability of early agreement. Hence, though there is a higher probability that a given offer will be accepted in the first period, the actual offer made will be less favorable. This may outweigh the direct effect of crisis and actually lead to greater delay, as is the case in Hsieh's model.

The argument that crisis may make groups more amenable to reform should be seen as complementary to arguments on perceptions of the need for a change in behavior. A crisis may not so much induce interest groups to see the world differently in intellectual terms, but to realize that their political interactions must change. As Williamson (1994b, p. 19) puts the point, "... a sufficiently acute crisis may also create a consensus that the old order has failed and needs to be replaced, leading individuals and groups to accept that their special interests need to be sacrificed (along with those of other special interest groups) on the altar of the general good." The last phrase makes Williamson's view very similar to the *ex-post* conflict of interests explanation of Drazen and Grilli.

Common property models of the sort considered in Section 10.7 also can be interpreted as giving a clear role to crisis. Groups agree to cease appropriative behavior only when there has been a large enough economic deterioration that defecting from cooperation is no longer individually optimal. Significant deterioration may be necessary, since appropriation is initially discretely better than cooperation for any level of economywide resources to be appropriated. Drazen (1999a) builds a model of selectivity in foreign aid, where aid is only effective after an economic crisis, on the basis of this type of argument.

---

[26] This argument depends on the specific role that a crisis plays in a war-of-attrition model and should not be taken to imply that crises increase welfare in general in economies where necessary reforms are delayed.

Empirical Evidence

For such a widely accepted argument, it is striking how little formal empirical testing there has been of the view that a crisis is necessary for significant policy change. Much of the existing empirical work is case studies, of which there are many excellent examples. There are also numerous excellent collections of case studies of reform in general, with the role of crisis in inducing specific reforms being commonly discussed. Such collections are briefly discussed at the beginning of Chapter 13, where we consider reform from a more applied perspective. Case studies, however, often seem to confirm the problems of tautology in studying the role of crisis, making it seem obvious that crisis was crucial to successful reform in the specific cases studied.

Econometric studies of the crisis hypothesis are rare. The basic problem is in finding implementable measures of crisis and reform (especially the former) and designing a formal empirical test in a way that leads to convincing results. A "crisis" is generally measured by a low value of some macroeconomic indicator (or set of indicators) relative to some reference level. An obvious problem with this approach is deciding how much deterioration constitutes a crisis; this parallels the point raised by Rodrik (1996) discussed earlier in this section, namely, that the absence of results may be taken simply to mean that the measure of crisis is not severe enough. Robustness tests or carefully designed tests may help get around this problem. "Reform" can be measured either by a change in policy variables or in macroeconomic outcomes.

Macroeconomic Performance over Time

Consistent with these measures of "crisis" and "reform," a simple test is to consider the effect of poor macroeconomic performance at date t (the crisis) on performance at some later date, taken to indicate the presence or absence of reform. Bruno and Easterly (1996), for example, consider the effect of inflation crises on growth and subsequent inflation in a wide cross section of countries. A high-inflation crisis is defined as inflation above 40% annually for two or more years. They find that growth falls sharply during high-inflation crises, but rises *above* its pre-crisis level after inflation comes down. They are particularly interested in the question of whether crisis makes countries more likely to reform. They find that high-inflation countries did undertake reforms, as measured by subsequent inflation performance. The correlation between inflation today and inflation tomorrow is not monotonically positive, but turns negative for high

inflation. At high enough inflation (150–200% per year), there is a negative relation between current inflation and inflation lagged five years. They
take this as evidence of the crisis hypothesis.

They also considered an empirical formalization of a debt crisis. They
identified 55 countries in their sample that rescheduled their foreign debt
payments. Of these, 19 had low inflation and no inflation stabilization.
Their per capita income continued to fall, their current account deficits
were higher than the other countries in the group, and they relied heavily
on overseas financing and foreign grants. Hence, there is nothing to
indicate that there is a mechanical increase in growth following a crisis.

Drazen and Easterly (1999) extend the Bruno–Easterly results in two
main ways: they consider a wider set of variables; and, for a given variable,
they consider alternative ways of how to define a reference level relative to
which a crisis is measured. As in Bruno and Easterly, the basic idea is to
look at an indicator of macroeconomic performance at t and at subsequent
dates $t + s$ for $s > 0$; the crisis hypothesis is represented by extremely
poor performance at t implying not simply good performance at $t + s$, but
performance at $t + s$ that is better if performance at t was very bad than if
it were just bad. For ease of later exposition, this may be termed a
"crossover." The indicators that are used are inflation, the black market
premium, the growth rate of per capita GDP, the current account deficit,
and the public sector deficit. Normally, an indicator will be positively
correlated across periods because policy indicators are persistent over
time. Drazen and Easterly consider a number of ways to "standardize"
macroeconomic performance, for example, measuring an indicator not
only in absolute terms at different points in time, but also relative to the
country mean and the global mean.

There are two general patterns that are seen: inflation and the black
market premium illustrate behavior consistent with the crisis hypothesis,
while growth rates, fiscal balance, and the current account balance do not.
These results are robust to how the variables are measured. Consider first
inflation. They consider yearly inflation rates over the period 1953–1996
for a sample of 123 countries. One test is to divide countries into
percentiles according to their inflation rates at t and to consider median
inflation in each percentile group five years later. The results are shown in
Table 10.1, following a similar table in Drazen and Easterly. Inflation
today is increasing in inflation five years ago until one reaches the 96th
percentile (which corresponds to median inflation of 68% *per annum*).
Above this level, inflation is decreasing in the level of inflation five years
ago. The results in the 99th percentile (median inflation 591%) are
particularly striking: not only is the median rate of inflation at $t + 5$ about
one-third of the corresponding figure for the 96th percentile, but the
confidence band (not shown in the table) is fairly narrow and lies entirely

TABLE 10.1
Worst Inflation Five Years Ago versus Today: 1953–96

Percentile of Median Inflation at t	Inflation at t Median Rate	Inflation at t + 5 Median Rate
90	27	23
91	29	22
92	32	24
93	36	32
94	45	36
95	55	43
96	68	70
97	94	36
98	133	32
99	591	25

below the confidence band on the peak at the 96th percentile. In other words, having inflation near 600% today is likely to lead to significantly lower inflation five years from now than is inflation near 70% today.[27] These results echo those of Bruno and Easterly (1996) and support the crisis hypothesis.

Another way of organizing the data is to divide countries into a small number of groups and trace inflation performance over subsequent years. For example, they consider countries in which inflation was between 40–100% in some year, 100–1000%, and over 1000%, and then look at inflation performance in years since inflation first passed the respective critical level. Looking at median inflation in each group, they find that the median rate of inflation for countries in the first (initial inflation of 40–100%) group did not show a significant change over the subsequent five years. The median rate of inflation for countries in the second (initial inflation of 100–1000%) group fell markedly over the subsequent five years, to a level which was insignificantly different from that of the first group. Median inflation for countries in the third (initial inflation above 1000%) group, however, fell far more, to about 15% median inflation rate after five years and about 10% after eight years. After five years, the median inflation rate in the group with initial inflation above 1000% was 33 percentage points *lower* than in the group with initial inflation between 100% and 1000%, a difference which they find to be statistically significant.

---

[27] Measuring inflation relative to country or global averages and considering an inflation crisis in terms of inflation more than two standard deviations from the mean tells a similar story.

Data on the black market premium tells a similar story. Again, the 99th percentile has a median black market rate five years from now that is below that of a lower percentile (the peak is at the 96th percentile). The confidence bands are wide for the other percentiles besides the 99th (and the 97th), although the median at the 99th percentile still lies below the confidence band of the 96th percentile. The 96th percentile corresponds to a black market premium of 309%, which predicts a black market premium in five years of 317%. The 99th percentile corresponds to a black market premium of 1038% (median for the percentile), which predicts a black market premium in five years of 69%. Similarly, countries with a black market premium of over 1000% at some date have a median black market premium significantly lower five years later than countries whose highest black market premium was between 100% and 1000%. These results also support the crisis hypothesis.

In contrast, they find no support for the crisis hypothesis for the other indicators in either sort of test. For example, for both the current account and fiscal balance, there is a positive correlation between values at t and five years later, whether one divides countries into percentiles or into broader classes. Both series display mean reversion, but do not display any "crossover." The 99th percentile of current account deficit as a percentage of GDP corresponds to a median deficit of 48%, falling to a still enormous median deficit of 34% after five years. The relation between the median deficit at t and five years later is fairly strongly monotonic as one moves down to the 90th percentile. Dividing countries into groups of initial current account deficit to GDP of 0 to -5%, -5 to -10%, and below -10% displays analogous monotonicity when one considers median values over the eight years since the initial episode. The behavior of fiscal deficit is qualitatively identical. Similarly, dividing countries with episodes of at least two years of negative growth into three groups (0 to -5%, -5 to -10%, and below -10%), Drazen and Easterly find a clear positive correlation between negative growth at t and median growth six to eight years later. The only difference is that the group of countries with the most negative (-10% or below) growth rates during the crisis show marginally better growth performance two to four years after the beginning of the crisis than those with less negative growth rates. However, this difference is not statistically significant and disappears after year 4.

How can one explain the difference in the behavior of the indicators? Drazen and Easterly present two, not inconsistent, explanations. First, the differing results for the different indicators may indicate a difference in the ease of adjustment. It may be very hard to reduce a current account deficit of 20–30% of GDP to a current account deficit of 5% of GDP (or to eliminate a government budget deficit of 28% of GDP, the 99th percentile of public sector balance figures), while reducing a high black market premium can happen overnight with a devaluation and exchange rate unification. That is, a "crisis" may be likely to lead to reform and economic improvement when the policy measures needed to improve are clear and relatively easy to implement, but have less of an effect for more difficult macroeconomic problems.

Second, Drazen and Easterly suggest that the extreme values of government budget or current account deficits may not correspond to a crisis in the following sense. For their sample of countries, they show there is a very high correlation between these two indicators and foreign aid received as a percentage of GDP. For example, as the ratio of the current account deficit to GDP rises from zero to 15%, aid rises almost monotonically from about 1% to about 6% of GDP. Countries with higher average current account deficits receive significantly more. This suggests that high budget and current account deficits may not be perceived as crises, because foreign aid cushions their effects. Hence, the failure of extreme values of deficits to induce reform may simply reflect that these episodes do not correspond to crises to the extent that the basic figures might suggest.

Direct Measures of Reform

An alternative empirical procedure is to measure policy change directly and to see how it correlates with extremely poor economic indicators. Lora (1998) constructs policy indices in five areas for 19 Latin American and Caribbean countries over the period 1985–1995. These are: trade reform (reduction in average tariffs and tariff variability); reform of the domestic financial system (reduction of controls on deposit and loan rates and reform of banking regulation); tax reform (reduction of basic value-added tax rates and marginal income tax rates for individuals and corporations); privatization (measured as the cumulative sum of revenue from privatization); and labor market reform (legislation allowing greater flexibility in hiring, firing, and wage payments). He is interested in testing the importance of a number of political and economic factors on the adoption of reform by regressing the reform indicators on political variables such as fragmentation and time the government has been in office, the extent of an apparatus to compensate losers from reform, measures of external variables such as capital flows, and economic crisis. As above, crisis is measured by macroeconomic indicators, including: the gap between real income per capita and its previous highest level; negative growth; high or variable inflation; and government budget deficits. Lora considers both reforms taken individually and an overall index of total structural reform, as a simple average of the five individual reform indices.

The strongest empirical result is the importance of crisis. It is consistently significant for the total reform index, no matter what other explanatory variables are included. For the total index, Lora finds the best crisis indicator to be the gap in per capita income relative to its peak. Individual reform indicators are sensitive to different crisis indicators. Negative GDP growth is especially important for trade and labor market reform. Past inflation (both level and variability) is quite important for financial sector reform. In contrast, he finds that privatization and tax reform do not appear to be facilitated by crisis, not even by fiscal crisis. The political variables he uses have little effect on the reform indices, while the effect of compensation schemes and external indicators is mixed.

To summarize, Lora's results are broadly consistent with those of Bruno and Easterly and Drazen and Easterly discussed above. Though imperfect, the tests indicate that empirically, crisis is important in inducing or facilitating reform, though much work is left to be done on matching of theory and actual experience. This is a major area for future development.

10.9. CONCLUSIONS

Our discussion of inaction, delay, and crisis concludes Part III of the book on models of explicit heterogeneity and conflict of interests in political economy. In Part IV of the book, we turn our attention to applications of the models of Parts II and III to specific areas. Chapter 10 serves as a good bridge between more general models and more specific applications for a number of reasons. First, as discussed in the introduction to the chapter, the failure to adopt socially beneficial economic reforms or their adoption only after long delays is a leading example of the divergence between the simple textbook models of economic policymaking and real-world experience. The argument that political factors lead to economically optimal policies not being enacted is the central theme of political economy as treated in this book. We have argued repeatedly that conflict of interests is key to understanding this outcome. In the analysis of inaction and delay, we have focused on the key role of a number of types of conflict of interests. Each important type of heterogeneity in earlier models found its reflection in some model of the failure to adopt socially beneficial policies in this chapter. Hence, the study of inaction and delay not only brings into sharp focus the subject matter of political economy as a whole, but also clearly illustrates the role of heterogeneity and conflict of interests as the key to understanding political economy.

A second reason why models of inaction and delay serve as a bridge to applications is that the material covered was somewhere between theory and application. Though the models themselves were often abstract and applicable to a wide range of questions, policy reform itself (that is, the adoption of superior policies) is a major applied area. We treat large-scale reform and transition as an applied question in Chapter 13. As argued in the introduction to the chapter, dividing material on reform into two separate chapters was done in the attempt to help bridge the often wide gap between the theory of reform and the practice. We will not repeat the arguments made for this division. It is hoped that the treatment in this chapter of nonadoption of superior policies made clear the benefit of a theoretical treatment. We now move on to applications.

PART IV

Application to Policy Issues

Factor Accumulation and Growth

> ...whoever could make two ears of corn, or two blades
> to grow upon a spot of ground where only one grew before,
> would deserve better of mankind, and do more
> essential service to his country than the whole race of
> politicians put together.
>
> —*Jonathan Swift,* Gulliver's Travels

11.1 INTRODUCTION

Political Economy and Growth

One of the most active areas of research in applied political economy is factor accumulation and growth, reflecting the very large interest in endogenous growth theory itself in the last decade. Interest in economic growth induces an interest in the political economy of growth in various ways. First of all, we are surely observing the phenomenon that "everything that rises, must converge." Both of these fields have witnessed intense activity in the past few years, and there is bound to be a cross-fertilization between areas of extreme research activity.

Interest in growth has induced considerable research on the political economy of growth not only because of the amount of research on growth, but also because of its nature. "New" growth theory has concentrated on endogenizing the underlying determinants of growth, that is, on models in which the "engine of growth" is endogenous to agents' decisions, rather than exogenous as in the typical growth model of the 1950s and 1960s. The main focus is on endogenous technical progress as the engine of growth, primarily via externalities in the process of research, human, and physical capital accumulation. The focus on externalities, and hence possible increasing returns to scale, implies the possibility of countries displaying widely divergent growth paths, in contrast to the emphasis on convergence and balanced growth that characterized earlier growth theory. New growth theory has thus been especially interested in explaining why some countries grow and flourish, while other countries appear to stagnate and not grow at all.[1]

These two characteristics of new growth theory—explaining growth as endogenous to agents' decisions, and explaining very different growth paths across countries—make it natural to consider the political economy of growth. Political economy models attempt to explain economic outcomes as reflecting endogenous political decisions which affect those outcomes; accumulation of physical and human capital should be significantly affected by political decisions, so the political economy of growth naturally fits into endogenous growth theory. Moreover, given the significant effects that political decisions may have on the incentive to accumulate capital, it is not surprising that politics is invoked as a cause of very different growth paths across countries, with rigorous political models being used to study that possibility.

Independent of new growth theory, the political economy of growth is a natural extension of the political economy of income redistribution, which was covered in Chapter 8. There, we saw that the tax-transfer policies associated with income redistribution tend to be distortionary, so that distortion of factor supplies is a principal effect of income redistribution programs. In a dynamic setting with accumulable factors, income redistribution programs will thus have important effects on growth. Almost all of the models of redistribution that we considered in Chapter 8 were essentially static in their implications for economic variables. Though some of the models (such as Tabellini [1991] or Fernandez and Rogerson [1995]) consider redistribution across time, few considered truly dynamic implications of redistributive programs. Focusing on the political-economic determinants and implications of such programs thus leads to a natural focus on growth. In studying the link between politics and growth, a main emphasis will be on the dynamic implications of redistribution.

The shift from static to dynamic models extends beyond effects of redistribution. Many of the models we considered in previous chapters either were static models of essentially dynamic phenomena, or were models in which the dynamics were modeled quite simply. Since many of the issues in political economy are truly dynamic, models should be explicitly dynamic as well. When rational, forward-looking agents choose policies with dynamic implications, they should take these implications into account in their political decisions. Once a voter considers dynamic effects, the policies he will currently support may be quite different than a static analysis would suggest.

Using truly dynamic models for analysis means that, in addition to the intertemporal effects of political decisions, we must also consider general equilibrium effects. Two stand out. First, there is a two-way feedback

[1] Two excellent recent texts on growth are Barro and Sala-i-Martin (1995) and Aghion and Howitt (1998).

between income distribution and growth. Not only does income distribution affect growth, but the dynamic evolution of the economy will affect the distribution of income, the composition of the electorate, and perhaps decisionmaking rules themselves. A number of these issues will be considered in Sections 11.3 and 11.4 below. Second, voting behavior should be forward-looking, which may put constraints on the set of policies over time that are time consistent. This issue has been considered in some detail by Krusell, Quadrini, and Rios-Rull (1997), and will be touched on several times in the chapter.

Politics, Redistribution, and Growth

The overwhelming focus of the literature on the political economy of growth is the effect of income inequality on growth via the implied pressure for redistribution. Three basic points may help put the literature in perspective, two concerning the connection between redistribution and growth, the third concerning the connection between income inequality and redistribution. First, other things equal, redistribution will depress growth if the instruments of redistribution are distortionary; second, redistribution may enhance growth in the presence of credit constraints or externalities; third, though inequality in the distribution of income is probably the major factor inducing pressure for redistribution, the linkage between inequality and redistribution is far from simple. We consider these three points in turn.

In arguing that redistribution will depress growth if the instruments of redistribution are distortionary, the starting point of the analysis is the importance of property rights, broadly defined, in the decision to accumulate factors of production. The incentive to accumulate physical or human capital will depend on the ability to retain the ownership of the accumulated factor and especially the returns to the factor. The less "secure" are these property rights to the accumulable asset, the lower is the incentive, *ceteris paribus*, to accumulate the factor. To the extent that the factor is a major input into the growth process, growth will be adversely affected. Political economy enters in, as the security of property rights reflects political decisions.

There are at least three aspects of the political nature of the security of property that are of interest. First, property rights can be considered in the narrow sense as applying to taxation of property: even in the absence of the threat of outright expropriation, societies can nonetheless legally expropriate the fruits of accumulation via taxation.[2] The same general argument applies: anticipated taxation of capital will lower the incentive to accumulate and thus may hamper growth. The specific argument is a

---

[2] We sidestep the philosophical (or perhaps semantic) debate on whether taxation of property should be interpreted as indicating that property rights are not "secure."

dynamic application of the Meltzer–Richard (1981) model discussed in Section 8.2 of Chapter 8, with its focus on the relation between income inequality and redistribution in a political equilibrium. When the distribution of income is skewed to the right, the median voter will have below average income and will favor redistribution, even if it is distortionary. Hence, if the Median Voter Theorem applies, majority voting will imply distortionary redistribution. Basic models of the negative effect of inequality on growth due to the distortionary nature of taxation needed to effect redistribution are considered in Section 11.2. Second, at the most basic level, the security of property may be *constitutional*, by which one means property rights protected by firm legal guarantees, not subject to change by the whim of the current government or of the majority. (See Chapter 5 for a discussion of constitutionalism.) This yields a linkage between *political institutions* and growth, as will be discussed in detail in Section 11.4 of this chapter. Third, the security of property guaranteed by laws and institutions depends on the security and stability of those laws and institutions themselves. Political instability may induce irresistible pressures for redistribution and expropriation. Hence, to the extent that political instability creates pressures for expropriation of principal or return, it will create a disincentive for accumulation and be inimical to growth. These issues will be discussed theoretically in Section 11.5 and empirically in Section 11.6.

The second basic point which is crucial in assessing the connection between redistribution and growth is that redistribution may enhance growth in the presence of credit constraints or externalities. That is, the above results on the negative relation between redistribution and growth can be overturned for at least two reasons. First, even if there are no externalities in the process of capital accumulation, credit constraints can lead to an underaccumulation of growth-enhancing factors of production. Redistribution of income to the poor helps them overcome the constraints implied by capital market imperfections, thereby increasing accumulation of productive factors and thus growth. The political aspect of this is that when income distribution is skewed, a majority of individuals may vote for redistribution, not only because of the direct income effects, but also to ease their credit constraints. If the redistribution can be done in a nondistortionary way and there are no externalities, growth will be enhanced, but aggregate welfare will not be affected. If redistribution is distortionary, redistribution will imply higher growth, but lower aggregate welfare in the absence of externalities.

The second reason why redistribution may enhance growth *and* welfare is the existence of externalities in the process of capital accumulation, so that the increased investment by the direct beneficiaries of redistribution can have a positive effect on those being taxed. This means that there can be both a significant positive growth effect and an aggregate welfare gain from redistribution. In both the theory and empirics of recent growth models, human capital is seen as especially important as an engine of growth. In line with a defining characteristic of current models of growth, significant externalities are associated with human capital accumulation. Hence, a full integration of political economy and endogenous growth would suggest a positive rather than a negative role for redistribution. Models of growth focusing on capital market imperfections and human capital externalities are considered in Section 11.3.

Finally, though inequality in the distribution of income is probably the major factor inducing pressure for redistribution, the linkage between inequality and redistribution is far from simple. The previous two paragraphs suggested why the economic linkage from redistribution to growth may yield either a positive or a negative effect. The political linkage from income inequality to redistribution is similarly ambiguous. The basic political linkage is an application of the median voter model to choice of tax-based redistribution schemes, where an increase in inequality induces a fall in the position of the median voter relative to the mean. There are a number of reasons for ambiguity. First, one must be careful in automatically associating higher inequality with a fall in the median relative to the mean; as Saint-Paul and Verdier (1996) point out, it is *not* a general result that skewness will increase for all mean-preserving spreads in the distribution of income. For example, if the higher dispersion is concentrated among the poor, the median could rise relative to the mean. Second, and more important, even if higher inequality implies a fall in the median-to-mean ratio, the median voter need not be the decisive voter, for example, if political participation is not complete, as the simple median voter model assumes. In many countries, participation increases with the level of income, so that the decisive voter is above the median. This may significantly weaken the effect of inequality on growth, a possibility we study in Section 11.4 below.

More generally, the connection between inequality and redistributive pressures will depend on the nature of the political process. For example, one may ask whether, for a given degree of inequality, growth will be higher in nondemocratic than in democratic regimes, due to inequality implying greater pressure for redistribution in more democratic regimes. The question itself is far more complex than may first appear and the answer is ambiguous, as will be discussed theoretically in Section 11.4 and examined empirically in Section 11.6.

11.2. BASIC MODELS OF FISCAL POLICY AND CAPITAL ACCUMULATION

We now turn to the first, and most widely discussed, linkage between income distribution and growth, namely, redistribution-oriented fiscal policy. As indicated, the basic model may be seen as a continuation of the material of Chapter 8, focusing on dynamic implications of redistributive programs.

A Basic Model

Persson and Tabellini (1994b) present a simple model that very clearly illustrates the basic mechanisms involved. A number of simplifications allow a rigorous, but tractable, solution. The model is one of overlapping generations in which only the young supply labor and only the old hold capital, with no bequests across generations. A very specific linear production structure is assumed, implying not only that pre-tax factor returns are independent of factor supplies, but also that the return to labor, but not the return to capital, is affected by an externality to capital accumulation. The linearity of the production function makes the problem easier to solve, but has no substantive implications. The assumptions on the nature of the externality, on the other hand, are crucial for the results when combined with the other assumptions. We return to this below. Only the young vote on the rate at which capital will be taxed in the second period. Combined with the assumptions about factor supply and the production structure, the voting decision then becomes simple, so that forward-looking voting behavior is easy to derive. Finally, utility is a homothetic function only of one's own consumption (yielding inelastic labor supply and no bequests), where homotheticity is assumed for tractability.

Key to the model is that individuals differ in their labor endowments and hence in their saving behavior, with this difference in saving leading to different preferences over capital taxation. As such, the model is very similar to Tabellini (1991), discussed in detail in Chapter 8, except that there are no bequests, a central component of the earlier model. The capital-taxation decision is crucial, as capital is the engine of growth. Though variables in the model are taken as functions of calendar time, the stationarity of all relevant parameters means that growth is constant over time. Hence, the basic results can be most easily illustrated in a two-period framework.

As in the basic overlapping generations model, the economy is composed of two nonaltruistic generations, assumed of equal size (say one unit), where the young supply one unit of labor inelastically and hold no capital, while the old supply no labor and consume all their income. Factors are paid their marginal products, net of taxes and transfers, where the aggregate production function in per capita terms is

$$y_t = w_t + Rk_t, \tag{11.1}$$

so that the pre-tax return to capital is a constant R, independent of the capital labor ratio k_t. The average wage w_t depends on the economywide stock of capital k_t (determined in the previous period); individual wages differ according to an individual-specific skill component ξ^i. Assume that ξ^i has a zero mean and a nonpositive median and is distributed in the population according to a known distribution $F(\xi)$ independent of k_t.

Hence, the individual specific wage at t, w_t^i, may be written

$$w_t^i = (w + \xi^i)k_t, \tag{11.2}$$

so that the economywide average wage is simply $w_t = wk_t$.

Since the old simply consume all their income and are assumed not to vote on capital taxation, Persson and Tabellini concentrate on the economic and political decisions of the young.[3] The economic problem of the young is the standard problem in the two-period OLG model, namely, how much to save, given expected returns in the following period. There is a linear tax on capital, with the returns distributed lump-sum to the old, so, as in Meltzer and Richard (1981), the political decision is over the linear tax rate τ on capital, given its known redistributive implications. The economic problem of a young consumer-voter i can be represented as choosing first- and second-period consumption c_1^i and c_2^i to maximize

$$\Omega^i = u(c_1^i, c_2^i), \tag{11.3}$$

subject to the budget constraints in the two periods:

$$c_1^i + k_2^i = w_1^i, \tag{11.4}$$

where k_2^i is saving to be carried over to the next period, and

$$c_2^i = (1 - \tau)Rk_2^i + v, \tag{11.5}$$

where v is a lump-sum transfer.

Maximization of (11.3) subject to (11.4) and (11.5) yields a first-order condition of the form

$$\frac{u_1(c_1^i, c_2^i)}{u_2(c_1^i, c_2^i)} = (1 - \tau)R, \tag{11.6}$$

where u_1, for example, represents the derivative of $u(\cdot, \cdot)$ with respect to its first argument. With homothetic preferences, (where demand rises proportionally with income), one can go further, since the ratio of consumption in the two periods is independent of income and depends only on

---

[3] Since their holding of capital is given and they have no concern about the welfare of their children, the voting decision of the old would be trivial. Under the system of linear taxes and lump-sum redistribution that Persson and Tabellini consider, all individuals with capital below the mean would vote for a tax rate of 1, while all individuals with capital above the mean would vote for a tax rate of zero. The outcome would depend on the distribution of abilities $F(\xi)$, which determines the distribution of saving. In order to concentrate on the effect of expected taxation on capital accumulation decisions, Persson and Tabellini limit voting to the young.

the intertemporal price $(1 - \tau)R$. Since individuals differ only in their level of wage income, we may write this relation as

$$\frac{c_2^i}{c_1^i} = \phi[(1 - \tau)R], \tag{11.6a}$$

where $\phi'(\cdot) > 0$. Substituting (11.4) into (11.5) and using (11.6a) to solve for consumption, one obtains

$$c_1^i = \frac{(1 - \tau)Rw_1^i + \nu}{\phi[(1 - \tau)R] + (1 - \tau)R},$$

$$c_2^i = \phi[(1 - \tau)R]c_1^i, \tag{11.7}$$

$$k_2^i = \frac{\phi(\cdot)w_1^i - \nu}{\phi[(1 - \tau)R] + (1 - \tau)R}.$$

Given (11.2), (11.7) makes clear how the distribution of skills F(ξ) induces a distribution of asset holding k_2^i, with more skilled (and hence higher-income) individuals accumulating more capital.

We can now derive the economy's growth rate and show how it depends on the rate of capital taxation τ. From (11.1) and the economywide version of (11.2), it is clear that output y_t grows at the same rate as k_t. To derive the growth rate of capital, one must first close the model with the government budget constraint connecting taxes and transfers, namely

$$\tau R k_2 = \nu, \tag{11.8}$$

where k_2 is the average level of saving, that is, capital accumulation in the economy. (Substituting (11.8) into the economywide aggregate analogue of (11.5), one sees that consumption will also grow at the same rate in an equilibrium.) Using the economywide analogues of (11.4) and (11.2) to write $k_2 = \Sigma_i w_1^i - \Sigma_i c_1^i = w k_1 - \Sigma_i c_1^i$ and (11.7) and (11.8) for c_1^i, we may (after some algebra) write the growth rate $\hat{y}$ as

$$\hat{y}(\tau; w, R) \equiv \frac{k_2}{k_1} - 1$$

$$= \frac{w\phi[(1 - \tau)R]}{\phi[(1 - \tau)R] + R} - 1. \tag{11.9}$$

One then immediately derives that $\partial \hat{y}/\partial \tau = -[wR^2\phi'/(\phi + R)^2] < 0$. Hence, an increase in the tax rate on capital discourages capital accumulation and hence lowers growth.

To complete the model, Persson and Tabellini determine the capital tax rate consistent with political-economic equilibrium in order to see what this tax rate depends on. As in the models of politically determined programs of redistribution in Chapter 8, such as Meltzer and Richard (1981) or Tabellini (1991), one begins with the preferred tax rate of each voter, found by differentiating (11.3) with respect to τ, subject to (11.4), (11.5), (11.6), and (11.8). That is, each voter calculates the tax rate he prefers consistent with economic optimization as given by (11.6), taking account of the effect of his tax choice on equilibrium transfers as determined by the government's budget constraint (11.8). Differentiating (11.3) with respect to τ, one derives

$$\frac{\partial \Omega^i}{\partial \tau} = Ru_2[\cdot,\cdot]\left((k_2 - k_2^i) + \tau\frac{\partial k_2}{\partial \tau}\right) \geq 0. \qquad (11.10)$$

From (11.10), one can see the two influences on an individual voter's desired capital tax rate. First, there is the level of his capital holdings k_2^i, relative to the economywide average k_2. This reflects the structure of the redistributive program, with an individual paying taxes according to his capital holdings k_2^i and receiving transfers in return as determined by the economywide average k_2. Hence, individuals with capital below the economywide average prefer as high a tax as possible, all else equal, while those with capital above the economywide average prefer a tax as low as possible, all else equal. However, all else is not equal, as indicated by the last term in large parentheses in (11.10). An increase in the tax rate τ discourages capital accumulation, thus reducing the base k_2 for income redistribution.

This second effect is the same for all voters, while the first effect differs across voters. Using (11.2), (11.7), and (11.9), one may derive

$$k_2^i - k_2 = \frac{\phi[(1-\tau)R]k_1}{\phi[(1-\tau)R] + (1-\tau)R}\xi^i, \qquad (11.11)$$

so that individuals' tax preferences depend on their skill endowment relative to the mean, with it being possible to rank their preferences for redistribution by their skill endowment. Since individual preferences over taxes are single peaked for each voter, Persson and Tabellini use the Median Voter Theorem to derive the political equilibrium policy as that favored by the median voter. Given the discussion immediately following (11.11), this is the voter with the median skill endowment, which we denote ξ^{med}.

One may then solve for the equilibrium tax rate by computing an expression for $\partial k_2/\partial \tau$ and substituting it and (11.11) into (11.10) evaluated for the median voter. The tax rate τ^* in a political equilibrium is thus implicitly defined by

$$\frac{\phi[(1 - \tau)R]\,\xi^{\text{med}}}{\phi[\cdot] + (1 - \tau)R} + \frac{\tau w R^2 \phi'[\cdot]}{(\phi[\cdot] + R)^2} = 0, \qquad (11.12)$$

where the first term represents the benefit of redistribution for the median voter, while the second captures the marginal cost of tax distortions. As in the Meltzer–Richard model, if the median voter has the mean skill level (i.e., $\xi^{\text{med}} = 0$), he strictly prefers a zero tax, because of the distortionary nature of taxation. If the income distribution is skewed to the right, meaning that the median income is below the mean income ($w + \xi^{\text{med}} < w$, or, equivalently, $\xi^{\text{med}} < 0$), the equilibrium tax rate on capital will be positive.

The relation between income inequality and growth follows immediately from the above discussion and from (11.9) above. If the median voter's income is above the mean and tax rates on capital are constrained to be nonnegative, there will be no program of redistribution, no matter how unequal the income distribution. Changes in the income distribution will have no effect on the amount of redistribution if the change does not reduce the median income below the mean. On the other hand, if the median voter's income is below the mean, he will choose a positive tax-transfer program, and a change in the distribution of income which lowers the median relative to the mean (which can be thought of as an increase in income inequality) will result in a higher τ. This will imply lower capital accumulation and, via (11.9), lower growth.

Some Alternative Models

The Persson–Tabellini model well represents the basic political economy model of growth and cleanly delivers a central result of this literature: higher inequality increases the pressure for redistribution, which in turn leads to higher capital taxation and lower growth. A number of questions may be raised: first, how general is the negative relation between inequality and growth; second, what technical assumptions are necessary to derive robust, unambiguous economic results; and, third, what empirical support does the fiscal mechanism receive?

As mentioned in the previous section, the intuitively attractive result that higher inequality will lead to lower growth in a world with redistributive fiscal policy will hold in some classes of models, but not in others. Once we drop the assumptions of essentially linear technologies and perfect capital markets, tax-based redistribution may increase growth, rather than retard it. In Section 11.3, we consider these points in greater detail. Moreover, even when redistribution decreases growth, an increase in income inequality does not necessarily increase redistributive pressures for reasons discussed in Section 11.1 above. All this being said, in linear growth models such as the Persson–Tabellini model, there will often be a clear connection between inequality and growth. This will be true for inequality not only in the size distribution of income across individuals, but also in the functional distribution of income, that is, where individuals differ in the composition of their income across factors, with the political decision being relative factor tax rates. (In Persson and Tabellini, all the old own capital and no labor, but differ in the size of their capital holdings.) This sort of model, as in Bertola (1993) and Alesina and Rodrik (1994), will be considered in this section. This same type of result could be derived in a model with a nonlinear production structure, but perfect credit markets, as in Benabou (1996), which is outlined in Section 11.3 below.

The simplicity of models relating inequality to growth is dictated by the problem of simultaneously solving for an economic and a political equilibrium. This is the second question above, namely, what are the technical (as opposed to economic) assumptions that are necessary to derive robust, unambiguous economic results. The standard approach is to consider a very simple economic environment, so that solving a forward-looking political choice problem becomes feasible. Possible approaches to this problem are discussed in Krusell, Quadrini, and Rios-Rull (1997). (See footnote 6 below for more details.) Among the simplifications of the economic environment generally used are either two periods or no transitional dynamics in a multiperiod model. Alternatively, there can be restrictions over policy choices, such as the constraint that a time-invariant policy must be chosen for all time at time zero, an unattractive assumption in a political model.

On the third question of what empirical support the fiscal mechanism receives, the short answer is: very little. Though the empirical evidence of a negative relation between inequality and growth is strong, there is almost no evidence that this effect is due to the fiscal mechanism outlined above, opposed to other possible linkages. We examine alternative approaches in the next three sections and empirical tests of the fiscal mechanism in Section 11.6 below. First, we consider models of the functional distribution of income.

The functional-distribution models of Bertola (1993) and of Alesina and Rodrik (1994), developed independently, are quite similar. We will exposit them by considering the latter in detail and then showing similarities and differences between the two models. In Alesina and Rodrik, the aggregate production function at time t is of the form

$$y_t = A k_t^\alpha g_t^{1-\alpha} l_t^{1-\alpha}, \tag{11.13}$$

where g_t is the aggregate level of government spending on productive services, financed by a constant linear tax on capital:

$$g_t = \tau k_t. \tag{11.14}$$

(The constancy of the tax rate will be discussed below.) Capital k_t is meant to represent all productive, accumulable factors, while labor l_t is meant to represent nonaccumulable factors. Factors are paid their marginal products. Hence, using (11.13) and (11.14) and normalizing aggregate labor input to unity, one derives the pre-tax returns to capital and labor:

$$r_t = \frac{\partial y_t}{\partial k_t} = \alpha A \tau^{1-\alpha} \equiv r(\tau),$$

$$w_t = \frac{\partial y_t}{\partial l_t} = (1 - \alpha) A \tau^{1-\alpha} k_t \equiv w(\tau) k_t, \tag{11.15}$$

where $r(\tau)$ and $w(\tau)$ are both increasing in τ. The net-of-tax return to capital is $r(\tau) - \tau$. Hence, given the crucial role of tax-financed government spending in the production function, both the net return to capital and the level of wage rates are affected by tax policy.

Individuals differ in their factor ownership due to differing labor endowments. Individual i's constant labor endowment is l^i, where $\int_i l^i = 1$. (Variables with a superscript i refer to individual values, while variables with no superscript refer to aggregate values.) Differences in relative factor ownership may be summarized by a parameter ξ^i defined by

$$\xi^i = \frac{l^i}{k_t^i/k_t}, \tag{11.16}$$

where $\xi^i \in [0, \infty]$. (Though ξ^i may in general change over time, the specification of preferences and technology implies that it does not in this case.) Using (11.15) and (11.16), individual after-tax income y^i may then be written

$$y_t^i = w(\tau)\xi^i k_t^i + (r(\tau) - \tau)k_t^i. \tag{11.17}$$

Individual utility is assumed to be of the family of instantaneous utility functions with a constant elasticity of intertemporal substitution (also termed constant relative risk aversion or CRRA utility functions). For simplicity, a unitary consumption elasticity of substitution is assumed, but the results will carry over to any CES utility function. The individual's utility over an infinite horizon is

$$\Omega^i = \int \ln c_t^i e^{-\rho t}\, dt, \tag{11.18}$$

where ρ is the (continuous-time) constant discount rate. The individual's problem is to maximize (11.18) subject to an equation on the evolution of individual capital holdings k^i, namely,

$$\dot{k}^i_t = w(\tau)\xi^i k^i_t + (r(\tau) - \tau)k^i_t - c^i_t, \qquad (11.19)$$

where a dot over a variable represents a time derivative. This maximization implies an Euler equation for the evolution of consumption of the form

$$\frac{\dot{c}^i}{c^i} = r(\tau) - \tau - \rho. \qquad (11.20)$$

(For simplicity of exposition, when no confusion is likely to result, we omit time subscripts from here on.) It is assumed that the tax rate τ is chosen so that $r - \tau > \rho$. If the tax rate τ is constant over time, capital holdings of each individual will then evolve according to

$$\frac{\dot{k}^i}{k^i} = \frac{\dot{c}^i}{c^i} = r(\tau) - \tau - \rho \equiv \hat{y}(\tau), \qquad (11.21)$$

where $\hat{y}(\tau)$ is the growth rate. Hence, all individuals accumulate capital at the same rate, independent of their factor endowment ξ^i. ξ^i therefore remains constant over time and $\hat{y}(\tau)$ also represents the growth rate for the economy as a whole.

The higher the after-tax rate of return on capital, the higher the growth rate. The after-tax return is maximized at an interior value of τ, namely,

$$\tau^* = ((1 - \alpha)\alpha A)^{1/\alpha}. \qquad (11.22)$$

The fact that the after-tax return (and the economy's growth rate) reaches its maximum at an interior value of τ may be explained intuitively as follows. For low tax rates, the productivity-enhancing effect of government expenditures g dominates, so that the after-tax return to capital *increases* in τ. For high enough τ, however, the negative direct effect dominates and the after-tax return falls. (For $w(\tau)$, there is only the productivity effect of higher tax-financed government expenditure, so that $w'(\tau)$ is positive for all values of τ.)

Along an optimal path, consumption c^i of individual i is a constant fraction of his wealth. Using (11.19) and (11.21), this may be written

$$c^i = y^i - \dot{k}^i_t$$

$$= (w(\tau)\xi^i + \rho)k^i. \qquad (11.23)$$

An individual therefore consumes all of his labor income and a fraction of his capital income.

To derive the preferences of an individual voter over tax rates, suppose that each individual chooses his preferred τ as if he were the decisive voter, taking into account the effect of his choice not only on his preferred tax rate, but also on the growth of the economy as a whole. Hence, an individual's choice of his preferred tax rate may be represented by choosing τ to maximize (11.18) subject to (11.23) and the constraint

$$\frac{\dot{k}^i}{k^i} = \frac{\dot{k}}{k} = r(\tau) - \tau - \rho \equiv \hat{y}(\tau). \qquad (11.24)$$

The individual's preferred tax rate τ^i is then defined implicitly by

$$(1 - (1-\alpha)\alpha A(\tau^i)^{-\alpha})\tau^i = (1-\alpha)\rho\frac{w(\tau^i)\xi^i}{w(\tau^i)\xi^i + \rho}, \qquad (11.25)$$

where the last term on the right-hand side is the share of labor income in total consumption spending.[4] Several observations about an individual's preferred tax rate will be useful. The preferred capital tax rate τ^i is increasing in the relative labor endowment ξ^i, with an individual who receives income only from capital ($\xi^i = 0$) preferring the tax rate which maximizes $r(\tau) - \tau$, which is τ^* in (11.22). This is also the tax rate that maximizes the growth rate $\hat{y}(\tau)$. Hence, any individual who receives part of his income from labor ($\xi^i > 0$), no matter how small a fraction of total income, prefers a tax rate above τ^*, that is, prefers a growth rate below the maximum. If all individuals were identical, so that $\xi^i = 1$, the welfare-maximizing tax rate would therefore *a fortiori* be above τ^*.

Why do almost all individuals in an economy (or the representative individual in an economy of identical individuals) prefer a tax rate that leads to growth below the maximum possible? The key to understanding this result (and hence the nature of the political equilibrium it implies) is to remember that the tax rate τ affects both the growth of consumption (from (11.20)) *and* its level (from (11.23)) for everyone except an individual who receives all his income from capital, whose level of consumption is independent of τ. For anyone with positive labor income, consider the effect of a marginal increase in τ above τ^*. Since the growth rate $\hat{y}$ is at a

---

[4] To derive this expression, note that (11.23) and (11.24) imply that (11.18) can be written

$$\Omega^i = \int \ln [(w(\tau)\xi^i + \rho)e^{\hat{y}(\tau)t}k_0^i]e^{-\rho t}\,dt,$$

for some initial k_0^i. Evaluating the integral and then differentiating with respect to τ yields (11.25).

maximum, the effect of this marginal increase in τ on $\hat{y}$ is second order, while the effect on instantaneous consumption is first order.

The political equilibrium in the Alesina and Rodrik model may then be easily derived. The conditions of the Median Voter Theorem are satisfied: there is voting over a single issue, namely, the capital tax rate τ, with single-peaked preferences that are monotonic in factor endowments. Hence, the equilibrium tax rate will be the tax rate preferred by the median voter, denoted τ^{med}. As the factor endowment does not change over time, neither will the identity of the median voter, nor his preferred tax rate. The equilibrium tax rate will be given by (11.25) for the median voter:

$$(1 - (1 - \alpha)\alpha A(\tau^{\text{med}})^{-\alpha})\tau^{\text{med}}$$
$$= (1 - \alpha)\rho\frac{w(\tau^{\text{med}})\xi^{\text{med}}}{w(\tau^{\text{med}})\xi^{\text{med}} + \rho}, \tag{11.26}$$

where ξ^{med} is the relative factor endowment of the median voter.

The growth rate in a political-economic equilibrium will then depend on the factor endowment ξ^{med} of the median voter, and the effect of increased inequality of income on growth will depend on how higher inequality affects ξ^{med}. Alesina and Rodrik point out that in observed functional income distributions, the labor/capital share of the median voter ($l^{\text{med}}/k^{\text{med}}$) is above the average share (l/k), that is, $\xi^{\text{med}} > 1$. Moreover, they argue that the greater the inequality of the functional distribution of income, the larger this difference between the median and the average is likely to be, that is, the higher will be ξ^{med}. This implies a higher equilibrium tax rate τ^{med} and hence a lower equilibrium growth rate $\hat{y}$, as the growth rate is monotonically falling in τ for $\tau > \tau^*$, as it will be if the median voter has any labor income. Hence, under the argument that an increase in the inequality of income will correspond to a fall in the income of the median voter relative to the mean income in the economy, Alesina and Rodrik derive the same result in a median voter model for the functional distribution of income that Persson and Tabellini (1994b) derived for the size distribution of income: *the more unequal the distribution of income and wealth, the lower the rate of growth*.[5] The more capital the median voter owns, the higher is the growth rate; for growth to be at its maximum possible level, the median voter must own only capital, thus preferring a tax rate that maximizes $r - \tau$ and hence the growth rate $\hat{y}$.

The Bertola (1993) model is similar to the Alesina and Rodrik model, highlighting some of the same issues and deriving many of the same

---

[5] Alesina and Rodrik point out that if we assume that all individuals have a common value of l^i (say 1), so that they differ only in their capital income, one may rewrite (11.17) as $y^i = (w + (r - \tau)(1/\xi^i))k$, so that there is a monotonic relation between the size and the factor composition of income.

results, but with some illuminating differences. Technically, the models are quite similar. Both use a continuous-time endogenous growth framework with an externality from capital accumulation to transform a production function with decreasing returns to capital into one with constant returns, thus allowing balanced growth. Whereas Alesina and Rodrik base this transformation on productive government expenditures, financed by a linear tax on capital, entering the production function, Bertola follows the endogenous growth literature in assuming that the index of technical progress depends on aggregate capital accumulation. That is, if the production function is of the form, $y_t = A_t k_t^{\alpha} l_t^{1-\alpha}$, the index of technical progress is of the form $A_t = k_t^{1-\alpha}$. Both papers consider inequality in the functional distribution of income, stressing the importance for the political economy of growth of the distinction between productive, accumulable factors, such as physical capital, and nonaccumulable factors, such as raw labor (or land). Bertola considers a general constant elasticity utility function, leading to an individually optimal growth path analogous to (11.21). Combined with the linear (inclusive of the externality) production function, factor shares are constant over time, as are saving and growth rates. That is, like other endogenous growth models with linear technology, one obtains steady-state growth with no transitional dynamics, with equilibrium growth being possible for any constant fiscal policy. As in Alesina and Rodrik, the constancy of factor shares combined with the lack of transitional dynamics implies that each individual's preferred fiscal policy is constant over time, and the Median Voter Theorem can be applied to the choice of constant tax rates over time.[6]

The models differ in the types of fiscal policy they study. Bertola first considers a subsidy to capital at rate τ_{π}, financed by flat tax on labor income τ_w (with a negative value of τ_{π} corresponding to a tax on capital). A balanced government budget implies that the capital subsidy and the labor tax are positively related, namely, $\tau_w = [\alpha/(1-\alpha)]\tau_{\pi}$. Since none of the income accruing to the nonaccumulated factor is saved, while a constant fraction ρ of capital income is saved, a transfer of income from labor to capital will increase the economy's saving rate and growth rate. Hence, the income transfer in Bertola is explicit, while the same sort of transfer between capital and labor is implicit in Alesina and Rodrik. However, the specific tax set-up that Bertola considers implies a monotonic positive relation between capital subsidy rates and growth, rather

---

[6] Krusell, Quadrini, and Rios-Rull (1997) argue that the time consistency of the constant tax paths derived in the Bertola (1993) and Alesina and Rodrik (1994) models depends not only on the fact that voters are infinitely lived (unlike the voters in the Persson and Tabellini [1994b] model, where it was assumed the government could precommit to the tax rate chosen by young voters), but also on the linearity of the growth model. More generally, the requirement of time consistency will imply that the tax path arising from voting period-by-period will not be identical to the one arising from a once-and-for-all choice of a constant tax rate at time zero, even if the former results in a constant tax rate.

than the analogous hump-shaped relationship in Alesina and Rodrik. As in the other models discussed so far in this section, the growth rate consistent with political-economic equilibrium in a median voter model is below the social optimum when the labor/capital share of the median voter is above the average labor/capital share. Unlike the results found in Alesina and Rodrik, however, the growth rate consistent with political equilibrium may be *larger* than the socially optimal one when investment subsidies are part of the policy menu. We will explore this type of result further in Section 11.3 below.

Another strong point of the Bertola model is that it allows for consideration of a wide range of tax policies. One must distinguish the economic consequences of a given tax policy from the political consequences in deriving the implications of a tax structure in a political equilibrium. From a purely economic point of view, the different propensities to consume out of labor and capital income imply that an investment subsidy financed by taxation of labor income (as considered in the previous paragraph) will increase saving and growth, while taxation of capital income to finance investment subsidies will be self-defeating. From a political point of view, however, financing investment subsidies by labor taxes need not increase growth in equilibrium, while other taxes may. As we saw, if the median voter is sufficiently capital-poor, significant subsidies will not gain political support if they are financed by labor taxation. Using a consumption tax to finance an investment subsidy has a less clear distributional, and hence growth, effect, once both political and economic factors are considered. A framework which allows consideration of a broad range of tax packages has a further, empirical advantage. The lack of empirical support for a model linking inequality to growth via redistributive taxation of capital may reflect the fact that systems of taxation, for redistribution and other reasons, are far more complicated than suggested by these simple models. One response to the lack of empirical support is that redistribution takes place via indirect means, rather than direct tax-transfer programs. A more persuasive argument is that the negative effects of redistributive taxation may be offset by investment subsidies, so that there is no simple empirical relation between taxation and investment.

One criticism of all of these models is that the lack of transitional dynamics. This is dictated, as discussed above, by the difficulty in solving for a simultaneous economic and political equilibrium if the economic model is not extremely simple. Considering more inherently dynamic models has other implications as well. When dynamic effects are taken into account, the long-run effects of tax-transfer programs on distribution may be quite different than the short-run effects. In terms of welfare, the dynamic implications of a tax-transfer program via its effect on capital accumulation may far outweigh any static effect. A tax on capital which reduces capital accumulation may benefit wage-earners in the short run, but harm them in the long run. (Diamond [1970] presents a dynamic model of the incidence of factor taxes which demonstrates this type of result.) Hence, when rational, forward-looking voters choose a redistribution program, the program that a voter of a given income level will currently support may be quite different not only than what might be suggested by the Meltzer–Richards model, but also by the basic Persson–Tabellini (1994b) model.

11.3. Imperfect Capital Markets, Externalities, and Endogenous Income Distribution

In this section, we consider some important extensions of the basic fiscal model of redistribution and growth, showing that the results can be much richer. As indicated above, once we introduce imperfect capital markets in a general model, the key result of the earlier model may easily be reversed, even in the absence of externalities. Allowing for the sort of externalities that are central to new growth models gives a strong reason why redistributive policies may enhance growth performance if the means used to redistribute income are not overly distortionary. Moreover, allowing these factors to come into play yields important feedbacks from growth to income distribution. We consider these issues in turn.

Capital Market Imperfections

Independent of the political economy literature, there have been several papers showing how income inequality may affect growth in the presence of capital market imperfections, as in Galor and Zeira (1993), Banerjee and Newman (1993), or Aghion and Bolton (1997). The general argument used in many papers is that a fixed cost in individual investment prevents individuals below a certain income level from taking advantage of investment opportunities in the presence of credit constraints. Greater equality in the distribution of income relaxes these constraints, thereby increasing capital accumulation and growth. The role of capital market imperfections in the relation between income inequality and growth may be illustrated in a version of the model of the previous section that follows Benabou (1996). The key difference from our earlier models is that individuals do not face constant returns in their investment decisions, so that income distribution matters for the aggregate level of accumulation, even taking the tax system as given.

Consider an overlapping generations model where an individual's utility function (11.3) is of the form

$$u^i = \ln c_1^i + \beta \ln c_2^i, \tag{11.27}$$

where β is the discount factor. An individual is born with an endowment of resources $w_1^i = w + \xi^i$, where ξ^i has a zero mean and a known distribution $F(\xi)$. Individuals save in the first period of life by investing in capital (physical or human) according to the technology:

$$y_{t+1}^i = \kappa w^{1-\alpha}(k_{t+1}^i)^\alpha, \tag{11.28}$$

where k_{t+1}^i is first-period saving (in period t), y_{t+1}^i is second-period before-tax income, κ is a constant, and $0 < \alpha < 1$. In contrast to (11.1), individuals face decreasing returns in their investment.

As a point of reference, assume that individuals face perfect credit markets, so they can borrow and lend from one another at an (endogenous) interest factor R. Denote the amount borrowed in the first period by b^i, where b^i can be positive or negative, but must be repaid with interest in the second period of life. The budget constraints in the two periods (where $t = 1$) become

$$
\begin{aligned}
c_1^i &= w_1^i + b^i - k_2^i, \\
c_2^i &= (1 - \tau)y_2^i + \nu - Rb^i.
\end{aligned} \tag{11.29}
$$

(For ease of exposition, we suppress the subscript 2 on y and k, these variables referring to second-period values.) Maximizing (11.27) subject to (11.28) and (11.29) yields the following first-order conditions with respect to b^i and k^i:

$$\frac{c_2^i}{c_1^i} = \beta R = \alpha\beta(1 - \tau)\frac{y^i}{k^i}. \tag{11.30}$$

Together with (11.28), the first-order conditions imply

$$k^i = \left[(1 - \tau)\frac{\alpha\kappa}{R}\right]^{1/1-\alpha} w \equiv k, \tag{11.31}$$

so that all individuals have the same investment independent of income. They also have the same second-period income y, so that no net transfers take place in equilibrium. The interest factor R can then be derived:

$$R = \alpha\kappa(1 - \tau)\left(\frac{w}{k}\right)^{1-\alpha} \equiv R(\tau). \tag{11.32}$$

The Euler equation $c_2^i = \beta R c_1^i$ then may be written

$$\kappa k^\alpha w^{1-\alpha} - Rb^i = \beta R(\tau)(w_1^i + b^i - k). \tag{11.33}$$

Combining (11.32), (11.33), and the condition for loan-market clearing, namely, $\int b^i\, di = 0$, one obtains

$$k = \frac{\beta\alpha(1-\tau)}{1+\beta\alpha(1-\tau)}w = s(\tau)w, \tag{11.34}$$

so that each individual invests the *same* fraction of *aggregate* resources. Though no net transfers take place in equilibrium, the *threat* of expropriation of part of the return to investment affects saving and growth. More specifically (11.34) implies that $\partial s(\tau)/\partial\tau < 0$, so that a higher tax on capital induces lower saving and capital accumulation. The growth rate of income within a generation is simply $\ln(y/w) = \ln\kappa + \alpha\ln s(\tau)$, so that the growth rate declines as τ rises.[7] Hence, a model with a nonlinear production function but perfect capital markets delivers the same results as the linear production models in Section 11.2.

Once we consider imperfect capital markets, the story will be quite different, depending on the nature of the tax system and of the nonlinear production function. Benabou (1996) presents a simple example with nonlinear taxation of investment expenditures (or of capital prior to production) according to

$$\underset{\sim}{k}^i = (k^i)^{1-\tau}(k^0)^\tau, \tag{11.35}$$

where $\underset{\sim}{k}^i$ is the after-tax level of investment and k^0 is defined by the balanced budget constraint $\int\underset{\sim}{k}^i\, di \equiv \int(k^i)^{1-\tau}(k^0)^\tau\, di = \int k^i\, di$.[8] This example corresponds to taxing large investments and subsidizing small ones: an individual investing k^i faces a price of $(k^i/k^0)^{\tau/(1-\tau)}$.

Imperfect capital markets may be represented simply by considering the above model when individuals have *no* access to a loan market, that is, where $b_i = 0$ for all i, so that an individual maximizes

$$u^i = \ln(w^i - k^i) + \beta\ln(\kappa w^{1-\alpha}(\underset{\sim}{k}^i)^\alpha), \tag{11.27a}$$

subject to (11.35), where second-period consumption is after-tax income. One derives optimal investment of

$$k^i = \frac{\beta\alpha(1-\tau)}{1+\beta\alpha(1-\tau)}w^i = s(\tau)w^i, \tag{11.34a}$$

---

[7] One can derive an explicit intergenerational growth equation if one assumes, as in the Persson and Tabellini model above, that the wage w_1^i is proportional to k_1, so that (11.34) becomes a capital accumulation equation.

[8] The previous results with perfect capital markets are the same if the income tax system were nonlinear analogous to (11.35) rather than linear. It is when capital markets are imperfect that the nonlinearity of the tax system is crucial to the results.

so that each individual invests a fraction s not of *aggregate* income (as in (11.34)), but of his *own* wage income w^i. Income distribution now matters. To determine economywide equilibrium magnitudes, we may use the balanced budget condition to define $k^0 = sw^0$, where

$$(w^0/w)^\tau = w^{1-\tau} / \int_i (w^i)^{1-\tau} \, di. \tag{11.35a}$$

Second-period individual income y^i as a function of w^i and economywide variables is then, from (11.28) and (11.35),

$$y^i = \kappa s^\alpha (w^i)^{\alpha(1-\tau)} (w^0)^{\alpha\tau} w^{1-\alpha}. \tag{11.36}$$

Summing over agents to obtain aggregate second-period income y, one derives the growth rate for aggregate income between periods:

$$\ln \frac{y}{w} = \ln \kappa + \alpha \ln s(\tau) - \ln \frac{\left(\int (w^i)^{1-\tau} \right)^\alpha di}{\int \left[(w^i)^{\alpha(1-\tau)} \right] di}, \tag{11.37}$$

where the first two terms equal the growth rate under perfect capital markets. The last term captures the effect of imperfect capital markets when the technology is nonlinear. This term is negative for $\alpha < 1$ due to Jensen's inequality and equal to zero when $\alpha = 1$.

A number of results thus emerge. *Given* the tax rate, an increase in income inequality (represented by a mean-preserving spread in w^i) reduces the growth rate, as long as $\alpha < 1$, while a more equal initial wage distribution implies higher growth. The reasoning is simple. Individuals face decreasing returns to investment, so that a distribution of income more favorable to the poor relaxes their credit constraints, allowing them to earn a higher return. However, if a more equal distribution is brought about by a greater redistribution (that is, a higher τ), there will be conflicting effects. A more equal income distribution will increase growth for the reason just given (an effect represented by the last term in (11.37)), but the higher tax rate necessary to effect the redistribution will reduce each individual's incentive to invest, as in the case of perfect capital markets. As in the models of Bertola (1993) and Alesina and Rodrik (1994) discussed in Section 11.2, there will be a growth-maximizing tax rate, which in the Benabou model will depend on the degree of pre-tax inequality.

This example makes clear that once we consider capital market imperfections in a world where the structure of production is not linear, it is no longer the case that redistribution reduces growth. Redistribution effected through the tax system will dampen the incentive to accumulate capital, the driving force of the models of Section 11.2, but may also ease credit constraints, thereby enhancing capital accumulation and growth. This is the main message of papers investigating the interaction of credit constraints and income inequality when the level of redistribution is *exogenous*, so that a more equal distribution of income generally has an unambiguously positive effect on growth.

A further difference between Benabou's model and the papers mentioned at the beginning of this section, such as Galor and Zeira (1993), is that in the latter, capital market imperfections interact with income inequality because of a fixed cost in investment that generates a threshold level of income or wealth. As Benabou (1996) points out and his model makes clear, while a nonconvexity of this sort was originally seen as crucial in generating the result that greater income equality may enhance growth in the presence of imperfect capital markets, the same result can arise solely through the feedback from distribution to factor prices. (Loury [1981] makes a similar point.)

Human Capital Externalities

We now consider externalities in the process of capital accumulation in the presence of capital market imperfections. When such externalities are important in the growth process, there may be a significant positive growth effect and an aggregate gain from redistribution. Whether tax-financed redistribution increases or decreases growth depends on whether or not the growth-enhancing effects of redistribution are greater than the distortionary effects of the taxation used to finance redistribution in depressing capital accumulation. These growth-enhancing effects may reflect both the role of redistribution in enabling the poor to overcome credit constraints and the positive spillovers that may result when they do. We consider two models to illustrate these effects. The first, due to Saint-Paul and Verdier (1993), assumes nondistortionary taxation and no explicit fixed costs in the investment process, allowing us to focus on the growth-enhancing effects of human capital externalities. In contrast to much of the literature on the political economy of growth, it implies an endogenous evolution of the distribution of income over time. In the second model, due to Perotti (1993), both fixed costs in the investment process and human capital externalities play a role in determining the relation between tax-financed redistribution and growth. Even with nondistortionary taxation, the initial distribution of income is central to whether or not redistribution enhances growth.

The Model of Saint-Paul and Verdier

Saint-Paul and Verdier (1993) present a model of an externality in the process of human capital accumulation in the presence of capital market imperfections, but where taxes are nondistortionary. Thus, redistribution unambiguously increases growth. Each generation is made up of a continuum of individuals, where total population is constant and normalized to 1. Each individual i lives for one period and has one child, also indexed by i. Generations are connected by altruism, in that each individual cares about his own consumption c_t^i and about his child's human capital h_{t+1}^i. Hence, individual i in generation t has a utility function of the form $u(c_t^i, h_{t+1}^i)$, which is increasing and strictly concave in each of its arguments, as well as homothetic. The marginal rate of substitution u_h/u_c is nonincreasing in h_{t+1}^i/c_t^i. The human capital of an individual in generation $t + 1$ depends on both public education g_t^{ed} and on inherited human capital, that is, on the human capital of their parents h_t^i, where this latter determinant is the only difference between individuals. Specifically, an individual's human capital is determined by

$$h_{t+1}^i = (1 - l)\gamma h_t^i + g_t^{ed}, \tag{11.38}$$

where $1 - l$ is the constant, exogenous fraction of time devoted to transmission of human capital across generations and $\gamma > 1$ is a parameter measuring increased productivity of human capital over time, implying aggregate economic growth. The formulation of g_t^{ed} is meant to represent that each individual is supplied with the same amount, rather than any inherent public good nature of public education. The aggregate production function is linear in human capital:

$$y_t = h_t, \tag{11.39}$$

where h_t is human capital used in production, namely, $h_t = l \int h_t^i \, di = \bar{l} h_t$. Equation (11.39) implies that the wage per unit of human capital is unity, so each individual's income is simply $l h_t^i$.

Public education in period t is financed by a proportional income tax τ_t, so that the amount of resources devoted to public education is $\tau_t \bar{l} h_t$. The production of public education benefits from the same productivity effect as private human capital transfers across generations, that is,

$$g_t^{ed} = \gamma l \tau_t \bar{h}_t. \tag{11.40a}$$

Hence, a social planner who is not concerned about the distribution of income *per se* will be indifferent as to whether education is publicly or privately provided. Private consumption is

$$c_t^i = (1 - \tau_t) l h_t^i. \tag{11.40b}$$

Note that the exogeneity of l, giving the division of time between working and human capital accumulation, means that the individual has no *eco-*

nomic choice problem. The proportional income tax is therefore nondistortionary.

The growth rate as a function of the tax rate may be easily derived. Aggregating (11.38) across individuals and using (11.40a), one derives

$$\bar{h}_{t+1} = \gamma(1 - l + \tau_t l)\bar{h}_t. \tag{11.41}$$

Given the production function (11.38), $\hat{h}(\tau) \equiv \gamma(1 - l + \tau l)$ is (one plus) the growth rate of the economy for a given tax rate τ. Hence, the economy's growth rate is unambiguously *increasing* in the tax rate τ, in contrast to the models of Section 11.2. Two characteristics of the model explain the difference. First as noted in the previous paragraph, the income tax is nondistortionary, since, by assumption, there is no investment choice in this model. This implies that there is no negative effect of taxation on asset accumulation. This characteristic alone, however, would not imply a *positive* effect of taxation on growth. It is the second characteristic, namely, tax-financed public education, which accounts for this positive effect. If human capital accumulation in (11.38) depended only on private inputs, (11.41) would imply growth of $\hat{h}(\tau) \equiv \gamma(1 - l)$, which would be independent of τ for an exogenous l and would be decreasing in τ if the investment versus consumption decision were endogenous, analogous to the models in Section 11.2. Tax-financed public education introduces a positive externality into the growth process, as an extra unit of income devoted to public education benefits all individuals. As public education must be financed by taxation in this model, higher taxes imply an increased growth effect. The assumption that taxes are nondistortionary due to exogenous l makes this effect unambiguous.

To complete the model, one then needs, first of all, to solve for the political equilibrium. Saint-Paul and Verdier, in line with much of the political economy of growth literature, consider a political system with majority voting over the tax rate. An individual's preferred tax rate is found by maximizing his utility $u(c_t^i, h_{t+1}^i)$, subject to the equations defining c_t^i, h_{t+1}^i, and g_t^{ed}. The first-order condition is

$$\frac{u_h\left[(1 - \tau_t)lh_t^i, (1 - l)\gamma h_t^i + \gamma\tau_t l\bar{h}_t\right]}{u_c\left[(1 - \tau_t)lh_t^i, (1 - l)\gamma h_t^i + \gamma\tau_t l\bar{h}_t\right]} \leq \frac{h_t^i}{\gamma\bar{h}_t}, \tag{11.42}$$

with desired $\tau_t > 0$ when (11.42) holds with equality, and equal to zero otherwise. Using the homotheticity of the utility function, one may write the solution to (11.42) with equality as a function $\tau(h_t^i/\bar{h}_t)$, and individual i's desired tax rate $\tilde{\tau}_t^i$ as

$$\tilde{\tau}_t^i = \max\left(0, \tau\left(h_t^i/\bar{h}_t\right)\right). \tag{11.43}$$

With further restrictions on the utility function, one may show that poorer individuals prefer higher tax rates, due to the redistributive nature of public education.[9] The concavity of the objective function in τ implies that preferences over tax rates are single peaked, with the preferred tax rate monotonically decreasing in an individual's relative position in the income distribution. The conditions of the Median Voter Theorem are thus satisfied, so that the actual tax rate in a political equilibrium will be the one preferred by the individual who is median in the income distribution.[10] Income is evolving over time according to (11.38), but this evolution will not change the ranking of individuals in the income distribution, so that the median voter will always come from the same dynasty. Hence, the tax rate will be determined by (11.43) for the individual with the median endowment h_t^{med}, which will evolve according to (11.38).

The impact of higher initial income inequality follows immediately from the relationship between relative income and the preferred tax rate, combined with the median voter result. With the median below the mean, an increase in income inequality may be associated with a lower initial value of the median endowment relative to the mean, that is, with a lower initial value of $h^{\text{med}}/\bar{h}$. This will mean higher taxes (as in the models of Section 11.2) and thus higher spending on public education, which implies, via (11.41), a higher growth rate. Hence, a country that starts with a more unequal income distribution will grow *faster* at each point of time than one with a more equal distribution. This is in sharp contrast to the basic fiscal model in the previous section, though the implication for tax rates is identical.

The model differs from the basic fiscal model in another way as well, since the income distribution is endogenously evolving over time. To see this, one may substitute (11.41) and (11.40a) into (11.38) to obtain (for any individual i)

$$\frac{h_{t+1}^i}{\bar{h}_{t+1}} = a_t \frac{h_t^i}{\bar{h}_t} + (1 - a_t), \qquad (11.44)$$

where $a_t = (1 - l)/(1 - l + l\tau_t) < 1$ as long as $\tau_t > 0$. Hence, the dispersion of income is shrinking over time. This reflects the "leveling" effect of public education in the model, where this effect will persist over time. Dynasties that are poorer than the mean will have human capital growth faster than the economy average; dynasties richer than the mean will

---

[9] Specifically, if we denote the left-hand side of (11.42) by a function $B(h_t^i/\bar{h}_t)$, with an inverse $\phi(\cdot) = B^{-1}(\cdot)$, one may show that a sufficient condition for $\tau(h_t^i/\bar{h}_t)$ to be decreasing in $h_t^i/\bar{h}_t$ is that $-x\phi'(x)/\phi(x) \geq 1$. See Saint-Paul and Verdier (1993).

[10] The interested reader may want to compare this model with the basic Meltzer and Richard model in Section 8.2 of Chapter 8, which delivers a similar relation between an individual's preferred tax rate and his skill endowment relative to the mean.

experience human capital growth slower than the economy average. The higher is taxation and thus spending on public education, the faster will be this income convergence process (as well as the overall growth rate itself being higher). On the other hand, if the median voter prefers $\tau_t = 0$, there will be no change in the dispersion of income both in the short run and in the long run, as this voter will remain the median voter.

Saint-Paul and Verdier consider the more realistic case in which the median voter is poorer than the mean, and ask to what political-economic equilibrium the economy will converge. With human capital below the mean, the median voter prefers a positive tax rate, so that income dispersion will shrink over time. As his income gets closer to the mean according to (11.44), he prefers lower spending on education, and growth slows down. As long as $u_h(\tau = 0)/u_c(\tau = 0) \geq 1/\gamma$, the economy will converge to full equality, with the steady-state tax rate τ_∞ defined by

$$\frac{u_h[(1 - \tau_\infty)l, (1 - l)\gamma + \gamma\tau_\infty l]}{u_c[(1 - \tau_\infty)l, (1 - l)\gamma + \gamma\tau_\infty l]} = \frac{1}{\gamma}. \tag{11.45}$$

The economy's growth factor will decline steadily to $\hat{h}_\infty \equiv \gamma(1 - l + l\tau_\infty)$. However, if the restriction on u_h/u_c evaluated at $\tau = 0$ is not satisfied, the income convergence process will stop before all inequality disappears, namely, it will stop as soon as the median voter's preferred tax rate equals zero. At that point, the economy will spend no further resources on public education, the income distribution will reproduce itself indefinitely, and the economy will grow according to $\hat{h} \equiv \gamma(1 - l)$.

Fixed Costs and Externalities in a Voting Equilibrium

We now consider a model of growth with imperfect capital markets closer to those of Galor and Zeira (1993) and Banerjee and Newman (1993), in that there is a fixed cost of investing in human capital, the factor which drives the growth process via externalities. Unlike these models, there is voting over the tax system, where in his voting decision, the decisive voter takes into account the effect of redistribution not only on his post-tax income (as in the most basic models of redistribution) and on his ability to invest (as a fixed-cost model would suggest), but also on the human capital externality, via its effect on the ability of *other* individuals to invest. In this respect, the message is similar to the message in the model of Saint-Paul and Verdier—not only may redistribution be good for growth, but the political endogeneity of tax rates implies that higher income inequality may be necessary for growth-enhancing redistribution to take place. The difference from the Saint-Paul and Verdier model in the previous subsection is that the nonconvexity in the investment process makes the choice of preferred tax rates much more complex for voters who internalize the growth externality in their individual voting (but not their individual investment) decision. As in other models with fixed costs and imperfect capital markets, the initial distribution of income plays a crucial role, though with added emphasis here, as it determines the nature of the political equilibrium.

The model is based on Perotti's (1993) model of growth with human capital externalities, though with some key changes. Because of the interaction of political and economic factors, the set of possible equilibria is far richer than in other models with fixed costs, credit constraints, and human capital externalities. In an economy that is very poor overall, only a very unequal distribution of income, which concentrates wealth in the hands of the rich, may be consistent with growth. This requires, however, that the middle class, which contains the decisive voters, be not too much poorer than the rich, for otherwise they will have an incentive to expropriate their wealth. In contrast, in a rich economy, where redistribution would significantly affect investment decisions only of the poor, growth is maximized for a more equal distribution of income. To achieve the growth-maximizing redistribution, however, the middle class and the poor must have similar incomes, for otherwise the decisive voters in the middle class will lack the incentive to enact the necessary redistributive program.

We consider a simplified version of Perotti's model, which will represent the main results. In some respects, it is similar in set-up to the Perotti model of redistribution and factor mobility considered in Section 8.7 of Chapter 8. There are two periods and three types of individuals, high income, middle income, and low income (denoted by initials H, M, and L, respectively), distinguished by their pre-tax labor income $w^H > w^M > w^L \geq 0$. Let us further assume that $w^H > 1, w^L < 1$, and w^M is "close" to $\bar{w}$, the mean of the income distribution. The importance of the first two assumptions will be clear shortly; the third assumption will play a role in characterizing possible equilibria. The number of individuals of type i is N_i, where it is assumed that the fraction of each group is strictly less than $1/2$ and that $N_H + N_M + N_L = 1$, so that the N_i can be interpreted as population fractions. The key assumption about relative sizes is that no group is large enough to form a majority by itself. For simplicity, it is assumed that there is no uncertainty and no discounting.

In period 1, individuals can invest either one or zero units in education. All investment must be financed out of first-period income—there is no capital market. Hence, in the absence of a program of redistribution to alleviate income inequality, high-income individuals would be able to invest in education, while poor individuals would not be able to invest. Second-period income y^i of an individual of type i is the sum of the pre-tax first-period wage w^i, the private return to human capital accumulation, and any spillover from the human capital investment of others. Denoting the decisions to invest or not invest by $\iota = 1$ and $\iota = 0$, respectively, and by N^{ed} the fraction of the population that invests in education

(N^{ed} can equal 0, N_{H}, $N_{\text{H}} + N_{\text{M}}$, or 1), the income y^i of an individual of type i in period 2 is

$$y^i = w^i + \gamma\iota^i + \gamma\kappa N^{\text{ed}}, \tag{11.46}$$

for $\gamma > 1$, and where $\gamma\kappa N^{\text{ed}}$ represents the externality from a fraction N^{ed} of other individuals investing in education, an effect that obtains even if the individual has not invested in education himself. κ, a parameter not in the original Perotti formulation, represents the strength of the spillover versus direct effect of human capital investment and will be useful in characterizing different possible political equilibria. As in Saint-Paul and Verdier, it is this externality from investment in education that drives the possible growth-enhancing effects of redistribution, but with the complication that the effect of redistribution on investment depends on the distribution of income.

Perotti considers a model with a deadweight cost in collecting taxes, an effect which may in itself depress growth in line with the models of Section 11.2. The nonlinearity of the tax system due to these collection costs makes the model quite complex. The main conceptual innovations may be represented with a linear tax system, greatly simplifying the exposition while retaining some of the key results on the relation between the initial distribution of income and economic growth. We will consider a nonlinear tax system in this type of model in Section 11.4 below, when we consider a model of an endogenous franchise.

With a linear tax-transfer scheme in the first period of life and making use of (11.46), consumption in the two periods of life is

$$\begin{aligned} c_1^i &= (1 - \tau)w^i + \tau\overline{w} - \iota^i, \\ c_2^i &= w^i + \gamma\iota^i + \gamma\kappa N^{\text{ed}}, \end{aligned} \tag{11.47}$$

where $\overline{w}$ is mean income, so that $\tau\overline{w}$ is the per capita transfer. Individual utility is linear in consumption, that is, $u^i = c_1^i + c_2^i$. With no capital markets, the only economic decision is whether or not to invest in education. Under the assumptions of $\gamma > 1$ and linear utility function with no discounting, all types would want to invest in human capital if they could. With no borrowing, investing in human capital in the first period requires that an individual's first-period, after-tax income inclusive of transfers is greater than or equal to 1. That is, an individual of income class i invests in human capital if and only if $w^i \geq \hat{w}$, where $\hat{w}$ is defined by $(1 - \tau)\hat{w} + \tau\overline{w} = 1$. This may be written

$$\iota^i = 1 \quad \text{if and only if } w^i \geq \hat{w}(\tau) \equiv \frac{1 - \tau\overline{w}}{1 - \tau}. \tag{11.48}$$

The decision of whether or not to invest may also be specified in terms of the tax rate τ. For each income type, there is a nonnegative critical tax rate, call it $\hat{\tau}^i$, consistent with first-period income net of taxes and transfers equal to 1, so that it is possible to invest in education. This critical rate may be written

$$\hat{\tau}^i = \max\left(0, \frac{1 - w^i}{\overline{w} - w^i}\right). \tag{11.49}$$

Given our assumptions that $w^H > 1$ and $w^L < \overline{w}$, $\hat{\tau}^H$ will be the maximum tax rate consistent with human capital investment by high-income individuals (that is, $\tau > \hat{\tau}^H$ chokes off their human capital investment), and $\hat{\tau}^L$ will be the minimum tax rate consistent with human capital investment by low-income individuals (that is, $\tau < \hat{\tau}^L$ implies that income redistribution will give them insufficient first-period income to invest in human capital).

Let us now consider each type's preferred tax rate as a basis for a political-economic equilibrium. The dependence of second-period income on the investment of others, which depends on the equilibrium tax rate via thresholds as in (11.48), means that an individual's preferred tax rate is far more complicated than in models without an externality, even when both the tax-transfer system and the utility function are linear. (This complication did not arise in the Saint-Paul and Verdier model because of the specification of the human capital externality.) In the absence of externalities, the linearity of both the tax-transfer system and the utility function implies that an individual's preferred tax rate would be either 0 or 1, depending on whether first-period pre-tax income w^i was below or above mean income $\overline{w}$. In the presence of externalities as specified in the last term of (11.46), an individual's preferred tax will depend on its effect on N^{ed}, the fraction of the population that invests in education. The key observation is that in a rich economy ($\overline{w} > 1$), middle- and high-income voters would be able to invest in education both with and without redistributive taxation, while low-income individuals would be able to invest only if the tax system raised their after-tax income above 1 (remember that pre-tax $w^L < 1$). In contrast, in a poor economy ($\overline{w} < 1$), only high-income voters are rich enough to invest in education, and this only in the absence of highly redistributive taxation, that is, τ close to 1. These observations assume that $w^M > 1$ when $\overline{w} > 1$ and $w^M < 1$ when $\overline{w} < 1$.

We now make these observations more precise in order to characterize the preferred tax rates $\tilde{\tau}^i$ for each type i. We do this by considering individual utility for each income type, depending on whether $\overline{w}$ is less than or greater than 1. When $\overline{w} > 1$, a high-income individual prefers a tax rate of zero (minimum redistribution), unless the externality from redistribution is strong enough that he prefers a tax rate allowing the poor to invest. Formally, when $\overline{w} > 1$ so that middle-income taxpayers are rich enough to invest in the absence of redistribution, the relevant tax rate choices for a high-income taxpayer are $\tau = 0$ (implying investment in education by a fraction $N^{\text{ed}} = N_{\text{H}} + N_{\text{M}}$ of the population) or $\tau = \tilde{\tau}^{\text{L}}$ (implying $N^{\text{ed}} = 1$). Using (11.46), (11.47), and $u^i = c_1^i + c_2^i$, the difference in utility may be written

$$u^{\text{H}}(\tau = 0) - u^{\text{H}}(\tau = \hat{\tau}^{\text{L}}) = \hat{\tau}^{\text{L}}(w^{\text{H}} - \overline{w}) - \gamma \kappa N_{\text{L}}, \qquad (11.50)$$

so that the preferred tax rate for type H is $\tilde{\tau}^{\text{H}} = 0$, unless κ is high, that is, unless the effect of the spillover from human capital investment of the poor is significant. When $\overline{w} < 1$, so that low-income individuals cannot invest for any level of redistribution, high-income taxpayers unambiguously prefer $\tau = 0$ to any other tax rate. For low-income taxpayers, the story is reversed. When $\overline{w} > 1$, they unambiguously prefer $\tau = 1$, as the highest possible tax rate has no adverse consequences for the investment of other groups, but maximizes their income. When $\overline{w} < 1$, so that low- and middle-income taxpayers could not invest for any program of redistribution, low-income individuals compare the tax rate that maximizes their first-period income ($\tau = 1$) with the tax rate that allows high-income individuals to accumulate human capital ($\tau = \hat{\tau}^{\text{H}}$, calculated for $\overline{w} < 1$). A low-income taxpayer prefers a tax rate of 1 (maximum redistribution), unless the externality from redistribution is strong enough that he prefers a tax rate allowing the rich to invest. Formally, when $\overline{w} < 1$, so that neither low- nor middle-income taxpayers can invest in any case, the relevant tax rate choices for a low-income taxpayer are $\tau = 1$ (implying $N^{\text{ed}} = 0$) or $\tau = \hat{\tau}^{\text{H}}$ (implying $N^{\text{ed}} = N_{\text{H}}$). The difference in utility may be written

$$u^{\text{L}}(\tau = 1) - u^{\text{L}}(\tau = \hat{\tau}^{\text{H}}) = (1 - \hat{\tau}^{\text{H}})(\overline{w} - w^{\text{L}}) - \gamma \kappa N_{\text{H}}, \quad (11.51)$$

so that the preferred tax rate $\tilde{\tau}^{\text{L}} = 1$, unless κ is high, that is, unless the effect of the spillover from human capital investment of the rich is significant. To summarize, for κ not too large, high- and low-income taxpayers will prefer their (diametrically opposed) extreme tax preferences. For κ large, the externality will lead rich taxpayers to soften their position in a rich economy and poor taxpayers to soften their position in a poor economy. Inspection of (11.49) indicates, however, that the farther apart are income levels, the weaker this effect will be.

In general, then, both when $\overline{w} > 1$ and when $\overline{w} < 1$, there will be a conflict between high-income and low-income taxpayers. The decisive voter (that is, the median voter in a majority voting system) will be the middle-income voter. Similar arguments can establish his preferred tax rate in the two cases. When $\overline{w} > 1$, so that the middle-income taxpayer can always invest, the analysis is similar to that summarized by (11.50), but with quite different implications. If $w^{\text{M}} < \overline{w}$ (the case of a positively skewed income distribution), the simple income redistribution and the human capital externality arguments push in the same direction, so that $\tilde{\tau}^M = 1$ for any value of κ. When $w^M > \bar{w}$, there is a conflict between the two objectives, with the decision over the preferred tax rate mirroring that of a high-income individual: when κ is large, the preferred tax rate $\tilde{\tau}^M = \hat{\tau}^L$, while when κ is small, $\tilde{\tau}^M = 0$. Hence, in the case of a rich economy, we note two key results. First, the preference of the middle-income voter is decisive. Second, this preference will be aligned with that of low-income voters if middle-income voters are relatively poor ($w^M < \bar{w}$) and aligned with the preference of high-income voters if $w^M > \bar{w}$.

When $\bar{w} < 1$, the middle-income taxpayer's choice is described by (11.51), with w^M replacing w^L. When $w^M < \bar{w}$, the relevant tax rate choices are $\tau = 1$ (implying $N^{ed} = 0$) or $\tau = \hat{\tau}^H$ (implying $N^{ed} = N_H$). The preferred tax rate is $\tilde{\tau}^M = 1$ if κ is small and $\tilde{\tau}^M = \hat{\tau}^H$ if κ is large. The determinants of the preferred tax rate are identical to low-income voters, except that the critical value of κ is lower. In contrast, when $1 > w^M > \bar{w}$, the preferred tax rate is $\tilde{\tau}^M = 0$ for any value of κ. Hence, we obtain the same two general results: the preference of the middle-income voter is decisive; and this preference is aligned with that of low-income voters if $w^M < \bar{w}$, and aligned with the preference of high-income voters if $w^M > \bar{w}$.

On the basis of this discussion, we may now calculate the relation between growth rates and income distribution in a political equilibrium. As should be clear, there are two cases to consider, depending on whether $\bar{w}$ is less than or greater than 1. In an economy with $\bar{w} < 1$, the political-economic equilibrium may be $\tau = 1$, $\tau = \hat{\tau}^H$, or $\tau = 0$, depending on the interest of the middle class, the decisive group of voters. Growth will be maximized (more precisely, it will be positive rather than zero) in the latter two cases, for only the lower, nonexpropriating tax rate will concentrate income in the hands of the rich, allowing growth-inducing investment to occur. If $w^M < \bar{w}$, this requires κ to be high enough so that middle-income individuals vote against their short-term interest in order to maximize growth explicitly. Alternatively, if the human capital externality is not large enough, growth is maximized only if $w^M > \bar{w}$, so that the middle class votes against any redistribution, because it hurts them directly. To summarize, if human capital externalities are not large, only a very unequal distribution of income, which concentrates wealth in the hands of the rich, may be consistent with growth. This is similar to the relation between inequality and growth stressed in the models in Section 11.2. The result, however, requires that the middle class is not too much poorer than the rich, for otherwise they will have an incentive to expropriate their wealth. Moreover, strong human capital externalities can overturn this conclusion.

In a rich economy, that is, one for which $\bar{w} > 1$ and $w^M > 1$, growth is maximized when the tax rate is $\hat{\tau}^L$ or above, allowing low-income, as well as middle- and high-income, individuals to invest. Unless the externality from human capital is large enough (that is, large κ), this requires

$w^M < \overline{w}$, so that the interests of the middle class are aligned with those of the poor. Hence, growth is maximized for a more equal distribution of income. To achieve this result, the middle class and the poor must have similar incomes, for otherwise the middle-income, decisive voters will lack the incentive to enact the necessary redistributive program.

11.4. POLITICAL INSTITUTIONS AND REGIMES

The principal result of Section 11.2 was that income inequality may depress growth in an economy in which the income of the median voter is below the average income level. This result depended on the specification of both the economic and the political processes linking inequality to economic outcomes. On the economic side, the specification of the growth process was crucial in determining the effect of redistribution on growth. This was examined in detail in the previous section. In this section, we consider more closely the political half of the linkage underlying the basic results on income inequality and growth. That is, we consider the role of political institutions in determining the effect of income inequality on the choice of redistributive policies. More generally, we will consider the relation between different types of political institutions on the one hand, and growth performance on the other.

There have been basically three strands of research addressing the question of how political institutions affect growth. The most extensive is empirical, as in Alesina and Perotti (1994), Barro (1996), and Perotti (1996a), to name just a few papers. We review this work in detail in Section 11.6, though a quick preview is probably useful. In short, the evidence of an empirical connection between democracy and growth seems mixed at best, with many researchers arguing one can find no significant, robust empirical evidence that democracy either encourages or retards growth. The empirical work is based on the other two strands of research. One is conceptual, using logical arguments that are not formalized in models to discuss why democracy may help or hinder growth relative to undemocratic or dictatorial regimes. The other strand, by far the least developed, uses formal, theoretical models to draw connections between democratic institutions and growth, with the causality running not only from democracy to growth, but in the other direction as well. In this section, we consider these two strands of argument, the conceptual and the theoretical, in turn.

The Conceptual Link between Political Institutions and Growth

The conceptual discussion of the effect of political institutions on policies affecting growth has been focused on three issues: the role of property rights; the susceptibility of the government to pressures, in particular for immediate consumption at the expense of investment, and, more generally, from special interest groups; and, the predatory nature of authoritarian leaders. The discussion of these issues is usually framed in terms of the question of the relation between democracy and growth. Will property rights, usually seen as essential for growth, be more secure under a democracy or a dictatorship? Will a democracy be more subject than a dictatorship to interest group pressure (especially pressure for redistribution that reduces investment, the main driving force in the models of the previous two sections)? On the other hand, will the autonomy of a dictatorship make it more likely than a democracy to follow policies enriching a small minority at the expense of the general good? There has been a wealth of articles and books concerning the relationship between democracy and growth, including a number of surveys of both the basic conceptual arguments and the empirical findings. To name but two, Przeworski and Limongi (1993) present a concise, but very clear, discussion; Sirowy and Inkeles (1990) present a longer review. Both papers contain very useful bibliographies.

Property Rights

There is widespread agreement that, broadly defined, "economic liberty" and "property rights" enhance growth. The term "property rights" is used in two closely related, but distinct, ways in the literature on the political economy of growth. The term is used to refer to institutions, sometimes very broadly defined, that secure the right to enjoy the fruits of one's labor, including policies which reduce restrictions on, and regulation of, economic transactions. It is also used to refer to the degree of security of property itself. Though the first usage seems more natural in discussing the importance of property rights in ensuring growth, the term is often used in the second, more general way, as in many of the models of Section 11.2. That is, the argument that property rights are less secure the more unequal the distribution of income is often not meant to imply that the institutions protecting property will be different, but that inequality makes income and wealth more subject to redistribution and expropriation, *given* the institutions that exist. This distinction may be useful, as it seems that the argument that democracy may be inimical to property rights is focused on the second, "equilibrium," concept, while that suggesting democracy fosters property rights is focused on the first, institutional concept.

As Przeworski and Limongi (1993) point out, the view that property rights are more secure in a democracy should not be taken for granted, with classical thinkers often arguing exactly the opposite. Specifically, to the extent that democracy is associated with a wider (or universal) voting franchise, democracy may be seen as threatening property, rather than making it more secure, since the previously disenfranchised tend to have far less property than those who vote when suffrage is limited. Przeworski and Limongi document that in the debate on extending the franchise to the poor in the nineteenth century, the view that greater democracy threatens property was held by both supporters and opponents of wider suffrage. We present a formal model of the effect of widening the franchise later in this section.

The basic problem may be put a bit more formally. Historically, political rights were extended to those who had accumulated wealth, that is, those who have economic power in a market system. To the extent that a greater degree of democracy is associated with giving more political rights to those who are less economically successful (for whatever reason), they will have a great incentive to use their political power to compensate themselves for their initial lack of economic power. This was exactly the phenomenon which lay behind the basic result in the models of Section 11.2: if the income or wealth of the median voter is below the mean, the outcome of the political process will be a redistribution from rich to poor.

More recent arguments have run in the opposite direction, namely, that property rights are more secure, rather than less secure, in democracies than in nondemocracies. One argument has to do with the ability to commit. (See also the general discussion in Chapter 5.) The argument is that in the absence of democratic controls on rulers, they will abrogate property rights when they view this as being to their benefit. As North and Weingast (1989, p. 803) put it in relating the importance of property rights to growth:

> The more likely it is that the sovereign will alter property rights for his or her own benefit, the lower the expected returns from investment and the lower in turn the incentive to invest. For economic growth to occur the sovereign or government must not merely establish the relevant set of rights, but make a credible commitment to them.

In contrast, dictators cannot commit to future policies, as Elster (1995) and Olson (1991) have stressed—if there are no limits on a ruler's power, he cannot make it credible that he will keep any commitment he makes. In the language of the time-consistency literature, he cannot credibly precommit. Another factor suggesting that property rights may be less secure in a dictatorship is that the regime itself may be less secure.

Though property rights are argued to be crucial to growth, there is little or no really convincing formal economic analysis of property rights with any degree of generality in the political economy literature. One way to formally analyze property rights and their evolution is as in the work of Grossman and Kim (1995, 1996a). This approach will be considered in Section 11.5 below.

Pressures for Redistribution

The second key conceptual issue concerns the role of political institutions in allowing pressures for redistribution by the poor to be translated into policies that reduce investment and growth. The basic argument is that in a democracy, the pressures for immediate consumption are far more difficult to resist than in a dictatorship. Dictatorships, it is argued, are better able to enact the painful policies needed to reduce consumption and increase national saving in order to free resources for investment in low-income economies. (See, for example, Rao [1984] or Sirowy and Inkeles [1990].) In a direct democracy, such policies would be defeated if put to popular vote; in a representative democracy, the attempt to enact difficult policies may simply lead to legislative delay, deadlock, and inaction, as in the models in Chapter 10. Moreover, politicians will cater to economic demands to increase their chances of re-election, as was studied in detail in Chapter 7. In short, as has been argued in many contexts, nondemocracies are less constrained in their choice of policies.[11]

The importance of insulation from interest group pressure is more general. It is argued that in order to pursue policies that enhance development, policymakers must be insulated not only from unions pressing for higher wages and consumption, but also from business interests pressing for policies favorable to their sectors or even individual firms. The state is seen as the only agent with maximization of the interests of society as a whole as its goal, as opposed to the interests of particular groups; to achieve this goal, it must not simply be shielded from interest group pressure, but even precommmitted in some cases not to respond to pressure. The state must have "autonomy" to pursue growth-enhancing policies. To complete the argument, some degree of authoritarianism in government is seen as crucial for this autonomy. (See, for example, the discussion in Sirowy and Inkeles [1990].)

There are a number of questions raised by this line of argument. First, even dictatorships need to please various constituencies, often including the poor. Pressures for redistribution that must be addressed can arise in nondemocratic systems as well as in democratic ones. In fact, in the absence of democratic ways to express such demands, they may be expressed in quite disruptive and violent ways, leading to significant political instability, itself harmful to growth. (Political instability is considered explicitly and formally in Section 11.5 below.) Hence, not only may dictatorships find that pressures for redistribution place constraints on policy choice; they may also be limited in their ability to enact extremely unpopular measures because the absence of democratic means of dissent implies that the regime's stability is threatened.

An even more basic question concerns the central assumption that authoritarian rulers are motivated by the social good, so that the autonomy

---

[11] A related argument leading to the same conclusion is focused on trade unions. If workers are free to organize trade unions, they will drive up wages at the expense of profits to provide themselves higher consumption, thus reducing investment. See Przeworski and Limongi (1993) for a discussion and trenchant critique of this argument.

provided by nondemocratic institutions will lead to superior policies.[12] But, why should they be motivated for the social, as opposed to their private, interest? The weakness of the unconditional argument that dictatorship enhances growth is the lack of convincing evidence, either theoretical or empirical, on why an autonomous state would act for the social good. In fact, evidence suggests that rulers who are not accountable to the electorate, even if they start out with the social good in mind, often become more predatory over time. Put a bit more formally, this approach crucially views the government as the safeguard against growth-retarding rent seeking by interest groups, rather than a rent seeker itself, but there is no strong reason to believe that this is the case. We will present a formal analysis of the effects of such rent seeking in Section 11.5.

Proponents of the argument that nondemocratic institutions may foster growth address this point by drawing a distinction between "predatory" or "kleptocratic" dictators versus "development-oriented" or "benevolent" dictators. While the former maximize their own (or their cronies') welfare, rather than social welfare, the latter follow policies favorable to growth and development, being willing to reduce the country's current consumption to increase welfare in the longer run. This response sounds tautological—dictatorship implies high growth if the dictator is growth oriented and low growth if he is not—though, carefully phrased, it is not. There is no reason to suppose that authoritarian governments are growth oriented. However, the question about insulation from interest group pressure really is: *conditional* on a government being growth oriented, will growth be higher if the government is less constrained by the democratic process? The point in the previous paragraph that pressures for redistribution may be manifest in disruptive ways in authoritarian governments suggests that the answer is not as obvious as it may seem. The argument that the effect differs across types of dictatorships implies that it will be difficult to resolve the point empirically, as we shall see.

Predatory Dictators

This leads us to the third major conceptual argument, namely, that governments that are more autonomous and less democratic are more likely to follow predatory policies harmful to growth. That is, in sharp contrast to the line of argument in the previous subsection, when government is autonomous and not accountable, it is more likely to enact policies that benefit a small minority at the expense of the general good. Only democratic institutions constrain the government to act in the general

---

[12] A related point is that one should not automatically assume that individuals are short-sighted, preferring consumption today to higher consumption tomorrow. This argument has received less attention since, as we saw above, pressures for redistribution can come from income inequality, rather than from high discount rates.

interest. To put the question starkly in terms of rent seeking, what if it is the autonomous government itself which is the predator on society, rather than the protector of society from predatory behavior?

One of the main arguments was already presented earlier in this section where we discussed property rights, and need not be repeated in detail here. In the absence of democratic controls, rulers will abrogate property rights when they view this as being to their benefit.[13] Olson (1991) has argued strongly in this direction. Those who argue that it is the absence of limits on an authoritarian ruler's power that is inimical to growth stress the overriding importance of property rights for the growth process. This is crucial not only for the incentive to invest in physical capital, but also for the incentive to innovate, central to new growth theory.

One should note that this is not simply an argument about regimes that limit "economic freedom." Many writers suggest that one should distinguish regimes that limit both political and economic freedoms from those that limit primarily the former but not the latter. The argument, already implied by the distinction between kleptocratic and development-oriented dictators in the previous subsection, is that our discussion only applies to the former type of dictator. Paralleling the discussion of property rights and democracy earlier in this section, however, the broader argument is that political freedom may be necessary to ensure the economic freedoms which are essential to high growth. Only when the political system is democratic and respects political rights will the related economic rights be secure.

Theoretical Models of Limited Franchise

Theoretical models of the relation between the extent of democracy and growth are rare, perhaps because of the difficulty in modeling the degree of democracy. A standard approach is to consider a voting system in which voting rights are limited in some dimension. For example, the franchise may be limited according to income, wealth, or some other observable criterion. Alternatively, all groups may be enfranchised, but instead of a "one man–one vote" rule, some groups may be given disproportionate weight in the decision process.

General Approaches

Benabou (1996) suggests the following general approach to changes in the extent of the franchise. Consider the model of the type presented in Section 11.2, but instead of assuming that the decisive voter is the one at the median, with half of the distribution of income or wealth below him,

---

[13] More generally, it is argued that authoritarian governments have a tendency towards corruption and waste.

let the decisive voter be the one with a fraction δ of the distribution below him. A system in which $\delta > 1/2$ is one in which the poor have less of a voice, due to a franchise restricted by wealth, to the influence of costly lobbying, or perhaps reflecting lower rates of electoral participation by the poor. In contrast, a decisive voter located at $\delta < 1/2$ could reflect, for example, lobbying by powerful unions who represent workers with incomes below the average. Suppose the distribution of initial endowments in a generation is lognormal, a reasonable empirical approximation, that is, ln w^i is normally distributed with mean w and variance σ^2. The decisive voter then is the voter with (log of) initial endowment w^{dec} defined by $F(w^{\text{dec}} - w/\sigma) = \delta$, where F is the cumulative distribution function of a standard normal. One may then show a number of basic results (see Benabou, Proposition 2 for details): the more "biased" the political system is against the poor (the larger is δ), the higher is growth in a model of distortionary redistribution; intertemporal efficiency will be maximized when the voter who is decisive is the one whose endowment is equal to the economywide mean w; and, the more unequal the income distribution, the higher must be δ to achieve intertemporal efficiency.

Benabou further points out that these results do not reflect the special assumption of a lognormal distribution. They hold for standard models of redistribution via capital taxation with complete markets. The basic insight is that under complete markets, heterogeneity of initial endowments has no consequences for efficiency. The net social benefit of taxation is maximized by maximizing the welfare of the representative individual. Therefore, if taxation is chosen by majority rule, maximum efficiency results from the individual with the average endowment being the representative voter. Furthermore, under complete markets, the steady-state rate of growth rises with the net return to capital, so that maximizing growth means maximizing this return. (This can be seen in both the Persson–Tabellini model and the Alesina–Rodrik model, in (11.22) in Section 11.2.)

On the basis of the sort of general results presented in the previous paragraph, several papers in the literature, beginning with Persson and Tabellini (1994), have argued that the effect of inequality on taxation and redistribution will be greater under democratic regimes than under non-democratic regimes. This is *not*, as in the above results, an argument about the effect of δ on growth for a *given* income distribution (as, for example, parameterized by w and σ for the lognormal above), but an argument about the effect of *changes* in the distribution (an increase in σ) for different values of δ. As Benabou argues, this claim, though perhaps intuitive, is not so easy to support on theoretical grounds. Since the tax rate in political equilibrium reflects the first-order conditions of the decisive voter, the argument that an increase in inequality will have different effects across political regimes reflects higher-order terms in the decisive voter's objective function, terms on which theory generally puts no restrictions. Using a simple model, Benabou argues that there is not an unambiguous theoretical presumption, unless one puts further restrictions on the nature of the regime. As we shall see in Section 11.6, with few exceptions, empirical work has found no statistically significant differential effect of inequality on growth across democratic and nondemocratic regimes.

What about causality in the opposite direction, that is, from growth or the level of development to the degree of democracy? There are a number of models that consider the possibility that the political decision mechanism may be endogenous to the growth process.[14] (In terms of the previous discussion, the question may be framed in terms of the endogeneity of δ.) Bourguignon and Verdier (1997) consider a model of endogenous *political participation*, the key assumption being that participation in voting is increasing in the level of income. In their model, income depends on human capital, which is the engine of growth. Gradstein and Justman (1995) assume that the franchise is (exogenously) limited by the level of income. Growth in income over time then extends the franchise and determines how the population eligible to vote will evolve. Ades and Verdier (1996) consider a similar phenomenon. Membership in the decisionmaking elite is limited by an exogenously fixed entry cost, so that political participation depends on income being above a certain level. Participation thus evolves over time with economic growth.

Acemoglu and Robinson (1996) allow the franchise or entry barrier to be endogenously determined, rather than being exogenously fixed. More specifically, those in power can determine the extent of the franchise by determining, for example, the minimum income level legally required for political participation. The poor, in the absence of the right to participate in the democratic process, may resort to expropriation or armed conflict to improve their economic lot. Hence, the rich may choose to extend the franchise to forestall or eliminate the threat of expropriation or insurrection. Higher income inequality thus leads to endogenously higher political participation by the poor, which may then translate into more redistributive policies. Acemoglu and Robinson's paper is closely related to Grossman and Kim (1996a) on predation discussed in Section 8.5 of Chapter 8, and specifically to Grossman's (1991) paper on insurrection. We consider some of this work in Section 11.5 below. As in Bourguignon and Verdier, the stress is on the endogeneity of the franchise *rule* and the implied effect of growth on political decisionmaking, rather than simply the endogeneity of the voting population for an exogenously specified rule about who may vote.

[14] The positive relation between income and participation can also be applied to the basic models of redistribution in a median voter model studied in Chapter 8.

A Model of Education and Endogenous Political Participation

The model of Bourguignon and Verdier illustrates a number of key points about endogenous political participation. They begin with the two-period model of Perotti (1993), considered in Section 11.3 above, but with distortionary taxes. At the beginning of the first period, there are only two classes of individuals, high- and low-income, where the initial endowments satisfy $w^H > 1 > w^L$. Earning ability is inherited from parents, an assumption used below in specifying endogenous political participation. The proportions of the two types are N_H and $N_L = 1 - N_H$, where $N_H < N_L$.

The key driving force, for *both* economic and political dynamics, is human capital accumulation. As in the model in Section 11.3, investment in education in the first period yields a private return γ which is greater than 1, the private cost of education. There is also a social return to education which is $\gamma \kappa N^{ed}$, where κ measures the strength of the educational externality and N^{ed} is the fraction of the population that has been educated. All investment must be financed out of first-period income—there is no capital market. Hence, in the absence of income transfers, high-income individuals would be able to invest in education, while poor individuals would not be able to invest, so that N^{ed} would equal N_H. It is assumed, for simplicity, that there is no uncertainty and no discounting.

The key difference from the model presented in Section 11.3 is that voting is not universal. Political participation is determined by education, with only the educated voting. Given the assumptions that the private return to education exceeds its costs and that education must be self-financed, this is equivalent to voting only by individuals whose initial income (or whose parent's initial endowment) was at least 1. Hence, in the first period, participation in the political process is determined by parent's education, so that only high-income individuals vote, a minority of the population. In the second period, the participation decision will depend on the level of education acquired in the first period. The endogeneity of the educational decision means that the political decision will also be endogenous in the second period. The positive correlation between participation and the level of income (or education) that is central to the model of Bourguignon and Verdier has found significant empirical support.

The limited franchise means that even though low-income individuals are a majority in the population in the first period, no redistribution will be necessarily imposed on the rich in a majority voting system. However, due to the existence of an externality in human capital accumulation, the rich may voluntarily transfer income to *some* of the poor, because it is in their own interests. More specifically, the rich can transfer funds $X = N_M(1 - w^L)$ to N_M poor, so that they become educated (and hence form the middle class), yielding an externality $\gamma \kappa N_M$ to the rich. There are two costs to such a transfer, beyond the loss of income. First, it is assumed that taxation is distortionary, where the distortion is represented very simply. In order to transfer an amount X, the rich must levy taxes equal to

$$\left(1 + \frac{dX}{\overline{w}_1}\right)X, \tag{11.52}$$

where $d > 0$ and where $\overline{w}_1 = N_L w^L + N_H w^H$, mean income in the first period.

The other cost to the rich of subsidizing education of the poor is dilution of its monopoly voting power in the second period. The middle class of size N_M created by education vote in the second period. If they are numerous enough, that is, if they outnumber the rich, they will be able to enact a program of redistribution of income away from the rich. Hence, high-income individuals as a class face a trade-off in helping the poor become educated. They gain from a more educated population, due to the externalities inherent in human capital accumulation. However, a more educated population is more "politically aware," and may use their voting power to tax away some of the income of the rich. Growth is maximized when all the poor are educated, the efficient solution if the distortionary cost of the required transfers (as measured by d) is not too high. However, such a widespread extension of the franchise would imply further income transfers away from the rich and would not be in their interests, if the human capital externality is not sufficiently large. The threat of redistribution inherent in giving voting rights to the poor yields a negative relation between inequality and growth related to, but conceptually distinct from, the mechanism discussed in length in Section 11.2. The more unequal the initial distribution of income, the more the rich have to lose from the poor getting educated and gaining political control. When the franchise is endogenized as it is here, more unequal limited-franchise societies may therefore develop more slowly both economically and politically; that is, they both grow and democratize more slowly.

Since the economic decision of whether or not to get educated is trivially determined by the level of first-period income, the key decision in the model is the decision of the rich of how widely to extend the franchise, that is, what fraction of the poor should be educated. The rich, who control the political mechanism in the first period, will choose the optimal educational subsidy to maximize their lifetime income. To solve this problem, however, one must note that there is a discontinuity, depending on whether the number of poor N_M who are educated (the new middle class) is less than or greater than the number of rich N_H. This discontinuity arises because of the possible difference in the outcome of voting in the two cases. Hence, we begin by deriving two types of second-period equilibria, distinguished by whether or not the rich remain a majority of the voting population. Which of these equilibria the rich find optimal, as well as the optimal value of N_M within each equilibrium, depends on parameter values. To better understand the role of income inequality, it will be useful, following Bourguignon and Verdier, to define a simple measure of it, namely, the difference Δ in initial endowments:

$$\Delta = w^H - w^L \quad \text{so that}$$

$$w^H = \overline{w} + (1 - N_H)\Delta \quad \text{and} \quad w^L = \overline{w} - N_H\Delta. \tag{11.53}$$

One type of equilibrium is where the number of poor who become educated is less than the initial number of rich, that is, $N_M < N_H$, so that the rich retain political power in the second period. There will then be no redistribution of income in the second period. With no discounting, lifetime income of a representative high-income individual is the sum of his endowment net of private education costs and transfers to the poor (his first-period income) and his second-period income, which is inclusive of private and social returns to education. Using (11.52), this may be written

$$y^H(N_M) = w^H - 1 - \frac{X(1 + dX/\overline{w})}{N_H}$$

$$+ w^H + \gamma(1 + \kappa(N_H + N_M)), \tag{11.54}$$

where the subsidy to the poor is $X = N_M(1 - w^L)$. As long as the marginal benefit to the rich of subsidizing education is positive at $N_M = 0$, that is, as long as $\kappa > (1 - w^L)/\gamma N_H$, the rich will subsidize the income of some of the poor. The optimal level of N_M from the point of view of the rich is found by maximizing (11.54), yielding

$$\tilde{N}_M = \frac{\gamma\kappa N_H - 1 + \overline{w} - N_H\Delta}{2d(1 - \overline{w} + N_H\Delta)}\overline{w}, \tag{11.55}$$

provided that this quantity is no greater than N_H.

The second type of equilibrium is where $N_M > N_H$, so that the new middle class can enact an income redistribution program in the second period. Bourguignon and Verdier assume that the middle class cannot target this policy simply towards themselves, but must include the uneducated poor $N_L - N_M$. Along the lines of Meltzer and Richard (1981), they assume that the redistribution policy is linear with a flat tax rate τ and a uniform, lump-sum transfer ν given by

$$\nu = \tau(1 - d\tau)(\overline{w} + \gamma[(1 + \kappa)(N_H + N_M)]), \tag{11.56}$$

where the term $(1 - d\tau)$ represents the distortionary effect of these taxes. The middle class choose a tax rate τ to maximize their second-period income net of taxes and transfers, which is $(1 - \tau)[w_L + \gamma(1 + \kappa(N_H + N_M))] + \nu$. This preferred tax rate is

$$\tilde{\tau} = 0 \qquad \text{if} \quad N_H\Delta \leq \gamma(N_L - N_M),$$

$$\tilde{\tau} = \frac{N_H\Delta - \gamma(N_L - N_M)}{2a[\overline{w} + \gamma(1 + \kappa)(N_H + N_M)]} \quad \text{if} \quad N_H\Delta > \gamma(N_L - N_M). \tag{11.57}$$

In words, the decisive middle-class voter will favor redistribution only if the net transfer he receives is positive; this will be the case if and only if his income is below average second-period income in the economy. This condition should have a familiar ring. There is then a critical value of N_M, namely,

$$\hat{N}_M = N_L\left(1 + \frac{\Delta}{\gamma}\right) - \frac{\Delta}{\gamma}, \tag{11.58}$$

which is the size of the middle class such that its income is equal to average income in the second period, so that the second-period redistributive tax rate τ is zero.

The optimal behavior of the rich is then described by choosing a level of N_M to maximize lifetime income. For $N_M \leq \hat{N}_M$, lifetime income is given by (11.54) with the income-maximizing value of N_M given by $\tilde{N}_M$ in (11.55). When $N_M > \hat{N}_M$, lifetime income of a high-income individual is no longer equal to $y^H(N_M)$ in (11.54), but to a lower value, call it $y^{TH}(N_M)$, reflecting the redistributive policy enacted in the second period. If $\tilde{N}_M > \hat{N}_M$ (so that $y^H(N_M)$ is still rising when $y^{TH}(N_M)$ becomes the relevant function), the optimal level of N_M is given not by $\tilde{N}_M$, but by the value that maximizes $y^{TH}(N_M)$.

On the basis of these calculations, Bourguignon and Verdier show that a number of cases are possible, where the most important determinants of the nature of the equilibrium are the size of the educational externality κ and the degree of initial income inequality Δ. The relation between income distribution, democracy, and growth is potentially complex because of the dynamic nature of the interactions, as well as the discontinuities induced by marginal changes in N_M in a voting equilibrium as N_M approaches N_H. We consider only a few examples (the interested reader is referred to the original article for the exact computations, which are a bit involved). When κ is high and Δ is low, we have a case most favorable to a wide franchise ("democracy"), where the rich agree to the education of a middle class that will outnumber them in order to achieve high growth, even though the rich lose political control, with this loss of political control known to imply redistribution in the second period. The more equal is the initial distribution of income, in the sense of a small gap between w^H and w^L (that is, small Δ), the lower the κ needs to be to induce democratization.

One especially interesting result concerns the effect of different levels of inequality on growth. As already indicated, for a given value of κ, low inequality (low Δ) implies an equilibrium with high growth and income redistribution away from the rich once the middle class gains control. (The positive association between redistribution and growth reflects the human capital externality which drove the models in Section 11.3 above.) Given κ, higher values of Δ will imply less redistribution (more exactly, *no* redistribution), exactly the opposite of the existing literature in which the extent of the franchise is fixed. The reason is that as the degree of inequality rises, so will the degree of redistribution *if* the rich cede power to a newly created middle class bent on redistribution. Either the rich will subsidize education for a number of the poor less than N_H, so that they will maintain political control, or (for certain combinations of low κ and low Δ) the rich will cede control to the new middle class because the latter will choose zero redistribution, given its distortionary costs. In short, higher inequality could lead to less redistribution, because it induces the rich to block the process of democratization.

11.5. Socio-Political Instability

In the models we have considered so far, focusing on specific political mechanisms, redistribution takes place through well-defined, orderly channels. As discussed in Section 8.5 of Chapter 8, an alternative approach to the political economy of redistribution is to abstract from the specific policy mechanism which is the vehicle for redistribution and, instead, consider more generally the phenomenon of expropriating resources and its implications. Following that approach, in this section, we consider some models of growth and redistribution that largely abstract from institutional details. Under this approach, specific redistributive mechanisms are replaced by a more general specification of the "technology" of redistribution, this specification limited only by reasonable assumptions on the relation between the attempt to expropriate resources and the outcome of the process. As in models of fiscal redistribution and growth under majority voting, there is a focus on the likelihood of expropriation depending on the characteristics of the income distribution. The role of political instability in the growth process seems especially important because, on the empirical level, there appears to be a significant relation between measures of political and/or social instability on the one hand and investment and growth on the other. We discuss such results in detail in Section 11.6.

This approach is connected to the models considered earlier in the chapter also in its focus on the security (or lack of it) of property rights as the key to determining the incentive to invest and, consequently, the possibility of growth. There are two strands of formal modeling here. One, discussed in Section 8.5 of Chapter 8, considers the allocation of resources to productive, predatory, or defensive activities. Grossman and Kim (1996b) provide an application of such models to growth. The second strand focuses on situations in which it is simply assumed that property rights are not secure, so that expropriation is possible, and considers the implications. These are common property models of the sort considered in Section 10.7 of Chapter 10. These models include Tornell and Velasco (1992), Lane and Tornell (1996), Benhabib and Rustichini (1996), and Tornell (1997).

On a more general level, the security of property guaranteed by laws and institutions depends on the security and stability of those laws and institutions themselves. Political instability may induce irresistible pressures for redistribution and expropriation. Hence, to the extent that political instability creates pressures for expropriation of principal or return, it will create a disincentive for accumulation and be inimical to growth. This approach can then be boiled down to two questions: what are the forces that create growth-retarding political instability; what is the political environment such that such instability will actually be translated into expropriation?

Rodrik (1997) considers the role of social conflict on a general level, arguing that domestic social conflicts are key to understanding growth collapses. He emphasizes the importance of both the ways in which social conflicts interact with external shocks, as well as the domestic institutions of conflict management which determine how these conflicts are resolved. Hence, one may think of two key determinants. The higher is "latent" social conflict (by which he means the "depth of pre-existing social cleavages in a society, along the lines of wealth, ethnic identity [and] geographical region") and the less developed or weaker are the institutions of conflict management, the greater is the negative growth effect of an unfavorable domestic shock. Operationally, there is a menu of responses to a shock, each with a different distributional consequence. The difference in equilibrium outcomes induced by different policy responses will depend on these two determinants; societies with high latent social conflict and weak conflict resolution mechanisms will exhibit political and social instability and low growth.

Let us now consider some theoretical models that formalize this connection.

Predation and Growth

Grossman and Kim (1996b) incorporate a model of predation of the sort discussed in Chapter 8 into a theory of growth. As the basic model of predation was discussed in detail there, here we simply sketch how it operates in a dynamic context. Inherited wealth can be allocated to one of three uses. As in standard growth models, it can be allocated to either consumption or accumulation of productive capital. It can also be allocated to activity associated with predation, either to offensive activity used to appropriate the wealth of others, or to defensive activity, that is, to defend against the predatory appropriation of others. Growth reflects the accumulation of productive capital, but predation can cause a redistribution of wealth at a point in time from prey to predator, or a destruction of wealth, in that resources may be used up in both offensive and defensive predatory activity. Hence, predation, and the defense against it, can affect the growth path, both for any dynasty and for the economy as a whole.

Identifying defensive activities as those that make property more secure, Grossman and Kim (1996b) provide a theory of the evolution of property rights in a model of growth. Property rights are fully secure if individuals or dynasties who are potential prey to predation allocate enough resources to deterring predation that none occurs in equilibrium. A key insight is that more secure property rights may actually *slow* growth, once one realizes that the security of property is not costless, but can be guaranteed only by expending costly resources. In fact, Grossman and Kim show examples where societies that tolerate predation (that is, where property rights are not fully secure) grow more quickly over intervals of time than those with fully secure property rights. This occurs when the deterrence of predation is itself a very costly activity.

Common Property Models with Constant Appropriation

In a common property model, as discussed in Section 10.7 of Chapter 10, there is common access to an aggregate stock of some valuable commodity. In a common property model of growth, the common commodity is output that either can be accumulated over time as productive capital or can be appropriated for private consumption; hence, appropriation is a growth-reducing activity. Rather than posit a specific institutional set-up by which appropriation takes place, it is simply assumed that there are groups or coalitions that have the power to extract resources (or transfers, if one likes) from the rest of society. Hence, society is seen as made up of powerful groups that can either cooperate or be in conflict. Social conflict is thus represented by the possibility of appropriating resources for one's own benefit, rather than cooperating for the social good.

A clear common property model of growth with simple strategies is that of Lane and Tornell (1996). By simple strategies, one means an optimal constant rate of appropriation of the common property, rather than wealth-dependent strategies, as in Velasco's (1998) model in Chapter 10. (We return to wealth-dependent strategies in the next subsection.) The simplicity of the strategy reflects assumptions on technology and preferences, in fact, the same assumptions that made the models in Section 11.2

simple: linear production technology combined with CES preferences. Unlike Velasco's model, there are no fixed costs associated with groups following appropriative strategies.

Lane and Tornell model common access quite simply. Aggregate output is linear in the aggregate capital stock k_t, and the change in the aggregate capital stock (in continuous time) is simply output minus the sum total of the consumption of powerful groups at each point in time. With J (> 1) groups, one has

$$\dot{k}_t = ak_t - \sum_{j=1}^{J} c_t^j, \tag{11.59}$$

where c_t^j is the consumption (that is, appropriation) of group j at time t. Hence, the modeling of appropriation as the growth-reducing activity is quite simple. The aggregate capital stock k_t is restricted to be positive at each point in time.

Each group's objective is to maximize the present discounted value of utility, where instantaneous utility is a CES function of consumption. The group's utility over an infinite horizon is

$$\Omega^j = \int_{s=t}^{\infty} \frac{\sigma}{\sigma - 1} (c_s^j)^{(\sigma-1)/\sigma} e^{-\rho(s-t)} \, ds, \tag{11.60}$$

where the elasticity of intertemporal substitution is $\sigma > 0$ and where $\rho < a$. There is an upper bound $\bar{\varsigma}$ on the rate of appropriation by each group, that is,

$$0 \leq c_t^j \leq \bar{\varsigma} k_t, \quad \text{where } 0 \leq \frac{a(1 - \sigma) + \rho\sigma}{J - \sigma(J - 1)} < \bar{\varsigma} < \infty. \tag{11.61}$$

In words, output cannot be appropriated all at once.[15] The value $[a(1 - \sigma) + \rho\sigma]/[J - \sigma(J - 1)]$ is the appropriation rate in an interior equilibrium, as we shall see below. Each group's strategy is to choose an optimal consumption stream $\tilde{c}_t^j$ to maximize (11.60) subject to (11.61) and the strategies of the other players. As in Section 10.7 of Chapter 10, Lane and Tornell consider Markov strategies, that is, strategies that are restricted to be functions only of the payoff-relevant state variables and are not allowed to be history dependent. In this case, this means that the c_t^j are functions only of k_t for each group j. The equilibrium concept is Markov Perfect Equilibrium (MPE). A J-component vector of Markov strategies $\{\tilde{c}^j(k_t)\}$ for $i = 1, \ldots, J$ forms a Markov Perfect Equilibrium if it is a subgame-perfect equilibrium for every realization of k_t. Formally, if the value of the

---

[15] Lane and Tornell also consider a lower bound on appropriation, but this plays a less critical conceptual role in their analysis and will be ignored.

payoff function (11.60) is denoted by $V(\cdot)$, a vector of strategies is an MPE if it satisfies, for all feasible $c^j(k_t)$,

$$V(\tilde{c}^j(k_t), \tilde{c}^{-j}(k_t), k_t) \geq V(c^j(k_t), \tilde{c}^{-j}(k_t), k_t) \quad \text{for all } j, t, \quad (11.62)$$

where $\tilde{c}^{-j} = (\tilde{c}^1, \ldots, \tilde{c}^{j-1}, \tilde{c}^{j+1}, \ldots, \tilde{c}^J)$. Using (11.59), (11.60), and (11.61), an MPE for this problem is then a solution to a set of J Hamiltonian equations, one for each group, of the form[16]

$$\mathcal{H}^j = \frac{\sigma}{\sigma - 1}(\tilde{c}_t^j)^{(\sigma-1)/\sigma} + \lambda_{jt}\left(ak_t - \tilde{c}_t^j - \sum_{i \neq j}\tilde{c}^i(k_t)\right)$$

$$+ \omega_{jt}(\bar{s}k_t - \tilde{c}_t^j). \quad (11.63)$$

To find an MPE, one must find a set of J optimal consumption strategies $\{\tilde{c}^j(k_t)\}$ for $j = 1, \ldots, J$ that simultaneously solve the J Hamiltonian problems (11.63). One first conjectures the form of the solution, and checks that this solution indeed solves the J Hamiltonian problems in (11.63). These J strategies are best responses to one another. One then shows that this candidate solution is indeed a Markov Perfect Equilibrium.

Given the form of the production and utility functions, one conjectures that consumption is a linear function of the state variable of the form

$$\tilde{c}_t^j = s_j k_t, \quad j = 1, \ldots, J, \quad (11.64)$$

where the s_i are coefficients to be determined. A solution to (11.63) must then satisfy the first-order conditions

$$\tilde{c}_t^j = (\lambda_{jt} + \omega_{jt})^{-\sigma}, \quad (11.65a)$$

$$\dot{\lambda}_{jt} = \lambda_{jt}\left(\rho - a + \sum_{i \neq j}s_i\right) - \omega_{jt}\bar{s}, \quad (11.65b)$$

$$\lim_{t \to \infty}\lambda_{jt}k_t e^{-\rho t} = 0, \quad (11.65c)$$

$$\omega_{jt}(\bar{s}k_t - \tilde{c}_t^j) = 0, \quad \omega_{jt} \geq 0. \quad (11.65d)$$

There are two MPEs: an interior Markov equilibrium in which $s_j < \bar{s}$ and an extreme Markov equilibrium in which $s_j = \bar{s}$. We consider them in turn.

To find an interior equilibrium, we must find consumption strategies $\{\tilde{c}^1(k_t), \ldots, \tilde{c}^J(k_t)\}$ solving (11.65) such that the constraint (11.61) does not

---

[16] For mathematical details on solving continuous-time optimization problems using Hamiltonians, one may refer to any treatment of calculus of variations. Takayama (1985) presents a highly accessible treatment.

bind. One show that this vector of is an admissible equilibrium in that it satisfies the first-order conditions (11.65) and implies a unique, continuously differentiable path for k_t which is nonnegative at every point in time. If (11.61) does not bind, then $\omega_{jt} = 0$ for all j and t. Equations (11.64) and (11.65a) then imply that the optimal consumption paths for each group must satisfy

$$\frac{\dot{\tilde{c}}_t^j}{\tilde{c}_t^j} = \frac{\dot{k}_t}{k_t} = -\sigma \frac{\dot{\lambda}_{jt}}{\lambda_{jt}}. \tag{11.66}$$

Using (11.59) to eliminate $\dot{k}_t$ and (11.65b) to eliminate $\dot{\lambda}_{jt}$, we obtain a set of J linearly independent equations in J unknowns:

$$\tilde{s}_j = a(1 - \sigma) + \rho\sigma - \sum_{i \neq j}(1 - \sigma)\tilde{s}_i, \qquad j = 1,\ldots,J. \tag{11.67}$$

These J equations have a unique solution:

$$\tilde{s}_j = \frac{a(1 - \sigma) + \rho\sigma}{J - \sigma(J - 1)}, \qquad j = 1,\ldots,J. \tag{11.68a}$$

Hence, the interior equilibrium is symmetric, in that all groups have identical optimal consumption paths. This path is found by substituting (11.68a) into (11.64), yielding

$$\tilde{c}_t^j = \frac{a(1 - \sigma) + \rho\sigma}{J - \sigma(J - 1)} k_t, \qquad j = 1,\ldots,J. \tag{11.68b}$$

The implied path for the aggregate capital stock is found by substituting (11.68b) into (11.59) and integrating the resulting expression. This yields

$$\tilde{k}_t = k_0 \exp\left(\frac{\sigma(a - J\rho)}{J - \sigma(J - 1)} t\right), \tag{11.69}$$

where $\tilde{k}_t$ represents the optimal path. Substituting (11.64), (11.65a), and (11.69) into the transversality condition (11.65c), one can show that the transversality condition is satisfied if and only if the $\tilde{s}_j$ are nonnegative. As (11.67) implies that $\tilde{s}_j < \bar{s}$ in (11.61), (11.65d) is clearly satisfied as well. Hence, all the first-order necessary conditions are satisfied.

To show that this solution is indeed an equilibrium, one must show that (11.62) is satisfied. This follows from maximizing a concave function (11.60) over a convex set (11.61), subject to a linear accumulation equation (11.59). Moreover, since $\tilde{s}$ from (11.68a) is the unique solution to this problem in the class of linear strategies (11.64), $\tilde{c}_t^j$ and $\tilde{k}_t$ given by (11.68b) and (11.69) define the unique interior MPE for this common property game. The present discounted value of utility to each group may be found by substituting (11.68b) and (11.69) into (11.60).

Lane and Tornell provide some intuition for the results by observing that with a CES utility function as in (11.60), optimal consumption will satisfy

$$c_t^j = \big((1 - \sigma)R_j + \sigma\rho\big)k_t, \tag{11.70}$$

where R_j is the return to capital faced by group j. In this common property set-up, the return to group j depends on the appropriation strategies of the other groups, that is, $R_j = a - \sum_{i \neq j} s_i$, which implies that a group's propensity to consume s_j is a function of the other groups' propensities to consume, that is, of the s_i, as long as $\sigma \neq 1$. (For log utility, the propensity to consume out of capital is simply ρ, independent of R_j, as we saw in (11.23) above.) In an interior equilibrium, the appropriation rates of other groups are such that s_j just equals s_i. One may also note that as the appropriation rates of other groups rise, R_j will fall. Whether consumption rises or falls as R_j falls, however, will depend on whether σ is less than or greater than 1, that is, whether the elasticity of intertemporal substitution is low or high. From (11.69), we can calculate the effect of parameter changes on the growth rate of capital and consumption in an interior equilibrium. An increase in the number J of powerful groups, for example, will imply a fall in the growth rate.

For the interior solution to satisfy the transversality condition, $\tilde{s}_j$ from (11.68a) must be nonnegative. Since $J > 1$, and σ, ρ, and a are all positive, Lane and Tornell point out that there are three combinations of parameters that satisfy the conditions for this solution to be optimal. They are

$$\text{I} \quad \sigma > \max\left(\frac{a}{a - \rho}, \frac{J}{J - 1}\right),$$

$$\text{II} \quad \sigma \in \left(1, \min\left(\frac{a}{a - \rho}, \frac{J}{J - 1}\right)\right), \tag{11.71}$$

$$\text{III} \quad \sigma \in (0, 1].$$

The alternative possibility to an interior equilibrium is an extreme equilibrium where $s_j = \bar{s}$ for each group j. This can be an equilibrium only for a sufficiently high elasticity of substitution, specifically, for $\sigma > J/(J - 1)$, corresponding to case I in (11.71). To see why this condition must hold for $s_j = \bar{s}$ to be an optimum, one considers the optimal propensity to consume $\tilde{s}_j$ for group j if all other groups i are choosing consumption propensities $s_i = \bar{s}$. More formally, one derives group j's optimal consumption propensities under these circumstances ignoring constraint

(11.61) and then checks whether the resulting ς_j are strictly less than $\bar{\varsigma}$ or not. If (11.61) does not bind, then $\omega_{jt} = 0$ for j, so that the path of c_t^j is described by (11.66). The optimal $\tilde{\varsigma}_j$ from (11.67) in this case are

$$\tilde{\varsigma}_j = \rho\sigma + (a - (J - 1)\bar{\varsigma})(1 - \sigma). \tag{11.72a}$$

When $J - \sigma(J - 1) > 0$ (that is, $\sigma < J/(J - 1)$), the inequality condition on $\bar{\varsigma}$ in (11.61) implies

$$\bar{\varsigma} > \rho\sigma + (a - (J - 1)\bar{\varsigma})(1 - \sigma). \tag{11.72b}$$

Combining (11.72a) and (11.72b), one sees that when $\sigma < J/(J - 1)$, $\tilde{\varsigma}_j < \bar{\varsigma}$, so that the extreme equilibrium does not exist. On the other hand, if $\sigma > J/(J - 1)$, the inequality in (11.72b) is reversed and $\tilde{\varsigma}_j > \bar{\varsigma}$, so the constraint (11.61) is binding. Therefore, there exists an MPE with $\tilde{\varsigma}_j = \bar{\varsigma}$ for all j. Intuitively, a high-appropriation MPE is possible only if there is a high enough intertemporal elasticity of substitution σ, so that the implied consumption path consistent with "fast" appropriation of the capital stock does not violate optimality conditions. Hence, if $\sigma > J/(J - 1)$, the common property model admits the possibility of multiple equilibria, one with a rate of appropriation of $(a(1 - \sigma) + \rho\sigma)/(J - (J - 1)\sigma)$, the other with a rate of appropriation equal to the maximum allowable level.

In a high-appropriation equilibrium, the path of the capital stock is

$$k_t = k_0 e^{(a - J\bar{\varsigma})t}. \tag{11.73}$$

In the high-appropriation equilibrium, the growth rate will be positive if $J\bar{\varsigma} < a$, and an increase in the number of interest groups J will lower the growth rate.

Common Property Models with Wealth-Dependent Appropriation and Growth

Benhabib and Rustichini (1996) present a common property model in the same spirit, but where the decision of whether to cooperate or appropriate may depend on the level of wealth. Appropriation of resources in the current period induces retaliation in the future in that defection by one player from cooperative behavior induces other players to follow noncooperative strategies in the future, leading to a total depletion of the capital stock. Their model is motivated by the observation that there is a robust negative relation between investment and various measures of political instability (see, for example, Venieris and Gupta [1986], Barro [1991], and Levine and Renelt [1992], as discussed in Section 11.6 below), and that investment-reducing instability appears to depend on the level of income. In their model, whether it is high or low levels of wealth that depress investment depends critically on the curvature of technology and preferences. Both cases are possible. Noncooperative behavior leading to no growth may manifest itself at low, but not high, levels of wealth, possibly leading to a "growth trap." This case is more likely when there are sufficiently high diminishing returns in utility, so that when wealth and consumption are high, the utility value of appropriating more consumption is unattractive, relative to the cost of future retaliation. When wealth and consumption are low, however, so that the marginal utility of consumption is high, the utility value of appropriating consumption today outweighs the cost of future retaliation.

Conversely, if the marginal utility of consumption does not diminish significantly as consumption rises, relative to the decreasing marginal productivity of capital, the opposite will be true. At low levels, capital is too valuable to risk the retaliation. As capital becomes more plentiful, fully cooperative behavior can no longer be sustained, and inefficiency will set in. Benhabib and Rustichini associate with Olson (1982) the possibility of inefficiencies arising only in a mature wealthy economy due to organized groups exerting redistributive pressures.[17]

Benhabib and Rustichini consider a discrete-time model of an appropriation game between two powerful groups. Analogous to (11.59), the players can consume out of a common resource pool. Unlike the Lane and Tornell model, in which there is an exogenous upper limit to the rate at which groups can appropriate resources, the only limit on appropriation is the total level of resources. Since there is no exogenously specified upper limit to appropriation, total consumption demands of the two players may exceed available output, so an allocation rule must be specified, relating the consumption demands of the two players to the allocation they receive. For player 1, for example, they specify the following rule:

$$
A_1(c^1, c^2, k) = \begin{cases} c^1 & \text{if } c^1 + c^2 \le f(k) \text{ or } c^1 \le \dfrac{f(k)}{2}, \\ f(k) - c^2 & \text{if } c^1 + c^2 \ge f(k) \text{ and } c^1 \ge \dfrac{f(k)}{2} \ge c^2, \\ \dfrac{f(k)}{2} & \text{if } c^1, c^2 \ge \dfrac{f(k)}{2}, \end{cases}
$$

$$(11.74)$$

with a similar allocation rule $A_2(\cdot)$ for group 2. One possibility is then that each player tries to appropriate as much as he can, in which case, all output is consumed in one period. More formally, Benhabib and Rusti-

---

[17] Olson's theory of stagnation in mature economies, and its representation by a common property model, was discussed in Section 10.3 of Chapter 10 in relation to models of nonadoption of socially beneficial policy changes.

chini consider the pair of *fast consumption* strategies $\bar{c}^{-1}(k) = \bar{c}^{-2}(k) = f(k)$. This will be a subgame-perfect equilibrium, and the value to player j of this equilibrium is

$$V_j^{\mathrm{D}}(k_0) = \sum_{t=0}^{\infty} \beta^t u\left(A_j\left[\bar{c}^{-1}(k_t), \bar{c}^{-2}(k_t), k_t\right]\right)$$

$$= u\left(f\left(\frac{k_0}{2}\right)\right), \tag{11.75}$$

where β is the discount factor and $u(\cdot)$ is the instantaneous utility function for both players.

Fast consumption strategies are important, for they are the punishment after a defection from a cooperative equilibrium. That is, after a defection from cooperation by one group, others will also cease cooperating and try to appropriate as much as they can, meaning they will follow a fast consumption strategy. Equation (11.75) defines the threat level in this trigger strategy equilibrium. Hence, any equilibrium must obey an *individual rationality constraint* of the form

$$\sum_{t=0}^{\infty} \beta^t u(c_t^j) \ge V_j^{\mathrm{D}}(k_0), \tag{11.76}$$

where c_t^j is the level of consumption in the equilibrium. To derive possible growth paths and from that, the possibilities for welfare-maximizing growth, Benhabib and Rustichini consider two other equilibrium concepts, and the associated infinite-horizon utility. In a first-best equilibrium, present discounted utility for each player $V^{\mathrm{FB}}(k)$ satisfies (we suppress the j subscripts, as the equilibrium is symmetric):

$$V^{\mathrm{FB}}(k) = \max_{c \le f(k)/2} u(c) + \beta V^{\mathrm{FB}}(f(k) - 2c), \tag{11.77}$$

while in a second-best equilibrium, present discounted utility $V^{\mathrm{SB}}(k)$ satisfies a similar equation:

$$V^{\mathrm{SB}}(k) = \max_{c \le f(k)/2} u(c) + \beta V^{\mathrm{SB}}(f(k) - 2c), \tag{11.78}$$

but where $V^{\mathrm{SB}}(k)$ must satisfy the additional constraint, $V^{\mathrm{SB}}(k) \ge V^{\mathrm{D}}(k)$. If the first-best solution satisfies this incentive compatibility constraint, then it is an equilibrium, and the first-best solution can be obtained in equilibrium. Otherwise, consumption is such that the incentive compatibility constraint for a second-best solution is satisfied with equality, that is, $V^{\mathrm{SB}}(k) = V^{\mathrm{D}}(k)$, where this equation defines the second-best level of

consumption (and hence capital accumulation) consistent with a cooperative (that is, no defection) equilibrium.

To make these concepts more concrete, let us first consider an example
as in Lane and Tornell, where the combination of CES utility and linear
production implies a propensity to consume which is independent of the
level of wealth. That is, we consider the appropriation game with the same
preferences and technology as in the previous section (albeit in discrete
rather than continuous time), but where we remove the restriction that
$c \leq \bar{s}k$. We begin by considering the first-best in this game. With preferences defined as in (11.60) and technology defined by $y = ak$, the individual's problem may be written

$$V(k) = \max_{c \leq y/2} \frac{\sigma}{\sigma - 1} c^{(\sigma-1)/\sigma} + \beta V(ak - 2c). \qquad (11.79)$$

Consumption paths are then of the form $c_s = sy_s$, so that y_t evolves
according to

$$y_{t+1} = a(y_t - 2c_t) = a(1 - 2s)y_t. \qquad (11.80)$$

Substituting $c_s = sy_s$ and (11.80) into value function $V(k) = \sum_{s=t}^{\infty} \beta^{s-t} u(c_s)$, we may derive a value function at time t for *any* s (not
only the first-best s) in terms of time-t aggregate output y:

$$V(k) = \frac{(\sigma/(\sigma - 1))s^{(\sigma-1)/\sigma}}{1 - \beta(a(1 - 2s))^{(\sigma-1)/\sigma}} y^{(\sigma-1)/\sigma} \equiv \Psi(s)y^{(\sigma-1)/\sigma}. \qquad (11.81)$$

This expression holds not only for paths along which consumption is
stationary, but also for paths along which it is nonstationary, that is, it
holds for any value $a\beta \neq 1$. To derive the optimal value of s, call it s^{FB},
one substitutes (11.81) and (11.80) into the envelope condition $V'(t) = a\beta V'(t + 1)$ relating the derivative of the value function V at two points of
time, to obtain

$$s^{FB} = \frac{1}{2}(1 - \beta^\sigma a^{\sigma-1}), \qquad (11.82)$$

where $\beta^\sigma a^{\sigma-1} < 1$ to avoid negative consumption. Call the associated
value function $V^{FB}(k)$.

Now consider defection against the first-best. A player who defects must
take into account that he will trigger punishment in the coming period.
That is, with the other player choosing $c^{FB} = s^{FB}y$, he chooses a consump-

tion level c^D in the current period which will trigger a reversion to a fast consumption strategy which exhausts all output in the next period if $c^D \neq c^{FB}$. Specifically, he maximizes

$$V^D(k, c^{FB}(k)) = \frac{\sigma}{\sigma - 1}(c^D)^{(\sigma-1)/\sigma}$$

$$+ \beta \frac{\sigma}{\sigma - 1}\left(\frac{a(y - s^{FB}y - c^D)}{2}\right)^{(\sigma-1)/\sigma}, \quad (11.83)$$

which implies a consumption level

$$c^D = s^D y \equiv \left(1 + \frac{2}{a}\left(\frac{a\beta}{2}\right)^\sigma\right)^{-1}(1 - s^{FB})y. \quad (11.84)$$

The associated value function is $V^D = \Psi^D y^{(\sigma-1)/\sigma}$, where

$$\Psi^D = \frac{\sigma}{\sigma - 1}(1 - s^{FB})^{(\sigma-1)/\sigma}\left(1 + \frac{2}{a}\left(\frac{a\beta}{2}\right)^\sigma\right)^{-1/\sigma}. \quad (11.85)$$

For the first-best consumption and capital accumulation path to constitute an equilibrium, it must be the case that the associated value must exceed the defection value, that is, $V^{FB}(k) \geq V^D(k)$ for all k along the equilibrium path. The nature of preferences and technology implies that this relation is either always satisfied or never satisfied. Hence, if $\Psi(s^{FB}) \geq \Psi^D(s^{FB})$, the first-best solution may be enforced. If, however, $\Psi(s^{FB}) < \Psi^D(s^{FB})$, then the first-best solution is not incentive compatible and the second-best solution will obtain. Consumption is given by $c = s^{SB}y$, where $s^{SB} \leq 1/2$ is defined by $\Psi(s^{SB}) = \Psi^D(s^{SB})$. In words, if the first-best path is not incentive compatible, in that there is an incentive to defect, consumption must be increased and accumulation slowed to the point at which it is no longer attractive to defect from this (second-best) solution.

We now consider wealth-dependent strategies. In the above case, the nature of preferences and technology implied that the ranking of strategies is independent of wealth (that is, c and V were linear in k). More generally, the possibility of enforcing a first-best equilibrium may depend on the level of wealth. One possibility, consistent with "poverty traps," is that first-best behavior, and hence first-best growth rates, are sustainable from high levels of wealth, but not from low levels, because of the incentive compatibility constraints. Benhabib and Rustichini explain this case intuitively as follows. As we saw, if the first-best level is not incentive compatible, consumption must be increased and accumulation slowed to prevent defection. When stocks of capital are low, the amount by which consumption must be increased to prevent defection is no longer feasible. Fixed costs of accumulation of the sort considered by Galor and Zeira (1993) can generate this case, but are not necessary. The interested reader is referred to Benhabib and Rustichini (1996) for some examples.

The alternative wealth-dependent case is where cooperative behavior is attainable from low levels of k, but not from high levels. Benhabib and Rustichini term this an "Olson" case, following Olson's (1982) influential study on the decline of growth rates in "mature" societies (that is, societies with relatively high levels of income), due to the rigidities imposed by entrenched interest groups trying to appropriate resources to themselves. To illustrate this case, they consider the equilibria that may emerge in the common property game when preferences imply a linear utility function of the form $u(c) = c$ and technology implies a Cobb–Douglas utility function $f(k) = k^\alpha$, where $0 < \alpha < 1$. The optimal steady state is given by the "modified" Golden rule $f'(k) = 1/\beta$, which implies a steady-state optimal capital stock k^* given by

$$k^* = (a\beta)^{1/(1-\alpha)}. \tag{11.86}$$

Given the linear utility function, the implied optimal policy is intuitive: for $y < k^*$, devote all output to capital accumulation and none to consumption; for $y \geq k^*$, set the sum of the two players' consumption such that k remains at k^*. Formally, one may write

$$
\begin{aligned}
c^{\text{FB}}(k) &= 0 && \text{if } k < k^{*(1/\alpha)}, \\
c^{\text{FB}}(k) &= \frac{k^\alpha - k^*}{2} && \text{if } k \geq k^{*(1/\alpha)},
\end{aligned}
\tag{11.87}
$$

with the value of the first-best steady state being for $V^{\text{FB}}(k^*) = (c^*(k^*))/(1 - \beta)$ for $c^*(k^*) = (k^{*\alpha} - k^*)/2$.

To determine whether the first-best path (11.87) can be sustained, Benhabib and Rustichini derive optimal defection behavior for any level of k. Consider the utility to a player from defecting when the capital stock is k and the other player is consuming c. We may write the value of defecting as

$$V^{\text{D}}(k, c) = \max_{c^{\text{D}} \geq 0} c^{\text{D}} + \frac{\beta}{2}(k^\alpha - c - c^{\text{D}})^\alpha, \tag{11.88}$$

where we have used the fact that defection triggers fast consumption strategies which exhaust output in the next period. Optimal defection consumption is then

$$c^D(k,c) = \begin{cases} 0 & \text{if } k^\alpha - c < (\alpha\beta/2)^{1(1-\alpha)}, \\ k^\alpha - c - (\alpha\beta/2)^{1/(1-\alpha)} & \text{if } k^\alpha - c \geq (\alpha\beta/2)^{1/(1-\alpha)}. \end{cases}$$

$$(11.89)$$

The associated value function is

$$V^D(k,c) = \begin{cases} \beta/2(k^\alpha - c)^\alpha & \text{if } k^\alpha - c < (\alpha\beta/2)^{1/(1-\alpha)}, \\ k^\alpha - c + \kappa & \text{if } k^\alpha - c \geq (\alpha\beta/2)^{1/(1-\alpha)}, \end{cases} \quad (11.90)$$

where $\kappa = (\beta/2)(\alpha\beta/2)^{\alpha/(1-\alpha)} - (\alpha\beta/2)^{1/(1-\alpha)}$. The optimal steady state k^* is not sustainable if $V^D(k^*, c^*) > (k^{*\alpha} - k^*)/(2(1 - \beta))$.

Let us consider an example. Suppose this inequality holds, so that incentive compatibility implies a second-best steady state such that $V^{SB}(k) = V^D(k)$, as discussed following (11.78). Call $\bar{k}$ the largest value of k satisfying this constraint, that is, the largest k such that $V^{SB}(\bar{k}) = V^D(\bar{k})$. In words, when the incentive compatibility constraint binds, $\bar{k} < k^*$, and the steady-state capital stock will be below k^*. (For example, following Benhabib and Rustichini, when $\alpha = .975$ and $\beta = .97$, $\bar{k} = .0906$ and $k^* = .1074$.) The optimal sustainable path will then be as follows. For $k < \bar{k}^{1/\alpha}$, optimal consumption in a symmetric equilibrium will be 0, so that the second-best and the first-best equilibrium will coincide. In words, an economy with output $y < \bar{k}$ will save all its income, identical to the optimal path. When $y \geq \bar{k}$, however, the incentive compatibility constraint will bind and consumption will follow

$$c^{SB}(k) = \frac{k^\alpha - \bar{k}}{2} < \frac{k^\alpha - k^*}{2} = c^{FB}(k). \quad (11.91)$$

Once $\bar{k}^{1/\alpha}$ is achieved, the economy will consume as much as needed to hit $\bar{k}$ in one step and will then stay at that capital level as a steady state. Capital accumulation will be below the first-best level associated with the steady state k^*.

11.6. EMPIRICAL DETERMINANTS OF GROWTH

In this section, we consider empirical testing of the above theories. The number of empirical studies of determinants of growth is immense, reflecting the great interest in endogenous growth in general. There are literally hundreds of papers empirically testing political determinants of growth. The literature is far too large to summarize here with any sense of completeness. Instead, the aim is to present some of the basic methodology that is used, as well as some of the basic results. A key purpose in reviewing the results (or, in some cases, the lack of them) is to put in better perspective the large number of theories discussed in this chapter. Sirowy and Inkeles (1990) provide a good survey of empirical work prior to 1990. Perotti (1996a) provides a more recent comprehensive survey of empirical research on political determinants of growth. Benabou (1996) also provides an excellent summary of recent work. Many leading papers are also published in the *Journal of Economic Growth*. For a general discussion of empirical determinants of growth, the reader is referred to Barro and Sala-i-Martin (1995) for a comprehensive treatment.

Almost all the empirical evidence on the political economy of growth is based on reduced-form estimation of the determinants of growth in a cross section of countries in which political variables are added to standard growth equations as potential explanatory variables. Hence, the basic regression is of the form

$$\hat{y}_i = a_0 + \sum_s a_s x_{si} + \sum_j b_j z_{ji} + \sum_m c_m DUM_{mi} + \epsilon_i, \qquad (11.92)$$

where $\hat{y}_i$ is the growth rate in country i at a given point in time t (or an average over a period of time), the x_s are economic variables that may affect growth (possibly including lagged values), the z_j are political variables which may affect the growth rate (possibly including interaction terms), and *DUM* refers to dummy variables (such as regional effects). Cross-section, rather than time-series, equations are generally run, due to the lack of variation in key explanatory variables over time, though depending on the variables used, there is also time-series or panel estimation. The specification of the political variables is a crucial issue. In addition to a basic reduced-form equation for the growth rate, models are tested by regressing intermediate variables, such as investment or saving rates, on a set of underlying determinants.

Inequality and Growth

The most basic result from an equation such as (11.92) is the negative effect of inequality on growth. In assessing such regressions, one must first consider measurement issues. Though many theories are concerned with the effect of the distribution of wealth on growth performance, such data are generally not available for a large number of countries. Hence, the distribution of income, more easily available, is used as a proxy. Jenkins (1991) provides an overview of measures of income inequality, including a detailed discussion of various measures and a review of the literature. Deininger and Squire (1996), in a highly influential article, argue that the existing measures on which much of the empirical work is based are highly flawed, and they present a new data set on income inequality which is both broader and of higher quality. They suggest that using improved data may call into question some basic results, as we shall discuss below. It has been argued that using inequality of income as a proxy for the inequality of wealth is not a serious empirical problem because the shapes of the two distributions are believed to vary together in cross sections of countries, though Deininger and Squire's (1998) results indicate that even though the distributions are highly correlated, it does make a difference whether one uses inequality of income or wealth. Note further that the distribution of wealth, however, is more skewed than the distribution of income, which matters for some of the above theories.

A second problem is choice of a summary measure for income inequality. One possibility is the Gini coefficient, measuring income dispersion in the population (see, for example, Ray [1998] for a precise definition). Other common measures begin with the division of the income distribution into quintiles, suggesting several possibilities: the ratio of the top to the bottom quintile; the percentage of income accruing to the third quintile, as suggested by a median voter model; or the combined share of middle quintiles, for example, the third and fourth quintiles, taken as a measure of the middle class, but argued to be less sensitive to measurement error than taking the third quintile alone. Theoretically, various characteristics of the shape of the income distribution may be important, and different summary measures do not always provide the same, unambiguous ranking of inequality, though they tend to be highly correlated.

The typical regression takes as the dependent variable the average rate of growth of per capita GDP over some long period of time (twenty to thirty years), which is regressed on some measure of initial inequality and a group of controls. Following the growth literature, these controls typically include: a measure of the initial level of income to capture conditional convergence, which always enters with a significant negative sign; a beginning-of-period measure of the stock of human capital, such as average years of secondary schooling, which is systematically positive; and, regional dummies, generally significantly negative for sub-Saharan Africa and positive for Southeast Asia. Other controls sometimes used are: measures of market distortions; additional measures of development (such as urbanization); additional human capital variables, on the argument that a single measure does not capture all relevant effects; and, demographic variables, such as the fraction of the population above a certain age. (We return to this last control in discussing fiscal theories of inequality and growth.) Perotti (1996a) presents a number of these basic regressions.

Prior to the work of Deininger and Squire (1998), which we will discuss shortly, the consensus was that no matter which measure of inequality is used, cross-section, reduced-form growth regressions yield a single message—higher initial inequality is associated with lower growth. Benabou

(1996), for example, surveys almost two dozen recent studies and reports not only a consistent negative effect of inequality on growth, but also a similar magnitude of effect across the studies. A one-standard-deviation decrease in inequality is found to raise the annual growth rate of per capita GDP by 0.5 to 0.8 percentage point. He points out that while this amounts to between 30% to 45% of the standard deviation in growth rates found in most samples, it does not come close to explaining the differential between high- and low-growth countries.

A very basic criticism of these results concerns the quality of the income distribution data, which are notoriously poor. There are two types of problems: the low quality of the underlying survey data and the possibility of very large measurement error; and, the noncomparability of inequality measures across countries, due to differences in the design of surveys from which income distribution data are computed. These differences include the definition of the unit receiving income, the definition of income itself, and the survey's coverage. Measurement problems are discussed in Jenkins (1991), Deininger and Squire (1996), and Perotti (1996a).

There is disagreement on the importance of possible measurement errors. On the one hand, Perotti (1996a) performs a number of robustness tests and concludes that the basic negative correlation between growth and income inequality is reasonably robust. On the other hand, based on careful construction of a new, more reliable data set, Deininger and Squire (1998) argue that the link between initial income inequality and growth is extremely weak. They do find a significant negative effect on growth of initial inequality in *assets*, as measured by the distribution of land, for a sample of 15 developing countries. In contrast, no significant effect is found for wealth inequality in OECD countries.

The work of Deininger and Squire calls into serious question many of the results on income inequality. For example, they report that if they rerun the regressions of Persson and Tabellini (1994b) eliminating the observations they believe are of dubious quality, the reported negative relation between income inequality and growth disappears. One outstanding empirical issue is thus seeing which results on income inequality remain when the theories are tested with better data. The results reported below should be read with this caveat in mind. On the other hand, the Deininger–Squire results on wealth inequality suggest that the basic result —that higher initial inequality reduces growth—is correct if we succeed in getting the right measure of inequality.

The theoretical models suggested political mechanisms by which the distribution of income may be endogenous to growth, for example, due to tax-financed human capital accumulation in a median voter model or due to the endogeneity of the voting franchise. Although there has been work on growth as a possible determinant of democracy (discussed later in this section), there has been little or no testing of these specific mechanisms. Of course, the empirical effects of growth on the distribution of income have been long discussed in the development literature, with the most well-known argument being the Kuznets (1955) Hypothesis: the relation between the level of income and inequality is U-shaped, with inequality first rising and then falling as a country becomes more developed. There is a large empirical literature on whether the Kuznets Hypothesis is observed in the data, with a largely, though not uniformly, negative finding. Deininger and Squire (1996) report no evidence for the U-shaped effect. Since our primary interest is in the political determinants, rather than the effects, of growth, we will not go into these studies.

One is then led to ask which of the political-economic theories suggesting a connection from income inequality to growth receives empirical support. The basic idea of this approach is to divide the reduced-form relation between income inequality and growth into two relationships: the effect of inequality on the variable central to the theory (for example, redistributive taxation), which for simplicity of exposition is termed the "political" mechanism; and the effect of that variable on growth, termed the "economic" mechanism. We now consider the tests for a number of the theories.

Fiscal Policy

We begin with the fiscal theories presented in Section 11.2, whereby higher inequality increases the pressure for redistribution, which reduces growth because of the distortionary nature of the instruments of redistribution. To test the first part, namely, the political mechanism, income inequality is regressed on various measures of fiscal redistribution: marginal and average tax rates; the share of transfers in GDP as a whole; or, categories of transfers, such as welfare, social security, health, or housing expenditures. Though different measures of inequality may be used, the share of the third quintile in the income distribution, or the combined share of the third and fourth quintiles (which we denote *MID* following Perotti) is often used. In his survey of results, Benabou (1996) finds that with the exception of Persson and Tabellini (1994b), most papers find little or no empirical support for the fiscal mechanism. The effect of income inequality on taxes or transfers is rarely significant, with the sign varying from one study to another. This lack of support is in accordance with the simple observation that countries with more income equality seem often to be characterized by more redistribution, not less.

Persson and Tabellini (1994b) criticize these tests of the theory as too narrow, since redistribution can take many forms in addition to simply tax-financed transfers, such as minimum wages, government regulations and restrictions, and targeted government expenditures. Benabou, however, argues that this criticism is not persuasive for a number of reasons. First of all, tests have been performed on a number of variables, generally with results unfavorable to the theory. For example, Perotti (1996a) regresses a number of fiscal variables on *MID*, the combined share of the third and fourth quintiles, plus a small number of explanatory economic variables including: the average marginal tax rate in a country over his sample period; average share of labor taxation in GDP; average share of income taxes in personal income; or average shares of government expenditure in GDP on social security and welfare or on health and housing. He finds that income distribution has little or no explanatory power for any of these variables. If the fiscal theory is correct, one should see at least some evidence in direct transfer mechanisms. It is difficult to see why redistributive pressures should be manifest *only* in indirect ways. Finally, if the Persson–Tabellini response is correct, one should see that such restrictions are higher in countries with more inequality, which does not appear to be true, at least in the OECD.

Testing the economic mechanism, whereby higher fiscal redistribution reduces growth, also provides little or no support for the theory. Easterly and Rebelo (1993) include various average and marginal tax rates in growth regressions and find that though the coefficients are negative as the theory predicts, they are almost never significant. Perotti (1996a) finds that the coefficient on the mean marginal tax rate in a basic growth regression is significantly *positive*.[18] Several studies, including Perotti (1992), and Sala-i-Martin (1992), find a significant positive relation between transfers and growth, consistent, for example, with the models of Section 11.4. For example, in a growth regression with the inequality variable *MID*, Perotti (1996a) includes the fraction of the population over 65, denoted *POP*65, as a proxy for larger old-age transfers per worker. He finds that it enters positively, with the coefficient on *MID* becoming statistically insignificant. (One possibility that Perotti suggests is that *POP*65 is a negative proxy for fertility, which is associated with lower growth.) As Perotti summarizes his findings in tests of both the economic and the political mechanism underlying the theory (p. 171), "these results are difficult to explain for virtually any of the existing standard economic and political models of fiscal policy." This conclusion sums up the bulk of the empirical work on the fiscal policy approach to the connection between inequality and growth.

A related question, which some argue explains the lack of empirical support for the fiscal mechanism in most cross-section regressions, is whether the effect is present in democracies but not in nondemocracies. We now turn to this issue; as we shall see, the evidence of a negative association between equality and fiscal variables specifically in democracies is weak.

---

[18] As Perotti's regression is estimated using instrumental variables, endogeneity of *MTAX* cannot explain the result.

Democracy and Growth

In Section 11.4, it was argued that democracy may have an effect on growth either directly, or interacted with the distribution of income. Under the latter argument, the pressures for redistribution induced by income inequality may be more likely to affect economic policy and hence growth in a democracy than in a dictatorship. To test the arguments, countries are separated into "democracies" and "nondemocracies" on the basis of an (often subjective) index of political rights, such as Gastil (1982–3 and subsequent). An equation such as (11.92) is then run separately for each subsample, or for the whole sample using a "democracy" index or dummy as discussed in the previous sentence, either alone or interacted with income distribution. Benabou (1996) reports that the results are generally negative—there is no consistent direct effect of democracy on growth. This may reflect the restriction of a linear effect in (11.92). For example, Barro (1996) finds a negative, but insignificant, effect in a linear regression, where democracy is measured by the Gastil index. He then considers a nonlinear specification, breaking a Gastil index normalized to 1 into thirds, and strongly rejects the hypothesis of a linear effect. He reports that the middle level of democracy is most favorable to growth, the lowest level comes second, and the highest level comes third. The highest and lowest thirds do not have significantly different growth rates from one another (given the levels of the other independent variables), while the middle level of democracy has a significantly higher growth rate than the other two levels.

Using an interaction term, Persson and Tabellini (1994b) find a statistically significant differential impact of inequality between democracies and nondemocracies (income inequality significantly affects growth in the former, but not the latter), but other studies have not reproduced this effect. Perotti's (1996a) analysis indicates why. He begins with a single growth regression of the form of (11.92) including the measure of equality *MID*, and adds an interactive term between *MID* and a 0–1 democracy indicator, *DEM*. (See the discussion after (11.93) below for an exact definition.) He finds that the coefficient on this interaction term is quite small and statistically insignificant. He then splits the sample into democracies and nondemocracies and runs the same regression without the interaction term. The coefficient on *MID* is significantly positive in democracies, but not in nondemocracies. The regressions, however, reveal another key difference: the coefficients on his human capital measures, average years of secondary schooling for males and females, are significantly larger in nondemocracies than in democracies, coefficients that were constrained to be the same in the regression run on the whole sample. He therefore adds interaction terms between the democracy indicator *DEM* and the human capital stock measures to the regression of all countries, a specification similar to that used by Persson and Tabellini (1994b) but for a different definition of the human capital proxy, and finds that the coefficient on $MID \cdot DEM$ is much larger and marginally significant.[19] Perotti argues that, in short, the effect of democracy on growth in empirical studies is very sensitive to specification. Moreover, he reports that the weakly positive effect he finds is not robust. The exclusion of one observation (Venezuela) from the favorable regression causes the coefficient on $MID \cdot DEM$ to fall by 40% and its t-statistic to drop to less than 1. Other robustness tests cast similar doubt on the robustness of the differential effect.

One especially serious problem in any empirical investigation of the effects of democracy on growth is the very high correlation between the level of GDP and a democracy dummy such as DEM. For example, of the 33 democracies in Perotti's sample of 67, only six had per capita GDP below the cut-off level defining them as poor. As many researchers have argued, "democracy" is an empirical proxy for "rich," an argument that Perotti confirms by running all the regressions using a rich-poor dummy rather than DEM and obtaining similar results. The crucial point in trying to assess the effect of democracy on growth is simple: it is not clear whether any effects that one finds should be attributed to a democracy effect rather than to a level of GDP effect.

One may also consider causation in the opposite direction, namely, what is the effect of the level of development on the propensity towards democracy? The argument that the more developed a country, the more likely that it is democratic is a hypothesis associated with Lipset (1959). Barro (1996) regresses the Gastil index of democracy averaged over a decade on a number of indicators of the standard of living, such as GDP, the infant mortality rate, educational attainment, and income inequality. He finds a significant effect for the first two variables: the estimated coefficient on log GDP is significantly positive, while that on the infant mortality rate is significantly negative. He surmises that the result that inequality is unimportant for the level of democracy may reflect the poor quality of the data. In contrast, Easterly (1997) finds little or no relation between growth and standard-of-living indicators, arguing that the effects may be too long term to be picked up with the statistical techniques commonly employed.

Borrowing Constraints and Human Capital Accumulation

A second key approach to the relation between inequality and growth, as discussed in Section 11.3, concerns investment in human capital in the

---

[19] Persson and Tabellini use a flow measure, primary school enrollment ratios, as a proxy for human capital, and obtain a larger positive coefficient on $MID \cdot DEM$ which is highly significant. Perotti discusses why the differences between these two measures are likely to produce a more significant effect in the Persson and Tabellini specification.

presence of imperfect capital markets. Human capital accumulation increases growth, but is limited by the borrowing constraints implied by imperfect capital markets. Government redistribution of income mitigates these borrowing constraints and hence increases growth. A related argument, following new growth theory, concerns the relationship between income distribution and growth via fertility. Fertility rates are argued to be high among the very poor, so that more unequal societies have higher average fertility, which in turn reduces per capita growth. Fertility may be thought of as a human capital variable, once one considers the quantity–quality trade-off in rearing children.

Empirically, human capital investment has been found to be a leading determinant of growth. Regressing male and female secondary school enrollment ratios on initial GDP, average years of secondary schooling (a stock variable), and *MID*, Perotti finds that a more equal distribution of income has a significant positive effect on an economy's accumulation of human capital. This correlation remains strong even when regional dummies are included in the regression to control for cultural factors. Many papers have also found a strong negative effect of fertility on growth. When one regresses fertility on measures of income inequality (for example, *MID* in Perotti) and initial GDP, one finds a negative coefficient on *MID* which is large in absolute value and highly significant statistically. Hence, the negative effect of inequality on growth may be a proxy for the effect of either fertility or human capital investment.

In many theories of human capital investment, fertility and schooling are jointly determined (see, for example, Becker, Murphy, and Tamura [1990]). Empirically, fertility and secondary school enrollment ratios are highly correlated. Perotti considers their interaction by including male and female secondary school enrollment ratios in a regression with fertility as the dependent variable and, conversely, by including fertility in regressions meant to explain secondary school enrollment ratios. In the fertility regression, one finds that the coefficient on *MID* falls, but still remains significant, both economically and statistically. In contrast, in the enrollment regression, the coefficient on fertility is negative and highly significant, and *MID* loses all explanatory power. Perotti interprets these results as suggesting that income distribution affects investment in education largely through its effects on fertility, but that even controlling for investment in education, income distribution still affects other determinants of fertility. To summarize, the empirical evidence is consistent with the argument that the connection between inequality and growth reflects the effects of human capital accumulation, as discussed in Section 11.3. More equal societies have significantly lower fertility rates and higher rates of investment in education, both of which are associated with higher rates of growth.

This evidence on the importance of human capital accumulation is also consistent with a role for borrowing constraints and imperfect capital markets, though such effects are difficult to test because of the difficulties of measuring such imperfections across countries. Perotti (1994) uses the ratio of loan size to house value for mortgages as an indicator of credit availability in an investment equation and finds a significant positive coefficient. There appear to be interactive effects as well: the negative effect of inequality rises with credit constraints, as theory predicts. The finding of a positive effect of transfers on growth, presented in our discussion of fiscal policy earlier in this section, can be seen as providing indirect evidence of the importance for growth of relaxing credit constraints. There is also a significant amount of microeconomic evidence in the development literature on the effect of credit constraints on individual agents, as in the work of Rosenzweig and Wolpin (1993) and Townsend (1995). Binswanger and Deininger (1995) provide a survey.

Social and Political Instability

As argued in Section 11.5, social and political instability is generally seen as detrimental to growth, with a highly unequal distribution of income and wealth being an important factor in creating such instability. As discussed in that section, the difficulty of modeling such instability in a convincing way which is not too abstract has led researchers to concentrate on empirical work. The standard approach, as presented at the end of the general discussion of inequality and growth earlier in this section, is to consider two empirical relations: first, the determinants of sociopolitical instability, especially income inequality; and, second, the connection between sociopolitical instability and either the determinants of growth, such as investment, or growth itself. Sociopolitical instability is argued to decrease investment for at least two reasons. First, it creates uncertainty both about the political environment, for example, the stability of the current political regime, and about the legal environment, for example, the security of property rights. Second, sociopolitical instability is seen as disrupting the workings of the market and of economic relations, having a direct adverse effect on productivity.

To carry out empirical work, one needs to provide a measure of instability. There are at least three types of measures. The most widely used emphasizes social unrest largely expressed outside standard political channels, such as violent demonstrations, strikes, political assassinations, or coups. Some studies, such as Londregan and Poole (1990), consider individual measures; more generally, an index is constructed, using several social and political indicators from world handbooks of these indicators, such as Banks (1987) or Jodice and Taylor (1988). This approach may be found in Venieris and Gupta (1986), Gupta (1990), Alesina and Perotti (1994, 1996b), Alesina, Özler, Roubini, and Swagel (1996), and Perotti (1996a). For example, Perotti (1996a) uses the following index of sociopolitical instability:

$$SPI = 1.60\,ASSASS + 2.33\,DEATH$$
$$+ 7.29\,SCOUP + 6.86\,UCOUP - 5.23\,DEM, \qquad (11.93)$$

where $ASSASS$ = number of political assassinations per million population per year; $DEATH$ = violent deaths per million population per year; $SCOUP$ = number of successful coups per year; $UCOUP$ = number of unsuccessful coups per year; and DEM = a dummy variable which is 1 for countries with an average value of Jodice and Taylor's democracy index greater than .5, and zero otherwise. The weights are chosen by the method of principal components.

A second measure of sociopolitical instability, suggested by Alesina and Perotti (1994), considers instability within the political system, of the sort discussed in Section 7.8 of Chapter 7. They suggest looking at a measure of executive instability, such as the frequency of government turnovers. A third measure, more directly linked to the security of property, is an indicator of "country risk" produced by specialized firms. Such indicators include: sovereign default risk; risk of nationalization or expropriation; measures of the "rule of law" and the enforceability of contracts; and, the level of bureaucracy and corruption. This approach has been used by Mauro (1995), Knack and Keefer (1995), and Svensson (1998a), among others.

The empirical results on the relation of sociopolitical instability to growth are quite impressive, both for the relation between inequality and instability and for the relation of sociopolitical instability to growth. Using a general index of sociopolitical instability, several papers find a significant positive relation between income inequality and instability. For example, Perotti reports that in a regression of SPI on MID and school enrollment ratios, the coefficient on MID is negative and statistically significant, both with and without the inclusion of regional dummies. Similar results are found for alternative indices of sociopolitical instability, such as the one suggested by Gupta (1990). Numerous papers have also found a significant negative relation between sociopolitical instability and growth. (See, for example, Veneiris and Gupta [1986], Alesina, Özler, Roubini, and Swagel [1996], Barro [1996], Knack and Keefer [1995], Perotti [1996a], and Svensson [1998a].) The effect is significant no matter which measure of instability is used, over a variety of samples and time periods. Londregan and Poole (1990) consider one measure of political instability, occurrence of coups d'etat, and also find results quite favorable to the hypothesis that sociopolitical instability significantly reduces growth.

There are some caveats to this line of work. First, the problem of simultaneity seems especially acute in considering the relation between growth and sociopolitical instability. Changes in growth rates may strongly influence political outcomes, even when one is defining instability in the narrow sense of a change in government. (Remember the results of Fair and others in Chapter 7 on the determinants of electoral outcomes.) Most studies use some sort of a simultaneous equations approach to address problems of simultaneity. Second, the distribution of indices of sociopolitical instability are quite disperse, so that their explanatory power could be coming from a small number of observations. For example, Perotti reports that *SPI* has a very fat left tail and a very thin, but long, right tail. In his sample of 64 countries, there are only eight with a value of *SPI* that exceeds the average by more than one standard deviation. Excluding countries with very high values of *SPI* from his growth equation, Perotti finds that in two-stage least-squares regressions, the coefficient on *SPI* remains high in absolute value, but is estimated quite imprecisely, due perhaps to a lack of variation of *SPI* in this case and problems of finding a good instrument. In OLS regressions, the coefficient on *SPI* remains both economically and statistically significant in the restricted sample. Perotti also finds that the estimated relation is much stronger in rich countries.

Third, the empirical effect of sociopolitical instability, especially in investment equations, depends on what controls are used in the regressions. Svensson (1998a) finds that when he includes both an instability index as in (11.93) and "country risk" variables in an investment equation, only the latter are significant. Knack and Keefer (1995) find that when one controls for initial GDP in an investment equation, political instability as measured by country risk is no longer significant.

The bottom line on all of this is that sociopolitical instability appears to be important both directly for growth and for explaining the effects of income inequality on growth, but far more work needs to be done both theoretically and empirically.

11.7. CONCLUSIONS

The study of factor accumulation and growth is an extremely active field in economics; and a significant part of this research activity is concerned with the role of political factors. Growth is an especially fruitful application of political economy for a number of reasons. First and foremost, as we hope this chapter has demonstrated, political economy is central to understanding the growth process both theoretically and empirically. Politics is a crucial factor in explaining why some countries grow more quickly and smoothly, while others grow hardly at all. Second, the techniques and models of modern political economy fit especially well into current research on growth. Basic models find applications in studying growth that seem natural rather than contrived, as they sometimes seem in other applications. Third, concepts and approaches in political economy that do not lend themselves easily to modeling (such as property rights or predatory behavior) also seem to fit comfortably into research on growth.

Finally, the empirical studies of political determinants of growth are far better developed than in other political economy applications. In short, from many angles, the study of factor accumulation and growth is almost a tailor-made application of political economy.

One should not, however, lose sight of the problems that remain. For all the effort put into growth theory and empirics in the last decade, there is still much that we do not understand, both in general and in relation to the political economy of growth. The wealth of theoretically clean models without a lot of loose ends tends to obscure this fact. So does the easy transition from model to model, as if everything is cut-and-dried, just waiting for presentation. The material in this chapter should be seen as an opening to the field, rather than as a body of work that closes the field. If it was not clear to the reader the first time through, another careful reading of the chapter will indicate just how many open questions there are.

The International Economy

Since talk of the globalization of the world's economy began
some 35 years ago, the demise of the nation-state has been
widely predicted.... But, whenever in the last 200 years
political passions and nation-state politics have
collided with economic rationality, political passions
and the nation-state have won.

—Peter F. Drucker,
"The Global Economy and the Nation-State,"
Foreign Affairs, 1997

12.1. INTRODUCTION

In this chapter, we apply the models of political economy derived in Parts
II and III to international macroeconomics. We concentrate on three
areas where political economy is especially relevant: exchange-rate arrangements; macroeconomic interdependence and policy coordination;
and, international capital flows, including sovereign borrowing and foreign
assistance programs. Each is treated in a separate section of the chapter.

The main challenge in analyzing the political economy of the open
economy is deciding how to limit the coverage. There are wide literatures
in both the political economy of trade and the political economy of
international macroeconomics. Even considering just the political economy
of international macroeconomics leaves a large number of areas. For any
area, there is often a substantial amount of research, including formal
modeling, more conceptual treatments, and extensive empirical work.

To address this problem, a number of expositional decisions have been
made; no doubt, they will not find favor in the eyes of every reader. First,
there will be no coverage of the political economy of international trade,
the "real" side of international economics. The field is growing rapidly
with much extremely exciting research, so it may seem a shame to exclude
it. However, that would be another long chapter in itself. Another strong
factor in this decision is comparative advantage: a careful treatment of the

political economy of trade is better left to someone specializing in the real side rather than the macro side of international economics.

Second, the chapter is not meant to be a self-contained introduction to open-economy macroeconomics to readers with no background in the area. Much of the material should be generally accessible, but there are some discussions in the chapter which assume familiarity with basic international macroeconomics. There are numerous excellent texts to provide a background for different areas covered in the chapter. A recent graduate-level text is Obstfeld and Rogoff (1996).

Third, in applications of political economy to the open economy, many of the formal models significantly overlap with analogous closed-economy models in earlier chapters. In the interest of covering more material without making the chapter unmanageable, this overlap is heavily exploited. Several models that are presented are exposited only skeletally, with references back to fuller treatments earlier in the book. Much research is presented only intuitively, with no formal modeling at all, but with references to earlier formal treatments. It is assumed that readers who are interested in learning more technical methods of analysis will make use of earlier chapters. This puts a burden on such readers, but one that should generally be manageable with a little creativity and a bit of hard work.

Fourth, the voluminous empirical literature is not covered, certainly not in the way empirical determinants of growth were covered in the previous chapter. However, there is an applied focus for a number of important issues, such as European Monetary Union, capital controls, and foreign assistance.

Let us now take a brief preliminary look at what will be covered in order to make clear the political nature of the topics covered. As indicated above, the chapter focuses on three main areas of international macroeconomics, which actually cover a significant part of the field as a whole. Topics are chosen both because of their importance in traditional international macroeconomics and because political economy is especially relevant in understanding them. The chapter is divided into three separate sections in a further attempt to make it more manageable. Some topics in different sections are largely unrelated; others, as we shall see, are closely related, so that the division may seem arbitrary at points.

The first part of the chapter considers the political economy of exchange rate arrangements, beginning in Section 12.2 with an analysis of fixed rates as a way to achieve political objectives. While choice of an exchange rate system may have several objectives, we concentrate on two political aims: establishing the credibility of the government's anti-inflationary commitment; and, as a means to more general political and economic integration. We begin with the first, considering issues surrounding pegging the exchange rate to gain anti-inflation credibility. This leads to the question of the credibility of the peg itself, as countries that have fixed their exchange rates often find their currencies coming under speculative attack. Though speculative attack appears to be a pure economic event, motivated by profit seeking by speculators, we argue that there are several political aspects to currency crises, which we explore in Section 12.3.

Analyzing the political economy of fixed exchange rates leads to an analysis of currency areas and monetary unions for at least two reasons. First, questions of the credibility of fixed rates lead naturally to examination of stronger institutional arrangements as a way to gain credibility for anti-inflation policy. Second, if the objective of fixed rates is greater political integration, one is naturally led to examine monetary union, both in the absence of political union and as a precursor to political union. The various aspects of monetary union are discussed in Section 12.4, concluding with a lengthy application to European integration and the recently formed European Monetary Union.

In Part II of the chapter, we consider macroeconomic interdependence more generally. A major issue in open-economy macroeconomics is the transmission of economic disturbances across countries, with government policy being a major source of such spillovers. When policy actions of sovereign governments affect one another, issues of policy coordination become central, which is the topic of Section 12.5. Coordination of policy between policymakers with heterogeneous objectives is itself a political question in a way that is at the heart of political economy—were there no difference in objectives, there would be no need for explicit coordination. Policy coordination has another political aspect as well—it may affect the behavior of the opportunistic or partisan policymakers who were so important in earlier chapters, due to either time-consistency constraints or partisan differences. In connection with these issues, we consider both welfare-enhancing cooperation, as well as ways that coordination can actually reduce welfare, in both monetary and fiscal policy. International policy cooperation has now become a standard topic in economics courses, and much of the literature covered here will be familiar in one form or another. Two newer topics are the formal analysis of institutions as a way to achieve policy cooperation and the analysis of interdependence using more stylized models of rent seeking. We summarize both approaches, using earlier material in the book on these topics and giving references to more complete treatments.

In Part III of the chapter, we consider a number of issues concerned with international capital flows, sovereign borrowing, and foreign assistance. Capital inflows and outflows are a major issue in open-economy macroeconomics, both theoretically and empirically, constituting a major macroeconomic "disturbance" of concern to policymakers. One response is the use of capital controls. In Section 12.7, we study political determinants of the imposition and removal of capital controls. On the theoretical level, we summarize two types of political models of controls, one reflecting ideological conflict between policymakers, the other the use of capital-account liberalization as a signal of commitment to economic reform. We also summarize the empirical research on political determinants of capital controls.

Another major issue in open-economy macroeconomics is sovereign debt, that is, the debt owed by a government to foreign creditors. Issues of sovereign debt are substantially different than those concerning nonsovereign debt and are inherently political. For example, since it is owed by the government, repayment decisions are not connected with any question of the ability to repay. With few exceptions, a borrower country has the technical ability to repay the debt, so that non-repayment is a political issue. In Section 12.8, we analyze basic models of sovereign borrowing and its repayment, especially the role of penalties in enforcing repayment. We also consider the importance of political versus nonpolitical penalties in the decision of whether to issue debt at home or abroad.

The final topic considered is foreign assistance, especially lending by governments and international financial organizations to developing countries for the purpose of structural adjustment. Our point of departure is the strikingly disappointing results that foreign aid programs have had in alleviating poverty and stimulating growth in the recipient countries, a failure that we argue reflects the political nature of aid. Foreign assistance is inherently political for a number of reasons. First, the incentives of the donors may be political, not only in the obvious sense that aid is often given for strategic political reasons, but also because the nature of aid (and especially its ineffectiveness) often reflects political and bureaucratic conflicts within the donor organizations. Second, the ineffectiveness of aid is also very much attributed to misappropriation by the recipients, where this is widely believed to reflect political factors. There are a number of models which formalize the role of political factors, as well as much empirical work detailing the role of political factors in explaining the ineffectiveness of aid.

PART I—EXCHANGE-RATE ARRANGEMENTS

12.2. Fixed versus Flexible Exchange Rates

The choice of optimal exchange rate arrangements has long been a key issue in open-economy macroeconomics. From an economic point of view, the general question may be put simply: which exchange rate arrangement is best for economic performance? The choice of the optimal regime from a purely economic point of view is beyond the scope and purpose of this chapter. Hence, we will simply review the key issues, suggesting that readers interested in the primarily economic arguments refer to the voluminous literature. The brief discussion of issues that are primarily economic is meant simply as a prelude to a discussion of political issues.

The main economic argument in favor of fixed nominal exchange rates is the reduced transaction costs for international trade that they imply. Floating exchange rates are seen as more volatile, implying more uncertain real exchange rates.[1] This uncertainty may reduce the volume of international trade, discourage investment, and reduce the possibilities for international diversification of risks. The role of fixed exchange rates in encouraging trade may extend to trade arrangements. In the European Union, for example, a fixed-rate system (or, more precisely, monetary union) is seen as maximizing the gains from unified goods and labor markets and eliminating the changes in competitiveness between countries stemming from persistent exchange rate movements, the latter tending to undermine support for a single market. This last argument suggests an important political argument for fixed exchange rates, namely, as increasing support for cooperative arrangements more generally. We explore connections between monetary and political union in Section 12.4.

Another argument often made for fixed rates is that pegging one's currency to that of a low-inflation country will help to restrain inflationary pressures. Hence, fixed rates are seen as providing discipline to enable a government to resist the temptation to follow inflationary policies. Viewing fixed rates as a commitment device brings us back to precisely the issues of commitment discussed in Chapter 5. We discuss this type of credibility argument below. A number of the issues discussed will mirror discussions in Chapters 4, 5, and 6, so that we rely at points on a more intuitive discussion, referring the reader who wants a more technical treatment to those chapters.

The main argument in favor of a flexible exchange rate is the monetary policy independence it allows, implying a greater ability to adjust to both domestic (or country-specific) and to foreign disturbances. The costs of giving up monetary sovereignty for purposes of economic stabilization in the face of country-specific shocks are considered explicitly in Section 12.4. Mussa (1979) and Marston (1985) present good surveys of the role of exchange rate regimes in optimal response to both domestic and foreign disturbances, arguing that though flexible rates are generally presumed to provide better insulation against foreign shocks, there are cases where this need not be true.

We now turn to primarily political aspects of the choice of exchange rate arrangements, which will be our focus.

---

[1] A key point to note is that fixing the exchange rate need not really reduce exchange rate risk, but simply greatly alter the form of the probability distribution of exchange rate changes, from continuous but small changes to infrequent jumps in the exchange rate. We return to this below in considering currency crises.

Pegging the Exchange Rate to Gain Credibility

Taken together with the economic arguments for flexible exchange rates, pegging the exchange rate to gain credibility for a low-inflation policy can be thought of as an application of the question of commitment versus flexibility introduced in Section 4.6 of Chapter 4 and further discussed in Chapter 5. Giavazzi and Pagano (1988) were perhaps the first to make explicit the argument for pegging the exchange rate to gain credibility. They consider a policymaker who has the same incentives towards surprise inflation that we first introduced in Chapter 4—unanticipated inflation may lower unemployment or may reduce the real value of the stock of outstanding debt. A social welfare-maximizing policymaker therefore has the temptation to engineer a surprise inflation; since this incentive to time-inconsistent behavior is understood by the public, the resulting equilibrium implies lower welfare than if he could commit himself to zero inflation. The problem is how to make such a commitment credible. Giavazzi and Pagano suggest joining an exchange rate mechanism with fixed but adjustable parities as a way to do so. They use the example of the European Monetary System (EMS), which we take as a representative of a fixed exchange rate system simply for expositional convenience.[2] With a fixed nominal exchange rate, inflation in excess of the EMS average translates into an appreciation of the real exchange rate, a real appreciation that would not occur if domestic inflation induced an equal nominal depreciation. The real exchange rate implications of high inflation thus change the governments' incentives to inflate.

One interesting aspect of the analysis is that it gives a specific real-world structure to the question of institutional commitment first raised in Chapter 5. The specific structure raises some new issues. For example, since inflation differentials between countries generally still exist in a fixed exchange rate system such as the EMS, fixing the exchange rate will imply a continually appreciating real exchange rate for the relatively high-inflation countries. Though inflation differentials may be far lower for these countries than if they did not join the EMS and let their exchange rates float, the flip side of the fixity of the nominal exchange rate is real overvaluation. If the cumulative real appreciation gets large enough, a realignment will be necessary, so that the welfare implications of commitment may be less clear.

Giavazzi and Pagano consider a continuous-time model in which the domestic policymaker in the EMS chooses a level of inflation π_t to maximize the welfare of the representative individual, where welfare

---

[2] There is a distinction between unilaterally pegging the exchange rate in the attempt to achieve anti-inflation credibility versus joining a multilateral fixed exchange rate system. As our main focus is on fixed rates as an anti-inflation device, we downplay this distinction here, but return to it in later sections.

depends on inflation and unemployment (as in the Barro–Gordon closed-economy model considered in Chapter 4), as well as the (log of the) real exchange rate z_t, defined as the foreign price level over the domestic price level. The inclusion of the real exchange rate is motivated by assuming that the domestic policymaker has the objective of increasing profits in the export sector, implying a desire for a higher real exchange rate. It is assumed that there is no capital mobility and a fixed period of time T between realignments, at which time a nominal devaluation returns the real exchange rate to its level at the last realignment, denoted z_0. With foreign inflation assumed to be zero, the (log of the) real exchange rate at each point of time is thus given by

$$z_t = z_0 - \int_{jT}^{t} \pi_s \, ds, \qquad t \in (jT, jT + T), \quad j = 1, 2, 3, \dots . \quad (12.1)$$

Both the return value of the real exchange rate z_0 and the time between realignments T are not choice variables of the domestic policymaker, but are determined by the EMS. In fact, if membership in the EMS is to be sustainable, these two parameters cannot be chosen independently of one another. Following Giavazzi and Pagano, we begin with the case where $z_0 = 0$, so that at each realignment the exchange rate is set back to the level consistent with purchasing power parity (PPP), and consider the effects of changes in T on welfare.

The domestic policymaker's objective is to minimize a loss function representing individual welfare. Given the discussion in the previous paragraph, the domestic policymaker's loss function may be represented by

$$\mathcal{L} = \sum_{j=0}^{\infty} \int_{jT}^{(j+1)T} e^{-\rho t} \left[-(\pi_t - \pi_t^e) + \frac{\theta}{2} \pi_t^2 - \kappa z_t \right] dt, \qquad (12.2)$$

where κ, $\theta > 0$.[3] This implies an optimal path for inflation under adjustable parities (where a "tilde" above an inflation rate implies an optimal value):

$$\tilde{\pi}_t^{\text{peg}} = \frac{1}{\theta} \left[1 - \frac{\kappa}{\rho} (1 - e^{-\rho(T-t)}) \right] \quad \text{for } t \in (0, T). \qquad (12.3)$$

Hence, under pegged rates with regular realignments, inflation along an optimal path rises monotonically between realignments and then falls back to its minimum level on the date of the realignment. The real exchange thus gradually falls from one realignment to the next, being always below PPP, except at realignment dates.

---

[3] Giavazzi and Pagano also consider the possibility that the collection of seigniorage is an additional incentive to inflate. Below, we consider seigniorage in a fixed-rate system.

In contrast, under flexible rates, Giavazzi and Pagano assume that PPP always holds and that the policymaker cannot affect the real exchange rate z_t. With exogenous z_t, the policymaker chooses a constant inflation rate:

$$\tilde{\pi}_t^{\text{flex}} = \frac{1}{\theta}. \tag{12.4}$$

Hence, $\tilde{\pi}_t^{\text{peg}} < \tilde{\pi}_t^{\text{flex}}$ for all $t < T$ with equality for $t = T$. The crucial question is not whether membership in an exchange rate system with an adjustable peg implies lower inflation, but whether it implies higher welfare. One may calculate the difference in equilibrium welfare under the two regimes, given the implications of the regimes for the dynamics of inflation and the real exchange rate. After some manipulation (the exact calculations for this expression, as well as for (12.6) and (12.8), may be found in Giavazzi and Pagano [1988]), one obtains the welfare difference Δ for a permanent choice between the two regimes:

$$\Delta = \tilde{\mathscr{L}}^{\text{flex}} - \tilde{\mathscr{L}}^{\text{peg}} = \frac{\kappa^2}{\theta \rho^3} \left[\frac{1}{2}(1 - e^{-\rho T}) - \frac{\rho T e^{-\rho T}}{1 - e^{-\rho T}} \right], \tag{12.5}$$

where this difference is nonnegative and uniformly increasing in T, the time between realignments, with a finite asymptote as T approaches infinity. Hence, as T increases and the system approaches one with permanently fixed rates, the welfare gain increases. In this open-economy version of the Barro–Gordon model, the incentive to inflate is the only source of inefficiency. The negative real exchange rate consequences of inflation attach an extra penalty to inflation, thus reducing the incentive to inflate. Since this disincentive is public knowledge, the low-inflation policy will be credible.

Giavazzi and Pagano point out that this disincentive system makes the fixed-rate regime unsustainable in the long run. Since the return point z_0 equals 0, the real exchange rate is always below PPP, except at realignment dates. Hence, in between realignments, a high-inflation country experiences a worsening trade balance; in the absence of capital mobility, it is either steadily losing foreign exchange reserves or steadily accumulating foreign debt. Hence, it would eventually have to abandon the fixed-rate regime. The calculation in (12.5) is thus misleading for a return point of $z_0 = 0$.

As one alternative, they consider the case in which, given $z_0 = 0$, the fixed-rate regime is known to collapse after a time interval of length $\bar{T}$. For temporary membership to yield a credibility benefit as discussed above, the commitment to remain in the system for an interval $\bar{T}$ must be credible, which it will be if the decision to join a temporary adjustable parity system improves the domestic policymaker's welfare. One may calculate that the welfare gain relative to flexible rates of membership for an interval $\overline{T}$ is

$$\Omega^{\mathrm{peg}}(\overline{T}) - \Omega^{\mathrm{flex}}(\overline{T}) = (1 - e^{-\rho\overline{T}})\Delta, \qquad (12.6)$$

where Δ is given by (12.5).

An even harsher set-up would be one where successive devaluations are insufficient to make up the entire loss of competitiveness cumulated since the last realignment. That is, in the adjustable peg mechanism, a relatively high-inflation country moves to a lower value of z_0, so that the real exchange fluctuates around a trend of real appreciation. Since the cost of inflation is now higher in the form of *persistent* real appreciation, the discipline conveyed by joining this system is higher. Hence, the welfare gain from joining is also higher, a point Giavazzi and Pagano show formally by means of a simple example. The flip side is that the accumulated loss of competitiveness means that the system may be viable for a shorter period of time. This is an essential trade-off in this set-up: a system with a greater penalty in terms of loss of competitiveness and hence loss of net foreign assets has a larger welfare gain (and is hence credible) as long as a country can afford to stay in, but it is sustainable for a shorter period of time.

To make a fixed nominal exchange rate permanently sustainable, the real exchange rate must be allowed to fluctuate *around* PPP, rather than below it. In this case, a high-inflation country will be allowed a sufficiently large depreciation at each realignment that in the early part of the interval between realignments they will run trade surpluses large enough to offset later trade deficits. Assuming that the trade balance (and hence the change in reserves) is a linear function of the log of z_t, Giavazzi and Pagano impose the following sustainability condition linking z_0 and T:

$$z_0 = \frac{1}{T}\int_0^T \int_0^t \tilde{\pi}_s^{\mathrm{peg}} \, ds \, dt, \qquad (12.7)$$

meaning that on the date of realignment, the real exchange rate must be above PPP by an amount exactly equal to the average loss of competitiveness until the next realignment. One obvious problem arises. From (12.7), one sees that, given T, the return point z_0 is an increasing function of domestic inflation in the interim: the higher is the chosen path $\tilde{\pi}_t^{\mathrm{peg}}$, the more the policymaker will be compensated in the subsequent nominal devaluation. If this can be exploited, the credibility-enhancing benefits of EMS membership would vanish, as the cost of real appreciation between realignments would be offset by the adjustment at realignment. (This problem is simply an analogue of the trade-off issue raised in the previous paragraph.) Giavazzi and Pagano therefore suggest that for EMS membership to be sustainable in the long run, but still yield credibility gains, domestic policymakers cannot view z_0 in (12.7) as manipulable. If z_0 is taken as given, the welfare gain from permanent membership as T approaches infinity can be derived as

$$\lim_{T \to \infty} \Delta + \frac{\kappa}{\theta\rho^2}\left(1 - \frac{\kappa}{\rho}\right), \tag{12.8}$$

where Δ is given by (12.5) and the last term is the discounted value of the initial competitiveness offset. When $\kappa/\rho > 1$, meaning the discounted value of the penalty for higher inflation exceeds the incentive to create inflation surprises, Giavazzi and Pagano argue that the EMS regime is no longer unambiguously superior. Though this may sound counterintuitive, an example will help explain why. As $T \to \infty$, (12.3) implies that $\tilde{\pi}_t^{\mathrm{peg}}$ is negative for $\kappa/\rho > 1$. Whereas this causes no problem in the earlier set-up with no competitiveness offset, it now implies that a country starts with a real appreciation, that is, with a competitiveness penalty to ensure long-run sustainability. If the cost associated with this penalty exceeds the benefit associated with reducing the temptation to inflate, the fixed-rate regime may be inferior to flexible rates. Giavazzi and Pagano suggest a similar argument will apply when T is finite.

Irrevocably Fixed Exchange Rates?

The sustainability issue that Giavazzi and Pagano raise has led some authors to question the commitment value of fixed rates. Tornell and Velasco (1995) argue that viewing fixed exchange rates as not irrevocably fixed may significantly change our view of credibility-enhancing properties of fixed rates. They in fact argue that flexible rates may be a stronger disciplining device than fixed rates. If the exchange rate cannot be fixed forever, fixed rates simply postpone the inflationary consequences of overexpansionary fiscal policy, while flexible rates mean that some of the inflation cost comes today. Bearing the costs currently may put a stronger constraint on fiscal authorities if they care about welfare primarily during their terms of office, rather than after.

Exchange Rate Pegs under Incomplete Information

The Giavazzi and Pagano model considers disciplining a policymaker with a known incentive to inflate. It is thus like the complete-information models considered in Chapter 4 and Section 6.3 of Chapter 6. An alternative is a model of incomplete information about a policymaker's preferences. Andersen and Risager (1991) consider a mimicking model of the sort presented in Section 6.4 of Chapter 6 to study the possible contractionary effects of pegging the exchange rate as a disinflationary device. As in the Backus and Driffill (1985a) model considered there, there are two types of policymakers: a tough type who assigns no loss to unemployment, caring only about reducing inflation, which is equal to the rate of exchange rate depreciation in their small open economy; and a weak type who assigns a loss to both unemployment and inflation, and who therefore sees a gain to an exchange rate devaluation as a means to increase employment. Uncertainty about the policymaker's type means that the announcement of a fixed exchange rate policy with the goal of price stability is not fully credible. The government's reputation is updated using Bayes' Law (see (6.9)), and over time the probability that the government is tough rises, implying a fall in expected inflation and in domestic interest rates. However, unlike the Backus–Driffill model, Andersen and Risager assume there is a positive probability that a weak type will abandon the peg and inflate (that is, devalue) in the first period. (In the model in Chapter 6, a weak type was certain to masquerade as tough with a sufficiently long horizon.) This makes a crucial difference. If the public is sure that a new government will choose zero inflation for a period of time at the beginning of its tenure, inflationary expectations will be zero immediately after the new government takes over, so that the move to zero inflation can be achieved with no output loss in the short term. In contrast, if there is a positive probability that a new government will initially inflate and break its fixed exchange rate promise almost immediately, the disinflationary fixed exchange rate policy will lead to a drop in output in the short term. Under this scenario, long-term interest rates will decline by less than short-term interest rates with the implementation of a program, reflecting its initial lack of full credibility.

12.3. CURRENCY CRISES AND CONTAGIOUS SPECULATIVE ATTACKS

In practice, countries that have chosen to fix their exchange rates often find their currencies coming under attack by speculators hoping to profit from a devaluation or a move to floating exchange rates. On the surface, a speculative attack appears to be a pure economic event, motivated by profit seeking by speculators, independent of political overtones. In fact, there are several political aspects to currency crises. The decision of whether or not to defend an exchange rate peg is a decision about trading off conflicting objectives. The decision to attack in turn depends on the credibility that speculators assign to the government's announced commitment to the peg. The importance of credibility leads to the possibility of self-fulfilling currency crises, whereby a given level of fundamentals may be consistent with either the maintenance of the fixed exchange rate or with its collapse. In this case, the expectation that the government is committed to defending the currency leads to this being an equilibrium and vice versa. Contagion in speculative attacks also has political aspects, not only because the decision to defend is political, but also because it may be political factors that link currencies together, so that crisis spreads across them. We consider these issues in turn.

Political Models of Speculative Attack

The seminal paper on speculative attack is Krugman (1979), in which an inconsistency in fundamentals induces a steady loss in reserves, ending in an abandonment of fixed rates. For example, the government is running a deficit, and is financing it by printing money. The rate of monetary expansion is inconsistent with the fixed exchange rate in the long run; in the short run, individuals do not want to hold the higher level of domestic currency, and they exchange it for foreign-currency-denominated assets. The peg rate must be abandoned when reserves hit a minimum level, which is common knowledge to all market participants. However, the peg collapses not at the date implied by simply extrapolating the steady decline of reserves, but in a speculative attack at some earlier date, namely, the first date at which optimal investor behavior implies such an attack will succeed.

In Krugman's "first-generation" model, policymakers are passive, sticking with current mutually inconsistent policies and abandoning the fixed rate reflexively when the critical minimum level is reached. An alternative approach to modeling currency collapse is to treat it not as inevitable, but as the result of a policy decision reflecting the weight the government places on the objective of maintaining a fixed ER, relative to other objectives. That is, a fixed rate collapses not because it is technically infeasible to maintain it, as in Krugman, but because the government no longer sees it as optimal in light of the costs of doing so and the importance of other objectives. In this approach, often referred to as a "second-generation" model, devaluation is a *political* decision, reflecting the balancing of conflicting objectives. More specifically, the government is modeled as having an objective function with more targets than instruments, as in the closed model of an output–inflation trade-off used extensively in Part II of the book or the model of Giavazzi and Pagano in the previous section. Examples include Obstfeld (1994), Drazen and Masson (1994), Masson (1995), Ozkan and Sutherland (1995), Obstfeld (1996), and Bensaid and Jeanne (1997).

In these models, speculator behavior is summarized by their expectations of a devaluation, rationally conditioned on the government's optimal response to a single underlying shock and on the common knowledge distribution of that shock. Drazen and Masson (1994) (which was discussed in detail in Section 6.8 of Chapter 6) and Masson (1995) add uncertainty about the policymaker's objectives (his "type"), and consider how it will interact with uncertainty about fundamentals. They show that when there is persistence in the effects of policy across periods, tough policy meant to defend a fixed exchange rate may actually make the peg less credible, as it is known to worsen the future trade-offs policymakers will face. Shocks that are not offset through a devaluation today have further unfavorable effects in the future, increasing the probability that a government of any type will devalue.

The result is descriptive of the sometimes failed attempts of governments to defend a fixed exchange rate via displays of toughness. Consider, for example, the experience of the United Kingdom or of Sweden in their attempts to maintain a fixed exchange rate in 1992 and the response of investors to their displays of toughness. In the case of the United Kingdom, in August and September of 1992, Prime Minister Major and Chancellor of the Exchequer Lamont vowed to defend the pound vigorously as speculative pressures mounted. Despite their tough statements, and the increases in short-term rates to back them up, reserves flowed out, with it being reported that the Bank of England may have spent half of its reserves in a single day in an unsuccessful attempt to defend the pound. In Sweden, when there was heavy pressure against the krona in September 1992, the Prime Minister and the Finance Minister both emphasized that they would defend the currency at any cost. Overnight interest rates were raised first to 24%, then to 75%, and finally to 500%, but the Riksbank had to engage in massive borrowing to meet the demand for foreign exchange. Though the September crisis passed, in November there was renewed speculation against the krona, with large capital outflows, followed by the Riksbank allowing the krona to float. In both cases, tough policy meant not simply to defend the exchange rate, but also to send the message that policymakers were firm in their commitment to the fixed exchange rate, appeared to have the opposite effect.

One may also expand this approach, in analogy to the closed-economy work on reputation, to models of speculators' optimal behavior in which they solve a more complicated, dynamic signal extraction problem in which there are several types of shocks. Bensaid and Jeanne (1997) and Drazen (1999b) present models in which the probability of devaluation is derived via Bayesian updating on the policymaker's type.

Self-Fulfilling Currency Crises

Models of self-fulfilling attacks, as in Obstfeld (1994, 1996), provide another political link, due to their emphasis on problems of credibility. In models of self-fulfilling crisis, a given level of fundamentals may be consistent with either the maintenance of the fixed exchange rate or with its collapse. The speculative attack equilibrium thus has a self-fulfilling characteristic, in that the exchange rate collapses if attacked, but survives if speculators do not attack. Hence, fundamentals do not unambiguously determine whether a peg can survive or not; market beliefs are critical.

The level of fundamentals will determine whether there are multiple possible equilibria or not.[4]

A Model of Multiple Equilibria and Escape Clauses

Obstfeld (1996) presents a simple model of multiplicity, based on the trade-off between unemployment and inflation that we have used repeatedly. Multiple equilibria can arise due to a fixed cost of a devaluation or revaluation of the exchange rate. Equilibria differ by the degree of market skepticism regarding the exchange rate peg, and the implications for unemployment, conditional on the maintenance of the current parity. Hence, different equilibria are associated with different probabilities of collapse. He considers a small open economy, where the exchange rate is identical to the domestic price level, so the change in the exchange rate is simply the rate of domestic inflation or deflation. In addition to the inflation and possible unemployment costs, changing the exchange rate parity implies a cost to the government $\zeta(\pi) = \bar{\zeta}$ for a devaluation (an upward change in the exchange rate) and $\zeta(\pi) = \underline{\zeta}$ for a revaluation.[5] Hence, the government's objective function may be written

$$\mathcal{L} = (U - \tilde{U})^2 + \theta\pi^2 + \zeta(\pi), \tag{12.9}$$

where both the unemployment rate U and the government's unemployment target $\tilde{U}$ are measured relative to the natural rate (so that $\tilde{U} < 0$), π is the rate of devaluation of the exchange rate (or revaluation if $\pi < 0$), and $\theta > 0$. Unemployment is determined by

$$U = (\pi^e - \pi) + \epsilon, \tag{12.10}$$

where π^e is the inflation expectation of domestic wage setters based on lagged information and ϵ is a mean-zero i.i.d. shock which is observed by the government before it chooses π, but by wage setters only after wages are set. For tractability of computation, assume that ϵ is uniformly distributed over $[-v, v]$.

If there were no fixed-cost term $\zeta(\pi)$, the rate of devaluation would be chosen to minimize (12.9) subject to (12.10), yielding an optimal rate of devaluation (or revaluation) as a function of the unemployment shock and

---

[4] A model based on an optimizing government is *not* identical to one with multiple equilibria and the resultant possibility of self-fulfilling crises. A "new" crisis model can have a unique equilibrium, as in Drazen and Masson (1994), whereas a nonoptimizing model can have multiple equilibria, as discussed by Krugman (1996).

[5] The costs of deviating from the fixed parity make this model an "escape-clause" model, as discussed in Section 4.6 of Chapter 4. The alternative formulation of an escape clause, as discussed in Section 6.8 of Chapter 6, yields a unique equilibrium, as indicated in the previous footnote.

the expected rate of inflation:

$$\pi = \frac{1}{1 + \theta}(\epsilon - \tilde{U} + \pi^e).\tag{12.11}$$

Substituting (12.11) and (12.10) into (12.9), one obtains the loss under discretion (*i.e.*, flexible rates) as a function of the unemployment shock and the expected rate of inflation:

$$\mathcal{L}^{\text{flex}} = \frac{\theta}{1 + \theta}(\epsilon - \tilde{U} + \pi^e)^2.\tag{12.12}$$

When the fixed rate is maintained, so that $\pi = 0$, the loss is

$$\mathcal{L}^{\text{fix}} = (\epsilon - \tilde{U} + \pi^e)^2.\tag{12.13}$$

If there is a fixed cost of changing the exchange rate, there will be a devaluation only if the shock ϵ is large enough that $\mathcal{L}^{\text{flex}} + \bar{\zeta} < \mathcal{L}^{\text{fix}}$ and a revaluation only if ϵ is small enough that $\mathcal{L}^{\text{flex}} + \underline{\zeta} < \mathcal{L}^{\text{fix}}$, in which case the change in the exchange rate will be determined by (12.11). That is, devaluation occurs when $\epsilon > \bar{\epsilon}$ and revaluation when $\epsilon < \underline{\epsilon}$, where

$$\bar{\epsilon} = \tilde{U} - \pi^e + ((1 + \theta)\bar{\zeta})^{1/2}$$
$$\underline{\epsilon} = \tilde{U} - \pi^e - ((1 + \theta)\underline{\zeta})^{1/2}.\tag{12.14}$$

Given this escape-clause rule, the rational expectation of π next period is

$$E(\pi) = E(\pi|\epsilon < \underline{\epsilon})\Pr(\epsilon < \underline{\epsilon}) + E(\pi|\epsilon > \bar{\epsilon})\Pr(\epsilon > \bar{\epsilon}),\tag{12.15}$$

which, using (12.11) and the uniform distribution for ϵ, may be written

$$E(\pi) = \frac{1}{1 + \theta}\left[\left(1 - \frac{\bar{\epsilon} - \underline{\epsilon}}{2v}\right)(\pi^e - \tilde{U}) - \frac{\bar{\epsilon}^2 - \underline{\epsilon}^2}{4v}\right].\tag{12.16}$$

In a rational-expectations equilibrium, $E(\pi) = \pi^e$. In the absence of the cost $\zeta(\pi)$, this would be determined simply by (12.11), leading to a unique devaluation expectation in equilibrium, namely, $\pi^e = -\tilde{U}/\theta$, and an associated actual change in the exchange rate for each realization of the shock ϵ. This is precisely the Barro–Gordon solution, derived in Section 4.4 of Chapter 4. The presence of a fixed cost, however, leads to an expectation $E(\pi)$ in (12.16) which is a nonlinear function of π^e. (Remember that, via (12.14), $\bar{\epsilon}$ and $\underline{\epsilon}$ are themselves decreasing functions of π^e.)

Specifically, for a low enough π^e, $\underline{\epsilon} > -v$, so that $\bar{\epsilon} - \underline{\epsilon}$ is independent of π^e. One may calculate $dE(\pi)/d\pi^e = 1/(1 + \theta)$. Similarly, for a high enough π^e, $\bar{\epsilon}$ is at the lower limit $-v$, so that the government's behavior is described by (12.11) and $dE(\pi)/d\pi^e = 1/(1 + \theta)$. (These correspond to the unique Barro–Gordon solution.) However, for "intermediate" values of π^e, $\underline{\epsilon} = -v$, $\bar{\epsilon}$ is interior to $[-v, v]$ and is described by (12.14), so that $E(\pi)$ is a quadratic function of π^e, implying the possibility of multiple intersections of (12.16) with the rational expectations line $E(\pi) = \pi^e$. Each of these intersections is an equilibrium.

Intuitively, if markets expect a low probability of a devaluation and hence a low π^e, a given (positive) unemployment shock is consistent with lower unemployment under fixed rates, so that the government is less likely in fact to devalue. Conversely, high devaluation expectations imply higher unemployment for any realization of ϵ, making the government more likely to incur the fixed cost ζ and devalue to improve welfare. Each of these expectations may be self-fulfilling. It is easy to show that if multiple equilibria exist, the devaluation expectation in the highest probability of devaluation equilibrium is equal to that under floating rates.

Among other things, the Obstfeld model provides a strong cautionary note on why fixing the exchange rate may not buttress the credibility of a government with an incentive to inflate. It may instead lead to self-fulfilling currency crises if the expectation of a devaluation remains high. The credibility-*reducing* effect of fixed exchange rates in this model is different than that stressed by Drazen and Masson (1994), in which there is a unique equilibrium. There, keeping with a fixed exchange rate today may so worsen the expected short-run trade-off tomorrow between inflation and unemployment that it makes the policy less credible.

Alternative Models of Multiple Equilibria

As Obstfeld (1996) points out, there are several other mechanisms which could lead to multiple equilibria. Multiplicity of equilibria is inherent to government debt or other assets if the return that one investor earns is an increasing, rather than a decreasing, function of the amount that other investors choose to invest. This phenomenon is important in the analysis of banking panics, as argued by Diamond and Dybvig (1983). Consider a bank that holds less than 100% reserves against deposits, whose redemption price is not allowed to vary. The belief that there will be a bank run can then be self-fulfilling on the part of rational depositors. If a depositor believes that a significant number of other depositors will withdraw their deposits, so that the bank must suspend convertibility, he will choose to withdraw his deposits as well. If many depositors share the initial belief, it will be self-fulfilling.

This idea may be applied to government debt if the attractiveness of holding the debt depends on the probability that it will be repaid in full, which in turn depends positively on the amount of debt which is held. In the simplest case, this would require that the repudiation cost rise more than proportionally to the amount of debt that is available to be repudiated. For example, suppose it was believed that sanctions for repudiation would be imposed only if the amount repudiated was above a certain level. It would then be optimal to buy government debt only if one believed enough other investors were doing the same, leading to the possibility of multiple equilibria. The key feature of this example, as for many models of multiple equilibria in financial markets, is that the set-up is such that individual investors perceive increasing returns to investment as a function of aggregate investment. These increasing returns are political in the sense that they arise because of some decision on the part of government affecting returns.

Calvo (1988) applies a similar idea to the determination of the interest rate on government debt to generate the possibility of multiple equilibria. He considers a two-period model in which debt issued in the first period can be partially repudiated (or equivalently, partially taxed away), at a cost proportional to the size of the default. Repudiation lowers the effective interest rate actually received in the second period for any interest rate contracted in the first period. Hence, the higher the probability of default that investors perceive, the greater the contract interest rate they demand in the first period. Calvo makes the further reasonable assumption that the probability of default depends on the government's budget position, the government being more likely to default on (or tax away the proceeds of) its debt the higher its level of expenditures. With debt service one component of government outlays, the optimal level of debt repudiation in the second period is an increasing function of the first-period interest rate. Hence, interest rates depend positively on expected repudiation, which in turn depends positively on interest rates. For reasonable parameter values, one gets two equilibria, one in which there is no repudiation of the debt, the other in which the debt is partially repudiated.

There are other mechanisms for multiple equilibria hinging on expected effective nominal interest rates. High nominal interest rates will put pressure on financial intermediaries, increasing the pressure for a government bailout. Increased expectations of the government stepping in as lender of last resort, and the associated monetary expansion, thus translate into increased expectations of a currency depreciation, thus ratifying market expectations.[6] Though empirical evidence on self-fulfilling crises due to credibility problems is still preliminary, there are a number of suggestive studies. Kaminsky and Reinhart (1999) suggest that banking crises and currency crises are strongly linked empirically. Rose and Svensson (1994) find that ERM credibility did not deteriorate until August 1992, just before the currency crises, which is taken as suggesting that the

---

[6] Or, the government may try to avoid a bailout by a quick devaluation.

pre-crisis parities were not viewed as unsustainable by market participants until the crisis occurred.

Contagious Currency Crises

Contagion of currency crises across countries has become a major focus of research, propelled in part by a number of seemingly contagious crises in the second half of the 1990s. Existence of contagion appears to be supported by solid empirical evidence,[7] and there is significant effort being devoted to construction of convincing theoretical models of contagion. Beyond starting with "second-generation" models of currency crisis stressing a trade-off of objectives, most current research on contagion gives little or no role to explicitly political factors.

"Contagion" is the phenomenon of a currency crisis *itself* in one country making a currency crisis (or currency weakness) in another country more likely.[8] The emphasis is meant to differentiate true contagion from a common shock (*other* than a currency crisis) which affects countries differentially because of their differential susceptibility to infection. When differential vulnerability to an unobserved common shock reflects unobserved characteristics, we may get what looks like true contagion, since a crisis in one country will be followed by a crisis in another, with no apparent explanation other than the original crisis itself.

Drazen (1998b) presents a model of intrinsically political contagion, in that the objectives which give rise to contagion are primarily political. In the absence of the political objective, devaluation in one country would not affect speculative pressure on another country's currency. Specifically, he considers a policy of holding the exchange rate fixed at a significant economic cost in order to further the objective of political integration. As discussed in Section 12.4 below, monetary union has often been adopted for political objectives, the move towards European Monetary Union being but the most recent example. One may think of membership in a "club,"[9] whether explicit or implicit, where the benefits of membership are heavily political and the condition for membership is the maintenance of a fixed exchange rate.

To obtain contagion, one must make the further assumption that the value of membership in the arrangement depends positively on who else is or may be a member. Hence, if a country learns that other potential

[7] See, for example, Eichengreen and Wyplosz (1993), Gerlach and Smets (1995), and, especially, Eichengreen, Rose, and Wyplosz (1995).

[8] Masson (1998), in contrast, argues that the term "contagion" should be applied only to cases where a crisis in one country triggers a crisis elsewhere for reasons *unexplained* by macroeconomic fundamentals, suggesting "spillover" be used when a crisis in one country affects the fundamentals in another country.

[9] The term "club" here is not used in the sense of Chapter 9, that is, primarily as a mechanism for provision of public goods.

members of the arrangement place less weight on meeting the conditions required to join, and hence are less likely to participate, it will find it less advantageous to join as well. It will therefore assign a lower value to maintaining a fixed exchange rate, especially when doing so requires sacrificing domestic goals. If speculators are uncertain about the value a country places on membership in the "club," but are aware of both the no-devaluation condition for membership and the dependence of this value on who else is a member, rational behavior on their part will then imply that a successful attack on one currency creates an externality in the form of a lower commitment of all other potential members. They will therefore be more vulnerable to attack, a phenomenon the paper terms "membership contagion." The paper further presents empirical evidence that membership contagion may have played a role in the 1992–1993 EMS crisis.

12.4. MONETARY UNIONS

Stronger Institutional Arrangements

One theme of the discussion so far is that comparing the political benefits of fixed versus flexible rates may be of limited relevance, as fixed exchange rates are, to use Obstfeld and Rogoff's (1995) term, a "mirage." The credibility-enhancing properties of committing to fixed rates require that fixed rates themselves be credible, with the discussion in previous sections suggesting a number of reasons why this may be open to question. The massive losses that central banks have suffered in trying to defend a fixed exchange rate when their commitment was less than fully credible suggests how costly fixed rates may be. As Obstfeld and Rogoff argue, the incidence of speculative attacks suggests that even systems with exchange rate bands pose problems so that, in their words (1995, p. 74), "there is little, if any, comfortable ground between floating rates and the adoption of a common currency." In short, since the announcement to maintain a fixed exchange rate need not itself be credible, countries that view it as crucial to demonstrate their commitment to fixed rates may opt for mechanisms that are stronger than simply turning exchange rate management over to an independent central bank that has an announced commitment to fixed rates. Basically, this means giving up control of the domestic currency—by joining a monetary union with other countries, by replacing domestic currency by foreign currency ("dollarization") as the medium of exchange,[10] or by adopting a currency board requiring that domestic currency be 100% backed by foreign currency assets. As in previous sections, we consider the

---

[10] Panama is the standard example of a dollarized economy, but the original decision to adopt the dollar as its currency was not an anti-inflation measure.

politics, rather than simply the economics, of these measures. From an economic point of view, joining a monetary union would imply a weaker commitment than dollarizing or adopting a currency board, as devaluations to deal with external imbalances are often allowed.

By giving up control of the currency, all three measures largely remove from public debate the possibility of a devaluation in response, for example, to a real appreciation. One way in which they are thought to differ is in their implications for sovereignty. Joining a monetary union implies an apparent loss of some national sovereignty in making policy, while adopting a currency board does not (at least explicitly) *appear* to cede sovereignty to other countries. On the other hand, to the extent that a country retains bargaining power within the monetary union, it can still affect its own monetary policy, however partially. Dollarization is seen as providing more credibility than a currency board since it is harder to undo the arrangement. Drazen (1999c) argues that both measures should be seen as examples of constitutionalism, as they make it difficult to revisit or reverse policy decisions.

Optimum Currency Areas

In a monetary union, countries adopt a single currency with a single central bank (and no internal exchange rates). As in the case of fixed versus flexible exchange rates, it is useful to distinguish the primarily economic arguments for a single-currency area from the more political ones. In discussing political-economic arguments about monetary unions, there is obviously significant overlap with the discussion of fixed exchange rates. When the argument is simply the same point but stronger, it will not be repeated. For example, if a credibly fixed exchange rate is a way to tie one's hands to gain anti-inflation credibility, giving up a single currency and joining a monetary union can be seen as credibility enhancing, only more so.

The economic arguments for a common currency are usually discussed in terms of *optimum currency areas*. The concept of an optimum currency area (OCA) was first developed by Mundell (1961), with other important early contributions being McKinnon (1963) and Kenen (1969). The move to European Monetary Union (EMU) has revived interest in optimum currency areas, with numerous recent papers. (See, for example, Bayoumi [1994], Bayoumi and Eichengreen [1996], and Frankel and Rose [1997]. Melitz [1995] presents a critical analysis of the state of research.) There are a number of factors that are central in determining the economic desirability of a common currency area. First, there is the extent of trade between the countries; the higher the volume of trade, the greater the saving in transaction costs resulting from the adoption of a common currency. Second, there is the question of how similar the countries are in the shocks they face and in the economy's response to these shocks. A common currency means adopting a common monetary policy; the loss in flexibility has low cost if the optimal monetary policy is the same across countries.[11] Third, similarity is less important the greater is the flexibility of wages and prices, so that the need for relative price adjustment can be accommodated by movement in domestic prices rather than exchange rate changes or increases in unemployment. Fourth, in a similar vein, the greater is the mobility of the labor force across countries, the better candidates the countries are to form a monetary union, since differential shocks within the area will then result in labor movement rather than unemployment. Finally, there is the question of the extent to which there is a system of compensatory fiscal transfers across regions differentially affected within the union (sometimes termed "fiscal federalism") and, more generally, the possibilities for risk sharing. (We return to this issue in Section 14.6 of Chapter 14.) Bayoumi and Eichengreen (1996) present a recent survey of these issues.

The Connection between Monetary and Political Union

Monetary sovereignty may be prized by a country as a sign of political sovereignty. As John Stuart Mill put it in an oft-quoted phrase, nations "assert their nationality by having, to their own inconvenience and that of their neighbors, a peculiar currency of their own." Political aspects of monetary sovereignty and monetary unification is both a classic topic and a very active area of current applied research in international economics, the latter because of EMU. We postpone a discussion of the politics of EMU until the very end of this section, after we have considered the broad range of research on the political economy of common currencies.

Related to the question of the connection between monetary and political sovereignty is the question of whether monetary union may be seen as a way to achieve political goals. Nineteenth-century Germany and Italy are often taken as examples, though the case is far from clear.[12] Bordo and Jonung (1997) point out that political unification in Italy was completed in 1861, but financial arrangements were quite disparate prior to this, with currency unification occurring only in 1862. This is similar to the United States, in which monetary unification followed soon after political union. They argue that in Germany, both political and monetary unification proceeded stepwise, with scholars disagreeing about when the most important step towards monetary unification occurred. Holtfereich (1993) suggests it was unification of coinage in 1857, while Kindleberger

---

[11] Frankel and Rose (1997) correctly point out that these criteria are not independent, since the correlation of business cycles across countries depends on the degree of trade integration.

[12] We return to economic determinants of the political union or breakup of nations in Chapter 14.

(1981) and others view the creation of the Reichsbank in 1875 as the crucial step. Hence, it is unclear whether monetary unification preceded political unification in 1871, or vice versa. In all these cases, one can argue that the creation of a national monetary union was closely associated with the creation of independent nation-states (or with reunification, as in the recent case of the former West and East Germany). All three national monetary unions were primarily arrangements to reduce seigniorage competition, standardize coinage, and set up a national unit of account.

There may be effects working in the other direction as well, from politics to the sustainability of the exchange rate arrangement. A difference between a monetary union and a fixed exchange rate (or even a currency board) concerns reversibility. Policy pronouncements notwithstanding, fixed exchange rates are never irrevocably fixed, as discussed in the previous section. Because leaving a true monetary union or a dollarization arrangement would mean reinventing a separate currency and central bank, that is, creating or resuscitating *institutions*, the commitment is more permanent. (It is for this reason that a currency board is more reversible than dollarization or a monetary union.) The breakup of strictly defined monetary unions has occurred because of the breakup of the associated sovereign state, never simply for monetary reasons. In contrast, those (multinational) monetary unions that have collapsed without the dissolution of the associated sovereign entities typically were not full in the sense given above, in that members maintained separate monetary authorities. This, in fact, facilitated the dissolution of the unions once the member countries were subject to large shocks.

Cohen (1993) suggests another link from politics to the sustainability of a currency union. He examines the history of a number of currency unions and argues that monetary cooperation within the union is most likely to be sustained either when there is a single dominant member who is willing and able to use its influence to sustain monetary cooperation or when there is a broad network of institutional linkages between members such that the loss of monetary autonomy is outweighed by the gains of cooperation. These two possibilities have obvious relevance for EMU.

Neumeyer (1998) suggests a different sort of link from politics to economics in a monetary union. The primary purpose of his paper is to give a choice-theoretic basis to the argument that an important benefit of a common currency is reduction of exchange rate uncertainty. Though it is widely believed that "excessive" exchange rate volatility reduces welfare, this is not easy to prove in a formal setting. The problem is that fluctuations in exchange rates in response to economic shocks (such as preference and technology shocks) generally are welfare improving relative to less exchange rate volatility in the face of the same shocks. However, exchange rates fluctuations caused by certain other, "nonfundamental" factors will indeed reduce the efficiency of financial markets.

To study the benefits of reducing exchange rate volatility, Neumeyer uses a general equilibrium model with incomplete asset markets to study the implications of a monetary union for hedging of risks; specifically, he is concerned with the benefit of the reduction of nominal volatility compared with the cost of reducing the number of currencies with which to hedge. Political influences on monetary policy, say in the timing of inflation stabilization, are a prime example of "nonfundamental" factors causing exchange rate volatility. The possibility of political interference implies that, given the realization of an economic shock, there is still uncertainty about monetary policy, as it will be influenced by future political events. The excess fluctuations in price levels that result are socially costly because they "contaminate" the real payoffs of nominal financial assets, thus reducing the ability of investors to use these assets to hedge against economic shocks. He thus argues that currency unions and permanently fixed exchange rate regimes may improve welfare by insulating money from domestic politics.

Monetary Union without Political Union—Policy Conflicts

If a group of countries form a full political and monetary union, so that not only is policy joint but so is the evaluation of policy, the issues within the union are basically identical to the monetary and fiscal policy issues in a closed economy. An alternative is the existence of a monetary union without a political union, so that there is a common monetary policy, but differences across countries in what the desired policy should be.

Stabilization Policy

Following Alesina and Grilli (1992), we begin with an analysis of policy conflicts within a monetary union in the absence of political union. Suppose there is a single monetary entity ("Europe") which sets policy to minimize a loss function trading off unemployment and inflation (as in (12.10), but with no devaluation cost $\zeta(\pi)$):

$$\mathscr{L}_{EU} = \left(U_{EU} - \tilde{U}_{EU}\right)^2 + \Theta\pi_{EU}^2, \tag{12.17}$$

where π_{EU} is the common inflation rate across members of the union, $\tilde{U}_{EU}$ is the central bank's unemployment target measured relative to the natural rate of unemployment (so that $\tilde{U}_{EU} < 0$ if the central bank's target is below the natural rate), and Θ is the relative weight put on inflation fluctuations. This is minimized subject to an unemployment relation for the entire union:

$$U_{EU} = (\pi_{EU}^e - \pi_{EU}) + \eta, \tag{12.18}$$

where π^e_{EU} is the expected common rate of inflation and η is a common European shock. The common European rate of inflation will be[13]

$$\pi_{EU} = -\frac{1}{\Theta}\tilde{U}_{EU} + \frac{1}{1+\Theta}\eta. \tag{12.19}$$

Each member country i evaluates the policy on the basis of its own loss function, identical to (12.17), but with Θ replaced by θ_i and $\tilde{U}_{EU}$ replaced by a country-specific target $\tilde{U}_i$, and with country-specific unemployment U_i depending on unanticipated European inflation and a country-specific shock ϵ_i, yielding an expected loss:

$$E\mathscr{L}_i = E\left[\left(\pi^e_{EU} - \pi_{EU} + \epsilon_i - \tilde{U}_i\right)^2 + \theta_i\pi^2_{EU}\right], \tag{12.20}$$

where E is the expectation operator. Hence, a country with $\theta_i < \Theta$ puts relatively more weight on unemployment fluctuations than the European central bank and thus has a higher temptation to inflate. When countries differ, the expected loss for membership can be found by substituting (12.19) into (12.20):

$$E\mathscr{L}_i^{\text{mem}} = E\left[\left(\epsilon_i - \frac{1}{1+\Theta}\eta - \tilde{U}_i\right)^2 + \theta_i\left(\frac{1}{1+\Theta}\eta - \frac{1}{\Theta}\tilde{U}_{EU}\right)^2\right]. \tag{12.21}$$

If instead each country were to choose its own optimal inflation policy autonomously, analogous to (12.19), the expected loss would be

$$E\mathscr{L}_i^{\text{aut}} = E\left[\left(\frac{\theta_i}{1+\theta_i}\epsilon_i - \tilde{U}_i\right)^2 + \theta_i\left(\frac{1}{1+\theta_i}\epsilon_i - \frac{1}{\theta_i}\tilde{U}_i\right)^2\right], \tag{12.22}$$

implying a difference of

$$
\begin{aligned}
E\mathscr{L}_i^{\text{mem}} - E\mathscr{L}_i^{\text{aut}} = {}& \theta_i\left(\frac{(\tilde{U}_{EU})^2}{\Theta^2} - \frac{(\tilde{U}_i)^2}{\theta_i^2}\right) \\
& + \frac{1}{1+\theta_i}\sigma_\epsilon^2 + \frac{1+\theta_i}{(1+\Theta)^2}\sigma_\eta^2 \\
& - \frac{2}{1+\Theta}\sigma_{\epsilon\eta},
\end{aligned} \tag{12.23}
$$

---

[13] These results are identical to those derived for the closed economy in Section 4.4 of Chapter 4.

where σ_ϵ^2 is the variance of ϵ_i and $\sigma_{\epsilon\eta}$ is the covariance between ϵ_i and η.

Differences in economic welfare from participating in a union versus retaining autonomy in policymaking stem from two sources: differences in objective functions, reflected in differences Θ and θ_i, as well as between $\tilde{U}_{EU}$ and $\tilde{U}_i$; and differences in shocks across economies, so that $\sigma_\epsilon^2 \neq \sigma_\eta^2$. Consider first the case where the shocks are identical across countries, that is, $\epsilon_i = \eta$, so that $\sigma_\eta^2 = \sigma_\epsilon^2 = \sigma_{\epsilon\eta} = \sigma^2$. In this case, the right-hand side of (12.23) may be written

$$\theta_i \left(\frac{(\tilde{U}_{EU})^2}{\Theta^2} - \frac{(\tilde{U}_i)^2}{\theta_i^2} \right) + \left(\frac{1}{1 + \Theta} - \frac{1}{1 + \theta_i} \right)^2 (1 + \theta_i)\sigma^2, \quad (12.24)$$

so that a country with an incentive to high inflation, namely, one for whom $\theta_i < \Theta$ and $|\tilde{U}_i| > |\tilde{U}_{EU}|$, will unambiguously benefit from participation in a monetary union because of the higher credibility it bestows. This is simply the Giavazzi–Pagano argument discussed in Section 12.2 above, extended to the case of an economy facing stochastic shocks.

In contrast, suppose that countries have identical objective functions, that is, $\theta_i = \Theta$ and $\tilde{U}_i = \tilde{U}_{EU}$ for all i, but face different shocks. The difference in objectives (12.23) becomes

$$\mathrm{E}\mathscr{L}_i^{\mathrm{mem}} - \mathrm{E}\mathscr{L}_i^{\mathrm{aut}} = \frac{1}{1 + \Theta} \left(\sigma_\epsilon^2 + \sigma_\eta^2 - 2\sigma_{\epsilon\eta} \right). \quad (12.25)$$

A number of results emerge. Suppose, for example, countries differ in the magnitude of their shocks, but shocks are perfectly correlated across countries, so that $\sigma_{\epsilon\eta} = \sigma_\epsilon \sigma_\eta$ and the term in parentheses in (12.25) becomes $(\sigma_\epsilon - \sigma_\eta)^2 > 0$. Thus, membership in a union is always welfare reducing. If the variance of shocks in country i exceeds the European average (so that $\sigma_\epsilon^2 > \sigma_\eta^2$), the European central bank will be stabilizing too little from country i's perspective, while if unemployment shocks show less variability than the European average, the central bank will be stabilizing too much. As a second possibility, suppose the variance of unemployment is the same across countries, but shocks are not perfectly correlated. The lower is the correlation between country-specific unemployment shocks and the common European shock, the greater will be the loss from participating in the union. In the polar case of perfect negative correlation with country i's shock, the European central bank will be contracting when country i experiences a negative shock and expanding when it experiences a positive shock.

Alesina and Grilli also consider the case where Θ, rather than being given, reflects the outcome of majority voting in the setting of the common European monetary policy, each country choosing its preferred Θ to minimize its own expected $\mathscr{L}_i$, that is, to minimize (12.21). One can then show that the lower is the variance of unemployment in a country, the more conservative a European central bank it will prefer. The same holds true the lower is the correlation between domestic and European unemployment fluctuations. When the correlation is low, a country would prefer a central bank which is relatively inactive, as it will generally stabilize in the wrong direction from country i's perspective. We return below both to specific application of these results to EMU and to general issues of choosing representatives in transnational organizations.

The Decision to Participate

Comparing the benefits from participation versus nonparticipation leads to a more explicit discussion of the incentives to participate. Casella (1992) considers the decision of whether to participate in a monetary union from the perspective of the distribution of power within the common central bank. Whereas most papers on international cooperation consider equal-sized countries, as in the previous subsection, Casella concentrates on the implications of unequal size for decisionmaking within the union, and, on the basis of that, for the decision to participate. Naively, one might think that a country's weight in decisionmaking should be proportional to its size, measured along some dimension. (This is implicit in the rule for splitting seigniorage revenues in EMU, whereby each member country's seigniorage share depends half on its population share and half on its GDP share in the total.) Suppose, however, that two countries contemplating a cooperative arrangement are of very different size. Under the proportionality rule, the much larger country would then basically determine the outcome in a cooperative arrangement, implying that the much smaller country would be worse off than in an equilibrium with no cooperation.[14] If participation in the union is voluntary (rather than required as a condition for something else, such as political union in), a small country may choose not to participate. It may then be in the interest of both countries to share power more equally than implied by the proportionality rule, so that the small country finds it optimal to participate. This point is shown formally in Section 12.5 below using reaction functions to illustrate noncooperative versus cooperative equilibria.

Fiscal Aspects and Seigniorage

Instead of considering the implications of a common monetary policy in terms of stabilization and response to shocks, one can consider the public

---

[14] Note that this is different than saying that noncooperation dominates *all* cooperative agreements from the point of view of each country. It only says that noncooperation dominates a specific cooperative agreement, namely, one where power is proportional to size, from the point of view of the small country.

finance implications of a common monetary policy and a common inflation tax rate. Giving up the right to print money means giving up the right to determine the level of seigniorage. Of course, seigniorage does not disappear; it simply accrues to a different entity.[15] Hence, there is the question of how the level of seigniorage is to be determined and how seigniorage revenues are to be split.

Canzoneri and Rogers (1990) reexamine criteria for an optimal currency area from a public finance perspective. Countries rely on seigniorage revenues to a different extent, even from the perspective of optimal tax packages. Hence, they recommend an additional criterion in specifying whether two countries should form a monetary union, namely, whether their optimal tax structures imply a similar reliance on the inflation tax. Among other things, this suggests that a high level of government spending may make it less likely that a group of countries will form an optimal currency area, as high revenue requirements may make it more likely that different countries will have different optimal tax packages.

Splitting the seigniorage has political implications as well. Casella (1992), as discussed above, considers the allocation of seigniorage revenues in partially determining the decision of whether to participate in a monetary union. Implicit in the rule for splitting seigniorage in EMU is the fact that a country's weight in decisionmaking should be proportional to its size, measured along some dimension. Hence, if participation is voluntary, a small country may choose not to participate. Allocating to it a more-than-proportional share of seigniorage revenues may then be necessary to induce its participation. With a common currency, more-than-proportional influence of the small country is equivalent to a transfer of seigniorage revenues in its favor.

Sibert (1994) argues that if the common central bank is able to choose both the level and the allocation of seigniorage, inflation will be suboptimally high. Suppose provision of public goods is financed with both income taxes set at the national level and seigniorage at the "European" level. If fiscal policy is set before monetary policy, a national fiscal authority has an incentive to set income taxes too low, as a welfare-maximizing common central bank will then give it more seigniorage revenues. In equilibrium, income taxes will be too low in each country and the community-wide inflation rate will be too high. In contrast, if the European central bank chooses *only* the level of inflation, Sibert argues that it may be too *low*, due to the negative spillover effects from income taxes. (Sibert assumes that the taxed factors are not mobile across countries, so there is no problem of tax competition, a phenomenon we discuss in Section 12.5 below.) An increase in a country's income tax rate lowers its disposable

---

[15] As the move to a single money will change the demand for money of the union relative to the sum of demands for individual countries' monies, total seigniorage can, of course, change. The direction of the effect could be positive or negative.

income and, ultimately, community-wide seigniorage revenues. In the Nash equilibrium between two fiscal authorities, their failure to internalize fiscal externalities leads to too high a level of income taxes and too low a level of inflation. Note the contrast with the situation where there are multiple issuers of money within a jurisdiction, in which the failure to internalize the externalities from monetary spillovers leads to an overissuance of money, as in Casella and Feinstein (1989) or Aizenman (1992).

The European Monetary Union

As indicated at the beginning of this section, a current area of research is the recently formed European Monetary Union, the EMU. The move to a common currency has been a major topic of research, especially in Europe, throughout the 1990s. The literature is literally voluminous; Wyplosz (1997) is but one of several excellent recent surveys.

The European Economic Community (EEC, sometimes simply denoted EC) as an entity dates to the 1957 Treaty of Rome. Since then, various plans for a single European currency were devised and discarded; real progress towards economic unification can probably be dated to 1986, with two key events. Three additional countries, Greece, Spain, and Portugal, joined the EEC; and, the Single European Act (SEA) was adopted, dictating a single market and removal over time of all barriers to the movement of goods, capital, and people within the EEC by the end of 1992. The Treaty of European Union (commonly referred to as the "Maastricht Treaty") in 1992 formally set out the goal of a European Union (EU) involving both economic and political union. The centerpiece of economic union (over and above the SEA) was the creation of EMU, a European Monetary Union. The nature of political union was left more vague by the Maastricht Treaty, the goal being eventual joint foreign and defense policies. "Convergence criteria" were also established requiring countries to show evidence of "good" macroeconomic behavior in order to be allowed to enter the future monetary union. Three criteria concerned monetary policy, two concerned fiscal policy. More specifically, the monetary criteria for a country to join the single-currency area were: first, that the inflation rate must be within $1\frac{1}{2}$ percentage points of the average of the three lowest EU countries; second, the long-term interest rate must be no greater than 2 percentage points higher than the interest rates of the three countries with the lowest inflation rates; third, the exchange rate must have remained within the exchange rate bands of the existing European Monetary System (EMS) "without severe tensions" for at least two years. The fiscal criteria were: first, a ceiling on the ratio of debt to GDP of 60%; and, second, a ceiling on the ratio of the government deficit to GDP of 3%.[16] When the Maastricht Treaty was signed, only Luxem-

---

[16] The "excessive deficit procedure" makes this last entry criterion permanent, except under "exceptional conditions" when a country is temporarily allowed to exceed the ceiling.

bourg met all five criteria. We return below to the politics of the convergence criteria.

The Maastricht Treaty contained an explicit timetable for EMU, envisioned as a three-stage process. Stage I, which began in 1992, comprised formal ratification of the treaty. Stage II, initiated in January 1994, was aimed at achieving various monetary and fiscal conditions for the establishment of a European Central Bank (ECB). First, national central banks were to be granted greater independence by their respective governments. Second, the European Monetary Institute was established, both to pave the way for the creation of a European central bank and to monitor the convergence criteria set out above. Stage III was the initiation of the monetary union itself, which was to take place no later than January 1, 1999, as it did, with 11 out of the current 15 EEC members (Austria, Belgium, Finland, France, Germany, Ireland, Italy, Luxembourg, Netherlands, Portugal, and Spain) joining the union. Exchange rates between the member countries were permanently fixed, both to one another and to a European currency unit, the euro. National currencies may still be used for a transition period, the euro starting to circulate as the medium of exchange after January 1, 2002, with national currencies losing legal tender status on July 1, 2002.

As in our discussion of fixed exchange rates in Section 12.2, we begin with a discussion of the economic arguments for EMU as a background for discussion of the political aspects. The common, though not universal, view is that the economic arguments in themselves do not make the case for EMU. First, there are the benefits from lower transaction costs from moving to a single currency, both in terms of lower costs of currency conversion and the effect of lower exchange rate uncertainty inducing greater trade and investment within the EEC. It is generally argued that the saving in transaction costs is not large (see, for example, the discussion in Eichengreen and Frieden [1993]), though Melitz (1997) argues that the economic case stands by itself, on the basis of the lower transaction costs it implies. A second argument is that the ECB will act as an anti-inflationary commitment mechanism as discussed in detail in Section 12.2 for fixed exchange rates and earlier in this section for stronger institutional arrangements. This is seen as a benefit especially to the high-inflation countries in the EEC. There are several reasons why this should be seen as a political, rather than simply an economic, argument. First, questions of credibility are inherently political, though the ultimate goal, of course, is to reduce inflation, that is, economic. Second, the decisionmaking process within the ECB (a board consisting of representatives from each member country, with "one-man, one-vote" decisionmaking) means that the common monetary policy need not be that of a "conservative central banker" as discussed in Section 5.4 of Chapter 5 above. Third, independent of institutional design, the choice of a common monetary policy will reflect the balancing of divergent country interests, as discussed in the model of Alesina and Grilli (1992) above. We return to this issue below.

A third economic argument for EMU is that the move to a truly integrated European market in goods, labor, and capital dictated by the SEA requires a single European currency. The removal of capital controls makes infeasible any exchange rate arrangement other than either a single currency or fully flexible rates between European countries, as discussed at the very beginning of this section. Flexible rates are seen as inducing high exchange rate uncertainty; more importantly, they are basically incompatible with the overall goal of an economically fully integrated Europe. This argument on the necessary relation between monetary union and true economic union more generally is persuasive; however, it simply shifts the focus to the economic benefits of full economic integration, which must be weighed against the economic costs.

The main economic cost of a common currency is the loss of autonomous monetary policy for individual countries, central in the discussion of optimum currency areas and considered more formally in the discussion of the Alesina–Grilli (1992) model earlier in this section. The general view is that Europe does not satisfy the standard conditions to constitute an optimum currency area. There is disagreement about the extent of asymmetry in the shocks hitting Europe: Bayoumi and Eichengreen (1994) argue that aggregate demand and supply shocks are much more asymmetrically distributed across the EEC than across the United States. On the other hand, many industries cut across Europe, so that industry-specific shocks affect countries in similar ways; Wyplosz (1997) suggests that European economies are well integrated. There is little disagreement about relatively low labor mobility across Europe, suggesting overall that the conditions for Europe to be an optimum currency area are not satisfied. Overall, it is not easy to make a clear case for EMU on purely economic grounds.

The Political Economy of EMU

As the above discussion makes clear, the issues surrounding EMU are not simply economic, but also political. Although the political nature of EMU is widely recognized, there has been relatively little formal political-economic analysis. A good reference is Eichengreen and Frieden (1993). As they point out, the decision to create a single currency is a political phenomenon, in that it was made not by a social planner, but is "the outcome of a political process of treaty negotiation, parliamentary ratification, and popular referenda. Interest groups support or oppose the initiative depending on how it is likely to affect their welfare, not the welfare of the nation or of the [European] Community as a whole." (p. 85) There are three general aspects to the political nature of EMU: its specifically political goals; the conflict over member countries' objectives; and, implications for the structure of EMU of the political process of resolving these conflicts. We consider these in turn.

The most basic political aspect of EMU is the importance that many observers put on monetary union specifically as a precursor to political union. That is, the argument for monetary union is that it helps to achieve the goal of political union. This issue was discussed generally earlier in this section; it is a major argument made for EMU, apparent not only in the Maastricht Treaty, but even in the whole process of economic integration beginning with the Treaty of Rome in 1957. A common argument is that economic union implies political cohesion, which will serve to prevent future military and political conflicts in Europe. Feldstein (1997), a vocal opponent of EMU, argues that the effect may actually be in the opposite direction, with the freedom to pursue their own economic, social, and international objectives that countries have in the absence of EMU serving to reduce conflict relative to a situation in which countries with diverse experiences are forced to pursue common policy. This argument gets to the heart of the issue, namely, whether enforcing economic cooperation will make political cooperation more or less easy.

Conflict over objectives is inherent in any economic union. This includes not simply the conflict between member countries over objectives, but also conflict among interest groups within member countries which will play out differently because the country has less autonomy in policymaking. For example, in responding to the attack on the pound in 1992 (see Section 12.3 above), the British government was limited in its ability to raise interest rates because the structure of mortgage lending meant that an increase in short-term rates would be passed on to mortgage rates. This would hurt property interests, a key constituency of the ruling Conservative party. Their influence on policy will obviously differ in the context of a monetary union. Similar examples can be given for other countries concerning the influence of domestic interest groups on monetary policy.

Distributional conflicts within countries are in turn reflected in policy differences across member countries of a monetary union. In EMU, the key policy conflict is over the degree of anti-inflation commitment. Germany and countries in its monetary sphere (such as Belgium, Luxembourg, and the Netherlands) favor a stronger commitment to price stability; some other EC countries favor a weaker commitment, with greater stress on other objectives. The Alesina–Grilli (1992) model above illustrates the nature of this conflict.

Interestingly, the move from the EMS to EMU can be seen as a move away from the highly anti-inflationary policies associated with the Bundesbank, rather than a move towards tougher monetary policy. With free capital flows within Europe, the EMS was compatible only with a single monetary policy for member countries, which increasingly became German monetary policy. (This reflected a number of factors, not simply Germany's economic size, but also the acceptance of its anti-inflationary leadership by like-minded countries.) For example, monetary tightness in the EMS in the 1991–1993 recession in Europe largely reflected the policy preferences of

Germany; other EMS members wanted less restrictive monetary policy, but the exchange rate system forced them to follow Germany's lead. Hence, countries such as France and Italy wanted to find a way to reassert a degree of control over the setting of their monetary policy. The creation of a European monetary authority that would supersede the Bundesbank and in which they would have a larger voice was seen as the way to regain some degree of monetary control. Hence, they strongly favored the creation of a European central bank with decisions made by majority vote, to which Germany was resistant. We return to this conflict below in considering how politics affected the nature of bargaining over EMU, as well as the outcome of this bargaining.

The conflict over objectives can also be seen in conflict over the nature of the transition. The length of stages I and II in the transition from Maastricht to monetary union reflected the resolution of a conflict between two different views of the relation between macroeconomic conditions and monetary union. One view, favored by central banks and especially the Bundesbank, was that low inflation and fiscal balance in member countries was a precondition for a successful monetary union. Otherwise, macroeconomic imbalances would make monetary union unsustainable. This "coronation approach" held that countries should satisfy strict convergence conditions before being allowed to join the single currency. The competing view was that convergence would be the *result* of the creation of a monetary union with an independent central bank, in line with the view that tough monetary institutions will impose a discipline on countries that would enable them to reduce inflation and fiscal deficits. The stress put on the five convergence conditions set out above, and the length of time given to allow them to be achieved, was the victory of the "coronation approach" over the "discipline from institutions" approach.

Finally, EMU can only be understood from a political perspective in that the nature of the transition, of its institutional structure, and of the policies that are expected to emerge, reflect the *process* by which the above conflicts of interests were and are resolved. German acceptance of the European Central Bank as it is structured in place of the Bundesbank provides a good example. The conventional wisdom is that the ECB recreates the Bundesbank at the EC level, with a similar single-minded commitment to price stability. The nature of the ECB governing board (numerically dominated by country representatives rather than members of the ECB Executive Board, with decisions made by majority rule) calls into question the argument that the ECB's institutional structure will automatically imply a tough anti-inflation outcome. (This is same point as made above, namely, that the move from EMS to EMU may imply a weakening of anti-inflationary policy.) Germany favored an institutional structure which would have implied a more anti-inflationary ECB, for example, more decisionmaking power in the hands of the Executive Board, and unanimity required for certain decisions, giving individual countries veto power. As structured, the ECB could be characterized as reflecting not a victory for German interests, but concessions on her part.

Garrett (1993) argues that Germany made such concessions because it had other goals that gave it a strong interest in making sure that EMU came into being, even if it meant giving up some of its economic objectives. Specifically, he argues that Germany was especially interested in gaining international acceptance of rapid reunification; that united Germany be accepted into the EC without treaty revisions; and, that both Europe and the United States not view reunification as presaging a more militaristic Germany. Making concessions was seen as smoothing European acceptance of reunification on terms Germany preferred; reunified Germany's tying itself to a united Europe was strongly seen as calming international fears that reunification might arouse. The nature of the CB can thus be understood only against the backdrop of the bargaining process that led up to it. This case provides but one example of a general phenomenon denoted **linkage politics** by political scientists, whereby otherwise unconnected objectives are tied together so that agreements can be reached. Parties make concessions in unrelated areas to reach agreements, so that the nature of outcomes reflects not only the different objectives of the parties, but also the process by which agreement is reached. Linkage politics played a crucial role in the formation of EMU.

The outcome of the conflict over whether macroeconomic convergence should precede or follow monetary union can now be better understood. Garrett argues that Germany viewed a strong anti-inflation commitment as deriving not only from the institutional characteristics of an independent monetary authority, but also from the interaction of these institutional features and a strong anti-inflationary constituency.[17] Hence, an independent ECB would be strongly anti-inflationary only if the members of EMU shared anti-inflationary objectives themselves. This view was the basis of Germany's insistence on "convergence before union," rather than vice versa. Moreover, once this German view on the nature of the transition to stage III was adopted, implying an EMU composed of members whose anti-inflation preferences have been demonstrated (or created), Germany was more willing to yield on the nature of decisionmaking within the ECB once established.

Alesina and Grilli (1993) show formally how the nature of decisionmaking within EMU can affect the relation between the composition of EMU and the policy outcome. They use the Alesina–Grilli (1992) model (exposited earlier in this section) of deciding whether to join a monetary union when countries differ in the relative weight they put on their inflation and unemployment goals, as summarized by a parameter θ_i for

---

[17] Posen (1995b) makes an analogous argument for the United States, namely, that the effectiveness of monetary institutions in providing anti-inflation credibility depends on the political support given to their goals. See Section 5.4 of Chapter 5.

country i. They define a feasible monetary union as one in which each member country is not worse off in the union than outside. With EMU's inflation policy defined by Θ, representing the weight the ECB puts on inflation fluctuations (see (12.17) and (12.19)), the benefit of joining EMU for country i depends on Θ relative to θ_i (see (12.23)). For concreteness, suppose that there are three potential members, say Italy, France, and Germany, with $\theta_{IT} < \theta_{FR} < \theta_{GE}$, and that both unemployment targets and the shocks are the same across countries. Therefore, conflict of interests reflects only different inflation preferences, as in (12.24), with $\tilde{U}_i = \tilde{U}_{EU}$ for all i. Note that in this case, the gain from membership is identically zero if $\theta_i = \Theta$. Hence, the minimum Θ for a country to join is θ_i, with $\Theta > \theta_i$ representing the gain from having monetary policy set by a central bank with less of an inflation bias than the government itself has. There is a maximum Θ consistent with it being optimal for country i to join, denoted $\overline{\Theta}_i$.

Feasibility depends on there being a nonempty range of possible values for Θ, such that membership is preferred to nonmembership. For example, when countries face identical shocks, feasibility requires that the highest Θ that the high-inflation country Italy would accept (that is, for which membership at $\overline{\Theta}_{IT}$ is preferred to nonmembership) is no less than θ_{GE}. That is, there exist values $\Theta \in [\theta_{GE}, \overline{\Theta}_{IT}]$. Which value of Θ will be chosen depends on the voting procedure and the nature of preferences. For example, if the preferred Θ of both France and Italy is below θ_{GE}, the outcome of majority voting will be $\Theta = \theta_{GE}$. Monetary policy will be made just tough enough to keep Germany in EMU. To the extent that the convergence criteria lead to a stronger anti-inflation constituency in France and Italy before EMU is inaugurated, as reflected in higher θ_{FR} and θ_{IT}, ECB monetary policy will be closer to Germany's preferred policy. Alesina and Grilli also consider cases where shocks are not identical across countries or where countries assign other benefits to EMU.

PART II—MACROECONOMIC INTERDEPENDENCE

12.5. INTERNATIONAL POLICY COOPERATION

A major issue in open-economy macroeconomics is the transmission of economic disturbances across countries. Policies undertaken by foreign governments are a main source of these disturbances. When policy actions of sovereign governments affect one another, the question of policy coordination becomes central. If the two governments had identical objectives, there would, of course, be no reason for coordination to be an issue. But since the two governments have, by definition, different constituencies, there is no reason to suppose that their objectives will overlap. As Hamada

(1976) observed in his pioneering contribution on international policy coordination, policymaking then becomes a noncooperative game, and there are likely to be gains from cooperation.

This reasoning implicitly assumes that countries are governed by benevolent social planners. Given the external effects from macroeconomic and trade policies, uncoordinated policies are likely to lead to inefficient outcomes, relative to what could be achieved under coordination. For example, if two countries each engage in expansionary monetary policy in order to depreciate their currency relative to the other in order to improve the current account, neither achieves the goal of a change in relative prices, and both end up with undesired inflation. Assuming that countries can make binding commitments, a more efficient outcome can be obtained.

There have been numerous papers on both theoretical and empirical aspects of policy coordination. Canzoneri and Henderson (1988) and Persson and Tabellini (1995) present excellent surveys of models of coordination, stressing political economy aspects. Coordination can take several forms. The most obvious form, which will be our focus of attention, is direct policy coordination. It is not, however, the only possibility. We begin with an alternative.

Policy Assignment

Following Mundell (1968), one can take the *policy assignment approach*, which, following Tinbergen (1952), considers the optimal assignment of instruments of economic policy to targets. By analogy, rather than two countries using all instruments to affect all targets, one could consider the assignment of instruments and targets to each country. For example Mundell (1971) advocates that under the then-prevailing dollar standard, the United States would adjust its money supply to peg the world price level, while the "rest of the world" would use monetary policy to keep the balance of payments in equilibrium. Such a view is based on the "redundancy" or "$N - 1$" problem, whereby $N - 1$ countries can achieve their balance of payments objective, with the Nth country acting as the residual country. (See also Swoboda and Dornbusch [1973] for an application of this approach.) Though the assignment approach is attractive in its simplicity, it can be misleading for a number of reasons. First, optimal policy often requires a mixing of instruments to achieve objectives. Second, under uncertainty, achieving policy goals may require more than simply having as many instruments as targets. (See, for example, Brainard [1967].) Furthermore, the simple assignment of objectives to countries ignores a basic incentive problem: will it be credible that a national authority will always have the incentive to use policy for the world good according to its assigned role? Hence, one wants to know whether an optimizing government would find it in its best interests to cooperate.[18]

Optimizing Governments—A Simple Monetary Model

Modeling interacting governments as optimizing agents suggests analyzing international policy coordination in terms of strategic behavior on the part of each country. That is, country behavior and the resultant equilibrium would be modeled by deriving reaction functions for countries on the basis of their own optimizing behavior. Another crucial reason for modeling governments as optimizing agents, already discussed in our treatment of currency crises, is that countries generally have fewer instruments than targets. It therefore seems more sensible to view them as having conflicting objectives that require trade-offs, as our heterogeneity paradigm suggests. All the more so *between* nations. This is the approach of Hamada (1976), who asks whether countries pursuing their national objectives in an interdependent world will lead to an equilibrium in which worldwide welfare is maximized, and who finds, not surprisingly, that it will not. He then asks whether this result will be altered by the adoption of international institutional changes ("rules of the game"). In Section 12.2, we considered the effect of institutions from the point of view of one country's welfare, ignoring strategic interactions; here, we include such interactions, as well as focusing more on worldwide welfare.

The basic arguments can be represented in terms of a simple model with quadratic loss functions and linear constraints. (We consider the implications of alternative specifications of objectives and economic structure in the next two subsections.) Suppose, for simplicity, that the world is made up of two "countries": the United States, denoted with a subscript US, and Europe, denoted with a subscript EU. The loss function for each country is, as above, a function of unemployment and inflation:

$$\mathscr{L}_i = U_i^2 + \theta_i \pi_i^2, \quad \text{for } i = US, EU, \tag{12.26}$$

where π is the rate of inflation of the consumer price index and, as always, the unemployment rate is measured relative to the natural rate of unemployment. Note that we have assumed that the policymaker's target unemployment rate is equal to the natural rate: he has no incentive to engineer a surprise inflation, an assumption that will be crucial for our simple results, and to which we return in detail below.

The consumer price index is a function of the domestic and foreign output price levels, which for simplicity we assume enter with equal

---

[18] Instrument assignment to different *levels* of government in a federal system (or a political union) is widely discussed in the public finance literature. We return to this issue in our discussion of fiscal unions in Section 14.6 of Chapter 14.

weights. Assume that the exchange rate is fixed and that output price inflation in each country is equal to the rate of domestic monetary growth, m_{US} for the United States and m_{EU} for Europe. Hence, the CPI inflation rate in each country is simply

$$\pi_i = .5m_{US} + .5m_{EU}, \quad \text{for } i = US, EU. \tag{12.27}$$

Unemployment in each country is related to unanticipated output price inflation according to

$$U_i = a_i(m_i^e - m_i) + \epsilon, \tag{12.28}$$

where $a_i > 0$ is a slope coefficient and ϵ is an unemployment shock common to both countries.

Each country has two targets but only one instrument, so that it cannot achieve its objectives independent of the action of the other country. In the absence of cooperation, the relevant solution concept is Nash noncooperative equilibrium. One begins by deriving reaction functions for each country, which give the optimal setting of the policy instrument under its control for each policy choice of the other country. In each country, we minimize the loss function (12.26) with respect to its own money growth rate, subject to (12.27) and (12.28), holding constant the other country's money growth rate. Taking expectations to eliminate m_{EU}^e and m_{US}^e (which will equal zero), this yields reaction functions

$$m_{US} = \Pi^{US}(\epsilon, m_{EU}) \equiv A_{US}\epsilon + D_{US}m_{EU}, \tag{12.29a}$$

$$m_{EU} = \Pi^{EU}(\epsilon, m_{US}) \equiv A_{EU}\epsilon + D_{EU}m_{US}, \tag{12.29b}$$

where

$$A_i = \frac{a_i}{a_i^2 + .25\theta_i}, \qquad D_i = -\frac{.25\theta_i}{a_i^2 + .25\theta_i}.$$

Solving (12.29a) and (12.29b) simultaneously, we derive the noncooperative Nash equilibrium:

$$m_{US}^N = \frac{A_{US} + D_{US}A_{EU}}{1 - D_{US}D_{EU}}\epsilon, \qquad m_{EU}^N = \frac{A_{EU} + D_{EU}A_{US}}{1 - D_{US}D_{EU}}\epsilon. \tag{12.30}$$

The solution and some of its properties are illustrated in Figure 12.1, which should be studied carefully. The reaction function of each country is given by the thick solid lines, with the most preferred point for the United States, for example, given by O_{US} (and similarly for Europe by O_{EU}). The Nash equilibrium is given by the intersection of the two reaction functions

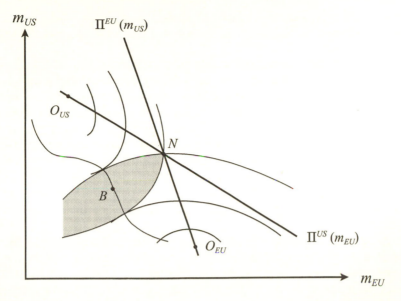

FIGURE 12.1. Reaction functions.

at N. Indifference curves centered on O_{US} and O_{EU} radiate outward, with utility being lower the farther away from O_i is the curve. The U.S. indifference curves are vertical when they intersect the US reaction function, since along the reaction function, m_{US} is chosen so that its marginal effect on US welfare is zero, given m_{EU}. Analogously, the European indifference curves are horizontal when they intersect the European reaction function.

In this simple example, the reaction functions are necessarily downward sloping, with the European reaction function steeper than the US reaction function for m_{EU} on the horizontal axis. More generally, in models of international spillovers, reaction functions could be either positively or negatively sloped. For example, in a model where a monetary expansion abroad increases unemployment at home via a depreciation of the foreign country's currency and a resultant trade balance improvement abroad, it would be easy to obtain a positively sloped reaction function. (Frankel and Rockett [1988] present a simple general mathematical representation of policy spillovers and reaction functions, and discuss the possibilities.) The case of negatively sloped reaction functions, where an increase in the setting of one country's policy instrument induces a decrease in the other country's policy instrument, is the case of *strategic substitutes*. When an increase in m_{US}, for example, induces an increase in m_{EU}, we have a case of *strategic complements*, where multiple intersections of the reaction functions, that is, multiple Nash equilibria, are possible. Independent of the possible existence of multiple equilibria, whether we have a case of strategic substitutes or complements will affect welfare considerations, as we shall see shortly.

The Nash equilibrium is clearly Pareto inefficient. The set of Pareto-efficient points is given by the set of tangencies of the two sets of indifference curves, the "contract curve" represented by the wavy line in the figure, lying to the southwest of the Nash equilibrium N. From our discussion above on the slopes of the indifference curves when they intersect the reaction functions, the indifference curves cannot be tangent at N, the intersection point of the U.S. and European reaction functions. The lens emanating from N (lightly shaded in the diagram) is the set of points Pareto superior to N. International cooperation between the two countries would imply a solution along the segment of the contract curve within this lens.

In economic terms, the inefficiency of the noncooperative solution in this model may be explained as follows. In response to a positive unemployment shock, each country expands without considering the effect of its policy on inflation abroad. Though some response to the unemployment shock is optimal (see below), in the uncoordinated equilibrium, inflation is too high relative to the Pareto-efficient solution.

If the countries can successfully cooperate, which point on the contract curve will be chosen? (Note there is a potential problem of how a given cooperative solution can be enforced. The basic literature on international policy does not address this point directly, though some later literature does, to which we return below.) Early discussions of international cooperation focused simply on the symmetric solution, which will arise from a more formal solution concept if the countries are identical. One may also consider the Nash bargaining solution, which is the solution where the product of the two countries' welfare gain over the noncooperative solution is maximized. The non-cooperative solution is seen as the "threat point," the point to which a country would revert in the absence of cooperation. One may also consider a solution where the sum of the utilities of the two countries is maximized. It may be worthwhile for the reader to compute one of these solutions, easily done for this simple model, to convince himself that in the cooperative solution, the shock is only partially accommodated.

Casella's (1992) argument on the implications of unequal size for the decision to participate in a union may be easily illustrated in terms of reaction functions. Referring back to Figure 12.1, one sees that not all points on the contract curve (the wavy line to the southwest of N) are preferred to the noncooperative equilibrium N, that is, not all points are inside the shaded lens. Different points on the contract curve correspond to different distributions of power between the two countries, with a point close to O_{US}, for example, corresponding to the United States having most of the bargaining power in striking a cooperative agreement. If the distribution of power were such that the bargaining point *B* ended up outside the lens, say above it, Europe would be better off not participating in a cooperative agreement and reverting to the noncooperative point. To participate, Europe would need to be given inducements (in Casella's example, a favorable distribution of seigniorage revenues) to put the solution at a point inside the lens.

As stressed in footnote 14, the argument is not that noncooperation dominates *all* cooperative equilibria from the point of view of each country, but only that noncooperation dominates some of them. Though this may seem obvious, it distinguishes this argument, which falls under the heading of potentially beneficial cooperation, from the arguments later in this section on counterproductive cooperation. The possibility of noncooperation dominating cooperation depends on policies being strategic substitutes and the reaction functions being negatively sloped. If policies were strategic complements, with the reaction functions upward sloping, all points on the contract curve would be in the lens of points Pareto dominating the noncooperative equilibrium.

Some Alternative Specifications of Monetary Models

We chose a very simple model of interdependence to illustrate the benefits of cooperation. There are numerous other specifications, leading to the same conclusion, often focusing on underadjustment to an unemployment shock. Given the shock, each country would like to expand, but chooses not to do so on its own because of the adverse effect such an expansion will have on its current account. If the two countries could agree to expand simultaneously, so that activity in both would be higher without adverse current account effects, both would be better off. In the uncoordinated equilibrium, economic activity is too low in the two countries. For example, Hamada's (1974) pioneering paper considered a fixed exchange rate model in which governments target their monetary policies to achieve balance-of-payments surpluses. In a noncooperative equilibrium, the uncoordinated use of contractionary monetary policy with a balance-of-payments goal leads to a suboptimal level of economic contraction. Cooper (1985) considers a model of monetary policy under flexible rates, each country trying to appreciate its currency to reduce inflation in the case of noncooperation. In equilibrium, there is no change in the real exchange rate or inflation, but a fall in output in each country. In these, as in many models of international policy cooperation, the focus is on the real exchange rate. Each country tries to change its terms of trade, but in equilibrium, the real exchange rate is unaffected. Such a model is presented below.

Canzoneri and Henderson distinguish "temporary" from "ongoing" conflict. In the former, the loss from noncooperation lasts only as long as policy surprises are effective in changing real activity. If monetary policy is ineffective once contracts have been renegotiated to take account of the change in the stance of monetary policy in response to a shock, the loss from noncooperation vanishes. In contrast, with ongoing conflict, countries have real exchange rate targets, in the case of Canzoneri and Henderson due to valuing increases in the purchasing power of full employment income. An ongoing conflict between policymakers in the two countries would exist even if there were no shocks and wages were perfectly flexible. Although there are economic differences, there is no real technical difference between these models and those we considered earlier. Hence, we will not treat them explicitly.

A Simple Model of Fiscal Coordination

A similar result on the optimality of coordination relative to the noncooperative equilibrium also arises in fiscal policy interdependence between countries. Though these can take many forms, one particularly relevant form of interaction between countries concerns taxation of capital that is mobile across countries. The harmful effects of tax competition across jurisdictions when factors are mobile has been often discussed; related · issues were discussed in Section 8.7 of Chapter 8. The formulation of the problem given here follows Persson and Tabellini (1995).

Consider a two-period model of capital taxation in two countries, where the representative consumer in the United States has a utility function of the form

$$\Omega_{US} = u(c_1) + c_2 + h(g_{US}) \tag{12.31}$$

where c_t is the representative consumer's consumption in period t (we have suppressed the country subscript), g_{US} is a public good supplied in the second period, and $u(\cdot)$ and $h(\cdot)$ are increasing concave functions. The representative consumer in the foreign country has an analogous utility function of the same form, specifically with the same functions $u(\cdot)$ and $h(\cdot)$, as well as the same capital mobility function $\phi(\cdot)$, defined below. The perfect symmetry of the problem in the two countries allow Persson and Tabellini to derive a very simple, clear solution.

The consumer receives an endowment e_{US} that can be consumed, invested at home, denoted k_{US}, or invested abroad, denoted k_{US}^*. One unit invested today yields one unit tomorrow in both countries, but foreign investment involves a mobility cost $\phi(k_{US}^*)$, borne in the second period. Capital invested at home is taxed at the domestic rate τ_{US}^k, while capital invested abroad is taxed at the foreign rate τ_{EU}^k. The representative consumer's budget constraints may be written

$$e_{US} = c_1 + s_{US},$$
$$c_2 = (1 - \tau_{US}^k)k_{US} + (1 - \tau_{EU}^k)k_{US}^* - \phi(k_{US}^*) \tag{12.32}$$
$$= (1 - \tau_{US}^k)s_{US} + (\tau_{US}^k - \tau_{EU}^k)k_{US}^* - \phi(k_{US}^*),$$

where total saving $s_{US} = k_{US} + k_{US}^*$ and where $\phi(0) = 0$, $\phi' > 0$ for $k^* > 0$, and $\phi'' > 0$. Foreign consumers have an analogous budget constraint. The government's second-period budget constraint is

$$g_{US} = \tau_{US}^k(k_{US} + k_{EU}^*), \tag{12.33}$$

where k_{EU}^* is investment by foreigners in the United States.

Crucial to the results of this type of model is the timing of government decisions over tax rates relative to consumers' decisions about how much and where to invest. Assume, therefore, that the governments in the two countries choose tax policy in period 1, after which consumers in each country choose how much to save and where to invest.

The individual decisions on saving and location of investment are derived by maximizing (12.31) subject to (12.32), given g_{US}, τ_{US}^k, and τ_{EU}^k. The resulting saving and foreign investment functions are

$$
\begin{aligned}
s_{US} &= S(\tau_{US}^k) \equiv e_{US} - (u')^{(-1)}(1 - \tau_{US}^k) \\
k_{US}^* &= K(\tau_{US}^k - \tau_{EU}^k) \equiv (\phi')^{(-1)}(\tau_{US}^k - \tau_{EU}^k),
\end{aligned}
\tag{12.34}
$$

where $(u')^{(-1)}(\cdot)$ and $(\phi')^{(-1)}(\cdot)$ are inverse functions and $K' > 0$, given the above assumptions on ϕ. The dependence of saving only on the tax rate in one's own country follows from the linearity of utility in second-period consumption. The foreign consumer's decision is characterized by similar conditions, where it is useful to note that the symmetry of the problem implies that foreign investment in the home country is characterized by the same functional relation, that is, $k_{EU}^* = K(\tau_{EU}^k - \tau_{US}^k)$, for $K(\cdot)$ defined as in (12.34). Note that an increase in the domestic tax rate τ_{US}^k, given the foreign tax rate τ_{EU}^k, decreases home investment in two ways: it reduces overall home saving, and it induces the consumer to place a higher fraction of saving in the foreign country.

In the noncooperative (Nash) equilibrium, each country chooses tax rates to maximize the relevant version of (12.31), subject to its budget constraint (12.33) and the consumer's first-order conditions (12.34), taking the other country's tax rate as given. For the United States, for example, one derives[19]

$$h'(g_{US}^N) = \left(1 + \frac{\tau_{US}^k}{S(\cdot)}\left(\frac{dS(\cdot)}{d\tau_{US}^k} - 2K'(\cdot)\right)\right)^{-1}, \tag{12.35}$$

---

[19] To derive this expression, set up an indirect utility function and differentiate with respect to τ_{US}^k, using the symmetry of the problem, including the facts that $k_{US}^* = K(\tau_{US}^k - \tau_{EU}^k) = -k_{EU}^*$ in evaluating the derivatives and that $k_{US}^* = k_{EU}^* = 0$ and $\tau_{EU}^k = \tau_{US}^k$ in equilibrium.

for $S(\cdot)$ and $K(\cdot)$ as defined in (12.34) and where $(\tau_{US}^k/S)(dS/d\tau_{US}^k)$ is the elasticity of saving with respect to the home tax rate.

In the cooperative equilibrium, tax rates for the two countries are chosen to maximize worldwide welfare. Following Persson and Tabellini, consider choosing τ_{US}^k and τ_{EU}^k to maximize the *sum* of welfare in the two countries. A similar exercise to that performed in the previous paragraph yields an optimal tax rate implicitly defined by

$$h'(g_{US}^C) = \left(1 + \frac{\tau_{US}^k}{S(\cdot)} \frac{dS(\cdot)}{d\tau_{US}^k}\right)^{-1}, \tag{12.36}$$

which is a standard optimal tax formula in the absence of capital flight. An identical formula describes fiscal policy in Europe in the two noncooperative and cooperative equilibria. Since $K' > 0$, the right-hand side of (12.35) is larger than the right-hand side of (12.36), due to the effect of higher domestic taxes inducing higher investment abroad, both increasing k_{US}^* and decreasing k_{EU}^*. (Hence, the factor of 2 in (12.35).) That is, in the absence of cooperation, the tax base is more elastic with respect to unilateral increases in capital taxation. Hence, the level of taxes and of government spending is higher in the cooperative equilibrium than in the noncooperative equilibrium, with a higher level of welfare as well.

Intuitively, in the noncooperative equilibrium, governments have the incentive to reduce capital taxation unilaterally, to attract foreign capital and to keep domestic capital at home. This incentive will be greater the greater is capital mobility between the two countries, that is, the greater is K'. As in the monetary models discussed earlier in the section, in equilibrium this will be unsuccessful, as tax rates will be equal at home and abroad. The attempt to attract net inflows, however, will lead to tax rates and government spending below the optimum. In the limit, if capital were perfectly mobile between countries, there would be zero taxation and zero government spending in the Nash equilibrium in both countries.

It would seem that as countries become small, the loss from noncooperation is small, as is often argued for tariff policy. Kehoe (1987) suggests this need not be the case for tax policy. He considers a simple overlapping generations model with taxation of labor to supply public goods, with a utility function of an individual in each generation analogous to (12.31). Capital is assumed to be perfectly mobile between countries. Since capital is accumulated from saving out of wage income by the young, a higher labor tax rate will reduce the world capital stock. As the number of countries becomes large, a single country which raises its tax rate unilaterally, taking the tax rates in other countries as given, will have little effect on the world capital stock. Given the world capital stock, however, an increase in its tax rate has a first-order effect on its revenues and hence on public consumption. The incentive to *raise* taxes in a noncooperative equilibrium rises as the number of countries becomes large, precisely because of the infinitesimal effect of the tax base, an effect (or more precisely, a lack of effect) not present if the number of countries is small. In the limit, as the number of countries becomes infinite, noncoordination would imply no capital accumulation and no public spending, while coordination would imply positive public consumption and higher utility.

Welfare-Reducing Policy Coordination—Credibility

That policy coordination should increase national welfare in a world of interdependency seems intuitive. There are, however, a number of reasons why policy coordination may reduce, rather than increase, the welfare of a country's citizens. The first reason, originally pointed out by Rogoff (1985b), concerns the sort of time-inconsistency problems first raised in Chapter 4. If each government has the incentive towards time-inconsistent behavior, and thus faces a credibility problem, the lack of policy coordination may act as a disciplining device. Hence, noncooperative behavior may lead governments closer to the first-best.

The basic result may be illustrated using the simple monetary model at the beginning of this section, but where we reintroduce an unemployment target below the natural rate for policymakers in each country, giving them the well-known incentive towards surprise inflation. Thus, we return to the model of international policy coordination above, but where we introduce a conflict between the domestic policymaker and the representative individual. That is, instead of (12.26), we assume that domestic policymakers have an objective function

$$\mathscr{L}_i = \left(U_i - \tilde{U}\right)^2 + \theta\pi_i^2, \quad \text{for } i = US, EU, \tag{12.37}$$

where $\tilde{U} < 0$. (We assume identical objective functions for simplicity of exposition.)

We slightly modify the structure of the economy from what was assumed earlier, both in order to illustrate the basic arguments as simply as possible, and in order to give an explicit role to the real exchange rate, as in the work of Giavazzi and Pagano (1988) and Cooper (1985) discussed above. Specifically, it is assumed that, in addition to the effect of unanticipated domestic inflation in reducing domestic unemployment, a change in the real exchange rate, defined as the foreign output price level over the domestic output price level, will affect the unemployment rate. (As above, we assume a fixed nominal exchange rate.) Because of the effect on competitiveness, it is assumed that an appreciation of the real exchange rate (a fall in the foreign output price relative to the domestic output price) leads to an increase in unemployment at home and to a decrease in unemployment abroad. It is the linkage of the two economies through the real exchange rate which makes them interdependent.

Working with the rate of change of the real exchange rate and assuming, as above, that the rate of output price inflation is equal to the rate of money growth, we assume a reduced-form equation for US unemployment of the form[20]

$$U_{US} = (m_{US}^e - m_{US}) - \omega(m_{EU} - m_{US}) + \epsilon, \qquad (12.38)$$

where $0 < \omega < 1$ represents the sensitivity of U.S. unemployment to an appreciation of the real exchange rate brought about by an increase in the rate of money growth in the United States relative to that in Europe. The European unemployment relation is identical, except that the change in the real exchange rate enters with the opposite sign. (As in the case of objective functions, the economic structure of the two countries is assumed identical for ease of exposition.) Finally, to close the model, we assume (again for simplicity of exposition) that it is output price inflation that enters the objective function (12.37), that is, that $\pi_i = m_i$.

Substituting (12.38) and $\pi_i = m_i$ into (12.37), the policymaker's objective (that is, loss) function for the United States may be written

$$\mathscr{L}_{US} = \left(m_{US}^e - (1 - \omega)m_{US} - \omega m_{EU} + \epsilon - \tilde{U}\right)^2 + \theta m_{US}^2, \quad (12.39)$$

with an analogous objective function for the European policymaker. In the noncooperative equilibrium, each policymaker minimizes his loss function by choice of a money growth rate, taking the money growth rate of the other policymaker as given. This would yield a pair of reaction functions, which could then be solved simultaneously to yield the noncooperative equilibrium. In this symmetric model, one obtains a noncooperative equilibrium of[21]

$$m_i^N = -\frac{1 - \omega}{\theta}\tilde{U} + \frac{1 - \omega}{1 - \omega + \theta}\epsilon, \quad \text{for } i = US, EU. \quad (12.40)$$

A cooperative equilibrium may be found by choosing m_{US} and m_{EU} to minimize the sum $\mathscr{L}_{US} + \mathscr{L}_{EU}$, which will imply an equilibrium:

$$m_i^C = -\frac{1}{\theta}\tilde{U} + \frac{1}{1 + \theta}\epsilon, \quad \text{for } i = US, EU. \quad (12.41)$$

---

[20] A derivation of this type of equation describing real activity may be found in Rogoff (1985b).

[21] One differentiates (12.40) and then takes expectations, using the fact $m_{US} = m_{EU}$ in equilibrium.

Comparing the noncooperative equilibrium in (12.40) and the cooperative equilibrium in (12.41), we see a trade-off. On the one hand, as in the monetary model at the beginning of this section, cooperation improves welfare in the face of stochastic shocks, in this case by increasing a policymaker's expansionary response to a positive unemployment shock. (Note that $1/(1 + \theta) > (1 - \omega)/(1 - \omega + \theta)$.) In the absence of cooperation, each policymaker is limited in his response to the shock by the adverse response of the real exchange rate to a unilateral monetary expansion. In equilibrium, of course, there is no change in the real exchange rate, but the fear of appreciation in the United States leads to an underresponse to the shock. In contrast, in the cooperative equilibrium, each policymaker can expand further without fear of a real appreciation.

The downside is that the inflation "bias" is higher in the cooperative equilibrium than in the noncooperative equilibrium, reflecting the greater possibility to respond to the incentive to reduce unemployment to $-\tilde{U}$. When policymakers coordinate their actions, they need not fear the real appreciation that would accompany unilateral expansion. Eliminating this problem thus cuts both ways as far as individual welfare, increasing welfare in response to shocks, but reducing it by raising the time-consistent average inflation rate. (This same trade-off between the average level of inflation and the ability to respond to shocks was seen in Section 5.4 of Chapter 5, when θ was treated as a choice variable in considering appointment of a conservative central banker.) It is the increase in the inflation bias under cooperation to which Rogoff (1985b) referred in arguing that policy cooperation can be counterproductive when policymakers face credibility problems.

This argument holds not only for monetary policy, but also for fiscal policy, as shown by Kehoe (1989), among others. As in the case of monetary policy, this problem occurs even if governments are benevolent, in the sense of maximizing social welfare. Kehoe's argument may be seen as an application of the time-consistency problem in capital taxation studied in detail in Section 4.2 of Chapter 4. It may be illustrated in a variant of the fiscal coordination model earlier in this section, but where labor supply is endogenous and both labor and capital can be taxed in the second period, and where the sequencing of individual and government decisions is changed. Earlier, we assumed that the governments in the two countries choose tax policy before consumers in each country choose how much to save and where to invest. Suppose instead that individuals first choose their total level of saving, governments choose their tax policies, after which, individuals choose where to invest. As in the closed-economy capital-taxation model, since investment is in place when tax rates are chosen, "benevolent" governments have the incentive to tax capital prohibitively in the second period to supply the public good. Hence, any pledge not to tax capital would lack credibility.

In the closed economy, the incentive towards prohibitive capital taxation induces consumers to underaccumulate capital, since they believe it will be taxed away. In the open economy, with the possibility of investing abroad and with the choice of *where* to invest made after tax rates are announced, a government that attempts to tax away capital will be met by capital flight. That is, capital flight acts as a disciplining device on governments. If there were no capital mobility costs, that is, $\phi(\kappa)$ in (12.32) is identically zero, individuals would invest in whichever country has the lower capital tax rate; if tax rates are equal, consumers would invest at home. In the noncooperative equilibrium, each country chooses a zero tax rate due to the possibility of full capital flight. In contrast, in a cooperative equilibrium, each country can choose positive tax rates if it knows its neighbors will coordinate on tax policy. In an equilibrium, $\tau_i^k = 1$ in each country, and we have the same problem of an inferior equilibrium as in the closed-economy model.

To summarize, in the models of a benevolent government with the incentive to be time inconsistent, as in Rogoff (1985b) or Kehoe (1989), the problem is one of the government's inability to commit; in an open economy, policy *competition* may have the effect of reputation or other commitment devices; it thus may bring the economy closer to the first-best equilibrium. International policy coordination can be welfare reducing if it removes this positive effect of competition.

Partisan Policymakers

A second reason for the possible nonoptimality of policy coordination is that policy is set by partisan policymakers, who use policy to constrain their successors, a possibility considered by Tabellini (1990a). His result is based on the closed-economy model of Alesina and Tabellini (1989) and Tabellini and Alesina (1990), which was discussed in detail in Section 7.9 of Chapter 7. In that model, policymakers differ in terms of the desired composition of public spending. Utility smoothing over time implies that if a policymaker were certain to remain in office, he would run a balanced budget. However, if he is uncertain as to whether or not he will be re-elected, he may run a deficit and issue debt, increasing spending today (dictated by his own preferences) relative to tomorrow (dictated by the preferences of tomorrow's policymaker, which may differ). By issuing debt which needs to be repaid tomorrow, today's policymaker can constrain tomorrow's policymaker.

Considering an open economy, Tabellini (1990a) uses the same type of model to show that the size of the deficit bias may be larger and individual welfare may be lower under international policy coordination than in a noncooperative equilibrium. The key effect is that in the absence of coordination, fiscal deficits imply a suboptimal time path of the real exchange rate, an effect that would tend to put a limit on deficits. Suppose two governments agree to pursue coordinated policies in the current period, neither, however, knowing whether it will be reappointed in the next period. By running the same deficit, they can eliminate any effect on the real exchange rate. In contrast, in the noncooperative equilibrium, a government that issues debt turns the terms of trade against itself. A government that cares about social welfare will therefore be induced to run a smaller deficit, coming closer to the zero-deficit result that voters would prefer if they did not know which party would be in power in the second period. As in the earlier models, a noncooperative solution may lead to lower rather than higher welfare. Higher fiscal deficits increase real interest rates, which can either increase or decrease consumer welfare. If the government is a net debtor to the private sector, a higher real interest rate implies a higher transfer to the consumer; if the marginal utility of private consumption is higher than the marginal utility of public consumption, this will be welfare improving. In the opposite case, a higher real interest rate reduces welfare of the representative agent. If the interest rate effect is positive and outweighs the terms-of-trade effect, consumer welfare will be higher under noncooperation. If the terms-of-trade effect dominates, or if both effects go in the same direction, policy coordination by partisan governments will lower social welfare.

Using a different sort of a model, Lohmann (1993) has demonstrated a similar result on the interaction between domestic political competition and international policy coordination. She begins with a model in which electoral competition generates a partisan business cycle (see Section 7.4 of Chapter 7) in which there is an election surprise in money growth (positive for a left-wing party, negative for a right-wing party) relative to what was rationally expected before the election. However, the difference between the expected and the actually implemented domestic money growth also enters the foreign objective function and affects foreign money growth and vice versa for the foreign money surprise, as in the simple monetary model at the beginning of this section. As a consequence of this feedback, money growth set by the left-wing (right-wing) party is even higher (lower).

Under international cooperation, the transmission of the political business cycle across countries is aggravated. When the foreign government sets the cooperative level of money growth, it takes into account the effect of its action on the utility level of the domestic party in power. After the election results are realized, foreign money growth is set higher (lower) if the left-wing (right-wing) party has won the elections. This monetary surprise, stronger than before, feeds back into domestic money growth. International cooperation eliminates the inflationary bias due to real exchange rate competition, but aggravates the international transmission and repercussion of the political cycle. The net effect is positive if the weight on the current account objective (that is, the weight on the real exchange rate) is sufficiently large, negative if the parties' difference in bliss points or the degree of international interdependence is sufficiently large.

These results on the possible negative effect of cooperation on the welfare of the representative citizen may be interpreted similarly to the results discussed above on the benefit of policy competition when a "benevolent" government has an incentive to be time inconsistent. Voters who are uncertain about the composition of future governments would like zero debt, implying expected utility smoothing. To use Tabellini's terminology, if the current government could enter into a binding agreement with future governments about the composition of public spending, the zero-debt solution would result. But governments not yet formed cannot commit themselves to a spending pattern. Policy competition across countries, as reflected in terms of trade effects, achieves some of this goal. International cooperation between current governments benefits them at the expense of future governments; it reduces the cost of strategically manipulating the debt meant to influence future policies.

Misperceptions

We quickly summarize a third reason for the possible nonoptimality of policy coordination, namely, policymakers may disagree about the structure of the economy. As Frankel and Rockett (1988) stress, when policymakers choose policy on the basis of an incorrect model, coordination may be counterproductive. Suppose that policymakers believe that the world is based on a model other than the true model (for example, they base their behavior on incorrect coefficients $\hat{a}_i$ in (12.28), rather than on the true a_i). The Nash solution would then be as in (12.30) but with hatted values of the parameters instead of unhatted values, denoted $(\hat{m}_{US}^N, \hat{m}_{EU}^N)$. The cooperative solution could be similarly derived, once again with the hatted parameters, and denoted $(\hat{m}_{US}^B, \hat{m}_{EU}^B)$. The welfare associated with these solutions is found by substituting them into the true equations (12.27) and (12.28), then in turn substituting the economic outcomes into the welfare functions (12.26). Frankel and Rockett show that for a general model of interactions between countries, it could be the case that, evaluated using the true indifference curves, welfare is lower with $(\hat{m}_{US}^B, \hat{m}_{EU}^B)$ than with $(\hat{m}_{US}^N, \hat{m}_{EU}^N)$. (In terms of Figure 12.1, the point associated with $(\hat{m}_{US}^N, \hat{m}_{EU}^N)$ and the point associated with $(\hat{m}_{US}^B, \hat{m}_{EU}^B)$ could both lie below the contract curve.)

In the case of misperceptions of the true model, cooperative policymakers can find a coordinated package that they *believe* is welfare improving, but the package actually reduces welfare. Based on simulations with a class of possible linear models, Frankel and Rockett argue that the gains from a country unilaterally discovering the true model and changing its policy accordingly are usually much greater than the potential gains from policy coordination. Cooperation over discovering the true model (as opposed to over policy using the incorrect model) should therefore yield large gains.

Frankel and Rockett also consider the perhaps more realistic case where policymakers in each country are uncertain about the true model and maximize expected utility based on the probability weight they assign to each possible model, as opposed to believing an incorrect model with certainty. A similar conclusion emerges about the possible welfare-reducing effect of policy coordination.

Misperceptions is not a political problem *per se*, that is, one reflecting a conflict of interests. This case, however, blends nicely with other examples of the welfare effects of conflict of interests. In standard models of coordination where all agents share a common economic model, the focus is on conflicting objectives between policymakers, or between policymakers and the public in addition, as in the previous two subsections. Frankel and Rockett consider both conflict of interests and conflict of perceptions between policymakers to show how coordination can be welfare reducing. Frankel (1986) considers the case of policymakers with identical objective functions who disagree *only* about the proper economic model and shows that the same results hold: policymakers are generally able to agree on a coordinated policy they believe is welfare improving relative to the noncooperative equilibrium; and, this package could easily reduce welfare rather than increase it.

How Can Cooperative Solutions Be Achieved?

Let us return to the models at the beginning of this section in which cooperation is productive. Though it is welfare improving, coordination in fact is not common. Cooper (1985) suggests that countries have done better in the creation and maintenance of rule-based regimes than in the coordination of specific policy actions. He points out, however, that it has proven extremely difficult to alter such regimes in an orderly way. He suggests a number of reasons for noncooperation. First, countries may not agree on the objectives of cooperation. Second, even with common overall objectives, countries may differ on their views of how the world works, as in the Frankel–Rockett model, or in their forecasts of the future. Third, there may be lack of trust (though this should be derived from primitives, which seems to be the whole point of a game-theoretic analysis). Fourth, as already indicated in discussing problems of monetary union, there is the ever-present desire of countries to retain their freedom of action. Cooper makes a very useful distinction between national sovereignty, that is, the "formal ability of a nation to act on its own rather than under instruction from another nation," and national autonomy, the "ability of a nation to attain its objectives through unilateral action." Macroeconomic interdependence implies a lack of autonomy, but, as he points out, this should not be confused with a loss of sovereignty.

One is then led to ask what solutions can be found, in the sense of attaining the better equilibrium. Though the problem is different than the time-consistency problem in Chapter 4, our discussion will, in a sense, mirror the discussion in Chapters 5 and 6, in that many of the same solutions will crop up.

Reputation

Canzoneri and Henderson (1988, 1991) discuss in detail the role of reputation in enforcing a cooperative solution. They consider repeated interactions between policymakers in two countries, focusing on trigger strategies in a repeated one-shot game to enforce better outcomes, as in the model of Section 6.3 in Chapter 6. The results are as in those models, but where the stochastic shock to real activity means that the temptation to defect varies period by period. If the shock is unbounded, there will be periods when the efficient solution cannot be enforced, as the temptation to defect is unbounded, while the loss from defecting is finite, as it depends on the discounted value of future *expected* shocks. The interested reader may apply the explicitly derived solutions in Chapter 4 to analogous open-economy models, or may refer to Canzoneri and Henderson (especially chapters 4 and 5 of [1991]) for details.

Institutions

A second general way to achieve the cooperative solution is via institutions. The basic idea here is to consider the use of institutions or other institutionalized choice mechanisms, rather than coordination of individual policy responses, to achieve better outcomes. Persson and Tabellini (1995) stress the importance of institutional mechanisms to achieve international cooperation, and their treatment of various possibilities is quite extensive.

In the realm of monetary policy, a primary institutional solution is a fixed exchange rate system to avoid manipulation of exchange rates to achieve national objectives. In the absence of cooperation about setting up a multilateral fixed exchange rate system, a single nation can set up a one-sided exchange rate peg to try to get closer to the cooperative system, much like countries can unilaterally decide to peg their exchange rate to that of a low-inflation country to try to enhance their credibility. Canzoneri and Gray (1985) study a fixed exchange rate regime in this respect, where one country makes a unilateral commitment to a specific monetary policy rule, while the other country chooses policy freely. Formally, this is a leader–follower model, with one policymaker precommitting his monetary policy, this being his "reaction function," the other choosing his monetary policy to maximize national welfare, given the precommitted "reaction function" of the first player. In the case where the countries are symmetric, including the shocks they face, this regime leads to the cooperative outcome, as long as the central bank chooses the reaction function optimally and remains with the peg. However, as Canzoneri and Henderson (1991) argue, the result is not robust to a more general framework.

THE INTERNATIONAL ECONOMY

When the two countries are not symmetric, or when the shocks they encounter are not perfectly correlated, this regime will not enforce the cooperative solution.

Canzoneri and Henderson argue that the basic problem with this solution is one common to leader–follower models: one of the players must be off his true reaction function, so that he has an incentive to deviate from the solution. Only in special cases will this incentive not exist. More generally, the pegging monetary authority has an incentive to act more aggressively (to deviate from its precommitted reaction) to impose a larger burden of adjustment to shocks on the nonpegging country.

What about multilateral commitments to fixed exchange rates to avoid manipulation of exchange rates to achieve national objectives? This was how its designers viewed the Bretton Woods system. Persson and Tabellini (1995) view Bretton Woods in terms of multilateral contracting theory, with a codified set of prospective rewards and sanctions tied to the behavior of national monetary authorities. We do not pursue the contracting approach here, referring the interested reader to the Persson and Tabellini article and to Section 5.4 of Chapter 5 for a discussion of the strengths and weaknesses of the contracting approach to the analysis of macroeconomic policy.

Other possible institutional solutions to problems of noncooperation include the creation of a monetary union, as discussed in detail in Section 12.4 of this chapter, and the reliance on international financial institutions (such as the IMF or the World Bank) or institutions designed to encourage international cooperation (such as the OECD) to help achieve policy coordination. On the former, one focus of some research is on institutional design, as in Casella and Feinstein (1989), Von Hagen and Süppel (1994), and Persson and Tabellini (1995). On the latter, there is much general discussion along these lines, but little formal analysis. One approach to the problem is the study of delegation in "two-level" games, to which we now turn.

Two-Level Games of International Cooperation

One promising line of formal study of cooperation among sovereign nations in international institutions is often done in terms of **two-level games** in which negotiators, each representing an organization (or country), bargain over an agreement, subject to the constraint that it must be ratified by their respective organizations. Putnam (1988) presents an especially insightful treatment of both the theory and the application of such two-level interactions. For analytical purposes, he decomposes the process of delegated negotiating and acceptance of international agreements into two stages: bargaining between the negotiators, leading to a tentative agreement (level I); and discussions within each group of constituents in the represented organizations about whether to ratify the agreement (level

II). He uses this decomposition to derive results about the outcome of such negotiations, specifically on the underlying political factors on which outcomes depend. Since an identical agreement must be ratified by both sides, a preliminary level-I agreement cannot be amended at level II without reopening the level-I negotiations—it must simply be voted "up" or "down." (In our earlier terminology, this is a closed-rule procedure.) A key concept is the *win-set*, which is, for a given level-II constituency, the set of all possible level-I agreements that would gain the necessary majority among constituents when simply voted up or down. The relative size of the level-II win-sets across constituencies will determine how the gains from bargaining are split; hence, win-sets can be thought of in terms of threat points in a noncooperative bargaining game. The size of the win-sets will depend on the characteristics of the respective level-II constituencies, their preferences and abilities to make collective choices, as well as on the bargaining rules and tactics in stage I.

Following Persson and Tabellini (1995), a simple two-level bargaining set-up can be represented in a version of the fiscal coordination policy model presented above. Consider a principal–agent model with two stages. In the first stage, each country chooses a policymaker; in the second stage, policymakers from each country choose tax policy noncooperatively, after which saving and investment take place. The two-stage game implies that we will get a result conceptually similar to the result for delegation of monetary policy in a closed economy discussed in Section 5.4 of Chapter 5: in the first stage, the electorate will choose a policymaker whose preferences are *different* from its own, due to the electorate's knowledge of the strategic interaction between policymakers in stage 2.

To make this more precise, suppose that each individual in each country has utility over consumption in the two periods and government spending similar to (12.31), but with individuals differing in the value they place on government spending. Hence, agent i has utility

$$\Omega^i = u(c_1^i) + c_2^i + \theta^i h(g_{US}), \tag{12.42}$$

where θ^i is the weight on government spending in agent i's utility function and where the country subscripts have generally been suppressed. The individual and government budget constraints are as in (12.32) and (12.33). Following the discussion in the earlier model, a policymaker of type θ_{US}^P will choose a domestic tax rate in the second stage that satisfies

$$\theta_{US}^P h'(g_{US}^N) = \left(l + \frac{\tau_{US}^k}{S} \left(\frac{\mathrm{d}S}{\mathrm{d}\tau_{US}^k} - 2\phi' \right) \right)^{-1}, \tag{12.43}$$

parallel to (12.35).

The choice of fiscal policy by the policymaker in the United States could be written as a reaction function for the domestic capital tax rate:

$$\tau_{US}^k = \Pi^{US}(\tau_{EU}^k; \theta_{US}^P), \qquad (12.44)$$

with a similar reaction function for the foreign capital tax rate. One can show that if $h(g)$ is not too concave, the reaction functions are upward sloping, with the position of the reaction functions depending on θ_{US}^P and θ_{EU}^P. The higher is θ_{US}^P (that is, the more weight the policymaker puts on government expenditures g), the higher will be τ_{US}^k, given τ_{EU}^k. Therefore, the higher are θ_{US}^P and θ_{EU}^P, the higher are equilibrium tax rates. Since tax competition between policymakers means inefficiently low tax rates in the noncooperative equilibrium in stage 2, the stage-1 median voter will choose a candidate with a higher preference for public spending than himself in order to raise equilibrium tax rates closer to his desired level.[22]

12.6. POLITICAL RESPONSES TO EXTERNAL SHOCKS

So far, we have considered political aspects of macroeconomic interdependence, focusing on specific political and economic arrangements. An alternative approach, as in Section 11.5 of Chapter 11, is to abstract from specific political and economic mechanisms and, instead, consider the politics of responses to external shocks from a more abstract perspective. Following this approach, in this section we quickly review some models of how conflict among interest groups affects the response to external shocks that largely abstract from institutional details. Two questions are especially interesting. First, how might political conflict magnify the effects of a negative shock, especially in reducing saving and investment? Second, how might problems of common access affect the response to an external shock? We consider these two issues in turn.

Investment Response

The effect of conflict of interests on the response of investment to an external shock has been considered in very similar models by Pazarbasioglu (1992) and Özler and Rodrik (1992), asking whether politically determined domestic policies will magnify or dampen the investment response. The key conflict is the distributive struggle between labor and capital. In response to a shock, workers can fight to tax capital more or less heavily; capitalists can invest more or less, including "negative" investment, that is, capital flight. Pazarbasioglu begins with the government's objective function, in which it attaches weights to the interests of capital and labor. These weights are affected by the redistributive political activity

[22] Technically, the voter maximizes his utility taking as given the foreign reaction function, $\Pi^{EU}(\tau_{US}^k; \theta_{EU}^P)$, rather than the foreign tax rate τ_{EU}^k.

of these two groups, implying that the equilibrium policies that are the result of maximizing the government's objective are similarly affected. Özler and Rodrik work directly with the policy functions, postulating an effect of redistributive political activity consistent with government decisionmaking in the face of political pressure. Key to their models is the pressure for redistribution, that is, *ex-post* heterogeneity. In both models, the effect of a shock could go either way. The political mechanism will dampen the effect of the shock if the initial level of redistributive activity is low, but may magnify its effect if the pre-shock level of redistributive activity is high.

Current Account Balance Response

More generally, one may ask about the response of total spending to an external shock. Representative-agent consumption theory implies that a temporary favorable shock to the terms of trade should lead to a current account surplus, as optimizing agents in the country save part of the windfall to smooth consumption and utility.[23] Tornell and Lane (1998) suggest, however, that when there are "common property" problems, a temporary terms-of-trade boom may result in a current account *deficit*, rather than a surplus, with an increase in government expenditure playing the major role. They consider an economy in which there are a number of strong interest groups whose interaction determines the size of government expenditures: each group makes demands on the government budget, viewed as a common pool as in Sections 10.7 of chapter 10 and 11.5 of Chapter 11. (The model is very similar to those presented earlier and hence it will not be exposited formally in this chapter.) Under certain circumstances, a positive terms-of-trade shock leads each group to increase its demands more than proportionally (which they term a "voracity" effect), so that a higher current account deficit results. Tornell and Lane further present several cases in which a temporary terms-of-trade boom had exactly the effect they hypothesize.

PART III—INTERNATIONAL CAPITAL AND AID FLOWS

12.7. CAPITAL CONTROLS

Flows of capital across borders is a major issue in open-economy macroeconomics, both theoretically and empirically. Capital inflows and outflows constitute a crucial macroeconomic "disturbance" of concern to policymakers. Concern about speculative attacks against the domestic currency,

---

[23] Kraay and Ventura (1997) suggest that this conventional wisdom about a favorable shock inducing a current account surplus may depend on whether the country is a net creditor or borrower.

as discussed in Section 12.3, is a leading example of this but certainly not the only one—capital flows which do not threaten the maintenance of an exchange rate peg may nonetheless lead to highly undesirable movements in the real exchange rate. The magnitude of capital flows is enormous. The Bank for International Settlements estimated that as of early 1998, the average *daily* turnover of "traditional" foreign exchange instruments (spot transactions, outright forwards, and foreign exchange swaps) was 1.5 *trillion* dollars, 25% higher than the comparable figure only three years earlier. Not surprisingly, a key focus of policymakers is somehow trying to manage such flows.

A leading response to capital flows is the use of capital controls. Controls on international capital flows are a common form of financial regulation. As in the case of exchange rate regimes discussed in Part I of the chapter, our interest is in the political, as opposed to simply economic, determinants of controls. To answer the question of why capital controls are imposed, it seems reasonable to begin with the question of what are their effects. For a number of reasons, the relation between the two questions is not as simple as may appear. First, capital-account liberalization is often only one element of broader reform programs, as was certainly the case in many recent liberalization episodes. Hence, the rationale for controls may be determined by the desire for an overall liberalization, rather than by the specific effects that the lifting of controls will have.

Viewing capital controls as part of a package suggests a second reason why the imposition of capital controls may reflect more than simply their pure economic effects: liberalization of the capital account may be adopted to signal a government's broader intentions. Imperfect information about a government's intentions may provide an incentive to use free capital mobility to enhance the credibility of a broader reform program. It is to a reformist government's advantage to engage in early commitment to an open capital account, by exposing itself to risks that less committed governments cannot afford. Finally, even as a stand-alone measure, the effects of capital controls are not always as simple theory would predict or what was expected by many market participants. As Bartolini and Drazen (1997a) document, a liberalization of restrictions on capital outflows has led to increased *inflows* in many countries, a fact they explain in terms of the signaling role of liberalization. Furthermore, as we have seen in Chapter 10, uncertainty about the effects of policy may have significant implications for its adoption.

Determinants of Capital Controls—A Theoretical Overview

Alesina, Grilli, and Milesi-Ferretti (1994) list four main motives for the use of capital controls: to limit volatile capital flows; to maintain the domestic tax base; to retain domestic savings; and to sustain structural reform.

Issues of structural reform will be treated in the next chapter. As maintaining the domestic tax base and retaining domestic savings are variants of the same general point, we consider here only two basic arguments: preventing capital outflows on average; and reducing the volatility of capital flows.

The second argument on volatility concerns very short-term capital flows and is motivated largely by the desire to insulate domestic markets from external shocks, possibly by means of differential treatment of short-term and long-term flows. Volatility of capital flows is seen as inducing volatility in exchange rates, a concern illustrated, for example, by the recent large inflows and subsequent outflows in Latin America in the late 1980s and early 1990s (culminating in the Mexican crisis of late 1994) or the even more recent turmoil in Asian financial markets. As such, this motivation for restricting capital flows turns on the costs of volatility, already discussed (albeit briefly) at the beginning of Section 12.2. By limiting the volatility of short-term capital flows, capital controls are also used to defend a fixed exchange rate regime, especially when it is inconsistent with current monetary and fiscal policies. The possibility of self-fulfilling speculative attacks even when the fundamentals are not inconsistent with the peg provides a further motivation for the imposition of controls on a nonpermanent basis. These issues were discussed in Section 12.3 above.

Having already discussed exchange rate issues, we concentrate on capital controls motivated by the desire to prevent capital outflows. From both an economic and a political point of view, the fiscal motive, namely, to maintain the domestic tax base for capital taxation, is especially important. We already touched on this motive in Section 12.5 in discussing the setting of capital tax policy in the presence of possible tax competition. There we assumed that the barriers to capital mobility were *not* due to government policy, governments choosing optimal tax policy taking the degree of capital mobility as given. Here, our focus is on policies that affect the degree of mobility as part tax revenue maximization. More specifically, the revenue motive reflects governments' attempts to collect revenue from financial repression, a point stressed by Giovannini and de Melo (1993), Aizenman and Guidotti (1994), and Alesina, Grilli, and Milesi-Ferretti (1994). For example, restrictions on holding assets denominated in foreign currency increase the base for the inflation tax. Another political dimension is that use of capital controls may reflect the strength of the government, or the general degree of social conflict and lack of cooperation among interest groups. Weak governments may resort to capital controls as a device for raising revenues if they lack the power to gain agreement on the imposition of other, presumably less distortionary, means of taxation.

Though restrictions on capital outflows are often used to increase the domestic tax base, the connection is not quite so simple. From a purely economic point of view, the removal of binding controls on capital outflows should lead to a capital outflow. As already indicated, however, many countries that have removed controls on *out*flows have experienced rapid and massive *in*flows of capital. A frequently advanced explanation, following Dooley and Isard (1980), is that controls which prevent investors from withdrawing capital from a host country act like investment irreversibility; their removal provides flexibility that makes investors more willing to bring capital into a country. This story is incomplete, for it gives no basis for the expectation that current policies will continue in the future, which is crucial to the argument. We address this issue below.

There is another reason why the connection between capital controls and capital accumulation is not simple. Empirically, capital controls have allowed governments to impose high reserve requirements to widen the revenue base. However, as Drazen (1989) points out, these measures may be detrimental to capital accumulation in the long run, because they imply that banks charge higher interest rates on loans, thus discouraging capital accumulation.

Empirical Determinants

Grilli and Milesi-Ferretti (1995) present empirical results on a large number of possible determinants of capital controls, as well as considering their political effects. They use a zero–one dummy variable across 20 OECD countries measuring whether capital controls are in place or not, based on the classification in the IMF's "Restrictions on Payments on Capital Transactions." They then regress this index on institutional and political factors, as in the work of Grilli, Masciandaro, and Tabellini (1991) discussed in Chapter 7, in the attempt to discover determinants of imposition of controls. They also regress macroeconomic outcomes on this dummy and a host of other possible explanatory variables.

The fiscal motive receives support, as they find that, empirically, inflation and seigniorage revenue are significantly higher in the presence of capital controls. In contrast to the simple association of government weakness and use of controls, however, they find that controls are more likely to be imposed by governments that have a relatively free hand over monetary policy, that is, when the central bank is not very independent. When the monetary authority is weak, governments can use controls to keep interest rates artificially low without interference of the central bank.

If capital controls are effectively used for financial repression, their use should have a significant *negative* effect on debt accumulation, a result for which Grilli and Milesi-Ferretti find empirical support. As already indicated, capital controls may serve not only to increase tax revenues via the seigniorage effect, making it easier to finance spending without debt accumulation, but also to keep real interest rates on government debt artificially low by limiting international arbitrage in asset markets. They find significant evidence that capital controls are associated with lower domestic interest rates, after controlling for the level of domestic debt.

Bartolini and Drazen (1997b) extend the approach of Grilli and Milesi-Ferretti to a sample of 73 developing countries over the period 1970–1994, constructing an index of restrictions on capital outflows. They concentrate on a single macroeconomic variable, the real interest rate in industrial countries, measured as an average of G-7 long-term nominal rates minus inflation rates. In a yearly time-series bivariate regression, they find a striking positive correlation, with the regression giving an r^2 of .65. They interpret as follows. A key determinant of the decision to liberalize the capital account across developing countries is the cost of liberalization, meaning the expected outflow in the case of removal of restrictions on outflows when world interest rates are high.

Partisan Conflict

Alesina and Tabellini (1989) present a model with an explicit theoretical link between the determinants of tax policy and the use of capital controls.[24] There are two factors, labor and capital; two groups, workers and capitalists; and two parties, each representing one of the groups. By assumption, each group's income is specialized to one factor—workers own no capital, while capitalists supply no labor—so that the parties that represent the groups have very different optimal policies regarding factor taxation. The accumulation of foreign assets is a way to avoid the risk of future taxation. Hence, the fear of a future left-wing government favoring labor could induce capital flight, so that a left-wing government would thus be inclined to impose capital controls.

Another partisan argument concerns inflation. For a number of the reasons discussed in Chapter 7, governments may have different preferences for inflation, depending on their ideological bent. If a left-wing government prefers higher public spending, it will prefer higher levels of seigniorage, and hence, given our earlier arguments, be more likely to impose controls. To the extent that controls allow a more inflationary policy without capital flight, preferences for different rates of inflation not related to seigniorage could also induce a partisan difference in the propensity to impose capital controls. If a left-wing party is more concerned about unemployment than a right-wing party and perceives a short-run inflation–unemployment trade-off, it may be more likely to impose controls. On the other hand, to the extent that inflation is a regressive form of taxation, a left-wing government may favor it less than a right-wing government.

---

[24] Checchi (1996) presents another type of model of politically motivated capital controls focusing on a conflict of interests between unions, firms, investors, and the government.

Capital Account Liberalization as a Signal

Bartolini and Drazen (1997a, 1997b) suggest that the effect of capital controls may stem from their role as a signal of future government behavior. If investors have imperfect information about a government's intentions and constraints, they will use the observation of current policies toward investment to infer the course of *future* policies. Specifically, a regime of free capital mobility may signal that imposition of controls is less likely to occur in the future and, more generally, that future policies are likely to be more favorable to investment.

We present here the intuitive argument, referring interested readers to the articles for the details of the precise technical formulation. In Bartolini and Drazen (1997a), the ultimate purpose of capital controls is to widen the tax base, consistent with the arguments given above. Countries with poorly developed tax systems often rely heavily on revenues from financial repression; countries that have nondistortionary revenue sources do not have to use capital controls to "trap" capital onshore. In their model, it is precisely a government that is most dependent on such a tax base that imposes controls, even though this may lead to a *lower expected* tax base. How exactly does this work? Investors have imperfect information about the government's revenue constraints and hence about whether it will impose capital controls in the future. Hence, the government's "type" is unobserved. Future imposition of controls on outflows, by making it more difficult to take capital out of the country, makes it less attractive to invest in the country currently. This gives "good" governments (specifically, those who have learned they will have little need to impose controls in the future) the incentive to allow free capital mobility in order to provide a good signal on future investment policies. If the signal is successful, capital flows in.

If adoption of a regime of free capital mobility is expected to lead to a capital inflow, why would a government most in need of these inflows not attempt to take advantage of this? That is, why is liberalization an informative signal in equilibrium? (Formally, the question is why a separating equilibrium prevails, rather than a pooling equilibrium in which all governments choose not to impose controls.) Thus, the key to the paper is showing that some governments choose to impose capital controls, *even though they know this is interpreted as a negative signal.*

The argument behind this result is straightforward. Consider a government that raises revenue from several sources, including capital taxation, to finance its expenditures. When welfare is highly concave in the level of expenditures, low expenditures imply very low welfare. If revenues (and hence expenditures) have a stochastic component, a government that foresees low revenues from other sources will therefore be especially sensitive to the possibility of low capital tax collection. It will then impose controls to insure itself against bad states of nature (when capital would flow out), thereby assuring a minimum level of revenues in *all* states of nature, even though, by imposing controls, it forgoes higher revenues on average. In a separating equilibrium, the observation of capital controls today raises the likelihood of capital controls in the future, for the government has revealed its inclination (or need) to use controls. The opposite is true for the adoption of an open capital account, which raises investors' confidence in their future ability to withdraw from the host country and thus may induce a capital inflow.

In Bartolini and Drazen (1997b), the argument is extended to simultaneous signaling by a group of countries, the focus being on external events that lead to opening the capital account in a signaling model. Specifically, the informativeness of a policy of free capital mobility depends on the path of world interest rates. Capital flows to "emerging markets" reflect investors' expectations of these countries' future policies and of world interest rates. With low interest rates, emerging markets experience a capital inflow and engage in a widespread policy of free capital mobility; with higher rates, only sufficiently committed countries allow free capital mobility, whereas others impose controls to trap capital onshore, thereby providing investors with a signal of future policies affecting capital mobility.

The argument can be applied to structural reform in general, as will be relevant to the issues treated in the next chapter. In deciding on policy reforms, the trade-off between costs and benefits depends on external circumstances. "Good" times reduce the costs of reforms and may induce their widespread adoption; "bad" times mean that only sufficiently motivated governments reform. Hence, if it is a favorable macroeconomic environment that leads many countries to adopt reforms, investors will be unable to distinguish governments truly committed to reform from those likely to renege on them in less favorable times. Conversely, the environment may be so unfavorable that no government implements reforms, making investors similarly unable to gather information on each country's commitment to reform (and hence on likely *future* policies) from the observation of *current* policies. Away from the two extremes, there is a separating equilibrium, so that current policies are informative about future policies. We return to these issues in the next chapter.

Technically, both papers use the stochastic version of Rogoff's (1987) model of reneging on a commitment presented at the end of Section 6.7 of Chapter 6. For example, in Bartolini and Drazen (1997b), it is assumed that the government assigns a one-time cost ζ to imposing controls for the first time, analogous to a one-time cost to breaking a commitment to zero inflation. ζ is not known to investors. There is a cut-off type ζ_t^o who is indifferent between imposing and not imposing controls at t; as in the stochastic version of the model of reneging on a commitment, the value of ζ_t^o depends on the realization of a shock, the stochastic world interest rate

r_t. The solution of the model, as in Chapter 6, is a sequence of the ζ_t^o, which may then be used to calculate the probability of controls being imposed in any period. The evolution of reputation thus depends on the observed history of policy, the current policy choice, and the realization of the stochastic shock.

While the intuition for these results is similar to that for other signaling models, the model has the interesting feature that the nature of the equilibrium (in particular, whether it is a pooling or separating equilibrium) varies over time in response to external shocks (an interest rate shock in this case). In the model, investors know the process driving interest rates, rationally anticipate potential changes in the type of equilibrium, and incorporate this knowledge in their investment decisions.

12.8. SOVEREIGN BORROWING

Issues of sovereign debt, namely, the debt owed by a government to foreign creditors, and its repayment is a major issue in international political economy. It is highly topical in light of the debt crisis of the early 1980s, in which numerous highly indebted countries rescheduled their debts, and similar crises in the 1990s.[25] There are two key features that distinguish sovereign debt from ordinary debt owed by nongovernment entities. First, the question of repayment is not connected with any question of the ability to repay. With few exceptions, a borrower country has the technical ability to repay the debt, so that non-repayment is a political issue, rather than one forced on a country by the infeasibility of repayment. Second, as Bulow and Rogoff (1989b) put it, collateral in the strict sense used in domestic debt contracts is "irrelevant." The assets of debtor countries that a creditor could reasonably seize in the event of default are generally worth only a fraction of outstanding debt. There are limited assets abroad and creditors cannot realistically seize assets within the debtor country.

Taken together, these two facts imply that for both debtors and creditors, issues connected with the decision to repay are substantially different than those concerning nonsovereign debt. The fact that sovereign debt contracts appear to be in an almost constant process of renegotiation are but one piece of evidence on the implications of this difference. Two key (closely) related questions then appear to be: what are the incentives for a

---

[25] Because of space limitations, we do not cover the empirical specifics of recent debt crises, nor institutional solutions that were devised to address the crises. The literature is enormous. Interested readers are referred to Sachs (1989b) for an excellent mixture of conceptual and applied studies, which includes Sachs (1989a). We also do not consider the role of international organizations in dealing with solutions to recent debt crises, but do consider adjustment lending by such organizations in Section 12.9 below, with some connections to problems of excessive debt.

debtor country to repay its sovereign debt? And, what is the optimal response of a creditor to non-repayment? In this section, we consider a number of issues connected with sovereign debt and these questions. The seminal paper in this area is Eaton and Gersovitz (1981). Bulow and Rogoff (1989a, 1989b) are extremely important contributions that also put political economy issues of sovereign debt in perspective. Eaton (1993) and Eaton and Fernandez (1995) provide excellent summaries.

Explicit Penalties for Default

We begin with explicit penalties for default by a sovereign government. As seizure of the sovereign's assets is not relevant, these penalties reflect the ability of creditors to impede or disrupt the international trade of a country that unilaterally defaults, preventing it from enjoying the gains from trade. As in many of our earlier models, it is the *threat* of punishment that is important. Punishment may never be carried out in equilibrium, but the threat of punishment will determine characteristics of contract.

We illustrate the basic results with a simple example based on Obstfeld and Rogoff (1996), in which sovereign borrowing is motivated by the desire to insure risk-averse citizens against country-specific shocks. They consider a two-period, representative-agent endowment model in which the representative individual consumes only in the second period, so that lifetime utility is the expected utility of second-period consumption as seen from period 1, namely, $\Omega(c_2) = Eu(c_2)$, where $u(\cdot)$ is a standard concave function. The first-period endowment, which equals first-period consumption, is zero, which implies that there is no saving or dissaving in the first period; the only activity in the first period is entering into insurance contracts with foreign insurers since second-period output is uncertain. Specifically, as of period 1, second-period output is $y_2 = \bar{y} + \epsilon$, where ϵ is a mean-zero shock specific to the home country with realizations $\underline{\epsilon} = \epsilon^1 < \epsilon^2 < \cdots < \epsilon^N = \bar{\epsilon}$ and $\bar{y} + \underline{\epsilon} > 0$. A realization ϵ_i occurs with probability $q(\epsilon_i)$.

The country can buy insurance abroad, where an insurance contract has a payment schedule $\mathscr{P}(\epsilon)$ to the insurer, which may be positive or negative. A positive value of $\mathscr{P}(\epsilon)$ is a premium the (home) country pays, a negative value a payout it receives. Insurers are risk neutral, so that in equilibrium, contracts must have zero expected profits, that is, $\sum_i^N q(\epsilon^i)\mathscr{P}(\epsilon^i) = 0$. For simplicity, assume for now that there is no possibility of rescheduling repayments, that is, no renegotiation of contracts.

As a point of reference, we first consider full insurance, which would be relevant if there were no risk of default. A borrower could commit itself to any contract such that $y_2 \geq \mathscr{P}(\epsilon)$, for all ϵ. The obvious contract is one where $\mathscr{P}(\epsilon) = \epsilon$, implying $c_2(\epsilon) = y_2 - \mathscr{P}(\epsilon) = \bar{y}$. However, a country that signs such a contract with insurers has an incentive to default when $\epsilon > 0$, that is, no incentive to make a payment in the second period if a good state of nature is realized, unless there is a cost to default. Formally, there is a problem of incentive compatibility, as discussed in Section 2.2 of Chapter 2. Let us therefore consider costs of default and incentive-compatible contracts.

The cost of default is that creditors impose trade sanctions of various sorts or the seizure of assets held abroad, where it is assumed for simplicity that a country loses a fraction α of output in the event of default. For an insurance contract to be incentive compatible, three conditions must be satisfied. First, the payment schedule $\mathcal{P}(\epsilon)$ satisfies an incentive-compatibility condition for *each* realization of ϵ, implying the insured is willing to pay the premium. Given the penalty for default, the incentive-compatibility condition is

$$\mathcal{P}(\epsilon^i) \leq \alpha(\bar{y} + \epsilon^i), \quad \forall i. \tag{12.45}$$

Second, the zero-profit condition for insurers, namely, $\sum_i^N q(\epsilon^i)\mathcal{P}(\epsilon^i) = 0$, must be satisfied. Third, the contract must be optimal for the insured country, given (12.45) and the zero-profit condition. Formally, this may be expressed as saying that the optimal incentive-compatible insurance contract maximizes $\sum_i^N q(\epsilon^i)\Omega(c_2(\epsilon^i))$ subject to (12.45), the zero-profit condition, and the N budget constraints:

$$c_2(\epsilon^i) = \bar{y} + \epsilon^i - \mathcal{P}(\epsilon^i). \tag{12.46}$$

Substituting (12.45) into the maximand, we write the objective as

$$
\begin{aligned}
\Omega = &\sum_{i=1}^N q(\epsilon^i)u(\bar{y} + \epsilon^i - \mathcal{P}(\epsilon^i)) \\
&- \sum_{i=1}^N \lambda(\epsilon^i)[\mathcal{P}(\epsilon^i) - \alpha(\bar{y} + \epsilon^i)] \\
&+ \mu \sum_{i=1}^N q(\epsilon^i)\mathcal{P}(\epsilon^i),
\end{aligned}
\tag{12.47}
$$

where λ and μ are Lagrange multipliers. Differentiating with respect to $\mathcal{P}(\epsilon^i)$ for each i, one obtains first-order conditions:

$$q(\epsilon^i)u'(c_2(\epsilon^i)) + \lambda(\epsilon^i) = \mu q(\epsilon^i), \tag{12.48}$$

(one condition for each ϵ_i) as well as complementary slackness conditions:

$$\lambda(\epsilon^i)[\alpha(\bar{y} + \epsilon^i) - \mathcal{P}(\epsilon^i)] = 0. \tag{12.49}$$

The multiplier $\lambda(\epsilon^i)$ is zero when the incentive-compatibility condition (12.45) holds with strict inequality. Nonzero $\lambda(\epsilon^i)$ induce unequal consumption across states according to (12.48).

What will an optimal contract look like in the presence of penalties for default? Following Obstfeld and Rogoff, we illustrate the nature of the contract by considering, for simplicity, the case where ϵ is continuous. For sufficiently low realizations of ϵ, the incentive-compatibility condition (12.45) will not bind, so that $\lambda(\epsilon) = 0$, implying constant c_2, irrespective of ϵ. In this case, (12.46) then implies $\mathscr{P}(\epsilon) = \mathscr{P}_0 + \epsilon$ for some constant $\mathscr{P}_0$. Hence, when $\lambda(\epsilon) = 0, c_2(\epsilon) = \bar{y} - \mathscr{P}_0$, where $\mathscr{P}_0$ is defined by $u'(\bar{y} - \mathscr{P}_0) = \mu$. Equations (12.46) and (12.48) then imply that, in states where (12.45) holds with equality, we have

$$u'(\bar{y} - \mathscr{P}_0) - u'(c_2(\epsilon)) = u'(\bar{y} - \mathscr{P}_0) - u'(\bar{y} + \epsilon - \mathscr{P}(\epsilon))$$

$$= u'(\bar{y} - \mathscr{P}_0) - u'((1 - \alpha)(\bar{y} - \epsilon))$$

$$= \frac{\lambda(\epsilon)}{q(\epsilon)} \geq 0. \tag{12.50}$$

Since the left-hand side of the last equality falls as ϵ falls, there exists a critical value of ϵ, call it $\hat{\epsilon}$, such that $u'(\bar{y} - \mathscr{P}_0) - u'((1 - \alpha)(\bar{y} - \hat{\epsilon})) = 0$, so that $\lambda(\epsilon) = 0$ is just satisfied at $\epsilon = \hat{\epsilon}$. For $\epsilon > \hat{\epsilon}$, $\lambda(\epsilon) > 0$ and $\mathscr{P}(\epsilon) = \alpha(\bar{y} + \epsilon)$, while for $\epsilon < \hat{\epsilon}$, $\lambda(\epsilon) = 0$ and $\mathscr{P}(\epsilon) = \mathscr{P}_0 + \epsilon$. Therefore, for $\epsilon = \hat{\epsilon}, \bar{y} - \mathscr{P}_0 = (1 - \alpha)(\bar{y} + \hat{\epsilon})$, so that $\mathscr{P}_0 = \alpha\bar{y} - (1 - \alpha)\hat{\epsilon}$. The payment schedule may then be written

$$\mathscr{P}(\epsilon) = \begin{cases} \alpha(\bar{y} + \hat{\epsilon}) + (\epsilon - \hat{\epsilon}) & \text{for } \epsilon < \hat{\epsilon}, \\ \alpha(\bar{y} + \hat{\epsilon}) + \alpha(\epsilon - \hat{\epsilon}) & \text{for } \epsilon > \hat{\epsilon}. \end{cases} \tag{12.51}$$

$\hat{\epsilon}$ is tied down by the zero-profit condition, requiring that expected positive payments equal expected negative payments. Below $\hat{\epsilon}$, payments $\mathscr{P}(\epsilon)$ rise one-for-one with ϵ, and consumption is $(1 - \alpha)(\bar{y} + \hat{\epsilon})$, below the first-best $\bar{y}$. Above $\hat{\epsilon}$, the incentive-compatibility constraint is binding. Payments rise less than proportionally to increases in ϵ; consumption is $(1 - \alpha)(\bar{y} + \epsilon)$, greater than the first-best level for sufficiently high ϵ. These characteristics of the payment schedule above $\hat{\epsilon}$ reflect the need for the contract to satisfy the incentive-compatibility constraint. The repayment schedule is illustrated in Figure 12.2.

Intuitively, the nature of the repayment schedule may be understood as follows. For low ϵ, there are no incentive-compatibility problems, so that full consumption smoothing can be achieved. For high ϵ, however, the temptation to default is too great under full insurance. The optimal contract therefore requires that only a portion α of the positive output shock be transferred to creditors. However, the limitation on how much a

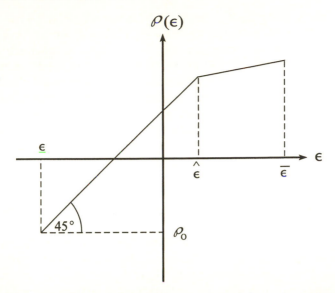

FIGURE 12.2. The incentive compatible payment schedule.

country can be required to transfer in a good state in order not to be tempted by default reduces the level of consumption that insurers can transfer in bad states, as creditors must make zero expected profits.

Note further that in equilibrium, no default takes place in any state of the world and the punishment of trade sanctions is never invoked. However, the severity of the threatened punishment (the size of α) is crucial in determining the nature of the equilibrium. The more severe is the punishment for default, meaning the larger is α, the larger is the range of ϵ over which a country can smooth consumption. As α approaches 1, the country can get closer to full consumption smoothing, implying higher expected utility. Extremely harsh punishments increase welfare because they allow a country to credibly commit to no default. This is similar to the models of Section 6.3 of Chapter 6, in which extremely harsh penalties for deviation can enforce good equilibria. The similarity in results is not surprising, as both the model presented here and the previous models assumed complete information about the temptation to deviate, or, in this case, default on borrowing.

There are at least two crucial ways in which this modeling of sovereign debt repayment is incomplete, both paralleling issues discussed in Chapter 6. First, implicit in the notion that harsh punishments increase welfare is the assumption that default can always be avoided if a country so desires. This reflects, among other things, the underlying presumption that with sovereign debt repayment, the basic problem is willingness rather than ability to repay, implying a credibility problem that the threat of punishment helps to mitigate. Formally, default in the model is a potential problem only in *good* times. In actual fact, default may reflect negative shocks, that is, very *bad* times, which call into question the ability to repay, or at least the political infeasibility of transferring resources abroad in the face of a severe negative shock at home. Once default may be unavoidable in some states of nature, it will generally not be the case that harsher punishments imply unambiguously higher expected welfare. There is a trade-off, harsh punishments increasing welfare if credibility is the problem, but reducing welfare if severe negative shocks are anticipated. This trade-off very much parallels similar trade-offs found earlier in the chapter: the trade-off between commitment to low inflation and flexibility to respond to shocks in the decision to join a monetary union in Section 12.4; and the gains and losses from international policy cooperation discussed in Section 12.5.

The possibility that a country may be forced into default and that harsh penalties for doing so may not be optimal raises a second problem with these simple insurance contracts. In deriving the results, it was assumed that penalties would always be enforced if a country defaults. In fact, rescheduling of interest payments, that is, the renegotiation of contracts, is quite common; one might say it is a defining characteristic of sovereign borrowing. When default actually occurs, creditors find it optimal to renegotiate the debt contract, rather than invoke sanctions. In the language of Chapter 6, carrying out the threatened punishment is not subgame perfect. Equilibria that depend on threats of trade sanctions which are not optimal to carry out are therefore suspect. We discuss below rescheduling of sovereign debt on the part of profit-maximizing creditors. Optimal punishment by sovereign *lenders*, either governments or international financial institutions, will also be central to our analysis of the politics of foreign aid in Section 12.9 below.

Exclusion from World Capital Markets

Suppose that there are no direct sanctions or costs that can be imposed on a defaulting country, but that its desire to have access to world capital markets is ongoing. Can reputational considerations, whereby a country that defaults is punished in the future by facing future capital market restrictions, enforce a no-default equilibrium? Prior to the late-1980s, it was widely believed that the threat of being cut off from further borrowing would induce a country to repay its debt. Bulow and Rogoff (1989a) showed convincingly that this is not the case, with Chari and Kehoe (1989) presenting a similar result. We illustrated the result by means of an example in Section 6.5 of Chapter 6. We demonstrate the argument more formally here, though the substance of the argument is identical to that given in the earlier chapter.

As in the previous subsection, consider a country with a stochastic income stream in which the government borrows abroad to smooth consumption of its citizens. Unlike that model, however, suppose that foreign creditors *cannot* punish default by trade sanctions or seizure of assets. The only punishment for default is that a country cannot borrow in the future with the sort of contract discussed in the previous section, which Bulow and Rogoff term a "reputation" contract. It can, however, lend abroad to smooth consumption in a "cash-in-advance" contract as follows. It makes a cash payout up front in exchange for receiving a (nonnegative), state-contingent payback next period, where the up-front payout is equal to the expected value of the payback it will receive next period. This payoff structure could arise, for example, if the borrowing country bought foreign assets whose payoffs were state contingent and negatively correlated with home income.

To make this argument precise, let the representative agent in a country have stochastic income $y_t = y(\epsilon_t)$ each period. The expected present discounted value of the stream of income is

$$E_t W_t = E_t \sum_{s=t}^{\infty} \frac{y(\epsilon_s)}{(1+r)^{s-t}}, \tag{12.52}$$

where r is the constant real interest rate. The expected present discounted value of repayments in a reputation contract is

$$E_t D_t = E_t \sum_{s=t}^{\infty} \frac{\mathscr{P}(\epsilon_s)}{(1+r)^{s-t}}. \tag{12.53}$$

For the contract to be feasible, D_t cannot exceed W_t for any realization of ϵ. That is, there must exist a constant κ, $0 \le \kappa \le 1$, such that, with probability 1 for all t and all ϵ,

$$D_t \le \kappa W_t, \tag{12.54}$$

where we assume κ is the smallest value such that a relation such as (12.54) holds.

If the country is not excluded from lending in international capital markets even after default on a reputation contract, it can still insure itself by writing a "cash-in-advance" contract in which it makes an up-front payment of A_t at the end of period t and receives a state-contingent repayment of $\mathscr{P}_{t+1}(\epsilon_{t+1})$ in $t+1$. Even if the sovereign offering the contract has defaulted in the past, a risk-neutral foreign investor will accept such a contract as long as the expected return equals the market return:

$$E_t(\mathscr{P}_{t+1}(\epsilon_{t+1})) = (1 + r)A_t. \qquad (12.55)$$

Moreover, there can be no state of nature in which the country is required to make a positive payment in $t + 1$:

$$(\mathscr{P}_{t+1}(\epsilon_{t+1})) \geq 0, \quad \forall \, \epsilon_{t+1}. \qquad (12.56)$$

By an arbitrage argument, Bulow and Rogoff prove that when it is possible to write cash-in-advance contracts, reputation contracts cannot be sustained in equilibrium, as there exist states of nature in which a country will default with certainty. That is, there exists a sufficiently good state of nature in which the country defaults on its reputation contract and uses the payment it would have made to foreign creditors to write a cash-in-advance contract. The proof consists of constructing a cash-in-advance contract in a good state of nature in which the country transfers less abroad in every state of nature in the ensuing period. The formal proof is as follows. Suppose that at time $s, y_s = y(\epsilon_s)$ is large so that $D_s < \kappa W_s$, but that $D_s > \kappa(W_s - y_s)$. The country then ceases payment on its reputation contract and uses $\mathscr{P}(\epsilon_s)$ instead to write a reputation contract with the following characteristics:

$$A_s(\epsilon_s) = \mathscr{P}(\epsilon_s) + \kappa(W_s - y(\epsilon_s)) - D_s, \qquad (12.57)$$

for the period-s up-front payment. For all periods $t > s$,

$$A_t(\epsilon_t) = \mathscr{P}_t(\epsilon_t) + \mathscr{P}(\epsilon_t) - \kappa y(\epsilon_t), \quad \forall \, \epsilon_t, \qquad (12.58)$$

$$\mathscr{P}_t(\epsilon_t) = \kappa W_t(\epsilon_t) - D_t(\epsilon_t), \quad \forall \, \epsilon_t. \qquad (12.59)$$

This contract must satisfy (12.55) and (12.56). The latter is satisfied, given (12.59); substituting iterated versions of (12.52) and (12.53) into (12.57) through (12.59), one can show that (12.55) is satisfied. In period s, the country makes a payment of $A_s < \mathscr{P}_s$, and in periods $t > s$, a net payment of $A_t - \mathscr{P}_t = \mathscr{P}_t - \kappa y_t < \mathscr{P}_t$. Hence, a reputation contract must include some state of nature in which the country is better off by defaulting and using the payment as initial collateral for a sequence of cash-in-advance contracts to smooth consumption.

In understanding the Bulow and Rogoff result, it is crucial to make a distinction between being cut off from renewed borrowing but being allowed to lend and being cut off entirely from international credit markets, both borrowing *and lending*, that is, being forced into complete financial autarky. The Bulow–Rogoff argument is that cutting off access to borrowing alone cannot enforce repayment (their "reputation contracts") if lending (that is, the ability to write "cash-in-advance" insurance contracts in international markets) is still allowed. Though their result has been misinterpreted to say that the threat of being cut off from all financial transactions cannot enforce repayment, their paper does not address that issue.

Autarky

Eaton (1993), among others, argues that it is unrealistic to assume that if a sovereign debtor defaults, it can still enforce a loan contract with a foreign borrower. The alternative to enforcement of contracts in both directions should not be enforcement in one direction (that is, for foreign lending but not borrowing), but enforcement in neither direction. That is, default on borrowing abroad will imply not only that foreign lenders will not lend to the borrower again but also that foreign lending by the borrower may itself not be repaid. Hence, he argues, default should be seen as leading to total financial autarky.

Grossman and Van Huyck (1988) and Chari and Kehoe (1989) show that the threat of being forced into autarky can enforce repayment of international loans, even without other explicit penalties. Chari and Kehoe, for example, consider a model in which the government borrows to smooth tax distortions in the face of random government expenditure. (For the basic result about when reputation can enforce repayment, it does not matter whether the government smooths utility via smoothing tax distortions in a model with labor supply or via smoothing consumption in a model without labor supply, as in the above example.) The results mirror our earlier results on using reputation to enforce "good behavior." For a sufficiently high discount factor, the threat of being forced into autarky, where utility fluctuates with government expenditure, can enforce repayment of sovereign debt. Not surprisingly, this result depends on the extent of variability of utility in autarky, that is, in the absence of utility smoothing. If utility is not too variable in autarky, then an equilibrium with repayment *cannot* be supported. Intuitively, in this case the benefit from access to international capital markets relative to autarky is not large enough to induce a country to repay its debts in all possible states, rather than being cut off. Furthermore, if randomness is high, but it is known that it will damp out, a reputational equilibrium can also not be supported. Suppose that at some T, the government believes it will face no further randomness in its expenditures. It can do no better than defaulting on its debt at T and balancing its budget forever after. But investors who realize that this is the government's optimal behavior will not lend at $T - 1$, so that the government will find it optimal to default at $T - 1$, and so on, so that the equilibrium unravels backwards.

Another way in which reputational considerations could enforce repayment is if there is a "spillover" of bad reputation from one area to another, a point conjectured by Bulow and Rogoff (1989a) and investigated by Cole and Kehoe (1996). They consider a reputational model with multiple relationships between debtors and creditors and spillovers between them and show that concern for reputation will *not* support borrowing if reputation spills over to other relationships with only transient benefits, but will if reputation spills over to a relationship with enduring benefits.

Rescheduling of Sovereign Debt

Rescheduling of payments on loans to banks by sovereign borrowers is extremely common. Bargaining between debtors and creditors over the flow of payments is basically ongoing. Hence, as Bulow and Rogoff (1989b) stress, renegotiation is a crucial feature of any complete model of sovereign borrowing. We present an intuitive discussion of their results, referring readers to the original article for technical details.

Suppose that creditors can impose various sorts of trade sanctions in the event of default. If they could commit themselves to "take-it-or-leave-it" offers (that is, commit themselves to no renegotiation in the event of default), the maximum a country can borrow will depend on the maximum loss it would suffer in trade autarky or under trade disruptions. With borrowing limited in this way, there will be no default in equilibrium.

When there is the possibility of renegotiation of the loan after a default, a debtor will in general be able to do better. The possibility of renegotiation after a default, and the inability of a defaulting country to precommit not to default and then reschedule in the future, make it far more difficult to calculate borrowing limits under renegotiation. To derive results, Bulow and Rogoff (1989b) use a specific model of bargaining, namely, Rubinstein's (1982) model of alternating offers. In this framework, Bulow and Rogoff consider subgame-perfect equilibria. In a perfect equilibrium of this bargaining game, either party will accept a rescheduling offer that gives it at least as much in present discounted value as it can expect to gain by waiting, given the optimal strategies of both parties. The outcome of bargaining will depend on both the relative patience of the two sides and the world interest rate. One interesting result is that the higher is the world interest rate r, the *less* the country will have to pay in the bargaining region! When world interest rates are high, creditors are anxious to get their money out of the country in order to invest elsewhere, a fact which a defaulting country exploits to its advantage. As in our earlier models, there is no debt repudiation in equilibrium, nor, for that matter, any delay in renegotiation. This reflects the assumption of complete information.

Adding asymmetric information would allow the possibility that suspension of payment and exclusion from capital markets is actually observed, but would obviously make modeling far more difficult. Cole, Dow, and English (1995) present a signaling model in which default and subsequent resumption of lending can be observed in equilibrium. The model is meant to explain the relatively quick readmittance of defaulting countries to international capital markets after partial repayment, where settlement of some outstanding claims appeared to be a prerequisite for obtaining new loans. Since settlements could not be legally compelled, they argue that debtors agreed to them to signal their intent to repay future loans. More precisely, there are two types of debtors, one more myopic than the other, with creditors unable to observe type. In equilibrium, the less myopic type services the debt, while the more myopic type defaults. The desire for readmittance is modeled by assuming that government type follows a Markov process, where changes in government type are unobservable. Hence, to signal its new preferences, a government that has become less myopic must make a large enough payment to separate itself from myopic types.

Foreign versus Domestic Debt

Suppose that in the simple punishment model at the beginning of this section, the government could borrow both abroad *and* at home. What are the political factors that determine how much sovereign borrowing to undertake? How will the penalties for default on foreign debt interact with the endogenous repudiation decision on domestic debt, as in Tabellini (1991)? Drazen (1998a) presents a model stressing that the crucial difference between domestic and foreign debt is the differential ability of domestic and foreign residents to "punish" a government that takes actions detrimental to the value of their holdings. This difference implies that effective cost of borrowing at home and abroad may differ substantially, so that the composition of the debt reflects the politically determined terms of borrowing.

The basic results may be derived in a simple two-period framework much like the Tabellini (1991) model in Section 8.6 of Chapter 8. Consider a two-period endowment economy where home and foreign capital markets are segmented. The government thus acts like a discriminating monopsonist in financing its expenditures, issuing either domestic debt b_{US} or foreign debt b_{EU} (both expressed in per capita terms), where it is assumed that all foreign debt comes from official lenders. In the first period, the government issues debt to finance government spending

$$b_{US} + b_{EU} = g, \qquad (12.60)$$

and repays the principal and interest, financing these payments by a tax which is uniform across all individuals. Denoting the interest rates (more exactly, one plus the interest rate) actually paid on domestic and foreign debt by R_{US} and R_{EU}, respectively, the second-period government budget constraint can be written

$$R_{US}b_{US} + R_{EU}b_{EU} = \tau, \qquad (12.61)$$

where τ is a nondistortionary tax in per capita terms, assumed equal across individuals. Repudiation of foreign borrowing is defined as repaying R_{EU} per dollar of debt below the world interest rate R^*, which can be thought of as the rate originally contracted. This brings on a perfectly anticipated penalty of $Z(R^* - R_{EU})$ per dollar of foreign debt b_{EU}, where $Z(\cdot)$ is an increasing, weakly concave function, and where $Z(0) = 0$. The nature of the penalty is determined by the foreign official lender; it may be a monetary penalty assessed *ex post*, or some other penalty that reduces utility. The latter is assumed, though in this framework, these two ways of modeling the penalty will be equivalent. The penalty implies a total effective cost of foreign borrowing of $R_{EU} + Z(R^* - R_{EU})$, which may be less than R^*, depending on the nature of the penalty function $Z(\cdot)$. Determination of the domestic interest factor R_{US} is discussed below.

Individuals live two periods and differ in their first-period endowment ξ, distributed in the population according to a cumulative distribution function $F(\xi)$, defined over $(0, \infty)$. Individuals have identical second-period endowments $\hat{\xi}$, assumed, for simplicity, to be at least as great as any second-period tax liabilities. For simplicity and without loss of generality, it is assumed they have perfect foresight about R_{US} and R_{EU}. The representative individual's utility function is identical to (12.31), but with the addition of the default penalty $Z(\cdot)$:

$$\Omega_{US} = u(c_1) + c_2 + h(g) - Z(R^* - R_{EU})b_{EU}. \qquad (12.62)$$

The budget constraints are

$$c_1 = \xi - s,$$
$$c_2 = R_{US}s + \hat{\xi} - \tau, \qquad (12.63)$$

where saving $s(\xi, R_{US})$ is constrained to be nonnegative. The linearity of the utility function in c_2 implies that saving will be zero for $\xi < u'^{(-1)}(R_{US})$, and rise one-for-one with ξ thereafter, as in (12.34).

The economic specification of the model is closed by a condition for domestic capital market equilibrium, namely, that the sum of individual saving is equal to the stock of debt (expressed in per capita terms):

$$b_{US} = \int_{\xi=0}^{\infty} s(\xi, R_{US}) \, dF(\xi). \qquad (12.64)$$

To derive the political equilibrium, one first derives an individual's most preferred fiscal policy and then aggregates preferences over all individuals. One may easily show that the conditions of the Median Voter Theorem are satisfied for this model, so that equilibrium fiscal policy will reflect the preferences of the median voter, who will turn out to be the individual with the median first-period endowment, ξ^{med}. From (12.62), the utility of the median voter may be written

$$\Omega^{\text{med}} = u\big(\xi^{\text{med}} - s(\xi^{\text{med}}, R_{US})\big) + R_{US}s(\xi^{\text{med}}, R_{US}) + \hat{\xi}$$
$$- \tau + h(g) - Z(R^* - R_{EU})b_{EU}. \tag{12.65}$$

The equilibrium values for g, R_{EU}, and R_{US} are found by differentiating (12.65) with respect to these three variables, subject to (12.60), (12.61), and (12.63). One obtains for g, R_{EU}, and R_{US}, respectively,

$$h'(g) = R_{EU} + Z(R^* - R_{EU}) \quad (< R^* \text{ for } Z'(0) < 1), \tag{12.66}$$

$$Z'(R^* - R_{EU}) = 1, \tag{12.67}$$

$$R_{US} = (R_{EU} + Z) + \frac{s(\xi^{\text{med}}, R_{US}) - b_{US}(R_{US})}{s'(\xi^{\text{med}}, R_{US})\big(1 - F\big[\xi^{\text{med}} - s(\xi^{\text{med}}, R_{US})\big]\big)}. \tag{12.68}$$

These equations have a simple interpretation. Equation (12.66) equates the marginal utility of government spending to its effective cost. As debt is financed by borrowing, its cost is the relevant interest factor, represented by the right-hand side of (12.65). A country that faces a low cost of repudiating its foreign debt will choose not only higher foreign borrowing to finance its expenditure, but higher government expenditure as well. Equation (12.67) determines the relevant interest factor, the net effective cost of foreign borrowing. A country will choose how much to repay, that is, R_{EU}, to minimize the total cost $R_{EU} + Z$, implying first-order condition (12.67). As long as $Z'(0) < 1$, a country can lower its net cost below R^* by repudiating some of its debt. (For $Z'(0) \geq 1$, $R_{EU} = R^*$.) The more lenient is the penalty for default, as represented by the $Z(\cdot)$ function, the lower will be R_{EU}. The determination of R_{EU} is represented in Figure 12.3.

The domestic interest factor R_{US} in a political-economic equilibrium is that preferred by the median voter,[26] given by (12.68). To rule out problems of time inconsistency, we assume that the government can commit to pay a domestic interest rate. To understand intuitively the

---

[26] Alternative political mechanisms for aggregating the preferences (such as lobbying, where richer voters would in essence have more weight) would yield a different equilibrium interest rate and a different level of domestic debt in equilibrium.

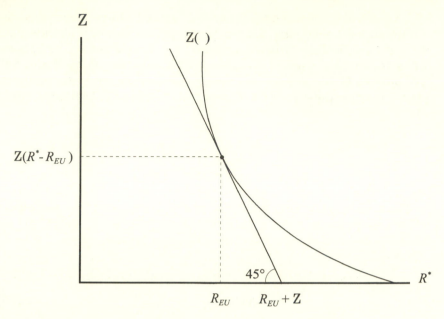

FIGURE 12.3. Political determination of the foreign interest factor.

preferred interest factor in (12.68), consider an individual with zero saving ($\xi < u'^{(-1)}(R_{US})$). In a rational-expectations equilibrium, his preferred interest factor is *not* zero, even though any positive payment on the domestic debt is a transfer of income away from him. A zero interest factor would imply zero domestic saving and zero domestic debt, so that all government spending would have to be financed by foreign borrowing. He would prefer a domestic interest factor that is positive but less than $R_{EU} + Z$ in order to induce positive domestic saving, so that part of desired government spending can be financed at a cost lower than the foreign interest rate. As long as an individual's saving is less than the economywide average, he prefers a domestic interest factor less than the foreign interest cost, due to the implicit income transfer. On the other hand, an individual whose saving is above the economywide average is willing to have a per-unit cost of government spending g above the foreign cost, since the excess represents a transfer to him. An interior preferred interest factor represents trading off the benefit (cost, if saving is below the average) of the transfer implicit in higher interest rates against the cost (benefit) of financing some government spending with domestic debt.

We see that a main determinant of the equilibrium solution would be characteristics of the income distribution. Given the world interest cost, a richer country would finance more of its spending by domestic debt. In a median voter model, a country with an income distribution skewed to the left would finance more of its spending via foreign borrowing than one with a more equal income distribution but the same average income. The lower is the effective foreign borrowing cost, the higher will be desired government spending. Moreover, in a median voter model, this will imply a lower domestic interest rate via (12.68), everything else equal, so the lower will be aggregate domestic saving and debt. Hence, a lower world interest cost implies that the amount a small economy borrows abroad increases, both from the side of desired government expenditure and from the side of lower desired domestic financing of spending. A country which expects to face a low effective foreign interest rate, because it does not expect to be forced to repay its foreign debts in full, will then be characterized by high government spending, a high government budget deficit, low domestic saving, and thus a high trade balance deficit. Put another way, the political feasibility of reneging on foreign debt would imply the domestic economy would look mismanaged in terms of a number of macroeconomic indicators.[27]

12.9. FOREIGN AID

The discussion of sovereign borrowing in the previous section leads naturally into a discussion of foreign assistance, that is, grants or loans that international financial institutions (IFIs) and richer countries give to poorer countries. Our point of departure is the strikingly disappointing results that foreign aid programs have had in alleviating poverty and stimulating growth in the recipient countries. For example, Boone (1996) shows empirically that aid does not significantly increase investment or benefit the poor (as measured by improvements in human development indicators), a general empirical result found by others as well. Similarly, many researchers have found no significant positive effect of aid on growth rates in cross-section studies.

Political factors no doubt play a central role in explaining this failure. (Boone [1996] provides a good overview of the politics of aid.) There are three general political explanations: noneconomic incentives on the part of donors in giving bilateral aid; incentives in donor organizations to give aid even though it is not productive; and, misappropriation by recipients. The first argument is that aid may appear ineffective in achieving economic goals because it is sometimes given for noneconomic reasons, that is, on

---

[27] This characterization seems quite descriptive of many countries in the African French franc zone (CFA), who financed their government spending with grants or loans which were never repaid from France. Until recently, France was willing to funnel money into these countries for presumably political reasons. In terms of the model, these countries knew they faced a very low effective foreign interest cost, implying high government expenditures, heavy foreign debt, and large trade balance deficits, as above. (These countries are discussed in Bruno and Easterly [1996].)

the basis of strategic or political considerations of the donor country, rather than in terms of need or efficiency. The second argument, applying to both bilateral and multilateral aid (but especially the latter), is based on the argument that donor organizations "push" aid onto recipients irrespective of the optimality of doing so. Moreover, there is a strong bias to making sure all funds are disbursed, generally to the originally designated recipient. Finally, it is argued that aid is often ineffective in improving economic conditions because it is grossly misappropriated by recipients. Once aid is given, governments "misbehave," backtracking on promises of economic reform and channeling funds to special interests and other nonproductive transfers.

A key feature of many grant and loan programs, instituted to help them better achieve their goals, is **conditionality**, meaning making aid conditional on countries pursuing a specific set of economic policies, or at least promising to pursue such policies. Conditionality is seen as greatly increasing the incentives of recipient countries to pursue behavior that will make aid successful. While this is certainly true in theory, conditionality in practice has had limited success at best. It often fails and is viewed as a limited tool to ensure that aid programs achieve their desired objectives. After discussing political reasons for aid being ineffective, we consider conditionality in theory and practice, including a consideration of the connection between aid and reform more generally.

Strategic Aid

Aid may appear ineffective in achieving economic goals because this is really not its objective, as it is given for strategic or political considerations of the donor or lender country. A main goal of aid in many cases is to build and strengthen political and military alliances. This argument applies primarily to *bilateral* aid, from one sovereign to another, rather than *multilateral* aid, from an IFI such as the World Bank or the IMF. To the extent that foreign aid may be meant to achieve strategic rather than economic goals, the lack of economic results need not indicate a lack of "success." It may mean simply that one needs to look at other indicators to measure the effectiveness of aid. It also means that economic mismanagement by recipients would not necessarily be punished by aid cutoffs, as aid programs have goals other than purely economic.

In the economics literature, work on strategic aid meant to maintain or strengthen ties between countries has been largely empirical. Good references include McKinlay and Little (1979), Maizels and Nissanke (1984), Burnside and Dollar (1997), and Ludborg (1998). The aim of this type of work is to discover country characteristics that help explain bilateral aid flows. In terms of political characteristics, one very strong result is that countries tend to give aid to former colonies. Countries with which donors have strong trade ties or investment interests are also more likely to receive aid. The political regime of the recipient does not appear to be a strong explanatory factor in overall aid flows, though changes in political policies are sometimes rewarded with increases or cuts in aid.

All of this is actually less sinister than it sounds. Political motives could include encouraging democracy in the recipient country, or perhaps encouraging longer-term social or structural reform, whose results would not be apparent over the short term. In transition economies, for example, democratization and broad structural reform are central policy issues, and aid flows are often meant to encourage these goals. There is as yet no significant econometric work to confirm or reject the view that adopting reform induces aid flows to these countries while not reforming induces aid cutoffs. There is some theoretical work on aid and reform, considering the effect of aid on the decision to undertake a macroeconomic stabilization program. We discuss this approach below.

Donor Institutions

Another political argument also focuses on donors, but in a quite different way, suggesting that inefficiency in donor organizations explains the ineffectiveness of aid. Specifically, the incentives within both bilateral and multilateral donor organizations are to "push aid out the door," making sure that it gets disbursed. Svensson (1998b), for example, argues that in donor organizations there is a strong bias towards giving loans to the originally designated recipient, regardless of government performance in that country and regardless of conditions in other potential recipient countries. Hence, aid is not necessarily given to countries where it can do the most good. Moreover, when recipient countries know the incentive of IFIs to push loans, threats to not disburse aid that has been committed (that is, conditionality) are not credible. There is almost no formal modeling, Svensson (1998b) being an exception.

There is significant evidence of such behavior in donor organizations, as reported by Svensson (1998b) for both bilateral and multilateral donors, where making sure the budget is spent has become the main goal. Mosley, Harrigan, and Toye (1995) argue that country loan officers in the World Bank are under pressure to meet disbursement targets regardless of country performance, an incentive strengthened by the fact that money not disbursed may often be returned to the Bank's general budget. Other objectives of the IFI, such as preventing default on existing loans, serves to exacerbate the problem.

Government Misappropriation

The most prevalent explanation of ineffectiveness of foreign aid focuses on recipients rather than donors, it being argued that aid is often grossly misappropriated by the recipient governments. Boone (1996) concludes that aid goes primarily to consumption of specific groups, with little evidence that it benefits the poor or that it goes to investment. He argues that the main effect is to increase the size of government, with government consumption rising by approximately three-quarters of total aid receipts. Similarly, Burnside and Dollar (1997) find a positive impact on growth in developing countries with sound fiscal, monetary, and trade policies, but no positive effect in the presence of poor policies.

Dollar and Svensson (1998) present striking evidence on the role of political variables in explaining the success or failure of World Bank structural adjustment lending, that is, loans conditioned on the recipient making significant changes (adjustment) in policy. They use data from the World Bank Operations Evaluation Department (OED) evaluating the success or failure of individual adjustment loans. (The OED is independent of the Bank's senior management, reporting directly to the board of directors.) Over the period 1980–1995, the OED found that about one-third of adjustment loans failed to achieve their objectives. Dollar and Svensson investigate the effects of two sets of variables on success or failure—political variables and variables measuring World Bank loan "inputs." Political variables include: whether the government is democratically elected; political instability (the number of government crises according to Banks [1994] during the implementation of the adjustment program); the degree of social divisions (as measured by the amount of ethnic fragmentation); and the length of government tenure (the number of years the incumbent that signed the loan agreement has been in power). World Bank inputs include: the amount of preparation that went into the loan, measured in various ways, and the amount of conditionality, both types and numbers of conditions. Using PROBIT analysis, Dollar and Svensson find that political variables are quite important in explaining the probability of loan success, while Bank input variables have *no* explanatory power in explaining loan success once political variables are included. We return to further discussion of their results below. Svensson (1998c) presents analogous empirical findings that the long-run impact of aid on growth depends on the degree of political and civil liberties in the recipient country.

A basic argument is that misappropriation reflects government intentions, specifically whether a government is redistributionist or development-oriented, with government type taken as given. There are also several models in which the use of foreign aid depends on domestic political conflicts. One approach is rent seeking, with Svensson (1999a) presenting a nice formalization using a common property model, an approach also used in Drazen (1999a). Another approach uses the war-of-attrition model, as in the work of Casella and Eichengreen (1996) or Fernandez-Arias (1997). We begin with models of government types.

Boone (1996) stresses the importance of the type of political regime for the effectiveness of aid programs. Classifying regimes is not simple, especially given the lack of a clear correlation between economic and political regime characteristics. To address this, Boone simply classifies regimes in terms of which citizens are in the government's utility function. He considers a model in which politicians use distortionary taxation and foreign aid to finance productive government spending and transfers to their political supporters. Specifically, he considers three extreme, alternative political regimes that such a framework suggests. An "elitist" government maximizes the welfare of its high-income supporters; an "egalitarian" government maximizes the welfare of low-income citizens, which will improve poverty indicators; finally, a "laissez-faire" government maximizes the welfare of the population by using aid to reduce distortionary taxes, leading to higher investment and higher income. The "elitist" model is consistent with the finding that aid has no significant empirical effect on either investment or quality of life for the poor. The basic result on the welfare-reducing role of redistribution parallels the results on redistribution and capital accumulation in the previous chapter. An increase in transfers implies a higher tax rate on capital, a lower capital stock, and lower output. The favored group that received the transfer will, however, have higher utility than in the case of no transfers.

Boone argues that cross-country patterns in macroeconomic performance (including saving and investment) are driven by underlying differences in political regimes. A rise in foreign aid permits a laissez-faire government to reduce tax distortions and increase income. In contrast, poor countries in his model are those with governments that have chosen redistributive policies, so that distortionary taxes need not fall. If these regimes have already chosen the tax rate to equate the benefits (higher infrastructure) and costs of distortionary taxes, aid goes to increase transfers, but does not affect distortionary taxes and output. An egalitarian government reduces poverty, while with an elitist government, foreign aid will have no effect on welfare of the poor. If foreign aid induces an increase in transfers exceeding the amount of aid, it will actually reduce output and make the poor worse off.

Rent Seeking and Economic Deterioration

A more realistic story of how aid may make a country worse off is that it induces rent seeking in the recipient country, as interest groups try to appropriate the aid for themselves. Svensson (1999a) makes this argument, formalizing it in a common property model much like those considered in earlier chapters. Since the basic common property model has been exposited in both Chapters 10 and 11 and Svensson's framework is quite similar, we only summarize his model. Interested readers may use the earlier models to derive results formally. As a background, Svensson considers a model where government revenue can go either to transfers to interest groups or to pure public goods that benefit all groups, where an extra unit of spending on the public good provides an extra unit of utility to all individuals. Transfers are pure private goods. The transfer that a group receives is proportional to its expenditure on rent seeking as a fraction of total expenditures on rent seeking by all groups. In a noncooperative equilibrium, rent-seeking activity implies that all government revenues go to transfers, with no spending on public goods. In a cooperative equilibrium, the allocation of government spending is chosen to maximize the joint utility of all groups. As in Benhabib and Rustichini (1996), a deviation from cooperation by one group triggers a punishment in the form of reversion to noncooperative behavior by all other groups. Punishment strategies imply the existence of second-best equilibria.

As in earlier models, Svensson is interested in the possible dependence of equilibrium on the state of the economy. However, unlike common property models of growth, in which the state of the economy is deterministically evolving, Svensson assumes that the state of the economy is stochastic. Specifically, government revenues τ are stochastic, with there being no possibility of storing goods between periods. He derives analogous state-dependent strategies to those found in the growth models. When government revenue is low, cooperation is sustainable and there is no rent seeking, while when revenue is above a critical level $\hat{\tau}$, the high income means a high incentive to deviate from cooperation so that rent seeking sets in.[28] All income gains above $\hat{\tau}$ are dissipated. In the second-best equilibrium, total appropriation rises more than the increase in income, so that provision of public goods falls with an increase in income above $\hat{\tau}$. Unlike the Tornell–Lane (1998) "voracity" effect in response to terms-of-trade shocks, which reflects a lack of coordination, overconsumption in response to favorable income shocks in the Svensson model is an optimal response, necessary to sustain the second-best equilibrium. The fall in public goods in response to a favorable shock suggests how aid increases may lower welfare.

Drazen (1999a) presents a common property model similar to Svensson's, but where the state of the economy is nonstochastic. Good economic performance requires an end to rent seeking by special interest groups, where the incentive to appropriate depends on the level of overall resources that may be appropriated. As the focus of the model is on the effects of selectivity in giving aid, we return to it after discussing conditionality more generally.

Conditionality and Aid Cutoffs

To the extent that the poor performance of aid programs reflects unsound policies in the recipient countries, it is often argued that conditionality

---

[28] Hence, in contrast to Boone (1996), the decision of whether aid goes to productive or "nonproductive" uses is endogenous, rather than being exogenously fixed by the type of government in power.

should be applied as a way to prevent misallocation of aid, so that it achieves its policy or project purposes. Mosley (1992, p. 129) argues that "since the establishment of the new international economic order at the Bretton Woods conference in 1944, conditionality ... has been an important component of the mechanism by which international financial institutions attempt to regulate the behavior of the world economy." Conditionality practices in the IMF developed in the 1950s and 1960s and underwent their first formal review in 1968, with a second general review in 1978–1979, culminating with the adoption of broad guidelines for use of IMF resources. (Guitián [1995] presents a general history and discussion of IMF conditionality.) Conditionality has become increasingly important in the World Bank since the beginning of the 1980s, with the shift from financing specific investment projects to structural adjustment loans promoting policy reform.

Sachs (1989a) argues that a theory of conditionality must explain three things. First, if the policies being recommended are beneficial to the recipient country, why must it be constrained to undertake them? Second, if the recipient must be constrained, what penalties does the lender have to enforce compliance? Third, why are IFIs better able to impose conditionality than are private capital markets? The answer we have given to the first question is that governments are not social welfare maximizers. Either, following Boone (1996), they have explicitly redistributionist goals encompassing only favored groups; or, more generally, interest group conflict and rent seeking imply that aid will be misappropriated.[29] Sachs, as well as Diwan and Rodrik (1992), present another argument, namely, that policies of recipient governments are time inconsistent. Recipient countries accept *ex ante* the need for policy change as a condition for receiving aid, but have a strong incentive to avoid the change in policy once aid has been received. Specifically, Sachs considers the choice between current consumption and investment. The latter has a high return, so that a country realizes the value of taking a loan to increase investment; however, the government's discount rate is even higher than the return on investment, so that once aid is received, it will be spent on current consumption. Conditionality binds a country to a course of investment and consumption postponement.

How is conditionality enforced? Conditionality sometimes takes the form of conditioning on *prior actions*, actions that are taken before the loan is disbursed, with the loan then given. More generally, policies relevant to the success of the loan have to be implemented after the loan

---

[29] Sachs (1989a) points out another sort of conflict that is quite relevant in practice. Programs are agreed upon in negotiations between the IFI and the executive branch, or more exactly, a small part of it, the finance ministry. There is often little assurance, however, that the finance minister will be able to gain the necessary approval from the legislature or even the rest of the executive branch.

has been agreed upon. The primary method of enforcement is cutting off further loans to governments that misappropriate the initial aid. In practice, this generally takes the form of *tranching* of loans, making the loan payments in installments, so that payments can be kept conditional on actions for longer, with later tranches not being disbursed if the necessary conditions have not been met.

There are several conceptual arguments why IFIs are better able to impose conditionality in lending than are private lenders. First, private lenders may face collective action problems, especially when there may be hundreds of creditors in allocating monitoring and enforcement costs and in coordinating their actions. When lending comes from an IFI, these coordination problems are lessened or eliminated. Second, the position of the IFI as an international political institution may give it the ability to dictate and enforce terms that private lenders cannot.[30] Finally, in practice, IMF conditionality is often a condition for other sorts of lending, a point stressed by Sachs (1989a). In theory, imposing conditionality and lending could be separated, with IFIs simply giving the "seal of approval" to catalyze private lending. (This type of argument has figured prominently in discussions of solutions to debt crises.) In practice, such financing is quite limited. The case for an IFI rather than private conditional lending is not all one-sided. Private banks have found ways to solve collective action problems. Moreover, the position of the IMF and the World Bank as international organizations often weakens their ability to impose strict conditionality because of objectives other than profit-maximization. Sachs (1989a) concludes that IFIs are probably better at imposing conditionality than private lenders, though the quantitative difference is far less than often argued.

The strongest conclusion of studies of conditionality is that empirical evidence clearly indicates that it works quite poorly, a conclusion that finds wide support. The most common type of research is case studies. Mosley, Harrigan, and Toye (1995) argue that conditionality has had little effect because of conflicting interests as discussed above. Sachs (1989a) similarly argues that conditionality has had very limited success. Spraos (1986) argues that conditionality makes sense in theory, but is "conceptually flawed" in practice because policy instruments rather than outcomes are targeted. Collier (1997) concludes simply that conditionality has failed, with the recipient governments' decisions of whether or not to reform being independent of the structure of assistance programs. Dollar and Svensson (1998) are, to my knowledge, the first to present econometric

---

[30] The practice of tough conditionality often leads to developing countries requesting IMF assistance only as a last resort, with the political landscape being decidedly anti-IMF. An IMF program is seen as cut from a single mold, hence poorly designed and inappropriate for a specific situation. Conditionality is viewed as a "straitjacket," to be avoided if at all possible. Though there is clearly an argument for careful program design, one lesson that has come up repeatedly in the book is that the issue of toughness versus flexibility is inherently difficult.

analysis of the effect of conditionality on the success of World Bank structural adjustment lending, based on quantitative measures of conditionality (see the above discussion). Their evidence is striking in showing that success or failure of structural adjustment loans appears to be independent of conditionality and measurable Bank inputs in loan preparation.

A key theme in the literature on the failure of conditionality is that the enforcement mechanism, namely, the threat of aid cutoff, is inherently weak and limited. There are several reasons for this. As the Bulow–Rogoff (1989a) model discussed in Section 12.8 above made clear, exclusion from foreign borrowing itself is insufficient to enforce repayment of loans (and hence conditionality even more so). A second reason is that conditionality is bound to be imperfect because a government's actions are imperfectly observable. IFI loans might fail for a variety of reasons other than clear misappropriation: bad luck, low government competence, or the government's ability to conceal actions that violate conditionality, causes that cannot be readily distinguished *ex ante*.[31] The multiplicity of potential causes for failure means that the cause of any particular failure is not necessarily identifiable. Mosley (1992) similarly argues that lenders may have good reason not to cut off further lending even if conditionality is not met. Third, conditionality may be difficult to enforce because of the complexity of negotiations that go into the giving of aid. Complexity and consequent lack of uniformity of reform programs complicates statistical inference about the causes of failure. Fourth, as Mosely *et al.* (1995) argue, the desire of IFIs to disburse loans also greatly weakens enforcement. Sachs (1989a) also argues that enforcement of conditionality is inherently limited, but adds that the problem is made worse by debt overhang. The requirement to pay extremely large debt service, he argues, greatly reduces the incentives of countries to comply with adjustment conditions, as the extra income produced goes to foreign banks rather than to improving the condition of the country's residents.

Formal Analysis of the Role of Donor Intentions and Conditionality

Theoretical models of conditionality are rare. Mosley (1992) presents a two-player (borrower and lender) bargaining model, in which a key element of the solution is the outcome of an internal conflict within the recipient country between winners and losers from the implementation of conditionality. There are two main conclusions in his analysis. First, some slippage is to be expected on any conditional loan contract, given the

---

[31] One can go a step further in the case where programs fail because of the desire of governments to make transfers to special interests. The use of conditionality to attempt to stop such transfers may lead to the transfers simply being *disguised* and made in inefficient ways, so that conditionality might actually lower the welfare of the representative citizen.

donor's desire to disburse; the optimal degree of slippage, from the recipient's point of view, depends on when it expects to emerge from the conditionality relation. Second, from the donor's point of view, random punishment of slippage as a threat strategy dominates punishment "according to the size of the crime." Mosley finds that slippage in conditionality is substantial in all types of international lending, even when the recipient country is financially weak and has little apparent bargaining power. This slippage is frequently pardoned, a finding consistent with the Bulow and Rogoff (1988a) model of renegotiating sovereign debt. Mosley argues that forgiveness has a compelling financial rationale for the lender, which becomes more compelling as the borrower's financial position deteriorates.

Svensson (1999b) argues that the incentive effects from allowing slippage based on the recipient's needs may lead it to be counterproductive. Specifically, he suggests that the poor performance of aid programs may reflect a *moral hazard* problem adversely affecting the incentive of recipients to undertake structural reforms. In principle, conditionality could improve recipient behavior, but only if the donor has a strong ability to precommit. In the absence of commitment, aid disbursement will be influenced by the needs of the poor, so that there will be low effort on the part of recipient governments to reduce poverty. Analogous to Rogoff's conservative central banker, delegation of disbursal of aid to an institution with *less* aversion to poverty may therefore *improve* the welfare of the poor.

Svensson (1999a) considers unconditional and conditional aid packages when aid reflects donor concerns about utility. Suppose aid is given in response to a country's perceived need, for example, to ensure that the utility of no individual falls below some critical level. (The opportunity cost of aid to the donor puts a floor on utility in the recipient country.) Since aid then lowers the cost of deviating from the cooperative equilibrium, it makes cooperation harder to sustain, that is, lowers the critical level $\hat{\tau}$ of government revenue above which cooperation is not sustainable. As a result, dissipation of rents increases. Hence, when it is impossible for a donor to commit aid cutoffs in advance, giving in response to need will undermine the mechanism that enforces good behavior by interest groups. Note that it is not so much the actual disbursement of aid when income is low that drives the result, but the expectation that this will happen in response to bad behavior.[32] Svensson then considers what happens if donors can enter into binding policy commitments *before* interest groups

---

[32] One interesting result in the paper is that aid is effective at the micro level (it is given directly as project aid where, by assumption, it is used as intended), but has adverse consequences at the macro level. The success of aid in raising income increases rent seeking and lowers the overall provision of public goods, as rent seeking increases more than one-to-one.

choose how much effort to devote to rent seeking, so that they can condition aid on the degree of rent seeking in equilibrium. The donor first chooses aid *a* as a function of the possible realizations of stochastic government revenue τ and rent-seeking expenditures by domestic interest groups. Then, after observing the aid schedule $a(\tau)$, interest groups choose the level of rent seeking. Equilibrium aid is computed by backwards induction. The main result is that a binding policy commitment will generally strengthen the mechanism that enforces cooperative behavior, thereby increasing the critical level $\hat{\tau}$.

Selectivity

The argument that conditionality does not work in practice has led to the argument for giving aid selectively, that is, refusing aid in cases where political factors suggest that it will be misappropriated. Dollar and Svensson (1998) argue for *selectivity* in IFI lending on the basis of their finding that political factors explain the success or failure of structural adjustment programs. As they put it, "the role of adjustment lending is to identify reformers, not to create them." Drazen (1999a) makes a similar argument for selectivity in lending. By providing no loans at all to a country for some time, the IFI may thereby produce an end to socially adverse behavior by the government, and ultimately benefit the average consumer. Selectivity is not meant as a permanent cutoff of lending, but to provide an incentive to improved loan management that simple conditionality itself could not provide.

Drazen's common property model is similar to Svensson's, but the state of the economy is nonstochastic and deteriorating over time. Economic deterioration plays a central role in the argument, as the incentive to appropriate depends on the level of overall resources that may be appropriated, as in Velasco's (1998) model of delayed stabilization discussed in Chapter 10. Cooperative behavior may not be sustainable at high levels of economywide income, but will be sustainable at lower levels. Hence, endogenous economic deterioration (that is, "crisis") is crucial to the change in the behavior of government and powerful interest groups. When the level of resources that can be appropriated becomes low enough, the promise of a resumption of lending conditional on acceptable economic behavior (reflecting economic reform and an end to gross misappropriation) is sufficient to induce groups not to engage in appropriative behavior. Aid cutoffs raise the cost of defection; aid resumptions raise the return to cooperation. Though economic deterioration will eventually imply that appropriation would no longer be optimal in the absence of selectivity, this deterioration might need to be quite extreme. Selective lending can induce a switch away from appropriative behavior when deterioration is far less extreme. The steeper is the aid or loan cutoff induced by appropriative behavior, the less the economy must deteriorate for cooperative behavior to be optimal.

Policy Reform as a Public Good

An alternative approach to the effect of foreign aid on recipient behavior is also based on domestic conflict of interests, but it is conflict over the public goods nature of policy reform. Suppose that a policy change generally seen as beneficial has not been adopted due to conflict over who will bear the cost of the policy change. This is the war-of-attrition paradigm used by Alesina and Drazen (1991) to study delayed fiscal stabilization. As shown in Chapter 10, changes in the level of utility associated with a policy change relative to the level of utility associated with the status quo will affect the expected date of policy change in this type of model. Casella and Eichengreen (1996) and Fernandez-Arias (1997) use this model of delayed fiscal stabilization to ask whether aid will accelerate or delay a stabilization. Intuitively, it would appear that either effect is possible, depending on how the aid program is structured. If external aid is given unconditionally, then it may simply serve to reduce the cost of not adopting the policy change, and hence delay reform. This is consistent with the findings of Drazen and Easterly (1999), discussed in Section 10.8 of Chapter 10. They find that extremely high current account or government budget deficits do not appear to induce reform (as a "crisis hastens reform" argument might suggest) and argue that this was because these indicators of poor macroeconomic performance induce greater foreign aid inflows, lessening the need to undertake macroeconomic adjustment. On the other hand, if the receipt of aid is made conditional on changing policy, it can hasten reform if the cause of no change in policy (and hence no aid disbursal) is a war of attrition between different interest groups.

Casella and Eichengreen (1996) introduce foreign aid into the Alesina–Drazen model and show that even aid conditioned on the adoption of policy reform can either accelerate or delay the expected date of a stabilization, depending on parameter values. The amount of aid is fixed in real terms as a fixed fraction of debt outstanding at the date of stabilization T, rather than at the date at which the aid package is announced or received. Since aid is fixed at T but delivered only at a later date, it appears that a country can get more aid if it stabilizes closer to the later date of actual receipt. Basically, the recipient country can manipulate the amount of aid it receives. This specific way of modeling aid appears to be crucial to the result that conditional aid can delay policy reform. Though the result is technically correct, the specification of aid disbursal does not seem to be an accurate specification of the donor country's behavior, that is, where the donor delivers more aid the later is the date of reform T relative to the date at which the aid package is announced. For example, if the donor decided on a fixed level of aid conditional on policy reform, rather than an amount that is *rising* if reform is delayed, a key incentive for delay would be eliminated and conditional aid would appear to unambiguously hasten a policy change.

Fernandez-Arias (1997) also considers possible ambiguous effects of receipt of aid on reform, concentrating more on the effect of aid on the relative cost of reforming versus not reforming. When aid is unconditional and not expected to be cut off, its effect is as predicted by a crisis model (for example, in the Drazen and Grilli [1993] model) but with the opposite sign. Receipt of aid is a "negative crisis." As with the crisis result in a war-of-attrition model, the welfare effect may be ambiguous, since not giving aid before a policy reform will result in a shorter, but more distorted, pre-reform period. An optimal unconditional aid package is the commitment to disburse aid at some point in the distant future, at a time when reform is expected to be already implemented.

Conditional aid is provided if and when a successful reform is implemented. Fernandez-Arias shows that with a linear loss function (the type used in Alesina–Drazen and Casella–Eichengreen), the commitment to provide aid in the future unambiguously accelerates reform, in contrast to Casella and Eichengreen's result. At first glance, it seems obvious that conditional aid will be a powerful mechanism to accelerate reform in general, as it internalizes the benefit of conceding. Fernandez-Arias argues, however, that conditional aid may have no effect, if the discounted value of the aid is time invariant. For a constant discounted value of aid, weak conditional aid (where the donor has no commitment ability) is equivalent to the optimal unconditional aid package. When the donor can commit, we can consider conditional aid in which the value of aid may vary over time. With commitment ability, the optimal conditional aid package strictly dominates unconditional aid packages.

These papers raise another issue. The real war of attrition connected to foreign aid for policy reform is probably not within a country, but between donor and recipient. In such a case, delay might be generated by a country purposely letting things get bad to induce the donor to be more responsive. To the best of my knowledge, there are no formal models of this type of waiting game, though the common property models with deterioration capture some of the flavor of this argument. Related models do exist in the literature on reform and transition, the subject of the next chapter.

12.10. CONCLUSIONS

This chapter has covered a lot of material; it has also left out a lot of material. The second characteristic is dictated by the first, since the volume of the material to be covered in the political economy of international macroeconomics made it necessary to limit the chapter in a number of ways. There was no coverage of the political economy of international trade, which is an extremely active and exciting area of research. Anyone wanting to specialize in political economy as applied to the open economy should become familiar with this literature as well.

Another limitation concerned the style of coverage, with material overlapping that presented in earlier chapters often covered only with skeletal modelling, or with no formal modelling at all. Readers interested in gaining expertise in the area may therefore want to treat this applications chapter as a source of "exercises" to improve their technical modelling ability. Those interested in a more conceptual approach are probably adequately served by the chapter as it stands.

Political economy issues in the open economy are not independent of the applications presented in the rest of the book, especially in the next chapter. Issues of sovereign borrowing and structural adjustment play an important role in the analysis of large-scale economic reform and transition in the next chapter. Issues of macroeconomic interdependence play a role in formal analysis of the union and break-up of nations, discussed in Chapter 14. We now turn to a detailed analysis of transition and reform.

CHAPTER THIRTEEN

Economic Reform and Transition

> Each day brings new problems, and each day we
> realize how interrelated they are, and how difficult
> it is to establish the proper order in which to deal with them.
>
> —*Vaclav Havel, "The New Year in Prague,"*
> The New York Review of Books, *1991*

> There is nothing more difficult to take in hand, more
> perilous to conduct, or more uncertain in its success, than to
> take the lead in the introduction of a new order of things.
>
> —*Machiavelli,* The Prince

13.1. INTRODUCTION

In this chapter, we apply earlier models of political economy to the question of large-scale reform and economic transition. By "reform," we mean any program or package of measures designed to enact a significant economic change. "Transition" can refer to a multistage process of significant economic transformation of an economy; the term is most commonly used to refer specifically to the process of transition from a centrally planned to a market economy in formerly socialist countries. In this specific context, there are a number of issues not found in the study of reform programs elsewhere. There are two shared characteristics of reform more generally and transition as applied to formerly socialist economies that suggest a unified treatment separate from the material presented in Chapter 10 on inaction and delay. These characteristics lead to combining these two areas in a single chapter.

The first feature common to reform and transition programs is their *magnitude* compared to many of the policies we have studied so far. This is the characteristic that distinguishes significant reform and transition programs from ordinary policy change. Magnitude has at least three dimensions. First, there is the significant *number* of policy changes that must be made for a reform or transition program to be successful. The multiplicity of policy changes implies that there are crucial issues of speed, sequencing, and possible complementarities not found in less ambitious policy changes. Second, there is the *scope* of reform and transition, both of the program and of its effects. Enormous changes in economic relations will lead to large changes in the economic and political situation in which agents find themselves, with significant political implications. In fact, many transition scholars argue that the nature of transition means that we are considering profound *qualitative* changes in economic and political relations that go beyond mere size or scope of the policy changes involved. Transition is seen as involving fundamental institutional or structural change, affecting things that would be taken as fixed in other economies. Third, the enormity of the changes implies extremely large *uncertainty* about outcomes, especially in the case of transition programs. Forming expectations of the post-reform environment is quite difficult, not only in aggregate, but also, and perhaps even more so, on the individual level. Hence, large-scale reform and transition are characterized by significant problems of incomplete and asymmetric information. To summarize, the *magnitude* of the policy changes and of their effects is the key to understanding the political economy of reform and transition.

The second common feature has to do with the literature itself. Anyone encountering the literature on reform and transition (especially the latter) for the first time must be struck by its chaotic nature, with the relation between articles often appearing quite puzzling. Two articles will come to opposite conclusions on the basis of different assumptions or models, with the reader having little sense of how they fit together. The apparent lack of connection between many articles reflects a number of phenomena. First, there is the newness of the problem of transition (not to mention the newness of formal political economy analysis). Moreover, it is often necessary to make assumptions about things of which we have little prior knowledge. Second, there are so many problems to tackle in transition, covering so many fields, that the appearance of chaos is not surprising. As a result, technical articles often address only one aspect of a far larger whole. One must also make judgements about which of many problems is most pressing. All of these dimensions of enormity of the transition problem lead to the appearance of lack of connectedness. Nonetheless, one is still left with the question, even after reading excellent survey articles, "How does it all fit together?"

Given the lack of connectedness in the literature, this chapter differs from previous chapters on applications in one key respect. Instead of attempting comprehensive coverage of a relatively well-organized set of questions, we first present a general framework of analysis, with the hope that it can be used to organize one's thinking about the political economy of reform and transition and to relate different approaches in the literature to one another. In so doing, it will be especially important to distinguish primarily economic problems in designing successful reform and transition programs from problems of a more political nature. The failure to make this distinction has very much contributed to confusion about the optimal strategies for reform and transition.

Concentrating on a theoretical framework of analysis runs the risk of missing crucial empirical points not conducive to modeling, as well as factors in the design of reform and transition programs that are country-specific. Though much of the literature is applied, referring to specific countries, the somewhat chaotic nature of the literature, especially on transition, suggests the approach taken here. Collections of applied studies of reform include Nelson (1990), Ranis and Mahmood (1992), Haggard and Kaufman (1992), Bates and Krueger (1993), Haggard and Webb (1994), and Williamson (1994a), to name a few. There are many excellent book-length studies of reform, including Grindle and Thomas (1991), Przeworski (1991), Krueger (1993b) and Graham (1994), as well as insightful overviews, including Krueger (1993a), Harberger (1993a, 1993b), Nelson (1994), Williamson (1994b), and Williamson and Haggard (1994) (both in the Williamson volume). Two excellent recent surveys are Rodrik (1996) and Tommasi and Velasco (1996). Work specifically on transition is, at this point, collected more in journals, including new journals specializing in transition economies. Murrell (1991) and the papers that follow constitute an enlightening symposium on transition, and Murrell (1996) provides a very good summary. The 1996 World Development Report is a longer, excellent introduction to problems of transition from an applied perspective.

The plan of this chapter is as follows. In the next section, we define the main issues. In Section 13.3, we outline the economic and political constraints that are crucial in understanding the dynamics of reform and transition. In Section 13.4, we present a general formal model of the implications of the magnitude of the changes associated with reform and transition, and in Section 13.5 we introduce heterogeneity to illustrate how the political constraints affect the choice of transition strategies. In Sections 13.6, 13.7, and 13.8, respectively, we discuss three key components of reform, namely, restructuring and labor reallocation, privatization, and price liberalization.

13.2. DEFINING THE ISSUES

Reform

What does one mean by "reform"? In Chapter 10, where the focus was on formal models of why socially beneficial policy changes are not adopted, or are adopted only with delay, we took reform to mean simply the adoption of a superior policy. In line with the more applied nature of this chapter, we here consider the question in more detail.

At the narrowest level, reform could mean any important policy change, such as a significant cut in the budget deficit. More deeply, one could think of a significant change in a policy *area*, such as a change in the whole tax or expenditure structure, with implications going beyond the effect on budget deficits. Or, more broadly, one could think of a *package* of policy changes, encompassing many areas, which are aimed at improving an economy's performance. The use of a package reflects the view that to be successful in significantly improving economic outcomes, reform must be comprehensive.

There is a qualitative as well as a quantitative aspect to the "magnitude" of reform, as indicated in the introduction. Many students of reform argue that true reform includes deeper institutional or structural change, so that beneficial policy changes can be consolidated and imbued with a greater degree of permanence.[1] These institutional changes are far more difficult both technically and politically, the latter difficulty reflecting the fact that they generally require the permanent elimination of advantages to some special interests.[2]

In speaking of the political economy of reform, most economists probably have in mind some notion of deep or broad reform as in the previous two paragraphs. There is some agreement on a number of elements in the package of broad policy changes which constitute reform, including removal of macroeconomic imbalances, trade liberalization, reduction of state intervention, and some degree of institutional reform. Williamson (1994b) presents a useful list of ten elements summarizing "the content of the policy reforms being urged by the most influential Washington institutions on Latin American countries in the late 1980s" (Williamson and Haggard, 1994, p. 529), hence dubbed the "Washington consensus." (In the late 1990s, there is probably less consensus on the optimal package of policy reforms.) These policy recommendations can be summarized as: fiscal reform on both the expenditure and the tax side; elimination of controls on exchange rates, capital, and current accounts; limiting market intervention by government; and, securing property rights. The complete list is reproduced as Table 13.1, based on the appendix in Williamson (1994b).

Transition

The "economics of transition" has come to cover a large number of topics. In general terms, a "transition" is the attempt to effect a significant

---

[1] To use Naim's (1994) terminology first discussed in Chapter 10, there are "stage-one" and "stage-two" reforms. The former are associated with the launching of reform programs; the latter generally concern deeper structural reform.

[2] A different notion of structural reform is a change in the policymaking *process* or decisionmaking apparatus. At points, we touch on reform of the policymaking process (as in discussions of the budgetary process in Chapter 14), but the analysis will be much more focused on changes in policies themselves.

TABLE 13.1
The "Washington" Consensus

1. **Fiscal Discipline**
   Budget deficits, properly measured to include provincial governments, state enterprises, and the central bank, should be small enough to be financed without recourse to the inflation tax, implying a primary surplus of several percent of GDP.

2. **Public Expenditure Priorities**
   Redirect expenditure from areas with low economic return (e.g., administration, defense, indiscriminate subsidies) to areas with high economic return and the potential to improve income distribution (e.g., primary health and education).

3. **Tax Reform**
   Broaden the tax base, cut marginal tax rates, and improve tax administration.

4. **Financial Liberalization**
   Eliminate preferential interest rates for privileged borrowers, achieve a positive real interest rate, with the ultimate objective of market-determined rates.

5. **Exchange Rates**
   A unified exchange rate (at least for trade transactions) to ensure export competitiveness.

6. **Trade Liberalization**
   Replace quantitative restrictions with tariffs, which should be progressively reduced until a uniform low tariff is achieved.

7. **Foreign Direct Investment**
   Abolish barriers on entry of foreign firms, with domestic and foreign firms allowed to compete on equal terms.

8. **Privatization**
   Private state enterprises.

9. **Deregulation**
   Abolish regulations that impede entry of new firms or restrict competition and ensure that all regulations are justified by criteria such as safety, environmental protection, or prudential supervision of financial institutions.

10. **Property Rights**
    A legal system that secures property rights throughout the economy without excessive costs.

qualitative economic change, where the magnitude of the change that is contemplated implies that reforms in many areas may be needed. In the context of the formerly socialist economies, transition refers to the process of moving from centrally planned to market-determined methods of allocating resources, making production decisions, and distribution.[3] The transition from socialism to capitalism has several components: macroeconomic *stabilization* (not unique to transition economies); *restructuring*, which means shifting to a new physical, organizational, or technological structure of production; *liberalization*, meaning reducing the level of government intervention in all spheres of economic activity; *privatization*, meaning both the transfer (by selling or some other means) of state-owned assets to private holders, and, more generally, the transfer of activities to private control; and, *construction of institutions*, especially of a legal and regulatory framework. To these changes, *democratization*, meaning moving to a democratic political system, is often added, since, from an economic point of view, the system of political decisionmaking will greatly affect economic outcomes.

Goals such as liberalization, privatization, and democratization are worthwhile in and of themselves; from an *economic* point of view, however, these may be seen as a means to an end, namely, more efficient use of resources. For example, reduced government intervention implies greater individual sovereignty in decisionmaking and hence higher individual utility; most economists, however, would probably base their argument for a reduction of intervention on efficiency grounds, rather than primarily on the increase in personal freedom it implies. This is the road taken in this chapter. That is, the economic problem of transition will be defined as an *efficiency* problem: *current economic arrangements imply a very large disparity between present use of resources and socially optimal (or at least Pareto-efficient) use, where eliminating this disparity requires a significant change in economic arrangements*.[4] Hence, the question is not whether to undertake the transition, or even what are the main components, but simply how it should be done.

---

[3] The political economy of transition is not limited to the specific question of the transition in formerly socialist economies. In many extremely poor LDCs, the process of transforming economic structures to modernize the economy is a transition problem of similar magnitude. We focus on the transition from socialism to capitalism both because of the great interest it is currently generating and because the most recent work in political economy has entered the transition literature to a far greater extent than it has entered the older literature on development.

[4] Consider, for example, labor reallocation undertaken to increase the efficiency with which resources are used. The majority of factories under socialism had a very low level of output per worker, especially when the output was adjusted for quality of the goods. Hence, factories were both inefficient, in terms of too much labor used per unit of output, and low quality. A major issue in transition is then how to move the least efficient workers out of the factory into alternative uses where they would be more efficient, defined to include retirement.

As with reform, there is the view that transition means a qualitative, rather than simply a very large quantitative, change in economic relations. One argument along these lines is that the significant political changes that are part of transition (either explicit or resulting from the reshuffling of interest groups that major economic changes will induce) make it qualitatively different than simply a package of broad economic reforms, even those including structural change. Changes in the political structure are seen to include (or even more so, to create and foster) interest groups which did not exist before the transition. Another argument is that transition in formerly socialist economies would affect institutional or structural elements that could be taken as given in other economies, making it fundamentally different than simply a package of reforms.

There is much to be said for the argument that transition is qualitatively different from simply designing far-reaching economic reform. The narrower focus put forward at the end of the next-to-last paragraph follows from a realistic assessment of what we can expect from economic analysis. Defining the focus as we do reflects not simply the desire to use tools that economists know best, but also the realization that no discipline is yet able to handle the issues raised in the previous paragraph in a really satisfying way. The chaotic nature of the literature discussed in the introduction may be a reflection of attempts to overreach the limits of our analytical capabilities.

13.3. ECONOMIC AND POLITICAL CONSTRAINTS

We begin with the above definition of the economic problem of major reform and transition as an efficiency problem requiring a significant change in economic arrangements. If the benefits of these programs are so large, it would seem that they should be enacted as fully and quickly as possible, as they would be in a frictionless, full-information world in which all decisions are made by a social planner. In understanding arguments for partial or gradual reform, it may therefore be useful to think about constraints on the reform process as a way of organizing the discussion of the political economy of reform and transition. In so doing, one must distinguish between constraints that are primarily economic from those which are more political. The theme of this section is that some of the confusion over the optimality of alternative transition strategies reflects the failure to make this distinction clearly.

To understand the distinction between economic and political constraints, consider the analogy of building a new house. There are purely economic considerations that influence both the speed with which the house is built and, even more obviously, the sequence in which things are done. A foundation must be laid before the walls are put up. How quickly should it be done? The theory of investment tells us that the marginal cost of investment will depend on the speed of investment: the faster we attempt to narrow the gap between the actual and desired capital stock, the higher may be the unit cost of investment. Building the house extremely quickly may make it quite costly, reflecting overtime wages paid to workers as well as premiums to obtain building materials without long delivery lags.

However, there are "political" considerations which could significantly affect the *technical* decision on how to build the house. Union work rules dictating wage scales may determine the composition of the work force that a contractor chooses to use. The agreement with the purchaser of the house over who will bear the cost of unforeseen design changes, or, more generally, cost overruns may affect choices of how to build when a contract covering all possible contingencies cannot be written. Uncertainties about building permits, or the possibility that building codes may be changed in the near future, so that approval of what may be built is uncertain, will affect the timing of building.

Economic Constraints

As with determinants of the optimal speed of investment, there are economic and political determinants of optimal speed and sequencing of reform and transition. We begin with a very quick and general discussion of those factors that are largely economic, not necessarily in order of empirical importance. This discussion mirrors the discussion in Section 10.2 of Chapter 10 on economic arguments for delay and inaction in adopting simple policy changes, though our focus here is on economic constraints involving the magnitude and multipart nature of reform programs.

First, there are technical limits on what reforms can be optimally implemented at a point in time. This can be qualitatively summarized as the constraint of a limited amount of the capital needed to implement reforms, where capital is defined broadly to include human, physical, or organizational capital. Optimal reform may then imply accumulation of the scarce capital as a precondition for successful transition. This technical constraint sometimes is summarized in terms of the *importance of initial conditions* in determining the optimal path of reform, where once again such a characterization reflects a broad definition of the term "initial conditions."

Second, if it is not possible to implement some welfare-improving policies immediately, for example due to a capital constraint as mentioned above, it may be optimal to postpone the removal of other distortions, even though immediate removal of these distortions is economically feasible. This is simply an application of the Theorem of the Second-Best. In the transition literature, arguments on the optimal bundling of reforms fall under the heading of "complementarity" of reforms. However, the Theorem of the Second-Best argues that welfare will be *lower* if some distortions are removed when others cannot be; this is an economic complementarity which differs from the argument that it may be *politically* wise to bundle reforms in a certain way, even though this implies *lower* economic welfare than an alternative. We return to this notion of political complementarity below.

Third, the enormity of the changes induced by a program of widespread economic reform and transition implies that problems of *incomplete information* will be significant. It may be quite difficult to form expectations of a post-reform environment, since the difference between the old and new systems is enormous. To help separate this argument from the political implications of incomplete information, consider a welfare-maximizing social planner who in his choice of policies has no political constraints, that is, no need to gain approval of his policies according to some collective choice mechanism. Even considering simple policy changes, what he adopts under incomplete information will obviously differ from what would be optimal if there were complete information. What additional problems are raised by the more complex nature of reform and transition programs? First, the magnitude of incomplete information about the effects of policy is so great that risk aversion would suggest shying away from too ambitious programs. This presumed tendency towards caution may be magnified by the fact that information about the effects of major reform programs may become available only over time. Combined with the multipart nature of reform programs, so that they need not be implemented all at once in their entirety, incomplete information thus implies the possible optimality of a "wait-and-see" approach, that is, of gradualism. Hence, even if decisions were made by the textbook enlightened social planner with wide-ranging powers, gradualism might be preferable to immediate reform.

In addition to the problem of incomplete information, whereby both the government and individuals do not know the effects of reforms, there is *asymmetric* information, where individuals may be differentially informed, or where individuals most affected by a program may possess crucial information not known to the government. As in the case of incomplete information, the problem is not unique to problems of reform and transition, but is probably more acute, given the nature of these programs. For example, in the case of labor reallocation introduced above, the government may lack information about the productivity of individual workers in their current job and their disutility of labor, a problem made severe by the distorted nature of production. And, as in the incomplete-information case, asymmetric information affects the choice of a social planner facing no political constraints.

All of these factors will imply an optimal economic transition program. The speed of our summary of economic determinants is not meant to downplay the importance of these factors in the design of reform and transition programs; they are not only crucial, but also form the basis of any discussion of the political economy of reform and transition. But, our goal is not the study of reform and transition in general, but specifically how political factors affect the nature of these programs. In assessing the effect of political considerations, therefore, we should compare the political equilibrium not to an immediate transition, but to the economically optimal transition program. Far more than in the case of investment in capital, however, in deciding on the optimal way to move to a market economy, these political considerations will play a major role.

The Political Problem Simply Stated

We are now ready to begin the material at the heart of the chapter, namely, how political constraints affect the nature of reform and transition programs. As in other parts of the book, "political constraints" is short-hand for the fact that decisions are made by a political mechanism, and hence may be quite different from those made by a social planner, subject to the same informational and technical constraints. The political problem in transition is that *for a program of reform and transition to succeed, it must have the necessary political support at crucial decision stages*. This support requires that those who are affected (the "principals") must perceive a benefit from continuing at each key stage, where "key stages" are defined by the specifics of the economic transition and the nature of the political mechanism. Stating the problem in this way allows us to summarize two components of satisfying the political constraint—the political mechanism, defining whose support is essential (that is, who are the "principals") and when it is essential; and, given the political mechanism, the principals' perception of sufficiently high net benefits from the program to warrant its continuation. As it does elsewhere in the study of political economy, *heterogeneity* plays a key role. Were there only a single type of consumer and no distributional issues, the design of a reform program would be based on the economic considerations listed above. Hence, the political constraint is thus gaining support when the economy is characterized by heterogeneity of interests. In the next section, we formalize these ideas. In the rest of this section, we very briefly set out some conceptual issues.

Uncertainty, Incomplete, and Asymmetric Information

One constraint on political support stems from uncertainty about the effects of a reform program and about the post-reform environment. This difficulty reflects a number of aspects of this uncertainty. The first is the problem of uncertainty about private benefits even if the society as a whole is expected to benefit, studied by Fernandez and Rodrik (1991) and analyzed in Chapter 10. As already indicated, the magnitude of the change induced by a transition program suggests that this uncertainty may be quite high. Second, the uncertainty generated by a transition program may not only be extremely large, but also of a sort with which individuals have little experience. Individuals who have lived in a centrally planned economy may have little or no way to form expectations about the transition to a market economy, since the extreme difference between the two systems.[5] Like high variance in possible outcomes, the difficulty in forming expectations about the post-transition economy may imply a strong bias for the status quo. The general model in Section 13.5 is built to highlight political problems arising from incomplete information.

Asymmetric information may also put a political (as opposed to a simply economic) constraint on the design of a reform or transition program. This is especially true in programs where the government must compensate individuals in the reform process, for example, in labor reallocation programs, discussed in detail in Section 13.6. If a program must gain unanimous or near-unanimous support, asymmetric information may mean that politically acceptable compensation packages are quite costly. A less strict political constraint, for example, requiring only majority support, implies that asymmetric-information problems may be less severe. In the literature, this is often referred to as the problem of *situation rents*, the value of one's position in the pre-reform environment. These may be quite large and not fully observable, so that if political acceptance of a package requires compensation, feasible programs are difficult to design.

Time Inconsistency

The multistage nature of reform and transition implies that there are significant problems of sequencing in designing a reform program. This, in turn, implies the possibility of significant potential time-consistency problems. However, as argued in Chapter 4 in our discussion of time consistency in general, the sequential nature of decisionmaking does not in itself mean time inconsistency will necessarily arise. Sequential decisionmaking is a necessary, not sufficient, condition for there to be a time-inconsistency problem. Two additional features make time inconsistency likely in reform and transition. First, given extremely large uncertainty associated with transition programs and the number of objectives relative to policy tools, manipulating expectations is likely to be an extra "instrument" in policy choice. Second, as we shall see, the combination of asymmetric information and majority rule will also give the government strong incentives toward time-inconsistent behavior. This may be thought of as a credibility

---

[5] This is analogous to Knight's (1921) famous distinction between risk and uncertainty, the former referring to situations in which individuals can assign probabilities to outcomes, the latter to situations in which they cannot. The nature of the transition from socialism to capitalism implies it is impossible to forecast what possible outcomes may be, much less to assign probabilities to them.

constraint in the design of a reform program, though credibility will have other meanings as well.

Complementarity of Reforms

Economic complementarity of reforms is another area that has political implications for the design of reform programs, over and above the economic implications. (As we shall see, there is some confusion even about the economic implications.) Complementarity of reforms may be central to building constituencies in favor of the reform process and widespread reform, and it may play a major role in the politics of reversal of reforms. A politically feasible multistage reform is one in which at each stage, the benefit of moving forward exceeds the benefit of not moving forward, whether that means staying put (if possible) or reverting to an earlier stage. Economic complementarity will affect these payoffs. This is closely related to the role of government as an agenda setter, where economic complementarity may significantly increase the value of being able to determine the reform agenda. In short, complementarity has many aspects; to make its role clearer, one must move to a formal model.

13.4. The Implications of Magnitude—A Formal Analysis

As argued above, the economic and political problems associated specifically with reform and transition programs flow from their magnitude. In Sections 13.6, 13.7, and 13.8, respectively, we discuss three key components of reform, namely, restructuring and labor reallocation, privatization, and price liberalization. As a background, in this section, we consider more general formal approaches. Dewatripont and Roland (1996) present a good overview of many issues from a general technical perspective.

Aggregate Uncertainty with Reversal Costs

Dewatripont and Roland (1995) suggest a general framework for studying the effects of uncertainty both on the aggregate and the individual level, and its implications for the speed and sequencing of reforms. The framework stresses two aspects, namely, the option value of reversal and the complementarity of reforms. We consider a variant of their framework. Following their approach, we begin by assuming *no* heterogeneity of interests, in order to set the stage for later analysis. That is, we begin with a model with no political problem as we have defined it.

Consider an infinite-horizon, discrete-time model with a representative individual with a discount factor $\beta < 1$. There are two possible reforms, denoted 1 and 2, with uncertain outcomes. Specifically, there are J outcomes for reform 1 and K possible outcomes for reform 2.[6] The net present discounted value of utility associated with implementing both reforms ("full reform") is V_{jk} if states j and k have been realized. (Dewatripont and Roland assume there is no path dependence, so that the outcome of full reform will be independent of whether both reforms were adopted simultaneously or sequentially, or of the order in which they were adopted.) The net present discounted value of utility associated with implementing only *one* of the reforms ("partial reform") is $O_j(1)$ for reform 1 if outcome j is realized and is $O_k(2)$ for reform 2 if outcome k is realized.[7] All three of these values may be positive or negative in a given state of nature, while the known value of the status quo is normalized to zero. This general framework is meant to be quite flexible. These values include many of the *economic* arguments on optimal reform and transition, in that they reflect the general problems of unfavorable "initial conditions" or (broadly defined) "insufficient capital" mentioned in Section 13.3 and central to applied discussions of reform and especially transition.

There is a cost of reversing reforms, ζ_i for each partial reform, ζ for full reform, where $\zeta_1 + \zeta_2 \geq \zeta > \max(\zeta_1, \zeta_2) > 0$, so that reversing partial reform is less costly than reversing full reform. Suppose that the outcome must be observed for one period, after which a reversal decision can be made. Implementing a single reform and observing the outcome is assumed to give information on the value of possible outcomes of full reform. For example, suppose reform 1 is implemented and outcome $O_j(1)$ is observed. This is informative for possible outcomes of full reform, in that the expectation of V_{jk} conditional on having observed the outcome of reform 1, that is, $E_k(V_{jk} \mid j)$, differs from the unconditional expectation $E_{j,k}(V_{jk})$.[8] For ease of exposition, it is useful to rank signals in terms of the

---

[6] For expositional purposes, not much is lost by assuming that each state of nature j (or k) is associated with a different outcome of reform 1 (or 2). More generally, we could allow the possibility that different states of nature imply the same outcome, so that observing the result of only reform 1, for example, need not perfectly reveal $j \in J$, and analogously for reform 2. In this case, we cannot speak of outcomes and states of nature j interchangeably, as we do here.

[7] One can work with net present values because the flow of benefits is constant per period and the time path of benefits is irrelevant (unlike the time path of information on the benefit of reform, which is central here). Hence, there is no problem connected with initial deterioration (the "J-curve" effect) *per se*. An optimizing government without political constraints simply cares about the expected present value of reform. All this can change with political constraints.

[8] More generally, one can think of a signal on possible outcomes of full reform conditional on observing $O_j(1)$, which may be uninformative, partially informative, or fully informative about realizations of V_{jk}. This more general formulation will be useful in certain cases, for example, where the outcome $O_j(1)$ does not fully reveal the state j, as in footnote 6.

expected return to full reform. If there are two signals j'' and j', then

$$j'' > j' \quad \Rightarrow \quad E_k(V_{jk} \mid j'') \geq E_k(V_{jk} \mid j'). \qquad (13.1)$$

Dewatripont and Roland assume strong complementarity of reforms, not only that $O_j(1)$ and $O_k(2)$ are much lower than V_{jk}, but further assuming that $O_j(1) < -\zeta_1$. (and analogously for $O_k(2)$). Hence, partial reform is never attractive *per se*, independent of its information revelation value. (The first assumption on the relative values of partial and full reform underlies the standard argument on why complementarity of reforms implies that full reform is optimal, though as Dewatripont and Roland point out, the implications of complementarity are more subtle.) Once one reform is implemented, the only possibilities are either to go forward with the second reform (full reform) or backward to the original status quo. Hence, in this simple set-up, the full-reform options are either gradualism (raising the further question of optimal sequencing), or doing things all at once (in a *big bang*, in analogy to the view that the universe was created in a "big bang"). The advantage of gradualism in this framework is that it allows the possibility of learning and of reversal at lower cost. (Make sure that the distinction between full reform and "big bang" is clear—the assumption on the magnitudes of $V_{jk}, O_j(1)$, and $O_k(2)$ is an argument for either full or no reform, but does not in itself determine the *speed* of reform, that is, big bang versus gradual.)

Optimal Speed of Reform

On the basis of this set-up, one can compare gradualism and big bang under uncertainty with reversal costs. Under big bang, both reforms are implemented simultaneously, and after one period it can be decided whether or not to reverse the entire package. Working with net present values, the expected utility of big bang is the sum of the current-period expected flow return to adopting both reforms plus the discounted value of returns from tomorrow onward, which is[9]

$$E(\Omega^{BB}) = (1 - \beta)E_{j,k}(V_{jk}) + \beta E_{j,k}(\max\{-\zeta, V_{jk}\}), \qquad (13.2)$$

where the expectations on the right-hand side are taken over all states of nature.

The expected value of gradualism depends on the payoff after the results of partial reform have been observed. If reform 1 has been

---

[9] Remember, a reform must stay in place for one period before it can be reversed. Since the expected single-period return from full reform is constant over time, the present discounted value of flows is the single-period return divided by $1 - \beta$, from which the first term follows.

implemented and state j' has been observed, the expected return from continuing with reform 2 conditional on this observation, denoted $R_2(j')$, is

$$R_2(j') = (1 - \beta)E_k(V_{jk} \mid j') + \beta E_k\big(\max\{-\zeta, V_{jk} \mid j'\}\big). \quad (13.3)$$

Since the assumption on the ranking of signals implies that $E_k(V_{jk} \mid j)$ is increasing in j, define $\hat{j}$ such that $j \geq \hat{j}$ if and only if $R_2(j) \geq -\zeta_1$, meaning reform 1 is reversed only for signals below $\hat{j}$. The *ex-ante* expected payoff starting with reform 1, denoted $E(\Omega^{12})$, is the current-period payoff plus the expected payoff from next period onward, which is the utility loss from reversal multiplied by the probability of reversal plus the expected utility from continuation, multiplied by the probability of continuation. Using (13.3), we may write

$$E(\Omega^{12}) = (1 - \beta)E_j\big(O_j(1)\big)$$
$$+ \beta\Big[\Pr\big(j < \hat{j}\big) \times (-\zeta_1) + \Pr\big(j \geq \hat{j}\big)R_2(j \mid j \geq \hat{j})\Big]. \quad (13.4)$$

(Gradualism with the reverse sequencing gives an analogous expression.) Using (13.2) and (13.3), the expected value of big bang may be written

$$E(\Omega^{BB}) = \Pr\big(j < \hat{j}\big)R_2(j \mid j < \hat{j}) + \Pr\big(j \geq \hat{j}\big)R_2(j \mid j \geq \hat{j}), \quad (13.2a)$$

so that (13.4) becomes

$$E(\Omega^{12}) = (1 - \beta)E_j\big(O_j(1)\big) + \beta E(\Omega^{BB})$$
$$+ \beta \Pr(j < \hat{j})\big(-R_2(j \mid j < \hat{j}) - \zeta_1\big). \quad (13.4a)$$

The difference between gradualism and big bang may then be expressed as

$$E(\Omega^{12}) - E(\Omega^{BB}) = (1 - \beta)\big(E_j\big(O_j(1)\big) - E(\Omega^{BB})\big)$$
$$+ \beta \Pr\big(j < \hat{j}\big)\big(-R_2(j \mid j < \hat{j}) - \zeta_1\big). \quad (13.5)$$

Equation (13.5), indicating the costs and benefits of gradualism, has a simple interpretation. The cost of gradualism is the current-period loss from implementing partial rather than immediate full reform. This is the first term on the right-hand side of (13.5). The gain from gradualism comes from the possibility of learning about bad expected outcomes of full reform, and hence being able to reverse the reform process at lower cost. (One may easily show that the optimality of gradualism requires our earlier assumption that $\zeta > \zeta_1$.) This gain is the utility gain from not going forward when there is a bad signal $j < \hat{j}$, that is, from "saving" $R_2(j < \hat{j}) <$

0 net of the reversal cost ζ_1. This is the last term in parentheses on the right-hand side of (13.5). (Note that when $j < \hat{j}$, $-R_2(j < \hat{j}) - \zeta_1 > 0$.) The probability that partial reform will be reversed, $\Pr(j < \hat{j})$, is the probability that the first reform is *informative*; given the utility gain from early reversal, the higher this probability, the higher the value of gradualism. Note that the informativeness of the reform refers not to the outcome of partial reform *per se* (the value of $O_j(1)$) but to the information about future outcomes $R_2(j)$.

If learning is very fast ($\beta \to 1$), then a necessary and sufficient condition for the optimality of gradualism under aggregate uncertainty is that $\Pr(j < \hat{j}) > 0$, that is, that the option of early reversal be exercised with positive probability. When learning takes time, gradualism is optimal when there is a positive probability of early reversal as long as learning is not too costly relative to either big bang or the status quo, that is, as long as $E_j(O_j(1))$ is not too negative.

To summarize, the Dewatripont–Roland framework and its results make clear the importance of the option value for early reversal in determining the optimality of gradualism relative to big bang under aggregate uncertainty. This option value depends on the first reform being potentially informative of the outcome of future reforms. If $\Pr(j < \hat{j}) = 0$, then either there would be no reform at all (if $E\Omega^{BB} < 0$) or a big bang (if $E\Omega^{BB} > 0$). Though it is the information value of partial reform that lies behind the results, an alternative specification could imply that the possibility of learning induces faster, rather than slower, implementation of reform. This would be true if there is a benefit to experimenting with reforms or if the government wants information on rates of change, for example, the rate of absorption of displaced workers under a new production structure.

This framework also clarifies the role of complementarity in a model without political constraints, often thought to be a sufficient condition for the optimality of big bang over gradualism. Here, we see that this is not the case: complementarity will be crucial in determining the optimality of partial reform over full or no reform as an *equilibrium*, but not necessarily the way in which equilibrium is reached. In fact, as Dewatripont and Roland stress, complementarity is *necessary* for gradualism to be optimal if aggregate uncertainty is the only constraint. Suppose that there is no complementarity, reforms being fully separable, so that $V_{jk} = O_j(1) + O_k(2)$. One may then easily show that gradualism is *never* optimal in this information-based framework. Since reforms can be assessed independently and there is no technical "budget constraint" on the number of reforms that can be simultaneously implemented, nor any political support constraint, each reform will either be tried immediately (if $E_j(O_j(1)) > 0$) or never (if $E_j(O_j(1)) < 0$). As we shall see in the next section, however, once we consider individual heterogeneity, and hence political support constraints, economic complementarities may play a major role in the choice of big bang versus gradualism.

Optimal Sequencing of Reform

Having established the argument for gradualism under aggregate uncertainty (that is, with no heterogeneity across agents), Dewatripont and Roland (1995) then consider optimal sequencing. This means, using the above notation, comparing $E(\Omega^{12})$ and $E(\Omega^{21})$. Following their exposition, we assume for simplicity that each reform can have only two possible outcomes: $H_s > 0$ with probability q_s and $L_s < 0$ with probability $1 - q_s$, for $s = 1, 2$, with $q_s H_s + (1 - q_s)L_s \equiv EO(s)$. Following (13.4), the expected utility of gradualism under a given sequencing may be written

$$E(\Omega^{sm}) = (1 - \beta)EO(s) + \beta[q_s \max\{-\zeta_s, R_m(H_s)\}$$
$$+ (1 - q_s) \max\{-\zeta_s, R_m(L_s)\}] \qquad (13.6)$$

for $s = 1, 2$ and $m \neq s$, where

$$R_m(H_s) = (1 - \beta)(H_s + EO(m))$$
$$+ \beta[q_m \max\{-\zeta, H_s + H_m\} + (1 - q_m) \max\{-\zeta, H_s + L_m\}], \quad (13.7)$$

with an analogous expression for $R_m(L_s)$.

If only one reform were informative, the optimal sequencing would be to implement this reform first. If neither reform were informative, there would be no argument for gradualism. Dewatripont and Roland therefore concentrate on the case in which both reforms are informative, which in this model can be expressed as

$$R_1(H_2) > -\zeta_2 > R_1(L_2) \quad \text{and} \quad R_2(H_1) > -\zeta_1 > R_2(L_1), \quad (13.8)$$

meaning that a good outcome implies continuation, while a negative outcome leads to reversal of partial reform. In order to derive results on sequencing, they also naturally assume that the outcome of partial reform is such that, combined with the above assumption, gradualism is optimal.

Using this framework, Dewatripont and Roland derive a number of results. (These may be easily demonstrated using the above methodology of computing expected values, as shown in Dewatripont and Roland [1995].) First, all else equal, including the probabilities of good and bad outcomes, reforms with a higher expected outcome should be implemented first, as long as $\beta < 1$. This result reflects the role of time preference, implying earlier implementation of reforms with higher expected returns. Second, abstracting from risk aversion and given identical expected outcomes and reversal costs, it is better to start with the riskier reform. (This may be demonstrated by supposing that the outcomes of reform 1 are a

mean-preserving spread of those for reform 2.) This follows from considering the option value of reversal. Starting with the riskier reform increases
the option value of reversibility and hence the expected outcome. When
both gains and losses of reform grow, a reform becomes more attractive if
losses can be avoided by reversal. As in the implications of complementarity in the absence of political constraints, this last result may be significantly affected by political factors.

13.5. HETEROGENEITY AND POLITICAL CONSTRAINTS

In the previous section, we considered the implications of uncertainty
about outcomes on speed and sequencing decisions of an optimizing
government facing no political constraints. That is, there was no heterogeneity across individuals leading them to have different preferred programs. We now consider the role of political factors by adding heterogeneity, where the political constraint is the need for the relevant groups to
view a program as welfare improving in terms of their own interests. We
concentrate on political implications of the "magnitude" of these programs, as defined in the introduction. We begin by considering the political
implications of problems of uncertainty and asymmetric information in the
general framework set out above.

"Communication Failures"

The first possibility is asymmetric information between government and
the public, that is, where the government believes a program to be optimal,
but cannot credibly communicate this to the public. Such models were
introduced in Section 10.5 of Chapter 10, where, for example, the government was assumed to have superior information about the state of the
world. We consider an asymmetric-information model of labor reallocation
in Section 13.6 below. Here, we consider the implications of the government having superior information for speed of reform more generally.

Consider the model at the beginning of this section, but where the
government and the public differ in the probabilities they assign to
different states of nature and thus to reform outcomes. Hence, expected
utility of reform will differ between the government and the public, where
we denote expectations by $E^{GOVT}(\cdot)$ and $E^{PUB}(\cdot)$, respectively. Specifically,
suppose that the public assigns a much higher probability to bad outcomes
than the government $(\mathrm{Pr}^{PUB}(j < \hat{j}) \gg \mathrm{Pr}^{GOVT}(j < \hat{j}))$, so that from
(13.2a), the government believes in the benefit of full reform (that is,
$E^{GOVT}(\Omega^{BB}) > 0$), while the public does not $(E^{PUB}(\Omega^{BB}) < 0)$. Since a
necessary political condition for a reform to be adopted is that it have a
positive expected value for the public, big bang is not a politically feasible
way to implement full reform.

In contrast to big bang, gradualism may be not only politically feasible (that is, $E^{PUB}(\Omega^{12}) > 0 > E^{PUB}(\Omega^{BB})$), but also likely to lead to full reform if the government's higher estimation of the probability of a good outcome is the correct one. To see this, consider (13.4a) evaluated for the public's expectations:

$$E^{PUB}(\Omega^{12}) = (1 - \beta)E_j^{PUB}(O_j(1)) + \beta E^{PUB}(\Omega^{BB})$$
$$+ \beta \Pr{}^{PUB}(j < \hat{j})(-R_2^{PUB}(j \mid j < \hat{j}) - \zeta_1).$$

(13.9)

If $-R_2^{PUB}(j \mid j < \hat{j}) - \zeta_1 > 0$ is high, a high value of $\Pr{}^{PUB}(j < \hat{j})$ yields $E^{PUB}(\Omega^{12}) > 0 > E^{PUB}(\Omega^{BB})$. The public will support continuation to full reform if the realized state $j' > \hat{j}$, which will be likely if the government's estimation of the probabilities is correct. Hence, asymmetric information between government and the public can lead to the political necessity of gradualism even though big bang is economically optimal (in an expected-value sense.) This is an often-cited political argument for gradualism.

Communication problems may also influence optimal sequencing under gradualism. As discussed in Section 10.5 of Chapter 10, when announcements are costless to make (when they are "cheap talk"), the ability of a policymaker to communicate information depends on how correlated are the preferences of the sender and the recipients of information. When they are more highly correlated, costless announcements may convey information. This suggests that programs may be sequenced to hit the policymaker's "informational constituency" first, that is, those to whom he finds it easiest to communicate information in order to help overcome the political constraint associated with asymmetric information between government and public. Austen-Smith (1990, 1993) has emphasizes this argument, as discussed in Chapter 10.

Uncertainty about Individual Benefits

A second important possibility is uncertainty on the individual level, where a reform or transition program affects individuals differentially, but in ways that are not fully known *ex ante*. This is as in the model of Fernandez and Rodrik (1991) of status quo bias discussed in Chapter 10, in which individuals or interest groups are uncertain about the benefits of a single policy change. They show that a policy that would end up benefitting a majority of the population is not adopted if there is sufficient uncertainty about its net benefits. In the case of multistage reform programs, individual uncertainty may be important for building constituencies over time in support of reform.

Dewatripont and Roland (1995) consider a version of the model presented in the previous section with uncertainty about individual benefits to heterogeneous agents. They consider a model with both individual and aggregate uncertainty. Both are necessary to illustrate the connection between individual uncertainty and the political importance of sequencing; in the absence of aggregate uncertainty, there is a status quo bias, but no general argument for gradualism, as there is no option value to reversal of partial reform. The set-up is very simple, with only two reforms, in order to focus on problems of sequencing when there are political constraints. Suppose each reform yields an aggregate (present discounted value) bene-fit $H > 0$ with probability q and an aggregate benefit $L < 0$ with probabil-ity $1 - q$. They assume that gradualism is optimal, which implies a neces-sary condition, namely, $2H > -\zeta_1 - \zeta_2 > H + L$.

Individual heterogeneity is modeled as follows. Whereas all individuals have similar expectations before either reform, once a reform is imple-mented, a fraction λ_s of the population receives, for any possible aggre-gate outcome $O(s)$ (positive or negative) of reform s, an individual payoff of $O(s) + H^i(s) > O(s)$, and a fraction $1 - \lambda_s$ receives an individual payoff of $O(s) + L^i(s) < O(s)$, where $\lambda_s H^i(s) + (1 - \lambda_s)L^i(s) = 0$ (so that if $\lambda_s > 1/2$, then $H^i(s) < -L^i(s)$). Hence, for both reforms, hetero-geneity of individual payoffs has no effect on the expected payoff for the population as a whole.[10] Though the two reforms do not affect *ex-ante* aggregate expected payoffs, they differ in the *number* of people who are expected to benefit. Under reform 1, a majority of the population benefits and a minority is hurt, while under reform 2, a minority benefits and a majority is hurt. This will be important, as continuation (or nonreversal) of reform must be supported by majority rule, which means here that it must benefit the median voter.

For simplicity, suppose that the two reforms are simply mirror images of one another in their idiosyncratic effects, in that $\lambda_1 = 1 - \lambda_2 > 1/2$, $H^i(1) = -L^i(2)$, and $L^i(1) = -H^i(2)$. Hence, the two reforms have identical expected payoff and riskiness, differing only in the distribution of payoffs across individuals. Note that in the absence of individual hetero-geneity, these reforms are obviously identical, with there being no implica-tions for optimal sequencing. Nor are there any implications of individual uncertainty under full reform. When both reforms are enacted, the median voter has experienced zero net gains. The expected payoff from a big bang strategy is thus unaffected by individual uncertainty.

Under gradualism, sequencing may make a difference. If the first reform has a negative aggregate outcome (i.e., L), then the median voter will not support continuation under either sequencing, as he knows reversal will take place in the following period. (Even if the outcome of the second reform is favorable, the assumption that $H + L < -\zeta_1 - \zeta_2$ means that

---

[10] There is no correlation of *individual* returns across the two reforms, so that an individual who received $H^i(1)$ from reform 1 has a zero expected idiosyncratic benefit from reform 2.

reversal is preferred.[11]) However, if the aggregate outcome of the first reform is favorable (i.e., H), the distribution of benefits may determine whether a reform process will be continued. If reform 1 (that is, the reform in which the majority has an idiosyncratic benefit) is enacted first, the payoff to the median voter from continuing is

$$R_2(H) = (1 - \beta)(H + H^i(1) + (qH + (1 - q)L))$$
$$+ \beta\big[(1 - q)(-\zeta_1 - \zeta_2) + q(2H + H^i(1))\big]$$
$$= \big[(1 - \beta)(H + (qH + (1 - q)L)) \qquad (13.10)$$
$$+ \beta[(1 - q)(-\zeta_1 - \zeta_2) + q2H]\big]$$
$$+ \big[(1 - \beta)H^i(1) + \beta qH^i(1)\big].$$

The first term in large brackets in the second line will be positive if full reform is optimal in an expected value sense. The last term in large brackets will also be positive since $H^i(1) > 0$. Hence, the median voter will want to continue with the reform process, with his *ex-post* stake in continuing being higher, the higher is $H^i(1)$. If reform 2 is enacted first, we get an analogous expression $R_1(H)$ for continuation in the case of a favorable outcome, with an identical first term in the second line of (13.10), but with the last term replaced by $[(1 - \beta)L^i(1) + \beta qL^i(1)] < 0$. If the whole expression is greater than $-\zeta_1$, then reform will be continued and sequencing does not matter. But, if $L^i(1)$ is sufficiently negative, the reform process will not be continued, even though the aggregate benefit of full reform is the same as under the alternative sequencing.

Intuitively, the difference between the two programs is in the position of the median voter. If reform 1, in which a majority benefit, is enacted first, the median voter will be an individual who has received an idiosyncratic positive shock, and hence will definitely favor continuation of reform if the aggregate outcome is positive. When reform 2 is enacted first, the median voter is an individual who has received an idiosyncratic negative shock, and hence may be reluctant to continue even if there is a favorable aggregate outcome. He has learned that he is among the relative expected losers from reform (as the *expected* idiosyncratic shock from reform 1 is zero), so that his stake in continuing the reform process is lessened relative to being one of the winners. But, this is the nature of reform 2, in which a majority, of all voters, and hence the median voter, are relative losers. Starting with a reform in which the individual net benefits are concentrated in a

---

[11] This statement would be exact under the previous assumptions if there were no discounting ($\beta = 1$). The condition $H + L < -\zeta_1 - \zeta_2$ means that a low outcome of reform makes reversal certain after the outcome of the second is realized. With discounting, the necessary condition is $-\zeta_1 > (1 - \beta)[L + H^i(1) + (qH + (1 - q)L)] - \beta(\zeta_1 + \zeta_2)$.

minority of the population runs a greater risk of reversal if the political constraint is majority rule, even if the aggregate outcome is favorable.[12]

The key point may be put as follows: appropriate sequencing can be crucial in *building constituencies* in favor of reform. Under majority rule, a transition process starting with a reform that benefits a majority if the aggregate outcome is favorable is more likely to be continued than one where the benefits are concentrated among a minority, since a larger group has a stake in continuation of the reform process. A transition process beginning with the "majority" reform may be politically feasible, while the opposite sequencing may not be. Under alternative arrangements, such as veto power by a specific minority, the politically feasible sequencing may be different, but the general result is the same. The need to gain and maintain support of specific groups, that is, to build constituencies for reform, during the multistage reform process puts a political constraint on the design of programs that would not be present in the absence of heterogeneity. This result is quite important. The need to build constituencies for reform by appropriate sequencing is a crucial political factor in the design of transition programs. We return to this issue in Section 13.6 when we consider the specific question of labor reallocation.

Creating Political Irreversibilities

Building a constituency for continuation of the reform process may be seen as an example of the more general strategy of creating *political irreversibility*. This often means taking advantage of favorable exogenous events in order to implement reforms, so that they are more likely to be sustained *ex post*. To use the vernacular, there are "windows of opportunity" for reform which can be utilized to create irreversibilities. Whereas sequencing to build constituencies often focuses on minimizing the possibility of reversal of reform and rollback to a previous stage of the transition process (what Dewatripont and Roland [1996] call the "*ex-post* political constraint"), exploiting favorable exogenous opportunities usually focuses on maximizing the probability of initially adopting a reform or of moving forward to the next stage of the transition process (what Dewatripont and Roland call the "*ex-ante* political constraint").

A political window of opportunity may reflect either changes over time in the composition of the "electorate," that is, groups whose support is crucial or anticipated changes in their preferences, such that there is a

---

[12] As in the Fernandez–Rodrik model, a crucial assumption in these models of *ex-post* heterogeneity is the impossibility of *ex-post* compensation from gainers to losers in the reform process. On an applied level, there are a number of reasons for the lack of *ex-post* compensation, including the distortionary taxation needed to finance such transfers, asymmetric information about the losses that are suffered in the reform process, and problems of the government committing to future schemes. We consider these last two problems explicitly in Section 13.6 below.

temporary opportunity to enact a program which will subsequently disappear.[13] (The latter opportunity is the "honeymoon" period, in which a majority is in favor of the government acting quickly at the beginning of the reform process.) Once a program is enacted, the new electorate may choose not to reverse it. This may arise because uncertainty has been favorably resolved, or because a "reform-monger" may take advantage of the characteristics of the existing electorate to create interest groups in favor of continuation once political conditions change, that is, to "tie the hands" of his successor.[14] The design of privatization schemes provides a good example. More generally, political windows of opportunity and the possibility of creating irreversibilities may very much dictate the optimal nature of reform strategies.

Majority Rule and Agenda Setting

In our earlier discussion focusing on uncertainty, gradualism was important in building support for large-scale reform because of its role in revealing information. The benefit of gradualism centered on the option value of early reversal. Once heterogeneity was introduced, building a constituency for reform implied initially adopting reforms expected to benefit a majority of the population. Aggregate information revelation was secondary to distributional considerations. In fact, creating a constituency in favor of a reform *ex post* means reducing the option value of early reversal. This gives rise to a tension between political feasibility *ex ante* (adopting a reform) and political feasibility *ex post* (not reversing the reform). It may be precisely because a reform is easier to reverse under a given sequencing that it is more acceptable *ex ante*.

When population groups have heterogeneous interests, a constituency for reform may be created, by playing groups off against each other. Wei (1997) presents a good example showing how a package of reforms that would not be accepted as a whole can be implemented gradually due to shifting majority coalitions. The model is based on the Fernandez–Rodrik (1991) model, but it is not uncertainty about individual benefits (that is, *ex-post* heterogeneity) that really drives the model; it is the known conflict of interests *across* sectors (that is, *ex-ante* heterogeneity) that enables gradualism to overcome majority opposition to full reform. It was this divergence of interest across sectors in the Fernandez–Rodrik model which implied that, even under risk neutrality, a reform benefitting a majority may be rejected by majority voting.

---

[13] Formally, a temporary change in the electorate will imply a temporary change in the expectation operator in the basic model at the beginning of this section, so that a big bang program would satisfy the relevant political constraint.

[14] This parallels the key result on debt nonrepudiation in Tabellini's (1991) model of intergenerational redistribution discussed in Section 8.6 of Chapter 8. One may also refer back to models of constraining one's successors in Section 7.9 of Chapter 7.

Wei presents a two-period model with three sectors, denoted *0*, *I*, and *II*, and two reforms, denoted 1 and 2. Workers (that is, voters) in sector *I* are hurt by reform 1 and helped by reform 2, while workers in sector *II* are hurt by reform 2 and helped by reform 1. Workers in sector *0* are helped by both reforms. (As in Fernandez and Rodrik, the specific model concerns trade reform, with two import-competing sectors, each hurt by a reform removing tariff protection for that sector, and an export sector, with workers in that sector unambiguously benefitting from both reforms.) Suppose there are an equal number of worker/voters in each sector before a reform, so that adoption of a reform under majority rule requires that it is supported by at least two types of voters.

To ensure that a reform, once adopted, will not be reversed, Wei assumes that after a reform is adopted, a small fraction of workers in the sector hurt by the reform can switch to the sector *0* (that is, to the sector that unambiguously gains from reform) at low cost. Enough workers switch to ensure that, once adopted, the reform is not reversed by majority vote. As in Fernandez–Rodrik, Wei assumes *ex-ante* uncertainty on the part of workers in sectors *I* and *II* as to who has a low cost of switching. It is the assumptions of *ex-ante* uncertainty combined with *ex-post* learning and switching on the part of some workers that allows this crucial difference in voting patterns *ex ante* and *ex post* by workers originally in a sector. As the purpose of these assumptions is simply to ensure that, once adopted, reforms will not be reversed, we simply assume here that, once adopted, a reform is irreversible. This allows us to concentrate on *ex-ante* coalition building via sequencing in a deterministic setting. As uncertainty is not material to this part of the model, such an approach focuses attention on the crucial factors that drive the results.

The deterministic present value payoffs of the reforms to workers in each sector may be represented by the payoff matrix in Table 13.2, where it is assumed that there is no discounting between the two periods.

Assume that in each period, the government can propose either the status quo (whose payoff is normalized to zero), one reform, or both reforms (that is, full reform, via "big bang"). The government is unable to precommit to future proposals, so that no conditional proposals are on the agenda.

Suppose that $H < L$, so that the "big bang" strategy of immediate full reform in either period will be opposed by workers in both sectors *I* and

TABLE 13.2
Net Payoffs to Reform

	Sector 0	*Sector I*	*Sector II*
Reform 1	H	$-L$	H
Reform 2	H	H	$-L$

II, and hence will fail under majority voting. What about a partial or gradual reform? If one reform has been (irreversibly) enacted, the other will then be accepted by majority rule, as it is opposed only by workers in that sector. This suggests the following backward induction argument. In the second period, it is clear from the payoff matrix in Table 13.2 that either reform individually would gain a majority, more exactly, two-thirds of the votes, as no further reform is possible. Given that one of the two reforms will be enacted in the second period, the other reform will be enacted in the first period, with the support of two-thirds of the voters. Hence, while full reform is not politically feasible via big bang, it can be achieved via gradualism, with the adoption first of one reform, and then the other.

Why was a backward induction argument necessary? Since each reform alone benefits two-thirds of the population, why not simply argue that enacting them sequentially will satisfy the political feasibility constraint? If voters in sectors *I* and *II* were myopic, this argument would be sufficient to show that gradualism can get around the majority-rule constraint on big bang adoption of full reform. Consider, however, forward-looking voters in an infinite-horizon world. If reform 1 alone, for example, is proposed and adopted with the votes of workers in sector *II*, these voters know that in the following period, reform 2 will be proposed and passed, over their objections. Given the payoffs ($H - L < 0$), they are worse off under full reform than they would have been under no reform. On the other hand, if voters in sector *II* vote against reform 1, so that it fails, reform 2 will not be automatically passed in the next period. If voters in sector *I* are similarly forward-looking, they would vote against reform 2 in the next period. Hence, voters in sector *II* can block reform 1 under majority voting, and if they are forward-looking, strategic voting will lead them to do so. There is no political "free lunch" under an infinite horizon with forward-looking voters. If full reform is not in their interests, rational voters will not enact it via the back door.[15] With a finite horizon, however, the strategic voting argument breaks down, as we demonstrated in the previous paragraph. It "unravels backwards," much as many equilibrium arguments unraveled backwards under a finite horizon in the reputational models in Chapter 6.

Wei justifies using a finite-horizon set-up by arguing that its implications on actual voting behavior are more sensible than the strategic voting implied by an infinite horizon set-up. Under strategic voting, voters in sector *I* must promise and convince voters in sector *II* that they will

---

[15] Though the relative payoffs and hence possible equilibria were different in our unanimity examples, note the similarity between this argument and the argument showing the political infeasibility of gradualism under unanimity. In those examples, a gradual reform will not be started because forward-looking voters realize the incentives which are set up once partial reform has been enacted.

protect their interests in the future. The credibility of such a commitment depends on sector-*II* voters being similarly forward-looking in the future. There is a tenuousness to the argument and potential time-consistency problems in the absence of commitment mechanisms. The absence of unraveling is based on a stationary environment. Wei points out that, in practice, even if a government remains in power, it does not offer the same set of policy options period after period into the indefinite future. The environment changes, so that bargains based on future cooperative behavior in the absence of formal commitment mechanisms are not fully credible, and results based on the existence of such bargains not fully believable. Moreover, governments change over time, casting further doubt on the willingness of voters to vote against their short-term interests in anticipation of future rewards.

Dewatripont and Roland (1996) suggest how certain exogenous foreseen events may induce the finite-horizon behavior crucial to the results on gradualism even in an infinite-horizon model. Suppose there are exogenous dates at which sectors are expected to "disappear," due to financial distress or early retirement of workers. Call t_1 the first date at which a sector, say sector *I*, will "disappear." The government can then enlist voters in sector *I* to join with voters in sector *0* in implementing reform 2, as they have no stake in preventing future implementation of reform 1. Voters in sector *II* thus know that at t_1, reform 2 will be implemented no matter what, so they will vote for reform 1 at time $t_1 - 1$, with full reform achieved by gradualism concluding no later than t_1. One could go a step further and continue the argument (with voters in sector *I* supporting reform 2 at $t_1 - 2$, *et cetera*), so that by backward iteration, one concludes that full reform could be completed in two periods via gradualism from any possible date.

Though very simple, these examples show the power that a government with control over the agenda may have to manage the multipart reform and transition in a majority-voting system. With more than two interest groups, none of whom has the power to block reform by itself, a skillful government can play groups off against one another, creating temporary coalitions to move the reform process forward towards full reform in a way that could not be done directly. Moreover, as the backward iteration argument showed, one of the tools that an agenda-setting government has in furthering reform is the ability to play groups off against the future. In Section 13.6, we examine this possibility in greater detail.

Unanimity and Irreversibility

When support for continuing reform must be unanimous at every stage, so that groups have veto power, heterogeneity of interests may imply that gradualism is not politically feasible and reform can only be implemented by big bang. We first consider *ex-ante* heterogeneity of interests, specifically, where individual reforms benefit some interest groups and harm other interest groups, though full reform is preferred by all groups. Suppose that complementarity of reforms is sufficiently weak that any partial reform is beneficial to some interest group; halting the full reform process is politically possible, given the unanimity constraint on either moving forward or back. Since groups that would be hurt realize that any further change (including rollback) will be blocked, they will block partial reform.[16] The only politically feasible strategy would be big bang, in which all groups unambiguously benefit.

This point can be easily illustrated using the deterministic model in the previous subsection with a simple example following Martinelli and Tommasi (1997). Suppose now that there are two distinct groups in the population, call them *I* and *II*, each with the power to block any reform, partial or full. (With this unanimity constraint, the relative size of the groups does not matter.) Reform 1 gives a net benefit of H to group *I* and of $-L$ to group *II*, where $H > L$. Reform 2 gives a net benefit of H to group *II* and $-L$ to group *I*. To give a role to gradualism but keep the example simple, we assume no discounting ($\beta = 1$), but suppose there is path dependence, in that the benefit of full reform depends on the sequencing. To capture the idea that gradualism is economically optimal, suppose that if reform 1 is implemented first and reform 2 only afterwards, the benefit of full reform to each group is $B_{12} = \gamma(H - L)$, where $1 < \gamma < H/(H - L)$; with the opposite sequencing or with simultaneous adoption, the benefit of full reform to each group is lower, but still positive, say $B_{21} = H - L > 0$. Suppose there are no economic reversal costs ζ.

The implications of unanimity on speed and sequencing are clear. Though gradualism with the adoption of reform 1 before reform 2 is optimal (assuming full reform will be eventually implemented), it is not politically feasible. If reform 1 were adopted alone, group *I* would block the adoption of full reform (and, analogously, group *II* would block the adoption of full reform if reform 2 were adopted alone). Knowing this, group *II* will block a partial reform in which reform 1 is adopted. Only an immediate, full reform is politically feasible. Though this example is quite stylized, it captures the essential elements of the political constraints on the design of reform and transition programs implied by the ability of interest groups to block reforms that are not in their individual interests.

---

[16] Any partial reform that benefitted all groups, that is, where heterogeneity of interests of the type specified here is not present, could of course be implemented.

The presence of special interest groups that can block reforms is an important political argument for big bang. Martinelli and Tommasi present a general equilibrium model of labor absorption which illustrates the same points in a less stylized model. The model of labor reallocation under the constraint of unanimity presented in Section 13.6 makes very similar points.

Gradualism and optimal sequencing may be politically infeasible even in the absence of interest groups with an *ex-ante* conflict of objectives. Consider the model of uncertainty about net benefits above in which individuals were identical *ex ante* but differed in the benefits they received from reform once it was implemented. This *ex-post* heterogeneity due to nonuniform distribution of benefits implied that once reform was implemented, individuals differed in their desire to continue the reform. Under majority rule, this implied that the choice of the sequencing of reforms affected the probability of continuing the reform process. Under unanimity, *ex-post* heterogeneity could imply the same political infeasibility of gradualism that we saw under *ex-ante* heterogeneity and majority rule. As above, it is crucial that partial reform is feasible as an equilibrium. Assume the same configuration of benefits as in the earlier example (H for "gainers," $-L$ for "losers"), except that individuals do not know *ex ante* whether they will be gainers or losers from a given reform. Though the identity of gainers and losers is not known beforehand, gradualism may nonetheless be politically infeasible. The key to the argument is that even though it is not known *ex ante* who will be a net gainer, it *is* known that there will be net gainers who can then block further reform. (One could think of these gainers as the vested interests in Olson's [1982] theory of stagnation who are created by changes which have strong distributional consequences even though they are beneficial in aggregate. See Section 10.3 of Chapter 10.) Knowing that there will be such groups, the population as a whole may block partial reform, so that only big bang is politically feasible.

The assumption of veto power brings into sharp relief a result derived above on the negative implication of building constituencies who can block further change, namely, the loss in flexibility. By considering the difficulty of undoing a policy once a constituency for it has been created, we see there are two sides to making it more difficult to reverse a reform; the downside is that the population as a whole may be less inclined to begin the process, even if the identity of the blocking constituency is not known *ex ante*. Using the analysis earlier in this section, the point may be put slightly more technically. Making reversal more difficult reduces the option value of early reversal, and hence implies a lower *ex-ante* expected value to the reform process. The realization that reform, once started, will be politically difficult to roll back may make groups hesitant to support it. A reform program may be more politically feasible *ex ante* precisely because it is easier to reverse.

13.6. LABOR REALLOCATION

In this and the following two sections, we consider specific areas of major structural reform, the first being the labor market. In systems which are mainly market-oriented, labor market reform means reducing government intervention in the labor markets, whether direct intervention or extremely restrictive labor legislation. In formerly socialist economies in which the government was the overly dominant authority, labor market reform means reallocation of labor to more productive uses. Though restructuring of production in these economies has many aspects, it has overwhelmingly taken the form of "labor shedding" as previously highly inefficient firms divest themselves of excess labor. In this section, we concentrate on the political economy of labor shedding and reallocation.

Restructuring via labor reallocation has a number of political implications. First, worker approval of programs of labor reallocation in formerly socialist economies is an important aspect of support for the transition process.[17] Second, shedding of inefficient labor has led to very high rates of unemployment in these economies, which becomes a significant political constraint in the design of transition programs. In the narrowest sense, it means the need for a "social safety net" to ensure political support for transition. A program of unemployment compensation has fiscal implications and feeds back into the speed of transition due to incentive effects.

Problems of political support due to unemployment and falling labor incomes resulting from labor reallocation do not apply only to former socialist economies. Income and unemployment effects imply pressure for transfers, a topic discussed at length in Chapter 8. They also have implications for elections. As argued in Chapter 7 for market democracies, changes in personal income and unemployment in the year before an election significantly affect election outcomes. Similarly, it is argued that in Poland, for example, the high unemployment associated with the first years of the transition was an important factor in the election outcome in 1993, in which the reformers were defeated. In the next several subsections, we take up a number of these points, such as implications of the need for worker support in the design of reallocation programs and of unemployment compensation as part of the reform process.

Labor Reallocation—A Basic Model

The general problem of labor reallocation in a transition economy is that a factory has workers who differ in their productivity or in the disutility of

---

[17] For example, as Aghion and Blanchard (1994, p. 287) put it for Poland, "Like every other decision involving state firms, privatization has required, de facto, worker's approval. This has largely determined both the—slow—speed as well as the shape of privatization." The role of worker veto-power is not as strong in other transition economies, however.

644

effort. Workers prefer working in the firm due to the high wages relative to the utility of their alternatives; the transition problem is to get the less productive workers to exit the firm. The government cannot observe worker characteristics, so it must induce less productive workers to self-select themselves out of the firm. Nonobservability means that there cannot be a "command optimum" in which the government simply orders all low-productivity workers to exit the factory. Instead, it must use a combination of wage and transfers for exit to induce self-selection.

Dewatripont and Roland (1992a, 1992b) present a simple two-period model of the political economy of labor reallocation in a given sector. Output per worker y is a function of effort ξ according to $y(\xi)$; suppose that there are two possible levels of effort, $\xi = 1, 2$, implying two levels of output per worker, $y(1) = y^1$ and $y(2) = y^2 > y^1$. In this model with two levels of productivity, Dewatripont and Roland assume that the government can control effort directly, but cannot observe the disutility of effort of individual workers, denoted z. Initially, there are three types of workers in the sector, each group of size one, made up of a continuum of atomistic workers. The disutility of effort of these three types is

$$z^H \geq z^M \geq z^L \geq 0. \tag{13.11}$$

Worker utility in each period is simply income (which is the sum of wages w and any transfers ν he may receive) minus ξ multiplied by the disutility of effort:

$$\Omega^i = w + \nu - \xi z^i, \tag{13.12}$$

where the effort after leaving the sector is normalized to zero, as is the outside opportunity of each type of worker. For simplicity, assume no discounting between periods.

Before restructuring, all workers are producing at level y^1, that is, at effort level $\xi = 1$; the wage is $w^{SQ} > z^H$ and transfers ν are zero. (Transfers to workers are paid to induce exit as part of a program of restructuring.) The excess of w^{SQ} over z^i is the "situation rent" associated with the inefficient status quo. This rent is negatively correlated with the disutility of effort in the sector. The aim of restructuring is to raise output per worker to y^2 with only type z^L remaining in the sector. This outcome is consistent with allocative efficiency under the assumption

$$z^M \geq y^1 \geq y^2 - y^1 \geq z^L. \tag{13.13}$$

This condition implies that the disutility of effort for type z^M (and hence for type z^H as well) is no less than output per worker for both output levels y^1 and y^2 (the first two inequalities) and that the gain in output in moving from $\xi = 1$ to $\xi = 2$ exceeds the greater disutility of effort for type

z^L (the last inequality). Hence, efficiency of labor allocation implies that only type z^L should remain in the sector at productivity level y^2.

As indicated, the key problem the government faces in restructuring is *asymmetric information*: it knows the values z^H, z^M, and z^L, as well as the proportion of each type of worker in the sector's work force, but it cannot observe an individual worker's disutility of effort. In order to achieve labor reallocation, it must induce low-effort workers to exit the sector by use of a package of wage w, transfer ν, and mandated effort level ξ offered to all workers in the sector at any date. In technical terms, the government offers an incentive-compatible package at each date to induce self-selection. (It is assumed that if a worker is indifferent between reform and the status quo, he votes for reform.) The government is an agenda setter, having the initiative in offering restructuring proposals. In period 1, the government thus offers a package $(w_1, \nu_1, \xi_1, w_2', \nu_2', \xi_2')$, where the subscripts refer to calendar time and the "prime" refers to an announced policy which, in the absence of government commitment across periods, need not carry out. In period 2, the government proposes a package (w_2, ν_2, ξ_2). In choosing packages, the government's objective is to maximize the net allocative surplus (the excess of total output per capita over total disutility of labor) minus the distortionary cost of government subsidies to firms meant to finance wage payments. For example, in the status quo before restructuring, the government is covering the sector's deficit of $3w^{SQ} - 3y^1$ by a subsidy to the sector financed by distortionary taxation. Denoting by d the distortionary cost per unit of the subsidy, the value of the government's objective in the status quo is

$$V^{SQ} = [3y^1 - (z^H + z^M + z^L)] - d[3w^{SQ} - 3y^1]. \qquad (13.14)$$

On the basis of this set-up, Dewatripont and Roland consider the optimality of alternative restructuring programs under two different political constraints: unanimity of worker approval, consistent with the crucial position of labor in some transition economies, and majority worker approval, which as we saw in the previous section, gives special importance to the government's role as an agenda setter.

Unanimity

Under the political constraint of unanimity of worker approval, a reform program must leave each worker at least as well off as he was under the status quo. This puts a strong constraint on what programs are politically feasible.[18] The seemingly most straightforward possibility for achieving

---

[18] Wyplosz (1993) considers a similar set of issues stemming from the constraint on restructuring programs implied by requiring that minority interests be taken into account. He stresses the importance of the ability to borrow abroad in order to finance compensation to the losers of the reform process, especially when reform is characterized by a "J-curve" of initial deterioration before the benefits of reform are realized.

efficiency is immediate full reform, that is, a big bang. Under an immediate full reform, efficiency is reached in the first period, with the package implying that types z^H and z^M exit immediately, and type z^L expends effort $\xi = 2$. Hence, given the constraint that a package must be incentive compatible and must satisfy the political constraint of unanimous support, the wage must compensate type z^L for the increase in effort he supplies, while the transfer for exit must be high enough to induce type z^M to exit and keep him as well off as the status quo in both periods, where his situation gave him net utility of $w^{SQ} - z^M$. Hence, immediate full reform yields a rent to the least able, that is, those with a high disutility of labor z^H. The least costly big bang program leading to immediate full reform, consistent with the incentive-compatibility and political constraints, is thus $(w_1, \nu_1, \xi_1)^{BB} = (w^{SQ} + z^L, 2(w^{SQ} - z^M), 2)$, with similar wage and mandated efficiency levels in period 2, and where exit bonus is given here as a lump sum paid in period 1 to cover both periods, conditional on not working in the sector in both periods.

When deriving the optimal behavior of the three types of workers, it may be useful to calculate the utility value of different actions. These are given in Table 13.3 for full immediate reform, and may be similarly calculated for other reforms. Using (13.12), Table 13.3 gives, for each type of worker, the utility of staying in the sector under the reform, denoted Ω^{stay}, the utility of exiting the sector under the reform, denoted Ω^{exit}, the utility of the status quo (hence, rejecting the reform), denoted Ω^{SQ}, the net gain from reform relative to the status quo under the optimal decision of staying or exiting, denoted Ω^{REF}, and the optimal decision (where this may be rejecting the reform, relevant under majority rule).

We can see the cost to immediate full reform. The desire to quickly remove inefficient workers implies rents to the least able, which may be quite high. The associated value of the government's single-period objective function is

$$V^{BB} = [y^2 - 2z^L] - d[3w^{SQ} + z^L - 2z^M - y^2]. \qquad (13.15)$$

In the attempt to save on costs of transfers and subsidies, the government may opt instead for a partial reform in the first period. They will accept lower productivity y^1 and keep type-z^M workers employed in the

TABLE 13.3
One-Period Worker Payoffs under Big Bang

Type	Ω^{stay}	Ω^{exit}	Ω^{SQ}	Ω^{REF}	Decision
z^L	$w^{SQ} - z^L$	$w^{SQ} - z^L$	$w^{SQ} - z^L$	0	Stay
z^M	$w^{SQ} + z^L - 2z^M$	$w^{SQ} - z^M$	$w^{SQ} - z^M$	0	Exit
z^H	$w^{SQ} + z^L - 2z^H$	$w^{SQ} - z^M$	$w^{SQ} - z^H$	$z^H - z^M$	Exit

sector, but save on wage payments and exit costs in the process. In this case, with effort unchanged relative to the status quo, they need not raise the wage, and the transfer for exit needed to keep type-z^H workers only as well off as the status quo, conceding no extra rents to these workers (over and above the "situation rents" associated with the inefficiencies that characterized the status quo). The lack of excess rents to type z^H reflects the fact that type z^M does not exit, implying that type z^H cannot skim off extra rents. The least costly program leading to this partial reform in the first period, consistent with the incentive-compatibility and political constraints, is $(w_1, v_1, \xi_1)^{PART} = (w^{SQ}, 2(w^{SQ} - z^H), 1)$, where, as in the case of full reform, the exit bonus is paid as a lump sum to cover both periods. Using a similar analysis to that presented in Table 13.3, one can show that each group is just indifferent between the status quo and reform conditional on their optimal strategy, which is to stay working in the sector for types and z^L, and z^M, and to exit for type z^H. The value of the government's (single-period) objective function under immediate partial reform is

$$V^{PART} = [2y^1 - z^M - z^L] - d[3w^{SQ} - z^H - 2y^1]. \quad (13.16)$$

Given z^H and z^M, partial reform will be preferable for z^M close to z^L, for then the efficiency loss from keeping type z^M working is small relative to the gain from lower rent extraction. Full reform gives excess rents (relative to situation rents in the status quo) of $z^H - z^M$ to workers of type z^H, and exit for type z^M workers. Given the trade-off between efficiency on the one hand and the cost of wage subsidies and transfers needed to satisfy the political and incentive constraints on the other, a parameter configuration like this will imply the preferability of partial over immediate full reform. Far lower financial cost of reform will compensate for lower efficiency of the results relative to more restructuring. Formally, the government will prefer partial to full reform in the first period if and only if $V^{PART} > V^{BB}$, which implies

$$z^M < \frac{1}{2}(z^L + z^H) - \frac{1}{2d}[(1 + d)(y^2 - 2y^1) + (z^M - z^L)]. \quad (13.17)$$

The problem is that this partial reform is not time consistent. Suppose that (13.17) is satisfied, so that the government prefers partial to full reform. Once the above program of partial reform has been implemented and group z^H has exited in the first period with the exit bonus $2(w^{SQ} - z^H)$, it becomes optimal for the government to offer another reform in period 2, namely, $(w_2, v_2, \xi_2) = (w^{SQ} + z^L, w^{SQ} - z^M, 2)$, the same package offered under full reform, but only for one period. This package will induce z^M to exit and is politically acceptable to both z^L and z^M, while increasing the value of the government's objective function. But since workers know the government's incentives to introduce a new package in the second period once type-z^H workers have exited in the first, they know that the immediate partial reform program is not time consistent. Hence, it cannot be implemented in the first period. Knowing the government's incentive towards time inconsistency, a type-z^H worker would not exit in the first period, preferring to work in the first period (enjoying utility of $w^{SQ} - z^H$ under the partial reform package) and to receive an exit transfer of $w^{SQ} - z^M$ in the second period.

The time inconsistency of a partial reform program should have a familiar ring. A sequence of (time-inconsistent) partial reform programs has the government acting like a discriminating monopsonist who is working his way up the supply curve period by period, paying an exit bonus just sufficient to induce the least able worker still remaining in the sector to exit in that period and promising no further reform in every period. Given the time inconsistency involved in the announcement of no further reform, the program is not an equilibrium and cannot be implemented from the first period. Partial reform would work if the government could commit to no further reform. One possibility is a reputational "spillover," as the government is likely to be restructuring more than one industry at the same time, so that reneging in one sector induces punishment elsewhere. (This sort of "spillover" of bad reputation across relationships has been suggested by Schelling [1960] and was investigated by Cole and Kehoe [1996] in the case of sovereign debt, as discussed in Section 12.8 of Chapter 12.) This argument would have to be worked out in greater detail.

An alternative is a time-consistent program of gradual reform, where enough rents are given to exiting workers to ensure time consistency. In the Dewatripont–Roland model, such a program would be $(w_1, \nu_1, \xi_1, w_2, \nu_2, \xi_2)^{GRAD} = (w^{SQ}, 2w^{SQ} - z^M - z^H, 1, w^{SQ} + z^L, w^{SQ} - z^M, 2)$. Type z^H exits in the first period, type z^M in the second. The value of the government's objective function under this two-stage program of gradual reform is (over both periods)

$$V^{GRAD} = [2y^1 - (z^M + z^L) + y^2 - 2z^L]$$
$$- d[6w^{SQ} + z^L - 2z^M - z^H - 2y^1 - y^2]. \quad (13.18)$$

Comparing (13.18) to (13.15) and (13.16), one sees that $V^{GRAD}/2$ is less than V^{PART}, the value of the government's objective function under (time-inconsistent) partial reform, but greater than V^{BB}, the value of the objective function under (costly) full reform. In fact, V^{GRAD} is the average of $2V^{PART}$ and $2V^{BB}$, the value of the government's objective when these latter two programs are maintained over both periods. Gradual exit of lower-productivity workers saves costs relative to achieving this efficiency immediately (that is, relative to achieving the same goal by big bang), because it concedes lower rents to less able workers who are reallocated over time. Under gradualism, the first-period exit bonus to z^H can be lower, as only these workers are reallocated at that time. However, the constraint of maintaining support for the program by all workers implies that for gradualism to be politically feasible, reallocated workers must be given some rents. From a purely economic perspective, the socially optimal program, that is, the program yielding the highest value of the government's objective function, is preferred because it works up the supply curve and minimizes the costly rents that are paid in the transition process, but the time-inconsistent nature of the program means it will not be supported and hence will not be feasible. Note that, as was stressed in the models of time inconsistency discussed in Chapter 4, heterogeneity of individuals is central to the problem of time inconsistency.

To summarize, asymmetric information combined with the fiscal costs of large-scale labor reallocation provides a rationale for gradualism in the presence of political constraints. The case for gradualism presented here is *not* based solely on economic considerations, neither on the simple economic argument that rapid restructuring is technically impossible, nor on the incentive-based argument that a gradual program simply forces individuals to reveal their private information and allows the government to minimize restructuring costs. The constraint of maintaining worker support for the program (here appearing as the requirement of time consistency) dictates a gradual program that is more costly than the government's most preferred gradual program, but is politically feasible.

Majority Rule

Under the requirement of needing to obtain the support of only a majority of the affected workers, the government is less politically constrained than under the requirement of unanimous support. Minorities can be hurt by reform programs, though of course economic and incentive-compatibility constraints must still be satisfied. More importantly, the government can play groups off not only against one another, but also against their future selves. This is the point that was explored in Section 12.4 above; Dewatripont and Roland (1992a, 1992b) apply these ideas to the case of labor reallocation in the process of restructuring. Their focus is on how the government, utilizing its power as an agenda setter, can dynamically exploit shifting majorities to extract more rents from workers, a procedure they term "divide and rule."

In order to investigate divide and rule tactics, Dewatripont and Roland (1992b) begin with two full reforms that are politically feasible under the majority-rule constraint, each hurting one type of worker. One is the second-period reform $(w_2, v_2, \xi_2)^{FL-} = (w^{SQ} - z^M + 2z^L, 2(w^{SQ} - z^M), 2)$, which gives z^L a wage just high enough to prevent them from exiting the sector, but leaves them worse off than the status quo (hence the labeling of the program $FL-$). The high exit bonus induces exit and support by types z^M and z^H. Group z^L opposes the reform, but they are in the minority. The other is the second-period reform $(w_2, \nu_2, \xi_2)^{FM-} = (w^{SQ} + z^L, 2(w^{SQ} - z^H), 2)$. The wage is such that group z^L remains employed, but at a higher effort level than the status quo, and is just indifferent between the status quo and full reform (and hence supports the program under the assumption that weak dominance of reform means it will be supported); the exit bonus is such that group z^H exits and supports the (weakly dominant) reform. The wage and exit bonus imply that type-z^M workers exit,[19] but are worse off than under the status quo. They oppose the reform, but are in the minority. These two programs imply the same allocative surplus $y^2 - 2z^L$, but differ in the distribution of payments across types of workers.

The importance of these policies is that they can be used by an agenda-setting government as threats to induce acceptance of reform programs that actually hurt a majority! Consider the first-period proposal $(w_1, \nu_1, \xi_1, w_2, \nu_2, \xi_2)^{FL-, M-} = (2w^{SQ} + 2z^L - z^M - z^H, 2w^{SQ} - z^M - z^H, 2, 2z^L, 0, 2)$. Relative to the status quo, this reform hurts z^M because of a bonus less than $2(w^{SQ} - z^M)$ and hurts z^L by giving them a wage just high enough to keep them in the sector but worse off than the status quo. The reform thus hurts a majority and would be expected to be rejected. Suppose, however, that if this proposal is rejected in the first period (so that we remain in the status quo), the government offers $FM-$, the full reform proposal hurting z^M, in the second period, which is a one-period optimum and is supported by the majority.[20] Group z^M loses $z^H - z^M$ under $FM-$ in the second period and thus would vote for $FL-, M-$ in the first period, as it leaves them better off. That is, the government uses a threat of an even less favorable reform in period 2 to induce z^M to support a reform in period 1 which is preferable to the government and which hurts z^M. This threat is credible, as was argued in the previous paragraph. Hence, by using its power as an agenda setter, the government can obtain majority support for a reform that hurts a majority relative to the status quo. A group is pitted against its future self, so that it agrees to unfavorable terms today in order to avoid a worse loss tomorrow.[21] This is what Dewatripont and Roland mean by "divide and rule" tactics; in (1992b), they present a detailed analysis of a number of such cases.

In terms of the government manipulating current voters, we may draw a number of analogies to earlier models. One analogy is to the possibility

---

[19] To yield the optimality of exit by type z^M, Dewatripont and Roland (1992a) assume that $2z^M \geq z^H + z^L$. Dewatripont and Roland (1992b) consider the alternative case, which requires a higher exit bonus.

[20] $FM-$ is more attractive to the government than $FL-$ under the assumption that $3z^M \leq 2z^H + z^L$. In the alternative case, the threat of implementing $FL-$ in the second period can be used to gain support for $FL-, M-$ in the first period.

[21] Note a similarity with the war-of-attrition model. A group accepts an unfavorable distribution of the burden of stabilization today because waiting implies the expectation of an even more unfavorable result, namely, the same distribution of burdens achieved at higher cost.

that good behavior today is enforced by the threat of punishment tomorrow, as in a number of models in Chapter 6. Since the threat of severe punishment, if believed, can enforce anything, we require such a threat to be credible. This was the requirement of subgame perfection in Chapter 6. Here, the requirement of credibility of the punishment means that the reform threatened in the next period must be optimal from the perspective of the government and must be supported by a majority. Another analogy is to Tabellini's (1991) model of nonrepudiation of the debt in a majority voting model, as discussed in Section 8.6 of Chapter 8. The previous generation issues debt to be repaid by the young of the current generation. The current young would have voted against debt issuance had they had a vote in the previous period, but given the existence of the debt, they vote to honor it. The previous generation, as agenda setters, have "created facts" which lead the young to support a policy which they would not have preferred *ex ante*. Here, the government may also be seen as "creating facts" by threats flowing from its agenda-setting powers.

On the other hand, passing reforms by threatening even worse policies may satisfy a credibility constraint, but certainly does not confer much *legitimacy* on the government. Support may be given for current programs at the cost of less support for some future program. Though such an idea is discussed in the literature on reform and transition, it has not, to the best of my knowledge, received any formal treatment. One possibility for modeling it would be in terms of a reputational argument when the government has unobserved preferences, as considered in Chapter 6.

Exogenously Fixed Unemployment Benefits

Though the level of unemployment benefits (exit bonuses in the above model) can be treated as an unconstrained policy choice, in reality political pressure implies that governments are required to provide a minimum level of benefits. Aghion and Blanchard (1994) present a simple model of labor reallocation that stresses the fiscal implications of unemployment benefits for the speed of the transition process. The dynamics are driven by job loss in the restructured state sector and job creation in the private sector. The fall in employment in the state sector is linearly increasing in the speed D at which the government chooses to pursue the transition. A higher speed of transition implies higher unemployment generated by the state sector. The amount of job creation H in the private sector is decreasing in labor cost, which is the sum of wages w and unemployment tax τ^U.[22] Assuming linearity with a factor of proportion a, the change in

---

[22] They also present a more sophisticated model in which job creation is forward-looking. The expectation of low profits in the future may lead to low current job creation, so that the pessimistic forecast becomes self-fulfilling.

U_t, the number unemployed, is

$$\frac{dU_t}{dt} = D - H_t$$

$$= D - a(y - \tau_t^U - w_t), \tag{13.19}$$

where y is the constant average product of labor in the private sector. Private sector wages are decreasing in unemployment according to

$$w_t = \nu^U + \gamma \frac{H_t}{U_t}, \tag{13.20}$$

where ν^U is the exogenously fixed level of unemployment benefits, H/U is the ratio of hires to unemployment, and γ is a constant. (A version of this equation including the real interest rate is derived from an optimizing model of choice between employment and unemployment in Aghion and Blanchard.) Taxes on employed workers finance a fixed level of unemployment benefits according to the government budget constraint

$$U_t \nu^U = \tau_t^U (1 - U_t), \tag{13.21}$$

so that higher unemployment raises τ_t^U, the unemployment tax per worker. Therefore the net effect of the level of unemployment on private job creation, and hence the rate of change of unemployment, is nonlinear. Substituting (13.20) and (13.21) into (13.19) to eliminate H_t, w_t, and τ_t^U, one obtains a nonlinear first-order differential equation in unemployment as a function of ν^U and D. A faster speed of transition D implies faster growth in unemployment.

This model of exogenously fixed unemployment benefits has a number of interesting implications. There is a maximum speed of restructuring. If the government opts for too high a rate of transition, the fiscal burden becomes so large that both the restructured state sector and the private sector become unprofitable and shut down. If the government chooses a lower, feasible speed of transition, an equilibrium is reached in which the flow into unemployment from the restructured state sector is just equal to the rate of job creation in the private sector, so that the unemployment rate is constant until the restructuring process is complete. A higher unemployment benefit ν^U implies a higher rate of unemployment during the transition, though given the structure of the model, leaves the speed of transition unchanged.

Insurance Aspects

Atkeson and Kehoe (1995) consider a model of unemployment benefits stressing the insurance aspect in the transition. As in the Dewatripont and

Roland model above, workers choose to leave the state sector as a function of their alternative opportunities and of the nature of social benefits. In contrast to the previous models in this section, Atkeson and Kehoe focus on the search process for employment in the private sector in transition process and on the incentives for efficient search implied by the structure of social insurance. Workers choose both the rate to exit the state sector, as in Dewatripont and Roland, with a higher rate of exit translating into a faster transition, and the intensity to search for good job matches in the private sector. Search is costly and uncertain from the individual point of view. It implies no wage income (and hence lower consumption in the absence of transfers) during the period of search, with consumption financed by borrowing against future expected income. The quality of the match found is uncertain *ex ante*, with higher search activity implying a higher probability, but not a certainty, of a better match.

Their main conclusion is that a more generous unemployment benefit package has ambiguous effects on the speed of transition. One might think that a more generous social insurance package would unambiguously increase the speed of transition, as it diminishes the income risk of job search and hence makes search more attractive. This is indeed what they conclude in a partial equilibrium framework, where one ignores the effect of higher search on aggregate resource constraints and hence on the cost of borrowing. However, in general equilibrium, greater social insurance can actually work in the opposite direction. Demand for consumption is equated to supply of output (produced by nonsearchers) by the interest rate. An increase in social insurance benefits implies a higher consumption demanded at each interest rate; in equilibrium, higher consumption demand must raise the interest rate and thereby decrease search activity. The net effect of an increase in social insurance benefits depends on the specification of the utility function. If agents have a strong precautionary demand for saving, adding social insurance to a system may actually decrease search and slow the speed of transition, even though it increases individual welfare.

The lesson of the Atkeson and Kehoe model is broader than their specific example. Independent of how one assesses its empirical relevance, it cautions against partial equilibrium analysis in evaluating the implications of labor market compensation programs on the speed of transition. It further suggests the value of carefully specifying the process by which workers find employment in the private sector after exiting the restructured state sector. Political pressure for a stronger social safety net may have ambiguous results for the speed of transition.

13.7. PRIVATIZATION

Another key structural reform is the privatization of state-owned industries. Privatization refers to two things at the firm level: the transfer from the government to private managers of the right to *control* the use of factors; and, the increase in the *ownership* of the income flows and profits by managers and private investors. Privatization is sometimes given broader meanings—the reduction in the influence of state-owned monopolies in the private sector; more generally, the extension of the private sector in the economy; or even the establishment of property rights in economies where the institution of private property was previously limited—but we concentrate on the narrower meanings.

As in the case of labor reallocation, while privatization is relevant for a range of economies, the issue has received the most attention in the case of the transition to market-oriented systems in formerly socialist economies. Privatization is sometimes discussed as if it were synonymous with restructuring; as we shall see, the two are connected in practice, though conceptually distinct. If the structure of production in a publicly owned firm is inefficient, it can (at least in theory) be restructured without being privatized (or restructured prior to being privatized in order to increase its selling price, as was done in many cases in Western Europe); conversely, it can be sold off to private sector owners without being restructured. To the extent that privatization and restructuring are considered together, the material of the previous section on labor reallocation becomes relevant in this section as well, as does the question of sequencing.

Transfer of Ownership and Transfer of Control

If privatization is viewed as transfer of ownership of income flows, questions of distribution are especially important, and they play a major role in determining political support for privatization. Privatization generally increases the inequality of the distribution of income and especially of wealth. To the extent that the questions involved are those of income and wealth redistribution, a number of issues were discussed on a general level in Chapter 8. For example, if redistribution is disguised, the discussion of disguised transfers in that chapter is relevant. More likely it is not disguised, with the outcome of the battle over how to privatize reflecting the strengths of the various combatants. A model of rent seeking may then be more applicable. Though ownership of income flows is not the only question, conflict over distribution of income and wealth is clearly one of the key political economy questions connected with privatization.

The distributional consequences are often a major factor in the design of actual privatization schemes.[23] Free distribution of shares to workers in their factories or the distribution of vouchers giving the right to buy shares

---

[23] One should note that there are also efficiency issues related to the effect of ownership structures on the ability of the firm to get financing, which may be crucial for restructuring. A key point is how the initial distribution of ownership affects the longer-term ownership structure.

is motivated in no small part by concerns about wealth inequality that other privatization programs may engender. As in many other government programs affecting income and wealth distribution, it is crucial to distinguish between short-run and long-run effects. This is especially true in privatization in formerly socialist economies, since the value of ownership of a firm will depend greatly on the structure of production, assumed highly inefficient under the old regime. Restructuring, however, will be affected by ownership, that is, who are the residual claimants to the income streams. Ownership structures will affect the ability of the firm to get financing, and the initial distribution of ownership may affect the longer-term ownership structure. Rapid and exclusive distribution of shares to workers may leave them worse off in the long run than alternatives which appear to be less favorable to them in the short run.

Control of firm decisions over resource use has a number of political aspects as well. Boycko, Shleifer, and Vishny (1993, 1996a, 1996b) and Shleifer and Vishny (1994) view state-owned enterprises as catering to the desires of politicians who want to increase employment in these firms and industries because of the political influence it gives them. Schmidt (1995) argues that privatization reduces the flow of this type of information to politicians, thus leading to restructuring, better allocation of labor, and a reduced resource drain on the public treasury.

The importance of establishing property rights in formerly socialist economies is seen as crucial to successful privatization and, more generally, to successful transition. As in other applications (see, for example, the discussion in Chapter 11 on property rights and economic growth), discussions of the role of property rights are not only informal as opposed to model-based, but also not always carefully thought out. In the context of transition economies, establishing property rights means establishing not only ownership and control rights, but also contract enforcement. Shleifer (1995) presents a very clear and insightful discussion of the issues involved.

There has been relatively little formal modeling of the political economy of privatization *per se*. This may reflect the view that the primary political economy question involved is redistribution, so that models of the conflict over redistribution are directly applicable. It may reflect the mistaken identification of privatization with restructuring, so that models of the latter are taken to be models of the former. There are, however, a number of promising lines of research.

A Model of Privatization Stressing Political Control

Boycko, Shleifer, and Vishny (1996a) present a simple linear model of political factors in privatization that captures a number of key considerations. (Shleifer and Vishny [1994] present a nonlinear version of the model with more stress on "bribes," i.e., transfers from firms to politicians.) The model concentrates on the gains from high employment that politicians see in state-owned enterprises, arguing that they are inefficient because they cater to the desires of politicians, rather than attempting to maximize efficiency. Politicians care about employment because high employment in the public sectors or in firms whose existence clearly depends on the government gives them votes and political influence. A money-losing firm which provides votes has a positive value to the government. Hence, a politician who controls the decisions of a public enterprise may force it to employ too much labor. Boycko, Shleifer, and Vishny are especially interested in the question of what are the circumstances under which privatization will lead to efficient restructuring of previously publicly owned enterprises.

Boycko, Shleifer, and Vishny consider a firm that chooses only the level of labor expenditures ω (that is, the wage bill, measured in dollars), which can take two values: an efficient amount ω^L or a higher amount $\omega^H > \omega^L$. Higher spending reflects excess wages and employment. There are three agents: the manager of the firm, representing the interests of private shareholders who have claim to a fraction γ of the firm's profits, a politician who cares about employment for political purposes, and the Treasury, which has claim to a fraction $1 - \gamma$ of the firm's profits and can give subsidies to the firm. Hence, public ownership is a continuous rather than a discrete variable, with a public firm being one with a value of γ close to zero. The politician and the manager of the firm have preferences over employment. We begin with a politician's objectives.

The politician favors high employment for political reasons, assigning a value $0 < \chi < 1$ to each dollar of employment expenditures. On the other hand, excess employment expenditures of the firm (that is, $\omega^H > \omega^L$) reduce the firm's, and hence the Treasury's, profits. The politician cares about this only indirectly, as lower Treasury profits may increase the pressure by the Treasury on the politician to stop programs of employment expansion. Assume that lower Treasury profits reduce politician welfare (measured in dollars) by a factor κ', where κ' is positive, but (perhaps significantly) less than 1. A low value of κ' represents a further bias the politician has towards high employment. The politician also assigns a cost to subsidies ν to the firm of κ'' per dollar of subsidies, where $\kappa'' < 1$. If the Treasury is fully aware of the politician's motivations and can fully see through disguised transfers in the form of overemployment and firm inefficiency, then κ'' should equal κ'. More likely, information asymmetries mean that it is easier for the politician to squander the firm's profits through overemployment and other inefficiencies than to get an extra dollar of subsidies for it, so that $\kappa' < \kappa''$. Boycko, Shleifer, and Vishny argue that there is also a political aspect to this difference, arising from competition among politicians (see the discussion of Boycko, Shleifer, and Vishny [1996b] below)—when a firm wastes resources, most politicians are unaware of the firm's potential profitability and hence do not attempt to appropriate these resources for themselves; in contrast, a politician who wants to give a transfer to the firm must compete for Treasury funds with other politicians who want to give subsidies to their own desired targets.

The politician's objective function may be represented by

$$\Omega^{\mathrm{Pol}} = \chi\omega - \kappa'(1 - \gamma)\omega - \kappa''\gamma\nu, \tag{13.22}$$

where the last term reflects the fact that, as part owner of the firm, the Treasury receives $1 - \gamma$ dollars back for every dollar of subsidies it gives, so that the effective subsidy is $\gamma\nu$. Subsidies are used by politicians to affect the manager's employment choices; before privatization, the politician chooses employment ω directly, implying no need to use subsidies in addition, so that ν would equal 0.[24]

The objective of the manager is to maximize his share of the profits inclusive of subsidies. In this simple formulation, profits from production are just a linear decreasing function of employment. Hence, the manager's objective function may be written

$$\Omega^{\mathrm{Man}} = -\gamma\omega + \gamma\nu. \tag{13.23}$$

Richer specifications could be used, but the conceptual results will be the same as long as the manager cares more about maximizing profits than does the politician.

Boycko, Shleifer, and Vishny (1996a) concentrate on privatization as a transfer of control of factor use from government to the private sector. The high value the politician puts on employment relative to other considerations is embodied in the assumption

$$\chi > (1 - \gamma)\kappa'. \tag{13.24}$$

This implies that the politician always prefers high employment ω^{H} to efficient low employment ω^{L}. When control of employment is turned over to managers and shareholders, their desire to maximize profits would lead them to choose $\omega = \omega^{\mathrm{L}}$ in the absence of other incentives. The politician may then use government subsidies to the firm to try to induce managers to choose a higher level of employment than is efficient. Boycko, Shleifer, and Vishny argue that the political use of transfers raises a key question about the effects of privatization: given the incentive of politicians to use subsidies to encourage overemployment, under what conditions will managers with rights of control choose to restructure (i.e., shed excess labor) rather than receive subsidies? That is, when will privatization be effective

---

[24] In their model with a continuum of employment levels, Shleifer and Vishny (1994) argue that if he controls employment directly, the politician will prefer higher private ownership, as it implies a greater amount that can be extracted from the firm via pushing for higher employment. (This article also draws a distinction between privatization as a transfer of claims over ownership rights and "corporatization" as a transfer of control.)

in inducing restructuring, even though politicians will use subsidies to try to prevent labor shedding?

The equilibrium level of employment and transfers after privatization, given the costs politicians face in extracting resources from the Treasury, depends on bargaining between the manager and the politician. In the absence of subsidies, the manager would choose ω^L. As a result of bargaining, he will choose ω^H if, conditional on the subsidy he receives for high employment, this choice makes him better off. Boycko, Shleifer, and Vishny compute the Nash bargaining solution (under equal bargaining power) given the objective functions (13.22) and (13.23). With only two possible employment levels, this solution maximizes the product of the gain in utility for the manager of switching from ω^L to ω^H and the gain in utility for the politician of switching from ω^L to ω^H, where these gains depend on the level of subsidies ν.[25] The equilibrium transfer consistent with the firm choosing high employment as a result of bargaining is the transfer that maximizes the product of the utility gains, namely,

$$\nu = \frac{\chi + \gamma\kappa'' - (1 - \gamma)\kappa'}{2\gamma\kappa''}(\omega^H - \omega^L). \tag{13.25}$$

If either party is worse off with ω^H and this transfer than he is with ω^L and no transfer, then a bargain will not be struck. Even with the prospect of transfers, the manager will restructure the firm and shed excess workers.

The condition for neither manager nor politician to benefit from high employment (i.e., for the utility gains from switching from ω^L to ω^H for both parties to be negative with ν given by (13.25)) is

$$\chi < \gamma\kappa'' + (1 - \gamma)\kappa'. \tag{13.26}$$

If (13.26) holds, privatization will lead to restructuring. The left-hand side of (13.26) is the benefit to the politician from high employment, the right-hand side is the cost in terms of direct and disguised transfers. When (13.26) holds, the politician will be unable to make it worthwhile to the firm not to restructure. Comparing (13.26) and (13.24), the difference is the term $\gamma\kappa''$. Privatization can lead to restructuring because, once privatized, the firm must be compensated by more for keeping excess labor—the politician must compensate the firm for profits foregone by private owners, which was not the case when the politician controlled employment decisions. Transfer of control makes the politician internalize the cost of inefficiently high employment, hence encouraging restructuring.

Transfer of ownership of income flows will have a similar effect. When $\kappa'' > \kappa'$, an increase in γ (i.e., greater private ownership) will raise the

---

[25] In the Shleifer and Vishny (1994) variant of this model, with a continuum of possible employment levels, there is a richer set of possible equilibria.

right-hand side of (13.26), making the condition more likely to hold, even when (13.24) holds as well. As ownership is transferred from the Treasury to the private sector, the politician must pay for excess employment not in terms of profits foregone, but in terms of subsidies, which are more expensive to him. This also encourages restructuring. Hence, both aspects of privatization are important in encouraging restructuring. Transfer of control makes politicians accountable for the profits lost due to excess employment, as the firm needs to be subsidized to be convinced to keep excess workers. Transfer of ownership forces politicians to give these subsidies directly rather than disguised in the form of lower profits for the Treasury. These direct subsidies are politically costly, as they must be extracted from a Treasury faced with many conflicting interests and demands, including groups pushing for lower taxes and a smaller government.

Boycko, Shleifer, and Vishny (1996b) suggest that the assertion that state-owned firms should be restructured before they are privatized depends on viewing the government as a social welfare maximizer. They argue quite forcefully that conflicts of interests within the government are at the center of the privatization debate. Once one views governments as made up of agents with sharply conflicting interests, rapid privatization with no restructuring [26] or other pre-privatization reforms emerges as the optimal policy. Specifically, they contend that in the typical formerly socialist economy, governments are often coalitions of sharply different political interests, with the ministry in charge of a state-owned firm or industry having an interest in maintaining state control. Consistent with the previous regime, these firms are the constituents of the ministry, who provide its base of power and who will lose their privileged position when the market economy develops. As they put it (1996, p. 768), "the traditional ministers are interested in maintaining state control over these sectors of the economy, continuing the flow of subsidies to them, as well as preserving the dependency of these sectors, and of the millions of voters they employ, on the ministries and the state more generally." Restructuring firms and breaking up state monopolies is generally contrary to their interests, as it implies a loss of resources and control. Hence, to the extent that the minister controls the decisions concerning the firm or industry, restructuring will not take place. More generally, any reform in that industry that lessens the rents the minister receives from his position will not be undertaken. For example, they will oppose various sorts of price deregulation, or the creation of independent regulators or authorities that would compete with the minister for control over firms.

---

[26] An important assumption here is that the initial ownership does not "lock in" the subsequent ownership structure.

Soft Budget Constraints

Kornai (1979, 1980) introduced the concept of "soft budget constraints," whereby the more money a firm loses, the higher are the subsidies it receives. Hence, firms will not have to face the full financial implications of inefficient production generally associated with a market system. There is a clear political aspect of soft budget constraints, as subsidies given to persistently inefficient, money-losing enterprises are presumably motivated by considerations other than economic efficiency. The model of Boycko, Shleifer, and Vishny (1996a) discussed above gives such a political motivation, namely, the maintenance of inefficiently high employment in order to generate votes and political support. This accords with Kornai's view that soft budget constraints are politically motivated by the desire of governments to avoid politically costly unemployment.

Dewatripont and Maskin (1995) present a very different argument in which soft budget constraints reflect not the sacrifice of economic efficiency maximization for political goals, but economic maximization in the presence of dynamic consistency problems. When there is asymmetric information *ex ante* and "sunk" investment costs *ex post*, subsidizing firms that have been unprofitable may be economically optimal. Their argument may be represented by a simple example. Suppose two types of project managers borrow one dollar for one period from the government: those with "good" (or "fast") projects that yield a (discounted) gross financial return of $R^H > 1$ after one period; and, those with "bad" (or "slow") projects, which generate no financial return after a single period. If refinanced for another period, a bad project has a (discounted) expected gross financial return of $R^L > 1$ at the end of the second period. Suppose further that when a project is successful ("good" projects after one period, "bad" projects after two periods), it yields a positive private benefit to the managers, while an unsuccessful project (a "bad" project if terminated after one period) yields a negative private benefit to the manager.

Suppose that $R^L < 2$. The government would then be better off if it were able to commit not to refinance bad, that is, money-losing, projects, since this will deter managers of these projects from applying for funding. However, since $R^L > 1$, it is optimal for the government to refinance at the end of one period, and optimal for managers of such projects to apply for refinancing. Termination of bad projects, that is, imposition of *hard* budget constraints, acts as a discipline device which leads to optimal self-selection, but it is not sequentially rational. Soft budget constraints reflect the problem that once the initial investment has been sunk, it is optimal to provide more funds as the continuation value is positive. This could easily be extended to many periods—in the absence of commitment, no matter how much has been invested in a project so far, further cash flows are optimal as long as the continuation value is positive. Nor is it necessarily a problem in government lending—a private lender faces the same dynamic consistency problem in his decision of whether to cut off loans, as in the case of banks lending to foreign sovereigns discussed in Chapter 12.

Multiple Equilibria in Privatization

So far, we have implicitly assumed that the efficiency gains from privatization are independent across firms. In fact, in the case of formerly socialist economies, the return to privatization of a single enterprise may depend positively on the results of privatizing other enterprises, rather than negatively as a model of limited financial capital might suggest. Increasing returns to privatization are not simply a possible feature of technology; they are inherent in privatization for at least two reasons. The first reason follows from what we argued is the defining characteristic of transition, namely, its scale and multipart nature. Privatization is most likely to succeed if it is part of an overall, comprehensive set of reforms, which is another way of stressing the complementarity of the economic reforms that constitute transition in the formerly socialist economies. By the same token, privatization of a single enterprise is more likely to succeed if it is part of a widespread privatization program. Given the nature of wholesale economic restructuring necessary to achieve efficiency in these economies, privatizing only a few enterprises is unlikely to be economically sustainable. In short, the economic efficiency of privatization is likely to increase with the scale of privatization.

The second argument for the existence of increasing returns is more explicitly political. Privatization is a policy with long run benefits, but short-run costs, such as increased unemployment, that are often high. For the policy of privatization to be continued, a large enough constituency must perceive benefits that outweigh these costs; otherwise, privatization will be abandoned. Expected returns from privatization will be higher if there is the expectation that the privatization program will be continued rather than abandoned. Hence, because of the political nature of the decision to continue as just outlined, a large-scale program (with a larger constituency for continuation) may have a higher rationally expected return than a smaller-scale program.

Labán and Wolf (1993) and Roland and Verdier (1994) investigate the implications of increasing returns, specifically the possibility of multiple equilibria consistent with rational investor beliefs.[27] Due to policy-based increasing returns, the same underlying production technology is consis-

---

[27] Coricelli and Milesi-Ferretti (1993) suggest a related argument concerning the tough reform policies. The short-run economic contraction which may accompany a tough reform will induce expectations that the government will abandon the policy, reducing its credibility and making an adverse output reaction more likely.

tent with a zero-privatization equilibrium and with a full-privatization equilibrium. Both papers argue that increasing returns to scale are central to the very slow progress of the privatization process in these economies relative to what was expected.

The multiple equilibria argument depends on the behavior of investors who must provide the capital to buy up enterprises that the government is attempting to privatize. When investors believe that small-scale privatization will yield low expected returns, they will be hesitant to invest, a hesitancy heightened by the rational expectation that the program will be abandoned. The lack of investment capital makes this expectation self-fulfilling. The policy question is then one of how the good, full-privatization equilibrium may be achieved. One possibility is to introduce other policy measures that eliminate the possibility of multiple equilibria; for example, if multiplicity reflects a self-fulfilling expectation of policy reversal due to a backlash from high unemployment, then an associated social welfare policy may be necessary to ensure the success of the privatization program. Another possibility is to choose policies that allow investors to coordinate on the good equilibrium.

Roland and Verdier suggest that privatization via free distribution of shares or vouchers for some firms to be privatized may reduce or eliminate the possibility of a policy reversal due to a backlash, as it reduces the unemployment consequences of privatization. However, as discussed in Section 13.7, this will increase the cost of restructuring after privatization and may lead to a Pareto-inferior outcome. In their model, it could also transform a unique full-privatization equilibrium into a situation with multiple equilibria. Laban and Wolf suggest minimum income guarantees to lessen the unemployment backlash, or privatization subsidies to allow coordination on the high-privatization equilibrium. As discussed in connection with restructuring in Section 13.6, the financing of these government assistance programs may be a crucial stumbling block. As in Wyplosz's (1993) model on restructuring when an initial deterioration (a "J-curve") is anticipated, the ability to finance these programs through foreign borrowing (or foreign assistance) can be critical in overcoming the political constraints.

Credible Privatization

Though we have touched on information asymmetries in discussing privatization, it has not been central to the analysis. Imperfect information about the commitment of the government to really privatizing state-owned enterprises may be crucial to the success of such efforts. For example, Schmidt (1997) argues that a key determinant of success in large-scale privatization is the belief that current (and future) governments will not expropriate future returns (or even renationalize the privatized firms or sectors). In the absence of such an assurance, restructuring and long-term investment may not take place. To safeguard against future policy reversals when policies are chosen democratically, Schmidt suggests giving away shares in state-owned enterprises to the general public. By lowering the probability of future policy reversals, free distribution of shares may actually induce more investment, higher expected profits, and higher revenues than a policy whereby shares are simply sold to the highest bidder.

Perotti (1995) suggests that imperfect information about the government's commitment to privatization may help explain why it is done only slowly and partially at first even though it is clear that privatization of a government-owned firm is optimal. Suppose that the government's commitment to not changing direction after the sale is unobserved.[28] A slow transition is used to signal a government's good intentions. Both "good" and "bad" governments have an interest in being perceived as the noninterfering type, as this belief on the part of investors will mean a higher sales price. A gradual sale (combined with immediate transfer of control of that part sold) is a signal that the government is patient and is willing to bear residual risk. A government planning to expropriate or otherwise reverse its policy is more impatient for two reasons. First, the sale price will fall once its policy preferences become known. Second, the retention of a large stake as implied by gradual sale reduces the gain from a policy reversal. Underpricing similarly reflects government "patience." Firms whose value is especially sensitive to public policy choices will be privatized with smaller initial sales, larger underpricing, and perhaps a longer period of time to complete privatization. As a government's reputation for commitment grows, we will observe larger share offerings.

13.8. PRICE LIBERALIZATION

A third component of major reform and the transition away from a centrally planned economy is price liberalization, meaning not only the decontrol of formerly controlled prices, but more generally, the introduction of the price mechanism as an allocative device in place of central planning. Exchange rate convertibility is sometimes included, though it is not a critical part of a liberalization package, at least in the early stages; numerous market economies have maintained exchange controls though relying on the price mechanism for allocation.

Income Distribution

Price liberalization (especially decontrol of artificially low prices) is seen as quite unpopular and hence politically difficult, even though it generally

---

[28] Shapiro and Willig (1990) also stress information aspects in modeling the political economy of privatization.

implies the end of queues and shortages of key commodities. This unpopularity may reflect not irrationality, but the very large distributional consequences of moving from centrally dictated to market-determined allocation. Though generally socially beneficial for the population as a whole in terms of improved allocation under a price system, price decontrol implies extremely large gains for some, smaller gains for others, and a loss in welfare for those who benefitted most from artificially low prices. This last group includes not only favored groups who were given disproportionately large rations of the controlled commodities, but also "ordinary" citizens whose consumption was concentrated on basic commodities with artificially very low prices. The effect of price liberalization on purchasing power of large groups of the population is therefore a key political issue which may greatly affect the speed of politically feasible decontrol programs. Income distribution is thus a major factor; as with labor reallocation and privatization, the political support constraint suggests that price liberalization must be combined with social welfare policies to be feasible and successful.

Credibility of Price Decontrol

The design of politically feasible price liberalization programs is also strongly affected by public uncertainty (and perhaps skepticism) about price liberalization. Will a program of price decontrol increase quantity supplied to market by enough to justify the higher prices? Consumers whose experience is limited to centrally planned systems where prices play a limited allocative role may be well aware of the shortcomings of the old regime, but nonetheless take a wait-and-see attitude to the market system. They are simply unsure about whether it will work. A low quantity response to price increases may significantly reduce support for a program of price liberalization if consumers are uncertain about whether this quantity response represents short-run or long-run elasticity of supply (or even unsure about the meaning of the concept "elasticity of supply"). If a program of price decontrol appears only partially successful in increasing the quantity of goods on the market, continuation of the program will be jeopardized.

Uncertainty combined with the need for public support does not, however, immediately imply a gradualist approach to price decontrol, as in some other areas of transition. A gradual program of decontrolling prices that are artificially low induces the expectation that current price increases will be followed by further price increases in the future. The expectation of future price increases induces firms producing durable goods to hold them off the market, leading to a low response of market supply to price. In fact, raising the price by a small amount may create the expectation of further significant decontrol, leading to a *fall* in supply to market. Hence, policy today induces a perverse response in current economic outcomes, not because of the intertemporal budget constraint as in the model in Section 2.5 of Chapter 2, but due to the gradualist nature of the program itself. It is much like the labor reallocation model of Section 13.6 above. The government faces a similar time-inconsistency problem. The expectation of future policy changes confounds the intended purpose of the current program, but the government cannot credibly commit to forgo further price decontrol. Perhaps paradoxically, expected abandonment of the program may induce a more favorable output response, if abandonment implies freezing prices at their current level or even reverting to the lower level of controlled prices.

The political-economic equilibrium consistent with price liberalization depends on the two-way connection between political support and expected program continuation on the one hand and output response on the other. Low supply response reduces support for a program of decontrolling prices; expectations of prices and program continuation in turn affects the price response. The nature of the program will thus be endogenous to economic developments, as well as those developments being strongly determined by expectations of the nature of the program. The question of how a program should be designed in order to maximize the probability of success will turn on the characteristics of the political-economic equilibrium.

Intertemporal Speculation and Program Abandonment

Van Wijnbergen (1992) presents a carefully worked-out, insightful model of political-economic equilibrium of price decontrol, with the aim of illuminating the positive and normative implications of a gradual versus a big bang approach. The two key variables are the supply response to and the credibility of a price-decontrol program, the latter defined as the probability that the program will be continued in the future.

Van Wijnbergen considers a two-period model of an economy producing both traded and nontraded goods. The traded goods sector, whose exogenous price is normalized to unity, uses only labor in a constant-returns-to-scale technology. The real wage w is thus fixed in terms of traded goods. The focus is on the nontraded goods sector, where there are decreasing returns, due to the existence of a fixed factor, say land. There are a large number of producers in the nontraded sector, so that no single producer can affect prices or (in the case of non-market-clearing prices) aggregate shortages. The production structure of the nontraded sector is represented by a cost function, giving the total cost ζ_t of producing output y_t at t:

$$\zeta_t = \zeta(y_t, w), \tag{13.27}$$

where the partial derivatives ζ_y, ζ_{yy}, and ζ_w are all positive. (The cost function is assumed to be the same in the first and second periods for simplicity.) Output produced in period 1 can either be sold in period 1 or stored for sale in period 2, where it will be entirely sold given the assumption of only two periods. Given possible spoilage, goods stored today yield stocks available for sale tomorrow according to

$$S_2 = \gamma(S_1),\qquad(13.28)$$

where $\gamma(0) = 0$, $0 < \gamma' < 1$, and $\gamma'' < 0$.

Prices in the traded goods sector are determined on the world market. Prices in the nontraded goods sector (expressed in terms of traded goods) are initially controlled at price $\bar{P}_0$ below the market-clearing price, P^*, which is assumed the same across periods. A big bang decontrol means allowing the price to rise to P^* immediately, so that $P_1 = P^*$. If a big bang program is continued, then $P_2 = P^*$ as well. If a big bang program is abandoned, van Wijnbergen assumes that prices revert to $\bar{P}_0$. A program of gradual price liberalization has the price increased only partially in period 1, to a level $\bar{P}_1$, where $P^* > \bar{P}_1 > \bar{P}_0$. Hence, a gradualist program will imply some rationing in period 1, the extent of rationing depending on the supply and hoarding response by producers to $\bar{P}_1$. If the gradualist program is continued, prices are fully decontrolled in period 2, so that $P_2 = P^*$. If the gradualist program is abandoned after one period, prices remain at their partially decontrolled level in period 2, that is, $P_2 = \bar{P}_1$. Denote by q^{BB} the probability that a big bang program will be abandoned at the end of one period and by q^{GR} the probability that a gradual program will be abandoned, where these will be endogenously determined. The "credibility" of a program is thus $1 - q^i$, i = BB, GR. Market participants take the relevant q^i as given.

We follow van Wijnbergen in focusing on the gradualist program. In the absence of a program of price decontrol, the price is $\bar{P}_0$ and is expected to remain there in both periods, with an associated level of output $\bar{y}_0$ in each period. All output is brought to market in each period, so that storage is zero in both periods. Under the gradual program, the producer's problem in period 1 is to choose output y_1 and storage S_1 given the current price $\bar{P}_1$ and expectation of next period's price, which is $\bar{P}_1$ with probability q^{GR} and P^* with probability $1 - q^{GR}$. In the second period, producers choose their output based on profit maximization, given the existing market price and the cost function (13.27). Since the price under either scenario is never greater than the market-clearing price, firms assume they will be able to sell all their output plus inventories in period 2, whether the program has collapsed or not. The second-period optimization can then be represented by choosing y_2 to maximize

$$P_2[y_2 + \gamma(S_1)] - \zeta(y_2, w),\qquad(13.29)$$

for given S_1. This yields a quantity of output produced $y_2 = \phi(P_2)$, where

$\phi() \equiv \zeta_y^{(-1)}()$ and $\phi'() = 1/\zeta_{yy} > 0$. The first-period production problem may then be written

$$\max_{y_1, S_1} \bar{P}_1(y_1 - S_1) - \zeta[y_1, w]$$
$$+ \beta E(P_2(\phi(P_2) + \gamma(S_1)) - \zeta[\phi(P_2), w]) \qquad (13.30)$$
$$+ \mu(y_1 - S_1) + \lambda S_1,$$

where the expectation is taken over values of P_2 and where μ and λ are the multipliers associated with $y_1 > S_1$ and $S_1 > 0$, respectively. The first-order conditions associated with the first-period producers problem are

$$\zeta_y[y_1, w] = \bar{P}_1 + \mu, \qquad (13.31)$$

for y_1, and

$$\bar{P}_1 - \lambda + \mu = \beta\big(q^{GR}\bar{P}_1 + (1 - q^{GR})P^*\big)\gamma'(S_1) \qquad (13.32)$$

for S_1. Equation (13.31) simply equates the cost of producing another unit of output to its value, including the shadow value of inventories if constrained by total production; (13.32) equalizes the value of an extra unit of inventories if sold today and the expected value if carried over and sold tomorrow. If either of the constraints is hit (so that either $\mu > 0$ if $S_1 = y_1$, or $\lambda > 0$ if $S_1 = 0$), this equality cannot be satisfied. As the definition of the function $\phi(\cdot)$ indicates, output will be increasing in price under any regime.

The first-order conditions (13.31) and (13.32) can be solved to yield output y_1 and storage S_1 as functions of $\bar{P}_1$ and q^{GR}. Consider first interior solutions for S_1. Output y_1 will be independent of q^{GR}, while S_1 will be decreasing in q^{GR}. Storage is decreasing in q^{GR} since a higher probability of program abandonment implies a lower expected price tomorrow, and hence a lower return to storage. Hence, given $\bar{P}_1$, quantity supplied to the market, namely $y_1 - S_1$, is rising in q^{GR}. A decontrol program that is "front-loaded," in that full decontrol is still achieved in two periods, but with a greater price increase in the first period, may be represented by a higher value of $\bar{P}_1$. Given q^{GR}, a higher $\bar{P}_1$ implies both higher y_1 for given S_1 (see (13.31)) and a smaller incentive to store output (see (13.32)), as it implies a lower capital gain between period 1 and period 2.[29] Hence, the quantity supplied to market increases with an increase in $\bar{P}_1$ at each value of q^{GR} when S_1 is interior.

---

[29] A lower value of $\bar{P}_1$ also means more rationing in period 1, hence more of an incentive for consumers to carry income over into period 2. This would raise the market-clearing price P^*, implying a further incentive for intertemporal speculation and further lowering $y_1 - S_1$.

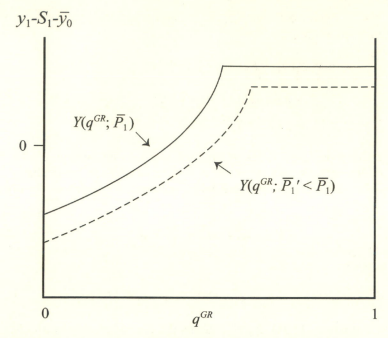

FIGURE 13.1. Output response and probability of program abandonment.

If the probability of abandonment q^{GR} is sufficiently close to 1 (that is, if the credibility of the price decontrol program being continued is sufficiently low), intertemporal speculation may not be optimal, so that $S_1 = 0$ and the quantity brought to market is independent of q^{GR}. For example, when $q^{GR} = 1$, there will be clearly no incentive to speculate, as expected $P_2 = \bar{P}_1$. Given spoilage of goods in storage, the same will be true for q^{GR} close to 1. When $S_1 = 0$, a higher value of $\bar{P}_1$ will imply an increase in the quantity of output brought to market, but the increase will be less than when $S_1 > 0$, as only y_1 is affected. These results may be represented as in Figure 13.1, based on a similar diagram in van Wijnbergen (1992), giving the change in output from the case of no decontrol, namely, $y_1 - S_1 - \bar{y}_0$, as a function of the probability of abandonment q^{GR} for a given $\bar{P}_1$. Call this curve $Y(q^{GR}; \bar{P}_1)$, where the dashed curve represents the relation for a lower value of $\bar{P}_1$. A key feature of this analysis is that for a given probability of abandonment q^{GR}, a "bolder" decontrol program, as represented by a higher value of $\bar{P}_1$, implies less hoarding of goods, more production, and hence smaller shortages.

Consumer Behavior

As in many of the models elsewhere in the book (consider the archetypical Meltzer–Richard model in Chapter 8), consumers play two roles in this model, both as economic and as political actors. As economic actors, they choose consumption demand as a function of the prices they face. The consumer divides his income in each period between traded and nontraded goods, where it is assumed that consumers have the ability to transfer income across periods. When prices clear markets, the consumer's problem is straightforward. Individual optimization aggregated across consumers implies demand functions for traded and nontraded goods; market clearing in the market for nontraded goods implies an equilibrium price P^* for nontraded goods. As this analysis is standard, we do not derive the equilibrium explicitly. For future use, denote by $C_1(P_1, E(P_2), 1)$ and $C_2(P_2, 1)$ the demand for consumption of nontraded goods as a function of current and expected future prices of nontraded and traded goods. (Remember that the price of traded goods is normalized to unity.)

What is novel relative to the analysis in the rest of the book is the case where prices do not clear markets, so that the consumer is rationed to consume a quantity $\bar{c}_t$ in period t. (For simplicity, suppose all consumers face the same ration.) To handle the case of rationing, define **virtual** price as the price at which consumers would willingly consume their allocated rations (see Neary and Roberts [1980] for an exposition of the approach of virtual prices). Hence, $\hat{P}_1$, the virtual price in period 1, satisfies

$$C(\hat{P}_1, EP_2, 1) = \bar{c}_1, \tag{13.33}$$

with a similar equation for $\hat{P}_2$, the virtual price if there is rationing in the second period. Virtual prices are useful in analyzing the welfare implications of rationing and changes in non-market-clearing prices. The welfare gain of a small increase in the allocated ration is proportional to the difference between the controlled and the virtual price, for example, to the difference $\hat{P}_1 - \bar{P}_1$. (As long as there is rationing at $\bar{P}_1$, the virtual price $\hat{P}_1 > \bar{P}_1$.) Under rationing, an increase in a non-market-clearing price has two opposite-signed effects on welfare. A marginal increase in a non-market-clearing price $\bar{P}$ means that the ration $\bar{c}$ costs more, but also increases the size of the ration. The total effect on utility $u(\cdot)$ of a marginal increase in $\bar{P}$ can be expressed as

$$\frac{du(\cdot)}{d\bar{P}} = -\bar{c} + (\hat{P} - \bar{P})\frac{d\bar{c}}{d\bar{P}}. \tag{13.34}$$

The last term represents the response of quantity brought to market with respect to a change in the partially decontrolled price.

In their political role, consumers vote at the beginning of period 2 on whether a price decontrol program should be continued, depending on their beliefs about the effect of decontrol on their welfare. The discussion at the end of the previous paragraph indicates that beliefs about the welfare effects of a decontrol program can be summarized by beliefs about the elasticity of market supply with respect to the market price, where individuals are uncertain about the true elasticity. Given his prior beliefs about this elasticity, each individual uses his observation of actual market supply and price changes in period 1 to form a posterior belief about this elasticity. Specifically, define by η the beliefs of individuals about the supply response $d(y_t - S_t)/dP_t$. Individuals begin with a prior over η and use their observations of $y_1 - S_1$ and $\bar{P}_1$ to form a posterior on η. Heterogeneity of individuals is characterized by a distribution of prior beliefs about η.

Whether or not an individual supports continuation of price decontrol depends on whether or not he believes it will improve his welfare. In general terms, this may be characterized as follows. Equation (13.34) defines a critical value at which an increase in prices has no effect on individual welfare, namely,

$$\eta^{\text{crit}} = \frac{\bar{c}}{\hat{P} - \bar{P}}. \tag{13.35}$$

A voter will support continuing a price decontrol program if his posterior value of η is greater than η^{crit} and will oppose continuation if it is less. This simple characterization of support or nonsupport means that the results of the Median Voter Theorem over two proposals may be applied. A proposal will pass if the median voter supports it and will fail if he does not. In this case, the program of price decontrol will be continued if the median voter's posterior beliefs over output response, denoted η^{med}, exceeds the relevant η^{crit} and will be abandoned otherwise.

To derive a probability q^{GR} of abandonment, let us suppose that individuals in the economy are uncertain about the median voter's η^{med}. All individuals are assumed to have common beliefs about the median voter's η^{med}, as summarized by a common density function $\Psi(\eta^{\text{med}})$ of possible values of η^{med}.[30] Given this distribution, the probability of program abandonment is given by

$$q^{\text{GR}} = \Pr(\eta^{\text{med}} < \eta^{\text{crit}}) = \int_{\eta^{\text{med}} = -\infty}^{\eta^{\text{crit}}} \Psi(\eta^{\text{med}}) \, d\eta^{\text{med}}. \tag{13.36}$$

It remains to determine how the observation of $y_1 - S_1$ affects beliefs about η^{med}. For any voter with any prior about η, the higher the value of $y_1 - S_1$ he observes at any $\bar{P}_1$, the higher should be his posterior η for a

---

[30] This technique, whereby an uncertain election outcome is derived in a median voter model by assuming uncertainty about the median voter's preferences, is commonly used. See, for example, Cukierman and Tommasi (1998a) in Chapter 10 or the electoral models in Chapter 7.

general distribution of possible values of $y_1 - S_1$.[31] The same will obviously be true for the median voter. Thus, for any $\bar{P}_1$, the higher is the observation $y_1 - S_1$, the higher is the belief about η^{med}. More exactly, one may think of a rightward shift in the density function $\Psi(\cdot)$ of possible values of η^{med}. Hence, by (13.35), the higher is $y_1 - S_1 - \bar{y}_0$, the smaller is q^{GR}. We thus get a downward sloping curve $q^{\text{GR}} = Q(y_1 - S_1 - \bar{y}_0)$, giving the probability of abandonment as a function of the observed outcome $y_1 - S_1 - \bar{y}_0$.

How will the $Q(\cdot)$ curve be affected by a smaller value of $\bar{P}_1$, representing a less "front- loaded" reform? One can show (see van Wijnbergen's article) that a lower value of $\bar{P}_1$ causes the curve to rotate counterclockwise around $y_1 - S_1 - \bar{y}_0 = 0$. The intuition is straightforward. When $y_1 - S_1 - \bar{y}_0 > 0$, the observed quantity response for a lower value of $\bar{P}_1$ implies a larger elasticity and hence a larger upward (or smaller downward) revision in η from any given prior. This then implies a rightward shift in the probability density function $\Psi(\eta^{\text{med}})$ and hence a lower value of q^{GR}. Conversely, when $y_1 - S_1 - \bar{y}_0 < 0$, a negative quantity response represents a more negative supply elasticity if observed for a lower $\bar{P}_1$, implying a larger downward revision in the prior η, a leftward shift in the probability density function $\Psi(\eta^{\text{med}})$ and hence a higher value of q^{GR}. The curve $q^{\text{GR}} = Q(y_1 - S_1 - \bar{y}_0, \bar{P}_1)$ and its rotation are represented in Figure 13.2, where the dashed $Q(\cdot)$ curve represents the relation for a lower value of $\bar{P}_1$.

Figure 13.2 (following a similar figure in van Wijnbergen [1992]), which shows both the $Y(q^{\text{GR}}, \bar{P}_1)$ and the $Q(y_1 - S_1 - \bar{y}_0, \bar{P}_1)$ curves, can be used to study the effects of gradualism in price decontrol on supply response and program credibility, meaning the probability that the program will be continued. (The same framework could be used to analyze a multistage decontrol program, to which we return below.) To summarize the above arguments about the curves, an increase in the probability q^{GR} of abandoning the price liberalization program implies a lower expected price next period and thus a lower incentive to stockpile goods rather than bring them to market. Hence, the $Y(q^{\text{GR}}, \bar{P}_1)$ curve slopes up. More stockpiling, that is, a higher S_1, means lower $y_1 - S_1 - \bar{y}_0$, implying a lower perceived supply elasticity and thus a stronger perception on the part of voters that the program of higher prices is *not* eliciting the desired increases in supply of goods. This reduces support for the program and increases the probability that the electorate will vote to abandon the program. Hence, the $Q(y_1 - S_1 - \bar{y}_0, \bar{P}_1)$ curve will be downward sloping.

---

[31] Somewhat more formally, given the price increase $\bar{P}_1 - \bar{P}_0$, an individual's prior on the supply response is $\eta(\bar{P}_1 - \bar{P}_0)$. For a general distribution of possible values $y_1 - S_1$, observing $y_1 - S_1 - \bar{y}_0 > \eta(\bar{P}_1 - \bar{P}_0)$ will lead him to increase his estimate of η, while observing $y_1 - S_1 - \bar{y}_0 < \eta(\bar{P}_1 - \bar{P}_0)$ will lead him to decrease his estimate. The higher is $y_1 - S_1$ either above or below the prior $\eta(\bar{P}_1 - \bar{P}_0)$, the higher is the posterior η. A more formal analysis can be found in van Wijnbergen (1992).

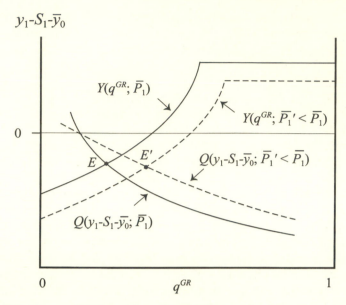

FIGURE 13.2. The equilibrium effect of gradualism.

In a rational-expectations equilibrium, the probability of program abandonment q^{GR} on which supply decisions are made is the actual probability
of the program being abandoned coming out of the political process, given
these supply decisions. This is represented by the intersection of the $Y(\cdot)$
and $Q(\cdot)$ curves, for example, at point E. The diagram is drawn so that
output supplied to market is actually less than what was supplied when
prices were controlled (i.e., at E, $y_1 - S_1 - \bar{y}_0 < 0$), due to a steeply falling
(from *right to left*) $Y(\cdot)$ curve as q^{GR} falls and the likelihood of a significant
price increase next period rises. This characteristic seems quite realistic—in
an economy where prices were kept at well below the market-clearing
levels (that is, $P^* \gg \bar{P}_1$), a partial decontrol still leaves the price well
below the market-clearing price, inducing expectations of a further large
price increase if it is anticipated that the program will be carried through
to completion. Hence, when prices were originally quite distorted, gradual
price decontrol induces expectations of large capital gains if firms wait to
sell their durable output, and hence large stockpiling of production. The
van Wijnbergen model thus captures a number of plausible features of the
effects of a program of gradual decontrol of artificially low prices. Considering point E, one sees that the decontrol program induces an increase in
production due to higher prices, but supply of goods on the market
actually falls. Though prices have risen, shortages get worse, so that with
uncertainty about how output responds to price increases in the new
market environment, there is a perceived negative elasticity of net supply.

Producers are accused of hoarding in order to make large profits, so that the program is seen as having adverse consequences for income distribution. These characteristics generate pressures for the program to be abandoned, as indicated by a probability of abandonment $q^{GR} > 1$.

What about a more "cautious" approach to decontrol? Consider first the case where the program is still scheduled to be completed in two periods, but is less "front-loaded," in that the first-period price is $\bar{P}_1' < \bar{P}_1$. (Van Wijnbergen labels this a more "gradual" approach, but see the discussion of multistage programs below.) A lower initial price implies greater hoarding of output by producers at each q^{GR}, as represented by the dashed upward-sloping curve in Figure 13.2, labeled $Y(q^{GR}, \bar{P}_1')$. However, q^{GR} is not constant, as consumers change their perceptions of the price elasticity of supply, given the *fall* in output (at any q^{GR}) in response to the lower price. This results in a rightward shift in the political support function, as represented by the dashed downward-sloping curve in the figure, labeled $Q(y_1 - S_1 - \bar{y}_0, \bar{P}_1')$. The new rational-expectations equilibrium is at E', where the probability of program abandonment is unambiguously higher. Hence, due to the inducement for greater intertemporal speculation in the presence of uncertainty about supply elasticities, a more cautious start to the program of price decontrol (a more "gradualist" program) actually leads to a greater probability of politically determined program collapse. This is one of the key results of the van Wijnbergen analysis.

An alternative way to define a more gradualist program is one stretching over more periods. Keeping the length of the program constant at two periods while choosing a lower first-period price $\bar{P}_1'$ implies that the "gradualist" program must have higher expected capital gains for any value of q^{GR}. Hence, by construction, making a two-period program more gradual will imply a greater incentive towards intertemporal speculation. Suppose, however, we consider a multistage decontrol program, where gradualism could affect both the length of the program and the way higher prices are phased in. The problem of intertemporal speculation in anticipation of future price increases may or may not be worse, depending on the rate of price decontrol relative to the rate of spoilage of goods and intertemporal discounting. (This may be seen by considering the right-hand side of (13.32).) Hence, a gradual program could be designed to allow learning as in the models discussed in Section 13.5 above without necessarily causing high intertemporal speculation. What is true, however, is that to the extent that gradualism induces the expectation of capital gains from storage, it will imply a greater incentive for voters to abandon the program. The conceptual analysis of decontrol, however, would be identical. This conceptual result is an important message of van Wijnbergen's analysis.

The point may be strengthened by comparing a two-period gradual program with a program of immediate decontrol of prices, that is, $P_1 = P^*$. With immediate price decontrol, there will be no incentive to hoard goods in the expectation of significantly higher prices in period 2. In fact, if there is any perceived probability that the program will be abandoned in the second period, with a reversion to the lower controlled price, there will be a strong incentive *not* to hold goods off market. Given that the higher period-1 price in a big bang program induces a large supply of goods to market, political support for the program based on updated beliefs about supply elasticities should also be high. Hence, though some economic considerations may argue for gradual decontrol, political constraints may imply the need for a rapid decontrol of prices.

13.9. CONCLUSIONS

Our approach to the political economy of reform and transition has been somewhere between the more theoretical approach to policy adoption in Chapter 10 and the very applied approach seen in much of the literature. Given the overwhelming importance of this topic, there is much to be said for the latter approach, in which one studies the political economy of specific reform and transition programs. The decision to begin with a more abstract model was dictated by the perception of a need to give some structure to the somewhat chaotic literature.

The formal structure presented in Sections 13.4 and 13.5 is only a tool. To those not working directly on problems of transition, it is meant to clarify the conceptual arguments on how programs should be structured. The general model, combined with the applications given in Sections 13.6, 13.7, and 13.8, should serve to introduce students of political economy (or of transition) to the political problems involved in transition, as well as providing a framework for analyzing those problems. Those who work (or who want to work) on problems of transition realize that what was covered here is an aid to analysis of, and not a substitute for, detail needed to understand specific country experiences.

CHAPTER FOURTEEN

The Size of Government and the Number of Nations

No matter what your religion, you should try to become a
government program, for then you will have everlasting life.

—Lynn Martin, former U.S. Representative

"Remember those days," McNally said,
"When we'd plan a map a month ahead,
And we'd know, if it came out at noon, let's say,
It was up to date the entire day?"

"Then the countries stayed as fixed by their founders,
And boundaries weren't made by bounders."
"Those days," said Rand, "are gone to *tally*."
"You said it, brother," said Mr. McNally.

*—Newman Levy, "I Wonder What Became
of Rand, McNally...."*

14.1. INTRODUCTION

In this chapter, we consider the political economy of government more
directly, both the size and scope of government, and the number of
governments, that is, nations. Discussion of the size of government based
on economic factors has a long history, dating back at least to Adam Smith
or perhaps well before. The topic has generated renewed interest due to
the significant growth of government in this century, one of the most
striking trends among macroeconomic variables. Tanzi and Schuknecht
(1995), for example, consider government expenditure as a percent of GDP
in a sample of 14 industrialized countries[1] from the later nineteenth

---

[1] Austria, Belgium, Canada, France, Germany, Italy, Japan, Netherlands, Norway, Spain,
Sweden, Switzerland, United Kingdom, and United States.

century until the late twentieth. Until World War I, the (unweighted) average was 8–9% of GDP, a figure which rose to 15.4% in 1920 and 18.3% in 1937.[2] The significant peacetime growth came after World War II, government expenditure averaged across these countries being 28.5% of GDP in 1960, 43.3% in 1980, and 49% in 1994 in their data. (There is a bit of a slowdown in the 1980s and 1990s, somewhat apparent in a closer look at their data and more apparent in some other compilations.) Similar postwar growth can be seen in many other countries as well.

Interest in economic determinants of the size of government has long been reflected in formal modeling. Some models were discussed in earlier chapters, and we review them here. The chapter focuses on recent political economy models, not because they are better than older work, but simply because they are more recent. Older work can be found in texts on public finance (for example, Atkinson and Stiglitz [1980]) and on public choice (for example, Mueller [1989]). Our treatment of the size of government will be largely integrative, exploiting our earlier extensive discussion of formal models. Where relevant, we refer the reader to earlier models, without rederiving the results. New material will, with some exceptions, be more conceptual and empirical.

In contrast to the long history of work on the size of governments, the study of the creation and dissolution of nations based on economic models is quite new. Models of the political economy of the number of nations tend to be relatively simple, stressing economic and political trade-offs in the size of a country, especially in the provision of public goods—the larger is a country in population, the more economies of scale it has in providing public goods, but the worse will be the match between the preferences of heterogeneous individuals and the nature of public spending. Interest in this topic no doubt partially reflects the rush of recent political events significantly changing the number of countries in the world. On the one hand, there is the breakup of the former Soviet Union into many countries, the breakup of some other former communist countries into smaller units, and demands for regional autonomy in other countries. On the other, there is the unification of Germany and the push for economic and perhaps ultimately political union in Europe. Research on the political economy of the number of nations also reflects the interest in the new political economy itself, that is, the interest in formal models of the interaction of political and economic factors. Other periods of rapid formation or dissolution of nations (in Europe after World War I, in Asia and Africa in the two decades after World War II) produced no similar interest in economic models to explain the phenomenon. The recent outburst of work, in my opinion, illustrates both the strengths and the

---

[2] This last figure excludes Germany, Japan, and Spain, all with heavy military expenditures at that time.

weaknesses of the new political economy. Given the novelty of this work, we will present a careful technical analysis.

14.2. THE SCOPE OF GOVERNMENT

A key determinant of the size of government is obviously its scope, meaning the range of functions assigned to the government. In this section, we present a very brief conceptual summary of this issue. The proper role of government in society has long interested not only economists, but also political philosophers, political scientists, and sociologists. The question has generated a significant amount of highly insightful work by non-economists. It is well worth keeping in mind the existence of these alternative approaches, for they often give a quite different and enlightening perspective on the issues we address.

In terms of implications for the changing size of government, views of the proper role of the state have changed considerably over the last two centuries. In reaction to the distorting effect of extremely regulative government in the eighteenth century, economists and political philosophers in the nineteenth century, beginning with Adam Smith, generally argued for a minimal role of the state. The primary role of the state was to provide various sorts of public goods, a view of the state underlying modern public choice theory (see, for example, chapter 2 of Mueller [1989]).[3]

Toward the end of the nineteenth century, some degree of redistribution was added to the legitimate functions of government, reflecting demands for some redistribution of wealth from the very rich to the poor in light of the popularity of socialism in many countries. Public primary education was already widespread at this time (combining public goods and redistribution functions) and the first, minimal social insurance systems were introduced, albeit with the purpose of ensuring social peace. (It is thus not so surprising that the first social security system was introduced by Bismarck in Germany in the 1880s). The role of government as a provider of social insurance was solidified in the Great Depression.

The growth in transfer payments has been one of the most dramatic changes in government spending in the last sixty years, growing from an average of less than 1% of GDP in the Tanzi–Schuknecht sample in about 1870, to just under 4% in about 1937 (far less if the United Kingdom is excluded) to over 20% of GDP in the early 1990s. Some of this growth in

---

[3] On public goods, Adam Smith writes on the importance of "erecting and maintaining those public institutions and those public works, which, though they may be in the highest degree advantageous to a great society, are however, of such a nature, that the profit could never repay the expense to any individual or small number of individuals." Compare this with the quote from Mueller (1997) in Section 3.3 of Chapter 3 on the public choice approach.

the post-World War II period reflects the political competition for transfers and subsidies, but, seen over a longer period, the order-of-magnitude change in transfers relative to GDP reflects a qualitative change in views of the role of government in the economy.

On a more formal level, one approach to explaining the mix between provision of public goods and transfer payments is to consider interest groups vying for transfer payments which are "financed" by cutting back spending on public goods rather than by raising taxes. That is, in most of the models of redistribution in Chapter 8, we considered political determination of the structure of transfers subject to a balanced budget condition equating total transfers to total taxes. Hence, the main effect of the competition for transfers is on the size of government, as discussed in the next section. Suppose instead that one held taxes constant so that higher transfers reduced spending on public goods dollar for dollar. The same models of redistribution would then serve as models of the composition of government spending. More generally, the competition for transfer payments would both increase the overall level of spending and change its composition, so that it would affect both the size and the scope of government. Examples of this approach are Dixit and Londregan (1998), discussed in Section 8.3 of Chapter 8, and Svensson (1999a), discussed in Section 12.9 of Chapter 12. Persson and Tabellini (1999) provide a general comparative politics approach to the division between transfers and public goods. Their work will be discussed in the next section.

A third function of government is stabilizing and regulating the macroeconomy. The Depression of the 1930s was seen by many at the time as indicating a failure of *laissez-faire* and led to a qualitative change in views about the proper role of government in this respect. Support for activist expenditure policies continued in the post-World War II period, which led to a rapid growth in government involvement in the economy. The wider role of government, and its implications for the growth of government expenditure, was encouraged by academic thinking in the Depression and the first two decades of the postwar period. *The General Theory* of Keynes and subsequent Keynesianism was seen as making the case for stabilization. Advances in the theory of public finance, such as Samuelson's treatment of the public goods problem and the theory of externalities, provided a basis for a larger allocative role of government. These strands were well summed up in Musgrave's (1959) description of the allocative, stabilizing, and redistributive functions of modern government, an influential book in the early 1960s. As Tanzi and Schuknecht point out, in many countries, the strong role of the state was written into law.

Beginning in the late 1960s and certainly by the 1980s, there has been a reversal in the enthusiasm for activist government that characterized the earlier postwar period. This disillusionment reflected a number of factors —apparent failures of large government programs targeted at specific social problems, the clearer disincentive effects of the tax programs necessary to support large government spending, problems with 1960s-style, Phillips-curve-based macroeconomic stabilization policies, and academic reexamination of the theoretical models underpinning highly activist government. The shift away from enthusiasm for activist government was solidified by (or, perhaps more accurately, led to) the election of conservatives in many countries (notably the United States and the United Kingdom in the 1980s) who forcefully advocated a smaller role for government. However, as many authors have pointed out, the strong calls for smaller government do not appear to be accompanied by equally strong actions in cutting the size of government. In the countries in the Tanzi–Schuknecht sample listed in footnote 1, over the period 1980–1994, public expenditure as a percent of GDP declined only in Belgium and (marginally) the Netherlands, and increased significantly in Canada, France, Italy, Norway, Spain, and Sweden. Government spending as a percent of GDP was flat in the United Kingdom and rose slightly in the United States over this period.

To summarize, changing perceptions of the proper role of government in the twentieth century played a large part in the growth of the size of government, but apparently less so in arresting and reversing that growth.

14.3. THE SIZE OF GOVERNMENT—GOVERNMENT SPENDING

In this section, we consider political determinants of the size of government (other than simply the "proper" functions of government), defined by flow values such as expenditures or taxes relative to national output. That is, taking as given a general conceptual view of the activities that government "should and should not" engage in, we ask what determines the size of these activities in practice. For example, given the view that governments should engage in income redistribution, what are the political factors that influence how large redistributive activity will be? Our treatment draws heavily on models covered in earlier chapters. A key result is that there are numerous convincing models of political determinants of government size, but none really explains the secular growth in the size of government discussed in the introduction.

Public Goods

The classic explanation for the existence of government is to provide public goods and eliminate externalities. The basic conceptual issues with viewing government as a provider of public goods were considered in Chapter 9. Here we consider the specific question of whether this function can explain the size and growth of government. Mueller (1989) addresses this question by considering government expenditure on public goods as a function of a basic set of determinants, namely, the relative price of public goods, income (of the median voter), and a vector of taste parameters. Expenditure on public goods (and hence the size of government) would rise over time if: the demand for public goods was inelastic and their price was rising; the demand for public goods was elastic and their price was falling; income was rising over time and the income elasticity of demand for public goods was greater than unity; or, tastes were shifting in the appropriate way.

Estimates of the price elasticity of demand for public goods suggest demand is inelastic, so that an increase in their relative price would lead to a growth in government as a provider. Baumol (1967) argues that an increasing relative price over time will be the case, as many government-provided goods are service intensive. (Baumol's underlying argument is that technical change will raise the price of labor-intensive goods relative to capital-intensive goods, so that the price of services will rise over time relative to manufactured and other capital-intensive goods.) Mueller points out that it is not immediately obvious that the Baumol hypothesis should apply to government-provided goods, as many are capital intensive, but, nonetheless, empirical studies indicate that productivity in the government sector has grown far less fast than in the private sector. He reports numerous studies that have found significant "Baumol effects" for the United States and several European countries, whereby the rise in the relative price of government-provided goods helps explain the growth in government. On the other hand, he argues that such effects can explain only about a quarter of the growth in goods and services provided by the government in the typical OECD country.

The other determinants seem to have relatively little explanatory power. Estimates of the income elasticity of demand for government expenditures are often less than 1 and rarely, according to Mueller, significantly greater than 1. A problem with "taste" variables is quantifying them. Mueller suggests that urbanization or population density is an obvious candidate, but reports surprisingly little empirical support for the hypothesis that increases in this variable significantly affected the size of government expenditures. Nor has strong empirical support for the influence of other taste variables been found.

Transfers and Subsidies

The basic argument of this section is that special interest groups use political mechanisms to increase transfers and subsidies that they receive. As indicated above, a very large part of the growth in government reflects increases in subsidies and transfers. Though some of this increase reflects changing views of the government's role in the economy, a large part of it does not. The most significant increase (as a percentage of GDP) in many countries occurred after 1960, when there were no substantial changes in views of the role of the government as a provider of social insurance.

Hence, political dynamics, rather than changing conceptions of government, played a major role in the growth of transfers.

We have already considered several models of transfers and subsidies, especially in Chapter 8 on redistribution. In the Meltzer–Richard (1981) model of income redistribution, each individual must receive the same transfer. The amount of redistribution in a political equilibrium is a function of the initial income distribution and the political decisionmaking mechanism. If each individual is self-interested and has no ideological taste for redistribution *per se*, his preferred tax rate is that which maximizes his utility. This desired tax rate is a nonincreasing function of his pre-tax income. An individual whose pre-tax income is at or above the mean will prefer a zero tax rate and no lump-sum redistribution, as he cannot gain from a positive tax-transfer scheme. Individuals with low enough income do not work and prefer the tax rate which maximizes the net transfer, taking into account the disincentive effects of taxation. The tax-transfer policy actually chosen will depend on the political mechanism by which preferences are aggregated. Under majority voting with no limit on the franchise, the tax-transfer program that is adopted reflects the preferences of the median voter. The lower is his income relative to the mean, the higher will be the tax rate, the level of transfers, and the size of the transfer program.

Another set of models presented in Chapter 8 allowed differential transfers that could be targeted at different political groups. The focus was on *who* gets targeted, rather than on the aggregate size of transfers, but the models considered, such as Dixit and Londregan (1996), have implications for the aggregate amount of transfers as well. For example, with competition between two parties, in equilibrium, a party chooses its promised transfers and taxes so that a change in the net transfers offered to any group will produce the same number of votes. Optimal party behavior implies (the reader may check (8.17) and the discussion that follows) that total transfers will be higher, for example, the more susceptible voters are to monetary transfers rather than ideology and the more effective are the parties in delivering (or extracting) income from voters, the larger is the group of voters near the point of ideological indifference between the two parties, the higher is the marginal utility of private consumption, *et cetera*.

Peltzman (1980) presents a theory of the connection between income inequality and the size of transfer programs of this sort. Candidates compete for votes by promising income transfers to groups that will support them. (Mueller and Murell [1986] similarly argue that growth in government expenditures reflects competition for votes). His key point is that the more equal is the distribution of income, the more bargaining power groups will have and hence the higher must be transfers in a political-economic equilibrium. Hence, his conclusion on the effect of higher inequality of income is the opposite of Meltzer and Richard. All of these models suggest why government may be too large; none really explains secular growth of government.

The growth of subsidies is subject to similar considerations to the growth of monetary transfers. Especially important in explaining the growth of government are nonmonetary redistribution and disguised transfers. As discussed in Chapter 8, there are many subsidy and transfer programs whose aim is redistributive, even though they are in the form of spending on goods and services rather than transfers. The classic "pork-barrel" public works programs come to mind. Public education also sometimes has strong redistributive implications, as do regulations restricting competition.

There is the widespread view that there is overprovision of such projects, implying total public works projects greater than is optimal. We discussed in Chapter 8 three general arguments for the overprovision of such programs: concentrated benefits and dispersed costs, so that those who bear the costs have no great incentive to oppose them (or are largely ignorant of these costs), whereas the beneficiaries have a strong incentive to push hard for their adoption; heavily political benefits of the programs, such as job creation in the recipient district; and, the nature of decision-making within the legislature leading to overprovision. Details of these arguments, including a formal presentation and a critical analysis, may be found in Section 8.4 of Chapter 8.

More generally, interest groups may expend resources in the attempt to transfer resources from others to themselves, a phenomenon generally labeled *rent seeking*. Here, we quickly review the implications of rent seeking on the aggregate size of government expenditures, based on the general model of rent seeking in Chapter 8. One question stressed in the literature on rent seeking is whether or not rents are totally dissipated by the socially wasteful expenditure of resources meant to capture them. Hence, among other things, there is a focus on aggregate resources absorbed by rent seeking; here, our concern is with one piece of the aggregate, namely, total government expenditures in rent-seeking contests, specifically, resources expended by government officials hoping to benefit from the expenditures of other rent-seeking groups. These resources may be significant relative to the size of the rent contested, but it is unclear whether it is a significant fraction of overall government spending. It may be significant in specific parts of government where there are potentially very large rents to be gained. In terms of aggregate government spending, the effect of rent seeking on the design of government programs is probably more significant than expenditures by officials trying to benefit from rent seeking. This may be especially true in the area of regulation, as for example in the work of Stigler (1971, 1975) and Posner (1975).

Comparative Politics

Another strand of research relates the size (and scope) of government to characteristics of the political system, such as the nature of the electoral system or the form of representation. Comparison of political systems and the implications of different decisionmaking mechanisms, the basis of comparative politics, was considered generally in Chapter 3. In the first part of Section 7.8 of Chapter 7, we discussed the empirical relation between the nature of the political system on the one hand and government deficits and debt accumulation on the other. Examples of the empirical comparative politics approach to government debt and deficits include Roubini and Sachs (1989a, 1989b) and Grilli, Masciandaro, and Tabellini (1991). The latter paper, for instance, relates debt accumulation to the nature of the party system, the electoral system, and whether a system is "presidential" (the president is elected directly into office and has significant independent authority) or "parliamentary" (the prime minister is accountable to the legislature), and, in parliamentary systems, the degree to which they are proportional. For example, they find a strong connection between representational political systems and a lack of fiscal discipline.

Formal modeling of the effects of electoral rules or regime types on government spending patterns is in its infancy.[4] Persson, Roland, and Tabellini (1998) and Persson and Tabellini (1999) present models of how political characteristics of regimes affect the size of government spending and its division between transfers and public goods. The latter paper, for example, considers targeted transfers by politicians and analyzes the effects of having a proportional versus a "first-past-the-post" electoral system for the legislature. They argue that the latter will generally result in larger government, more redistributive spending, and lower provision of public goods. Their modeling of targeted transfers is broadly similar to that of Dixit and Londregan (1996), presented in detail in Section 8.3 of Chapter 8, and the interested reader may find it useful to review the general structure of that model.

In Persson and Tabellini (1999), two parties, R and L, compete in an election by their choice of platforms which have several components. Elected politicians can tax voters to finance three types of spending: "rents" to themselves which provide no benefit to any voter; a public good g benefitting all voters; and, transfers which may be targeted at specific groups of voters. Voters prefer more public goods, lower taxes, and higher transfers to themselves; they also have an ideological preference over the two parties. This ideological preference differs across voters, where the preference of voter i is denoted η^i. The higher is η^i, the stronger is the ideological preference for party R, where a voter with $\eta^i = 0$ is ideologically indifferent between the two parties. Unlike the Dixit and Londregan model, voters are assumed identical in their willingness to trade off utility from consumption and ideology, and parties are assumed to have no differential ability to target transfers or taxes across groups of voters. These assumptions mean that redistribution is driven simply by the

---

[4] Another new and related approach is the use of "transaction-cost politics" (see Chapter 3) to help explain fiscal structures. An example is Saiegh and Tommasi (1998).

density of voters in groups whose ideological position makes them most susceptible to being influenced by transfers. A voter votes for the party whose platform gives him the higher utility inclusive of his ideological preference η^i, as in the Rogoff and Sibert (1988) model in Chapter 7 (see (7.29)) or the Dixit and Londregan model (see (8.14)).

There are three voter groups, where it is assumed that everyone in group i must receive the same transfer, ν^i. Groups differ in the distributions of their ideological preferences, both the mean ideological position $\overline{\eta}^h$ ($h = 1, 2, 3$) and the dispersion of the η^i around $\overline{\eta}^h$, as indexed by a parameter σ^h, where a lower σ^h corresponds to a tighter distribution, and hence more ideological homogeneity. Groups may be ranked by their average ideology; without loss of generality, assume that $\overline{\eta}^1 < \overline{\eta}^2 < \overline{\eta}^3$, where $\overline{\eta}^1 < 0$ and $\overline{\eta}^3 > 0$, but where each group contains voters for whom $\eta^i = 0$, that is, voters who are ideologically indifferent between the two parties. The assumptions on $\overline{\eta}^1$ and $\overline{\eta}^3$ imply that the two parties have "natural" constituencies, with group-2 voters being "swing" voters. For simplicity, it is assumed that $\overline{\eta}^2 = 0$, so that the mean ideological position of group 2 implies indifference between the two parties. Persson and Tabellini then make the substantive assumption that group 2 also has the lowest dispersion σ^2, that is, the tightest distribution around its ideological mean.

Given the underlying distribution of voter preferences, how will the electoral system affect the equilibrium fiscal policy in a political-economic equilibrium? Under a system of proportional representation, parties receive seats in strict proportion to their overall vote total, so that the entire country can be viewed as a single, multiple-seat constituency. A party must therefore win a majority of total votes to be elected. The assumptions about the distribution of voters implies that in equilibrium, transfers will be given only to group-2 voters, reflecting the high density of voters close to ideological indifference. (Consider (8.17) in Chapter 8 and the discussion that follows). These transfers are financed by lower public goods and higher taxes. Group-2 voters are net beneficiaries from this policy, while group-1 and group-3 voters are net losers. Hence, the political cost of courting group-2 voters is the loss of electoral support from other groups, with the choice between public goods and transfers being determined by equating the marginal gain in votes from the favored group with the marginal loss in votes from other groups. This is the essential trade-off that determines the size and scope of government. The greater is the gain from influencing swing voters (due, for example, to a greater concentration near the point of ideological indifference), the more they will be courted, so that provision of public goods will be lower and taxes will be higher.

In contrast, suppose that for the same distribution of voters' ideological preferences, the electoral system is "first-past-the-post," with single-member districts elected by plurality vote. Electoral victory means winning a majority of districts. The key observation is that under this system, voter preferences may imply that some districts are not contested. That is, some districts lean so heavily to one party that neither party chooses to expend any resources to influencing voters in those districts. Only swing districts are contested. In this case, not only do some voters receive no transfers (as in the case with proportional voting), but the cost of *not* paying attention to them (and hence potentially losing their votes) is also ignored. Hence, the cost of giving transfers to swing voters is less, so that in equilibrium they receive more transfers, with a lower level of public goods being provided than in the case of a proportional electoral system.

To illustrate this argument clearly, Persson and Tabellini consider the case in which there are three electoral districts, with a perfect overlap between the groups and the districts, and assume that the mean ideological preferences of groups 1 and 3 are so far from zero (far to the left for group 1, far to the right for group 3) that their districts are not contested. All transfers are then given to district 2, made up solely of group-2 voters. In choosing the level of transfers, taxes, and public goods, parties compete for the same voters as under the proportional electoral system, but now ignore the electoral costs on groups 1 and 3 of targeted transfers to group 2. Hence, transfers are higher and public goods provision is lower under a first-past-the post electoral system. The result is more general than the case of perfect overlap, in that other population distribution can imply that electoral competition may be limited to a subset of districts, with the implied difference for the size and scope of government under proportional versus first-past-the-post systems.

The clarity of the results depends on the assumptions and characteristics of the model. Foremost are the crucial assumptions about the distribution of ideological preferences across voting groups and the distribution of voters across districts. Less obviously, the assumptions that parties have no differential ability to target transfers across groups of voters (that is, to their "core" supporters, in the terminology of Dixit and Londregan [1996]) or even that utility is linear in transfers received could affect the results. For example, suppose that a large fraction of the voters had distinct ideological preferences though were still relatively close to the ideological center, but that the population distribution was such that relatively few voters lived in districts contested in a first-past-the-post system. With decreasing marginal utility of consumption, the size of transfer a party found optimal to direct to any individual voter would be limited, so that a proportional electoral system might lead to higher aggregate transfers and lower public goods supply. The interested reader may want to experiment with other configurations to see the implications of different electoral systems under alternative assumptions.

The great attraction of the Persson–Tabellini comparative politics approach is that it allows us to map political systems into outcomes for the size and composition of government spending in a rigorous but flexible way. They also consider the implications of presidential versus parliamentary regimes when politicians cannot commit to platforms, with the two types of regimes implying differences in competition among different legislators and agenda-setters and hence in the size and mix of government spending. Similarly, Persson, Roland, and Tabellini (1998) investigate implications of separation of powers or coalitions for economic outcomes.

Fiscal Illusion

"Fiscal illusion" as an explanation of big government refers to the possibility that voters can be led to underestimate the size of government expenditures, thereby accepting a government larger than they would if their perceptions were correct. Hence, fiscal illusion is not simply an empirical statement about misperceptions about government size, but a hypothesis about how policymakers may succeed in deceiving voters about the true size of government. It is argued that voters measure the size of government by their tax bill and policymakers can disguise taxes so that voters underestimate the true tax bill. The key question is then: what are the specific mechanisms by which taxes are disguised? For example, a standard argument is that indirect taxes are more disguised than direct taxes.

Fiscal illusion may be thought of more generally, Oates (1988) presents a survey of the extensive empirical literature and summarizes it in terms of five basic hypotheses: the more complex the tax structure, the harder it is to perceive the true tax burden; automatic tax increases due to the progressivity of the tax structure are harder to perceive than legislated tax changes; the implicit tax burden associated with debt issuance is harder to perceive than current taxes; property tax burdens are less obvious to renters than to homeowners; and, lump-sum transfers to governmental units are spent very differently than equivalent lump-sum transfers to individuals in those jurisdictions. On examining the evidence for these arguments, Oates concludes that none of them receives compelling empirical support. We present further negative evidence below and return to fiscal illusion in discussing deficit spending.

Bureaucracy

Anecdotal evidence suggests a particular dislike of "bureaucracy" by voters, where "bureaucracy" is simply a code word either for large government or for inefficient government. A more sophisticated view of bureaucracy, and of attitudes towards it, is that bureaucracy refers to a way of conducting government business. When government is large in both size and scope, when it is responsible for a myriad of functions, it must be subdivided into a large number of agencies or "bureaus," each responsible for specialized (but often overlapping and conflicting) functions. Bureaucracy is the administrative apparatus of the modern state, without which it could not function. Weber (1946b) argues that where the rule of law prevails, the hierarchy that characterizes bureaucracy is necessary, but must be governed by a number of principles, including rules of procedure, restrictions on authority through stipulated rules, supervision of the exercise of authority, and separation of office and the incumbent. Wilson (1989b), in his comprehensive study, analyzes government agencies in terms of the incentives faced by different types of agents within the bureaucracy. He "define[s] a bureaucrat as someone whose occupational incentives come entirely from within the agency." (p. 60)

There is much good work on bureaucracy defined as the necessary apparatus of government, especially in the sociology and political science literature, with the beginnings of more formal analysis in economics. The classic and seminal work on bureaucracy is that of Weber (1946b), originally published in 1922. More recently, Niskanen (1971) has been quite influential. A modern classic is Wilson (1989b), a must-read for any serious student of bureaucracy. Crozier (1964) is another excellent study of bureaucracy in action, if such a phrase is appropriate. Formal economic studies include Fiorina and Noll (1978), Tirole (1986), Legros and Newman (1993), and Banerjee (1997), to name only a few.

We begin with the view of "bureaucracy" as a code word for government inefficiency. A distinguishing feature of much of government output is its nonmarket nature. Government agencies supply many activities which can be only imperfectly measured by units of output (think of the Department of Defense providing "national defense"), making it inherently difficult to measure efficiency and hence to monitor it. Niskanen (1971) attempts to formalize the tendency to inefficiency. He points out that incentives to inefficiency are compounded by other features of bureaucracies. First, government bureaus are often monopoly producers of their services. With a monopoly position, and if there is no threat of entry, the bureau faces no competitive pressures which would push towards efficient provision, a point also stressed by Wilson (1989b). Second, the structure of public sector compensation means that the bureaucrat's salary does not reflect efficiency gains and cost savings. In fact, the bureaucrat's salary may fall as a result of producing the same activity with fewer inputs. This, too, mitigates against efficient provision of services.

Niskanen argues that bureaucratic behavior may be explained by *budget maximization*, which translates into both higher salaries and more power. He views bureaucratic behavior as a principal–agent problem under asymmetric information. In brief, his theory is that the bureau receives a budget (say, from the legislature) as an increasing, concave function of the output g it is perceived as producing. The bureau's budget, but not its true output, is observed by the principal (here, the legislature), which takes the budget itself as a measure of the benefits from the bureau's activities. The bureau's costs are an increasing, convex function of g, where the cost function is known only to the bureau. Given the asymmetric information problems, the principal cannot monitor whether the bureau is efficient in providing services. Nonobservability allows the bureau to maximize its budget, subject only to the constraint of covering costs. The resultant maximization implies a higher level of g and a higher budget than would be implied by maximizing net benefits, that is, by setting marginal benefit equal to marginal cost.

Niskanen's model may be extended in a number of directions. These include alternative institutional arrangements, for example, requiring the bureau to provide the principal with a cost schedule for a range of output levels; alternative goals, such as personnel expansion; or more complex bargaining between the bureau and its principal. Mueller (1989) provides a concise summary.

Niskanen's theory, as attractive as it may be to those convinced of the inefficiency and budget-maximizing tendencies of bureaucracies, is subject to several criticisms. In fact, bureaus may be quite constrained in their ability to maximize their budgets, as detailed quite persuasively by Wilson (1989b). He shows with several case studies that Niskanen's presumption of budget maximization and larger government is often not the case. Second, bureaucrats at the top of agencies, whose salaries are constrained, may not benefit from budget maximization as the basic theory suggests. To the extent that dislike of "bureaucracy" is dislike of perceived government inefficiency, the political implication of attitudes towards bureaucracy for the size of government is largely an empirical question, likely to benefit from the same sort of analysis as that presented in the following subsection. However, given the measurement problems we have discussed, the results of such an analysis would probably not be very clear-cut.

Taking the view that bureaucracy refers to a way of conducting government business, dislike of "bureaucracy" is dislike of the nature of interaction between citizens and government that the bureaucratic form of government implies. As Weber puts it, there is the public desire for guarantees against bureaucratic arbitrariness. The necessity of bureaucracy as an administrative apparatus suggests another perspective on the relation between bureaucracy and the growth of government. Growth in the size of government reflects the growth in complexity of the tasks that government is assigned to undertake. We do not pursue a discussion of greater complexity of government because it is largely a technical, as opposed to a political, explanation, which appears to miss what may be important reasons for the growth of government.

A more political view, consistent with our above discussion of rent seeking, is that the modern state is characterized by a struggle for power not only between different parties or between executive and legislative branches, but also between elected officials and the bureaucracy and between different bureaus. Wilson (1989b) presents numerous examples. Weber views such bureaucratic struggles as one of the major issues of the bureaucratic state and devotes significant effort to analyzing its implications. In his view, success in other political struggles must be coupled with effective control over administrative implementation.

Do Voters Penalize Heavy Spending at the Polls?

The main argument on overspending on "pork-barrel" projects was the concentration of benefits in a small group and the dispersion of costs over a larger group, such that the political mechanism has a bias to overspending. However logical, this argument for overprovision is incomplete, for it does not address the question of why legislators or voters agree to programs that yield only costs for them, albeit small ones. The theoretical arguments are discussed in detail in Section 8.4 of Chapter 8.

Is there evidence, other than purely anecdotal, that voters penalize high government spending? In Chapter 7, we considered in detail the theoretical and empirical relation between macroeconomic performance and election outcomes. Following the work of Kramer (1971), Tufte (1975), and especially Fair (1978, 1982, 1988), we concluded that economic fluctuations have an important influence on the results of congressional and presidential elections. The growth rate of real per capita income or GNP and the rate of inflation appear to be significant determinants of vote totals. The general conclusion is that voters hold the incumbent party accountable for economic events. What about the growth in government spending?

Niskanen (1975) analyzes US presidential elections from 1896 to 1972 and finds that, holding macroeconomic performance constant, increases in federal spending imply lower vote totals for the incumbent party. Peltzman (1992) argues that there is strong econometric evidence on several levels of government. Analyzing US elections for president, senators, and state governors in the period 1950–1988, he finds that voters penalize growth in federal and state spending at the polls, but the composition of federal spending growth appears to be irrelevant: the vote loss to the incumbent President's party at the polls is the same whether defense or nondefense spending rises. In contrast, at the US state level, composition appears to matter: in state governors' elections, increases in spending on welfare payments are especially heavily punished. Peltzman also finds that it is high spending rather than high taxes that appears to bother voters. In contrast to the implications of the models of opportunism in Chapter 7, he argues that voters are not easily "bought off" by election year spending —spending just prior to an election is especially heavily punished at the polls in his results.

In short, Peltzman argues that voters are informed about government spending and vote accordingly. If spending is punished at the polls, why has government grown so much over this century? He argues that the political cost of government spending is too weak to constrain incumbent politicians because of the advantage of incumbency. That is, the electoral advantage conferred by being an incumbent is sufficiently great that even with the negative reaction to high spending at the polls, the net result is a larger government. He argues, however, consistent with our discussion above of changing views of the proper role of government, that expenditure growth has slowed since 1980. He concludes that voters are learning, but it takes time.

14.4. GOVERNMENT DEBT AND DEFICITS

Parallel to the secular growth in the size of government is the existence of persistent government deficits and growth in government debt in a large number of countries since 1960. Among industrialized countries, Austria, Greece, Spain, Netherlands, Italy, Ireland, and Belgium all saw their government debt-to-GDP ratios rise severalfold from 1960 to 1990, with the ratio going above 100% in the last three countries. In contrast, in a number of other countries in the Tanzi–Schuknecht sample (France, Germany, Japan, United Kingdom, and the United States, to name a few), the ratio has been stable over these three decades, but has shown some tendency to rise in the late 1980s. Though debt-to-GDP ratios have historically risen significantly during wartime, until the 1960s this was reversed in peacetime, with the ratio falling fairly steadily. The sharp, continued increase in the debt in a number of countries during peacetime is historically unprecedented.

As in Section 14.3 on government spending, we ask the question of whether political economy models can help explain evolution of debt and deficits, including how it has changed over time. Parallel to that section, we both rely on models that appeared in earlier chapters and present a number of new arguments. Political economy explanations of deficits have a long history. Alesina and Perotti (1995a) present an overview of some of the questions discussed in this section.

Deficit Illusion

Parallel to the discussion of "fiscal illusion" above as an explanation of big government, one may consider explanations of persistent deficits in terms of misperceptions about deficits. A classic argument is that individuals favor expenditures, but do not want to pay for them. Wagner (1976) and Buchanan and Wagner (1977) have formalized this point in the notion of a "deficit illusion," whereby voters do not understand the government's intertemporal budget constraint.[5] Faced with deficit-financed expenditure, voters overestimate the value of the expenditure side and underestimate

[5] Buchanan, Rowley, and Tollison (1986) present a collection of papers on this approach to deficits.

the future tax burden. Opportunistic incumbents take advantage of this misperception, running deficits to win the favor of voters.

Though some may find this theory attractive as a rough description of reality, there are logical problems, as there were with fiscal illusion as an explanation of government size. It does not fit well with theories of rational individual behavior, nor does it correlate with empirical studies such as Peltzman (1992). Further, it does not explain why persistent deficits are a relatively recent phenomenon. Buchanan and Wagner (1977) suggest that fiscal illusion reflects the complexity of tax structures, though far more work needs to be done to evaluate this argument.

Debt as a Strategic Variable

In Section 7.9 of Chapter 7, we considered issuance of debt as a strategic variable, that is, issuance to constrain one's possible successors or to influence election outcomes. Persson and Svensson (1989), Alesina and Tabellini (1990), and Tabellini and Alesina (1990) suggest that partisan policymakers issue debt to "tie the hands" of a possible successor with different preferences, which may lead to an overissuance of government debt relative to what is optimal. To summarize the argument, policymakers, though partisan, care about social welfare. Only distortionary taxes are available to finance public spending and to service the debt, with the level of distortion rising with the tax burden. Hence, the spending a government would find optimal would depend on the level of debt (via debt service) existing when it began office: the higher is level of debt, the lower will be desired spending for given preferences. If a government knew it would be retained in office, utility smoothing would imply no issuance of debt in their nonstochastic models. In contrast, under certain reasonable parameter configurations, the probability of being replaced leads to debt issuance in order to reduce the spending of a successor government, with the debt issuance higher, the higher is the probability of being replaced. The models do not convincingly explain the growth of debt in the last decades relative to earlier times. First, reelection probabilities have not fallen uniformly and significantly since the 1960s; second, parties have not become more partisan in their spending preferences.

A related theory of debt issuance, also discussed in detail in the same section, concerns strategic use of debt to affect endogenous election outcomes. The basic idea is that by choosing the environment that one's electoral opponent will inherit if he is elected (thus constraining his policy choices), an opportunistic incumbent can affect the electorate's expectations of macroeconomic performance under that opponent. Strategic choice of debt will thus influence an incumbent's reelection chances not because it affects the current state of the economy, but because it affects voters' perceptions of the post-election state of the economy under possible election outcomes. Aghion and Bolton (1990), for example, consider a model in which partisan differences among policymakers lead to different propensities to default on the debt. Interesting as the model is, it also does not explain why deficits and debt started rising in many countries in the last decades, nor why it stayed stable in seemingly similar countries over the same period.

Intergenerational Arguments

Debt is a way of transferring resources both within and across generations (often simultaneously). In Chapter 8, we considered models of intergenerational redistribution, often accomplished by issuing debt. Since there is an extensive discussion of the political economy of intergenerational redistribution there, we will not discuss it in detail here, simply pointing out how it may apply to the growth in debt in ways not covered in Sections 14.2 and 14.3 above. (For example, since "pay-as-you-go" or unfunded social security is an intergenerational transfer and akin to accumulating debt, expansion of such a program implies expansion of the debt.) Formal models are presented by Browning (1975) and Tabellini (1990b, 1991), both covered explicitly in Chapter 8. In Tabellini's (1991) model of government debt, a generation exploits the fact that the following generation, which must repay any debt issued, is not present when a vote is taken on issuing the debt. However, in a majority voting system, a majority of voters at each point in time must support a tax-transfer scheme for it to be continued. Thus, a generation will choose a scheme which enough voters in the next generation will support so that it gains the support of a majority of voters overall, that is, one that is "politically viable." In the case of government debt, the old and the children of the wealthy (who hold a quantity of debt above the mean) vote to repay the debt.

Cukierman and Meltzer (1989) present a model of debt accumulation similar in spirit to Tabellini's, focusing on "rich" and "poor" voters within a generation, but where an operative bequest motive plays a central role. (In Tabellini's model, there is intergenerational altruism, but the bequest motive is not operative, a fact that is central to his results.) The rich plan to leave bequests, so that with perfect markets they are indifferent to debt policy—they can offset any change in debt and deficit policy by adjusting the size of the bequest they leave. The poor, on the other hand, would like to leave negative bequests, but this is legally impossible. The transfer inherent in issuance of government debt to be repaid by the next generation implies that they favor issuance of government debt. In a voting model, they would favor issuance of debt, though it should be noted that a social planner faced with the same constraints would also favor issuance of debt. As in several of our earlier models, these models do not adequately address the question of why there has been an apparent change in attitudes to deficits after World War II in so many countries.

Deficits and Policy Delay

Another reason why deficits may persist (or may rise) is conflict over the burden of eliminating the deficit. In Section 10.6 of Chapter 10, we considered the war-of-attrition model of delayed stabilization of Alesina and Drazen (1991), in which it was argued that disagreement about the burden of taxation leads to the failure to close the deficit. This model has been used to explain the apparent propensity of coalition governments to run deficits. Spolaore (1993), for example, formalizes this point in a war-of-attrition model applied to coalition governments. When a fiscal shock hits, a coalition government delays adjustment relative to what a single-party government would do. Spolaore argues that the inefficiency associated with delayed closing of the deficit is increasing in the number of parties in the coalition.

However, one should be careful in arguing that the war-of-attrition model clearly ties certain types of governments to deficit policies. Though it seems intuitive that larger coalition governments find it more difficult to make painful decisions, expected delay in eliminating a deficit could either rise or fall as the number of parties rises. As the discussion of coalition government in Chapter 7 indicated, the interactions, and subsequent dynamics, within a coalition government are far more complicated than in the war-of-attrition model. If the only possible options for a coalition partner are either to accept a proposal on the table, or to veto it, an increase in the number of partners may in fact increase delay. On the other hand, in practice, the range of behavior is far wider. For example, as the number of parties increases (both within and outside of the coalition), the possibility of forming alliances, that is, subcoalitions, within the coalition may increase as well, as shown in the theoretical literature.

A similar result on failure to eliminate government deficits and endogenous growth of debt arose in the common property models studied in Section 10.7 of Chapter 10 (and applied to a range of issues thereafter). Conceptually, these are similar to models of rent seeking, where interest groups expend resources to try to appropriate a larger share of some common property. A difference is their explicitly dynamic nature, making them especially relevant to questions of debt accumulation. As discussed in Chapter 10, Velasco (1998) presents an explicit common property model of delayed fiscal reform. Common property models are quite stylized, even more than war-of-attrition models. Like war-of-attrition models, they are therefore most useful to present a conceptual argument about deficits and growth of debt, rather than as an underpinning for very specific institutional models. Like many of the models discussed in the last few sections, neither model suggests why the appearance of persistent deficits is a relatively recent phenomenon.

Expansionary Effects of Fiscal Contraction

We conclude this section by examining recent research on the macroeconomic effects of fiscal adjustment. We focus on two questions. The first, in this subsection, asks what is the effect of fiscal adjustment on economic activity. Specifically, we ask whether fiscal contraction is necessarily contractionary, or whether it may in fact be expansionary. The second, addressed in the next subsection concerns the relation of the composition of fiscal adjustment on its permanence.

To anyone who has studied macroeconomics, the answer to the first question is obvious. Conventional wisdom, consistent with the basic Keynesian model, is that deficit spending is generally expansionary, while a fiscal contraction leads to a contraction in economic activity. This follows simply from the effect of the fiscal adjustment on aggregate demand and hence on economic activity in a demand-based model. Most macroeconomists would add two caveats to this conventional wisdom. First, if economic agents are forward-looking and internalize the government's intertemporal budget constraint, a current change in nondistortionary taxes will have no effect on their consumption decisions in the absence of any change in government spending, either current or anticipated. This is Ricardian equivalence, first discussed in Chapter 2; the reader may refer back to Section 2.5 of that chapter for a formal analysis of the effect of anticipated changes in components of the government budget. Such a change has no effect on the present discounted value of taxes that individuals anticipate having to pay, and hence no effect on their economic decisions. Second, if taxes are distortionary, there may be a supply-side effect, whereby a cut in factor taxation may increase factor supply and thus increase economic activity. This does not change the qualitative relation between cuts in taxes and increases in economic activity, but may reverse the sign of the correlation between deficits and economic activity. If the cut in taxes leads to a significant increase in the supply of the taxed factor (usually labor), it would imply an *increase* in tax revenues and hence a *fall* in the deficit, so that an observed fiscal contraction would go along with an economic expansion. This is the (in)famous "Laffer Curve" effect, much discussed in the 1980s. Two observations help put this argument in perspective. First, the general (but not universal) view is that empirically, the Laffer effect is unlikely to hold. It depends on a tax elasticity of labor supply greater than unity, which most careful empirical studies of labor supply do not support. Second, the nonstandard prediction concerns the correlation of economic activity with the deficit, not with the underlying fiscal stimulus. Even if the Laffer effect holds, so that a fiscal consolidation, let us say due to a tax increase, leads to a higher deficit, it still implies a negative correlation between changes in tax rates and changes in economic activity. That is, supply-side effects, even if they are strong, do not change the presumption that a fiscal contraction is contractionary.

Recent research has challenged this presumption. In an important paper, Giavazzi and Pagano (1990) examine the two largest fiscal consolidations in Europe in the 1980s, Denmark in 1983–1986 and Ireland in 1987–1989, in which the cyclically adjusted government budget deficit fell by 9.7 and 5.2% of GDP, respectively, and show that they led to a sharp *increase* in private consumption and economic activity, not to a decrease. Bertola and Drazen (1993) find similar results not only for Denmark and Ireland, but also for Belgium, Sweden, and the United Kingdom, all of which enacted programs of fiscal austerity in the 1980s. Alesina and Perotti (1995b, 1997) consider several large and protracted fiscal adjustments in OECD countries in the 1980s and find that they did not lead to significantly lower GDP growth rates or higher unemployment rates.

To explain the expansionary effect of fiscal contraction, Giavazzi and Pagano suggest that a cut in government consumption that is anticipated to be permanent implies an expectation of permanently lower taxes, thus increasing private wealth. If the cut is unanticipated, private wealth jumps with the implementation of the fiscal contraction, implying an analogous jump in private consumption. Hence, they explain the expansion by the effect of the fiscal contraction on permanent income when consumers are forward-looking and internalize the government's intertemporal budget constraint. An analogous positive effect on investment follows from a cut in government consumption inducing the expectation of permanently lower distortionary tax rates coupled with a forward-looking investment function.

Suppose a fiscal consolidation based on tax increases *without* a significant change in current government consumption leads to a similar economic expansion. The basic permanent income argument given in the previous paragraph is no longer sufficient to explain the result. Blanchard (1990) and Drazen (1990) suggest that a sharp fiscal adjustment may signal a change in the *process* generating fiscal deficits, so that more than simple intertemporal accounting is at work. More specifically, a sharp fiscal contraction today leads market participants to believe that the conflicts that induced high deficit spending have been resolved, so that they expect lower deficits in the future beyond what simple intertemporal balance predicts. Giavazzi and Pagano's (1995) finding that a boom in private consumption is more likely if the deficit cut is large, no matter how achieved, is consistent with this argument. To expand on the point, a fiscal adjustment may be taken as a signal of a *political* consolidation, as in the models of Alesina and Drazen (1991) or Velasco (1998) discussed in Chapter 10. The political change induces a sharp revision in expectations of future fiscal policy, implying what appears to be a disproportional effect of the current consolidation. This last link is exactly as predicted by the models in Section 2.5 of Chapter 2, whereby expectations of future economic policy depend on current policy often in a nonlinear way.

Bertola and Drazen (1993) consider such a signaling effect of fiscal adjustment in a fully worked-out model of permanent-income consumers and nondistortionary taxes. The initial policy process is assumed to imply that the ratio of government consumption to output, denoted g/y, drifts upward over time. (More precisely, it follows Brownian motion with a positive drift.) Hence, to maintain intertemporal government budget balance, there must be a change in fiscal policy when government consumption becomes too high. They suggest, consistent with what was observed in numerous OECD countries in the mid- to late-1980s, that government spending as a percentage of GDP is cut when it hits a critical high level. Modeling the ratio of government spending relative to output as following Brownian motion (subject to government intervention) allows them to solve for explicit time paths of consumption using techniques of regulated Brownian motion.[6] When a discrete cut in government spending is anticipated when g/y hits a critical level, the relation between private consumption and the growth of government spending may have interesting nonlinearities. At low levels of g/y, increases in this ratio are associated with decreases in c/y, the ratio of private consumption to GDP. This reflects permanent income consumption behavior when individuals internalize the government budget constraint, and it represents the basic Giavazzi–Pagano explanation of expansionary fiscal contraction. However, when the ratio g/y becomes high enough, the sign of this relation reverses, higher g/y implying *higher* c/y. The reason is that when g/y gets closer to the critical value at which a discrete adjustment will occur (implying a large discrete increase in permanent income), this anticipated change in the fiscal policy process dominates the calculation of permanent income, so that permanent income, and hence consumption, rise rather than fall with increases in g/y. Bertola and Drazen show that this predicted nonlinear relation is actually observed in a number of European countries which did ultimately enact discrete fiscal consolidations. They further argue that the richness of the possible outcomes when changes in current fiscal policy are taken as signals of future policy in a sophisticated way should lead one to expect such nonlinear responses. Simple linear extrapolation to form expectations of future fiscal policy (and the sustainability of current policy), for example by linear vector autoregressions (VARs), are likely to be misleading.

The Composition of Adjustment and Its Persistence

Fiscal adjustments, even sharp ones, are often only temporary. Extending the reasoning of the political models of inaction and delay presented in Chapter 10 suggests that the persistence of a fiscal adjustment depends on whether it is associated with an underlying political adjustment. However,

---

[6] As solving models with regulated Brownian motion processes is technically sophisticated, it is not presented here. The interested reader is referred to the original article.

the characteristics of political changes are generally far harder to observe than the nature of the fiscal adjustment itself. Alesina and Perotti (1995b, 1997) explore this issue by considering the relation between the composition of a fiscal adjustment and its subsequent persistence. For example, in the earlier paper, they look at a sample of 20 OECD countries in the period 1960–1992 that undertook a significant fiscal contraction, defined as a cut in the cyclically adjusted primary government budget deficit of at least 1.5% of GDP in any year. They find that the more persistent fiscal adjustments (in terms of the ratio of either debt or cyclically adjusted deficits to GDP in the subsequent three years) are those that were concentrated on cutting two specific types of outlays: expenditures on social programs and the wage component of government consumption. In contrast, fiscal adjustments that relied on increased labor taxation and cuts in capital expenditures were less likely to persist.

Their explanation is a political one. Because cuts in public employment and transfers are politically far more difficult than capital spending cuts and some types of tax increases, only governments seriously committed to lasting deficit reduction are likely to carry them out. That is, individuals take the type of deficit reduction as a signal of the government's unobserved commitment to deficit reduction. They further note that the political support for fiscal consolidation will also depend critically on its effects on the distribution of income, where they stress the functional distribution of income. It may also depend on the effects on the size distribution of income or wealth. A possible relation between the political support for a policy and its effects on the income distribution was raised in general terms in Chapter 11 on growth and in specific terms in Chapter 13 in discussing political support for privatization and price decontrol programs.

14.5. BUDGETARY RULES AND INSTITUTIONS

A final political explanation of the size of government debt and deficits concerns the budget *process*, including the rules and institutions by which the budget is made. Under this view, recent secular growth in government deficits reflects changes in budgetary rules and institutions. Persistent deficits, implying secular growth of debt, would suggest that lasting reduction or elimination of deficits requires structural changes in the nature of budgetary policymaking.

The literature on the effect of budget institutions on the size of government deficits and debt may be divided into two general areas: the effect of legislated quantitative limits on fiscal variables; and the effect of procedural rules. Legislated limits include: restrictions on deficit financing, including balanced budget laws; expenditure ceilings; numerical targets for fiscal variables; and, restrictions on issuance of debt. Procedural rules concern, among other things: the extent to which the process of formulating the budget is "hierarchical"; effective requirements for "transparency" in the budget document; rules of amendment in both the formulation and approval of the budget; the nature of voting in the approval process; and, rules concerning supplementary budgets and open-ended appropriations in the implementation of the budget. Analysis of the effects of quantitative rules in restricting the growth of deficits and debts has been largely empirical rather than conceptual or theoretical, and has concentrated on balanced budget and debt restrictions, rather than numerical fiscal targets.

Balanced Budget Restrictions

A balanced budget restriction is probably the most widely discussed quantitative fiscal rule, at least in the United States, though certainly not the only rule. The Maastricht criteria in Europe for the transition to EMU are, qualitatively at least, restrictions of the same sort. On the national level in the United States, the attempt to control budget deficits by a legislated balanced budget restriction culminated in the Gramm–Rudman–Hollings Deficit Reduction Act of 1985, which contained deficit targets implying a deficit falling to zero over five years. In any year in which the target was not met, "Gramm–Rudman" (as it was commonly referred to) legislated an equal cut in defense and nondefense expenditures to meet the target. The act did not have its desired effect, in part because when the targets became binding, the Congress passed new legislation to modify the targets. (See Gramlich [1995] for an overview of this and other budget restriction measures.) The failure of Gramm–Rudman to enforce a balanced budget has led to widespread discussion of balanced budget amendments to the US Constitution to achieve a balanced budget by law (see Chapter 5 for a discussion of "constitutionalizing" a law to make it more binding), a possibility which is unlikely to occur.

In contrast, balanced budget restrictions are ubiquitous at the state level in the United States. US states have been the "laboratory" in which the effects of balanced budget restrictions have been studied. Every state except for Vermont has such a legal restriction, 41 of them in the state constitution, the other eight in legislation. These restrictions vary across states (see, for example, Poterba [1996] for a concise summary and further references). The differences may be summarized by the stage of the budget process at which budget balance is required—*formulation* of the budget by the executive; *approval* of the budget by the legislature; and *implementation* of the budget. Most states (44, according to the National Association of State Budget Officers [1992]) require that the executive submit a balanced budget to the legislature. A stronger requirement (in 37 states) is that the legislature enact a balanced budget. Under this requirement, there may still be a deficit if the assumptions on which the budget is formulated are not realized. The most stringent requirement is at the implementation stage: 24 states not only require that the legislature enact a balanced budget, but also prohibit a deficit actually being carried forward over some time interval. In some states it cannot be carried over into the next fiscal year; in others it can be carried over, but must be corrected in the following fiscal year.

Balanced budget restrictions in the US states typically apply to only part of the budget. Public investment is often exempt from the requirement, with it usually applying to the "general fund" or operating budget. Special or earmarked funds (such as social insurance or highway funds) are often exempt as well. This application to only part of the budget is in sharp contrast to what has been proposed at the national level for the United States.

Debt Limits

In addition to explicit deficit restrictions, many US state constitutions have restrictions on the amount of debt a state may issue. This limit may be in nominal terms, or relative to state revenues, the property tax base, state assets, or the general fund. These limits may apply to borrowing for specific or for general purposes, and they may be combined with requirements about how debt issuance is authorized (such as by a public vote authorizing a bond issue). Debt issuance above the constitutional limit generally requires constitutional amendment. However, these limits typically refer to debt with the explicit backing of the state government, that is, guaranteed by the state's power to raise revenue ("full faith and credit" debt). Debt restrictions do not apply to special authorities or public corporations created to issue debt for specific projects, debt that is not guaranteed, that is, not officially backed by the "full faith and credit" of the state. However, as in the case of bailouts by central banks of financial intermediaries that are not formally insured, there is the realistic expectation by holders of nonguaranteed debt issues by special authorities that state governments will stand behind it. In this sense, the debt becomes identical to "full faith and credit" debt, so that issuance of debt by special authorities becomes a way to circumvent the constitutional restrictions. Von Hagen (1991) provides a good summary of the issue.

Theoretical Considerations

The basic conceptual question concerning deficit restrictions is how much flexibility should such restrictions optimally have. This question encompasses questions such as: whether a rule itself is optimal; and, at what stage in the budget process should a rule be imposed. The answer depends in part on what is the purpose of retaining flexibility in fiscal policy, for example, to retain some ability to respond to unforeseen revenue needs, or to be able to use fiscal policy for economic stabilization over the cycle.

The lack of extensive theoretical work on balanced budget rules may stem from the fact that this basic conceptual question is more general than balanced budget rules; it concerns the trade-off between flexibility and commitment which concerns other aspects of policy as well, such as monetary policy. This issue was first raised in Chapter 4, and has come up repeatedly in following chapters. Our general conclusions from discussion of the trade-off in constraining monetary policy are applicable here as well; the interested reader is referred to earlier discussions, especially Section 4.6 of Chapter 4. Particularly relevant for fiscal rules is the argument that state-contingent quantitative rules are generally preferable, but they are not always workable. First of all, it is impossible to specify all possible contingencies *ex ante*. Second, given private information, it is often difficult to verify if the government has reneged on a state-contingent rule or not.[7]

The difficulty of verifying whether the government has abided by a numerical fiscal restriction suggests that to be credible, numerical fiscal rules must be simple. This requirement is usually labeled *transparency* of fiscal rules; transparency is generally thought to be central for quantitative fiscal restrictions to be effective in controlling the growth of deficits. Among the methods used to thwart the effectiveness of balanced budget rules are (see Alesina and Perotti [1996a] for a summary): overoptimistic predictions of key macroeconomic variables; strategic use of what is kept on- or off-budget; measuring fiscal adjustment relative to an inflated baseline; and, multiyear budgeting, in which difficult changes are postponed, with the budget being revised before the "day of reckoning." Quantitative restrictions may increase the incentives for "creative accounting" and hence could actually lead to worse outcomes in terms of welfare. Another aspect of transparency is the difficulty of measuring fiscal variables, much more so than for inflation. (See, for example, Blejer and Cheasty [1991] on problems of measuring the fiscal position.) Not only is there disagreement about which measure of the deficit is the "correct" one, but even when there is agreement about which measure to use, the ease with which deficit measures may be manipulated makes verification especially difficult.

Empirical Analysis

In contrast to the relatively small amount of theoretical work, there is a significant amount of empirical work on the effect of quantitative deficit and debt restrictions, primarily, though not exclusively, using US states. A first question concerns attempts to circumvent these rules by "creative accounting," the problem of transparency raised in the previous paragraph. It has been argued that the failure of quantitative restrictions to reduce budget deficits in several countries stems from measurement problems.

[7] See the discussion of Canzoneri (1985) in Section 6.4 of Chapter 6.

Laws were supposedly complied with, but manipulation of the numbers meant that, in fact, the laws had little real effect. Poterba (1996, p. 396) points out that the experience of US states suggests that "a wide range of accounting changes and related techniques can be used to satisfy balanced-budget rules." Nonetheless, he finds that such changes are quantitatively less important than tax increases and spending cuts in meeting the requirements, so that the rules do have real effects. In contrast, Alesina and Perotti (1996a) suggest that the lack of transparency in the budget process was critical in problems in enforcing fiscal discipline in Italy.

Another type of empirical analysis looks at the effect of the rules on measured outcomes. A number of results emerge, using measures of the stringency of balanced budget restrictions and of debt limits across US states. Von Hagen (1991) uses two types of measures: dummies for types of debt limits (such as nominal or percentage limits); and, an index of stringency from the Advisory Council of Intergovernmental Relations (ACIR [1987]), which ranks state balanced budget restrictions from zero (no restriction) to ten (very stringent restriction). State debt per capita and debt–income ratios are *not* significantly different in states with and without debt limits; such limits appear to affect only the ratio of nonguaranteed to guaranteed debt, it being significantly larger on average in states with debt limits.

Measurements of the stringency of balanced budget restrictions tell a similar story. Von Hagen divides states into three groups—low, medium, and high stringency—and finds that average debt per capita in 1985 was significantly higher in states with low stringency than in states with high stringency, with there being no statistically significant difference between medium- and high-stringency states. Debt–income ratios and debt growth from 1975 to 1985 are not significantly different across the three groups. The ratio of nonguaranteed to guaranteed state debt is significantly higher in states with very stringent balanced budget restrictions. Taken together, these results suggest that in terms of average performance, quantitative fiscal restrictions are not especially effective in restraining the growth of debt. The restrictions affect the debt mix, that is, *which* type of debt instrument to issue, rather than *whether* to issue debt, nonguaranteed debt being used to evade debt limits.

Von Hagen further points out, however, that these results do not give a complete picture, because of the large dispersion of debt indicators across states. Looking at the dispersion of debt indicators across states (rather than the average level of debt) conditional on the indicators of quantitative restrictions, he finds that distributions of per capita debt, debt–income ratios, and the debt mix are affected by quantitative restrictions. For example, median state debt per capita is significantly lower in states with debt limits and a high stringency index than in states without debt limits or with a low stringency index, with similar effects found in the distribution of debt–income ratios. The difference between these results and those using average levels of debt indicators reflects the fact that quantitative restrictions affect the frequency distribution of debt indicators, but not the mean. The distributions become more skewed towards low debt indicators in groups of states with debt limits or stringent balanced budget restrictions. However, the distribution of debt indicators in the group with debt limits or stringent balanced budget restrictions contain the states with the highest debt indicators. Von Hagen suggests that this indicates the quantitative restrictions do little to lessen the likelihood of extreme outcomes. It may reflect instead a selection bias, a state with a really extreme deficit problem being highly likely to adopt a balanced budget restriction or debt limit. The restriction might be quite important in limiting growth of debt and deficits relative to what it would be in its absence, though the equilibrium level of debt would still be quite large. More generally, Poterba (1996) suggests that correlations between quantitative fiscal rules and outcomes may reflect an "omitted third variable," namely, voter tastes for fiscal restraint. The endogeneity of fiscal institutions is crucial in interpreting the results.

Another empirical question concerns the effect of balanced budget rules on the persistence of deficits. As indicated above, even with a balanced budget requirement (for example, at the proposal stage), states can still run deficits. Poterba (1994) finds that U.S. states with restrictive quantitative rules respond to unexpected deficits with faster fiscal adjustment than states with less restrictive quantitative rules. Moreover, deficit adjustment in response to balanced budget rules is much faster when a single party controls both the executive and the state legislature than when control is divided. This result correlates with the results on fiscal restraint in coalition governments in Europe found by Grilli, Masciandaro, and Tabellini (1991) discussed in Section 7.8 of Chapter 7. Alt and Lowry (1994) also report a significant effect of quantitative restrictions in the response to shocks with a partisan aspect, but find that it depends on which party controls the legislature, rather than on whether the government is divided. In states that prohibit deficit carryovers, a one-dollar state deficit induces a 77-cent response in the following year, either through tax increases or spending cuts, in states in which the legislature is Republican-controlled, compared to a 34-cent response in states with such a restriction in which the legislature is Democratic-controlled. In states without a restriction on deficit carryovers, the analogous figures are 31 cents and 40 cents for the two parties, respectively.

Procedural Rules

The other main area in the study of the effect of budget institutions on the size of government deficits and debt concerns the effect of procedural rules, that is, the effect of the nature of the budgetary process on the size of deficits. The budgetary process can be characterized as a system of rules and regulations, formal and informal, which determine the fiscal decisions made. One needs to consider the effect of procedural rules at all three stages of the budget process, namely, formulation, approval, and implementation of the budget. Theoretical studies of the effects of procedural rules on budget outcomes are abundant in the political science literature, less numerous (though growing) in the economics literature. On the empirical side, there are a few studies of the effects of characteristics of the budget process in the economics literature, similar in approach to empirical analyses of the effects of quantitative restrictions discussed above.

Budget Formulation

We begin with the theoretical work. The first budget formulation stage, in which the budget is prepared via negotiation within the executive branch, itself consists of substages. An important institutional detail is the extent to which the drafting of the budget is centralized. A key issue is the relative influence of agents representing specific constituencies, such as cabinet ministers with specific constituencies, versus agents whose function it is to represent the populace as a whole in the process of budget negotiations, such as the finance minister or the prime minister. A *"hierarchical"* process is one where the latter have relatively more power in the preparation of the budget, there being a defined hierarchy in the process; a *"collegial"* process is one where individual ministers have significant power, decisions being made more democratically. Von Hagen and Harden (1995) present a formal model of individual ministers, each with his own constituency, bargaining over the budget. Each minister maximizes his utility, taking the bids of the others as given, a process that results in large budget bias. They then compare this outcome with one in which ministers without constituencies (such as treasury minister) are given special powers in the budget process, such as the right to veto proposals of individual ministers, the power to set the agenda for budget negotiations, and the power to set binding limits on allocations. They then show how the equilibrium spending will be lower in the second scenario. Their conclusion is that at the stage of formulating the budget, spending will be lower with procedural rules devised to strengthen the collective interest of the government as a whole over the (selfish) interests of individual ministers. The drawback of hierarchical rules is that they may produce budget proposals that do not protect minority interests.

Legislative Approval Rules

There has been significant theoretical work on the effect of procedural rules at the legislative approval stage in the political science literature. Procedural rules in the legislature concern several dimensions of the nature of voting on the budget, such as rules of agenda (including whether the size of the budget is set first or emerges as a residual) and rules of amendment. Many of these papers have two basic goals: first, to show how the effect of procedural rules may be analyzed formally (rather than simply intuitively), using game-theoretic bargaining models; and, second, to show via formal analysis how (and why) intuitive conclusions may be incorrect.

Ferejohn and Krehbiel (1987) consider the effect on the overall size of the budget of whether it is determined as a residual in the process, after individual appropriations are chosen (a "piecemeal appropriations" process) or chosen first, after which appropriations are chosen subject to the overall constraint (an "overall budget" process). The former resembles the process used by the U.S. Congress prior to 1974, the latter the Congressional process instituted by the 1974 Budget Implementation and Control Act. One might naturally think (as did the framers of the 1974 act) that the latter process would impose more budget discipline and hence lead to lower budgets. Ferejohn and Krehbiel show this is not necessarily the case. Depending on the preferences of individual legislators, a piecemeal appropriations process may yield a *lower* overall budget. The two processes are modeled as sequential two-stage games, where the vote of a legislator in the first stage in each of the two processes is influenced by the known preferences of other legislators and by the known consequences of a vote at the second stage. Suppose there are two goods, military spending g and domestic spending d, where each legislator i has a most preferred bundle $(\tilde{g}^i, \tilde{d}^i)$. Values of other bundles are given by distance from $(\tilde{g}^i, \tilde{d}^i)$ in two-dimensional space, where it is assumed that each legislator knows the preferences of other legislators, and, for simplicity, there are only three legislators. In an appropriation process, spending on one good (say, military) is first chosen as the median of the three legislators' most preferred values of g, say at g^{med}. Given g^{med}, legislators have preferences over d, implying a chosen level of domestic spending, and a total budget, the sum of $g + d$.[8] Under the piecemeal appropriation process, the equilibrium does not depend on the order of voting on the two individual spending categories.

In an overall budget process, the legislators choose the total budget (the sum $g + d$), knowing the preferences of each legislator for g and d at the second, appropriations stage for any total budget. Given majority voting at the appropriations stage, legislators thus know the outcome of the second-stage appropriations process given their choice of the budget in stage one (it is the median of the most preferred points projected onto the overall

---

[8] The interested reader can derive the exact appropriation by drawing a set of "circular" indifference curves in two dimensions implied by the nature of preferences for three legislators and deriving the majority winners for each appropriation, chosen sequentially.

budget line[9]). Legislators choose a budget size by majority vote in the first stage knowing these outcomes. Hence, a small budget may be defeated if two legislators realize that a larger budget will give them higher utility under the implied majority appropriation in the second stage.

The size of the budget which emerges does *not* depend unambiguously on the process; which budget process yields a lower total budget depends on the nature of preferences of the legislators. Ferejohn and Krehbiel show that the overall budget process may actually lead to a higher overall budget, and they derive necessary and sufficient conditions for this to be the case in a legislature with a large number of members. It will depend on the proportion of legislators with different combinations of preference intensities over the two goods, and the agreements that result over the total level of spending. The exact details are somewhat complex and the interested reader is referred to the original article. However, the basic message is straightforward: once we consider sophisticated legislators who both have different preferences over spending bundles and who realize the implications of their decisions in an overall budget process for subsequent appropriations, a procedural "reform" such as voting on the total budget first need not lower the size of the budget in equilibrium.

When one considers the amendment process, similar results emerge, whereby conclusions that seem intuitive do not necessarily stand up to careful scrutiny. Voting on the budget in the legislature may be subject to a *closed* rule on amendments, whereby once a proposal is made, it must be either passed or voted down (in which case another proposal is made and voted on), but may not be amended. Under an *open* rule, amendments may be offered to proposals. For example, under a simple open rule, an unlimited number of amendments may be proposed, but they must be put up one at a time against the proposal on the floor. A legislator may propose an amendment or may make a motion that the amendment process be closed, subject to majority vote. If that motion is passed, the proposal on the floor is voted on; if an amendment is proposed, it is voted on against the proposal on the floor, the winner becoming the new proposal on the floor.

Intuitively, one might think that an open rule would lead to higher or more wasteful spending than one where a proposal must be simply voted up or down, as the latter limits the possibility of adding extra provisions favorable to special interests. In fact, the theoretical effect of amendment rules on the size of the budget is not so clear. Baron (1991), for example, shows in a carefully worked-out bargaining model that more wasteful programs may be adopted under a closed rule than under an open rule.

---

[9] In a diagram similar to that suggested in the previous footnote, draw an overall budget line in two dimensions (a downward-sloping 45° line) and the preferred bundle for each legislator as the tangent of their indifference curves with the budget line. Majority voting yields the equilibrium appropriation.

The reason is that a more generous budget will be proposed under a closed rule because of the need to gain majority support when no amendments are allowed. Simple intuition fails if it ignores the fact that legislators are forward-looking and sophisticated in making and voting on budget proposals. In deciding to vote for or against a proposal, a legislator considers the consequences of the proposal being adopted versus it being rejected and other proposals being made. A legislator supports a program not simply if it provides benefits in excess of the tax burden to his constituents, but if the net benefits are at least as great as what could be expected if the current proposal is defeated and the budget process continues. To put the point more prosaically, if the proposed budget must be passed as is without amendment or voted down with the need to formulate a new budget, the budget may be formulated to contain "something for everyone" to ensure passage.

Budget Implementation

At the implementation stage, there are also a number of conceptual issues concerning procedural rules. One concerns the issue of flexibility versus commitment already discussed above. If there are unforeseen events, there is a trade-off between how much the budget should bind the government's actions during the fiscal year and how much flexibility the government has to respond to unforeseen events. As Von Hagen and Harden (1995) point out, the binding force of the budget law depends on the government's ability to enact supplementary budgets during the fiscal year, on the use of open-ended appropriations in the budget, and on the power of the executive to enforce the original budget.

The effects of procedural rules at different stages may be independent. Lax rules at one stage will undo the effect of tight rules at another stage. Two further general conceptual issues are important in assessing the effectiveness of institutions in enforcing budget discipline. The first is that institutions themselves are endogenous. Countries that want fiscal discipline develop institutions to support these preferences. Second, political factors may determine budget outcomes independent of fiscal institutions and legal restraints.

Empirical Analysis

In the economics literature, empirical analysis of the effects of procedural rules considers indices of such rules and correlates them with fiscal outcomes. The methodology is similar to the work of Grilli, Masciandaro, and Tabellini (1991), relating the legal form of government[10] to fiscal

---

[10] For example: is a system "presidential," in that the president is elected directly into office and has significant independent authority, or "parliamentary," in which the prime minister is accountable to the legislature? Within a parliamentary system, there is the question of the degree to which it is proportional.

indicators, as was discussed above. Von Hagen (1992) constructs an index of institutional characteristics of the budget process in the (then) 12 European Union countries, based on an analysis of budget legislation. This index includes: the strength of the prime minister in budget negotiations; the degree of limits on amendments in the budget approval process; the nature of the legislative voting process on the budget (for example, whether a vote is taken on the global size of the budget at the beginning of legislative debate); the degree of transparency in the budget, and, the degree of flexibility in implementing the budget. A high value of the index corresponds to procedural rules that should limit the size of deficits.[11] Von Hagen regresses fiscal performance measures on this index for the 1980s and finds that countries with high values of his index have significantly lower deficit and debt (as a percentage of GDP) than countries with a low value of the index.

14.6. THE NUMBER OF NATIONS

There have been a number of recent papers using formal economic models to study the formation and breakup of countries and political unions. The use of economic models is substantive rather than methodological, meaning that the focus is primarily on economic determinants of the number of countries, rather than on using tools of economic analysis to study noneconomic factors. These papers stress fiscal issues in determining the number of countries that would emerge from the political process in a world of fixed population size, but where individuals in different geographic locations differ from one another. These fiscal issues include: the provision of public goods; income redistribution, both in nonstochastic and stochastic settings; and factor mobility in the face of different fiscal policies across jurisdictions. In this approach, the size of a country reflects various trade-offs in fiscal policy.

What Is a Nation?

A first question is: what defines a nation or country (we use the terms interchangeably), at least in economic or political-economic terms? By this one means what are the political-economic (as opposed to sociological, cultural, or ethnological) characteristics we associate with, for example, two regions forming a single country rather than two separate countries. From a political point of view, a nation has sovereignty in its choice of

---

[11] The theoretical discussion on legislative approval rules indicates that, for example, an overall budget process need not lead to a lower budget theoretically than a piecemeal appropriation process. To test the effect of budget procedures on outcomes, it is necessary to make an assumption about the direction of the effect in general, and Von Hagen makes the intuitive assumptions about the general direction of effects.

policies, that is, the formal ability to act on its own rather than under the instruction of another nation. Three types of economic characteristics of countries appear in the literature. First, certain economic relations may be more efficient in a single country than in two separate countries. These include factors such as ease of trade (broadly defined) and contract enforcement. In the macroeconomic literature on country formation, these differences are not derived from fundamentals, but simply posited, as in the pathbreaking paper of Bolton and Roland (1997) discussed below. Not deriving these characteristics from first principles is a good strategy, since the focus is on the economic effects of unification or breakup on these economic relations.

A second approach, reflecting the literature on monetary unions, is that a country, through some political process, has an aggregate macroeconomic objective function, while a "policy union" of different countries is a group of countries who have chosen to have a common policy, even though their national objectives do not fully coincide. For example, Alesina and Grilli (1992), in their model of a European central bank discussed in Chapter 12, distinguish monetary union with and without political union. The adoption of common objectives within a country reflects the political mechanism by which preferences are aggregated.

A third approach, characterizing all the papers in the most recent macroeconomic literature on country formation, is that from an economic standpoint a country is defined by some degree of commonality in *fiscal* policy. That is, a nation is a fiscal union. This union may be complete, with all individuals in a country facing identical tax and expenditure structures. More likely, it may be only partial, with some tax, redistribution, and expenditure policies differing across regions in the country, a phenomenon known as "regional autonomy." In any system with both national and local governments, with some fiscal autonomy for the latter, such differences will arise without calling into question the economic sovereignty of the national government. (In fact, as we shall see, regional autonomy may be crucial for a country to remain unified rather than break up into subunits.) This being said, the literature assumes that *within* a country some characteristics of fiscal policy must be the same for all individuals, whereas these may be different *across* countries. The typical assumption in the literature, which is the most sensible, is that in economic terms countries are characterized by their level of supply of some (largely nonrival) public goods. This way of characterizing a "nation" dovetails with the first argument, as the efficiency aspects of having a single rather than multiple countries may arise from the common public goods within the country.

One may be tempted to dismiss these economic theories of the formation and breakup of countries by arguing that what defines a nation is not economic characteristics or common economic policies, but things such as language, ethnicity, and especially culture. To the extent that a paper argues that economic factors are determinate, one would probably be correct in viewing the paper as somewhat misguided. These models should instead be viewed as conceptual investigations of the possible contribution of economic factors to the formation or breakup of countries, or of the contribution of economic factors to the optimal size of nations. This leaves unanswered the question of just how important the economic factors are relative to other factors.[12] Theoretical papers are mute on this question, and there has been no empirical work on this in the economics literature. One's guess is that on the national level, the arguments that recent papers present are not extremely important empirically. In contrast, these models may be far more relevant for the formation or dissolution of local jurisdictions, an issue discussed briefly in Section 8.7 of Chapter 8 and in great detail in the theory of local public finance. The greater relevance of the models to formation of localities is especially true for the models of endogenous incremental borders discussed below, an approach that seems especially ill-suited for understanding the formation of nations.[13]

How much can simple economic models really tell us about the determinants of the creation and breakup of nation states? Noneconomic factors almost certainly played the major role in decisions on the recent breakup of a number of formerly socialist economies and on the union of others. In fact, as argued in Chapter 12, political considerations may even be primary in the formation of economic or monetary unions, as many argue is the case for European Monetary Union currently. It would be too much to suggest that economists should incorporate the range of important political and sociological factors into models of nation formation. The theory of comparative advantage suggests this is a bad idea, not only because economists would be treading on ground with which they are largely unfamiliar, but also because what economists do have to offer to understanding the number and size of nations would be obscured. Realization of the relative importance (or nonimportance) of economic factors helps to put the contribution of these models in perspective.[14]

Economies of Scale versus Diversity of Preferences in Public Goods Provision

Suppose that we accept the economic approach. If one defines a country by provision of public goods, size of a country is seen as reflecting a basic

[12] There is also a question of whether, even if we concentrate simply on common fiscal policy, these models really provide a theory of geographical nations, or only a theory of formation of clubs for the provision of public goods. We consider this below.

[13] The city of Takoma Park, Maryland seceded from Prince Georges County and joined Montgomery County to take advantage of better schools, even though this meant higher taxes.

[14] There are many insightful treatments of nationalism and the formation of nation-states in the political science literature. One especially interesting recent work on the formation of nations and their borders is Anderson (1991), including a fascinating discussion of the formation of national borders in Latin America which provides a sharp contrast to the theories discussed here.

trade-off. On the one hand, a large jurisdiction can benefit from greater economies of scale in the provision of public goods. It can also internalize the externalities reflected in tax competition, an issue discussed in detail in our treatment of local public finance in Chapter 8. On the other hand, the larger is the jurisdiction, the less the choice of public goods will "match" the tastes of residents of the jurisdiction. In the theory of local public finance, the desire for "specificity" in the provision of public goods is a major factor in community formation. The optimal trade-off between these factors will determine the optimal number of countries; the collective choice on this trade-off arising out of a specific political mechanism will determine the number of countries in practice in this type of model. As is obvious from the above discussion, the models which are used bear some similarities to models of community formation of Tiebout (1956) and subsequent writers in local public finance. One issue we will address is the similarities and differences between models of formation and dissolution of localities and models of formation and dissolution of countries.

Both the optimal and the politically determined size and number of countries will also be affected by trade-offs in redistribution. Suppose that the reach of a redistributive system corresponds to a country. Though this assumption is not literally true, redistribution within a jurisdiction is generally politically easier than redistribution across jurisdictions. Hence, let us take this as a working assumption. If shocks are not perfectly correlated across regions, then a larger jurisdiction may be better able to insure against these shocks, that is, better able to share risks. On the other hand, the lack of specificity argument in the case of public goods applies here as well, at least when applied to a political mechanism.[15] A larger jurisdiction encompassing more regions has a greater diversity of incomes, so that the amount of redistribution coming out of the political mechanism may be inferior from the point of view of some of the electorate to what would arise in a smaller jurisdiction. We discuss models of redistribution as a determinant of the size and number of countries below.

Even if we accept the proposition that factors such as trade-offs in the supply of public goods are key factors in the formation of national (as opposed to local) jurisdictions, the models do not really provide a theory of geographical nations, but rather a theory of formation of clubs for the provision of public goods. This is exactly the theory of clubs presented in Chapter 9, in which individuals with similar tastes join together for the provision of an excludable public good. The questions set out above are questions of the optimal size and number of clubs, especially when we allow "mixed" clubs, namely, clubs with heterogeneous members. In order

---

[15] Redistribution itself may be a public good, as suggested by Hochman and Rodgers (1969). Pauly (1973) then suggests that if individuals value redistribution *per se*, standard implications of models on community formation may no longer be correct in either their positive or normative predictions. See Chapter 8, and the application below.

to turn the theory of clubs into a theory of nations as we know them, one must make further assumptions to make a club geographically contiguous. For example, one could assume that there are very high administrative costs of a club whose members are geographically dispersed or that geographical location and preferences for public goods are highly correlated. Either assumption will turn a theory of clubs into a theory of geographically contiguous nations. Whether use of these assumptions suggests that a theory of clubs actually explains the existence of nations is another question entirely. As it stands, many recent models of nation formation based on club theory seem more an attempt to apply an existing theory to an area where its applicability is far from clear, rather than a source of significant insights.

Union or Breakup of Well-Defined Regions

We begin with the case in which the borders of regions are well defined, so that one concentrates on whether preexisting regions will choose to unite or not. Specifically, we consider a model in which geographical areas differ in factor endowments and the income distribution of the (immobile) population, following Bolton and Roland's (1997) model of the economic determinants of whether two regions will choose to unite into a single nation or not.

Consider two regions, say A and B, in a nation, where factors are fully immobile across borders. There are two factors of production, capital and labor, with a common production technology across regions. Hence, output in region j is given by $Y_j = K_j^\alpha N_j^{1-\alpha}$, where $0 < \alpha < 1$. Factors are paid competitively, so that in region j, the equilibrium wage rate w_j and the equilibrium return on capital r_j are given by

$$w_j = (1 - \alpha)y_j \quad \text{and} \quad r_j = \alpha\frac{y_j}{k_j}, \tag{14.1}$$

where y_j is per capita output in region j and k_j is the capital–labor ratio. Hence, an individual i in region j with capital and labor endowment of K_j^i and N_j^i will have income of

$$y_j^i = w_j N_j^i + r_j K_j^i. \tag{14.2}$$

The distribution of income in each region is represented by a probability density function $\phi_j(y^i)$ with support $[0, y^{\max}]$, so that income distribution in the nation as a whole is represented by $\phi(y^i) = \frac{1}{2}(\phi_A(y^i) + \phi_B(y^i))$. Per capita national income is given by $y = \int y^i\phi(y^i)\,dy^i$. The differences between regions are fully summed up by differences in factor returns (reflecting the absence of factor mobility) and differences in the distribution of income.

Following Bolton and Roland, we assume there is an efficiency loss in the nation breaking up into two separate regions, which they model simply by assuming that under separation, an individual with capital and labor endowment of K_j^i and N_j^i will realize a pre-tax income of only κy_j^i, where $\kappa < 1$. This assumption implies that no individual can increase his pre-tax income simply by political separation. (Remember that factors are immobile across regions whether they are separated or united, so that factor returns are independent of the political arrangement.) Separation can, of course, affect the relation of pre-tax and post-tax income.

Individuals consume a private good c and receive transfers v, financed by a proportional tax on total income at rate τ. To model the deadweight loss from taxation, Bolton and Roland assume that a dollar of aggregate tax revenue provides only $(1 - \tau/2)$ dollars of transfers, so that if total per capita tax revenues in the nation are τy (where y is mean income), after-tax income (and hence consumption) of individual i is

$$c^i = (1 - \tau)y^i + (\tau - \tau^2/2)y. \qquad (14.3)$$

It is assumed that preferences are the same across regions. For simplicity, utility is linear in consumption, that is, $u(c) = c$, so that (14.3) also represents utility of an individual with pre-tax income y^i when the tax rate is τ.[16] The preferred tax rate for an individual with income y^i is that which maximizes consumption, namely,

$$\tilde{\tau}(y^i) = \max(0, (y - y^i)/y), \qquad (14.4)$$

when national income is y.

Individual preferences over tax rates are clearly single-peaked, so that under majority voting, the equilibrium tax rate is that preferred by the median voter, that is, the voter with median income, assumed to be below mean income in each region and in the nation as a whole. (Note that it is assumed that the median voter chooses the tax rate assuming that the nation stays unified, rather than acting strategically to forestall separation. We return to this below.) When the two regions form a single nation and the tax rate is that preferred by the median voter with income y^{med}, the utility of an individual with income y^i is

$$u(y^i) = y^i + \frac{1}{2}\frac{(y - y^{\mathrm{med}})}{y}[(y - y^i) + (y^{\mathrm{med}} - y^i)], \qquad (14.5)$$

---

[16] Alternatively, one could assume that the tax finances a publicly provided private good g, where taxes have the same deadweight cost as with the provision of transfers. If, as in Bolton and Roland (1997), utility is linear in the sum $c + g$, we get identical results.

so that the utility of the median voter is

$$u(y^{\text{med}}) = y^{\text{med}} + \frac{1}{2}\frac{(y - y^{\text{med}})^2}{y}. \tag{14.6}$$

When the regions constitute separate nations, expressions analogous to (14.4) through (14.6) for desired taxes and utility obtain, with mean and median income being at their regional values. Under separation, one may denote the equilibrium tax rate in region j by τ_j and the associated utility of an individual with income y^i by $u^j(y^i)$ for $j = A, B$.

Separation and Integration

Bolton and Roland assume that separation occurs when a majority of voters in either region is in favor of separation. The assumption that unilateral succession is possible reflects not only the underlying assumption that a national government is too weak to prevent a secession of a region, but also that integration requires the support of all regions involved. The latter argument is motivated by the interest in using the model to study the economic determinants of political union of a group of countries. The preference for separation or unification of a voter in region j with income y^i depends on the sign of $u^j(y^i) - u(y^i)$. One can easily show that $u^j(y^i) - u(y^i)$ is either always increasing or always decreasing in y^i. This implies (combined with the assumption that separation occurs if a majority in either region favors it) that separation will be the political equilibrium if the median voter in either region prefers separation to unification.[17] The median voter in region j, with income y_j^{med}, prefers separation when $u^j(y_j^{\text{med}}) - u(y_j^{\text{med}}) > 0$. Using $\tilde{\tau}_j = (y_j - y_j^{\text{med}})/y_j$, where y_j is average income in region j, one obtains

$$u^j\left(y_j^{\text{med}}\right) - u\left(y_j^{\text{med}}\right) = \frac{1}{2}\frac{\left(y^{\text{med}} - y_j^{\text{med}}\right)^2}{y}$$

$$+ \frac{1}{2}\left[\left(\kappa y_j - \frac{\left(y_j^{\text{med}}\right)^2}{y}\right) - \left(y - \frac{\kappa\left(y_j^{\text{med}}\right)^2}{y_j}\right)\right]. \tag{14.7}$$

---

[17] When $u^j(y^i) - u(y^i)$ is increasing in y^i, every voter in region j prefers separation when the voter with the median income in that region prefers separation, and all voters with income below the median income prefer unification when the median voter prefers unification. When $u^j(y^i) - u(y^i)$ is decreasing in y^i, the reverse will be true.

Equation (14.7) summarizes the forces determining separation or unification of regions. When it is positive in either region A or region B, separation occurs. Bolton and Roland suggest three types of effects summarized by (14.7). First, there is a *fiscal policy preference* effect (which they term a *political* effect) corresponding to the first term of (14.7), reflecting a difference in desired fiscal policy between the median voter in region j and the median voter in the unified nation. Second, there is an *efficiency* effect, reflecting the efficiency loss from separation when $\kappa < 1$. The smaller is κ, the lower is $u^j(y_j^{med}) - u(y_j^{med})$ and the lower is the benefit from separation to the median voter, all else equal. Finally, there is a *tax base* effect, reflecting the difference between regional per capita income and national per capita income. Even if $\kappa = 1$ and $y_j^{med} = y^{med}$, a difference in the tax base will induce a preference for separation or unification. The median voter in the richer region, in which $y_j > y$, will prefer separation, as unification implies a transfer to the other region, while the median voter in the poorer region that receives the transfer will prefer unification.

The "pure" effect of different preferences over fiscal policy may be seen by setting $\kappa = 1$ and $y_j = y$. In this case, only the first right-hand-side term of (14.7) is nonzero, and separation is preferred whenever the median income in the two regions differs. This is a strong result, for it implies that separation would always occur under democracy (except in the zero-probability case in which median income in the two regions is exactly the same), even though there are no net transfers between the two regions. In fact, a majority of voters in both regions prefer separation. With no cost to separation for either region (either efficiency losses or loss of transfer revenues by the poorer region), any difference in preferred redistributive policy between the two regions induces separation. Viewing redistribution as a public good, this result represents the general argument that different tastes for public goods is a key economic determinant of the desire for separation. As Bolton and Roland put it, this effect represents the desire for "government closer to the people" as crucial in the decision of regions to form independent nations.

If we retain the assumption of different income distributions but equal per capita income across regions, but recognize the efficiency losses of separation (here represented by $\kappa < 1$), we can represent a key economic trade-off in the separation decision discussed in the introduction to this section. Separation into independent nations yields government policy closer to the preferences of a majority of voters, but at an efficiency cost. Given the income distributions in the two regions, the greater is the efficiency loss inherent in separation (the smaller is κ), the greater is the incentive to remain unified. Conversely, given κ, the greater is the difference in income distribution across regions, the greater is the incentive for separation.

In discussions of the politics of separation, differences across regions in a country in the within-region distribution of income are generally far less important than differences in *average* income across regions. To the extent that these differences induce transfers across regions, they provide an incentive for a rich region to separate itself from a poor region, efficiency losses of separation notwithstanding. This incentive will be quite strong when income differences are large across regions, a prediction of the model quite consistent empirically with numerous cases of pressures for regional separatism.

Compensatory Fiscal Policy

Though this analysis is quite illuminating as far as economic causes of the possible breakup of nations, Bolton and Roland point out that it overstates the pressure for separation. In the face of a possible secession, national tax policy could be changed to forestall separation. Such accommodation towards a separatist region might be expected if there are significant costs to separation and could result in a nation remaining unified that would otherwise break apart. They use the above model to ask both how tax policy in a unified nation might change in response to the threat of secession, and when there will or will not be accommodating tax policy that will preclude separation.

To address these questions, they consider a two-stage game. In the first stage, the unified nation votes on a national tax rate τ; in the second stage, voters in each region decide whether or not to separate taking τ as given, in which case each region chooses its own tax rate by majority vote. This tax rate is the tax rate preferred by the median voter in region j, namely, $(y_j - y_j^{\text{med}})/y_j$. The tax rate τ is chosen in the first stage knowing the implications of the choice for the second stage. There may be two types of subgame-perfect equilibria: one in which unification is the outcome, the other in which the outcome is separation.

A nonseparation condition is that a majority of voters in *each* region prefers union with tax rate τ to separation. One may easily show that the nonseparation condition is satisfied as long as it holds for the median voter in each region. For the median voter, this necessary nonseparation condition is

$$(1 - \tau)y_j^{\text{med}} + (\tau - \tau^2/2)y$$

$$\geq \kappa \left[y_j^{\text{med}} + \frac{1}{2} \frac{\left(y_j - y_j^{\text{med}}\right)^2}{y_j} \right] \quad \text{for } j = A, B. \quad (14.8)$$

This condition will also be sufficient, any tax rate not satisfying this condition being defeated by a tax rate that does in the first stage of voting. Hence, when (14.8) holds in both regions for some tax rate τ, then the only political equilibrium is union, with a tax rate satisfying (14.8) being the equilibrium tax rate. It may, however, be the case that there is no τ that satisfies (14.8).

To explore this case, as well as the determination of taxes when (14.8) is satisfied, Bolton and Roland consider a specific example, with other possibilities being analyzed in the same way. Specifically, suppose that average per capita income is higher in region A than in region B $(y_A > y_B)$ and that income distribution in the regions is such that $y_A^{\text{med}}/y_A > y^{\text{med}}/y > y_B^{\text{med}}/y_B$, implying that $\tilde{\tau}_A < \tilde{\tau} < \tilde{\tau}_B$. The analysis of possibilities can be demonstrated by a diagram such as Figure 14.1 (drawn for the case where there are tax rates that satisfy (14.8)), based on Figure Ia in Bolton and Roland (1997). Tax rates are plotted on the horizontal axis, payoffs to the median voter in each region and in the unified nation on the vertical axis. The curves joining the endpoints (representing $\tau = 0$ and $\tau = 1$) represent the payoffs to the three median voters in a unified nation as a function of τ, defined by $(1 - \tau)y_j^{\text{med}} + (\tau - \tau^2/2)y$. When $\tau = 0$, these payoffs are simply pre-tax incomes, with the ranking of the payoffs (that is, incomes) representing the above assumptions about income distributions. When $\tau = 1$, all payoffs are equal. The straight lines intersecting these curves, $u^A(y_A^{\text{med}})$ and $u^B(y_B^{\text{med}})$, are the payoffs to the median voter in each region under separation, that is, the right-hand side of (14.8).

The set of tax rates such that the median voter in region A prefers union to separation (that is, such that (14.8) is satisfied for $j = A$) is the set of rates such that $(1 - \tau)y_A^{\text{med}} + (\tau - \tau^2/2)y \geq u^A(y_A^{\text{med}})$, as indicated in Figure 14.1. Similarly, the set of tax rates such that the median voter in region B prefers union to separation is the set of rates such that $(1 - \tau)y_B$

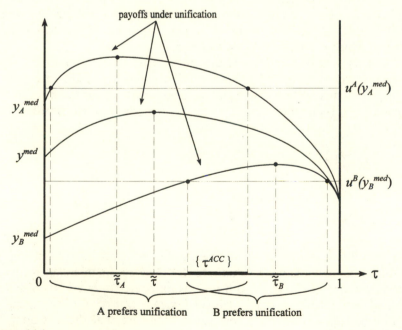

FIGURE 14.1

$+ (\tau - \tau^2/2)y \geq u^B(y_B^{\text{med}})$, similarly indicated. The set of tax rates τ consistent with a majority supporting union in both regions is the intersection of these two sets, call it $\{\tau^{\text{ACC}}\}$. Since welfare for any tax rate contained in $\{\tau^{\text{ACC}}\}$ exceeds $u^A(y_A^{\text{med}})$ and $u^B(y_B^{\text{med}})$ by definition of the set of intersections, it is clear that (14.8) is both a necessary and a sufficient condition for union rather than separation. The set $\{\tau^{\text{ACC}}\}$ may be empty; if it is not empty, it may or may not contain $\tilde{\tau}$, the tax rate the median voter would prefer if separation were not a credible threat. The tax rate that would be chosen in a unified nation facing the possibility of separation is the tax rate that maximizes the welfare of the median voter in the unified nation, subject to the constraint that it lies in $\{\tau^{\text{ACC}}\}$. In terms of the diagram, it will be the highest point in the shaded region of the middle curve, which is the utility of the median voter in a unified nation. When $\{\tau^{\text{ACC}}\}$ contains $\tilde{\tau}$, it will be the tax rate chosen in a political equilibrium with a unified nation. In this case, the threat of succession requires no tax accommodation. If $\{\tau^{\text{ACC}}\}$ is nonempty but does not contain $\tilde{\tau}$ (the case drawn in Figure 14.1), the threat of succession requires accommodation, but accommodating fiscal policy can prevent separation. On the other hand, if $\{\tau^{\text{ACC}}\}$ is empty, separation is inevitable even with the possibility of accommodating fiscal policy.

An increase in κ, that is, less of an efficiency loss from separation, induces an increase in $u^A(y_A^{\text{med}})$ and $u^B(y_B^{\text{med}})$ (that is, an upward shift in the straight lines in the diagram) and a corresponding reduction in the size of the set of feasible accommodating tax rates for the median voter in each region, and hence in $\{\tau^{\text{ACC}}\}$. Conversely, if separation induces large efficiency losses (a low value of κ), the set of taxes consistent with union will be large and will contain $\tilde{\tau}$. These results, easily illustrated by means of the figure, should be intuitive. When κ is close to unity, so that separation has low cost to at least one region, accommodating fiscal policy will not forestall separation. When κ is small, on the other hand, no accommodation will be necessary to forestall separation, since it is so costly.

One might think that accommodating fiscal policy will generally take the form of lower taxes to induce a rich region not to secede from the political union. This is the argument of Buchanan and Faith (1987), who suggest that the threat of separation will always lead to lower accommodating taxes. Bolton and Roland's analysis makes clear this is not always the case. For example, if one region requires higher redistribution than would be implied by $\tilde{\tau}$ as the price of remaining in the union, then accommodating fiscal policy would imply an equilibrium tax rate above $\tilde{\tau}$. This possibility is the one illustrated in Figure 14.1.

The analysis can also be used to consider opt-out clauses in the process of unification, as in the process of European unification. Bolton and Roland suggest adding a stage 0 to the above game, a stage in which two previously independent countries vote on unification. Adding this stage to stages 1 and 2 above then represents voting for unification with an opt-out clause. When $\{\tau^{ACC}\}$ contains $\tilde{\tau}$, the possibility of opting out *ex post* has no effect; however, when $\{\tau^{ACC}\}$ does not contain $\tilde{\tau}$, unification would take place only with such a clause. In this nonstochastic model in which the outcome of stage-1 and stage-2 votes can be foreseen with certainty, the opt-out clause will not be exercised even in this latter case, but its existence is crucial for the process of unification to take place. The reason is that the opt-out clause places a constraint on fiscal policy in stage 1; without this constraint, the equilibrium tax rate in a union would be $\tilde{\tau}$, which would be inconsistent with (politically feasible) union when $\tilde{\tau}$ is not in $\{\tau^{ACC}\}$. The threat of secession induces choice of a value of τ in $\{\tau^{ACC}\}$ in stage 1.

In a nonstochastic setting, the argument that union may be facilitated by making exit easier refers to the effect of the opt-out clause on the threat points of potential members. In a stochastic setting, the focus would be not so much on threat points as on the possibility of responding to especially adverse shocks by breaking previous commitments. An opt-out clause is thus conceptually similar to an escape clause. Another analogy to the argument that union may be facilitated by making exit easier is the role of a liberalization of restrictions on capital outflows in inducing a capital inflow, as discussed in Chapter 12.

The possibility of stochastic shocks is also important in considering different tastes for redistribution across the regions. In the Bolton–Roland model, factor returns and factor endowments are nonstochastic, with the income distribution being fully characterized by an individual's total income y_i, independent of its source. Suppose instead that in a world of factor immobility, factor returns were stochastic, with the statistical properties of the wage and the return to capital being different. Two regions in which individuals have different factor endowments may then have a strong reason for separation, as the optimal fiscal response to external shocks may be quite different. This parallels the first driving force determining incentives for separation following (14.7), namely, the "fiscal policy preference effect," though it arises for a somewhat different reason. Different sensitivities to external shocks as an argument for political separation is analogous to the basically identical point made in Section 12.4 of Chapter 12 for the case of currency areas or monetary unions. Many of the same arguments apply, and it should not be difficult to include such an analysis in the determination of political separation or unification. We return to some of these questions below.

Factor Mobility

The analysis so far has assumed that neither capital nor labor is mobile between the two regions. In relaxing this assumption, a natural starting point is to assume that capital is more mobile than labor; we therefore begin by assuming that while there is no labor mobility across regions, capital is fully mobile between the two regions. Perfect capital mobility between regions A and B means that the return to capital is equalized across the regions, which, given the structure of factor returns in (14.1), means equal capital–labor ratios k_A and k_B in the two regions. This, in turn, implies that wage rates and per capita incomes are the same across regions. However, the distribution of income can still be different in the two regions, so that the key ratios of median-to-average income y_A^{med}/y and y_B^{med}/y in the two regions will not be equal. Hence, differences in desired fiscal policies will generally still be present.

The effect of factor mobility across countries (or of the absence of factor mobility) will also very much depend on the nature of differences in preferred fiscal policies, a point stressed by Bolton and Roland (1996). In contrast to the standard Tiebout (1956) model of local public expenditure, in which mobility of individuals across jurisdictions allows them to express diversity of tastes for public expenditure (see Section 8.7 of Chapter 8), Bolton and Roland (1996) argue that it may be *absence* of mobility that is a condition for diversity of public policies. When individuals differ only in their taxable incomes and intensity of preferences for public goods, perfect mobility will lead to equalization of tax rates and public goods provision across countries and to the removal of obstacles to political integration. In the absence of mobility, fiscal policies will be different across countries, so that political obstacles to integration will be greater. Tiebout-type results may obtain when individuals differ in their preferences over the *composition* of public goods. In this case, mobility may increase diversity of public goods supply, as it allows for individual sorting and more specialized provision across countries.

The importance of the nature of preferences for the effect of mobility may be seen by considering a variant of the above model. Suppose there are two publicly provided goods, with the bundle of publicly provided goods in country j given by $g_j = \{g_j^X, g_j^Z\}$. The utility of a representative resident of country j is

$$u\left(c^i, g_j\right) = c^i + \theta^i \cdot g_j, \tag{14.9}$$

where $\theta^i = \{\theta^{iX}, \theta^{iZ}\}$ is the intensity of individual i's preferences for the two public goods. Bolton and Roland consider two polar cases: the first in which individuals differ in the intensity of their preferences for public goods, but agree on the composition of the optimal bundle; the second in which individuals differ in their preferences over the composition of public goods, but not in the intensity of these preferences. The first case is represented by $\theta^{iZ} = 0$ for all individuals i in both countries, and θ^{iX} equal to either θ^H or $\theta^L < \theta^H$. The second case is also represented by there being two types of individuals, one type with $\theta^{iX} = \theta$ and $\theta^{iZ} = 0$, the other type with $\theta^{iX} = 0$ and $\theta^{iZ} = \theta$.

As in the above model, individuals also differ in their income, with the distribution of income in each country represented by a probability density function $\phi_j(y^i)$ with support $[0, y^{max}]$. For simplicity, Bolton and Roland assume that there is the same fraction of individuals of each type within each income class. The two countries may differ in their income distributions and in the proportion of types in the population. The supply of public goods in a region is financed by a linear tax on income, with there being a deadweight cost of taxation. The total supply of public goods in country j is given by

$$g_j^X + g_j^Z = \left(\tau_j - \tau_j^2/2\right)y_j, \tag{14.10}$$

where y_j is average income and τ_j is the tax rate in country j (and where $\kappa = 1$ for any political arrangement). In each country, tax rates and public goods supply are determined by majority vote. Unification of the two countries into a single nation takes place if it is favored by a majority of voters in each country.

Consider first the case of differences in the intensity of preferences for public goods with agreement over the composition. The utility of an individual of type θ^h ($h = H, L$) in country j may be written

$$u\left(y^i; \tau_j | \theta^i = \theta^h\right) = (1 - \tau_j)y^i + \theta^h\left(\tau_j - \frac{\tau_j^2}{2}\right)y_j. \tag{14.11}$$

It is clear from (14.11) that all individuals have single-peaked preferences over τ_j, no matter their income or intensity of preferences. The modeling of preferences means that heterogeneity in the two dimensions of income and intensity of preferences can be reduced to a single dimension $\hat{y}^i \equiv y^i/\theta^i$ for individual i, which Bolton and Roland term "hedonic income." The median voter in country j is the one with median hedonic income, with the equilibrium tax rate being that preferred by the median voter. The tax rate in country j is then

$$\tilde{\tau}_j = 1 - \frac{\hat{y}_j^{med}}{y_j} = 1 - \frac{y_j^{med}/\theta_j^{med}}{y_j}, \tag{14.12}$$

where y_j^{med} is the income of the median voter in country j and θ_j^{med} is his type.

An analogous expression for the equilibrium tax holds in a union of the two countries, where the analogous variables are denoted without a subscript j (so that the tax is $\tilde{\tau}$, national income is y, etc.). Suppose that individual and aggregate incomes remain unaffected by unification (that is, $\kappa = 1$), so that y is simply the average of y_A and y_B, weighted by the respective relative populations of the two countries. Suppose further, without loss of generality, that $\hat{y}_A^{\text{med}} > \hat{y}_B^{\text{med}}$, with $\hat{y}^{\text{med}}$ that in the unified country between these two values. Because median income in the unified nation is different than median income in either of the original countries, desired tax policy will be different as well. The change in the utility of the median voter in each country j as a result of union is given by an expression analogous to (14.7), namely,

$$
u\left(y_j^{\text{med}}; \tilde{\tau}/\theta_j^{\text{med}}\right) - u^j\left(y_j^{\text{med}}; \tilde{\tau}_j/\theta_j^{\text{med}}\right)
$$

$$
= \frac{1}{2}\left[\left(1 - \frac{\left(\hat{y}_j^{\text{med}}\right)^2}{y_j y}\right)(y - y_j) - \frac{\left(\hat{y}^{\text{med}} - \hat{y}_j^{\text{med}}\right)^2}{y}\right]. \quad (14.13)
$$

Unification takes place if this quantity is positive for both countries A and B. As in (14.7), this equation summarizes the forces determining separation or unification of the two countries. The second right-hand-side term in brackets represents the *fiscal policy preference* effect, reflecting the difference in desired fiscal policy between the median voter in region j and the median voter in the unified nation. The first term is the *tax base* effect, reflecting the difference between regional per capita income and national per capita income, implying transfers between the two regions.

If individuals are mobile between the two countries, an individual, depending on his characteristics, will move to the other country either to lower his tax burden or to benefit from higher supply of public goods. National governments setting tax policy must take this into account. As in the model of redistribution across jurisdictions in Section 8.7 of Chapter 8, equilibrium must satisfy certain conditions in the face of perfect mobility: no individual has the incentive to move from one country to the other; and, fiscal policy in each country is optimal, given fiscal policy in the other country. With perfect mobility of factors between the two countries, an individual with income y_i in country A will have exactly the same income in country B. Hence, the equilibrium tax vector $\{\tau_A, \tau_B\}$ must be such that an individual i with income y^i and preferences θ^i in country A must (weakly) prefer to stay in A, that is,

$$
(1 - \tau_A)y^i + \theta^i\left(\tau_A - \frac{\tau_A^2}{2}\right)y_A \geq (1 - \tau_B)y^i + \theta^i\left(\tau_B - \frac{\tau_B^2}{2}\right)y_B, \quad (14.14)
$$

for all (y^i, θ^i). Similarly, an individual i in country B must prefer to stay in B:

$$
(1 - \tau_B)y^i + \theta^i\left(\tau_B - \frac{\tau_B^2}{2}\right)y_B \geq (1 - \tau_A)y^i + \theta^i\left(\tau_A - \frac{\tau_A^2}{2}\right)y_A, \quad (14.15)
$$

for all (y^i, θ^i). Combining these two equilibrium conditions, Bolton and Roland obtain a rather striking result: any fiscal equilibrium under perfect mobility is such that $\tau_A = \tau_B \geq 0$ and $y_A = y_B$ if $\tau_A = \tau_B > 0$. That is, if there is perfect mobility, the two countries must offer the same tax and public goods package even though agents differ in their preferences, since with any overlap of types in the two countries, individuals must be indifferent as to their location.[18] Because of the nature of preferences, mobility does not lead to sorting. On the contrary, individual mobility prevents the emergence of fiscal diversity across countries. If there is the same fiscal policy across countries, there will obviously be no barrier to political union.

Now, suppose that diversity of preferences over public goods is over composition of the bundle of public goods, with all individuals having the same intensity of preferences. Bolton and Roland consider the polar case set out above in which there are two types of individuals, one with $\theta^{iX} = \theta$ and $\theta^{iZ} = 0$ (call them type-X individuals), the other with $\theta^{iX} = 0$ and $\theta^{iZ} = \theta$ (type-Z individuals). Suppose, without loss of generality, that there is a majority of type-X individuals in country A, a majority of type-Z individuals in country B, and a majority of type-X individuals in the two countries together.

If there is no mobility between countries, the above assumptions imply that there is a political equilibrium with $g^Z = 0$ in country A, $g^X = 0$ in country B, and the equilibrium tax rate determined by the median voter in each country. The stronger the minority in each country, the closer to zero will be the equilibrium tax rate. In contrast, with perfect mobility, there exists an equilibrium with perfect sorting of types and the same tax rate in both countries. With perfect sorting, each country has the same income distribution (given the above assumption that there is the same fraction of individuals of each type within each income class) and hence the same median voter, from which the same tax rate in both countries follows. The tax rate will be higher than in the case with no mobility, with more diversity of public goods in equilibrium than in the case with no mobility. This mirrors the standard Tiebout results.

Regional Autonomy in a Federal State

Regional autonomy refers to the possibility that the two regions may choose different fiscal policies while remaining part of the same country.

---

[18] Formally, the proof is that with individuals in both countries, any overlap of the "hedonic" income distributions requires that individuals with the same "hedonic" income must satisfy both (14.13) and (14.14), which can be easily shown to imply $\tau_A = \tau_B \geq 0$ and $y_A = y_B$ if $\tau_A = \tau_B > 0$. If the distributions do not overlap and $\tau_A \neq \tau_B$, then individuals are partitioned so that all those with incomes below a critical level live in the high-tax country and all those with incomes above the critical level live in the low-tax country. No other partition can satisfy (14.13) and (14.14). However, this cannot be an equilibrium, as the highest income person in the high-tax country has an incentive to move to the other country.

That is, in addition to the possibilities of either union of the two regions into a single country with a single fiscal policy, or breakup into two different countries, there is a third political arrangement: the two regions are joined in a *federal* state in which each region has some degree of independence or autonomy in setting its own fiscal policies. This possibility is considered by Bolton and Roland (1997) in terms of the trade-offs involved. Consistent with their views of the benefits of unification, they assume that the efficiency losses associated with separation can be (largely) avoided in a federal state. It would then seem that from an economic standpoint, autonomy of the regions in a single country would always dominate separation, so that it would be optimal to have a world with a single, federal nation.

The economic drawback of a unified federal state relative to separate countries concerns the possible differences in factor mobility under the two arrangements. In comparing a single nonfederal state with separate countries, Bolton and Roland assume that mobility between two separate countries is limited relative to mobility in a single country. They argue that the key question in considering a federal state is the degree of mobility between the autonomous regions. If the mobility of factors between regions in a federal state were the same as between two separate countries, then regional autonomy would in fact always dominate separation. If, however, factors are more mobile between regions in a federal state than between the same two regions as separate countries (as would likely be the case), there may be a downside to autonomy relative to either separation or unification with a common fiscal policy—autonomy can trigger factor movements across regions, inducing costly fiscal competition between regions. Capital would move to where it is taxed the least, while labor may move to where its net benefit is the highest. Tax competition is a major problem in many federal systems, as discussed in the theory of local public finance. The choice of voters in a democratic system then depends on the costs of fiscal competition under autonomy against the efficiency gains from being part of a single nation. If the efficiency gains from unification are high and/or the possibility for factor flight is low (for example, if labor is immobile between regions and capital is low), then autonomy will be the preferred option. If the efficiency gains from unification are high, but large potential capital flight would induce significant fiscal competition between regions in a federal state, unification without autonomy will be preferred.

Bolton and Roland (1997) consider the possibility of federal states in the model of the previous sections, in which capital, but not labor, is assumed to be mobile between regions in a unified state, whether federal or centralized, while being immobile between independent countries. Decisions on the political structure are determined in multistage voting. In a unified nation, there is first a vote on a countrywide fiscal policy. A vote in each region then takes place on autonomy, with autonomy being adopted if it is favored by a majority of voters in at least one region. No matter how this vote comes out, there is then a third stage vote in which, conditional on the decision of whether regions will have autonomy in a unified nation, they decide whether they want to be fully independent, similar to what was analyzed above. If autonomy is chosen at the second stage, each region sets its own tax rate; once tax rates are set, individuals choose how to allocate their capital across regions, where capital is taxed only at source. Perfect mobility of capital between the two regions A and B implies that the after-tax rates of return are equalized. Denoting the tax rate in region j under federalism by τ_{Fj}, one has

$$(1 - \tau_{FA})/k_A^{1-\alpha} = (1 - \tau_{FB})/k_B^{1-\alpha}, \tag{14.16}$$

where we have used $r_j = \alpha k_j^{\alpha-1}$.

Given the multistage nature of voting and the nature of decisions on allocation of capital across regions under autonomy, the model gets quite complicated. We give only a summary of the results here, with the reader interested in fuller details being referred to the original article. To analyze fiscal competition between the two regions in a federal system, Bolton and Roland consider a Nash equilibrium in regional fiscal policies, that is, a pair of tax rates $\{\tau_{FA}, \tau_{FB}\}$ such that each region's tax rate is the best response of that region's median voter, given the other region's choice of tax rate. Hence, for any τ_{FB}, region A's tax rate is the rate τ_{FA} that is the solution to

$$\max\left[(1 - \tau_{FA})y_A^{\text{med}} + (\tau_{FA} - \tau_{FA}^2/2)y_A\right], \tag{14.17}$$

subject to (14.16).

If the two regions are identical, so that the median income is the same in each region, then there is a unique Nash equilibrium with the equilibrium tax rate τ_F below what it would be in a centralized state. Intuitively, the lower tax rate is the result of fiscal competition to attract capital. If there were no efficiency losses to separation ($\kappa = 1$), so that voters were indifferent between unification and separation in this case, the political effect of fiscal competition is clear. Federalism would never be preferred as fiscal competition drives the tax rate below what is optimal and could be achieved under an alternative political structure. When the income distributions are different across regions, the results are more complicated, but the possible political implications of fiscal competition can still be shown. The interested reader is referred to Bolton and Roland (1997) for exact details.

Fiscal federalism is also relevant when income is stochastic, so that fiscal policy is used for risk sharing, a possibility to which we return below.

Endogenous Incremental Borders

An alternative approach to the formation of nations is to begin with the geographical distribution of an immobile population, but no preexisting regions, and consider how borders would be optimally drawn and how they would be drawn under different political choice mechanisms. Countries would then be collections of individuals, rather than regions, with the possibility of marginal changes in borders as individuals switch countries, "taking their location" with them. Without further assumptions, a country would be a club, that is, a collection of individuals with similar preferences but no constraints on their location. One way to obtain geographically connected political jurisdictions is to impose a correlation between geographical location and preferences on public goods. The paradigm of country formation would then be the Hotelling (1929) model of spatial competition, with the variant of the model depending on the specific assumption of how location and preferences are correlated. This approach has been used by Casella and Feinstein (1990), Wei (1992), and, most notably, by Alesina and Spolaore (1997).

Alesina and Spolaore consider a continuum of otherwise identical individuals distributed uniformly on an interval, say $[0, 1]$. A "country" is a segment of this interval, with the government located at one point along the segment. The utility of individuals in the country depends on the absolute value of their distance from the government. Hence, within a country, the utility of an individual i is

$$u^i = g(1 - \kappa \delta^i) + y - \tau, \tag{14.18}$$

where δ^i is the distance between i's location and the seat of government, g is the maximum possible utility from public goods, obtained by an individual located at the seat of government where $\delta^i = 0$, y is pre-tax income, assumed exogenous and equal for all individuals, τ is the tax an individual pays to finance government, also assumed equal across individuals, and κ is a positive constant. Government is a nonrival public good, with cost ζ independent of the size of the country.

This formulation of the model shows very clearly the trade-off in the size of nations discussed at the beginning of this section. The cost of government per capita (or of the public goods it provides) decreases with the number of people in a country. However, as a nation gets larger, the distance of people from their government (in both a figurative and a literal sense) increases. This represents the less good match between the actual and desired public goods supply that characterizes larger nations that was central to the models in the previous section as well.

Alesina and Spolaore then compare the world social planner's solution for the population size and number of nations (given the assumptions about the characteristics of world population, these are identical questions) with the population size that would emerge under different political systems. The world social planner chooses the number of nations J by maximizing world utility (the sum of the utilities (14.18) for each individual in the continuum $[0, 1]$), subject to the constraint that total taxes equal $J\zeta$, the cost of running J governments. Utility depends on the location of the government; it is obvious that in any given country, it will be optimal to put the government in the center of the country, that is, at the midpoint of the line segment that defines the country.

Deriving the number of nations that would arise from decentralized democracy is far more complicated, as one must carefully specify the rules under which nations are formed or eliminated. Alesina and Spolaore suggest a number of possible rules for setting borders. First, individuals at the border between two countries can choose which country to join. Second, a new country can be created, or an existing one eliminated, if the modification is approved by majority rule in each of the existing countries affected by the redrawing of borders. An alternative is that a group of individuals can secede from existing nations and form a new nation when they vote unanimously to do so. They then consider the stable number of nations that would emerge. (Seats of government are assumed to be chosen by majority rule within a country after the borders are established. With equal taxes for all citizens, the result will be the same as with a social planner, with the government located in the center of the country.) We do not pursue the details here because of doubts about the realism, and hence relevance, of this approach to nation formation and dissolution. The interested reader is referred to Alesina and Spolaore (1997) for precise details.

A main result that emerges in Alesina and Spolaore (1997) is that a benevolent world social planner chooses to have fewer nations than in the democratic equilibrium. Intuitively, this is most easily understood in terms of externalities, in that (for example) the formation of a new nation has effects on existing nations that residents of the new nation do not take into account when choosing to form the nation. The benevolent social planner chooses the size of nations taking all individuals into account, optimally trading off economies of scale in public goods provision and satisfying the public goods preferences of a (geographically) diverse population. He compensates individuals who are far from the seat of government with transfers. These transfers, however, would not be supported by majority rule in a democracy. In the absence of transfers, individuals who are far from the seat of government choose to form their own country, though this leads to a suboptimally large number of nations. This result on democracy leading to too many nations when secession is possible mirrors results found by Bolton and Roland. It has a strong ring of plausibility, independent of the precise details of the Alesina–Spolaore model.

A second type of result concerns the relation between country size and economic integration. In a world of trade barriers, the population size of a country influences the size of the market. Other things equal, a correlation between country and market size may push towards the formation of larger countries. With increasing economic integration, which would sever the connection between country and trade boundaries, this incentive towards large political size is weakened, so that the equilibrium size of countries in this sort of model would fall. Alesina and Spolaore point out that this prediction of the model, that economic integration and fewer trade barriers will be accompanied by greater pressures for political separatism, is consistent with current trends, at least in some parts of the world.

To summarize, the Alesina and Spolaore model of the number and size of nations, based on the Hotelling model of location, has a number of predictions that are plausible. A deeper question is whether the underlying "marginalist" approach to the formation of nations is plausible. As indicated above (see, for example, footnote 13 and the discussion surrounding it), the marginalist approach may be sometimes relevant for localities like cities or counties. They will make marginal adjustments in their borders for purely economic reasons by absorbing an unincorporated area or (more rarely) giving up a small area to another city or county. At the national level, making marginal adjustments for economic reasons, as opposed to political or socio-ethnic reasons, does not seem especially descriptive of reality.

Redistribution and Risk Sharing at the National Level

The discussion so far of economic arguments for union, separation, or autonomy has been made in the context of certainty. A crucial consideration in the formation of "policy unions" is insulation against shocks, an issue which arose in our discussion of optimum currency areas in Chapter 12. In that discussion, it was argued that, other things equal, the less similar countries are in the shocks that they face, the stronger is the argument against adopting a common currency. With the stress on monetary rather than fiscal policy, the argument was that changes in the exchange rate between countries would then be required to combat the effects of different shocks to the countries. When one allows compensatory fiscal transfers across regions in a monetary union, the argument that countries facing uncorrelated shocks cannot form a viable union is no longer necessarily true. With the possibility of transfers across countries or regions, conclusions opposite to those of the literature on optimum currency areas may hold. Suppose there were no scope for discretionary monetary policy, the burden of adjustment falling on fiscal policy. A negative shock specific to one country would be optimally met by a net transfer from another country. If fiscal transfers across countries are politically infeasible, but transfers within countries can be made, such redistribution would require uniting the countries under a single fiscal authority. By combining regions facing uncorrelated shocks into a single fiscal jurisdiction, there is greater scope for risk sharing. If the feasibility of such transfers depends on political arrangements, the characteristics of the shocks hitting different regions will affect the case for separation or union.

728

A first question to be addressed in analyzing the risk-sharing benefits of *fiscal federalism*, as it is called, is whether regional governments can achieve the same benefits on their own. Specifically, could regional governments self-insure against shocks without federal fiscal redistribution by running countercyclical deficits? Sachs and Sala-i-Martin (1992), for example, conclude that countercyclical regional fiscal policy is likely to be far less effective for stabilizing stochastic income streams than cross-regional transfers for a number of reasons. First, countercyclical regional fiscal policy means that budget deficits have to be repaid by higher taxes or lower spending at the regional level at some point in the future. If individuals incorporate the expectation of higher future taxes into their intertemporal budget constraints, as implied by Ricardian equivalence, the stabilizing effect of countercyclical policy is lessened or even eliminated. Sachs and Sala-i-Martin point out that Ricardian equivalence need not frustrate regional stabilization in the presence of cross-regional transfers, as such transfers have a nonzero value to the region even in present discounted value terms. Second, interregional mobility within a nation means that factors may migrate when tax rates are high, greatly limiting the ability of regions to smooth income out of their own tax base over time. The fear of such migration and the fiscal difficulties it would imply for a countercyclical policy may make regions quite hesitant to engage in income smoothing via countercyclical fiscal policy. To the extent that migration across national borders is generally far smaller than across regional borders, the same caveat need not apply to programs of national redistribution across regions over time.

Persson and Tabellini (1996a) present a theoretical analysis of the political economy determinants of regional transfers within a country. The regions are taken as given and it is assumed that there is no mobility between regions. (Interregional mobility of factors was central to the analysis of redistribution across regions in Section 8.7 of Chapter 8, where we saw it may very much limit the effectiveness of tax-transfer policy.) A key result is that if there is a rich enough menu of fiscal instruments, the risk-sharing and redistributive aspects of transfers across asymmetric regions can be kept separate, but there is a trade-off between redistribution and risk sharing when the set of fiscal instruments is limited. In the absence of moral hazard, an issue discussed in Persson and Tabellini (1996b), full insurance against shocks will be optimal. To make this point concrete, they consider a model of two regions of equal size composed of risk-averse individuals who face both individual idiosyncratic income shocks and regional income shocks. Regional shocks are perfectly negatively correlated between regions, so that there is no aggregate risk at the countrywide level. The two regions are asymmetric in that there is a higher probability of a positive shock in one of them (and hence of a negative shock in the other). There is both regional policy, consisting of a tax (subsidy) on individual income accompanied by a lump-sum transfer (tax) to each individual in the region, and a federal policy, consisting of transfers across regions which may take several forms, including transfers that depend on the difference in *ex-post* regional income and possibly a lump-sum transfer across regions. Let the transfer rate on the former be τ, the lump-sum transfer be γ. The federal budget balances in that positive values of τ or γ in one region are matched by negative values in the other.

In the case of no limitations on fiscal instruments, a fully state-contingent redistributive policy is chosen before the shock is realized, including nonzero values of both τ and γ. The setting of the policy variables is found as the solution to a Nash bargaining problem. In equilibrium, full insurance is achieved, with the high-risk region paying a lump-sum transfer to the low-risk region to compensate for its higher risk. The greater is the asymmetry between the two regions, the larger is the compensatory transfer γ.

In practice, fully state-contingent transfers are difficult to implement for a number of reasons. First, it is difficult to specify all states of nature *ex ante*, and often difficult to verify them *ex post*. Second, if the shocks hitting regions are very asymmetric, achieving complete risk sharing may require that residents of different regions be treated quite asymmetrically, which would violate equal-treatment provisions that characterize countries' constitutions. When political factors constrain the use of policy instruments, full risk sharing may not be achievable.

To address the issue of political constraints, Persson and Tabellini analyze what outcomes can be achieved with limitations on transfers between the regions. One possibility is a constraint of non-state-contingent fiscal policy between regions, meaning that the interregional transfer rate τ is set before the state is realized and the lump-sum cross-region transfer γ is constrained to be zero. This constraint on the use of policy instruments implies a trade-off between the goals of risk sharing and redistribution and a conflict of interests over this trade-off between asymmetric regions. All individuals in the low-risk region want less insurance against aggregate regional shocks, that is, a lower τ (since there is no compensating lump-sum transfer), whereas all individuals in the high-risk region want more insurance against regional shocks. One possible choice mechanism is voting over τ in a federal election before the regional shock is realized, along with voting in a regional election over the *regional* social insurance scheme to insure individuals within the region against idiosyncratic shocks.

Given the identity of interests within a region, but the conflict between regions, Persson and Tabellini argue that the policy choice should be made not by countrywide voting, but by bargaining between regional representatives. To study the possible outcomes, they consider a bargaining solution between two regions, as in the case of fully state-contingent transfers. In this case, the bargaining is not over the size of the cross-regional lump-sum transfer, but over the extent of insurance against regional shocks. If autarky (i.e., political separation) is the threat point in the bargain, there will be incomplete regional insurance in equilibrium, since the low-risk region, which prefers less insurance, has more bargaining power. The more asymmetric are the regions, the lower will be the amount of risk sharing in the Nash bargaining solution.

They contrast this solution with one where there is federal social insurance that transfers income from rich to poor individuals across regions. That is, insurance against individual income shocks is a function assigned to federal government either in place of or in addition to regional government. The political constraint of equal treatment of individuals with the same income across regions means that there is no cross-regional lump-sum transfer, that is, γ is constrained to be zero. Technically, interregional income-based transfers at rate τ can be thought of as going directly to individuals. With $\gamma = 0$, net transfer *rates* are not state contingent, as in the previous constrained-transfer case. This scheme is therefore economically equivalent to that described in the previous paragraph, in that any outcome achieved under the previous constrained scheme can be achieved here. The political implications, however, are quite different, so that the political-economic equilibrium may be different as well. Federal insurance implies that there is redistribution across regions from rich to poor, so that heterogeneous interests cut across regions.

When policy choices are made by Nash bargaining, the economic equivalence of the constrained-transfer schemes translates into political equivalence, with the equilibrium policy being identical. Hence, under bargaining, there is underinsurance relative to the case of no constraints on fiscal policy, as was the case of only regional insurance against individual income shocks and constrained interregional transfers. This equivalence vanishes if federal policy on social insurance is chosen by nationwide voting, since there are cross-region voting coalitions that were not present in the previous case. In fact, Persson and Tabellini show that the results in the previous constrained-transfer case can be exactly the opposite under voting, depending on the distribution of individual income risk.[19] Under voting and a federal social insurance scheme, they argue, under plausible assumptions about the distribution of individual income risk, that the interests of the median voter in the two regions combined will be aligned with the interests of the high-risk region. This implies overinsurance relative to the case of fully state-contingent fiscal policy. Furthermore, the greater is the asymmetry between regions, the higher is the degree of (over)insurance.

Intuitively, the difference between the outcomes of the two constrained fiscal schemes may be explained as follows. Under the first system of non-state-contingent net transfers and regional social insurance, federal transfers are simply across regions, so that the conflict between regions is

---

[19] The demonstration is somewhat complex, so interested readers are referred to the original article.

clear. The region less in need of cross-regional fiscal transfers has more bargaining power, so unambiguously, there is underinsurance of regional risks. Under the second system of federal social insurance, federal transfers are both directly across regions (with a clear conflict of interests across regions) and from rich to poor individuals across regions. This second characteristic of fiscal transfers implies that there will be coalitions of voters across regions, and the conflict of interests between regions is no longer unambiguous. There are plausible distributions of individual income risk such that voting leads to overinsurance.

One may also consider interregional risk sharing via redistribution between regions hit by different shocks from a more empirical perspective. There are several such studies. To take but one, Sachs and Sala-i-Martin (1992) ask what may be learned from the U.S. federal system of fiscal transfers. Specifically, they ask how much a region's disposable income falls given the transfer system in response to a one-dollar negative shock to the region's income. They divide the United States into nine economically diverse regions and estimate two elasticities for the time period 1970–1988: a tax elasticity, measuring the percent increase in taxes paid to the U.S. Treasury in response to a 1% increase in regional income; and a transfer elasticity, measuring the percent increase in transfers received from the U.S. Treasury in response to a 1% decrease in regional income. These elasticities are found, not surprisingly, to differ and to be sensitive to estimation methods. Nonetheless, they find these elasticities to be generally significant. In summary, they report that a one-dollar fall in a region's disposable per capita income triggers a fall in federal taxes of about 34 cents and an increase in transfers of about 6 cents. That is, a negative income shock of one dollar implies a fall in a region's disposable income of only about 60 cents, somewhere between one-third and one-half of the shock absorbed by the federal tax-transfer system. They further point out that this figure is largely capturing the nondiscretionary component of the progressive tax-transfer system in the United States, and does not include large one-time transfers given to cushion severe one-time shocks. These figures suggest that transfers at the national level may be quite effective for risk sharing in a well-designed system of fiscal federalism.

14.7. CONCLUSIONS

In this chapter, we have considered political economy explanations of both the size of government and the creation and breakup of nations. As will be obvious to the reader, the treatment of the former topic has relied heavily on models presented in earlier chapters. Though constant reference to material in earlier chapters may have been annoying, it is unavoidable in a later chapter of the book, even more so in the book's final chapter. It is also in the nature of applications and hence serves as a lesson in itself.

Readers who have familiarized themselves with the models in Parts II and III of the book will, it is hoped, find those models useful in a wide variety of applications.

There are general lessons about political economy in macroeconomics to be learned from considering the topics and results in this chapter from a very broad perspective. These lessons apply to much of the field and are brought into sharp contrast by the material covered in the chapter. Both topics—the size of government and the formation of nations—are at the same time both classical and long-standing questions of political economy and questions at the forefront of new or modern political economy. Like much of the new political economy, the material in both areas can be seen as a reexamination of long-standing questions from a new perspective. Recent work on the formation of nations, for example, treats a key question in politics, but in a way quite different from the treatment political philosophers have traditionally used or that political scientists use today. The models we considered give a clear picture of the technical nature of the new political economy in general, and a sampling of techniques in particular. Comparing earlier topics in the book to more traditional treatments presents a similar contrast.

The contrast between the approach of the new political economy and traditional approaches gives a sense of both some of the strengths and some of the weaknesses of the new political economy. The work on formation and dissolution of nations presents an excellent example. The technical models on this topic (and more generally in the book as a whole) allow us to give more precise answers to many questions. For example, the decision of two regions to stay united or to break apart depends on the strengths of conflicting factors. Formal models give a sense of how strong a given factor such as the loss from separate markets must be to offset another factor such as the gain from having government "closer to the people." Formal models also allow us to make concrete what "closer to the people" may mean, such as greater specificity of public goods. This point—that formal models both clarify what the trade-offs are and give more substance to the factors being traded off—applies to the models used throughout the book.

The material on formation of nations in this chapter should also have illustrated potential weaknesses of the technical approach that characterizes the new political economy. Obviously, there are limits to what can be explained, as the formal models on the creation and breakup of nations make clear. Factors not amenable to formal modeling are crucial in the formation of nations; our inability to model them should not make us lose sight of them and of how they interact with economic factors. Second, the attempt to put things in a formal framework may sometimes obscure rather than illuminate, especially if a formalization is chosen not for its relevance to the problem at hand, but for its tractability or elegance. At some points in our discussion, this problem was pointed out for models of creation of nations. More generally, it has been pointed out numerous times in other parts of the book. It is hoped that the reader, in considering the material in the book as a whole, is impressed by two things. One is the usefulness and power of the technical approach in general and the formal models in particular to address important questions. The second is the limitations of existing models and technical approaches. If one can combine these two impressions in the right proportions, one should be able to make significant progress in extending the field even further.

Acemoglu, D. and J. Robinson (1996), "Why Did the West Extend the Franchise? Democracy, Inequality and Growth in Historical Perspective," working paper, Massachusetts Institute of Technology.

Ades, A. and T. Verdier (1996), "The Rise and Fall of Elites: Economic Development and Social Polarization in Rent-Seeking Societies," CEPR Discussion Paper, 1495.

Advisory Council on Intergovernmental Relations (1987), *Fiscal Discipline in the Federal System*: *National Reform and the Experience of States*, Washington, DC: Advisory Council on Intergovernmental Relations.

Aghion, P. and O. Blanchard (1994), "On the Speed of Transition in Central Europe," in S. Fischer and J. Rotemberg, eds., *NBER Macroeconomics Annual*, Cambridge, MA: MIT Press.

Aghion, P. and P. Bolton (1990), "Government Domestic Debt and the Risk of Default: A Political-economic Model of the Strategic Role of Debt," in R. Dornbusch and M. Draghi, eds., *Public Debt Management*: *Theory and History*, Cambridge: Cambridge University Press.

_____ (1997), "A Theory of Trickle-Down Growth and Development," *Review of Economic Studies* 64, 151–72.

Aghion, P. and P. Howitt (1998), *Endogenous Growth Theory*, Cambridge, MA: MIT Press.

Aizenman, J. (1992), "Competitive Externalities and the Optimal Seigniorage," *Journal of Money, Credit and Banking* 24, 61–71.

Aizenman, J. and P. Guidotti (1994), "Capital Controls, Collection Costs and Domestic Public Debt," *Journal of International Money and Finance* 13, 41–54.

Akerlof, G. (1991), "Procrastination and Obedience," *American Economic Review* 81, 1–19.

Alesina, A. (1987), "Macroeconomic Policy in a Two-Party System as a Repeated Game," *Quarterly Journal of Economics* 102, 651–78.

_____ (1988a), "Credibility and Policy Convergence in a Two-Party System with Rational Voters," *American Economic Review* 78, 796–805.

_____ (1988b), "Macroeconomics and Politics," in O. Blanchard and S. Fischer, eds., *NBER Macroeconomics Annual*, Cambridge, MA: MIT Press.

_____ (1995), "Elections, Party Structure, and the Economy," in J. Banks and E. Hanushek, eds., *Modern Political Economy*: *Old Topics, New Directions*, Cambridge: Cambridge University Press.

Alesina, A., G. Cohen, and N. Roubini (1992), "Macroeconomic Policy and Elections in OECD Democracies," *Economics and Politics* 4, 1–30.

_____ (1993), "Electoral Business Cycles in Industrial Democracies," *European Journal of Political Economy* 23, 1–25.

Alesina, A. and A. Cukierman (1990), "The Politics of Ambiguity," *Quarterly Journal of Economics* 105, 829–50.

Alesina, A. and A. Drazen (1991), "Why are Stabilizations Delayed?," *American Economic Review* 81, 1170–88.

Alesina A. and R. Gatti (1995), "Independent Central Banks: Low Inflation at No Cost?," *American Economic Review Papers and Proceedings* 85, 196–200.

Alesina, A. and V. Grilli (1992), "The European Central Bank: Reshaping Monetary Policies in Europe," in M. Canzoneri, V. Grilli, and P. Masson, eds., *Establishing a Central Bank, Issues in Europe and Lessons from the U.S.*, Cambridge: Cambridge University Press.

———— (1993), "On The Feasibility of a One-Speed or Multi-Speed European Monetary Union," *Economics and Politics* 5, 145–65.

Alesina, A., V. Grilli, and G.-M. Milesi-Ferretti (1994), "The Political Economy of Capital Controls," in L. Leiderman and A. Razin, eds., *Capital Mobility: The Impact on Consumption, Investment, and Growth*, Cambridge: Cambridge University Press.

Alesina, A., S. Ozler, N. Roubini, and P. Swagel (1996), "Political Instability and Economic Growth," *Journal of Economic Growth* 1, 193–215.

Alesina, A. and R. Perotti (1994), "The Political Economics of Growth: A Selective Survey and Some New Results," *World Bank Economic Review* 8, 351–71.

———— (1995a), "The Political Economy of Budget Deficits," *IMF Staff Papers* 42, 1–37.

———— (1995b), "Fiscal Expansions and Adjustments in OECD Economies," *Economic Policy* 21, 205–40.

———— (1996a), "Fiscal Discipline and the Budget Process," *American Economic Review Papers and Proceedings* 86, 401–7.

———— (1996b), "Income Distribution, Political Instability, and Investment," *European Economic Review* 40, 1203–28.

———— (1997), "Fiscal Adjustments in OECD Countries: Composition and Macroeconomic Effects," *IMF Staff Papers* 44, 210–48.

Alesina, A. and D. Rodrik (1994), "Distributive Politics and Economic Growth," *Quarterly Journal of Economics* 109, 465–90.

Alesina, A. and H. Rosenthal (1995), *Partisan Politics, Divided Government, and the Economy*, Cambridge: Cambridge University Press.

———— (1996), "A Theory of Divided Government," *Econometrica* 64, 1311–41.

Alesina, A. and N. Roubini (1992), "Political Cycles in OECD Economies," *Review of Economic Studies* 59, 663–88.

Alesina, A., N. Roubini, and G. Cohen (1997), *Political Cycles and the Macroeconomy*, Cambridge, MA: MIT Press.

Alesina, A. and S. Spear (1988), "An Overlapping Generations Model of Electoral Competition," *Journal of Public Economics* 37, 359–79.

Alesina, A. and E. Spolaore (1997), "On the Number and Size of Nations," *Quarterly Journal of Economics* 112, 1027–56.

Alesina, A. and L. Summers (1993), "Central Bank Independence and Macroeconomic Performance," *Journal of Money, Credit, and Banking* 25, 151–62.

Alesina, A. and G. Tabellini (1989), "External Debt, Capital Flight and Political Risk," *Journal of International Economics* 27, 199–220.

———— (1990), "A Positive Theory of Budget Deficits and Government Debt," *Review of Economic Studies* 57, 403–14.

Alt, J. and A. Chrystal (1983), *Political Economy*, Berkeley, CA: Berkeley University Press.

Alt, J. and R. Lowry (1994), "Divided Government, Fiscal Institutions, and Budget Deficits: Evidence from States," *American Political Science Review* 88, 811–28.

Alt, J. and K. Shepsle (1990), *Perspectives on Positive Political Economy*, Cambridge: Cambridge University Press.

Andersen, T. and O. Risager (1991), "The Role of Credibility for the Effects of a Change in Exchange-Rate Policy," *Oxford Economic Papers* 43, 85–98.

Anderson, B. (1991), *Imagined Communities: Reflections on the Origin and Spread of Nationalism*, London: Verso.

Arcelus, F. and A. Meltzer (1975), "The Effect of Aggregate Economic Variables on Congressional Elections," *American Political Science Review* 69, 1232–39.

Archer, D. (1997), "The New Zealand Approach to Rules and Discretion in Monetary Policy," *Journal of Monetary Economics* 39, 3–15.

Arnold, R. (1990), *The Logic of Congressional Action*, New Haven, CT: Yale University Press.

——— (1979), *Congress and the Bureaucracy: A Theory of Influence*, New Haven, CT: Yale University Press.

Atkeson, A. and P. Kehoe (1995), "Social Insurance and Transition," Research Department Staff Report 202, Federal Reserve Bank of Minneapolis.

Atkinson A. and N. Stern (1974), "Pigou, Taxation and Public Goods," *Review of Economic Studies* 41, 119–28.

Atkinson A. and J. Stiglitz (1980), *Lectures on Public Economics*, New York: Mc-Graw Hill.

Auernheimer, L. (1974), "The Honest Government's Guide to the Revenue from the Creation of Money," *Journal of Political Economy* 82, 598–606.

Austen-Smith, D. (1986), "Legislative Coalitions and Electoral Equilibrium," *Public Choice* 50, 185–210.

——— (1987), "Interest Groups, Campaign Contributions and Probabilistic Voting," *Public Choice* 54, 123–39.

——— (1990), "Credible Debate Equilibria," *Social Choice and Welfare* 7, 75–93.

——— (1993), "Information and Influence: Lobbying for Agendas and Votes," *American Journal of Political Science* 37, 799–833.

——— (1997), "Interest Groups: Money, Information, and Influence," in D. Mueller, ed., *Perspectives on Public Choice: A Handbook*, Cambridge: Cambridge University Press.

Austen-Smith, D. and J. Banks (1988), "Elections, Coalitions, and Legislative Outcomes," *American Political Science Review* 82, 405–22.

——— (1990), "Stable Governments and the Allocation of Policy Portfolios," *American Political Science Review* 84, 891–906.

Backus, D. and J. Driffill (1985a), "Inflation and Reputation," *American Economic Review* 75, 530–38.

——— (1985b), "Rational Expectations and Policy Credibility Following a Change in Regime," *Review of Economic Studies* 52, 211–21.

Bade, R. and M. Parkin (1988), "Central Bank Laws and Monetary Policy," working paper, University of Western Ontario.

Baldwin, R. (1985), *The Political Economy of U.S. Import Policy*, Cambridge, MA: MIT Press.

Banerjee, A. (1997), "A Theory of Misgovernance," *Quarterly Journal of Economics* 112, 1289–1332.

Banerjee, A. and A. Newman (1993), "Occupational Choice and the Process of Development," *Journal of Political Economy* 101, 274–98.

Banks A. (1987, 1994), *A Political Handbook of the World*, Binghamton, NY: CSA Publications, SUNY-Binghamton.

Baron, D. (1989), "Service-Induced Campaign Contributions and the Electoral Equilibrium," *Quarterly Journal of Economics* 104, 45–72.

_____ (1991), "Majoritarian Incentives, Pork Barrel Programs, and Procedural Control," *American Journal of Political Science* 35, 57–90.

_____ (1994), "Electoral Competition with Informed and Uninformed Voters," *American Political Science Review* 88, 33–47.

Baron, D. and J. Ferejohn (1989), "Bargaining in Legislatures," *American Political Science Review* 81, 1181–1206.

Barro, R. (1973), "The Control of Politicians: An Economic Model," *Public Choice* 14, 19–42.

_____ (1986), "Reputation in a Model of Monetary Policy with Incomplete Information," *Journal of Monetary Economics* 17, 3–20.

_____ (1991), "Economic Growth in a Cross-Section of Countries," *Quarterly Journal of Economics* 106, 407–44.

_____ (1995), "Optimal Debt Management," NBER Working Paper #5327.

_____ (1996), "Democracy and Growth," *Journal of Economic Growth* 1, 1–28.

Barro, R. and D. Gordon (1983a), "Rules, Discretion, and Reputation in a Model of Monetary Policy," *Journal of Monetary Economics* 12, 101–21.

_____ (1983b), "A Positive Theory of Monetary Policy in a Natural Rate Model," *Journal of Political Economy* 91, 589–610.

Barro, R. and X. Sala-i-Martin (1995), *Economic Growth*, New York: McGraw-Hill.

Bartolini, L. and A. Drazen (1997a), "Capital Account Liberalization as a Signal," *American Economic Review* 87, 138–54.

_____ (1997b), "When Liberal Policies Reflect External Shocks, What Do We Learn?," *Journal of International Economics* 42, 249–73.

Bates, R. and A. Krueger, eds. (1993), *Political and Economic Interactions in Economic Policy Reform: Evidence from Eight Countries*, Oxford: Basil Blackwell.

Baumol, W. (1952), *Welfare Economics and the Theory of the State*, Cambridge, MA: Harvard University Press.

_____ (1967), "Macroeconomics of Unbalanced Growth: The Anatomy of Urban Crisis," *American Economic Review* 57, 415–26.

Bayoumi, T. (1994), "A Formal Model of Optimum Currency Areas," *International Monetary Fund Staff Papers* 41, 537–54.

Bayoumi, T. and B. Eichengreen (1994), "Shocking Aspects of European Monetary Union," in F. Torres and F. Giavazzi, eds., *The Transition to Economic and Monetary Union*, Cambridge: Cambridge University Press.

_____ (1996), "Optimum Currency Areas and Exchange Rate Volatility: Theory and Evidence," working paper, International Monetary Fund.

Beck, N. (1987), "Elections and the Fed: Is There a Political Monetary Cycle?," *American Journal of Political Science* 31, 194–216.

Becker, G. (1983), "A Theory of Competition among Interest Groups for Political Influence," *Quarterly Journal of Economics* 98, 371–400.

_____ (1985), "Public Policies, Pressure Groups, and Deadweight Costs," *Journal of Public Economics* 28, 329–47.

Becker G., K. Murphy, and R. Tamura (1990), "Human Capital, Fertility, and Economic Growth," *Journal of Political Economy* 98, S12–S37.

Becker, G. and G. Stigler (1974), "Law Enforcement, Malfeasance, and the Compensation of Enforcers," *Journal of Legal Studies* 1, 1–18.

Benabou, R. (1996), "Inequality and Growth," in B. Bernanke and J. Rotemberg, eds., *NBER Macroeconomics Annual*, Cambridge, MA: MIT Press.

Benhabib, J. and A. Rustichini (1996), "Social Conflict and Growth," *Journal of Economic Growth* 1, 125–42.

Benoit, J.- P. and V. Krishna (1985), "Finitely Repeated Games," *Econometrica* 53, 905–22.

Ben-Porath, Y. (1975), "The Years of Plenty and the Years of Famine—A Political Business Cycle?," *Kyklos* 28, 400–403.

Bensaid, B. and O. Jeanne (1997), "The Instability of Fixed Exchange Rate Systems When Raising the Nominal Interest Rate is Costly," *European Economic Review* 41, 1461–78.

Bernanke, B., T. Laubach, F. Mishkin, and A. Posen (1999), *Inflation Targeting: Lessons from the International Experience*, Princeton, NJ: Princeton University Press.

Bernheim, D. and M. Whinston (1986), "Menu Auctions, Resource Allocation, and Economic Influence," *Quarterly Journal of Economics* 101, 1–31.

Bertola, G. (1993), "Market Structure and Income Distribution in Endogenous Growth Models," *American Economic Review* 83, 1184–99.

Bertola, G. and A. Drazen (1993), "Trigger Points and Budget Cuts: Explaining the Effects of Fiscal Austerity," *American Economic Review* 83, 11–26.

Besley, T. and S. Coate (1995), "Efficient Policy Choice in a Representative Democracy: A Dynamic Analysis," working paper.

Bhagwati, J. (1982), "Directly Unproductive Profit-Seeking (DUP) Activities," *Journal of Political Economy* 90, 988–1002.

Bhagwati, J. and T. Srinivasan (1980), "Revenue Seeking: A Generalization of the Theory of Tariffs," *Journal of Political Economy* 88, 1069–87.

Bhattacharya, U. and P. Weller (1997), "The Advantage to Hiding One's Hand: Speculation and Central Bank Intervention in the Foreign Exchange Market," *Journal of Monetary Economics* 39, 251–77.

Binswanger, H. and K. Deininger (1995), "Towards a Political Economy of Agriculture and Agrarian Relations," working paper, The World Bank.

Black, D. (1948), "On the Rationale of Group Decision Making," *Journal of Political Economy* 56, 23–34.

Blanchard, O. (1985), "Credibility, Disinflation, and Gradualism," *Economics Letters* 17, 211–17.

_____ (1990), "Comments on Giavazzi and Pagano," in O. Blanchard and S. Fischer, eds., *NBER Macroeconomics Annual* 1990, Cambridge, MA: MIT Press.

Blejer, M. and A. Cheasty (1991), "The Measurement of Fiscal Deficits: Analytical and Methodological Issues," *Journal of Economic Literature* 29, 1644–78.

Blinder, A. (1998), *Central Banking in Theory and Practice*, Cambridge, MA: MIT Press.

Bloom, H. and H. Price (1975), "Voter Response to Short-Run Economic Conditions: The Asymmetric Effect of Prosperity and Recession," *American Political Science Review* 69, 1240–54.

Bolton, P. and G. Roland (1996), "Distributional Conflicts, Factor Mobility, and Political Integration," *American Economic Review Papers and Proceedings* 86, 99–104.

_____ (1997), "The Breakup of Nations: A Political Economy Analysis," *Quarterly Journal of Economics* 112, 1057–90.

Boone, P. (1996), "Politics and the Effectiveness of Foreign Aid," *European Economic Review* 40, 289–329.

Bordo, M. and L. Jonung (1997), "The History of Monetary Regimes—Some Lessons for Sweden and the EMU," *Swedish Economic Policy Review* 4, 285–358.

Bourguignon, F. and T. Verdier (1997), "Oligarchy, Democracy and Growth," DELTA working paper.

Boycko, M., A. Shleifer, and R. Vishny (1993), "Privatizing Russia," *Brookings Papers in Economic Activity* 2, 139–92.

_____ (1996a), "A Theory of Privatization," *Economic Journal* 106, 309–19.

_____ (1996b), "Second-Best Economic Policy for a Divided Government," *European Economic Review* 40, 767–74.

Brainard, W. (1967), "Uncertainty and the Effectiveness of Policy," *American Economic Review Papers and Proceedings* 67, 411–25.

Brander, J. and B. Spencer (1983), "International R & D Rivalry and Industrial Strategy," *Review of Economic Studies* 50, 707–22.

Breyer, F. (1994), "The Political Economy of Intergenerational Redistribution," *European Journal of Political Economy* 10, 61–84.

Browning, E. K. (1975), "Why the Social Insurance Budget is Too Large in a Democracy," *Economic Inquiry* 13, 373–88.

Bruce, N. and M. Waldman (1991), "Transfers in Kind: Why They Can Be Efficient and Nonpaternalistic," *American Economic Review* 81, 1345–51.

Bruno, M. and W. Easterly (1996), "Inflation's Children: Tales of Crises that Beget Reforms," *American Economic Review Papers and Proceedings* 86, 213–17.

Buchanan, J. M. (1965), "An Economic Theory of Clubs," *Economica* 32, 1–14.

_____ (1970), "Notes for an Economic Theory of Socialism," *Public Choice* 8, 29–43.

Buchanan, J. M. and R. Faith (1987), "Secession and the Limits of Taxation: Towards a Theory of Internal Exit," *American Economic Review* 77, 1023–31.

Buchanan, J. M., C. Rowley, and R. Tollison, eds. (1986), *Deficits*, Oxford: Basil Blackwell.

Buchanan, J., R. Tollison, and G. Tullock, eds. (1980), *Toward a Theory of the Rent-Seeking Society*, College Station: Texas A & M Press.

Buchanan, J. and G. Tullock (1962), *The Calculus of Consent, Logical Foundations of Constitutional Democracy*, Ann Arbor, MI: University of Michigan Press.

Buchanan, J. and R. Wagner (1977), *Democracy in Deficit: The Political Legacy of Lord Keynes*, New York: Academic Press.

Bulow J. and K. Rogoff (1989a), "Sovereign Debt: Is To Forgive To Forget?," *American Economic Review* 79, 43–50.

_____ (1989b), "A Constant Recontracting Model of Sovereign Debt," *Journal of Political Economy* 97, 155–78.

Burnside, C. and D. Dollar (1997), "Aid, Policies and Growth," Policy Research Working Paper No. 1777, The World Bank, Washington, DC.

Calvert, R. and J. Ferejohn (1983), "Coattail Voting in Recent Presidential Elections," *American Political Science Review* 77, 407–16.

Calvo, G. (1978), "On the Time Consistency of Optimal Policy in a Monetary Economy," *Econometrica* 46, 1411–28.

_____ (1988), "Servicing Public Debt: The Role of Expectations," *American Economic Review* 78, 647–61.

Calvo, G. and A. Drazen (1998), "Uncertain Duration of Reform: Dynamic Implications," *Macroeconomic Dynamics* 2, 443–55.

Calvo, G. and P. Guidotti (1990), "Indexation and Maturity of Government Bonds: An Exploratory Model," in R. Dornbusch and M. Draghi, eds., *Public Debt Management: Theory and History*, Cambridge: Cambridge University Press.

_____ (1993), "On the Flexibility of Monetary Policy: The Case of the Optimal Inflation Tax," *Review of Economic Studies* 60, 667–87.

Calvo, G. and M. Obstfeld (1990), "Time Consistency of Fiscal and Monetary Policy: A Comment," *Econometrica* 58, 1245–47.

Cameron, C. and J. Jung (1992), "Strategic Endorsements," working paper, Department of Political Science, Columbia University.

Campbell, A. (1960), "Surge and Decline: A Study of Electoral Change," *Public Opinion Quarterly* 24, 397–418.

_____ (1964), "Voters and Elections: Past and Present," *Journal of Politics* 26, 745–57.

Campbell, A., P. Converse, W. Miller, and D. Stokes (1966), *Elections and the Political Order*, New York: Wiley.

Campbell, J. (1987), "The Revised Theory of Surge and Decline," *American Journal of Political Science* 31, 965–79.

_____ (1993), *The Presidential Pulse of Congressional Elections*, Lexington, KY: The University Press of Kentucky.

Canavan, C. and M. Tommasi (1996), "Visibility and Credibility: On Nominal Anchors and Other Ways to Send Clear Signals," working paper.

Canzoneri, M. (1985), "Monetary Policy Games and the Role of Private Information," *American Economic Review* 75, 1056–70.

Canzoneri, M. and J. Gray (1985), "Monetary Policy Games and the Consequences of Non-Cooperative Behavior," *International Economic Review* 26, 547–64.

Canzoneri, M. and D. Henderson (1988), "Is Sovereign Policymaking Bad?," *Carnegie-Rochester Conference Series on Public Policy* 28, 93–140.

_____ (1991), *Monetary Policy in Interdependent Economies: A Game-Theoretic Approach*, Cambridge, MA: MIT Press.

Canzoneri, M. and C. Rogers (1990), "Is the European Community an Optimal Currency Area? Optimal Taxation Versus the Cost of Multiple Currencies," *American Economic Review* 80, 419–33.

Caplin, A. and B. Nalebuff (1991), "On 64% Majority Rule," *Econometrica* 56, 787–814.

Casella, A. (1992), "Participation in a Currency Union," *American Economic Review* 82, 847–63.

Casella, A. and B. Eichengreen (1996), "Can Foreign Aid Accelerate Stabilization?," *Economic Journal* 106, 605–19.

Casella, A. and J. Feinstein (1989), "Management of a Common Currency," in M. DeCecco and A. Giovannini, eds., *A European Central Bank?*, Cambridge: Cambridge University Press.

_____ (1990), "Public Goods in Trade: On the Formation of Markets and Political Jurisdictions," NBER Working Paper #3554.

Chappell, H. and W. Keech (1986), "Party Differences in Macroeconomic Policies and Outcomes," *American Economic Review, Papers and Proceedings* 76, 71–74.

Chari, V. and H. Cole (1993), "A Contribution to the Theory of Pork Barrel Spending," Research Department Staff Report 156, Federal Reserve Bank of Minneapolis.

Chari, V. and P. Kehoe (1989), "Sustainable Plans and Debt," Federal Reserve Bank of Minneapolis working paper.

_____ (1990), "Sustainable Plans," *Journal of Political Economy* 98, 783–802.

Chari, V., P. Kehoe, and E. Prescott, (1989), "Time Consistency and Policy," in R. Barro, ed., *Modern Business Cycle Theory*, Cambridge, MA: Harvard University Press.

Checchi, D. (1996), "Capital Controls and Conflict of Interests," *Economics and Politics* 8, 33–50.

Cho, I.-K. and D. Kreps (1987), "Signaling Games and Stable Equilibria," *Quarterly Journal of Economics* 102, 179–221.

Chowdhury, A. (1993), "Political Surfing over Economic Waves: Parliamentary Election Timing in India," *American Journal of Political Science* 37, 1100–1118.

Clarke, E. (1971), "Multipart Pricing of Public Goods," *Public Choice* 11, 17–33.

_____ (1972), Multipart Pricing of Public Goods: An Example," in S. Mushkin, ed., *Public Prices for Public Products*, Urban Institute, Washington, DC.

Coase, R. (1937), "The Nature of the Firm," *Economica N.S.* 4, 386–405.

Coate, S. and S. Morris (1995), "On the Form of Transfers to Special Interests," *Journal of Political Economy* 103, 1210–35.

Cohen, B. J. (1993), "Beyond EMU: The Problem of Sustainability," *Economics and Politics* 5, 187–203.

Cole, H., J. Dow, and W. English (1995), "Default, Settlement, and Signaling: Lending Resumption in a Reputational Model of Sovereign Debt," *International Economic Review* 36, 365–85.

Cole, H. and P. Kehoe (1996), "Reputation Spillover Across Relationships: Reviving Reputation Models of Debt," Research Department Staff Report 209, Federal Reserve Bank of Minneapolis.

Collier, P. (1997), "The Failure of Conditionality," in C. Gwin and J. Nelson, eds., *Perspectives on Aid and Development*, Washington, DC: Overseas Development Council.

Condorcet, Marquis de (1785), "Essay on the Application of Mathematics to the Theory of Decision Making" (translated), in K. Baker, ed., *Condorcet: Selected Writings*, Indianapolis, IN: Bobbs-Merrill, 1976.

Cooper, R. (1985), "Economic Interdependence and Coordination of Economic Policies," in R. Jones and P. Kenen, eds., *Handbook of International Economics*, vol. II, Amsterdam: North-Holland, 1195–1234.

Coricelli, F. and G.-M. Milesi-Ferretti (1993), "On the Credibility of 'Big Bang' Programs," *European Economic Review* 37, 387–95.

Cornes, R. and T. Sandler (1986), *The Theory of Externalities, Public Goods, and Club Goods*, Cambridge: Cambridge University Press.

Cox, G. and M. McCubbins (1986), "Electoral Politics as a Redistributive Game," *Journal of Politics* 48, 370–89.

Crawford, V. and J. Sobel (1982), "Strategic Information Transmission," *Econometrica* 50, 1431–51.

Cremer, J. (1986), "Cooperation in Ongoing Organizations," *Quarterly Journal of Economics* 101, 33–49.

Crozier, M. (1964), *The Bureaucratic Phenomenon*, Chicago: University of Chicago Press.

Cukierman, A. (1992), *Central Bank Strategy, Credibility and Independence: Theory and Evidence*, Cambridge, MA: MIT Press.

Cukierman, A., M. Kiguel, and N. Liviatan (1992), "How Much to Commit to an Exchange Rate Rule? Balancing Credibility and Flexibility," *Revista de Analisis Economico* 7, 73–90.

Cukierman, A. and N. Liviatan (1991), "Optimal Accommodation by Strong Policy-makers Under Incomplete Information," *Journal of Monetary Economics* 27, 99–127.

Cukierman, A. and A. Meltzer (1986), "A Positive Theory of Discretionary Policy, The Cost of Democratic Government, and the Benefits of a Constitution," *Economic Inquiry* 24, 367–88.

_____ (1989), "A Political Theory of Government Debt and Deficits in a Neo-Ricardian Framework," *American Economic Review* 79, 713–32.

_____ (1990), "A Theory of Ambiguity, Credibility and Inflation Under Discretion and Asymmetric Information," *Econometrica* 54, 1099–1128.

Cukierman, A. and M. Tommasi (1998a), "When Does It Take Nixon to Go to China," *American Economic Review* 88, 180–97.

_____ (1998b), "Credibility of Policymakers and of Economic Reforms," in F. Sturzenegger and M. Tommasi, eds., *The Political Economy of Reform*, Cambridge, MA: MIT Press.

Cukierman, A., S. Webb, and B. Neyapti (1992), "Measuring the Independence of Central Banks and Its Effect on Policy Outcomes," *World Bank Economic Review* 6, 353–98.

Debelle, G. and S. Fischer (1994), "How Independent Should A Central Bank Be?," in J. Fuhrer, ed., *Goals, Guidelines, and Constraints Facing Monetary Policymakers*, Federal Reserve Bank of Boston Conference Series, no. 38, Boston: Federal Reserve Bank of Boston.

Deininger K. and L. Squire (1996), "A New Data Set Measuring Income Inequality," *World Bank Economic Review*, 10, 569–91.

_____ (1998), "New Ways of Looking at Old Issues: Inequality and Growth," *Journal of Development Economics* 57, 259–87.

Denzau, A. and M. Munger (1986), "Legislators and Interest Groups: How Unorganized Interests Get Represented," *American Political Science Review* 80, 89–106.

Dewatripont, M. and E. Maskin (1995), "Credit and Efficiency in Centralized and Decentralized Economies," *Review of Economic Studies* 62, 541–55.

Dewatripont, M. and G. Roland (1992a), "Economic Reform and Dynamic Political Constraints," *Review of Economic Studies* 59, 703–30.

_____ (1992b), "The Virtues of Gradualism and Legitimacy in the Transition to a Market Economy," *Economic Journal* 102, 291–300.

_____ (1995), "The Design of Reform Packages under Uncertainty," *American Economic Review* 85, 1207–23.

_____ (1996), "Transition as a Process of Large-Scale Economic Change," *Economics of Transition* 4, 1–30.

Diamond, D. and P. Dybvig (1983), "Bank Runs, Deposit Insurance, and Liquidity," *Journal of Political Economy* 91, 401–19.

Diamond, P. (1965), "National Debt in a Neoclassical Growth Model," *American Economic Review* 55, 1125–50.

_____ (1970), "The Incidence of an Interest Income Tax," *Journal of Economic Theory* 2, 211–24.

Diwan, I. and D. Rodrik (1992), "External Debt, Adjustment, and Burden Sharing: A Unified Framework," *Princeton Studies in International Finance* No. 73, Princeton: Princeton University.

Dixit, A. (1996), *The Making of Economic Policy: A Transaction-Cost Politics Perspective*, Cambridge, MA: MIT Press.

Dixit, A. and J. Londregan (1995), "Redistributional Politics and Economic Efficiency," *American Political Science Review* 89, 856–66.

_____ (1996), "The Determinants of Success of Special Interests in Redistributive Politics," *Journal of Politics* 58, 1132–55.

_____ (1998), "Ideology, Tactics, and Efficiency in Redistributive Politics," *Quarterly Journal of Economics* 113, 497–529.

Dollar, D. and J. Svensson (1998), "What Explains the Success of Failure of Structural Adjustment Programs?," Policy Research Working Paper No. 1938, The World Bank, Washington, DC.

Dooley, M. and P. Isard (1980), "Capital Controls, Political Risk, and Deviations from Interest-Rate Parity," *Journal of Political Economy* 88, 370–84.

Dornbusch, R. and S. Edwards (1990), "Macroeconomic Populism," *Journal of Development Economics* 32, 247–77.

Downs, A. (1957), *An Economic Theory of Democracy*, New York: Harper and Row.

Drazen, A. (1985), "Tight Money and Inflation: Further Results," *Journal of Monetary Economics* 15, 113–20.

_____ (1989), "Monetary Policy, Capital Controls, and Seigniorage in an Open Economy," in M. DeCecco and A. Giovannini, eds., *A European Central Bank?*, Cambridge: Cambridge University Press.

_____ (1990), "Comments on Giavazzi and Pagano," in O. Blanchard and S. Fischer, eds., *NBER Macroeconomics Annual 1990*, Cambridge, MA: MIT Press.

_____ (1996), "The Political Economy of Delayed Reform," *Journal of Policy Reform* 1, 25–46.

_____ (1998a), "Towards A Political Economic Theory of Domestic Debt," in G. Calvo and M. King, eds., *The Debt Burden and its Consequences for Monetary Policy*, London: Macmillan.

_____ (1998b), "Political Contagion in Currency Crises," forthcoming in P. Krugman, ed., *Currency Crises*, Cambridge, MA: National Bureau of Economic Research.

_____ (1999a), "What Does One Gain By Cutting Off Foreign Aid?," working paper.

_____ (1999b), "Interest Rate Defense Against Speculative Attack under Asymmetric Information," working paper.

_____ (1999c), "Central Bank Independence, Democracy, and Dollarization," working paper.

Drazen, A. and W. Easterly (1999), "Do Crises Induce Reform?: Simple Empirical Tests of Conventional Wisdom," working paper.

Drazen, A. and V. Grilli (1993), "The Benefit of Crises for Economic Reforms," *American Economic Review* 83, 598–607.

Drazen, A. and E. Helpman (1987), "Stabilization with Exchange Rate Management," *Quarterly Journal of Economics* 102, 835–55.

_____ (1988), "Stabilization with Exchange Rate Management under Uncertainty," in E. Helpman, A. Razin, and E. Sadka, eds., *Economic Effects of the Government Budget*, Cambridge, MA: MIT Press, 310–27.

_____ (1990), "Inflationary Consequences of Uncertain Macroeconomic Policy," *Review of Economic Studies* 57, 147–64.

Drazen, A. and S. Hubrich (1999), "Comment on Cukierman and Tommasi, 'When Does it Take Nixon to Go to China'," working paper.

Drazen, A. and P. Masson (1994), "Credibility of Policies versus Credibility of Policymakers," *Quarterly Journal of Economics* 109, 735–54.

Easterly, W. (1997), "Life After Growth," working paper, The World Bank.

Easterly, W. and S. Rebelo (1993), "Fiscal Policy and Economic Growth," *Journal of Monetary Economics* 32, 417–58.

Eaton, J. (1993), "Sovereign Debt: A Primer," *World Bank Economic Review* 7, 137–72.

Eaton, J. and R. Fernandez (1995), "Sovereign Debt," in G. Grossman and K. Rogoff, eds., *Handbook of International Economics*, vol. III, Amsterdam: North-Holland.

Eaton, J. and M. Gersovitz (1981), "Debt with Potential Repudiation," *Review of Economic Studies* 48, 289–309.

Eichengreen, B. (1990), "The Capital Levy in Theory and Practice," in R. Dornbusch and M. Draghi, eds., *Public Debt Management: Theory and History*, Cambridge: Cambridge University Press.

Eichengreen, B. and J. Frieden (1993), "The Political Economy of European Monetary Unification: An Analytical Introduction," *Economics and Politics* 5, 85–104.

Eichengreen, B., A. Rose, and C. Wyplosz (1995), "Exchange Market Mayhem: The Antecedents and Aftermath of Speculative Attacks," *Economic Policy* 21, 249–312.

Eichengreen, B. and C. Wyplosz (1993), "The Unstable EMS," *Brookings Papers on Economic Activity* 1, 51–143.

Eijffinger, S. and J. De Haan (1996), *The Political Economy of Central Bank Independence*, Special Papers in International Economics No. 19, Princeton University.

Elster, J. (1984), "Imperfect Rationality: Ulysses and the Sirens," in J. Elster, *Ulysses and the Sirens: Studies in Rationality and Irrationality*, Cambridge: Cambridge University Press.

_____ (1988), "Introduction," in J. Elster and R. Slagstad, eds., *Constitutionalism and Democracy*, Cambridge: Cambridge University Press.

_____ (1989), *The Cement of Society, A Study in Social Order*, Cambridge: Cambridge University Press.

_____ (1995), "The Impact of Constitutions on Economic Performance," *Proceedings of the 1994 World Bank Annual Conference on Development Economics*, 209–39.

Elster, J. and R. Slagstad, eds. (1988), *Constitutionalism and Democracy*, Cambridge: Cambridge University Press.

Enelow, J. (1997), "Cycling and Majority Rule," in D. Mueller, ed., *Perspective on Public Choice: A Handbook*, Cambridge: Cambridge University Press, 149–62.

Enelow, J. and M. Hinich (1984), *The Spatial Theory of Voting: An Introduction*, Cambridge: Cambridge University Press.

Epple, D. and T. Romer (1991), "Mobility and Redistribution," *Journal of Political Economy* 99, 828–58.

Erikson, R. (1988), "The Puzzle of Midterm Loss," *Journal of Politics* 50, 1012–29.

Fair, R. (1978), "The Effect of Economic Events on Votes for President," *Review of Economics and Statistics* 60, 159–72.

_____ (1982), "The Effect of Economic Events on Votes for President: 1980 Results," *Review of Economics and Statistics* 64, 322–25.

_____ (1988), "The Effects of Economic Events on Votes for President: 1984 Update," *Political Behavior* 10, 168–79.

Farell, J. and M. Rabin (1996), "Cheap Talk," *Journal of Economic Perspectives* 10, 103–18.

Faust, J. (1996), "Whom Can We Trust to Run the Fed? Theoretical Support for the Founders' Views," *Journal of Monetary Economics* 37, 267–83.

Feldstein, M. (1997), "The Political Economy of the European Economic and Monetary Union: Political Sources of an Economic Liability," *Journal of Economic Perspectives* 11, 23–42.

Ferejohn, J. (1986), "Incumbent Performance and Electoral Control," *Public Choice* 50, 5–26.

Ferejohn, J. and K. Krehbiel (1987), "The Budget Process and the Size of the Budget," *American Journal of Political Science* 31, 296–320.

Fernandez, R. and D. Rodrik (1991), "Resistance to Reform: Status Quo Bias in the Presence of Individual Specific Uncertainty," *American Economic Review* 81, 1146–55.

Fernandez, R. and R. Rogerson (1993), "Zoning and the Political Economy of Local Redistribution," NBER Working Paper 4456.

Fernandez, R. and R. Rogerson (1995), "On the Political Economy of Education Subsidies," *Review of Economic Studies* 62, 249–62.

Fernandez-Arias, E. (1997), "Crisis, Foreign Aid, and Macroeconomic Reform," working paper, Inter-American Development Bank.

Fershtman, C. and K. Judd (1987), "Equilibrium Incentives in Oligopoly," *American Economic Review* 77, 927–40.

Fiorina, M. (1981a), *Retrospective Voting in American National Elections*, New Haven, CT: Yale University Press.

_____ (1981b), "Universalism, Reciprocity, and Distributive Policymaking in Majority Rule Institutions," in J. Crecine, ed., *Research in Public Policy Analysis and Management*, vol. 1, Greenwich, CT: JAI Press.

Fiorina, M. and R. Noll (1978), "Voters, Bureaucrats and Legislators: A Rational Choice Perspective on the Growth of Bureaucracy," *Journal of Public Economics* 9, 239–54.

Fischer, S. (1980), "Dynamic Inconsistency, Cooperation, and the Benevolent Dissembling Government," *Journal of Economic Dynamics and Control* 2, 93–107.

_____ (1995), "Central-Bank Independence Revisited," *American Economic Review* 85, 201–6.

Flood, R. (1983), "Comment on Buiter and Miller," in J. Frenkel, ed., *Exchange Rates and International Macroeconomics*, Chicago, IL: University of Chicago Press, 359–65.

Flood, R. and P. Isard (1989), "Monetary Policy Strategies," *IMF Staff Papers* 36, 612–32.

Frankel, J. (1986), "The Implications of Conflicting Models for Coordination Between Monetary and Fiscal Policy-Makers," working paper.

Frankel, J. and K. Rockett (1988), "International Macroeconomic Policy Coordination When Policymakers Do Not Agree On the True Model," *American Economic Review* 78, 318–40.

Frankel, J. and A. Rose (1997), "The Endogeneity of Optimum Currency Area Criteria," *Swedish Economic Policy Review* 4, 489–512.

Fratianni, M., J. von Hagen, and C. Waller (1997), "Central Banking as a Principal Agent Problem," *Economic Inquiry* 35, 378–93.

Frey, B. and F. Schneider (1978), "An Empirical Study of Politico-Economic Interaction in the United States," *Review of Economics and Statistics* 60, 174–83.

Friedman, J. (1971), "A Noncooperative Equilibrium for Supergames," *Review of Economic Studies* 38, 1–12.

Friedman, M. (1968), "The Role of Monetary Policy," *American Economic Review* 58, 1–17.

_____ (1969), "The Optimum Quantity of Money," in M. Friedman, *The Optimum Quantity of Money, and Other Essays*, Chicago, IL: Aldine Pub. Co.

Fudenberg, D. and J. Tirole (1991), *Game Theory*, Cambridge, MA: MIT Press.

Galor, O. and J. Zeira (1993), "Income Distribution and Macroeconomics," *Review of Economic Studies* 60, 35–52.

Garfinkel, M. and A. Glazer (1994), "Does Electoral Uncertainty Cause Economic Fluctuations?," *American Economic Review* 84, 169–73.

Garrett, G. (1993), "The Politics of Maastricht," *Economics and Politics* 5, 105–23.

Gärtner, M. (1994), "The Quest for Political Cycles in OECD Economies," *European Journal of Political Economy* 10, 427–40.

Gerlach, S. and F. Smets (1995), "Contagious Speculative Attacks," *European Journal of Political Economy* 11, 5–63.

Giavazzi, F. and M. Pagano (1988), "The Advantage of Tying One's Hands: EMS Discipline and Central Bank Credibility," *European Economic Review* 32, 1055–82.

_____ (1990), "Can Severe Fiscal Adjustments Be Expansionary?," in O. Blanchard and S. Fischer, eds., *NBER Macroeconomics Annual 1990*, Cambridge, MA: MIT Press.

_____ (1995), "Non-Keynesian Effects of Fiscal Policy Changes: International Evidence and the Swedish Experience," NBER Working Paper #5332.

Giovannini, A. and M. de Melo (1993), "Government Revenue from Financial Repression," *American Economic Review* 83, 953–63.

Glazer, A. (1991), "The Politics of Delay," working paper.

Golden, D. and J. Poterba (1980), "The Price of Popularity: The Political Business Cycle Reexamined," *American Journal of Political Science* 24, 696–714.

Gradstein, M. and M. Justman (1995), "A Political Interpretation of the Kuznets Curve," working paper, Ben-Gurion University, Israel.

Graham, C. (1994), *Safety Nets, Politics, and the Poor: Transitions in Market Economies*, Washington, DC: The Brookings Institution.

Gramlich, E. (1995), The Politics and Economics of Budget Deficit Control: Policy Questions and Research Questions," in J. Banks and E. Hanushek, eds., *Modern Political Economy: Old Topics, New Directions*, Cambridge: Cambridge University Press.

Green, E. and R. Porter (1984), "Noncooperative Collusion under Imperfect Price Information," *Econometrica* 52, 87–100.

Green, J. and J-J. Laffont (1977), "Characterization of Satisfactory Mechanisms for the Revelation of Preferences for Public Goods," *Econometrica* 45, 427–38.

Grier, K. (1989), "On the Existence of a Political Monetary Cycle," *American Journal of Political Science* 33, 376–89.

Grilli, V., D. Masciandaro, and G. Tabellini (1991), "Political and Monetary Institutions and Public Financial Policies in the Industrial Countries," *Economic Policy* 13, 341–92.

Grilli, V. and G.-M. Milesi-Ferretti (1995), "Economic Effects and Structural Determinants of Capital Controls," *IMF Staff Papers* 42, 517–51.

Grindle, M. and J. Thomas (1991), *Public Choices and Policy Change: The Political Economy of Reform in Developing Countries*, Baltimore, MD: Johns Hopkins University Press.

Groenewegen, P. (1987), "'Political Economy' and 'Economics'," in J. Eatwell, M. Milgate and P. Newman, eds., *The New Palgrave—A Dictionary of Economics*, vol. 3, London: The Macmillan Press Limited, 904–7.

Grofman, B. and B. Norrander (1990), "Efficient Use of Reference Group Cues in a Single Dimension," *Public Choice* 64, 213–28.

Grossman, G. and E. Helpman (1994), "Protection for Sale," *American Economic Review* 84, 833–50.

_____ (1996a), "Electoral Competition and Special Interest Politics," *Review of Economic Studies* 63, 265–86.

_____ (1996b), "Competing for Endorsements," Harvard Institute for Economic Research Working Paper 1784.

Grossman, H. (1991), "A General Equilibrium Model of Insurrections," *American Economic Review* 81, 912–21.

_____ (1995), "Robin Hood and the Redistribution of Property Income," *European Journal of Political Economy* 11, 1275–88.

Grossman, H. and M. Kim (1995), "Swords or Plowshares? A Theory of the Security of Claims to Property," *Journal of Political Economy* 103, 1275–88.

_____ (1996a), "Predation and Production," in M. Garfinkel and S. Skaperdas, *The Political Economy of Conflict and Appropriation*, Cambridge: Cambridge University Press.

_____ (1996b), "Predation and Accumulation," *Journal of Economic Growth* 1, 333–51.

Grossman, H. and J. Van Huyck (1988), "Sovereign Debt as a Contingent Claim: Excusable Default, Repudiation, and Reputation," *American Economic Review* 78, 1088–97.

Groves, T. (1970), Ph.D. Dissertation, University of California, Berkeley.

_____ (1973), "Incentives in Teams," *Econometrica* 41, 617–31.

Groves, T. and J. Ledyard (1977), "Some Limitations of Demand Revealing Processes," *Public Choice* 29-2 (Special Supplement), 107–24.

Guitián, M. (1995), "Conditionality: Past, Present, and Future," *International Monetary Fund Staff Papers* 42, 792–835.

Gupta, D. (1990), *The Economics of Political Violence*, New York: Praeger.

Gustafsson, B. and N. Klevmarken, eds. (1989), *The Political Economy of Social Security*, Amsterdam: North-Holland.

Haggard, S. and R. Kaufman, eds. (1992), *The Politics of Economic Adjustment*, Princeton, NJ: Princeton University Press.

Haggard, S. and S. Webb, eds. (1994), *Voting for Reform: Democracy, Political Liberalization, and Economic Adjustment*, New York: Oxford University Press.

Hamada, K. (1974), "Alternative Exchange Rate Systems and the Interdependence of Monetary Policy," in R. Aliber, ed., *National Monetary Policies and the International Financial System*, Chicago, IL: University of Chicago Press.

_____ (1976), "A Strategic Analysis of Monetary Interdependence," *Journal of Political Economy* 84, 677–700.

Hammond, P. (1975), "Charity: Altruism or Cooperative Egoism?" in Edmund Phelps, ed., *Altruism, Morality, and Economic Theory*, New York: Russell Sage, 115–31.

Harberger, A. C. (1954), "Monopoly and Resource Allocation," *American Economic Review* 44, 77–87.

_____ (1993a), "Secrets of Success: A Handful of Heroes," *American Economic Review Papers and Proceedings* 83, 343–50.

_____ (1993b), "The Search for Relevance in Economics," *American Economic Review Papers and Proceedings* 83, 1–17.

Hardin, R. (1982), *Collective Action*, Baltimore, MD: Johns Hopkins University Press.

_____ (1995), *One for All*, Baltimore, MD: Johns Hopkins University Press.

Harrington, J. (1992), "The Revelation of Information through the Electoral Process: An Exploratory Model," *Economics and Politics* 4, 255–75.

_____ (1993), "The Impact of Reelection Pressures on the Fulfillment of Campaign Promises," *Games and Economic Behavior* 5, 71–97.

Harsanyi, J. (1967–8), "Games with Incomplete Information Played by Bayesian Players," *Management Science* 14, 159–82, 320–34, 486–502.

Harsanyi, J. and R. Selten (1988), *A General Theory of Equilibrium Selection in Games*, Cambridge, MA: MIT Press.

Havrilesky, T. (1987), "A Partisanship Theory of Fiscal and Monetary Policy," *Journal of Money, Credit, and Banking* 19, 308–25.

_____ (1993), *The Pressures of American Monetary Policy*, Boston, MA: Kluwer.

Haynes, S. and J. Stone (1989), "Political Models of the Business Cycle Should Be Revived," *Economic Inquiry* 28, 442–65.

Hess, G. and A. Orphanides (1995), "War Politics: An Economic, Rational Voter Framework," *American Economic Review* 85, 828–46.

Hibbs, D. (1977), "Political Parties and Macroeconomic Policy," *American Political Science Review* 71, 1467–87.

_____ (1987), *The American Political Economy: Macroeconomics and Electoral Politics in the United States*, Cambridge, MA: Harvard University Press.

_____ (1992), "Partisan Theory After Fifteen Years," *European Journal of Political Economy* 8, 361–73.

_____ (1994), "The Partisan Model of Macroeconomic Cycles: More Theory and Evidence for the United States," *Economics and Politics* 6, 1–24.

Hillman, A. (1989), *The Political Economy of Protection*, Chur, Switzerland: Harwood Academic Publishers.

Hillman, A. and J. Riley (1989), "Politically Contested Rents and Transfers," *Economics and Politics* 1, 17–39.

Hirschman, A. (1970), *Exit, Voice, and Loyalty*, Cambridge, MA: Harvard University Press.

Hirshleifer, J. (1991), "The Paradox of Power," *Economics and Politics* 3, 177–200.

Hochman, H. and J. Rodgers (1969), "Pareto Optimal Redistribution," *American Economic Review* 59, 542–57.

Holtfereich, C.-L. (1993), "Did Monetary Unification Precede or Follow Political Unification of Germany in the 19th Century?," *European Economic Review* 37, 518–24.

Hotelling, H. (1929), "Stability in Competition," *Economic Journal* 39, 41–57.

Hsieh, C.-T. (1997), "Bargaining over Reform," working paper.

Ito, T. (1990), "The Timing of Elections and Political Business Cycles in Japan," *Journal of Asian Economics* 1, 135–56.

Jacobson, G. and S. Kernell (1981), *Strategy and Choice in Congressional Elections*, New Haven, CT: Yale University Press.

Jenkins, S. (1991), "The Measurement of Income Inequality," in L. Osbert, ed., *Economic Inequality and Poverty: International Perspectives*, Armonk, NY: Sharpe, 3–38.

Jodice, D. and D. Taylor (1988), *World Handbook of Social and Political Indicators*, New Haven, CT: Yale University Press.

Johansen, L. (1977), "The Theory of Public Goods: Misplaced Emphasis?," *Journal of Public Economics* 7, 147–52.

Kalecki, M. (1943), "Political Aspects of Full Employment," reprinted in M. Kalecki, *Selected Essays on the Dynamics of the Capitalist Economy*, Cambridge, Cambridge University Press, 1971.

Kaminsky, G. and C. Reinhart (1999), "The Twin Crises: The Causes of Banking and Balance-of-Payments Problems," *American Economic Review* 89, 473–500.

Kane, E. (1990), "Bureaucratic Self-Interest as an Obstacle to Monetary Reform," in T. Mayer, ed., *The Political Economy of American Monetary Policy*, Cambridge: Cambridge University Press.

Keech, W. (1995), *Economic Politics: The Costs of Democracy*, Cambridge: Cambridge University Press.

Keech, W. and K. Pak (1989), "Electoral Cycles and Budgetary Growth in Veterans' Benefit Programs," *American Journal of Political Science* 33, 901–11.

Kehoe, P. (1987), "Coordination of Fiscal Policies in a World Economy," *Journal of Monetary Economics* 19, 349–76.

_____ (1989), "Policy Cooperation Among Benevolent Governments May Be Undesirable," *Review of Economic Studies* 56, 289–96.

Kenen, P. (1969), "The Theory of Optimum Currency Areas: An Eclectic View," in R. Mundell and A. Swoboda, eds., *Monetary Problems of the International Economy*, Chicago, IL: University of Chicago Press.

Keohane, R. (1984), *After Hegemony*, Princeton, NJ: Princeton University Press.

Kernell, S. (1977), "Presidential Popularity and Negative Voting: An Alternative Explanation of the Midterm Congressional Decline of the President's Party," *American Political Science Review* 71, 44–66.

Key, V. O. Jr. (1966), *The Responsible Electorate: Rationality in Presidential Voting 1936–60*, Cambridge, MA: Harvard University Press.

Kindleberger, C. (1981), *A Financial History of Western Europe*, London: George Allen and Unwin.

King, M. (1997), "Changes in UK Monetary Policy: Rules and Discretion in Practice," *Journal of Monetary Economics* 39, 81–87.

Knack, S. and P. Keefer (1995), "Institutions and Economic Performance: Cross-Country Tests Using Alternative Institutional Measures," *Economics and Politics* 7, 207–27.

Knight, F. (1921), "Risk, Uncertainty, and Profit," New York: Harper and Row.

Kornai, J. (1979), "Resource-Constrained versus Demand-Constrained Systems," *Econometrica* 47, 801–19.

_____ (1980), *Economics of Shortage*, Amsterdam: North-Holland.

Kotlikoff, L., T. Persson, and L.E.O. Svensson (1988), "Social Contracts: A Possible Solution to the Time-Inconsistency Problem," *American Economic Review* 78, 662–77.

Kraay, A. and J. Ventura (1997), "Current Accounts in Debtor and Creditor Countries," working paper, The World Bank.

Kramer, G. (1971), "Short-Term Fluctuations in U.S. Voting Behavior, 1896–1964," *American Political Science Review* 65, 131–43.

Kreps, D. (1990), *Game Theory and Economic Modelling*, Oxford: Oxford University Press.

Kreps, D. and R. Wilson (1982), "Reputation and Imperfect Information," *Journal of Economic Theory* 27, 253–79.

Krueger, A. (1974), "The Political Economy of the Rent-Seeking Society," *American Economic Review* 64, 291–303.

_____ (1993a), "Virtuous and Vicious Circles in Economic Development," *American Economic Review Papers and Proceedings* 83, 351–55.

_____ (1993b), *Political Economy of Policy Reform in Developing Countries*, Cambridge, MA: MIT Press.

Krugman, P. (1979), "A Model of Self-Fulfilling Balance of Payments Crises," *Journal of Money Credit and Banking* 11, 311–25.

_____ (1996), "Are Currency Crises Self-Fulfilling?" *NBER Macroeconomics Annual*, 345–78.

Krusell, P., V. Quadrini, and J-V. Rios-Rull (1997), "Politico-Economic Equilibrium and Economic Growth," *Journal of Economic Dynamics and Control* 21, 243–72.

Krusell, P. and J.-V. Rios-Rull (1996), "Vested Interests in a Positive Theory of Stagnation and Growth," *Review of Economic Studies* 63, 301–29.

Kuznets, S. (1955), "Economic Growth and Income Inequality," *American Economic Review* 45, 1–28.

Kydland F. and E. Prescott (1977), "Rules Rather than Discretion: The Inconsistency of Optimal Plans," *Journal of Political Economy* 85, 473–91.

Labán, R. and F. Sturzenegger (1994a), "Distributional Conflict, Financial Adaptation and Delayed Stabilization," *Economics and Politics* 6, 257–76.

_____ (1994b), "Fiscal Conservatism as a Response to the Debt Crisis," *Journal of Development Economics* 45, 305–24.

Labán, R. and H. Wolf (1993), "Large Scale Privatization in Transition Economies," *American Economic Review* 83, 1199–1210.

Lane, P. and A. Tornell (1996), "Power, Growth and the Voracity Effect," *Journal of Economic Growth* 1, 213–41.

Laver, M. and N. Schofield (1991), *Multiparty Government, The Politics of Coalition in Europe*, Oxford: Oxford University Press.

Laver, M. and K. Shepsle (1990), "Coalitions and Cabinet Government," *American Political Science Review* 84, 873–90.

Legros, P. and A. Newman (1993), "Wealth Effects, Distribution, and the Theory of Organization," working paper.

Leiderman, L. and L.E.O. Svensson, eds. (1995), *Inflation Targets*, Cambridge: Cambridge University Press.

Levine, R. and D. Renelt (1992), "A Sensitivity Analysis of Cross-Country Growth Regressions," *American Economic Review* 82, 942–63.

Lewis, D. (1969), *Convention*, Cambridge, MA: Harvard University Press.

Lewis-Beck, M. (1988), *Economics and Elections*, Ann Arbor: University of Michigan Press.

Lindahl, E. (1919), "Just Taxation—A Positive Solution" (translated), reprinted in R. Musgrave and A. Peacock, eds., *Classics in the Theory of Public Finance*, New York: St. Martin's Press, 1967.

Lindbeck, A. (1976), "Stabilization Policy in Open Economies with Endogenous Politicians," *American Economic Review Papers and Proceedings* 66, 1–19.

Lindbeck, A., S. Nyberg, and J. Weibull (1999), "Social Norms and Economic Incentives in the Welfare State," *Quarterly Journal of Economics* 114, 1–35.

Lindbeck, A. and J. Weibull (1987), "Balanced Budget Redistribution as the Outcome of Political Competition," *Public Choice* 52, 272–97.

Lindblom, C. (1977), *Politics and Markets*, New York: Basic Books.

Lipset, S. (1959), "Some Social Requisites of Democracy: Economic Development and Political Development," *American Political Science Review* 53, 69–105.

Liviatan, N. (1984), "Tight Money and Inflation," *Journal of Monetary Economics* 13, 5–15.

Lockwood, B. (1997), "State-Contingent Inflation Contracts and Unemployment Persistence," *Journal of Money, Credit and Banking* 29, 286–99.

Lohmann, S. (1990), "Monetary Policy Strategies—A Correction," *IMF Staff Papers* 37, 440–45.

_____ (1992), "Optimal Commitment in Monetary Policy: Credibility versus Flexibility," *American Economic Review* 82, 273–86.

_____ (1993), "Electoral Cycles and International Policy Cooperation," *European Economic Review* 37, 1373–91.

_____ (1995), "A Signaling Model of Competitive Political Pressures," *Economics and Politics* 7, 181–206.

Londregan, J. and K. Poole (1990), "Poverty, the Coup Trap, and the Seizure of Executive Power," *World Politics* 92, 1–24.

Lora, E. (1998), "What Makes Reform Likely?: Timing and Sequencing of Structural Reforms in Latin America," working paper, Office of the Chief Economist, Inter-American Development Bank.

Loury, G. (1981), "Intergenerational Transfers and the Distribution of Earnings," *Econometrica* 49, 843–67.

Lowi, T. (1964), "American Business, Public Policy, Case Studies, and Political Theory," *World Politics* 16, 677–715.

Lucas, R. (1976), "Econometric Policy Evaluation: A Critique," *Journal of Monetary Economics* 1, Supplementary Series 1976, 19–46.

Lucas, R. and N. Stokey (1983), "Optimal Fiscal and Monetary Policy in an Economy without Capital," *Journal of Monetary Economics* 12, 53–93.

Ludborg, P. (1998), "Foreign Aid and International Support as a Gift Exchange," *Economics and Politics* 10, 127–41.

Lupia, A. (1992), "Busy Voters, Agenda Control, and the Power of Information," *American Political Science Review* 869, 390–403.

Lupia, A. and K. Strøm (1995), "Coalition Termination and the Strategic Timing of Parliamentary Elections," *American Political Science Review* 89, 648–65.

Madsen, H. (1980), "Electoral Outcomes and Macroeconomic Policies: The Scandinavian Cases," in P. Whitely, ed., *Models of Political Economy*, London: Sage, 15–46.

Magee, S. (1997), "Endogenous Protection: The Empirical Evidence," in D. Mueller, ed., *Perspectives on Public Choice: A Handbook*, Cambridge: Cambridge University Press, 526–61.

Maizels, A. and M. Nissanke (1984), "Motivation for Aid to Developing Countries," *World Development* 12, 879–900.

Marston, R. (1985), "Stabilization Policies in Open Economies," in R. Jones and P. Kenen, eds., *Handbook of International Economics*, vol. II, Amsterdam: North-Holland, 859–916.

Martinelli, C. and M. Tommasi (1997), "Sequencing of Economic Reforms in the Presence of Political Constraints," *Economics and Politics* 9, 115–31.

Masson, P. (1995), "Gaining and Losing EMS Credibility: The Case of the United Kingdom," *The Economic Journal* 105, 571–82.

_____ (1998), "Contagion: Monsoonal Effects, Spillovers, and Jumps Between Multiple Equilibria," working paper, IMF Research Department.

Matthews, S. (1989), "Veto Threats: Rhetoric in a Bargaining Game," *Quarterly Journal of Economics* 104, 347–69.

Mauro, P. (1995), "Corruption and Growth," *Quarterly Journal of Economics* 110, 681–712.

McCallum, B. (1978), "The Political Business Cycle: An Empirical Test," *Southern Economic Journal* 42, 504–15.

_____ (1995), "Two Fallacies Concerning Central-Bank Independence," *American Economic Review* 85, 207–10.

_____ (1997), "Crucial Issues Concerning Central Bank Independence," *Journal of Monetary Economics* 39, 99–112.

McKinlay, R.D. and R. Little (1979), "The U.S. Aid Relationship: A Test of the Recipient and Donor Interest Models," *Political Studies* 27, 236–50.

McKinnon, R. (1963), "Optimum Currency Areas," *American Economic Review* 53, 717–24.

McRae, D.C. (1977), "A Political Model of the Business Cycle," *Journal of Political Economy* 85, 239–63.

Melitz, J. (1995), "The Current Impasse on Research in Optimum Currency Areas," *European Economic Review* 39, 492–500.

_____ (1997), "The Evidence about the Costs and Benefits of EMU," *Swedish Economic Policy Review* 4, 359–410.

Meltzer, A. and S. Richard (1981), "A Rational Theory of the Size of Government," *Journal of Political Economy* 89, 914–27.

Milesi-Ferretti, G.-M. (1995a), "The Disadvantage of Tying Their Hands: On the Political Economy of Policy Commitments," *Economic Journal* 105, 1381–1402.

_____ (1995b), "Do Good or Do Well? Public Debt Management in a Two-Party Economy," *Economics and Politics* 7, 59–78.

Milesi-Ferretti, G.-M. and E. Spolaore (1993), "How Cynical Can An Incumbent Be? Strategic Policy in a Model of Government Spending," working paper.

Milgrom, P. and J. Roberts (1982), "Predation, Reputation, and Entry Deterrence," *Journal of Economic Theory* 27, 280–312.

Mondino, G., F. Sturzenegger, and M. Tommasi (1996), "Recurrent High Inflation and Stabilization: A Dynamic Game," *International Economic Review* 37, 981–96.

Mosley, P. (1992), "A Theory of Conditionality," in P. Mosley, ed., *Development Finance and Policy Reform Essays in the Theory and Practice of Conditionality in Less Developed Countries*, New York: St. Martin's Press.

Mosley, P., J. Harrigan, and J. Toye (1995), *Aid and Power*, Volume 1, Second edition, London: Routledge.

Mueller, D. (1989), *Public Choice II*, Cambridge: Cambridge University Press.

―――― (1997), "Constitutional Public Choice," in D. Mueller, ed., *Perspectives in Public Choice: A Handbook*, Cambridge: Cambridge University Press, 124–46.

Mueller, D. and P. Murrell (1986), "Interest Groups and the Size of Government," *Public Choice* 48, 125–45.

Mundell, R. (1961), "A Theory of Optimum Currency Areas," *American Economic Review* 51, 509–17.

―――― (1968), *International Economics*, New York: Macmillan.

―――― (1971), *Monetary Theory: Inflation, Interest, and Growth in the World Economy*, Pacific Palisades, CA: Goodyear Publishing Co.

Murrell, P., ed. (1991), "Symposium on Economic Transition in the Soviet Union and Eastern Europe," *Journal of Economic Perspectives* 5.

―――― (1996), "How Far Has the Transition Progressed?," *Journal of Economic Perspectives* 10, 25–44.

Musgrave, R. (1959), *The Theory of Public Finance*, New York: McGraw-Hill.

Mussa, M. (1979), "Macroeconomic Independence and the Exchange Rate Regime," in J. Frenkel and R. Dornbusch, eds., *International Economic Policy: Theory and Evidence*, Baltimore, MD: Johns Hopkins University Press.

Naím, M. (1994), "Latin America: The Second Stage of Reform," *Journal of Democracy* 54.

National Association of State Budget Officers (1992), *State Balanced Budget Requirements: Provisions and Practice*, Washington, DC: National Association of State Budget Officers.

Neary, P. and K. Roberts (1980), "The Theory of Household Behavior Under Rationing," *European Economic Review* 13, 25–42.

Nelson, J., ed. (1990), *Economic Crisis and Policy Choice: The Politics of Adjustment in the Third World*, Princeton, NJ: Princeton University Press.

―――― (1994), "The Political Economy Of Policy Reform: Panel Discussion," in J. Williamson, ed., *The Political Economy of Policy Reform*, Washington DC: Institute for International Economics, 472–77.

Neumeyer, P. (1998), "Currencies and the Allocation of Risk: The Welfare Effects of a Monetary Union," *American Economic Review* 88, 246–59.

Neustadt, Richard (1960), *Presidential Power*, New York: Wiley.

Niskanen, W. (1971), *Bureaucracy and Representative Government*, Chicago: Aldine-Atherton.

―――― (1975), "Bureaucrats and Politicians," *Journal of Law and Economics* 18, 617–43.

Nitzan, S. (1994), "Modelling Rent-Seeking Contests," *European Journal of Political Economy* 10, 41–60.

Nordhaus, W. (1975), "The Political Business Cycle," *Review of Economic Studies* 42, 169–90.

―――― (1989), "Alternative Approaches to the Political Business Cycle," *Brookings Papers on Economic Activity* 2, 1–68.

North, D. (1990a), *Institutions, Institutional Change and Economic Performance*, Cambridge: Cambridge University Press.

_____ (1990b), "A Transaction Cost Theory of Politics," *Journal of Theoretical Politics* 2, 555–67.

North, D. and B. Weingast (1989), "Constitutions and Commitment: The Evolution of Institutions Governing Public Choice in Seventeenth Century England," *Journal of Economic History* 69, 802–30.

Oates, W. (1972), *Fiscal Federalism*, New York: Harcourt Brace.

_____ (1977), "An Economist's Perspective on Fiscal Federalism," in W. Oates, ed., *The Political Economy of Fiscal Federalism*, Lexington, MA: Heath.

Obstfeld, M. (1994), "The Logic of Currency Crises," *Cahiers Économiques et Monétaires* (Banque de France, Paris) 43, 189–213.

_____ (1996), "Models of Currency Crises with Self-fulfilling Features," *European Economic Review* 40, 1037–48.

_____ (1997), "Destabilizing Effects of Exchange Rate Escape Clauses," *Journal of International Economics* 43, 61–77.

Obstfeld, M. and K. Rogoff (1995), "The Mirage of Fixed Exchange Rates," *Journal of Economic Perspectives* 9, 73–96.

_____ (1996), *Foundations of International Macroeconomics*, Cambridge, MA: MIT Press.

Okun, A. (1973) "Comments on Stigler's Paper," *American Economic Review* 63, 172–77.

Olsen, E. (1969), "A Normative Theory of Transfers," *Public Choice* 6, 39–58.

Olson, M. (1965), *The Logic of Collective Action*, Cambridge, MA: Harvard University Press.

_____ (1982), *The Rise and Decline of Nations*, New Haven, CT: Yale University Press.

_____ (1991), "Autocracy, Democracy and Prosperity," in R. Zeckhauser, ed., *Strategy and Choice*, Cambridge, MA and London: MIT Press, 131–57.

Ordeshook, P. (1986), *Game Theory and Political Theory*, Cambridge: Cambridge University Press.

Orphanides, A. (1992), "The Timing of Stabilizations," Finance and Economics Discussion Series No. 194, Washington DC: Federal Reserve Board.

Osborne, M. and A. Rubinstein (1994), *A Course in Game Theory*, Cambridge, MA: MIT Press.

Ozkan, F. and A. Sutherland, (1995) "Policy Measures to Avoid a Currency Crisis," *Economic Journal* 105, 510–19.

Özler, S. and D. Rodrik (1992), "External Shocks, Politics, and Private Investment," *Journal of Development Economics* 39, 141–62.

Paldam, M. (1979), "Is There an Electoral Cycle? A Comparative Study of National Accounts," *Scandinavian Journal of Economics* 81, 323–42.

Pareto, V. (1935), *The Mind and Society*, A. Livingston, ed., New York: Harcourt Brace.

Pauly, M. (1973), "Income Redistribution as a Local Public Good," *Journal of Public Economics* 2, 35–58.

Pazarbasioglu, C. (1992), "Private Investment in the Presence of Political Uncertainty," Ph.D. Dissertation, Georgetown University.

Peltzman, S. (1980), "The Growth of Government," *Journal of Law and Economics* 23, 209–88.

_____ (1992), "Voters as Fiscal Conservatives," *Quarterly Journal of Economics* 107, 327–61.

Perotti, E. (1995), "Credible Privatization," *American Economic Review* 85, 847–59.

Perotti, R. (1992), "Income Distribution, Politics, and Growth," *American Economic Review Papers and Proceedings* 82, 311–16.

_____ (1993), "Political Equilibrium, Income Distribution, and Growth," *Review of Economic Studies* 60, 755–76.

_____ (1996a), "Income Distribution, Democracy, and Growth: What the Data Say," *Journal of Economic Growth* 1, 149–87.

_____ (1996b), "Redistribution and Non Consumption Smoothing in an Open Economy," *Review of Economic Studies* 63, 411–33.

Persson, M., T. Persson, and L. Svensson (1988), "Time Consistency of Monetary and Fiscal Policy," *Econometrica* 55, 1419–32.

Persson, T. (1988), "Credibility of Macroeconomic Policy: An Introduction and Broad Survey," *European Economic Review*, 32, 519–32.

Persson, T., G. Roland, and G. Tabellini (1997), "Separation of Powers and Accountability: Towards a Formal Approach to Comparative Politics," *Quarterly Journal of Economics* 112, 1163–1202.

_____ (1998), "Towards Micropolitical Foundations of Public Finance," *European Economic Review* 42, 685–94.

Persson, T. and L.E.O. Svensson (1989), "Why a Stubborn Conservative Would Run a Deficit: Policy with Time-Inconsistent Preferences," *Quarterly Journal of Economics* 104, 325–45.

Persson, T. and G. Tabellini (1990), *Macroeconomic Policy, Credibility and Politics*, London: Harwood.

_____ (1993), "Designing Institutions for Monetary Stability," *Carnegie-Rochester Series on Public Policy* 39, 53–84.

_____ (1994a), *Monetary and Fiscal Policy. Volume I: Credibility; Volume II: Politics*, Cambridge, MA: MIT Press.

_____ (1994b), "Is Inequality Harmful for Growth?," *American Economic Review* 84, 600–621.

_____ (1995), "Double-Edged Incentives: Institutions and Policy Coordination," in G. Grossman and K. Rogoff, eds., *Handbook of International Economics*, vol. III, Amsterdam: North-Holland.

_____ (1996a), "Federal Fiscal Constitutions: Risk Sharing and Redistribution," *Journal of Political Economy* 104, 979–1009.

_____ (1996b), "Federal Fiscal Constitutions: Risk Sharing and Moral Hazard," *Econometrica* 64, 623–46.

_____ (1999), "The Size and Scope of Government: Comparative Politics with Rational Politicians," *European Economic Review* 43, 699–735.

Phelps, E. (1970), "Phillips Curves, Expectations of Inflation and Optimal Unemployment Over Time," *Economica* 34, 254–81.

Posen, A. (1993), "Why Central Bank Independence Does Not Cause Low Inflation: There Is No Institutional Fix For Politics," in R. O'Brien, ed., *Finance and the International Economy*, vol. 7, Oxford: Oxford University Press, 40–65.

_____ (1995a), "Central Bank Independence and Disinflationary Credibility: A Missing Link?," *Federal Reserve Bank of New York Staff Reports* 1.

_____ (1995b), "Declarations Are Not Enough: Financial Sector Sources of Central Bank Independence," in B. Bernanke and J. Rotemberg, eds., *NBER Macroeconomics Annual 1995*, Cambridge, MA: MIT Press.

Posner, R. (1975), "The Social Costs of Monopoly and Regulation," *Journal of Political Economy* 83, 807–27.

Poterba, J. (1994), "State Responses to Fiscal Crises: The Effects of Budgetary Institutions and Politics," *Journal of Political Economy* 102, 799–821.

_____ (1996), "Budget Institutions and Fiscal Policy in the U.S. States," *American Economic Review Papers and Proceedings* 86, 395–400.

Przeworski, A. (1991), *Democracy and the Market: Political and Economic Reforms in Eastern Europe and Latin America*, Cambridge: Cambridge University Press.

Przeworski A. and F. Limongi (1993), "Political Regimes and Economic Growth," *Journal of Economic Perspectives* 7, 51–70.

Putnam, R. (1988), "Diplomacy and Domestic Politics: The Logic of Two-Level Games," *International Organization* 42, 427–60.

Ranis, G. and S. Mahmood (1992), *The Political Economy of Development Policy Change*, Oxford: Basil Blackwell.

Rao, V. (1984), "Democracy and Economic Development," *Studies in Comparative International Development* 19, 67–81.

Ray, D. (1998), *Development Economics*, Princeton, NJ: Princeton University Press.

Riker, W. (1962), *The Theory of Political Coalitions*, New Haven, CT: Yale University Press.

Robbins, L. (1932), *An Essay on the Nature and Significance of Economic Science*, London: Macmillan.

Roberts, K. (1977), "Voting Over Income Tax Schedules," *Journal of Public Economics* 8, 329–40.

Rodriguez, F. (1998), "Inequality, Redistribution and Rent-Seeking," unpublished manuscript, University of Maryland.

Rodrik, D. (1989), "Promises, Promises: Credible Policy Reform via Signaling," *The Economic Journal* 99, 756–72.

_____ (1993), "The Positive Economics of Policy Reform," *American Economic Review Papers and Proceedings* 83, 356–61.

_____ (1996), "Understanding Economic Policy Reform," *Journal of Economic Literature* 34, 9–41.

_____ (1997), "Where Did All the Growth Go? External Shocks, Social Conflict and Growth Collapses," working paper, Harvard University.

Rogoff, K. (1985a), "The Optimal Degree of Commitment to an Intermediate Monetary Target," *Quarterly Journal of Economics* 100, 1169–90.

_____ (1985b), "Can International Monetary Policy Cooperation Be Counterproductive?," *Journal of International Economics* 14, 199–217.

_____ (1987), "Reputational Constraints on Monetary Policy," *Carnegie-Rochester Conference Series on Public Policy* 26, 141–81.

_____ (1988), "Comment on 'Macroeconomics and Politics'," *NBER Macroeconomics Annual*, Cambridge, MA: MIT Press.

_____ (1990), "Equilibrium Political Budget Cycles," *American Economic Review* 80, 21–36.

Rogoff, K. and A. Sibert (1988), "Elections and Macroeconomic Policy Cycles," *Review of Economic Studies* 55, 1–16.

Roland, G. and T. Verdier (1994), "Privatization in Eastern Europe: Irreversibility and Critical Mass Effects," *Journal of Public Economics* 54, 161–83.

Romer, C. and D. Romer (1989), "Does Monetary Policy Matter—A New Test in the Spirit of Friedman and Schwartz," in O. Blanchard and S. Fischer, eds., *1989 NBER Macroeconomics Annual*, Cambridge, MA: MIT Press.

Romer, D. (1997), "Misconceptions and Political Outcomes," NBER Working Paper #6117.

Romer, T. (1975), "Individual Welfare, Majority Voting, and the Properties of a Linear Income Tax," *Journal of Public Economics* 4, 163–85.

Romer, T. and H. Rosenthal (1978), "Political Resource Allocation, Controlled Agendas and the Status Quo," *Public Choice* 33, 27–43.

———— (1979), "Bureaucrats versus Voters: On the Political Economy of Resource Allocation by Direct Democracy," *Quarterly Journal of Economics* 93, 563–87.

Rose, A. and L.E.O. Svensson (1994), "European Exchange Rate Credibility Before the Fall," *European Economic Review* 38, 1185–1216.

Rosenzweig, M. and K. Wolpin (1993), "Credit Market Constraints, Consumption Smoothing, and the Accumulation of Durable Production Assets in Low Income Countries: Investments in Bullocks in India," *Journal of Political Economy* 101, 223–44.

Roubini, N and J. Sachs (1989a), "Political and Economic Determinants of Budget Deficits in the Industrial Democracies," *European Economic Review* 33, 903–38.

———— (1989b), "Government Spending and Budget Deficits in the Industrial Countries," *Economic Policy* 8, 99–132.

Rubinstein, A. (1982), "Perfect Equilibrium in a Bargaining Model," *Econometrica* 50, 97–109.

Sachs, J. (1989a), "Conditionality, Debt Relief and Developing Country Debt Crisis," in J. Sachs, ed., *Developing Country Debt and Economic Performance, Vol. 1. The International Financial System*, Chicago: University of Chicago Press.

————, ed. (1989b), *Developing Country Debt and the World Economy*, Chicago: University of Chicago Press.

Sachs, J. and X. Sala-i-Martin (1992), "Fiscal Federalism and Optimum Currency Areas: Evidence for Europe from the United States," in M. Canzoneri, V. Grilli, and P. Masson, eds., *Establishing a Central Bank, Issues in Europe and Lessons from the U.S.*, Cambridge: Cambridge University Press.

Safire, W. (1978), *Safire's Political Dictionary*, New York: Random House.

Saiegh, S. and M. Tommasi (1998), "Argentina's Federal Fiscal Institutions: A Case Study in the Transaction Cost Theory of Politics," working paper.

Saint-Paul, G. and T. Verdier (1993), "Education, Democracy and Growth," *Journal of Development Economics* 42, 399–407.

———— (1996), "Inequality, Redistribution and Growth: A Challenge to the Conventional Political Economy Approach," *European Economic Review* 40, 719–28.

Sala-i-Martin, X. (1992), "Transfers," NBER Working Paper #4186.

Samuelson, P. (1954), "The Pure Theory of Public Expenditure," *Review of Economics and Statistics* 36, 387–89.

———— (1955), "Diagrammatic Exposition of a Theory of Public Expenditure," *Review of Economics and Statistics* 37, 350–56.

———— (1958), "An Exact Consumption Loan Model of Interest with or without the Social Contrivance of Money," *Journal of Political Economy* 66, 467–82.

Sandler, T. and J. Tschirhart (1980), "The Economic Theory of Clubs: An Evaluative Survey," *Journal of Economic Literature* 18, 1488–1521.

Sargent, T. and N. Wallace (1981), "Some Unpleasant Monetarist Arithmetic," *Federal Reserve Bank of Minneapolis Review* Fall, 1–19.

Schelling, T. (1960), *The Strategy of Conflict*, Cambridge, MA: Harvard University Press.

_____ (1978), *Micromotives and Macrobehavior*, New York: W.W. Norton.

Schmidt, K. (1995), "The Costs and Benefits of Privatization: An Incomplete Contracts Approach," mimeo, University of Bonn.

_____ (1997), "The Political Economy of Privatization and the Risk of Expropriation," CEPR Discussion Paper No. 1542.

Schumpeter, J. (1939), *Business Cycles: A Theoretical, Historical and Statistical Analysis of the Capitalist Process*, New York: McGraw-Hill.

Selten, R. (1975), "Reexamination of the Perfectness Concept for Equilibrium Points in Extensive Games," *International Journal of Game Theory* 4, 25–55.

_____ (1978), "The Chain Store Paradox," *Theory and Decision* 9, 127–59.

Shapiro, C. and R. Willig (1990), "Economic Rationale for the Scope of Privatization," in E. Suleiman and J. Waterbury, eds., *The Political Economy of Public Sector Reform and Privatization*, London: Westview Press, 55–87.

Sheffrin, S. (1989), "Evaluating Rational Partisan Business Cycle Theory," *Economics and Politics* 1, 239–59.

Shepsle, K. and B. Weingast (1981), "Political Preferences for the Pork Barrel: A Generalization," *American Journal of Political Science* 25, 96–112.

_____ (1984), "Political Solutions to Market Problems," *American Political Science Review* 78, 417–34.

Shleifer, A. (1995), "Establishing Property Rights," *Proceedings of the 1994 World Bank Annual Conference on Development Economics*, 93–117.

Shleifer, A. and R. Vishny (1994), "Politicians and Firms," *Quarterly Journal of Economics* 109, 995–1025.

Sibert, A. (1994), "The Allocation of Seigniorage in a Common Currency Area," *Journal of International Economics* 37, 111–22.

Simon, H. (1969), *The Sciences of the Artificial*, Cambridge, MA: MIT Press.

Sirowy, L. and A. Inkeles (1990), "The Effects of Democracy on Economic Growth and Inequality: A Review," *Studies in Comparative International Development* 25, 126–57.

Sjoblom, K. (1985), "Voting for Social Security," *Public Choice* 45, 225–40.

Smith, A. (1996), "Endogenous Election Timing in Majoritarian Parliamentary Systems," *Economics and Politics* 8, 85–110.

Snyder, J. (1990), "Campaign Contributions as Investments: The US House of Representatives 1980–86," *Journal of Political Economy* 98, 1125–1227.

_____ (1991), "On Buying Legislatures," *Economics and Politics* 3, 93–109.

Spolaore, E. (1993), "Macroeconomic Policy, Institutions and Efficiency," Ph.D. Dissertation, Harvard University.

Spraos, J. (1986), "IMF Conditionality: Ineffectual, Inefficient, Mistargeted," *Essays in International Finance* No. 166, Princeton: Princeton University Press.

Stein, J. (1989), "Cheap Talk and the Fed: A Theory of Imprecise Policy Announcements," *American Economic Review* 79, 32–42.

Stigler, G. (1957), "The Tenable Range of the Functions of Local Government," in *Federal Expenditure Policy for Economic Growth and Stability*, Joint Economic Committee, Subcommittee on Fiscal Policy, Washington, DC.

––––– (1971), "The Theory of Economic Regulation," *Bell Journal of Economics* 2, 3–21.

––––– (1973), "General Economic Conditions and National Elections," *American Economic Review* 63, 160–67.

––––– (1975), *The Citizen and the State: Essays on Regulation*, Chicago, IL: University of Chicago Press.

Stokey, N. and R. E. Lucas, Jr. (1989), *Recursive Methods in Economic Dynamics*, Cambridge, MA: Harvard University Press.

Strotz, R. (1956), "Myopia and Inconsistency in Dynamic Utility Maximization," *Review of Economic Studies* 23, 165–80.

Sugden, R. (1984), "Reciprocity: The Supply of Public Goods Through Voluntary Contributions," *Economic Journal* 94, 772–87.

––––– (1986), *The Economics of Rights, Co-operation and Welfare*, Oxford: Basil Blackwell.

Svensson, J. (1998a), "Investment, Property Rights, and Political Instability: Theory and Evidence," *European Economic Review* 42, 1317–41.

––––– (1998b), "Reforming Donor Institutions: Aid Tournaments," working paper, The World Bank.

––––– (1998c), "Aid, Growth and Democracy," working paper, The World Bank.

––––– (1999a), "Foreign Aid and Rent-Seeking," *Journal of Development Economics*, forthcoming.

––––– (1999b), "When is Foreign Aid Policy Credible? Aid Dependence and Conditionality," *Journal of International Economics*, forthcoming.

Svensson, L.E.O. (1997a), "Optimal Inflation Targets, 'Conservative' Central Banks, and Linear Inflation Contracts," *American Economic Review* 87, 98–114.

––––– (1997b), "Inflation Forecast Targeting: Implementing and Monitoring Inflation Targets," *European Economic Review* 41, 1111–46.

Swoboda, A. and R. Dornbusch (1973), "Adjustment, Policy, and Monetary Equilibrium in a Two-Country Model," in M. Connolly and A. Swoboda, eds., *International Trade and Money*, London: George Allen and Unwin.

Tabellini, G. (1990a), "Domestic Politics and the International Coordination of Fiscal Policies," *Journal of International Economics* 28, 245–65.

––––– (1990b), "A Positive Theory of Social Security," NBER Working Paper #3272.

––––– (1991), "The Politics of Intergenerational Redistribution," *Journal of Political Economy* 99, 335–57.

Tabellini, G. and A. Alesina (1990), "Voting on the Budget Deficit," *American Economic Review* 80, 37–49.

Takayama, A. (1985), *Mathematical Economics*, Cambridge: Cambridge University Press.

Tanzi, V. and L. Schuknecht (1995), "The Growth of Government and the Reform of the State in Industrial Countries," Working Paper 95/130, Fiscal Affairs Department, International Monetary Fund.

Taylor, J. (1983), "Comment," *Journal of Monetary Economics* 12, 123–5.

Tiebout, C. (1956), "A Pure Theory of Local Expenditures," *Journal of Political Economy* 64, 416–24.

Tinbergen, J. (1952), *On the Theory of Economic Policy*, Amsterdam: North-Holland.

Tirole, J. (1986), "Hierarchies and Bureaucracies: On the Role of Collusion in Organizations," *Journal of Law, Economics and Organizations* 2, 181–214.

de Tocqueville, A. (1835), *Democracy in America*, New York: Harper and Row, 1966.

Tommasi, M. and A. Velasco (1996), "Where are We in the Political Economy of Reform" *Journal of Policy Reform* 1, 187–238.

Tornell, A. (1997), "Economic Growth and Decline with Endogenous Property Rights," *Journal of Economic Growth* 2, 219–50.

_____ (1998), "Reform from Within," NBER Working Paper #6497.

Tornell, A. and P. Lane (1998), "Are Windfalls a Curse? A Non-Representative Agent Model of the Current Account and Fiscal Policy," *Journal of International Economics* 44, 83–112.

Tornell, A. and A. Velasco (1992), "The Tragedy of the Commons and Economic Growth: Why Does Capital Flow From Poor to Rich Countries?," *Journal of Political Economy* 100, 1208–31.

_____ (1995), "Fiscal Discipline and the Choice of Exchange Rate Regime," *European Economic Review* 39, 759–70.

Townsend, R. (1995), "Financial Systems in Northern Thai Villages," *Quarterly Journal of Economics* 110, 1011–46.

Tufte, E. (1975), "Determinants of the Outcomes of Midterm Congressional Elections," *American Political Science Review* 69, 812–26.

_____ (1978), *Political Control of the Economy*, Princeton, NJ: Princeton University Press.

Tullock, G. (1959), "Some Problems of Majority Voting," *Journal of Political Economy* 67, 571–79.

_____ (1967), "The Welfare Cost of Tariffs, Monopolies, and Theft," *Western Economic Journal* 5, 224–32.

_____ (1970), "A Simple Algebraic Logrolling Model," *American Economic Review* 60, 419–26.

_____ (1980), "Efficient Rent-Seeking," in J. Buchanan, R. Tollison and G. Tullock, eds., *Towards A Theory of the Rent-Seeking Society*, College Station, TX: Texas A & M University Press, 97–112.

_____ (1983), *Economics of Income Redistribution*, Boston, MA: Kluwer-Nijhoff.

Van Wijnbergen, S. (1992), "Intertemporal Speculation, Shortages and the Political Economy of Price Reform," *Economic Journal* 102, 1395–1406.

Velasco, A. (1998), "A Model of Fiscal Deficits and Delayed Fiscal Reforms," in J. Poterba and J. Von Hagen, eds., *Fiscal Institutions and Fiscal Performance*, Chicago: University of Chicago Press.

Venieris, Y. and D. Gupta (1986), "Income Distribution and Sociopolitical Instability as Determinants of Savings: A Cross-Sectional Model," *Journal of Political Economy* 94, 873–83.

Vickers, J. (1986), "Signaling in a Model of Monetary Policy with Incomplete Information," *Oxford Economic Papers* 38, 443–55.

Vickrey, W. (1961), "Counterspeculation, Auctions, and Competitive Sealed Tenders," *Journal of Finance* 16, 8–37.

Von Hagen, J. (1991), "A Note on the Empirical Effectiveness of Formal Fiscal Restraints," *Journal of Public Economics* 44, 199–210.

_____ (1992), "Budgeting Procedures and Fiscal Performance in the European Community," Economic Paper No. 96, Commission of The European Communities, Directorate General for Economic and Financial Affairs.

Von Hagen, J. and I. Harden (1995), "Budget Processes and the Commitment to Fiscal Discipline," *European Economic Review* 39, 771–79.

Von Hagen, J. and R. Süppel (1994), "Central Bank Constitutions for Federal Monetary Unions," *European Economic Review* 38, 774–82.

Wagner, R. E. (1976), "Revenue Structure, Fiscal Illusion, and Budgetary Choice," *Public Choice* 25, 45–61.

Waller, C. (1989), Monetary Policy Games and Central Bank Politics," *Journal of Money, Credit and Banking* 21, 422–31.

_____ (1992), "A Bargaining Model of Partisan Appointments to the Central Bank," *Journal of Monetary Economics* 29, 411–28.

Walsh, C. (1994), "Central Bank Independence and the Costs of Disinflation in the EC," working paper, University of California, Santa Cruz.

_____ (1995a), "Optimal Contracts for Central Bankers," *American Economic Review* 85, 150–67.

_____ (1995b), "Recent Central Bank Reforms and the Role of Price Stability as the Sole Objective of Monetary Policy," in B. Bernanke and J. Rotemberg, eds., *NBER Macroeconomics Annual 1995*, Cambridge, MA: MIT Press.

Weber, M. (1946a), "Politics as a Vocation," in H. Gerth and C. Mills, eds., *From Max Weber: Essays in Sociology*, New York: Oxford University Press.

_____ (1946b), "Bureaucracy," chapter 6, part III of *Wirtschaft und Gesellschaft*, in H. Gerth and C. Mills, eds., *From Max Weber: Essays in Sociology*, New York: Oxford University Press.

_____ (1947), *The Theory of Social and Economic Organization*, translated by A.M. Henderson and T. Parsons, New York: Oxford University Press.

Wei, S.-J. (1992), "To Divide or To Unite: A Theory of Secessions," working paper, Kennedy School, Harvard University.

_____ (1997), "Gradualism versus Big Bang: Speed and Sustainability of Reforms," *Canadian Journal of Economics* 30, 1234–47.

Weingast, B. (1979), "A Rational Choice Perspective on Congressional Norms," *American Journal of Political Science* 23, 245–62.

Weingast, B. and W. Marshall (1988), "The Industrial Organization of Congress: Or, Why Legislatures, Like Firms, are Not Organized as Markets," *Journal of Political Economy* 96, 132–63.

Weingast, B., K. Shepsle, and C. Johnsen (1981), "The Political Economy of Benefits and Costs: A Neoclassical Approach to Distributive Politics," *Journal of Political Economy* 89, 642–64.

Wicksell, K. (1896), "A New Principle of Just Taxation," reprinted in R. Musgrave and A. Peacock, eds., *Classics in the Theory of Public Finance*, New York: St. Martin's Press, 1967.

Wildasin, D. (1991), "Income Redistribution in a Common Labor Market," *American Economic Review* 81, 757–74.

Williams, J. (1990), "The Political Manipulation of Macroeconomic Policy," *American Political Science Review* 84, 767–95.

Williamson, J., ed. (1994a), *The Political Economy of Economic Reform*, Washington, DC: Institute for International Economics.

Williamson, J. (1994b), "In Search of a Manual for Technopols" in J. Williamson, ed., *The Political Economy of Economic Reform*, Washington, DC: Institute for International Economics.

Williamson, J. and S. Haggard (1994), "The Political Conditions for Economic Reform," in J. Williamson, ed., *The Political Economy of Economic Reform*, Washington, DC: Institute for International Economics.

Williamson, O. (1989), "Transaction Cost Economics," in R. Schmalensee and R. Willig, eds., *Handbook of Industrial Organization*, Vol. I, Amsterdam: North-Holland.

Wilson, J. (1989a), *American Government* (4th edition), Lexington, MA: D.C. Heath and Company.

_____ (1989b), *Bureaucracy: What Government Agencies Do and Why They Do It*, New York: Basic Books.

Wilson, R. (1969), "An Axiomatic Model of Logrolling," *American Economic Review* 59, 331–41.

Wittman, D. (1989), "Why Democracies Produce Efficient Results," *Journal of Political Economy* 97, 1395–1424.

Woolley, J. (1986), *Monetary Politics: The Federal Reserve and the Politics of Monetary Policy*, Cambridge: Cambridge University Press.

Wyplosz, C. (1993), "After the Honeymoon: On the Economics and Politics of Economic Transformation," *European Economic Review* 37, 379–86.

_____ (1997), "EMU: Why and How It Might Happen," *Journal of Economic Perspectives* 11, 3–22.

Young, P. (1993), "The Evolution of Conventions," *Econometrica* 61, 57–84.

Zarazaga, C. (1993), "Megainflations as Hyperinflation Avoidance," working paper.

SUBJECT INDEX

Page numbers in **boldface** refer to definitions of concepts. Page numbers followed by an "n" indicate footnotes.